LITERATURE AND SOCIETY

An Introduction to Fiction, Poetry, Drama, Nonfiction

——————— Fourth Edition ———————

PAMELA J. ANNAS

University of Massachusetts/Boston

ROBERT C. ROSEN

William Paterson University

PEARSON

Prentice
Hall

Upper Saddle River, New Jersey 07458

Library of Congress Cataloging-in-Publication Data

Annas, Pamela J.
  Literature and society : an introduction to fiction, poetry,
    drama, nonfiction / Pamela J. Annas, Robert C. Rosen.—4th ed.
      p. cm.
  Includes bibliographical references.
  ISBN 0–13–153457–2
  1. Literature—History and criticism.   2. Literature and society.
  I. Rosen, Robert C.   II. Title
  PN51.A55 2006
  808—dc22   2005037879

Editorial Director: Leah Jewell
Acquisitions Editor: Vivian Garcia
Editorial Assistant: Christina Volpe
Production Liaison: Fran Russello
Director of Marketing: Brandy Dawson
Assistant Marketing Manager: Andrea Messineo
Marketing Assistant: Vicki DeVita
Manufacturing Buyer: Christina Amato
Cover Art Director: Jayne Conte
Cover Design: Bruce Kenselaar
Cover Image: Jonathan Green, Colored Clothes, 1988. Oil on Masonite 23.5″ x 23.5″. Jonathan
Green Studios, Inc. Private Collection. Photography by Tim Stamm.
Photo Researcher: Sheila Norman
Director, Image Resource Center: Melinda Reo
Manager, Rights and Permissions: Zina Arabia
Manager, Visual Research: Beth Brenzel
Manager, Cover Visual Research & Permissions: Karen Sanatar
Image Permission Coordinator: Richard Rodrigues
Composition/Full-Service Project Management: Bruce Hobart/Pine Tree Composition, Inc.
Printer/Binder: The Courier Companies
Cover Printer: Phoenix Color Corp.

Credits and acknowledgments borrowed from other sources and reproduced, with permission, in
this textbook appear on page 1535.

Pearson Education LTD., London
Pearson Education Singapore, Pte. Ltd
Pearson Education, Canada, Ltd
Pearson Education—Japan
Pearson Education Australia PTY, Limited

Pearson Education North Asia Ltd
Pearson Educación de Mexico, S.A. de C.V.
Pearson Education Malaysia, Pte. Ltd
Pearson Education, Upper Saddle River,
  New Jersey

10 9 8 7 6 5 4 3 2 1
ISBN 0-13-153457-2

CONTENTS

FICTION   52

POETRY   151

❀ ❀ ❀

DRAMA **207**

   An old man listens to and talks back at tape recordings about his life that
   he made when he was younger.

POETRY   380

DRAMA   **436**

DRAMA   730

DRAMA   1050

Life in New York City today intersects with life in Hiroshima the day the bomb fell.

NONFICTION   1093

An old medicine man tells the story of the famous 1890 massacre of Native American men, women, and children by U.S. soldiers.

In this 1967 speech, King argues that the United States should get out of Vietnam.

In the last chapter of her graphic (visual) memoir about growing up in Iran in a time of war, 14 year old outspoken Marjane is sent into exile to keep her safe.

"No one knows who they were: husband and wife, lovers, dear friends, colleagues, strangers thrown together at the window there at the lip of hell." Brian Doyle gives us a powerful witness to the tragedy of September 11, 2001.

VARIETIES OF PROTEST   1127

❀ ❀ ❀

DRAMA   1302

    Her traitorous brother has been killed and the King has decreed he shall
    be denied burial, but Antigone puts the laws of the gods above those of
    the state.

    Corporate Hollywood and the U.S. government tried to suppress this
    1953 film about a zinc miners' strike in New Mexico.

NONFICTION 1423

HOW FICTION WORKS 1467

HOW POETRY WORKS 1483

CONTENTS BY GENRE

FICTION

POETRY

DRAMA

NONFICTION

PREFACE

Growing Up and Growing Older, Women and Men, Money and Work, Peace and War, and Varieties of Protest: we have organized the fourth edition of *Literature and Society,* as we did its predecessors, around five major social issues or themes and have selected for each theme literary works—stories, poems, plays, creative nonfiction—that embody a diversity of perspectives and bring to life a variety of experiences.

Growing Up and Growing Older are, of course, universal human experiences. But they are also profoundly particular social experiences, different, for example, for people of different genders, sexual orientations, races, ethnicities, or social classes, as the wide variety of literary works in this section reveal. On the theme of Women and Men, the selections range from love poems to poems of protest, from tragedy to satiric essay and comic fiction, but all illuminate the ways society shapes an individual's experience and gender identity. The issues involving Money and Work are nearly universal in human experience, but, as the literature in this section illustrates, the social conditions within which a person labors can make work fulfilling or alienating, exciting or tedious, life sustaining or life destroying; and the manner in which a society uses and distributes wealth shapes the lives of those who have money and those who do not in subtle as well as obvious ways. We devote a section to Peace and War because war and the need for peace continue to be central to modern existence; even those who have never experienced war directly are profoundly affected by the legacy of past wars, by the militarization of culture, and by the nightmare prospects of nuclear war and terrorism. Finally, in every society, people have engaged in protest, whether spontaneous or planned, whether as individuals or in groups, against what they have perceived as injustice; the selections that explore Varieties of Protest are not simply works *of* protest but works *about* protest, about the act of standing up (or perhaps sitting down) for what one believes is right.

The stories, poems, plays, and works of creative nonfiction grouped around these five themes provide a broad and accessible introduction to the ways literature can enrich our understanding of self and society. The themes, of course, overlap. Literary works are complex; they are rarely about just one thing. Arthur Miller's play *Death of a Salesman* is about growing up and growing older as well as money and work; Pamela Zoline's science fiction story "The Heat Death of the Universe" explores relationships between women and men as well as a very interesting variety of protest. The thematic categories are meant not to limit but to overlap in ways that stimulate thinking and discussion.

Within each thematic category, *Literature and Society* offers a heterogeneous selection of literary works, representing a great many different experiences and perspectives. In addition to works from the canon of American and English literature, we have included a range of selections by women, working-class, gay or lesbian, ethnic, African-American, Native American, post colonial and other writers whose presence in a literature course will not only mean class discussions that are more varied and more exciting, but also an introduction to literature that truly reflects the extraordinary diversity of the society students live in. Close to half of the featured selections in this fourth edition of *Literature and Society* are by women and more than forty percent of the selections are by "minorities." We have not only maintained a strong commitment to the inclusion of African American writers, but, since the first edition, have increased representation by Asian American, Native American, and Latino and Latina writers. We have also added work by writers from a number of countries, including Iraq, Ireland, Turkey, Germany, Norway, Spain, Pakistan, Israel, Senegal, South Africa, Russia, Palestine, Iran, and Chile. The more than forty stories, two hundred poems, ten plays (including one screenplay), and twenty works of nonfiction included will enable students to hear a wide range of voices, differing from one another in gender, age, sexual orientation, race, ethnicity, nationality, and social class.

The editorial apparatus of *Literature and Society* is designed to help students understand both the social meanings and the formal elements of the literary works included. Though we have organized the book by theme rather than by literary genre or literary concept, we give serious attention to matters of form and to the ways literary technique serves larger purposes—the re-creation of experience, the testing of ideas, the exploration of social issues. Four detailed chapters—on fiction, on poetry, on drama, and on nonfiction prose—introduce key literary concepts and approaches and develop them through numerous examples. A long chapter on "Literature and the Writing Process" offers a number of techniques to help students think about their own writing process and uses sample papers, paragraphs, and journal entries to guide students through the stages of that process, from generating ideas to revising and editing.

A preface to each of the five thematic sections introduces the theme that unifies the section and raises some of the key questions the works included explore. Study and discussion questions, suggestions for writing, and author biographies accompany all short stories, plays, and works of nonfiction, and about one third of the poems in each section. The study and discussion questions are concerned with both content and form; they lead students toward a basic understanding of each work. The suggestions for writing (meant to take from five to thirty minutes each) are more subjective and open-ended, intended to stimulate thinking about the larger meanings of the works; they encourage students to explore their own responses in creative ways and to articulate their own opinions. At the end of each thematic section are a number of suggested topics for longer papers, usually involving a comparison of two or more works; these questions offer students the chance to integrate what they have learned. For research paper assignments, each featured selection includes three to five suggestions of critical resources as starting points for a research paper. All selections, including the "additional poems," are covered in the *Instructor's Manual.* Additional helpful material, including definitions of major schools of literary criticism, a glossary of literary terms, and a critical casebook on a poem, are available on the *Literature and Society* Webpage.

Literature and Society is adaptable to a variety of instructional possibilities. Though designed specifically for an introductory literature course, the book can easily be used in a writing course, for its five thematic sections and many suggestions for writing generate a wide range of formal and informal writing assignments; and its process-oriented chapter, "Literature and the Writing Process," is detailed and thorough, even including a section on how to write essay exams. There are far more selections in *Literature and Society* than one could ever use in one or even two semesters of a literature or writing course, so the instructor will find a great deal of freedom to adapt the text to his or her own purposes. A careful mix of well-known, canonical works and equally teachable and formally interesting non-canonical works invites the instructor to combine the familiar and the new in any proportion suited to the design of the course. The instructor might opt for a thorough exploration of any one of the five themes offered or, alternatively, might choose to design a course which selects among the many texts offered across the book as a whole. And should an instructor wish to organize a course by literary genre rather than by theme, there is an alternate table of contents. However it is used, we think *Literature and Society* introduces students to a wide and exciting variety of literature in a way that will consistently engage their interest and that will help them understand that literature is about the very things—money, work, growing up and growing older, civic responsibility and protest, war and peace, what it means to be male or female—that matter in their own lives.

We could never have completed this book without the suggestions, help, and support of many people. We owe thanks to Barbara Apfelbaum, Michael Conlon, Robert Crossley, Fred Danker, Lennard Davis, Linda Dittmar, Penny Dugan, Mary Anne Ferguson, Emily Filardo, Marilyn Frankenstein, Bruce Franklin, Gill Gane, Steve Golin, Linda Hamalian, Russ Hart, Jim Hauser, Esther Iwanaga, Reamy Jansen, Jay Jordan, Louis Kampf, Mary Jane Karp, Stan Karp, Suzanne Kistler, Kathy Koch, Paul Lauter, Robert Lee, Lucye Millerand, Virginia Ramey Mollenkott, Charlotte Nekola, Thomas O'Grady, Richard Ohmann, Susan O'Malley, Donna Perry, Elliot Podwill, Susan Radner, Neill Rosenfeld, Carolyn Rothschild, Pancho Savery, Ron Schreiber, Stephen Rosskamm Shalom, Roger Shatzkin, Wally Sillanpoa, George Slover, Rajini Srikanth, John Tobin, Leonard Vogt, Abdurrahman Wahab, Jack Weston, and the friends who rarely let on how tired they were of hearing about this project. Thanks also to my teenage son, Chris, who provided computer support and stand-up comedy.

Special thanks to students at the University of Massachusetts/Boston in Introductory Composition, Practical Criticism, Nature of Literature: Poetry, Writing as Women, The Modern Period, Contemporary Women Poets, Personal Narrative, and Working-Class Literature; to Christian Pulver for biographic and bibliographic research; and to Michael LeBlanc and Laura Krier for editorial assistance.

We would also like to thank a few people at Prentice Hall: Phil Miller, who gave us encouragement and valuable criticism from the start; fourth edition editor Vivian Garcia, whose patience and good humor helped ease this edition from conception to production; Michael Farmer, who worked on permissions; and Bruce Hobart, production editor.

The following reviewers offered helpful suggestions for the fourth edition: Elyce Ray Helford, Middle Tennessee State University; Carol A. Galbus, Winona State University; Michele Graham, Olive-Harvey College; Suzanne Moore, St. Clair County Community College; Paul Lindholdt, Eastern Washington University.

Pamela J. Annas
University of Massachusetts/Boston

Robert C. Rosen
William Paterson University

LITERATURE AND THE WRITING PROCESS

When you are first learning how to read and write about a work of literature, its very completeness and solidity might be intimidating, rather as though you were standing at the edge of a dense, green tropical jungle. Its façade is a solid and tangled mass of leaves. It smells of rain and shadows. You hear as-yet-unidentified creatures calling to one another from branch to branch and crashing through the undergrowth. How are you going to find or make a path into the jungle of the text? What are you going to discover there? Will you be able to identify and make sense of it and describe it when you come out on the other side?

In some ways, reading and writing about a work of literature—a poem, a story, a novel, a play, creative nonfiction—is easier than working on a nonliterary subject. At least your subject, the literary text, is right there in front of you in all its glorious and annoying entirety, on your desk or on the kitchen table or maybe on your lap as you ride home from school on the subway. It often has a beginning, a middle, and an end; it certainly has a shape. It offers a world for you to visit and describe.

BEGINNING, DISCOVERING, INVENTING, PLANNING, DRAFTING

Ideally, you have had time enough to read the story, poem, essay, or play once through for enjoyment before you have to begin work on it. Now read it again, looking for a way in. This time, read with a pen or pencil in hand. Mark passages (lines, scenes, images, words) that particularly strike you. Perhaps this is where some insight about the whole clicks into place for you. Perhaps you notice recurrences and connections that will add up to a pattern you will be able to write about, like images of housework and aging in Pamela Zoline's "The Heat Death of the Universe," or the repeated use of sibilant sounds ("s") in Langston Hughes's poem "Harlem." Maybe you have noticed some aspect of this text that reminds you of another literary work you've read, perhaps one about a similar type of social experience, such as growing up immigrant and female in America or fighting in a war, and you can note where and how the writers deal similarly and differently with various aspects of that experience. Or you might mark passages that remind you of something in your own life, such as beginning school, looking for a new job, or falling in love. And you should certainly note any part of a literary work that particularly moves you, that evokes an emotional response or a sudden increase in attention that strongly pulls you into the words, even if you can't yet express why.

Generally speaking, your first impulses are good and can be trusted. If you are drawn to an image or a scene or an exchange of dialogue, the chances are very good that either (1) it is an important passage, you are meant to notice it, and most other readers will too; or (2) it catches your particular interest because of who you are, and so you will probably have something original and unusual and particularly your own to say about it. Either way, you have (to return to our opening metaphor) discerned a break in the wall of leaves that may well be a path into this literary jungle.

Taking Notes

So here you sit or stand or lie, reading the text for the second or twelfth time, pen in hand. As well as marking parts of the work with a check, an asterisk, or brackets (or using whatever notational system you like), you will also want to be making notes about your associations and reactions—personal, political, social, and literary. Some people make marginal notes in the text itself, but margins can very quickly become cluttered and the notes hard to read. You might instead keep a note pad with you and write down your reactions and insights as you read, identifying them by page number or key word or phrase from the text. Some people prefer note cards; 5″ × 8″ cards provide more room to write than 3″ × 5″ cards, and it's a good idea to write only on one side of the card. Have confidence; assume that you will fill the cards with brilliant or at least usable insights. The advantage of using note cards is that you can shuffle them around until you find a sequence that makes organizational sense to you; then your deck of cards can either substitute for or help you to write an outline.

Exploratory Writing

You might want to do some exploratory writing at this point in the writing process. Try *freewriting,* or free associating, on the topic for five to ten minutes. Simply write whatever comes into your mind, without worrying about grammar, spelling, organization, or logic. This form of uncensored writing usually has the effect of loosening you up and getting words onto the page, and so it is of particular use to writers who find themselves blocked at the point in the writing process when they first face a blank sheet of paper. Your freewriting may be mostly about your struggles with what you have been reading. That too is useful, if only to get those struggles out of the way now so that they don't creep into the paper itself. Much of what you freewrite may turn out to be garbage; often, though, you will produce a valuable insight or the beginnings of an approach to your text. Besides, even garbage, if you compost it, is useful. Some association or fragmentary comment that initially seems irrelevant may turn out to be the key to your paper. Because freewriting is exploratory writing—not the paper itself but potential material for the paper—you need not care at all about how it sounds or how grammatically or formally "correct" it is, or even how close to truth, whatever that is. Kick your critical, editorial self out of the room during the initial stages of writing. You can also use the initial freewriting to express any feelings you might be having about the text, the topic, the instructor, your boss, your boyfriend/girlfriend, or the weather so that, refreshed, you can get on with the job at hand. You might even discover, in the process of venting what you probably thought of as remarks inappropriate to the task of writing an essay, that there is some provocative connection between, for example, your current job situation and the story or poem about which you are trying to write an essay.

In addition to freewriting—which you can do again at any point in the writing process where you feel stuck, blocked, up in a tree, or down in the mud—another helpful exploratory exercise is to *divide* the topic into parts or categories and to make lists of characteristics about each one. You might do this with the characters in a story. As well as dividing, you might *connect*—make notes about the relations between the parts into which you have previously divided the topic. Your exploratory writing is still that part of the process where you are gathering material for your paper. Here the material may or may not be less centered on the text than on your own thoughts, responses, associations to the poem, story, play, or work of nonfictional prose with which you are engaged. If your paper is to come alive and to have your voice, it needs to have a great deal of you in the writing and behind the writing. In order for your paper to be engaging *to* your readers, it must be engaged *with* the literature you are writing about. If the paper is not in some way a record of your passionate (or at least involved) relationship with the text, it's likely to be a detached and therefore dull piece of writing.

Inventing an Approach

Have you been given a paper topic by your instructor, or are you devising one of your own? If you have been given a topic, then your reading, note taking, and organizing of your material will be influenced by that topic. In some ways, having a topic given to you makes life easier because it aids you in the necessary task of limitation. You needn't say everything there is to say about a play or poem; you need only address yourself to the specific question.

Here is an example. How do Denise Levertov's images in her poem "Life at War" add up to an argument about war, and what is that argument? Such a question gives you clues about what to look for and how to organize your paper. You have been given certain information: (1) that there *is* an argument about war in the poem, that the poem is making a point, and (2) that the images in the poem—

that is, the representations of visual or other sense perceptions—are in the service of its argument. You are given certain directions about what to look at, the images, and what to look for, the argument. You might want to begin by listing the various images of war in the poem: disasters like pebbles in the brain; a feeling like "lumps of raw dough" in a child's stomach; the mutilation of breasts, eyes, penises; the smell of "burned human flesh." Also list the images of human potential when we are at peace, such as "delicate Man, whose flesh/ responds to a caress, whose eyes/ are flowers that perceive the stars." Now, what are your own visceral and emotional responses to these two sets of images? We can say pretty conclusively, even from the few images we've listed here, that this is an antiwar poem. But why is Levertov against the war, here specifically the Vietnam War? What is it she says we are losing or perverting when we engage in this war, in any war?

It may seem more difficult and fraught with potential dangers to come up with your own topic for a literary work, but doing so can also be more fun. As with any other paper you write, a paper about a work of literature needs to have a central point, a thesis, that is large enough to engage something important and exciting in the text but small enough that you don't get lost in it. Most of us are far more likely to choose too large a topic, thinking in our modesty or lack of confidence that we will never find enough to say to fill up the required number of pages. A sense of what size topic fits what size essay is a skill that you will develop with practice. In the meantime, if you have two ideas for a paper, it is generally safer to choose the smaller, more limited topic. One simple way to limit yourself is to choose a formal aspect of the work to write about: with poetry, perhaps the image pattern, the sounds, the speaker of the poem; with fiction, the style, atmosphere, setting, the function of one of the characters, not necessarily the main character; with drama, the tension or conflict between two of the characters, how a subplot illuminates the main plot, the stage directions; with nonfictional prose, the rhetorical or narrative devices the writer uses to build an argument, or the tone and the audience of the piece. In writing about any kind of literature, a good way to provide a workable limitation is to pick a passage to analyze in detail and show how that small part sheds light on the work as a whole.

If you are free to come up with a topic of your own, you might well take this opportunity to explore a social or personal issue that interests you. Try ten minutes of freewriting your personal responses to the text. How males and females are socialized into gender and sexual roles is the subject of several stories, poems, and memoirs, from Jamaica Kincaid's "Girl" to Tommy Avicolli Mecca's "He Defies You Still: The Memoirs of a Sissy." Are you amused, angry, afraid when you read one of these prose pieces? What in the text evokes that response? Do you have memories of parental voices and school bullying that are triggered by Kincaid's or Mecca's texts? What in the way each of these texts is written—images, voice, characters, scenes—brings up your response? Point to specific examples. Or you might choose two literary works on a similar theme and compare/contrast them—perhaps T. S. Eliot's "The Love Song of J. Alfred Prufrock" and Irena Klepfisz's "they did not build wings for them," both about aging, identity, and self-esteem but written from different gender perspectives. Any of these approaches might be of use to you in working out your own ideas on a subject that has relevance to your own life. If you choose a topic that interests you and to which you have some personal connection, you are more likely to enjoy writing the paper, to learn something from writing it, and to find time in your life to do it. Also, the paper is likely to be better.

Outlining

Okay. You have provided yourself with or been given a focus for your essay on a literary work, you've read and reread the text carefully (and if it is a poem, read it out loud), you've made some notes and gathered some evidence, you've had some insights, and perhaps you've made a brief outline or in some other way begun to arrange your material. This outline does not need to be the elaborate, detailed kind that notes every point and subpoint and sub-subpoint, but rather a brief *notational outline* that lists what you think are the most important insights you've come up with so far, with evidence under each point in the form of a page number or a few words to remind you where in the poem or story or play or essay or memoir you found something to support that insight. Then you can experiment with arranging those insights in the order in which you think, at least for now, it makes most sense to proceed.

Drafting

The chapters in this book on how fiction, poetry, drama, and nonfiction work suggest approaches to each of the genres. There is, alas, no formula for writing about literature, or any other subject, that will work for everyone or that will inevitably produce a good paper. At some point you, personally, have to put pen to paper or fingers to keyboard and begin. Perhaps it would help if you discarded the notion that there is a right answer, a "correct" reading or interpretation of any given literary text. In fact, the more you reproduce the actual meeting, friendship, love affair, or confrontation between you and what you have been reading, the stronger your paper is likely to be. (Of course, you do need to back up what you're saying with textual evidence.) Although a book like this can offer you suggestions about gathering evidence and generating ideas, about revising and editing, the actual production of a piece of writing, sentence by sentence, is creative and mysterious and depends a great deal on the kind of experience you are having with your subject. You may have a general idea of what you plan to say before you start, but what you actually *do* say may very well surprise you, since writing is exploring a new country composed of you and your subject.

A few cautions. Do not wait until the night before the paper is due to begin writing it. Although it is true that many of us work best under pressure, you are less likely to be satisfied with what you turn in if you leave no time to revise. Most people begin to have ideas as soon as the assignment is given. Take five minutes right then and write those ideas down before you lose them. Read (or reread) the work you are going to be writing about early in the space of time given for the assignment so that it will be available for thinking about while you are driving, riding the subway or bus, walking, working, or making dinner. When you have ideas, make a note of them immediately. You may find when you do begin to write that your accumulated notes and thoughts about the text add up to quite a bit of work already done.

Writing Block Syndrome can happen when the first (or rough) draft of your paper has to carry too much weight, especially (1) if you have left yourself no time to revise, so that your first draft is of necessity also your last draft, and everything is riding on this one version, which is an anxiety- and often paralysis-inducing experience; or (2) if you have done very little thinking or prewriting about your subject, so that when you confront the blank page your mind is also blank.

Even under the best conditions, sitting down to the task of the first complete draft of your paper is often accompanied by a certain amount of apprehension: Can I pull it off this time? Do I really have anything worthwhile to say? Hasn't it all been said before—and better? Is what I think this story (poem, play, essay) is about what it really is about? How do I start? How do I end? How many words was this supposed to be anyway? This nervous anticipation, a sort of writing stage fright, is quite normal and afflicts experienced writers as well as relative beginners. The trick is to harness the nervous energy to the task of making sentences and prevent it from escalating into panic. If you have allowed yourself some time to write and then to revise, and if you have given yourself the time to think about your subject, to discuss it with whomever will listen, to freewrite some responses, to reread the text and mark passages that interest you, and to make a brief notational outline, then writing your first draft will not feel so much like a scary first step but rather like just one more stage in the writing process.

In the first draft, you find, explore, and settle on the main focus on your paper. Some people have a fairly clear idea of their thesis when they begin the first draft; others find themselves modifying their hypothesis as they think through their subject. You may find yourself writing for a while before you write a sentence that seems to be your true beginning, where you, your subject, and language finally connect. Don't fret if the first few paragraphs of your draft feel more like freewriting than formal writing. Keep writing.

As you move through your first draft, write as long as the words are flowing; when they stop, take a break, move around, then sit back down again and refer (1) to your notational outline to remind you of the next major section of your paper, (2) to your notes for your main points on that aspect of the subject, and (3) to the text for evidence and examples to support your points. Keep doing this until you reach the end. You will have the chance to rewrite everything that needs revising, including the introduction and conclusion.

SURVIVING THE WRITING PROCESS

Both beginning and experienced writers go through a series of struggles with (1) their subject—the topic and the text; (2) themselves—including perfectionism on the one hand and crises of confidence about the worth of what they have to say on the other; (3) the world—finding time and space, and perhaps support from the other people in their lives, in order to write; (4) their audience—often the teacher, who will be sitting in judgment on their work; and (5) language and form—how to say what they want to say. Just as there are organizational stages to the writing process, there seem to be psychological stages as well, though perhaps "stages" is too structured a concept for something as various and initially messy as the fertile chaos of creativity. One student wrote about her struggle with the beginning of writing in this way:

> It's almost as though I have to figure out the mystery of the universe prior to writing anything about anything. Everything seems to be related somehow, in some way, in varying degrees to a certain extent. The mystery of the universe inevitably appears and needs to be resolved before I can make any valid assumptions about whatever it is that I'm supposed to write about.

In the beginning is the assignment, followed almost immediately by modes of avoidance and procrastination truly amazing in their variety and ingenuity. "I may finally decide to clean the cupboards or the oven," writes one student, "or throw a small addition on my house." Most students also note, however, that avoiding writing doesn't bring the hoped-for relief: "These activities of delay ... are a ritual of sorts. I go through the motions of avoidance before I allow myself to come face to face with the process of writing." Another student characterizes the first stage of her writing process not as avoidance or denial but as "... hysteria. This manifests itself by my repeating to everyone and anyone who will listen, 'I have a paper to write. I have a paper to write.' To be fair to myself, I sometimes vary this with 'I have to write a paper. I have to write a paper.'"

Sooner or later, we hope not too late, you do have to sit down and write the paper. But perhaps the time spent procrastinating isn't all bad, if we redefine procrastination as part of the prewriting stage, that space in between the assignment's dropping into your life and the actual production of the paper. And, after all, your room does get cleaned when a paper is due, your socks get sorted, and all your overdue correspondence and telephone messages get answered. (See the preceding section on "drafting" for some practical suggestions on how to use this prewriting time productively.)

Once the writing begins, it can become a totally engrossing activity: "The next thing I knew I was sleeping and waking up surrounded by little balls of paper which contained ideas." Or as another student, a little further on in her paper, said, "I sit here writing, crossing out, tearing out pages from the notebook, squinting at words I have substituted over others. It's coming, slowly, but this is very hard work. I feel like I'm climbing a hill in three feet of mud." Writing does take a lot of energy. Perhaps this, as well as anxiety, is why many people eat constantly while they are writing, munching their way through vast bowls of popcorn, mounds of chocolate chip cookies or raw carrots, or drinking pots of coffee, cans of soda, or cup after cup of herbal tea.

The fact is that writing *is* hard work, and even painful, a fair amount of the time. Producing something coherent, whole, and your own out of fragments, out of thin air, out of the meeting between yourself and your subject is like making a universe, like giving birth. And, as one student remarked about the final stages of her own writing process: "one of the enabling factors in writing, I think, is our native ability to forget the pain. . . . The endless hours lugging heavy images and clunky phraseology to and fro vanish in my fantasies, all agony and frustration forgotten."

Counterbalancing both the pain and the slogging-up-the-mountain-through-the-mud feeling is the exhilaration of writing, in those moments when you have surrendered yourself to the process and have hit your stride. As one student eloquently put it,

```
    I have to confess: it's the words I love. . . .
They feel good rolling off the tongue. Their patterns
on the page please the eye. They congregate, like old
Southern ladies at church, into sentences and para-
graphs. The rise and fall of their cadences is punc-
tuated by exclamations (Yes, Jesus!) and commas
(Mmmhmm), and question marks (Ain't it so). In their
silences, their hushed pauses, a quiet hymn as soft
as magnolias rises from their lips.
```

Just as there is no one "correct answer" when you are writing about literature, there is no one correct *way* to write about literature or any other subject. Depending on your temperament and on the topic, one method or another of writing may prove most productive and comfortable for you. Whatever your method of writing, whether you spin your sentences out like a silkworm, accrete words around a stimulating irritant in the way an oyster makes a pearl, piece your paragraphs together like a quilt maker, or compose from the materials at hand like someone constructing a magnificent pot of soup, the process of writing a paper is a creative as well as critical, psychological as well as intellectual experience. It has moments of frustration and of self-searching, and you may have to struggle with a writing block at some point in the process. It also has moments of intense satisfaction and delight—when the words are flowing, when you've produced a particularly good insight or constructed an elegant sentence, and, finally, when you are looking with relief at the completed paper. You might try sometime, either as a narrative or as a series of day-by-day journal entries, to write about your own particular writing process, from the moment you receive a writing assignment until the time you turn it in. Writers, like the students quoted here, often find it demystifying and empowering to trace just what it is they do when they write and how they work writing into their lives. For writing is not something that happens outside of you; it is not separate from who you are or the life you live.

REVISING AND EDITING

Revising a paper is not simply a matter of correcting the spelling and strewing commas like chocolate sprinkles over the pages. Revising involves a reengagement with your ideas and words and often with the literary text you are writing about. It may involve substantial rethinking and rewriting. Revising is not only editorial and critical; it continues to be creative. However, you do have a complete text of your own to work with at this stage, and this raises interesting possibilities for becoming an engaged reader of your own text. How is your relation to *your* text like and unlike your relation to the text you are writing about? Try writing a one- or two-paragraph response to your own completed first draft.

Let your draft sit for a day or two so that you acquire some distance from it. If you can coax someone you trust to be honest to read your first draft and make constructively critical suggestions, this will aid you in revising. Here is where work in pairs and small groups in class can be very valuable. Experiment with letting someone else in the group read your paper aloud to the group, so that you become a relatively detached audience for your own prose. Along with the other group members, offer constructive suggestions for revising that paper which just happens to be yours. During this exercise, flag any place where a listener's attention wanders; this generally indicates a problem area, either because the prose is clunky and people have turned away in embarrassment or because the writing has become unclear and the audience has lost the thread of the argument. Working in groups on a piece of your writing reminds you that you are not writing to yourself. An essay is a public rather than a private document. That *you* understand what you have written is not enough; your readers need to be able to follow it as well. Following are some questions and suggestions to consider as you revise.

The Whole Paper

1. Think about your audience. Your audience may be your instructor and also the rest of your writing community, the class you are in. What is the *tone* of your paper and the stance you are taking toward your audience? Do you need to anticipate objections? Are you aiming for gentle

persuasion? Note that you *do* have a tone; check that your tone is consistent throughout the paper. A related issue is level of formality. Your instructor may have a preference about the appropriate level of formality for the assignment, whether "I" is allowed, for example.

2. How much do you need to put in your paper? How much is obvious and needn't be said? As a general rule, it is better to say too much and risk being obvious than to say too little and risk being obscure. In writing about a literary text, you might imagine that your audience read that work, very carefully, a year ago; that is, they are not ignorant of it, but they may need to be reminded of the details.

3. What is the main point of your paper? Is it clearly stated? Does your paper say what you want it to say?

4. Go through the paper paragraph by paragraph. Does everything in the paper support or in some way clearly connect with your main point? If not, you may have to leave something out, as much as you may like it.

5. Do your ideas and your overall argument or thesis develop from beginning to end? Or do you just keep repeating the same point in different words or, worse yet, in the same words? You may want to make a new outline between first draft and second, to clarify the paper's development.

6. Have you used evidence from the literary work to support your assertion, either by reference or in quotations? Remember that what you write about a quoted passage ought to aim at being at least as long as the quotation itself. There are times when it makes sense to include a substantial quotation and say something substantial about it. There are other times when you can incorporate a few quoted words from the text into your own sentences to give the flavor of a writer's style or thinking, without losing your own.

7. Have you considered using figurative language and narrative or dramatic devices in your own prose along with the perhaps more philosophical development of your argument to provide variety and vividness?

8. Does your paper have moments of interest and excitement? Build on these. Try to make the rest of the paper come up to the standard you have set for yourself in your best moments.

9. Does your paper have your voice? Does it sound like you? Think about how a letter you write to a friend sounds like you and nobody else. An essay you write should have that much personality.

10. Title your paper. A good title is interesting in itself, is inviting to a reader, and in some way characterizes the paper as a whole.

11. A mnemonic: The final draft should be clear, comprehensive, concise, convincing, and, if you can manage it, compelling.

12. Revise as many times as necessary. Each revision will be easier than the previous one.

Paragraphs

1. Does each paragraph cover one main point, however complex?
2. Does each paragraph have some version of a main or topic sentence?

3. Does each contain (and contain only) sentences that are relevant to the subject of that paragraph? Sentences that don't fit still may be relevant to the paper as a whole; they probably either belong in some other paragraph already written or could become the topic sentence or in some way part of a new paragraph yet to be written.
4. You may find in your paper paragraphs that are wonderful but that do not belong in this paper. Remove them from this paper and store them in your Brilliant Paragraph Box for use in a future paper. Or you might need to recast your paper so that the wonderful paragraph is integral to the paper.
5. Vary the structure and rhythm of your paragraphs. Don't make them all the same in length and format, or you will lose your reader to a deep slumber.

Beginnings and Endings

Opening paragraphs should be interesting and compelling and should invite the reader into the paper. They should say something substantial about the subject of the paper either directly or indirectly and should be as graceful, as powerful, and as polished as you can manage. If you find yourself with any extra time before the paper is due, you might spend it going over your opening paragraph one more time. But be careful not to hypnotize yourself out of clarity with the beauty of your own prose. However gorgeous it sounds, it still has to mean something.

Following are the effective opening paragraphs of three different short papers on the same assignment: "Is 'The Love Song of J. Alfred Prufrock' really a love song? Pay attention to how Prufrock sees himself and to the world T. S. Eliot has fashioned for Prufrock to walk around in."

1. "The Love Song of J. Alfred Prufrock" is a poem that is far removed from the subject of love. The absence of romance in the world of Prufrock is so ostensive that the poem actually mocks its title. Prufrock is as disillusioned by his tedious life as anyone who has ridden through life in the back seat.

2. "The Love Song of J. Alfred Prufrock" describes the journey of T. S. Eliot's symbol of modern man through the character's personal images of his society. This trip supposedly leads to the "overwhelming question" (1. 10) in everyone's life, but in fact, it only explains why Prufrock is not able to answer this question—at least not out loud. The cause of this suppression of true self which leads to Prufrock's false, unmeaningful, and most importantly, loveless life is

```
his society—or, instead, his impressions of his so-
ciety.
```

```
   3. SHOULD I SPIT OUT THE BUTT-ENDS?
Dear J.A.,
   You were leading me to an overwhelming question.
You told me you were going to sing a love song, and
I, unseasoned, did as you bid and unquestioningly
(. . . do not ask, "What is it?" 1. 11) followed you,
thinking all the while that you were leading me into
romance. I know you can tell me that you warned me
by quoting Dante, but I didn't understand your use of
his epigraph until after we had made our visit.
```

The first of these three gets right to the main point by directly answering the question the instructor has posed with a firm "no"—this poem is not a love poem. The writer goes on to suggest that the absence of romance is so striking as to suggest irony or satire: "the poem actually mocks its title." The third and last sentence addresses itself to the rest of the topic by beautifully characterizing Prufrock's sense of self and relation to his world in the metaphor of riding through life in the back seat of a car. The vivid metaphor catches a reader's attention, pulling us into the paper in hope of more vivid images. It also embodies an apt and accurate insight about Prufrock. The use of metaphor, the compressed and concise language of poetry, allows this writer to say something significant in a very few words.

The second of these writers chooses to begin with the secondary rather than the main question the instructor has posed, that is, with Prufrock's relation to his world. He characterizes this relation as a journey and, further, asserts that Prufrock stands for all of us and his world for modern society. Though this writer does not create a metaphor, as did the first, he does quote from the poem ("overwhelming question") and gives us an image of Prufrock's avoidance of this question. The final sentence tells us that Prufrock's life is loveless as well as false and meaningless, and it loops back to the opening sentence in his comment that the lack of love in Prufrock's life is tangled up with his vision of the world.

The third writer takes a more daring approach by addressing herself directly to Prufrock, casting her essay in the form of a letter to the protagonist of the poem. Here the title of the paper is an adaptation of a quote from the poem and certainly captures a reader's attention, as does the letter format. Because the poem itself is addressed to an invisible companion, it is reasonable and clever to assume a cloak of invisibility oneself and to enter the world of the poem. The writer quotes from the poem, she mentions the warning epigraph of Dante's *Inferno,* and, though she doesn't come right out and say, as the other two writers do, that this is not a love song, you are pretty sure by the end of the paragraph that she thinks it is not.

All three of these opening paragraphs address themselves to the assigned paper topic. They all mix abstraction and idea with vivid imagery or narration and are interesting and provocative enough to encourage one to read on. There are many ways of beginning a paper about a work of literature; give yourself permission to play with the possibilities so that you can move beyond a formula opening or a simple restatement of the question.

Closing paragraphs should say something substantial but not introduce new information; and, although they can be quietly powerful, they need not sound like Wagnerian opera. Mainly, they should leave readers with a sense of completion and with confidence in the writer, not hanging in mid-air wondering where they are going to fall. Here is the concluding paragraph of a nine-paragraph paper on Alan Sillitoe's "The Loneliness of the Long-distance Runner."

```
    Sillitoe's intent is to demonstrate the hypocrisy
of a system that condemns the antisocial behavior of
those it excludes. He succeeds in showing that, for
some, being an Out-law is the only means to a sense
of self-worth.
```

The paper has been about the tension between the individual protagonist and the society he lives in. This writer's conclusion says something about both protagonist and setting and about how the tension between the two is resolved. He speaks both of the author's intent and of his achievement. He restates his thesis and succinctly summarizes his argument, though you'll have to take that on faith. The tone of this closing paragraph is confident but quiet, comprehensive as well as concise.

Sentences and Words

As you revise, look closely at your sentences. Read them aloud or have someone read them to you. Are they varied in length and complexity? You don't want the same sentence structure over and over. Is there a rhythm to the prose? Look for unnecessary repetitions of phrases or words and edit them out; pare the sentences down to their essentials, even if that means losing part of your count toward the required number of words. Are the main and subordinate clauses connected to one another in a way that makes sense? If you have incorporated quotations into your own sentences, they are now subject to the laws of your grammatical universe; that is, they must syntactically meld into the rest of the sentence they are in. We necessarily become more aware of our own style when we write about literature, because style is part of what we are writing about. Do at least a few of your sentences approach elegance? Pick out your very best sentence and use that as the standard to aim for in your paper.

Mark Twain, roasting one of his literary predecessors, offers us a number of practical suggestions. In "Fenimore Cooper's Literary Offenses" Twain remarks that the writer should "say what he is proposing to say, not merely come near it"; "use the right word, not its second cousin"; "eschew surplusage"; "not omit necessary details"; "avoid slovenliness of form"; "use good grammar"; and "employ a simple and straightforward style." Have you selected the word with the exact nuance you want? Think about the word you've chosen. Look up in a dictionary or a thesaurus any word whose connotations you don't fully understand. If a word doesn't seem quite right, take a separate sheet of paper and brainstorm or free associate for a few minutes on the word, writing down every alternative word that comes to mind. Try not to censor yourself in the exercise—the most bizarre association might in the end turn out to be the freshest and most apt substitute for the word you are dissatisfied with, making your reader sit up and take notice. Be economical with words; use one appropriate word instead of six or seven vague ones. Words are the basis, the ground of language, where the potential for power and clarity chiefly resides. This is certainly true in the literature you are writing about and can be increasingly true in your own writing. Each well-written literary work we read and study enriches our vocabulary and our own sense of style.

REVISING AND EDITING: AN EXAMPLE

Here is an example, in its original and revised versions, of the opening paragraph of a comparison/contrast essay of about 800 words. The paper assignment was this: Compare and contrast Meridel Le Sueur's "Women on the Breadlines" and Richard Wright's "The Man Who Went to Chicago" for what they have to say about the experiences and the problems of working and not working during the Great Depression. Le Sueur and Wright variously consider issues of gender, race, and social class entwined with the subject of work. Find three points of similarity and three points of difference in their prose pieces. You may find these in *what* they say and/or in *how* they say what they say; that is, you may want to discuss the form of their essays as well as the content. Use *specific evidence* from the two essays to support your analysis.

After reading and commenting on each other's papers in class and reading the instructor's extensive written comments, students were asked to choose *one* paragraph in their paper that needed work and to revise it. The two versions of the opening paragraph included here were one student's choice. After getting feedback on their revised paragraphs, students went on to revise the entire paper.

First Version

```
Wright/Le Sueur comparison/contrast

    "Never had I felt so much the slave as when I
scoured those stone steps each afternoon." Richard
```

Wright (page 906) makes this statement when he is speaking about cleaning the stairs and the white people keep stepping on the clean stairs and making a mess.

It reminded me of the final passage in Meridel Le Sueur's essay ". . . being a slave without the security of a slave." (page 885). They are both comparing themselves to slaves. They are both feeling some of the same emotions. I found this among some of the other similarities in the two essays.

Revised Version

The (not so) Great Depression

"Never had I felt so much the slave as when I scoured those stone steps each afternoon." Richard Wright (p. 906) makes this statement when he is speaking about cleaning the stairs and how the white people keep stepping on the clean stairs and making a mess. It reminded me of the final passage in Meridel Le Sueur's essay, ". . . being a slave without the security of a slave." (p. 885) They are both comparing themselves to slaves. Wright because no matter how easy he makes it for white people, they continuously step on his clean stairs, as if he and his work are so insignificant that there is no need for them to go out of their way for him. Le Sueur is feeling like a slave because no matter how hard she tries (and the other women in her story) her work is always viewed as temporary. The jobs do not last long enough for the women to become valued employees. They are hungry and tired. One day they have a job and the next that job is over. I took Le Sueur's statement to mean the women didn't have the security of knowing their jobs would still be there tomorrow. They didn't have the security of whatever little food the slaves had being available to them. Both Le Sueur and Wright are feeling some of the same emotions. They are both feeling the anger, the exhaustion, and the sheer frustration of trying to survive during the Depression.

Revision happens here in a number of ways, beginning with the title. Titles are important: A title is an eye catcher and lead-in to the opening paragraph. In addition, titles should have some personality, characterizing your particular approach and voice. The title of the first version here ("Wright/Le Sueur comparison/contrast") is anemic; it only restates the assignment in a hurried kind of way and gives us no hint of what the writer's approach to the topic will be. Also, the writer misspells one author's name. Her revised title ("The [not so] Great Depression") is much better: It has both an approach and an attitude; it has more specificity and a wry humor that makes us want to read on.

What is good about the writer's first version is that she begins, inductively, with the two texts, with specific comparison/contrast evidence the assignment asks for. She then goes on to make the beginning of a thesis or at least a focusing statement—that both Le Sueur and Wright compare themselves to slaves—and she has found examples in which they use similar language. We see her deciding to begin by discussing similarities (she will also talk about how both Wright and Le Sueur are members of groups discriminated against and that both stories are set in cities in the United States during the 1930s); she will then go on to discuss differences (male/female; family/no family; personal narration/third person account).

In her revision, the writer puts together into a substantial introductory paragraph what had originally been two very short paragraphs, each little more than a quote and a gloss on the quote. Putting the two quotes together shows the writer at work on significant comparison/contrast. She then discusses each of the quotes in the context of the essays they come from. Throughout the revision, the writer is more specific and detailed. For example, rather than saying "They are both feeling some of the same emotions" and leaving it at that, in the revision the writer tells us just what emotions are being felt in a couple of detailed sentences that provide a strong ending to this opening paragraph: "Both Le Sueur and Wright are feeling some of the same emotions. They are both feeling the anger, the exhaustion, and the sheer frustration of trying to survive during the Depression." In spite of the differences she will get to later in her essay, she sees important similarities, especially in emotional content, in these accounts by a black man and a white woman of trying to survive in the United States during the Great Depression.

Revision is not necessarily something a writer does once and is done with. Very rarely does a piece of writing feel completely satisfactory the second time or even the third. For example, what further revisions might the writer of "The (not so) Great Depression" undertake? People who write for a living are well aware of the ongoing improvability of their writing and revise anywhere from three to thirty or more times. The more complex the project, the more factors and components you are trying to fit into place, the more tinkering may be required before you get it the way you want it. Revising can be as creative and absorbing as the production of a first draft. Revision (re-visioning) is an essential stage in the writing process. See "Sample Paper: Original and Revision" later in this chapter for more on revising and a look at two drafts of an entire paper.

WRITING UNDER PRESSURE: THE ESSAY EXAM

Sometimes we feel a strong need to write a letter to a friend or family member; to write to our congressperson or the editor of our local paper on a subject about which we feel intensely; to write a poem or short story about an experience we want to explore or to preserve; to write in our journals, if we keep journals, in order to work through our feelings about an event. We often go to such internally motivated writing with eagerness and/or relief and rise from it soothed and refreshed. This is *not* the kind of writing this section is about.

The writing we generally find more difficult to do is writing done under outside pressure: writing not for ourselves but for someone else, writing whose parameters some other person has set, writing by which our worth will be judged in some way with fairly immediate consequences, writing done under time constraints. The epitome of this type of writing is the essay exam.

There are at least three major differences between a paper and an exam. First is the time you have in which to accomplish the task. With an exam, you generally have one to three hours in which to write one or more essays, though you might sometimes be given a take-home exam to complete within a few days. In contrast, you usually have a few days to a few weeks in which to write a paper. (Of course, if you are one of those people who wait until the night before a paper is due to begin writing, then all your papers might feel like exams.) Second, in an exam situation, the process of writing, from pondering the topic to polishing the sentences, is much more harried and condensed than in writing a paper. This is not to say that you can't go through many of the stages we discussed previously; you will just have to do them in fast forward.

Third, the psychology of the exam situation is not the same as the relatively leisured and sometimes unpressured process of writing a paper. And different people respond differently to exams. Some people are energized, exhilarated, and put into top intellectual gear by the sight of a blue book; others freeze, lose focus, stare at the questions and their blank pages while the clock ticks and the scratch of other students' pens on paper fills their ears. One school of thought has it that what exams (multiple choice as well as essay) test is not so much knowledge of the subject but simply the ability to take exams—to demonstrate grace under pressure. We tend to agree with this view, but life as it is currently arranged is full of exams. Therefore, it behooves us to learn the skill of taking them and doing as well as we can on them. If you do have immense difficulty in exam situations, you might ask your professor if an alternative way of proving competence in the material is available. Or you could check with your school's academic support service, which might offer a workshop in exam-taking skills.

Following are some suggestions for making the essay exam a less stressful, more successful experience.

1. Study for the exam. Read through your class notes, highlighting significant points, recurrent themes or issues, and connections between readings that have come up in class discussions or in the instructor's lectures. Take a close look at

the syllabus. Is there an overall theoretical or developmental framework that has structured the course? Have you read all the assigned material? You might reread passages you marked or that were pointed out in class as important. After you have done all of this, studying with a classmate is often helpful. Don't spend much time trying to "psych out" the potential questions. As in judo or tae kwon do, focus on your internal balance and be ready to move in any direction.

2. If possible, get a good night's sleep and eat a light meal. Have with you at least two pens and some scratch paper on which to write preliminary notes. Bring along an apple, a cookie, or a box of raisins for quick energy.

3. Read each question carefully. This point cannot be overemphasized. You may know the material backward and forward, but if you do not answer the question directly and fully, you will be graded down. Your grade depends on what you put on the page, not on what is in your head. Look for key words such as *compare/contrast, define, evaluate, discuss, analyze, distinguish.* Organize your essay to answer what the question asks you to do.

Here are two examples of essay questions:

a. "An image is an intellectual and emotional complex in an instant of time."— Ezra Pound. Discuss this definition in terms of one or more of the Imagist poems we have been reading. You could do a detailed explication of one poem, a comparison of two poems, or a more wide-ranging essay in which you use a number of poems to support your discussion. In the last case, the focus would be less on the poems themselves than on the concept of Imagism.

b. Select two of the following short stories ("The Yellow Wallpaper," "A Mistaken Charity," "I Stand Here Ironing," "The Lesson") and compare/contrast the writer's use of point of view. What does each writer's particular choice allow her to do? How does point of view affect the presentation of character and the reader's relation to the characters and their world? Support your argument with specific references to the two stories.

In the first exam question, you are given a quotation that is a definition and basically asked to test ("discuss this definition in terms of") that definition against your choice of evidence. You will need to know which of the poems you have been reading are the Imagist poems. You are given three options for proceeding and asked to choose one of them.

In the second question, you are given a choice of materials to cover (the four specific stories) and asked to choose two (not one, three, or four) and to compare/contrast them. That means you must discuss them in direct relation to one another. As is often the case, the instructor has given you a couple of secondary or subquestions to help you get started and organize your essay. Unless instructed otherwise, you must answer those additional questions.

4. Before you begin writing, take five minutes or so to make some preliminary notes on scratch paper. Outline the main points you are going to make, perhaps the order in which you are going to make them, and how you are going to respond to each part of the question, making sure that you have all the parts covered.

5. Pace yourself. If you must answer two questions in three hours, allow yourself one and a half hours for each question. Keep an eye on the clock. Try not to get carried away by the first question and thus end up giving yourself only half an hour for the second. Occasionally, take a ten-second break and stretch, or at least flex your writing hand.

6. Pause occasionally to ask yourself whether you have stayed "on track," whether you are answering the question directly and completely, whether you have stated your main points clearly, whether you have avoided digressing, whether you are dealing with all parts of the question. Look back at your preliminary notes.

7. Make sure you are referring to the readings, both primary and secondary, sufficiently but not excessively. If you have access to the material (if, for example, this is an open-book exam), do not overquote but do quote appropriately where the quotation supports your argument. Attribute all quotations and paraphrases accurately. If you are expressing a literary critic's idea in your own words, for example, you must give the writer credit for it—otherwise, it is plagiarism. In your writing about the literary texts, avoid summaries or "book reports."

8. Give yourself ten minutes or so before the end of the exam period to read through your essay(s), checking grammar, spelling, sentence structure, attribution of quotations or paraphrases, and development of your argument. If something needs to be added to make the development of your argument clear, write it in the margin with an arrow indicating where it belongs. If something seems irrelevant, cross it out neatly. As long as the pages are reasonably clear and legible, there is no need to waste time by copying the exam over. And hasty recopying may introduce errors.

9. In essay exams, what is important is to answer the question fully and directly. Clarity is more important than eloquence, though the occasional well-turned phrase does no harm. Forget rhetoric and b.s.—ninety-six times out of a hundred they won't work. What your professor wants is evidence, analysis, thoroughness—proof that you have adequately learned the material and the concepts of the course and can articulate your knowledge.

KINDS OF WRITING

Freewriting.   Your instructor may give you a prompt—"Write for ten minutes on jealousy in Shakespeare's *Othello*" or "Free associate in writing for five minutes on the word 'waitress' as a prelude to reading Judy Grahn's poem "Ella, in a square apron, along Highway 80." In a freewriting or timed writing, you brainstorm or free associate on a topic, writing as fast as you can, trying not to censor your writing, trying to write down everything that passes through your mind in relation to the text. The point of the exercise is to connect with fresh, original, and unedited thoughts, words, images, insights. The rush to write in the exercise is meant to bypass the sometimes stultifying conventionality of our editorial selves here at the origins of a piece of our own writing. The short amount of time, five or ten minutes usually, is meant to be nonintimidating. Surely, you think, I can write for five minutes on this topic; it's not like I'm committing an entire evening or weekend—it's not like I'm really starting this paper. That we are generally not sharing these primal thoughts with anyone else means we are free to take risks. Finally, a freewrite breaks through what can be an initial writing block on an assignment, getting at least some words down on paper; sometimes it even can happen that a revised freewrite ends up as part of a finished essay. See the earlier section on "Exploratory Writing" for further discussion of freewriting.

Explication.   In an explication, you go through the work line by line or sentence by sentence, sometimes word by word, unpacking the meanings of the text piece by piece. An explication of a literary work can easily be longer than the work itself, so this approach is usually confined to fairly short poems or to passages in a work of prose or poetry. In an explication, details are crucial and so is the relation of each detail to other details and to the work as a whole. A good explication depends on extremely close reading and although in itself it may seem of limited interest, doing one is a valuable exercise in learning how to focus on what is there in the literary text. In any writing about literature, explication is a useful tool. See the appendix at the end of "How Poetry Works" for a set of explication questions that will guide you through explicating a poem.

Response.   Whereas explication is primarily text centered, a response is primarily reader centered. For example, did Levertov's poem "Life at War," mentioned earlier in this chapter, make you feel nauseated, angry, and sad about the waste of human potential in war? Write down the specific associations the poem evoked in you. If you responded to W. B. Yeats's "The Lake Isle of Innisfree" with nostalgic memories of nature and a fierce desire to quit the urban rat race, then you are launched into a response piece of writing. Your responses to a work of literature and what in the text evoked them are information for you as a writer about literature and, in a response paper, are the main focus. In a response essay you might discuss as well any personal associations the poem pulled from you. Like explication, a response paper can be an enjoyable and useful writing project in itself. As techniques, both explication and response are also likely to provide ideas and material that you can use in other types of writing.

Analysis.   To analyze means (1) to separate something into its parts to find out their nature, proportion, function, interrelationship; (2) to examine something in detail to determine its nature or tendencies. An analysis of a literary work usually focuses on some particular aspect of the work that will illuminate for your readers the work as a whole. What you choose to analyze needs to be limited enough that you can fully explore it and significant enough that your analysis will advance our understanding of the poem, story, play, or nonfictional work. You might decide that a good way to approach Marc Kaminsky's play *In the Traffic of a Targeted City* would be to write down the characteristics of the two settings in the play—New York in the 1980s and Hiroshima the day the atomic bomb was dropped—and how they are similar and different, keeping in mind that the same two actors play all the characters. Or you might first list and then analyze the importance of the "stuff" that someone almost stole in ntozake shange's choreopoem "somebody almost walked off wid alla my stuff" (p. 426).

Comparison/Contrast. Comparison/contrast is a specific type of analysis. Here you are working with at least two literary works or at least two aspects of one text. You might compare and contrast the experience of women in the Depression as presented in Le Sueur's "Women on the Breadlines" and the experience of men during the Depression as it appears in the selection from Tom Kromer's *Waiting for Nothing*. It is generally helpful as an early step in comparison/contrast writing to make lists of similarities and differences and to decide which are most important and which less so. You will need to decide whether you find the similarities or the differences more striking; that will help give you your thesis. You might be asked to compare and/or contrast characters within one literary work; for example, the hero and the villain, Othello and Iago, in Shakespeare's tragedy *Othello*. Contrast would seem the likely place to begin this topic, but you might ask yourself if the two men have anything in common. In structuring a comparison/contrast paper, you might choose to interpret or characterize each work or character in turn, then analyze the differences. This approach works best in a short paper. Or you might choose to write a point-by-point analysis, each paragraph taking one aspect of the topic and discussing both in relation to that topic. For example, one paragraph on Le Sueur and Kromer might discuss starving quietly versus begging for one's supper. Another might explore what options for survival are open to Le Sueur's characters versus Kromer's, and so on. In this kind of analysis, as in any other, you need to deal with all the relevant evidence. That is, you cannot ignore some aspect of the work simply because it doesn't fit your theory.

Review. If you are writing on a whole book (or play or film), try writing a review. Unlike the usual essay on literature, a review assumes that your reader has not yet read the book (or seen the play or film) under consideration. So you need to provide enough information about the plot, characters, or overall structure so that your reader can follow you, but you don't want to say so much that your review turns into pure summary or that you leave nothing to your reader's imagination. As well as describing a book, a review makes a judgment, an evaluation. Was it good or bad, moving or boring, significant or trivial? Why and how? Further, you might want to tell your readers what is singular or special about this book for *you:* characters, language or style, images, politics, balance or arrangement of elements. Give your readers a sense of the texture of the work by quoting from it, but briefly. You might want to put the particular work into a context such as the writer's other work, similar work by the writer's contemporaries, the literary tradition out of which she or he is writing, or the history of the issue written about. You might praise the book, pan it, or write a response somewhere in between, weighing the pros and cons; your judgment of the work will affect the tone of your review. Whatever your opinion, it needs to be backed up with evidence. Be true to your own response and try to write the complexity of that response (far beyond "I liked it" or "I hated it") into the review itself. A *review article,* usually longer than a simple review, does all the foregoing, pays more attention to matters of context, and, in some cases, covers more than one book.

Research Paper.   You might be asked to write a paper that takes into account more than the literary text, you as reader, and your social context. A research assignment might ask that you find out more about a particular writer's life and times and put the literary work into a context that is biographical, social and historical, philosophical and political, or literary historical. Or a research paper might require you to read what other literary critics and historians have said about a particular play, poem, or story: (a) to compare/contrast their ideas about the text and/or (b) to yourself enter the critical dialogue about the text. In *Literature and Society,* each short story, play, nonfiction work, and featured poem is prefaced by biographical and bibliographical information. Following the study questions and writing exercises for each of these are three to five critical references. Both the prefaces and the critical resources will give you starting points for your research. Go to the *Literature and Society* Web site to see a Critical Casebook, an array of responses to a single poem.

When you have been assigned to write a research paper, try to develop a few ideas and a thesis or main point of your own about the literary work before you begin your research. It is hard not to be overwhelmed by the fully worked-through analyses you will encounter in contrast to your own tentative insights at this stage. If you have a good idea of what you want to say about the text (subject to evolution, of course), then you can engage in dialogue with other literary critics rather than feel squashed by their finished, multiply revised, authoritatively-in-print discussions. You may use or discard, agree or disagree with what others have said about a literary work, but remember that the paper you are writing is your own. And, of course, remember to cite your sources for every idea not your own, both when you quote the other writer's words and when you borrow his or her insights, even though you might cast them into your own language. See the section on "Manuscript Form" at the end of this chapter for the technical details of citation.

Critical Reading Journal.   It can be extremely useful to keep an ongoing journal on your reading in a literature course. Such a journal can function on a number of levels, either separately or simultaneously: (1) explication and analysis of individual texts; (2) your responses—emotional, intellectual, political—to works of literature; (3) the connections you make, as the semester and your reading go on, among the literary texts you are reading—comparisons and contrasts between characters, issues, ways of writing, recurring themes, social issues; (4) connections between the literature and your own life; (5) arguments with or further explorations of points brought up in class discussion; and (6) experiments in creative writing of your own, perhaps in the mode of a writer you are studying. Following the last suggestion, you might write an opening paragraph that provides a setting and an atmosphere, or try a character sketch, or write a short poem based on one extended image. If you write two or three pages a week in your journal, you will have by the end of the semester a substantial amount of writing and a record of your thinking about the literature. The journal is also a valuable source for any papers you might be asked to write. The trick here is to keep up with your journal week by week and not fall behind. If you find yourself trying to write eight or nine pages of your reading journal on three weeks of reading and class discussion the night before the journal is due, you will feel harassed and sorry for yourself and will have defeated the purpose of the assignment, which is to give you a cumulative experience.

The writing in a critical reading journal tends to be less formal than in most essays, but it still needs to be clearly organized with the sentences well constructed. You might explore a topic such as the importance of having a job in three poems by working-class writers for a couple of paragraphs, then leave a space and move on to something else, like how Tillie Olsen's "I Stand Here Ironing" made you wonder how your own mother thought about you or how reading Sandra Cisneros's "The Family of Little Feet" or Dorothy Allison's "Gun Crazy" made you think about how the end of childhood was marked in your own life.

PASSAGES FROM STUDENT CRITICAL
READING JOURNALS

Following are several examples of passages from critical reading journals, all of them written in a course on American working-class literature. They exemplify the way a reading journal can include many different types of writing, from explication to response and from analysis to experiments in creative writing. These excerpts also demonstrate the way in which the more relaxed format of the reading journal encourages an authentic, lively, and individual writing voice.

1. A response to Tillie Olsen's short story "I Stand Here Ironing," in which the student identifies with the character of Emily and remembers her own experience as the oldest child in a working-class family:

> In the story Olsen describes the desperate situa-
> tion many working class mothers find themselves in
> when they have young children or babies who need their

attention and not enough time or energy to give that attention. The situation of course is an economic one, in which the type of care a mother gives her child is controlled by economic factors. As a woman who has not had children, yet is the oldest of six in a working class family I can identify more with some of Emily's experiences. In a large working class family early childhood responsibilities often fall to the oldest child, especially if that child is female. As a child of six or seven I was standing on a chair pulled up to the sink in order to wash dishes, by the age of eleven I was cooking meals for four younger siblings. There were more than a few times when I had been left in charge that every strange sound in a house devoid of adults became sinister and amplified beyond measure. On Friday nights when both our parents were working we had frozen food for supper. As keeper of the peace, it was always my responsibility to count the contents of every box and make sure that each person got their fair share.

Early childhood responsibility is something which I think is typical of most working class families. I had occasion to talk one day with a woman who was 94 years old. As I fed her her breakfast she talked about her childhood. She was one of nine children and she had left school in the seventh grade to work. "If I wanted a pair of new shoes, I had to work for them," she said with a mixture of pride and wistfulness. "Black patent leather shoes with cloth tops and seven buttons. That was real class in those days."

2. An analysis of Alice Walker's "Everyday Use" in which the student disagrees with the class discussion of the story:

It was said in class that Dee wanted certain things from her mother's home only because being aware of one's roots was a fashionable thing to do. The story actually backs up this line of reasoning; after all, Dee wants to use the quilts for wall coverings and the churn top for a centerpiece. She only wants to use them as showpieces, examples of her "heritage." Dee is more interested in how the pieces will make her look more chic than she is about how much the family really depends on those things for survival. As much as the story backs up this opinion there is

something in me that tends to disagree with it. I believe (and don't ask me why) that Dee really needs
those things almost as much as her family does. She
needs them in order to remember her working class
background even though it appears that she despises
it. She is caught between a rock and a hard place.
As much as she wants to despise her background she
cannot deny the existence of it. Using her family's
furniture as quaint showpieces is her way of coping
with this strange paradox.

I am not completely satisfied with my own explanation of this story and Dee. This uneasiness on my part
is probably due to the ambivalence I feel toward the
character of Dee. I can't really figure out what I
think. I read the story and look at the character one
way. Then I read it again and I look at her in another way. I decided I can't figure her out because
she can't figure herself out.

3. An analysis of two lines of Judy Grahn's poem about a truck-stop waitress, "Ella, in a square apron, along Highway 80":

In Ella's poem, her message or image came in two
lines: "Like some isolated lake, her flat blue eyes
take care of their own stark bottoms./ Her hands are
nervous, curled, ready/ to scrape." Grahn delivers
Ella to me on a few different levels: she is alone
and self sufficient, unafraid to take care of herself
and ready to strike out at those who try to stand in
her way, and yet, at the same time she is not a cruel
or malicious person, for she is likened to the beauty
of a solemn lake. She is a woman who understands self-
preservation and also the price one must pay for it.

4. One student's response to and analysis of a class discussion of Richard
Wright's "The Man Who Went to Chicago" followed by another student's reaction to that same episode in Wright's essay:

(a) . . . the question which arose in class the
other day about whether or not Richard Wright was
writing as an angry man seems rhetorical (some of my
classmates conjecturing that, indeed, he didn't
"sound that angry"—that Wright was surprisingly measured and analytical when discussing his experience
as a black man in America in the 1930s and '40s). But

all one had to do was to give pause to Wright's allusion to the stair washing incident in order to imagine the incredible rage he must have felt: Hell, I
got pissed off just reading about it, never mind experiencing it. To think that people could discount a
man's labor to such a degree that they openly mocked
his efforts (and they were educated people—part of the
medical community) and even sought to vandalize his
work is enough to make the reader scream out in angry protest and frustration. So how must Mr. Wright
have felt when "a sadistically observant white man
would notice that he had tracked dirty water up the
steps, and he would look back down at me and smile
and say: Boy, we sure keep you busy, don't we? And I
would not be able to answer . . . ."? Angry? We must
be kidding. There are times when I truly believe that
if I were a black person in America that I would go
out, buy a rifle, and shoot every white person that
I saw. I mean, to be black and to be aware of the
legacy that America has foisted upon people of color
and not want to destroy America—burn it to the ground—
takes an incredible amount of self-control, probably
unfathomable to most of us who have lived in the favored role, as the Western European descendants of
privilege.

And so, again, the point is not whether or not
Wright was angry, but rather it's how was he able to
focus this anger in such a way as to illuminate the
American experience in his brilliant manner. It is
part of his genius that he is able to take the stuff
of which rage is made and fashion it into works of
both power and intelligence.

(b) Why bother washing the stairs if White America
keeps walking over it?

The answer is simple, either stop washing the stairs
or stop White America from walking over them. Simple,
right? Oh, wait a minute, I forgot about discrimination, powerlessness, self-hate, ambiguous feelings
about who the enemy really is, and inability to change
the system.

5. Two examples of creative writing, one poem and one prose piece, inspired
by the literature students were reading that semester:

(a)

My other job

Familiar faces every day
Some say "The usual."
I grab their brand of cigarettes
before they ask for it.
Megabucks
The Numbers Game
"Gimme 3674 across the board"
I finish punching the numbers.
"Three dollars please."
I know all their names.
I can tell you whether they like
Coke or Pepsi.
I know everything
about them. When I go home
I forget they exist.

(b)

Going Up

I have never lived in a house that had an upstairs. Sure I've walked up the stairs, two flights, eleven steps each, of gray gritty cement to get to my family's apartment, but I have never gone upstairs. Many times I've wished that I could say, "Goodnight, I'm going upstairs." It sounds so homey, so damn middle class comfortable. My family has always lived in multiple unit dwellings. First, a three family my father purchased or, more correctly, mortgaged when he was fresh out of the Navy, then a six family (the very house my father's father bought when he was fresh out of the Army), and then a two family. Never, never a house that was ours and ours alone. I hate mailboxes that have more than one name on them. I guess that going up the stairs instead of upstairs was a symptom, a brand that shouted obscenely our economic situation. We were poor. Not cabbage soup poor, not cardboard bottom shoe poor, not even uncle sam could you spare some change poor. We were ugly day to day getting by poor.

SAMPLE EXPLICATION PAPER: ORIGINAL AND REVISION

The assignment was to write a three-page (600–800 word) explication of a poem, concentrating on sound and image patterns. This student chose to write on Carolyn Forché's prose poem, "The Colonel." The revisions here do not involve large reorganizations of the paper, moving paragraphs from one place to another or filling in holes in the argument. With a good basic structure and line of argument in the original draft, the writer here works, paragraph by paragraph, on strengthening her focus: by stating her argument more clearly and strongly throughout the paper, by selecting and arranging her evidentiary quotes to maximum effect, and by cutting out some unnecessary or rambling remarks, replacing them with fewer and more concise words that attend directly to the paper assignment—to explicate the poem, concentrating on image and sound patterns. The writer here emphasizes an exploration of the poem's sound as her primary focus. Notice, for example, how her revision begins in the second half of her first draft's opening paragraph, where she replaces some random examples of sound patterns with an authoritative thesis statement: "Forché uses alliteration, assonance, consonance and repetition to enhance the poem's meaning and mood." This has a confident sound; we feel we are in good hands. The exemplary details of the original first paragraph are not lost; the writer moves them to the second paragraph where their compression into a separate supportive unit gives them more force.

Look again at the suggestions for revision given earlier in this chapter. Specifically, how and where has this writer edited and rethought her paper? Are there any further revisions you would want to add?

First Version

```
                                                        Smith 1

      Sarah Smith
      Professor Annas
      English 212
      20 February 2005


          Have You Heard What the Colonel Said?


      Carolyn Forché's poem "The Colonel" is presented
      to the reader in a blank verse prose form. A prose
      poem is written in a short block form resembling a
```

paragraph except for the density of the poem and the lack of indentation. The prose form allows us to concentrate on the serious subject and tone of the poem. Using brief yet explicit sentences, Forché creates the tense act and impression that is repeatedly heard through her choice of words and form that describes the situation. The words and sounds are entirely significant to the poem because they develop and create very sensuous and concrete images and also include many strong connotations. They describe the environment, the mood, the characters and their feelings. Some of the sounds in "The Colonel" are hard and cacaphonic. There were "daily papers, pet dogs, a pistol on the cushion beside him." Here Forché is using alliteration of the cacaphonic "p" sound to emphasize the pistol which suddenly upsets the regularity of the image we start to create when we read: ". . . daily papers, pet dogs . . ." There is a subtle rhythm to the poem, giving it an even tone that reflects the emotional state- ment of the narrator.

In short successions of sentences the poem builds until it reveals the dreadfullness of the encounter and the revulsion displayed by the colonel's message to his visitors. "What you have heard is true. I was in his house." We are in- troduced to the narrator as she speaks to her fel- low comrades perhaps, recalling the incident involving a dinner at a colonel's home one evening. The narrator goes on to briefly describe the colonel's family. "His wife carried a tray of coffee and sugar. His daughter filed her nails, his son went out for the night." In this brief introduction the narrator declares much about the attitudes of the family. Clearly the ignorance to the violence at hand is displayed through the sim- ple unmoving actions displayed by his family. The syntactical repetition of the pronoun "his" in these two sentences emphasize the powerful image of the colonel in his home.

The narrator describes the exterior of the house in a jagged manner. There is violence, illustrated all around from the impression given. "The moon swung bare on its black cord over the house. On the television was a cop show. It was in English. Broken bottles were embedded in the walls around the house to scoop the kneecaps from a man's legs or cut his hands to lace. On the windows there were gratings like those in a liquor store." From these images I see the moon perceived with a sense of gloom, hanging on a black cord like the execution that takes place during the night. There is the blood of the poor and desperate dried on the walls of the colonel's house and on his living soul. Even the television show is violent.

They dine on. . . . "We had dinner, rack of lamb, good wine. A gold bell was on the table for calling the maid. The maid brought green mangoes, salt, a type of bread." The repetition of the initial consonant sound as in good, gold, and green connects the dinner in a flowing manner. This image seems very civilized and festive, with all the ingredients of a nice well mannered meal so this image adds a twist to the violent scene and heightens the tension of the poem.

Following dinner, the narrator is asked how he enjoyed the country. "There was a brief commercial in Spanish. His wife took everything away. There was some talk about how difficult it had become to govern." Each sentence here is linked together yet separate. While the narrator is asked how she enjoys the country, our attention is suddenly focused on the "brief commercial in Spanish," as if there was nothing she could say truthfully about the situation of the country to this imposing colonel without creating a violent reaction. Then there is "talk" of how difficult it has become to govern. There seems to be no real conversation, just "talk" and I assume from the statement that the colonel is doing all the speaking. The mood is too heavy at the colonel's home for an open discussion of opposing political views.

"The parrot said hello on the terrace. The colonel told him to shut up, and pushed himself from the table. My friend said to me with his eyes: say nothing." At this moment the tension is thick and the turning point is descending upon us. The colonel is obviously about to reveal something of great significance. The colonel comes back carrying a sack. He empties its contents, human ears. He shook an ear in their face and forced them to watch as he soaks the dried ear as if he wanted the dead among the living native people to hear his message "As for the rights of your people tell them to go fuck themselves." Here the brutality of the colonel is fully manifested. Like Forché says, "There is no other way to say this." The simplicity of the statement is intentional, because there is no other way to say this. The gruesome horror exposed through the colonel's actions and statement strikes us in the face with brutal force. The colonel is almost finished with his guest as he said, "Something for your poetry, no? Some of the ears on the floor caught this scrap in his voice. Some of the ears on the floor were pressed to the ground." The last two lines imply that some of the persecuted people knew why they were being executed while others did not. In the last sentence I picture the victims' ears literally being pressed to the ground.

The poetic craft displayed in "The Colonel" is Forché's use of the narrative voice which allows the reader to interact with the poem. The brief yet explicit sentences lead us through the sequences of the evening stating clearly the tone, atmosphere, and meaning of "The Colonel."

Smith 5

Work Cited

Forché, Carolyn. "The Colonel." *Literature and Society: An Introduction to Fiction, Poetry, Drama, Nonfiction.* Eds. Pamela J. Annas and Robert C. Rosen. 4th Ed. Upper Saddle River: Prentice Hall, 2006. 967.

Revision

Smith 1

Sarah Smith
Professor Annas
English 212
20 February 2005

Have You Heard What the Colonel Said?

Carolyn Forché's poem "The Colonel" is presented to the reader in a blank verse prose form. A prose poem is written in a short block form resembling a paragraph except for the density of the poem and lack of indentation. The prose form allows us to concentrate on the serious subject and tone of the poem. Using brief yet explicit sentences, Forché creates the tense act and impression that is repeatedly heard through her choice of words and form that describe the situation. The words and sounds are entirely significant to the poem because they develop and create very sensuous and concrete images and also include many strong connotations. Forché uses alliteration, assonance, consonance and repetition to enhance the poem's meaning and mood. There is a subtle rhythm to the poem, giving it an even tone that reflects the emotional statement of the narrator.

Smith 2

In the sound pattern of "The Colonel," the use of alliteration is smooth and balanced throughout the poem to reveal the horror and accentuate the revulsion of this visit to the colonel's home. For example: "There were daily papers, pet dogs, a pistol on the cushion beside him." Here Forché is using alliteration of the cacophonic plosive sounds to emphasize the pistol which suddenly upsets the regularity of the image we start to create when we read: ". . . daily papers, pet dogs . . . ."

"What you have heard is true. I was in his house." We are introduced to the narrator as she speaks to her fellow comrades perhaps, recalling the incident involving a dinner at the colonel's home one evening. The narrator goes on to briefly describe the colonel's family. "His wife carried a tray of coffee and sugar. His daughter filed her nails, his son went out for the night." The family's tranquil attitude is contrasted to the hardened feelings towards violence displayed by the colonel. This gives the sense that his family is protected by his violent actions. The syntactical repetition of the pronoun "his" in these two sentences emphasizes the powerful image of the colonel in his home.

The narrator describes the house in a frightening manner. The impression of violence that surrounds the house is described in:

The moon swung bare on its black cord over the house. On the television was a cop show. It was in English. Broken bottles were embedded in the walls around the house to scoop the kneecaps from a man's legs or cut his hands to lace. On the windows there were gratings like those in liquor stores.

From these images the moon is cast in a shadow of gloom, hanging on a black cord like the execution that takes place during the night. There is blood

of the poor and desperate dried on the walls of
the colonel's house and on his living soul. Even
the television show is violent. Combining concrete
images and serious alliteration, the sound heightens our senses to the imagery of the exterior.

They dine: "We had dinner, rack of lamb, good
wine. A gold bell was on the table for calling
the maid. The maid brought green mangoes, salt, a
type of bread." The repetition of the initial consonant sound, as in good, gold, and green, connects the dinner in a flowing manner. Also using
commas to enhance the alliteration and build up
to a climax, Forché adds a twist to the violent
scene by adding civilized festive images to the
underlying hostility of this meeting with the
colonel.

Following dinner, the narrator is asked how she
enjoys the country. "There was a brief commercial
in Spanish. His wife took everything away. There
was some talk of how difficult it had become to
govern." Each sentence here is linked together yet
separate. While the narrator is asked how she enjoys the country, our attention is suddenly focused on the brief commercial in Spanish, as if
there were nothing she could say truthfully about
the situation of the country to this imposing
colonel without creating a violent reaction.

The colonel returns to the table carrying a
sack. He empties its contents. At this moment the
tension is thick and the climax is descending upon
us. Human ears of the colonel's victims are
spilled on the table in front of his visitors. He
shook an ear in their faces and forced them to
watch as he soaked the dried ear as if he wanted
the dead among the living native people to hear
his message: "As for the rights of your people,
tell them to go fuck themselves." Here the brutality of the colonel is fully manifested. Like
Forché says, "There is no other way to say this."
The gruesome horror exposed through the colonel's

Smith 4

actions and statement strikes us in the face with brutal force.

Forché uses repetition in these two sentences: "Some of the ears on the floor caught this scrap in his voice. Some of the ears on the floor were pressed to the ground." The repetition of these images reemphasize the persecution of the native people. It seems to me the connotation implied by these two sentences is that some of the people knew why they were being executed while others did not. In the last sentence I picture the victims' ears literally being pressed to the ground by the colonel and his men.

In short successions of sentences the poem builds until it reveals the dreadfulness of the encounter and revulsion displayed by the colonel's message to his visitors. The simple sentence structure and concrete sounds intermingle and produce very real and concrete images. The tone of "The Colonel" is flat and unobtrusive. This sound pattern enhances the sequences of events by letting the sounds and word choices increase the tension. If this poem were written in verse it would make too much of an appeal on our emotions towards the colonel and the subject of the poem. The simple sentences disclose the violence and anger that is felt by the narrator and addressed to the audience. The sound pattern, using alliteration, consonance, assonance and repetition, adds to the development of this prose poem.

Smith 5

Work Cited

Forché, Carolyn. "The Colonel." *Literature and Society: An Introduction to Fiction, Poetry, Drama, Nonfiction*. Ed. Pamela J. Annas and Robert C. Rosen. 4th Ed. Upper Saddle River: Prentice Hall, 2006. 967.

DOCUMENTATION AND MANUSCRIPT FORM

Academic Honesty

Why do we document the words and ideas of others when we write? The following is adapted from the English Department of the University of Massachusetts/Boston's "Academic Honesty Statement."[1] All students should be familiar with the specific definitions and regulations concerning Academic Honesty contained in the code of their own particular school or university:

Intrinsically, the reading of literature involves a "conversation" between author and reader. "It takes two to speak the truth," Thoreau once noted: "one to speak, and another to hear." When we read, we are active: We speak back to the author, who may not literally "hear" us but whose writing nonetheless operates as a sounding board for our responses to the world of words and ideas opened up by the text. The study of literature also involves a conversation—between reader and reader. At the most immediate level, this conversation takes place in the classroom, in the exchange of responses between readers—between teachers and students, between student and student. Ideally, this conversation continues outside the classroom: in the hallways, in the cafeteria, in offices, at home, online—wherever inquiring minds come together.

In fact, this conversation extends far beyond the classroom and is, almost always, part of a larger "critical dialogue"—another world of words and ideas— that we also participate in each time we write a paper or an exam or otherwise present our work for consideration or evaluation by others. That dialogue takes place in the realm of inquiry into the processes of literature undertaken through academic scholarship and criticism recorded via various media: in books, articles, and reviews in print, on radio and television, on CD-ROM, on the Web. Participation in this dialogue is an important dimension of the learning experience for all students of literature: Our learning increases through consideration of what others have learned and have made available to us as readers and students.

But with such participation comes the responsibility of identifying—and of acknowledging appropriately—which aspects of the critical dialogue (or even the classroom conversation) originate with us individually, which aspects are general common knowledge, and which originate with a scholar or a critic or another student. Students meet that responsibility by thoroughly documenting all sources consulted—regardless of whether they are quoted from directly, paraphrased, rephrased, or otherwise "borrowed from."

Faculty take very seriously the obligation of students, in presenting work (whether written or oral) for evaluation, to give full credit to others where and when such credit is due. In commitment to the very integrity of the academic enterprise—the pursuit of knowledge and truth—all faculty hold students accountable for any instances of "plagiarism" (that is, the misrepresentation of an-

---

[1]Thomas O'Grady, 2003.

other's words or original ideas as one's own) or for any other form of academic dishonesty. The penalties for violations may range from, minimally, a grade of "F" on the assignment in question to a grade of "F" in the course to academic suspension to outright dismissal from the academic institution.

Citation of Sources

Don't worry about the citation form for quoting passages and documenting sources until near the end of the writing process. It would be a shame to lose your writing momentum, to derail an interesting and productive train of thought, in order to work out the exact form for a footnote or to ponder whether the comma goes before or after the quotation mark in the middle of a sentence. But these matters must be faced eventually and, if you handle them correctly, your paper will be more readable for the effort.

Titles

In general, titles of books, full-length plays, films, and periodicals—works that are published as independent physical entities—are italicized in print or underlined when typed: *Pride and Prejudice* or *Death of a Salesman,* for example. On the other hand, titles of *parts of* books or periodicals—such as poems, short stories, essays, and one-act plays—are enclosed in quotation marks: "Everyday Use," "Krapp's Last Tape," and so on. (If you read newspapers often, you may find this confusing; since newspapers generally do not use italics, they enclose *all* titles in quotation marks.) For your own title of your paper, use neither underlining nor quotation marks. And with any title, capitalize the first word, the last word, and all other words except prepositions, coordinating conjunctions, and articles.

Quotations

Quotations from the work or works of literature you are discussing can often clarify and enrich your writing. Quotations can serve as evidence for points you want to argue and can help give your readers a feel for the work itself. But you should avoid quoting too often and should only quote a passage at length if you discuss it in some detail, for at least as long as the quotation itself. Your own words should provide adequate context and identification for whatever you quote, so that your reader does not get lost.

Generally, quotations of more than four typed lines of prose or more than two or three lines of poetry should be set off from your own text. Indent each line of these "block" quotations five spaces from the left margin, and do not use quotation marks (except any that appear in the original), since the indenting itself indicates that you are quoting. Poetry should be reproduced exactly as it is in the printed source—linebreaks, layout and so on. Shorter quotations should simply be integrated into your text, with quotation marks at the beginning and at the end of the quotation:

> The narrator in "A Drop in the Bucket" remembers Cousin Tryphena's "somnolent, respectable, unprofitable life."

Short quotations of poetry that span the break between lines should preserve any capitalization at the beginning of a new line and should use a slash to indicate where each new line begins:

> Death had entered the Garden of Love, for the speaker "saw it was filled with graves,/ And tomb-stones where flowers should be."

If you are quoting from a longer poem, say longer than 14 lines, include the line number(s) in parentheses following the quote, for example, (ll. 15–16).

It is essential to quote your original source accurately, but you may sometimes want to insert or delete words for the sake of clarity, brevity, or smooth integration of the quotation into your own text. An insertion is enclosed in square brackets and a deletion is indicated with an ellipsis (three dots):

> "He [Nelson Reed] was a steady husband . . . and a deacon in the Baptist church," we learn early in the story.

Generally, when a quote is in the middle of a sentence the page numbers can go at the end of the sentence, before the period, for example, ". . . the Baptist church," we learn early in the story (12).

In a block quotation, the deletion of a paragraph or more of prose or a line or more of poetry is indicated by a line of spaced dots:

> We are warned to be especially careful this time of year:
>
> > He knows if you are sleeping.
> > . . . .
> > He knows if you've been bad or good.

Here, though literally only two lines of poetry are quoted, the block format is preferable because otherwise the combination of ellipsis and line breaks would be awkward.

Punctuating short quotations that are merged with your own text takes some care. Periods and commas go inside (that is, before) closing quotation marks, unless the quotation is followed by page number, line number, or other information about the source of the quotation:

> Owen describes the dying soldier's face as "like a devil's sick of sin."

But

Kingsolver writes of "the years it took to be home again" (line 24).

Punctuation marks other than periods and commas go outside the quotation marks, unless they belong to the quoted material:

What does the chief engineer mean by "irresponsible victims"?

But

Hayden ends with a question that gains force through repetition: "What did I know, what did I know/ of love's austere and lonely offices?"

Finally, in short quotations, when the quoted material itself contains quotation marks, they are replaced by *single* quotation marks:

Her mother, the narrator, says that Maggie "thinks her sister has held life always in the palm of one hand, that 'no' is a word the world never learned to say to her."

Documentation

A source may be classified as either a primary source, that is, a work of literature you are writing about; or a secondary source, a work related to or about the primary source, such as a biography, a history, or a work of literary criticism. The mechanics of quoting are the same for secondary sources as they are for primary sources, as described earlier. Your writing should indicate what sources you used and how you used them. If you quote from a source, you need to indicate where in that source you quoted from. If you borrow ideas from a secondary source—even if you don't copy the language of that source—you need to document that borrowing as well. Documentation can help an interested reader pursue your ideas further or a skeptical reader check up on you. Documentation can also serve to distinguish your own ideas from those you discovered in secondary sources, a distinction most instructors consider very important.

There are two major systems for documenting sources. Traditionally, a raised number in the text points to a numbered note at the bottom of the page (a footnote) or at the end of an essay (an endnote) that provides bibliographical information about the source. However, since 1984 the Modern Language Association, borrowing from the sciences and the social sciences, has recommended a "Works Cited" approach, in which a single alphabetical list at the end of an essay provides bibliographical data about all sources, and brief parenthetical references in the text point to particular items in the list. The endnote/footnote method is probably easier for readers, while the Works Cited method is undoubtedly easier for writers. Though the endnote/footnote method is falling out of favor, both methods are still in use and both will be explained here, at least briefly. For a fuller explanation of both methods, see Joseph Gibaldi's *MLA Handbook for Writers of Research Papers,* 5th edition.

1. The Works Cited Approach

A list of works cited should come after the end of your text and begin on a new page, headed simply: Works Cited. The list should include every work explicitly cited in the text and no others. Works should be listed alphabetically, by author's last name or, if the name is unknown, by title. If there are two or more works by one author, they should be listed one after another, arranged in reverse chronological order by publication date; and in entries after the first, the author's name should be replaced by three hyphens. Each entry should begin at the left margin and lines after the first line of an entry should be indented five spaces.

The list that follows illustrates the form for several common types of Works Cited entries:

A book by one author
Williams, Raymond. *Drama From Ibsen to Brecht.* New York: Oxford UP, 1969.
(Note that periods follow the author's name, the title, and the publication data; a colon follows the place of publication; and a comma follows the publisher's name. "UP" stands for "University Press.")

A book by two authors
Gilbert, Sandra M., and Susan Gubar. *The Madwoman in the Attic: The Woman Writer and the Nineteenth-Century Literary Imagination.* New Haven: Yale UP, 1979.
(Note that the name of the second author is in normal order: first name, then last name.)

A work in an anthology or collection
McKay, Claude. "The White House." *Call and Response: The Riverside Anthology of the African American Literary Tradition.* Ed. Patricia Liggins Hill et al. Boston: Houghton Mifflin, 1998. 885.
("Ed." means "edited by"; "et al." means "and others" and is sometimes used when there are more than three authors. The number after the date indicates the page on which the poem appears.)

Multiple works in an anthology or collection
Hill, Patricia Liggins, et al., eds. *Call and Response: The Riverside Anthology of the African American Literary Tradition.* Boston: Houghton Mifflin, 1998.

Bambara, Toni Cade. "My Man Bovanne." Hill et al. 1789–1792.
(If you are citing more than one work from an anthology, you can either
(1) provide a full citation, like the preceding McKay citation, for each
work or (2) provide one full citation, under the editor's name, for the anthology itself and then use a shortened citation, like the Bambara citation
here, for each work in the anthology that you want to refer to.)

An introduction, preface, foreword, or afterword
Aaron, Daniel. Introduction. *The Disinherited.* By Jack Conroy. New
York: Hill and Wang, 1963. vii–xiv.

A translation
Duras, Marguerite. *The War: A Memoir.* Trans. Barbara Bray. New York:
Pantheon, 1986.

A journal article
Booth, Wayne C. "The Ethics of Teaching Literature." *College English* 61
(1998): 41–55.
(The number immediately after the title of the journal is the volume number. *College English* numbers pages continuously; there are six monthly
issues per volume and each new volume, rather than each new issue, begins with page 1. If, instead, a journal begins each new *issue* with page 1,
then the year and page number[s] alone will usually not suffice to point
to a unique place in the volume and a more precise date such as "[Sep-
tember 1998]" or "[Spring 1999]" is necessary.)

A film, DVD, or video recording
Casablanca. Dir. Michael Curtiz. Perf. Humphrey Bogart and Ingrid
Bergman. Warner Bros., 1942.

A song
Shakur, Tupac. "Dear Mama." *Me Against the World.* Amaru/Jive, 1995.

Electronic Resources

An entire Web site

Poets.org. The Academy of American Poets. 15 Sept. 2003. http://www.poets.org/

A full online citation should include the following information in order:

- title of Web site (italicized or underlined)
- the author or organization who has created and maintains the site
- the date the site was created (if possible)
- the date visited for information
- the complete URL (address)

Due to the ever-changing conventions of Web pages, you may not always find all of the information noted above, especially the actual date a Web site was created (see above example). If this is the case, then provide as much information as you can so that a reader would be able to find the site.

An Online book
Elbow, Peter. *Writing With Power.* New York: Oxford University Press, 1998. *Questia.* 23 August 2005 http://www.questia.com/

An Online article
Lawton, Lee. Rev. of *Foxfire,* by Joyce Carol Oates. *Women's Book On-line.* 16 August 1998 <http://home.cybergrrl.com/review>.
(Internet documentation form is still evolving, but citations should probably include the author, title, print source if the Web source derives from one, date the source was accessed, and Web address and/or database service name.)

An article or essay through your library databases
Jarraway, Daviod. "Montage of an Otherness Deferred: Dreaming Subjectivity in Langston Hughes." *American Literature* 44(1996): 819–847. JSTOR—*The Scholarly Journal Archive.* University of Massachusetts Boston, Healey Library, 20 August 2005. http://www.jstor.org.
Your library subscribes to various online databases and journals with access to the complete texts of articles. When you find a source through your library's services, often the link will be a temporary link—meaning the link is different every time a new search is instigated. If this is the case, simply provide the home page address for the service accessed.

Citing in your Paper

The overall as well as common sense criterion of good documentation is this: Can someone else find your source? You need to provide sufficient information so that anyone can follow up on your citations and find the article or other document.

Parenthetical references in your text will indicate that you have quoted from or used ideas or information from specific sources in the Works Cited list. The items in this list are whole works (books, articles, poems, and so on), but you will usually want to cite particular pages of these works, so your parenthetical citations should indicate page numbers as well as sources. In general, a parenthetical citation should include the minimum information necessary to point to a specific place in a unique work on the list.

If your Works Cited list contains only one work by the author in question, you can simply provide the author's last name and the page number(s) you wish to cite:

She sees "a supernatural weariness in his smile" (Duras 54).

The parenthetical citation here tells us that the quote appears on page 54 of the work by Duras on the list of Works Cited. If your text itself indicates the author you are citing, you can simply supply the page number:

Duras sees "a supernatural weariness in his smile" (54).

If two authors on your list have the same last name, supply the first name as well in parenthetical citations. If the work cited has two authors, use the last name of each: (Gilbert and Gubar 26). If there is no known author, supply the full or a shortened version of the title. If the list contains more than one work by the same author, use the author's name together with a full or shortened version of the title: (Williams, *Drama* 147).

2. The Endnote/Footnote Approach

This method of documenting sources uses raised numbers in the text, each of which corresponds to a numbered footnote at the bottom of the page or endnote at the end of the essay. The 1995 *MLA Handbook* recommends endnotes over footnotes, but footnotes still have their champions. Notes of either kind are numbered consecutively, beginning with "1," and the raised number in the text follows any punctuation except a dash.

Here is the text:

She sees "a supernatural weariness in his smile."[1]

Here is the corresponding note:

[1]Marguerite Duras, *The War: A Memoir,* trans. Barbara Bray (New York: Pantheon, 1986) 54.

This approach differs from the Works Cited approach in several ways. The page number here is provided not in the text but in the note, along with the rest of the bibliographical information. Since there is no Works Cited list to be alphabetized by last name, the author's name appears in normal order in notes. And the first line of each note is indented five spaces, while any lines that follow begin at the left margin.

Note 1 illustrates the form for a translated book. Following are other examples from the earlier discussion of the Works Cited approach, but recast as notes. Each illustrates the form for a common type of source:

[2]Raymond Williams, *Drama From Ibsen to Brecht* (New York: Oxford UP, 1969) 147.

[3]Sandra M. Gilbert and Susan Gubar, *The Madwoman in the Attic: The Woman Writer and the Nineteenth-Century Literary Imagination* (New Haven: Yale UP, 1979) 36.

[4]Claude McKay, "The White House," *Call and Response: The Riverside Anthology of the African American Literary Tradition,* ed. Patricia Liggins Hill et al. (Boston: Houghton Mifflin, 1998) 885.

[5]Daniel Aaron, introduction, *The Disinherited,* by Jack Conroy (New York: Hill and Wang, 1963) ix.

[6]Wayne C. Booth, "The Ethics of Teaching Literature," *College English* 61 (1998): 49.

Full documentation need not be provided in references after the first reference to a particular work. Generally, the author's last name and the appropriate page number(s) will suffice, though more information (such as a first name or a shortened title) may sometimes be necessary to avoid ambiguity. A second reference to the article cited in note 6 might use a note like this:π

[7]Booth 44–45.

If the same work is cited many times in succession in the text, as it well may be in an essay about a single literary work, citations after the first may be given parenthetically (simply the page number) rather than in notes. This can reduce the needless clutter of a series of notes that are identical except for page numbers. And if the same work is cited repeatedly, but not successively, the author's last name plus the page number(s) can substitute for a note.

Explanatory Footnotes

An explanatory footnote may be used by a writer to provide additional information to clarify or expand on a thought that might otherwise impede the flow of the writer's ideas if inserted into the main body of a text. In the following passage from Barry Lopez's nonfiction work *Arctic Dreams* (1986), the explanatory footnote is marked by an asterisk (*) to signify to the reader that more information related to the current paragraph can be found at the bottom of the page. Lopez is writing about the "oscillation" of the Alaskan landscape during the transition from winter to spring.

> The spring silence is broken by pistol reports of cracking on the river, and then the sound of breaking branches and the whining pop of a falling tree as the careening blocks of ice gouge the riverbanks. A related but far eerier phenomenon occurs in the coastal ice. Suddenly in the middle of winter

and without warning a huge piece of sea ice surges hundreds of feet inland, like something alive. The Eskimo call it *ivu*.*

---

*Eskimo descriptions of this phenomenon were not taken seriously until 1982, when archeologists working at Utqiagvik, a prehistoric village site near Barrow, Alaska, discovered a family of five people that had been crushed to death in such an incident.

The line above the footnote isn't always used, but it aids in telling the reader that this footnote is complementary to the main body of text. In this case, Lopez adds an important anecdote that vividly expands his ideas without hindering the coherency of his ideas.

Explanatory footnotes may be numbered consecutively throughout a text or marked by an asterisk (as above) or other symbol that tells the reader there is more information at the bottom of the page. Asterisks tend to be used when there are very few explanatory footnotes, certainly no more than one per page, and numbers used when there are several such explanatory footnotes. Barbara Ehrenreich's footnotes in *Nickel and Dimed: On (Not) Getting By in America* (2001) are extensive and provide a parallel and authoritative commentary on the personal narrative of her investigation of minimum wage work in the United States at the end of the twentieth century. Ehrenreich's goal was, through personal experience, to discover whether she could in fact work a minimum wage job and make enough to live. She looks for jobs, works them, and spends a lot of time trying to find an affordable place to live. Here, she has just been offered a job, but "Now thoroughly unnerved, I tell him I'm not working an eleven-hour shift, not without time and a half after eight. I don't tell him about the generations of workers who fought and sometimes died for the ten hour day and then the eight, although this is very much on my mind." (4) Her footnote reads:

> [4] Under the Fair Labor Standards Act it is in fact illegal not to pay time and a half for hours worked above forty hours per week. Certain categories of workers—professionals, managers, and farmworkers—are not covered by the FLSA, but retail workers are not among them.

Ehrenreich has a total of thirteen footnotes in this one chapter. Most of them are explanatory or a combination of explanatory and citation and so she is using the footnote rather than Works Cited approach to include both, and putting those notes at the bottom of the appropriate page rather than in a Notes section at the back of her book. This makes sense, since *Nickel and Dimed* is aimed at a nonacademic audience and since her footnotes are in continual dialogue with her narrative.

In contrast, Alicia Ostriker, in *Stealing the Language: The Emergence of Women's Poetry in America* (1986), is writing more to an academic audience of students and literary scholars, so her combination of explanatory and citational footnotes is placed at the end of her book and takes the place of a Works Cited section. It is also possible to have a Works Cited section at the end of your paper and to include occasional explanatory footnotes, using either a number system or an asterisk.

Final Manuscript Preparation

Unless your instructor tells you otherwise, try to follow these general guidelines. If it is at all possible, type or word process your essay; otherwise, write neatly with dark ink. Double space your entire essay, including block quotations, footnotes, and the list of Works Cited, and, if you have a choice, select a clear, simple, 12 point font. Use white, $8\frac{1}{2} \times 11$-inch paper, type or print on one side only, and leave top, bottom, left, and right margins of at least an inch. Make sure your typewriter or printer prints reasonably darkly, and if your printer has more than one print mode, use the highest quality mode.

Put a title and your name at the top of the first page. Number each page and put your last name before the page number on each page after the first, in case your pages get separated. Proofread your paper carefully and, if you can't type or print it out again, make corrections neatly in pen. Keep a photocopy or extra printout of your paper in case the original is lost or your computer dies. Last, simply paper clip the pages together; avoid binders or staples and save your instructor a headache or a puncture wound trying to undo them.

At this point, you can congratulate yourself: Your paper is done.

GROWING UP
AND GROWING OLDER

Velino "Shije" Herrera. Story Teller, ca. 1925–1935, gouache and pencil on artist's board,
10¹/₁₆″ × 15¹/₁₆″. National Museum of American Art, Washington, D.C./Art Resource, NY.

Birth, childhood, puberty, adolescence, adulthood, pregnancy, childbirth, parenting, middle age, aging and old age, death whether it comes early or late: stretching behind us and before us are the stages of life, as well as the one we are currently struggling with and enjoying. Writers of all sorts have celebrated, explored, and puzzled about the entire continuum of human life, sometimes focusing on a moment somewhere in the journey between birth and death, sometimes merging events and images from different stages (as when on the brink of adulthood we might look back at a significant moment in our childhood that helps us understand whom we are now), sometimes telling in circular, linear, or fragmented fashion the story of an entire life. As readers, our own sense of the variety, complexity, and continuity of human life is enriched by the array of human lives we touch through literature. More often than we might suspect, a life stage is the subject of a work of literature—the realization, for example, that might be at the center of the main character's or persona's sudden awareness of the slide from middle to old age, from childhood to adult understanding.

How do people, in life and in literature, construct and maintain an identity as they move through the stages of life, growing up and growing older? What provides continuity? What provokes change? How do people cope with the changes that different life stages bring? How we as individuals experience the various stages of life is inextricably tied to our social context.

What would the experience of birth and infancy be like if we had all been test-tube babies? In the opening scenes of *Brave New World,* Aldous Huxley shows us an assembly line of bottled babies and their early conditioning, before and after they are "decanted," for the social roles from laborer through technician to ruler that they will be expected to fill as adults. Huxley's "brave new world," his totally planned society, represents an extreme example of social conditioning, but, like all dystopian (that is, anti-utopian) writers, he shows us through extrapolation and exaggeration the tendencies and possibilities of our own present world. A second science fiction story, Octavia Butler's "Bloodchild," imagines a socially and biologically symbiotic relationship between humans and an alien species that needs humans in order to reproduce. Coming to adulthood for the protagonist involves the realization of what his role will be in this process and a decision whether he will accept it.

We are all conditioned, however subtly, by the social expectations and assumptions of and about our gender, race, social class, and culture and the historical period in which we live. We are continually pushed toward our "proper" role, and sometimes the conditioning or socialization works and sometimes it doesn't. Jamaica Kincaid's "Girl" captures the voice one young girl from the West Indies hears as she grows up, the admonitions and instructions that encode proper social behavior for a female in her particular culture. The voice in "Girl" may sometimes annoy its recipient, but it is basically loving. Toni Morrison's preadolescent protagonist, Claudia, in the excerpt from her novel *The Bluest Eye,* rebels against the white American cultural standards of beauty represented by the "big blue-eyed Baby Doll" she receives for Christmas. When three girls on the edge of adolescence, in Sandra Cisneros's "The Family of Little Feet," try on dress-up high heels and walk around their urban neighborhood, everyone sees and treats them differently. They discover the excitement and danger of sexual symbols—and it makes them a little sick. Tommy Avicolli Mecca, in "He Defies You Still: The Memoirs of a Sissy," brings us into the world of a young man struggling toward his homosexual identity in a hostile family, school, and church environment.

An important aspect of childhood and adolescence is the relation we have to previous generations—parents, grandparents, and other relatives are important figures for us in early life. The speaker of Theodore Roethke's poem "My Papa's Waltz" remembers how, when he was a small child, his father would come home from work and a few drinks at the bar and dance him into bed. There is love in this poem, but also fear, for the dance is as rough as the life his father leads outside the home. The smell of whiskey on his father's breath, his mother's frown, his father beating time on his head—all these details, along with the poem's sense of breathless energy, add up to a poignant but complicated memory. A lyric poem will often capture one intense moment in a life, while the narrative nature of prose lends itself more easily to the gradual unfolding of a substantial portion of a character's life. James Baldwin's short story "Sonny's Blues" tells us much about the life, from childhood through adulthood, of a young black jazz musician, from the point of view of his older brother—who loves Sonny, is frustrated by him, and finally comes to understand him through listening to the blues music he plays. Nathaniel Hawthorne takes us through one long night with his protagonist, Goodman Brown, as that young man comes to a whole new view of the people in his community he had thought of as role models.

As we enter the twenty-first century, we have fewer rituals marking the passage from one life stage to another than many other times and cultures have had. For example, we do not, as do some cultures, remove young boys from their mother's to their father's house at a prescribed age. We do not send adolescents out into the desert to have a vision and find a name in order to become adults. However, an important rite of passage in many parts of the American South and West traditionally has been the gift to twelve- to thirteen-year-old boys of a gun, which symbolizes independence, responsibility, maturity, and the ability to provide for and to protect your family. In the current social climate, this can be a scary thought and is certainly a topic for discussion. However, in Dorothy Allison's "Gun Crazy," a girl sees no reason why she can't have a gun too. Though young men and women usually leave home to go to college, get married, go to war, or take a job, we rarely mark that change with a recognizable ritual that says to all concerned that one part of your life is over and another is beginning. And what if what is supposed to come next, such as a job, does not? Gwendolyn Brooks's poem "We Real Cool" captures in eight lines the chilly alienation of a gang of unemployed black youths hanging around outside a pool hall. There is an assumption of continuity in contemporary Western life that means, perhaps, that when we move into a new stage we are sometimes confused and unprepared, and in order to maintain an equilibrium, we may have to construct our own meaning for the event, as Wakako Yamauchi's young female protagonist, in

the play "And the Soul Shall Dance," tries to do growing up in her Asian American community. Krapp, the aging protagonist of Samuel Beckett's play, "Krapp's
Last Tape," seems to be struggling with the continuity of the stages of his life by
listening to earlier versions of himself on his tape recorder.

The change from childhood to adulthood is particularly confusing in its current lack of ritual. Female puberty, where the onset of menstruation is a definite
marker of the passage from one life stage to another, is the subject of two nonfiction prose pieces in this section. "No Name Woman," from Maxine Hong
Kingston's *The Woman Warrior,* begins with a cautionary tale from a Chinese
American girl's mother about what can happen to her now that she is able to
get pregnant. She, like her nameless aunt in China, her mother tells her, could
bear a child in shame, be outcast by her village, and be driven to suicide: "Now
that you have started to menstruate, what happened to her could happen to you.
Don't humiliate us. You wouldn't like to be forgotten as if you had never been
born. The villagers are watchful." Welcome to being a woman! If we are female,
we probably remember the warnings we received. And if we are male, we may
remember being told to be careful about getting a girl "in trouble," because we
might then have to marry her.

What makes Kingston's piece so fascinating is in part its particular cultural
context: the young protagonist not only has to cope with growing up female in
America; she carries the weight of her Chinese cultural tradition on her back as
well. How she handles her mother's cautionary tale, how she rewrites it to her
own needs and fits it, in a formally circular way, into the construction of her own
identity, is much of the interest of this story. Kingston takes a "universal" situation (puberty), makes it concrete and specific to a particular cultural tradition,
and shows how a young girl comes to a strong sense of personal identity in spite
of her mother's warnings of female powerlessness and vulnerability. For Audre
Lorde, writing out of her Barbadian American background in *Zami,* puberty is
a cause for relief and celebration; it also provides a rare moment of closeness
and shared female identity with the protagonist's overworked and often unap-
proachable mother. Here, too, though in a more celebratory way, the young
woman's self-image is expressed in terms of her cultural heritage—through the
lushly sensual description of the mortar and pestle her mother brought with
them to the United States.

Brave New World aside, the process of pregnancy and giving birth, like menstruation, is so far an exclusively female experience, (though Octavia Butler's
"Bloodchild" moves into male territory). Of all the major life stages, this one may
be the least written about. Why do you suppose that is the case? Toi Derricotte's
"Transition" is an excerpt from her book-length poem about pregnancy and
childbirth. (Transition is the intense stage of labor immediately preceding the actual birth.) Sharon Olds's "The Language of the Brag" explores in particularly
American terms the heroism of giving birth, while Pat Mora's "Immigrants"
looks at immigrant parents' hopes for their "American" children. Gwendolyn
Brooks's poem "the mother" takes up the issue of abortion. Joy Harjo's personal
essay, "Three Generations of Native American Women's Birth Experience,"

examines cultural traditions around giving birth as well as the intrusion of technology, racism, and classism into what should be a joyful and intimate event.

If giving birth is a woman's experience, aging is something we can all anticipate. Several of the poems, stories, and plays in this section are about middle age and old age. They run the gamut of feeling: from the sense of loss and missed opportunity in T. S. Eliot's "The Love Song of J. Alfred Prufrock" and John Updike's "Ex-Basketball Player" through the acceptance of aging in W. B. Yeats's "Sailing to Byzantium" and Gwendolyn Brooks's "The Bean Eaters" to William Carlos Williams's portrait of sensual enjoyment in "To a Poor Old Woman" and the redefinition of the concept of "old maid" in Irena Klepfisz's "they did not build wings for them." Essex Hemphill in "June 25" and Ron Schreiber in "diagnosis (4-10-86)" consider AIDS, from the perspectives of a sufferer and a partner respectively, and what that disease can do to identity and to personal relations. Shakespeare's sonnet "That time of year thou mayst in me behold" and Lloyd Schwartz's "Leaves" find in natural images matter for contemplation of aging, wisdom, love and self love. Patricia Smith's "Undertaker" views death in the contemporary social and political context of an urban African American community.

Gender, race, culture, social class, national or regional identity, and the time we live in affect how individuals experience every stage of life from birth to death. They shape the details of our separate biographies, particularize experience, and provide vivid and immediate interest. Two final and vividly particular examples: the two main characters in Mary E. Wilkins Freeman's "A Mistaken Charity" are not only old; they are female, they are disabled, they are poor, they come from a long line of poor white and working-class people, and they are proud. All these particulars affect their response to attempts by the charity-minded of their town to put them, "for their own good," into a genteel old ladies' home. At the other end of life, the Native American young man in Sherman Alexie's "Jesus Christ's Half Brother Is Alive and Well on the Spokane Indian Reservation" has adopted an orphaned infant. In vivid journal entries he tells us the story of his and the child's first six years—Will James ever speak? What will he say?—and the protagonist's struggle, in the midst of poverty and low expectations, to become a responsible father. Though all humanity may share certain aspects of each life stage, finally there is no such thing as a "universal" experience of childhood, of adolescence, of parenting, of aging, or of any of the other stages of life. If our experiences were truly universal, life and literature would be excruciatingly boring.

Fiction

ALDOUS HUXLEY (1894–1963)

Grandson of renowned biologist T. H. Huxley, Aldous Huxley was born in Godalming, England, and studied at Eton and Oxford. Unlike his grandfather, Huxley chose not to study science and instead took to reading and analyzing English literature. Initially a poet, Huxley soon found his writing niche in satire and social criticism. By the early 1920s, Huxley was traveling extensively and writing essays, novels and plays critiquing the folly of human behavior. In 1932, Huxley published Brave New World—*an innovative science fiction novel which explores the modernist notion of "dystopia" and a future society deluded by the promise of scientific progress. Among his many writings, other notable works include* Antic Hay *(1923),* Point Counter Point *(1928),* Eyeless in Gaza *(1936), and* Island *(1962). The excerpt below, from* Brave New World, *introduces the reader to "Bokanovsky's Process"—a supposed scientific breakthrough where human twins can be cloned by the thousands.*

FROM *Brave New World* (1932)

A squat grey building of only thirty-four stories. Over the main entrance the words, CENTRAL LONDON HATCHERY AND CONDITIONING CENTRE, and, in a shield, the World State's motto, COMMUNITY, IDENTITY, STABILITY.

The enormous room on the ground floor faced towards the north. Cold for all the summer beyond the panes, for all the tropical heat of the room itself, a harsh thin light glared through the windows, hungrily seeking some draped lay figure, some pallid shape of academic goose-flesh, but finding only the glass and nickel and bleakly shining porcelain of a laboratory. Wintriness responded to wintriness. The overalls of the workers were white, their hands gloved with a pale corpse-coloured rubber. The light was frozen, dead, a ghost. Only from the yellow barrels of the microscopes did it borrow a certain rich and living substance, lying along the polished tubes like butter, streak after luscious streak in long recession down the work tables.

"And this," said the Director opening the door, "is the Fertilizing Room."

Bent over their instruments, three hundred Fertilizers were plunged, as the Director of Hatcheries and Conditioning entered the room, in the scarcely breathing silence, the absent-minded, soliloquizing hum or whistle, of absorbed concentration. A troop of newly arrived students, very young, pink and callow, followed nervously, rather abjectly, at the Director's heels. Each of them carried a notebook, in which, whenever the great man spoke, he desperately scribbled.

Straight from the horse's mouth. It was a rare privilege. The D.H.C. for Central London always made a point of personally conducting his new students round the various departments.

"Just to give you a general idea," he would explain to them. For of course some sort of general idea they must have, if they were to do their work intelligently—though as little of one, if they were to be good and happy members of society, as possible. For particulars, as every one knows, make for virtue and happiness; generalities are intellectually necessary evils. Not philosophers but fretsawyers and stamp collectors compose the backbone of society.

"To-morrow," he would add, smiling at them with a slightly menacing geniality, "you'll be settling down to serious work. You won't have time for generalities. Meanwhile . . ."

Meanwhile, it was a privilege. Straight from the horse's mouth into the notebook. The boys scribbled like mad.

Tall and rather thin but upright, the Director advanced into the room. He had a long chin and big, rather prominent teeth, just covered, when he was not talking, by his full, floridly curved lips. Old, young? Thirty? Fifty? Fifty-five? It was hard to say. And anyhow the question didn't arise; in this year of stability, A.F. 632, it didn't occur to you to ask it.

"I shall begin at the beginning," said the D.H.C. and the more zealous students recorded his intention in their notebooks: *Begin at the beginning.* "These," he waved his hand, "are the incubators." And opening an insulated door he showed them racks upon racks of numbered test-tubes. "The week's supply of ova. Kept," he explained, "at blood heat; whereas the male gametes," and here he opened another door, "they have to be kept at thirty-five instead of thirty-seven.[1] Full blood heat sterilizes." Rams wrapped in theremogene beget no lambs.

Still leaning against the incubators he gave them, while the pencils scurried illegibly across the pages, a brief description of the modern fertilizing process; spoke first, of course, of its surgical introduction—"the operation undergone voluntarily for the good of Society, not to mention the fact that it carries a bonus amounting to six months' salary"; continued with some account of the technique for preserving the excised ovary alive and actively developing; passed on to a consideration of optimum temperature, salinity, viscosity; referred to the liquor in which the detached and ripened eggs were kept; and, leading his charges to the work tables, actually showed them how this liquor was drawn off from the test-tubes; how it was let out drop by drop onto the specially warmed slides of the microscopes; how the eggs which it contained were inspected for abnormalities, counted and transferred to a porous receptacle; how (and he now took them to watch the operation) this receptacle was immersed in a warm bouillon containing free-swimming spermatozoa—at a minimum concentration of one hundred thousand per cubic centimetre, he insisted; and how, after ten minutes, the container was lifted out of the liquor and its contents re-examined; how, if

---

[1]35 and 37 degrees Centigrade are 95 and 98.6 degrees Fahrenheit, respectively.

any of the eggs remained unfertilized, it was again immersed, and, if necessary, yet again; how the fertilized ova went back to the incubators; where the Alphas and Betas remained until definitely bottled; while the Gammas, Deltas and Epsilons were brought out again, after only thirty-six hours, to undergo Bokanovsky's Process.

"Bokanovsky's Process," repeated the Director, and the students underlined the words in their little notebooks.

One egg, one embryo, one adult—normality. But a bokanovskified egg will bud, will proliferate, will divide. From eight to ninety-six buds, and every bud will grow into a perfectly formed embryo, and every embryo into a full-sized adult. Making ninety-six human beings grow where only one grew before. Progress.

"Essentially," the D.H.C. concluded, "bokanovskification consists of a series of arrests of development. We check the normal growth and, paradoxically enough, the egg responds by budding."

Responds by budding. The pencils were busy.

He pointed. On a very slowly band a rack-full of test-tubes was entering a large metal box, another rack-full was emerging. Machinery faintly purred. It took eight minutes for the tubes to go through, he told them. Eight minutes of hard X-rays being about as much as an egg can stand. A few died; of the rest, the least susceptible divided into two; most put out four buds; some eight; all were returned to the incubators, where the buds began to develop; then, after two days, were suddenly chilled, chilled and checked. Two, four, eight, the buds in their turn budded; and having budded were dosed almost to death with alcohol; consequently burgeoned again and having budded—bud out of bud out of bud—were thereafter—further arrest being generally fatal—left to develop in peace. By which time the original egg was in a fair way to becoming anything from eight to ninety-six embryos—a prodigious improvement, you will agree, on nature. Identical twins—but not in piddling twos and threes as in the old viviparous days, when an egg would sometimes accidentally divide; actually by dozens, by scores at a time.

"Scores," the Director repeated and flung out his arms, as though he were distributing largesse. "Scores."

But one of the students was fool enough to ask where the advantage lay.

"My good boy!" The Director wheeled sharply round on him. "Can't you see? Can't you *see?*" He raised a hand; his expression was solemn. "Bokanovsky's Process is one of the major instruments of social stability!"

Major instruments of social stability.

Standard men and women; in uniform batches. The whole of a small factory staffed with the products of a single bokanovskified egg.

"Ninety-six identical twins working ninety-six identical machines!" The voice was almost tremulous with enthusiasm. "You really know where you are. For the first time in history." He quoted the planetary motto. "Community, Identity, Stability." Grand words. "If we could bokanovskify indefinitely the whole problem would be solved."

Solved by standard Gammas, unvarying Deltas, uniform Epsilons. Millions of identical twins. The principle of mass production at last applied to biology.

"But, alas," the Director shook his head, "we *can't* bokanovskify indefinitely."

Ninety-six seemed to be the limit; seventy-two a good average. From the same ovary and with gametes of the same male to manufacture as many batches of identical twins as possible—that was the best (sadly a second best) that they could do. And even that was difficult.

"For in nature it takes thirty years for two hundred eggs to reach maturity. But our business is to stabilize the population at this moment, here and now. Dribbling out twins over a quarter of a century—what would be the use of that?"

Obviously, no use at all. But Podsnap's Technique had immensely accelerated the process of ripening. They could make sure of at least a hundred and fifty mature eggs within two years. Fertilize and bokanovskify—in other words, multiply by seventy-two—and you get an average of nearly eleven thousand brothers and sisters in a hundred and fifty batches of identical twins, all within two years of the same age.

"And in exceptional cases we can make one ovary yield us over fifteen thousand adult individuals."

Beckoning to a fair-haired, ruddy young man who happened to be passing at the moment, "Mr. Foster," he called. The ruddy young man approached. "Can you tell us the record for a single ovary, Mr. Foster?"

"Sixteen thousand and twelve in this Centre," Mr. Foster replied without hesitation. He spoke very quickly, had a vivacious blue eye, and took an evident pleasure in quoting figures. "Sixteen thousand and twelve; in one hundred and eighty-nine batches of identicals. But of course they've done much better," he rattled on, "in some of the tropical Centres. Singapore has often produced over sixteen thousand five hundred; and Mombasa has actually touched the seventeen thousand mark. But then they have unfair advantages. You should see the way a negro ovary responds to pituitary! It's quite astonishing, when you're used to working with European material. Still," he added, with a laugh (but the light of combat was in his eyes and the lift of his chin was challenging), "still, we mean to beat them if we can. I'm working on a wonderful Delta-Minus ovary at this moment. Only just eighteen months old. Over twelve thousand seven hundred children already, either decanted or in embryo. And still going strong. We'll beat them yet."

"That's the spirit I like!" cried the Director, and clapped Mr. Foster on the shoulder. "Come along with us and give these boys the benefit of your expert knowledge."

Mr. Foster smiled modestly. "With pleasure." They went.

In the Bottling Room all was harmonious bustle and ordered activity. Flaps of fresh sow's peritoneum ready cut to the proper size came shooting up in little lifts from the Organ Store in the sub-basement. Whizz and then, click! the lift-hatches flew open; the bottle-liner had only to reach out a hand, take the flap, insert, smooth-down, and before the lined bottle had had time to travel out of reach along the endless band, whizz, click! another flap of peritoneum had shot up from the depths, ready to be slipped into yet another bottle, the next of that slow interminable procession on the band.

Next to the Liners stood the Matriculators. The procession advanced; one by one the eggs were transferred from their test-tubes to the larger containers; deftly the peritoneal lining was slit, the morula dropped into place, the saline solution poured in . . . and already the bottle had passed, and it was the turn of the labellers. Heredity, date of fertilization, membership of Bokanovsky Group—details were transferred from test-tube to bottle. No longer anonymous, but named, identified, the procession marched slowly on; on through an opening in the wall, slowly on into the Social Predestination Room.

"Eighty-eight cubic metres of card-index," said Mr. Foster with relish, as they entered.

"Containing *all* the relevant information," added the Director.

"Brought up to date every morning."

"And co-ordinated every afternoon."

"On the basis of which they make their calculations."

"So many individuals, of such and such quality," said Mr. Foster.

"Distributed in such and such quantities."

"The optimum Decanting Rate at any given moment."

"Unforeseen wastages promptly made good."

"Promptly," repeated Mr. Foster. "If you knew the amount of overtime I had to put in after the last Japanese earthquake!" He laughed good-humouredly and shook his head.

"The Predestinators send in their figures to the Fertilizers."

"Who give them the embryos they ask for."

"And the bottles come in here to be predestinated in detail."

"After which they are sent down to the Embryo Store."

"Where we now proceed ourselves."

And opening a door Mr. Foster led the way down a staircase into the basement.

The temperature was still tropical. They descended into a thickening twilight. Two doors and a passage with a double turn insured the cellar against any possible infiltration of the day.

"Embryos are like photograph film," said Mr. Foster waggishly, as he pushed open the second door. "They can only stand red light."

And in effect the sultry darkness into which the students now followed him was visible and crimson, like the darkness of closed eyes on a summer's afternoon. The bulging flanks of row on receding row and tier above tier of bottles glinted with innumerable rubies, and among the rubies moved the dim red spectres of men and women with purple eyes and all the symptoms of lupus. The hum and rattle of machinery faintly stirred the air.

"Give them a few figures, Mr. Foster," said the Director, who was tired of talking.

Mr. Foster was only too happy to give them a few figures.

Two hundred and twenty metres long, two hundred wide, ten high. He pointed upwards. Like chickens drinking, the students lifted their eyes towards the distant ceiling.

Three tiers of racks: ground floor level, first gallery, second gallery.

The spidery steel-work of gallery above gallery faded away in all directions into the dark. Near them three red ghosts were busily unloading demijohns from a moving staircase.

The escalator from the Social Predestination Room.

Each bottle could be placed on one of fifteen racks, each rack, though you couldn't see it, was a conveyor travelling at the rate of thirty-three and a third centimetres an hour. Two hundred and sixty-seven days at eight metres a day. Two thousand one hundred and thirty-six metres in all. One circuit of the cellar at ground level, one on the first gallery, half on the second, and on the two hundred and sixty-seventh morning, daylight in the Decanting Room. Independent existence—so called.

"But in the interval," Mr. Foster concluded, "we've managed to do a lot to them. Oh, a very great deal." His laugh was knowing and triumphant.

"That's the spirit I like," said the Director once more. "Let's walk round. You tell them everything, Mr. Foster."

Mr. Foster duly told them.

Told them of the growing embryo on its bed of peritoneum. Made them taste the rich blood surrogate on which it fed. Explained why it had to be stimulated with placentin and thyroxin. Told them of the *corpus luteum* extract. Showed them the jets through which at every twelfth metre from zero to 2040 it was automatically injected. Spoke of those gradually increasing doses of pituitary administered during the final ninety-six metres of their course. Described the artificial maternal circulation installed on every bottle at Metre 112; showed them the reservoir of blood-surrogate, the centrifugal pump that kept the liquid moving over the placenta and drove it through the synthetic lung and waste-product filter. Referred to the embryo's troublesome tendency to anæmia, to the massive doses of hog's stomach extract and foetal foal's liver with which, in consequence, it had to be supplied.

Showed them the simple mechanism by means of which, during the last two metres out of every eight, all the embryos were simultaneously shaken into familiarity with movement. Hinted at the gravity of the so-called "trauma of decanting," and enumerated the precautions taken to minimize, by a suitable training of the bottled embryo, that dangerous shock. Told them of the tests for sex carried out in the neighbourhood of metre 200. Explained the system of labelling—a T for the males, a circle for the females and for those who were destined to become freemartins a question mark, black on a white ground.

"For of course," said Mr. Foster, "in the vast majority of cases, fertility is merely a nuisance. One fertile ovary in twelve hundred—that would really be quite sufficient for our purposes. But we want to have a good choice. And of course one must always leave an enormous margin of safety. So we allow as many as thirty per cent. of the female embryos to develop normally. The others get a dose of male sex-hormone every twenty-four metres for the rest of the course. Result: they're decanted as freemartins—structurally quite normal (except," he had to admit, "that they *do* have just the slightest tendency to grow beards), but sterile. Guaranteed sterile. Which brings us at last," continued Mr. Foster, "out of the realm of mere slavish imitation of nature into the much more interesting world of human invention."

He rubbed his hands. For of course, they didn't content themselves with merely hatching out embryos: any cow could do that.

"We also predestine and condition. We decant our babies as socialized human beings, as Alphas or Epsilons, as future sewage workers or future . . ." He was going to say "future World controllers," but correcting himself, said "future Directors of Hatcheries," instead.

The D.H.C. acknowledged the compliment with a smile.

They were passing Metre 320 on rack II. A young Beta-Minus mechanic was busy with screwdriver and spanner on the blood-surrogate pump of a passing bottle. The hum of the electric motor deepened by fractions of a tone as he turned the nuts. Down, down . . . A final twist, a glance at the revolution counter, and he was done. He moved two paces down the line and began the same process on the next pump.

"Reducing the number of revolutions per minute," Mr. Foster explained. "The surrogate goes round slower; therefore passes through the lung at longer intervals; therefore gives the embryo less oxygen. Nothing like oxygen-shortage for keeping an embryo below par." Again he rubbed his hands.

"But why do you want to keep the embryo below par?" asked an ingenuous student.

"Ass!" said the Director, breaking a long silence. "Hasn't it occurred to you that an Epsilon embryo must have an Epsilon environment as well as an Epsilon heredity?"

It evidently hadn't occurred to him. He was covered with confusion.

"The lower the caste," said Mr. Foster, "the shorter the oxygen." The first organ affected was the brain. After that the skeleton. At seventy per cent. of normal oxygen you got dwarfs. At less than seventy eyeless monsters.

"Who are no use at all," concluded Mr. Foster.

Whereas (his voice became confidential and eager), if they could discover a technique for shortening the period of maturation what a triumph, what a benefaction to Society!

"Consider the horse."

They considered it.

Mature at six; the elephant at ten. While at thirteen a man is not yet sexually mature; and is only full-grown at twenty. Hence, of course, that fruit of delayed development, the human intelligence.

"But in Epsilons," said Mr. Foster very justly, "we don't need human intelligence."

Didn't need and didn't get it. But though the Epsilon mind was mature at ten, the Epsilon body was not fit to work till eighteen. Long years of superfluous and wasted immaturity. If the physical development could be speeded up till it was as quick, say, as a cow's, what an enormous saving to the Community!

"Enormous!" murmured the students. Mr. Foster's enthusiasm was infectious.

He became rather technical; spoke of the abnormal endocrine coordination which made men grow so slowly; postulated a germinal mutation to account for it. Could the effects of this germinal mutation be undone? Could the individual Epsilon embryo be made a revert, by a suitable technique, to the normality of dogs and cows? That was the problem. And it was all but solved.

Pilkington, at Mombasa, had produced individuals who were sexually mature at four and full-grown at six and a half. A scientific triumph. But socially useless. Six-year-old men and women were too stupid to do even Epsilon work. And the process was an all-or-nothing one; either you failed to modify at all, or else you modified the whole way. They were still trying to find the ideal compromise between adults of twenty and adults of six. So far without success. Mr. Foster sighed and shook his head.

Their wanderings through the crimson twilight had brought them to the neighbourhood of Metre 170 on Rack 9. From this point onwards Rack 9 was enclosed and the bottles performed the remainder of their journey in a kind of tunnel, interrupted here and there by openings two or three metres wide.

"Heat conditioning," said Mr. Foster.

Hot tunnels alternated with cool tunnels. Coolness was wedded to discomfort in the form of hard X-rays. By the time they were decanted the embryos had a horror of cold. They were predestined to emigrate to the tropics, to be miners and acetate silk spinners and steel workers. Later on their minds would be made to endorse the judgment of their bodies. "We condition them to thrive on heat," concluded Mr. Foster. "Our colleagues upstairs will teach them to love it."

"And that," put in the Director sententiously, "that is the secret of happiness and virtue—liking what you've *got* to do. All conditioning aims at that: making people like their unescapable social destiny."

In a gap between two tunnels, a nurse was delicately probing with a long fine syringe into the gelatinous contents of a passing bottle. The students and their guides stood watching her for a few moments in silence.

"Well, Lenina," said Mr. Foster, when at last she withdrew the syringe and straightened herself up.

The girl turned with a start. One could see that, for all the lupus and the purple eyes, she was uncommonly pretty.

"Henry!" Her smile flashed redly at him—a row of coral teeth.

"Charming, charming," murmured the Director and, giving her two or three little pats, received in exchange a rather deferential smile for himself.

"What are you giving them?" asked Mr. Foster, making his tone very professional.

"Oh, the usual typhoid and sleeping sickness."

"Tropical workers start being inoculated at Metre 150," Mr. Foster explained to the students. "The embryos still have gills. We immunize the fish against the future man's diseases." Then, turning back to Lenina, "Ten to five on the roof this afternoon," he said, "as usual."

"Charming," said the Director once more, and, with a final pat, moved away after the others.

On Rack 10 rows of next generation's chemical workers were being trained in the toleration of lead, caustic soda, tar, chlorine. The first of a batch of two hundred and fifty embryonic rocket-plane engineers was just passing the eleven hundred metre mark on Rack 3. A special mechanism kept their containers in constant rotation. "To improve their sense of balance," Mr. Foster explained. "Doing repairs on the outside of a rocket in mid-air is a ticklish job. We slacken off the circulation when they're right way up, so that they're half starved, and double the flow of surrogate when they're upside down. They learn to associate topsy-turvydom with well-being; in fact, they're only truly happy when they're standing on their heads.

"And now," Mr. Foster went on, "I'd like to show you some very interesting conditioning for Alpha Plus Intellectuals. We have a big batch of them on Rack 5. First Gallery level," he called to two boys who had started to go down to the ground floor.

"They're round about Metre 900," he explained. "You can't really do any useful intellectual conditioning till the foetuses have lost their tails. Follow me."

But the Director had looked at his watch. "Ten to three," he said. "No time for the intellectual embryos, I'm afraid. We must go up to the Nurseries before the children have finished their afternoon sleep."

Mr. Foster was disappointed. "At least one glance at the Decanting Room," he pleaded.

"Very well then." The Director smiled indulgently. "Just one glance."

II

Mr. Foster was left in the Decanting Room. The D.H.C. and his students stepped into the nearest lift and were carried up to the fifth floor.

INFANT NURSERIES. NEO-PAVLOVIAN CONDITIONING ROOMS, announced the notice board.

The Director opened a door. They were in a large bare room, very bright and sunny; for the whole of the southern wall was a single window. Half a dozen nurses, trousered and jacketed in the regulation white viscose-linen uniform, their hair aseptically hidden under white caps, were engaged in setting out bowls of roses in a long row across the floor. Big bowls, packed tight with blossom. Thousands of petals, ripe-blown and silkily smooth, like the cheeks of innumerable little cherubs, but of cherubs, in that bright light, not exclusively pink and Aryan, but also luminously Chinese, also Mexican, also apoplectic with too much blowing of celestial trumpets, also pale as death, pale with the posthumous white-ness of marble.

The nurses stiffened to attention as the D.H.C. came in.

"Set out the books," he said curtly.

In silence the nurses obeyed his command. Between the rose bowls the books were duly set out—a row of nursery quartos opened invitingly each at some gaily coloured image of beast or fish or bird.

"Now bring in the children."

They hurried out of the room and returned in a minute or two, each pushing a kind of tall dumbwaiter laden, on all its four wire-netted shelves, with eight-month-old babies, all exactly alike (a Bokanovsky Group, it was evident) and all (since their caste was Delta) dressed in khaki.

"Put them down on the floor."

The infants were unloaded.

"Now turn them so that they can see the flowers and books."

Turned, the babies at once fell silent, then began to crawl towards those clus-ters of sleek colours, those shapes so gay and brilliant on the white pages. As they approached, the sun came out of a momentary eclipse behind a cloud. The roses flamed up as though with a sudden passion from within; a new and pro-found significance seemed to suffuse the shining pages of the books. From the ranks of the crawling babies came little squeals of excitement, gurgles and twit-terings of pleasure.

The Director rubbed his hands. "Excellent!" he said. "It might almost have been done on purpose."

The swiftest crawlers were already at their goal. Small hands reached out un-certainly, touched, grasped, unpetaling the transfigured roses, crumpling the il-luminated pages of the books. The Director waited until all were happily busy. Then, "Watch carefully," he said. And, lifting his hand, he gave the signal.

The Head Nurse, who was standing by a switchboard at the other end of the room, pressed down a little lever.

There was a violent explosion. Shriller and ever shriller, a siren shrieked. Alarm bells maddeningly sounded.

The children started, screamed; their faces were distorted with terror.

"And now," the Director shouted (for the noise was deafening), "now we pro-ceed to rub in the lesson with a mild electric shock."

He waved his hand again, and the Head Nurse pressed a second lever. The screaming of the babies suddenly changed its tone. There was something des-perate, almost insane, about the sharp spasmodic yelps to which they now gave utterance. Their little bodies twitched and stiffened; their limbs moved jerkily as if to the tug of unseen wires.

"We can electrify that whole strip of floor," bawled the Director in explana-tion. "But that's enough," he signalled to the nurse.

The explosions ceased, the bells stopped ringing, the shriek of the siren died down from tone to tone into silence. The stiffly twitching bodies relaxed, and what had become the sob and yelp of infant maniacs broadened out once more into a normal howl of ordinary terror.

"Offer them the flowers and the books again."

The nurses obeyed; but at the approach of the roses, at the mere sight of those gaily-coloured images of pussy and cock-a-doodle-doo and baa-baa black sheep, the infants shrank away in horror; the volume of their howling suddenly increased.

"Observe," said the Director triumphantly, "observe."

Books and loud noises, flowers and electric shocks—already in the infant mind these couples were compromisingly linked; and after two hundred repetitions of the same or a similar lesson would be wedded indissolubly. What man has joined, nature is powerless to put asunder.

"They'll grow up with what the psychologists used to call an 'instinctive' hatred of books and flowers. Reflexes unalterably conditioned. They'll be safe from books and botany all their lives." The Director turned to his nurses. "Take them away again."

Still yelling, the khaki babies were loaded on to their dumb-waiters and wheeled out, leaving behind them the smell of sour milk and a most welcome silence.

One of the students held up his hand; and though he could see quite well why you couldn't have lower-caste people wasting the Community's time over books, and that there was always the risk of their reading something which might undesirably decondition one of their reflexes, yet . . . well, he couldn't understand about the flowers. Why go to the trouble of making it psychologically impossible for Deltas to like flowers?

Patiently the D.H.C. explained. If the children were made to scream at the sight of a rose, that was on grounds of high economic policy. Not so very long ago (a century or thereabouts), Gammas, Deltas, even Epsilons, had been conditioned to like flowers—flowers in particular and wild nature in general. The idea was to make them want to be going out into the country at every available opportunity, and so compel them to consume transport.

"And didn't they consume transport?" asked the student.

"Quite a lot," the D.H.C. replied. "But nothing else."

Primroses and landscapes, he pointed out, have one grave defect: they are gratuitous. A love of nature keeps no factories busy. It was decided to abolish the love of nature, at any rate among the lower classes; to abolish the love of nature, but *not* the tendency to consume transport. For of course it was essential that they should keep on going to the country, even though they hated it. The problem was to find an economically sounder reason for consuming transport than a mere affection for primroses and landscapes. It was duly found.

"We condition the masses to hate the country," concluded the Director. "But simultaneously we condition them to love all country sports. At the same time, we see to it that all country sports shall entail the use of elaborate apparatus. So that they consume manufactured articles as well as transport. Hence those electric shocks."

"I see," said the student, and was silent, lost in admiration.

There was a silence; then, clearing his throat, "Once upon a time," the Director began, "while our Ford was still on earth, there was a little boy called Reuben Rabinovitch. Reuben was the child of Polish-speaking parents." The Director interrupted himself. "You know what Polish is, I suppose?"

"A dead language."

"Like French and German," added another student, officiously showing off his learning.

"And 'parent'?" questioned the D.H.C.

There was an uneasy silence. Several of the boys blushed. They had not yet learned to draw the significant but often very fine distinction between smut and pure science. One, at last, had the courage to raise a hand.

"Human beings used to be . . ." he hesitated; the blood rushed to his cheeks. "Well, they used to be viviparous."

"Quite right." The Director nodded approvingly.

"And when the babies were decanted . . ."

"'Born',," came the correction.

"Well, then they were the parents—I mean, not the babies, of course; the other ones." The poor boy was overwhelmed with confusion.

"In brief," the Director summed up, "the parents were the father and the mother." The smut that was really science fell with a crash into the boys' eye-avoiding silence. "Mother," he repeated loudly rubbing in the science; and, leaning back in his chair, "These," he said gravely, "are unpleasant facts; I know it. But then most historical facts *are* unpleasant."

He returned to Little Reuben—to Little Reuben, in whose room, one evening, by an oversight, his father and mother (crash, crash!) happened to leave the radio turned on.

("For you must remember that in those days of gross viviparous reproduction, children were always brought up by their parents and not in State Conditioning Centres.")

While the child was asleep, a broadcast programme from London suddenly started to come through; and the next morning, to the astonishment of his crash and crash (the more daring of the boys ventured to grin at one another), Little Reuben woke up repeating word for word a long lecture by that curious old writer ("one of the very few whose works have been permitted to come down to us"), George Bernard Shaw,[2] who was speaking, according to a well-authenticated tradition, about his own genius. To Little Reuben's wink and snigger, this lecture was, of course, perfectly incomprehensible and, imagining that their child had suddenly gone mad, they sent for a doctor. He, fortunately, understood English, recognized the discourse as that which Shaw had broadcasted the previous evening, realized the significance of what had happened, and sent a letter to the medical press about it.

"The principle of sleep-teaching, or hypnopædia, had been discovered." The D.H.C. made an impressive pause.

---

[2](1856–1960), British playwright

The principle had been discovered; but many, many years were to elapse before that principle was usefully applied.

"The case of Little Reuben occurred only twenty-three years after Our Ford's first T-Model was put on the market." (Here the Director made a sign of the T on his stomach and all the students reverently followed suit.) "And yet . . ."

Furiously the students scribbled. "*Hypnopædia, first used officially in A.F. 214. Why not before? Two reasons. (a) . . .*"

"These early experimenters," the D.H.C. was saying, "were on the wrong track. They thought that hypnopædia could be made an instrument of intellectual education . . ."

(A small boy asleep on his right side, the right arm stuck out, the right hand hanging limp over the edge of the bed. Through a round grating in the side of a box a voice speaks softly.

"The Nile is the longest river in Africa and the second in length of all the rivers of the globe. Although falling short of the length of the Mississippi-Missouri, the Nile is at the head of all rivers as regards the length of its basin, which extends through 35 degrees of latitude . . ."

At breakfast the next morning, "Tommy," some one says, "do you know which is the longest river in Africa?" A shaking of the head. "But don't you remember something that begins: The Nile is the . . ."

"The-Nile-is-the-longest-river-in-Africa-and-the-second-in-length-of-all-the-rivers-of-the-globe . . ." The words come rushing out. "Although-falling-short-of . . ."

"Well now, which is the longest river in Africa?"

The eyes are blank. "I don't know."

"But the Nile, Tommy."

"The-Nile-is-the-longest-river-in-Africa-and-second . . ."

"Then which river is the longest, Tommy?"

Tommy bursts into tears. "I don't know," he howls.)

That howl, the Director made it plain, discouraged the earliest investigators. The experiments were abandoned. No further attempt was made to teach children the length of the Nile in their sleep. Quite rightly. You can't learn a science unless you know what it's all about.

"Whereas, if they'd only started on *moral* education," said the Director, leading the way towards the door. The students followed him, desperately scribbling as they walked and all the way up in the lift. "Moral education, which ought never, in any circumstances, to be rational."

"Silence, silence," whispered a loud speaker as they stepped out at the fourteenth floor, and "Silence, silence," the trumpet mouths indefatigably repeated at intervals down every corridor. The students and even the Director himself rose automatically to the tips of their toes. They were Alphas, of course; but even Alphas have been well conditioned. "Silence, silence." All the air of the fourteenth floor was sibilant with the categorical imperative.

Fifty yards of tiptoeing brought them to a door which the Director cautiously opened. They stepped over the threshold into the twilight of a shuttered dormitory. Eighty cots stood in a row against the wall. There was a sound of light regular breathing and a continuous murmur, as of very faint voices remotely whispering.

A nurse rose as they entered and came to attention before the Director.

"What's the lesson this afternoon?" he asked.

"We had Elementary Sex for the first forty minutes," she answered. "But now it's switched over to Elementary Class Consciousness."

The Director walked slowly down the long line of cots. Rosy and relaxed with sleep, eighty little boys and girls lay softly breathing. There was a whisper under every pillow. The D.H.C. halted and, bending over one of the little beds, listened attentively.

"Elementary Class Consciousness, did you say? Let's have it repeated a little louder by the trumpet."

At the end of the room a loud speaker projected from the wall. The Director walked up to it and pressed a switch.

". . . all wear green," said a soft but very distinct voice, beginning in the middle of a sentence, "and Delta Children wear khaki. Oh no, I don't want to play with Delta children. And Epsilons are still worse. They're too stupid to be able to read or write. Besides they wear black, which is such a beastly colour. I'm *so* glad I'm a Beta."

There was a pause; then the voice began again.

"Alpha children wear grey. They work much harder than we do, because they're so frightfully clever. I'm really awfully glad I'm a Beta, because I don't work so hard. And then we are much better than the Gammas and Deltas. Gammas are stupid. They all wear green, and Delta children wear khaki. Oh no, I *don't* want to play with Delta children. And Epsilons are still worse. They're too stupid to be able . . ."

The Director pushed back the switch. The voice was silent. Only its thin ghost continued to mutter from beneath the eighty pillows.

"They'll have that repeated forty or fifty times more before they wake; then again on Thursday, and again on Saturday. A hundred and twenty times three times a week for thirty months. After which they go on to a more advanced lesson."

Roses and electric shocks, the khaki of Deltas and a whiff of asafœtida—wedded indissolubly before the child can speak. But wordless conditioning is crude and wholesale; cannot bring home the finer distinctions, cannot inculcate the more complex courses of behaviour. For that there must be words, but words without reason. In brief, hypnopædia.

"The greatest moralizing and socializing force of all time."

The students took it down in their little books. Straight from the horse's mouth.

Once more the Director touched the switch.

". . . so frightfully clever," the soft, insinuating, indefatigable voice was saying. "I'm really awfully glad I'm a Beta, because . . ."

Not so much like drops of water, though water, it is true, can wear holes in the hardest granite; rather, drops of liquid sealing-wax, drops that adhere, incrust, incorporate themselves with what they fall on, till finally the rock is all one scarlet blob.

"Till at last the child's mind *is* these suggestions, and the sum of the suggestions *is* the child's mind. And not the child's mind only. The adult's mind too— all his life long. The mind that judges and desires and decides—made up of these suggestions. But all these suggestions are *our* suggestions!" The Director almost shouted in his triumph. "Suggestions from the State." He banged the nearest table. "It therefore follows ..."

A noise made him turn around.

"Oh, Ford!" he said in another tone, "I've gone and woken the children."

Study and Discussion Questions

1. Why, in the world of *Brave New World,* are babies manufactured rather than born? Why are they conditioned so thoroughly once they've been made?
2. Who is "Our Ford" and why is the present year called "A.F. 632"? Why does the Director (when he is explaining the discovery of hypnopaedia) make "a sign of the T on his stomach" when he mentions "Our Ford"?
3. Why does Huxley repeatedly emphasize the diligence with which the students copy down the Director's every word?
4. What are some of the ways Huxley shapes our attitude toward the society he describes? Begin by looking at the imagery in the second paragraph.
5. What can we infer, from these first two chapters, about the political and economic structure of the society depicted in *Brave New World?*

Suggestions for Writing

1. Critics often discuss science fiction and utopian or dystopian literature in terms of "extrapolation," that is, a projection of current social trends into a distant future. What aspects of twentieth-century society are illuminated (and satirized) in this extrapolation?
2. The society of *Brave New World,* we learn later, provides its inhabitants with material abundance, unlimited physical pleasure, and freedom from unhappiness. Then what exactly is wrong with this society?
3. Is social conditioning always bad? What criteria could you suggest for deciding when it is good and when it is not? And how it should be accomplished?

Critical Resources

1. Baker, Robert. *Brave New World: History, Science and Dystopia.* Boston: Twayne, 1990.
2. Meckier, Jerome, ed. *Critical Essays on Aldous Huxley.* London: Prentice Hall, 1996.
3. Murray, Nicholas. *Aldous Huxley.* New York: St. Martin's Press, 2003.
4. Sexton, James. "Aldous Huxley's Bokanovsky" *Science Fiction Studies.* March 1989: 84–89.

❀ ❀ ❀

JAMAICA KINCAID (b. 1950)

Elaine Potter Richardson (Kincaid's original name) was born in St. John's, Antigua, in the Caribbean. The only daughter in a family of four children, Richardson left Antigua for the United States in 1966 at the age of 17 and entered the New School for Social Research in New York City to study photography and began to write. In 1973, Richardson changed her name to Jamaica Kincaid so she could write anonymously and in 1976 landed a job as a staff writer at The New Yorker, *a job she held until 1995. While at* The New Yorker, *Kincaid published a collection of short stories,* At the Bottom of the River *(1983), as well as the novels* Annie John *(1985),* Lucy *(1990), and* A Small Place *(1988)—a book-length essay on the British legacy in Antigua after independence in 1981. Since 1995, Kincaid's works include* Autobiography of My Mother *(1996),* My Brother *(1997),* My Favorite Plant *(1988), and* My Garden Book *(1999). She currently teaches and lives in Bennington, Vermont. "Girl" is an early example of a recurring theme in Kincaid's work: the complex relationship between mothers and daughters.*

Girl (1983)

Wash the white clothes on Monday and put them on the stone heap; wash the color clothes on Tuesday and put them on the clothesline to dry; don't walk barehead in the hot sun; cook pumpkin fritters in very hot sweet oil; soak your little cloths right after you take them off; when buying cotton to make yourself a nice blouse, be sure that it doesn't have gum on it, because that way it won't hold up well after a wash; soak salt fish overnight before you cook it; is it true that you sing benna[1] in Sunday school?; always eat your food in such a way that it won't turn someone else's stomach; on Sundays try to walk like a lady and not like the slut you are so bent on becoming; don't sing benna in Sunday school; you mustn't speak to wharf-rat boys, not even to give directions; don't eat fruits on the street—flies will follow you; *but I don't sing benna on Sundays at all and never in Sunday school;* this is how to sew on a button; this is how to make a buttonhole for the button you have just sewed on; this is how to hem a dress when you see the hem coming down and so to prevent yourself from looking like the slut I know you are so bent on becoming; this is how you iron your father's khaki shirt so that it doesn't have a crease; this is how you iron your father's khaki pants so that they don't have a crease; this is how you grow okra—far from the house, because okra tree harbors red ants; when you are growing dasheen, make sure it gets plenty of water or else it makes your throat itch when you are eating it; this is how you sweep a corner; this is how you sweep a whole house; this is how you sweep a yard; this is how you smile to someone you don't like too

---

[1]Calypso or rock and roll.

much; this is how you smile to someone you don't like at all; this is how to smile to someone you like completely; this is how you set a table for tea; this is how you set a table for dinner; this is how you set a table for dinner with an important guest; this is how you set a table for lunch; this is how you set a table for breakfast, this is how to behave in the presence of men who don't know you very well, and this way they won't recognize immediately the slut I have warned you against becoming; be sure to wash every day, even if it is with your own spit: don't squat down to play marbles—you are not a boy, you know; don't pick people's flowers—you might catch something; don't throw stones at blackbirds, because it might not be a blackbird at all; this is how to make a bread pudding; this is how to make doukona; this is how to make pepper pot; this is how to make a good medicine for a cold; this is how to make a good medicine to throw away a child before it even becomes a child; this is how to catch a fish; this is how to throw back a fish you don't like, and that way something bad won't fall on you; this is how to bully a man; this is how a man bullies you; this is how to love a man, and if this doesn't work there are other ways, and if they don't work don't feel too bad about giving up; this is how to spit up in the air if you feel like it, and this is how to move quick so that it doesn't fall on you; this is how to make ends meet; always squeeze bread to make sure it's fresh; *but what if the baker won't let me feel the bread?;* you mean to say that after all you are really going to be the kind of woman who the baker won't let near the bread?

Study and Discussion Questions

1. Who is speaking? To whom? How old do you think the girl being addressed is?
2. Categorize and characterize the advice given.
3. What seems to be the speaker's main concern? What evidence is there that she has it in mind even when she's not talking about it directly?
4. Analyze the impact of the narrator's stringing so many words of advice together. What else makes the story funny?

Suggestions for Writing

1. What would the girl grow up to be like if the followed all the advice given? Discuss the story as a comment on women's roles in society.
2. Choose someone—a parent, older sibling, employer, teacher—who gives too much advice and write a short piece modeled on "Girl."

Critical Resources

1. Ferguson, Moira. *Jamaica Kincaid: Where the Land Meets the Body.* Charlottesville, VA: U of Virginia P, 1994.
2. Paravisini, Moira. *Jamaica Kincaid: A Critical Companion.* Westport, CT: Greenwood, 1999.

3. Vorda, Allan. "An Interview with Jamaica Kincaid." *Mississippi Review* 20
    1.2 (1991): 7–26.

TONI MORRISON (b. 1931)

*Born in Lorain, Ohio, Toni Morrison received a B.A. in English from Howard
University and her M.A. in English at Cornell. Yet it was her early life experiences
in Ohio that would become a cornerstone of her writing: "No matter what I write,
I begin there . . . Ohio offers an escape from the stereotyped black settings. It is
neither plantation or ghetto"* (Black Women Writers at Work, *1986). From such
a vantage point, Morrison has sought to offer a more complicated version of the
African American experience—one infused with myth and folklore, race and identity. After teaching for a few years, Morrison accepted a position as a book editor
at Random House in New York in 1964. In 1969, Morrison published her first
book,* The Bluest Eye, *at the age of 38. She spent the next 25 years at Random
House, helping raise public awareness of other black writers as well as publishing
her own work:* Sula *(1973);* Song of Solomon *(1977);* Tar Baby *(1981);* Beloved
(1987), which won the Pulitzer Prize for Fiction; Jazz *(1992);* Paradise *(1998); and
her most recent novel,* Love *(2003). In addition to her novels Morrison has written and edited several critical works, including* Playing in the Dark: Whiteness and
the Literary Imagination *(1992), and coauthored several children's books with her
son Slade Morrison. In 1993, Morrison became the first African American to win
the Nobel Prize for literature. The excerpt below, taken from* The Bluest Eye,
*looks at a young black girl's reaction to the "blue-eyed, yellow-haired, pink-
skinned doll" given to her for Christmas.*

FROM *The Bluest Eye*   (1970)

It had begun with Christmas and the gift of dolls. The big, the special, the loving gift was always a big, blue-eyed Baby Doll. From the clucking sounds of
adults I knew that the doll represented what they thought was my fondest wish.
I was bemused with the thing itself, and the way it looked. What was I supposed
to do with it? Pretend I was its mother? I had no interest in babies or the concept of motherhood. I was interested only in humans my own age and size, and
could not generate any enthusiasm at the prospect of being a mother. Motherhood was old age, and other remote possibilities. I learned quickly, however, what
I was expected to do with the doll: rock it, fabricate storied situations around it,
even sleep with it. Picture books were full of little girls sleeping with their dolls.
Raggedy Ann dolls usually, but they were out of the question. I was physically

revolted by and secretly frightened of those round moronic eyes, the pancake face, and orangeworms hair.

The other dolls, which were supposed to bring me great pleasure, succeeded in doing quite the opposite. When I took it to bed, its hard unyielding limbs resisted my flesh—the tapered fingertips on those dimpled hands scratched. If, in sleep, I turned, the bone-cold head collided with my own. It was a most uncomfortable, patently aggressive sleeping companion. To hold it was no more rewarding. The starched gauze or lace on the cotton dress irritated any embrace. I had only one desire: to dismember it. To see of what it was made, to discover the dearness, to find the beauty, the desirability that had escaped me, but apparently only me. Adults, older girls, shops, magazines, newspapers, window signs—all the world had agreed that a blue-eyed, yellow-haired, pink-skinned doll was what every girl child treasured. "Here," they said, "this is beautiful, and if you are on this day 'worthy' you may have it." I fingered the face, wondering at the single-stroke eyebrows; picked at the pearly teeth stuck like two piano keys between red bowline lips. Traced the turned-up nose, poked the glassy blue eyeballs, twisted the yellow hair. I could not love it. But I could examine it to see what it was that all the world said was lovable. Break off the tiny fingers, bend the flat feet, loosen the hair, twist the head around, and the thing made one sound—a sound they said was the sweet and plaintive cry "Mama," but which sounded to me like the bleat of a dying lamb, or, more precisely, our icebox door opening on rusty hinges in July. Remove the cold and stupid eyeball, it would bleat still, "Ahhhhhh," take off the head, shake out the sawdust, crack the back against the brass bed rail, it would bleat still. The gauze back would split, and I could see the disk with six holes, the secret of the sound. A mere metal roundness.

Grown people frowned and fussed: "You-don't-know-how-to-take-care-of-nothing. I-never-had-a-baby-doll-in-my-whole-life-and-used-to-cry-my-eyes-out-for-them. Now-you-got-one-a-beautiful-one-and-you-tear-it-up-what's-the-matter-with-you?"

How strong was their outrage. Tears threatened to erase the aloofness of their authority. The emotion of years of unfulfilled longing preened in their voices. I did not know why I destroyed those dolls. But I did know that nobody ever asked me what I wanted for Christmas. Had any adult with the power to fulfill my desires taken me seriously and asked me what I wanted, they would have known that I did not want to have anything to own, or to possess any object. I wanted rather to feel something on Christmas day. The real question would have been, "Dear Claudia, what experience would you like on Christmas?" I could have spoken up, "I want to sit on the low stool in Big Mama's kitchen with my lap full of lilacs and listen to Big Papa play his violin for me alone." The lowness of the stool made for my body, the security and warmth of Big Mama's kitchen, the smell of the lilacs, the sound of the music, and, since it would be good to have all of my senses engaged, the taste of a peach, perhaps, afterward.

Instead I tasted and smelled the acridness of tin plates and cups designed for tea parties that bored me. Instead I looked with loathing on new dresses that required a hateful bath in a galvanized zinc tub before wearing. Slipping around on the zinc, no time to play or soak, for the water chilled too fast, no time to enjoy one's nakedness, only time to make curtains of soapy water careen down between the legs. Then the scratchy towels and the dreadful and humiliating absence of dirt. The irritable, unimaginative cleanliness. Gone the ink marks from legs and face, all my creations and accumulations of the day gone, and replaced by goose pimples.

I destroyed white baby dolls.

But the dismembering of dolls was not the true horror. The truly horrifying thing was the transference of the same impulses to little white girls. The indifference with which I could have axed them was shaken only by my desire to do so. To discover what eluded me: the secret of the magic they weaved on others. What made people look at them and say, "Awwwww," but not for me? The eye slide of black women as they approached them on the street, and the possessive gentleness of their touch as they handled them.

If I pinched them, their eyes—unlike the crazed glint of the baby doll's eyes—would fold in pain, and their cry would not be the sound of an icebox door, but a fascinating cry of pain. When I learned how repulsive this disinterested violence was, that it was repulsive because it was disinterested, my shame floundered about for refuge. The best hiding place was love. Thus the conversion from pristine sadism to fabricated hatred, to fraudulent love. It was a small step to Shirley Temple. I learned much later to worship her, just as I learned to delight in cleanliness, knowing, even as I learned, that the change was adjustment without improvement.

Study and Discussion Questions

1. Why do adults give dolls to little girls?
2. Why does Claudia hate Shirley Temple?
3. What's wrong with the Christmas baby doll Claudia is given?
4. What would Claudia really like for Christmas?
5. How does Claudia's description of the doll undermine its purported beauty? What words and images does Morrison use?
6. What does the paragraph about taking a bath have to do with the subject of baby dolls?
7. Claudia says she transferred her destructive impulses toward dolls "to little white girls." How do you think this happens? Is she justified in feeling this way?
8. Why is love the best hiding place for shame?

Suggestions for Writing

1. Select one of the substantial paragraphs in this excerpt and analyze Morrison's imagery, her language, and how she makes a small unified episode out of the paragraph.
2. Were you given a Christmas or birthday present you hated when you were a child? Write a letter to the giver saying how and why you hated the present.

3. Make an argument for or against giving children toys that socialize them into gender-specific roles as adults. You might pick a particular toy to use as an example.
4. What is "adjustment without improvement" in the context of this piece of writing? What do you think Morrison is saying about how children are socialized—and particularly about how black children are socialized into a white world?

Critical Resources

1. *Beloved.* Dir. Johnathan Demme. Perf. Oprah Winfrey, Danny Glover. Touchstone Pictures, 1998.
2. Gates, Henry Louis and K. Appiah, eds. *Toni Morrison: Critical Perspectives Past and Present.* New York: Amistad, 1993.
3. Gutherie, Danille. *Conversations with Toni Morrison.* Jackson: U of Mississippi P, 1994.
4. Middleton, David. *Toni Morrison's Fiction: Contemporary Criticism.* New York: Garland, 2000.

SANDRA CISNEROS (b. 1954)

Sandra Cisneros spent much of her young life moving with her family back and forth between Chicago, where she was born, and Mexico City. In an often repeated quote, she describes her independent feminine self as the "daughter of a Mexican father and a Mexican-American mother . . . sister to six brothers . . . nobody's mother and nobody's wife" (Introduction, The House on Mango Street, *1991). Cisneros draws frequently on her adolescent experience as a Latina in a working-class household of boys to explore issues of gender and race in both her poetry and prose. Her writings include the poetry collections* Bad Boys *(1980),* My Wicked, Wicked Ways *(1987), and* Loose Woman *(1994); the award-winning* The House on Mango Street *(1984) and* Woman Hollering Creek and Other Stories *(1991); the bilingual juvenile novel* Hairs/Pelitos *(1994); and her most recent prose work,* Caramelo *(2002). The short piece "The Family of Little Feet" is taken from* The House on Mango Street.

The Family of Little Feet   (1984)

There was a family. All were little. Their arms were little, and their hands were little, and their height was not tall, and their feet very small.

The grandpa slept on the living room couch and snored through his teeth. His feet were fat and doughy like thick tamales, and these he powdered and stuffed into white socks and brown leather shoes.

The grandma's feet were lovely as pink pearls and dressed in velvety high heels that made her walk with a wobble, but she wore them anyway because they were pretty.

The baby's feet had ten tiny toes, pale and see-through like a salamander's, and these he popped into his mouth whenever he was hungry.

The mother's feet, plump and polite, descended like white pigeons from the sea of pillow, across the linoleum roses, down down the wooden stairs, over the chalk hopscotch squares. 5, 6, 7, blue sky.

Do you want this? And gave us a paper bag with one pair of lemon shoes and one red and one pair of dancing shoes that used to be white but were now pale blue. Here, and we said thank you and waited until she went upstairs.

Hurray! Today we are Cinderella because our feet fit exactly, and we laugh at Rachel's one foot with a girl's grey sock and a lady's high heel. Do you like these shoes? But the truth is it is scary to look down at your foot that is no longer yours and see attached a long long leg.

Everybody wants to trade. The lemon shoes for the red shoes, the red for the pair that were once white but are now pale blue, the pale blue for the lemon, and take them off and put them back on and keep on like this a long time until we are tired.

Then Lucy screams to take our socks off and yes, it's true. We have legs. Skinny and spotted with satin scars where scabs were picked, but legs, all our own, good to look at, and long.

It's Rachel who learns to walk the best all strutted in those magic high heels. She teaches us to cross and uncross our legs, and to run like a double-dutch rope, and how to walk down to the corner so that the shoes talk back to you with every step. Lucy, Rachel, me tee-tottering like so. Down to the corner where the men can't take their eyes off us. We must be Christmas.

Mr. Benny at the corner grocery puts down his important cigar: Your mother know you got shoes like that? Who give you those?

Nobody.

Them are dangerous, he says. You girls too young to be wearing shoes like that. Take them shoes off before I call the cops, but we just run.

On the avenue a boy on a home-made bicycle calls out: Ladies, lead me to heaven.

But there is nobody around but us.

Do you like these shoes? Rachel says yes, and Lucy says yes, and yes I say, these are the best shoes. We will never go back to wearing the other kind again. Do you like these shoes?

In front of the laundromat six girls with the same fat face pretend we are invisible. They are the cousins, Lucy says, and always jealous. We just keep strutting.

Across the street in front of the tavern a bum man on the stoop.

Do you like these shoes?

Bum man says, Yes, little girl. Your little lemon shoes are so beautiful. But come closer. I can't see very well. Come closer. Please.

You are a pretty girl, bum man continues. What's your name, pretty girl?

And Rachel says Rachel, just like that.

Now you know to talk to drunks is crazy and to tell them your name is worse, but who can blame her. She is young and dizzy to hear so many sweet things in one day, even if it is a bum man's whiskey words saying them.

Rachel, you are prettier than a yellow taxi cab. You know that.

But we don't like it. We got to go, Lucy says.

If I give you a dollar will you kiss me? How about a dollar. I give you a dollar, and he looks in his pocket for wrinkled money.

We have to go right now, Lucy says taking Rachel's hand because she looks like she's thinking about that dollar.

Bum man is yelling something to the air but by now we are running fast and far away, our high heel shoes taking us all the way down the avenue and around the block, past the ugly cousins, past Mr. Benny's, up Mango Street, the back way, just in case.

We are tired of being beautiful. Lucy hides the lemon shoes and the red shoes and the shoes that used to be white but are now pale blue under a powerful bushel basket on the back porch, until one Tuesday her mother, who is very clean, throws them away. But no one complains.

Study and Discussion Questions

1. About how old do you think Lucy, Rachel, and the speaker of this first-person plural story, Esperanza, are? What clues lead you to think this?
2. How are the high heels "magic"? Discuss the journey of these talismans through the girls' day—how they arrive, how they depart, and what the nature of their magic is.
3. Give examples of Cisneros's use of imagery, literal or figurative, in this story. What effect do these images have?
4. In one sense, this is a children's game of "dress up." What are the girls playing at?
5. How are the three girls seen differently by others after they take off their socks and put on the high heels? Give some examples.
6. Mr. Benny at the corner grocery comments that the shoes "are dangerous." Is he correct? How are the shoes dangerous?
7. "We are tired of being beautiful," begins the last paragraph of the story. What do you think the three girls learned from the high-heels game? What does the experience Lucy, Rachel, and Esperanza have with the high heels suggest about the passage from girlhood to womanhood?

Suggestions for Writing

1. Cisneros could have chosen to tell this story in the past tense and in the voice of an adult remembering an incident from her childhood. Instead, she gives us a young girl's voice and present tense. Do you find this per-

spective effective? What does Cisneros gain from choosing the child's voice? What might she be losing?

2. Write about an experience from your own childhood/youth when you got a glimpse, whether welcome or not, into the adult world or into your own future as a grown-up.

Critical Resources

1. Cisneros, Sandra. Interview with Ray Suarez. *The News Hour Online.* <www.pbs.org/newshour>. October 2002.
2. Cruz, Felicia. "On the 'Simplicity' of Sandra Cisneros' The House on Mango Street." *Modern Fiction Studies.* Winter (2001): 910–40.
3. Doyle, Jacqueline. "More Room of Her Own: Sandra Cisneros's The House on Mango Street." *Melus.* 19.4 (1994): 5–35.
4. Olivares, Juliana. "Sandra Cisneros' *The House on Mango Street* and the Poetics of Space." *Chicana Creativity and Criticism: Charting New Frontiers in American Literature.* Ed. Maria Herrera-Sobek and Helena Viramontes. Houston: Arte Publico, 1988. 160–70.
5. *Sandra Cisneros: In Conversation with Dorothy Allison.* Lannan Foundation 1999, 60 minutes.

OCTAVIA BUTLER (b. 1947)

*Octavia Butler grew up as an only child in Pasadena, California. Rather awkward (she was 6 feet tall as a teenager) and lonely (*Authors and Artists for Young Adults, *2003), Butler turned to books and writing. She submitted her first science fiction story to a magazine when she was thirteen years old. After obtaining her associates degree from Pasadena City College, she enrolled at UCLA, where she continued to nurture her craft through writing workshops. Although she published her first short stories in 1970, it was the publication of her novel* Patternmaster *(1976) that established her as a new voice in science fiction. As one of the few African American women writing science fiction, Butler has become a pioneer in the genre, exploring how concepts of race, sex, and power play out and transform when set in futuristic worlds. Within these contexts, Butler explores their impact not only on human relationships, but how relationships develop between humans and more advanced forms of life. Butler's other works include* Mind of My Mind *(1977), the* Xenogenesis *trilogy (1987–1989),* Bloodchild and Other Stories *(1995),* Parable of the Sower *(1995), and* Lilith's Brood *(2000). "Bloodchild," first published in 1985, was the winner of the Hugo and Nebula awards for science fiction.*

Bloodchild   (1984)

My last night of childhood began with a visit home. T'Gatoi's sister had given us two sterile eggs. T'Gatoi gave one to my mother, brother, and sisters. She insisted that I eat the other one alone. It didn't matter. There was still enough to leave everyone feeling good. Almost everyone. My mother wouldn't take any. She sat, watching everyone drifting and dreaming without her. Most of the time she watched me.

I lay against T'Gatoi's long, velvet underside, sipping from my egg now and then, wondering why my mother denied herself such a harmless pleasure. Less of her hair would be gray if she indulged now and then. The eggs prolonged life, prolonged vigor. My father, who had never refused one in his life, had lived more than twice as long as he should have. And toward the end of his life, when he should have been slowing down, he had married my mother and fathered four children.

But my mother seemed content to age before she had to. I saw her turn away as several of T'Gatoi's limbs secured me closer. T'Gatoi liked our body heat and took advantage of it whenever she could. When I was little and at home more, my mother used to try to tell me how to behave with T'Gatoi—how to be respectful and always obedient because T'Gatoi was the Tlic government official in charge of the Preserve, and thus the most important of her kind to deal directly with Terrans. It was an honor, my mother said, that such a person had chosen to come into the family. My mother was at her most formal and severe when she was lying.

I had no idea why she was lying, or even what she was lying about. It *was* an honor to have T'Gatoi in the family, but it was hardly a novelty. T'Gatoi and my mother had been friends all my mother's life, and T'Gatoi was not interested in being honored in the house she considered her second home. She simply came in, climbed onto one of her special couches, and called me over to keep her warm. It was impossible to be formal with her while lying against her and hearing her complain as usual that I was too skinny.

"You're better," she said this time, probing me with six or seven of her limbs. "You're gaining weight finally. Thinness is dangerous." The probing changed subtly, became a series of caresses.

"He's still too thin," my mother said sharply.

T'Gatoi lifted her head and perhaps a meter of her body off the couch as though she were sitting up. She looked at my mother, and my mother, her face lined and old looking, turned away.

"Lien, I would like you to have what's left of Gan's egg."

"The eggs are for the children," my mother said.

"They are for the family. Please take it."

Unwillingly obedient, my mother took it from me and put it to her mouth. There were only a few drops left in the now-shrunken, elastic shell, but she squeezed them out, swallowed them, and after a few moments some of the lines of tension began to smooth from her face.

"It's good," she whispered. "Sometimes I forget how good it is."

"You should take more," T'Gatoi said. "Why are you in such a hurry to be old?"

My mother said nothing.

"I like being able to come here," T'Gatoi said. "This place is a refuge because of you, yet you won't take care of yourself."

T'Gatoi was hounded on the outside. Her people wanted more of us made available. Only she and her political faction stood between us and the hordes who did not understand why there was a Preserve—why any Terran could not be courted, paid, drafted, in some way made available to them. Or they did understand, but in their desperation, they did not care. She parceled us out to the desperate and sold us to the rich and powerful for their political support. Thus, we were necessities, status symbols, and an independent people. She oversaw the joining of families, putting an end to the final remnants of the earlier system of breaking up Terran families to suit impatient Tlic. I had lived outside with her. I had seen the desperate eagerness in the way some people looked at me. It was a little frightening to know that only she stood between us and that desperation that could so easily swallow us. My mother would look at her sometimes and say to me, "Take care of her." And I would remember that she too had been outside, had seen.

Now T'Gatoi used four of her limbs to push me away from her onto the floor. "Go on, Gan," she said. "Sit down there with your sisters and enjoy not being sober. You had most of the egg. Lien, come warm me."

My mother hesitated for no reason that I could see. One of my earliest memories is of my mother stretched alongside T'Gatoi, talking about things I could not understand, picking me up from the floor and laughing as she sat me on one of T'Gatoi's segments. She ate her share of eggs then. I wondered when she had stopped, and why.

She lay down now against T'Gatoi, and the whole left row of T'Gatoi's limbs closed around her, holding her loosely, but securely. I had always found it comfortable to lie that way, but except for my older sister, no one else in the family liked it. They said it made them feel caged.

T'Gatoi meant to cage my mother. Once she had, she moved her tail slightly, then spoke. "Not enough egg, Lien. You should have taken it when it was passed to you. You need it badly now."

T'Gatoi's tail moved once more, its whip motion so swift I wouldn't have seen it if I hadn't been watching for it. Her sting drew only a single drop of blood from my mother's bare leg.

My mother cried out—probably in surprise. Being stung doesn't hurt. Then she sighed and I could see her body relax. She moved languidly into a more comfortable position within the cage of T'Gatoi's limbs. "Why did you do that?" she asked, sounding half asleep.

"I could not watch you sitting and suffering any longer."

My mother managed to move her shoulders in a small shrug. "Tomorrow," she said.

"Yes. Tomorrow you will resume your suffering—if you must. But just now, just for now, lie here and warm me and let me ease your way a little."

"He's still mine, you know," my mother said suddenly.

"Nothing can buy him from me." Sober, she would not have permitted herself to refer to such things.

"Nothing," T'Gatoi agreed, humoring her.

"Did you think I would sell him for eggs? For long life? My son?"

"Not for anything," T'Gatoi said, stroking my mother's shoulders, toying with her long, graying hair.

I would like to have touched my mother, shared that moment with her. She would take my hand if I touched her now. Freed by the egg and the sting, she would smile and perhaps say things long held in. But tomorrow, she would remember all this as a humiliation. I did not want to be part of a remembered humiliation. Best just be still and know she loved me under all the duty and pride and pain.

"Xuan Hoa, take off her shoes," T'Gatoi said. "In a little while I'll sting her again and she can sleep."

My older sister obeyed, swaying drunkenly as she stood up. When she had finished, she sat down beside me and took my hand. We had always been a unit, she and I.

My mother put the back of her head against T'Gatoi's underside and tried from that impossible angle to look up into the broad, round face. "You're going to sting me again?"

"Yes, Lien."

"I'll sleep until tomorrow noon."

"Good. You need it. When did you sleep last?"

My mother made a wordless sound of annoyance. "I should have stepped on you when you were small enough," she muttered.

It was an old joke between them. They had grown up together, sort of, though T'Gatoi had not, in my mother's lifetime, been small enough for any Terran to step on. She was nearly three time my mother's present age, yet would still be young when my mother died of age. But T'Gatoi and my mother had met as T'Gatoi was coming into a period of rapid development—a kind of Tlic adolescence. My mother was only a child, but for a while they developed at the same rate and had no better friends than each other.

T'Gatoi had even introduced my mother to the man who became my father. My parents, pleased with each other in spite of their different ages, married as T'Gatoi was going into her family's business—politics. She and my mother saw each other less. But sometime before my older sister was born, my mother promised T'Gatoi one of her children. She would have to give one of us to someone, and she preferred T'Gatoi to some stranger.

Years passed. T'Gatoi traveled and increased her influence. The Preserve was hers by the time she came back to my mother to collect what she probably saw as her just reward for her hard work. My older sister took an instant liking to her and wanted to be chosen, but my mother was just coming to term with me and T'Gatoi liked the idea of choosing an infant and watching and taking part in all the phases of development. I'm told I was first caged within T'Gatoi's many limbs only three minutes after my birth. A few days later, I was given my first taste of egg. I tell Terrans that when they ask whether I was ever afraid of her. And I tell it to Tlic when T'Gatoi suggests a young Terran child for them and they, anxious and ignorant, demand an adolescent. Even my brother who had somehow grown up to fear and distrust the Tlic could probably have gone smoothly into one of their families if he had been adopted early enough. Sometimes, I think for his sake he should have been. I looked at him, stretched out on the floor across the room, his eyes open, but glazed as he dreamed his egg dream. No matter what he felt toward the Tlic, he always demanded his share of egg.

"Lien, can you stand up?" T'Gatoi asked suddenly.

"Stand?" my mother said. "I thought I was going to sleep."

"Later. Something sounds wrong outside." The cage was abruptly gone.

"What?"

"Up, Lien!"

My mother recognized her tone and got up just in time to avoid being dumped on the floor. T'Gatoi whipped her three meters of body off her couch, toward the door, and out at full speed. She had bones—ribs, a long spine, a skull, four sets of limb bones per segment. But when she moved that way, twisting, hurling herself into controlled falls, landing running, she seemed not only boneless, but aquatic—something swimming through the air as though it were water. I loved watching her move.

I left my sister and started to follow her out the door, though I wasn't very steady on my own feet. It would have been better to sit and dream, better yet to find a girl and share a waking dream with her. Back when the Tlic saw us as not much more than convenient, big, warm-blooded animals, they would pen several of us together, male and female, and feed us only eggs. That way they could be sure of getting another generation of us no matter how we tried to hold out. We were lucky that didn't go on long. A few generations of it and we would have *been* little more than convenient, big animals.

"Hold the door open, Gan," T'Gatoi said. "And tell the family to stay back."

"What is it?" I asked.

"N'Tlic."

I shrank back against the door. "Here? Alone?"

"He was trying to reach a call box, I suppose." She carried the man past me, unconscious, folded like a coat over some of her limbs. He looked young—my brother's age perhaps—and he was thinner than he should have been. What T'Gatoi would have called dangerously thin.

"Gan, go to the call box," she said. She put the man on the floor and began stripping off his clothing.

I did not move.

After a moment, she looked up at me, her sudden stillness a sign of deep impatience.

"Send Qui," I told her. "I'll stay here. Maybe I can help."

She let her limbs begin to move again, lifting the man and pulling his shirt over his head. "You don't want to see this," she said. "It will be hard. I can't help this man the way his Tlic could."

"I know. But send Qui. He won't want to be of any help here. I'm at least willing to try."

She looked at my brother—older, bigger, stronger, certainly more able to help her here. He was sitting up now, braced against the wall, staring at the man on the floor with undisguised fear and revulsion. Even she could see that he would be useless.

"Qui, go!" she said.

He didn't argue. He stood up, swayed briefly, then steadied, frightened sober.

"This man's name is Bram Lomas," she told him, reading from the man's armband. I fingered my own armband in sympathy. "He needs T'Khotgif Teh. Do you hear?"

"Bram Lomas, T'Khotgif Teh," my brother said. "I'm going." He edged around Lomas and ran out the door.

Lomas began to regain consciousness. He only moaned at first and clutched spasmodically at a pair of T'Gatoi's limbs. My younger sister, finally awake from her egg dream, came close to look at him, until my mother pulled her back.

T'Gatoi removed the man's shoes, then his pants, all the while leaving him two of her limbs to grip. Except for the final few, all her limbs were equally dexterous. "I want no argument from you this time, Gan," she said.

I straightened. "What shall I do?"

"Go out and slaughter an animal that is at least half your size."

"Slaughter? But I've never—"

She knocked me across the room. Her tail was an efficient weapon whether she exposed the sting or not.

I got up, feeling stupid for having ignored her warning, and went into the kitchen. Maybe I could kill something with a knife or an ax. My mother raised a few Terran animals for the table and several thousand local ones for their fur. T'Gatoi would probably prefer something local. An achti, perhaps. Some of those were the right size, though they had about three times as many teeth as I did and a real love of using them. My mother, Hoa, and Qui could kill them with knives. I had never killed one at all, had never slaughtered any animal. I had spent most of my time with T'Gatoi while my brother and sisters were learning the family business. T'Gatoi had been right. I should have been the one to go to the call box. At least I could do that.

I went to the corner cabinet where my mother kept her large house and garden tools. At the back of the cabinet there was a pipe that carried off waste water from the kitchen—except that it didn't anymore. My father had rerouted the waste water below before I was born. Now the pipe could be turned so that one half slid around the other and a rifle could be stored inside. This wasn't our only gun, but it was our most easily accessible one. I would have to use it to shoot one of the biggest of the achti. Then T'Gatoi would probably confiscate it. Firearms were illegal in the Preserve. There had been incidents right after the Preserve was established—Terrans shooting Tlic, shooting N'Tlic. This was before the joining of families began, before everyone had a personal stake in keeping the peace. No one had shot a Tlic in my lifetime or my mother's, but the law still stood—for our protection, we were told. There were stories of whole Terran families wiped out in reprisal back during the assassinations.

I went out to the cages and shot the biggest achti I could find. It was a handsome breeding male, and my mother would not be pleased to see me bring it in. But it was the right size, and I was in a hurry.

I put the achti's long, warm body over my shoulder—glad that some of the weight I'd gained was muscle—and took it to the kitchen. There, I put the gun back in its hiding place. If T'Gatoi noticed the achti's wounds and demanded the gun, I would give it to her. Otherwise, let it stay where my father wanted it.

I turned to take the achti to her, then hesitated. For several seconds, I stood in front of the closed door wondering why I was suddenly afraid. I knew what was going to happen. I hadn't seen it before but T'Gatoi had shown me diagrams and drawings. She had made sure I knew the truth as soon as I was old enough to understand it.

Yet I did not want to go into that room. I wasted a little time choosing a knife from the carved, wooden box in which my mother kept them. T'Gatoi might want one, I told myself, for the tough, heavily furred hide of the achti.

"Gan!" T'Gatoi called, her voice harsh with urgency.

I swallowed. I had not imagined a single moving of the feet could be so difficult. I realized I was trembling and that shamed me. Shame impelled me through the door.

I put the achti down near T'Gatoi and saw that Lomas was unconscious again. She, Lomas, and I were alone in the room—my mother and sisters probably sent out so they would not have to watch. I envied them.

But my mother came back into the room as T'Gatoi seized the achti. Ignoring the knife I offered her, she extended claws from several of her limbs and slit the achti from throat to anus. She looked at me, her yellow eyes intent. "Hold this man's shoulders, Gan."

I stared at Lomas in panic, realizing that I did not want to touch him, let alone hold him. This would not be like shooting an animal. Not as quick, not as merciful, and, I hoped, not as final, but there was nothing I wanted less than to be part of it.

My mother came forward. "Gan, you hold his right side," she said. "I'll hold his left." And if he came to, he would throw her off without realizing he had done it. She was a tiny woman. She often wondered aloud how she had produced, as she said, such "huge" children.

"Never mind," I told her, taking the man's shoulders. "I'll do it." She hovered nearby.

"Don't worry," I said. "I won't shame you. You don't have to stay and watch."

She looked at me uncertainly, then touched my face in a rare caress. Finally, she went back to her bedroom.

T'Gatoi lowered her head in relief. "Thank you, Gan," she said with courtesy more Terran than Tlic. "That one . . . she is always finding new ways for me to make her suffer."

Lomas began to groan and make choked sounds. I had hoped he would stay unconscious. T'Gatoi put her face near his so that he focused on her.

"I've stung you as much as I dare for now," she told him. "When this is over, I'll sting you to sleep and you won't hurt anymore."

"Please," the man begged. "Wait . . ."

"There's no more time, Bram. I'll sting you as soon as it's over. When T'Khotgif arrives she'll give you eggs to help you heal. It will be over soon."

"T'Khotgif!" the man shouted, straining against my hands.

"Soon, Bram." T'Gatoi glanced at me, then placed a claw against his abdomen slightly to the right of the middle, just below the left rib. There was movement on the right side—tiny, seemingly random pulsations moving his brown flesh, creating a concavity here, a convexity there, over and over until I could see the rhythm of it and knew where the next pulse would be.

Lomas's entire body stiffened under T'Gatoi's claw, though she merely rested it against him as she wound the rear section of her body around his legs. He might break my grip, but he would not break hers. He wept helplessly as she used his pants to tie his hands, then pushed his hands above his head so that I could kneel on the cloth between them and pin them in place. She rolled up his shirt and gave it to him to bite down on.

And she opened him.

His body convulsed with the first cut. He almost tore himself away from me. The sound he made . . . I had never heard such sounds come from anything human. T'Gatoi seemed to pay no attention as she lengthened and deepened the cut, now and then pausing to lick away blood. His blood vessels contracted, reacting to the chemistry of her saliva, and the bleeding slowed.

I felt as though I were helping her torture him, helping her consume him. I knew I would vomit soon, didn't know why I hadn't already. I couldn't possibly last until she was finished.

She found the first grub. It was fat and deep red with his blood—both inside and out. It had already eaten its own egg case but apparently had not yet begun to eat its host. At this stage, it would eat any flesh except its mother's. Let alone, it would have gone on excreting the poisons that had both sickened and alerted Lomas. Eventually it would have begun to eat. By the time it ate its way out of Lomas's flesh, Lomas would be dead or dying—and unable to take revenge on the thing that was killing him. There was always a grace period between the time the host sickened and the time the grubs began to eat him.

T'Gatoi picked up the writhing grub carefully and looked at it, somehow ignoring the terrible groans of the man.

Abruptly, the man lost consciousness.

"Good," T'Gatoi looked down at him. "I wish you Terrans could do that at will." She felt nothing. And the thing she held . . .

It was limbless and boneless at this stage, perhaps fifteen centimeters long and two thick, blind and slimy with blood. It was like a large worm. T'Gatoi put it into the belly of the achti, and it began at once to burrow. It would stay there and eat as long as there was anything to eat.

Probing through Lomas's flesh, she found two more, one of them smaller and more vigorous. "A male!" she said happily. He would be dead before I would. He would be through his metamorphosis and screwing everything that would hold still before his sisters even had limbs. He was the only one to make a serious effort to bite T'Gatoi as she placed him in the achti.

Paler worms oozed to visibility in Lomas's flesh. I closed my eyes. It was worse than finding something dead, rotting, and filled with tiny animal grubs. And it was far worse than any drawing or diagram.

"Ah, there are more," T'Gatoi said, plucking out two long, thick grubs. You may have to kill another animal, Gan. Everything lives inside you Terrans."

I had been told all my life that this was a good and necessary thing Tlic and Terran did together—a kind of birth. I had believed it until now. I knew birth was painful and bloody, no matter what. But this was something else, something worse. And I wasn't ready to see it. Maybe I never would be. Yet I couldn't not see it. Closing my eyes didn't help.

T'Gatoi found a grub still eating its egg case. The remains of the case were still wired into a blood vessel by their own little tube or hook or whatever. That was the way the grubs were anchored and the way they fed. They took only blood until they were ready to emerge. Then they ate their stretched, elastic egg cases. Then they ate their hosts.

T'Gatoi bit away the egg case, licked away the blood. Did she like the taste? Did childhood habits die hard—or not die at all?

The whole procedure was wrong, alien. I wouldn't have thought anything about her could seem alien to me.

"One more, I think," she said. "Perhaps two. A good family. In a host animal these days, we would be happy to find one or two alive." She glanced at me. "Go outside, Gan, and empty your stomach. Go now while the man is unconscious."

I staggered out, barely made it. Beneath the tree just beyond the front door, I vomited until there was nothing left to bring up. Finally, I stood shaking, tears streaming down my face. I did not know why I was crying, but I could not stop. I went further from the house to avoid being seen. Every time I closed my eyes I saw red worms crawling over redder human flesh.

There was a car coming toward the house. Since Terrans were forbidden motorized vehicles except for certain farm equipment, I knew this must be Lomas's Tlic with Qui and perhaps a Terran doctor. I wiped my face on my shirt, struggled for control.

"Gan," Qui called as the car stopped. "What happened?" He crawled out of the low, round, Tlic-convenient car door. Another Terran crawled out the other

side and went into the house without speaking to me. The doctor. With his help
and a few eggs, Lomas might make it.

"T'Khotgif Teh?" I said.

The Tlic driver surged out of her car, reared up half her length before me.
She was paler and smaller than T'Gatoi—probably born from the body of an
animal. Tlic from Terran bodies were always larger as well as more numerous.

"Six young," I told her. "Maybe seven, all alive. At least one male."

"Lomas?" she said harshly. I liked her for the question and the concern in her
voice when she asked it. The last coherent thing he had said was her name.

"He's alive," I said.

She surged away to the house without another word.

"She's been sick," my brother said, watching her go. "When I called, I could
hear people telling her she wasn't well enough to go out even for this."

I said nothing. I had extended courtesy to the Tlic. Now I didn't want to talk
to anyone. I hoped he would go in—out of curiosity if nothing else.

"Finally found out more than you wanted to know, eh?"

I looked at him.

"Don't give me one of *her* looks," he said. "You're not her. You're just her
property."

One of her looks. Had I picked up even an ability to imitate her expressions?

"What'd you do, puke?" He sniffed the air. "So now you know what
you're in for."

I walked away from him. He and I had been close when we were kids. He
would let me follow him around when I was home, and sometimes T'Gatoi
would let me bring him along when she took me into the city. But something
had happened when he reached adolescence. I never knew what. He began keeping out of T'Gatoi's way. Then he began running away—until he realized there
was no "away." Not in the Preserve. Certainly not outside. After that he concentrated on getting his share of every egg that came into the house and on looking out for me in a way that made me all but hate him—a way that clearly said,
as long as I was all right, he was safe from the Tlic.

"How was it, really?" he demanded, following me.

"I killed an achti. The young ate it."

"You didn't run out of the house and puke because they ate an achti."

"I had . . . never seen a person cut open before." That was true, and enough
for him to know. I couldn't talk about the other. Not with him.

"Oh," he said. He glanced at me as though he wanted to say more, but he
kept quiet.

We walked, not really headed anywhere. Toward the back, toward the cages,
toward the fields.

"Did he say anything?" Qui asked. "Lomas, I mean."

Who else would he mean? "He said 'T'Khotgif.' "

Qui shuddered. "If she had done that to me, she'd be the last person I'd call for."

"You'd call for her. Her sting would ease your pain without killing the
grubs in you."

"You think I'd care if they died?"

No. Of course he wouldn't. Would I?

"Shit!" He drew a deep breath. "I've seen what they do. You think this thing with Lomas was bad? It was nothing."

I didn't argue. He didn't know what he was talking about.

"I saw them eat a man," he said.

I turned to face him. "You're lying!"

"*I saw them eat a man.*" He paused. "It was when I was little. I had been to the Hartmund house and I was on my way home. Halfway here, I saw a man and a Tlic and the man was N'Tlic. The ground was hilly. I was able to hide from them and watch. The Tlic wouldn't open the man because she had nothing to feed the grubs. The man couldn't go any further and there were no houses around. He was in so much pain, he told her to kill him. He begged her to kill him. Finally, she did. She cut his throat. One swipe of one claw. I saw the grubs eat their way out, then burrow in again, still eating."

His words made me see Lomas's flesh again, parasitized, crawling. "Why didn't you tell me that?" I whispered.

He looked startled as though he'd forgotten I was listening. "I don't know."

"You started to run away not long after that, didn't you?"

"Yeah. Stupid. Running inside the Preserve. Running in a cage."

I shook my head, said what I should have said to him long ago. "She wouldn't take you, Qui. You don't have to worry."

"She would . . . if anything happened to you."

"No. She'd take Xuan Hoa. Hoa . . . wants it." She wouldn't if she had stayed to watch Lomas.

"They don't take women," he said with contempt.

"They do sometimes." I glanced at him. "Actually, they prefer women. You should be around them when they talk among themselves. They say women have more body fat to protect the grubs. But they usually take men to leave the women free to bear their own young."

"To provide the next generation of host animals," he said, switching from contempt to bitterness.

"It's more than that!" I countered. Was it?

"If it were going to happen to me, I'd want to believe it was more, too."

"It *is* more!" I felt like a kid. Stupid argument.

"Did you think so while T'Gatoi was picking worms out of that guy's guts?"

"It's not supposed to happen that way."

"Sure it is. You weren't supposed to see it, that's all. And his Tlic was supposed to do it. She could sting him unconscious and the operation wouldn't have been as painful. But she'd still open him, pick out the grubs, and if she missed even one, it would poison him and eat him from the inside out."

There was actually a time when my mother told me to show respect for Qui because he was my older brother. I walked away, hating him. In his way, he was gloating. He was safe and I wasn't. I could have hit him, but I didn't think I would be able to stand it when he refused to hit back, when he looked at me with contempt and pity.

He wouldn't let me get away. Longer legged, he swung ahead of me and made me feel as though I were following him.

"I'm sorry," he said.

I strode on, sick and furious.

"Look, it probably won't be that bad with you. T'Gatoi likes you. She'll be careful."

I turned back toward the house, almost running from him.

"Has she done it to you yet?" he asked, keeping up easily. "I mean, you're about the right age for implantation. Has she—"

I hit him. I didn't know I was going to do it, but I think I meant to kill him. If he hadn't been bigger and stronger, I think I would have.

He tried to hold me off, but in the end, had to defend himself. He only hit me a couple of times. That was plenty. I don't remember going down, but when I came to, he was gone. It was worth the pain to be rid of him.

I got up and walked slowly toward the house. The back was dark. No one was in the kitchen. My mother and sisters were sleeping in their bedrooms—or pretending to.

Once I was in the kitchen, I could hear voices—Tlic and Terran from the next room. I couldn't make out what they were saying—didn't want to make it out.

I sat down at my mother's table, waiting for quiet. The table was smooth and worn, heavy and well crafted. My father had made it for her just before he died. I remembered hanging around underfoot when he built it. He didn't mind. Now I sat leaning on it, missing him. I could have talked to him. He had done it three times in his long life. Three clutches of eggs, three times being opened up and sewed up. How had he done it? How did anyone do it?

I got up, took the rifle from its hiding place, and sat down again with it. It needed cleaning, oiling.

All I did was load it.

"Gan?"

She made a lot of little clicking sounds when she walked on bare floor, each limb clicking in succession as it touched down. Waves of little clicks.

She came to the table, raised the front half of her body above it, and surged onto it. Sometimes she moved so smoothly she seemed to flow like water itself. She coiled herself into a small hill in the middle of the table and looked at me.

"That was bad," she said softly. "You should not have seen it. It need not be that way."

"I know."

"T'Khotgif—Ch'Khotgif now—she will die of her disease. She will not live to raise her children. But her sister will provide for them, and for Bram Lomas." Sterile sister. One fertile female in every lot. One to keep the family going. That sister owed Lomas more than she could ever repay.

"He'll live then?"

"Yes."

"I wonder if he would do it again."

"No one would ask him to do that again."

I looked into the yellow eyes, wondering how much I saw and understood there, and how much I only imagined. "No one ever asks us," I said. "You never asked me."

She moved her head slightly. "What's the matter with your face?"

"Nothing. Nothing important." Human eyes probably wouldn't have noticed the swelling in the darkness. The only light was from one of the moons, shining through a window across the room.

"Did you use the rifle to shoot the achti?"

"Yes."

"And do you mean to use it to shoot me?"

I stared at her, outlined in the moonlight—coiled, graceful body. "What does Terran blood taste like to you?"

She said nothing.

"What are you?" I whispered. "What are we to you?"

She lay still, rested her head on her topmost coil. "You know me as no other does," she said softly. "You must decide."

"That's what happened to my face," I told her.

"What?"

"Qui goaded me into deciding to do something. It didn't turn out very well." I moved the gun slightly, brought the barrel up diagonally under my own chin. "At least it was a decision I made."

"As this will be."

"Ask me, Gatoi."

"For my children's lives?"

She would say something like that. She knew how to manipulate people, Terran and Tlic. But not this time.

"I don't want to be a host animal," I said. "Not even yours."

It took her a long time to answer. "We use almost no host animals these days," she said. "You know that."

"You use us."

"We do. We wait long years for you and teach you and join our families to yours." She moved restlessly. "You know you aren't animals to us."

I stared at her, saying nothing.

"The animals we once used began killing most of our eggs after implantation long before your ancestors arrived," she said softly. "You know these things, Gan. Because your people arrived, we are relearning what it means to be a healthy, thriving people. And your ancestors, fleeing from their homeworld, from their own kind who would have killed or enslaved them—they survived because of us. We saw them as people and gave them the Preserve when they still tried to kill us as worms."

At the word "worms," I jumped. I couldn't help it, and she couldn't help noticing it.

"I see," she said quietly. "Would you really rather die than bear my young, Gan?"

I didn't answer.

"Shall I go to Xuan Hoa?"

"Yes!" Hoa wanted it. Let her have it. She hadn't had to watch Lomas. She'd be proud. . . . Not terrified.

T'Gatoi flowed off the table onto the floor, startling me almost too much.

"I'll sleep in Hoa's room tonight," she said. "And sometime tonight or in the morning, I'll tell her."

This was going too fast. My sister Hoa had had almost as much to do with raising me as my mother. I was still close to her—not like Qui. She could want T'Gatoi and still love me.

"Wait! Gatoi!"

She looked back, then raised nearly half her length off the floor and turned to face me. "These are adult things, Gan. This is my life, my family!"

"But she's . . . my sister."

"I have done what you demanded. I have asked you!"

"But—"

"It will be easier for Hoa. She has always expected to carry other lives inside her."

Human lives. Human young who should someday drink at her breasts, not at her veins.

I shook my head. "Don't do it to her, Gatoi." I was not Qui. It seemed I could become him, though, with no effort at all. I could make Xuan Hoa my shield. Would it be easier to know that red worms were growing in her flesh instead of mine?

"Don't do it to Hoa," I repeated.

She stared at me, utterly still.

I looked away, then back at her. "Do it to me."

I lowered the gun from my throat and she leaned forward to take it.

"No," I told her.

"It's the law," she said.

"Leave it for the family. One of them might use it to save my life someday."

She grasped the rifle barrel, but I wouldn't let go. I was pulled into a standing position over her.

"Leave it here!" I repeated. "If we're not your animals, if these are adult things, accept the risk. There is risk, Gatoi, in dealing with a partner."

It was clearly hard for her to let go of the rifle. A shudder went through her and she made a hissing sound of distress. It occurred to me that she was afraid. She was old enough to have seen what guns could do to people. Now her young and this gun would be together in the same house. She did not know about the other guns. In this dispute, they did not matter.

"I will implant the first egg tonight," she said as I put the gun away. "Do you hear, Gan?"

Why else had I been given a whole egg to eat while the rest of the family was left to share one? Why else had my mother kept looking at me as though I were going away from her, going where she could not follow? Did T'Gatoi imagine I hadn't known?

"I hear."

"Now!" I let her push me out of the kitchen, then walked ahead of her toward my bedroom. The sudden urgency in her voice sounded real. "You would have done it to Hoa tonight!" I accused.

"I must do it to someone tonight."

I stopped in spite of her urgency and stood in her way. "Don't you care who?"

She flowed around me and into my bedroom. I found her waiting on the couch we shared. There was nothing in Hoa's room that she could have used. She would have done it to Hoa on the floor. The thought of her doing it to Hoa at all disturbed me in a different way now, and I was suddenly angry.

Yet I undressed and lay down beside her. I knew what to do, what to expect. I had been told all my life. I felt the familiar sting, narcotic, mildly pleasant. Then the blind probing of her ovipositor. The puncture was painless, easy. So easy going in. She undulated slowly against me, her muscles forcing the egg from her body into mine. I held on to a pair of her limbs until I remembered Lomas holding her that way. Then I let go, moved inadvertently, and hurt her. She gave a low cry of pain and I expected to be caged at once within her limbs. When I wasn't, I held on to her again, feeling oddly ashamed.

"I'm sorry," I whispered.

She rubbed my shoulders with four of her limbs.

"Do you care?" I asked. "Do you care that it's me?"

She did not answer for some time. Finally, "You were the one making the choices tonight, Gan. I made mine long ago."

"Would you have gone to Hoa?"

"Yes. How could I put my children into the care of one who hates them?"

"It wasn't . . . hate."

"I know what it was."

"I was afraid."

Silence.

"I still am." I could admit it to her here, now.

"But you came to me . . . to save Hoa."

"Yes." I leaned my forehead against her. She was cool velvet, deceptively soft. "And to keep you for myself," I said. It was so. I didn't understand it, but it was so.

She made a soft hum of contentment. "I couldn't believe I had made such a mistake with you," she said. "I chose you. I believed you had grown to choose me."

"I had, but . . ."

"Lomas."

"Yes."

"I had never known a Terran to see a birth and take it well. Qui has seen one, hasn't he?"

"Yes."

"Terrans should be protected from seeing."

I didn't like the sound of that—and I doubted that it was possible. "Not protected," I said. "Shown. Shown when we're young kids, and shown more than once. Gatoi, no Terran ever sees a birth that goes right. All we see is N'Tlic—pain and terror and maybe death."

She looked down at me. "It is a private thing. It has always been a private thing."

Her tone kept me from insisting—that and the knowledge that if she changed her mind, I might be the first public example. But I had planted the thought in her mind. Chances were it would grow, and eventually she would experiment.

"You won't see it again," she said. "I don't want you thinking any more about shooting me."

The small amount of fluid that came into me with her egg relaxed me as completely as a sterile egg would have, so that I could remember the rifle in my hands and my feelings of fear and revulsion, anger and despair. I could remember the feelings without reviving them. I could talk about them.

"I wouldn't have shot you," I said. "Not you." She had been taken from my father's flesh when he was my age.

"You could have," she insisted.

"Not you." She stood between us and her own people, protecting, interweaving.

"Would you have destroyed yourself?"

I moved carefully, uncomfortable. "I could have done that. I nearly did. That's Qui's 'away.' I wonder if he knows."

"What?"

I did not answer.

"You will live now."

"Yes." *Take care of her,* my mother used to say. Yes.

"I'm healthy and young," she said. "I won't leave you as Lomas was left—alone, N'Tlic. I'll take care of you."

Afterword

It amazes me that some people have seen "Bloodchild" as a story of slavery. It isn't. It's a number of other things, though. On one level, it's a love story between two very different beings. On another, it's a coming-of-age story in which a boy must absorb disturbing information and use it to make a decision that will affect the rest of his life.

On a third level, "Bloodchild" is my pregnant man story. I've always wanted to explore what it might be like for a man to be put into that most unlikely of all positions. Could I write a story in which a man chose to become pregnant *not* through some sort of misplaced competitiveness to prove that a man could do anything a woman could do, not because he was forced to, not even out of curiosity? I wanted to see whether I could write a dramatic story of a man becoming pregnant as an act of love—choosing pregnancy in spite of as well as because of surrounding difficulties.

Also, "Bloodchild" was my effort to ease an old fear of mine. I was going to travel to the Peruvian Amazon to do research for my Xenogenesis books (*Dawn, Adulthood Rites,* and *Imago*), and I worried about my possible reactions to some of the insect life of the area. In particular, I worried about the botfly—an insect with, what seemed to me then, horror-movie habits. There was no shortage of botflies in the part of Peru that I intended to visit.

The botfly lays its eggs in wounds left by the bites of other insects. I found the idea of a maggot living and growing under my skin, eating my flesh as it grew, to be so intolerable, so terrifying that I didn't know how I could stand it if it happened to me. To make matters worse, all that I heard and read advised botfly victims not to try to get rid of their maggot passengers until they got back home to the United States and were able to go to a doctor—or until the fly finished the larval part of its growth cycle, crawled out of its host, and flew away.

The problem was to do what would seem to be the normal thing, to squeeze out the maggot and throw it away, was to invite infection. The maggot becomes literally attached to its host and leaves part of itself behind, broken off, if it's squeezed or cut out. Of course, the part left behind dies and rots, causing infection. Lovely.

When I have to deal with something that disturbs me as much as the botfly did, I write about it. I sort out my problems by writing about them. In a high school classroom on November 22, 1963, I remember grabbing a notebook and beginning to write my response to news of John Kennedy's assassination. Whether I write journal pages, an essay, a short story, or weave my problems into a novel, I find the writing helps me get through the trouble and get on with my life. Writing "Bloodchild" didn't make me like botflies, but for a while, it made them seem more interesting than horrifying.

There's one more thing I tried to do in "Bloodchild." I tried to write a story about paying the rent—a story about an isolated colony of human beings on an inhabited, extrasolar world. At best, they would be a lifetime away from reinforcements. It wouldn't be the British Empire in space, and it wouldn't be *Star Trek.* Sooner or later, the humans would have to make some kind of accommodation with their um . . . their hosts. Chances are this would be an unusual accommodation. Who knows what we humans have that others might be willing to take in trade for a livable space on a world not our own?

Study and Discussion Questions

1. Science fiction writers, whether they are imagining an alien species or extrapolating a utopian or dystopian world from the one we currently live in, have a task in addition to most realistic or mainstream writers: they must fairly quickly give their readers enough information to form a bridge between our own world and the imagined world in which the story will take place. How does Butler do this in the first few paragraphs of "Bloodchild"? List the information you receive in the first couple of pages that help build this bridge for the reader.

2. Why do you think Butler begins the story with this sentence: "My last night of childhood began with a visit home"? What do you learn about the tensions that will motivate the plot from this sentence? Finally, why is it Gan's last night of childhood?
3. What is going on with the protagonist's (Gan's) mother in the beginning scene? Note some of the tensions between the mother and T'Gatoi.
4. What is T'Gatoi's history with this family? How do they feel about her? How does she feel about them?
5. There are two, possibly three, crisis points in "Bloodchild." What are they?
6. Discuss your reaction and the reaction of various characters to the "birth" scene.
7. What is the function of the scene between Gan and his brother?
8. What are the decisions Gan makes in "Bloodchild"? How do they move him from childhood to adulthood?
9. How is this a story about pregnancy? Does it give you a new or different perspective on pregnancy?
10. How is this a story about difficult choices?
11. Discuss the story's title, "Bloodchild."

Suggestions for Writing

1. In the "Afterword" to "Bloodchild," Octavia Butler advances five themes or motifs of this story. What are they? Choose one of these and write about how she develops that motif in the story.
2. Butler begins the "Afterword" by writing, "It amazes me that some people have seen "Bloodchild" as a story of slavery. It isn't." As an African American writer and author of *Kindred,* her best known and closest to mainstream novel in which a modern Black woman inadvertently time travels to the pre-Emancipation South, it is not surprising some readers would see a connection between the human/T'Lic relation and slavery in this country. In your opinion, how is the human/T'Lic relation like and/or unlike slavery?
3. Write a short short story about a human encounter with an alien species.

Critical Resources

1. Allison, Dorothy. "The Future of Female: Octavia Butler's Mother Lode." *Reading Black, Reading Feminist: A Critical Anthology.* Ed, Henry Louis Gates. New York: Meridian, 1990. 471–78
2. Fry, Joan. "An Interview With Octavia Butler." *Poets and Writers Magazine.* March/April 1997, 58–69.
3. Helford, Elyce Rae. "'Would You Really Rather Die than Bear My Young?': The Construction of Gender, Race and Species in Octavia Butler's 'Bloodchild.'" *African American Review.* Summer (1994): 259–71.
4. Zaki, Hoda. "Utopia, Dystopia, and Ideology in the Science Fiction of Octavia Butler." *Science Fiction Studies* 17.2 (1990): 239–51.

❋ ❋ ❋

JAMES BALDWIN (1924–1987)

Son of a Harlem preacher, Baldwin himself began preaching at age 14; this experience and his early religious training would have an enduring effect on his writing style. Throughout the 1950s and 1960s, Baldwin was a voice for civil rights, speaking and writing in protest of racial hatred. In both his essays and novels, he seeks to understand the social and psychological effects of racism and the role of love in combating such forces. He is perhaps best known for his nonfiction essays, collected in Notes of a Native Son *(1955),* Nobody Knows My Name *(1961), and* The Fire Next Time *(1963), and for his fiction* Go Tell It On The Mountain *(1953), a coming-of-age story about a young black man in Harlem;* Giovanni's Room *(1956), a novel about gay life in Paris; and* Going to Meet the Man *(1965), a collection of short stories. He has also won acclaim as a dramatist, with* The Amen Corner *(1955) and* Blues for Mister Charlie *(1964). "Sonny's Blues," published in 1957, is demonstrative of the emotional, lyrical prose found in much of Baldwin's work.*

Sonny's Blues (1957)

I read about it in the paper, in the subway, on my way to work. I read it, and I couldn't believe it, and I read it again. Then perhaps I just stared at it, at the newsprint spelling out his name, spelling out the story. I stared at it in the swinging lights of the subway car, and in the faces and bodies of the people, and in my own face, trapped in the darkness which roared outside.

It was not to be believed and I kept telling myself that, as I walked from the subway station to the high school. And at the same time I couldn't doubt it. I was scared, scared for Sonny. He became real to me again. A great block of ice got settled in my belly and kept melting there slowly all day long, while I taught my classes algebra. It was a special kind of ice. It kept melting, sending trickles of ice water all up and down my veins, but it never got less. Sometimes it hardened and seemed to expand until I felt my guts were going to come spilling out or that I was going to choke or scream. This would always be at a moment when I was remembering some specific thing Sonny had once said or done.

When he was about as old as the boys in my classes his face had been bright and open, there was a lot of copper in it; and he'd had wonderfully direct brown eyes, and great gentleness and privacy. I wondered what he looked like now. He had been picked up, the evening before, in a raid on an apartment downtown, for peddling and using heroin.

I couldn't believe it: but what I mean by that is that I couldn't find any room for it anywhere inside me. I had kept it outside me for a long time. I hadn't wanted to know. I had had suspicions, but I didn't name them, I kept putting them away. I told myself that Sonny was wild, but he wasn't crazy. And he'd always been a good boy, he hadn't ever turned hard or evil or disrespectful, the way kids can, so quick, so quick, especially in Harlem. I didn't want to believe that I'd ever see my brother going down, coming to nothing, all that light in his face gone out, in the condition I'd already seen so many others. Yet it had happened and here I was, talking about algebra to a lot of boys who might, every one of them for all I knew, be popping off needles every time they went to the head. Maybe it did more for them than algebra could.

I was sure that the first time Sonny had ever had horse, he couldn't have been much older than these boys were now. These boys, now, were living as we'd been living then, they were growing up with a rush and their heads bumped abruptly against the low ceiling of their actual possibilities. They were filled with rage. All they really knew were two darknesses, the darkness of their lives, which was now closing in on them, and the darkness of the movies, which had blinded them to that other darkness, and in which they now, vindictively, dreamed, at once more together than they were at any other time, and more alone.

When the last bell rang, the last class ended, I let out my breath. It seemed I'd been holding it for all that time. My clothes were wet—I may have looked as though I'd been sitting in a steam bath, all dressed up, all afternoon. I sat alone in the classroom a long time. I listened to the boys outside, downstairs, shouting and cursing and laughing. Their laughter struck me for perhaps the first time. It was not the joyous laughter which—God knows why—one associates with children. It was mocking and insular, its intent was to denigrate. It was disenchanted, and in this, also, lay the authority of their curses. Perhaps I was listening to them because I was thinking about my brother and in them I heard my brother. And myself.

One boy was whistling a tune, at once very complicated and very simple, it seemed to be pouring out of him as though he were a bird, and it sounded very cool and moving through all that harsh, bright air, only just holding its own through all those other sounds.

I stood up and walked over to the window and looked down into the courtyard. It was the beginning of the spring and the sap was rising in the boys. A teacher passed through them every now and again, quickly, as though he or she couldn't wait to get out of that courtyard, to get those boys out of their sight and off their minds. I started collecting my stuff. I thought I'd better get home and talk to Isabel.

The courtyard was almost deserted by the time I got downstairs. I saw this boy standing in the shadow of a doorway, looking just like Sonny. I almost called his name. Then I saw that it wasn't Sonny, but somebody we used to know, a boy from around our block. He'd been Sonny's friend. He'd never been mine, having been too young for me, and, anyway, I'd never liked him. And now, even though he was a grown-up man, he still hung around that block, still spent hours on the street corners, was always high and raggy. I used to run into him from time to time and he'd often work around to asking me for a quarter or fifty cents. He always had some real good excuse, too, and I always gave it to him, I don't know why.

But now, abruptly, I hated him. I couldn't stand the way he looked at me, partly like a dog, partly like a cunning child. I wanted to ask him what the hell he was doing in the school courtyard.

He sort of shuffled over to me, and he said, "I see you got the papers. So you already know about it."

"You mean about Sonny? Yes, I already know about it. How come they didn't get you?"

He grinned. It made him repulsive and it also brought to mind what he'd looked like as a kid. "I wasn't there. I stay away from them people."

"Good for you." I offered him a cigarette and I watched him through the smoke. "You come all the way down here just to tell me about Sonny?"

"That's right." He was sort of shaking his head and his eyes looked strange, as though they were about to cross. The bright sun deadened his damp dark brown skin and it made his eyes look yellow and showed up the dirt in his kinked hair. He smelled funky. I moved a little away from him and I said, "Well, thanks. But I already know about it and I got to get home."

"I'll walk you a little ways," he said. We started walking. There were a couple of kids still loitering in the courtyard and one of them said goodnight to me and looked strangely at the boy beside me.

"What're you going to do?" he asked me. "I mean, about Sonny?"

"Look. I haven't seen Sonny for over a year, I'm not sure I'm going to do anything. Anyway, what the hell *can* I do?"

"That's right," he said quickly, "ain't nothing you can do. Can't much help old Sonny no more, I guess."

It was what I was thinking and so it seemed to me he had no right to say it.

"I'm surprised at Sonny, though," he went on—he had a funny way of talking, he looked straight ahead as though he were talking to himself—"I thought Sonny was a smart boy, I thought he was too smart to get hung."

"I guess he thought so too," I said sharply, "and that's how he got hung. And how about you? You're pretty goddamn smart, I bet."

Then he looked directly at me, just for a minute. "I ain't smart," he said. "If I was smart, I'd have reached for a pistol a long time ago."

"Look. Don't tell *me* your sad story, if it was up to me, I'd give you one." Then I felt guilty—guilty, probably, for never having supposed that the poor bastard *had* a story of his own, much less a sad one, and I asked, quickly, "What's going to happen to him now?"

He didn't answer this. He was off by himself some place. "Funny thing," he said, and from his tone we might have been discussing the quickest way to get to Brooklyn, "when I saw the papers this morning, the first thing I asked myself was if I had anything to do with it. I felt sort of responsible."

I began to listen more carefully. The subway station was on the corner, just before us, and I stopped. He stopped, too. We were in front of a bar and he ducked slightly, peering in, but whoever he was looking for didn't seem to be there. The juke box was blasting away with something black and bouncy and I

half watched the barmaid as she danced her way from the juke box to her place
behind the bar. And I watched her face as she laughingly responded to something someone said to her, still keeping time to the music. When she smiled one
saw the little girl, one sensed the doomed, still-struggling woman beneath the
battered face of the semiwhore.

"I never *give* Sonny nothing," the boy said finally, "but a long time ago I
come to school high and Sonny asked me how it felt." He paused, I couldn't
bear to watch him, I watched the barmaid, and I listened to the music which
seemed to be causing the pavement to shake. "I told him it felt great." The music stopped, the barmaid paused and watched the juke box until the music began again. "It did."

All this was carrying me some place I didn't want to go. I certainly didn't want
to know how it felt. It filled everything, the people, the houses, the music, the
dark, quicksilver barmaid, with menace; and this menace was their reality.

"What's going to happen to him now?" I asked again.

"They'll send him away some place and they'll try to cure him." He shook his
head. "Maybe he'll even think he's kicked the habit. Then they'll let him loose"—
he gestured, throwing his cigarette into the gutter. "That's all."

"What do you mean, that's *all?*"

But I knew what he meant.

"I *mean,* that's *all.*" He turned his head and looked at me, pulling down the
corners of his mouth. "Don't you know what I mean?" he asked, softly.

"How the hell *would* I know what you mean?" I almost whispered it, I
don't know why.

"That's right," he said to the air, "how would *he* know what I mean?" He
turned toward me again, patient and calm, and yet I somehow felt him shaking,
shaking as though he were going to fall apart. I felt that ice in my guts again, the
dread I'd felt all afternoon; and again I watched the barmaid, moving about the
bar, washing glasses, and singing. "Listen. They'll let him out and then it'll just
start all over again. That's what I mean."

"You mean—they'll let him out. And then he'll just start working his way back
in again. You mean he'll never kick the habit. Is that what you mean?"

"That's right," he said, cheerfully. "*You* see what I mean."

"Tell me," I said at last, "why does he want to die? He must want to die, he's
killing himself, why does he want to die?"

He looked at me in surprise. He licked his lips. "He don't want to die. He
wants to live. Don't nobody want to die, ever."

Then I wanted to ask him—too many things. He could not have answered, or
if he had, I could not have borne the answers. I started walking. "Well, I guess
it's none of my business."

"It's going to be rough on old Sonny," he said. We reached the subway station.
"This is your station?" he asked. I nodded. I took one step down. "Damn!" he
said, suddenly. I looked up at him. He grinned again. "Damn it if I didn't leave
all my money home. You ain't got a dollar on you, have you? Just for a couple
of days, is all."

All at once something inside gave and threatened to come pouring out of me. I didn't hate him any more. I felt that in another moment I'd start crying like a child.

"Sure," I said. "Don't sweat." I looked in my wallet and didn't have a dollar, I only had a five. "Here," I said. "That hold you?"

He didn't look at it—he didn't want to look at it. A terrible, closed look came over his face, as though he were keeping the number on the bill a secret from him and me. "Thanks," he said, and now he was dying to see me go. "Don't worry about Sonny. Maybe I'll write him or something."

"Sure," I said. "You do that. So long."

"Be seeing you," he said. I went on down the steps.

And I didn't write Sonny or send him anything for a long time. When I finally did, it was just after my little girl died, he wrote me back a letter which made me feel like a bastard.

Here's what he said:

Dear brother,

You don't know how much I needed to hear from you. I wanted to write you many a time but I dug how much I must have hurt you and so I didn't write. But now I feel like a man who's been trying to climb up out of some deep, real deep and funky hole and just saw the sun up there, outside. I got to get outside.

I can't tell you much about how I got here. I mean I don't know how to tell you. I guess I was afraid of something or I was trying to escape from something and you know I have never been very strong in the head (smile). I'm glad Mama and Daddy are dead and can't see what's happened to their son and I swear if I'd known what I was doing I would never have hurt you so, you and a lot of other fine people who were nice to me and who believed in me.

I don't want you to think it had anything to do with me being a musician. It's more than that. Or maybe less than that. I can't get anything straight in my head down here and I try not to think about what's going to happen to me when I get outside again. Sometime I think I'm going to flip and *never* get outside and sometime I think I'll come straight back. I tell you one thing, though, I'd rather blow my brains out than go through this again. But that's what they all say, so they tell me. If I tell you when I'm coming to New York and if you could meet me, I sure would appreciate it. Give my love to Isabel and the kids and I was sure sorry to hear about little Gracie. I wish I could be like Mama and say the Lord's will be done, but I don't know it seems to me that trouble is the one thing that never does get stopped and I don't know what good it does to blame it on the Lord. But maybe it does some good if you believe it.

Your brother,
Sonny

Then I kept in constant touch with him and I sent him whatever I could and I went to meet him when he came back to New York. When I saw him many things

I thought I had forgotten came flooding back to me. This was because I had begun, finally, to wonder about Sonny, about the life that Sonny lived inside. This life, whatever it was, had made him older and thinner and it had deepened the distant stillness in which he had always moved. He looked very unlike my baby brother. Yet, when he smiled, when we shook hands, the baby brother I'd never known looked out from the depths of his private life, like an animal waiting to be coaxed into the light.

"How you been keeping?" he asked me.

"All right. And you?"

"Just fine." He was smiling all over his face. "It's good to see you again."

"It's good to see you."

The seven years' difference in our ages lay between us like a chasm: I wondered if these years would ever operate between us as a bridge. I was remembering, and it made it hard to catch my breath, that I had been there when he was born; and I had heard the first words he had ever spoken. When he started to walk, he walked from our mother straight to me. I caught him just before he fell when he took the first steps he ever took in this world.

"How's Isabel?"

"Just fine. She's dying to see you."

"And the boys?"

"They're fine, too. They're anxious to see their uncle."

"Oh, come on. You know they don't remember me."

"Are you kidding? Of course they remember you."

He grinned again. We got into a taxi. We had a lot to say to each other, far too much to know how to begin.

As the taxi began to move, I asked, "You still want to go to India?"

He laughed. "You still remember that. Hell, no. This place is Indian enough for me."

"It used to belong to them," I said.

And he laughed again. "They damn sure knew what they were doing when they got rid of it."

Years ago, when he was around fourteen, he'd been all hipped on the idea of going to India. He read books about people sitting on rocks, naked, in all kinds of weather, but mostly bad, naturally, and walking barefoot through hot coals and arriving at wisdom. I used to say that it sounded to me as though they were getting away from wisdom as fast as they could. I think he sort of looked down on me for that.

"Do you mind," he asked, "if we have the driver drive alongside the park? On the west side—I haven't seen the city in so long."

"Of course not," I said. I was afraid that I might sound as though I were humoring him, but I hoped he wouldn't take it that way.

So we drove along, between the green of the park and the stony, lifeless elegance of hotels and apartment buildings, toward the vivid, killing streets of our childhood. These streets hadn't changed, though housing projects jutted up out of them now like rocks in the middle of a boiling sea. Most of the houses in which we had grown up had vanished, as had the stores from which we had stolen, the basements in which we had first tried sex, the rooftops from which we had hurled tin cans and bricks. But houses exactly like the houses of our past yet dominated the landscape, boys exactly like the boys we once had been found themselves smothering in these houses, came down into the streets for light and air and found themselves encircled by disaster. Some escaped the trap, most didn't. Those who got out always left something of themselves behind, as some animals amputate a leg and leave it in the trap. It might be said, perhaps, that I had escaped, after all, I was a school teacher; or that Sonny had, he hadn't lived in Harlem for years. Yet, as the cab moved uptown through streets which seemed, with a rush, to darken with dark people, and as I covertly studied Sonny's face, it came to me that what we both were seeking through our separate cab windows was that part of ourselves which had been left behind. It's always at the hour of trouble and confrontation that the missing member aches.

We hit 110th Street and started rolling up Lenox Avenue. And I'd known this avenue all my life, but it seemed to me again, as it had seemed on the day I'd first heard about Sonny's trouble, filled with a hidden menace which was its very breath of life.

"We almost there," said Sonny.

"Almost." We were both too nervous to say anything more.

We live in a housing project. It hasn't been up long. A few days after it was up it seemed uninhabitably new, now, of course, it's already rundown. It looks like a parody of the good, clean, faceless life—God knows the people who live in it do their best to make it a parody. The beat-looking grass lying around isn't enough to make their lives green, the hedges will never hold out the streets, and they know it. The big windows fool no one, they aren't big enough to make space out of no space. They don't bother with the windows, they watch the TV screen instead. The playground is most popular with the children who don't play at jacks, or skip rope, or roller skate, or swing, and they can be found in it after dark. We moved in partly because it's not too far from where I teach, and partly for the kids; but it's really just like the houses in which Sonny and I grew up. The same things happen, they'll have the same things to remember. The moment Sonny and I started into the house I had the feeling that I was simply bringing him back into the danger he had almost died trying to escape.

Sonny has never been talkative. So I don't know why I was sure he'd be dying to talk to me when supper was over the first night. Everything went fine, the oldest boy remembered him, and the youngest boy liked him, and Sonny had remembered to bring something for each of them; and Isabel, who is really much nicer than I am, more open and giving, had gone to a lot of trouble about dinner and was genuinely glad to see him. And she's always been able to tease Sonny in a way that I haven't. It was nice to see her face so vivid again and to hear her laugh and watch her make Sonny laugh. She wasn't, or, anyway, she didn't seem to be, at all uneasy or embarrassed. She chatted as though there were no subject which had to be avoided and she got Sonny past his first, faint stiff-ness. And thank God she was there, for I was filled with that icy dread again. Everything I did seemed awkward to me, and everything I said sounded freighted with hidden meaning. I was trying to remember everything I'd heard about dope addiction and I couldn't help watching Sonny for signs. I wasn't do-ing it out of malice. I was trying to find out something about my brother. I was dying to hear him tell me he was safe.

"Safe!" my father grunted, whenever Mama suggested trying to move to a neighborhood which might be safer for children. "Safe, hell! Ain't no place safe for kids, nor nobody."

He always went on like this, but he wasn't, ever, really as bad as he sounded, not even on weekends, when he got drunk. As a matter of fact, he was always on the lookout for "something a little better," but he died before he found it. He died suddenly, during a drunken weekend in the middle of the war, when Sonny was fifteen. He and Sonny hadn't ever got on too well. And this was partly be-cause Sonny was the apple of his father's eye. It was because he loved Sonny so much and was frightened for him, that he was always fighting with him. It doesn't do any good to fight with Sonny. Sonny just moves back, inside himself, where he can't be reached. But the principal reason that they never hit it off is that they were so much alike. Daddy was big and rough and loud-talking, just the op-posite of Sonny, but they both had—that same privacy.

Mama tried to tell me something about this, just after Daddy died. I was home on leave from the army.

This was the last time I ever saw my mother alive. Just the same, this picture gets all mixed up in my mind with pictures I had of her when she was younger. The way I always see her is the way she used to be on a Sunday afternoon, say, when the old folks were talking after the big Sunday dinner. I always see her wearing pale blue. She'd be sitting on the sofa. And my father would be sitting in the easy chair, not far from her. And the living room would be full of church folks and relatives. There they sit, in chairs all around the living room, and the night is creeping up outside, but nobody knows it yet. You can see the darkness growing against the windowpanes and you hear the street noises every now and again, or maybe the jangling beat of a tambourine from one of the churches close by, but it's real quiet in the room. For a moment nobody's talking, but every face looks darkening, like the sky outside. And my mother rocks a little from the waist, and my father's eyes are closed. Everyone is looking at something a child can't see. For a minute they've forgotten the children. Maybe a kid is lying on the rug, half asleep. Maybe somebody's got a kid in his lap and is absent-mindedly stroking the kid's head. Maybe there's a kid, quiet and big-eyed, curled up in a big chair in the corner. The silence, the darkness coming, and the dark-ness in the faces frightens the child obscurely. He hopes that the hand which strokes his forehead will never stop—will never die. He hopes that there will never come a time when the old folks won't be sitting around the living room, talking about where they've come from, and what they've seen, and what's hap-pened to them and their kinfolk.

But something deep and watchful in the child knows that this is bound to end, is already ending. In a moment someone will get up and turn on the light. Then the old folks will remember the children and they won't talk any more that day. And when the light fills the room, the child is filled with darkness. He knows that every time this happens he's moved just a little closer to that darkness outside. The darkness outside is what the old folks have been talking about. It's what they've come from. It's what they endure. The child knows that they won't talk any more because if he knows too much about what's happened to *them,* he'll know too much too soon, about what's going to happen to *him.*

The last time I talked to my mother, I remember I was restless. I wanted to get out and see Isabel. We weren't married then and we had a lot to straighten out between us.

There Mama sat, in black, by the window. She was humming an old church song, *Lord, you brought me from a long ways off.* Sonny was out somewhere. Mama kept watching the streets.

"I don't know," she said, "if I'll ever see you again, after you go off from here. But I hope you'll remember the things I tried to teach you."

"Don't talk like that," I said, and smiled. "You'll be here a long time yet."

She smiled, too, but she said nothing. She was quiet for a long time. And I said, "Mama, don't you worry about nothing. I'll be writing all the time, and you be getting the checks. . . ."

"I want to talk to you about your brother," she said, suddenly. "If anything happens to me he ain't going to have nobody to look out for him."

"Mama," I said, "ain't nothing going to happen to you *or* Sonny. Sonny's all right. He's a good boy and he's got good sense."

"It ain't a question of his being a good boy," Mama said, "nor of his having good sense. It ain't only the bad ones, nor yet the dumb ones that gets sucked under." She stopped, looking at me. "Your Daddy once had a brother," she said, and she smiled in a way that made me feel she was in pain. "You didn't never know that, did you?"

"No," I said, "I never knew that," and I watched her face.

"Oh, yes," she said, "your Daddy had a brother." She looked out of the window again. "I know you never saw your Daddy cry. But *I* did—many a time, through all these years."

I asked her, "What happened to his brother? How come nobody's ever talked about him?"

This was the first time I ever saw my mother look old.

"His brother got killed," she said, "when he was just a little younger than you are now. I knew him. He was a fine boy. He was maybe a little full of the devil, but he didn't mean nobody no harm."

Then she stopped and the room was silent, exactly as it had sometimes been on those Sunday afternoons. Mama kept looking out into the streets.

"He used to have a job in the mill," she said, "and, like all young folks, he just liked to perform on Saturday nights. Saturday nights, him and your father would drift around to different places, go to dances and things like that, or just sit

around with people they knew, and your father's brother would sing, he had a
fine voice, and play along with himself on his guitar. Well, this particular Saturday night, him and your father was coming home from some place, and they were
both a little drunk and there was a moon that night, it was bright like day. Your
father's brother was feeling kind of good, and he was whistling to himself, and
he had his guitar slung over his shoulder. They was coming down a hill and beneath them was a road that turned off from the highway. Well, your father's
brother, being always kind of frisky, decided to run down this hill, and he did,
with that guitar banging and clanging behind him, and he ran across the road,
and he was making water behind a tree. And your father was sort of amused at
him and he was still coming down the hill, kind of slow. Then he heard a car
motor and that same minute his brother stepped from behind the tree, into the
road, in the moonlight. And he started to cross the road. And your father started
to run down the hill, he says he don't know why. This car was full of white men.
They was all drunk, and when they seen your father's brother they let out a great
whoop and holler and they aimed the car straight at him. They was having fun,
they just wanted to scare him, the way they do sometimes, you know. But they
was drunk. And I guess the boy, being drunk, too, and scared, kind of lost his
head. By the time he jumped it was too late. Your father says he heard his brother
scream when the car rolled over him, and he heard the wood of that guitar when
it give, and he heard them strings go flying, and he heard them white men shouting, and the car kept on a-going and it ain't stopped till this day. And, time your
father got down the hill, his brother weren't nothing but blood and pulp."

Tears were gleaming on my mother's face. There wasn't anything I could say.

"He never mentioned it," she said, "because I never let him mention it before
you children. Your Daddy was like a crazy man that night and for many a night
thereafter. He says he never in his life seen anything as dark as that road after
the lights of that car had gone away. Weren't nothing, weren't nobody on that
road, just your Daddy and his brother and that busted guitar. Oh, yes. Your
Daddy never did really get right again. Till the day he died he weren't sure but
that every white man he saw was the man that killed his brother."

She stopped and took out her handkerchief and dried her eyes and
looked at me.

"I ain't telling you all this," she said, "to make you scared or bitter or to make
you hate nobody. I'm telling you this because you got a brother. And the world
ain't changed."

I guess I didn't want to believe this. I guess she saw this in my face. She turned
away from me, toward the window again, searching those streets.

"But I praise my Redeemer," she said at last, "that He called your Daddy
home before me. I ain't saying it to throw no flowers at myself, but, I declare, it
keeps me from feeling too cast down to know I helped your father get safely
through this world. Your father always acted like he was the roughest, strongest
man on earth. And everybody took him to be like that. But if he hadn't had *me*
there—to see his tears!"

She was crying again. Still, I couldn't move. I said, "Lord, Lord, Mama, I didn't know it was like that."

"Oh, honey," she said, "there's a lot that you don't know. But you are going to find it out." She stood up from the window and came over to me. "You got to hold on to your brother," she said, "and don't let him fall, no matter what it looks like is happening to him and no matter how evil you gets with him. You going to be evil with him many a time. But don't you forget what I told you, you hear?"

"I won't forget," I said. "Don't you worry, I won't forget. I won't let nothing happen to Sonny."

My mother smiled as though she were amused at something she saw in my face. Then, "You may not be able to stop nothing from happening. But you got to let him know you's *there.*"

Two days later I was married, and then I was gone. And I had a lot of things on my mind and I pretty well forgot my promise to Mama until I got shipped home on a special furlough for her funeral.

And, after the funeral, with just Sonny and me alone in the empty kitchen, I tried to find out something about him.

"What do you want to do?" I asked him.

"I'm going to be a musician," he said.

For he had graduated, in the time I had been away, from dancing to the juke box to finding out who was playing what, and what they were doing with it, and he had bought himself a set of drums.

"You mean, you want to be a drummer?" I somehow had the feeling that being a drummer might be all right for other people but not for my brother Sonny.

"I don't think," he said, looking at me very gravely, "that I'll ever be a good drummer. But I think I can play a piano."

I frowned. I'd never played the role of the older brother quite so seriously before, had scarcely ever, in fact, *asked* Sonny a damn thing. I sensed myself in the presence of something I didn't really know how to handle, didn't understand. So I made my frown a little deeper as I asked: "What kind of musician do you want to be?"

He grinned, "How many kinds do you think there are?"

"Be *serious,*" I said.

He laughed, throwing his head back, and then looked at me. "I *am* serious."

"Well, then, for Christ's sake, stop kidding around and answer a serious question. I mean, do you want to be a concert pianist, you want to play classical music and all that, or—or what?" Long before I finished he was laughing again. "For Christ's *sake,* Sonny!"

He sobered, but with difficulty. "I'm sorry, But you sound so—*scared!*" and he was off again.

"Well, you may think it's funny now, baby, but's not going to be so funny when you have to make your living at it, let me tell you *that.*" I was furious because I knew he was laughing at me and I didn't know why.

"No," he said, very sober now, and afraid, perhaps, that he'd hurt me, "I don't want to be a classical pianist. That isn't what interests me. I mean"—he paused, looking hard at me, as though his eyes would help me to understand, and then gestured helplessly, as though perhaps his hand would help—"I mean, I'll have a lot of studying to do, and I'll have to study *everything,* but, I mean, I want to play *with*—jazz musicians." He stopped. "I want to play jazz," he said.

Well, the word had never before sounded as heavy, as real, as it sounded that afternoon in Sonny's mouth. I just looked at him and I was probably frowning a real frown by this time. I simply couldn't see why on earth he'd want to spend his time hanging around nightclubs, clowning around on bandstands, while people pushed each other around a dance floor. It seemed—beneath him, somehow. I had never thought about it before, had never been forced to, but I suppose I had always put jazz musicians in a class with what Daddy called "good-time people."

"Are you *serious?*"

"Hell, *yes,* I'm serious."

He looked more helpless than ever, and annoyed, and deeply hurt.

I suggested, helpfully: "You mean—like Louis Armstrong?"

His face closed as though I'd struck him. "No. I'm not talking about none of that old-time, down home crap."

"Well, look, Sonny, I'm sorry, don't get mad. I just don't altogether get it, that's all. Name somebody—you know, a jazz musician you admire."

"Bird."

"Who?"

"Bird! Charlie Parker! Don't they teach you nothing in the goddamn army?"

I lit a cigarette. I was surprised and then a little amused to discover that I was trembling. "I've been out of touch," I said. "You'll have to be patient with me. Now. Who's this Parker character?"

"He's just one of the greatest jazz musicians alive," said Sonny, sullenly, his hands in his pockets, his back to me. "Maybe *the* greatest," he added, bitterly, "that's probably why *you* never heard of him."

"All right," I said, "I'm ignorant. I'm sorry. I'll go out and buy all the cat's records right away, all right?"

"It don't," said Sonny, with dignity, "make any difference to me. I don't care what you listen to. Don't do me no favors."

I was beginning to realize that I'd never seen him so upset before. With another part of my mind I was thinking that this would probably turn out to be one of those things kids go through and that I shouldn't make it seem important by pushing it too hard. Still, I didn't think it would do any harm to ask: "Doesn't all this take a lot of time? Can you make a living at it?"

He turned back to me and half leaned, half sat, on the kitchen table. "Everything takes time," he said, "and—well, yes, sure, I can make a living at it. But what I don't seem to be able to make you understand is that it's the only thing I want to do."

"Well, Sonny," I said, gently, "you know people can't always do exactly what they *want* to do—"

"*No,* I don't know that," said Sonny, surprising me. "I think people *ought* to do what they want to do, what else are they alive for?"

"You getting to be a big boy," I said desperately, "it's time you started thinking about your future."

"I'm thinking about my future," said Sonny, grimly. "I think about it all the time."

I gave up. I decided, if he didn't change his mind, that we could always talk about it later. "In the meantime," I said, "you got to finish school." We had already decided that he'd have to move in with Isabel and her folks. I knew this wasn't the ideal arrangement because Isabel's folks are inclined to be dicty[1] and they hadn't especially wanted Isabel to marry me. But I didn't know what else to do. "And we have to get you fixed up at Isabel's."

There was a long silence. He moved from the kitchen table to the window. "That's a terrible idea. You know it yourself."

"Do you have a *better* idea?"

He just walked up and down the kitchen for a minute. He was as tall as I was. He had started to shave. I suddenly had the feeling that I didn't know him at all.

He stopped at the kitchen table and picked up my cigarettes. Looking at me with a kind of mocking, amused defiance, he put one between his lips. "You mind?"

"You smoking already?"

He lit the cigarette and nodded, watching me through the smoke. "I just wanted to see if I'd have the courage to smoke in front of you." He grinned and blew a great cloud of smoke to the ceiling. "It was easy." He looked at my face. "Come on, now. I bet you was smoking at my age, tell the truth."

I didn't say anything but the truth was on my face, and he laughed. But now there was something very strained in his laugh. "Sure. And I bet that ain't all you was doing."

He was frightening me a little. "Cut the crap," I said. "We already decided that you was going to go and live at Isabel's. Now what's got into you all of a sudden?"

"*You* decided it," he pointed out. "*I* didn't decide nothing." He stopped in front of me, leaning against the stove, arms loosely folded. "Look, brother. I don't want to stay in Harlem no more, I really don't." He was very earnest. He looked at me, then over toward the kitchen window. There was something in his eyes I'd never seen before, some thoughtfulness, some worry all his own. He rubbed the muscle of one arm. "It's time I was getting out of here."

"Where do you want to *go,* Sonny?"

"I want to join the army. Or the navy, I don't care. If I say I'm old enough, they'll believe me."

Then I got mad. It was because I was so scared. "You must be crazy. You goddamn fool, what the hell do you want to go and join the *army* for?"

---

[1]Having upper-class pretensions.

"I just told you. To get out of Harlem."

"Sonny, you haven't even finished *school.* And if you really want to be a musician, how do you expect to study if you're in the *army?*"

He looked at me, trapped, and in anguish. "There's ways. I might be able to work out some kind of deal. Anyway, I'll have the G.I. Bill when I come out."

"*If* you come out." We stared at each other. "Sonny, please. Be reasonable. I know the setup is far from perfect. But we got to do the best we can."

"I ain't learning nothing in school," he said. "Even when I go." He turned away from me and opened the window and threw his cigarette out into the narrow alley. I watched his back. "At least, I ain't learning nothing you'd want me to learn." He slammed the window so hard I thought the glass would fly out, and turned back to me. "And I'm sick of the stink of these garbage cans!"

"Sonny," I said, "I know how you feel. But if you don't finish school now, you're going to be sorry later that you didn't." I grabbed him by the shoulders. "And you only got another year. It ain't so bad. And I'll come back and I swear I'll help you do *whatever* you want to do. Just try to put up with it till I come back. Will you please do that? For me?"

He didn't answer and he wouldn't look at me.

"Sonny. You hear me?"

He pulled away. "I hear you. But you never hear anything *I* say."

I didn't know what to say to that. He looked out of the window and then back at me. "OK," he said, and sighed. "I'll try."

Then I said, trying to cheer him up a little, "They got a piano at Isabel's. You can practice on it."

And as a matter of fact, it did cheer him up for a minute. "That's right," he said to himself. "I forgot that." His face relaxed a little. But the worry, the thoughtfulness, played on it still, the way shadows play on a face which is staring into the fire.

But I thought I'd never hear the end of that piano. At first, Isabel would write me, saying how nice it was that Sonny was so serious about his music and how, as soon as he came in from school, or wherever he had been when he was supposed to be at school, he went straight to that piano and stayed there until suppertime. And, after supper, he went back to that piano and stayed there until everybody went to bed. He was at the piano all day Saturday and all day Sunday. Then he bought a record player and started playing records. He'd play one record over and over again, all day long sometimes, and he'd improvise along with it on the piano. Or he'd play one section of the record, one chord, one change, one progression, then he'd do it on the piano. Then back to the record. Then back to the piano.

Well, I really don't know how they stood it. Isabel finally confessed that it wasn't like living with a person at all, it was like living with sound. And the sound didn't make any sense to her, didn't make any sense to any of them—naturally. They began, in a way, to be afflicted by this presence that was living in their home. It was as though Sonny were some sort of god, or monster. He moved in an atmosphere which wasn't like theirs at all. They fed him and he ate, he washed himself, he walked in and out of their door; he certainly wasn't nasty or unpleasant or rude, Sonny isn't any of those things; but it was as though he were all wrapped up in some cloud, some fire, some vision all his own; and there wasn't any way to reach him.

At the same time, he wasn't really a man yet, he was still a child, and they had to watch out for him in all kinds of ways. They certainly couldn't throw him out. Neither did they dare to make a great scene about that piano because even they dimly sensed, as I sensed, from so many thousands of miles away, that Sonny was at that piano playing for his life.

But he hadn't been going to school. One day a letter came from the school board and Isabel's mother got it—there had, apparently, been other letters but Sonny had torn them up. This day, when Sonny came in, Isabel's mother showed him the letter and asked where he'd been spending his time. And she finally got it out of him that he'd been down in Greenwich Village, with musicians and other characters, in a white girl's apartment. And this scared her and she started to scream at him and what came up, once she began—though she denies it to this day—was what sacrifices they were making to give Sonny a decent home and how little he appreciated it.

Sonny didn't play the piano that day. By evening, Isabel's mother had calmed down but then there was the old man to deal with, and Isabel herself. Isabel says she did her best to be calm but she broke down and started crying. She says she just watched Sonny's face. She could tell, by watching him, what was happening with him. And what was happening was that they penetrated his cloud, they had reached him. Even if their fingers had been a thousand times more gentle than human fingers ever are, he could hardly help feeling that they had stripped him naked and were spitting on that nakedness. For he also had to see that his presence, that music, which was life or death to him, had been torture for them and that they had endured it, not at all for his sake, but only for mine. And Sonny couldn't take that. He can take it a little better today than he could then but he's still not very good at it and, frankly, I don't know anybody who is.

The silence of the next few days must have been louder than the sound of all the music ever played since time began. One morning, before she went to work, Isabel was in his room for something and she suddenly realized that all of his records were gone. And she knew for certain that he was gone. And he was. He went as far as the navy would carry him. He finally sent me a postcard from some place in Greece and that was the first I knew that Sonny was still alive. I didn't see him any more until we were both back in New York and the war had long been over.

He was a man by then, of course, but I wasn't willing to see it. He came by the house from time to time, but we fought almost every time we met. I didn't like the way he carried himself, loose and dreamlike all the time, and I didn't like his friends, and his music seemed to be merely an excuse for the life he led. It sounded just that weird and disordered.

Then we had a fight, a pretty awful fight, and I didn't see him for months. By and by I looked him up, where he was living, in a furnished room in the Village, and I tried to make it up. But there were lots of other people in the room and Sonny just lay on his bed, and he wouldn't come downstairs with me, and he treated these other people as though they were his family and I weren't. So I got mad and then he got mad, and then I told him that he might just as well be dead as live the way he was living. Then he stood up and he told me not to worry about him any more in life, that he *was* dead as far as I was concerned. Then he pushed me to the door and the other people looked on as though nothing were happening, and he slammed the door behind me. I stood in the hallway, staring at the door. I heard somebody laugh in the room and then the tears came to my eyes. I started down the steps, whistling to keep from crying. I kept whistling to myself, *You going to need me, baby, one of these cold, rainy days.*

I read about Sonny's trouble in the spring. Little Grace died in the fall. She was a beautiful little girl. But she only lived a little over two years. She died of polio and she suffered. She had a slight fever for a couple of days, but it didn't seem like anything and we just kept her in bed. And we would certainly have called the doctor, but the fever dropped, she seemed to be all right. So we thought it had just been a cold. Then, one day, she was up, playing, Isabel was in the kitchen fixing lunch for the two boys when they'd come in from school, and she heard Grace fall down in the living room. When you have a lot of children you don't always start running when one of them falls, unless they start screaming or something. And, this time, Grace was quiet. Yet, Isabel says that when she heard that *thump* and then that silence, something happened in her to make her afraid. And she ran to the living room and there was little Grace on the floor, all twisted up, and the reason she hadn't screamed was that she couldn't get her breath. And when she did scream, it was the worst sound, Isabel says, that she'd ever heard in all her life, and she still hears it sometimes in her dreams. Isabel will sometimes wake me up with a low, moaning, strangled sound and I have to be quick to awaken her and hold her to me and where Isabel is weeping against me seems a mortal wound.

I think I may have written Sonny the very day that little Grace was buried. I was sitting in the living room in the dark, by myself, and I suddenly thought of Sonny. My trouble made his real.

One Saturday afternoon, when Sonny had been living with us, or, anyway, been in our house, for nearly two weeks, I found myself wandering aimlessly about the living room, drinking from a can of beer, and trying to work up the courage to search Sonny's room. He was out, he was usually out whenever I was home, and Isabel had taken the children to see their grandparents. Suddenly I was standing still in front of the living room window, watching Seventh Avenue. The idea of searching Sonny's room made me still. I scarcely dared to admit to myself what I'd be searching for. I didn't know what I'd do if I found it. Or if I didn't.

On the sidewalk across from me, near the entrance to a barbecue joint, some people were holding an old-fashioned revival meeting. The barbecue cook, wearing a dirty white apron, his conked[2] hair reddish and metallic in the pale sun, and a cigarette between his lips, stood in the doorway, watching them. Kids and older people paused in their errands and stood there, along with some older men and a couple of very tough-looking women who watched everything that happened on the avenue, as though they owned it, or were maybe owned by it. Well, they were watching this, too. The revival was being carried on by three sisters in black, and a brother. All they had were their voices and their Bibles and a tambourine. The brother was testifying and while he testified two of the sisters stood together, seeming to say, amen, and the third sister walked around with the tambourine outstretched and a couple of people dropped coins into it. Then the brother's testimony ended and the sister who had been taking up the collection dumped the coins into her palm and transferred them to the pocket of her long black robe. Then she raised both hands, striking the tambourine against the air, and then against one hand, and she started to sing. And the two other sisters and the brother joined in.

It was strange, suddenly, to watch, though I had been seeing these street meetings all my life. So, of course, had everybody else down there. Yet, they paused and watched and listened and I stood still at the window. "*Tis the old ship of Zion,*" they sang, and the sister with the tambourine kept a steady, jangling beat, "*it has rescued many a thousand!*" Not a soul under the sound of their voices was hearing this song for the first time, not one of them had been rescued. Nor had they seen much in the way of rescue work being done around them. Neither did they especially believe in the holiness of the three sisters and the brother, they knew too much about them, knew where they lived, and how. The woman with the tambourine, whose voice dominated the air, whose face was bright with joy, was divided by very little from the woman who stood watching her, a cigarette between her heavy, chapped lips, her hair a cuckoo's nest, her face scarred and swollen from many beatings, and her black eyes glittering like coal. Perhaps they both knew this, which was why, when, as rarely, they addressed each other, they addressed each other as Sister. As the singing filled the air the watching, listening faces underwent a change, the eyes focusing on something within; the music seemed to soothe a poison out of them; and time seemed, nearly, to fall away from the sullen, belligerent, battered faces, as though they were fleeing back to their first condition, while dreaming of their last. The barbecue cook half shook his head and smiled, and dropped his cigarette and disappeared into his joint. A man fumbled in his pockets for change and stood holding it in his hand impatiently, as though he had just remembered a pressing appointment further up the avenue. He looked furious. Then I saw Sonny, standing on the edge of the crowd. He was carrying a wide, flat notebook with a green cover, and it made him look, from where I was standing, almost like a schoolboy. The coppery sun brought out the copper in his skin, he was very faintly smiling, standing very still. Then the singing stopped, the tambourine turned into a collection plate again. The furious man dropped in his coins and vanished, so did a couple of the women, and Sonny

---

[2]Straightened.

dropped some change in the plate, looking directly at the woman with a little smile. He started across the avenue, toward the house. He has a slow, loping walk, something like the way Harlem hipsters walk, only he's imposed on this his own half-beat. I had never really noticed it before.

I stayed at the window, both relieved and apprehensive. As Sonny disappeared from my sight, they began singing again. And they were still singing when his key turned in the lock.

"Hey," he said.

"Hey, yourself. You want some beer?"

"No. Well, maybe." But he came up to the window and stood beside me, looking out. "What a warm voice," he said.

They were singing *If I could only hear my mother pray again!*

"Yes," I said, "and she can sure beat that tambourine."

"But what a terrible song," he said, and laughed. He dropped his notebook on the sofa and disappeared into the kitchen. "Where's Isabel and the kids?"

"I think they went to see their grandparents. You hungry?"

"No." He came back into the living room with his can of beer. "You want to come some place with me tonight?"

I sensed, I don't know how, that I couldn't possibly say no. "Sure. Where?"

He sat down on the sofa and picked up his notebook and started leafing through it. "I'm going to sit in with some fellows in a joint in the Village."

"You mean, you're going to play, tonight?"

"That's right." He took a swallow of his beer and moved back to the window. He gave me a sidelong look. "If you can stand it."

"I'll try," I said.

He smiled to himself and we both watched as the meeting across the way broke up. The three sisters and the brother, heads bowed, were singing *God be with you till we meet again.* The faces around them were very quiet. Then the song ended. The small crowd dispersed. We watched the three women and the lone man walk slowly up the avenue.

"When she was singing before," said Sonny, abruptly, "her voice reminded me for a minute of what heroin feels like sometimes—when it's in your veins. It makes you feel sort of warm and cool at the same time. And distant. And—and sure." He sipped his beer, very deliberately not looking at me. I watched his face. "It makes you feel—in control. Sometimes you've got to have that feeling."

"Do you?" I sat down slowly in the easy chair.

"Sometimes." He went to the sofa and picked up his notebook again. "Some people do."

"In order," I asked, "to play?" And my voice was very ugly, full of contempt and anger.

"Well"—he looked at me with great, troubled eyes, as though, in fact, he hoped his eyes would tell me things he could never otherwise say—"they *think* so. And *if* they think so—!"

"And what do *you* think?" I asked.

He sat on the sofa and put his can of beer on the floor. "I don't know," he said, and I couldn't be sure if he were answering my question or pursuing his thoughts. His face didn't tell me. "It's not so much to *play*. It's to *stand* it, to be able to make it at all. On any level." He frowned and smiled: "In order to keep from shaking to pieces."

"But these friends of yours," I said, "they seem to shake themselves to pieces pretty goddamn fast."

"Maybe." He played with the notebook. And something told me that I should curb my tongue, that Sonny was doing his best to talk, that I should listen. "But of course you only know the ones that've gone to pieces. Some don't—or at least they haven't *yet* and that's just about all *any* of us can say." He paused. "And then there are some who just live, really, in hell, and they know it and they see what's happening and they go right on. I don't know." He sighed, dropped the notebook, folded his arms. "Some guys, you can tell from the way they play, they on something *all* the time. And you can see that, well, it makes something real for them. But of course," he picked up his beer from the floor and sipped it and put the can down again, "they *want* to, too, you've got to see that. Even some of them that say they don't—*some,* not all."

"And what about you?" I asked—I couldn't help it. "What about you? Do *you* want to?"

He stood up and walked to the window and remained silent for a long time. Then he sighed. "Me," he said. Then: "While I was downstairs before, on my way here, listening to that woman sing, it struck me all of a sudden how much suffering she must have had to go through—to sing like that. It's *repulsive* to think you have to suffer that much."

I said: "But there's no way not to suffer—is there, Sonny?"

"I believe not," he said and smiled, "but that's never stopped anyone from trying." He looked at me. "Has it?" I realized, with this mocking look, that there stood between us, forever, beyond the power of time or forgiveness, the fact that I had held silence—so long!—when he had needed human speech to help him. He turned back to the window. "No, there's no way not to suffer. But you try all kinds of ways to keep from drowning in it, to keep on top of it, and to make it seem—well, like *you*. Like you did something, all right, and now you're suffering for it. You know?" I said nothing. "Well you know," he said, impatiently, "why *do* people suffer? Maybe it's better to do something to give it a reason, *any* reason."

"But we just agreed," I said, "that there's no way not to suffer. Isn't it better, then, just to—take it?"

"But nobody just takes it," Sonny cried, "that's what I'm telling you! *Everybody* tries not to. You're just hung up on the *way* some people try—it's not *your* way!"

The hair on my face began to itch, my face felt wet. "That's not true," I said, "that's not true. I don't give a damn what other people do, I don't even care how they suffer. I just care how *you* suffer." And he looked at me. "Please believe me," I said, "I don't want to see you—die—trying not to suffer."

"I won't," he said, flatly, "die trying not to suffer. At least, not any faster than anybody else."

"But there's no need," I said, trying to laugh, "is there? in killing yourself."

I wanted to say more, but I couldn't. I wanted to talk about will power and how life could be—well, beautiful. I wanted to say that it was all within; but was it? or, rather, wasn't that exactly the trouble? And I wanted to promise that I would never fail him again. But it would all have sounded—empty words and lies.

So I made the promise to myself and prayed that I would keep it.

"It's terrible sometimes, inside," he said, "that's what's the trouble. You walk these streets, black and funky and cold, and there's not really a living ass to talk to, and there's nothing shaking, and there's no way of getting it out—that storm inside. You can't talk it and you can't make love with it, and when you finally try to get with it and play it, you realize *nobody's* listening. So *you've* got to listen. You got to find a way to listen."

And then he walked away from the window and sat on the sofa again, as though all the wind had suddenly been knocked out of him. "Sometimes you'll do *anything* to play, even cut your mother's throat." He laughed and looked at me. "Or your brother's." Then he sobered. "Or your own." Then: "Don't worry. I'm all right now and I think I'll *be* all right. But I can't forget—where I've been. I don't mean just the physical place I've been, I mean where I've *been*. And *what* I've been."

"What have you been, Sonny?" I asked.

He smiled—but sat sideways on the sofa, his elbow resting on the back, his fingers playing with his mouth and chin, not looking at me. "I've been something I didn't recognize, didn't know I could be. Didn't know anybody could be." He stopped, looking inward, looking helplessly young, looking old. "I'm not talking about it now because I feel *guilty* or anything like that—maybe it would be better if I did, I don't know. Anyway, I can't really talk about it. Not to you, not to anybody," and now he turned and faced me. "Sometimes, you know, and it was actually when I was most *out* of the world, I felt that I was in it, that I was *with* it, really, and I could play or I didn't really have to *play*, it just came out of me, it was there. And I don't know how I played, thinking about it now, but I know I did awful things, those times, sometimes, to people. Or it wasn't that I *did* anything to them—it was that they weren't real." He picked up the beer can; it was empty; he rolled it between his palms: "And other times—well, I needed a fix, I needed to find a place to lean, I needed to clear a space to *listen*—and I couldn't find it, and I—went crazy, I did terrible things to *me*, I was terrible *for* me." He began pressing the beer can between his hands, I watched the metal begin to give. It glittered, as he played with it, like a knife, and I was afraid he would cut himself, but I said nothing. "Oh well. I can never tell you. I was all by myself at the bottom of something, stinking and sweating and crying and shaking, and I smelled it, you know? *my* stink, and I thought I'd die if I couldn't get away from it and yet, all the same, I knew that everything I was doing was just locking me in with it. And I didn't know," he paused, still flattening the beer can, "I didn't know, I still *don't* know, something kept telling me that maybe it was good to smell your own stink, but I didn't think that *that* was what I'd been trying to do—and—who can stand it?" and he abruptly dropped the ruined beer can, looking at me with a small, still smile, and then rose, walking to the window as though it were the lodestone rock. I watched his face, he watched the avenue. "I couldn't tell you when Mama died—but the reason I wanted to leave Harlem so bad was to get away from drugs. And then, when I ran away, that's what I was running from—really. When I came back, nothing had changed, *I* hadn't changed, I was just—older." And he stopped, drumming with his fingers on the windowpane. The sun had vanished, soon darkness would fall. I watched his face. "It can come again," he said, almost as though speaking to himself. Then he turned to me. "It can come again," he repeated. "I just want you to know that."

"All right," I said, at last. "So it can come again, All right."

He smiled, but the smile was sorrowful. "I had to try to tell you," he said.

"Yes," I said. "I understand that."

"You're my brother," he said, looking straight at me, and not smiling at all.

"Yes," I repeated, "yes. I understand that."

He turned back to the window, looking out. "All that hatred down there," he said, "all that hatred and misery and love. It's a wonder it doesn't blow the avenue apart."

We went to the only nightclub on a short, dark street, downtown. We squeezed through the narrow, chattering, jampacked bar to the entrance of the big room, where the bandstand was. And we stood there for a moment, for the lights were very dim in this room and we couldn't see. Then, "Hello, boy," said a voice and an enormous black man, much older than Sonny or myself, erupted out of all that atmospheric lighting and put an arm around Sonny's shoulder. "I been sitting right here," he said, "waiting for you."

He had a big voice, too, and heads in the darkness turned toward us.

Sonny grinned and pulled a little away, and said, "Creole, this is my brother. I told you about him."

Creole shook my hand. "I'm glad to meet you, son," he said, and it was clear that he was glad to meet me *there,* for Sonny's sake. And he smiled, "You got a real musician in *your* family," and he took his arm from Sonny's shoulder and slapped him, lightly, affectionately, with the back of his hand.

"Well. Now I've heard it all," said a voice behind us. This was another musician, and a friend of Sonny's, a coal-black, cheerful-looking man, built close to the ground. He immediately began confiding to me, at the top of his lungs, the most terrible things about Sonny, his teeth gleaming like a lighthouse and his laugh coming up out of him like the beginning of an earthquake. And it turned out that everyone at the bar knew Sonny, or almost everyone; some were musicians, working there, or nearby, or not working, some were simply hangers-on, and some were there to hear Sonny play. I was introduced to all of them and they were all very polite to me. Yet, it was clear that, for them, I was only Sonny's brother. Here, I was in Sonny's world. Or, rather: his kingdom. Here, it was not even a question that his veins bore royal blood.

They were going to play soon and Creole installed me, by myself, at a table in a dark corner. Then I watched them, Creole, and the little black man, and Sonny, and the others, while they horsed around, standing just below the bandstand. The light from the bandstand spilled just a little short of them and, watching them laughing and gesturing and moving about, I had the feeling that they, nevertheless, were being most careful not to step into that circle of light too suddenly: that if they moved into the light too suddenly, without thinking, they would perish in flame. Then, while I watched, one of them, the small, black man, moved into the light and crossed the bandstand and started fooling around with his drums. Then—being funny and being, also, extremely ceremonious—Creole took Sonny by the arm and led him to the piano. A woman's voice called Sonny's name and a few hands started clapping. And Sonny, also being funny and being ceremonious, and so touched, I think, that he could have cried, but neither hiding it nor showing it, riding it like a man, grinned, and put both hands to his heart and bowed from the waist.

Creole then went to the bass fiddle and a lean, very bright-skinned brown man jumped up on the bandstand and picked up his horn. So there they were, and the atmosphere on the bandstand and in the room began to change and tighten. Someone stepped up to the microphone and announced them. Then there were all kinds of murmurs. Some people at the bar shushed others. The waitress ran around, frantically getting in the last orders, guys and chicks got closer to each other, and the lights on the bandstand, on the quartet, turned to a kind of indigo. Then they all looked different there. Creole looked about him for the last time, as though he were making certain that all his chickens were in the coop, and then he—jumped and struck the fiddle. And there they were.

All I know about music is that not many people ever really hear it. And even then, on the rare occasions when something opens within, and the music enters, what we mainly hear, or hear corroborated, are personal, private, vanishing evocations. But the man who creates the music is hearing something else, is dealing with the roar rising from the void and imposing order on it as it hits the air. What is evoked in him, then, is of another order, more terrible because it has no words, and triumphant, too, for that same reason. And his triumph, when he triumphs, is ours. I just watched Sonny's face. His face was troubled, he was working hard, but he wasn't with it. And I had the feeling that, in a way, everyone on the bandstand was waiting for him, both waiting for him and pushing him along. But as I began to watch Creole, I realized that it was Creole who held them all back. He had them on a short rein. Up there, keeping the beat with his whole body, wailing on the fiddle, with his eyes half closed, he was listening to everything, but he was listening to Sonny. He was having a dialogue with Sonny. He wanted Sonny to leave the shoreline and strike out for the deep water. He was Sonny's witness that deep water and drowning were not the same thing—he had been there, and he knew. And he wanted Sonny to know. He was waiting for Sonny to do the things on the keys which would let Creole know that Sonny was in the water.

And, while Creole listened, Sonny moved, deep within, exactly like someone in torment. I had never before thought of how awful the relationship must be between the musician and his instrument. He has to fill it, this instrument, with the breath of life, his own. He has to make it do what he wants it to do. And a piano is just a piano. It's made out of so much wood and wires and little hammers and big ones, and ivory. While there's only so much you can do with it, the only way to find this out is to try; to try and make it do everything.

And Sonny hadn't been near a piano for over a year. And he wasn't on much better terms with his life, not the life that stretched before him now. He and the piano stammered, started one way, got scared, stopped; started another way, panicked, marked time, started again; then seemed to have found a direction, panicked again, got stuck. And the face I saw on Sonny I'd never seen before. Everything had been burned out of it, and, at the same time, things usually hidden were being burned in, by the fire and fury of the battle which was occurring in him up there.

Yet, watching Creole's face as they neared the end of the first set, I had the feeling that something had happened, something I hadn't heard. Then they finished, there was scattered applause, and then, without an instant's warning, Creole started into something else, it was almost sardonic, it was *Am I Blue*. And, as though he commanded, Sonny began to play. Something began to happen. And Creole let out the reins. The dry, low, black man said something awful on the drums, Creole answered, and the drums talked back. Then the horn insisted, sweet and high, slightly detached perhaps, and Creole listened, commenting now and then, dry, and driving, beautiful and calm and old. Then they all came together again, and Sonny was part of the family again. I could tell this from his face. He seemed to have found, right there beneath his fingers, a damn brand-new piano. It seemed that he couldn't get over it. Then, for awhile, just being happy with Sonny, they seemed to be agreeing with him that brand-new pianos certainly were a gas.

Then Creole stepped forward to remind them that what they were playing was the blues. He hit something in all of them, he hit something in me, myself, and the music tightened and deepened, apprehension began to beat the air. Creole began to tell us what the blues were all about. They were not about anything very new. He and his boys up there were keeping it new, at the risk of ruin, destruction, madness, and death, in order to find new ways to make us listen. For, while the tale of how we suffer, and how we are delighted, and how we may triumph is never new, it always must be heard. There isn't any other tale to tell, it's the only light we've got in all this darkness.

And this tale, according to that face, that body, those strong hands on those strings, has another aspect in every country, and a new depth in every generation. Listen, Creole seemed to be saying, listen. Now these are Sonny's blues. He made the little black man on the drums know it, and the bright, brown man on the horn. Creole wasn't trying any longer to get Sonny in the water. He was wishing him Godspeed. Then he stepped back, very slowly, filling the air with the immense suggestion that Sonny speak for himself.

Then they all gathered around Sonny and Sonny played. Every now and again one of them seemed to say, amen. Sonny's fingers filled the air with life, his life.

But that life contained so many others. And Sonny went all the way back, he really began with the spare, flat statement of the opening phrase of the song. Then he began to make it his. It was very beautiful because it wasn't hurried and it was no longer a lament. I seemed to hear with what burning he had made it his, with what burning we had yet to make it ours, how we could cease lamenting. Freedom lurked around us and I understood, at last, that he could help us to be free if we would listen, that he would never be free until we did. Yet, there was no battle in his face now. I heard what he had gone through, and would continue to go through until he came to rest in earth. He had made it his: that long line, of which we knew only Mama and Daddy. And he was giving it back, as everything must be given back, so that, passing through death, it can live forever. I saw my mother's face again, and felt, for the first time, how the stones of the road she had walked on must have bruised her feet. I saw the moonlit road where my father's brother died. And it brought something else back to me, and carried me past it, I saw my little girl again and felt Isabel's tears again, and I felt my own tears begin to rise. And I was yet aware that this was only a moment, that the world waited outside, as hungry as a tiger, and that trouble stretched above us, longer than the sky.

Then it was over. Creole and Sonny let out their breath, both soaking wet, and grinning. There was a lot of applause and some of it was real. In the dark, the girl came by and I asked her to take drinks to the bandstand. There was a long pause, while they talked up there in the indigo light and after awhile I saw the girl put a Scotch and milk on top of the piano for Sonny. He didn't seem to notice it, but just before they started playing again, he sipped from it and looked toward me, and nodded. Then he put it back on top of the piano. For me, then, as they began to play again, it glowed and shook above my brother's head like the very cup of trembling.

Study and Discussion Questions

1. In what ways are Sonny and his brother different? How, for example, do their relationships to the Harlem community differ? What might account for these differences?
2. Why does Baldwin begin the story with the narrator reading about Sonny in the newspaper? Why does the narrator have so little interest in his brother at first? What is he afraid of? Why does he feel guilty?
3. How were the narrator and Sonny able to grow up together and yet remain such strangers?
4. What experiences bring the narrator closer to Sonny and help him understand his brother better?
5. Why does Sonny use heroin? Why does his music mean so much to him? Why the blues?
6. What has the narrator learned by the end of the story?
7. Events in the story are narrated out of chronological order. What is the effect of the story's structure?

Suggestions for Writing

1. What do you think Sonny's future might be? Write a brief narrative of the next five or ten years.
2. Listen to some instrumental music and try to put into words what is going on in it, in the way Baldwin does at the end of the story.
3. Imagine that, at the end of Sonny's performance, the narrator were, for some reason, swept off to another country, never to see or talk to his brother again. Write the letter he might have written, telling Sonny how he now feels about him.

Critical Resources

1. Lemming, David. *James Baldwin: A Biography.* New York: Alfred Knopf, 1994.
2. Reid, Robert. "The Powers of Darkness in 'Sonny's Blues.' " *CLA Journal* 43.4 (2000): 443–453.
3. Standley, Fred and Nancy Burt, eds. *Critical Essays on James Baldwin.* Boston: Hall, 1988.
4. Standley, Fred and Louis Pratt, eds. *Conversations with James Baldwin.* Jackson: UP of Mississippi, 1989.

NATHANIAL HAWTHORNE (1804–1864)

Nathaniel Hawthorne was born into an established Puritan family in Salem, Massachusetts. After graduating from Bowdoin College in 1825, Hawthorne aspired to literary fame and returned to Salem to begin writing stories. For the next decade, he irregularly sold his work to literary magazines. Finally, in 1837, Hawthorne published his first collection of short stories (then called "romances") Twice-Told Tales, which would bring him the literary acknowledgment he was seeking, but not the income necessary to support his new family. To supplement his income, Hawthorne was forced to take on other work, serving as a customs inspector in Boston for a few years, then as the American consul to Liverpool, appointed by his close friend President Franklin Pierce. Throughout these years, he continued to write, crafting short stories and novels that probed the individual's struggle with conscience and the weight of Puritan guilt. In a lush prose style, and with the frequent use of allegory, his works tend to move in and out of ambiguity, creating multiple levels of meaning. His other works include Mosses from an Old Manse *(1846),* The Scarlet Letter *(1850),* The House of the Seven Gables *(1851),* The Blithedale Romance *(1852), and* The Marble Faun *(1860). "Young Goodman Brown," first published in* Mosses from an Old Manse, *is a prime example of the gothic and Puritan influences in Hawthorne's writing and "has provoked perhaps more discussion than any other short story in American fiction"* (Nathaniel Hawthorne, *Introduction, 1979).*

Young Goodman Brown   (1846)

Young Goodman[1] Brown came forth at sunset into the street at Salem village; but put his head back, after crossing the threshold, to exchange a parting kiss with his young wife. And Faith, as the wife was aptly named, thrust her own pretty head into the street, letting the wind play with the pink ribbons of her cap while she called to Goodman Brown.

"Dearest heart," whispered she, softly and rather sadly, when her lips were close to his ear, "prithee put off your journey until sunrise and sleep in your own bed to-night. A lone woman is troubled with such dreams and such thoughts that she's afeard of herself sometimes. Pray tarry with me this night, dear husband, of all nights in the year."

"My love and my Faith," replied young Goodman Brown, "of all nights in the year, this one night must I tarry away from thee. My journey, as thou callest it, forth and back again, must needs be done 'twixt now and sunrise. What, my sweet, pretty wife, dost thou doubt me already, and we but three months married?"

"Then God bless you!" said Faith, with the pink ribbons; "and may you find all well when you come back."

"Amen!" cried Goodman Brown. "Say thy prayers, dear Faith, and go to bed at dusk, and no harm will come to thee."

So they parted; and the young man pursued his way until, being about to turn the corner by the meeting-house, he looked back and saw the head of Faith still peeping after him with a melancholy air, in spite of her pink ribbons.

"Poor little Faith!" thought he, for his heart smote him. "What a wretch am I to leave her on such an errand! She talks of dreams, too. Methought as she spoke there was trouble in her face, as if a dream had warned her what work is to be done to-night. But no, no; 'twould kill her to think it. Well, she's a blessed angel on earth; and after this one night I'll cling to her skirts and follow her to heaven."

With this excellent resolve for the future, Goodman Brown felt himself justified in making more haste on his present evil purpose. He had taken a dreary road, darkened by all the gloomiest trees of the forest, which barely stood aside to let the narrow path creep through, and closed immediately behind. It was all as lonely as could be; and there is this peculiarity in such a solitude, that the traveller knows not who may be concealed by the innumerable trunks and the thick boughs overhead; so that with lonely footsteps he may yet be passing through an unseen multitude.

"There may be a devilish Indian behind every tree," said Goodman Brown to himself; and he glanced fearfully behind him as he added, "What if the devil himself should be at my very elbow!"

His head being turned back, he passed a crook of the road, and, looking forward again, beheld the figure of a man, in grave and decent attire, seated at the

---

[1]Goodman and Goody (used later) were respectful terms of address for men and women not of the upper classes.

foot of an old tree. He arose at Goodman Brown's approach and walked onward side by side with him.

"You are late, Goodman Brown," said he. "The clock of the Old South was striking as I came through Boston, and that is full fifteen minutes agone."

"Faith kept me back a while," replied the young man, with a tremor in his voice, caused by the sudden appearance of his companion, though not wholly unexpected.

It was now deep dusk in the forest, and deepest in that part of it where these two were journeying. As nearly as could be discerned, the second traveller was about fifty years old, apparently in the same rank of life as Goodman Brown, and bearing a considerable resemblance to him, though perhaps more in expression than features. Still they might have been taken for father and son. And yet, though the elder person was as simply clad as the younger, and as simple in manner too, he had an indescribable air of one who knew the world, and who would not have felt abashed at the governor's dinner table or in King William's court, were it possible that his affairs should call him thither. But the only thing about him that could be fixed upon as remarkable was his staff, which bore the likeness of a great black snake, so curiously wrought that it might almost be seen to twist and wriggle itself like a living serpent. This, of course, must have been an ocular deception, assisted by the uncertain light.

"Come, Goodman Brown," cried his fellow-traveller, "this is a dull pace for the beginning of a journey. Take my staff, if you are so soon weary."

"Friend," said the other, exchanging his slow pace for a full stop, "having kept covenant by meeting thee here, it is my purpose now to return whence I came. I have scruples touching the matter thou wot'st of."

"Sayest thou so?" replied he of the serpent, smiling apart. "Let us walk on, nevertheless, reasoning as we go; and if I convince thee not thou shalt turn back. We are but a little way in the forest yet."

"Too far! too far!" exclaimed the goodman, unconsciously resuming his walk. "My father never went into the woods on such an errand, nor his father before him. We have been a race of honest men and good Christians since the days of the martyrs; and shall I be the first of the name of Brown that ever took this path and kept"—

"Such company, thou wouldst say," observed the elder person, interpreting his pause. "Well said, Goodman Brown! I have been as well acquainted with your family as with ever a one among the Puritans; and that's no trifle to say. I helped your grandfather, the constable, when he lashed the Quaker woman so smartly through the streets of Salem; and it was I that brought your father a pitch-pine knot, kindled at my own hearth, to set fire to an Indian village, in King Philip's war.[2] They were my good friends, both; and many a pleasant walk have we had along this path, and returned merrily after midnight. I would fain be friends with you for their sake."

---

[2]War between Indians and New England colonists, 1675–1676.

"If it be as thou sayest," replied Goodman Brown, "I marvel they never spoke of these matters; or, verily, I marvel not, seeing that the least rumor of the sort would have driven them from New England. We are a people of prayer, and good works to boot, and abide no such wickedness."

"Wickedness or not," said the traveller with the twisted staff, "I have a very general acquaintance here in New England. The deacons of many a church have drunk the communion wine with me; the selectmen of divers towns make me their chairman; and a majority of the Great and General Court are firm supporters of my interest. The governor and I, too—But these are state secrets."

"Can this be so?" cried Goodman Brown, with a stare of amazement at his undisturbed companion. "Howbeit, I have nothing to do with the governor and council; they have their own ways, and are no rule for a simple husbandman like me. But, were I to go on with thee, how should I meet the eye of that good old man, our minister, at Salem village? Oh, his voice would make me tremble both Sabbath day and lecture day."

Thus far the elder traveller had listened with due gravity; but now burst into a fit of irrepressible mirth, shaking himself so violently that his snake-like staff actually seemed to wriggle in sympathy.

"Ha! ha! ha!" shouted he again and again; then composing himself, "Well, go on, Goodman Brown, go on; but, prithee, don't kill me with laughing."

"Well, then, to end the matter at once," said Goodman Brown, considerably nettled, "there is my wife, Faith. It would break her dear little heart; and I'd rather break my own."

"Nay, if that be the case," answered the other, "e'en go thy ways, Goodman Brown. I would not for twenty old women like the one hobbling before us that Faith should come to any harm."

As he spoke he pointed his staff at a female figure on the path, in whom Goodman Brown recognized a very pious and exemplary dame, who had taught him his catechism in youth, and was still his moral and spiritual adviser, jointly with the minister and Deacon Gookin.

"A marvel, truly, that Goody Cloyse should be so far in the wilderness at nightfall," said he. "But with your leave, friend, I shall take a cut through the woods until we have left this Christian woman behind. Being a stranger to you she might ask whom I was consorting with and whither I was going."

"Be it so," said his fellow-traveller. "Betake you the woods, and let me keep the path."

Accordingly the young man turned aside, but took care to watch his companion, who advanced softly along the road until he had come within a staff's length of the old dame. She, meanwhile, was making the best of her way, with singular speed for so aged a woman, and mumbling some indistinct words—a prayer, doubtless—as she went. The traveller put forth his staff and touched her withered neck with what seemed the serpent's tail.

"The devil!" screamed the pious old lady.

"Then Goody Cloyse knows her old friend?" observed the traveller, confronting her and leaning on his writhing stick.

"Ah, forsooth, and is it your worship indeed?" cried the good dame. "Yea, truly is it, and in the very image of my old gossip, Goodman Brown, the grandfather of the silly fellow that now is. But—would your worship believe it?—my broomstick hath strangely disappeared, stolen, as I suspect, by that unhanged witch, Goody Cory, and that, too, when I was all anointed with the juice of smallage, and cinquefoil, and wolf's bane"—

"Mingled with fine wheat and the fat of a new-born babe," said the shape of old Goodman Brown.

"Ah, your worship knows the recipe," cried the old lady, cackling aloud. "So, as I was saying, being all ready for the meeting, and no horse to ride on, I made up my mind to foot it; for they tell me there is a nice young man to be taken into communion to-night. But now your good worship will lend me your arm, and we shall be there in a twinkling."

"That can hardly be," answered her friend. "I may not spare you my arm, Goody Cloyse; but here is my staff, if you will."

So saying, he threw it down at her feet, where, perhaps, it assumed life, being one of the rods which its owner had formerly lent to the Egyptian magi. Of this fact, however, Goodman Brown could not take cognizance. He had cast up his eyes in astonishment, and, looking down again, beheld neither Goody Cloyse nor the serpentine staff, but this fellow-traveller alone, who waited for him as calmly as if nothing had happened.

"That old woman taught me my catechism," said the young man; and there was a world of meaning in this simple comment.

They continued to walk onward, while the elder traveller exhorted his companion to make good speed and persevere in the path, discoursing so aptly that his arguments seemed rather to spring up in the bosom of his auditor than to be suggested by himself. As they went, he plucked a branch of maple to serve for a walking stick, and began to strip it of the twigs and little boughs, which were wet with evening dew. The moment his fingers touched them they became strangely withered and dried up as with a week's sunshine. Thus the pair proceeded, at a good free pace, until suddenly, in a gloomy hollow of the road, Goodman Brown sat himself down on the stump of a tree and refused to go any farther.

"Friend," said he, stubbornly, "my mind is made up. Not another step will I budge on this errand. What if a wretched old woman do choose to go to the devil when I thought she was going to heaven: is that any reason why I should quit my dear Faith and go after her?"

"You will think better of this by and by," said his acquaintance, composedly. "Sit here and rest yourself a while; and when you feel like moving again, there is my staff to help you along."

Without more words, he threw his companion the maple stick, and was as speedily out of sight as if he had vanished into the deepening gloom. The young man sat a few moments by the roadside, applauding himself greatly, and thinking with how clear a conscience he should meet the minister in his morning walk, nor shrink from the eye of good old Deacon Gookin. And what calm sleep would be his that very night, which was to have been spent so wickedly, but so purely and sweetly now, in the arms of Faith! Amidst these pleasant and praise-worthy meditations, Goodman Brown heard the tramp of horses along the road, and deemed it advisable to conceal himself within the verge of the forest, conscious of the guilty purpose that had brought him thither, though now so happily turned from it.

On came the hoof tramps and the voices of the riders, two grave old voices, conversing soberly as they drew near. These mingled sounds appeared to pass along the road, within a few yards of the young man's hiding-place; but, owing doubtless to the depth of the gloom at that particular spot, neither the travellers nor their steeds were visible. Though their figures brushed the small boughs by the wayside, it could not be seen that they intercepted, even for a moment, the faint gleam from the strip of bright sky athwart which they must have passed. Goodman Brown alternately crouched and stood on tiptoe, pulling aside the branches and thrusting forth his head as far as he durst without discerning so much as a shadow. It vexed him the more, because he could have sworn, were such a thing possible, that he recognized the voices of the minister and Deacon Gookin, jogging along quietly, as they were wont to do, when bound to some ordination or ecclesiastical council. While yet within hearing, one of the riders stopped to pluck a switch.

"Of the two, reverend sir," said the voice like the deacon's, "I had rather miss an ordination dinner than to-night's meeting. They tell me that some of our community are to be here from Falmouth and beyond, and others from Connecticut and Rhode Island, besides several of the Indian powwows, who, after their fashion, know almost as much deviltry as the best of us. Moreover, there is a goodly young woman to be taken into communion."

"Mighty well, Deacon Gookin!" replied the solemn old tones of the minister. "Spur up, or we shall be late. Nothing can be done, you know, until I get on the ground."

The hoofs clattered again; and the voices, talking so strangely in the empty air, passed on through the forest, where no church had ever been gathered or solitary Christian prayed. Wither, then, could these holy men be journeying so deep into the heathen wilderness? Young Goodman Brown caught hold of a tree for support, being ready to sink down on the ground, faint and overburdened with the heavy sickness of his heart. He looked up to the sky, doubting whether there really was a heaven above him. Yet there was the blue arch, and the stars brightening in it.

"With heaven above and Faith below, I will yet stand firm against the devil!" cried Goodman Brown.

While he still gazed upward into the deep arch of the firmament and had lifted his hands to pray, a cloud, though no wind was stirring, hurried across the zenith and hid the brightening stars. The blue sky was still visible, except directly overhead, where this black mass of cloud was sweeping swiftly northward. Aloft in the air, as if from the depths of the cloud, came a confused and doubtful sound of voices. Once the listener fancied that he could distinguish the accents of towns-people of his own, men and women, both pious and ungodly, many of whom he had met at the communion table, and had seen others rioting at the tavern. The next moment, so indistinct were the sounds, he doubted whether he had heard aught but the murmur of the old forest, whispering without a wind. Then came a stronger swell of those familiar tones, heard daily in the sunshine at Salem village, but never until now from a cloud of night. There was one voice, of a young woman, uttering lamentations, yet with an uncertain sorrow, and entreating for some favor, which, perhaps, it would grieve her to obtain; and all the unseen multitude, both saints and sinners, seemed to encourage her onward.

"Faith!" shouted Goodman Brown, in a voice of agony and desperation; and the echoes of the forest mocked him, crying, "Faith! Faith!" as if bewildered wretches were seeking her all through the wilderness.

The cry of grief, rage, and terror was yet piercing the night, when the unhappy husband held his breath for a response. There was a scream, drowned immediately in a louder murmur of voices, fading into far-off laughter, as the dark cloud swept away, leaving the clear and silent sky above Goodman Brown. But something fluttered lightly down through the air and caught on the branch of a tree. The young man seized it, and beheld a pink ribbon.

"My Faith is gone!" cried he, after one stupefied moment. "There is no good on earth; and sin is but a name. Come, devil; for to thee is this world given."

And, maddened with despair, so that he laughed loud and long, did Goodman Brown grasp his staff and set forth again, at such a rate that he seemed to fly along the forest path rather than to walk or run. The road grew wilder and drearier and more faintly traced, and vanished at length, leaving him in the heart of the dark wilderness, still rushing onward with the instinct that guides mortal man to evil. The whole forest was peopled with frightful sounds—the creaking of the trees, the howling of wild beasts, and the yell of Indians; while sometimes the wind tolled like a distant church bell, and sometimes gave a broad roar around the traveller, as if all Nature were laughing him to scorn. But he was himself the chief horror of the scene, and shrank not from its other horrors.

"Ha! ha! ha!" roared Goodman Brown when the wind laughed at him. "Let us hear which will laugh loudest. Think not to frighten me with your deviltry. Come witch, come wizard, come Indian powwow, come devil himself, and here comes Goodman Brown. You may as well fear him as he fear you."

In truth, all through the haunted forest there could be nothing more frightful than the figure of Goodman Brown. On he flew among the black Pines, brandishing his staff with frenzied gestures, now giving vent to an inspiration of horrid blasphemy, and now shouting forth such laughter as set all the echoes of the forest laughing like demons around him. The fiend in his own shape is less hideous than when he rages in the breast of man. Thus sped the demoniac on his course, until, quivering among the trees, he saw a red light before him, as when the felled trunks and branches of a clearing have been set on fire, and throw up their lurid blaze against the sky, at the hour of midnight. He paused, in a lull of the tempest that had driven him onward, and heard the swell of what seemed a hymn, rolling solemnly from a distance with the weight of many voices. He knew the tune; it was a familiar one in the choir of the village meeting-house. The verse died heavily away, and was lengthened by a chorus, not of human voices, but of all the sounds of the benighted wilderness pealing in awful harmony together. Goodman Brown cried out, and his cry was lost to his own ear by its unison with the cry of the desert.

In the interval of silence he stole forward until the light glared full upon his eyes. At one extremity of an open space, hemmed in by the dark wall of the forest, arose a rock, bearing some rude, natural resemblance either to an altar or a pulpit, and surrounded by four blazing pines, their tops aflame, their stems untouched, like candles at an evening meeting. The mass of foliage that had overgrown the summit of the rock was all on fire, blazing high into the night and fitfully illuminating the whole field. Each pendent twig and leafy festoon was in a blaze. As the red light arose and fell, a numerous congregation alternately shone forth, then disappeared in shadow, and again grew, as it were, out of the darkness, peopling the heart of the solitary woods at once.

"A grave and dark-clad company," quoth Goodman Brown.

In truth they were such. Among them, quivering to and fro between gloom and splendor, appeared faces that would be seen next day at the council board of the province, and others which, Sabbath after Sabbath, looked devoutly heavenward, and benignantly over the crowded pews, from the holiest pulpits in the land. Some affirm that the lady of the governor was there. At least there were high dames well known to her, and wives of honored husbands, and widows, a great multitude, and ancient maidens, all of excellent repute, and fair young girls, who trembled lest their mothers should espy them. Either the sudden gleams of light flashing over the obscure field bedazzled Goodman Brown, or he recognized a score of the church members of Salem village famous for their especial sanctity. Good old Deacon Gookin had arrived, and waited at the skirts of that venerable saint, his revered pastor. But, irreverently consorting with these grave, reputable, and pious people, these elders of the church, these chaste dames and dewy virgins, there were men of dissolute lives and women of spotted fame, wretches given over to all mean and filthy vice, and suspected even of horrid crimes. It was strange to see that the good shrank not from the wicked, nor were the sinners abashed by the saints. Scattered also among their pale-faced enemies were the Indian priests, or powwows, who had often scared their native forest with more hideous incantations than any known to English witchcraft.

"But where is Faith?" thought Goodman Brown; and as hope came into his heart, he trembled.

Another verse of the hymn arose, a slow and mournful strain, such as the pious love, but joined to words which expressed all that our nature can conceive of sin, and darkly hinted at far more. Unfathomable to mere mortals is the lore of fiends. Verse after verse was sung; and still the chorus of the desert swelled between like the deepest tone of a mighty organ; and with the final peal of that dreadful anthem there came a sound, as if the roaring wind, the rushing streams, the howling beasts, and every other voice of the unconcerted wilderness were mingling and according with the voice of guilty man in homage to the prince of all. The four blazing pines threw up a loftier flame, and obscurely discovered shapes and visages of horror on the smoke wreaths above the impious assembly. At the same moment the fire on the rock shot redly forth and formed a glowing arch above its base, where now appeared a figure. With reverence be it spoken, the figure bore no slight similitude, both in garb and manner, to some grave divine of the New England churches.

"Bring forth the converts!" cried a voice that echoed through the field and rolled into the forest.

At the word, Goodman Brown stepped forth from the shadow of the trees and approached the congregation, with whom he felt a loathful brotherhood by the sympathy of all that was wicked in his heart. He could have well-nigh sworn that the shape of his own dead father beckoned him to advance, looking downward from a smoke wreath, while a woman, with dim features of despair, threw out her hand to warn him back. Was it his mother? But he had no power to retreat one step, nor to resist, even in thought, when the minister and good old Deacon Gookin seized his arms and led him to the blazing rock. Thither came also the slender form of a veiled female, led between Goody Cloyse, that pious teacher of the catechism, and Martha Carrier, who had received the devil's promise to be queen of hell. A rampant hag was she. And there stood the proselytes beneath the canopy of fire.

"Welcome, my children," said the dark figure, "to the communion of your race. Ye have found thus young your nature and your destiny. My children, look behind you!"

They turned; and flashing forth, as it were, in a sheet of flame, the fiend worshippers were seen; the smile of welcome gleamed darkly on every visage.

"There," resumed the sable form, "are all whom ye have reverenced from youth. Ye deemed them holier than yourselves, and shrank from your own sin, contrasting it with their lives of righteousness and prayerful aspirations heavenward. Yet here are they all in my worshipping assembly. This night it shall be granted you to know their secret deeds: how hoary-bearded elders of the church have whispered wanton words to the young maids of their households; how many a woman, eager for widows' weeds, has given her husband a drink at bedtime and let him sleep his last sleep in her bosom; how beardless youths have made haste to inherit their fathers' wealth; and how fair damsels—blush not, sweet ones—have dug little graves in the garden, and bidden me, the sole guest, to an infant's funeral. By the sympathy of your human hearts for sin ye shall scent out all the places—whether in church, bed-chamber, street, field, or forest—where crime has been committed, and shall exult to behold the whole earth one stain of guilt, one mighty blood spot. Far more than this. It shall be yours to penetrate, in every bosom, the deep mystery of sin, the fountain of all wicked arts, and which inexhaustibly supplies more evil impulses than human power—than my power at its utmost—can make manifest in deeds. And now, my children, look upon each other."

They did so; and, by the blaze of the hell-kindled torches, the wretched man beheld his Faith, and the wife her husband, trembling before that unhallowed altar.

"Lo, there ye stand, my children," said the figure, in a deep and solemn tone, almost sad with its despairing awfulness, as if his once angelic nature could yet mourn for our miserable race. "Depending upon one another's hearts, ye had still hoped that virtue were not all a dream. Now are ye undeceived. Evil is the nature of mankind. Evil must be your only happiness. Welcome again, my children, to the communion of your race."

"Welcome," repeated the fiend worshippers, in one cry of despair and triumph.

And there they stood, the only pair, as it seemed, who were yet hesitating on the verge of wickedness in this dark world. A basin was hollowed, naturally, in the rock. Did it contain water, reddened by the lurid light? or was it blood? or, perchance, a liquid flame? Herein did the shape of evil dip his hand and prepare to lay the mark of baptism upon their foreheads, that they might be partakers of the mystery of sin, more conscious of the secret guilt of others, both in deed and thought, than they could now be of their own. The husband cast one look at his pale wife, and Faith at him. What polluted wretches would the next glance show them to each other, shuddering alike at what they disclosed and what they saw.

"Faith! Faith!" cried the husband, "look up to heaven, and resist the wicked one."

Whether Faith obeyed he knew not. Hardly had he spoken when he found himself amid calm night and solitude, listening to a roar of the wind which died heavily away through the forest. He staggered against the rock, and felt it chill and damp; while a hanging twig, that had been all on fire, besprinkled his cheek with the coldest dew.

The next morning young Goodman Brown came slowly into the street of Salem village, staring around him like a bewildered man. The good old minister was taking a walk along the graveyard to get an appetite for breakfast and meditate his sermon, and bestowed a blessing, as he passed, on Goodman Brown. He shrank from the venerable saint as if to avoid an anathema. Old Deacon Gookin was at domestic worship, and the holy words of his prayer were heard through the open window. "What God doth the wizard pray to?" quoth Goodman Brown. Goody Cloyse, that excellent old Christian, stood in the early sunshine at her own lattice, catechizing a little girl who had brought her a pint of morning's milk. Goodman Brown snatched away the child as from the grasp of the fiend himself. Turning the corner by the meeting-house, he spied the head of Faith, with the pink ribbons, gazing anxiously forth, and bursting into such joy at sight of him that she skipped along the street and almost kissed her husband before the whole village. But Goodman Brown looked sternly and sadly into her face, and passed on without a greeting.

Had Goodman Brown fallen asleep in the forest and only dreamed a wild dream of a witch-meeting?

Be it so if you will; but, alas! it was a dream of evil omen for young Goodman Brown. A stern, a sad, a darkly meditative, a distrustful, if not a desperate man did he become from the night of that fearful dream. On the Sabbath day, when the congregation were singing a holy psalm, he could not listen because an anthem of sin rushed loudly upon his ear and drowned all the blessed strain. When the minister spoke from the pulpit with power and fervid eloquence, and, with his hand on the open Bible, of the sacred truths of our religion, and of saint-like lives and triumphant deaths, and of future bliss or misery unutterable, then did Goodman Brown turn pale, dreading lest the roof should thunder down upon the gray blasphemer and his hearers. Often, awaking suddenly at midnight, he shrank from the bosom of Faith; and at morning or eventide, when the family knelt down at prayer, he scowled and muttered to himself, and gazed sternly at his wife, and turned away. And when he had lived long, and was borne to his grave a hoary corpse, followed by Faith, an aged woman, and children and grand-children, a goodly procession, besides neighbors not a few, they carved no hope-ful verse upon his tombstone, for his dying hour was gloom.

Study and Discussion Questions

1. Think about the names of the characters. What is the significance of these names?
2. Who is the person young Goodman Brown meets in the forest? Why does Hawthorne mention that the two resemble each other?
3. What is young Goodman Brown's errand this night? Why doesn't he tell his wife what it is?
4. What are the travelling companion's means of persuasion?
5. What finally causes Goodman Brown to go on with his journey?
6. Who is at the meeting in the woods? In what ways does that community differ from the one Goodman Brown (a) comes from and (b) expected to find there?
7. What does this story suggest is the "real" nature of human beings?

Suggestions for Writing

1. Write about a time you discovered something (or thought you discovered something) that caused a major shift in the way you saw the world.
2. How would the story and your response to it have been changed if Hawthorne had left out the suggestion that all this might have been a dream?

Critical Resources

1. Berkove, Lawrence. "'Reasoning as We Go': The Flawed Logic of Young Goodman Brown." *Nathaniel Hawthorne Review* 24.1 (1998): 46–52.
2. Frank, Albert von. *Critical Essays on Hawthorne's Short Stories.* Boston: G. K. Hall, 1991.
3. Keil, James. "Hawthorne's 'Young Goodman Brown': Early 19th Century and Puritan Constructions of Gender." *New England Quarterly* 69.1 (1996): 33–55.
4. Reynolds, Larry. *A Historical Guide to Nathaniel Hawthorne.* Oxford: Oxford UP, 2001.

❀ ❀ ❀

SHERMAN ALEXIE (b. 1966)

Sherman Alexie was born on the Spokane Indian Reservation in the state of Wash-ington. Learning to read by the age of three, Alexie excelled at the BIA (Bureau of Indian Affairs) reservation school, but decided to attend Reardon High School, 32 miles from the reservation because he thought he would receive a stronger education there. Alexie, "The only Indian . . . except for the school mascot" (shermanalexie.com), graduated with honors. After receiving his B.A. in Ameri-can Studies, Alexie was granted a National Endowment for the Arts Poetry Fel-lowship in 1992. Whether in poetry, prose or drama, Alexie has sought to bring the realities of modern reservation life to the public. His work is laden with dark hu-mor—a humor full of irony that is both critical of the dominant culture and hope-ful of a better future for all Native Americans. Alexie has also gained notoriety as a slam poet and screenplay writer. His writings include the poetry collections The Business of Fancydancing *(1991),* I Would Steal Horses *(1993), and* The Man Who Loves Salmon *(1998); the short story collection* The Lone Ranger and Tonto Fistfight in Heaven *(1993); the novels* Reservation Blues *(1995) and* Indian Killer *(1996); and the screenplays* Smoke Signals *(1998) and* The Business of Fancy-dancing *(2003). His latest work is the collection of short stories* Ten Little Indians *(2003). The following piece is taken from* The Lone Ranger and Tonto Fistfight in Heaven.

Jesus Christ's Half-Brother Is Alive and Well on the Spokane Indian Reservation (1993)

1966

Rosemary MorningDove gave birth to a boy today and seeing as how it was nearly Christmas and she kept telling everyone she was still a virgin even though Frank Many Horses said it was his we all just figured it was an accident. Any-how she gave birth to him but he came out all blue and they couldn't get him to breathe for a long time but he finally did and Rosemary MorningDove named him ———— which is unpronounceable in Indian and English but it means: *He Who Crawls Silently Through the Grass with a Small Bow and One Bad Arrow Hunting for Enough Deer to Feed the Whole Tribe.*

We just call him James.

1967

Frank Many Horses and Lester FallsApart and I were drinking beers in the Breakaway Bar playing pool and talking stories when we heard the sirens. Indians get all excited when we hear sirens because it means fires and it means they need firefighters to put out the fires and it means we get to be firefighters and it means we get paid to be firefighters. Hell somebody always starts a fire down at the Indian burial grounds and it was about time for the Thirteenth Annual All-Indian Burial Grounds Fire so Frank and Lester and I ran down to the fire station expecting to get hired but we see smoke coming from Commodity Village where all the really poor Indians live so we run down there instead and it was Rosemary MorningDove's house that was on fire. Indians got buckets of water but this fire was way too big and we could hear a baby crying and Frank Many Horses gets all excited even though it's Lillian Many's baby right next to us. But Frank knows James is in the house so he goes running in before any of us can stop him and pretty soon I see Frank leaning out the upstairs window holding James and they're both a little on fire and Frank throws James out the window and I'm running my ass over to catch him before he hits the ground making like a high school football hero again but I miss him just barely slipping through my fingers and James hits the ground hard and I pick him up right away and slap the flames out with my hands all the while expecting James to be dead but he's just looking at me almost normal except the top of his head looks all dented in like a beer can.

He wasn't crying.

1967

I went down to the reservation hospital to see how James and Frank and Rosemary were doing and I got drunk just before I went so I wouldn't be scared of all the white walls and the sound of arms and legs getting sawed off down in the basement. But I heard the screams anyway and they were Indian screams and those can travel forever like all around the world and sometimes from a hundred years ago so I close my ears and hide my eyes and just look down at the clean clean floors. Oh Jesus I'm so drunk I want to pray but I don't and before I can change my mind about coming here Moses MorningDove pulls me aside to tell me Frank and Rosemary have died and since I saved James's life I should be the one who raises him. Moses says it's Indian tradition but somehow since Moses is going on about two hundred years old and still drinking and screwing like he was twenty I figure he's just trying to get out of his grandfatherly duties. I don't really want any of it and I'm sick and the hospital is making me sicker and my heart is shaking and confused like when the nurse wakes you up in the middle of the night to give you a sleeping pill but I know James will end up some

Indian kid at a welfare house making baskets and wearing itchy clothes and I'm only twenty myself but I take one look at James all lumpy and potato looking and I look in the mirror and see myself holding him and I take him home.

Tonight the mirror will forgive my face.

1967

All dark tonight and James couldn't sleep and just kept looking at the ceiling so I walk on down to the football field carrying James so we can both watch the stars looking down at the reservation. I put James down on the fifty-yard line and I run and run across the frozen grass wishing there was snow enough to make a trail and let the world know I was there in the morning. Thinking I could spell out my name or James's name or every name I could think of until I stepped on every piece of snow on the field like it was every piece of the world or at least every piece of this reservation that has so many pieces it might just be the world. I want to walk circles around James getting closer and closer to him in a new dance and a better kind of healing which could make James talk and walk before he learns to cry. But he's not crying and he's not walking and he's not talking and I see him sometimes like an old man passed out in the back of a reservation van with shit in his pants and a battered watch in his pocket that always shows the same damn time. So I pick James up from the cold and the grass that waits for spring and the sun to change its world but I can only walk home through the cold with another future on my back and James's future tucked in my pocket like an empty wallet or a newspaper that feeds the fire and never gets read.

Sometimes all of this is home.

1968

The world changing the world changing the world. I don't watch the TV anymore since it exploded and left a hole in the wall. The woodpile don't dream of me no more. It sits there by the ax and they talk about the cold that waits in corners and surprises you on a warm almost spring day. Today I stood at the window for hours and then I took the basketball from inside the wood stove and shot baskets at the hoop nailed to a pine tree in the yard. I shot and shot until the cold meant I was protected because my skin was too warm to feel any of it. I shot and shot until my fingertips bled and my feet ached and my hair stuck to the skin of my bare back. James waited by the porch with his hands in the dirt and his feet stuck into leather shoes I found in the dump under a washing machine. I can't believe the details I am forced to remember with each day that James comes closer to talking. I change his clothes and his dirty pants and I wash his face and the crevices of his little body until he shines like a new check.

This is my religion.

1968

Seems like the cold would never go away and winter would be like the bottom of my feet but then it is gone in one night and in its place comes the sun so large and laughable. James sitting up in his chair so young and he won't talk and the doctors at the Indian clinic say it's way too early for him to be talking anyhow but I see in his eyes something and I see in his eyes a voice and I see in his eyes a whole new set of words. It ain't Indian or English and it ain't cash register and it ain't traffic light or speed bump and it ain't window or door. Late one day James and I watch the sun fly across the sky like a basketball on fire until it falls down completely and lands in Benjamin Lake with a splash and shakes the ground and even wakes up Lester Falls-Apart who thought it was his father come back to slap his face again.

Summer coming like a car from down the highway.

1968

James must know how to cry because he hasn't cried yet and I know he's waiting for that one moment to cry like it was five hundred years of tears. He ain't walked anywhere and there are no blisters on his soles but there are dreams worn clean into his rib cage and it shakes and shakes with each breath and I see he's trying to talk when he grabs at the air behind his head or stares up at the sky so hard. All of this temperature rising hot and I set James down in the shade by the basketball court and I play and I play until the sweat of my body makes it rain everywhere on the reservation. I play and I play until the music of my shoes against pavement sounds like every drum. Then I'm home alone and I watch the cockroaches live their complicated lives.

I hold James with one arm and my basketball with the other arm and I hold everything else inside my whole body.

1969

I take James to the Indian clinic because he ain't crying yet and because all he does sometimes is stare and stare and sometimes he'll wrap his arms around the stray dogs and let them carry him around the yard. He's strong enough to hold his body off the ground but he ain't strong enough to lift his tongue from the bottom of his mouth to use the words for love or anger or hunger or good morning. Maybe he's only a few years old but he's got eyes that are ancient and old and dark like a castle or a lake where the turtles go to die and sometimes even to live. Maybe he's going to howl out the words when I least expect it or want it and he'll yell out a cuss word in church or a prayer in the middle of a grocery store. Today I moved through town and walked and walked past the people who hadn't seen me in so long maybe for months and they asked questions about me and James and no one bothered to knock on the door and look for the answers. It's just me and James walking and walking except he's on my back and his eyes are looking past the people who are looking past us for the coyote of our soul and the wolverine of our heart and the crazy crazy man that touches every Indian who spends too much time alone. I stand in the Trading Post touching the canned goods and hoping for a vision of all the miles until Seymour comes in with a twenty-dollar bill and buys a couple cases of beer and we drink and drink all night long. James gets handed from woman to woman and from man to man and a few children hold this child of mine who doesn't cry or recognize the human being in his own body. All the drunks happy to see me drunk again and back from the wagon and I fell off that wagon and broke my ass and dreams and I wake up the next morning in a field watching a cow watch me. With piss in my pants I make the long walk home past the HUD houses and abandoned cars and past the powwow grounds and the Assembly of God where the sinless sing like they could forgive us all. I get home and James is there with Suzy Song feeding him and rocking him like a boat or a three-legged chair.

I say no and I take James away and put him in his crib and I move into Suzy's arms and let her rock and rock me away from my stomach and thin skin.

1969

Long days and nights mean the sky looks the same all the time and James has no words yet but he dreams and kicks in his sleep and sometimes kicks his body against my body as he sleeps in my arms. Nobody dreams all the time because it would hurt too much but James keeps dreaming and sleeping through a summer rainstorm and heat lightning reaching down a hand and then a fist to tear a tree in half and then to tear my eyes in half with the light. We had venison for dinner. We ate deer and its wild taste shook me up and down my spine. James spit his mouthful out on the floor and the dogs came to finish it up and I ate and ate and the dogs ate and ate what they could find and the deer grew in my stomach. The deer grew horns and hooves and skin and eyes that pushed at my rib cage and I ate and ate until I could not feel anything but my stomach expanding and stretched full.

All my life the days I remember most with every detail sharp and clear are the days when my stomach was full.

1969

We played our first basketball game of the season tonight in the community center and I had Suzy Song watch James while I played and all of us warriors roaring against the air and the nets and the clock that didn't work and our memories and our dreams and the twentieth-century horses we called our legs. We played some Nez Percé team and they ran like they were still running from the cavalry and they were kicking the shit out of us again when I suddenly steal the ball from their half-white point guard and drive all the way to the bucket. I jump in the air planning to dunk it when the half-white point guard runs under me knocking my ass to the floor and when I land I hear a crunch and my leg bends in half the wrong way. They take me to the reservation hospital and later on they tell me my leg has exploded and I can't play ball for a long time or maybe forever and when Suzy comes by with James and they ask me if this is my wife and son and I tell them yes and James still doesn't make a noise and so they ask me how old he is. I tell them he's almost four years old and they say his physical development is slow but that's normal for an Indian child. Anyhow I have to have an operation and all but since I don't have the money or the strength or the memory and it's not covered by Indian Health I just get up and walk home almost crying because my leg and life hurt so bad. Suzy stays with me that night and in the dark she touches my knee and asks me how much it hurts and I tell her it hurts more than I can talk about so she kisses all my scars and she huddles up close to me and she's warm and she talks into my ear close. She isn't always asking questions and sometimes she has the answers. In the morning I wake up before her and I hobble into the kitchen and make some coffee and fix a couple of bowls of cornflakes and we sit in bed eating together while James lies still in his crib watching the ceiling so Suzy and I watch the ceiling too.

The ordinary can be like medicine.

1970

Early snow this year and James and I sit at home by the stove because I can't walk anywhere with my bad knee and since it is snowing so hard outside nobody could drive out to get us but I know somebody must be thinking about us because if they weren't we'd just disappear just like those Indians who used to climb the pueblos. Those Indians disappeared with food still cooking in the pot and air waiting to be breathed and they turned into birds or dust or the blue of the sky or the yellow of the sun.

There they were and suddenly they were forgotten for just a second and for just a second nobody thought about them and then they were gone.

1970

I took James down to the reservation hospital again because he was almost five years old and still hadn't bothered to talk yet or crawl or cry or even move when I put him on the floor and once I even dropped him and his head was bleeding and he didn't make a sound. They looked him over and said there was nothing wrong with him and that he's just a little slow developing and that's what the doctors always say and they've been saying that about Indians for five hundred years. Jesus I say don't you know that James wants to dance and to sing and to pound a drum so hard it hurts your ears and he ain't ever going to drop an eagle feather and he's always going to be respectful to elders at least the Indian elders and he's going to change the world. He's going to dynamite Mount Rushmore or hijack a plane and make it land on the reservation highway. He's going to be a father and a mother and a son and a daughter and a dog that will pull you from a raging river.

He'll make gold out of commodity cheese.

1970

Happy birthday James and I'm in the Breakaway Bar drinking too many beers when the Vietnam war comes on television. The white people always want to fight someone and they always get the dark-skinned people to do the fighting. All I know about this war is what Seymour told me when he came back from his tour of duty over there and he said all the gooks he killed looked like us and Seymour said every single gook he killed looked exactly like someone he knew on the reservation. Anyhow I go to a Christmas party over at Jana Wind's house and leave James with my auntie so I could get really drunk and not have to worry about coming home for a few days or maybe for the rest of my life. We all get really drunk and Jana's old man Ray challenges me to a game of one-on-one since he says I'm for shit now and was never any good anyway but I tell him I can't since my knee is screwed up and besides there's two feet of snow on the ground and where are we going to play anyhow? Ray says I'm chickenshit so I tell him come on and we drive over to the high school to the outside court and there's two feet of snow on the court and we can't play but Ray smiles and pulls out a bottle of kerosene and pours it all over the court and lights it up and pretty soon the snow is all melted down along with most of Lester FallsApart's pants since he was standing too close to the court when Ray lit the fire. Anyhow the court is clear and Ray and I go at it and my knee only hurts a little and everyone was cheering us on and I can't remember who won since I was too drunk and so was everyone else. Later I hear how Ray and Joseph got arrested for beating some white guy half to death and I say that Ray and Joseph are just kids but Suzy says nobody on the reservation is ever a kid and that we're all born grown up anyway. I look at James and I think maybe Suzy is wrong about Indian kids being born adults and that maybe James was born this way and wants to stay this way like a baby because he doesn't want to grow up and see and do everything we all do?

There are all kinds of wars.

1971

So much time alone with a bottle of one kind or another and James and I remember nothing except the last drink and a drunk Indian is like the thinker statue except nobody puts a drunk Indian in a special place in front of a library. For most Indians the only special place in front of a library might be a heating grate or a piece of sun-warmed cement but that's an old joke and I used to sleep with my books in piles all over my bed and sometimes they were the only thing keeping me warm and always the only thing keeping me alive.

Books and beer are the best and worst defense.

1971

Jesse WildShoe died last night and today was the funeral and usually there's a wake but none of us had the patience or energy to mourn for days so we buried Jesse right away and dug the hole deep because Jesse could fancydance like God had touched his feet. Anyhow we dug the hole all day and since the ground was still a little frozen we kept doing the kerosene trick and melting the ice and frost and when we threw a match into the bottom of the grave it looked like I suppose hell must look and it was scary. There we were ten little Indians making a hell on earth for a fancydancer who already had enough of that shit and probably wouldn't want to have any more of it and I kept wondering if maybe we should just take his body high up in the mountains and bury him in the snow that never goes away. Maybe we just sort of freeze him so he doesn't have to feel anything anymore and especially not some crazy ideas of heaven or hell. I don't know anything about religion and I don't confess my sins to anybody except the walls and the wood stove and James who forgives everything like a rock. He ain't talking or crying at all and sometimes I shake him a little too hard or yell at him or leave him in his crib for hours all alone but he never makes a sound. One night I get so drunk I leave him at somebody's house and forget all about him and can you blame me? The tribal police drag me into the cell for abandonment and I'm asking them who they're going to arrest for abandoning me but the world is spinning and turning back on itself like a snake eating its own tail. Like a snake my TV dinner rises from the table the next day and snaps at my eyes and wrists and I ask the tribal cop how long I've been drunk and he tells me for most of a year and I don't remember any of it. I've got the DT's so bad and the walls are Nazis making lampshades out of my skin and the toilet is a white man in a white hood riding me down on horseback and the floor is a skinny man who wants to teach me a trick he's learned to do with a knife and my shoes squeal and kick and pull me down into the dead pig pit of my imagination. Oh Jesus I wake up on the bottom of that mass grave with the bones of generations of slaughter and I crawl and dig my way up through layers and years of the lunch special. I dig for hours through the skin and eyes and the fresh blood soon enough and pull myself through the eye of a sow and pluck the maggots from my hair and I want to scream but I don't want to open my mouth and taste and taste and taste.

Like the heroin addict said I just want to be pure.

1971

Been in A.A. for a month because that was the only way to keep James with me and my auntie and Suzy Song both moved into the house with me to make sure I don't drink and to help take care of James. They show the same old movies in A.A. and it's always the same white guy who almost destroys his life and his wife and his children and his job but finally realizes the alcohol is killing him and he quits overnight and spends the rest of the movie and the rest of his whole life at a picnic with his family and friends and boss all laughing and saying we didn't even recognize you back then Bob and we're glad to have you back Daddy and we'll hire you back at twice the salary you old dog you. Yesterday I get this postcard from Pine Ridge and my cousin says all the Indians there are gone and do I know where they went? I write back and tell him to look in the A.A. meeting and then I ask him if there are more birds with eyes that look like his and I ask him if the sky is more blue and the sun more yellow because those are the colors we all become when we die. I tell him to search his dreams for a man dressed in red with a red tie and red shoes and a hawk head. I tell him that man is fear and will eat you like a sandwich and will eat you like an ice cream cone and will never be full and he'll come for you in your dreams like he was a bad movie. I tell him to turn his television toward the wall and to study the walls for imperfections and those could be his mother and father and the stain on the ceiling could be his sisters and maybe the warped floorboard squeaking and squeaking is his grandfather talking stories.

Maybe they're all hiding on a ship in a bottle.

1972

Been sober so long it's like a dream but I feel better somehow and Auntie was so proud of me she took James and me into the city for James's checkup and James still wasn't talking but Auntie and James and I ate a great lunch at Woolworth's before we headed back to the reservation. I got to drive and Auntie's uranium money Cadillac is a hell of a car and it was raining a little and hot so there were rainbows rainbows rainbows and the pine trees looked like wise men with wet beards or at least I thought they did. That's how I do this life sometimes by making the ordinary just like magic and just like a card trick and just like a mirror and just like the disappearing. Every Indian learns how to be a magician and learns how to misdirect attention and the dark hand is always quicker than the white eye and no matter how close you get to my heart you will never find out my secrets and I'll never tell you and I'll never show you the same trick twice.

I'm traveling heavy with illusions.

1972

Every day I'm trying not to drink and I pray but I don't know who I'm praying to and if it's the basketball gathering ash on the shelf or the blank walls crushing me into the house or the television that only picks up public channels. I've seen only painters and fishermen and I think they're both the same kind of men who made a different choice one time in their lives. The fisherman held a rod in his hand and said yes and the painter held a brush in his hand and said yes and sometimes I hold a beer in my hand and say yes. At those moments I want to drink so bad that it aches and I cry which is a strange noise in our house because James refuses tears and he refuses words but sometimes he holds a hand up above his head like he's reaching for something. Yesterday I neatly trip over Lester FallsApart lying drunk as a skunk in front of the Trading Post and I pick him up and he staggers and trembles and falls back down. Lester I say you got to stand up on your own and I pick him up and he falls down again.

Only a saint would have tried to pick him up the third time.

1972

The streetlight outside my house shines on tonight and I'm watching it like it could give me vision. James ain't talked ever and he looks at that streetlight like it was a word and maybe like it was a verb. James wanted to streetlight me and make me bright and beautiful so all the moths and bats would circle me like I was the center of the world and held secrets. Like Joy said that everything but humans keeps secrets. Today I get my mail and there's a light bill and a postcard from an old love from Seattle who asks me if I still love her like I used to and would I come to visit?

I send her my light bill and tell her I don't ever want to see her again.

1973

James talked today but I had my back turned and I couldn't be sure it was real. He said potato like any good Indian would because that's all we eat. But maybe he said I love you because that's what I wanted him to say or maybe he said geology or mathematics or college basketball. I pick him up and ask him again and again what did you say? He just smiles and I take him to the clinic and the doctors say it's about time but are you sure you didn't imagine his voice? I said James's voice sounded like a beautiful glass falling off the shelf and landing safely on a thick shag carpet.

The doctor said I had a very good imagination.

1973

I'm shooting hoops again with the younger Indian boys and even some Indian girls who never miss a shot. They call me old man and elder and give me a little bit of respect like not running too fast or hard and even letting me shoot a few more than I should. It's been a long time since I played but the old feelings and old moves are there in my heart and in my fingers. I see these Indian kids and I know that basketball was invented by an Indian long before that Naismith guy ever thought about it. When I play I don't feel like drinking so I wish I could play twenty-four hours a day seven days a week and then I wouldn't wake up shaking and quaking and needing just one more beer before I stop for good. James knows it too and he sits on the sideline clapping when my team scores and clapping when the other team scores too. He's got a good heart. He always talks whenever I'm not in the room or I'm not looking at him but never when anybody else might hear so they all think I'm crazy. I am crazy. He says things like I can't believe. He says $E = MC^2$ and that's why all my cousins drink themselves to death. He says the earth is an oval marble that nobody can win. He says the sky is not blue and the grass is not green.

He says everything is a matter of perception.

1973

Christmas and James gets his presents and he gives me the best present of all when he talks right at me. He says so many things and the only thing that matters is that he says he and I don't have the right to die for each other and that we should be living for each other instead. He says the world hurts. He says the first thing he wanted after he was born was a shot of whiskey. He says all that and more. He tells me to get a job and to grow my braids. He says I better learn how to shoot left-handed if I'm going to keep playing basketball. He says to open a fireworks stand.

Every day now there are little explosions all over the reservation.

1974

Today is the World's Fair in Spokane and James and I drive to Spokane with a few cousins of mine. All the countries have exhibitions like art from Japan and pottery from Mexico and mean-looking people talking about Germany. In one little corner there's a statue of an Indian who's supposed to be some chief or another. I press a little button and the statue talks and moves its arms over and over in the same motion. The statue tells the crowd we have to take care of the earth because it is our mother. I know that and James says he knows more. He says the earth is our grandmother and that technology has become our mother and that they both hate each other. James tells the crowd that the river just a few yards from where we stand is all we ever need to believe in. One white woman asks me how old James is and I tell her he's seven and she tells me that he's so smart for an Indian boy. James hears this and tells the white woman that she's pretty smart for an old white woman. I know this is how it will all begin and how the rest of my life will be. I know when I am old and sick and ready to die that James will wash my body and take care of my wastes. He'll carry me from HUD house to sweathouse and he will clean my wounds. And he will talk and teach me something new every day.

But all that is so far ahead.

Study and Discussion Questions

1. Discuss the title of Alexie's story. (*Note:* Jesus did have a brother or cousin named James.) What possibilities for redemption exist in the story?
2. Consider the child's two names.
3. How does Alexie's narrator become a (single) parent? How does this change his life? How does he change in response? Note several examples of the narrator's development throughout the story.
4. What do we learn about life on the Reservation from this story? List at least five points, citing evidence from the text.
5. Discuss the structure of the story. Why do you think Alexie chose to narrate the story in short, date-headed sections? Why the pattern of the substantial paragraph followed by a short one-sentence paragraph? Do you find this an effective way of telling this particular story?
6. Choose a few *images* (literal or figurative) that particularly strike you and discuss each. What does each image evoke for you? How and why are they effective?
7. Alexie said in a 1996 talk, (November 9, 1996, University of Massachusetts/Boston) "The most revolutionary thing I can do is raise a kid that loves him or her self." Discuss Alexie's statement in relation to this story.
8. How is Alexie's narrator as a parent? List positive and negative qualities, citing examples for each.
9. If it takes a village to raise a child, how is the Spokane Indian community as parenting support for the narrator?
10. Discuss both the religious (in the sense of allusions to the story of Christ) and the spiritual (e.g., the circumstances of the adoption, James's "strangeness," the language Alexie uses) implications of "Jesus Christ's Half-Brother Is Alive and Well on the Spokane Indian Reservation."
11. Does James finally talk? Give evidence from the story to support your opinion.

12. As it happens, 1966, the year the story of James begins, is also the year Sherman Alexie was born. How might this biographical fact add to your interpretation of the story?

Suggestions for Writing

1. Do some reading and research on life on Indian reservations in the United States. Then discuss this story along with the three Sherman Alexie poems "Futures," "The Reservation Cab Driver," and "The Powwow at the End of the World".
2. In the Bible (the King James translation, if possible), read the Epistle of James in the New Testament. Also read Acts XV, where James makes an important speech to the Apostles. How do some of the issues and themes connected with the Biblical James resonate with the story of James and his adoptive father in Alexie's story?
3. Consider Alexie's choice to structure his story in short titled sections. Compare/contrast to Pamela Zoline's use of an analogous form in her story "The Heat Death of the Universe" (Varieties of Protest). How are their purposes different, and how does this structure support each?
4. Exercise in form/technique: Try writing a short story in numbered or labeled sections.
5. See *Smoke Signals,* a film based on Sherman Alexie's short stories, and write a paper on film adaptation—how the film uses material and themes from this short story. You might want to read the other stories in Alexie's 1993 collection, *The Lone Ranger and Tonto Fistfight in Heaven.*

Critical Resources

1. City Lore and Poets House. *People's Poetry Gathering.* April 18, 2005. <http://www.peoplespoetry.org/pg_clips_audvid.html>.
2. Fraser, Joelle. "An Interview with Sherman Alexie." *Iowa Review.* (2000): 59–70.
3. *shermanalexie.com.* 18 April 2005. <http://www.shermanalexie.com>.
4. Spencer, Russ. "What It Means to Be Sherman Alexie." *Book Magazine.com.* 18 April 2005. <http://www.bookmagazine.com/archive/issue11/alexie.shtml>.

❋ ❋ ❋

MARY E. WILKINS FREEMAN (1852–1930)

Mary Eleanor Wilkins was born and lived much of her life in Randolph, Massachusetts. After high school, she spent a year at Mount Holyoke Female Seminary and soon began earning a living writing. She married Dr. Charles Freeman in 1902, when she was almost fifty, and moved with him to New Jersey, but their marriage fell apart due to his growing alcoholism. Freeman was widely read during her lifetime, but her work fell into obscurity after her death. Although she wrote children's books, poetry, novels, and plays, it is her short fiction that brought a revaluation of her work in the 1980s. Working within a realist mode, Freeman was a protofeminist voice from the nineteenth century—questioning the sentimental fiction of her day as well as the limited roles available to women. Her most well-known story collections are A Humble Romance *(1887) and* A New England Nun *(1891). "A Mistaken Charity" looks at the struggle of two aging women and their desire to be independent.*

A Mistaken Charity   (1887)

There were in a green field a little, low, weather-stained cottage, with a foot-path leading to it from the highway several rods distant, and two old women—one with a tin pan and old knife searching for dandelion greens among the short young grass, and the other sitting on the doorstep watching her, or, rather, having the appearance of watching her.

"Air there enough for a mess, Harriét?" asked the old woman on the door-step. She accented oddly the last syllable of the Harriet, and there was a curious quality in her feeble, cracked old voice. Besides the question denoted by the arrangement of her words and the rising inflection, there was another, broader and subtler, the very essence of all questioning, in the tone of her voice itself; the cracked, quavering notes that she used reached out of themselves, and asked, and groped like fingers in the dark. One would have known by the voice that the old woman was blind.

The old woman on her knees in the grass searching for dandelions did not reply; she evidently had not heard the question. So the old woman on the door-step, after waiting a few minutes with her head turned expectantly, asked again, varying her question slightly, and speaking louder:

"Air there enough for a mess, do ye s'pose, Harriét?"

The old woman in the grass heard this time. She rose slowly and laboriously; the effort of straightening out the rheumatic old muscles was evidently a painful one; then she eyed the greens heaped up in the tin pan, and pressed them down with her hand.

"Wa'al, I don't know, Charlotte," she replied, hoarsely. "There's plenty on 'em here, but I 'ain't got near enough for a mess; they do bile down so when you get 'em in the pot; an' it's all I can do to bend my j'ints enough to dig 'em."

"I'd give consider'ble to help ye, Harriét," said the old woman on the door-step.

But the other did not hear her; she was down on her knees in the grass again, anxiously spying out the dandelions.

So the old woman on the door-step crossed her little shrivelled hands over her calico knees, and sat quite still, with the soft spring wind blowing over her.

The old wooden door-step was sunk low down among the grasses, and the whole house to which it belonged had an air of settling down and mouldering into the grass as into its own grave.

When Harriet Shattuck grew deaf and rheumatic, and had to give up her work as tailoress, and Charlotte Shattuck lost her eyesight, and was unable to do any more sewing for her livelihood, it was a small and trifling charity for the rich man who held a mortgage on the little house in which they had been born and lived all their lives to give them the use of it, rent and interest free. He might as well have taken credit to himself for not charging a squirrel for his tenement in some old decaying tree in his woods.

So ancient was the little habitation, so wavering and mouldering, the hands that had fashioned it had lain still so long in their graves, that it almost seemed to have fallen below its distinctive rank as a house. Rain and snow had filtered through its roof, mosses had grown over it, worms had eaten it, and birds built their nests under its eaves; nature had almost completely overrun and obliterated the work of man, and taken her own to herself again, till the house seemed as much a natural ruin as an old treestump.

The Shattucks had always been poor people and common people; no especial grace and refinement or fine ambition had ever characterized any of them; they had always been poor and coarse and common. The father and his father before him had simply lived in the poor little house, grubbed for their living, and then unquestioningly died. The mother had been of no rarer stamp, and the two daughters were cast in the same mould.

After their parents' death Harriet and Charlotte had lived along in the old place from youth to old age, with the one hope of ability to keep a roof over their heads, covering on their backs, and victuals in their mouths—an all-sufficient one with them.

Neither of them had ever had a lover; they had always seemed to repel rather than attract the opposite sex. It was not merely because they were poor, ordinary, and homely; there were plenty of men in the place who would have matched them well in that respect; the fault lay deeper—in their characters. Harriet, even in her girlhood, had a blunt, defiant manner that almost amounted to surliness, and was well calculated to alarm timid adorers, and Charlotte had always had the reputation of not being any too strong in her mind.

Harriet had gone about from house to house doing tailorwork after the primitive country fashion, and Charlotte had done plain sewing and mending for the neighbors. They had been, in the main, except when pressed by some temporary anxiety about their work or the payment thereof, happy and contented, with that negative kind of happiness and contentment which comes not from gratified ambition, but a lack of ambition itself. All that they cared for they had had in tolerable abundance, for Harriet at least had been swift and capable about her work. The patched, mossy old roof had been kept over their heads, the coarse, hearty food that they loved had been set on their table, and their cheap clothes had been warm and strong.

After Charlotte's eyes failed her, and Harriet had the rheumatic fever, and the little hoard of earnings went to the doctors, times were harder with them, though still it could not be said that they actually suffered.

When they could not pay the interest on the mortgage they were allowed to keep the place interest free; there was as much fitness in a mortgage on the little house, anyway, as there would have been on a rotten old apple-tree; and the people about, who were mostly farmers, and good friendly folk, helped them out with their living. One would donate a barrel of apples from his abundant harvest to the two poor old women, one a barrel of potatoes, another a load of wood for the winter fuel, and many a farmer's wife had bustled up the narrow footpath with a pound of butter, or a dozen fresh eggs, or a nice bit of pork. Besides all this, there was a tiny garden patch behind the house, with a straggling row of currant bushes in it, and one of gooseberries, where Harriet contrived every year to raise a few pumpkins, which were the pride of her life. On the right of the garden were two old apple-trees, a Baldwin and a Porter, both yet in a tolerably good fruit-bearing state.

The delight which the two poor old souls took in their own pumpkins, their apples and currants, was indescribable. It was not merely that they contributed largely towards their living; they were their own, their private share of the great wealth of nature, the little taste set apart for them alone out of her bounty, and worth more to them on that account, though they were not conscious of it, than all the richer fruits which they received from their neighbors' gardens.

This morning the two apple-trees were brave with flowers, the currant bushes looked alive, and the pumpkin seeds were in the ground. Harriet cast complacent glances in their direction from time to time, as she painfully dug her dandelion greens. She was a short, stoutly built old woman, with a large face coarsely wrinkled, with a suspicion of a stubble of beard on the square chin.

When her tin pan was filled to her satisfaction with the sprawling, spidery greens, and she was hobbling stiffly towards her sister on the door-step, she saw another woman standing before her with a basket in her hand.

"Good-morning, Harriet," she said, in a loud, strident voice, as she drew near. "I've been frying some doughnuts, and I brought you over some warm."

"I've been tellin' her it was real good in her," piped Charlotte from the door-step, with an anxious turn of her sightless face towards the sound of her sister's footstep.

Harriet said nothing but a hoarse "Good-mornin', Mis' Simonds." Then she took the basket in her hand, lifted the towel off the top, selected a doughnut, and deliberately tasted it.

"Tough," said she. "I s'posed so. If there is anything I 'spise on this airth it's a tough doughnut."

"Oh, Harriét!" said Charlotte, with a frightened look.

"They air tough," said Harriet, with hoarse defiance, "and if there is anything I 'spise on this airth it's a tough doughnut."

The woman whose benevolence and cookery were being thus ungratefully received only laughed. She was quite fleshy, and had a round, rosy, determined face.

"Well, Harriet," said she, "I am sorry they are tough, but perhaps you had better take them out on a plate, and give me my basket. You may be able to eat two or three of them if they are tough."

"They air tough—turrible tough," said Harriet, stubbornly; but she took the basket into the house and emptied it of its contents nevertheless.

"I suppose your roof leaked as bad as ever in that heavy rain day before yesterday?" said the visitor to Harriet, with an inquiring squint towards the mossy shingles, as she was about to leave with her empty basket.

"It was turrible," replied Harriet, with crusty acquiescence—"turrible. We had to set pails an' pans everywheres, an' move the bed out."

"Mr. Upton ought to fix it."

"There ain't any fix to it; the old ruff ain't fit to nail new shingles on to; the hammerin' would bring the whole thing down on our heads," said Harriet, grimly.

"Well, I don't know as it can be fixed, it's so old. I suppose the wind comes in bad around the windows and doors too?"

"It's like livin' with a piece of paper, or mebbe a sieve, 'twixt you an' the wind an' the rain," quoth Harriet, with a jerk of her head.

"You ought to have a more comfortable home in your old age," said the visitor, thoughtfully.

"Oh, it's well enough," cried Harriet, in quick alarm, and with a complete change of tone; the woman's remark had brought an old dread over her. "The old house'll last as long as Charlotte an' me do. The rain ain't so bad, nuther is the wind; there's room enough for us in the dry places, an' out of the way of the doors an' windows. It's enough sight better than goin' on the town." Her square, defiant old face actually looked pale as she uttered the last words and stared apprehensively at the woman.

"Oh, I did not think of your doing that," she said, hastily and kindly. "We all know how you feel about that, Harriet, and not one of us neighbors will see you and Charlotte go to the poorhouse while we've got a crust of bread to share with you."

Harriet's face brightened. "Thank ye, Mis' Simonds," she said, with reluctant courtesy. "I'm much obleeged to you an' the neighbors. I think mebbe we'll be able to eat some of them doughnuts if they air tough," she added, mollifyingly, as her caller turned down the foot-path.

"My, Harriét," said Charlotte, lifting up a weakly, wondering, peaked old face, "what did you tell her them doughnuts was tough fur?"

"Charlotte, do you want everybody to look down on us, an' think we ain't no account at all, just like any beggars, 'cause they bring us in vittles?" said Harriet, with a grim glance at her sister's meek, unconscious face.

"No, Harriét," she whispered.

"Do you want *to go to the poor-house?*"

"No, Harriét." The poor little old woman on the door-step fairly cowered before her aggressive old sister.

"Then don't hender me agin when I tell folks their doughnuts is tough an' their pertaters is poor. If I don't kinder keep up an' show some sperrit, I sha'n't think nothing of myself, an' other folks won't nuther, and fust thing we know they'll kerry us to the poorhouse. You'd 'a been there before now if it hadn't been for me, Charlotte."

Charlotte looked meekly convinced, and her sister sat down on a chair in the doorway to scrape her dandelions.

"Did you git a good mess, Harriét?" asked Charlotte, in a humble tone.

"Toler'ble."

"They'll be proper relishin' with that piece of pork Mis' Mann brought in yesterday. O Lord, Harriét, it's a chink!"

Harriet sniffed.

Her sister caught with her sensitive ear the little contemptuous sound. "I guess," she said, querulously, and with more pertinacity than she had shown in the matter of the doughnuts, "that if you was in the dark, as I am, Harriét, you wouldn't make fun an' turn up your nose at chinks. If you had seen the light streamin' in all of a sudden through some little hole that you hadn't known of before when you set down on the doorstep this mornin', and the wind with the smell of the apple blows in it came in your face, an' when Mis' Simonds brought them hot doughnuts, an' when I thought of the pork an' greens jest now—O Lord, how it did shine in! An' it does now. If you was me, Harriét, you would know there was chinks."

Tears began starting from the sightless eyes, and streaming pitifully down the pale old cheeks.

Harriet looked at her sister, and her grim face softened.

"Why, Charlotte, hev it that thar *is* chinks if you want to. Who cares?"

"Thar *is* chinks, Harriét."

"Wa'al, thar *is* chinks, then. If I don't hurry, I sha'n't get these greens in in time for dinner."

When the two old women sat down complacently to their meal of pork and dandelion greens in their little kitchen they did not dream how destiny slowly and surely was introducing some new colors into their web of life, even when it was almost completed, and that this was one of the last meals they would eat in their old home for many a day. In about a week from that day they were established in the "Old Ladies' Home" in a neighboring city. It came about in this wise: Mrs. Simonds, the woman who had brought the gift of hot doughnuts, was a smart, energetic person, bent on doing good, and she did a great deal. To be sure, she always did it in her own way. If she chose to give hot doughnuts, she gave hot doughnuts; it made not the slightest difference to her if the recipients of her charity would infinitely have preferred ginger cookies. Still, a great many would like hot doughnuts, and she did unquestionably a great deal of good.

She had a worthy coadjutor in the person of a rich and childless elderly widow in the place. They had fairly entered into a partnership in good works, with about an equal capital on both sides, the widow furnishing the money, and

Mrs. Simonds, who had much the better head of the two, furnishing the active schemes of benevolence.

The afternoon after the doughnut episode she had gone to the widow with a new project, and the result was that entrance fees had been paid, and old Harriet and Charlotte made sure of a comfortable home for the rest of their lives. The widow was hand in glove with officers of missionary boards and trustees of charitable institutions. There had been an unusual mortality among the inmates of the "Home" this spring, there were several vacancies, and the matter of the admission of Harriet and Charlotte was very quickly and easily arranged. But the matter which would have seemed the least difficult—inducing the two old women to accept the bounty which Providence, the widow, and Mrs. Simonds were ready to bestow on them—proved the most so. The struggle to persuade them to abandon their tottering old home for a better was a terrible one. The widow had pleaded with mild surprise, and Mrs. Simonds with benevolent determination; the counsel and reverend eloquence of the minister had been called in; and when they yielded at last it was with a sad grace for the recipients of a worthy charity.

It had been hard to convince them that the "Home" was not an almshouse under another name, and their yielding at length to anything short of actual force was only due probably to the plea, which was advanced most eloquently to Harriet, that Charlotte would be so much more comfortable.

The morning they came away, Charlotte cried pitifully, and trembled all over her little shrivelled body. Harriet did not cry. But when her sister had passed out the low, sagging door she turned the key in the lock, then took it out and thrust it slyly into her pocket, shaking her head to herself with an air of fierce determination.

Mrs. Simonds's husband, who was to take them to the depot, said to himself, with disloyal defiance of his wife's active charity, that it was a shame, as he helped the two distressed old souls into his light wagon, and put the poor little box, with their homely clothes in it, in behind.

Mrs. Simonds, the widow, the minister, and the gentleman from the "Home" who was to take charge of them, were all at the depot, their faces beaming with the delight of successful benevolence. But the two poor old women looked like two forlorn prisoners in their midst. It was an impressive illustration of the truth of the saying "that it is more blessed to give than to receive."

Well, Harriet and Charlotte Shattuck went to the "Old Ladies' Home" with reluctance and distress. They stayed two months, and then—they ran away.

The "Home" was comfortable, and in some respects even luxurious; but nothing suited those two unhappy, unreasonable old women.

The fare was of a finer, more delicately served variety than they had been accustomed to; those finely flavored nourishing soups for which the "Home" took great credit to itself failed to please palates used to common, coarser food.

"O Lord, Harriét, when I set down to the table here there ain't no chinks," Charlotte used to say. "If we could hev some cabbage, or some pork an' greens, how the light would stream in!"

Then they had to be more particular about their dress. They had always been tidy enough, but now it had to be something more; the widow, in the kindness of her heart, had made it possible, and the good folks in charge of the "Home," in the kindness of their hearts, tried to carry out the widow's designs.

But nothing could transform these two unpolished old women into two nice old ladies. They did not take kindly to white lace caps and delicate neckerchiefs. They liked their new black cashmere dresses well enough, but they felt as if they broke a commandment when they put them on every afternoon. They had always worn calico with long aprons at home, and they wanted to now; and they wanted to twist up their scanty gray locks into little knots at the back of their heads, and go without caps, just as they always had done.

Charlotte in a dainty white cap was pitiful, but Harriet was both pitiful and comical. They were totally at variance with their surroundings, and they felt it keenly, as people of their stamp always do. No amount of kindness and attention—and they had enough of both—sufficed to reconcile them to their new abode. Charlotte pleaded continually with her sister to go back to their old home.

"O Lord, Harriét," she would exclaim (by the way, Charlotte's "O Lord," which, as she used it, was innocent enough, had been heard with much disfavor in the "Home," and she, not knowing at all why, had been remonstrated with concerning it), "let us go home. I can't stay here no ways in this world. I don't like their vittles, an' I don't like to wear a cap; I want to go home and do different. The currants will be ripe, Harriét. O Lord, thar was almost a chink, thinking about 'em. I want some of 'em; an' the Porter apples will be gettin' ripe, an' we could have some apple-pie. This here ain't good; I want merlasses fur sweeting. Can't we get back no ways, Harriét? It ain't far, an' we could walk, an' they don't lock us in, nor nothin'. I don't want to die here; it ain't so straight up to heaven from here. O Lord, I've felt as if I was slantendicular from heaven ever since I've been here, an' it's been so awful dark. I ain't had any chinks. I want to go home, Harriét."

"We'll go to-morrow mornin'," said Harriet, finally; "we'll pack up our things an' go; we'll put on our old dresses, an' we'll do up the new ones in bundles, an' we'll jest shy out the back way to-morrow mornin'; an' we'll go. I kin find the way, an' I reckon we kin git thar, if it is fourteen mile. Mebbe somebody will give us a lift."

And they went. With a grim humor Harriet hung the new white lace caps with which she and Charlotte had been so pestered, one on each post at the head of the bedstead, so they would meet the eyes of the first person who opened the door. Then they took their bundles, stole slyly out, and were soon on the high-road, hobbling along, holding each other's hands, as jubilant as two children, and chuckling to themselves over their escape, and the probable astonishment there would be in the "Home" over it.

"O Lord, Harriét, what do you s'pose they will say to them caps?" cried Charlotte, with a gleeful cackle.

"I guess they'll see as folks ain't goin' to be made to wear caps agin their will in a free kentry," returned Harriet, with an echoing cackle, as they sped feebly and bravely along.

The "Home" stood on the very outskirts of the city, luckily for them. They would have found it a difficult undertaking to traverse the crowded streets. As it was, a short walk brought them into the free country road—free comparatively, for even here at ten o'clock in the morning there was considerable traveling to and from the city on business or pleasure.

People whom they met on the road did not stare at them as curiously as might have been expected. Harriet held her bristling chin high in air, and hobbled along with an appearance of being well aware of what she was about, that led folks to doubt their own first opinion that there was something unusual about the two old women.

Still their evident feebleness now and then occasioned from one and another more particular scrutiny. When they had been on the road a half-hour or so, a man in a covered wagon drove up behind them. After he had passed them, he poked his head around the front of the vehicle and looked back. Finally he stopped, and waited for them to come up to him.

"Like a ride, ma'am?" said he, looking at once bewildered and compassionate.

"Thankee," said Harriet, "we'd be much obleeged."

After the man had lifted the old women into the wagon, and established them on the back seat, he turned around, as he drove slowly along, and gazed at them curiously.

"Seems to me you look pretty feeble to be walking far," said he. "Where were you going?"

Harriet told him with an air of defiance.

"Why," he exclaimed, "it is fourteen miles out. You could never walk it in the world. Well, I am going within three miles of there, and I can go on a little farther as well as not. But I don't see—Have you been in the city?"

"I have been visitin' my married darter in the city," said Harriet, calmly.

Charlotte started, and swallowed convulsively.

Harriet had never told a deliberate falsehood before in her life, but this seemed to her one of the tremendous exigencies of life which justify a lie. She felt desperate. If she could not contrive to deceive him in some way, the man might turn directly around and carry Charlotte and her back to the "Home" and the white caps.

"I should not have thought your daughter would have let you start for such a walk as that," said the man. "Is this lady your sister? She is blind, isn't she? She does not look fit to walk a mile."

"Yes, she's my sister," replied Harriet, stubbornly: "an' she's blind; an' my darter didn't want us to walk. She felt reel bad about it. But she couldn't help it. She's poor, and her husband's dead, an' she's got four leetle children."

Harriet recounted the hardships of her imaginary daughter with a glibness that was astonishing. Charlotte swallowed again.

"Well," said the man, "I am glad I overtook you, for I don't think you would ever have reached home alive."

About six miles from the city an open buggy passed them swiftly. In it were seated the matron and one of the gentlemen in charge of the "Home." They never thought of looking into the covered wagon—and indeed one can travel in one of those vehicles, so popular in some parts of New England, with as much privacy as he could in his tomb. The two in the buggy were seriously alarmed, and anxious for the safety of the old women, who were chuckling maliciously in the wagon they soon left far behind. Harriet had watched them breathlessly until they disappeared on a curve of the road; then she whispered to Charlotte.

A little after noon the two old women crept slowly up the foot-path across the field to their old home.

"The clover is up to our knees," said Harriet; "an' the sorrel and the white-weed; an' there's lots of yaller butterflies."

"O Lord, Harriét, thar's a chink, an' I do believe I saw one of them yaller butterflies go past it," cried Charlotte, trembling all over, and nodding her gray head violently.

Harriet stood on the old sunken door-step and fitted the key, which she drew triumphantly from her pocket, in the lock, while Charlotte stood waiting and shaking behind her.

Then they went in. Everything was there just as they had left it. Charlotte sank down on a chair and began to cry. Harriet hurried across to the window that looked out on the garden.

"The currants air ripe," said she; "*an'* them pumpkins hev run all over everything."

"O Lord, Harriét," sobbed Charlotte, "thar is so many chinks that they air all runnin' together!"

Study and Discussion Questions

1. Look at the paragraphs that describe the Shattuck sisters' house and yard. How does the setting of this story mirror the characters?
2. What are the "chinks" referred to in the story? Why does Charlotte say at the end: "thar is so many chinks that they air all runnin' together"?
3. List the different kinds of charity in the story. Which ones are "mistaken" and which are not?
4. Why are Charlotte and Harriet uncomfortable in the Old Ladies' Home?
5. Describe the relationship between the two sisters.
6. What do you think is the author's attitude toward the Shattuck sisters?
7. Why does Harriet tell Mrs. Simonds that her doughnuts are "turrible tough"?
8. "It is more blessed to give than to receive." Is there any irony in Freeman's use of this maxim?

Suggestions for Writing

1. This story was published in 1887. What are some of the issues it raises that are still very much with us today?

2. Have you ever been either a recipient or a giver of charity? (Being taken to the movies by a friend when you couldn't afford it and volunteering your time and labor to help someone in need are examples.) Describe the situation and how you felt in it.

3. Define *charity*. Give some examples from your own experience or knowledge. Which of these are "mistaken" and which are not? Why?

Critical Resources

1. Glasser, Leah Blatt. *In the Closet Hidden: The Life and Work of Mary E. Wilkins Freeman.* Amherst: U of Massachusetts P, 1996.
2. Marchalonis, Shirley, ed. *Critical Essays on Mary Wilkins Freeman.* Boston: G. K. Hall, 1991.
3. Reichardt, Mary. *Mary Wilkins Freeman: A Study of the Short Fiction.* New York: Twayne, 1997.

POETRY

WALT WHITMAN (1819–1892)

Walt Whitman was born in West Hills, New York. At an early age, his family moved to Brooklyn, where he attended grammar school until, at the age of 12, he was apprenticed to a printer to help meet the financial needs of his family. This early experience in the world of printing inevitably exposed the young Whitman to journalism and to a life of writing and publishing. In 1855, Whitman anonymously published Leaves of Grass, *a book of poetry that he continued to revise, expand, and republish throughout his life. At the time, Whitman's effusive free verse radically challenged traditional notions of democracy, race, and religion. In like manner, his explicit treatment of sexuality, both heterosexual and homosexual, also engendered controversy, prompting several areas of the country to ban the book on grounds of obscenity. As Whitman evolved as a poet, so did later versions of* Leaves of Grass, *most notably the poems he wrote as a volunteer nurse during the Civil War that demonstrate a turn toward a more simplified, realist verse. Often referred to as the father of modern American poetry, Whitman's pioneering break from conventional poetic forms and themes has inspired generations of subsequent writers. His prose works include* Democratic Vistas *(1871). "We Two Boys Together Clinging" is taken from the 1860 version of* Leaves of Grass.

We Two Boys Together Clinging (1860)

We two boys together clinging,
One the other never leaving,
Up and down the roads going, North and South excursions making,
Power enjoying, elbows stretching, fingers clutching,
Arm'd and fearless, eating, drinking, sleeping, loving,   5
No law less than ourselves owning, sailing, soldiering, thieving, threatening,
Misers, menials, priests alarming, air breathing, water drinking, on the turf or
        the sea-beach dancing,
Cities wrenching, ease scorning, statutes mocking, feebleness chasing,
Fulfilling our foray.

Study and Discussion Questions

1. What is the mood of the poem? Why does Whitman bother to include "air breathing, water drinking"?

2. What is the boys' attitude toward society?
3. What does the last line mean?
4. What is the poem's grammatical structure? How does this help create its meaning?

Suggestions for Writing

1. How old are these two boys? Describe their relationship.
2. Copying the poem's grammatical structure, try writing a poem of your own about a youthful enthusiasm.

Critical Resources

1. Greenspan, Ezra. *Cambridge Companion to Walt Whitman.* Cambridge: Cambridge UP, 1995.
2. Kaplan, Justin. *Walt Whitman: A Life.* New York: Simon & Schuster, 1980.
3. Woodress, James. *Critical Essays on Walt Whitman.* Boston: G. K. Hall, 1983.

AUDRE LORDE (1934–1992)

Born in Harlem of West Indian parents, Audre Lorde began writing poetry at the age of 12, publishing her first poem in Seventeen *magazine as a teenager. She obtained her B.A. in English from Hunter College (New York) in 1961 and a M.A. in Library Science from Columbia University. Lorde described herself as a "black, lesbian, mother, warrior, poet" (Contemporary Authors Online), who, after several years as a librarian, realized that writing and teaching were her true vocations. From 1968 until her death in 1992 (after a long battle with cancer), Lorde held teaching positions at several universities. She eventually returned in 1981 to Hunter College as Professor of English. Her poetry and prose is grounded in the deep sense of her identity as a black, lesbian feminist, and is often driven by conflicting emotions of anger and love. Her works include the poetry collections* The First Cities *(1968),* New York Headshop and Museum *(1974),* The Black Unicorn *(1978),* Our Dead Behind Us *(1986), and* The Marvelous Arithmetics of Distance *(1993, published posthumously); the autobiographical works* The Cancer Journals *(1980) and* Zami: A New Spelling of My Name: A Biomythography *(1982); and the essay collections* Sister Outsider *(1984) and* A Burst of Light *(1988). Lorde was a founding editor of Kitchen Table: Women of Color Press. "From the House of Yemanji" articulates Lorde's ambivalent relationship with her mother, as well as the desire to reconnect with her African roots.*

From the House of Yemanjá[1]   (1978)

My mother had two faces and a frying pot
where she cooked up her daughters
into girls
before she fixed our dinner.
My mother had two faces   5
and a broken pot
where she hid out a perfect daughter
who was not me
I am the sun and moon and forever hungry
for her eyes.   10

I bear two women upon my back
one dark and rich and hidden
in the ivory hungers of the other
mother
pale as a witch   15
yet steady and familiar
brings me bread and terror
in my sleep
her breasts are huge exciting anchors
in the midnight storm.   20
All this has been
before
in my mother's bed
time has no sense
I have no brothers   25
and my sisters are cruel.

Mother I need
mother I need
mother I need your blackness now
as the august earth needs rain.   30
I am

---

[1]"Mother of the other *Orisha* [Yoruban deities], Yemanjá is also the goddess of oceans.
Rivers are said to flow from her breasts. One legend has it that a son tried to rape her. She
fled until she collapsed, and from her breasts, the rivers flowed. Another legend says that
a husband insulted Yemanjá's long breasts, and when she fled with her pots he knocked
her down. From her breasts flowed the rivers, and from her body then sprang forth all the
other *Orisha*. River-smooth stones are Yemanjá's symbol, and the sea is sacred to her fol-
lowers. Those who please her are blessed with many children" [Lorde's note].

the sun and moon and forever hungry
the sharpened edge
where day and night shall meet
and not be   35
one.

Study and Discussion Questions

1. List the characteristics of the two faces, the two women, that the speaker's mother is (or at least appears to her daughter to be).
2. What does the speaker need from her mother now? What did she need from her mother earlier?
3. Why is she "forever hungry"?
4. What does it imply to describe yourself as "a sharpened edge"?

Suggestion for Writing

1. The speaker of the poem says her mother "cooked up her daughters/ into girls." Come up with one or more images for your own upbringing.

Critical Resources

1. *A Litany for Survival: The Life and Work of Audre Lorde.* Directors Ada G. Griffin and Michelle Parkerson. New York: Third World Newsreel, 1996. 60 minutes. For more information go to <http://www.pbs.org/pov/pov1996/ alitanyforsurvival/index.html>
2. Burr, Zofia. *Of Women, Poetry and Power: Strategies of Address in Dickinson, Miles, Brooks, Lorde and Angelou.* Urbana: U of Illinois P, 2002.
3. Dhairyam, Sagri. "Artifacts for Survival: Remapping the Contours of Poetry with Audre Lorde." *Feminist Studies* 18.2 (1992): 228–56.
4. Provost, Kara. "Becoming Afrekete: The Trickster in The Work of Audre Lorde-Maskers and Tricksters." *MELUS* 20.4 (1995): 45–59.

ROBERT HAYDEN (1913–1980)

Placed in a foster home as an infant, Robert Hayden grew up in a Detroit ghetto ironically called "Paradise Valley" by its residents. He attended Wayne State University for a short time but left in 1936 to work for the Federal Writer's Project, researching African American history and folklore that had been neglected by conventional history books. This experience with alternative historical narratives would have a profound impact on his poetry. In 1941, he entered Michigan University and studied under the poet W. H Auden, honing the technical aspects of his writing. In 1946, Hayden began teaching at Fisk University and would remain there for the next 23 years. Although he published his first poetry collection,

Heart-Shape in the Dust *in 1940, it wasn't until* Selected Poems *(1966) that Hayden was recognized as a skilled poet with his own poetic vision. In 1976, he was appointed as Consultant in Poetry to the Library of Congress (later retitled Poet Laureate). His other works include* Figure of Time: Poems *(1955),* A Ballad of Remembrance *(1962),* Words of Mourning Time *(1970),* The Night-Blooming Cereus *(1972), and* Angel of Ascent *(1975). "Those Winter Sundays," first published in* Selected Poems, *takes on the appearance of a loose sonnet, exploring the hard realizations of childhood.*

Those Winter Sundays   (1962)

Sundays too my father got up early
and put his clothes on in the blueblack cold,
then with cracked hands that ached
from labor in the weekday weather made
banked fires blaze. No one ever thanked him.   5

I'd wake and hear the cold splintering, breaking.
When the rooms were warm, he'd call,
and slowly I would rise and dress,
fearing the chronic angers of that house,

Speaking indifferently to him,   10
who had driven out the cold
and polished my good shoes as well.
What did I know, what did I know
of love's austere and lonely offices?

Study and Discussion Questions

1. Is the contrast in the poem between coldness and warmth only physical?
2. What is the significance of "and polished my good shoes as well"?
3. What, besides simply growing up, seems to have happened to change the speaker's attitude toward his father?
4. What does the last word of the poem mean? Why does Hayden use that word? Explain the last two lines.

Suggestion for Writing

1. Given the subject of the poem, how does Hayden avoid sentimentality?

Critical Resources

1. Fetrow, Fred. *Robert Hayden.* Boston: Twayne, 1984.

2. Goldstein, Laurence and Robert Chrisman, eds. *Robert Hayden: Essays of the Poetry.* Ann Arbor: U of Michigan P, 2001.
3. Hatcher, John. *From the Auroral Darkness: The Life and Poetry of Robert Hayden.* Oxford: George Ronald, 1984.
4. Williams, Pontheolla. *Robert Hayden: A Critical Analysis of His Poetry.* Urbana: U of Illinois P, 1987.

SYLVIA PLATH (1932–1963)

In the barely 30 years of her life, Sylvia Plath created a body of poetry that broke through the mannerly conventions of post World War II American verse into intense, personal, passionately imaged lyrics that helped to revolutionize poetry in England and the United States. Born in Boston, she published her first poem at age eight; by the time she was 17, she was regularly sending poems and stories out to magazines. Her autographical novel, The Bell Jar *(1963), is based on the year she both won a* Seventeen *magazine student editor contest and made her first suicide attempt. Plath graduated from Smith College and then went to England to study at Cambridge University. There she met and married British poet Ted Hughes, whose poems were as intense and convention breaking as her own. Before their marriage shattered, Plath and Hughes had two children. She committed suicide on February 11, 1963. Plath published one volume of poetry before her death,* The Colossus *(1960), the title poem of which is included here. "The Colossus" seems to refer to her relation to her father, Otto Plath, an entomologist who published a book on bumblebees and who died when Sylvia was a child. Her famous poem "Daddy" (included in Varieties of Protest) references her father as well as Ted Hughes.* Ariel *(1965), containing poems written in the last two or three years of her life, established Sylvia Plath's reputation in what critics were then calling the "confessional" school of poetry, which also included Robert Lowell and Anne Sexton. In 1962, Plath's radio play in verse,* Three Women, *was broadcast on the BBC in London. Other books by Sylvia Plath published posthumously include a prose collection,* Johnny Panic and the Bible of Dreams, The Journals of Sylvia Plath, Letters Home, *a children's story in verse,* The Bed Book, *and three volumes of poetry—*Ariel, Crossing the Water, *and* Winter Trees, *all now included in* The Collected Poems of Sylvia Plath.*

The Colossus   (1960)

I shall never get you put together entirely,
Pieced, glued, and properly jointed.
Mule-bray, pig-grunt and bawdy cackles

Proceed from your great lips.
It's worse than a barnyard.   5

Perhaps you consider yourself an oracle,
Mouthpiece of the dead, or of some god or other.
Thirty years now I have laboured
To dredge the silt from your throat.
I am none the wiser.   10

Scaling little ladders with gluepots and pails of lysol
I crawl like an ant in mourning
Over the weedy acres of your brow
To mend the immense skull-plates and clear
The bald, white tumuli of your eyes.   15

A blue sky out of the Oresteia
Arches above us. O father, all by yourself
You are pithy and historical as the Roman Forum.
I open my lunch on a hill of black cypress.
Your fluted bones and acanthine hair are littered   20

In their old anarchy to the horizon-line.
It would take more than a lightning-stroke
To create such a ruin.
Nights, I squat in the cornucopia
Of your left ear, out of the wind,   25

Counting the red stars and those of plum-colour.
The sun rises under the pillar of your tongue.
My hours are married to shadow.
No longer do I listen for the scrape of a keel
On the blank stones of the landing.   30

Study and Discussion Questions

1. Look up "colossus" and "The Colossus of Rhodes" in a dictionary/ency-
   clopedia. In this poem, who is the Colossus? What is the narrator's relation to him?
2. Look up all other allusions and words you don't know all the meanings
   of (e.g., "tumuli")—don't guess at what a word means in a poem.
3. What, literally, is happening in this poem? What is the setting? Who is the
   speaker of the poem and what is she spending her time doing?
4. List the images in the poem. Which of the five (or six, if we add kinetic)
   senses is Plath evoking?

5. "Mule-bray, pig-grunt and bawdy cackles/ Proceed from your great lips./ It's worse than a barnyard." Discuss these lines from the first stanza. What does this poem say to us about language and creativity?
6. What is the particular tension in this poem between the "characters"?
7. What is the speaker of the poem's quest? Why does she need to do this?
8. Is she succeeding? Pick two images from the poem that suggest her success or failure.
9. What does "The Colossus" say about family and its effects on us? What does it say in particular about developing our creative potential?

Suggestion for Writing

1. Compare/contrast "The Colossus" with "Daddy" (Varieties of Protest). How far has the speaker of the poem traveled in three years in terms of her relation with the memory of her father? (Plath's father actually died close to her ninth birthday.) How far has the poet traveled in terms of her art? Discuss the language, images, structure, and rhythms of each poem as well as the story or quest of each poem.

Critical Resources

1. The Academy of American Poets, Inc. <www.poets.org/poet.php/prm PID/11>.
2. Brennan, Claire, ed. *The Poetry of Sylvia Plath*. New York: Columbia UP, 2001.
3. Middlebrook, Diane. *Her Husband*. New York: Viking, 2003.
4. Rosenblatt, Jon. *The Poetry of Initiation*. Chapel Hill: U of North Carolina P, 1979.
5. Wagner, Linda. *Critical Essays on Sylvia Plath*. Boston: G. K. Hall, 1984.

PHILIP LEVINE (b. 1928)

Philip Levine was born the son of Russian-Jewish immigrants in Detroit, Michigan, and grew up in the industrial world of the auto factories. From the time he was 14 and on through his 20s, Levine worked on the assembly lines as he made his way through college. It was during this time that he began reading poetry and aspired to give a poetic voice to the blue-collar experience. In 1957, he received his M.F.A. from the University of Iowa and began a teaching career. Six years later he published his first volume of poetry, On the Edge, *and has since published over 20 collections in 4 decades. Levine has made his reputation on verse that resists extravagant language and traditional poetic devices and is concentrated on the essence of the sincere, unadorned image. While some critics have questioned his lack of rhyme and meter, Levine has forged his own style of free-verse poetry—a "narrative poetry" that attempts to tell the stories of working people and to render this experience in a vernacular that is both common and perceptive. He was awarded the Pulitzer Prize for* The Simple Truth *in 1994. Other notable poetry collections include* Not This Pig *(1968),* 5 Detroits *(1970),* They Feed They Lion *(1972),* 7 Years From Somewhere *(1979),* Sweet Will *(1985),* A Walk With Tom Jefferson *(1988),* What Work Is *(1991, National Book Award), and his latest collection,* Breath: Poems *(2004).*

✸ ✸ ✸

PHILIP LEVINE (b. 1928)

Among Children   1991

I walk among the rows of bowed heads—
the children are sleeping through fourth grade
so as to be ready for what is ahead,
the monumental boredom of junior high
and the rush forward tearing their wings   5
loose and turning their eyes forever inward.
These are the children of Flint, their fathers
work at the spark plug factory or truck
bottled water in 5 gallon sea-blue jugs
to the widows of the suburbs. You can see   10
already how their backs have thickened,
how their small hands, soiled by pig iron,
leap and stutter even in dreams. I would like
to sit down among them and read slowly
from *The Book of Job* until the windows   15
pale and the teacher rises out of a milky sea
of industrial scum, her gowns streaming
with light, her foolish words transformed
into song, I would like to arm each one
with a quiver of arrows so that they might   20
rush like wind there where no battle rages
shouting among the trumpets, Ha! Ha!
How dear the gift of laughter in the face
of the 8 hour day, the cold winter mornings
without coffee and oranges, the long lines   25
of mothers in old coats waiting silently
where the gates have closed. Ten years ago
I went among these same children, just born,

in the bright ward of the Sacred Heart and leaned
down to hear their breaths delivered that day,   30
burning with joy. There was such wonder
in their sleep, such purpose in their eyes
closed against autumn, in their damp heads
blurred with the hair of ponds, and not one
turned against me or the light, not one   35
said, I am sick, I am tired, I will go home,
not one complained or drifted alone
unloved, on the hardest day of their lives.
Eleven years from now they will become
the men and women of Flint or Paradise,   40
the majors of a minor town, and I
will be gone into smoke or memory,
so I bow to them here and whisper
all I know, all I will never know.

Study and Discussion Questions

1. What has been, is, and will be the lives of these children, according to Philip Levine? List details.
2. What is Levine saying about being working class in the United States?
3. List and discuss the *images* Levine uses to literally and figuratively present the children.
4. Why does the poet want to read to the fourth-grade children "from *The Book of Job*"?
5. What is the relation of the poet/speaker of the poem to these children?
6. Industrial life has often been depicted in opposition to nature. Note where and how Levine uses images of nature in this poem.
7. Analyze the structure of "Among Children." Outline the stages of Levine's argument. Why do you think he chooses to begin the poem when the children are 9 or 10 years old?
8. Why do you think Levine wrote this poem in one long stanza instead of breaking it up into shorter stanzas? Note the length of his lines. Note also his use of enjambment, how and where he chooses to break his lines.

Suggestions for Writing

1. Choose an image or passage that is particularly moving or powerful for you in "Among Children" and write a paragraph discussing it—both your own individual response and an analysis of the sounds and connotations of words, the mood created, the people evoked, and whatever else seems important to you.
2. Find a copy of W. B. Yeats's poem "Among School Children." How has Levine used Yeats's famous poem as a starting point for his own? How

and where do the two poems differ? Give specific examples from the poems. How is Levine's poem a political, spiritual, human, and poetic response to Yeats's poem? How is Levine's focus different from Yeats's?
Note: Levine was 60 years old when his poem was published.
3. How might Philip Levine's poems been influenced by earlier poets like
Whitman, Yeats, Sandburg, Lorca, and Neruda? See poems by each of
these poets in this book.

Critical Resources

1. Buckley, Christopher, ed. *On the Poetry of Philip Levine: Stranger to Nothing.* Ann Arbor: U of Michigan P, 1991.
2. Levine, Philip. *The Bread of Time: Toward an Autobiography.* Ann Arbor:
U of Michigan P, 2001.
3. Levine, Philip. *So Ask: Essays, Conversations, and Interviews.* Ann Arbor:
U of Michigan P, 2002.
4. Hirsh, Edward. "The Visionary Poetics of Philip Levine and Charles
Wright." *The Columbia History of American Poetry,* ed, Jay Parini. New
York: Columbia P, 1993.
5. Yeats, William Butler, "Among School Children." *Collected Poems of
W. B. Yeats.* New York: Macmillan, 1956.

❀ ❀ ❀

GWENDOLYN BROOKS (1917–2000)

*Gwendolyn Brooks grew up in Chicago. She began writing poetry at an early age,
publishing her first poem at age thirteen. After receiving her B.A. in English from
Wilson Junior College in 1936, Brooks worked for the NAACP Youth Council.
During this time, Brooks was greatly influenced by poet Langston Hughes and
other writers from the Harlem Renaissance, who encouraged her to study the modernist poetry of Eliot and Pound. As is evident in much of her early work, Brooks
combines the technical skill and form of modernist poetry with the imagery and
rhythms of African American life and language. In 1950, she became the first
African American to win the Pulitzer Prize for her poetry collection* Annie Allen
*(1950). In 1967, Brooks's visit to Fisk University was a transformative moment
for her as a poet and African American. Impressed by the energy of young black
poets like Leroi Jones, Brooks's penchant for formal structures (she was a master
of the sonnet) and themes loosened. While her devotion to the African-American
experience remained, her poetry increasingly became more political, more contentious, as she became aware of her role as a black feminist in the Civil Rights
Movement. In 1985, she was appointed poetry consultant to the Library of Congress (Poet Laureate). She has written several poetry collections, including* A
Street in Bronzeville *(1945),* Annie Allen *(1950),* The Bean Eaters *(1960),* In

the Mecca *(1968),* Beckonings *(1975),* Black Love *(1982), and* In Montgomery
(2001, posthumously); the novel Maud Martha *(1953); and the autobiography*
Report from Part One *(1972).*

the mother   (1945)

Abortions will not let you forget.
You remember the children you got that you did not get,
The damp small pulps with a little or with no hair,
The singers and workers that never handled the air.
You will never neglect or beat   5
Them, or silence or buy with a sweet.
You will never wind up the sucking-thumb
Or scuttle off ghosts that come.
You will never leave them, controlling your luscious sigh,
Return for a snack of them, with gobbling mother-eye.   10

I have heard in the voices of the wind the voices of my dim
　　　　killed children.
I have contracted. I have eased
My dim dears at the breasts they could never suck.
I have said, Sweets, if I sinned, if I seized
Your luck   15
And your lives from your unfinished reach,
If I stole your births and your names,
Your straight baby tears and your games,
Your stilted or lovely loves, your tumults, your marriages,
　　　　aches, and your deaths,
If I poisoned the beginnings of your breaths,   20
Believe that even in my deliberateness I was not deliberate.
Though why should I whine,
Whine that the crime was other than mine?—
Since anyhow you are dead.
Or rather, or instead,   25
You were never made.
But that too, I am afraid,
Is faulty: oh, what shall I say, how is the truth to be said?
You were born, you had body, you died.
It is just that you never giggled or planned or cried.   30

Believe me, I loved you all.

Believe me, I knew you, though faintly, and I loved, I loved you
All.

Study and Discussion Questions:

1. List the ways Brooks makes these never-born children come alive in her poem.
2. What is the mother's relation to these unborn children? How does she image motherhood?
3. Look at the rhyme scheme in each of the three stanzas. Label the end rhymes with a new letter of the alphabet for each new rhyme, beginning with A for "forget/get." Words don't have to rhyme exactly (e.g., "seized/reach"); they can be slant or off rhymes.
4. Are there any lines which don't seem to have an end rhyme with any other word? Check to see if there is an internal rhyme, a rhyme within the line that rhymes with the end of the line.
5. Discuss the use of repetition in the poem, especially in the last stanza but also throughout the poem. What effect does the repetition have?
6. Why do you think Brooks uses second person point of view in the first stanza and then switches to first person?
7. How do the opening and closing lines of the poem respond to each other?

Suggestions for Writing

1. Brooks, without taking a position herself, has remarked that advocates on both sides of the abortion debate have claimed this poem as expressing their particular position. What in the poem could cause proponents of each stance to make this claim?
2. "the mother" allows us inside the thoughts, experiences, and feelings of a woman who has had choices to make and has made them. How does she work through the complexity of her actions and feelings as the poem develops?
3. Have you ever had to make a difficult decision, one that would "not let you forget"? Write about it, working through the memories and feelings in vivid images.

Critical Resources

1. Bloom, Harold, ed. *Gwendolyn Brooks*. Philadelphia: Chelsea House, 2000.
2. Brooks, Gwendolyn. *Report from Part One: An Autobiography*. Detroit: Broadside P, 1972.
3. Gayles, Gloria Wade. *Conversation with Gwendolyn Brooks*. Jackson: UP of Mississippi, 2003.
4. Mootry, Maria, ed. *A Life Distilled: Gwendolyn Brooks, Her Poetry and Fiction*. Urbana: U of Illinois P, 1987.

❀ ❀ ❀

SHARON OLDS (b. 1942)

Sharon Olds was born in San Francisco. She earned her Ph.D. from Columbia in 1972. Eight years later, at the age of 37, Olds published her first volume of poetry, Satan Says *(1980), followed by* The Dead and the Living *(1984), which won the National Book Critics' Circle Award. Olds's work has attracted a large audience— a rarity for contemporary poets. Much of her popularity is due to the accessible nature of her verse. Sometimes compared to Walt Whitman, Olds's poetry frequently centers on the sensations of the human body—the living, sensual experiences of death, birth, violence, sex, and love. She wrote in 1980, "Is there anything that shouldn't or can't be written about in a poem? What has never been written in a poem?" Olds explores those taboo areas of physical life that all humans share, but which often lie silent in the public sphere. Her vivid images and stark language have prompted critics to both praise her work as "unexpected, bold and deeply rewarding" as well as condemn it as "pornographic." Olds currently teaches at New York University. Subsequent poetry collections include* The Sign of Saturn *(1991),* The Father *(1992),* Blood, Tin, Straw *(1999), and* The Unswept Room *(2002). "The Language of the Brag," first published in* Satan Says, *frankly portrays the physical and emotional event of giving birth.*

The Language of the Brag   (1980)

I have wanted excellence in the knife-throw,
I have wanted to use my exceptionally strong and accurate arms
and my straight posture and quick electric muscles
achieve something at the center of a crowd,
the blade piercing the bark deep,   5
the shaft slowly and heavily vibrating like the cock.

I have wanted some epic use for my excellent body,
some heroism, some American achievement
beyond the ordinary for my extraordinary self,
magnetic and tensile, I have stood by the sandlot   10
and watched the boys play.

I have wanted courage, I have thought about fire
and the crossing of waterfalls, I have dragged around
my belly big with cowardice and safety,
my stool black with iron pills,   15
my huge breasts oozing mucus,
my legs swelling, my hands swelling,
my face swelling and darkening, my hair
falling out, my inner sex stabbed again and again with terrible pain

like a knife. 20
I have lain down.

I have lain down and sweated and shaken
and passed blood and feces and water and
slowly alone in the center of a circle I have
passed the new person out 25
and they have lifted the new person free of the act
and wiped the new person free of that
language of blood like praise all over the body.

I have done what you wanted to do, Walt Whitman,
Allen Ginsberg, have done this thing, 30
I and the other women this exceptional
act with the exceptional heroic body,
this giving birth, this glistening verb,
and I am putting my proud American boast
right here with the others. 35

Study and Discussion Questions

1. Write down the opening words of each of the poem's five stanzas. What is the progression here?
2. When pregnancy and childbirth are represented in literature or discussed in nonfiction, the tone is frequently sentimental. Show two or three ways in which Sharon Olds's poem is not sentimental about pregnancy and childbirth.
3. What does the speaker of the poem say in the first dozen lines of the poem that she wanted? How are these gender specific aspirations in western culture?
4. Why do you think Olds chooses in describing childbirth the phrase "the-new person" rather than "The baby"?
5. Discuss the lines "that / language of blood like praise all over the body" and "this giving birth, this glistening verb." Why and how is she connecting language and this very female act of childbirth?
6. Discuss the title of the poem in relation to the last stanza.

Suggestions for Writing

1. How has Sharon Olds redefined the concepts of "hero" and "heroism" from a woman's perspective in "The Language of the Brag"? First look up some definitions of both words and think about traditional and currently popular conceptions of heroism and characteristics of the hero.
2. Look up poems by Walt Whitman and Allen Ginsberg in this book and discuss how and why the speaker of the poem and/or the poet Sharon Olds has done what she "wanted to do."

3. Even though there are more literary works about pregnancy now than there were 20 years ago, this major life experience of women is still not that often the subject of literature. Why do you think this is so? List other major experiences specific to females, those specific to males, and those common to both genders. From your own knowledge, rank how often each of these experiences is the subject of literature, film, visual art.

Critical Resources

1. Argyros, Ellen. "'Some Epic Use of My Excellent Body': Redefining Childbirth as Heroic in *Beloved* and 'The Language of The Brag.'" *This Giving Birth: Pregnancy and Childbirth in American Woman's Writing.* Eds. Susan Whitcomb-McCallum and Julie Thorpe. Bowling Green, KY: Popular, 2000.
2. Spalding, Esta. "The Earthly Matter: A Conversation with Sharon Olds." *Brick* 67 (2001): 85–92.
3. *Sharon Olds.* The Lannon Foundation, 1991. 60 minutes. For more information go to <http://www.lannan.org/lf/lit/search_detail/sharon-olds>.

JOHN UPDIKE (b. 1932)

John Updike was born in Shilington, Pennsylvania. He graduated from Harvard in 1954 and then moved to Oxford, England, to study art for a year. He later returned to the United States to work for the New Yorker *magazine, which began publishing his work. Updike eventually settled in Ipswich, Massachusetts. Updike's subjects are the values and problems of middle-class America. In this fiction, Updike seeks to problematize this seemingly mundane world, addressing such themes as family, religion, morality, sports, and the dynamics of intimate relationships. His novels include* Rabbit, Run, *(1960),* Couples *(1968),* Rabbit Redux *(1971),* Rabbit Is Rich *(1981),* The Witches of Eastwick *(1984),* Roger's Version *(1986),* Rabbit at Rest *(1990),* In the Beauty of the Lilies *(1996) and* Gertrude and Cladius *(2000). See critical resources under Updike's story "A & P." For further acquaintance with Updike's poetry, see his* Collected Poems: 1953–1993.

Ex-Basketball Player   (1957)

Pearl Avenue runs past the high-school lot,
Bends with the trolley tracks, and stops, cut off
Before it has a chance to go two blocks,
At Colonel McComsky Plaza. Berth's Garage

Is on the corner facing west, and there,   5
Most days, you'll find Flick Webb, who helps Berth out

Flick stands tall among the idiot pumps—
Five on a side, the old bubble-head style,
Their rubber elbows hanging loose and low
One's nostrils are two S's, and his eyes   10
An E and O. And one is squat, without
A head at all—more of a football type.

Once Flick played for the high-school team, the Wizards.
He was good: in fact, the best. In '46
He bucketed three hundred ninety points,   15
A county record still. The ball loved Flick.
I saw him rack up thirty-eight or forty
In one home game. His hands were like wild birds.

He never learned a trade, he just sells gas,
Checks oil, and changes flats. Once in a while,   20
As a gag, he dribbles an inner tube,
But most of us remember anyway.
His hands are fine and nervous on the lug wrench.
It makes no difference to the lug wrench, though.

Off work, he hangs around Mae's luncheonette   25
Grease-gray and kind of coiled, he plays pinball,
Smokes those thin cigars, nurses lemon phosphates.
Flick seldom says a word to Mae, just nods
Beyond her face toward bright applauding tiers
Of Necco Wafers, Nibs, and JuJu Beads.   30

Study and Discussion Questions

1. What are the various indications that Flick is diminished in the present?
2. What is the significance of the first four lines?
3. Analyze the imagery of the second stanza.
4. What is the meaning of the last line of the fourth stanza?

Suggestions for Writing

1. Is Flick unhappy now?
2. Describe someone you knew in high school whom you think is or soon
   will be somehow less than he or she then was. Is social class a factor?

T. S. ELIOT (1888–1965)

Thomas Stearns Eliot was born in St. Louis into a well-to-do family with roots in New England. At a young age, Eliot was encouraged to write poetry by his mother. He received both his B.A. and M.A. at Harvard and spent time studying at Oxford and at the Sorbonne in Paris. Eliot is considered a key figure in modernist poetry and criticism. His major work, The Waste Land *(1922), is considered one of the most important poems of the twentieth century, influencing and influenced by both the symbolist and imagist schools of poetry which sought to create layers of meaning through simplified language and concrete images. Eliot's other major volumes of poetry are* Prufrock and Other Observations *(1917) and* Four Quartets *(1943). Eliot's early, influential critical essays are collected in* The Sacred Wood *(1920), and he wrote several verse plays, including* Murder in the Cathedral *(1935) and* The Cocktail Party *(1949). He received the Nobel Prize for literature in 1948. "The Love Song of J. Alfred Prufrock" is an example of Eliot's early style and the beginnings of modernist poetry.*

The Love Song of J. Alfred Prufrock   (1917)

> *S'io credesse che mia risposta fosse*
> *A persona che mai tornasse al mondo,*
> *Questa fiamma staria senza piu scosse.*
> *Ma perciocche giammai di questo fondo*
> *Non torno vivo alcun, s'i'odo il vero,*
> *Senza tema d'infamia ti rispondo.[1]*

Let us go then, you and I,
When the evening is spread out against the sky
Like a patient etherised upon a table;
Let us go, through certain half-deserted streets,
The muttering retreats   5
Of restless nights in one-night cheap hotels
And sawdust restaurants with oyster-shells:
Streets that follow like a tedious argument
Of insidious intent
To lead you to an overwhelming question . . .   10
Oh, do not ask, "What is it?"
Let us go and make our visit.
In the room the women come and go
Talking of Michelangelo.

---

[1]From Dante's *Inferno*, spoken to Dante by Guido da Montelfeltro, who is wrapped in flame: "If I thought that my reply were to someone who could ever return to the world, this flame would shake no more. But since no one has ever returned alive from this place, if what I hear is true, without fear of infamy I answer you."

The yellow fog that rubs its back upon the window-panes,   15
The yellow smoke that rubs its muzzle on the window-panes
Licked its tongue into the corners of the evening,
Lingered upon the pools that stand in drains,
Let fall upon its back the soot that falls from chimneys,
Slipped by the terrace, made a sudden leap,   20
And seeing that it was a soft October night,
Curled once about the house, and fell asleep.

And indeed there will be time
For the yellow smoke that slides along the street,
Rubbing its back upon the window-panes;   25
There will be time, there will be time
To prepare a face to meet the faces that you meet;
There will be time to murder and create,
And time for all the works and days of hands
That lift and drop a question on your plate;   30
Time for you and time for me,
And time yet for a hundred indecisions,
And for a hundred visions and revisions,
Before the taking of a toast and tea.

In the room the women come and go   35
Talking of Michelangelo.

And indeed there will be time
To wonder, "Do I dare?" and, "Do I dare?"
Time to turn back and descend the stair,
With a bald spot in the middle of my hair—   40
[They will say: "How his hair is growing thin!"]
My morning coat, my collar mounting firmly to the chin,
My necktie rich and modest, but asserted by a simple pin—
[They will say: "But how his arms and legs are thin!"]
Do I dare   45
Disturb the universe?
In a minute there is time
For decisions and revisions which a minute will reverse.

For I have known them all already, known them all:—
Have known the evenings, mornings, afternoons,   50
I have measured out my life with coffee spoons;
I know the voices dying with a dying fall
Beneath the music from a farther room.
    So how should I presume?

And I have known the eyes already, known them all—   55
The eyes that fix you in a formulated phrase,
And when I am formulated, sprawling on a pin,
When I am pinned and wriggling on the wall,
Then how should I begin
To spit out all the butt-ends of my days and ways?   60
    And how should I presume?

And I have known the arms already, known them all—
Arms that are braceleted and white and bare
[But in the lamplight, downed with light brown hair!]
Is it perfume from a dress   65
That makes me so digress?
Arms that lie along a table, or wrap about a shawl.
    And should I then presume?
    And how should I begin?
                                                        . . . . .

Shall I say, I have gone at dusk through narrow streets   70
And watched the smoke that rises from the pipes
Of lonely men in shirt-sleeves, leaning out of windows? . . .

I should have been a pair of ragged claws
Scuttling across the floors of silent seas.

                                                        . . . . .

And the afternoon, the evening, sleeps so peacefully!   75
Smoothed by long fingers,
Asleep . . . tired . . . or it malingers,
Stretched on the floor, here beside you and me.
Should I, after tea and cakes and ices,
Have the strength to force the moment to its crisis?   80
But though I have wept and fasted, wept and prayed,
Though I have seen my head [grown slightly bald] brought in upon a platter,
I am no prophet—and here's no great matter;
I have seen the moment of my greatness flicker,   85
And I have seen the eternal Footman hold my coat, and snicker,
And in short, I was afraid.

And would it have been worth it, after all,
After the cups, the marmalade, the tea,
Among the porcelain, among some talk of you and me,   90
Would it have been worth while,
To have bitten off the matter with a smile,

To have squeezed the universe into a ball
To roll it toward some overwhelming question,
To say: "I am Lazarus, come from the dead,   95
Come back to tell you all, I shall tell you all"—
If one, settling a pillow by her head,
  Should say: "That is not what I meant at all.
  That is not it, at all."

And would it have been worth it, after all,   100
Would it have been worth while,
After the sunsets and the dooryards and the sprinkled streets,
After the novels, after the teacups, after the skirts that trail along the floor—
And this, and so much more?—   105
It is impossible to say just what I mean!
But as if a magic lantern threw the nerves in patterns on a screen:
Would it have been worth while
If one, settling a pillow or throwing off a shawl,
And turning toward the window, should say: 110
  "That is not it at all,
  That is not what I meant, at all."

. . . . .

No! I am not Prince Hamlet, nor was meant to be;
Am an attendant lord, one that will do
To swell a progress, start a scene or two,   115
Advise the prince; no doubt, an easy tool,
Deferential, glad to be of use,
Politic, cautious, and meticulous;
Full of high sentence, but a bit obtuse;
At times, indeed, almost ridiculous—   120
Almost, at times, the Fool.

I grow old . . . I grow old . . .
I shall wear the bottoms of my trousers rolled.

Shall I part my hair behind? Do I dare to eat a peach?
I shall wear white flannel trousers, and walk upon the beach.   125
I have heard the mermaids singing, each to each.

I do not think that they will sing to me.

I have seen them riding seaward on the waves
Combing the white hair of the waves blown back
When the wind blows the water white and black.   130

We have lingered in the chambers of the sea
By sea-girls wreathed with seaweed red and brown
Till human voices wake us, and we drown.

Study and Discussion Questions

1. Who are the "you and I" in line 1? What are they doing?
2. How does what Prufrock comments on in the first 69 lines reveal his state of mind? What different emotions do you see him feeling throughout the poem?
3. Characterize Prufrock. What is his self-image? What are his fears?
4. What kind of world does Prufrock live in? Describe the setting(s) of Prufrock's journey.
5. Prufrock is concerned with the past and future. He says, "For I have known them all already," and, though he says he is no prophet, he does look into the future and speculate about what will happen to him. How do what Prufrock sees in the past and fears in the future affect his present behavior?
6. Is this poem about love?
7. How does the allusion to Dante's *Inferno* help in understanding the poem? The allusion to John the Baptist? to Lazarus? to Hamlet?
8. How does Eliot use repetition in the poem? Note slight changes in some of the repeated phrases.

Suggestions for Writing

1. List every question Prufrock asks in the poem. Do they have anything in common?
2. Choose one image from the poem and explain what it adds to your knowledge of Prufrock.
3. What advice would you give Prufrock?

Critical Resources

1. Eliot, T. S. "Tradition and the Individual Talent (1919)." *Contemporary Literary Criticism: Literary and Cultural Studies.* Eds. Robert Con Davis and Ronald Schleifer. New York: Longman, 1998.
2. Hayman, Bruch. "How Old Is Prufrock? Does He Want To Get Married?" *College Language Association Journal* 38.1 (1994): 59–68.
3. Jain, Manju. *A Critical Reading of the Selected Poetry of TS Eliot.* New York: Oxford UP, 2001.
4. Sharpe, Tony. *TS Eliot: A Literary Life.* New York: St. Martin's, 1992.

❄ ❄ ❄

WILLIAM BUTLER YEATS (1865–1939)

William Butler Yeats was born in Dublin, Ireland, and studied art in college until he turned to writing. It is often said that Yeats was the greatest poet of the twentieth century, even though he preferred to work within more traditional poetics of rhyme and form in contrast to the modernist poets (such as Eliot) who were bringing such traditions into question. Yeats's marriage to Georgie Hyde-Lees, and her "automatic writing," "... in which [the] hand and pen presumably serve as unconscious instruments for the spirit world to send information" (Artists and Authors for Young Adults), helped him codify his interest in the occult and mysticism. He was active in Irish nationalist causes, helped found an Irish national theater, and served as a senator of the new Irish Free State. In 1933, he carefully shaped his many volumes of poetry into the definitive Collected Poems *(1933). He received the Nobel Prize for literature in 1923. "Sailing to Byzantium" is one of several Yeats poems in this anthology.*

Sailing to Byzantium[1]   (1927)

I

That is no country for old men. The young
In one another's arms, birds in the trees
—Those dying generations—at their song,
The salmon-falls, the mackerel-crowded seas,
Fish, flesh, or fowl, commend all summer long   5
Whatever is begotten, born, and dies.
Caught in that sensual music all neglect
Monuments of unageing intellect.

II

An aged man is but a paltry thing,
A tattered coat upon a stick, unless   10
Soul clap its hands and sing, and louder sing
For every tatter in its mortal dress,

---

[1]Now called Istanbul, Byzantium was the capital and cultural center of the Byzantine Empire.

Nor is there singing school but studying
Monuments of its own magnificence;
And therefore I have sailed the seas and come   15
To the holy city of Byzantium.

III

O sages standing in God's holy fire
As in the gold mosaic of a wall,
Come from the holy fire, perne in a gyre,[2]
And be the singing-masters of my soul.   20
Consume my heart away; sick with desire
And fastened to a dying animal
It knows not what it is; and gather me
Into the artifice of eternity.

IV

Once out of nature I shall never take   25
My bodily form from any natural thing,
But such a form as Grecian goldsmiths make
Of hammered gold and gold enamelling
To keep a drowsy Emperor awake;
Or set upon a golden bough to sing   30
To lords and ladies of Byzantium
Of what is past, or passing, or to come.

Study and Discussion Questions

1. *What* is "no country for old men"? Why?
2. What about Byzantium appeals to the speaker?
3. How does the speaker of the poem feel about aging?
4. How do people spend their time in the country of the young? How do
   they spend their time in Byzantium?
5. What constitutes immortality in this poem? What does the speaker mean
   when he asks to be gathered "into the artifice of eternity"?
6. Why, having left the world, will he sing "of what is past, or passing, or to
   come"?

---

[2]Unwind down a spiral.

Suggestions for Writing

1. Contrast Byzantium and the world the speaker of the poem has left in terms of the images used to describe each.
2. Write a sentence stating the main point of each stanza.

Critical Resources

1. Jeffares, Norman A. *A Commentary on the Collected Poems of W. B. Yeats.* London: Macmillan, 1968.
2. Smith, Stan, ed. *W. B. Yeats: A Critical Introduction.* Dublin: Gill and Macmillan, 1990.
3. Yeats, W. B. *The Autobiography of William Butler Yeats.* First Macmillan Hudson River edition. New York: Macmillan, 1987, c1965.

WILLIAM SHAKESPEARE (1564–1616)

Born in Stratford-on-Avon in England, William Shakespeare attended the free grammar school there, married Anne Hathaway when he was eighteen, and soon after went to live in London. Once there, Shakespeare began working as an actor and playwright, his first plays being presented in 1589. As a member of the acting company Lord Chamberlain's Men, Shakespeare established himself as the most popular playwright in London. Eventually the company had the resources to build The Globe Theater and, with Shakespeare as the principal playwright, established themselves as the leading troupe in London. While Shakespeare is considered the most important dramatist in the English language, his sonnets, published in 1609, have acquired renown based on their own literary merit. Patterned after the traditional Petrarchan sonnet and arranged as a dialogue between the poet and two central figures (a "friend" and the "Dark Lady"), Shakespeare's sonnets explore notions of beauty, friendship, and the uncertainty of human feelings. Sonnet 73, "That time of year thou mayst in me behold," utilizes stark images and precise metaphors to create a palpable sense of time.

That time of year thou mayst in me behold   (1609)

LXXIII

That time of year thou mayst in me behold
When yellow leaves, or none, or few, do hang
Upon those boughs which shake against the cold,
Bare ruined choirs where late the sweet birds sang:

In me thou see'st the twilight of such day   5
As after sunset fadeth in the west,
Which by and by black night doth take away,
Death's second self that seals up all in rest:
In me thou see'st the glowing of such fire
That on the ashes of his youth doth lie   10
As the death-bed whereon it must expire,
Consumed with that which it was nourished by:
　This thou perceivest, which makes thy love more strong
　To love that well which thou must leave ere long.

Study and Discussion Questions

1. Who is speaking, and to whom? What are the relative ages of the two?
2. Explain line 12.
3. Explain in detail each of the three metaphors for growing old. How are they similar and how do they differ? What is the meaning of the order in which they appear?
4. How confident does the speaker seem in the assertion the final couplet makes?

Suggestions for Writing

1. Write a prose paragraph or two describing the speaker's attitude toward growing older.
2. What other metaphors might one use to describe aging? What are the associations and implications of each?

Critical Resources

1. Booth, Stephen. *Shakespeare's Sonnets: Edited with Analytical Commentary.* New Haven: Yale UP, 2001.
2. Tetsumaro, Hiyashi. *Shakespeare's Sonnets: A Record of 20th Century Criticism.* Metchuen, NJ: Scarecrow, 1972.
3. Vendler, Helen. *The Art of Shakespeare's Sonnets.* Cambridge, MA: Belknap Press of Harvard UP, 1997.

WILLIAM CARLOS WILLIAMS (1883–1963)

Born of an English father and a Puerto Rican mother, William Carlos Williams grew up in Rutherford, New Jersey. Although his father introduced him to Shakespeare and Dante, the young Williams was more interested in math and science. While a medical student at the University of Pennsylvania, Williams began reading the poetry of John Keats and Walt Whitman; however, it was his friendship with

Ezra Pound and other Imagist poets that helped him break from traditional, structured poetry and move toward a more precise, compact verse that sought to render images as they are perceived by the poet. With the publication of Eliot's "Wasteland" in 1922, Williams began to dislike the shape contemporary poetry was taking. In contrast to the angst of modernism, he was more concerned with creating a distinctively American poetry—a poetry that was intimately connected to locale. As a doctor in a small town (Paterson, New Jersey), he was privy to a side of ordinary life not traditionally seen as poetic. The real, human experience of his patients and townspeople were what Williams believed poetry should communicate. Although not widely known during his lifetime, Williams's work has had a considerable influence on American poetry. The more than 20 volumes of poetry he wrote during his lifetime have been gathered in the two-volume The Collected Poems of William Carlos Williams *(1986), edited by A. Walton Litz and Christopher MacGowan. He was also a prolific writer of nonfiction essays and fiction (novels and short stories). For a complete bibliography, see the* Guide to the Poetry of William Carlos Williams *(1995). "To a Poor Old Woman" was published in* The Earlier Poems *(1951).*

To a Poor Old Woman

munching a plum on
the street a paper bag
of them in her hand

They taste good to her
They taste good   5
to her. They taste
good to her

You can see it by
the way she gives herself
to the one half   10
sucked out in her hand

Comforted
a solace of ripe plums
seeming to fill the air
They taste good to her   15

Study and Discussion Questions

1. Discuss the sounds in and the sound of the poem. List the repeated consonant sounds (consonance). What effect do these sounds have?
2. In stanza two the same sentence is used three times. Why? How is the sentence changed by breaking the lines in different places?

3. If this four-stanza poem were a four-paragraph essay, what would be the main point of each paragraph? How does Williams gradually develop our understanding of the experience he is describing?
4. Is the first stanza really only three lines?
5. Discuss the dynamic tension between the title "To a Poor Old Woman" and the experience the poem presents. What images does the title conjure up for you? What images and sensations does the poem actually present? Is there any irony here and, if so, who is it directed at?
6. Why do you think Williams titles his poem "To A Poor Old Woman" rather than "A Poor Old Woman"?

Suggestion for Writing

1. Characterize someone through **images** of his or her relation to a particular food. This could end up as a poem in lines or as a short vivid prose piece. It could be serious, funny, or in any mood you choose.

Critical Resources

1. Deese, Helen and Steven Gould Axelrod, eds. *Critical Essays on William Carlos Williams.* New York: G. K. Hall, 1995.
2. Larson, Kelli. *Guide to the Poetry of William Carlos Williams.* London: Prentice Hall, 1995.
3. Wagner, Linda Welshimer, ed. *Interviews With William Carlos Williams: "Speaking Straight Ahead."* New York: New Directions, 1976.
4. Williams, William Carlos. *I Wanted to Write a Poem: The Autobiography of The Works of A Poet.* Boston: Beacon, 1968.

IRENA KLEPFISZ (b. 1941)

Irena Klepfisz was born in Warsaw, Poland, at the peak of World War II and Nazi occupation. Her parents were secular, working-class Jews active in the resistance to German aggression. Her father would be killed before the war ended, but she and her mother escaped to safety, eventually immigrating to Sweden and then to the United States when she was eight years old. Klepfisz received her Ph.D. in English from the University of Chicago in 1968. In 1975, she published her first book of poetry, Periods of Stress, *in which she explores her experiences as both a Jewish lesbian and Holocaust survivor. This book, and much of her subsequent writing (poetry and essays), is infused with a political charge and looks at questions of identity, memory, and place. In addition, Klepfisz's use of Yiddish in her writing and her translations of Yiddish writers into English have created an awareness of Yiddish culture in mainstream America. Her works of poetry include* Periods of Stress *(1975),* Keeper of Accounts *(1982),* Different Enclosures *(1985) and* A Few Words in the Mother Tongue: Poems Selected and New (1971–1990) *(1990); and the nonfiction* Dreams of an Insomniac: Jewish Feminist Essays, Speeches, and Diatribes. *She has also coedited several works, including* The Tribe of Dina: A Jewish Women's Anthology *(1989). Her poem "they did not build wings for them" was published in* Periods of Stress.

they did not build wings for them   (1974)

they did not build wings for them
the unmarried aunts;   instead they
crammed them into old maids' rooms
or placed them as nannies with
the younger children;   mostly they   5
ate in the kitchen, but sometimes
were permitted to dine with the family
for which they were grateful and
smiled graciously as the food was passed.
they would eat slowly never filling   10
their plates and their hearts would
sink at the evening's end when it was
time to retreat into an upstairs corner.

but there were some who did not smile
who never wished to be grafted on   15
the bursting houses.   these few remained
indifferent to the family gatherings
preferring the aloneness of their small rooms
which they decorated with odd objects
found on long walks.   they collected   20
bird feathers and skulls unafraid to clean
them to whiteness;   stones which resembled
humped bears or the more common tiger and
wolf;   dried leaves whose brilliant colors
never faded;   pieces of wood still covered   25
with fresh moss and earth which retained
their moisture and continued flourishing.
these they placed by their dresser mirrors
in arrangements reminiscent of secret rites
or hung over delicate watercolors of unruly   30
trees whose branches were about to snap
with the wind.

it happened sometimes that among these
one would venture even further.   periodically
would be heard vague tales of a woman   35
withdrawn and inaccessible suddenly disappearing
one autumn night leaving her room bare
of herself.   women gossiped about a man.
but eventually word would come back
she had moved north to the ocean and lived   40
alone.   she was still collecting
but now her house was filled with crab
and lobster shells; discolored claws
which looked like grinning south american
parrots trapped in fish nets decorated   45
the walls; skulls of unidentifiable
creatures were arranged in geometric patterns
and soft reeds in tall green bottles
lined the window sills.   one room
in the back with totally bare walls   50
was a workshop.   here she sorted colored
shells and pasted them on wooden boards
in the shape of common flowers.   these she sold
without sentiment.

such a one might also disappear inland.   55
rumor would claim she had travelled in
men's clothing.   two years later it would
be reported she had settled in the woods
on some cleared land.   she ran a small farm
mainly for supplying herself with food   60
and wore strangely patched dresses and shawls
of oddly matched materials.   but aloneness
was her real distinction.   the house was neat
and the pantry full.   seascapes and pastoral
scenes hung on the walls.   the garden was   65
well kept and the flower beds clearly defined
by color: red   yellow   blue.   in the woods
five miles from the house she had an orchard.
here she secretly grafted and crossed varieties
creating singular fruit of shades and scents   70
never thought possible.   her experiments rarely
failed and each spring she waited eagerly to see
what new forms would hang from the trees.
here the world was a passionate place and she
would visit it at night baring her breasts   75
to the moon.

Study and Discussion Questions

1. How are the "unmarried aunts" treated by their families?
2. Klepfisz uses the word *grafted* twice. What is she doing with the word in each instance?
3. Why are we told in the third stanza that the woman sells what she makes "without sentiment"?
4. What do all the women in stanzas two, three, and four have in common?
5. How does the second stanza of the poem function as a transition between the first stanza and the last two stanzas?

Suggestion for Writing

1. Write a new definition of *old maid* or *spinster* based on this poem. (You might decide to come up with a new word as well as a new definition.)

Critical Resources

1. Klepfisz, Irena. *On the Poem's Other Side.* Audio. People's Poetry Gathering. <http://www.peoplespoetry.org/clips/pg_klepfisz.html>. 3 minutes.
2. Hedley, Jane. "Nepantilist Poetics: Narrative and Cultural Identity in the Mixed-Language Writings of Irena Klepfisz and Gloria Anzaldua." *Narrative* 4.1 (1996): 36–54.
3. Peterson, Nancy J, ed. *Against Amnesia: Contemporary Women Writers and the Crises Of Historical Memory.* Philadelphia: University of Pennsylvania Press, 2001.

PATRICIA SMITH (b. 1955)

Born on the West Side of Chicago, Patricia Smith would go to sleep at night listening to her father, a factory worker, read stories from the local newspaper. After graduating from high school, Smith entered Southern Illinois University in hopes of studying journalism, but soon left and took a job as a typist at the Chicago Daily News. *Over time, Smith began writing entertainment reviews for the paper and in 1978 was hired at the* Chicago Sun-Times *as an entertainment writer. Smith would eventually become the first African American woman to write a weekly column at the* Boston Globe. *During these years as a journalist, Smith was also busy writing and performing poetry in both Chicago's and Boston's rising "slam" scene, of which she would become one of its central figures, winning the National Poetry Slam four times. Slam poetry has since taken hold throughout the country as one of our most vibrant and contemporary poetic forms. Smith has published three books of poetry,* Life According to Motown *(1991),* Big Towns, Big Talk *(1992), and* Close to Death *(1993). After her falling out with the* Boston Globe, *Smith coauthored with novelist* Charles Johnson Africans in America: America's*

Journey Through Slavery *(1998). Smith's live performance of "Undertaker" (dir. Angelica Brisk, Tied to the Tracks Films) was the subject of an award-winning short film on slam poetry.*

Undertaker   (1993)

For Floyd Williams

When a bullet enters the brain, the head explodes.
I can think of no softer warning for the mothers
who sit doubled before my desk,
knotting their smooth brown hands,
and begging, fix my boy, fix my boy.   5
Here's his high school picture.
And the smirking, mildly mustachioed player
in the crinkled snapshot
looks nothing like the plastic bag of boy
stored and dated in the cold room downstairs.   10
In the picture, he is cocky and chiseled,
clutching the world by the balls. I know the look.
Now he is flaps of cheek,
slivers of jawbone, a surprised eye,
assorted teeth, bloody tufts of napped hair.   15
The building blocks of my business.
So I swallow hard, turn the photo face down
and talk numbers instead. The high price
of miracles startles the still-young woman,
but she is prepared. I know that she has sold   20
everything she owns, that cousins and uncles
have emptied their empty bank accounts,
that she dreams of her baby
in tuxedoed satin, flawless in an open casket,
a cross or blood red rose tacked to his fingers,   25
his halo set at a cocky angle.
I write a figure on a piece of paper
and push it across to her
while her chest heaves with hoping.
She stares at the number, pulls in   30
a slow weepy breath: *"Jesus."*

But Jesus isn't on this payroll. I work alone
until the dim insistence of morning,

bent over my grisly puzzle pieces, gluing,
stitching, creating a chin with a brushstroke.   35
I plop glass eyes into rigid sockets,
then carve eyelids from a forearm, an inner thigh.
I plump shattered skulls, and paint the skin
to suggest warmth, an impending breath.
I reach into collapsed cavities to rescue   40
a tongue, an ear. Lips are never easy to recreate.

And I try not to remember the stories,
the tales the mothers must bring me
to ease their own hearts. *Oh,* they cry,
my Ronnie, my Willie, my Michael, my Chico.   45
It was self-defense. He was on his way home,
a dark car slowed down, they must have thought
he was someone else. He stepped between
two warring gang members at a party.
Really, he was trying to get off the streets,   50
trying to pull away from the crowd.
He was just trying to help a friend.
He was in the wrong place at the wrong time.
Fix my boy; he was a good boy. Make him the way he was.

But I have explored the jagged gaps   55
in the boy's body, smoothed the angry edges
of bulletholes. I have touched him in places
no mother knows, and I have birthed
his new face. I know he believed himself
invincible, that he most likely hissed   60
"Fuck you, man" before the bullets lifted him
off his feet. I try not to imagine
his swagger, his lizard-lidded gaze,
his young mother screaming into the phone.

She says she will find the money, and I know   65
this is the truth that fuels her, forces her
to place one foot in front of the other.
Suddenly, I want to take her down
to the chilly room, open the bag
and shake its terrible bounty onto the   70
gleaming steel table. I want her to see him,
to touch him, to press her lips to the flap of cheek.
The woman needs to wither, finally, and move on.

We both jump as the phone rattles in its hook.
I pray it's my wife, a bill collector, a wrong number.   75

But the wide, questioning silence on the other end
is too familiar. Another mother needing a miracle.
Another homeboy coming home.

Study and Discussion Questions

1. How is "Undertaker" a *dramatic* poem (look up the definition of dramatic poetry in "How Poetry Works"), both (a) technically and (b) emotionally?
2. How many "characters" are there in this poem? Who are they? What do we know about each one?
3. How does money come into the story this poem presents? Discuss "the high price of miracles."
4. What does the mother want? What does the undertaker want? Discuss the dramatic tension between the two characters.
5. Look up the word *irony* in an unabridged dictionary and in a dictionary of literary terms. Then discuss at least three ironies in Smith's poem.
6. The speaker of this poem is the undertaker himself. What do we see him doing in the poem? How does he feel about his job? What is the speaker's *tone?*

Suggestions for Writing

1. Imagine this dramatic poem being performed. How would you stage "Undertaker"?
2. Write a paragraph discussing what you think Smith means by the undertaker's last line: "Another homeboy coming home."
3. What figures from myth, fiction, history, and/or popular culture does the undertaker remind you of? How do these associations add to the poem's resonance?

Critical Resources

1. Glazner, Gary, ed. *Poetry Slam: The Competitive Art of Performance Poetry.* San Francisco: Manic D Press, 2000.
2. Holman, Bob. "Patricia Smith, Journalism and Poetry: Shall We Meditate on Truth." *Modern American Poetry Online.* Department of English, University of Illinois at Urbana-Champaign. 18 April 2005. <http://www.english.uiuc.edu/maps/poets/s_z/p_smith/about.htm>.
3. Schmid, Julie. "What's Going On: Poetics, Performance and Patricia's Smith's "Close to Death." *Modern American Poetry Online.* Department of English, University of Illinois at Urbana-Champaign. 18 April 2005. <http://www.english.uiuc.edu/maps/poets/s_z/p_smith/about.htm>.
4. *Slamnation.* Dir. Paul Devlin. Documentary. 90 minutes, 1996. For more information go to <http://www.slamnation.com>.

❀ ❀ ❀

GWENDOLYN BROOKS (1917–2000)

Gwendolyn Brooks grew up in Chicago. She began writing poetry at an early age, publishing her first poem at age thirteen. After receiving her B.A. in English from Wilson Junior College in 1936, Brooks worked for the NAACP Youth Council. During this time, Brooks was greatly influenced by poet Langston Hughes and other writers from the Harlem Renaissance, who encouraged her to study the modernist poetry of Eliot and Pound. As is evident in much of her early work, Brooks combines the technical skill and form of modernist poetry with the imagery and rhythms of African American life and language. In 1950, she became the first African American to win the Pulitzer Prize for her poetry collection Annie Allen *(1950). In 1967, Brooks's visit to Fisk University was a transformative moment for her as a poet and African American. Impressed by the energy of young black poets like Leroi Jones, Brooks's penchant for formal structures (she was a master of the sonnet) and themes loosened. While her devotion to the African American experience remained, her poetry increasingly became more political, more contentious, as she became aware of her role as a black feminist in the Civil Rights Movement. In 1985, she was appointed poetry consultant to the Library of Congress (Poet Laureate). She has written several poetry collections, including* A Street in Bronzeville *(1945),* Annie Allen *(1950),* The Bean Eaters *(1960),* In the Mecca *(1968),* Beckonings *(1975),* Black Love *(1982), and* In Montgomery *(2001, posthumously); the novel* Maud Martha *(1953); and the autobiography* Report from Part One *(1972).*

The Bean Eaters   (1960)

They eat beans mostly, this old yellow pair.
Dinner is a casual affair.
Plain chipware on a plain and creaking wood,
Tin flatware.

Two who are Mostly Good.   5
Two who have lived their day,
But keep on putting on their clothes
And putting things away.

And remembering ...
Remembering, with twinklings and twinges,   10
As they lean over the beans in their rented back room that
       is full of beads and receipts and dolls and cloths,
          tobacco crumbs, vases and fringes.

Study and Discussion Questions

1. Speculate on the social class of this couple. Make a list of details from the poem to provide evidence for your conclusion.
2. Why does Brooks call the pair "the bean eaters"? How does this characterize them?
3. Discuss the use of rhyme and repetition in the poem. Show where Brooks uses each and what the effect is.
4. What do you think the poet's attitude is toward the characters in this poem? In what light does she present them? How does she want us to see them?
5. What's going on in the final stanza of the poem? Describe how Brooks varies the form in the last stanza and speculate on what effect she might be after.
6. What is the significance of the items this couple has saved and stored?
7. Are these two people, "this old yellow pair," contented and fulfilled with their lives? How do you think they feel about the way their life together has turned out?

Suggestions for Writing

1. Compare/contrast "The Bean Eaters" with another Gwendolyn Brooks poem in *Literature and Society* (there are several).
2. Write a poem or a vivid prose paragraph on your grandparents or another older person or persons you know well.
3. Imagine yourself as an old man or woman and describe your life then.

Critical Resources

1. Bloom, Harold, ed. *Gwendolyn Brooks.* Philadelphia: Chelsea House, 2000.
2. Brooks, Gwendolyn. *Report from Part One: An Autobiography.* Detroit: Broadside, 1972.
3. Gayles, Gloria Wade. *Conversation with Gwendolyn Brooks.* Jackson: UP of Mississippi, 2003.
4. Mootry, Maria, ed. *A Life Distilled: Gwendolyn Brooks, Her Poetry and Fiction.* Urbana: U of Illinois P, 1987.

❋ ❋ ❋

JOY HARJO (b. 1951)

Joy Harjo was born in Tulsa, Oklahoma, and grew up there and in New Mexico. She is Muskeegee/Creek and of mixed descent—her mother Cherokee, French and Irish, her father full-blooded Cherokee. Harjo has described her childhood as "tempestuous." At the age of 16 she was thrown out of her house and forced to survive on her own. Despite such hardships, Harjo entered the University of New Mexico to study medicine, though she soon switched to creative writing and began writing poetry: "I don't believe I would be alive today if it hadn't been for

writing ... writing helped me give voice to turn around a terrible silence that was
killing me. And on a larger level, if we, as Indian people, Indian woman, keep
silent, then we will disappear" (The Spiral of Memory: Interviews: Joy Harjo
1996). Harjo's poetry reflects this sentiment, often politically charged and speak-
ing out against the violence and oppression of Native-American women. Harjo
has taught creative writing at several colleges and universities. She also writes mu-
sic and plays the saxophone. Native Joy for Real *is her 1997 CD with her band,*
Poetic Justice. Her poetry collections include The Last Song *(1975),* She Had
Some Horses *(1983),* In Mad Love and War *(1990),* The Woman Who Fell From
the Sky *(1996),* A Map to the Next World: Poetry and Tales *(2000), and* How
We Become Human *(2002). "Remember" was first published in* She Had Some
Horses.

Remember (1983)

Remember the sky that you were born under,
know each of the star's stories.
Remember the moon, know who she is. I met her
in a bar once in Iowa City.
Remember the sun's birth at dawn, that is the   5
strongest point of time. Remember sundown
and the giving away to night.
Remember your birth, how your mother struggled
to give you form and breath. You are evidence of
her life, and her mother's, and hers.   10
Remember your father. He is your life, also.
Remember the earth whose skin you are:
red earth, black earth, yellow earth, white earth
brown earth, we are earth.
Remember the plants, trees, animal life who all have their   15
tribes, their families, their histories, too. Talk to them,
listen to them. They are alive poems.
Remember the wind. Remember her voice. She knows the
origin of this universe. I heard her singing Kiowa[1] war
dance songs at the corner of Fourth and Central once.   20
Remember that you are all people and that all people are you.
Remember that you are this universe and that this universe is you.
Remember that all is in motion, is growing, is you.

---

[1]American Indian people of the Southern Great Plains.

Remember that language comes from this.
Remember the dance that language is, that life is.   25
Remember.

Study and Discussion Questions

1. What does the speaker of the poem remember? What categories do these memories fall into?
2. What do you learn about the identity of the speaker of the poem through her memories?
3. What grammatical form is the poem cast in? What is the point of view of the poem? What effect do both of these have on the reader?
4. Why should we remember? What is the purpose of bringing back these kinds of memories?

Suggestion for Writing

1. Write a series of lines, beginning each line with "remember." Don't worry about whether this is a poem or not. Concentrate on making each line as specific and as vivid as you can. Do this initially as a free writing exercise. That is, write as fast and free associatively as you can for ten minutes, remembering what is important to you. Then revise, add to, and arrange your lines.

Critical Resources

1. Coltelli, Laura, ed. *The Spiral of Memory: Interviews: Joy Harjo.* Ann Arbor: U of Michigan P, 1996.
2. Goodman, Jenny. "Politics and the Personal Lyric in the Poetry of Joy Harjo and C.D Wright." *The Journal of the Society for the Study of the Multi-Ethnic Literature of the United States.* Summer (1994): 35–56.
3. *Joy Harjo.* The Lannan Foundation, Los Angeles, 1996. 60 minutes. For more information go to <http://www.lannan.org/lf/lit/search_detail/joy-harjo>.
4. Strom, Karen and Joy Harjo. *Joy Harjo.* 18 April 2005. <http://www.hanksville.org/storytellers/joy/>.
5. Whitehead, Kim. *The Feminist Poetry Movement.* Jackson: UP of Mississippi, 1996.
6. Wilson, Nancy, ed. *The Nature of Native American Poetry.* Albuquerque: U of New Mexico P, 2001.

❀ ❀ ❀

Additional Poems

JOHN KEATS (1795–1821)

When I Have Fears   (1818)

When I have fears that I may cease to be
  Before my pen has glean'd my teeming brain,
Before high-piled books, in charact'ry,[1]
  Hold like rich garners the full-ripen'd grain;
When I behold, upon the night's starr'd face,   5
  Huge cloudy symbols of a high romance,
And think that I may never live to trace
  Their shadows, with the magic hand of chance;
And when I feel, fair creature of an hour!
  That I shall never look upon thee more,   10
Never have relish in the faery[2] power
  Of unreflecting love!—then on the shore
Of the wide world I stand alone, and think
  Till Love and Fame to nothingness do sink.

WALT WHITMAN (1819–1892)

FROM *Leaves of Grass*   (1855)

A child said *What is the grass?* fetching it to me with full hands;
How could I answer the child? I do not know what it is any more than he.

I guess it must be the flag of my disposition, out of hopeful green stuff woven.

Or I guess it is the handkerchief of the Lord,
A scented gift and remembrancer designedly dropt,   5
Bearing the owner's name someway in the corners, that we may see and
        remark, and say *Whose?*

Or I guess the grass is itself a child, the produced babe of the vegetation.

---

[1]Printed characters expressing thought.
[2]Magical.

Or I guess it is a uniform hieroglyphic,
And it means, Sprouting alike in broad zones and narrow zones,
Growing among black folks as among white,   10

Kanuck, Tuckahoe, Congressman. Cuff[1] I give them the same, I receive
      them the same.

And now it seems to me the beautiful uncut hair of graves.

Tenderly will I use you curling grass,
It may be you transpire from the breasts of young men,
It may be if I had known them I would have loved them,   15
It may be you are from old people, or from offspring taken soon out of their
      mothers' laps,
And here you are the mothers' laps

This grass is very dark to be from the white heads of old mothers,
Darker than the colorless beards of old men,
Dark to come from under the faint red roofs of mouths   20

O I perceive after all so many uttering tongues,
And I perceive they do not come from the roofs of mouths for nothing.
I wish I could translate the hints about the dead young men and women,
And the hints about old men and mothers, and the offspring taken soon out of
      their laps.

What do you think has become of the young and old men?   25
And what do you think has become of the women and children?

They are alive and well somewhere,
The smallest sprout shows there is really no death,
And if ever there was it led forward life, and does not wait at the end to arrest it,
And ceas'd the moment life appear'd.   30

All goes onward and outward, nothing collapses,
And to die is different from what any one supposed, and luckier.

---

[1]Kanuck, a French Canadian; Tuckahoe, someone from Virginia; Cuff, a black person

GERARD MANLEY HOPKINS (1844–1889)

Spring and Fall   (1880)

to a young child

Márgarét, áre you gríeving
Over Goldengrove unleaving?
Leáves, like the things of man, you
With your fresh thoughts care for, can you?
Áh! ás the heart grows older   5
It will come to such sights colder
By and by, nor spare a sigh
   Though worlds of wanwood leafmeal lie;[1]
And yet you *will* weep and know why.
Now no matter, child, the name: 10
Sórrow's spríngs áre the same.
Nor mouth had, no nor mind, expressed
What heart heard of, ghost[2] guessed:
It is the blight man was born for,
It is Margaret you mourn for.   15

EDNA ST. VINCENT MILLAY (1892–1950)

Grown-up   (1920)

Was it for this I uttered prayers,
And sobbed and cursed and kicked the stairs,
That now, domestic as a plate,
I should retire at half-past eight?

---

[1]Pale woods; like "piecemeal," in pieces.
[2]Soul.

EDNA ST. VINCENT MILLAY (1892–1950)

What Lips My Lips Have Kissed   (1923)

What lips my lips have kissed, and where, and why,
I have forgotten, and what arms have lain
Under my head till morning; but the rain
Is full of ghosts tonight, that tap and sigh
Upon the glass and listen for reply,   5
And in my heart there stirs a quiet pain
For unremembered lads that not again
Will turn to me at midnight with a cry.
Thus in the winter stands the lonely tree,
Nor knows what birds have vanished one by one,   10
Yet knows its boughs more silent than before:
I cannot say what loves have come and gone,
I only know that summer sang in me
A little while, that in me sings no more.

e. e. cummings (1894–1962)

in Just—   (1923)

in Just—
springwhen the world is mud—
luscious the little
lame balloonman
whistlesfarand wee   5

and eddieandbill come
running from marbles and
piracies and it's
spring

when the world is puddle-wonderful   10

the queer
old balloonman whistles
farandwee
and bettyandisbel come dancing

from hop-scotch and jump-rope and   15

it's
spring
and
the
goat-footed   20

balloonManwhistles
far
and
wee

MARGARET WALKER (1915–1998)

Lineage   (1942)

My grandmothers were strong.
They followed plows and bent to toil.
They moved through fields sowing seed.
They touched earth and grain grew.
They were full of sturdiness and singing.   5
My grandmothers were strong.

My grandmothers are full of memories
Smelling of soap and onions and wet clay
With veins rolling roughly over quick hands
They have many clean words to say.   10
My grandmothers were strong.
Why am I not as they?

THEODORE ROETHKE (1908–1963)

My Papa's Waltz   (1948)

The whiskey on your breath
Could make a small boy dizzy;
But I hung on like death:
Such waltzing was not easy.

We romped until the pans   5

Slid from the kitchen shelf;
My mother's countenance
Could not unfrown itself.

The hand that held my wrist
Was battered on one knuckle;   10
At every step you missed
My right ear scraped a buckle.

You beat time on my head
With a palm caked hard by dirt,
Then waltzed me off to bed   15
Still clinging to your shirt.

DYLAN THOMAS (1914–1953)

Do Not Go Gentle Into That Good Night   (1952)

Do not go gentle into that good night,
Old age should burn and rave at close of day;
Rage, rage against the dying of the light.

Though wise men at their end know dark is right,
Because their words had forked no lightning they   5
Do not go gentle into that good night.

Good men, the last wave by, crying how bright
Their frail deeds might have danced in a green bay,
Rage, rage against the dying of the light.

Wild men who caught and sang the sun in flight   10
And learn, too late, they grieved it on its way,
Do not go gentle into that good night.

Grave men, near death, who see with blinding sight
Blind eyes could blaze like meteors and be gay,
Rage, rage against the dying of the light.   15

And you, my father, there on the sad height,
Curse, bless, me now with your fierce tears, I pray.
Do not go gentle into that good night.
Rage, rage against the dying of the light.

GWENDOLYN BROOKS (b. 1917)

We Real Cool   (1960)

THE POOL PLAYERS
SEVEN AT THE GOLDEN SHOVEL.

We real cool. We
Left school. We

Lurk late. We
Strike straight. We

Sing sin. We
Thin gin. We

Jazz June. We
Die soon.

JAMES WRIGHT (1927–1980)

Autumn Begins in Martins Ferry, Ohio   (1963)

In the Shreve High football stadium,
I think of Polacks nursing long beers in Tiltonsville,

And gray faces of Negroes in the blast furnace at Benwood,
And the ruptured night watchman of Wheeling Steel,
Dreaming of heroes.   5

All the proud fathers are ashamed to go home.
Their women cluck like starved pullets,
Dying for love.

Therefore,
Their sons grow suicidally beautiful
At the beginning of October,   10
And gallop terribly against each other's bodies.

PATRICIA SMITH (b. 1955)

Discovering Country   (1993)

For Emmett Till

How giddy wide the country opened its arms to him,
giggling green from the first; feathery branches
arching above his head, blessings and sweet shade.
He could run, laughing and tripping until chest ached
and rusty bowlegs tangled; he could run   5
with no schoolyard bullies, storefronts or curbs
forcing his path. Whole mouthfuls of air,
smelling like free—and sidearmed stones,
always flat, kissing the river five or six times,
seven if the ripples whispered.   10
Even the name of this world, Greenwood,
open and fresh like sun shining in his mouth.
And everywhere, fat pods threatening juice,
fruit drooping from trees, bushes wild with roses—
nothing like Chicago, a city of gray and glass   15
with all its life potted in kitchenette windows,
crammed into dirty streetcorner parks.

He had the whole summer to be dazzled
by this new talk, sluggish as the river,
slurred like a radio with old batteries.   20
There was time to savor thick warm chunks
of buttered cornbread, paint a clown mouth
on top of his own with the juice from berries.
He slept with fresh air teasing his skin
while buzzing pressed at the screen   25
begging to taste him. He woke to bacon slabs
and singing. And as soon as he could,
he would begin to run, gulping difference,
until his eyes were full. He would run
that way until his mother received him in August,   30
blacker, gushing and bug-bitten.
And what was he to the men with pink grizzled faces,
the skinny women with cockleburrs caught in their hair?
Nothing but another boy running as fast as he could,
filling his chest with summer He was a big boy,   35
brown and strong, almost to their shoulders.
No harm in whistling them a big of city

before the last of it shook loose,
jostled by running, washed away by the river.

The buzzing rocked him that night, and any cover   40
was too much. His dreams were jumbled.
He was taken back to Chicago in chains.
He sang badly at the top of his lungs.
He went blind.
He pulled his stubby fingers through a woman's hair.   45
He dreamed that there was nothing running wouldn't solve,
and when he woke he would call his mother,
tell her that here was forever.

It was then that rough hands
pulled him from summer sleep   50
and men with earth in their mouths
ran with him through the moonwash,
leaving no time for bacon or gospel.

TOI DERRICOTTE (b. 1941)

Transition   (1983)

the meat rolls up and moans on the damp table.
my body is a piece of cotton over another
woman's body.   some other woman, all muscle and nerve, is
tearing apart and opening under me,
i move with her like skin, not able to do anything else,
i am just watching her, not able to believe what her   5
body can do, what it *will* do, to get this thing accomplished.

this muscle of a lady, this crazy ocean in my teacup.
she moves the pillars of the sky.   i am stretched into
fragments, tissue paper thin.   the light shines through   10
to her goatness, her blood-thick heart that thuds like
one drum in the universe emptying its stars.

she is
that heart
larger   15
than my life
stuffed
in

me
like sausage
black sky
bird
pecking
at the bloody
ligament

trying
to get
in, get
out
i am
holding out with
everything i
have
holding out
the evil thing

when i see there is
no answer
to the screamed
word
GOD
nothing i can do,
no use,
i have to let her in,
open the door,
put down the mat
welcome her
as if she
might be the
called for death,
the final
abstraction.
she comes
like a tunnel
fast
coming into
blackness
with my headlights
off

you can push ...

i hung there, still hurting, not knowing what to do.

if you push too early, it hurts more.   i called the
doctor back again.   *are you sure i can push?   are you sure?*

i couldn't believe that pain was over, that the punishment was enough, that the wave, the huge blue mind i
was living inside, was receding.   i had forgotten there   65
ever was a life without pain, a moment when pain wasn't
absolute as air.

why weren't the nurses and doctors rushing toward me?
why weren't they wrapping me in white? white for respect,
white for triumph, white for the white light i was being   70
accepted into after death?   why was it so simple as saying
you can push?   why were they walking away from me into
other rooms as if this were not the end the beginning of
something which the world should watch?

i felt something pulling me inside, a soft call, but i   75
could feel her power.   something inside me i could go
with, wide and deep and wonderful.   the more i gave
to her, the more she answered me.   i held this conversation
in myself like a love that never stops.   i pushed toward
her, she came toward me, gently, softly, sucking like a   80
wave.   i pushed deeper and she swelled wider, darker when
she saw i wasn't afraid.   then i saw the darker glory
of her under me.
why wasn't the room bursting with lilies?   why was
everything the same with them moving so slowly as if   85
they were drugged?   why were they acting the same when,
suddenly, everything had changed?

we were through with pain, would never suffer in our
lives again.   put pain down like a rag, unzipper skin,
step out of our dead bodies, and leave them on the   90
floor.   glorious spirits were rising, blanched with
light, like thirsty women shining with their thirst.

JOY HARJO (b. 1951)

Rainy Dawn   1990

I can still close my eyes and open them four floors up looking south and west
from the hospital, the approximate direction of Acoma, and farther on to the
roofs of the houses of the gods who have learned there are no endings, only

beginnings. That day so hot, heat danced in waves off bright car tops, we
both stood poised at that door from the east, listened for a long time to the   5
sound of our grandmothers' voices, the brushing wind of sacred wings, the
rattle of raindrops in dry gourds. I had to participate in the dreaming of you
into memory, cupped your head in the bowl of my body as ancestors lined up
to give you a name made of their dreams cast once more into this stew of
precious spirit and flesh. And let you go, as I am letting you go once more   10
in this ceremony of the living, thirteen years later. And when you were born
I held you wet and unfolding, like a butterfly newly born from the chrysalis of
my body. And breathed with you as you breathed your first breath. Then was
your promise to take it on like the rest of us, this immense journey, for love,
for rain.

TINO VILLANUEVA (b. 1941)

Not Knowing, in Aztlan[1]   (1984)

the way they look at you
                    the schoolteachers
the way they look at you
                    the City Hall clerks
the way they look at you   5
            the cops
            the airport marshals
the way they look at you

you don't know if it's something you did

                    or something you are   10

LLOYD SCHWARTZ

Leaves   (1992)

1

Every October it becomes important, no, *necessary,*
to see the leaves turning, to be surrounded

---

[1]Mythical place in northwestern Mexico, where Aztecs believe they originated.

by leaves turning; it's not just the symbolism,
to confront in the death of the year your death,
one blazing farewell appearance, though the irony   5
isn't lost on you that nature is most seductive
when it's about to die, flaunting the dazzle of its
incipient exit, an ending that at least so far
the effects of human progress (pollution, acid rain)
have not yet frightened you enough to make you believe   10
is real; that is, you know this ending is a deception
because of course nature is always renewing itself—
    the trees don't *die,* they just pretend,
     go out in style, and return in style: a new style.

2

Is it deliberate how far they make you go   15
especially if you live in the city to get far
enough away from home to see not just trees
but only trees? The boring highways, roadsigns, high
speeds, 10-axle trucks passing you as if they were
in an even greater hurry than you to look at leaves: 20
so you drive in terror for literal hours and it looks
like rain, or *snow,* but it's probably just clouds,
(too cloudy to see any color?) and you wonder,
given the poverty of your memory, which road had the
most color last year, but it doesn't matter since   25
you're probably too late anyway, or too early—
    whichever road you take will be the wrong one
    and you've probably come all this way for nothing.

3

You'll be driving along depressed when suddenly
a cloud will move and the sun will muscle through   30
and ignite the hills. It may not last. Probably
won't last. But for a moment the whole world
comes to. Wakes up. Proves it lives. It lives—
red, yellow, orange, brown, russet, ocher, vermilion,
gold. Flame and rust. Flame and rust, the permutations   35
of burning. You're on fire. Your eyes are on fire.
It won't last, you don't want it to last. You
can't stand any more. But you don't want it to stop.
It's what you've come for. It's what you'll

come back for. It won't stay with you, but you'll   40
    remember that it felt like nothing else you've felt
    or something you've felt that also didn't last.

PAT MORA (b. 1942)

Immigrants   (1986)

wrap their babies in the American flag,
feed them mashed hot dogs and apple pie,
name them Bill and Daisy,
buy them blonde dolls that blink blue
eyes or a football and tiny cleats   5
before the baby can even walk,
speak to them in thick English,
        hallo, babee, hallo,
whisper in Spanish or Polish
when the babies sleep, whisper   10
in a dark parent bed, that dark
parent fear, "Will they like
our boy, our girl, our fine american
boy, our fine american girl?"

SIMON J. ORTIZ (b. 1941)

My Father's Song   (1988)

Wanting to say things,
I miss my father tonight,
His voice, the slight catch,
the depth from his thin chest,
the tremble of emotion   5
in something he has just said
to his son, his song:

We planted corn one spring at Acu—
we planted several times
but this one particular time   10

I remember the soft damp sand
in my hand.

My father had stopped at one point
to show me an overturned furrow;
the plowshare had unearthed   15
the burrow nest of a mouse
in the soft moist sand.

Very gently, he scooped tiny pink animals
into the palm of his hand
and told me to touch them.   20
We took them to the edge
of the field and put them in the shade
of a sand moist clod.

I remember the very softness
of cool and warm sand and tiny alive mice   25
and my father saying things.

RON SCHREIBER (b. 1934)

diagnosis (4-10-86)   (1989)

we'll call it an "especially
virulent form of pneumonia,"

ironically an accurate way
of saying both what it is

& what it is not. I am   5
stunned. what about co-

factors! I want to scream.
what about the incubation

period! Period. I have been
happy for eight and a half   10

years. John will be, we hope,
35 in June. June 10. two

months from now. Now.
it's a hospital bed, coughing.

vomiting unappetizing food　　　　　　　　　　　　　　　　15
& red medicine that looks like

blood. especially virulent.
eight years of happiness is

more than most people get,
more than I had before. "I　　　　　　　　　　　　　　　　20

have been happy & I won't be
happy anymore" is the ironic

-ally accurate way I phrase it
to myself. I'm 52. this

happiness—with this unusual &　　　　　　　　　　　　　　25
particular man—won't happen

to me again.

ESSEX HEMPHILL (1957–1995)

June 25　　　　　　　　　　　　　　　　　　　　　　(1994)

Yesterday, my new doctor, based in short-skirted, fashionable
Los Angeles, on trendy, palm-tree-lined Wilshire Boulevard, informed me that I now possess only twenty-three T cells.[1] Needless to say, my face cracked, but I'm a show boy, I learned long
ago how to keep things together even under the most strained　　　5
and pressing of circumstances. I haven't always known how to
use this facility, but of late it comes in handy, although I think
it costs something internally to hold oneself in check in the
face of provocation and overwhelming emotions.

---

[1]T cells are part of the immune system; a declining T cell count is an indication of the
progression of AIDS.

By the end of my visit, I was armed with prescriptions for six   10
different medications, which the pharmacist assured me will
not interact violently. Quite frankly, I don't know whether I
should calculate my remaining T cells into nanoseconds and
minutes, days and weeks, or hours and years.

Some of the T cells I am without are not here through my   15
own fault. I didn't lose all of them foolishly, and I didn't lose all
of them erotically. Some of the missing T cells were lost to racism, a well-known transmittable disease. Some were lost to
poverty because there was no money to do something about
the plumbing before the pipes burst and the room flooded.   20
Homophobia killed quite a few, but so did my rage and my
pointed furies, so did the wars at home and the wars within, so
did the drugs I took to remain calm, cool, collected.

There are T cells lying dead by the roadside, slain by the guise
of friendship, the pettiness and jealousy of minds and talent in   25
the process of wasting to nothingness due to envy, gazing into
other yards instead of looking closely at and tending to their
own. There are T cells sacrificed between the love and anger
my mother and I hold for one another, T cells that have simply
exploded due to the decibel of our screeching.   30

There are countless wasted T cells between my father and me,
the result of painful, subterranean silences that I cannot resolve
with only twenty-three T cells, nor should I really be expected
to, nor should I try, since it was his violence I witnessed and remain scarred from. I am forced to remember him in certain   35
ways, to always see him punching and pushing, slapping and
yelling, not because I want to, I just haven't learned how to
make so many scars into things of beauty, and I don't know if I
ever will.

Actually, there are T cells scattered all about me, at doorways   40
where I was denied entrance because I was a faggot or a nigga
or too poor or too black. There are T cells spilling out of my
ashtrays from the cigarettes I have anxiously smoked. There are
T cells all over the floors of several bathhouses, coast to coast,
and halfway around the world, and in numerous parks, and in   45
countless bars, and in places I am forgetting to make room for
other memories. My T cells are strewn about like the leaves of
a mighty tree, like the fallen hair of an old man, like the stars of
a collapsing universe.

That is who I am now, *one of them,* one of *them.* A single strand,   50
a curling leaf, a burning star foretelling grief. I say this only to
dispel such gloom. I say this loud to kill death's bloom.

OLAV H. HAUGE

I Pass the Arctic Circle   (2003)

Translated by Robert Hadin from Norwegian

A man on the train points to the cairn on the mountain.
We're passing the Arctic Circle, he says.
At first we don't see any difference,
to the north the land looks the same,
but we know what we go toward.   5
I wouldn't have noticed this little event myself
if I hadn't, one of these days, passed seventy.

ORY BERNSTEIN

A Son Seeing His Mother Seeing Death   (1995)

Translated from Hebrew by Richard Flantz From: With Death

A son seeing his mother seeing death.
She still blocking the sight from him.
On the pillow life still going on, wild.

There she grasps the edge of the blanket, the purse,
and doesn't let go, as if urging on horses.   5
And when she stops, nothing more will block my view.

Drama

SAMUEL BECKETT (1906–1989)

Samuel Beckett was born in Dublin, Ireland, studied there at Trinity College, and then moved to France, where he lived most of his life and where he served in the anti-Nazi resistance during World War II. His early experimental fiction and poetry were greatly influenced by his friend, novelist James Joyce. Beckett wrote most of his plays in French and later translated them into English. His play Waiting for Godot *(1953) was a major event in the development of the Theater of the Absurd. Among his other plays are* Endgame *(1957),* How It Is *(1961), and* Happy Days *(1961). Beckett also wrote several novels, including* Molloy *(1951),* Malone Dies *(1951),* Watt *(1953), and* The Unnamable *(1953). In 1969 he won the Nobel Prize for literature.*

Krapp's Last Tape (1958)

A late evening in the future.

Krapp's den.

Front centre a small table, the two drawers of which open towards audience.

Sitting at the table, facing front, i.e. across from the drawers, a wearish old man: Krapp.

Rusty black narrow trousers too short for him. Rusty black sleeveless waistcoat, four capacious pockets. Heavy silver watch and chain. Grimy white shirt open at neck, no collar. Surprising pair of dirty white boots, size ten at least, very narrow and pointed.

White face. Purple nose. Disordered grey hair. Unshaven.

Very near-sighted (but unspectacled). Hard of hearing.

Cracked voice. Distinctive intonation.

Laborious walk.

On the table a tape-recorder with microphone and a number of cardboard boxes containing reels of recorded tapes.

Table and immediately adjacent area in strong white light. Rest of stage in darkness.

Krapp remains a motionless moment, heaves a great sigh, looks at his watch, fumbles in his pockets, takes out an envelope, puts it back, fumbles, takes out a small bunch of keys, raises it to his eyes, chooses a key, gets up and moves to front of table. He stoops, unlocks first drawer, peers into it, feels about inside it, takes out a reel tape, peers at it, puts it back, locks drawer, unlocks second drawer, peers into it, feels about inside it, takes out a large banana, peers at it, locks drawer, puts keys back in his pocket. He turns, advances to edge of stage, halts, strokes banana, peels it, drops skin at his feet, puts end of banana in his mouth and remains motionless, staring vacuously before him. Finally he bites off the end, turns aside and begins pacing to and fro at edge of stage, in the light, i.e. not more than four or five paces either way, meditatively eating banana. He treads on skin, slips, nearly falls, recovers himself, stoops and peers at skin and finally pushes it, still stooping, with his foot over the edge of stage into pit. He resumes his pacing, finishes banana, returns to table, sits down, remains a moment motionless, heaves a great sigh, takes keys from his pockets, raises them to his eyes, chooses key, gets up and moves to front of table, unlocks second drawer, takes out a second large banana, peers at it, locks drawer, puts back keys in his pocket, turns, advances to edge of stage, halts, strokes banana, peels it, tosses skin into pit, puts end of banana in his mouth and remains motionless, staring vacuously before him. Finally he has an idea, puts banana in his waistcoat pocket, the end emerging, and goes with all the speed he can muster backstage into darkness. Ten seconds. Loud pop of cork. Fifteen seconds. He comes back into light carrying an old ledger and sits down at table. He lays ledger on table, wipes his mouth, wipes his hands on the front of his waistcoat, brings them smartly together and rubs them.

KRAPP: Ah! *(He bends over ledger, turns the pages, finds the entry he wants, reads.)* Box ... thrree ... spool ... five. *(He raises his head and stares front. With relish.)* Spool! *(Pause.)* Spooool! *(Happy smile. Pause. He bends over table, starts peering and poking at the boxes.)* Box ... thrree ... thrree ... four ... two ... (with surprise) nine! good God! ... seven ... ah! the little rascal! *(He takes up box, peers at it.)* Box thrree. *(He lays it on table, opens it and peers at spools inside.)* Spool ... *(he peers at ledger)* ... five ... *(he peers at spools)* ... five ... five ... ah! the little scoundrel! *(He takes out a spool, peers at it.)* Spool five. *(He lays it on table, closes box three, puts it back with the others, takes up the spool.)* Box thrree, spool five. *(He bends over the machine, looks up. With relish.)* Spooool! *(Happy smile. He bends, loads spool on machine, rubs his hands.)* Ah! *(He peers at ledger, reads entry at foot of page.)* Mother at rest at last ... Hm ... The black ball ... *(He raises his head, stares blankly front. Puzzled.)* Black ball? ... *(He peers again at ledger, reads.)* The dark nurse

. . . *(He raises his head, broods, peers again at ledger, reads.)* Slight improvement in bowel condition . . . Hm . . . Memorable . . . what? *(He peers closer.)* Equinox, memorable equinox. *(He raises his head, stares blankly front. Puzzled.)* Memorable equinox? . . . *(Pause. He shrugs his shoulders, peers again at ledger, reads.)* Farewell to—*(he turns the page)*—love.

He raises his head, broods, bends over machine, switches on and assumes listening posture, i.e. leaning forward, elbows on table, hand cupping ear towards machine, face front.

TAPE: *(strong voice, rather pompous, clearly Krapp's at a much earlier time.)* Thirty-nine today, sound as a—*(Settling himself more comfortably he knocks one of the boxes off the table, curses, switches off, sweeps boxes and ledger violently to the ground, winds tape back to beginning, switches on, resumes posture.)* Thirty-nine today, sound as a bell, apart from my old weakness, and intellectually I have now every reason to suspect at the . . . *(hesitates)* . . . crest of the wave—or thereabouts. Celebrated the awful occasion, as in recent years, quietly at the Winehouse. Not a soul. Sat before the fire with closed eyes, separating the grain from the husks. Jotted down a few notes, on the back of an envelope. Good to be back in my den, in my old rags. Have just eaten I regret to say three bananas and only with difficulty refrained from a fourth. Fatal things for a man with my condition. *(Vehemently.)* Cut 'em out! *(Pause.)* The new light above my table is a great improvement. With all this darkness round me I feel less alone. *(Pause.)* In a way. *(Pause.)* I love to get up and move about in it, then back here to . . . *(hesitates)* . . . me. *(Pause.)* Krapp. *Pause.*

The grain, now what I wonder do I mean by that, I mean . . . *(hesitates)* . . . I suppose I mean those things worth having when all the dust has—when all *my* dust has settled. I close my eyes and try and imagine them. *Pause. Krapp closes his eyes briefly.*

Extraordinary silence this evening, I strain my ears and do not hear a sound. Old Miss McGlome always sings at this hour. But not tonight. Songs of her girlhood, she says. Hard to think of her as a girl. Wonderful woman though. Connaught, I fancy. *(Pause.)* Shall I sing when I am her age, if I ever am? No. *(Pause.)* Did I sing as a boy? No. *(Pause.)* Did I ever sing? No. *Pause.*

Just been listening to an old year, passages at random. I did not check in the book, but it must be at least ten or twelve years ago. At that time I think I was still living on and off with Bianca in Kedar Street. Well out of that, Jesus yes! Hopeless business. *(Pause.)* Not much about her, apart from a tribute to her eyes. Very warm. I suddenly saw them again. *(Pause.)* Incomparable! *(Pause.)* Ah well . . . *(Pause.)* These old P.M.s are gruesome, but I often find them—*(Krapp switches off, broods, switches on)*—a help before embarking on a new . . . *(hesitates)* . . . retrospect. Hard to believe I was ever that young whelp. The voice! Jesus! And the aspirations! *(Brief laugh in which Krapp joins.)* And the resolutions! *(Brief laugh in which Krapp joins.)* To drink less, in particular. *(Brief laugh of Krapp alone.)* Statistics. Seventeen hundred hours, out of the preceding eight thousand odd, consumed on licensed premises alone. More than 20%, say 40% of his waking life. *(Pause.)* Plans for a less . . . *(hesitates)* . . . engrossing sexual life. Last illness of his father. Flagging pursuit of happiness. Unattainable laxation. Sneers at what he calls his youth and thanks to God that it's over. *(Pause.)* False ring there. *(Pause.)* Shadows of the opus . . . magnum. Closing with a—*(brief laugh)*—yelp to Providence. *(Prolonged laugh in which Krapp joins.)* What remains of all that misery? A girl in a shabby green coat, on a railway-station platform? No? *Pause.*   When I look—

Krapp switches off, broods, looks at his watch, gets up, goes backstage into darkness. Ten seconds. Pop of cork. Ten seconds. Second cork. Ten seconds. Third cork. Ten seconds. Brief burst of quavering song.

KRAPP: *(sings)*

> Now the day is over,
> Night is drawing nigh-igh,
> Shadows—

Fit of coughing. He comes back into light, sits down, wipes his mouth, switches on, resumes his listening posture.

TAPE: —back on the year that is gone, with what I hope is perhaps a glint of the old eye to come, there is of course the house on the canal where mother lay a-dying, in the late autumn, after her long viduity *(Krapp gives a start)*, and the—*(Krapp switches off, winds back tape a little, bends his ear closer to machine, switches on)*—a-dying, after her long viduity, and the—

Krapp switches off, raises his head, stares blankly before him. His lips move in the syllables of "viduity." No sound. He gets up, goes backstage into darkness, comes back with an enormous dictionary, lays it on table, sits down and looks up the word.

KRAPP: *(reading from dictionary).* State—or condition of being—or remaining—a widow—or widower. *(Looks up. Puzzled.)* Being—or remaining? . . . *(Pause. He peers again at dictionary. Reading.)* "Deep weeds of viduity" . . . Also of an animal, especially a bird . . . the vidua or weaver-bird . . . Black plumage of male . . . *(He looks up. With relish.)* The vidua-bird!

Pause. He closes dictionary, switches on, resumes listening posture.

TAPE: —bench by the weir from where I could see her window. There I sat, in the biting wind, wishing she were gone. *(Pause.)* Hardly a soul, just a few

regulars, nursemaids, infants, old men, dogs. I got to know them quite well—
oh by appearance of course I mean! One dark young beauty I recollect particularly, all white and starch, incomparable bosom, with a big black hooded
perambulator, most funereal thing. Whenever I looked in her direction she
had her eyes on me. And yet when I was bold enough to speak to her—not
having been introduced—she threatened to call a policeman. As if I had designs on her virtue! *(Laugh. Pause.)* The face she had! The eyes! Like . . .
(hesitates) . . . chrysolite! *(Pause.)* Ah well . . . *(Pause.)* I was there when—
(Krapp switches off, broods, switches on again)—the blind went down, one of
those dirty brown roller affairs, throwing a ball for a little white dog, as chance
would have it. I happened to look up and there it was. All over and done with,
at last. I sat on for a few moments with the ball in my hand and the dog yelping and pawing at me. *(Pause.)* Moments. Her moments, my moments. *(Pause.)*
The dog's moments. *(Pause.)* In the end I held it out to him and he took it in
his mouth, gently, gently. A small, old, black, hard, solid rubber ball. *(Pause.)*
I shall feel it, in my hand, until my dying day. *(Pause.)* I might have kept it.
(Pause.) But I gave it to the dog. *Pause.*   Ah well . . .   *Pause.*

Spiritually a year of profound gloom and indigence until that memorable night
in March, at the end of the jetty, in the howling wind, never to be forgotten,
when suddenly I saw the whole thing. The vision, at last. This I fancy is what
I have chiefly to record this evening, against the day when my work will be
done and perhaps no place left in my memory, warm or cold, for the miracle
that . . . *(hesitates)* . . . for the fire that set it alight. What I suddenly saw then
was this, that the belief I had been going on all my life, namely—*(Krapp
switches off impatiently, winds tape forward, switches on again)*—great granite rocks the foam flying up in the light of the lighthouse and the wind-gauge
spinning like a propellor, clear to me at last that the dark I have always struggled to keep under is in reality my most—*(Krapp curses, switches off, winds
tape forward, switches on again)*—unshatterable association until my dissolution of storm and night with the light of the understanding and the fire—
*(Krapp curses louder, switches off, winds tape forward, switches on
again)*—my face in her breasts and my hand on her. We lay there without
moving. But under us all moved, and moved us, gently, up and down, and
from side to side. *Pause.*

Past midnight. Never knew such silence. The earth might be uninhabited.
Pause.
Here I end—

Krapp switches off, winds tape back, switches on again.

—upper lake, with the punt, bathed off the bank, then pushed out into the stream
and drifted. She lay stretched out on the floorboards with her hands under
her head and her eyes closed. Sun blazing down, bit of a breeze, water nice
and lively. I noticed a scratch on her thigh and asked her how she came by it.

Picking gooseberries, she said. I said again I thought it was hopeless and no good going on, and she agreed, without opening her eyes. *(Pause.)* I asked her to look at me and after a few moments—*(pause)*—after a few moments she did, but the eyes just slits, because of the glare. I bent over her to get them in the shadow and they opened. *(Pause. Low.)* Let me in. *(Pause.)* We drifted in among the flags and stuck. The way they went down, sighing, before the stem! *(Pause.)* I lay down across her with my face in her breasts and my hand on her. We lay there without moving. But under us all moved, and moved us, gently, up and down, and from side to side. *Pause.* Past midnight. Never knew—

Krapp switches off, broods. Finally he fumbles in his pockets, encounters the banana, takes it out, peers at it, puts it back, fumbles, brings out the envelope, fumbles, puts back envelope, looks at his watch, gets up and goes backstage into darkness. Ten seconds. Sound of bottle against glass, then brief siphon. Ten seconds. Bottle against glass alone. Ten seconds. He comes back a little unsteadily into light, goes to front of table, takes out keys, raises them to his eyes, chooses key. Unlocks first drawer, peers into it, feels about inside, takes out reel, peers at it, locks drawer, puts keys back in his pocket, goes and sits down, takes reel off machine, lays it on dictionary, loads virgin reel on machine, takes envelope from his pocket, consults back of it, lays it on table, switches on, clears his throat and begins to record.

KRAPP: Just been listening to that stupid bastard I took myself for thirty years ago, hard to believe I was ever as bad as that. Thank God that's all done with anyway. *(Pause.)* The eyes she had! *(Broods, realizes he is recording silence, switches off, broods. Finally.)* Everything there, everything, all the—*(Realizes this is not being recorded, switches on.)* Everything there, everything on this old muckball, all the light and dark and famine and feasting of . . . *(hesitates)* . . . the ages! *(In a shout.)* Yes! *(Pause.)* Let that go! Jesus! Take his mind off his homework! Jesus! *(Pause. Weary.)* Ah maybe he was right. *(Pause.)* Maybe he was right. *(Broods. Realizes. Switches off. Consults envelope.)* Pah! *(Crumples it and throws it away. Broods. Switches on.)* Nothing to say, not a squeak. What's a year now? The sour cud and the iron stool. *(Pause.)* Revelled in the word spool. *(With relish.)* Spooool! Happiest moment of the past half million. *(Pause.)* Seventeen copies sold, of which eleven at trade price to free circulating libraries beyond the seas. Getting known. *(Pause.)* One pound six and something, eight I have little doubt. *(Pause.)* Crawled out once or twice, before the summer was cold. Sat shivering in the park, drowned in dreams and burning to be gone. Not a soul. *(Pause.)* Last fancies. *(Vehemently.)* Keep 'em under! *(Pause.)* Scalded the eyes out of me reading *Effie* again, a page a day, with tears again. Effie . . . *(Pause.)* Could have been happy with her, up there on the Baltic, and the pines, and the dunes. *(Pause.)* Could I? *(Pause.)* And she? *(Pause.)* Pah! *(Pause.)* Fanny came in a couple of times. Bony old ghost of a whore. Couldn't do much, but I suppose better than a kick in the crutch. The last time wasn't so bad. How do you manage it, she said, at your age? I told her I'd been saving up for her all my life. *(Pause.)* Went to Vespers once, like when I was in short trousers. *(Pause. Sings.)*

> Now the day is over,
> Night is drawing nigh-igh,
> Shadows—*(coughing, then almost
> inaudible)*—of the evening
> Steal across the sky.

(Gasping.) Went to sleep and fell off the pew. *(Pause.)* Sometimes wondered in the night if a last effort mightn't—*(Pause.)* Ah finish your booze now and get to your bed. Go on with this drivel in the morning. Or leave it at that. *(Pause.)* Leave it at that. *(Pause.)* Lie propped up in the dark—and wander. Be again in the dingle on a Christmas Eve, gathering holly, the red-berried. *(Pause.)* Be again on Croghan on a Sunday morning, in the haze, with the bitch, stop and listen to the bells. *(Pause.)* And so on. *(Pause.)* Be again, be again. *(Pause.)* All that old misery. *(Pause.)* Once wasn't enough for you. *(Pause.)* Lie down across her.

Long pause. He suddenly bends over machine, switches off, wrenches off tape, throws it away, puts on the other, winds it forward to the passage he wants, switches on, listens staring front.

TAPE: —gooseberries, she said. I said again I thought it was hopeless and no good going on, and she agreed, without opening her eyes. *(Pause.)* I asked her to look at me and after a few moments—*(Pause.)*—after a few moments she did, but the eyes just slits, because of the glare. I bent over her to get them in the shadow and they opened. *(Pause. Low.)* Let me in. *(Pause.)* We drifted in among the flags and stuck. The way they went down, sighing before the stem! *(Pause.)* I lay down across her with my face in her breasts and my hand on her. We lay there without moving. But under us all moved, and moved us, gently, up and down, and from side to side.

Pause. Krapp's lips move. No sound.

Past midnight. Never knew such silence. The earth might be uninhabited. *Pause.*

Here I end this reel. Box—*(Pause.)*—three, spool—*(pause)*—five. *(Pause.)* Perhaps my best years are gone. When there was a chance of happiness. But I wouldn't want them back. Not with the fire in me now. No, I wouldn't want them back.

Krapp motionless staring before him. The tape runs on in silence.

CURTAIN

Study and Discussion Questions

1. About how old is Krapp now? How old is he in the tape he listens to? On tape, he talks of listening to himself on an earlier tape. How old is he on that tape?
2. What was Krapp's life like in earlier years? What is it like now?
3. Why did Krapp end his relationship with the woman in the punt? How does he feel about her now?
4. Discuss the staging and lighting of the play. How do they help shape the play's meaning?
5. Why is Krapp having so much trouble recording this year's tape? Why might this be Krapp's last tape?
6. What is the significance of Krapp's ignorance of the meaning of "viduity," a word he hears on his tape?
7. Krapp, we learn, is a writer. What is the importance of this?
8. What is the significance of all those bananas Krapp eats?
9. Explain the significance of Krapp's last words in the play, when he says, of his earlier years, "No, I wouldn't want them back."

Suggestions for Writing

1. Describe the younger Krapp from the point of view of the woman in the punt.
2. What do you think Krapp's book was like? Write a brief review of it.
3. What (besides the existence of tape recorders) makes this a modern, twentieth-century play?
4. If you once kept a journal or diary, read through it and describe how you feel about your earlier self.

Critical Resources

1. Fletcher, John, ed. *Beckett: A Study of His Plays.* London: Methuen, 1978, 1986.
2. Gusson, Mel. *Conversations With and About Beckett.* New York: Grove, 1996.
3. Knowlson, James. *Damned to Fame: The Life of Samuel Beckett.* New York: Simon & Schuster, 1996.
4. Worth, Katharine. *Samuel Beckett's Theater: Life Journeys.* New York: Oxford UP, 1999.

WAKAKO YAMAUCHI (1924)

Wakako Yamauchi grew up in California during the Great Depression as a "Nisei"—a Japanese-American child of Japanese immigrants. With the onset of

*World War II, Yamauchi and her family were uprooted and placed in a govern-
ment internment camp in Poston, Arizona, where they were forced to stay until
the war ended 18 months later. Coincidentally, Yamauchi was interned with Hisaye
Yamamoto and the two became friends, writing and contributing artwork to a local newspaper. After leaving the internment camp, Yamauchi moved to Chicago,
where she became an avid play-goer while taking correspondent writing classes
from UC Berkeley. During the next several years she published a few short stories
but found that she preferred drama to prose. Yamauchi has since established herself as an important Japanese American playwright who explores the political implications of government decisions and the impact they have on the internal lives
of her characters. In addition to being a poet and gifted artist, Yamauchi has written several plays, including* The Chairman's Wife *(1993),* 12-1-A *(1993),* The Music Lessons *(1994), and the mixed-genre* Songs My Mother Taught Me: Stories,
Plays and Memoir *(1994). "And the Soul Shall Dance," first written as a short
story, became one of Yamauchi's most successful plays.*

And the Soul Shall Dance

The first production of And the Soul Shall Dance *was February 23–April 16, 1977
(extended run), at East-West Players. It was produced by Rae Creavy and Clyde Kusatsu
and directed by Mako and Alberto Issac.*

Double Cast

Shizuko Hoshi, Haunani Minn	EMIKO
J. Maseras Pepito, Pat Li	HANA
Jim Ishida, Sab Shimono	MURATA
Keone Young, Yuki Shimoda	OKA
Mimosa Iwamatsu, Denice Kumagai	MASAKO
Susan Inouye, Diane Takei	KIYOKO

Characters
MURATA, 40, Issei farmer
HANA, 35, Issei wife of Murata
MASAKO, 11, Nisei daughter of the Muratas
OKA, 45, Issei farmer
EMIKO, 30, wife of Oka
KIYOKO, 14, Oka's daughter

ACT I   *Scene i Summer afternoon, 1935. Muratas' kitchen
Scene ii That evening. Okas' yard and beyond
Scene iii The same evening. Okas' yard*

ACT II   *Scene i Mid-September afternoon. Muratas' kitchen and yard*
                  Scene ii November night. Muratas' kitchen
                  Scene iii The next morning. Muratas' yard
                  Scene iv The following spring afternoon. Okas' yard
                  Scene v Same day, late afternoon. Muratas' yard
                  Scene vi Same evening. Desert

Kokoro Ga Odoru	*And the Soul Shall Dance*
Akai kuchibiru	Red lips
Kappu ni yosete	Press against a glass
Aoi sake nomya	Drink the green wine
Kokoro ga odoru	And the soul shall dance
Kurai yoru no yume	In the dark night
Setsu nasa yo	Dreams are unbearable
Aoi sake nomya	Drink the green wine
Yume ga odoru	And the dreams will dance
Asa no munashisa	The morning's truth
Yume wo chirasu	Scatter the dreams
Sora to kokoro wa	Sky and soul
Sake shidai	Are suspended by wine
Futari wakare no	In the separation
Samishisa yo	The desolation
Hitori sake nomya	Drink the wine
Kokoro ga odoru	And the soul shall dance

ACT I

Scene i

Summer afternoon, 1935

ON RISE: *Interior of the Murata house. The set is spare. There are a
                  kitchen table, four chairs, a bed, and on the wall, a calen-
                  dar indicating the year and month: June 1935. A doorway
                  leads to the other room. Props are: a bottle of sake, two
                  cups, a dish of chiles, a phonograph, and two towels hang-
                  ing on pegs on the wall. A wide wooden bench is outside.*

                  *The bathhouse has just burned to the ground due to
                  MASAKO's carelessness. Offstage there are sounds of
                  MURATA putting out the fire.*

Inside, HANA MURATA, in a drab housedress, confronts MASAKO (in summer dress). MASAKO is sullen and defiant.

HANA: How could you be so careless, Masako? You know you should be extra careful with fire. How often have I told you? Now the whole bathhouse is gone. I told you time and again—when you stoke a fire, you must see that everything is swept into the fireplace.

> *[MURATA enters. He is in old work clothes. He suffers from heat and exhaustion.]*

MURATA *[coughing]*: Shack went up like a matchbox. This kind of weather dries everything . . . just takes a spark to make a bonfire out of that dry timber.

HANA: Did you save any of it?

MURATA: No. Couldn't.

HANA *[to MASAKO]*: How many times have I told you . . .

> *[MASAKO moves nervously.]*

MURATA: No use crying about it now. *Shikata ga nai.* It's gone now. No more bathhouse. That's all.

HANA: But you've got to tell her. Otherwise she'll make the same mistake. You'll be building a bathhouse every year.

> *[MURATA removes his shirt and wipes off his face. He throws his shirt on a chair and sits at the table.]*

MURATA: *Baka!* Ridiculous!

MASAKO: I didn't do it on purpose.

> *[MASAKO goes to the bed. She opens a book. HANA follows her.]*

HANA: I know that, but you know what this means? It means we bathe in a bucket . . . inside the house. Carry water in from the pond, heat it on the stove . . . we'll use more kerosene.

MURATA: Tub's still there. And the fireplace. We can still build a fire under the tub.

HANA *[shocked]*: But no walls! Everyone in the country can see us!

MURATA: Wait till dark then. Wait till dark.

HANA: We'll be using a lantern. They'll still see us.

MURATA: Angh! Who? Who'll see us? You think everyone in the country waits to watch us take a bath? Hunh! You know how stupid you sound? Who cares about a couple of farmers taking a bath at night?

HANA *[defensively]*: It'll be inconvenient.

[HANA is saved by a rap on the door. OKA enters. He is short and stout. He wears faded work clothes.]

OKA: Hello! Hello! *Oi!* What's going on here? Hey! Was there some kind of fire?

[HANA rushes to the door to let OKA in. He stamps the dust from his shoes and enters.]

HANA: Oka-san! You just wouldn't believe . . . We had a terrible thing happen.

OKA: Yeah. Saw the smoke from down the road. Thought it was your house. Came rushing over. Is the fire out?

[MURATA half rises and sits back again. He's exhausted.]

MURATA *[gesturing]*:   *Oi, oi.* Come in. Sit down. No big problem. It was just our bathhouse.

OKA: Just the *furoba*, eh?

MURATA: Just the bath.

HANA: Our Musako was careless, and the *furoba* caught fire. There's nothing left but the tub.

[MASAKO looks up from her book, pained. She makes a small sound.]

OKA: Long as the tub's there, no problem. I'll help you with it.

[He starts to roll up his sleeves.]

MURATA: What . . . now? Now?

OKA: *[heh-heh]* Long as I'm here.

HANA: Oh, Papa. Aren't we lucky to have such friends?

MURATA *[to HANA]*:   We can't work on it now. The ashes are still hot. I just now put the damned fire out. Let me rest a while. *[to OKA] Oi,* how about a little sake? *[gesturing to HANA]* Make sake for Oka-san.

[OKA sits at the table. HANA goes to prepare the sake. She heats it, gets out the cups, and pours it for the men.]

MURATA *[continuing]*:   I'm tired . . . I am *tired.*

HANA: Oka-san has so generously offered his help. . . .

[OKA is uncomfortable. He looks around and sees MASAKO sitting on the bed.]

OKA: Hello, there, Masako-chan. You studying?

MASAKO: No, it's summer vacation.

MURATA [*sucking in his breath*]:   Kids nowadays . . . no manners.

HANA: She's sulking because I had to scold her.

[*MASAKO makes a small moan.*]

MURATA: Drink, Oka-san.

OKA [*sipping*]:   Ahhhh . . . That's good.

MURATA: Eh, you not working today?

OKA: No-no. I took the afternoon off today. I was driving over to Nagata-san's when I saw this big black cloud of smoke coming from your yard.

HANA: It went up so fast.

MURATA: What's up at Nagata-kun's? [*to* HANA] Get out the chiles. Oka-san loves chiles.

[*HANA opens a jar of chiles and puts them on a plate. She serves them and gets out her mending basket and walks to MASAKO. MASAKO makes room for her.*]

OKA [*helping himself*]:   Ah, chiles.

[*MURATA waits for an answer.*]

OKA [*continuing*]:   Well, I want to see him about my horse. I'm thinking of selling my horse.

MURATA: Sell your horse?

OKA [*scratching his head*]:   The fact is, I need some money. Nagata-san's the only one around made money this year, and I'm thinking he might want another horse.

MURATA: Yeah, he made a little this year. And he's talking big . . . big! Says he's leasing twenty more acres this fall.

OKA: Twenty acres?

MURATA: Yeah. He might want another horse.

OKA: Twenty acres, eh?

MURATA: That's what he says. But you know his old woman makes all the decisions at that house.

[*OKA scratches his head.*]

HANA: They're doing all right.

MURATA: Heh. Nagata-kun's so henpecked, it's pathetic. Peko-peko. [*He makes henpecking motions.*]

OKA [*feeling the strain*]:   I better get over there.

MURATA: Why the hell you selling your horse?

OKA: Well ... a ... I need cash.

MURATA: Oh yeah. I could use some too. Seems like everyone's getting out of the depression but the poor farmers. Nothing changes for us. We go on and on planting our tomatoes and summer squash and eating them. Well, at least it's healthy.

HANA: Papa, do you have lumber?

MURATA: Lumber? For what?

HANA: The bath ...

MURATA *[impatiently]*:   Don't worry about that. We need more sake now.

[HANA rises wearily.]

OKA: You sure Nagata-kun's working twenty more?

MURATA: Last I heard. What the hell, if you need a few bucks, I can loan (you) ...

OKA: A few hundred. I need a few hundred dollars.

MURATA: Oh, a few hundred. But what the hell you going to do without a horse? Out here a man's horse is as important as his wife.

OKA *[seriously]*:   I don't think Nagata will buy my wife.

[The men laugh, but HANA doesn't find it so funny. MURATA glances at her. She fills the cups again. OKA makes a half-hearted gesture to stop her. MASAKO watches the pantomime carefully. OKA finishes his drink.]

OKA *[continuing]*:   I better get moving.

MURATA: What's the big hurry?

OKA: Like to get the horse business done.

MURATA: Eh ... relax. Do it tomorrow. He's not going to die, is he?

OKA *[laughing]*:   Hey, he's a good horse. I want to get it settled today. If Nagatakun won't buy, I got to find someone else.

OKA *[continuing]*:   You think maybe Kawaguchi-kun ...?

MURATA: No-no. Not Kawaguchi. Maybe Yamamoto.

HANA: What is all the money for, Oka-san? Does Emiko-san need an operation?

OKA: No-no. Nothing like that.

HANA: Sounds very mysterious.

OKA: No mystery, Missus. No mystery. No sale, no money, no story.

MURATA *[laughing]*:   That's a good one. "No sale, no money, no . . ." Eh, Mama ... *[He points to the empty cups.]*

HANA *[filling the cups, muttering]*:   I see we won't be getting any work done today. *[to MASAKO]* Are you reading again? Maybe we'd still have a bath if you ...

MASAKO: I didn't do it on purpose.

MURATA *[loudly]*: I sure hope you know what you're doing, Oka-kun. What'd you do without a horse?

OKA: I was hoping you'd lend me yours now and then. *[He looks at HANA.]* I'll pay for some of the feed.

MURATA: Sure! Sure!

OKA: The fact is, I need that money. I got a daughter in Japan, and I just got to send for her this year.

[HANA leaves her mending and sits at the table.]

HANA: A daughter? You have a daughter in Japan? Why, I didn't know you had children. Emiko-san and you . . . I thought you were childless.

OKA *[scratching his head]*: We are. I was married before.

MURATA: You son-of-a-gun!

HANA *[overlapping]*: Is that so? How old is your daughter?

OKA: Kiyoko must be . . . fifteen now. Yeah, fifteen.

HANA: Fifteen! Oh, that *would* be too old for Emiko-san, child. Is Kiyoko-san living with relatives in Japan?

OKA *[reluctantly]*: With grandparents. Shizue's parents. *[pause]* Well, the fact is, Shizue—that's my first wife—Shizue and Emiko were sisters. They come from a family with no sons. I was a boy when I went to work for them . . . as an apprentice. They're blacksmiths. Later I married Shizue and took on the family name—you know, *yoshi*—because they had no sons. My real name is Sakakihara.

MURATA: Sakakihara! That's a great name!

HANA: A magnificent name!

OKA: No one knows me by that here.

MURATA: Should have kept that—Sakakihara.

OKA *[muttering]*: I don't even know myself by that name.

HANA: And Shizue-san passed away and you married Emiko-san?

OKA: Oh. Well, Shizue and I lived with the family for a while, and we had the baby—you know, Kiyoko. *[He gets looser with the liquor.]* Well, while I was serving apprentice with the family, they always looked down their noses at me. After I married, it got worse.

HANA *[distressed]*: Worse!

OKA: That old man . . . *[unnnnh!]* Always pushing me around, making me look bad in front of my wife and kid. That old man was the meanest . . . ugliest . . .

MURATA: Yeah, I heard about that apprentice work—*detchi-boko*. Heard it was damned humiliating.

OKA: That's the God's truth!

MURATA: Never had to do it myself. I came to America instead. They say *detchiboko* is blood work.

OKA: The work's all right. I'm not afraid of work. It's the humiliation! I hated them! Pushing me around like I was still a boy. Me, a grown man! And married to their daughter!

[MURATA and HANA groan in sympathy.]

OKA *[continuing]*:   Well, Shizue and I talked it over, and we decided the best thing was to get away. We thought if I came to America and made some money . . . you know, send her money until we had enough, and I'd go back and we'd leave the family . . . you know, move to another province . . . start a small business, maybe in the city . . . a noodle shop or something.

MURATA: That's everyone's dream. Make money, go home, and live like a king.

OKA: I worked like a dog. Sent every penny to Shizue. And then she dies. She died on me!

[HANA and MURATA observe a moment of silence in respect for OKA's anguish.]

HANA: And you married Emiko-san.

OKA: I didn't marry her. They married her to me! Right after Shizue died.

HANA: But Oka-san, you were lu(cky) . . .

OKA: Before the body was cold! No respect. By proxy. The old man wrote me that they were arranging a marriage by proxy for me and Emiko. They said she'd grown to be a beautiful woman and would serve me well.

HANA: Emiko-san *is* a beautiful woman.

OKA: And they sent her to me. Took care of everything! Immigration, fare, everything.

HANA: But she's your sister-in-law. Kiyoko's aunt. It's good to keep the family together.

OKA: That's what I thought. But hear this: Emiko was the favored one. Shizue was not so pretty, not so smart. They were grooming Emiko for a rich man—his name was Yamato—lived in a grand house in the village. They sent her to schools; you know, the culture thing: the dance, tea ceremony, you know, all that. They didn't even like me, and suddenly they married her to me.

MURATA: Yeah. You don't need all that formal training to make it over here. Just a strong back.

HANA: And a strong will.

OKA: It was all arranged. I couldn't do anything about it.

HANA: It'll be all right. With Kiyoko-san coming . . .

OKA *[dubiously]*:   I hope so. *[pause]* I never knew human beings could be so cruel. You know how they mistreated my daughter? After Emiko came here, things got from bad to worse, and I *never* had enough money to send to Kiyoko and . . .

MURATA: They don't know what it's like here. They think money's picked off the ground here.

OKA: And they treated Kiyoko so bad. They told her I forgot about her. They told her I didn't care . . . said I abandoned her. Well, she knew better. She wrote to me all the time, and I always told her I'd send for her . . . as soon as I got the money. *[He shakes his head.]* I just got to do something this year.

HANA: She'll be happier here. She'll know her father cares.

OKA: Kids tormented her for being an orphan.

MURATA: Kids are cruel.

HANA: Masako will help her. She'll help her get started at school. She'll make friends. She'll be all right.

OKA: I hope so. She'll need friends. *[He tries to convince himself he's making the right decision.]* What could I say to her? Stay there? It's not what you think over here? I can't help her? I just have to do this thing. I just have to do this one thing for her.

MURATA: Sure.

HANA: Don't worry. It'll work out fine.

[MURATA gestures to HANA. She gets the sake.]

MURATA: You talk about selling your horse, I thought you were pulling out.

OKA: I wish I could. But there's nothing else I can do.

MURATA: Without money, yeah.

OKA: You can go into some kind of business with money, but a man like me . . . no education . . . there's no kind of job I can do. I'd starve in the city.

MURATA: Dishwashing, maybe. Janitor.

OKA: At least here we can eat. Carrots, maybe, but we can eat.

[They laugh. HANA starts to pour more wine.]

OKA: I better not drink anymore. Got to drive to Nagata-san's yet. *[He walks over to MASAKO.]* You study hard, don't you? You'll teach Kiyoko English, eh? When she gets here . . .?

HANA: Oh, yes, she will.

MURATA: Kiyoko-san could probably teach her a thing or two.

OKA: She won't know about American ways.

MASAKO: I'll help her.

HANA: Don't worry, Oka-san. She'll have a good friend in our Masako.

[They move to the door.]

OKA: Well, thanks for the sake. I guess I talk too much when I drink. *[He scratches his head and laughs.]* Oh. I'm sorry about the fire. By the way, come to my house for your bath . . . until you build yours again.

HANA: Oh, a . . . thank you. I don't know if . . .

MURATA: Good, good! I need a good hot bath tonight.

OKA: Tonight, then.

MURATA: We'll be there.

HANA *[bowing]*:   Thank you very much. *Sayonara.*

OKA *[nodding]*:   See you tonight.

[OKA leaves. HANA faces MURATA as soon as the door closes.]

HANA: Papa, I don't know about going over there.

MURATA *[surprised]*: Why?

HANA: Well, Emiko-san . . .

MURATA *[irritated]*: What's the matter with you? We need a bath and Oka's invited us over.

HANA *[to MASAKO]*: Help me clear the table.

[MASAKO reluctantly leaves her book.]

HANA *[continuing]*: Papa, you know we've been neighbors already three, four years, and Emiko-san's never been very hospitable.

MURATA: She's shy, that's all.

HANA: Not just shy. She's strange. I feel like she's pushing me off. She makes me feel like—I don't know—like I'm prying or something.

MURATA: Maybe you are.

HANA: And never puts out a cup of tea . . . If she had all that training in the graces . . . why, a cup of tea . . .

MURATA: So if you want tea, ask for it.

HANA: I can't do that, Papa. *[pause]* She's strange. . . . I don't know . . . *[to MASAKO]* When we go there, be very careful not to say anything wrong.

MASAKO: I never say anything anyway.

HANA *[thoughtfully]*: Would you believe the story Oka-san just told? Why, I never knew . . .

MURATA: There're lots of things you don't know. Just because a man don't . . . don't talk about them, don't mean he don't feel . . . don't think about . . .

HANA *[looking around]*: We'll have to take something. There's nothing to take. Papa, maybe you can dig up some carrots.

MURATA: God, Mama, be sensible. They got carrots. Everybody's got carrots.

HANA: Something . . . Maybe I should make something.

MURATA: Hell, they're not expecting anything.

HANA: It's not good manners to go empty-handed.

MURATA: We'll take the sake.

[HANA grimaces. MASAKO sees the phonograph.]

MASAKO: I know, Mama. We can take the Victrola! We can play records for Mrs. Oka. Then nobody has to talk.

[MURATA laughs.]

[Fade out]

ACT I
Scene ii

That evening

ON RISE: *The exterior wall of the Okas' weathered house. There is a workable screen door and a large screened window. Outside there is a wide wooden bench that can accommodate three or four people. There is one separate chair, and a lantern stands against the house.*

The last rays of the sun light the area in a soft golden glow. This light grows gray as the scene progresses, and it is quite dark by the end of the scene.

Through the screened window, EMIKO can be seen walking erratically back and forth. She wears drab cotton but her grace and femininity come through. Her hair is bunned back in the style of the Issei women of the era.

OKA sits cross-legged on the bench. He wears a Japanese summer robe (yukata) and fans himself with a round Japanese fan.

The MURATAS enter. MURATA carries towels and a bottle of sake. HANA carries the Victrola, and MASAKO, a package containing their yukata.

OKA *[standing to greet the MURATAS]*:   Oh, you've come. Welcome!
MURATA: *Yah . . .* Good of you to ask us.
HANA *[bowing]*:   Yes, thank you very much. *[to MASAKO]* Say hello, Masako.
MASAKO: Hello.
HANA: And thank you.
MASAKO: Thank you.

[OKA makes motions of protest. EMIKO stops her pacing and watches from the window.]

HANA *[glancing briefly at the window]*:   And how is Emiko-san this evening?
OKA *[turning to the house]*:   Emi! Emiko!
HANA: That's all right. Don't call her out. She must be busy.
OKA: Emiko!

[EMIKO comes to the door. HANA starts a bow toward the house.]

MURATA: *Konbanwa!* (Good evening)

HANA: *Konbanwa,* Emiko-san. I feel so badly about this intrusion. *[pause]* Your husband has told you our bathhouse was destroyed by fire, and he graciously invited us to come use yours.

[EMIKO shakes her head.]

OKA: I didn't have a chance to . . .

[HANA recovers and nudges MASAKO.]

HANA: Say hello to Mrs. Oka.
MASAKO: Hello, Mrs. Oka.

[HANA lowers the Victrola to the bench.]

OKA: What's this? You brought a phonograph?
MASAKO: It's a Victrola.
HANA *[laughing indulgently]*:   Yes. Masako wanted to bring this over and play some records.
MURATA *[extending the wine]*:   Brought a little sake too.
OKA *[taking the bottle]*:   Ah, now that I like. Emiko, bring out the cups.

[OKA waves at his wife, but she doesn't move. He starts to ask again but decides to get them himself. He enters the house and returns with two cups.]

[EMIKO seats herself on the single chair. The MURATAS unload their paraphernalia; OKA pours the wine, the men drink, HANA chatters and sorts the records. MASAKO stands by helping her.]

HANA: Yes, our Masako loves to play records. I like records too, and Papa, he . . .
MURATA *[watching EMIKO]*:   They take me back home. The only way I can get there. In my mind.
HANA: Do you like music, Emiko-san?

[EMIKO looks vague, but smiles.]

HANA *[continuing]*:   Oka-san, you like them, don't you?
OKA: Yeah. But I don't have a player. No chance to hear them.
MURATA: I had to get this for them. They wouldn't leave me alone until I got it. Well . . . a phonograph . . . what the hell; they got to have *some* fun.
HANA: We don't have to play them, if you'd rather not.
OKA: Play. Play them.

HANA: I thought we could listen to them and relax. *[She extends some records to EMIKO.]* Would you like to look through these, Emiko-san?

> *[EMIKO doesn't respond. She pulls out a sack of Bull Durham and begins to roll a cigarette. HANA pushes MASAKO to her.]*

HANA *[continuing]*:   Take these to her.

> *[MASAKO goes to EMIKO with the records. She stands watching her as EMIKO lights a cigarette.]*

HANA *[continuing]*:   Some of these are very old. You might know them, Emiko-san. *[She sees MASAKO watching EMIKO.]* Masako, bring those over here. *[She laughs uncomfortably.]* You might like this one, Emiko-san. *[She starts the player.]* Do you know it?

> *[The record whines out "Kago No Tori." EMIKO listens with her head cocked.]*

> *[She smokes her cigarette. She is wrapped in nostalgia and memories of the past. MASAKO watches her carefully.]*

MASAKO *[whispering]*:   Mama, she's crying.

> *[Startled, HANA and MURATA look toward EMIKO.]*

HANA *[pinching MASAKO]*:   Shhh. The smoke is in her eyes.
MURATA: Did you bring the record I like, Mama?

> *[EMIKO rises abruptly and enters the house.]*

MASAKO: They're tears, Mama.
HANA: From yawning, Masako. *[regretfully to OKA]* I'm afraid we offended her.
OKA *[unaware]*:   Hunh? Aw . . . no . . . pay no attention. No offense.

> *[MASAKO looks toward the window. EMIKO stands forlornly and slowly drifts into a dance.]*

HANA: I'm very sorry. Children, you know . . . they'll say anything. Anything that's on their minds.

> *[MURATA notices MASAKO looking through the window and tries to divert her attention.]*

MURATA: The needles. Masako, where're the needles?

MASAKO *[still watching]*:   I forgot them.

[HANA sees what's going on. OKA is unaware.]

HANA: Masako, go take your bath now. Masako . . .

[MASAKO reluctantly takes her towel and leaves.]

OKA: Yeah, yeah. Take your bath, Masako-chan.
MURATA *[sees EMIKO still dancing]*:   Change the record, Mama.
OKA *[still unaware]*:   That's kind of sad.
MURATA: No use to get sick over a record. We're supposed to enjoy.

[HANA stops the record. EMIKO disappears from the window. HANA selects a lively ondo ("Tokyo Ondo").]

HANA: We'll find something more fun.

[The three tap to the music.]

HANA *[continuing]*:   Can't you just see the festival? The dancers, the bright kimonos, the paper lanterns bobbing in the wind, the fireflies . . . How nostalgic. Oh, how nostalgic.

[EMIKO appears from the side of the house. Her hair is down; she wears an old straw hat. She dances in front of the MURATAS. They are startled.]

[After the first shock, they watch with frozen smiles. They try to join EMIKO's mood, but something is missing. OKA is grieved. He finally stands as though he's had enough. EMIKO, now close to the door, ducks into the house.]

HANA: That was pretty. Very nice.

[OKA settles down and grunts. MURATA clears his throat, and MASAKO returns from her bath.]

MURATA: You're done already? *[He's glad to see her.]*
MASAKO: I wasn't very dirty. The water was too hot.
MURATA: Good! Just the way I like it.
HANA: Not dirty?
MURATA *[picking up his towel]*:   Come on, Mama . . . scrub my back.
HANA *[laughing with embarrassment]*:   Oh, oh . . . well . . . *[She stops the player.]*
Masako, now don't forget. Crank the machine and change the needle now and then.

MASAKO: I didn't bring them.

HANA: Oh. Oh ... all right. I'll be back soon. Don't forget ... Crank. *[She leaves with her husband.]*

> *[OKA and MASAKO are alone. OKA is awkward and falsely hearty.]*

OKA: So! So you don't like hot baths, eh?

MASAKO: Not too hot.

OKA *[laughing]*:   I thought you like it real hot. Hot enough to burn the house down.

> *[MASAKO doesn't laugh.]*

OKA *[continuing]*:   That's a little joke.

> *[MASAKO busies herself to conceal her annoyance.]*

OKA *[continuing]*:   I hear you're real good in school. Always top of the class.

MASAKO: It's a small class. Only two of us.

OKA: When Kiyoko comes, you'll help her in school, yeah? You'll take care of her ... a favor for me, eh?

MASAKO: Okay.

OKA: You'll be her friend, eh?

MASAKO: Okay.

OKA: That's good. That's good. You'll like her. She's a nice girl too.

> *[OKA stands, yawns, and stretches.]*

OKA *[continuing]*:   I'll go for a little walk now. *[He touches his crotch to indicate his purpose.]*

> *[MASAKO turns her attention to the records and selects one, "And the Soul Shall Dance," and begins to sway with the music. The song draws EMIKO from the house. She looks out the window, sees MASAKO is alone, and slips into a dance.]*

EMIKO: Do you like that song, Masa-chan?

> *[MASAKO is startled. She remembers her mother's warning. She doesn't know what to do. She nods.]*

EMIKO *[continuing]*:   That's one of my favorite songs. I remember in Japan I used to sing it so often. My favorite song. *[She sings along with the record.]*

Akai kuchibiru / Kappu yosete / Aoi sake nomya / Kokoro ga ordoru. Do you
know what that means, Masa-chan?

MASAKO: I think so. The soul will dance?

EMIKO: Yes, yes, that's right. The soul shall dance. Red lips against a glass, drink
the green . . .

MASAKO: Wine?

EMIKO *[nodding]:*   Drink the green wine . . .

MASAKO: Green? I thought wine was purple.

EMIKO: Wine is purple, but this is a green liqueur.

> *[EMIKO holds up one of the cups as though it were crystal
> and looks at the light that would shine through the green
> liquid.]*

EMIKO *[continuing]:*   It's good. It warms your heart.

MASAKO: And the soul dances.

EMIKO: Yes . . .

MASAKO: What does it taste like? The green wine?

EMIKO: Oh, it's like . . . it's like . . .

> *[The second verse starts: Kurai yoru noy ume / Setsu nasa
> yo / Aoi sake nomya / Yume ga odoru.]*

MASAKO: In the dark night . . .

EMIKO: Dreams are unbearable . . .

MASAKO: Drink the . . .

EMIKO: Drink the green wine . . .

MASAKO: And the dreams will dance.

EMIKO *[softly]:*   I'll be going back one day.

MASAKO: Where?

EMIKO: My home. Japan. My real home. I'm going back one day.

MASAKO: By yourself?

EMIKO: Oh, yes. It's a secret. You can keep a secret?

MASAKO: Un-hunh. I have lots of secrets. All my own.

> *[The music stops. EMIKO sees OKA approaching and dis-
> appears into the house. MASAKO attends to the record and
> does not know EMIKO is gone.]*

MASAKO *[continuing]:*   Secrets I never tell anyone . . .

OKA: Secrets? What kind of secrets? What did she say?

MASAKO *[startled]:*   Oh! Nothing.

OKA: What did you talk about?

MASAKO: Nothing. Mrs. Oka was talking about the song. She was telling me
what it meant . . . about the soul.

OKA *[scoffing]*: Heh! What does she know about soul? *[calming down]* Ehhh ... Some people don't have them—souls.

MASAKO *[timidly]*: I thought ... I thought everyone has a soul. I read in a book ...

OKA *[laughing]*: Maybe ... maybe you're right. I'm not an educated man, you know. I don't know too much about books. When Kiyoko comes you can talk to her about it. Kiyoko is very ...

> *[From inside the house, we hear EMIKO begin to sing loudly at the name KIYOKO as though trying to drown it out. OKA stops talking, then resumes.]*

OKA *[continuing]*: Kiyoko is very smart. You'll have a good time with her. She'll learn your language fast. How old did you say you are?

MASAKO: Almost twelve.

> *[By this time OKA and MASAKO are shouting to be heard above EMIKO's singing.]*

OKA: Kiyoko is fifteen. Kiyoko ...

> *[OKA is exasperated. He rushes into the house seething. MASAKO hears OKA's muffled rage. "Behave yourself" and "Kitchigai" come through. MASAKO slinks to the window and looks in. OKA slaps EMIKO around. MASAKO reacts to the violence. OKA comes out. MASAKO returns to the bench in time. He pulls his fingers through his hair and sits next to MASAKO. She draws away.]*

OKA: Want me to light a lantern?

MASAKO *[shaken]*: No ... ye ... okay.

OKA: We'll get a little light here.

> *[He lights the lantern as the MURATAS return from their bath. They are in good spirits.]*

MURATA: Ahhh ... Nothing like a good hot bath.

HANA: So refreshing.

MURATA: A bath should be taken hot and slow. Don't know how Masako gets through so fast.

HANA: She probably doesn't get in the tub.

MASAKO: I do.

> *[Everyone laughs.]*

MASAKO *[continuing]*:   Well, I do.

> *[EMIKO comes out. She has a large purple welt on her face. She sits on the separate chair, hands folded, quietly watching the MURATAS. They look at her with alarm. OKA engages himself with his fan.]*

HANA: Oh! Emiko-san . . . what . . . a . . . a . . . whaa . . . *[She draws a deep breath.]* What a nice bath we had. Such a lovely bath. We do appreciate your hos . . . pitality. Thank you so much.

EMIKO: Lovely evening, isn't it?

HANA: Very lovely. Very. Ah, a little warm, but nice. Did you get a chance to hear the records? *[turning to MASAKO]* Did you play the records for Mrs. Oka?

MASAKO: Ye . . . no. The needle was . . .

EMIKO: Yes, she did. We played the records together.

MURATA: Oh, you played the songs together?

EMIKO: Yes . . . yes.

MURATA: That's nice. Masako can understand pretty good, eh?

EMIKO: She understands everything. Everything I say.

MURATA *[withdrawing]*:   Oh, yeah? Eh, Mama, we ought to be going. *[He closes the player.]* Hate to bathe and run but . . .

HANA: Yes, yes. Tomorrow is a busy day. Come, Masako.

EMIKO: Please . . . stay a little longer.

MURATA: Eh, well, we got to be going.

HANA: Why, thank you, but . . .

EMIKO: It's still quite early.

OKA *[ready to say good-bye]*:   Enjoyed the music. And the sake.

EMIKO: The records are very nice. Makes me remember Japan. I sang those songs . . . those very songs . . . Did you know I used to sing?

HANA *[politely]*:   Why, no. No. I didn't know that. You must have a very lovely voice.

EMIKO: Yes.

HANA: No, I didn't know that. That's very nice.

EMIKO: Yes, I sang. My parents were very strict. They didn't like it. They said it was frivolous. Imagine?

HANA: Yes, I can imagine. Things were like that . . . in those days singing was not considered proper for nice . . . I mean, only for women in the profess . . .

MURATA: We better get home, Mama.

HANA: Yes, yes. What a shame you couldn't continue with it.

EMIKO: In the city I did do some classics: the dance, and the koto, and the flower, and of course, the tea. *[She makes the gestures for the disciplines.]* All those. Even some singing. Classics, of course.

HANA *[politely]*:   Of course.

EMIKO: All of it is so disciplined . . . so disciplined. I was almost a *natori*.

HANA: How nice!

EMIKO: But everything changed.

HANA: Oh!

EMIKO: I was sent here to America. *[She glares at OKA.]*

HANA: Oh, too bad. I mean, too bad about your *natori*.

MURATA *[loudly to OKA]*: So did you see Nagata-san today?

OKA: Oh, yeah, yeah.

MURATA: What did he say? Is he interested?

OKA: Yeah. Yeah. He's interested.

MURATA: He likes the horse, eh?

OKA: Ah . . . yeah.

MURATA: I knew he'd like him. I'd buy him myself if I had the money.

OKA: Well, I have to take him over tomorrow. He'll decide then.

MURATA: He'll buy. He'll buy. You'd better go straight over to the ticket agent and get that ticket. Before you *[ha-ha]* spend the money.

OKA: *[ha-ha]* Yeah.

HANA: It'll be so nice when Kiyoko-san comes to join you. I know you're looking forward to it.

EMIKO *[confused]*: Oh . . . oh . . .

HANA: Masako is so happy. It'll be good for her too.

EMIKO: I had more freedom in the city. I lived with an aunt and she let me . . . she wasn't so strict.

> *[MURATA and MASAKO have their gear together and are ready to leave.]*

MURATA: Good luck on the horse tomorrow.

OKA: Yeah.

HANA *[bowing]*: Many, many thanks.

OKA: Thanks for the sake.

HANA *[bowing again]*: Good night, Emiko-san. We'll see you again soon. We'll bring the records too.

EMIKO *[softly]*: Those songs. Those very songs.

MURATA: Let's go, Mama.

> *[The MURATAS pull away. Light follows them and grows dark on the OKAS. The MURATAS begin walking home.]*

HANA: That was uncomfortable.

MASAKO: What's the matter with . . .

HANA: Shhh!

MURATA: I guess Oka has his problems.

MASAKO: Is she really *kitchigai*?

HANA: Of course not. She's not crazy. Don't say that word.

MASAKO: I heard Mr. Oka call her that.

HANA: He called her that?

MASAKO: I . . . I think so.

HANA: You heard wrong, Masako. Emiko-san isn't crazy. She just likes her drinks. She had too much to drink tonight.

MASAKO: Oh.

HANA: She can't adjust to this life. She can't get over the good times she had in Japan. Well, it's not easy. But one has to know when to bend . . . like the bamboo. When the winds blow, bamboo bends. You bend or crack. Remember that, Masako.

MURATA *[wryly]*:   Bend, eh? Remember that, Mama.

HANA *[softly]*:   You don't know. It isn't ever easy.

MASAKO: Do you want to go back to Japan, Mama?

HANA: Everyone does.

MASAKO: Do you, Papa?

MURATA: I'll have to make some money first.

MASAKO: I don't. Not me. Not Kiyoko.

HANA: After Kiyoko-san comes, Emiko will have company and things will straighten out. She has nothing to live on but memories. She doesn't have any friends. At least I have my friends at church. At least I have that. She must get awful lonely. . . .

MASAKO: I know that. She tried to make friends with me.

HANA: She did? What did she say?

MASAKO: Well, sort of . . .

HANA: What did she say?

MASAKO: She didn't say anything. I just felt it. Maybe you should be her friend, Mama.

MURATA: Poor woman. We could have stayed longer.

HANA: But you wanted to leave. I tried to be friendly. You saw that. It's not easy to talk to Emiko. She either closes up, you can't pry a word from her, or else she goes on and on. All that . . . that . . . about the koto and tea and the flower . . . I mean, what am I supposed to say? She's so unpredictable. And the drinking . . .

MURATA: All right, all right, Mama.

MASAKO: Did you see her black eye?

HANA *[calming down]*:   She probably hurt herself. She wasn't very steady.

MASAKO: Oh, no. Mr. Oka hit her.

HANA: I don't think so.

MASAKO: He hit her. I saw him.

HANA: You saw? Papa, do you hear that? She saw them. That does it. We're not going there again.

MURATA: Aw . . . Oka wouldn't do that. Not in front of a kid.

MASAKO: Well, they didn't do it in front of me. They were in the house.

MURATA: You see?

HANA: That's all right. You just have to fix the bathhouse. Either that or we're going to bathe at home . . . in a bucket, if we have to. We're not going . . . we'll bathe at home.

[MURATA mutters to himself.]

HANA: What?

MURATA: I said all right, it's the bucket then. I'll get to it when I can.

> *[HANA passes MURATA and walks ahead.]*
>
> *[Fade out]*

ACT I

Scene iii

> *The same evening*

ON RISE: The exterior of the Oka house. The MURATAS have just left. EMIKO sits on the bench, her back to OKA. OKA, still standing, looks at her contemptuously as she pours herself a drink.

OKA: Nothing more disgusting than a drunk woman.

> *[EMIKO ignores him.]*

OKA *[continuing]*:   You made a fool of yourself. You made a fool of *me!*

EMIKO: One can only make a fool of one's self.

OKA: You learn that in the fancy schools, eh?

> *[EMIKO examines the pattern of her cup.]*

OKA *[continuing]*:   Eh? Ehhh? *[pause]* Answer me!

> *[EMIKO ignores him.]*

OKA *[continuing]*:   I'm talking to you. Answer me! *[threatening]* You don't get away with that. You think you're so fine. . . .

> *[EMIKO looks off at the horizon. OKA roughly turns her around.]*

OKA *[continuing]*:   When I talk, you listen!

> *[EMIKO turns away again. OKA pulls the cup from her hand.]*

OKA *[continuing]*:   Goddammit! What'd you think my friends think of you? What kind of ass they think I am?

[He grabs her shoulders.]

EMIKO: Don't touch me. Don't touch (me) . . .

OKA: Who the hell you think you are? "Don't touch me, don't touch me." Who the hell! High and mighty, eh? Too good for me, eh? Don't put on the act for me. I know who you are.

EMIKO: Tell me who I am, Mister Smart Peasant.

OKA: Shut your fool mouth, goddammit! Sure. I'll tell you. I know all about you. Shizue told me. The whole village knows.

EMIKO: Shizue!

OKA: Yeah, Shizue. Embarrassed the hell out of her, your own sister.

EMIKO: Embarrassed? I have nothing to be ashamed of. I don't know what you're talking about.

OKA *[derisively]*:   You don't know what I'm talking about. I know. The whole village knows. They're all laughing at you. At me! Stupid Oka got stuck with a secondhand woman. I didn't say anything because . . .

EMIKO: I'm not secondhand!

OKA: Who you trying to fool? I know. Knew long time ago. Shizue wrote me all about your . . . your affairs in Tokyo. The men you were mess(ing) . . .

EMIKO: Affairs? Men?

OKA: That man you were messing with. I knew all along. I didn't say anything because you . . . I . . .

EMIKO: I'm not ashamed of it.

OKA: You're not ashamed! What the hell! Your father thought he was pulling a fast one on me . . . thought I didn't know nothing . . . thought I was some kind of dumb ass . . . I didn't say nothing because Shizue's dead. Shizue's dead. I was willing to give you a chance.

EMIKO *[laughing]*:   A chance? Give me a chance?

OKA: Yeah. A chance! Laugh! Give a *joro* another chance. Sure, I'm stupid . . . dumb.

EMIKO: I'm not a whore. I'm true. He knows I'm true.

OKA: True! *[Hah!]*

EMIKO: You think I'm untrue just because I let . . . let you . . . There's only one man for me.

OKA: Let me *[obscene gesture]*? I can do what I want with you. Your father palmed you off on me—like a dog or cat—animal. Couldn't do nothing with you. Even the rich dumb Yamato wouldn't have you. Your father—greedy father—so proud . . . making big plans for you . . . for himself. *[Humh!]* The whole village laughing at him.

[EMIKO hangs her head.]

OKA *[continuing]*:   Shizue told me. And she was working like a dog ... trying to keep your goddam father happy ... doing my work and yours.

EMIKO: My work?

OKA: Yeah, your work too! She killed herself working. She killed herself. *[He has tender memories of his uncomplaining wife.]* Up in the morning getting the fires started, working the bellows, cleaning the furnace, cooking, and late at night working with the sewing ... tending the baby. *[He mutters.]* The goddam family killed her. And you ... you out there in Tokyo with the fancy clothes, doing the *[sneering]* dance, the tea, the flower, the *[obscene gesture]* ...

EMIKO *[hurting]*:   Ahhhhh ...

OKA: Did you have fun? Did you have fun on your sister's blood?

[EMIKO doesn't answer.]

OKA *[continuing]*:   Did you? He must have been a son-of-a-bitch. What would make that goddam greedy old man send his prize mare to a plow horse like me? What kind of bum was he that your father would ...

EMIKO: He's not a bum. He's not a bum.

OKA: Was he Korean? Was he *Etta?* That's the only thing I could figure.

EMIKO: I'm true to him. Only him.

OKA: True? You think he's true to you? You think he waits for you? Remembers you? *Aho!* Think he cares?

EMIKO: He does.

OKA: And waits ten years? *Baka!* Go back to Japan and see. You'll find out. Go back to Japan. *Kaire!*

EMIKO: In time.

OKA: In time. How about now?

EMIKO: I can't now.

OKA: *[Hah!]* Now! Go now! Who needs you? Who needs you? You think a man waits ten years for a woman? You think you're some kind of ... of diamond ... treasure ... he's going to wait his life for you? Go to him. He's probably married with ten kids. Go to him. Get out! Goddam *joro.* Go! Go!

[OKA sweeps EMIKO off the bench.]

EMIKO: Ahhh! I ... I don't have the money. Give me money to ...

OKA: If I had money I would give it to you ten years ago. You think I been eating this *kuso* for ten years because I like it?

EMIKO: You're selling the horse. Give me the (money) ...

OKA *[scoffing]*:   That's for Kiyoko. I owe you nothing.

EMIKO: Ten years, you owe me.

OKA: Ten years of what? Misery? You gave me nothing. I give you nothing. You want to go, pack your bag and start walking. Try cross the desert. When you get dry and hungry, think about me.

EMIKO: I'd die out there.

OKA: Die? You think I didn't die here?

EMIKO: I didn't do anything to you.

OKA: No, no, you didn't. All I wanted was a little comfort and you . . . no, you didn't. No. So you die. We all die. Shizue died. If she was here, she wouldn't treat me like this. Ah, I should have brought her with me. She'd be alive now. We'd be poor but happy like . . . like Murata and his wife . . . and the kid.

EMIKO: I wish she were alive too. I'm not to blame for her dying. I didn't know. I was away. I loved her. I didn't want her to die. I . . .

OKA *[softening]*:   I know that. I'm not blaming you for that. And it's not my fault what happened to you either.

> *[OKA is encouraged by EMIKO's silence which he mistakes for a change of attitude.]*

OKA *[continuing]*:   You understand that, eh? I didn't ask for you. It's not my fault you're here in this desert with . . . with me.

> *[EMIKO weeps. OKA reaches out.]*

OKA *[continuing]*:   I know I'm too old for you. It's hard for me too. But this is the way it is. I just ask you be kinder . . . understand it wasn't my fault. Try make it easier for me. For yourself too.

> *[OKA touches her and she shrinks from his hand.]*

EMIKO: Ach!

OKA *[humiliated again]*:   Goddam it! I didn't ask for you! *Aho!* If you was smart, you'da done as your father said . . . cut out that *saru shibai* with the *Etta* . . . married the rich Yamato. Then you'd still be in Japan. Not here to make my life so miserable.

> *[EMIKO is silent.]*

OKA *[continuing]*:   And you can have your *Etta* . . . or anyone else you want. Take them all on.

> *[OKA is worn out. It's hopeless.]*

OKA *[continuing]*:   God, why do we do this all the time? Fighting all the time. There must be a better way to live. There must be another way.

> *[OKA waits for a response, gives up, and enters the house. EMIKO watches him leave and pours another drink. The storm has passed, the alcohol takes over.]*

EMIKO: I must keep the dream alive. The dream is all I live for. I am only in exile now. If I give in, all I've lived before will mean nothing . . . will be for nothing. Nothing. If I let you make me believe this is all there is to my life, the dream would die. I would die.

[*She pours another drink and feels warm and good.*]

[*Fade out*]

ACT II

Scene i

Mid-September afternoon

ON RISE: *Muratas' kitchen. The calendar reads September. MASAKO is at the kitchen table with several books. She thumbs through a Japanese magazine. HANA is with her sewing.*]

MASAKO: Do they always wear kimonos in Japan, Mama?
HANA: Most of the time.
MASAKO: I wonder if Kiyoko will be wearing a kimono like this.
HANA [*looking at the magazine*]:   They don't dress like that. Not for every day.
MASAKO: I wonder what she's like.
HANA: Probably a lot like you. What do you think she's like?
MASAKO: She's probably taller.
HANA: Mr. Oka isn't tall.
MASAKO: And pretty.
HANA [*laughing*]:   Mr. Oka . . . Well, I don't suppose she'll look like her father.
MASAKO: Mrs. Oka is pretty.
HANA: She isn't Kiyoko-san's real mother, remember?
MASAKO: Oh, that's right.
HANA: But they are related. Well, we'll soon see.
MASAKO: I thought she was coming in September. It's already September.
HANA: Papa said Oka-san went to San Pedro a few days ago. He should be back soon with Kiyoko-san.
MASAKO: Didn't Mrs. Oka go too?
HANA [*glancing toward the Oka house*]:   I don't think so. I see lights in their house at night.
MASAKO: Will they bring Kiyoko over to see us?
HANA: Of course. First thing, probably. You'll be very nice to her, won't you?

[*MASAKO finds another book.*]

MASAKO: Sure. I'm glad I'm going to have a friend. I hope she likes me.

HANA: She'll like you. Japanese girls are very polite, you know.

MASAKO: We have to be or our mamas get mad at us.

HANA: Then I should be getting mad at you more often.

MASAKO: It's often enough already, Mama. *[She opens the book.]* Look at this, Mama. I'm going to show her this book.

HANA: She won't be able to read at first.

MASAKO: I love this story. Mama, this is about people like us—settlers—it's about the prairie. We live in a prairie, don't we?

HANA: Prairie? Does that mean desert?

MASAKO: I think so.

HANA *[looking at the bleak landscape]*:   We live in a prairie.

MASAKO: It's about the hardships and the floods and droughts and how they have nothing but each other.

HANA: We have nothing but each other. But these people . . . they're white people.

MASAKO: Sure, Mama. They come from the east. Just like you and Papa came from Japan.

HANA: We come from the far far east. That's different. White people are different from us.

MASAKO: I know that.

HANA: White people among white people . . . that's different from Japanese among white people. You know what I'm saying?

MASAKO: I know that. How come they don't write books about us . . . about Japanese people?

HANA: Because we're nobodies here.

MASAKO: If I didn't read these, there'd be nothing for me.

HANA: Some of the things you read, you're never going to know.

MASAKO: I can dream though.

HANA *[sighing]*:   Sometimes the dreaming makes the living harder. Better to keep your head out of the clouds.

MASAKO: That's not much fun.

HANA: You'll have fun when Kiyoko-san comes. You can study together, you can sew, and sometime you can try some of those fancy American recipes.

MASAKO: Oh, Mama. You have to have chocolate and cream and things like that.

HANA: We'll get them.

> *[We hear the sound of Oka's old car. MASAKO and HANA pause and listen. MASAKO runs to the window.]*

MASAKO: I think it's them!

HANA: Oka-san?

MASAKO: It's them! It's them!

> *[HANA stands and looks out. She removes her apron and puts away her sewing.]*

HANA: Two of them. Emiko-san isn't with them. *[pause]* Let's go outside.

> *[OKA and KIYOKO enter. OKA is wearing his going-out clothes: a sweater, white shirt, dark pants, but no tie. KIYOKO walks behind him.]*
>
> *[KIYOKO is short, broad-chested, and very self-conscious. Her hair is straight and banded into two shucks. She wears a conservative cotton dress, white socks, and two-inch heels.]*
>
> *[OKA is proud. He struts in, his chest puffed out.]*

OKA: Hello, hello! We're here. We made it! *[He pushes KIYOKO forward.]* This my daughter, Kiyoko. *[to KIYOKO]* Murata-san. Remember, I was talking about? My friends . . .

KIYOKO *[bowing deeply]*:   Hajime mashite yoroshiku onegai shimasu.

HANA *[also bowing deeply]*:   I hope your journey was pleasant.

OKA *[pushing KIYOKO to MASAKO while she still bows]*:   This is Masako-chan; I told you about her.

> *[MASAKO is shocked at KIYOKO's appearance. The girl she expected is already a woman. She stands with her mouth agape and withdraws noticeably. HANA rushes in to fill the awkwardness.]*

HANA: Say hello, Masako. My goodness, where are your manners? *[She laughs apologetically.]* In this country they don't make much to-do about manners. *[She stands back to examine KIYOKO.]* My, my, I didn't picture you so grown up. My, my . . . Tell me, how was your trip?

OKA *[proudly]*:   We just drove in from Los Angeles this morning. We spent the night in San Pedro, and the next two days we spent in Los Angeles . . . you know, Japanese town.

HANA: How nice!

OKA: Kiyoko was so excited. Twisting her head this way and that—couldn't see enough with her big eyes. *[He imitates her fondly.]* She's from the country, you know . . . just a big country girl. Got all excited about the Chinese dinner— we had a Chinese dinner. She never ate it before.

> *[KIYOKO covers her mouth and giggles.]*

HANA: Chinese dinner!

OKA: Oh, yeah. Duck, *pakkai*, chow mein, seaweed soup . . . the works!

HANA: A feast!

OKA: Oh, yeah. Like a holiday. Two holidays. Two holidays in one.

[HANA pushes MASAKO forward.]

HANA: Two holidays in one! Kiyoko-san, our Masako has been looking forward
  to meeting you.
KIYOKO *[bowing again]*:   *Hajime mashite . . .*
HANA: She's been planning all sorts of things she'll do with you: sewing, cook-
  ing . . .
MASAKO: Oh, Mama . . .

[KIYOKO covers her mouth and giggles.]

HANA: It's true, Kiyoko-san. She's been looking forward to having a best friend.

[KIYOKO giggles and MASAKO pulls away.]

OKA: Kiyoko, you shouldn't be so shy. The Muratas are my good friends, and
  you should feel free with them. Ask anything, say anything. Right?
HANA: Of course, of course. *[She is annoyed with MASAKO.]* Masako, go in and
  start the tea.

[MASAKO enters the house.]

HANA *[continuing]*:   I'll call Papa. He's in the yard. Papa! Oka-san is here! *[to
  KIYOKO]* Now tell me, how was your trip? Did you get seasick?
KIYOKO *[bowing and nodding]*:   Eh *[affirmative]*. A little.
OKA: Tell her. Tell her how sick you got.

[KIYOKO covers her mouth and giggles.]

HANA: Oh, I know, I know. I was too. That was a long time ago. I'm sure things
  are improved now. Tell me about Japan. What is it like now? They say it's so
  changed . . . modern.
OKA: Kiyoko comes from the country . . . backwoods. Nothing changes much
  there from century to century.
HANA: Ah! That's true. That's why I love Japan. And you wanted to leave. It's
  unbelievable. To come here!
OKA: She always dreamed about it.
HANA: Well, it's not really that bad.
OKA: No, it's not that bad. Depends on what you make of it.
HANA: That's right. What you make of it. I was just telling Masako today . . .

*[MURATA enters. He rubs his hands to remove the soil and
  comes in grinning. He shakes OKA's hand.]*

MURATA: *Oi, oi . . .*

OKA: *Yah* . . . I'm back. This is my daughter.

MURATA: No! She's beautiful!

OKA: Finally made it. Finally got her here.

MURATA *[to KIYOKO]*:   Your father hasn't stopped talking about you all summer.

HANA: And Masako too.

KIYOKO *[bowing]*:   *Hajime mashite* . . .

MURATA *[with a short bow]*:   *Yah.* How'd you like the trip?

OKA: I was just telling your wife . . . had a good time in Los Angeles. Had a couple of great dinners, took in the cinema—Japanese pictures, bought her some American clothes . . .

HANA: Oh, you bought that in Los Angeles.

MURATA: Got a good price for your horse, eh? Lots of money, eh?

OKA: Nagata-kun's a shrewd bargainer. Heh. It don't take much money to make her happy. She's a country girl.

MURATA: That's all right. Country's all right. Country girl's the best.

OKA: Had trouble on the way back.

MURATA: Yeah?

OKA: Fan belt broke.

MURATA: That'll happen with these old cars.

OKA: Lucky I was near a gasoline station. We were in the mountains. Waited in a restaurant while it was getting fixed.

HANA: Oh, that was good.

OKA: Guess they don't see Japanese much. Stare? Terrible! Took them a long time to wait on us. Dumb waitress practically threw the food at us. Kiyoko felt bad.

HANA: Ah! That's too bad . . . too bad. That's why I always pack a lunch when we take trips.

MURATA: They'll spoil the day for you . . . those barbarians!

OKA: Terrible food too. Kiyoko couldn't swallow the dry bread and bologna.

HANA: That's the food they eat!

MURATA: Let's go in . . . have a little wine. Mama, we got wine? This is a celebration.

HANA: I think so. A little.

[They enter the house talking. MASAKO has made tea and HANA serves the wine.]

HANA *[continuing]*:   How is your mother? Was she happy to see you?

KIYOKO: Oh, she . . . yes.

HANA: I just know she was surprised to see you so grown up. Of course, you remember her from Japan, don't you?

KIYOKO *[nodding]*:   *Eh* (affirmative). I can barely remember. I was very young.

HANA: Of course. But you do, don't you?

KIYOKO: She was gone most of the time . . . at school in Tokyo. She was very
   pretty, I remember that.
HANA: She's still very pretty.
KIYOKO: Yes. She was always laughing. She was much younger then.
HANA: Oh, now, it hasn't been that long ago.

> *[MASAKO goes outside. The following dialogue continues*
> *muted as the light goes dim in the house and focuses on*
> *MASAKO. EMIKO enters, is drawn to the Murata window,*
> *and listens.]*

OKA: We stayed at an inn on East First Street. *Shizuokaya.* Whole inn filled
   with Shizuoka people . . . talking the old dialect. Thought I was in Japan again.
MURATA: That right?
OKA: Felt good. Like I was in Japan again.
HANA *[to KIYOKO]*:   Did you enjoy Los Angeles?
KIYOKO: Yes.
OKA: That's as close as I'll get to Japan.
MURATA: *Mattakuna!* That's for sure. Not in this life.

[Outside MASAKO is aware of EMIKO.]

MASAKO: Why don't you go in?
EMIKO: Oh. Oh. Why don't you?
MASAKO: They're all grown-ups in there. I'm not grown up.
EMIKO *[softly]*:   All grown-ups. Maybe I'm not either. *[Her mood changes.]*
   Masachan, do you have a boyfriend?
MASAKO: I don't like boys. They don't like me.
EMIKO: Oh, that will change. You will change. I was like that too.
MASAKO: Besides, there's none around here . . . Japanese boys. There are some
   at school, but they don't like girls.
HANA *[calling from the kitchen]*:   Masako . . .

[MASAKO doesn't answer.]

EMIKO: Your mother is calling you.
MASAKO *[to her mother]*:   *Nani?* (What?)
HANA *[from the kitchen]*:   Come inside now.
EMIKO: You'll have a boyfriend one day.
MASAKO: Not me.
EMIKO: You'll fall in love one day. Someone will make the inside of you light
   up, and you'll know you're in love. Your life will change . . . grow beautiful.
   It's good, Masa-chan. And this feeling you'll remember the rest of your
   life . . . will come back to you . . . haunt you . . . keep you alive . . . five, ten
   years . . . no matter what happens. Keep you alive.

HANA *[from the house]*:   Masako . . . Come inside now.

[MASAKO turns aside to answer and EMIKO slips away.]

MASAKO: What, Mama?

[HANA comes out.]

HANA: Come inside. Don't be so unsociable. Kiyoko wants to talk to you.

MASAKO *[watching EMIKO leave]*:   She doesn't want to talk to me. You're only saying that.

HANA: What's the matter with you? Don't you want to make friends with her?

MASAKO: She's not my friend. She's your friend.

HANA: Don't be silly. She's only fourteen.

MASAKO: Fifteen. They said fifteen. She's your friend. She's an old lady.

HANA: Don't say that.

MASAKO: I don't like her.

HANA: Shhh! Don't say that.

MASAKO: She doesn't like me either.

HANA: Ma-chan. Remember your promise to Mr. Oka? You're going to take her to school, teach her the language, teach her the ways of Americans.

MASAKO: She can do it herself. You did.

HANA: That's not nice, Ma-chan.

MASAKO: I don't like the way she laughs. *[She imitates KIYOKO holding her hand to her mouth and giggling and bowing.]*

HANA: Oh, how awful! Stop that. That's the way the girls do in Japan. Maybe she doesn't like your ways either. That's only a difference in manners. What you're doing now is considered very bad manners. *[She changes her tone.]* Machan, just wait: when she learns to read and speak, you'll have so much to say to each other. Come on, be a good girl and come inside.

MASAKO: It's just old people in there, Mama. I don't want to go in.

[HANA calls to KIYOKO inside.]

HANA: Kiyoko-san, please come here a minute. Maybe it's better for you to talk to Masako alone.

[KIYOKO dutifully goes outside.]

HANA *[continuing]*:   Masako has a lot of things to tell you . . . about what to expect in school and . . . things.

MURATA *[calling from the table]*:   Mama, put out something . . . chiles—for Oka-san.

[HANA enters the house. KIYOKO and MASAKO stand awkwardly facing each other, KIYOKO glancing shyly at MASAKO.]

MASAKO: Do you like it here?
KIYOKO *[nodding]*:   *Eh* (affirmative).

> *[There is an uncomfortable pause.]*

MASAKO: School will be starting next week.
KIYOKO *[nodding]*:   *Eh.*
MASAKO: Do you want to walk to school with me?
KIYOKO *[nodding]*:   *Hai.*

> *[MASAKO rolls her eyes and tries again.]*

MASAKO: I leave at 7:30.
KIYOKO: *Eh.*

> *[There's a long pause. MASAKO gives up and moves off-stage.]*

MASAKO: I have to do something.

> *[KIYOKO watches her leave and uncertainly moves back to the house. HANA looks up at KIYOKO coming in alone, sighs, and quietly pulls out a chair for her.]*

> *[Fade out]*

ACT II
Scene ii

November night

ON RISE: Interior of the Murata home. Lamps are lit. The family is at the kitchen table. HANA sews, MASAKO does her homework, MURATA reads the paper. They're dressed in warm robes and are having tea.

Outside, thunder rolls in the distance and lightning flashes.

HANA: It'll be *ohigan* (autumn festival) soon.
MURATA: Something to look forward to.
HANA: We'll need sweet rice for *omochi* (rice cakes).
MURATA: I'll order it next time I go to town.
HANA *[to MASAKO]*:   How is school? Getting a little harder?
MASAKO: Not that much. Sometimes the arithmetic is hard.

HANA: How is Kiyoko-san doing? Is she getting along all right?

MASAKO: She's good in arithmetic. She skipped a grade already.

HANA: Already? That's good news. Only November and she skipped a grade! At this rate she'll be through before you.

MASAKO: Well, she's older.

MURATA: Sure, she's older, Mama.

HANA: Has she made any friends?

MASAKO: No. She follows me around all day. She understands okay, but she doesn't talk. She talks like, you know . . . she says "ranchi" for lunch and "ranchi" for ranch too, and like that. Kids laugh and copy behind her back. It's hard to understand her.

HANA: You understand her, don't you?

MASAKO: I'm used to it.

HANA: You should tell the kids not to laugh. After all, she's trying. Maybe you should help her practice those words . . . show her what she's doing wrong.

MASAKO: I already do. Our teacher told me to do that.

MURATA [*looking up from his paper*]: You ought to help her all you can.

HANA: And remember, when you started school, you couldn't speak English either.

MASAKO: I help her.

> [*MURATA goes to the window. The night is cold. Lightning flashes and the wind whistles.*]

MURATA: Looks like a storm coming up. Hope we don't have a freeze.

HANA: If it freezes, we'll have another bad year. Maybe we ought to start the smudge pots.

MURATA [*listening*]: It's starting to rain. Nothing to do now but pray.

HANA: If praying is the answer, we'd be in Japan now. Rich.

MURATA [*wryly*]: We're not dead yet. We still have a chance.

> [*HANA glares at the small joke.*]

MURATA [*continuing*]: Guess I'll turn in.

HANA: Go to bed, go to bed. I'll sit up and worry.

MURATA: If worrying was the answer, we'd be around the world twice and in Japan. Come on, Mama. Let's go to bed. It's too cold tonight to be mad.

> [*There's an urgent knock on the door. The MURATAS react.*]

MURATA [*continuing*]: *Dareh da!* (Who is it?)

> [*MURATA goes to the door and hesitates.*]

MURATA [*continuing*]: Who is it!

KIYOKO *[weakly]*:   It's me ... help me ...

> *[MURATA opens the door and KIYOKO stumbles in. She wears a kimono with a shawl thrown over. Her legs are bare except for a pair of straw zori. Her hair is wet and stringy, and she trembles uncontrollably.]*

MURATA: My God! Kiyoko-san! What's the matter?

HANA *[overlapping]*:   Kiyoko-san! What is it?

MURATA: What happened?

KIYOKO: They're fighting, they're fighting!

MURATA: Oh, don't worry. Those things happen. No cause to worry. Mama, make tea for her. Sit down and catch your breath. Don't worry. I'll take you home when you're ready.

HANA: Papa, I'll take care of it.

MURATA: Let me know when you're ready to go home.

HANA: It must be freezing out there. Try to get warm. Try to calm yourself.

MURATA: Kiyoko-san, don't worry. *[He puts his robe around her.]*

> *[HANA waves MASAKO and MURATA off. MURATA leaves. MASAKO goes to her bed in the kitchen.]*

HANA: Papa, I'll take care of it.

KIYOKO *[looking at Murata's retreating form]*:   But I came to ask your help. . . .

HANA: You ran down here without a lantern? You could have fallen and hurt yourself.

KIYOKO: I don't care ... I don't care ...

HANA: You don't know, Kiyoko-san. It's treacherous out there—snakes, spiders ...

KIYOKO: I must go back! I ... I ... you ... please come with me. . . .

HANA: First, first we must get you warm. Drink your tea.

KIYOKO: But they'll kill each other. They're fighting like animals. Help me stop them!

> *[HANA warms a pot of soup.]*

HANA *[calmly]*:   I cannot interfere in a family quarrel.

KIYOKO: It's not a quarrel. It's a ... a ...

HANA: That's all it is. A family squabble. You'll see. Tomorrow ...

> *[KIYOKO pulls at HANA's arm.]*

KIYOKO: Not just a squabble! Please ... please ...

> *[KIYOKO starts toward the door, but HANA stops her.]*

HANA: Now listen. Listen to me, Kiyoko-san. I've known your father and mother a little while now. I suspect it's been like this for years. Every family has some kind of trouble.

KIYOKO: Not like this, not like this.

HANA: Some have it better, some worse. When you get married, you'll understand. Don't worry. Nothing will happen. *[She takes a towel and dries KIYOKO's hair.]* You're chilled to the bone. You'll catch your death.

KIYOKO: I don't care. . . . I want to die.

HANA: Don't be silly. It's not that bad.

KIYOKO: It is! They started drinking early in the afternoon. They make some kind of brew and hide it somewhere in the desert.

HANA: It's illegal to make it. That's why they hide it. That home brew is poison to the body. The mind too.

KIYOKO: It makes them crazy. They drink it all the time and quarrel constantly. I was in the other room studying. I try so hard to keep up with school.

HANA: We were talking about you just this evening. Masako says you're doing so well. You skipped a grade?

KIYOKO: It's hard . . . hard. I'm too old for the class and the children . . .

[She remembers all her problems and starts crying again.]

HANA: It's always hard in a new country.

KIYOKO: They were bickering and quarreling all afternoon. Then something happened. All of a sudden they were on the floor . . . hitting and . . . and . . . He was hitting her in the stomach, the face . . . I tried to stop them, but they were so . . . drunk.

HANA: There, there. It's probably all over now.

KIYOKO: Why does it happen like this? Nothing is right. Everywhere I go. Masachan is so lucky. I wish my life was like hers. I can hardly remember my real mother.

HANA: Emiko-san is almost a real mother to you. She's blood kin.

KIYOKO: She hates me. She never speaks to me. She's so cold. I want to love her, but she won't let me. She hates me.

HANA: I don't think so, Kiyoko-san.

KIYOKO: She does! She hates me.

HANA: No. I don't think you have anything to do with it. It's this place. She hates it. This place is so lonely and alien.

KIYOKO: Then why didn't she go back? Why did they stay here?

HANA: You don't know. It's not so simple. Sometimes I think . . .

KIYOKO: Then why don't they make the best of it here? Like you?

HANA: That isn't easy either. Believe me. *[She leaves KIYOKO to stir the soup.]* Sometimes . . . sometimes the longing for home . . . the longing fills me with despair. Will I never return again? Will I never see my mother, my father, my sisters again? But what can one do? There are responsibilities here . . . children

... *[pause]* And another day passes ... another month ... another year. *[She takes the soup to KIYOKO.]* Did you have supper tonight?

KIYOKO *[bowing]*:   Ah. When my ... my aunt gets like this, she doesn't cook. No one eats. I don't get hungry anymore.

HANA: Cook for yourself. It's important to keep your health.

KIYOKO: I left Japan for a better life.

HANA: It isn't easy for you, is it? But you must remember your filial duty.

KIYOKO: It's so hard.

HANA: But you can make the best of it here, Kiyoko-san. And take care of yourself. You owe that to yourself. Eat. Keep well. It'll be better, you'll see. And sometimes it'll seem worse. But you'll survive. We do, you know.

HANA *[continuing]*:   It's getting late.

KIYOKO *[apprehensively]*:   I don't want to go back.

HANA: You can sleep with Masako tonight. Tomorrow you'll go back. And you'll remember what I told you. *[She puts her arm around KIYOKO.]* Life is never easy, Kiyoko-san. Endure. Endure. Soon you'll be marrying and going away. Things will not always be this way. And you'll look back on this ... this night and you'll ...

> *[There is a rap on the door. HANA exchanges glances with KIYOKO and opens the door a crack.]*
>
> *[OKA has come looking for KIYOKO. He wears an overcoat and holds a wet newspaper over his head.]*

OKA: Ah! I'm sorry to bother you so late at night—the fact is ...

HANA: Oka-san.

OKA *[jovially]*:   Good evening, good evening. *[He sees KIYOKO.]* Oh, there you are. Did you have a nice visit?

HANA *[irritated]*:   Yes, she's here.

OKA *[still cheerful]*:   Thought she might be. Ready to come home now?

HANA: She came in the rain.

OKA *[ignoring HANA's tone]*:   That's foolish of you, Kiyoko. You might catch cold.

HANA: She was frightened by your quarreling. She came for help.

OKA *[laughing with embarrassment]*:   Oh! Kiyoko, that's nothing to worry about. It's just we had some disagreement.

HANA: That's what I told her, but she was frightened just the same.

OKA: Children are ...

HANA: Not children, Oka-san. Kiyoko. Kiyoko was terrified. I think that was a terrible thing to do to her.

OKA *[rubbing his head]*:   Oh, I ... I ...

HANA: If you had seen her a few minutes ago ... hysterical ... shaking ... crying ... wet and cold to the bone ... out of her mind with worry.

OKA *[rubbing his head]*:   Oh, I don't know what she was so worried about.

HANA: You. You and Emiko fighting like you were going to kill each other.

OKA *[lowering his head in penitence]*:   Aaaaaaahhhhhhhh . . .

HANA: I know I shouldn't tell you this, but there's one or two things I have to say: You sent for Kiyoko-san, and now she's here. You said yourself she had a bad time in Japan, and now she's having a worse time. It's not easy for her in a strange country; the least you can do is try to keep from worrying her . . . especially about yourselves. I think it's terrible what you're doing to her . . . terrible!

OKA *[bowing in deep humility]*:   I am ashamed.

HANA: I think she deserves better. I think you should think about that.

OKA *[still bowing]*:   I thank you for this reminder. It will never happen again. I promise.

HANA: I don't need that promise. Make it to Kiyoko-san.

OKA: Come with Papa now. He did a bad thing. He'll be a good Papa from now. He won't worry his little girl again. All right?

> *[They move toward the door. KIYOKO tries to return MURATA's robe.]*

KIYOKO: Thank you so much.

OKA: Thank you again.

HANA *[to KIYOKO]*:   That's all right. You can bring it back tomorrow. Remember . . . remember what we talked about. *[loudly]* Good night, Oka-san.

> *[They leave. HANA goes to MASAKO, who pretends to sleep. She covers her. MURATA appears from the bedroom. He's heard it all. He and HANA exchange a quick glance and together they retire to their room.]*
>
> *[Fade out]*

ACT II

Scene iii

The next morning

ON RISE: The Murata house and yard. HANA and MURATA have already left the house to examine the rain damage in the fields.

MASAKO prepares to go to school. She puts on a coat and gets her books and lunch bag. Meanwhile, KIYOKO slips quietly into the yard. She wears a coat and carries Murata's robe and sets it on the outside bench.

MASAKO walks out and is surprised to see KIYOKO.

MASAKO: Hi. I thought you'd be . . . sick today.

KIYOKO: Oh. I woke up late.

MASAKO *[scrutinizing KIYOKO's face]*:   Your eyes are red.

KIYOKO *[averting her face]*:   Oh. I . . . got . . . sand in it. Yes.

MASAKO: Do you want eye drops? We have eye drops in the house.

KIYOKO: Oh, no. That's all right.

MASAKO: That's what's called bloodshot.

KIYOKO: Oh.

MASAKO: My father gets it a lot. When he drinks too much.

KIYOKO: Oh.

[MASAKO notices KIYOKO doesn't carry a lunch.]

MASAKO: Where's your lunch bag?

KIYOKO: I . . . forgot it.

MASAKO: Did you make your lunch today?

KIYOKO: Yes. Yes, I did. But I forgot it.

MASAKO: Do you want to go back and get it?

KIYOKO: No. *[pause]* We will be late.

MASAKO: Do you want to practice your words?

KIYOKO *[thoughtfully]*:   Oh . . .

MASAKO: Say, "My."

KIYOKO: My?

MASAKO: Eyes . . .

KIYOKO: Eyes.

MASAKO: Are . . .

KIYOKO: Are.

MASAKO: Red.

KIYOKO: Red.

MASAKO: Your eyes are red.

[KIYOKO will not repeat it.]

MASAKO *[continuing]*:   I . . .

[KIYOKO doesn't cooperate.]

MASAKO *[continuing]*:   Say, "I."

KIYOKO: I.

MASAKO: Got . . .

KIYOKO: Got.

MASAKO: Sand . . .

[KIYOKO balks.]

MASAKO *[continuing]*:   Say, "I."
KIYOKO *[sighing]*:   I.
MASAKO: Reft . . .
KIYOKO: Reft.
MASAKO: My . . .
KIYOKO: My.
MASAKO: Runch.
KIYOKO: Run . . . Lunch. *[pause]* Masako-san, you are mean. You are hurting me.
MASAKO: It's a joke! I was just trying to make you laugh!
KIYOKO: I cannot laugh today.
MASAKO: Sure you can. You can laugh. Laugh! Like this! *[She makes a hearty laugh.]*
KIYOKO: I cannot laugh when you make fun of me.
MASAKO: Okay, I'm sorry. We'll practice some other words then, okay?

[KIYOKO doesn't answer.]

MASAKO *[continuing]*:   Say, "Okay."
KIYOKO *[reluctantly]*:   Okay.
MASAKO: Okay, then . . . um . . . um . . . Say . . . um . . . *[rapidly]* "She sells seashells by the seashore."

[KIYOKO turns away indignantly.]

MASAKO *[continuing]*:   Aw, come on, Kiyoko! It's just a joke. Laugh!
KIYOKO *[sarcastically]*:   Ha-ha-ha. Now you say, "*Kono kyaku wa yoku kaki ku kyaku da!*"
MASAKO: Sure! I can say it. *Kono kyaku waki ku kyoku kaku* . . .
KIYOKO: That's not right.
MASAKO: *Koki kuki kya* . . .
KIYOKO: No. No-no-no.
MASAKO: Okay, then. You say, "Sea sells she shells . . . shu . . . sh."

[They both laugh, KIYOKO with her hands over her mouth. MASAKO takes KIYOKO's hands away.]

MASAKO: Not like that. Like this! *[She makes a big laugh.]*
KIYOKO: Like this? *[She imitates MASAKO.]*
MASAKO: Yeah, that's right! *[pause]* You're not mad anymore?
KIYOKO: I'm not mad anymore.
MASAKO: Okay. You can share my lunch because we're . . .
KIYOKO: "Flends?"

[MASAKO looks at KIYOKO. They giggle and move on.]

[HANA and MURATA come in from assessing the storm's damage. They are dressed warmly. HANA is depressed. MURATA tries to be cheerful.]

MURATA: It's not so bad, Mama.

HANA: Half the ranch is flooded. At least half.

MURATA: No-no. Quarter, maybe. It's sunny today. It'll dry.

HANA: The seedlings will rot.

MURATA: No-no. It'll dry. It's all right. Better than I expected.

HANA: If we have another bad year, no one will lend us money for the next crop.

MURATA: Don't worry. If it doesn't drain by tomorrow, I'll replant the worst places. We still have some seed left. Yeah, I'll replant.

HANA: More work.

MURATA: Don't worry, Mama. It'll be all right.

HANA *[quietly]*: Papa, where will it end? Will we always be like this—always at the mercy of the weather . . . prices . . . always at the mercy of the Gods?

MURATA *[patting HANA's back]*: Things will change. Wait and see. We'll be back in Japan by . . . in two years. Guarantee. Maybe sooner.

HANA *[dubiously]*: Two years . . .

MURATA *[finding the robe on the bench]*: Ah, look, Mama. Kiyoko-san brought back my robe.

HANA *[sighing]*: Kiyoko-san . . . poor Kiyoko-san. And Emiko-san . . .

MURATA: Ah, Mama. We're lucky. We're lucky, Mama.

[Fade out]

ACT II

Scene iv

The following spring afternoon

ON RISE: *Exterior of the Oka house. OKA is dressed to go out. He wears a sweater, long-sleeved white shirt, dark pants, no tie. He puts his foot to the bench to wipe off his shoe with the palm of his hand. He straightens his sleeve, removes a bit of lint, and runs his fingers through his hair. He hums softly.*

      KIYOKO comes from the house. Her hair is frizzled in a permanent wave, she wears a gaudy new dress and a pair of new shoes. She carries a movie magazine.

OKA *[appreciatively]*: Pretty. Pretty.

KIYOKO *[turning for him]*:   It's not too *hadeh?* I feel strange in colors.

OKA: Oh, no. Young girls should wear bright colors. Time enough to wear gray when you get old. Old-lady colors.

[KIYOKO giggles.]

OKA *[continuing]*:   Sure you want to go to the picture show? It's such a nice day . . . shame to waste in a dark hall.

KIYOKO: Where else can we go?

OKA: We can go to Murata-san's.

KIYOKO: All dressed up?

OKA: Or Nagata-san's. I'll show him what I got for my horse.

KIYOKO: I love the pictures.

OKA: We don't have many nice spring days like this. Here the season is short. Summer comes in like a dragon . . . right behind . . . breathing fire . . . like a dragon. You don't know the summers here. They'll scare you.

[He tousles KIYOKO's hair and pulls a lock of it. It springs back. He shakes his head in wonder.]

OKA *[continuing]*:   Goddam. Curly hair. Never thought curly hair could make you so happy.

KIYOKO *[giggling]*:   All the American girls have curly hair.

OKA: Your friend Masako like it?

KIYOKO *[nodding]*:   She says her mother will never let her get a permanent wave.

OKA: She said that, eh? Bet she's wanting one.

KIYOKO: I don't know about that.

OKA: Bet she's wanting some of your pretty dresses too.

KIYOKO: Her mother makes all her clothes.

OKA: Buying is just as good. Buying is better. No trouble that way.

KIYOKO: Masako's not interested in clothes. She loves the pictures, but her mother won't let her go. Someday, can we take Masako with us?

OKA: If her mother lets her come. Her mother's got a mind of her own. Stiff back.

KIYOKO: But she's nice.

OKA *[dubiously]*:   Oh, yeah. Can't be perfect, I guess. Kiyoko, after the harvest I'll have money, and I'll buy you the prettiest dress in town. I'm going to be lucky this year. I feel it.

KIYOKO: You're already too good to me . . . dresses, shoes, permanent wave . . . movies . . .

OKA: That's nothing. After the harvest, just wait . . .

KIYOKO: . . . magazines. You do enough. I'm happy already.

OKA: You make me happy too, Kiyoko. You make me feel good . . . like a man again. *[That bothers him.]* One day you're going to make a young man happy.

[KIYOKO giggles.]

OKA *[continuing]*:   Someday we going to move from here.

KIYOKO: But we have good friends here, Papa.

OKA: Next year our lease will be up and we got to move.

KIYOKO: The ranch is not ours?

OKA: No. In America Japanese cannot own land. We lease and move every two to three years. Next year we going go someplace where there's young fellows. There's none good enough for you here. Yeah. You going to make a good wife. Already a good cook. I like your cooking.

KIYOKO *[a little embarrassed]*:   Shall we go now?

OKA: Yeah. Put the magazine away.

KIYOKO: I want to take it with me.

OKA: Take it with you?

KIYOKO: Last time, after we came back, I found all my magazines torn in half. Even the new ones.

OKA *[looking toward the house]*:   Torn?

KIYOKO: This is the only one I have left.

OKA: All right, all right.

> *[The two prepare to leave when EMIKO lurches through the door. Her hair is unkempt—she looks wild. She holds an empty can in one hand, the lid in the other.]*

EMIKO: Where is it?

> *[OKA tries to make a hasty departure.]*

KIYOKO: Where is what?

> *[OKA pushes KIYOKO ahead of him, still trying to make a getaway.]*

EMIKO: Where is it? Where is it? What did you do with it?

> *[EMIKO moves toward OKA.]*

OKA *[with false unconcern to KIYOKO]*:   Why don't you walk on ahead to Muratasan's.

KIYOKO: We're not going to the pictures?

OKA: We'll go. First you walk to Murata-san's. Show them your new dress. I'll meet you there.

> *[KIYOKO enters the house, pushing past EMIKO, emerges with a small package, and exits, looking worriedly back at OKA and EMIKO. OKA sighs and shakes his head.]*

EMIKO *[shaking the can]*:   Where is it? What did you do with it?

OKA *[feigning surprise]*:   With what?

EMIKO: You know what. You stole it. You stole my money.

OKA: *Your* money?

EMIKO: I've been saving that money.

OKA: Yeah? Well, where'd you get it? Where'd you get it, eh? You stole it from me! Dollar by dollar! You stole it from me! Out of my pocket!

EMIKO: I saved it!

OKA: From *my* pocket!

EMIKO: It's mine! I saved for a long time. Some of it I brought from Japan.

OKA: *Bakayuna!* What'd you bring from Japan? Nothing but some useless kimonos.

[OKA tries to leave, but EMIKO hangs on to him.]

EMIKO: Give back my money! Thief!

[OKA swings around and balls his fists but doesn't strike.]

OKA: Goddam! Get off me!

EMIKO *[now pleading]*:   Please give it back . . . please . . . please . . .

[EMIKO strokes his legs, but OKA pulls her hands away and pushes her from him.]

EMIKO *[continuing]*:   Oni!

OKA *[seething]*:   Oni? What does that make you? *Oni-baba?* Yeah, that's what you are . . . a devil!

EMIKO: It's mine! Give it back!

OKA: The hell! You think you can live off me and steal my money too? How stupid you think I am?

EMIKO *[tearfully]*:   But I've paid. I've paid . . .

OKA: With what?

EMIKO: You know I've paid.

OKA *[scoffing]*   You call that paying?

EMIKO: What did you do with it?

OKA: I don't have it.

EMIKO: It's gone? It's gone?

OKA: Yeah! It's gone. I spent it. The hell! Every last cent.

EMIKO: The new clothes . . . the curls . . . restaurants . . . pictures . . . shoes . . . My money. My going-home money.

OKA: You through?

EMIKO: What will I do? What (will) . . .

OKA: I don't care what you do. Walk. Use your feet. Swim to Japan. I don't care.
I give you no more than you gave me. Now I don't want anything. I don't care
what you do. *[He walks away.]*

> *[EMIKO still holds the empty can. Offstage we hear Oka's
> car start off. Accustomed to crying alone, she doesn't utter
> a sound. Her shoulders shake, her dry soundless sobs turn
> to a silent laugh. She wipes the dust gently from the can as
> though comforting a friend. Her movements grow sensu-
> ous, her hands move to her own body, around her throat,
> over her breasts, to her hips, caressing, soothing, remind-
> ing her of her lover's hands.]*

> *[Fade out]*

ACT II

Scene v

Same day, late afternoon

> ON RISE: Exterior of the Murata house. The light is soft. HANA
> sweeps the yard; MASAKO hangs a glass wind chime on the
> wall.]

HANA *[directing MASAKO]*:   There. There. That's a good place.
MASAKO: Here?
HANA *[nodding]*:   It must catch the slightest breeze. *[sighing and listening]* It
brings back so much. That's the reason I never hung one before. I guess it
doesn't matter much anymore.
MASAKO: I thought you liked to think about Japan.
HANA *[laughing softly]*:   I didn't want to hear that sound too often . . . get too
used to it. Sometimes you hear something too often, after a while you don't
hear it anymore. I didn't want that to happen. The same thing happens to feelings too, I guess. After a while, you don't feel anymore. You're too young to
understand that yet.
MASAKO: I understand, Mama.
HANA: Wasn't it nice of Kiyoko-san to give you the *furin*?
MASAKO: I love it. I don't know anything about Japan, but it makes me feel
something too.
HANA: Maybe someday when you're grown up, gone away, you'll hear it and
remember yourself as this little girl . . . remember this old house, the ranch,
and . . . your old mama.
MASAKO: That's kind of scary.

[EMIKO enters unsteadily. She carries a bundle wrapped in a colorful scarf (furoshiki). In the package are two beautiful kimonos.]

HANA: Emiko-san! What a pleasant surprise! Please sit down. We were just hanging the wind chime. It was so sweet of Kiyoko-san to give it to Masako. She loves it.

[EMIKO looks mildly interested. She acts as normal as she can throughout the scene, but at times drops the facade, revealing her desperation.]

EMIKO: Thank you. *[She sets the bundle on the bench but keeps her hand on it.]*
HANA: Your family was here earlier.

[EMIKO smiles vaguely.]

HANA *[continuing]*:   On their way to the pictures, I think. Make tea for us, Machan.
EMIKO: Please don't.
HANA: Kiyoko-san was looking so nice . . . her hair all curly. Of course, in our day, straight black hair was desirable. Of course, times change.
EMIKO: Yes . . .
HANA: But she did look fine. My, my, a colorful new dress, new shoes, a permanent wave—looked like a regular American girl. Did you choose her dress?
EMIKO: No . . . I didn't go.
HANA: You know, I didn't think so. Very pretty though. I liked it very much. Of course, I sew all Masako's clothes. It saves money. It'll be nice for you to make things for Kiyoko-san too. She'd be so pleased. I know she'd be pleased.

[While HANA talks, EMIKO plucks nervously at the package. She waits for HANA to stop.]

HANA *[continuing]*:   Emiko-san, is everything all right?
EMIKO *[smiling nervously]*:   Yes.
HANA: Masako, please go make tea for us. See if there aren't any more of those crackers left. Or did you finish them? *[to EMIKO]* We can't keep anything in this house. She eats everything as soon as Papa brings it home. You'd never know it, she's so skinny. We never have anything left for company.
MASAKO: We hardly ever have company anyway.

[HANA gives MASAKO a strong look before MASAKO leaves. EMIKO is lost in her own thoughts.]

HANA: Is there something you . . . I can help you with? *[very gently]* Emiko-san?

EMIKO *[suddenly frightened]*:   Oh, no. I was thinking . . . Now that . . . now that
. . . Masa-chan is growing up . . . older . . .

HANA: Oh, yes.

EMIKO: I was thinking . . .

> *[She stops, puts the package on her lap, and is lost again.]*

HANA: Yes, she *is* growing. Time goes so fast. I think she'll be taller than me
soon. *[She laughs weakly but looks puzzled.]*

EMIKO: Yes . . .

> *[EMIKO's depression pervades the atmosphere. HANA is af-
> fected by it. The two women sit in silence. A small breeze
> moves the wind chimes. At the moment, light grows dim on
> the two lonely figures.]*

> *[MASAKO brings the tray of tea. The light returns to nor-
> mal.]*

HANA *[gently]*:   You're a good girl.

> *[MASAKO looks first to EMIKO, then to her mother. She sets
> the tray on the bench and stands near EMIKO. EMIKO seems
> to notice her for the first time.]*

EMIKO: How are you?

> *[HANA pours the tea.]*

HANA: Emiko-san, is there something I can do for you?

EMIKO: There's . . . I was . . . I . . . Masa-chan will be a young lady soon . . .

HANA: Well, I don't know about "lady."

EMIKO: Maybe she would like a nice . . . nice . . . *[She unwraps the package.]* I
have kimonos I wore in Japan for dancing. Maybe she can . . . if you like, I
mean. They'll be nice on her. She's so slim.

> *[EMIKO shakes out a robe. HANA and MASAKO are im-
> pressed.]*

HANA: Ohhh! Beautiful!

MASAKO: Oh, Mama! Pretty!

> *[They touch the material.]*

MASAKO *[continuing]*:   Gold threads, Mama.

HANA: Brocade!

EMIKO: Maybe Masa-chan would like them. I mean for her school programs . . . Japanese school.

HANA: Oh, no! Too good for country. People will be envious of us . . . wonder
where we got them.

EMIKO: I mean for festivals. *Obon, Hana Matsuri* . . .

HANA: Oh, but you have Kiyoko-san now. You should give them to her. Has
she seen them?

EMIKO: Oh. No.

HANA: She'll love them. You should give them to her—not our Masako.

EMIKO: I thought . . . I mean, I was thinking of . . . if you could give me a little
. . . if you could pay . . . manage to give me something for . . .

HANA: But these gowns, Emiko-san—they're worth hundreds.

EMIKO: I know, but I'm not asking for that. Whatever you can give. Only as
much as you can give.

MASAKO: Mama?

HANA: Masako, Papa doesn't have that kind of money.

EMIKO: Anything you can give. Anything . . .

MASAKO: Ask Papa.

HANA: There's no use asking. I *know* he can't afford it.

EMIKO *[looking at MASAKO]*:   A little at a time . . .

MASAKO: Mama?

HANA *[firmly]*:   No, Masako. This is a luxury.

> *[HANA folds the gowns and puts them away. EMIKO is dec-
> imated. HANA sees this and tries to find a way to help.]*

HANA *[continuing]*:   Emiko-san, I hope you understand.

> *[EMIKO is silent, trying to gather her resources.]*

HANA *[continuing]*:   I know you can sell them and get the full price somewhere. Let's see . . . a family with lots of growing daughters . . . someone who
did well last year. Nagata-san has no girls. Umeda-san has girls but no money.
Well, let's see . . . Maybe not here in this country town. Ah . . . you can take
them to the city—Los Angeles—and sell them to a store. Or terminal Island.
Lots of wealthy fishermen there. Yes, that would be the place. Why, it's no
problem, Emiko-san. Have your husband take them there. I know you'll get
your money. He'll find a buyer. I know he will.

EMIKO: Yes . . . *[She ties the bundle and sits quietly.]*

HANA: Please have your tea. I'm sorry. I really would like to take them for
Masako, but it just isn't possible. You understand, don't you?

> *[EMIKO nods.]*

HANA *[continuing]*:   Please don't feel so . . . so bad. It's not really a matter of
life or death, is it? Emiko-san?

> *[EMIKO nods again. HANA sips her tea.]*

MASAKO: Mama? If you could ask Papa . . .
HANA: Oh, the tea is cold. Masako, could you heat the kettle?
EMIKO: No more. I must be going. *[She picks up her package and rises slowly.]*
HANA *[helplessly]*:   So soon? Emiko-san, please stay.

[EMIKO starts to go.]

HANA *[continuing]*:   Masako will walk with you. *[She pushes MASAKO forward.]*
EMIKO: It's not far.
HANA: Emiko-san? You'll be all right?
EMIKO: Yes . . . yes . . . yes . . .
HANA *[calling after EMIKO]*:   I'm sorry, Emiko-san.
EMIKO: Yes.

[MASAKO and HANA watch as EMIKO leaves. The light grows dim as though a cloud passed over. HANA strokes MASAKO's hair.]

HANA: Your hair is so black and straight . . . nice.

[They stand close. The wind chimes tinkle; light grows dim. Light returns to normal.]

[MURATA enters. He sees the tableau of mother and child and is puzzled.]

MURATA: What's going on here?

[The women part.]

HANA: Oh . . . nothing. Nothing.
MASAKO: Mrs. Oka was here. She had two kimo(nos) . . .
HANA *[putting her hand on MASAKO's shoulder]*:   It was nothing.
MURATA: Eh? What'd she want?
HANA: Later, Papa. Right now, I'd better fix supper.
MURATA *[looking at the sky]*:   Strange how that sun comes and goes. Maybe I didn't need to irrigate . . . looks like rain. *[He remembers.]* Ach! I forgot to shut the water!
MASAKO: I'll do it, Papa.
HANA: Masako, that gate's too heavy for you.
MURATA: She can handle it. Take out the pin and let the gate fall all the way down. All the way. And put the pin back. Don't forget to put the pin back.
HANA: And be careful. Don't fall in the canal.

[MASAKO leaves.]

MURATA: What's the matter with that girl?
HANA: Nothing. Why?
MURATA: Usually have to *beg* her to (do) . . .

HANA: She's growing up.

MURATA: Must be that time of the month.

HANA: Oh, Papa, she's too young for that yet.

MURATA [*genially as they enter the house*]:   Got to start sometime. Looks like I'll be outnumbered soon. I'm outnumbered already.

> [*HANA glances at him and quietly begins preparations for supper. MURATA removes his shirt and picks up a paper. Light fades slowly.*]

> [*Fade out*]

ACT II

Scene vi

Same evening

ON RISE: *Exterior, desert. There is at least one shrub, a tumbleweed maybe. MASAKO walks slowly. From a distance we hear EMIKO singing the song, "And the Soul Shall Dance." MASAKO looks around, sees the shrub, and crouches by it. EMIKO appears. She wears her beautiful kimono tied loosely at her waist. She carries a branch of sage. Her hair is loose.*]

EMIKO: *Akai kuchibiru / Kappu ni yosete / Aoi sake nomya / Kokoro ga odoru Kurai yoru no yume / Setsu nasa yo. . . .*

> [*EMIKO breaks into a dance, laughs mysteriously, turns round and round acting out a fantasy. MASAKO stirs uncomfortably. EMIKO senses a presence. She stops, drops her branch, empties out her sleeve of imaginary flowers at MASAKO, and exits singing.*]

EMIKO [*continuing*]:   *Aoi sake nomya / Yume ga odoru. . . .*

> [*MASAKO watches as EMIKO leaves. She rises slowly and picks up the branch EMIKO has left. She moves forward a step and looks off to the point where EMIKO disappeared.*]

> [*Light slowly fades on MASAKO, and the image of her forlorn form remains etched on the retina.*]

> [*Fade out*]

Study and Discussion Questions

1. What is the setting of this play in time and place? How does the setting help shape what happens?

2. What are the differences between the two wives, Hana and Emiko? What role models does Masako have for becoming a woman?

3. The 13-year-old Masako is the only character Emiko makes a connection with in the play. Why do you think she is drawn to Masako? What is Yamauchi trying to do by creating this connection between Masako and Emiko? How does the final scene change or enhance your thoughts about this connection?

4. How are Kiyoko, Mr. Ota's daughter, and Masako different when Kiyoko first comes to California? How does their relationship evolve? How is the incident of the tongue twisters important? How does Kiyoko change through the course of the play?

5. How do economic conditions constrain different characters in the play? List at least three instances in which money (or the lack of it) is of major importance.

6. Discuss some of the tensions the women in this story encounter being Japanese and living in the United States.

7. What role does music play in *And the Soul Shall Dance?* Read again the lyrics for the song, *And the Soul Shall Dance,* that preface the play. Discuss the events of the play in light of the poem.

Suggestions for Writing

1. Most of the characters experience conflict between wanting to remember Japan, perhaps even return to Japan, and wanting to put Japan out of their minds. Write an exploratory essay about this conflict of immigration, using aspects of the play to illustrate and ground your ideas.

2. Compare/contrast *And the Soul Shall Dance* with Hisaye Yamamoto's short story, "Seventeen Syllables" in terms of the expectations and possibilities for Japanese-American women.

3. Research laws pertaining to Japanese immigrants to the United States prior to World War II, specifically the land ownership laws mentioned in the play. What were the justifications for these laws? What were the effects on the immigrants?

4. Choose one of the six characters and discuss his or her role or function in *And the Soul Shall Dance.*

Critical Resources

1. McDonald, Dorothy Newman and Katherine Newman. "Relocation and Dislocation: The Writings of Hisaye Yamamoto and Wakako Yamauchi." *MELUS* 7 (1980): 21–38.

2. Osborn, William and Slyvia A. Watanabe. "A MELUS Interview: Wakako Yamauchi—Japanese-American Writer." *MELUS* Summer (1998).

3. Yamauchi, Wakako. *Songs my Mother Taught Me: Stories, Plays and a Memoir.* New York: Feminist Press at City University, 1994.

4. Yogi, Stan. "Rebels and Heroines: Subversive Narratives in the Stories of Wakako Yamauchi and Hisaye Yamamoto." *Reading the Literatures of Asian America.* Eds. Shirley Geok-lin Lim and Amy Ling. Philadelphia: Temple UP, 1992. 131–150.

❋ ❋ ❋

NONFICTION

MAXINE HONG KINGSTON (b. 1940)

Maxine Hong Kingston was born in Stockton, California. Her mother, a midwife in China, and her father, a scholar in China, took jobs in a laundrymat after immigrating to the United States. Maxine was the first child of six. Growing up, she was a good student, writing poetry in elementary school and graduating from high school with honors. She received her B.A. in English from the University of California Berkeley in 1962. Soon afterward she moved to Hawaii, where she began to teach and write, sporadically publishing her stories in magazines and newspapers, then publishing a collection of these stories as The Woman Warrior *(1976). Kingston's blending of fiction and nonfiction, as well as her establishment of a much needed Chinese-American literary voice, garnered public attention and strong reviews by critics. Her next book,* China Men *(1980), won the American Book Award for general nonfiction. Other essay collections include* Hawaii's One Summer *(1989). She has experimented with other genres—the novel* Tripmaster Monkey: His Fake Book *(1988), and a collection of poetry* To Be the Poet *(2002). Her most recent work is* The Fifth Book of Peace *(2003). "No Name Woman" is the introductory chapter of* The Woman Warrior.

No Name Woman (1976)

"You must not tell anyone," my mother said, "what I am about to tell you. In China your father had a sister who killed herself. She jumped into the family well. We say that your father has all brothers because it is as if she had never been born.

"In 1924 just a few days after our village celebrated seventeen hurry-up weddings—to make sure that every young man who went 'out on the road' would responsibly come home—your father and his brothers and your grandfather and his brothers and your aunt's new husband sailed for America, the Gold Mountain. It was your grandfather's last trip. Those lucky enough to get contracts waved goodbye from the decks. They fed and guarded the stowaways and helped them off in Cuba, New York, Bali, Hawaii. 'We'll meet in California next year,' they said. All of them sent money home.

"I remember looking at your aunt one day when she and I were dressing; I had not noticed before that she had such a protruding melon of a stomach. But I did not think, 'She's pregnant,' until she began to look like other pregnant women, her shirt pulling and the white tops of her black pants showing. She could not have been pregnant, you see, because her husband had been gone for years. No one said anything. We did not discuss it. In early summer she was ready to have the child, long after the time when it could have been possible.

"The village had also been counting. On the night the baby was to be born the villagers raided our house. Some were crying. Like a great saw, teeth strung with lights, files of people walked zigzag across our land, tearing the rice. Their lanterns doubled in the disturbed black water, which drained away through the broken bunds. As the villagers closed in, we could see that some of them, probably men and women we knew well, wore white masks. The people with long hair hung it over their faces. Women with short hair made it stand up on end. Some had tied white bands around their foreheads, arms, and legs.

"At first they threw mud and rocks at the house. Then they threw eggs and began slaughtering our stock. We could hear the animals scream their deaths—the roosters, the pigs, a last great roar from the ox. Familiar wild heads flared in our night windows; the villagers encircled us. Some of the faces stopped to peer at us, their eyes rushing like searchlights. The hands flattened against the panes, framed heads, and left red prints.

"The villagers broke in the front and the back doors at the same time, even though we had not locked the doors against them. Their knives dripped with the blood of our animals. They smeared blood on the doors and walls. One woman swung a chicken, whose throat she had slit, splattering blood in red arcs about her. We stood together in the middle of our house, in the family hall with the pictures and tables of the ancestors around us, and looked straight ahead.

"At that time the house had only two wings. When the men came back, we would build two more to enclose our courtyard and a third one to begin a second courtyard. The villagers pushed through both wings, even your grandparents' rooms, to find your aunt's, which was also mine until the men returned. From this room a new wing for one of the younger families would grow. They ripped up her clothes and shoes and broke her combs, grinding them underfoot. They tore her work from the loom. They scattered the cooking fire and rolled the new weaving in it. We could hear them in the kitchen breaking our bowls and banging the pots. They overturned the great waist-high earthenware jugs; duck eggs, pickled fruits, vegetables burst out and mixed in acrid torrents. The old woman from the next field swept a broom through the air and loosed the spirits-of-the-broom over our heads. 'Pig.' 'Ghost.' 'Pig,' they sobbed and scolded while they ruined our house.

"When they left, they took sugar and oranges to bless themselves. They cut pieces from the dead animals. Some of them took bowls that were not broken and clothes that were not torn. Afterward we swept up the rice and sewed it back up into sacks. But the smells from the spilled preserves lasted. Your aunt gave birth in the pigsty that night. The next morning when I went for the water, I found her and the baby plugging up the family well.

"Don't let your father know what I told you. He denies her. Now that you have started to menstruate, what happened to her could happen to you. Don't humiliate us. You wouldn't like to be forgotten as if you had never been born. The villagers are watchful."

Whenever she had to warn us about life, my mother told stories that ran like this one, a story to grow up on. She tested our strength to establish realities. Those in the emigrant generations who could not reassert brute survival died young and far from home. Those of us in the first American generations have had to figure out how the invisible world the emigrants built around our childhoods fit in solid America.

The emigrants confused the gods by diverting their curses, misleading them with crooked streets and false names. They must try to confuse their offspring as well, who, I suppose, threaten them in similar ways—always trying to get things straight, always trying to name the unspeakable. The Chinese I know hide their names; sojourners take new names when their lives change and guard their real names with silence.

Chinese-Americans, when you try to understand what things in you are Chinese, how do you separate what is peculiar to childhood, to poverty, insanities, one family, your mother who marked your growing with stories, from what is Chinese? What is Chinese tradition and what is the movies?

If I want to learn what clothes my aunt wore, whether flashy or ordinary, I would have to begin, "Remember Father's drowned-in-the-well sister?" I cannot ask that. My mother has told me once and for all the useful parts. She will add nothing unless powered by Necessity, a riverbank that guides her life. She plants vegetable gardens rather than lawns; she carries the odd-shaped tomatoes home from the fields and eats food left for the gods.

Whenever we did frivolous things, we used up energy; we flew high kites. We children came up off the ground over the melting cones our parents brought home from work and the American movie on New Year's Day—*Oh, You Beautiful Doll* with Betty Grable one year, and *She Wore a Yellow Ribbon* with John Wayne another year. After the one carnival ride each, we paid in guilt; our tired father counted his change on the dark walk home.

Adultery is extravagance. Could people who hatch their own chicks and eat the embryos and the heads for delicacies and boil the feet in vinegar for party food, leaving only the gravel, eating even the gizzard lining—could such people engender a prodigal aunt? To be a woman, to have a daughter in starvation time was a waste enough. My aunt could not have been the lone romantic who gave up everything for sex. Women in the old China did not choose. Some man had commanded her to lie with him and be his secret evil. I wonder whether he masked himself when he joined the raid on her family.

Perhaps she encountered him in the fields or on the mountain where the daughters-in-law collected fuel. Or perhaps he first noticed her in the marketplace. He was not a stranger because the village housed no strangers. She had to have dealings with him other than sex. Perhaps he worked an adjoining field, or he sold her the cloth for the dress she sewed and wore. His demand must have surprised, then terrified her. She obeyed him; she always did as she was told.

When the family found a young man in the next village to be her husband, she stood tractably beside the best rooster, his proxy, and promised before they met that she would be his forever. She was lucky that he was her age and she would be the first wife, an advantage secure now. The night she first saw him, he had sex with her. Then he left for America. She had almost forgotten what he looked like. When she tried to envision him, she only saw the black and white face in the group photograph the men had had taken before leaving.

The other man was not, after all, much different from her husband. They both gave orders: she followed. "If you tell your family, I'll beat you. I'll kill you. Be here again next week." No one talked sex, ever. And she might have separated the rapes from the rest of living if only she did not have to buy her oil from him or gather wood in the same forest. I want her fear to have lasted just as long as rape lasted so that the fear could have been contained. No drawn-out fear. But women at sex hazarded birth and hence lifetimes. The fear did not stop but permeated everywhere. She told the man, "I think I'm pregnant." He organized the raid against her.

On nights when my mother and father talked about their life back home, sometimes they mentioned an "outcast table" whose business they still seemed to be settling, their voices tight. In a commensal tradition, where food is precious, the powerful older people made wrongdoers eat alone. Instead of letting them start separate new lives like the Japanese, who could become samurais and geishas, the Chinese family, faces averted but eyes glowering sideways, hung on to the offenders and fed them leftovers. My aunt must have lived in the same house as my parents and eaten at an outcast table. My mother spoke about the raid as if she had seen it, when she and my aunt, a daughter-in-law to a different household, should not have been living together at all. Daughters-in-law lived with their husbands' parents, not their own; a synonym for marriage in Chinese is "taking a daughter-in-law." Her husband's parents could have sold her, mortgaged her, stoned her. But they had sent her back to her own mother and father, a mysterious act hinting at disgraces not told me. Perhaps they had thrown her out to deflect the avengers.

She was the only daughter; her four brothers went with her father, husband, and uncles "out on the road" and for some years became western men. When the goods were divided among the family, three of the brothers took land, and the youngest, my father, chose an education. After my grandparents gave their daughter away to her husband's family, they had dispensed all the adventure and all the property. They expected her alone to keep the traditional ways, which her brothers, now among the barbarians, could fumble without detection. The heavy, deep-rooted women were to maintain the past against the flood, safe for returning. But the rare urge west had fixed upon our family, and so my aunt crossed boundaries not delineated in space.

The work of preservation demands that the feelings playing about in one's guts not be turned into action. Just watch their passing like cherry blossoms. But perhaps my aunt, my forerunner, caught in a slow life, let dreams grow and fade and after some months or years went toward what persisted. Fear at the enormities of the forbidden kept her desires delicate, wire and bone. She looked at a man because she liked the way the hair was tucked behind his ears, or she liked the question-mark line of a long torso curving at the shoulder and straight at the hip. For warm eyes or a soft voice or a slow walk—that's all—a few hairs, a line, a brightness, a sound, a pace, she gave up family. She offered us up for a charm that vanished with tiredness, a pigtail that didn't toss when the wind died. Why, the wrong lighting could erase the dearest thing about him.

It could very well have been, however, that my aunt did not take subtle enjoyment of her friend, but, a wild woman, kept rollicking company. Imagining her free with sex doesn't fit, though. I don't know any women like that, or men either. Unless I see her life branching into mine, she gives me no ancestral help.

To sustain her being in love, she often worked at herself in the mirror, guessing at the colors and shapes that would interest him, changing them frequently in order to hit on the right combination. She wanted him to look back.

On a farm near the sea, a woman who tended her appearance reaped a reputation for eccentricity. All the married women blunt-cut their hair in flaps about their ears or pulled it back in tight buns. No nonsense. Neither style blew easily into heart-catching tangles. And at their weddings they displayed themselves in their long hair for the last time. "It brushed the backs of my knees," my mother tells me. "It was braided, and even so, it brushed the backs of my knees."

At the mirror my aunt combed individuality into her bob. A bun could have been contrived to escape into black streamers blowing in the wind or in quiet wisps about her face, but only the older women in our picture album wear buns. She brushed her hair back from her forehead, tucking the flaps behind her ears. She looped a piece of thread, knotted into a circle between her index fingers and thumbs, and ran the double strand across her forehead. When she closed her fingers as if she were making a pair of shadow geese bite, the string twisted together catching the little hairs. Then she pulled the thread away from her skin, ripping the hairs out neatly, her eyes watering from the needles of pain. Opening her fingers, she cleaned the thread, then rolled it along her hairline and the tops of her eyebrows. My mother did the same to me and my sisters and herself. I used to believe that the expression "caught by the short hairs" meant a captive held with a depilatory string. It especially hurt at the temples, but my mother said we were lucky we didn't have to have our feet bound when we were seven. Sisters used to sit on their beds and cry together, she said, as their mothers or their slaves removed the bandages for a few minutes each night and let the blood gush back into their veins. I hope that the man my aunt loved appreciated a smooth brow, that he wasn't just a tits-and-ass man.

Once my aunt found a freckle on her chin, at a spot that the almanac said predestined her for unhappiness. She dug it out with a hot needle and washed the wound with peroxide.

More attention to her looks than these pullings of hairs and pickings at spots would have caused gossip among the villagers. They owned work clothes and good clothes, and they wore good clothes for feasting the new seasons. But since a woman combing her hair hexes beginnings, my aunt rarely found an occasion to look her best. Women looked like great sea snails—the corded wood, babies, and laundry they carried were the whorls on their backs. The Chinese did not admire a bent back; goddesses and warriors stood straight. Still there must have been a marvelous freeing of beauty when a worker laid down her burden and stretched and arched.

Such commonplace loveliness, however, was not enough for my aunt. She dreamed of a lover for the fifteen days of New Year's, the time for families to exchange visits, money, and food. She plied her secret comb. And sure enough she cursed the year, the family, the village, and herself.

Even as her hair lured her imminent lover, many other men looked at her. Uncles, cousins, nephews, brothers would have looked, too, had they been home between journeys. Perhaps they had already been restraining their curiosity, and they left, fearful that their glances, like a field of nesting birds, might be startled and caught. Poverty hurt, and that was their first reason for leaving. But another, final reason for leaving the crowded house was the never-said.

She may have been unusually beloved, the precious only daughter, spoiled and mirror gazing because of the affection the family lavished on her. When her husband left, they welcomed the chance to take her back from the in-laws; she could live like the little daughter for just a while longer. There are stories that my grandfather was different from other people, "crazy ever since the little Jap bayoneted him in the head." He used to put his naked penis on the dinner table, laughing. And one day he brought home a baby girl, wrapped up inside his brown western-style greatcoat. He had traded one of his sons, probably my father, the youngest, for her. My grandmother made him trade back. When he finally got a daughter of his own, he doted on her. They must have all loved her, except perhaps my father, the only brother who never went back to China, having once been traded for a girl.

Brothers and sisters, newly men and women, had to efface their sexual color and present plain miens. Disturbing hair and eyes, a smile like no other threatened the ideal of five generations living under one roof. To focus blurs, people shouted face to face and yelled from room to room. The immigrants I know have loud voices, unmodulated to American tones even after years away from the village where they called their friendships out across the fields. I have not been able to stop my mother's screams in public libraries or over telephones. Walking erect (knees straight, toes pointed forward, not pigeon-toed, which is Chinese-feminine) and speaking in an inaudible voice, I have tried to turn myself American-feminine. Chinese communication was loud, public. Only sick people had to whisper. But at the dinner table, where the family members came nearest one another, no one could talk, not the outcasts nor any eaters. Every word that falls from the mouth is a coin lost. Silently they gave and accepted food with both hands. A preoccupied child who took his bowl with one hand got a sideways glare. A complete moment of total attention is due everyone alike. Children and lovers have no singularity here, but my aunt used a secret voice, a separate attentiveness.

She kept the man's name to herself throughout her labor and dying; she did not accuse him that he be punished with her. To save her inseminator's name she gave silent birth.

He may have been somebody in her own household, but intercourse with a man outside the family would have been no less abhorrent. All the village were kinsmen, and the titles shouted in loud country voices never let kinship be forgotten. Any man within visiting distance would have been neutralized as a lover—"brother," "younger brother," "older brother"—one hundred and fifteen relationship titles. Parents researched birth charts probably not so much to assure good fortune as to circumvent incest in a population that has but one hundred surnames. Everybody has eight million relatives. How useless then sexual mannerisms, how dangerous.

As if it came from an atavism deeper than fear, I used to add "brother" silently to boys' names. It hexed the boys, who would or would not ask me to dance, and made them less scary and as familiar and deserving of benevolence as girls.

But, of course, I hexed myself also—no dates. I should have stood up, both arms waving, and shouted out across libraries, "Hey, you! Love me back." I had no idea, though, how to make attraction selective, how to control its direction and magnitude. If I made myself American-pretty so that the five or six Chinese boys in the class fell in love with me, everyone else—the Caucasian, Negro, and Japanese boys—would too. Sisterliness, dignified and honorable, made much more sense.

Attraction eludes control so stubbornly that whole societies designed to organize relationships among people cannot keep order, not even when they bind people to one another from childhood and raise them together. Among the very poor and the wealthy, brothers married their adopted sisters, like doves. Our family allowed some romance, paying adult brides' prices and providing dowries so that their sons and daughters could marry strangers. Marriage promises to turn strangers into friendly relatives—a nation of siblings.

In the village structure, spirits shimmered among the live creatures, balanced and held in equilibrium by time and land. But one human being flaring up into violence could open up a black hole, a maelstrom that pulled in the sky. The frightened villagers, who depended on one another to maintain the real, went to my aunt to show her a personal, physical representation of the break she had made in the "roundness." Misallying couples snapped off the future, which was to be embodied in true offspring. The villagers punished her for acting as if she could have a private life, secret and apart from them.

If my aunt had betrayed the family at a time of large grain yields and peace, when many boys were born, and wings were being built on many houses, perhaps she might have escaped such severe punishment. But the men—hungry, greedy, tired of planting in dry soil, cuckolded—had had to leave the village in order to send food-money home. There were ghost plagues, bandit plagues, wars with the Japanese, floods. My Chinese brother and sister had died of an unknown sickness. Adultery, perhaps only a mistake during good times, became a crime when the village needed food.

The round moon cakes and round doorways, the round tables of graduated size that fit one roundness inside another, round windows and rice bowls—these talismen had lost their power to warn this family of the law: a family must be whole, faithfully keeping the descent line by having sons to feed the old and the dead, who in turn look after the family. The villagers came to show my aunt and her lover-in-hiding a broken house. The villagers were speeding up the circling of events because she was too shortsighted to see that her infidelity had already harmed the village, that waves of consequences would return unpredictably, sometimes in disguise, as now, to hurt her. This roundness had to be made coin-sized so that she would see its circumference: punish her at the birth of her baby. Awaken her to the inexorable. People who refused fatalism because they could invent small resources insisted on culpability. Deny accidents and wrest fault from the stars.

After the villagers left, their lanterns now scattering in various directions toward home, the family broke their silence and cursed her. "Aiaa, we're going to die. Death is coming. Death is coming. Look what you've done. You've killed us. Ghost! Dead ghost! Ghost! You've never been born." She ran out into the fields, far enough from the house so that she could no longer hear their voices, and pressed herself against the earth, her own land no more. When she felt the birth coming, she thought that she had been hurt. Her body seized together. "They've hurt me too much," she thought. "This is gall, and it will kill me." Her forehead and knees against the earth, her body convulsed and then released her onto her back. The black well of sky and stars went out and out and out forever; her body and her complexity seemed to disappear. She was one of the stars, a bright dot in blackness, without home, without a companion, in eternal cold and silence. An agoraphobia rose in her, speeding higher and higher, bigger and bigger; she would not be able to contain it; there would be no end to fear.

Flayed, unprotected against space, she felt pain return, focusing her body. This pain chilled her—a cold, steady kind of surface pain. Inside, spasmodically, the other pain, the pain of the child, heated her. For hours she lay on the ground, alternately body and space. Sometimes a vision of normal comfort obliterated reality: she saw the family in the evening gambling at the dinner table, the young people massaging their elders' backs. She saw them congratulating one another, high joy on the mornings the rice shoots came up. When these pictures burst, the stars drew yet further apart. Black space opened.

She got to her feet to fight better and remembered that old-fashioned women gave birth in their pigsties to fool the jealous, pain-dealing gods, who do not snatch piglets. Before the next spasms could stop her, she ran to the pigsty, each step a rushing out into emptiness. She climbed over the fence and knelt in the dirt. It was good to have a fence enclosing her, a tribal person alone.

Laboring, this woman who had carried her child as a foreign growth that sickened her every day, expelled it at last. She reached down to touch the hot, wet, moving mass, surely smaller than anything human, and could feel that it was human after all—fingers, toes, nails, nose. She pulled it up on to her belly, and it lay curled there, butt in the air, feet precisely tucked one under the other. She opened her loose shirt and buttoned the child inside. After resting, it squirmed and thrashed and she pushed it up to her breast. It turned its head this way and that until it found her nipple. There, it made little snuffling noises. She clenched her teeth at its preciousness, lovely as a young calf, a piglet, a little dog.

She may have gone to the pigsty as a last act of responsibility: she would protect this child as she had protected its father. It would look after her soul, leaving supplies on her grave. But how would this tiny child without family find her grave when there would be no marker for her anywhere, neither in the earth nor the family hall? No one would give her a family hall name. She had taken the child with her into the wastes. At its birth the two of them had felt the same raw pain of separation, a wound that only the family pressing tight could close. A child with no descent line would not soften her life but only trail after her, ghostlike, begging her to give it purpose. At dawn the villagers on their way to the fields would stand around the fence and look.

Full of milk, the little ghost slept. When it awoke, she hardened her breasts against the milk that crying loosens. Toward morning she picked up the baby and walked to the well.

Carrying the baby to the well shows loving. Otherwise abandon it. Turn its face into the mud. Mothers who love their children take them along. It was probably a girl; there is some hope of forgiveness for boys.

"Don't tell anyone you had an aunt. Your father does not want to hear her name. She has never been born." I have believed that sex was unspeakable and words so strong and fathers so frail that "aunt" would do my father mysterious harm. I have thought that my family, having settled among immigrants who had also been their neighbors in the ancestral land, needed to clean their name, and a wrong word would incite the kinspeople even here. But there is more to this silence: they want me to participate in her punishment. And I have.

In the twenty years since I heard this story I have not asked for details nor said my aunt's name; I do not know it. People who can comfort the dead can also chase after them to hurt them further—a reverse ancestor worship. The real punishment was not the raid swiftly inflicted by the villagers, but the family's deliberately forgetting her. Her betrayal so maddened them, they saw to it that she would suffer forever, even after death. Always hungry, always needing, she would have to beg food from other ghosts, snatch and steal it from those whose living descendants give them gifts. She would have to fight the ghosts massed at crossroads for the buns a few thoughtful citizens leave to decoy her away from village and home so that the ancestral spirits could feast unharassed. At peace, they could act like gods, not ghosts, their descent lines providing them with paper suits and dresses, spirit money, paper houses, paper automobiles, chicken, meat, and rice into eternity—essences delivered up in smoke and flames, steam and incense rising from each rice bowl. In an attempt to make the Chinese care for people outside the family, Chairman Mao encourages us now to give our paper replicas to the spirits of outstanding soldiers and workers, no matter whose ancestors they may be. My aunt remains forever hungry. Goods are not distributed evenly among the dead.

My aunt haunts me—her ghost drawn to me because now, after fifty years of neglect, I alone devote pages of paper to her, though not origamied into houses and clothes. I do not think she always means me well. I am telling on her, and she was a spite suicide, drowning herself in the drinking water. The Chinese are always very frightened of the drowned one, whose weeping ghost, wet hair hanging and skin bloated, waits silently by the water to pull down a substitute.

Study and Discussion Questions

1. What is the occasion on which the narrator's mother tells her the story? What is her reason for doing so?
2. What does the title of this piece signify?
3. Why do the villagers raid the house? What were they trying to accomplish at the time? What were they afraid of? What does the narrator say was the "real punishment" they inflicted on her aunt?
4. What are the different stories the narrator makes up to account for her aunt's pregnancy?
5. How does Kingston characterize Chinese immigrants to America?
6. How does the narrator say she has contributed to her aunt's punishment?
7. What does Kingston say about ghosts? What function do they play in the lives of the Chinese villagers?
8. What are the ghosts in the narrator's own life?

Suggestions for Writing

1. What stories were you told, what warnings were you given, at the beginning of puberty?
2. Why does the narrator refuse any longer to participate in her aunt's punishment? How does she act out this refusal?
3. What do we learn from "No Name Woman" about the position of women in prerevolutionary Chinese village society? What do we learn about the position of women today?

Critical Resources

1. Huntley, E. D. *Maxine Hong Kingston: A Critical Companion.* Westport, CT. Greenwood, 2001.
2. Skenasy, Ted and Terra Martin, eds. *Conversations with Maxine Hong Kingston.* Jackson: UP of Mississippi, 1998.
3. *Stories of Maxine Hong Kingston.* Bill Moyers, World of Ideas Series, 1994. 52 minutes. For more information go to <http://www.films.com/id/7649>.
4. Trombley, Laura, ed. *Critical Essays on Maxine Hong Kingston.* New York: G. K. Hall, 1998.

❀ ❀ ❀

AUDRE LORDE (1934–1992)

Born in Harlem of West Indian parents, Audre Lorde began writing poetry at the age of 12, publishing her first poem in Seventeen *magazine as a teenager. She obtained her B.A. in English from Hunter College (New York) in 1961 and a M.A. in Library Science from Columbia University. Lorde described herself as a "black, lesbian, mother, warrior, poet" (Contemporary Authors Online), who, after several years as a librarian, realized that writing and teaching were her true vocations. From 1968 until her death in 1992 (after a long battle with cancer), Lorde held teaching positions at several universities. She eventually returned in 1981 to Hunter College as Professor of English. Her poetry and prose is grounded in the deep sense of her identity as a black, lesbian feminist and is often driven by conflicting emotions of anger and love. Her works include the poetry collections* The First Cities *(1968),* New York Headshop and Museum *(1974),* The Black Unicorn *(1978),* Our Dead Behind Us *(1986), and* The Marvelous Arithmetics of Distance *(1993, published posthumously); the autobiographical works* The Cancer Journals *(1980) and* Zami: A New Spelling of My Name: A Biomythography *(1982); and the essay collections* Sister Outsider *(1984) and* A Burst of Light *(1988). Lorde was a founding editor of Kitchen Table: Women of Color Press. "From the House of Yemanji" articulates Lorde's ambivalent relationship with her mother, as well as the desire to reconnect with her African roots.*

FROM *Zami: A New Spelling of My Name*   (1982)

When I was growing up in my mother's house, there were spices you grated and spices you pounded, and whenever you pounded spice and garlic or other herbs, you used a mortar. Every West Indian woman worth her salt had her own mortar. Now if you lost or broke your mortar, you could, of course, buy another one in the market over on Park Avenue, under the bridge, but those were usually Puerto Rican mortars, and even though they were made out of wood and worked exactly the same way, somehow they were never really as good as West Indian mortars. Now where the best mortars came from I was never really sure, but I knew it must be in the vicinity of that amorphous and mystically perfect place called "home." And whatever came from "home" was bound to be special.

My mother's mortar was an elaborate affair, quite at variance with most of her other possessions, and certainly with her projected public view of herself. It stood, solid and elegant, on a shelf in the kitchen cabinet for as long as I can remember, and I loved it dearly.

The mortar was of a foreign fragrant wood, too dark for cherry and too red for walnut. To my child eyes, the outside was carved in an intricate and most enticing manner. There were rounded plums and oval indeterminate fruit, some long and fluted like a banana, others ovular and end-swollen like a ripe alligator pear. In between these were smaller rounded shapes like cherries, lying in batches against and around each other.

I loved to finger the hard roundness of the carved fruit, and the always surprising termination of the shapes as the carvings stopped at the rim and the bowl sloped abruptly downward, smoothly oval but suddenly businesslike. The heavy sturdiness of this useful wooden object always made me feel secure and somehow full; as if it conjured up from all the many different flavors pounded into the inside wall, visions of delicious feasts both once enjoyed and still to come.

The pestle was long and tapering, fashioned from the same mysterious rose-deep wood, and fitted into the hand almost casually, familiarly. The actual shape reminded me of a summer crook-necked squash uncurled and slightly twisted. It could also have been an avocado, with the neck of the alligator pear elongated and the whole made efficient for pounding, without ever losing the apparent soft firmness and the character of the fruit which the wood suggested. It was slightly bigger at the grinding end than most pestles, and the widened curved end fitted into the bowl of the mortar easily. Long use and years of impact and grinding within the bowl's worn hollow had softened the very surface of the wooden pestle, until a thin layer of split fibers coated the rounded end like a layer of velvet. A layer of the same velvety mashed wood lined the bottom inside the sloping bowl.

My mother did not particularly like to pound spice, and she looked upon the advent of powdered everything as a cook's boon. But there were some certain dishes that called for a particular savory blending of garlic, raw onion, and pepper, and souse was one of them.

For our mother's souse, it didn't matter what kind of meat was used. You could have hearts, or beefends, or even chicken backs and gizzards when we were really poor. It was the pounded-up saucy blend of herb and spice rubbed into the meat before it was left to stand so for a few hours before cooking that made that dish so special and unforgettable. But my mother had some very firm ideas about what she liked best to cook and about which were her favorite dishes, and souse was definitely not one of either.

On the very infrequent occasions that my mother would allow one of us three girls to choose a meal—as opposed to helping to prepare it, which was a daily routine—on those occasions my sisters would usually choose one of those proscribed dishes so dear to our hearts remembered from our relatives' tables, contraband, and so very rare in our house. They might ask for hot dogs, perhaps, smothered in ketchup sauce, or with crusty Boston-baked beans; or american chicken, breaded first and fried crispy the way the southern people did it; or creamed something-or-other that one of my sisters had tasted at school; whathave-you croquettes or anything fritters; or once even a daring outrageous request for slices of fresh watermelon, hawked from the back of a rickety wooden pickup truck with the southern road-dust still on her slatted sides, from which a young bony Black man with a turned-around baseball cap on his head would hang and half-yell, half-yodel—"Wahr—deeeeeee-mayyyyyyy-lawnnnnnnn."

There were many american dishes I longed for too, but on the one or two occasions a year that I got to choose a meal, I would always ask for souse. That way, I knew that I would get to use my mother's mortar, and this in itself was more treat for me than any of the forbidden foods. Besides, if I really wanted hot dogs or anything croquettes badly enough, I could steal some money from my father's pocket and buy them in the school lunch.

"Mother, let's have souse," I'd say, and never even stop to think about it. The anticipated taste of the soft spicy meat had become inseparable in my mind from the tactile pleasures of using my mother's mortar.

"But what makes you think anybody can find time to mash up all that stuff?" My mother would cut her hawk-grey eyes at me from beneath their heavy black brows. "Among-you children never stop to think," and she'd turn back to whatever it was she had been doing. If she had just come from the office with my father, she might be checking the day's receipts, or she might be washing the endless plies of dirty linen that always seemed to issue from rooming-houses.

"Oh, I'll pound the garlic, Mommy!" would be my next line in the script written by some ancient and secret hand, and off I'd go to the cabinet to get down the heavy wooden mortar and pestle.

I took a head of garlic out from the garlic bottle in the icebox, and breaking off ten or twelve cloves from the head, I carefully peeled away the tissue lavender skin, slicing each stripped peg in half lengthwise. I dropped them piece by piece into the capacious waiting bowl of the mortar. Taking a slice from a small onion, I put the rest aside to be used later over the meat, and cutting the slice into quarters, I tossed it into the mortar also. Next came the coarsely ground fresh black pepper, and then a lavish blanketing cover of salt over the whole. Last, if we had any, a few leaves from the top of a head of celery. My mother sometimes added a slice of green pepper, but I did not like the texture of the pepper-skin under the pestle, and preferred to add it along with the sliced onion later on, leaving it all to sit over the seasoned and resting meat.

After all the ingredients were in the bowl of the mortar, I fetched the pestle and placing it into the bowl, slowly rotated the shaft a few times, working it gently down through all the ingredients to mix them. Only then would I lift the pestle, and with one hand firmly pressed around the carved side of the mortar caressing the wooden fruit with my aromatic fingers, I thrust sharply downward, feeling the shifting salt and the hard little pellets of garlic right up through the shaft of the wooden pestle. Up again, down, around, and up—so the rhythm began.

The *thud push rub rotate up* repeated over and over. The muted thump of the pestle on the bed of grinding spice as the salt and pepper absorbed the slowly yielding juices of the garlic and celery leaves.

Thud push rub rotate up. The mingling fragrances rising from the bowl of the mortar.

Thud push rub rotate up. The feeling of the pestle held between my curving fingers, and the mortar's outside rounding like fruit into my palm as I steadied it against my body.

All these transported me into a world of scent and rhythm and movement and sound that grew more and more exciting as the ingredients liquefied.

Sometimes my mother would look over at me with that amused annoyance which passed for tenderness.

"What you think you making there, garlic soup? Enough, go get the meat now." And I would fetch the lamb hearts, for instance, from the icebox and begin to prepare them. Cutting away the hardened veins at the top of the smooth firm muscles, I divided each oval heart into four wedge-shaped pieces, and taking a bit of the spicy mash from the mortar with my fingertips, I rubbed each piece with the savory mix, the pungent smell of garlic and onion and celery enveloping the kitchen.

The last day I ever pounded seasoning for souse was in the summer of my fifteenth year. It had been a fairly unpleasant summer for me. I had just finished my first year in high school. Instead of being able to visit my newly found friends, all of whom lived in other parts of the city, I had had to accompany my mother on a round of doctors with whom she would have long whispered conversations. Only a matter of utmost importance could have kept her away from the office for so many mornings in a row. But my mother was concerned because I was fourteen and a half years old and had not yet menstruated. I had breasts but no period, and she was afraid there was something "wrong" with me. Yet, since she had never discussed this mysterious business of menstruation with me, I was certainly not supposed to know what all this whispering was about, even though it concerned my own body.

Of course, I knew as much as I could have possibly found out in those days from the hard-to-get books on the "closed shelf" behind the librarian's desk at the public library, where I had brought a forged note from home in order to be allowed to read them, sitting under the watchful eye of the librarian at a special desk reserved for that purpose.

Although not terribly informative, they were fascinating books, and used words like *menses* and *ovulation* and *vagina*.

But four years before, I had had to find out if I was going to become pregnant, because a boy from school much bigger than me had invited me up to the roof on my way home from the library and then threatened to break my glasses if I didn't let him stick his "thing" between my legs. And at that time I knew only that being pregnant had something to do with sex, and sex had something to do with that thin pencil-like "thing" and was in general nasty and not to be talked about by nice people, and I was afraid my mother might find out and what would she do to me then? I was not supposed to be looking at the mailboxes in the hallway of that house anyway, even though Doris was a girl in my class at St. Mark's who lived in that house and I was always so lonely in the summer, particularly that summer when I was ten.

So after I got home I washed myself up and lied about why I was late getting home from the library and got a whipping for being late. That must have been a hard summer for my parents at the office too, because that was the summer that

I got a whipping for something or other almost every day between the Fourth of July and Labor Day.

When I wasn't getting whippings, I hid out at the library on 135th Street, and forged notes from my mother to get books from the "closed shelf," and read about sex and having babies, and waited to become pregnant. None of the books were very clear to me about the relationship between having your period and having a baby, but they were all very clear about the relationship between penises and getting pregnant. Or maybe the confusion was all in my own mind, because I had always been a very fast but not a very careful reader.

So four years later, in my fifteenth year, I was a very scared little girl, still half-afraid that one of that endless stream of doctors would look up into my body and discover my four-year-old shame and say to my mother, "Aha! So that's what's wrong! Your daughter is about to become pregnant!"

On the other hand, if I let Mother know that I knew what was happening and what these medical safaris were all about, I would have to answer her questions about how and wherefore I knew, since she hadn't told me, divulging in the process the whole horrible and self-incriminating story of forbidden books and forged library notes and rooftops and stairwell conversations.

It was a year after the rooftop incident, when we had moved farther uptown. The kids at St. Catherine's seemed to know a lot more about sex than at St. Mark's. In the eighth grade, I had stolen money and bought my classmate Adeline a pack of cigarettes and she had confirmed my bookish suspicions about how babies were made. My response to her graphic descriptions had been to think to myself, *there obviously must be another way that Adeline doesn't know about, because my parents have children and I know they never did anything like that!* But the basic principles were all there, and sure enough they were the same as I had gathered from *The Young People's Family Book.*

So in my fifteenth summer, on examining table after examining table, I kept my legs open and my mouth shut, and when I saw blood on my pants one hot July afternoon, I rinsed them out secretly in the bathroom and put them back on wet because I didn't know how to break the news to my mother that both her worries and mine were finally over. (All this time I had at least understood that having your period was a sign you were not pregnant.)

What then happened felt like a piece of an old and elaborate dance between my mother and me. She discovers finally, through a stain on the toilet seat left there on purpose by me as a mute announcement, what has taken place; she scolds, "Why didn't you tell me about all of this, now? It's nothing to get upset over, you are a woman, not a child anymore. Now you go over to the drugstore and ask the man for . . ."

I was just relieved the whole damn thing was over with. It's difficult to talk about double messages without having a twin tongue. Nightmarish evocations and restrictions were being verbalized by my mother:

"This means from now on you better watch your step and not be so friendly with every Tom, Dick, and Harry . . ." (which must have meant my staying late after school to talk with my girlfriends, because I did not even know any boys); and, "Now remember, too, after you wrap up your soiled napkins in newspaper, don't leave them hanging around on the bathroom floor where your father has to see them, not that it's anything shameful but all the same, remember . . ."

Along with all of these admonitions, there was something else coming from my mother that I could not define. It was the lurking of that amused/annoyed brow-furrowed half-smile of hers that made me feel—all her nagging words to the contrary—that something very good and satisfactory and pleasing to her had just happened, and that we were both pretending otherwise for some very wise and secret reasons. I would come to understand these reasons later, as a reward, if I handled myself properly. Then, at the end of it all, my mother thrust the box of Kotex at me (I had fetched it in its plain wrapper back from the drugstore, along with a sanitary belt), saying to me,

"But look now what time it is already, I wonder what we're going to eat for supper tonight?" She waited. At first I didn't understand, but I quickly picked up the cue. I had seen the beefends in the icebox that morning.

"Mommy, please let's have some souse—I'll pound the garlic." I dropped the box onto a kitchen chair and started to wash my hands in anticipation.

"Well, go put your business away first. What did I tell you about leaving that lying around?" She wiped her hands from the washtub where she had been working and handed the plain wrapped box of Kotex back to me.

"I have to go out, I forgot to pick up tea at the store. Now make sure you rub the meat good."

When I came back into the kitchen, my mother had left. I moved toward the kitchen cabinet to fetch down the mortar and pestle. My body felt new and special and unfamiliar and suspect all at the same time.

I could feel bands of tension sweeping across my body back and forth, like lunar winds across the moon's face. I felt the slight rubbing bulge of the cotton pad between my legs, and I smelled the delicate breadfruit smell rising up from the front of my print blouse that was my own womansmell, warm, shameful, but secretly utterly delicious.

Years afterward when I was grown, whenever I thought about the way I smelled that day, I would have a fantasy of my mother, her hands wiped dry from the washing, and her apron untied and laid neatly away, looking down upon me lying on the couch, and then slowly, thoroughly, our touching and caressing each other's most secret places.

I took the mortar down, and smashed the cloves of garlic with the edge of its underside, to loosen the thin papery skins in a hurry. I sliced them and flung them into the mortar's bowl along with some black pepper and celery leaves. The white salt poured in, covering the garlic and black pepper and pale chartreuse celery fronds like a snowfall. I tossed in the onion and some bits of green pepper and reached for the pestle.

It slipped through my fingers and clattered to the floor, rolling around in a semicircle back and forth, until I bent to retrieve it. I grabbed the head of the wooden stick and straightened up, my ears ringing faintly. Without even wiping it, I plunged the pestle into the bowl, feeling the blanket of salt give way, and the broken cloves of garlic just beneath. The downward thrust of the wooden pestle slowed upon contact, rotated back and forth slowly, and then gently altered its rhythm to include an up and down beat. Back and forth, round, up and down, back, forth, round, round, up and down.... There was a heavy fullness at the root of me that was exciting and dangerous.

As I continued to pound the spice, a vital connection seemed to establish itself between the muscles of my fingers curved tightly around the smooth pestle in its insistent downward motion, and the molten core of my body whose source emanated from a new ripe fullness just beneath the pit of my stomach. That invisible thread, taut and sensitive as a clitoris exposed, stretched through my curled fingers up my round brown arm into the moist reality of my armpits, whose warm sharp odor with a strange new overlay mixed with the ripe garlic smells from the mortar and the general sweat-heavy aromas of high summer.

The thread ran over my ribs and along my spine, tingling and singing, into a basin that was poised between my hips, now pressed against the low kitchen counter before which I stood, pounding spice. And within that basin was a tiding ocean of blood beginning to be made real and available to me for strength and information.

The jarring shocks of the velvet-lined pestle, striking the bed of spice, traveled up an invisible pathway along the thread into the center of me, and the harshness of the repeated impacts became increasingly more unbearable. The tidal basin suspended between my hips shuddered at each repetition of the strokes which now felt like assaults. Without my volition my downward thrusts of the pestle grew gentler and gentler, until its velvety surface seemed almost to caress the liquefying mash at the bottom of the mortar.

The whole rhythm of my movements softened and elongated, until, dreamlike, I stood, one hand tightly curved around the carved mortar, steadying it against the middle of my body; while my other hand, around the pestle, rubbed and pressed the moistening spice into readiness with a sweeping circular movement.

I hummed tunelessly to myself as I worked in the warm kitchen, thinking with relief about how simple my life would be now that I had become a woman. The catalogue of dire menstruation-warnings from my mother passed out of my head. My body felt strong and full and open, yet captivated by the gentle motions of the pestle, and the rich smells filling the kitchen, and the fullness of the young summer heat.

I heard my mother's key in the lock.

She swept into the kitchen briskly, like a ship under full sail. There were tiny beads of sweat over her upper lip, and vertical creases between her brows.

"You mean to tell me no meat is ready?" My mother dropped her parcel of tea onto the table, and looking over my shoulder, sucked her teeth loudly in weary disgust. "What do you call yourself doing, now? You have all night to stand up there playing with the food? I go all the way to the store and back already and still you can't mash up a few pieces of garlic to season some meat? But you know how to do the thing better than this! Why you vex me so?"

She took the mortar and pestle out of my hands and started to grind vigorously. And there were still bits of garlic left at the bottom of the bowl.

"Now you do, so!" She brought the pestle down inside the bowl of the mortar with dispatch, crushing the last of the garlic. I heard the thump of wood brought down heavily upon wood, and I felt the harsh impact throughout my body, as if something had broken inside of me. Thump, thump, went the pestle, purposefully, up and down in the old familiar way.

"It was getting mashed, Mother," I dared to protest, turning away to the icebox. "I'll fetch the meat." I was surprised at my own brazenness in answering back.

But something in my voice interrupted my mother's efficient motions. She ignored my implied contradiction, itself an act of rebellion strictly forbidden in our house. The thumping stopped.

"What's wrong with you, now? Are you sick? You want to go to your bed?"

"No, I'm all right, Mother."

But I felt her strong fingers on my upper arm, turning me around, her other hand under my chin as she peered into my face. Her voice softened.

"Is it your period making you so slow-down today?" She gave my chin a little shake, as I looked up into her hooded grey eyes, now becoming almost gentle. The kitchen felt suddenly oppressively hot and still, and I felt myself beginning to shake all over.

Tears I did not understand started from my eyes, as I realized that my old enjoyment of the bone-jarring way I had been taught to pound spice would feel different to me from now on, and also that in my mother's kitchen there was only one right way to do anything. Perhaps my life had not become so simple, after all.

My mother stepped away from the counter and put her heavy arm around my shoulders. I could smell the warm herness rising from between her arm and her body, mixed with the smell of glycerine and rosewater, and the scent of her thick bun of hair.

Study and Discussion Questions

1. What words in Lorde's description of the mortar evoke a sensual response? Group the words under the various senses: taste, touch, smell, sight, sound.
2. Do the same with the first description of pounding the spice.
3. Make a list of words to characterize the narrator's mother.
4. Why are both the narrator and her mother silent with each other on the subject of menstruation?
5. How and to what extent does her mother's behavior toward the narrator change when she begins menstruating?
6. How does the narrator feel when her mother takes over the mortar and pestle?
7. What does the narrator say she has learned about herself?

Suggestions for Writing

1. Describe an object or an activity important to you, using sensual detail as Lorde does in her description of the mortar or in her description of pounding the spice.
2. Describe the process of making a favorite meal in that same kind of vivid detail.
3. Compare/contrast the two scenes Lorde gives us of using the mortar. How do they differ? What is the tone of each one? What do you think the writer's purpose was in including two such scenes? What is the effect on you of the repetition?

Critical Resources

1. *A Litany for Survival: The Life and Work of Audre Lorde.* Directors Ada G. Griffin and Michelle Parkerson. New York: Third World Newsreel, 1996. 60 minutes. For more information go to <http://www.pbs.org/pov/pov1996/alitanyforsurvival/index.html>.
2. Burr, Zofia. *Of Women, Poetry and Power: Strategies of Address in Dickinson, Miles, Brooks, Lorde and Angelou.* Urbana: U of Illinois P, 2002.
3. Dhairyam, Sagri. "Artifacts for Survival: Remapping the Contours of Poetry with Audre Lorde." *Feminist Studies* 18.2 (1992): 228–56.
4. Provost, Kara. "Becoming Afrekete: The Trickster in The Work of Audre Lorde-Maskers and Tricksters." *MELUS* 20.4 (1995): 45–59.

TOMMI AVICOLLI MECCA (b. 1951)

Tommi Avicolli Mecca is a self-described "longtime southern Italian queer writer, activist, and performer" who was born in working-class South Philadelphia in 1951. Whether he is writing prose, poetry, or drama, Avicolli Mecca's work frequently explores his struggles growing up gay in a conservative, working-class southern Italian-American family. Working against main-stream stereotypes of southern Italian-American life, Avicolli Mecca's direct and sincere writing style seeks to give a voice to the gay male experience. He has published Between Little Rock and a Hard Place *(1993) and coedited* Hey Paesan: Writings by Lesbians and Gay Men of Italian Descent *(1999). His work has appeared in numerous anthologies, including* Gay and Lesbian Poetry in Our Time *(1988),* That's Revolting! *(2004), and* Speaking for Our Lives and The Whole World Was Watching *(2004). A former editor of the* Philadelphia Gay News, *he currently does occasional op eds. for the* SF Bay Guardian *and writes a regular column for* www.sanfranciscosentinel.com. *He recently wrote and starred in a one-man show,* Italian. Queer. Dangerous *(2005), based on the stories he has written for his weekly column. In "He Defies You Still: Memoirs of a Sissy," first published in 1985, Avicolli Mecca moves between literary genres to recount some difficult past experiences. He has since published a longer, more detailed version entitled "Memoirs of a South Philly Sissy" (1991).*

He Defies You Still: The Memoirs of a Sissy   (1985)

Scene One:

A homeroom in a Catholic high school in South Philadelphia. The boy sits quietly in the first aisle, third desk, reading a book. He does not look up, not even for a moment. He is hoping no one will remember he is sitting there. He wishes he were invisible. The teacher is not yet in the classroom so the other boys are talking and laughing loudly.

Suddenly, a voice from beside him: "Hey, you're a faggot, ain't you?"

The boy does not answer. He goes on reading his book, or rather pretending he is reading his book. It is impossible to actually read now.

"Hey, I'm talking to you!"

The boy still does not look up. He is so scared his heart is thumping madly. But he can't look up.

"Faggot, I'm talking to you!"

To look up is to meet the eyes of the tormentor.

Suddenly a sharp pencil point is thrust into the boy's arm. He jolts, shaking off the pencil, aware that there is blood seeping from the wound.

"What did you do that for?" he asks timidly.

"Cause I hate faggots," the other boy says, laughing. Some other boys begin to laugh, too. A symphony of laughter. The boy feels as if he's going to cry. But he must not cry. Must not cry. So he holds back the tears and tries to read the book again. He must read the book. Read the book.

When the teacher arrives a few minutes later, the class quiets down. The boy does not tell the teacher what has happened. He spits on the wound to clean it, dabbing it with a tissue until the bleeding stops. For weeks he fears some dreadful infection from the lead in the pencil point.

Scene Two:

The boy is walking home from school. A group of boys (two, maybe three, he is not certain) grab him from behind, drag him into an alley and beat him up. When he gets home, he races up to his room, refusing dinner ("I don't feel well," he tells his mother through the locked door) and spends the night alone in the dark wishing he would die. . . .

These are not fictitious accounts—I *was* that boy. Having been branded a sissy by neighborhood children because I preferred jump rope to baseball and dolls to playing soldiers, I was often taunted with "hey sissy" or "hey faggot" or "yoo hoo, honey" when I left the house.

To avoid harassment, I spent many summers alone in my room. I went out on rainy days when the street was empty.

I came to like being alone. I didn't need anyone, I told myself over and over. I was an island. Contact with others meant pain. Alone, I was protected. I began writing poems, then short stories. There was no reason to go outside anymore. I had a world of my own.

> In the schoolyard today
> they'll single you out
> Their laughter will leave your ears ringing
> like the church bells
> that once awed you . . .[1]

School was one of the more painful experiences of my youth. The neighborhood bullies could be avoided. The taunts of the children living in those endless row houses could be evaded by staying in my room. But school was something I had to face day after day for some two hundred mornings a year.

I had few friends in school. Some kids would talk to me, but few wanted to be known as my close friend. Afraid of labels. If I was a sissy, then they would be sissies, too. I was condemned to loneliness.

Fortunately, a new boy moved into our neighborhood and befriended me; he wasn't afraid of the labels. He protected me when the other guys threatened to beat me up. He walked me home from school; he broke through the terrible loneliness. We were in third or fourth grade at the time.

We spent a summer or two together. Then his parents sent him to camp and I was once again confined to my room.

Scene Three:

High school lunchroom. The boy sits at a table near the back of the room. Without warning, his lunch bag is grabbed and tossed to another table. Someone opens it and confiscates a package of Tastykakes; another boy takes the sandwich. The empty bag is tossed back to the boy who stares at it, dumbfounded. He should be used to this; it has happened before.

Someone says, "Faggot," laughing. There is always laughter. It does not annoy him anymore.

There is no teacher nearby. There is never a teacher around. And what would he say if there were? Could he report the crime? He would be jumped

---

[1]From the poem "Faggot," by Tommi Avicolli, published in *GPU News,* September 1979. [Author's note]

after school if he did. Besides, it would be his word against theirs. Teachers never noticed anything. They never heard the taunts. Never heard the word, "faggot." They were the great deaf mutes, pillars of indifference; a sissy's pain was not relevant to history and geography and god made me to love honor and obey him, amen.

The boy reaches into his pocket for some money, but there's only a few coins. Always just a few coins. He cleans windshields at his father's gas station on Saturdays and Sundays to earn money. But it's never much. Only enough now to buy a carton of milk and some cookies. Only enough to watch the other boys eat and laugh, hoping they'll choke on their food. . . .

Scene Four:

High school religion class. Someone has a copy of *Playboy*. Father N. is not in the room yet; he's late, as usual. Someone taps the boy roughly on the shoulder. He turns. A finger points to the centerfold model, pink fleshy body, thin and sleek. Almost painted. Not real. The other asks in a mocking voice, "Hey, does she turn you on? Look at those tits!"

The boy smiles, nodding meekly; turns away.

The other jabs him harder on the shoulder, "Hey, what'samatter, don't you like girls?"

Laughter. Thousands of mouths; unbearable din of laughter. In the arena: thumbs down. Don't spare the queer.

"Wanna suck my dick, huh? That turn you on, faggot!"

What did being a sissy really mean? It was a way of walking (from the hips rather than the shoulders); it was a way of talking (often with a lisp or in a high-pitched voice); it was a way of relating to others (gently, not wanting to fight, or hurt anybody's feelings). It was being intelligent ("an egghead" they called it sometimes); getting good grades. It meant not being interested in sports, not playing football in the street after school; not discussing teams and scores and play-offs. And it involved not showing a fervent interest in girls, not talking about scoring or tits or *Playboy* centerfolds. Not concealing pictures of naked women in your history book; or porno books in your locker.

On the other hand, anyone could be a "faggot." It was a catchall. If you did something that didn't conform to the acceptable behavior of the group, then you risked being called a faggot. It was the most commonly used put-down. It kept guys in line. They became angry when somebody called them a faggot. More fights started over calling someone a faggot than anything else. The word had power. It toppled the male ego, shattered his delicate facade, violated the image he projected. He was tough. Without feeling. Faggot cut through all this. It made him vulnerable. Feminine. And feminine was the worst thing he could possibly be. Girls were fine for fucking, but no boy in his right mind wanted to be like them. A boy was the opposite of a girl. He was not feminine. He was not feeling. He was not weak.

Just look at the gym teacher who growled like a dog; or the priest with the black belt who threw kids against the wall in rage when they didn't know their Latin. They were men, they got respect.

But not the physics teacher who preached pacificism during lectures on the nature of atoms. Everybody knew what he was—and why he believed in the antiwar movement.

Scene Five:

FATHER: I wanna see you walk, Mark.
MARK: What do you mean?
FATHER: Just walk, Mark.
MARK: (Starts to walk) I don't understand.
FATHER: That's it, just walk.
MARK: (Walks back and forth)
FATHER: Now come here.

(Mark approaches; father slaps him across the face, hard)

MARK: What was that for?
FATHER: I want you to walk right now.
MARK: What do you mean?
FATHER: Stop fooling around, Mark, I want you to walk like a man.
MARK: Dad, I . . .
FATHER: (Interrupting) Don't say another word. Just get over there and walk right—walk like a man.[2]

My parents only knew that the neighborhood kids called me names. They begged me to act more like the other boys. My brothers were ashamed of me. They never said it, but I knew. Just as I knew that my parents were embarassed by my behavior.

At times, they tried to get me to act differently. Once my father lectured me on how to walk right. I'm still not clear on what that means. Not from the hips, I guess; don't "swish" like faggots do.

A nun in elementary school told my mother at open house that there was "something wrong with me." I had draped my sweater over my shoulders like a girl, she said. I was a smart kid, no complaints about my grades, but I should know better than to wear my sweater like a girl.

My mother stood there, mute. I wanted her to say something, to chastise the nun, to defend me. But how could she? This was a nun talking—representative of Jesus, protector of all that was good and decent.

---

[2]From the play *Judgement of the Roaches,* by Tommi Avicolli, produced in Philadelphia at the Gay & Lesbian Coffee house, the Painted Bride Arts Center, and the University of Pennsylvania; aired over WXPN-FM in four parts; and presented at the Lesbian/Gay Conference in Norfolk, VA, July 1980. [Author's note]

An uncle once told me I should start "acting like a boy" instead of a girl. Everybody seemed ashamed of me. And I guess I was ashamed of myself, too. It was hard not to be.

Scene Six:

PRIEST: Do you like girls, Mark?
MARK: Uh-huh.
PRIEST: I mean REALLY like them?
MARK: Yeah—they're okay.
PRIEST: There's a role they play in your salvation. Do you understand it, Mark?
MARK: Yeah.
PRIEST: You've got to like girls. Even if you should decide to enter the seminary, it's important to keep in mind God's plan for a man and a woman. . . .[3]

Catholicism of course condemned homosexuality. Effeminacy was tolerated as long as the effeminate person did not admit to being gay. Thus, priests could be effeminate because they weren't gay.

As a sissy, I couldn't count on support from the church. A male's sole purpose in life was to father children—souls for the church to save. The only hope a homosexual had of attaining salvation was to remain totally celibate. Don't even think of touching another boy. To think of a sin was a sin. And to sin was to put a mark on the soul. Sin—led to hell. There was no way around it. If you sinned, you were doomed.

Realizing I was gay wasn't an easy task. Although I knew I was attracted to boys by the time I was about eleven, I didn't connect this attraction to homosexuality. I was not queer. Not I. I was merely appreciating a boy's good looks, his fine features, his proportions. It didn't seem to matter that I didn't appreciate a girl's looks in the same way. There was no twitching in my thighs when I gazed upon a beautiful girl. But I wasn't queer.

We sat through endless English classes, and history courses about the wars between men who were not allowed to love each other. No gay history was ever taught. You're just a faggot. Homosexuals had never contributed to the human race. God destroyed the queers in Sodom and Gommorrah.

I resisted that label—queer—for the longest time. Even when everything pointed to it, I refused to see it. I was certainly not queer. Not I.

Near the end of my junior year in high school, most of the teasing and taunting had let up. Now I was just ignored. Besides, I was getting a reputation for being a hippie, since I spoke up in social studies classes against the war, and wore my hair as long as I could without incurring the wrath of the administration. When your hair reached a certain length, you were told to get a hair cut.

---

[3]Ibid. [Author's note]

If you didn't, you were sent down to the vice principal's office where you were given a hair cut.

I had a friend toward the end of junior year; his name was Joe. He introduced me to Jay at the bowling alley in South Philadelphia. I knew immediately I was in love with Jay.

A relationship developed. It was all very daring; neither of us understood what was happening. I still rejected the label. I wasn't queer. He wasn't queer. But I knew I was in love with him. I told myself that all the time. Yet I wasn't a homosexual.

Franny was a queer. He lived a few blocks away. He used to dress in women's clothes and wait for the bus on the corner. Everybody laughed at Franny. Everybody knew he was queer.

Then, one night, Halloween, a chilly October night, Jay called:

Scene Seven:

. . ."What?"

"It's wrong."

"What's wrong."

Tossing in my sleep—sweating. It was the winter of '69. The heavy woolen cover became a thick shroud on top of me. The heat pricked me like so many needles.

"Why can't I see you tonight?"

"We can't see each other anymore. . . ."

My heart was an acrobat. It leaped like a frog. Landed in a deep puddle. Help, it shouted. It was going down for the third time.

"Why?" I felt nauseous. I was going to vomit.

"We can't. I've got to go."

"Wait—!"

"What?"

There were tears running down my cheeks in streams that left a salty residue at the corners of my lips. The record player in the background shut off, closing me in. The walls of the room collapsed. I was entombed.

"Please, talk to me. I can't let you go like this. I want to know what's wrong. Please . . ."

"I can't see you anymore. It's over. It was a mistake."

"It wasn't a mistake, Jay. I—I love you."

"Don't say that!" Voice quivering; don't force me to see things I don't want to see right now.

"But I do. And you love me. Admit it. Don't break it off now. Admit it. Admit that you love me."

"I've got to go."

"You can't go. Admit it!"

"Goodbye."

"Jay?"

Silence.[4]

We learned about Michelangelo, Oscar Wilde, Gertrude Stein—but never that they were queer. They were not queer. Walt Whitman, the "father of American poetry," was not queer. No one was queer. I was alone, totally unique. One of a kind. Except for Franny who wore dresses and makeup. Where did Franny go every night? Were there others like me somewhere? Another planet, perhaps?

In school, they never talked of queers. They did not exist. The only hint we got of this other species was in religion class. And even then it was clouded in mystery—never spelled out. It was a sin. Like masturbation. Like looking at *Playboy* and getting a hard-on. A sin.

Once a progressive priest in senior-year religion class actually mentioned homosexuals—he said the word, broke the silence—but he was talking about homosexuals as pathetic and sick. Fixated at some early stage; penis, anal, whatever. Only heterosexuals passed on to the nirvana of sexual development.

No other images from the halls of the Catholic high school except those the other boys knew: swishy faggot sucking cock in an alley somewhere, grabbing asses in the bathroom. Never mentioning how straight boys craved blow jobs, too.

It was all a secret. You were not supposed to talk about queers. Whisper maybe. Laugh about them, yes. But don't be open, honest; don't try to understand. Don't cite their accomplishments. No history faces you this morning. You're a faggot. No history—a faggot.

Epilogue:

The boy marching down Spruce Street. Hundreds of queers. Signs proclaiming gay pride. Speakers. Tables with literature from gay groups. A miracle, he is thinking. Tears are coming loose now. Someone hugs him.

> You could not control
> the sissy in me
> nor could you exorcise him
> nor electrocute him
> You declared him illegal illegitimate
> insane and immature
> but he defies you still.[5]

Study and Discussion Questions

1. List the eight scenes Avicolli presents to the reader.
2. What were the narrator's responses to being tormented by his classmates in elementary school?

---

[4]From the novel *Deaf Mute's Final Dance*, by Tommi Avicolli. [Author's note]
[5]From the poem "Sissy Poem," published in *Magic Doesn't Live Here Anymore*, Spruce Street Press, 1976. [Author's note]

3. List the words and/or labels for homosexual used in this essay. Add others you know of. How does this list make you feel.
4. What is the distinction between "sissy" and "faggot," according to Avicolli?
5. How did the narrator's parents cope with his "difference"?
6. Most of us went through the experience of having our first teenage romance end in failure. Why is the narrator's experience of this common phenomenon even more devastating than most of ours?
7. Discuss the poem in the epilogue.
8. Discuss voice and tone in this personal narrative.

Suggestions for Writing

1. How and why did the narrator resist accepting who he was? What mores in the Church, the school curriculum, and society in general guided him toward this resistance?
2. Describe an experience in which you were seen as different in some way.
3. Avicolli says no gay history or literature was taught when he was in school; for example, the fact that Michelangelo, Oscar Wilde, Gertrude Stein, and Walt Whitman were gay was never mentioned. Can you remember occasions in your own educational experience when homosexuality was a subject, even in passing? Discuss.

Critical Resources

1. Avicolli Mecca, Tommi. "Queer's Eye View." *SanfranciscoSentinel.com.* April 22, 2005 http://www.sanfranciscosentinel.com/id274.htm. A biweekly online column written by Avicolli Mecca.
2. Cappelo, Mary and Wallace Sillanpoa. "Compagna/Compagno: A Conversation." *Melus* Spring (1977): 55–88.
3. Rigoglioso, Marguerite. "Bowing to Mecca: An Interview with Playwright Tommi Avicolli Mecca." *Women Visionaries.* April 22, 2005. http://www .womenvisionaries.com/marguerite/index.html.

DOROTHY ALLISON (b. 1949)

Dorothy Allison was born in Greenville, South Carolina, and was the first person from her family to finish high school. She studied at Florida Presbyterian College (now Eckerd College) and the New School for Social Research in New York City. Working in the tradition of other southern writers such as Flannery O'Connor and William Faulkner, Allison's writings offer a more contemporary and complex picture of southern, working-class culture. In both her poetry and fiction, Allison's working-class, female characters struggle to find understanding as they grapple with issues of class, gender and sexuality. Her work includes The Women Who Hate Me: Poetry 1980–1990 *(1991); the novels* Bastard Out of Carolina *(1992), and* Cavedweller *(1998); a collection of short stories,* Trash *(1988); an essay collection,* Skin: Talking About Sex, Class and Literature *(1993); and the mem-oir,* One or Two Things I Know for Sure *(1995). She is currently working on a science fiction trilogy. "Gun Crazy," first printed in* Skin, *tells the story of one girl's experience learning to shoot a real gun.*

Gun Crazy (1993)

When we were little, my sister and I would ride with the cousins in the back of my uncle Bo's pickup truck when he drove us up into the foothills where we could picnic and the men could go shooting. I remember standing up behind the cab, watching the tree branches filter the bright Carolina sunshine, letting the wind push my hair behind me, and then wrestling with my cousin, Butch, until my aunt yelled at us to stop.

"Ya'll are gonna fall out," she was always screaming, but we never did.

Every stop sign we passed was pocked with bullet holes.

"Fast flying bees," Uncle Jack told us with a perfectly serious expression.

"Hornets with lead in their tails," Bo laughed.

My mama's youngest brother, Bo, kept his guns, an ought-seven rifle and a lovingly restored old Parker shotgun, wrapped in a worn green army blanket. A fold of the blanket was loosely stitched down a third of its length to make a cloth bag, the only sewing Bo ever did in his life. He kept his cleaning kit—a little bag of patches and a plastic bottle of gun oil—in the blanket pouch with the guns. Some evenings he would spread the blanket out in front of the couch and sit there happily cleaning his guns slowly and thoroughly. All the while he would sip cold beer and talk about what a fine time a man could have with his weapons out in the great outdoors. "You got to sit still, perfectly still," he'd say, nod, and sip again, then dab a little more gun oil on the patch he was running through the rifle barrel.

"Oh, you're good at that," someone would always joke.

"The man an't never shot an animal once in his life," Bo's wife, Nessa, told us. "Shot lots of bottles, whiskey bottles, beer bottles, coke-cola bottles. The man's one of the great all-time bottle destroyers."

I grinned. Stop signs and bottles, paper targets and wooden fences. My uncles loved to shoot, it was true, but the only deer they ever brought home was one found drowned in a creek and another that Uncle Jack hit head-on one night when he was driving his Pontiac convertible with the busted headlights.

"Let me help you," I begged my uncle Bo one night when he had pulled out his blanket kit and started the ritual of cleaning his gun. I was eleven, shy but fearless. Bo just looked at me over the angle of the cigarette jutting out of the corner of his mouth. He shook his head.

"I'd be careful," I blurted.

"Nessa, you hear this child?" Bo yelled in the direction of the kitchen and then turned back to me. "An't no such thing as careful where girls and guns are concerned." He took the cigarette out of his mouth and gave me another of those cool, distant looks. "You an't got no business thinking about guns."

"But I want to learn to shoot."

He laughed a deep throaty laugh, coughed a little, then laughed again. "Girls don't shoot," he told me with a smile. "You can do lots of things, girl, but not shooting. That just an't gonna happen."

I glared at him and said, "I bet Uncle Jack will teach me. He knows how careful I can be."

Bo shook his head and tucked the cigarette back in the corner of his mouth. "It an't about careful, it's about you're a girl. You can whine and wiggle all you wont. An't nobody in this family gonna teach you to shoot." His face was stern, his smile completely gone. "That just an't gonna happen."

When I was in high school my best girlfriend was Anne, whose mama worked in the records division at the local children's hospital. One Sunday Anne invited me to go over to the woods out behind the mental hospital, to a hollow there where we could do some plinking.

"Plinking?"

"You know, plinking. Shooting bottles and cans." She pushed her hair back off her face and smiled at me. "If there's any water we'll fill the bottles up and watch it shoot up when the glass breaks. That's my favorite thing."

"You got a gun?" My mouth was hanging open.

"Sure. Mama gave me a rifle for my birthday. Didn't I tell you?"

"I don't think so." I looked away, so she wouldn't see how envious I felt. Her mama had given her a gun for her sixteenth birthday! I had always thought Anne's mama was something special, but that idea was simply amazing.

Anne's mama refused to cook, smoked Marlboros continuously, left the room any time any of her three children mentioned their dead father, and drank cocktails every evening while leaning back in her Lazy-Boy lounge chair and wearing dark eyeshades. "Don't talk to me," she'd hiss between yellow stained teeth. "I got crazy people and drunken orderlies talking at me all day long. I come home, I want some peace and quiet."

"My mama thinks a woman should be able to take care of herself," Anne told me.

"Right," I agreed. "She's right." Inside, I was seething with envy and excitement. Outside, I kept my face smooth and noncommittal. I wanted to shoot, wanted to shoot a shotgun like all my uncles, pepper stop signs and scare dogs. But I'd settle for a rifle, the kind of rifle a woman like Anne's mama would give her sixteen-year-old daughter.

That Sunday I watched closely as Anne slid a bullet into the chamber of her rifle and sighted down the gully to the paper target we had set up thirty feet away. Anne looked like Jane Fonda in *Cat Ballou*[1] after she lost her temper—fierce, blonde, and competent. I swallowed convulsively and wiped sweaty palms on my jeans. I would have given both my big toes to have been able to stand like that, legs apart, feet planted, arms up, and the big rifle perfectly steady as the center circle target was fissured with little bullet holes.

Anne was myopic, skinny, completely obsessed with T. E. Lawrence,[2] and neurotically self-conscious with boys, but holding that rifle tight to her shoulder and peppering the target, she looked different—older and far more interesting. She looked sexy, or maybe the gun looked sexy, I wasn't sure. But I wanted that look. Not Anne, but the power. I wanted to hold a rifle steady, the stock butting my shoulder tightly while I hit the target dead center. My mouth went dry. Anne showed me how to aim the gun a little lower than the center of the target.

"It shoots a little high," she said. "You got to be careful not to let it jump up when it fires." She stood behind me and steadied the gun in my hands. I put the little notch at the peak of the barrel just under the target, tightened my muscles, and pulled the trigger. The rifle still jerked up a little, but a small hole appeared at the outer edge of the second ring of the target.

"Goddamn!" Anne crowed. "You got it, girl." I let the barrel of the rifle drop down, the metal of the trigger guard smooth and warm under my hand.

You got to hold still, I thought. Perfectly still. I sighted along the barrel again, shifting the target notch to the right of the jars Anne had set up earlier. I concentrated, focused, felt my arm become rigid, stern and strong. I pulled back on the trigger slowly, squeezing steadily, the way in the movies they always said it was supposed to be done. The bottle exploded, water shooting out in a wide fine spray.

"Goddamn!" Anne shouted again. I looked over at her. Her glasses had slipped down on her nose and her hair had fallen forward over one eye. Sun shone on her sweaty nose and the polished whites of her teeth. She was staring at me like I had stared at her earlier, her whole face open with pride and delight.

Sexy, yeah. I pointed the barrel at the sky and let my mouth widen into a smile.

"Goddamn," I said, and meant it with all my heart.

Study and Discussion Questions

1. List some details Allison gives us to establish the physical and social setting of her narrative. What do we learn about her family, her locale, and her social class in the first few paragraphs?
2. What does the second short section, about Bo, tell us about the place and use of guns in the lives of Allison's people?

---

[1] Actor (b. 1937) in 1965 American movie about a school teacher turned outlaw.
[2] British scholar and soldier (1888–1935), known as "Lawrence of Arabia."

3. Why does the eleven-year-old first person narrator want to learn to shoot? How does her uncle respond to this yearning and why does he respond the way he does?

4. How is Anne's mama "something special"? Who is she set in contrast to? What are the two contrasting philosophies about girls and guns we see in "Gun Crazy"?

5. In the fifth section, seven years or so after the narrative begins, the narrator finally does get to shoot a rifle. List several details that demonstrate how she feels about this.

Suggestions for Writing

1. Allison deftly and succinctly builds the narrative through five short sections. Consider Allison's "Gun Crazy" as an argument as well as a story. Trace the development of her argument from section one through section five. What does she establish in each of the five sections?

2. a. Guns and learning to shoot or handle them become in this autobiographical story a "contested symbol." What function does knowing how to shoot and care for a gun have in Allison's Southern white working-class culture? What is skill with a gun symbolic of; who are the contestants in the story for this symbol; what is the contest about; how is it waged; what is the prize?

   b. Think of one other symbol in contemporary culture that you see as contested, and discuss.

3. In the fifth and last section of "Gun Crazy," Allison mentions Jane Fonda in the film *Cat Ballou* as well as T. E. Lawrence (Lawrence of Arabia). Why is she invoking these two figures and how is she using them? How are both of them cultural icons? Think of other figures in the popular imagination that you might evoke and discuss what meanings these have.

Critical Resources

1. Connie Griffin, "Going Naked into the World: Recovery and Representation in the Works of Dorothy Allison." *Concerns* 26.3 (1999): 6–20.

2. Sandell, Jillian. "Telling Stories of 'Queer White Trash': Race, Class, and Sexuality in the Work of Dorothy Allison." *White Trash: Race and Class in America*. Wray, Matt and Annalee Newitz, eds. New York: Routledge, 1997. 211–330.

3. *Two or Three Things But Nothing For Sure*. A documentary based on Allison's work *Two or Three Things I Know for Sure*. Director Tina DiFeliciantonia and Jane C. Wagner. Naked Eye Productions, 1998. See http://nakedeyeproductions.com/ for more information.

❀ ❀ ❀

JOY HARJO (b. 1951)

Joy Harjo was born in Tulsa, Oklahoma, and grew up there and in New Mexico. She is Muskeegee/Creek and of mixed descent—her mother Cherokee, French and Irish, her father full-blooded Cherokee. Harjo has described her childhood as "tempestuous." At the age of 16 she was thrown out of her house and forced to survive on her own. Despite such hardships, Harjo entered the University of New Mexico to study medicine, though she soon switched to creative writing and began writing poetry: "I don't believe I would be alive today if it hadn't been for writing . . . writing helped me give voice to turn around a terrible silence that was killing me. And on a larger level, if we, as Indian people, Indian woman, keep silent, then we will disappear" (The Spiral of Memory: Interviews: Joy Harjo *1996). Harjo's poetry reflects this sentiment, often politically charged and speaking out against the violence and oppression of Native-American women. Harjo has taught creative writing at several colleges and universities. She also writes music and plays the saxophone.* Native Joy for Real *is her 1997 CD with her band,* Poetic Justice. *Her poetry collections include* The Last Song *(1975),* She Had Some Horses *(1983),* In Mad Love and War *(1990),* The Woman Who Fell From the Sky *(1996),* A Map to the Next World: Poetry and Tales *(2000), and* How We Become Human *(2002). "Remember" was first published in* She Had Some Horses.

Three Generations of Native American Women's Birth Experience

It was still dark when I awakened in the stuffed back room of my mother-in-law's small rented house with what felt like hard cramps. At 17 years of age I had read everything I could from the Tahlequah Public Library about pregnancy and giving birth. But nothing prepared me for what was coming. I awakened my child's father and then ironed him a shirt before we walked the four blocks to the Indian hospital because we had no car and no money for a taxi. He had been working with another Cherokee artist silk-screening signs for specials at the supermarket and making $5 a day, and had to leave me alone at the hospital because he had to go to work. We didn't awaken his mother. She had to get up soon enough to fix breakfast for her daughter and granddaughter before leaving for her job at the nursing home. I knew my life was balanced at the edge of great, precarious change and I felt alone and cheated. Where was the circle of women to acknowledge and honor this birth?

It was still dark as we walked through the cold morning, under oaks that symbolized the stubbornness and endurance of the Cherokee people who had made Tahlequah their capital in the new lands. I looked for handholds in the misty gray sky, for a voice announcing this impending miracle. I wanted to change everything; I wanted to go back to a place before childhood, before our tribe's removal to Oklahoma. What kind of life was I bringing this child into? I was a poor, mixed-blood woman heavy with a child who would suffer the struggle of poverty, the legacy of loss. For the second time in my life I felt the sharp tug of my own birth cord, still connected to my mother. I believe it never pulls away, until death, and even then it becomes a streak in the sky symbolizing that most important warrior road. In my teens I had fought my mother's weaknesses with all my might, and here I was at 17, becoming as my mother, who was in Tulsa, cooking breakfasts and preparing for the lunch shift at a factory cafeteria as I walked to the hospital to give birth. I should be with her; instead, I was far from her house, in the house of a mother-in-law who later would try to use witchcraft to destroy me.

After my son's father left me I was prepped for birth. This meant my pubic area was shaved completely and then I endured the humiliation of an enema, all at the hands of strangers. I was left alone in a room painted government green. An overwhelming antiseptic smell emphasized the sterility of the hospital, a hospital built because of the U.S. government's treaty and responsibility to provide health care to Indian people.

I intellectually understood the stages of labor, the place of transition, of birth—but it was difficult to bear the actuality of it, and to bear it alone. Yet in some ways I wasn't alone, for history surrounded me. It is with the birth of children that history is given form and voice. Birth is one of the most sacred acts we take part in and witness in our lives. But sacredness seemed to be far from my lonely labor room in the Indian hospital. I heard a woman screaming in the next room with her pain, and I wanted to comfort her. The nurse used her as a bad example to the rest of us who were struggling to keep our suffering silent.

The doctor was a military man who had signed on this watch not for the love of healing or out of awe at the miracle of birth, but to fulfill a contract for medical school payments. I was another statistic to him; he touched me as if he were moving equipment from one place to another. During my last visit I was given the option of being sterilized. He explained to me that the moment of birth was the best time to do it. I was handed the form but chose not to sign it, and am amazed now that I didn't think too much of it at the time. Later I would learn that many Indian women who weren't fluent in English signed, thinking it was a form giving consent for the doctor to deliver their babies. Others were sterilized without even the formality of signing. My light skin had probably saved me from such a fate. It wouldn't be the first time in my life.

When my son was finally born I had been deadened with a needle in my spine. He was shown to me—the incredible miracle nothing prepared me for—then taken from me in the name of medical progress. I fell asleep with the weight of chemicals and awoke yearning for the child I had suffered for, had anticipated in the months proceeding from his unexpected genesis when I was still 16 and a student at Indian school. I was not allowed to sit up or walk because of the possibility of paralysis (one of the drug's side effects), and when I finally got to hold him, the nurse stood guard as if I would hurt him. I felt enmeshed in a system in which the wisdom that had carried my people from generation to generation was ignored. In that place I felt ashamed I was an Indian woman. But I was also proud of what my body had accomplished despite the rape by the bureaucracy's machinery, and I got us out of there as soon as possible. My son would flourish on beans and fry bread, and on the dreams and stories we fed him.

My daughter was born four years later, while I was an art student at the University of New Mexico. Since my son's birth I had waitressed, cleaned hospital rooms, filled cars with gas (while wearing a miniskirt), worked as a nursing assistant, and led dance classes at a health spa. I knew I didn't want to cook and waitress all my life, as my mother had done. I had watched the varicose veins grow branches on her legs, and as they grew, her zest for dancing and sports dissolved into utter tiredness. She had been born with a caul over her face, the sign of a gifted visionary.

My earliest memories are of my mother writing songs on an ancient Underwood typewriter after she had washed and waxed the kitchen floor on her hands and knees. She too had wanted something different for her life. She had left an impoverished existence at age 17, bound for the big city of Tulsa. She was shamed in a time in which to be even part Indian was to be an outcast in the great U.S. system. Half her relatives were Cherokee full-bloods from near Jay, Oklahoma, who for the most part had nothing to do with white people. The other half were musically inclined "white trash" addicted to country-western music and Holy Roller fervor. She thought she could disappear in the city; no one would know her family, where she came from. She had dreams of singing and had once been offered a job singing on the radio but turned it down because she was shy. Later one of her songs would be stolen before she could copyright it and would make someone else rich. She would quit writing songs. She and my father would divorce and she would be forced to work for money to feed and clothe four children, all born within two years of each other.

As a child growing up in Oklahoma, I liked to be told the story of my birth. I would beg for it while my mother cleaned and ironed. "You almost killed me," she would say. "We almost died." That I could kill my mother filled me with remorse and shame. And I imagined the push-pull of my life, which is a legacy I deal with even now when I am twice as old as my mother was at my birth. I loved to hear the story of my warrior fight for my breath. The way it was told, it had been my decision to live. When I got older, I realized we were both nearly casualties of the system, the same system flourishing in the Indian hospital where later my son Phil would be born.

My parents felt lucky to have insurance, to be able to have their children in the hospital. My father came from a fairly prominent Muscogee Creek family. *His* mother was a full-blood who in the early 1920s got her degree in art. She was a painter. She gave birth to him in a private hospital in Oklahoma City; at least that's what I think he told me before he died at age 53. It was something of which they were proud.

This experience was much different from my mother's own birth. She and five of her six brothers were born at home, with no medical assistance. The only time a doctor was called was when someone was dying. When she was born her mother named her Wynema, a Cherokee name my mother says means beautiful woman, and Jewell, for a can of shortening stored in the room where she was born.

I wanted something different for my life, for my son, and for my daughter, who later was born in a university hospital in Albuquerque. It was a bright summer morning when she was ready to begin her journey. I still had no car, but I had enough money saved for a taxi for a ride to the hospital. She was born "naturally," without drugs. I could look out of the hospital window while I was in labor at the bluest sky in the world. I had support. Her father was present in the delivery room—though after her birth he disappeared on a drinking binge. I understood his despair, but did not agree with the painful means to describe it. A few days later Rainy Dawn was presented to the sun at her father's pueblo and given a name so that she will always be recognized as a part of the people, as a child of the sun.

That's not to say that my experience in the hospital reached perfection. The clang of metal against metal in the delivery room had the effect of a tuning fork reverberating fear in my pelvis. After giving birth I held my daughter, but they took her from me for "processing." I refused to lie down to be wheeled to my room after giving birth; I wanted to walk out of there to find my daughter. We reached a compromise and I rode in a wheelchair. When we reached the room I stood up and walked to the nursery and demanded my daughter. I knew she needed me. That began my war with the nursery staff, who deemed me unknowledgeable because I was Indian and poor. Once again I felt the brushfire of shame, but I'd learned to put it out much more quickly, and I demanded early release so I could take care of my baby without the judgment of strangers.

I wanted something different for Rainy, and as she grew up I worked hard to prove that I could make "something" of my life. I obtained two degrees as a single mother. I wrote poetry, screenplays, became a professor, and tried to live a life that would be a positive influence for both of my children. My work in this life has to do with reclaiming the memory stolen from our peoples when we were dispossessed from our lands east of the Mississippi; it has to do with restoring us. I am proud of our history, a history so powerful that it both destroyed my father and guarded him. It's a history that claims my mother as she lives not far from the place her mother was born, names her as she cooks in the cafeteria of a small college in Oklahoma.

When my daughter told me she was pregnant, I wasn't surprised. I had known it before she did, or at least before she would admit it to me. I felt despair, as if nothing had changed or ever would. She had run away from Indian school with her boyfriend and they had been living in the streets of Gallup, a border town notorious for the suicides and deaths of Indian peoples. I brought her and her boyfriend with me because it was the only way I could bring her home. At age 16, she was fighting me just as I had so fiercely fought my mother. She was making the same mistakes. I felt as if everything I had accomplished had been in vain. Yet I felt strangely empowered, too, at this repetition of history, this continuance, by a new possibility of life and love, and I steadfastly stood by my daughter.

I had a university job, so I had insurance that covered my daughter. She saw an obstetrician in town who was reputed to be one of the best. She had the choice of a birthing room. She had the finest care. Despite this, I once again battled with a system in which physicians are taught the art of healing by dissecting cadavers. My daughter went into labor a month early. We both knew intuitively the baby was ready, but how to explain that to a system in which numbers and statistics provide the base of understanding? My daughter would have her labor interrupted; her blood pressure would rise because of the drug given to her to stop the labor. She would be given an unneeded amniocentesis and would have her labor induced—after having it artificially stopped! I was warned that if I took her out of the hospital so her labor could occur naturally my insurance would cover nothing.

My daughter's induced labor was unnatural and difficult, monitored by machines, not by touch. I was shocked. I felt as if I'd come full circle, as if I were watching my mother's labor and the struggle of my own birth. But I was there in the hospital room with her, as neither my mother had been for me, nor her mother for her. My daughter and I went through the labor and birth together.

And when Krista Rae was born she was born to her family. Her father was there for her, as were both her grandmothers and my friend who had flown in to be with us. Her paternal great-grandparents and aunts and uncles had also arrived from the Navajo Reservation to honor her. Something *had* changed.

Four days later, I took my granddaughter to the Saguaro forest before dawn and gave her the name I had dreamed for her just before her birth. Her name looks like clouds of mist settling around a sacred mountain as it begins to speak. A female ancestor approaches on a horse. We are all together.

Study and Discussion Questions

1. The birth of Harjo's first child was a miserable experience for her. List the factors that made it so.
2. How was the birth of Harjo's daughter, four years later, different from the birth of her son? How was it similar?
3. "Something *had* changed," Harjo writes, comparing her daughter's experience giving birth to her own experiences. What had changed? What hadn't?
4. Harjo also discusses the birth of her mother and her own birth. Why does she describe them in the middle of her essay, not (since they came first) at the start?
5. List instances where Harjo mentions social class and/or her Native American ethnicity as being factors in the options for birth and treatment she receives.
6. Note where Harjo mentions "shame." What about the situations she was in provoked shame in her?
7. Give instances of Harjo's pride in her family and her heritage.
8. What are the differences, according to Harjo, between the traditional Native American or natural childbirth experience and the typical birth experience available through Western medicine?

9. "Three Generations of Native American Women's Birth Experience" is a personal narrative essay. Discuss how Harjo puts together elements of memoir and argument to make a case for a more natural, less technological experience of giving birth.

Suggestions for Writing

1. Describing the birth of her son, Harjo writes, "I felt enmeshed in a system in which the wisdom that had carried my people from generation to generation was ignored." Write as much as you can about what that wisdom might be.
2. Narrate the story of your own birth, as you might have heard it from your mother or other family members. If you don't know or remember the story, ask for this important piece of your own history. You can tell the story however you like, making choices about point of view, characters, setting, dialogue, and plot.
3. If you hope some day to be involved in a birth experience (as mother, father, family, close friend), what would you like it to be like? What role should medical science and medical technology play?

Growing Up and Growing Older Paper Topics

1. Compare two works that provide insight into the social context of birth. (Suggestions: Huxley, *Brave New World;* Olds, "The Language of the Brag"; Harjo, "Three Generations of Native American Women's Birth Experience")
2. Discuss the socialization of young people into racial, ethnic, social class, and/or gender roles in one or more works. (Suggestions: Kingston, "No Name Woman"; Kincaid, "Girl"; Allison, "Gun Crazy"; Avicolli Mecca, "He Defies You Still: The Memoirs of a Sissy"; Morrison, *The Bluest Eye*)
3. Discuss the portrayal of growing up in terms of the closing off of possibilities in one or more works. (Suggestions: Huxley, *Brave New World;* Brooks, "We Real Cool"; Levine, "Among Children")
4. Discuss the portrayal of growing *older* in terms of the closing off of possibilities in one or more works. (Suggestions: Updike, "Ex-Basketball Player"; Beckett, "Krapp's Last Tape"; Eliot, "The Love Song of J. Alfred Prufrock"; Shakespeare, "That time of year thou mayst in me behold")
5. Discuss the portrayal of growing old in terms of the opening up of possibilities in one or more works. (Suggestions: Williams, "To a Poor Old Woman"; Yeats, "Sailing to Byzantium"; Klepfisz, "they did not build wings for them")
6. Discuss one or more works as explorations of what it means to be an adult. (Suggestions: Hawthorne, "Young Goodman Brown"; Cisneros, "The Family of Little Feet"; Millay, "Grown-Up"; Alexie, "Jesus Christ's Half-Brother Is Alive and Well on the Spokane Indian Reservation")
7. Compare the treatment of their subject in two poems by the same author. (Suggestions: Yeats, Brooks, Millay, Plath, Smith, Grahn, cummings)

8. Discuss the struggle to grow and thrive in environments characterized by poverty and prejudice. (Suggestions: Baldwin, "Sonny's Blues"; Alexie, "Jesus Christ's Half-Brother is Alive and Well on the Spokane Indian Reservation"; Levine, "Among Children")

9. Discuss the poet's use of sound and imagery to express his or her feelings about death in one or more works. (Suggestions: Thomas, "Do Not Go Gentle Into That Good Night"; Hemphill, "June 25"; Smith, "Undertaker")

10. Discuss growing up as a search for identity in one or more works. (Suggestions: Allison, "Gun Crazy"; Kingston, "No Name Woman"; Brooks, "We Real Cool"; Yamauchi, "And the Soul Shall Dance")

11. Discuss the connections between identity, memory, and spiritual wholeness in one or more works. (Suggestions: Harjo, "Remember"; Hawthorne, "Young Goodman Brown", Lorde, "From The House of Yemanja")

12. Compare the writer's portrayal of illness in relation to identity, social attitudes, and/or aging. (Suggestions: Schreiber, "diagnosis (4-10-86)"; Hemphill, "June 25"; Freeman, "A Mistaken Charity")

13. Discuss the portrayal of pregnancy and/or childbirth in one or more works. (Suggestions: Derricotte, "Transition"; Olds, "The Language of the Brag"; Brooks, "the mother"; Butler, "Bloodchild"; Harjo, "Three Generations of Native American Women's Birth Experience")

14. Discuss self-image and old age in one or more works. (Suggestions: Freeman, "A Mistaken Charity"; Beckett, "Krapp's Last Tape"; Yeats, "Sailing to Byzantium")

15. How are parents and childhood years remembered in one or more literary works? (Suggestions: Lorde, "From the House of Yemanja" and *Zami: A New Spelling of My Name;* Hayden, "Those Winter Sundays"; Plath, "The Colossus"; Roethke, "My Papa's Waltz")

WOMEN AND MEN

Sidney Goodman (1936–), "Ann and Andrew Dintenfass" (1971). Charcoal, 27 × 32½ in.
Courtesy of Terry Dintenfass, Inc., New York.

From "The Song of Solomon" to the stories of Ernest Hemingway and the poems of Adrienne Rich, the politics of sexuality has been a major subject of literature. Different cultures and historical eras have written into their drama, fiction, poetry, and nonfiction their sexual/social codes: what it means to be a woman, what it means to be a man, what behavior is appropriate and permissible for each gender, how men and women are expected to meet and marry or not, and how women and men form bonds with members of their own sex. Gender and sexuality are political, in the larger sense of that term, because they justify and exemplify the distribution and management of power.

Karl Shapiro's "Buick," a love poem to a car, makes us think of other instances in which men have assigned female gender to objects they control and direct. Olgo Broomas's poem, "Cinderella," considers the plight of the token woman. Jo Carson, in "I Cannot Remember All the Times" (Varieties of Protest), and Barbara Kingsolver, in "This House I Cannot Leave," write about violence against women. And Christina Garcia's story "Ines in the Kitchen" focuses on the shaping of a young wife by her husband to be exactly the type of woman he requires. We see a further example of sexual politics as power relations in Charlotte Perkins Gilman's 1892 short story, "The Yellow Wallpaper," in which a woman is confined to her room (of weird yellow wallpaper) by her physician husband for a "rest cure." The first person narrator writes: "There comes John, and I must put this away—he hates to have me write a word."

The different ways women and men perceive the world and the conflict, trouble, tragedy, and sometimes comedy that result have been the subject of much literature. From Shakespearean drama to television sitcoms, misunderstandings that arise when males and females look at the same event and interpret it in widely divergent ways have been a source of laughter and of anger, of tragedy, and of comedy. The way men and women see and judge each other's behavior is central to many of the works included in this section. Muriel Rukeyser's poem "Waiting for Icarus" retells with sardonic humor the Greek myth of the man who stole his father's wings and flew too high. Rukeyser provides us the perspective of the woman who waits for Icarus, increasingly annoyed as the day wears on. Susan Glaspell's play *Trifles* is a murder mystery that turns on the amazingly different data women and men gather when they look at the same crime scene. Tragic misperception (helped along by treachery) is certainly central to Shakespeare's great tragedy about jealousy and love, *Othello*. Why are we so ready to believe the worst about those we love the best? The malicious Iago easily manipulates Othello into a belief that his beloved Desdemona has betrayed him. In *Othello*, not only gender differences but also cultural differences lead to tragic mistakes of perception; Othello is a Moor trying and often failing to understand the Venetian society he has moved into. Woman as the embodiment of mysterious and inexplicable yearnings of the puzzled male consciousness is central to Jean Toomer's "Fern," an attempt by a northern black man to come to terms with the pain and beauty of the South.

The roles women and men are trained to assume can be comfortable or entrapping. Irish playwright J. M. Synge's one-act play *Riders to the Sea* explores the traditional kinds of work, the differing dangers and expectations, in the lives of men and women in the bleak Aran Islands off the coast of Ireland in 1904, while a number of the selections included in this section, written in the second half of the twentieth century, explore the meaning of gender identity. Tupac Shakur's rap song "Keep Ya Head Up" and John Updike's "A & P" both deal with what it means "to be a man" and with the associated social concepts of "honor," "responsibility" and maybe "bravery." But what is a woman's place? How are women defined? Judy Grahn's story "Boys at the Rodeo" looks at one example of twentieth-century ritualized machismo, an afternoon at the rodeo, from a feminist perspective. The narrator's point of view, both inside and outside the system she observes, is crucial to the story's meaning and power. Judy Brady's satiric essay "I Want a Wife" defines the nurturing, supporting, and mirroring functions of the role of a wife in terms that are simultaneously comic and furious, whereas Kate Chopin's ironic "The Story of an Hour," published in 1894, considers the life of a wife versus that of a woman alone. Escaped slave Sojourner Truth's speech "Ain't I a Woman" reminds readers that gender roles have a racial (and, by implication, class) component. Her speech challenges the definition of "woman" as a white and middle-class lady: "I could work as much and eat as much as a man—when I could get it—and bear the lash as well! And ain't I a woman?" Richard Rodriguez's personal essay "Huck Finn, Dan Quayle, and the Value of Acceptance" ponders what is involved in "coming out" to one's immigrant parents.

Some of the selections included here focus on women characters testing the limits of their socially defined roles. Virginia Woolf's sketch of Shakespeare's hypothetical sister, Judith, shows what might have happened in the Elizabethan Age to a young woman rebelling against social convention. Marge Piercy's "The woman in the ordinary" describes a woman on the verge of breaking out of her socially defined limitations: "in you bottled up is a woman peppery as curry." Irena Klepfisz's "they did not build wings for them (Growing Up and Growing Older) transforms social stereotypes of old women, in her poem they disappear, move north to the ocean to become artists or move inland to the woods, "where the world was a passionate place." It is useful to compare these two poems from the second wave of feminism (roughly 1967 to the present) with an example from an earlier era of feminist writing (roughly 1875 to 1919), Charlotte Perkins Gilman's 1892 short story "The Yellow Wallpaper," which chronicles an ambiguous breakthrough that is also a breakdown and that raises important questions about social conventions and the social definition of madness. Poems by Alma Luz Villanueva, "Crazy Courage," and Stefanie Malis, "Transsexual Cloud," focus on transgender identity.

Beyond the sexual politics of gender (which we consider from other perspectives in Growing Up and Growing Older and Varieties of Protest), the most common crisis we encounter in the realm of sexual politics begins when we fall in love. The meaning and the experience of love have traditionally been subjects of lyric poetry: from Shakespeare's sonnets to Adrienne Rich's *Twenty-One Love Poems;* from Ted Hughes's view of a failed and destructive marriage

in "The Lovepet" to ntozake shange's choreopoem about a relationship she
managed to get out of just in time, "somebody almost walked off wid alla my
stuff," from Edna St. Vincent Millay's "Love is not all: it is not meat nor drink"
to D. H. Lawrences's gorgeous morning after portrait of a lover, "Gloire de
Dijon"; from John Donne's comic poem "The Flea" to Langston Hughes's brief
and chilling "Mellow," from Alice Bloch's progress report on a lesbian relationship, "Six Years," to Elizabeth Bishop's villanelle about loss, "One Art." These
poems present a variety of relations between lovers—ritualized equality or inequality, conflict and hostility, romance and reverence, presence and absence—
and they include realistic as well as idealistic explorations of human relations in
the realm of love. In each case, the images that the poet uses to express or describe love are a clue to the sexual politics of the poem. Not all writing about
love, of course, is in the form of poetry. Written from the point of view of the
teenage protagonist, Hisaye Yamamoto's "Seventeen Syllables" explores how
one comes to an understanding about one's own parents' marriage. Ernest Hemingway's very short story "Hills Like White Elephants" and Raymond Carver's
"Signals" each present a relationship in trouble and crisis—one is set in a railroad waiting station in post World War I Spain, the other in an upscale restaurant in post World War II U.S.A. The style of both Hemingway's and Carver's
short stories is typically understated and spare with a minimum of description
and authorial musing and a lot of dialogue. How might these stylistic choices in
themselves say something about the love relationships in trouble that are at the
center of the two stories?

The poems, plays, songs, short stories, and nonfiction included in this section
offer a wide range of attitudes, expressed in content and through form, about
gender, sexuality, friendship, and love; about the limitations and the possibilities
for human growth. In a successful literary work, what we think of as form is not
separable from meaning. Formal elements—including character, imagery, setting,
plot structure, and point of view—are where the assumptions, "meaning," and
resonance of a work reside. That the play *Trifles* is set entirely in the disordered
kitchen of Minnie Wright's farmhouse is crucial to the women characters' "reading" of the mystery of John Wright's murder. That we stay entirely inside the
point of view of Tahira Naqui's protagonist, a Pakistani physician and husband,
as he tries to figure out who is sending love letters to his office adds an anxious,
slightly claustrophobic, slightly surreal quality to this crisis of middle age and his
taken-for-granted marriage. The image of deer hunting at night is as crucial to
our understanding of Louise Erdrich's poem "Jacklight" as a ravenous imaginary
animal as the personification of marriage is in Ted Hughes's "The Love Pet." Sexual politics is an arena in which we struggle with other issues—of identity, spirituality, power, autonomy, need, and the limiting or the realization of our
freedom and potential.

FICTION

CHARLOTTE PERKINS GILMAN (1860–1935)

Soon after Charlotte Perkins Gilman's birth in Hartford, Connecticut, her father abandoned his wife and two children, leaving them in poverty. In need, Gilman's mother sought the help of relatives, in particular, Harriet Beecher Stowe and her sisters, all prominent writers and feminists during the era. In such an environment, Gilman developed a strong and independent sense of her self-worth as a woman. Early on in her career she worked as a teacher and a commercial artist. After becoming deeply depressed after the birth of her first child, a famous neurologist ordered complete bed rest, which made matters worse. Eventually, Gilman left her husband, moved to California, and began writing and speaking on economics and feminism. She edited The Forerunner, *a feminist journal, from 1909 until 1916. Among Gilman's writings are* Women and Economics *(1898);* Herland *(1915), a utopian novel; and* The Living of Charlotte Perkins Gilman *(1935), her autobiography. The short story "The Yellow Wallpaper," considered one of Gilman's finest works, was written out of her encounter with the late-nineteenth-century medical profession's misdiagnosis of women's physiology and psychology.*

The Yellow Wallpaper (1892)

It is very seldom that mere ordinary people like John and myself secure ancestral halls for the summer.

A colonial mansion, a hereditary estate, I would say a haunted house and reach the height of romantic felicity—but that would be asking too much of fate!

Still I will proudly declare that there is something queer about it.

Else, why should it be let so cheaply? And why have stood so long untenanted?

John laughs at me, of course, but one expects that.

John is practical in the extreme. He has no patience with faith, an intense horror of superstition, and he scoffs openly at any talk of things not to be felt and seen and put down in figures.

John is a physician, and *perhaps*—(I would not say it to a living soul, of course, but this is dead paper and a great relief to my mind)—*perhaps* that is one reason I do not get well faster.

You see, he does not believe I am sick! And what can one do?

If a physician of high standing, and one's own husband, assures friends and relatives that there is really nothing the matter with one but temporary nervous depression—a slight hysterical tendency—what is one to do?

My brother is also a physician, and also of high standing, and he says the same thing.

So I take phosphates or phosphites—whichever it is—and tonics, and air and exercise, and journeys, and am absolutely forbidden to "work" until I am well again.

Personally, I disagree with their ideas.

Personally, I believe that congenial work, with excitement and change, would do me good.

But what is one to do?

I did write for a while in spite of them; but it *does* exhaust me a good deal—having to be so sly about it, or else meet with heavy opposition.

I sometimes fancy that in my condition, if I had less opposition and more society and stimulus—but John says the very worst thing I can do is to think about my condition, and I confess it always makes me feel bad.

So I will let it alone and talk about the house.

The most beautiful place! It is quite alone, standing well back from the road, quite three miles from the village. It makes me think of English places that you read about, for there are hedges and walls and gates that lock, and lots of separate little houses for the gardeners and people.

There is a *delicious* garden! I never saw such a garden—large and shady, full of box-bordered paths, and lined with long grape-covered arbors with seats under them.

There were greenhouses, but they are all broken now.

There was some legal trouble, I believe, something about the heirs and co-heirs; anyhow, the place has been empty for years.

That spoils my ghostliness, I am afraid, but I don't care—there is something strange about the house—I can feel it.

I even said so to John one moonlight evening, but he said what I felt was a draught, and shut the window.

I get unreasonably angry with John sometimes. I'm sure I never used to be so sensitive. I think it is due to this nervous condition.

But John says if I feel so I shall neglect proper self-control; so I take pains to control myself—before him, at least, and that makes me very tired.

I don't like our room a bit. I wanted one downstairs that opened onto the piazza and had roses all over the window, and such pretty old-fashioned chintz hangings! But John would not hear of it.

He said there was only one window and not room for two beds, and no near room for him if he took another.

He is very careful and loving, and hardly lets me stir without special direction.

I have a schedule prescription for each hour in the day; he takes all care from me, and so I feel basely ungrateful not to value it more.

He said he came here solely on my account, that I was to have perfect rest and all the air I could get. "Your exercise depends on your strength, my dear," said he, "and your food somewhat on your appetite; but air you can absorb all the time." So we took the nursery at the top of the house.

It is a big, airy room, the whole floor nearly, with windows that look all ways, and air and sunshine galore. It was nursery first, and then playroom and gymnasium, I should judge, for the windows are barred for little children, and there are rings and things in the walls.

The paint and paper look as if a boys' school had used it. It is stripped off—the paper—in great patches all around the head of my bed, about as far as I can reach, and in a great place on the other side of the room low down. I never saw a worse paper in my life. One of those sprawling, flamboyant patterns committing every artistic sin.

It is dull enough to confuse the eye in following, pronounced enough constantly to irritate and provoke study, and when you follow the lame uncertain curves for a little distance they suddenly commit suicide—plunge off at outrageous angles, destroy themselves in unheard-of contradictions.

The color is repellent, almost revolting: a smouldering unclean yellow, strangely faded by the slow-turning sunlight. It is a dull yet lurid orange in some places, a sickly sulphur tint in others.

No wonder the children hated it! I should hate it myself if I had to live in this room long.

There comes John, and I must put this away—he hates to have me write a word.

We have been here two weeks, and I haven't felt like writing before, since that first day.

I am sitting by the window now, up in this atrocious nursery, and there is nothing to hinder my writing as much as I please, save lack of strength.

John is away all day, and even some nights when his cases are serious.

I am glad my case is not serious!

But these nervous troubles are dreadfully depressing.

John does not know how much I really suffer. He knows there is no reason to suffer, and that satisfies him.

Of course it is only nervousness. It does weigh on me so not to do my duty in any way!

I meant to be such a help to John, such a real rest and comfort, and here I am a comparative burden already!

Nobody would believe what an effort it is to do what little I am able—to dress and entertain, and order things.

It is fortunate Mary is so good with the baby. Such a dear baby!

And yet I *cannot* be with him, it makes me so nervous.

I suppose John never was nervous in his life. He laughs at me so about this wallpaper!

At first he meant to repaper the room, but afterward he said that I was letting it get the better of me, and that nothing was worse for a nervous patient than to give way to such fancies.

He said that after the wallpaper was changed it would be the heavy bedstead, and then the barred windows, and then that gate at the head of the stairs, and so on.

"You know the place is doing you good," he said, "and really, dear, I don't care to renovate the house just for a three months' rental."

"Then do let us go downstairs," I said. "There are such pretty rooms there."

Then he took me in his arms and called me a blessed little goose, and said he would go down cellar, if I wished, and have it whitewashed into the bargain.

But he is right enough about the beds and windows and things.

It is as airy and comfortable a room as anyone need wish, and, of course, I would not be so silly as to make him uncomfortable just for a whim.

I'm really getting quite fond of the big room, all but that horrid paper.

Out of one window I can see the garden—those mysterious deep-shaded arbors, the riotous old-fashioned flowers, and bushes and gnarly trees.

Out of another I get a lovely view of the bay and a little private wharf belonging to the estate. There is a beautiful shaded lane that runs down there from the house. I always fancy I see people walking in these numerous paths and arbors, but John has cautioned me not to give way to fancy in the least. He says that with my imaginative power and habit of story-making, a nervous weakness like mine is sure to lead to all manner of excited fancies, and that I ought to use my will and good sense to check the tendency. So I try.

I think sometimes that if I were only well enough to write a little it would relieve the press of ideas and rest me.

But I find I get pretty tired when I try.

It is so discouraging not to have any advice and companionship about my work. When I get really well, John says we will ask Cousin Henry and Julia down for a long visit; but he says he would as soon put fireworks in my pillow-case as to let me have those stimulating people about now.

I wish I could get well faster.

But I must not think about that. This paper looks to me as if it *knew* what a vicious influence it had!

There is a recurrent spot where the pattern lolls like a broken neck and two bulbous eyes stare at you upside down.

I get positively angry with the impertinence of it and the everlastingness. Up and down and sideways they crawl, and those absurd unblinking eyes are everywhere. There is one place where two breadths didn't match, and the eyes go all up and down the line, one a little higher than the other.

I never saw so much expression in an inanimate thing before, and we all know how much expression they have! I used to lie awake as a child and get more entertainment and terror out of blank walls and plain furniture than most children could find in a toy-store.

I remember what a kindly wink the knobs of our big old bureau used to have, and there was one chair that always seemed like a strong friend.

I used to feel that if any of the other things looked too fierce I could always hop into that chair and be safe.

The furniture in this room is no worse than inharmonious, however, for we had to bring it all from downstairs. I suppose when this was used as a playroom they had to take the nursery things out, and no wonder! I never saw such ravages as the children have made here.

The wallpaper, as I said before, is torn off in spots, and it sticketh closer than a brother—they must have had perseverance as well as hatred.

Then the floor is scratched and gouged and splintered, the plaster itself is dug out here and there, and this great heavy bed, which is all we found in the room, looks as if it had been through the wars.

But I don't mind it a bit—only the paper.

There comes John's sister. Such a dear girl as she is, and so careful of me! I must not let her find me writing.

She is a perfect and enthusiastic housekeeper, and hopes for no better profession. I verily believe she thinks it is the writing which made me sick!

But I can write when she is out, and see her a long way off from these windows.

There is one that commands the road, a lovely shaded winding road, and one that just looks off over the country. A lovely country, too, full of great elms and velvet meadows.

This wallpaper has a kind of sub-pattern in a different shade, a particularly irritating one, for you can only see it in certain lights, and not clearly then.

But in the places where it isn't faded and where the sun is just so—I can see a strange, provoking, formless sort of figure that seems to skulk about behind that silly and conspicuous front design.

There's sister on the stairs!

Well, the Fourth of July is over! The people are all gone, and I am tired out. John thought it might do me good to see a little company, so we just had Mother and Nellie and the children down for a week.

Of course I didn't do a thing. Jennie sees to everything now.

But it tired me all the same.

John says if I don't pick up faster he shall send me to Weir Mitchell[1] in the fall.

But I don't want to go there at all. I had a friend who was in his hands once, and she says he is just like John and my brother, only more so!

Besides, it is such an undertaking to go so far.

I don't feel as if it was worthwhile to turn my hand over for anything, and I'm getting dreadfully fretful and querulous.

I cry at nothing, and cry most of the time.

Of course I don't when John is here, or anybody else, but when I am alone.

And I am alone a good deal just now. John is kept in town very often by serious cases, and Jennie is good and lets me alone when I want her to.

So I walk a little in the garden or down that lovely lane, sit on the porch under the roses, and lie down up here a good deal.

I'm getting really fond of the room in spite of the wallpaper. Perhaps *because* of the wallpaper.

It dwells in my mind so!

---

[1]American neurologist (1829–1914) who treated Gilman.

I lie here on this great immovable bed—it is nailed down, I believe—and follow that pattern about by the hour. It is as good as gymnastics, I assure you. I start, we'll say, at the bottom, down in the corner over there where it has not been touched, and I determine for the thousandth time that I *will* follow that pointless pattern to some sort of a conclusion.

I know a little of the principle of design, and I know this thing was not arranged on any laws of radiation, or alternation, or repetition, or symmetry, or anything else that I ever heard of.

It is repeated, of course, by the breadths, but not otherwise.

Looked at in one way, each breadth stands alone; the bloated curves and flourishes—a kind of "debased Romanesque" with delirium tremens—go waddling up and down in isolated columns of fatuity.

But, on the other hand, they connect diagonally, and the sprawling outlines run off in great slanting waves of optic horror, like a lot of wallowing sea-weeds in full chase.

The whole thing goes horizontally, too, at least it seems so, and I exhaust myself trying to distinguish the order of its going in that direction.

They have used a horizontal breadth for a frieze, and that adds wonderfully to the confusion.

There is one end of the room where it is almost intact, and there, when the crosslights fade and the low sun shines directly upon it, I can almost fancy radiation after all—the interminable grotesque seems to form around a common center and rush off in headlong plunges of equal distraction.

It makes me tired to follow it. I will take a nap, I guess.

I don't know why I should write this.

I don't want to.

I don't feel able.

And I know John would think it absurd. But I *must* say what I feel and think in some way—it is such a relief!

But the effort is getting to be greater than the relief.

Half the time now I am awfully lazy, and lie down ever so much. John says I mustn't lose my strength, and has me take cod liver oil and lots of tonics and things, to say nothing of ale and wine and rare meat.

Dear John! He loves me very dearly, and hates to have me sick. I tried to have a real earnest reasonable talk with him the other day, and tell him how I wish he would let me go and make a visit to Cousin Henry and Julia.

But he said I wasn't able to go, nor able to stand it after I got there; and I did not make out a very good case for myself, for I was crying before I had finished.

It is getting to be a great effort for me to think straight. Just this nervous weakness, I suppose.

And dear John gathered me up in his arms, and just carried me upstairs and laid me on the bed, and sat by me and read to me till it tired my head.

He said I was his darling and his comfort and all he had, and that I must take care of myself for his sake, and keep well.

He says no one but myself can help me out of it, that I must use my will and self-control and not let any silly fancies run away with me.

There's one comfort—the baby is well and happy, and does not have to occupy this nursery with the horrid wallpaper.

If we had not used it, that blessed child would have! What a fortunate escape! Why, I wouldn't have a child of mine, an impressionable little thing, live in such a room for worlds.

I never thought of it before, but it is lucky that John kept me here after all; I can stand it so much easier than a baby, you see.

Of course I never mention it to them any more—I am too wise—but I keep watch for it all the same.

There are things in that wallpaper that nobody knows about but me, or ever will.

Behind that outside pattern the dim shapes get clearer every day.

It is always the same shape, only very numerous.

And it is like a woman stooping down and creeping about behind that pattern. I don't like it a bit. I wonder—I begin to think—I wish John would take me away from here!

It is so hard to talk with John about my case, because he is so wise, and because he loves me so.

But I tried it last night.

It was moonlight. The moon shines in all around just as the sun does.

I hate to see it sometimes, it creeps so slowly, and always comes in by one window or another.

John was asleep and I hated to waken him, so I kept still and watched the moonlight on that undulating wallpaper till I felt creepy.

The faint figure behind seemed to shake the pattern, just as if she wanted to get out.

I got up softly and went to feel and see if the paper *did* move, and when I came back John was awake.

"What is it, little girl?" he said. "Don't go walking about like that—you'll get cold."

I thought it was a good time to talk, so I told him that I really was not gaining here, and that I wished he would take me away.

"Why, darling!" said he. "Our lease will be up in three weeks, and I can't see how to leave before.

"The repairs are not done at home, and I cannot possibly leave town just now. Of course, if you were in any danger, I could and would, but you really are better, dear, whether you can see it or not. I am a doctor, dear, and I know. You are gaining flesh and color, your appetite is better, I feel really much easier about you."

"I don't weigh a bit more," said I, "nor as much; and my appetite may be better in the evening when you are here but it is worse in the morning when you are away!"

"Bless her little heart!" said he with a big hug. "She shall be as sick as she pleases! But now let's improve the shining hours by going to sleep, and talk about it in the morning!"

"And you won't go away?" I asked gloomily.

"Why, how can I, dear? It is only three weeks more and then we'll take a nice little trip of a few days while Jennie is getting the house ready. Really, dear, you are better!"

"Better in body perhaps—" I began, and stopped short, for he sat up straight and looked at me with such a stern, reproachful look that I could not say another word.

"My darling," said he, "I beg of you, for my sake and for our child's sake, as well as for your own, that you will never for one instant let that idea enter your mind! There is nothing so dangerous, so fascinating, to a temperament like yours. It is a false and foolish fancy. Can you not trust me as a physician when I tell you so?"

So of course I said no more on that score, and we went to sleep before long. He thought I was asleep first, but I wasn't, and lay there for hours trying to decide whether that front pattern and the back pattern really did move together or separately.

On a pattern like this, by daylight, there is a lack of sequence, a defiance of law, that is a constant irritant to a normal mind.

The color is hideous enough, and unreliable enough, and infuriating enough, but the pattern is torturing.

You think you have mastered it, but just as you get well under way in following, it turns a back-somersault and there you are. It slaps you in the face, knocks you down, and tramples upon you. It is like a bad dream.

The outside pattern is a florid arabesque, reminding one of a fungus. If you can imagine a toadstool in joints, an interminable string of toadstools, budding and sprouting in endless convolutions—why, that is something like it.

That is, sometimes!

There is one marked peculiarity about this paper, a thing nobody seems to notice but myself, and that is that it changes as the light changes.

When the sun shoots in through the east window—I always watch for that first long, straight ray—it changes so quickly that I never can quite believe it.

That is why I watch it always.

By moonlight—the moon shines in all night when there is a moon—I wouldn't know it was the same paper.

At night in any kind of light, in twilight, candlelight, lamplight, and worst of all by moonlight, it becomes bars! The outside pattern, I mean, and the woman behind it is as plain as can be.

I didn't realize for a long time what the thing was that showed behind, that dim sub-pattern, but now I am quite sure it is a woman.

By daylight she is subdued, quiet. I fancy it is the pattern that keeps her so still. It is so puzzling. It keeps me quiet by the hour.

I lie down ever so much now. John says it is good for me, and to sleep all I can.

Indeed he started the habit by making me lie down for an hour after each meal.

It is a very bad habit, I am convinced, for you see, I don't sleep.

And that cultivates deceit, for I don't tell them I'm awake—oh, no!

The fact is I am getting a little afraid of John.

He seems very queer sometimes, and even Jennie has an inexplicable look.

It strikes me occasionally, just as a scientific hypothesis, that perhaps it is the paper!

I have watched John when he did not know I was looking, and come into the room suddenly on the most innocent excuses, and I've caught him several times *looking at the paper!* And Jennie too. I caught Jennie with her hand on it once.

She didn't know I was in the room, and when I asked her in a quiet, a very quiet voice, with the most restrained manner possible, what she was doing with the paper, she turned around as if she had been caught stealing, and looked quite angry—asked me why I should frighten her so!

Then she said that the paper stained everything it touched, that she had found yellow smooches on all my clothes and John's and she wished we would be more careful!

Did not that sound innocent? But I know she was studying that pattern, and I am determined that nobody shall find it out but myself.

Life is very much more exciting now than it used to be. You see, I have something more to expect, to look forward to, to watch. I really do eat better, and am more quiet than I was.

John is so pleased to see me improve! He laughed a little the other day, and said I seemed to be flourishing in spite of my wallpaper.

I turned it off with a laugh. I had no intention of telling him it was *because* of the wallpaper—he would make fun of me. He might even want to take me away.

I don't want to leave now until I have found it out. There is a week more, and I think that will be enough.

I'm feeling so much better!

I don't sleep much at night, for it is so interesting to watch developments; but I sleep a good deal during the daytime.

In the daytime it is tiresome and perplexing.

There are always new shoots on the fungus, and new shades of yellow all over it. I cannot keep count of them, though I have tried conscientiously.

It is the strangest yellow, that wallpaper! It makes me think of all the yellow things I ever saw—not beautiful ones like buttercups, but old, foul, bad yellow things.

But there is something else about that paper—the smell! I noticed it the moment we came into the room, but with so much air and sun it was not bad. Now we have had a week of fog and rain, and whether the windows are open or not, the smell is here.

It creeps all over the house.

I find it hovering in the dining-room, skulking in the parlor, hiding in the hall, lying in wait for me on the stairs.

It gets into my hair.

Even when I go to ride, if I turn my head suddenly and surprise it—there is that smell!

Such a peculiar odor, too! I have spent hours in trying to analyze it, to find what it smelled like.

It is not bad—at first—and very gentle, but quite the subtlest, most enduring odor I ever met.

In this damp weather it is awful. I wake up in the night and find it hanging over me.

It used to disturb me at first. I thought seriously of burning the house—to reach the smell.

But now I am used to it. The only thing I can think of that it is like is the *color* of the paper! A yellow smell.

There is a very funny mark on this wall, low down, near the mopboard. A streak that runs round the room. It goes behind every piece of furniture, except the bed, a long, straight, even *smooch,* as if it had been rubbed over and over.

I wonder how it was done and who did it, and what they did it for. Round and round and round—round and round and round—it makes me dizzy!

I really have discovered something at last.

Through watching so much at night, when it changes so, I have finally found out.

The front pattern *does* move—and no wonder! The woman behind shakes it!

Sometimes I think there are a great many women behind, and sometimes only one, and she crawls around fast, and her crawling shakes it all over.

Then in the very bright spots she keeps still, and in the very shady spots she just takes hold of the bars and shakes them hard.

And she is all the time trying to climb through. But nobody could climb through that pattern—it strangles so; I think that is why it has so many heads.

They get through, and then the pattern strangles them off and turns them upside down, and makes their eyes white!

If those heads were covered or taken off it would not be half so bad.

I think that woman gets out in the daytime!

And I'll tell you why—privately—I've seen her!

I can see her out of every one of my windows!

It is the same woman, I know, for she is always creeping, and most women do not creep by daylight.

I see her in that long shaded lane, creeping up and down. I see her in those dark grape arbors, creeping all around the garden.

I see her on that long road under the trees, creeping along, and when a carriage comes she hides under the blackberry vines.

I don't blame her a bit. It must be very humiliating to be caught creeping by daylight!

I always lock the door when I creep by daylight. I can't do it at night, for I know John would suspect something at once.

And John is so queer now that I don't want to irritate him. I wish he would take another room! Besides, I don't want anybody to get that woman out at night but myself.

I often wonder if I could see her out of all the windows at once.

But, turn as fast as I can, I can only see out of one at one time.

And though I always see her, she *may* be able to creep faster than I can turn! I have watched her sometimes away off in the open country, creeping as fast as a cloud shadow in a wind.

If only that top pattern could be gotten off from the under one! I mean to try it, little by little.

I have found out another funny thing, but I shan't tell it this time! It does not do to trust people too much.

There are only two more days to get this paper off, and I believe John is beginning to notice. I don't like the look in his eyes.

And I heard him ask Jennie a lot of professional questions about me. She had a very good report to give.

She said I slept a good deal in the daytime.

John knows I don't sleep very well at night, for all I'm so quiet!

He asked me all sorts of questions, too, and pretended to be very loving and kind.

As if I couldn't see through him!

Still, I don't wonder he acts so, sleeping under this paper for three months.

It only interests me, but I feel sure John and Jennie are affected by it. Hurrah! This is the last day, but it is enough. John is to stay in town over night, and won't be out until this evening.

Jennie wanted to sleep with me—the sly thing; but I told her I should undoubtedly rest better for a night all alone.

That was clever, for really I wasn't alone a bit! As soon as it was moonlight and that poor thing began to crawl and shake the pattern, I got up and ran to help her.

I pulled and she shook. I shook and she pulled, and before morning we had peeled off yards of that paper.

A strip about as high as my head and half around the room.

And then when the sun came and that awful pattern began to laugh at me, I declared I would finish it today!

We go away tomorrow, and they are moving all my furniture down again to leave things as they were before.

Jennie looked at the wall in amazement, but I told her merrily that I did it out of pure spite at the vicious thing.

She laughed and said she wouldn't mind doing it herself, but I must not get tired.

How she betrayed herself that time!

But I am here, and no person touches this paper but Me—not *alive!*

She tried to get me out of the room—it was too patent! But I said it was so quiet and empty and clean now that I believed I would lie down again and sleep all I could, and not to wake me even for dinner—I would call when I woke.

So now she is gone, and the servants are gone, and the things are gone, and there is nothing left but that great bedstead nailed down, with the canvas mattress we found on it.

We shall sleep downstairs tonight, and take the boat home tomorrow.

I quite enjoy the room, now it is bare again.

How those children did tear about here!

This bedstead is fairly gnawed!

But I must get to work.

I have locked the door and thrown the key down into the front path.

I don't want to go out, and I don't want to have anybody come in, till John comes.

I want to astonish him.

I've got a rope up here that even Jennie did not find. If that woman does get out, and tries to get away, I can tie her!

But I forgot I could not reach far without anything to stand on!

This bed will *not* move!

I tried to lift and push it until I was lame, and then I got so angry I bit off a little piece at one corner—but it hurt my teeth.

Then I peeled off all the paper I could reach standing on the floor. It sticks horribly and the pattern just enjoys it! All those strangled heads and bulbous eyes and waddling fungus growths just shriek with derision!

I am getting angry enough to do something desperate. To jump out of the window would be admirable exercise, but the bars are too strong even to try.

Besides I wouldn't do it. Of course not. I know well enough that a step like that is improper and might be misconstrued.

I don't like to *look* out of the windows even—there are so many of those creeping women, and they creep so fast.

I wonder if they all come out of that wallpaper as I did?

But I am securely fastened now by my well-hidden rope—you don't get *me* out in the road there!

I suppose I shall have to get back behind the pattern when it comes night, and that is hard!

It is so pleasant to be out in this great room and creep around as I please!

I don't want to go outside. I won't, even if Jennie asks me to.

For outside you have to creep on the ground, and everything is green instead of yellow.

But here I can creep smoothly on the floor, and my shoulder just fits in that long smooch around the wall, so I cannot lose my way.

Why, there's John at the door!

It is no use, young man, you can't open it!

How he does call and pound!

Now he's crying to Jennie for an axe.

It would be a shame to break down that beautiful door!

"John, dear!" said I in the gentlest voice. "The key is down by the front steps, under a plantain leaf!"

That silenced him for a few moments.

Then he said, very quietly indeed, "Open the door, my darling!"

"I can't," said I. "The key is down by the front door under a plantain leaf!" And then I said it again, several times, very gently and slowly, and said it so often that he had to go and see, and he got it of course, and came in. He stopped short by the door.

"What is the matter?" he cried. "For God's sake, what are you doing!"

I kept on creeping just the same, but I looked at him over my shoulder.

"I've got out at last," said I, "in spite of you and Jane. And I've pulled off most of the paper, so you can't put me back!"

Now why should that man have fainted? But he did, and right across my path by the wall, so that I had to creep over him every time!

Study and Discussion Questions

1. What do the narrator and the woman in the wallpaper have in common?
2. Is the narrator right to be suspicious of her husband or is her suspicion simply a manifestation of her nervous ailment?
3. Why is the narrator so tired?
4. What kind of person does John want his wife to be? How does he try to maneuver her into being that?
5. What is the significance of the fact that the narrator's room was originally a nursery?
6. "There comes John, and I must put this away—he hates to have me write a word." Why doesn't John want her to write? Why does she disagree with him?
7. How does the way the narrator sees and feels about the yellow wallpaper change during the story?

Suggestions for Writing

1. Who is John? List the words that describe him. Write a brief character sketch.
2. Gilman wrote this story in 1890 as a warning about a treatment for nervous depression fashionable then. Gilman herself was told to "live as domestic a life as possible," to "have but two hours' intellectual life a day" and "never to touch pen, brush, or pencil again." Discuss the way in which the treatment which is supposed to cure the narrator worsens her condition, and speculate about the reasons.
3. What is wrong with this marriage?

Critical Resources

1. Dock, Julie, ed. *"The Yellow Wallpaper" and the History of Its Publication and Reception: A Critical Edition and Casebook.* University Park: U of Pennsylvania P, 1998.
2. Golden, Catherine, ed. *The Captive Imagination: A Casebook on The Yellow Wallpaper.* New York: Feminist Press at City University, 1992.
3. Karpinsky, Joanne, ed. *Critical Essays on Charlotte Perkins Gilman.* Toronto: G.K. Hall, 1992.

❀ ❀ ❀

ERNEST HEMINGWAY (1899–1961)

Ernest Hemingway was born in Oak Park, Illinois. As a boy he went on frequent hunting and fishing trips in northern Michigan with his father, a doctor. He boxed and played football in high school and, after graduating, worked as a newspaper reporter. Near the end of World War I, Hemingway was a volunteer ambulance driver and then a soldier in Italy, where he was wounded. He spent much of the 1920s in Paris and the 1930s in Key West, Florida. He was an active supporter of the Republican Revolutionary Cause in the Spanish Civil War and worked as a war correspondent during World War II. His writings include the novels The Sun Also Rises *(1926),* A Farewell to Arms *(1929), and* The Old Man and The Sea *(1952); the collections* In Our Time *(1925) and* The Fifth Column and the First Forty-Nine Stories *(1938); and the memoir* A Moveable Feast *(1964, posthumously). In 1954, he received the Nobel Prize for literature. "Hills Like White Elephants," taken from the short story collection* Men Without Women *(1927), demonstrates Hemingway's concise use of dialogue.*

Hills Like White Elephants (1927)

The hills across the valley of the Ebro were long and white. On this side there was no shade and no trees and the station was between two lines of rails in the sun. Close against the side of the station there was the warm shadow of the building and a curtain, made of strings of bamboo beads, hung across the open door into the bar, to keep out flies. The American and the girl with him sat at a table in the shade, outside the building. It was very hot and the express from Barcelona would come in forty minutes. It stopped at this junction for two minutes and went on to Madrid.

"What should we drink?" the girl asked. She had taken off her hat and put it on the table.

"It's pretty hot," the man said.

"Let's drink beer."

"*Dos cervezas,*" the man said into the curtain.

"Big ones?" a woman asked from the doorway.

"Yes. Two big ones."

The woman brought two glasses of beer and two felt pads. She put the felt pads and the beer glasses on the table and looked at the man and the girl. The girl was looking off at the line of hills. They were white in the sun and the country was brown and dry.

"They look like white elephants," she said.

"I've never seen one," the man drank his beer.

"No, you wouldn't have."

"I might have," the man said. "Just because you say I wouldn't have doesn't prove anything."

The girl looked at the bead curtain. "They've painted something on it," she said. "What does it say?"

"Anis del Toro. It's a drink."

"Could we try it?"

The man called "Listen" through the curtain. The woman came out from the bar.

"Four reales."

"We want two Anis del Toro."

"With water?"

"Do you want it with water?"

"I don't know," the girl said. "Is it good with water?"

"It's all right."

"You want them with water?" asked the woman.

"Yes, with water."

"It tastes like licorice," the girl said and put the glass down.

"That's the way with everything."

"Yes," said the girl. "Everything tastes of licorice. Especially all the things you've waited so long for, like absinthe."

"Oh, cut it out."

"You started it," the girl said. "I was being amused. I was having a fine time."

"Well, let's try and have a fine time."

"All right. I was trying. I said the mountains looked like white elephants. Wasn't that bright?"

"That was bright."

"I wanted to try this new drink. That's all we do, isn't it—look at things and try new drinks?"

"I guess so."

The girl looked across at the hills.

"They're lovely hills," she said. "They don't really look like white elephants. I just meant the coloring of their skin through the trees."

"Should we have another drink?"

"All right."

The warm wind blew the bead curtain against the table.

"The beer's nice and cool," the man said.

"It's lovely," the girl said.

"It's really an awfully simple operation, Jig," the man said. "It's not really an operation at all."

The girl looked at the ground the table legs rested on.

"I know you wouldn't mind it, Jig. It's really not anything. It's just to let the air in."

The girl did not say anything.

"I'll go with you and I'll stay with you all the time. They just let the air in and then it's all perfectly natural."

"Then what will we do afterward?"

"We'll be fine afterward. Just like we were before."

"What makes you think so?"

"That's the only thing that bothers us. It's the only thing that's made us unhappy."

The girl looked at the bead curtain, put her hand out and took hold of two of the strings of beads.

"And you think then we'll be all right and be happy."

"I know we will. You don't have to be afraid. I've known lots of people that have done it."

"So have I," said the girl. "And afterward they were all so happy."

"Well," the man said, "if you don't want to you don't have to. I wouldn't have you do it if you don't want to. But I know it's perfectly simple."

"And you really want to?"

"I think it's the best thing to do. But I don't want you to do it if you don't really want to."

"And if I do it you'll be happy and things will be like they were and you'll love me?"

"I love you now. You know I love you."

"I know. But if I do it, then it will be nice again if I say things are like white elephants, and you'll like it?"

"I'll love it. I love it now but I just can't think about it. You know how I get when I worry."

"If I do it you won't ever worry?"

"I won't worry about that because it's perfectly simple."

"Then I'll do it. Because I don't care about me."

"What do you mean?"

"I don't care about me."

"Well, I care about you."

"Oh, yes. But I don't care about me. And I'll do it and then everything will be fine."

"I don't want you to do it if you feel that way."

The girl stood up and walked to the end of the station. Across, on the other side, were fields of grain and trees along the banks of the Ebro. Far away, beyond the river, were mountains. The shadow of a cloud moved across the field of grain and she saw the river through the trees.

"And we could have all this," she said. "And we could have everything and every day we make it more impossible."

"What did you say?"

"I said we could have everything."

"We can have everything."

"No, we can't."

"We can have the whole world."

"No, we can't."

"We can go everywhere."

"No, we can't. It isn't ours any more."

"It's ours."

"No, it isn't. And once they take it away, you never get it back."

"But they haven't taken it away."

"We'll wait and see."

"Come on back in the shade," he said. "You mustn't feel that way."

"I don't feel any way," the girl said. "I just know things."

"I don't want you to do anything that you don't want to do—"

"Nor that isn't good for me," she said. "I know. Could we have another beer?"

"All right. But you've got to realize—"

"I realize," the girl said. "Can't we maybe stop talking?"

They sat down at the table and the girl looked across at the hills on the dry side of the valley and the man looked at her and at the table.

"You've got to realize," he said, "that I don't want you to do it if you don't want to. I'm perfectly willing to go through with it if it means anything to you."

"Doesn't it mean anything to you? We could get along."

"Of course it does. But I don't want anybody but you. I don't want any one else. And I know it's perfectly simple."

"Yes, you know it's perfectly simple."

"It's all right for you to say that, but I do know it."

"Would you do something for me now?"

"I'd do anything for you."

"Would you please please please please please please please stop talking?"

He did not say anything but looked at the bags against the wall of the station. There were labels on them from all the hotels where they had spent nights.

"But I don't want you to," he said, "I don't care anything about it."

"I'll scream," the girl said.

The woman came out through the curtains with two glasses of beer and put them down on the damp felt pads. "The train comes in five minutes," she said.

"What did she say?" asked the girl.

"That the train is coming in five minutes."

The girl smiled brightly at the woman, to thank her.

"I'd better take the bags over to the other side of the station," the man said. She smiled at him.

"All right. Then come back and we'll finish the beer."

He picked up the two heavy bags and carried them around the station to the other tracks. He looked up the tracks but could not see the train. Coming back, he walked through the barroom, where people waiting for the train were drinking. He drank an Anis at the bar and looked at the people. They were all waiting reasonably for the train. He went out through the bead curtain. She was sitting at the table and smiled at him.

"Do you feel better?" he asked.

"I feel fine," she said. "There's nothing wrong with me. I feel fine."

Study and Discussion Questions

1. What is this couple arguing about? What clues let you know? Why do you think Hemingway doesn't allow his characters to say directly what they are talking about?

2. What is the balance of power between the man and the woman in this story? How does Hemingway construct this balance of power? What factors are involved in the situation? What factors are involved in Hemingway's stylistic choices, including how the two characters are referred to?
3. What effects do the descriptions of the setting have in the midst of this couple's argument?
4. Why this particular title—"Hills Like White Elephants"? What does that mean to you? How does it fit the story?
5. The "girl" says: "That's all we do, isn't it—look at things and try new drinks?" Describe the life they seem to be leading. When do you think this story is set?
6. What is the man's argument? What does he want? Is he conflicted? How is he trying to get his way?
7. What is the woman's argument, or defense? What does she want—Is it possible that she wants more than one thing?
8. How does the lack of attribution in the dialogue affect the story and the way you perceive the characters?

Suggestions for Writing:

1. Write about communication and miscommunication between men and women, or between couples, from your own experience. How is communication and miscommunication happening in "Hills Like White Elephants"?
2. Jump to six months later and write a scene between the two characters in this story.

Critical Resources

1. Benson, Jackson, ed. *New Critical Approaches to the Short Stories of Ernest Hemingway.* Durham, NC: Duke UP, 1990.
2. Broer, Lawerence and Gloria Holland, eds. *Hemingway and Women: Female Critics and Female Voices.* Tuscaloosa: U of Alabama P, 2002.
3. Brucolli, Matthew. *Conversations with Ernest Hemingway.* Jackson: U of Mississippi P, 1986.
4. Lynn, Kenneth. *Hemingway.* Cambridge: Harvard UP, 1995.
5. Tyler, Lisa. *Student Companion to Ernest Hemingway.* Westport: Greenwood, 2001.

RAYMOND CARVER (1938–1988)

Raymond Carver was born in Clatskanie, Oregon, but spent the bulk of his childhood and adolescence in Yakima, Washington. Carver would be the first one in his family to graduate from high school. He married in 1957 and immediately started a family. During the following decade, he and his wife moved from town to town

seeking work to support the family while trying to attend college. Carver gradu-
ated from Humboldt State College (California) in 1963. In 1967, his short story
"Will You Please Be Quiet, Please?" was published in Best American Short
Stories—*his first story to gain national recognition. As his publications and repu-*
tation as a writer began to grow, Carver was also dealing with growing alcoholism,
brought on by the pressure to support a family while trying to write. Although
many biographers have focused on Carver's propensity to drink (a habit he over-
came by 1977), Carver's spare, spirited stories of modern working-class people are
some of the best examples of a generation of American writing often called
"minimalism"—a prose style "loosely characterized by equanimity of surface, 'or-
dinary' subjects, recalcitrant narrators and deadpan narratives, slightness of story
and characters who don't think out loud" (Raymond Carver, 1994). His writings
include the poetry collections Near Klamath *(1968),* Winter Insomnia *(1970), and*
Where Water Comes Together With Other Water *(1985); and the short story col-*
lections Will You Please Be Quiet, Please? *(1976),* Furious Seasons and Other
Stories *(1977),* What We Talk About When We Talk About Love *(1981),* Fires:
Essays, Poems, Stories *(1983), and* Cathedral *(1983). "Signals," taken from* Will
You Please Be Quiet, Please?, *is a prime example of Carver minimalism.*

Signals

(1976)

As their first of the extravagances they had planned for that evening, Wayne
and Caroline went to Aldo's, an elegant new restaurant north a good distance.
They passed through a tiny walled garden with small pieces of statuary and were
met by a tall graying man in a dark suit who said, "Good evening, sir. Madam,"
and who swung open the heavy door for them.

Inside, Aldo himself showed them the aviary—a peacock, a pair of Golden
pheasants, a Chinese ring-necked pheasant, and a number of unannounced birds
that flew around or sat perched. Aldo personally conducted them to a table,
seated Caroline, and then turned to Wayne and said, "A lovely lady," before moving off—a dark, small, impeccable man with a soft accent.

They were pleased with his attention.

"I read in the paper," Wayne said, "that he has an uncle who has some kind
of position in the Vatican. That's how he was able to get copies of some of these
paintings." Wayne nodded at a Velasquez reproduction on the nearest wall. "His
uncle in the Vatican," Wayne said.

"He used to be *maître d'* at the Copacabana in Rio," Caroline said. "He knew
Frank Sinatra, and Lana Turner was a good friend of his."

"Is that so?" Wayne said. "I didn't know that. I read that he was at the Victo-
ria Hotel in Switzerland and at some big hotel in Paris. I didn't know he was at
the Copacabana in Rio."

Caroline moved her handbag slightly as the waiter set down the heavy goblets. He poured water and then moved to Wayne's side of the table.

"Did you see the suit he was wearing?" Wayne said. "You seldom see a suit like that. That's a three-hundred-dollar suit." He picked up his menu. In a while, he said, "Well, what are you going to have?"

"I don't know," she said. "I haven't decided. What are you going to have?"

"I don't know," he said. "I haven't decided, either."

"What about one of these French dishes, Wayne? Or else this? Over here on this side." She placed her finger in instruction, and then she narrowed her eyes at him as he located the language, pursed his lips, frowned, and shook his head.

"I don't know," he said. "I'd kind of like to know what I'm getting. I just don't really know."

The waiter returned with card and pencil and said something Wayne couldn't quite catch.

"We haven't decided yet," Wayne said. He shook his head as the waiter continued to stand beside the table. "I'll signal you when we're ready."

"I think I'll just have a sirloin. You order what you want," he said to Caroline when the waiter had moved off. He closed the menu and raised his goblet. Over the muted voices coming from the other tables Wayne could hear a warbling call from the aviary. He saw Aldo greet a party of four, chat with them as he smiled and nodded and led them to a table.

"We could have had a better table," Wayne said. "Instead of right here in the center where everyone can walk by and watch you eat. We could have had a table against the wall. Or over there by the fountain."

"I think I'll have the beef Tournedos," Caroline said.

She kept looking at her menu. He tapped out a cigaret, lighted it, and then glanced around at the other diners. Caroline still stared at her menu.

"Well, for God's sake, if that's what you're going to have, close your menu so he can take our order." Wayne raised his arm for the waiter, who lingered near the back talking with another waiter.

"Nothing else to do but gas around with the other waiters," Wayne said.

"He's coming," Caroline said.

"Sir?" The waiter was a thin pock-faced man in a loose black suit and a black bow tie.

". . . And we'll have a bottle of champagne, I believe. A small bottle. Something, you know, domestic," Wayne said.

"Yes, sir," the waiter said.

"And we'll have that right away. Before the salad or the relish plate," Wayne said.

"Oh, bring the relish *tray,* anyway," Caroline said. "Please."

"Yes, madam," the waiter said.

"They're a slippery bunch," Wayne said. "Do you remember that guy named Bruno who used to work at the office during the week and wait tables on weekends? Fred caught him stealing out of the petty-cash box. We fired him."

"Let's talk about something pleasant," Caroline said.

"All right, sure," Wayne said.

The waiter poured a little champagne into Wayne's glass, and Wayne took the glass, tasted, and said, "Fine, that will do nicely." Then he said, "Here's to you, baby," and raised his glass high. "Happy birthday."

They clinked glasses.

"I like champagne," Caroline said.

"I like champagne," Wayne said.

"We could have had a bottle of Lancer's," Caroline said.

"Well, why didn't you say something, if that's what you wanted?" Wayne said.

"I don't know," Caroline said. "I just didn't think about it. This is fine, though."

"I don't know too much about champagnes. I don't mind admitting I'm not much of a . . . connoisseur. I don't mind admitting I'm just a lowbrow." He laughed and tried to catch her eye, but she was busy selecting an olive from the relish dish. "Not like the group you've been keeping company with lately. But if you wanted Lancer's," he went on, "you should have ordered Lancer's."

"Oh, shut up!" she said. "Can't you talk about something else?" She looked up at him then and he had to look away. He moved his feet under the table.

He said, "Would you care for some more champagne, dear?"

"Yes, thank you," she said quietly.

"Here's to us," he said.

"To us, my darling," she said.

They looked steadily at each other as they drank.

"We ought to do this more often," he said.

She nodded.

"It's good to get out now and then. I'll make more of an effort, if you want me to."

She reached for celery. "That's up to you."

"That's not true! It's not me who's . . . who's . . ."

"Who's what?" she said.

"I don't care what you do," he said, dropping his eyes.

"Is that true?"

"I don't know why I said that," he said.

The waiter brought the soup and took away the bottle and the wineglasses and refilled their goblets with water.

"Could I have a soup spoon?" Wayne asked.

"Sir?"

"A soup spoon," Wayne repeated.

The waiter looked amazed and then perplexed. He glanced around at the other tables. Wayne made a shoveling motion over his soup. Aldo appeared beside the table.

"Is everything all right? Is there anything wrong?"

"My husband doesn't seem to have a soup spoon," Caroline said. "I'm sorry for the disturbance," she said.

"Certainly. *Une cuiller, s'il vous plaît*," Aldo said to the waiter in an even voice. He looked once at Wayne and then explained to Caroline. "This is Paul's first night. He speaks little English, yet I trust you will agree he is an excellent waiter. The boy who set the table forgot the spoon." Aldo smiled. "It no doubt took Paul by surprise."

"This is a beautiful place," Caroline said.

"Thank you," Aldo said. "I'm delighted you could come tonight. Would you like to see the wine cellar and the private dining rooms?"

"Very much," Caroline said.

"I will have someone show you around when you have finished dining," Aldo said.

"We'll be looking forward to it," Caroline said.

Aldo bowed slightly and looked again at Wayne. "I hope you enjoy your dinner," he said to them.

"That jerk," Wayne said.

"Who?" she said. "Who are you talking about?" she said, laying down her spoon.

"The waiter," Wayne said. "The waiter. The newest and the dumbest waiter in the house, and we got him."

"Eat your soup," she said. "Don't blow a gasket."

Wayne lighted a cigaret. The waiter arrived with salads and took away the soup bowls.

When they had started on the main course, Wayne said, "Well, what do you think? Is there a chance for us or not?" He looked down and arranged the napkin on his lap.

"Maybe so," she said. "There's always a chance."

"Don't give me that kind of crap," he said. "Answer me straight for a change."

"Don't snap at me," she said.

"I'm asking you," he said. "Give me a straight answer," he said.

She said, "You want something signed in blood?"

He said, "That wouldn't be such a bad idea."

She said, "You listen to me! I've given you the best years of my life. The best years of my life!"

"The best years of *your* life?" he said.

"I'm thirty-six years old," she said. "Thirty-seven tonight. Tonight, right now, at this minute, I just can't say what I'm going to do. I'll just have to see," she said.

"I don't care what you do," he said.

"Is that true?" she said.

He threw down his fork and tossed his napkin on the table.

"Are you finished?" she asked pleasantly. "Let's have coffee and dessert. We'll have a nice dessert. Something good."

She finished everything on her plate.

"Two coffees," Wayne said to the waiter. He looked at her and then back to the waiter. "What do you have for dessert?" he said.

"Sir?" the waiter said.

"Dessert!" Wayne said.

The waiter gazed at Caroline and then at Wayne.

"No dessert," she said. "Let's not have any dessert."

"Chocolate mousse," the waiter said. "Orange sherbet," the waiter said. He smiled, showing his bad teeth. "Sir?"

"And I don't want any guided tour of this place," Wayne said when the waiter had moved off.

When they rose from the table, Wayne dropped a dollar bill near his coffee cup. Caroline took two dollars from her handbag, smoothed the bills out, and placed them alongside the other dollar, the three bills lined up in a row.

She waited with Wayne while he paid the check. Out of the corner of his eye, Wayne could see Aldo standing near the door dropping grains of seed into the aviary. Aldo looked in their direction, smiled, and went on rubbing the seeds from between his fingers as birds collected in front of him. Then he briskly brushed his hands together and started moving toward Wayne, who looked away, who turned slightly but significantly as Aldo neared him. But when Wayne looked back, he saw Aldo take Caroline's waiting hand, saw Aldo draw his heels smartly together, saw Aldo kiss her wrist.

"Did madam enjoy her dinner?" Aldo said.

"It was marvelous," Caroline said.

"You will come back from time to time?" Also said.

"I shall," Caroline said. "As often as I may. Next time, I should like to have your permission to check things out a little, but this time we simply must go."

"Dear lady," Aldo said. "I have something for you. One moment, please." He reached to a vase on a table near the door and swung gracefully back with a long-stemmed rose.

"For you, dear lady," Aldo said. "But caution, please. The thorns. A very lovely lady," he said to Wayne and smiled at him and turned to welcome another couple.

Caroline stood there.

"Let's get out of here," Wayne said.

"You can see how he could be friends with Lana Turner," Caroline said. She held the rose and turned it between her fingers.

"Good night!" she called out to Aldo's back.

But Aldo was occupied selecting another rose.

"I don't think he ever knew her," Wayne said.

Study and Discussion Questions

1. Give two reasons why this is an important evening for Wayne and Caroline.
2. Why is Wayne uncomfortable at Aldo's? List three or four instances of his discomfort.

3. A good bit of the tension in Carver's story is expressed in terms of social class. In addition to the examples of Wayne's discomfort addressed in question 2, what is going on between Caroline and Wayne that has social class implications?
4. This is a marriage that seems to be in trouble. How do we know this? Do you think the marriage will survive? Why or why not?
5. What does the restaurant owner, Aldo, represent to Wayne? To Caroline?
6. Why is the story titled "Signals"? List as many signals in the story as you can find. What are these signals conveying?
7. The title of this story, "Signals," is a good word to describe Carver's signature literary style: "characterized by flatness of narrative tone, extreme spareness of story, an obsession with the drab and quotidian, a general avoidance of extensive rumination on the page, and, in sum, a striking restraint in prose style. This movement, whose most notable practitioners also include Ann Beattie, Elizabeth Tallent, Tobias Wolff, Mary Robison, and Frederick Barthelme, is typically referred to as 'minimalism,' a designation that highlights the Spartan technique and the focus on the tiny fault lines that threaten to open out into violence or defeat" (Arthur Saltzman, *Understanding Raymond Carver*).

   Give some examples in "Signals" of the characteristics of minimalism Saltzman mentions.
8. Carver himself comments, in a 1981 essay "On Writing," (*Fires*, 1983),

   > What creates tension in a piece of fiction is partly the way the concrete words are linked together to make up the visible actions of the story. But it's also the things that are left out, that are implied, the landscape just under the smooth (but sometimes broken and unsettled) surface of things.

   In "Signals," what is left out or implied?

Suggestions for Writing

1. Write a scene in a restaurant or at a dinner table that captures some conflict or tension in the participants/characters. Try to convey the conflict without *telling* us what it is.
2. Compare/contrast Carver's "Signals" with Hemingway's "Hills Like White Elephants." What do the two stories have in common in terms of situation and style? How do they differ?
3. Raymond Carver comments in "On Writing,"

   > It's possible, in a poem or a short story, to write about commonplace things and objects using commonplace but precise language, and to endow those things—a chair, a window curtain, a fork, a stone, a woman's earring—with immense, even startling power. It is possible to write a line of seemingly innocuous dialogue and have it send a chill along the reader's spine. . . .

   a. Choose a passage in "Signals" and discuss Carver's use of language.
   b. Write a passage of prose or poetry yourself in which you consciously work at using "commonplace but precise language." Or revise a previous piece of writing of your own to achieve what Carver suggests.

Critical Resources

1. Kirk, Nesset. *The Stories of Raymond Carver: A Critical Study.* Athens: Ohio UP, 1995.
2. Meyer, Adam. *Raymond Carver.* New York: Twayne Publishers, 1995.
3. *Short Cuts.* Director Robert Altman. Avenue Picture Productions, 1993. Based on the stories of Raymond Carver.
4. Stull, William, ed. *Conversations with Raymond Carver.* Jackson: UP of Mississippi, 1990.

HISAYE YAMAMOTO (b. 1921)

Hisaye Yamamoto was born in Redondo Beach, California, the daughter of immigrant farmers. While studying languages at Compton Junior College, Yamamto, along with 100,000 other Japanese Americans, was interned in a wartime detention camp in Poston, Arizona, where she become friends with writer Wakabo Yamauchi ("And The Soul Shall Dance"). During her internment she began publishing stories for the Poston Chronicle. After her release, she started a family and worked as a journalist. In 1952, she declined a writing fellowship from Stanford University to work instead on a Catholic community farm on Staten Island, New York. Yamamoto gained national fame with the publication of her collected short stories Seventeen Syllables and Other Stories *(1998), which was republished in 2001 with four new stories. The title piece of the collection (printed here) exemplifies Yamamoto's unique use of silence as a powerful means of communication.*

Seventeen Syllables (1949)

The first Rosie knew that her mother had taken to writing poems was one evening when she finished one and read it aloud for her daughter's approval. It was about cats, and Rosie pretended to understand it thoroughly and appreciate it no end, partly because she hesitated to disillusion her mother about the quantity and quality of Japanese she had learned in all the years now that she had been going to Japanese school every Saturday (and Wednesday, too, in the summer). Even so, her mother must have been skeptical about the depth of Rosie's understanding, because she explained afterwards about the kind of poem she was trying to write.

See, Rosie, she said, it was a *haiku*, a poem in which she must pack all her meaning into seventeen syllables only, which were divided into three lines of five, seven, and five syllables. In the one she had just read, she had tried to capture the charm of a kitten, as well as comment on the superstition that owning a cat of three colors meant good luck.

"Yes, yes, I understand. How utterly lovely," Rosie said, and her mother, either satisfied or seeing through the deception and resigned, went back to composing.

The truth was that Rosie was lazy; English lay ready on the tongue but Japanese had to be searched for and examined, and even then put forth tentatively (probably to meet with laughter). It was so much easier to say yes, yes, even when one meant no, no. Besides, this was what was in her mind to say: I was looking through one of your magazines from Japan last night, Mother, and towards the back I found some *haiku* in English that delighted me. There was one that made me giggle off and on until I fell asleep—

I lie awake, comme il faut,
sighing for some dough.

Now, how to reach her mother, how to communicate the melancholy song? Rosie knew formal Japanese by fits and starts, her mother had even less English, no French. It was much more possible to say yes, yes.

It developed that her mother was writing the *haiku* for a daily newspaper, the *Mainichi Shimbun,* that was published in San Francisco. Los Angeles, to be sure, was closer to the farming community in which the Hayashi family lived and several Japanese vernaculars were printed there, but Rosie's parents said they preferred the tone of the northern paper. Once a week, the *Mainichi* would have a section devoted to *haiku,* and her mother became an extravagant contributor, taking for herself the blossoming pen name, Ume Hanazono.[1]

So Rosie and her father lived for awhile with two women, her mother and Ume Hanazono. Her mother (Tome Hayashi by name) kept house, cooked, washed, and, along with her husband and the Carrascos, the Mexican family hired for the harvest, did her ample share of picking tomatoes out in the sweltering fields and boxing them in tidy strata in the cool packing shed. Ume Hanazono, who came to life after the dinner dishes were done, was an earnest, muttering stranger who often neglected speaking when spoken to and stayed busy at the parlor table as late as midnight scribbling with pencil on scratch paper or carefully copying characters on good paper with her fat, pale green Parker.

The new interest had some repercussions on the household routine. Before, Rosie had been accustomed to her parents and herself taking their hot baths early and going to bed almost immediately afterwards, unless her parents challenged each other to a game of flower cards or unless company dropped in. Now if her father wanted to play cards, he had to resort to solitaire (at which he always cheated fearlessly), and if a group of friends came over, it was bound to

---

[1]Ume, a flowering tree; Hanazono, a flower garden.

contain someone who was also writing *haiku,* and the small assemblage would be split in two, her father entertaining the nonliterary members and her mother comparing ecstatic notes with the visiting poet.

If they went out, it was more of the same thing. But Ume Hanazono's life span, even for a poet's, was very brief—perhaps three months at most.

One night they went over to see the Hayano family in the neighboring town to the west, an adventure both painful and attractive to Rosie. It was attractive because there were four Hayano girls, all lovely and each one named after a season of the year (Haru, Natsu, Aki, Fuyu[2]), painful because something had been wrong with Mrs. Hayano ever since the birth of her first child. Rosie would sometimes watch Mrs. Hayano, reputed to have been the belle of her native village, making her way about a room, stooped, slowly shuffling, violently trembling (*always* trembling), and she would be reminded that this woman, in this same condition, had carried and given issue to three babies. She would look wonderingly at Mr. Hayano, handsome, tall, and strong, and she would look at her four pretty friends. But it was not a matter she could come to any decision about.

On this visit, however, Mrs. Hayano sat all evening in the rocker, as motionless and unobtrusive as it was possible for her to be, and Rosie found the greater part of the evening practically anaesthetic. Too, Rosie spent most of it in the girls' room, because Haru, the garrulous one, said almost as soon as the bows and other greetings were over. "Oh, you must see my new coat!"

It was a pale plaid of grey, sand, and blue, with an enormous collar, and Rosie, seeing nothing special in it, said, "Gee, how nice."

"Nice?" said Haru, indignantly. "Is that all you can say about it? It's gorgeous! And so cheap, too. Only seventeen-ninety eight, because it was a sale. The saleslady said it was twenty-five dollars regular."

"Gee," said Rosie. Natsu, who never said much and when she said anything said it shyly, fingered the coat covetously and Haru pulled it away.

"Mine," she said, putting it on. She minced in the aisle between the two large beds and smiled happily. "Let's see how your mother likes it."

She broke into the front room and the adult conversation and went to stand in front of Rosie's mother, while the rest watched from the door. Rosie's mother was properly envious. "May I inherit it when you're through with it?"

Haru, pleased, giggled and said yes, she could, but Natsu reminded gravely from the door, "You promised me, Haru."

Everyone laughed but Natsu, who shamefacedly retreated into the bedroom. Haru came in laughing, taking off the coat. "We were only kidding, Natsu," she said. "Here, you try it on now."

After Natsu buttoned herself into the coat, inspected herself solemnly in the bureau mirror, and reluctantly shed it, Rosie, Aki, and Fuyu got their turns, and Fuyu, who was eight, drowned in it while her sisters and Rosie doubled up in

---

[2]Spring; Summer; Fall; Winter.

amusement. They all went into the front room later, because Haru's mother quaveringly called to her to fix the tea and rice cakes and open a can of sliced peaches for everybody. Rosie noticed that her mother and Mr. Hayano were talking together at the little table—they were discussing a *haiku* that Mr. Hayano was planning to send to the *Mainichi,* while her father was sitting at one end of the sofa looking through a copy of *Life,* the new picture magazine. Occasionally, her father would comment on a photograph, holding it toward Mrs. Hayano and speaking to her as he always did—loudly, as though he thought someone such as she must surely be at least a trifle deaf also.

The five girls had their refreshments at the kitchen table, and it was while Rosie was showing the sisters her trick of swallowing peach slices without chewing (she chased each slippery crescent down with a swig of tea) that her father brought his empty teacup and untouched saucer to the sink and said, "Come on, Rosie, we're going home now."

"Already?" asked Rosie.

"Work tomorrow," he said.

He sounded irritated, and Rosie, puzzled, gulped one last yellow slice and stood up to go, while the sisters began protesting, as was their wont.

"We have to get up at five-thirty," he told them, going into the front room quickly, so that they did not have their usual chance to hang onto his hands and plead for an extension of time.

Rosie, following, saw that her mother and Mr. Hayano were sipping tea and still talking together, while Mrs. Hayano concentrated, quivering, on raising the handleless Japanese cup to her lips with both her hands and lowering it back to her lap. Her father, saying nothing, went out the door, onto the bright porch, and down the steps. Her mother looked up and asked, "Where is he going?"

"Where is he going?" Rosie said. "He said we were going home now."

"Going home?" Her mother looked with embarrassment at Mr. Hayano and his absorbed wife and then forced a smile. "He must be tired," she said.

Haru was not giving up yet. "May Rosie stay overnight?" she asked, and Natsu, Aki, and Fuyu came to reinforce their sister's plea by helping her make a circle around Rosie's mother. Rosie, for once having no desire to stay, was relieved when her mother, apologizing to the perturbed Mr. and Mrs. Hayano for her father's abruptness at the same time, managed to shake her head no at the quartet, kindly but adamant, so that they broke their circle and let her go.

Rosie's father looked ahead into the windshield as the two joined him. "I'm sorry," her mother said. "You must be tired." Her father, stepping on the starter, said nothing. "You know how I get when its *haiku,*" she continued, "I forget what time it is." He only grunted.

As they rode homeward silently, Rosie, sitting between, felt a rush of hate for both—for her mother for begging, for her father for denying her mother. I wish this old Ford would crash, right now, she thought, then immediately, no, no, I wish my father would laugh, but it was too late: already the vision had passed through her mind of the green pick-up crumpled in the dark against one of the mighty eucalyptus trees they were just riding past, of the three contorted, bleeding bodies, one of them hers.

Rosie ran between two patches of tomatoes, her heart working more rambunctiously than she had ever known it. How lucky it was that Aunt Taka and Uncle Gimpachi had come tonight, though, how very lucky. Otherwise she might not have really kept her half-promise to meet Jesus Carrasco. Jesus was going to be a senior in September at the same school she went to, and his parents were the ones helping with the tomatoes this year. She and Jesus, who hardly remembered seeing each other at Cleveland High where there were so many other people and two whole grades between them, had become great friends this summer—he always had a joke for her when he periodically drove the loaded pick-up up from the fields to the shed where she was usually sorting while her mother and father did the packing, and they laughed a great deal together over infinitesimal repartee during the afternoon break for chilled watermelon or ice cream in the shade of the shed.

What she enjoyed most was racing him to see who could finish picking a double row first. He, who could work faster, would tease her by slowing down until she thought she would surely pass him this time, then speeding up furiously to leave her several sprawling vines behind. Once he had made her screech hideously by crossing over, while her back was turned, to place atop the tomatoes in her green-stained bucket a truly monstrous, pale green worm (it had looked more like an infant snake). And it was when they had finished a contest this morning, after she had pantingly pointed a green finger at the miniature tomatoes evident in the lugs at the end of his row and he had returned the accusation (with justice), that he had startlingly brought up the matter of their possibly meeting outside the range of both their parents' dubious eyes.

"What for?" she had asked.

"I've got a secret I want to tell you," he said.

"Tell me now," she demanded.

"It won't be ready till tonight," he said.

She laughed. "Tell me tomorrow then."

"It'll be gone tomorrow," he threatened.

"Well, for seven hakes, what is it?" she had asked, more than twice, and when he had suggested that the packing shed would be an appropriate place to find out, she had cautiously answered maybe. She had not been certain she was going to keep the appointment until the arrival of mother's sister and her husband. Their coming seemed a sort of signal of permission, of grace, and she had definitely made up her mind to lie and leave as she was bowing them welcome.

So as soon as everyone appeared settled back for the evening, she announced loudly that she was going to the privy outside, "I'm going to the *benjo!*" and slipped out the door. And now that she was actually on her way, her heart pumped in such an undisciplined way that she could hear it with her ears. It's because I'm running, she told herself, slowing to a walk. The shed was up ahead, one more patch away, in the middle of the fields. Its bulk, looming in the dimness, took on a sinisterness that was funny when Rosie reminded herself that it was only a wooden frame with a canvas roof and three canvas walls that made a slapping noise on breezy days.

Jesus was sitting on the narrow plank that was the sorting platform and she went around to the other side and jumped backwards to seat herself on the rim of a packing stand. "Well, tell me," she said without greeting, thinking her voice sounded reassuringly familiar.

"I saw you coming out the door," Jesus said. "I heard you running part of the way, too."

"Uh-huh," Rosie said. "Now tell me the secret."

"I was afraid you wouldn't come," he said.

Rosie delved around on the chicken-wire bottom of the stall for number two tomatoes, ripe, which she was sitting beside, and came up with a left-over that felt edible. She bit into it and began sucking out the pulp and seeds. "I'm here," she pointed out.

"Rosie, are you sorry you came?

"Sorry? What for?" she said. "You said you were going to tell me something."

"I will, I will," Jesus said, but his voice contained disappointment, and Rosie fleetingly felt the older of the two, realizing a brand-new power which vanished without category under her recognition.

"I have to go back in a minute," she said, "My aunt and uncle are here from Wintersburg. I told them I was going to the privy."

Jesus laughed. "You funny thing," he said. "You slay me!"

"Just because you have a bathroom *inside,*" Rosie said. "Come on, tell me."

Chuckling, Jesus came around to lean on the stand facing her. They still could not see each other very clearly, but Rosie noticed that Jesus became very sober again as he took the hollow tomato from her hand and dropped it back into the stall. When he took hold of her empty hand, she could find no words to protest; her vocabulary had become distressingly constricted and she thought desperately that all that remained intact now was yes and no and oh, and even these few sounds would not easily out. Thus, kissed by Jesus, Rosie fell for the first time entirely victim to a helplessness delectable beyond speech. But the terrible, beautiful sensation lasted no more than a second, and the reality of Jesus' lips and tongue and teeth and hands made her pull away with such strength that she nearly tumbled.

Rosie stopped running as she approached the lights from the windows of home. How long since she had left? She could not guess, but gasping yet, she went to the privy in back and locked herself in. Her own breathing deafened her in the dark, close space, and she sat and waited until she could hear at last the nightly calling of the frogs and crickets. Even then, all she could think to say was oh, my, and the pressure of Jesus' face against her face would not leave.

No one had missed her in the parlor, however, and Rosie walked in and through quickly, announcing that she was next going to take a bath. "Your father's in the bathhouse," her mother said, and Rosie, in her room, recalled that she had not seen him when she entered. There had been only Aunt Taka and Uncle Gimpachi with her mother at the table, drinking tea. She got her robe and straw sandals and crossed the parlor again to go outside. Her mother was telling them about the *haiku* competition in the *Mainichi* and the poem she had entered.

Rosie met her father coming out of the bathhouse. "Are you through, Father?" she asked. "I was going to ask you to scrub my back."

"Scrub your own back," he said shortly, going toward the main house.

"What have I done now?" she yelled after him. She suddenly felt like doing a lot of yelling. But he did not answer, and she went into the bathhouse. Turning on the dangling light, she removed her denims and T-shirt and threw them in the big carton for dirty clothes standing next to the washing machine. Her other things she took with her into the bath compartment to wash after her bath. After she had scooped a basin of hot water from the square wooden tub, she sat on the grey cement of the floor and soaped herself at exaggerated leisure, singing "Red Sails in the Sunset" at the top of her voice and using da-da-da where she suspected her words. Then, standing up, still singing, for she was possessed by the notion that any attempt now to analyze would result in spoilage and she believed that the larger her volume the less she would be able to hear herself think, she obtained more hot water and poured it on until she was free of lather. Only then did she allow herself to step into the steaming vat, one leg first, then the remainder of her body inch by inch until the water no longer stung and she could move around at will.

She took a long time soaking, afterwards remembering to go around outside to stoke the embers of the tin-lined fireplace beneath the tub and to throw on a few more sticks so that the water might keep its heat for her mother, and when she finally returned to the parlor, she found her mother still talking *haiku* with her aunt and uncle, the three of them on another round of tea. Her father was nowhere in sight.

At Japanese school the next day (Wednesday, it was), Rosie was grave and giddy by turns. Preoccupied at her desk in the row for students on Book Eight, she made up for it at recess by performing wild mimicry for the benefit of her friend Chizuko. She held her nose and whined a witticism or two in what she considered was the manner of Fred Allen; she assumed intoxication and a British accent to go over the climax of the Rudy Vallee recording of the pub conversation about William Ewart Gladstone; she was the child Shirley Temple piping, "On the Good Ship Lollipop"; she was the gentleman soprano of the Four Inkspots[3] trilling, "If I Didn't Care." And she felt reasonably satisfied when Chizuko wept and gasped, "Oh, Rosie, you ought to be in the movies!"

---

[3]Fred Allen (1894–1956), American radio and television humorist; Rudy Vallee, (1901–1986), American singer and bandleader; William Ewart Gladstone (1809–1898), nineteenth-century British prime minister; Shirley Temple (b. 1928), a child movie actor; Four Inkspots, American vocal quartet.

Her father came after her at noon, bringing her sandwiches of minced ham and two nectarines to eat while she rode, so that she could pitch right into the sorting when they got home. The lugs were piling up, he said, and the ripe tomatoes in them would probably have to be taken to the cannery tomorrow if they were not ready for the produce haulers tonight. "This heat's not doing them any good. And we've got no time for a break today."

It *was* hot, probably the hottest day of the year, and Rosie's blouse stuck damply to her back even under the protection of the canvas. But she worked as efficiently as a flawless machine and kept the stalls heaped, with one part of her mind listening in to the parental murmuring about the heat and the tomatoes and with another part planning the exact words she would say to Jesus when he drove up with the first load of the afternoon. But when at last she saw that the pick-up was coming, her hands went berserk and the tomatoes started falling in the wrong stalls, and her father said, "Hey, hey! Rosie, watch what you're doing!"

"Well, I have to go to the *benjo*," she said, hiding panic.

"Go in the weeds over there," he said, only halfjoking.

"Oh, Father!" she protested.

"Oh, go on home," her mother said. "We'll make out for awhile."

In the privy Rosie peered through a knothole toward the fields, watching as much as she could of Jesus. Happily she thought she saw him look in the direction of the house from time to time before he finished unloading and went back toward the patch where his mother and father worked. As she was heading for the shed, a very presentable black car purred up the dirt driveway to the house and its driver motioned to her. Was this the Hayashi home, he wanted to know. She nodded. Was she a Hayashi? Yes, she said, thinking that he was a good-looking man. He got out of the car with a huge, flat package and she saw that he warmly wore a business suit. "I have something here for your mother then," he said, in a more elegant Japanese than she was used to.

She told him where her mother was and he came along with her, patting his face with an immaculate white handkerchief and saying something about the coolness of San Francisco. To her surprised mother and father, he bowed and introduced himself as, among other things, the *haiku* editor of the *Mainichi Shimbun*, saying that since he had been coming as far as Los Angeles anyway, he had decided to bring her the first prize she had won in the recent contest.

"First prize?" her mother echoed, believing and not believing, pleased and overwhelmed. Handed the package with a bow, she bobbed her head up and down numerous times to express her utter gratitude.

"It is nothing much," he added, "but I hope it will serve as a token of our great appreciation for your contributions and our great admiration of your considerable talent."

"I am not worthy," she said, falling easily into his style. "It is I who should make some sign of my humble thanks for being permitted to contribute."

"No, no, to the contrary," he said, bowing again.

But Rosie's mother insisted, and then saying that she knew she was being unorthodox, she asked if she might open the package because her curiosity was so great. Certainly she might. In fact, he would like her reaction to it, for personally, it was one of his favorite *Hiroshiges.*[4]

Rosie thought it was a pleasant picture, which looked to have been sketched with delicate quickness. There were pink clouds, containing some graceful calligraphy, and a sea that was a pale blue except at the edges, containing four sampans with indications of people in them. Pines edged the water and on the far-off beach there was a cluster of thatched huts towered over by pine-dotted mountains of grey and blue. The frame was scalloped and gilt.

After Rosie's mother pronounced it without peer and somewhat prodded her father into nodding agreement, she said Mr. Kuroda must at least have a cup of tea after coming all this way, and although Mr. Kuroda did not want to impose, he soon agreed that a cup of tea would be refreshing and went along with her to the house, carrying the picture for her.

"Ha, your mother's crazy!" Rosie's father said, and Rosie laughed uneasily as she resumed judgment on the tomatoes. She had emptied six lugs when he broke into an imaginary conversation with Jesus to tell her to go and remind her mother of the tomatoes, and she went slowly.

Mr. Kuroda was in his shirtsleeves expounding some *haiku* theory as he munched a rice cake, and her mother was rapt. Abashed in the great man's presence, Rosie stood next to her mother's chair until her mother looked up inquiringly, and then she started to whisper the message, but her mother pushed her gently away and reproached, "You are not being very polite to our guest."

"Father says the tomatoes . . ." Rosie said aloud, smiling foolishly.

"Tell him I shall only be a minute," her mother said, speaking the language of Mr. Kuroda.

When Rosie carried the reply to her father, he did not seem to hear and she said again, "Mother says she'll be back in a minute."

"All right, all right," he nodded, and they worked again in silence. But suddenly, her father uttered an incredible noise, exactly like the cork of a bottle popping, and the next Rosie knew, he was stalking angrily toward the house, almost running in fact, and she chased after him crying, "Father! Father! What are you going to do?"

He stopped long enough to order her back to the shed. "Never mind!" he shouted. "Get on with the sorting!"

And from the place in the fields where she stood, frightened and vacillating, Rosie saw her father enter the house. Soon Mr. Kuroda came out alone, putting on his coat. Mr. Kuroda got into his car and backed out down the driveway onto the highway. Next her father emerged, also alone, something in his arms (it was the picture, she realized), and, going over to the bathhouse woodpile, he threw the picture on the ground and picked up the axe. Smashing the picture, glass and all (she heard the explosion faintly), he reached over for the kerosene

---

[4]Ando Hiroshige (1797–1858), wood block print artist.

that was used to encourage the bath fire and poured it over the wreckage. I am dreaming, Rosie said to herself, I am dreaming, but her father, having made sure that his act of cremation was irrevocable, was even then returning to the fields.

Rosie ran past him and toward the house. What had become of her mother? She burst into the parlor and found her mother at the back window watching the dying fire. They watched together until there remained only a feeble smoke under the blazing sun. Her mother was very calm.

"Do you know why I married your father?" she said without turning.

"No," said Rosie. It was the most frightening question she had ever been called upon to answer. Don't tell me now, she wanted to say, tell me tomorrow, tell me next week, don't tell me today. But she knew she would be told now, that the telling would combine with the other violence of the hot afternoon to level her life, her world to the very ground.

It was like a story out of the magazines illustrated in sepia, which she had consumed so greedily for a period until the information had somehow reached her that those wretchedly unhappy autobiographies, offered to her as the testimonials of living men and women, were largely inventions: Her mother, at nineteen, had come to America and married her father as an alternative to suicide.

At eighteen she had been in love with the first son of one of the well-to-do families in her village. The two had met whenever and wherever they could, secretly, because it would not have done for his family to see him favor her—her father had no money; he was a drunkard and a gambler besides. She had learned she was with child; an excellent match had already been arranged for her lover. Despised by her family, she had given premature birth to a stillborn son, who would be seventeen now. Her family did not turn her out, but she could no longer project herself in any direction without refreshing in them the memory of her indiscretion. She wrote to Aunt Taka, her favorite sister in America, threatening to kill herself if Aunt Taka would not send for her. Aunt Taka hastily arranged a marriage with a young man of whom she knew, but lately arrived from Japan, a young man of simple mind, it was said, but of kindly heart. The young man was never told why his unseen betrothed was so eager to hasten the day of meeting.

The story was told perfectly, with neither groping for words nor untoward passion. It was as though her mother had memorized it by heart, reciting it to herself so many times over that its nagging vileness had long since gone.

"I had a brother then?" Rosie asked, for this was what seemed to matter now; she would think about the other later, she assured herself, pushing back the illumination which threatened all that darkness that had hitherto been merely mysterious or even glamorous. "A half-brother?"

"Yes."

"I would have liked a brother," she said.

Suddenly, her mother knelt on the floor and took her by the wrists. "Rosie," she said urgently, "Promise me you will never marry!" Shocked more by the request than the revelation, Rosie stared at her mother's face. Jesus, Jesus, she called silently, not certain whether she was invoking the help of the son of the Carrascos or of God, until there returned sweetly the memory of Jesus' hand, how it had touched her and where. Still her mother waited for an answer, holding her wrists so tightly that her hands were going numb. She tried to pull free. Promise, her mother whispered fiercely, promise. Yes, yes, I promise, Rosie said. But for an instant she turned away, and her mother, hearing the familiar glib agreement, released her. Oh, you, you, you, her eyes and twisted mouth said, you fool. Rosie, covering her face, began at last to cry, and the embrace and consoling hand came much later than she expected.

Study and Discussion Questions

1. What are some of the things that separate Rosie and her mother?
2. "Rosie and her father lived for awhile with two women, her mother and Ume Hanazono." What differences are there between these two sides of Rosie's mother?
3. List as many different things as you can that Mrs. Hayashi gets out of writing *haiku.*
4. Why is Rosie's father so bothered by his wife's interest in *haiku?*
5. What might Mrs. Hayano represent to Rosie? To Rosie's mother?
6. In what ways do social class and class differences enter into the lives of the characters in "Seventeen Syllables"?
7. Why does Rosie fear that the story of her mother's marrying will "level her life, her world to the very ground"?
8. What does Yamamoto achieve by telling this story from Rosie's point of view?
9. What are the meaning and significance of the last line of "Seventeen Syllables"?

Suggestions for Writing

1. Describe the various forces pushing on Rosie. Outline what you think the next five or ten years of her life might hold.
2. "Seventeen Syllables" was first published in 1949, not long after the wartime internment of Japanese-Americans. Does that history cast any shadow over the story?
3. Explicate the last paragraph of "Seventeen Syllables."

Critical Resources

1. Cheng, Ming. "The Unrepentent Fire: Tragic Limitations in Hisaye Yamaoto's 'Seventeen Syllables.' " *MELUS* Winter (1994): 91–107.
2. Cheung, King-Kok. *Words Matter: Conversations with Asian American Writers.* Honolulu: U of Hawaii P and UCLA, 2000.
3. King-Kok, Cheung. *Articulate Silences: Hisaye Yamaoto, Maxine Hong Kingston, Joy Kogawa.* Ithaca, NY: Cornell UP, 1993.
4. *Rabbit in the Moon.* (documentary) Director Emiko Omori. Wabi-Sabi Productions, 1999. See <http://www.newday.com> for more information.

❀ ❀ ❀

CRISTINA GARCIA (b. 1958)

Born in Havana in 1958, during the Cuban Revolution, Cristina Garcia was taken to the United States by her parents at the age of two. Garcia grew up in Brooklyn and would receive her B.A. in political science from Barnard College in 1979, followed by a degree in Latin American Studies from John Hopkins in 1981. After spending several years as a reporter and researcher for Time *magazine, Garcia resigned her position to write fiction full time. In 1993 she published her first novel,* Dreaming in Cuban, *which became a finalist for the National Book Award and established her as a respected contemporary novelist.* Dreaming in Cuban *was followed by* The Aguero Sisters *(1997) and* Monkey Hunting *(2003). These generational epics explore Cuban American identity (with a focus on the feminine) and are characterized by dramatic shifts from realism to magical realism. Garcia's poetic prose style eloquently shows the connections between history and character. "Inés in the Kitchen," one of her few short stories, was first published in* Little Havana Blues: A Cuban-American Literature Anthology *(1996).*

Inés in the Kitchen   (1996)

Inés Maidique is twelve weeks pregnant and nauseous. Her back hurts, her breasts are swollen, and her feet no longer fit into her dressy shoes. Although she is barely showing, she walks around in sneakers to ease the soreness that has settled in every corner of her body. The eleven pounds she's gained feel like fifty.

When her husband returns home he'll expect her trussed up in a silk dress and pearls and wearing make-up and high heels. It's Friday and Richard likes for her to make a fuss over him at the end of the week. He'll be home in two hours so Inés busies herself preparing their dinner—a poached loin of lamb with mint chutney, cumin rice, ratatouille, and spiced bananas for dessert.

Richard will question her closely about what she's eaten that day. Inés will avoid telling him about the fudge cookies she devoured that morning in the supermarket parking lot. She hadn't wanted to eat the whole box, but bringing it home was unthinkable. Richard scoured the kitchen cabinets for what he called "illegal foods" and she was in no mood for his usual harangue.

With a long length of string Inés ties together the eye of loin and tenderloin at one inch intervals, leaving enough string at the ends to suspend the meat from the handles of the kettle. She slits the lamb in several places and inserts slivers of garlic. Then she sets about preparing the stock, skimming the froth as it simmers. Inés thinks about the initial excitement she'd felt when the blood test came back positive. She always knew, or thought she knew, she wanted a child, but now she is less certain.

The mint leaves give off a tart scent that clears her head with each pulse of the food processor. She adds fresh coriander, minced garlic, ginger root, honey, and a little lemon until the chutney congeals. Then she whisks it together with

plain yogurt in a stainless steel bowl. Inés remembers the abortion she'd had
the month before her college graduation. She was twenty-one and, like now,
twelve weeks pregnant. The baby's father was Cuban, like her, a hematology
resident at the hospital where Inés was finishing her practicum. Manolo Espada
was not opposed to having the baby, only against getting married. This was un-
acceptable to Inés. After the abortion, she bled for five days and cramped so
hard she passed out. Inés spent the summer working a double shift at an emergency room in Yonkers. Her child would have been eight years old by now. Inés
thinks of this often.

Shortly before she was to marry Richard, Inés tracked down her old lover to
San Francisco, where he'd been doing AIDS research with an eminent name in
the field. Over the phone, Manolo told her he was leaving for Africa the following month on a two-year grant from the Department of Health. Inés abruptly
forgot everything she had planned to say. Even if she'd wanted him again, it was
too late. She'd already sent out her wedding invitations and Richard had put a
down payment on the colonial house across from the riding stables. Manolo was
going to Africa. It would have never worked out.

Ratatouille is one of Inés's favorite dishes. It's easy to prepare and she cooks
big batches of it at a time then freezes it. The red peppers give the ratatouille a
slightly sweetish taste. Inés heats the olive oil in a skillet then tosses in the garlic and chopped onion. She adds the cubed egg-plants and stirs in the remaining
ingredients one at a time. On another burner she prepares the rice with chicken
broth, cuminseed, and fresh parsley. If she times it right, dinner will be ready just
as Richard walks through the door.

Her husband doesn't know about Inés's abortion, and only superficially about
Manolo Espada. It is better this way. Richard doesn't like it when Inés's attention is diverted from him in any significant way. How, she wonders, will he get
used to having a baby around? Richard was the only boy in a family of older sisters, and accustomed to getting his way. His father died when Richard was eight
and his three sisters had worked as secretaries to put him through medical
school. Richard had been the great hope of the Roth family. When he told them
he was marrying a Catholic, his mother and sisters were devastated. Janice, the
oldest, told him point-blank that Inés would ruin his life. Perhaps, Inés thinks,
his sister was right.

Inés strains the stock through a fine sieve into an enormous ceramic bowl, dis-
carding the bones and scraps. She pours the liquid back into the kettle and turns
on the burner to moderately high. Carefully, she lowers the lamb into the stock
without letting it touch the sides or the bottom of the kettle, then she ties the
string to the handles, and sets the timer for twelve minutes.

Other things concern Inés. She's heard about men running off when their
wives become pregnant and she's afraid that Richard, who places such a premium on her looks, will be repelled by her bloating body. As it is, Inés feels that
Richard scrutinizes her for nascent imperfections. He abhors cellulite and vari-
cose veins, the corporal trademarks of his mother and sisters, and so Inés works
hard to stay fit. She swims, plays tennis, takes aerobics classes, and works out

twice a week on the Nautilus machines at her gym. Her major weakness is a
fondness for sweets. Inés loves chocolate, but Richard glares at her in restaurants
if she so much as asks to see the dessert menu. To him a lack of self-discipline
on such small matters is indicative of more serious character flaws.

What of her husband's good qualities? Richard takes her to the Bahamas
every winter, although he spends most of the time scuba-diving, a sport which
Inés does not share. And he is intelligent and well-informed and she believes he
is faithful. Also, he isn't a tightwad like so many of her friends' husbands, watching every penny, and he doesn't hang out with the boys or play poker or anything
like that. Richard is an adequate lover, too, although he lacks imagination. He
likes what he likes, which does not include many of the things that Inés likes.
Once, in bed, she asked Richard to pretend he was Henry Kissinger. The request
offended him deeply. If Richard rejected so harmless a game, what would he say
to the darker, more elaborate rituals she'd engaged in with Manolo?

The loin of lamb is medium rare, just the way Richard likes it. Inés lets it cool
off on the cutting board for a few minutes before slicing it diagonally into thick,
juicy slabs. She sets the table with their wedding linen and china and wedges two
white candles into squat crystal holders. Inés thinks back on the five years she
worked as a nurse. She was good at what she did and was sought after for the
most important cardiology cases. More than one surgeon had jokingly proposed
to her after she'd made a life-saving suggestion in the operating room. But like
most men, they assumed she was unavailable. Someone so pretty, so self-
contained, they thought, must already be spoken for.

When Richard first started working at the hospital, Inés felt drawn to him.
There was something about his manner, about his nervous energy that appealed
to her. It certainly wasn't his looks. Richard was skinny and tall with fleecy colorless hair, not at all like the mesomorphic Manolo whose skin seemed more of
a pelt. For three months she and Richard worked side by side on coronary by-
passes, ventricular aneurysm resections, mitral valve replacements. Their manner
was always cordial and efficient, with none of the macabre bantering one often
hears in operating rooms. One day, Richard looked up at her from a triple bypass and said, "Marry me, Inés." And so she did.

When Inés was a child, her father had predicted wistfully that she would never
marry, while her mother seemed to gear her for little else. Inés remembers the
beauty pageants she was forced to enter from an early age, the banana curls that
hung from her skull like so many sausages. She'd won the "Little Miss Latin New
York" pageant in 1964, when she was seven years old. Her mother still considers this to be Inés's greatest achievement. Inés had sung and played the piano to
"Putting on the Ritz," which she'd translated to Spanish herself. Gerardo complained to his wife about sharing Inés with an auditorium full of leering strangers,
but Haydée would not budge. "This is better than a dowry, Gerardo." But
Gerardo preferred to have his daughter, dolled up in her starched Sunday dress
and ruffled anklets, all to himself.

Gerardo expected Inés to drop everything to play the piano for him, and for
many years she complied. This became more and more difficult as she got older.

Her parents separated and her father would call at all hours on the private phone line he'd installed in Inés's bedroom, pleading with her to come play the white baby grand he had rented just for her. Sometimes he would stroke her hair or tickle her spine as she played, tease her about her tiny new breasts or affectionately pat her behind. Inés remembers how the air seemed different during those times, charged and hard to swallow. Now her father is dead. And what, she asks herself, does she really know about him?

Inés turns off all the burners and pours herself a glass of whole milk. She is doing all the right things to keep the life inside her thriving. But she accomplishes this without anticipation, only a sense of obligation. Sometimes she has a terrible urge to pour herself a glass of rum, although she hates the taste, and she knows what it would do to the baby, or to burn holes in the creamy calfskin upholstery of her husband's sports car. Other times, mostly in the early afternoons, she feels like setting fire to the damask curtains that keep their living room in a perpetual dusk. She dreams about blowing up her herb garden with its fragrant basil leaves, then stealing a thoroughbred from the stable across the street and riding it as fast as she can.

Inés finishes the last of her milk. She rinses the glass and leans against the kitchen sink. There is a jingling of keys at the front door. Richard is home.

Study and Discussion Questions

1. What do we suspect about Inés's state of mind from the title and the opening sentence of the story?
2. List four or five significant *facts* we learn about Inés during the course of the story.
3. Who are the men in Inés's life that we hear about? Characterize her relation with each one.
4. How and why does being pregnant become a crisis point for Inés?
5. Garcia intersperses Inés's musings with vivid detailed paragraphs on what she is cooking for dinner. Why? What is the function of these paragraphs in the story? What effect do they have on the reader?
6. How does Inés feel about her pregnancy? Locate and discuss three passages in the story that may bear on her attitude toward being pregnant.
7. Discuss Inés's fantasies of escape in the second to last paragraph.
8. How might ethnicity be a factor in this story? Locate passages where Inés's Cuban identity (or her husband's Anglo identity) is explicitly or implicitly part of the story's tension.
9. Does Inés develop and change, however subtly, as the story progresses? Has she come to some realization by the end of the story?

Suggestions for Writing

1. Is Inés feeling trapped in her life? What evidence do you have either way? What do you think she will do next?
2. Write a postscript to "Inés in the Kitchen" set sometime later—you choose the time.

3. Write a couple of paragraphs from Richard's point of view.
4. Why and how do you think pregnancy is an important transitional event, perhaps even a rite of passage, in the lives of women? If you haven't been pregnant or had children yourself, talk to a few women who have gone through that experience and discuss with them any ponderings about or crises of identity they had during their pregnancy or any significant realizations they came to.
5. Is there a comparably significant "rite of passage" event in the lives of men? (This rite of passage doesn't have to be biological.) Discuss its components and compare to pregnancy as a rite of passage.

Critical Resources

1. Arujo, Nara. "I Came All the Way from Cuba So I Could Speak Like This? Cuban and Cuban- American Literatures in the US." *Comparing Postcolonial Literatures: Dislocations.* Ed. Ashok Bery. New York: Macmillan, St. Martin's, 2000.
2. Gomez-Vega, Ibis. "The Journey Home: Defining Identity in Cristina Garcia's *Dreaming in Cuban.*" *Voices: A Journal of Chicana/Latina Studies* 1.2 (1997): 71–100.
3. López, Iraida H. "'. . . And There Is Only My Imagination Where Our History Should Be': An Interview with Cristina García." *Bridges to Cuba/Puentes a Cuba.* Ed. Ruth Behar. Ann Arbor: U of Michigan P, 1995. 102–114.

JOHN UPDIKE (b. 1932)

John Updike was born in Shilington, Pennsylvania. He graduated from Harvard in 1954 and then moved to Oxford, England, to study art for a year. He later returned to the United States to work for the New Yorker *magazine, which began publishing his work. Updike eventually settled in Ipswich, Massachusetts. Updike's subjects are the values and problems of middle-class America. In this fiction, Updike seeks to problematize this seemingly mundane world, addressing such themes as family, religion, morality, sports, and the dynamics of intimate relationships. His novels include* Rabbit, Run *(1960),* Couples *(1968),* Rabbit Redux *(1971),* Rabbit Is Rich *(1981),* The Witches of Eastwick *(1984),* Roger's Version *(1986) and* Rabbit at Rest *(1990),* In the Beauty of the Lilies *(1996), and* Gertrude and Claudius *(2000). In "A & P," first published in* Pigeon Feathers and Other Stories *(1962), Updike's rare use of humor adds to the ambiguity of the story's meaning.*

A & P   (1962)

In walks these three girls in nothing but bathing suits. I'm in the third check-out slot, with my back to the door, so I don't see them until they're over by the bread. The one that caught my eye first was the one in the plaid green two-piece. She was a chunky kid, with a good tan and a sweet broad soft-looking can with those two crescents of white just under it, where the sun never seems to hit, at the top of the backs of her legs. I stood there with my hand on a box of HiHo crackers trying to remember if I rang it up or not. I ring it up again and the customer starts giving me hell. She's one of these cash-register-watchers, a witch about fifty with rouge on her cheekbones and no eyebrows, and I know it made her day to trip me up. She'd been watching cash registers for fifty years and probably never seen a mistake before.

By the time I got her feathers smoothed and her goodies into a bag—she gives me a little snort in passing, if she'd been born at the right time they would have burned her over in Salem—by the time I get her on her way the girls had circled around the bread and were coming back, without a pushcart, back my way along the counters, in the aisle between the checkouts and the Special bins. They didn't even have shoes on. There was this chunky one, with the two-piece—it was bright green and the seams on the bra were still sharp and her belly was still pretty pale so I guessed she just got it (the suit)—there was this one, with one of those chubby berry-faces, the lips all bunched together under her nose, this one, and a tall one, with black hair that hadn't quite frizzed right, and one of these sunburns right across under the eyes, and a chin that was too long—you know, the kind of girl other girls think is very "striking" and "attractive" but never quite makes it, as they very well know, which is why they like her so much—and then the third one, that wasn't quite so tall. She was the queen. She kind of led them, the other two peeking around and making their shoulders round. She didn't look around, not this queen, she just walked straight on slowly, on these long white primadonna legs. She came down a little hard on her heels, as if she didn't walk in her bare feet that much, putting down her heels and then letting the weight move along to her toes as if she was testing the floor with every step, putting a little deliberate extra action into it. You never know for sure how girls' minds work (do you really think it's a mind in there or just a little buzz like a bee in a glass jar?) but you got the idea she had talked the other two into coming in here with her, and now she was showing them how to do it, walk slow and hold yourself straight.

She had on a kind of dirty-pink—beige maybe, I don't know—bathing suit with a little nubble all over it and, what got me, the straps were down. They were off her shoulders looped loose around the cool tops of her arms, and I guess as a result the suit had slipped a little on her, so all around the top of the cloth there was this shining rim. If it hadn't been there you wouldn't have known there could have been anything whiter than those shoulders. With the straps pushed off, there was nothing between the top of the suit and the top of her head except just *her,* this clean bare plane of the top of her chest down from the shoulder bones like a dented sheet of metal tilted in the light. I mean, it was more than pretty.

She had sort of oaky hair that the sun and salt had bleached, done up in a bun that was unravelling, and a kind of prim face. Walking into the A & P with your straps down, I suppose it's the only kind of face you *can* have. She held her head so high her neck, coming up out of those white shoulders, looked kind of stretched, but I didn't mind. The longer her neck was, the more of her there was.

She must have felt in the corner of her eye me and over my shoulder Stokesie in the second slot watching, but she didn't tip. Not this queen. She kept her eyes moving across the racks, and stopped, and turned so slow it made my stomach rub the inside of my apron, and buzzed to the other two, who kind of huddled against her for relief, and then they all three of them went up the cat-and-dog-food-breakfast-cereal-macaroni-rice-raisins-seasonings-spreads-spaghetti-soft-drinks-crackers-and-cookies aisle. From the third slot I look straight up this aisle to the meat counter, and I watched them all the way. The fat one with the tan sort of fumbled with the cookies, but on second thought she put the package back. The sheep pushing their carts down the aisle—the girls were walking against the usual traffic (not that we have one-way signs or anything)—were pretty hilarious. You could see them, when Queenie's white shoulders dawned on them, kind of jerk, or hop, or hiccup, but their eyes snapped back to their own baskets and on they pushed. I bet you could set off dynamite in an A & P and the people would by and large keep reaching and checking oatmeal off their lists and muttering "Let me see, there was a third thing, began with A, as-paragus, no, ah, yes, applesauce!" or whatever it is they do mutter. But there was no doubt, this jiggled them. A few houseslaves in pin curlers even looked around after pushing their carts past to make sure what they had seen was correct.

You know, it's one thing to have a girl in a bathing suit down on the beach, where what with the glare nobody can look at each other much anyway, and an-other thing in the cool of the A & P, under the fluorescent lights, against all those stacked packages, with her feet paddling along naked over our checkerboard green-and-cream rubber-tile floor.

"Oh Daddy," Stokesie said beside me. "I feel so faint."

"Darling," I said. "Hold me tight." Stokesie's married, with two babies chalked up on his fuselage already, but as far as I can tell that's the only difference. He's twenty-two, and I was nineteen this April.

"Is it done?" he asks, the responsible married man finding his voice. I forgot to say he thinks he's going to be manager some sunny day, maybe in 1990 when it's called the Great Alexandrov and Petrooshki Tea Company or something.

What he meant was, our town is five miles from a beach, with a big summer colony out on the point, but we're right in the middle of town, and the women generally put on a shirt or shorts or something before they get out of the car into the street. And anyway these are usually women with six children and vari-cose veins mapping their legs and nobody, including them, could care less. As I say, we're right in the middle of town, and if you stand at our front doors you can see two banks and the Congregational church and the newspaper store and three real-estate offices and about twenty-seven old freeloaders tearing up Central Street because the sewer broke again. It's not as if we're on the Cape; we're north of Boston and there's people in this town haven't seen the ocean for twenty years.

The girls had reached the meat counter and were asking McMahon something. He pointed, they pointed, and they shuffled out of sight behind a pyramid of Diet Delight peaches. All that was left for us to see was old McMahon patting his mouth and looking after them sizing up their joints. Poor kids, I began to feel sorry for them, they couldn't help it.

Now here comes the sad part of the story, at least my family says it's sad, but I don't think it's so sad myself. The store's pretty empty, it being Thursday afternoon, so there was nothing much to do except lean on the register and wait for the girls to show up again. The whole store was like a pinball machine and I didn't know which tunnel they'd come out of. After a while they come around out of the far aisle, around the light bulbs, records at discount of the Caribbean Six or Tony Martin Sings or some such gunk you wonder they waste the wax on, sixpacks of candy bars, and plastic toys done up in cellophane that fall apart when a kid looks at them anyway. Around they come, Queenie still leading the way, and holding a little gray jar in her hands. Slots Three through Seven are unmanned and I could see her wondering between Stokes and me, but Stokesie with his usual luck draws an old party in baggy gray pants who stumbles up with four giant cans of pineapple juice (what do these bums *do* with all that pineapple juice? I've often asked myself) so the girls come to me. Queenie puts down the jar and I take it into my fingers icy cold. Kingfish Fancy Herring Snacks in Pure Sour Cream: 49¢. Now her hands are empty, not a ring or a bracelet, bare as God made them, and I wonder where the money's coming from. Still with that prim look she lifts a folded dollar bill out of the hollow at the center of her nubbled pink top. The jar went heavy in my hand. Really, I thought that was so cute.

Then everybody's luck begins to run out. Lengel comes in from haggling with a truck full of cabbages on the lot and is about to scuttle into that door marked MANAGER behind which he hides all day when the girls touch his eye. Lengel's pretty dreary, teaches Sunday school and the rest, but he doesn't miss that much. He comes over and says, "Girls, this isn't the beach."

Queenie blushes, though maybe it's just a brush of sunburn I was noticing for the first time, now that she was so close. "My mother asked me to pick up a jar of herring snacks." Her voice kind of startled me, the way voices do when you see the people first, coming out so flat and dumb yet kind of tony, too, the way it ticked over "pick up" and "snacks." All of a sudden I slid right down her voice into her living room. Her father and the other men were standing around in ice-cream coats and bow ties and the women were in sandals picking up herring snacks on toothpicks off a big glass plate and they were all holding drinks the color of water with olives and sprigs of mint in them. When my parents have somebody over they get lemonade and if it's a real racy affair Schlitz in tall glasses with "They'll Do It Every Time" cartoons stencilled on.

"That's all right," Lengel said. "But this isn't the beach." His repeating this struck me as funny, as if it had just occurred to him, and he had been thinking all these years the A & P was a great big dune and he was the head lifeguard. He didn't like my smiling—as I say he doesn't miss much—but he concentrates on giving the girls that sad Sunday-school-superintendent stare.

Queenie's blush is no sunburn now, and the plump one in plaid, that I liked better from the back—a really sweet can—pipes up. "We weren't doing any shopping. We just came in for the one thing."

"That makes no difference," Lengel tells her, and I could see from the way his eyes went that he hadn't noticed she was wearing a two-piece before. "We want you decently dressed when you come in here."

"We *are* decent," Queenie says suddenly, her lower lip pushing, getting sore now that she remembers her place, a place from which the crowd that runs the A & P must look pretty crummy. Fancy Herring Snacks flashed in her very blue eyes.

"Girls, I don't want to argue with you. After this come in here with your shoulders covered. It's our policy." He turns his back. That's policy for you. Policy is what the kingpins want. What the others want is juvenile delinquency.

All this while, the customers had been showing up with their carts but, you know, sheep, seeing a scene, they had all bunched up on Stokesie, who shook open a paper bag as gently as peeling a peach, not wanting to miss a word. I could feel in the silence everybody getting nervous, most of all Lengel, who asks me, "Sammy, have you rung up their purchase?"

I thought and said "No" but it wasn't about that I was thinking. I go through the punches, 4, 9, GROC, TOT—it's more complicated than you think, and after you do it often enough, it begins to make a little song, that you hear words to, in my case "Hello (bing) there, you (gung) happy pee-pul (splat)!"—the splat being the drawer flying out. I uncrease the bill, tenderly as you may imagine, it just having come from between the two smoothest scoops of vanilla I had ever known there were, and pass a half and a penny into her narrow pink palm, and nestle the herrings in a bag and twist its neck and hand it over, all the time thinking.

The girls, and who'd blame them, are in a hurry to get out, so I say "I quit" to Lengel quick enough for them to hear, hoping they'll stop and watch me, their unsuspected hero. They keep right on going, into the electric eye; the door flies open and they flicker across the lot to their car, Queenie and Plaid and Big Tall Goony-Goony (not that as raw material she was so bad), leaving me with Lengel and a kink in his eyebrow.

"Did you say something, Sammy?"

"I said I quit."

"I thought you did."

"You didn't have to embarrass them."

"It was they who were embarrassing us."

I started to say something that came out "Fiddle-de-doo." It's a saying of my grandmother's, and I know she would have been pleased.

"I don't think you know what you're saying," Lengel said.

"I know you don't," I said. "But I do." I pull the bow at the back of my apron and start shrugging it off my shoulders. A couple customers that had been heading for my slot begin to knock against each other, like scared pigs in a chute.

Lengel sighs and begins to look very patient and old and gray. He's been a friend of my parents for years. "Sammy, you don't want to do this to your Mom and Dad," he tells me. It's true, I don't. But it seems to me that once you begin a gesture it's fatal not to go through with it. I fold the apron, "Sammy" stitched in red on the pocket, and put it on the counter, and drop the bow tie on top of it. The bow tie is theirs, if you've ever wondered. "You'll feel this for the rest of your life," Lengel says, and I know that's true, too, but remembering how he made that pretty girl blush makes me so scrunchy inside I punch the No Sale tab and the machine whirs "pee-pul" and the drawer splats out. One advantage to this scene taking place in summer, I can follow this up with a clean exit, there's no fumbling around getting your coat and galoshes, I just saunter into the electric eye in my white shirt that my mother ironed the night before, and the door heaves itself open, and outside the sunshine is skating around on the asphalt.

I look around for my girls, but they're gone, of course. There wasn't anybody but some young married screaming with her children about some candy they didn't get by the door of a powder-blue Falcon station wagon. Looking back in the big windows, over the bags of peat moss and aluminum lawn furniture stacked on the pavement, I could see Lengel in my place in the slot, checking the sheep through. His face was dark gray and his back stiff, as if he'd just had an injection of iron, and my stomach kind of fell as I felt how hard the world was going to be to me hereafter.

Study and Discussion Questions

1. What does the story gain from being narrated by Sammy rather than, say, by Stokesie, or even by an omniscient narrator?
2. Characterize Sammy's attitude toward "girls" and toward women. Does the way he views Queenie change?
3. What evidence is there of a difference in social class between Sammy and the three young women? Does this difference in any way help explain his quitting?
4. Aside from his desire to impress Queenie and her friends, why *does* Sammy quit? Explain the significance of his last words in the story: "I felt how hard the world was going to be to me hereafter."

Suggestions for Writing

1. Briefly retell of the story from Queenie's point of view.
2. "A & P" was published in 1962 and, presumably, takes place around then, before the women's liberation movement that began in the late 1960s. What, if anything, would likely be different if the story took place today?

Critical Resources

1. De Bellis, Jack. *The John Updike Encyclopedia*. Westport, CT: Greenwood, 2000.
2. Dessner, Lawrence Jay. "Irony and Innocence in John Updike's 'A & P.'" *Studies in Short Fiction* 25.3 (1988): 315–17.
3. Saldivar, Toni. "The Art of John Updike's 'A & P.'" *Studies in Short Fiction* 34.2 (1997): 215–25.
4. Updike, John. *Self Conscious: Memoirs*. New York: Knopf, 1989.

JUDY GRAHN (b. 1940)

Judy Grahn grew up in a working-class family in New Mexico. She began writing poetry at the age of 10, but it didn't occur to her to become a full-time writer until the age of 25. She joined the Air Force when she was 19, but was discharged for being a lesbian (see her long poem "A Women Is Talking to Death"). Grahn became an important figure in the lesbian/feminist movements of the late 1960s and helped found the Women's Press Collective—an independent press that gave women authors and women's issues an outlet for publication. In addition to raising the public awareness of feminism, Grahn has endeavored in her writing to redefine perceptions of gay and lesbian life, researching the histories of gay culture and its unacknowledged influence on modern society. Her works include the poetry collections A Woman Is Talking to Death *(1974, Varieties of Protest), The* Work of a Common Woman *(1978), and* The Queen of Wands *(1982); the nonfiction* Another Mother Tongue: Gay Words, Gay Worlds *(1984), The Highest* Apple: Sappho and the Lesbian Poetic Tradition *(1985), Blood and Bread and* Roses *(1986), and* Really Reading Gertrude Stein *(1989); and the novel* Mundane's World *(1988). She has also coauthored* Inanna, Lady of Largest Heart: Poems of the Sumerian High Priestess Enheduanna *(2001). "Boys at the Rodeo" first appeared in* True-to-Life Adventure Stories *(1978).*

Boys at the Rodeo (1978)

A lot of people have spent time on some women's farm this summer of 1972 and one day six of us decide to go to the rodeo. We are all mature and mostly in our early thirties. We wear levis and shirts and short hair. Susan has shaved her head.

The man at the gate, who looks like a cousin of the sheriff, is certain we are trying to get in for free. It must have been something in the way we are walking. He stares into Susan's face. "I know you're at least fourteen," he says. He slaps her shoulder, in that comradely way men have with each other. That's when we know he thinks we are boys.

"You're over thirteen," he says to Wendy.

"You're over thirteen," he says to me. He examines each of us closely, and sees only that we have been outdoors, are muscled, and look him directly in the eye. Since we are too short to be men, we must be boys. Everyone else at the rodeo are girls.

We decide to play it straight, so to speak. We make up boys' names for each other. Since Wendy has missed the episode with Susan at the gate, I slap her on the shoulder to demonstrate. "This is what he did." Slam. She never missed a step. It didn't feel bad to me at all. We laugh uneasily. We have achieved the status of fourteen year old boys, what a disguise for travelling through the world. I split into two pieces for the rest of the evening, and have never decided if it is worse to be 31 years old and called a boy or to be 31 years old and called a girl.

Irregardless, we are starved so we decide to eat, and here we have the status of boys for real. It seems to us that all the men and all the women attached to the men and most of the children are eating steak dinner plates; and we are the only women not attached to men. We eat hot dogs, which cost one tenth as much. A man who has taken a woman to the rodeo on this particular day has to have at least $12.00 to spend. So he has charge of all of her money and some of our money too, for we average $3.00 apiece and have taken each other to the rodeo.

Hot dogs in hand we escort ourselves to the wooden stands, and first is the standing up ceremony. We are pledging allegiance for the way of life—the competition, the supposed masculinity and pretty girls. I stand up, cursing, pretending I'm in some other country. One which has not been rediscovered. The loudspeaker plays Anchors Aweigh, that's what I like about rodeos, always something unexpected. At the last one I attended in another state the men on horses threw candy and nuts to the kids, chipping their teeth and breaking their noses. Who is it, I wonder, that has put these guys in charge. Even quiet mothers raged over that episode.

Now it is time for the rodeo queen contest, and a display of four very young women on horses. They are judged for queen 30% on their horse*man*ship and 70% on the number of queen tickets which people bought on their behalf to 'elect' them. Talk about stuffed ballot boxes. I notice the winner as usual is the one on the registered thoroughbred whose daddy owns tracts and tracts of something—lumber, minerals, animals. His family name is all over the county.

The last loser sits well on a scrubby little pony and lives with her aunt and uncle. I pick her for the dyke even though it is speculation without clues. I can't help it, it's a pleasant habit. I wish I could give her a ribbon. Not for being a dyke, but for sitting on her horse well. For believing there ever was a contest, for not being the daughter of anyone who owns thousands of acres of anything.

Now the loudspeaker announces the girls' barrel races, which is the only grown women's event. It goes first because it is not really a part of the rodeo, but more like a mildly athletic variation of a parade by women to introduce the real thing. Like us boys in the stand, the girls are simply bearing witness to someone else's act.

The voice is booming that barrel racing is a new, modern event, that these young women are the wives and daughters of cowboys, and barrel racing is a way for them to participate in their own right. How generous of these northern cowboys to have resurrected barrel racing for women and to have forgotten the hard roping and riding which women always used to do in rodeos when I was younger. Even though I was a town child, I heard thrilling rumors of the all-women's rodeo in Texas, including that the finest brahma bull rider in all of Texas was a forty year old woman who weighed a hundred pounds.

Indeed, my first lover's first lover was a big heavy woman who was normally slow as a cold python, but she was just hell when she got up on a horse. She could rope and tie a calf faster than any cowboy within 500 miles of Sweetwater, Texas. That's what the West Texas dykes said, and they never lied about anything as important to them as calf roping, or the differences between women and men. And what about that news story I had heard recently on the radio, about a bull rider who was eight months pregnant? The newsman just had apoplectic fits over her, but not me. I was proud of her. She makes me think of all of us who have had our insides so overly protected from jarring we cannot possibly get through childbirth without an anesthetic.

While I have been grumbling these thoughts to myself, three barrels have been set up in a big triangle on the field, and the women one by one have raced their horses around each one and back to start. The trick is to turn your horse as sharply as possible without overthrowing the barrel.

After this moderate display, the main bulk of the rodeo begins, with calf roping, bronco riding, bull riding. It's a very male show during which the men demonstrate their various abilities at immobilizing, cornering, maneuvering and conquering cattle of every age.

A rodeo is an interminable number of roped and tied calves, ridden and unridden broncoes. The repetition is broken by a few antics from the agile, necessary clown. His long legs nearly envelope the little jackass he is riding for the satire of it.

After a number of hours they produce an event I have never seen before—goat tying. This is for the girls eleven and twelve. They use one goat for fourteen participants. The goat is supposed to be held in place on a rope by a large man on horseback. Each girl rushes out in a long run half way across the field, grabs the animal, knocks it down, ties its legs together. Sometimes the man lets his horse drift so the goat pulls six or eight feet away from her, something no one would allow to happen in a male event. Many of the girls take over a full minute just to do their tying, and the fact that only one goat has been used makes everybody say, 'poor goat, poor goat,' and start laughing. This has become the real comedy event of the evening, and the purpose clearly is to show how badly girls do in the rodeo.

Only one has broken through this purpose to the other side. One small girl is not disheartened by the years of bad training, the ridiculous crossfield run, the laughing superior man on his horse, *or* the shape-shifting goat. She downs it in a beautiful flying tackle. This makes me whisper, as usual, 'that's the dyke,' but for the rest of it we watch the girls look ludicrous, awkward, outclassed and totally dominated by the large handsome man on horse. In the stands we six boys drink beer in disgust, groan and hug our breasts, hold our heads and twist our faces at each other in embarrassment.

As the calf roping starts up again, we decide to use our disguises to walk around the grounds. Making our way around to the cowboy side of the arena, we pass the intricate mazes of rail where the stock is stored, to the chutes where they are loading the bull riders onto the bulls.

I wish to report that although we pass by dozens of men, and although we have pressed against wild horses and have climbed on rails overlooking thousands of pounds of angry animal flesh, though we touch ropes and halters, we are never once warned away, never told that this is not the proper place for us, that we had better get back for our own good, are not safe, etc., none of the dozens of warnings and threats we would have gotten if we had been recognized as thirty one year old girls instead of fourteen year old boys. It is a most interesting way to wander around the world for the day.

We examine everything closely. The brahma bulls are in the chutes, ready to be released into the ring. They are bulky, kindly looking creatures with rolling eyes; they resemble overgrown pigs. One of us whispers, "Aren't those the same kind of cattle that walk around all over the streets in India and never hurt anybody?"

Here in the chutes made exactly their size, they are converted into wild antagonistic beasts by means of a nasty belt around their loins, squeezed tight to mash their most tender testicles just before they are released into the ring. This torture is supplemented by a jolt of electricity from an electric cattle prod to make sure they come out bucking. So much for the rodeo as a great drama between man and nature.

A pale, nervous cowboy sits on the bull's back with one hand in a glove hooked under a strap around the bull's midsection. He gains points by using his spurs during the ride. He has to remain on top until the timing buzzer buzzes a few seconds after he and the bull plunge out of the gate. I had always considered it the most exciting event.

Around the fence sit many eager young men watching, helping, and getting in the way. We are easily accepted among them. How depressing this can be.

Out in the arena a dismounted cowboy reaches over and slaps his horse fiercely on the mouth because it has turned its head the wrong way.

I squat down peering through the rails where I see the neat, tight-fitting pants of two young men standing provocatively chest to chest.

"Don't you think Henry's a queer," one says with contempt.

"Hell, I *know* he's a queer," the other says. They hold an informal spitting contest for the punctuation. Meantime their eyes have brightened and their fronts are moving toward each other in their clean, smooth shirts. I realize they are flirting with each other, using Henry to bring up the dangerous subject of themselves.

I am remembering all the gay cowboys I ever knew. This is one of the things I like about cowboys. They don't wear those beautiful pearl button shirts and tight levis for nothing.

As the events inside the arena subside, we walk down to a roped off pavillion where there is a dance. The band consists of one portly, bouncing enthusiastic man of middle age who is singing with great spirit into the microphone. The rest of the band are three grim, lean young men over fourteen. The drummer drums angrily, while jerking his head behind himself as though searching the air for someone who is already two hours late and had seriously promised to take him away from here. The two guitar players are sleepwalking from the feet up with their eyes so glassy you could read by them.

A redhaired man appears, surrounded by redhaired children who ask, "Are you drunk, Daddy?"

"No, I am not drunk," Daddy says.

"Can we have some money?"

"No," Daddy says, "I am not drunk enough to give you any money."

During a break in the music the redhaired man asks the bandleader where he got his band.

"Where did I get this band?" the bandleader puffs up, "I raised this band myself. These are all my sons—I raised this band myself." The redhaired man is so very impressed he is nearly bowing and kissing the hand of the bandleader, as they repeat this conversation two or three times. "This is *my* band," the bandleader says, and the two guitar players exchange grim and glassy looks.

Next the bandleader has announced "Okie From Muskogee," a song intended to portray the white country morality of cowboys. The crowd does not respond but he sings enthusiastically anyway. Two of his more alert sons drag themselves to the microphone to wail that they don't smoke marijuana in Muskogee—as those hippies down in San Francisco do, and they certainly don't. From the look of it they shoot hard drugs and pop pills.

In the middle of the song a very drunk thirteen year old boy has staggered up to Wendy, pounding her on the shoulder and exclaiming, "Can you dig it, brother?" Later she tells me she has never been called brother before, and she likes it. Her first real identification as one of the brothers, in the brotherhood of man.

We boys begin to walk back to our truck, past a cowboy vomiting on his own pretty boots, past another lying completely under a car. Near our truck, a young man has calf-roped a young woman. She shrieks for him to stop, hopping weakly along behind him. This is the first bid for public attention I have seen from any woman here since the barrel race. I understand that this little scene is a re-enactment of the true meaning of the rodeo, and of the conquest of the west. And oh how much I do not want to be her; I do not want to be the conquest of the west.

I am remembering how the clown always seems to be tall and riding on an ass, that must be a way of poking fun at the small and usually dark people who tried to raise sheep or goats or were sod farmers and rode burros instead of tall handsome blond horses, and who were driven under by the beef raisers. And so today we went to a display of cattle handling instead of a sheep shearing or a goat milking contest—or to go into even older ghost territory, a corn dance, or acorn gathering. . . .

As we reach the truck, the tall man passes with the rodeo queen, who must surely be his niece, or something. All this non-contest, if it is for anyone, must certainly be for him. As a boy, I look at him. He is his own spitting image, of what is manly and white and masterly, so tall in his high heels, so *well horsed*. His manner portrays his theory of life as the survival of the fittest against wild beasts, and all the mythical rest of us who are too female or dark, not straight, or much too native to the earth to now be trusted as more than witnesses, flags, cheerleaders and unwilling stock.

As he passes, we step out of the way and I am glad we are in our disguise. I hate to step out of his way as a full grown woman, one who hasn't enough class status to warrant his thinly polite chivalry. He has knocked me off the sidewalk of too many towns, too often.

Yet somewhere in me I know I have always wanted to be manly, what I mean is having that expression of courage, control, coordination, ability I associate with men. To *provide*.

But here I am in this truck, not a man at all, a fourteen year old boy only. Tomorrow is my thirty second birthday. We six snuggle together in the bed of this rickety truck which is our world for the time being. We are headed back to the bold and shakey adventures of our all-women's farm, our all-women's households and companies, our expanding minds, ambitions and bodies, we who are neither male nor female at this moment in the pageant world, who are not the rancher's wife, mother earth, Virgin Mary or the rodeo queen—we who are really the one who took her self seriously, who once took an all out dive at the goat believing that the odds were square and that she was truly in the contest.

And now that we know it is not a contest, just a play—we have run off with the goat ourselves to try another way of life.

Because I certainly do not want to be a 32 year old girl, or calf either, and I certainly also do always remember Gertrude Stein's[1] beautiful dykely voice saying, what is the use of being a boy if you grow up to be a man.

Study and Discussion Questions

1. Why does the man at the gate decide the women are boys?
2. What kind of freedom does being seen as 14-year-old boys give to these women in their thirties?
3. By providing a narrator who is an outsider to the scene, Grahn is able to penetrate the mystique of the rodeo. Discuss how this works in the section on the brahma bull riding.

---

[1]American writer (1874–1946).

4. Is Grahn only talking about the rodeo in this story or are there larger implications?
5. Why does the narrator award the word *dyke* to one of the losers of the queen contest and to the one girl who takes the goat-tying event seriously?
6. What is the tone of "Boys at the Rodeo"?

Suggestions for Writing

1. What does Grahn suggest about the rodeo as a male ritual?
2. If these six women had been seen as "girls," what would their day at the rodeo have been like?
3. Discuss the depiction of the goat-tying event as an example of social criticism.

Critical Resources

1. Felstiner, John. "Judy Grahn." *Women Writers of the West Coast: Speaking of Their Lives and Careers.* Ed. Marilyn Yalom. Santa Barbara, CA: Capra, 1983. 92–102
2. *Stolen Moments.* (documentary) Director Margaret Wescott. Appearing: Judy Grahn, Audre Lorde, Joan Nestle. 1997. 90 minutes.
3. Whitehead, Kim. *The Feminist Poetry Movement.* Jackson: UP of Mississippi, 1996.

KATE CHOPIN (1851–1904)

Katherine O'Flaherty Chopin was born and raised in St. Louis, Missouri. When Chopin was 4 years old, her father died, and Chopin's care rested solely in the hands of her mother and great grandmother, both independent and strong-willed women. Under their guidance, the middle-class Chopin studied literature and music, developing her own sense of feminine independence. In 1870, at the age of 19, she married Oscar Chopin and moved to New Orleans. After his death in 1883, Chopin returned to St. Louis, where she began to write to support her six children, publishing her first novel, At Fault, *in 1890. During the next 14 years she would write two more novels, dozens of short stories, poetry, reviews, and criticism. While popular during her life as a writer of "local color," composing vivid depictions of New Orleans life, Chopin's early feminist vision, controversial at the time, has solidified her place in American fiction. In addition to skillful use of dialect and dialogue, Chopin questioned the oppressive nature of conventional marriage for women. Even more radical was her exploration of female passion and sexual desire—central themes in her best-known work,* The Awakening *(1899), a novel that was condemned as immoral during her lifetime but is now mandatory reading in*

English classes throughout the United States. In addition to the novels already mentioned, Chopin's short story collections include Bayou Folk *(1894) and* A Night in Acadie *(1897). "The Story of an Hour" was originally included in the collection* A Vocation and A Voice *(1897).*

The Story of an Hour   (1894)

Knowing that Mrs. Mallard was afflicted with a heart trouble, great care was taken to break to her as gently as possible the news of her husband's death.

It was her sister Josephine who told her, in broken sentences, veiled hints that revealed in half concealing. Her husband's friend Richards was there, too, near her. It was he who had been in the newspaper office when intelligence of the railroad disaster was received, with Brently Mallard's name leading the list of "killed." He had only taken the time to assure himself of its truth by a second telegram, and had hastened to forestall any less careful, less tender friend in bearing the sad message.

She did not hear the story as many women have heard the same, with a paralyzed inability to accept its significance. She wept at once, with sudden, wild abandonment, in her sister's arms. When the storm of grief had spent itself she went away to her room alone. She would have no one follow her.

There stood, facing the open window, a comfortable, roomy armchair. Into this she sank, pressed down by a physical exhaustion that haunted her body and seemed to reach into her soul.

She could see in the open square before her house the tops of trees that were all aquiver with the new spring life. The delicious breath of rain was in the air. In the street below a peddler was crying his wares. The notes of a distant song which some one was singing reached her faintly, and countless sparrows were twittering in the eaves.

There were patches of blue sky showing here and there through the clouds that had met and piled above the other in the west facing her window.

She sat with her head thrown back upon the cushion of the chair quite motionless, except when a sob came up into her throat and shook her, as a child who has cried itself to sleep continues to sob in its dreams.

She was young, with a fair, calm face, whose lines bespoke repression and even a certain strength. But now there was a dull stare in her eyes, whose gaze was fixed away off yonder on one of those patches of blue sky. It was not a glance of reflection, but rather indicated a suspension of intelligent thought.

There was something coming to her and she was waiting for it, fearfully. What was it? She did not know; it was too subtle and elusive to name. But she felt it, creeping out of the sky, reaching toward her through the sounds, the scents, the color that filled the air.

Now her bosom rose and fell tumultuously. She was beginning to recognize this thing that was approaching to possess her, and she was striving to beat it back with her will—as powerless as her two white slender hands would have been.

When she abandoned herself a little whispered word escaped her slightly parted lips. She said it over and over under her breath: "Free, free, free!" The vacant stare and the look of terror that had followed it went from her eyes. They stayed keen and bright. Her pulses beat fast, and the coursing blood warmed and relaxed every inch of her body.

She did not stop to ask if it were not a monstrous joy that held her. A clear and exalted perception enabled her to dismiss the suggestion as trivial.

She knew that she would weep again when she saw the kind, tender hands folded in death; the face that had never looked save with love upon her, fixed and gray and dead. But she saw beyond that bitter moment a long procession of years to come that would belong to her absolutely. And she opened and spread her arms out to them in welcome.

There would be no one to live for during those coming years; she would live for herself. There would be no powerful will bending her in that blind persistence with which men and women believe they have a right to impose a private will upon a fellow-creature. A kind intention or a cruel intention made the act seem no less a crime as she looked upon it in that brief moment of illumination.

And yet she had loved him—sometimes. Often she had not. What did it matter! What could love, the unsolved mystery, count for in face of this possession of self-assertion which she suddenly recognized as the strongest impulse of her being!

"Free! Body and soul free!" she kept whispering.

Josephine was kneeling before the closed door with her lips to the keyhole, imploring for admission. "Louise, open the door! I beg; open the door—you will make yourself ill. What are you doing, Lousie? For heaven's sake open the door."

"Go away. I am not making myself ill." No; she was drinking in a very elixir of life through that open window.

Her fancy was running riot along those days ahead of her. Spring days, and summer days, and all sorts of days that would be her own. She breathed a quick prayer that life might be long. It was only yesterday she had thought with a shudder that life might be long.

She arose at length and opened the door to her sister's importunities. There was a feverish triumph in her eyes, and she carried herself unwittingly like a goddess of Victory. She clasped her sister's waist, and together they descended the stairs. Richards stood waiting for them at the bottom.

Some one was opening the front door with a latchkey. It was Brently Mallard who entered, a little travel-stained, composedly carrying his grip-sack and umbrella. He had been far from the scene of accident, and did not even know there had been one. He stood amazed at Josephine's piercing cry; at Richards' quick motion to screen him from the view of his wife.

But Richards was too late.

When the doctors came they said she had died of heart disease—of joy that kills.

Study and Discussion Questions

1. Does Louise Mallard love her husband?
2. Why is it important that Louise goes to her room alone immediately after she hears the news of her husband's death?
3. Look at paragraphs 4, 5, and 6. How do the language, tone, and imagery in this section begin to prepare us (and Louise) for Louise's shift in feeling?
4. When Louise begins to recognize "the thing that was approaching to possess her," why does she initially try to will it out of existence? Also, think about that quote. Why do you think she describes the new feeling in this way?
5. What kind of life does Louise envision as a widow, as a woman who "would live for herself"?
6. Though the point of view in this story is that of a woman, is Chopin blaming men for what is wrong with marriage?

Suggestions for Writing

1. Discuss the narrator's attitude toward the institution of marriage.
2. Irony refers to the recognition of a reality different from appearance. How is the situation of "The Story of an Hour" ironic in several ways?
3. What, if anything, has changed about marriage in the hundred years since this story was written? If you think much has changed, how would you rewrite the story for a contemporary audience?

Critical Resources

1. Beer, Janet. *Kate Chopin, Edith Wharton, and Charlotte Perkins Gilman: Studies in Short Fiction.* New York: St. Martin's, 1997.
2. Berkove, Lawrence. "Fatal Self-Assertion in Kate Chopin's The Story of An Hour." *Literary Realism* 32.2 (2000): 152–58.
3. *Five Stories of an Hour.* Director Paul Kafno et al. Princeton: Films for the Humanities and Sciences, 1999. 26 minutes. For more information go to <http://www.films.com/id/3992>.
4. Petry, Alice, ed. *Critical Essays on Kate Chopin.* New York: G. K. Hall, 1996.
5. Toth, Emily. *Unveiling Kate Chopin.* Jackson: UP of Mississippi, 1999.

JEAN TOOMER (1894–1967)

Nathan Eugene Toomer grew up in Washington, D.C. He attended several universities after graduating from high school but was unable to stay at one university long enough to obtain a degree. In 1921, Toomer took a job as headmaster of a black school in Georgia. It was here that Toomer experienced black southern culture for the first time. Its contrast with his northern upbringing would provide the material necessary for his master-work, Cane *(1923), a three-part*

compilation of mixed-form, including short stories, poetry, and a drama. Al-
though Cane *and its author were well received at publication and "hailed as . . .*
the promise of a new day for black literature in America" (Notable Black American Men), *both soon disappeared from the public consciousness. It wasn't until*
the 1960s that scholars rediscovered Cane *and Toomer's influence on the Harlem*
Renaissance of the 1920s. Although he continued to write after 1923, it is Cane,
with its rich, sensual prose and modern synthesis of genres, that Toomer is most
known for. He also wrote Essentials *(1931) and* The Flavor of Man *(1949). In*
"Fern," taken from Cane, *Toomer's use of questions invites readers to engage in*
dialogue with the narrator.

Fern (1923)

Face flowed into her eyes. Flowed in soft cream foam and plaintive ripples, in
such a way that wherever your glance may momentarily have rested, it immediately thereafter wavered in the direction of her eyes. The soft suggestion of down
slightly darkened, like the shadow of a bird's wing might, the creamy brown color
of her upper lip. Why, after noticing it, you sought her eyes, I cannot tell you.
Her nose was aquiline, Semitic. If you have heard a Jewish cantor sing, if he has
touched you and made your own sorrow seem trivial when compared with his,
you will know my feeling when I follow the curves of her profile, like mobile
rivers, to their common delta. They were strange eyes. In this, that they sought
nothing—that is nothing that was obvious and tangible and that one could see,
and they gave the impression that nothing was to be denied. When a woman
seeks, you will have observed, her eyes deny. Fern's eyes desired nothing that you
could give her; there was no reason why they should withhold. Men saw her eyes
and fooled themselves. Fern's eyes said to them that she was easy. When she was
young, a few men took her, but got no joy from it. And then, once done, they felt
bound to her (quite unlike their hit and run with other girls), felt as though it
would take them a lifetime to fulfill an obligation which they could find no name
for. They became attached to her, and hungered after finding the barest trace of
what she might desire. As she grew up, new men who came to town felt as almost everyone did who ever saw her: that they would not be denied. Men were
everlastingly bringing her their bodies. Something inside of her got tired of them,
I guess, for I am certain that for the life of her she could not tell why or how she
began to turn them off. A man in fever is no trifling thing to send away. They began to leave her, baffled and ashamed, yet vowing to themselves that some day
they would do some fine thing for her: send her candy every week and not let
her know whom it came from, watch out for her wedding-day and give her a
magnificent something with no name on it, buy a house and deed it to her, rescue her from some unworthy fellow who had tricked her into marrying him. As
you know, men are apt to idolize or fear that which they cannot understand,

especially if it be a woman. She did not deny them, yet the fact was that they were denied. A sort of superstition crept into their consciousness of her being somehow above them. Being above them meant that she was not to be approached by anyone. She became a virgin. Now a virgin in a small southern town is by no means the usual thing, if you will believe me. That the sexes were made to mate is the practice of the South. Particularly, black folks were made to mate. And it is black folks whom I have been talking about thus far. What white men thought of Fern I can arrive at only by analogy. They let her alone.

Anyone, of course, could see her, could see her eyes. If you walked up the Dixie Pike most any time of day, you'd be most like to see her resting listless-like on the railing of her porch, back propped against a post, head tilted a little forward because there was a nail in the porch post just where her head came which for some reason or other she never took the trouble to pull out. Her eyes, if it were sunset, rested idly where the sun, molten and glorious, was pouring down between the fringe of pines. Or maybe they gazed at the gray cabin on the knoll from which an evening folk-song was coming. Perhaps they followed a cow that had been turned loose to roam and feed on cotton-stalks and corn leaves. Like as not they'd settle on some vague spot above the horizon, though hardly a trace of wistfulness would come to them. If it were dusk, then they'd wait for the search-light of the evening train which you could see miles up the track before it flared across the Dixie Pike, close to her home. Wherever they looked, you'd follow them and then waver back. Like her face, the whole countryside seemed to flow into her eyes. Flowed into them with the soft listless cadence of Georgia's South. A young Negro, once, was looking at her, spellbound, from the road. A white man passing in a buggy had to flick him with his whip if he was to get by without running him over. I first saw her on her porch. I was passing with a fellow whose crusty numbness (I was from the North and suspected of being prejudiced and stuck-up) was melting as he found me warm. I asked him who she was. "That's Fern," was all that I could get from him. Some folks already thought that I was given to nosing around; I let it go at that, so far as questions were concerned. But at first sight of her I felt as if I heard a Jewish cantor sing. As if his singing rose above the unheard chorus of a folk-song. And I felt bound to her. I too had my dreams: something I would do for her. I have knocked about from town to town too much not to know the futility of mere change of place. Besides, picture if you can, this cream-colored solitary girl sitting at a tenement window looking down on the indifferent throngs of Harlem. Better that she listen to folk-songs at dusk in Georgia, you would say, and so would I. Or, suppose she came up North and married. Even a doctor or a lawyer, say, one who would be sure to get along—that is, make money. You and I know, who have had experience in such things, that love is not a thing like prejudice which can be bettered by changes of town. Could men in Washington, Chicago, or New York, more than the men of Georgia, bring her something left vacant by the bestowal of their bodies? You and I who know men in these cities will have to say, they could not. See her out and out a prostitute along State Street in Chicago. See her move into a southern town where white men are more aggressive. See her become a white man's concubine. . . . Something I must do for her. There was myself. What could

I do for her? Talk, of course. Push back the fringe of pines upon new horizons. To what purpose? and what for? Her? Myself? Men in her case seem to lose their self-ishness. I lost mine before I touched her. I ask you, friend (it makes no difference if you sit in the Pullman or the Jim Crow as the train crosses her road), what thoughts would come to you—that is, after you'd finished with the thoughts that leap into men's minds at the sight of a pretty woman who will not deny them; what thoughts would come to you, had you seen her in a quick flash, keen and intuitively, as she sat there on her porch when your train thundered by? Would you have got off at the next station and come back for her to take her where? Would you have completely forgotten her as soon as you reached Macon, Atlanta, Augusta, Pasadena, Madison, Chicago, Boston, or New Orleans? Would you tell your wife or sweetheart about a girl you saw? Your thoughts can help me, and I would like to know. Something I would do for her ...

One evening I walked up the Pike on purpose, and stopped to say hello. Some of her family were about, but they moved away to make room for me. Damn if I knew how to begin. Would you? Mr. and Miss So-and-So, people, the weather, the crops, the new preacher, the frolic, the church benefit, rabbit and possum hunting, the new soft drink they had at old Pap's store, the schedule of the trains, what kind of town Macon was, Negro's migration north, bollweevils, syrup, the Bible—to all these things she gave a yassur or nassur, without further comment. I began to wonder if perhaps my own emotional sensibility had played one of its tricks on me. "Lets take a walk," I at last ventured. The suggestion, coming af-ter so long an isolation, was novel enough, I guess, to surprise. But it wasn't that. Something told me that men before me had said just that as a prelude to the of-fering of their bodies. I tried to tell her with my eyes. I think she understood. The thing from her that made my throat catch, vanished. Its passing left her vis-ible in a way I'd thought, but never seen. We walked down the Pike with people on all the porches gaping at us. "Doesn't it make you mad?" She meant the row of petty gossiping people. She meant the world. Through a canebrake that was ripe for cutting, the branch was reached. Under a sweet-gum tree, and where red-dish leaves had dammed the creek a little, we sat down. Dusk, suggesting the al-most imperceptible procession of giant trees, settled with a purple haze about the cane. I felt strange, as I always do in Georgia, particularly at dusk. I felt that things unseen to men were tangibly immediate. It would not have surprised me had I had vision. People have them in Georgia more often than you would sup-pose. A black woman once saw the mother of Christ and drew her in charcoal on the courthouse wall ... When one is on the soil of one's ancestors, most any-thing can come to one ... From force of habit, I suppose, I held Fern in my arms—that is, without at first noticing it. Then my mind came back to her. Her eyes, unusually weird and open, held me. Held God. He flowed in as I've seen the countryside flow in. Seen men. I must have done something—what, I don't know, in the confusion of my emotion. She sprang up. Rushed some distance from me. Fell to her knees, and began swaying, swaying. Her body was tortured with something it could not let out. Like boiling sap it flooded arms and fingers till she shook them as if they burned her. It found her throat, and spattered inarticulately in plaintive, convulsive sounds, mingled with calls to Christ Jesus. And then she sang, brokenly. A Jewish cantor singing with a broken voice. A child's voice, uncertain, or an old man's. Dusk hid her; I could hear only her song. It seemed to me as though she were pounding her head in anguish upon the ground. I rushed to her. She fainted in my arms.

There was talk about her fainting with me in the canefield. And I got one or two ugly looks from town men who'd set themselves up to protect her. In fact, there was talk of making me leave town. But they never did. They kept a watch-out for me, though. Shortly after, I came back North. From the train window I saw her as I crossed her road. Saw her on her porch, head tilted a little forward where the nail was, eyes vaguely focused on the sunset. Saw her face flow into them, the countryside and something that I call God, flowing into them ... Nothing ever really happened. Nothing ever came to Fern, not even I. Something I would do for her. Some fine unnamed thing ... And, friend, you? She is still living, I have reason to know. Her name, against the chance that you might happen down that way, is Fernie May Rosen.

Study and Discussion Questions

1. What is it about Fern's eyes?
2. What is the history of Fern's relationships with men? How do men feel about her?
3. How does the narrator, who is an outsider to Fern's community, see her? Is his view any different from that of the men who live there?
4. Who is the audience the narrator is imagining when he says "you and I"?
5. How is Fern's southern setting important to the narrator's sense of her?
6. List examples of imagery in this story. What mood do they evoke?

Suggestions for Writing

1. Discuss the power of point of view in this story.
2. Write a paragraph from Fern's point of view.
3. What does Fern represent or symbolize to the narrator?

Critical Resources

1. Boelhower, William. "Not Free Gifts: Toomer's 'Fern' and the Harlem Renaissance." *Temples for Tomorrow: Looking Back at the Harlem Renaissance.* Bloomington: Indiana UP, 2001.
2. Fabre, Genevieve and Michel Feith, eds. *Jean Toomer and the Harlem Renaissance.* New Brunswick, NJ: Rutgers UP, 2001.
3. Jones, Robert, *Jean Toomer: Selected Essays and Literary Criticism.* Knoxville: U of Tennessee P, 1996.
4. Toomer, Jean. *Essentials.* Ed by Rudolph Byrd. Athens: U of Georgia P, 1991.

❀ ❀ ❀

TAHIRA NAQVI (b. 1948)

Tahira Naqvi was born and raised in Lahore, Pakistan. After receiving a dual Master's in Psychology and English Education at Government College in Lahore, she immigrated to the United States in 1971. While the past decade has seen a rising awareness of South-Asian writers, Naqvi's writing and identity as a Pakistani/Muslim woman has added a balancing point of view to the abundance of Indian/Hindu narratives in South-Asian literature: "Pakistani immigrant life, women or rather their stories are different from the stories of Indian women ... I as a Pakistani writer with a Pakistani writer's and a Muslim woman's sensibility come with a built in restraint that works itself into the narrative" (Mehraab, www.mehraab.com). This restraint can be seen in the subtle way Naqvi meshes common Pakistani life with political settings. As a consequence, her stories offer a strong contrast to Western stereotypes of Muslim women. Her works include the short story collections The Attar of Roses *(1998) and* Dying in a Strange Country *(2001). In addition to her fiction, Naqvi is also a prolific translator of Urdu (the national language of Pakistan) writers. "A Man of Integrity" was published in* The Attar of Roses.

A Man of Integrity (1998)

The letter came in an ordinary white envelope, the kind one can buy fifty of for ten rupees. Somewhat transparent, crumpled because it was thin and flimsy, it was obviously not an official envelope, which was why he looked at it anxiously. Why was a personal letter posted to his office address? Was it bad news?

He tore open the envelope and removed the piece of paper that, unlike the envelope, was more expensive looking, heavy, unlined, with a watermark—special writing paper. The ink was Mont Blanc blue, the writing, in English, neat and ordered. He began reading:

Dear Sami *Sahib:*
You will be surprised no doubt when you get this letter. You will wonder who is writing to you at the office, why the handwriting doesn't look familiar, if it's a personal letter, etc., etc. The letter itself is harmless, I will say right away, so don't worry unnecessarily. And it's from a stranger. You don't know me. We have never met. Perhaps we have seen each other, as people walking in the streets see each other, but we have never met. Although a meeting may have taken place, the sort that takes place at a crowded party where people who don't know each other are randomly introduced. Anyway, this is all conjecture. The fact is I know you quite well, but you know nothing about me.

Sami quickly turned over the letter to see who had signed it. Nadira. A woman. He knew no one of that name. His heart began thumping against his ribs and he felt sweat gather on his forehead like prickly heat. Surely this meant trouble. These were turbulent times. People were often singled out for no obvious reason and made to suffer in the most humiliating ways. He had an enemy. Someone who wished to degrade him. And this was a common ploy. A woman appears from nowhere and places at his door an accusation, says for example that she is with child, that the child is his. Just recently poor Kamil Khan, the famous cricketer and now politician, had suffered such a fate. But he, Sami Ahmed, M.B.B.S, general practitioner, was neither famous nor a politician. Why him? Brushing a hand across his brow, he flipped over the sheet and resumed reading.

> For a strange woman to be writing to a man, especially one who is married, is beyond the bounds of good behavior, I agree, but I have written to you after much thought. This is not the act of a thoughtless, insensitive woman. For a whole year I have wondered what to do. Can I be candid? You seem like a lonely man. You stay long hours in your clinic, even when you have no patients. Why do you not go home to your wife, your two children? I do not wish to be rude, but I think you are running from them. Perhaps you need a friend. Perhaps I can be your friend. Is it possible that we meet somewhere?

There was no mention of a child. As yet. The paper in Sami's hands shook and his breath came fast, as if he had been running. Nevertheless, this had all the signs of a conspiracy to dishonor him. Doctors were common targets for such scandal. It was a patient. A woman who had been coming to him for some time and now had seen her chance for extortion. Would she want only money? The letter had ended. The last sentence said, "I will write again," and she had signed it, simply, "Nadira."

"Doctor *saab*, shall I send in the next patient?" Sami's attendant, Rafi, a young man given to illusions of superiority because he worked in a doctor's office, showed his head through the door.

"No, no, wait a few minutes." Sami dismissed him with a wave of his hand. He wanted to concentrate. Who was this woman, this . . . this Nadira? He had seen innumerable women in the last six years of practice. Which one was she? His mind refused to work. Other, unrelated images pushed for his attention. Again and again he saw pictures of the young girl for whom he had harbored a pubescent passion when he was fifteen. A long-necked, sprightly girl, she was seventeen, perhaps, or eighteen, and came to hang up her family's wash on the roof of the house next door. Bending, lifting up her arms, reaching up on her toes, turning, stretching her lithe body, she strung the clothes on the line with the grace and energy of a dancer. Bewitched the first time he saw her, the kite he had been flying forgotten, Sami watched her in a daze, the string in his hand suddenly loose, the kite swelling away from him, tugging at his hand as it rose and plunged, his mouth dry, his groin burning with desire.

"Doctor *saab*, it's Mrs. Niazi, she says she's in a rush." The thickly mustached face of his attendant appeared behind the door again.

"*Acha, acha,* send her in. How many more do we have?"

"Just two, Doctor *saab,* the old *mai* with a stomach ache and Bashir, Kamal *saab*'s gardener. He has fever today and he can barely move, his whole body is aching he says and I told him he will need Disprin . . ."

"*Acha,* go now," Sami said impatiently. Rafi sometimes fancied himself a nurse.

Mrs. Niazi was, like Sami, in her late thirties. As with so many of her counterparts, she had little to do, far too much to eat, and subsequently had put on weight. Now she was complaining of shortness of breath along with her frequent headaches. She was convinced she had high blood pressure and suspected that Sami deliberately withheld the information from her. Her large black shawl hanging carelessly from her shoulders and nearly trailing the floor as was the custom, she walked in and greeted Sami in the manner patients greet their family doctors, as if they are uncles, brothers, or at least old friends. Sami looked at her closely. She was stout, her face was puffy, there were dark bluish circles under her eyes, and her hair, cut short, was pinned away from her face, revealing gray streaks at the hairline. How beautiful she must have been once, when the eyes were bright, the skin taut and smooth, the body and spirit untarnished by neglect and apathy. She deposited herself in the chair across from his desk with a sigh, crossed her legs and shook her head despondently.

"Doctor *saab,* you have to give me something for my headaches," she said, pressing down on her forehead with one heavily ringed, plump hand. "Like this I'll die."

No, it could not be her. She depended too much on him. It was someone who had no fear in her heart, who was daring and presumptuous. Who then? The image of the girl from his youth rose up in his mind again. Why, after all these years, did he have to think of her? It wasn't a memory he was very proud of. He had behaved foolishly. He wouldn't want his own son to be so enamored.

He had written a letter to her, calling her 'queen of my dreams,' because he did not know her name, secured the letter to a jewelled plastic comb with a rubber band and had then thrown his gift and the letter over the parapet when she was pulling down laundry one afternoon. She knew she had an admirer on the rooftop across from hers and she had smiled enchantingly at him more than once. But the letter, a fervid, incoherent admission of his passion, fell into the wrong hands. Just as she stooped to pick up his epistle, her fingers still clutching a white sheet that she had partly dislodged from the line, an older woman, probably an aunt or her mother, appeared as if from nowhere from behind the white billowing bedsheet that flapped noisily in the wind, and grabbed the comb along with the letter still attached to it.

Sami knew that the disaster he had courted for so long had finally arrived at his door. A complaint was lodged with his mother, who, in turn, warned his father, who then boxed his ears and threatened to break his legs if he went up to the rooftop again. Love had clutched at his heart many times in later years, but none of his other attachments had generated the excitement this one had.

"No, no, Mrs. Niazi, you won't die, we won't let you," Sami said, smiling benevolently at his patient. "Now what seems to be the trouble?"

That afternoon, driving home in his red Suzuki that needed tuning and stalled and coughed frequently, he continued to think of the letter, which was now snug in his left pocket. Zaheen, his wife, should be warned, he decided. She should be told about the letter and the danger it carried. There was no reason to conceal it from her. He was not a man of secrets and there wasn't much in his life his wife or any one in his family didn't know about. After all, his was an uneventful life. Every morning, after a ritual of bathing and shaving, reading the paper and eating a breakfast that was always the same, he left for his clinic, saw patients until one, then came home for lunch and a long nap, returned to the clinic at five, saw more patients, read for an hour from the medical journals from America he subscribed to faithfully, and left for home around ten. If the Lahore traffic, which was particularly murderous at that time, didn't slow him down too much he made it back to his home in Shadman around ten-thirty. Zaheen didn't seem to mind that he came home so late so he wasn't worried if the traffic delayed him further. On Fridays he took the evening off and that was when he took Zaheen and the two boys, aged six and four, to visit his parents who lived on the other side of town, in Samanabad. Zaheen could drive and on the days she wanted to do her shopping, he left the car with her and took a taxi or bus to work.

He tried to think of Zaheen's face as she heard from him the story of the strange letter. It surprised him that he couldn't form a picture of her in his head. Was this a sign? Perhaps he shouldn't tell her any of this. Women are suspicious by nature and she might create a mountain out of a molehill. She might think he had done or said something to encourage the writer of this letter to make such an overture. The writing was indeed bold. One might be led to believe that the woman already knew what his response was to be. Just then, as a cloud of dust blew across his windshield while he waited at a red light, Sami reached into his pocket with his left hand, withdrew the letter, crunched it into a ball and threw it out of the window of his car. A gust of wind blew it away.

The second letter arrived on a day when he had been away from the clinic. His father had suffered a mild stroke and he was with him all day at Mayo Hospital. In the evening, just as the evening *azaans* were being relayed from the loudspeakers of the mosques ubiquitously scattered about in the city, he arrived at his clinic. Five or six patients with long-suffering expressions sat in the waiting room, among them a young woman he did not remember having seen before. For a few seconds he paused at the door of his office. His heart missed a beat. He remembered the letter. Rafi, relieved to see the doctor arrive, ran toward him. Sami slammed the door quickly.

With his characteristic persistence Rafi stuck his head through the opening in the door. "Doctor *saab,* the post is on your table and today we have three new patients. Mrs. Niazi's sister is also here. Should I send her in?" Rafi had obviously planned the order of the visits already. Relatives, then friends, acquaintances next followed by their relatives, and finally the others. That was the standard procedure at any doctor's office.

"Just wait a few minutes. I'll ring when I'm ready." Sami picked up the mail. The envelope, the handwriting on it already familiar, peeped from under a newsletter from the Pakistan Medical Association and some correspondence from Pfizer, a drug company. White, small, so different from the rest.

He sat down. Today he was not as nervous. A certain excitement seemed to take hold of him, a feeling of anticipation nibbled at his thoughts. He ripped open the envelope. The same paper, the same dark blue ink, the same neat and or-dered handwriting. But the heading had been changed. "My dear Sami *Sahib*," it now said. He was reminded of his adolescent letter. 'Queen of my dreams.' What foolishness.

He became aware of noises in the waiting room. The patients were com-plaining. He heard Rafi say that Doctor *saab*'s father had been ill, they must show some deference. A solicitous chorus arose. Rafi proceeded with details. He had taken charge.

Sami started reading.

I have seen you look worried. Is it because of my letter? I do not wish to upset you, to make you feel anxious. My greatest desire is to give you some-thing you do not have. A woman's friendship, her trust, her companionship. Do you not want all of these things? Think of what we can have, together. I will be in your office one day. Of course you will not know me. This se-crecy is important because I am placing my honor at stake and I cannot reveal myself until I am sure you want what I do.

Why were women always so preoccupied with notions of friendship and com-panionship with men? How they liked to complicate their lives by yearning for something they wanted only in principle instead of being grateful for what they actually had: a man to protect them, to take care of them, to give them children. For friendship they had friends, sisters, cousins, that whole noisy lot a man had so little patience with.

This time the letter ended with the words "Yours, Nadira." Yours. The word tickled his heart, his body was suffused with a warmth he had not felt in a long time. What was this! Folding the letter carefully, he slipped it back into the en-velope and placed it in his desk drawer, the one he always kept locked.

Sami Ahmed deemed himself a man of integrity. He was also a faithful husband. He had not so much as even looked at another woman with lust in his heart ex-cept perhaps some of those American actresses in the movies who made it very difficult for any man to keep his thoughts completely on track. His practice brought him into close contact with women of all ages and all types. Some were young and extremely attractive, some middle-aged and extremely attractive, oth-ers not so attractive but very attentive, like Mrs. Niazi, and those other women who wore *burkas* and hid themselves from the world, but thought nothing of lifting their veils in his presence to talk to him about their innermost thoughts and who believed he was as near to God as they would get in this life. Not once had he been tempted, nor had he given any of these women more than professional attention.

At home, he had a good relationship with his wife. There were periods of lovemaking when he wasn't too tired, and he had never imagined that he and his wife didn't have good sex. Zaheen had never complained, but then women don't like to talk much about such things. Anyway, there was nothing to complain about. He was a good husband, was he not? Did he not provide his family with all the comforts they needed? And he didn't embroil himself in scandalous affairs like some men he knew, like his best friend Hanif, for example, who had been seeing a married woman for three years and was now on the verge of breaking the news to his wife. Sami suspected she already knew and had no choice but to remain silent, for the sake of the children of course.

And so, being the man he was, Sami was agitated by the letters. What made matters worse was the knowledge that he experienced what he guiltily recognized to be an unwholesome excitement from this curious correspondence. The woman (if she was that and not a man pretending to be a woman and out to dishonor the doctor for some imagined grievance) had not suggested a meeting as yet nor had she offered to speak to him on the phone. But he knew, the agitation growing to disturbing proportions, that a phone call would come soon. Such was the nature of life in the city. Letters belonged to an older, slower time. Now it was the telephone, that instrument of immediate gratification, which generated communication. This knowledge brought in its wake further trepidation. What if she chose to call at home? He remembered a cousin whose wife left him simply because a strange woman who never disclosed her identity kept calling her to offer details of a sordid romance involving her husband. The couple began to quarrel. Ugly scenes ensued. She accused him of infidelity. He protested, violently, and before long they were throwing things at each other and one day a side table he had flung at her struck her on the side of her forehead and she fainted. The children, a boy only seven, and a girl nearly ten, ran out of the house in terror. The father went after them and dragged them home only to find his wife bleeding from the spot that had received the impact of the chair. She had to be hospitalized. In a month a divorce followed. The whole family was torn apart.

Sami shuddered as the details of that unhappy, miserable incident returned to him. His wife must never know of the letters. He must destroy the one in his drawer the very next morning. Having made that resolve, he found himself wondering, somewhat foolishly, when the third letter would be coming and what it would say. That night Sami tossed and turned in bed with no peace in his heart.

"Are you all right?" Zaheen asked him. "Are you worried about Abba?" Her voice was tinged with sympathy.

He was suddenly, ashamedly, relieved that he could respond hastily with "Yes, I am worried. A stroke, under the best of circumstances, is a horrible thing, and he's old and so weak." How easily the lie came to him, he thought as he shut his eyes and beckoned sleep to come to him.

The next day the phone call arrived just as he had finished prescribing antibiotics to his last patient. Rafi informed him irately that it was some '*Begum saab*' who didn't want to speak to the receptionist but wanted only to speak to 'Doctor *saab*.' His patient, an older man who had bronchitis and looked frail and helpless, fumbled as he folded the prescription that had been handed to him, slipped it into his front coat pocket, and touching his forehead in a *salaam*, left the room.

Sami picked up the receiver and feigned a disinterested "Hallo."

"Hallo." The voice did not sound familiar. Sami was not given to easily recognizing people's voices on the phone. Always, he was too distracted, his mind was elsewhere, so that unless the voice at the other end identified itself, he failed to connect it to anyone he knew.

"*Salaamalekum.*"

"*Walekumsalaam.* Who is this?" He bravely maintained a wooden inflection. Inside his chest his heart rocked as if it were a boat cast on turbulent waters.

"It's me." The voice quivered. Sami could picture a smile, a slight curling of the lips.

"Who is this please? I'm very busy today. Is it Mrs. Niazi?" Sami attempted to sound brusque.

"No, you know it's not Mrs. Niazi, it's Nadira. Can you talk?"

"Look, I don't know any Nadira and if you are sick please make an appointment with the receptionist." He felt he had taken charge.

"Of course you know me." The voice was smooth, a little husky, perhaps because she was speaking in a hushed voice. Sometimes she spoke English and once in a while she lapsed into Urdu.

"What do you want?" The words fell out of his mouth without his volition. He sat back in his chair and looked straight at the door of his office, noticing that the paint was peeling in one corner, wondering foolishly at that moment if Rafi could hear him.

"I want only to be with you. But what do you want?"

"I don't want anything. This is not proper. Writing to me and calling me like this is not proper at all. You know I'm married, I'm happily married, so why bother with me, hunh?" He decided the direct approach would be the best.

"If you're so happy why do you sit here in the office, long after the last patient's gone?"

"I stay in the office to read. Reading at home is difficult . . . anyway, it has nothing to do with being happy or not being happy. But what you are suggesting is impossible. I want to tell you right away I will not be drawn into this trap you're trying to plan for me. Please don't call here again and please don't write." He injected his tone with as much disapproval as he could muster. He also raised his voice a little. After this he should have banged the receiver down. Instead he kept it to his ear. There was silence for a few seconds at the other end.

"How much better if we sat across from each other and had this conversation. Then you could see I was not out to trap you. You would see I was sincere." His

show of anger had not produced the desired effect. She did not appear to be ruffled by either his words or his tone. Her persistence proved unnerving.

"Look," Sami erupted impatiently, aware with a sick feeling that he should
end this conversation before it went further, "I don't know what it will take for
you to understand that what you want is impossible. However . . ." What was he
doing? The voice of caution reared its head. Stop! "If you have a problem that
you wish to discuss, come to the office. You obviously know the clinic hours.
Make an appointment with my receptionist . . ."

"Can I come now?" She cut him short. He imagined the smile becoming co-
quettish. His heart raced.

A glance at his watch showed it was past nine already. Rafi was closing up the
office. The receptionist would come in with the next day's appointments and she
and Rafi would leave together in another ten minutes.

"No, I will be leaving soon. If you wish to see me come tomorrow around one.
Rafi, my attendant, will show you in. Tell him . . . tell him you're my wife's
cousin." The words slipped out without effort.

She didn't say anything. There was a click and she was gone. Sami replaced
the receiver on the cradle. His hands were clammy, even though it was mid-
December and tonight was particularly chilly. Would she come?

She didn't come, or if she was among the five or six new female patients he had
that week, she didn't reveal herself nor could he guess if it was one or the other.
In his heart he suspected that she was one of them. For a while the tall, slim
woman who complained of stomach pains, whose fingers were long and bare of
rings, whose eyes were thickly edged with sooty-black lashes, whose full, red lips
curved in a bashful smile when she presented her symptoms, and who was wearing some kind of perfume that seemed to insinuate itself in his brain and excite his thoughts, seemed to be the one. She glanced at him sideways, as if she
couldn't raise her eyes and look at him squarely. As he listened to her complaints
he felt a familiar warmth creeping up along his thighs. His chest constricted with
some emotion he could not name.

"Doctor *saab*, I have these shooting pains," she said in English, the voice
trained at an English-medium school. "They start from here," she pointed to the
lower left side of her abdomen, "and go up all along my arm." There was such
detachment in her eyes, they were so devoid of anything except a concern for
the shooting pains that Sami cursed himself for his stupidity and, feeling once
again as if he were the boy with the kite string slipping from his hands again, he
adjusted the knobs of the stethoscope in his ears and bent forward attentively.

At night, unable to sleep, he picked up a medical journal from his bedside
table and started flipping through it. "Risk Determinants in Survivors of
Myocardial Infarction" caught his eye and he told himself he should read it.
Zaheen was putting the boys to bed. He could hear her talking to them in the
low, hushed voice she reserved for bedtime conversations with them. With a feeling of dismay he realized he didn't know what she said to them as she tucked

them in. Did she tell them stories? Did she read to them from story books or did she tell them the old tales that were handed down orally from one generation to another? The story of the flea that greedily downed a whole stream and suffered from catastrophic indigestion, the parrot that could never keep a secret, the princess who lived in the flower of the pomegranate fruit and waited eternally for her prince. Perhaps she read to them. With a twinge of guilt he realized he had never seen the story books in his children's room. When was the last time he was there?

The phone rang with a loud, jarring sound and he jumped. The journal slipped from his hands and fell off the bed and his mouth became dry.

He fumbled with the receiver. "Hallo," he croaked.

"Doctor *saab, salaamalekum,* it's Jamal Syed. My wife is complaining of severe pain in her right leg, she's unable to sleep." The husband's voice sounded troubled, apprehensive.

Swept over by a wave of relief that almost took his breath away, Sami transferred the receiver to his other hand and lifted himself on his elbow. "Does it come and go, Jamal *sahib,* or is it continuous?" Calming his nerves, he assumed his professional tone.

Jamal spoke to his wife. Sami heard the sick woman's voice in the background. "Doctor *saab,*" Jamal continued, "she says it starts whenever she moves her leg and it spreads all along the side, she's in terrible discomfort."

Sciatica. Can't do much about it. "She should rest, avoid sudden movements and tomorrow I'll see her in the clinic. It's not serious." Sami comforted the distraught husband.

When Zaheen returned to the room he was lying on his side with his eyes closed. Phone calls were normal at any time of the night in a doctor's house, but he was stricken with the thought that Zaheen might ask who it was and he would then be forced to talk to her. He didn't wish to talk to her. There was too much on his mind.

She moved under the covers unhurriedly, sighing gently. Why was she sighing? Was something wrong? Did she suspect anything? How could she, unless . . . His heart lurched. Zaheen sighed again and turned so husband and wife lay back to back, facing away from each other. Sleep evaded him; like a kite caught in sudden strong wind, tugging, pulling, it ran from him.

The sun was just a dash of orange on a shadowy horizon when he awoke the next morning. For a few minutes he stared at the sky through the gap between the window curtains, seized with a strangeness he couldn't account for. He felt as if he was someone else, not the man he was yesterday or the day before that, a man who should not be in this bed, in this room. The clock on his nightstand said 6:30. In another half hour Zaheen would be up. Slowly he slipped out of bed. For a few seconds he stood still, not sure of what it was that he wanted to do. Ignoring the impulse to return to a warm bed he left the room and walked over to the boys' bedroom.

The children were sleeping soundly. He could hear the soft, rhythmic murmur of their breathing. The room looked different. The beds were new and Zaheen had put up framed pictures on the walls, animals and scenery, prints she must have cut out of calendars. A small white bookcase held the boys' store of books. Sami bent down to examine them, fingering the spines while he peered at the titles. As his gaze traveled lower he observed that the second shelf contained books that were not children's books at all. *Jane Eyre, Lady Chatterley's Lover, Wuthering Heights, Rebecca, Gone with the Wind, Pride and Prejudice,* and Urdu novels as well, *Dastak na do, Terhi Lakir,* other titles not so familiar, also newer works in English perhaps by American and British authors. These were Zaheen's books. She had been reading.

Sami was surprised. Why, he didn't know. After all, Zaheen was a well-educated woman. She had a B.A. from Kinnaird College, one of the most prestigious colleges for women in Lahore, she spoke English fluently, and she also had once been fond of painting. Sami remembered how taken he was with the fact that his wife-to-be was so talented. Some of the paintings she had done before she was married now hung in their drawing room and their bedroom. One, a still life with roses in a vase and books had been Sami's favorite in the days he was engaged to her. He couldn't remember why she had stopped painting. Of course. The children, she said once. They would get into the tubes of paint no matter where she set up her easel.

After some thought he realized he was surprised to see the books because he had never had occasion to find Zaheen sitting with a book propped in her lap. Always she was running around the house, doing this or that. Maybe she also read the newspaper after he left for work.

He tiptoed back into bed just when Zaheen was stirring.

Suddenly, just as he had anticipated, the letters stopped. Instead, Nadira now called him regularly, every night soon after he had finished with his last patient. It was as if she had a clairvoyant view of how many patients he had and when he was seeing the last one. After the third telephone call he sent off Rafi and the receptionist, telling them he would lock up himself. "I have some reading to do," he told them, pointing to a pile of journals on his desk. Rafi, the conscientious caretaker that he was, exhibited reluctance to let the doctor do what he had been doing himself for five years. "But Doctor *saab,* I'll stay as long as you want, I'll take care of it, don't worry," he said in a worried tone. Sami persuaded him it was all right, he should go and not worry. The pile of journals on the doctor's desk grew and Rafi finally realized his employer meant business.

Tonight, when the phone rang he was alone in the office, riffling idly through *Cardiology Update*s, having paused at "Anthracyclines and the Heart" several times with the intent of reading it.

"Were you waiting for my call?" Nadira asked with a quick laugh. There was something about the manner in which the tiny laugh came at the end of a word quickly, almost as a part of it, that made it sound familiar, as if he heard it every day. But, despite all his efforts, he was hard pressed to link it to anyone he knew.

"Yes, I was. But I don't have much time. Yesterday I got home at ten-thirty and if this continues, Zaheen . . . my wife will know something is wrong." So now he was plotting to deceive his wife.

"Perhaps she doesn't really care. After all, you're a doctor, doctors have emergencies and can be held up by sick patients without any notice."

"Yes, that's true. But still . . . anyway, when are you coming to see me? Are you going to be a mystery woman forever?" Sami heard her laugh in response to his daring query. Was she laughing at him?

"Soon, be patient. So how was your day today?"

"It was all right. The same old routine, nothing different."

"Are you bored with your work?"

"I used to find it exciting, but now it's just all the same. There's no challenge in seeing patients suffering from the flu, from pains and aches, from diarrhea, men and women who seem to court sickness just so they can have some change in their lives." Why was he telling her all this? He had never even admitted any of this to himself. Not once had he openly admitted that he missed the excitement and challenge of real medicine. Diseases with long, complex names sprang at him from his journals, and he read about them as if they were exotic tales from faraway lands, with avid eagerness and hunger. He envied doctors who made life and death decisions, who pulled despairing patients out of the darkness of death and hopelessness, who walked around with a swagger, arrogantly. Set aside for him seemed to be the commonplace—flu, skin rashes, diarrhea, aches and pains—illnesses that often needed no more than placebos and pep talk to evince a cure.

"Why don't you do something about it?"

"Like what? Life is a drudge, I have to make money, the family has to be provided for, and there's no other choice, is there?"

"Isn't there?" Nadira's query was like herself. A distant, mysterious, enigmatic suggestion.

They talked, he more than she, and when he closed up the office it was nearly ten-thirty. He should have called Zaheen to tell her he had been held up.

She opened the door for him when he rang the doorbell. The houseboy was nowhere in sight. Perhaps he was already asleep. It was past eleven. Sami began mumbling about a troublesome patient, keeping his eyes away from Zaheen's face as he recounted the problems the patient was having. Zaheen listened without amazement, nor did she complain about the lateness of the hour, which surprised him. Was she going to be surly because he was late?

"And the traffic, even this late, was awful. I don't understand where people are off to at this hour of night." He grumbled, irked by her silence.

"Well, those who work late have only this time for some recreation," Zaheen said, making her way to the kitchen. "Not everyone is eager to get home and to bed," she added with a cheerful smile. So, she wasn't angry. Relief flooded over him.

The next morning Sami felt he was coming down with a cold. The hazards of his profession. A cold was such a nasty business, especially for a doctor, especially when one could do little about a perpetually runny nose and sniffles. To his patients he'd say, take two aspirins, inhale some steam, drink lots of liquids, and keep warm. To himself he said none of those things, because nothing helped.

Only time took care of the common cold. Everything else was a well-intended deception. He called the office, told Rafi to cancel the morning patients and gave orders that if someone seriously ill put in a call to the office, he was to be contacted at home at once.

Zaheen was still in the kitchen. The boys had left for school. Sami showered, standing a long time under the hot water, letting the steaming warmth seep into every pore of his body. His eyes were closed and his head was filled with reflections of Nadira and when he would see her and how she would look. Suddenly he was gripped with a fearful thought. It was as if the water had been turned off suddenly and he had been doused with an icy cold splash. What if she was an ugly hag of a woman? He froze. Steeped in the vanity of his own desire, he had not thought for a second that Nadira was anything but beautiful and young. Like his rooftop beloved. Unable to shrug the thought away, he shut off the water and came out of the shower quickly. As he rubbed himself with a towel the image of a woman unlike any of the pictures he had formed in his mind of Nadira arose like a specter before him. Could that soft-textured, sugary, teasing voice belong to anyone whose face was not like the moon? Yes, it could. And she might also be fat, like Mrs. Niazi, whose voice was soft and sugary as well. What had he done!

Sami sat down on his bed as if someone dear to him had just died. He shivered and his nose began to run. Within minutes he was sneezing. He stood up, restless and anguished by what was now passing through his head. Perhaps she was Mrs. Niazi, after all. Oh God, no!

His eyes burned and brimmed over as his nose filled up again. He looked for the box of tissues Zaheen kept on her dresser. It wasn't there. Opening the top drawer of his wife's dresser, he searched for and found another box. As he was struggling with a Kleenex his glance fell on a sketch pad lying among Zaheen's toiletries. Was she sketching again? And what was the pad doing here, in this drawer, nestled among Zaheen's cosmetics, her ornate jewelry box, her hair clips and combs, her hair brushes? Sami removed the pad out of the drawer and lifted the cover. A pencil portrait of their younger son, Arif, stared at him. Had she been practicing? The drawing was good, well-executed, a faithful resemblance. He turned over the page. A blank page. But his eyes fell on something stuck to the white emptiness of the thick grainy paper that he thought at first was an illusion. No, not that, something else. Perhaps Zaheen was preparing to create a collage.

He was wrong. What he saw was no illusion, no collage. It just sat there, as if it were meant to be there, snug, unmoving, still. An ordinary white envelope, harmless in its appearance, so familiar. His heart missed a beat. So misery had already crossed his doorstep. What did this letter say? Why had Nadira betrayed him? How long had Zaheen known? Why hadn't she said something last night? What was she waiting for? Why had fate played this trick on him? The questions buzzed in his ears as if they were harsh, cacophonous voices.

Just as he had lifted the envelope from its place of hiding he heard footsteps behind him. Turning, he saw Zaheen standing in the doorway. Their eyes met.

The envelope fluttered to the floor from his hand like the last eddying leaf broken off from a bare-limbed, autumn tree. He noted that a look of astonishment spread over her face like a slow blush. So, she had not planned on telling him about the letter. Why? He was puzzled.

She made no attempt to move. One hand firmly on the doorknob, she returned his gaze silently, without flinching, her face suddenly pale, her eyes brimming with tears of accusation.

Study and Discussion Questions

1. It is generally a good idea to pause for a moment on the title of a literary work before you go on reading and think about your reactions to the title and what you think, initially, it might mean. Seeing this one, "A Man of Integrity," what did you think the story would be about?
2. Look up the word "integrity" in an unabridged dictionary and note the denotations of the word that you think apply to the story. What other words or associations does "integrity" suggest to you?
3. What do we come to learn about the protagonist, Sami? List his "vital statistics." Also any speculations you have about him.
4. Discuss the two paragraphs that begin "That afternoon, driving home in his red Suzuki . . ." and end "A gust of wind blew it away." How is this scene the first crisis point in the story? What do we learn about Sami's life and his marriage? What choice does Sami make here?
5. Note references to and discuss Sami's recurring memory of the girl "on the roof of the house next door." What function do these memories have in the story?
6. Contrast Sami's reaction to the first and second letters from "Nadira."
7. "Sami Ahmed deemed himself a man of integrity. He was also a faithful husband." Discuss.
8. What do we learn about Sami's wife Zaheen? What about her art? What about the books on her bookshelf?
9. Why do you think Nadira's voice sounds familiar to Sami?

Suggestions for Writing

1. What do you make of the ending of the story? Has Nadira sent a letter to Zaheen? Is Zaheen having a flirtation with someone as well? Is Zaheen Nadira? Has Sami simply found an unrelated blank envelope that triggers his guilt? Choose one of the above or come up with your own interpretation of the ending and find evidence in the story to make your case.
2. What do you think "the Nadira incident" will do to Sami and Zaheen Ahmed's marriage?
3. "A Man of Integrity" is set in a city in Pakistan among the professional middle class in the 1990s. Would the story have played out differently if it were set in the United States or some other country? If the social class of the characters were different? If the time period were different?
4. Write about (an essay) or narrate (a story) a challenge to your own integrity.

Critical Resources

1. Devi, Gayatru. "Tahira Naqvi: Sprinkling the Attar of Pakistan Over Amreeka and the World." *Monsoon Interviews.* 22 April 2005. <http://www.monsoonmag.com/interviews/i3inter_naqvi.html>.
2. Leach, Laurie. "Conflict over Privacy in Indo-American Short Fiction." *Ethnicity and the American Short Story.* Ed. Julie Brown. New York: Garland, 1997. 197–211.
3. Srikanth, Rajini. *The World Next Door: South Asian American Literature and the Idea of America.* Philadelphia: Temple UP, 2004 (see pp. 136–44; 159–60; 227–29).

POETRY

JOHN DONNE (1572–1631)

John Donne was born in London into a prominent Roman Catholic family. Because of his religion, he was prevented from taking a degree at Oxford; he became an Anglican convert soon after. He participated in naval expeditions and upon return to England studied law and was appointed secretary to Sir Thomas Egerton. But his secret marriage to Egerton's niece cost him his position and led to brief imprisonment. Donne struggled to earn a living for a number of years, but eventually found a patron to support his writing. In 1615, he was ordained an Anglican priest and his sermons became immensely popular. Only after his death did he gain a reputation as the leading "metaphysical" poet. His Poems *were published by his son in 1633.*

The Flea   (1633)

Mark but this flea, and mark in this,
How little that which thou deny'st me is;
It sucked me first, and now sucks thee,
And in this flea, our two bloods mingled be;
Thou know'st that this cannot be said   5
A sin, or shame, or loss of maidenhead,
   Yet this enjoys before it woo,
    And pampered swells with one blood made of two,
    And this, alas, is more than we would do.

Oh stay, three lives in one flea spare,   10
Where we almost, yea more than married are.
This flea is you and I, and this
Our marriage bed, and marriage temple is;
Though parents grudge, and you, we are met,
And cloistered in these living walls of jet.   15
   Though use make you apt to kill me,
    Let not to this, self murder added be,
    And sacrilege, three sins in killing three.

Cruel and sudden, hast thou since
Purpled thy nail, in blood of innocence?   20
Wherein could this flea guilty be,

Except in that drop which it sucked from thee?
Yet thou triumph'st, and say'st that thou
Find'st not thyself, nor me the weaker now;
    'Tis true, then learn how false, fears be;   25
    Just so much honour, when thou yield'st to me,
    Will waste, as this flea's death took life from thee.

Study and Discussion Questions

1. To whom is the poem addressed?
2. "The Flea" is an example of a *conceit,* an ingenious metaphor. What does the speaker of the poem mean when he says: "This flea is you and I, and this/ Our marriage bed, and marriage temple is"?
3. What literally is happening in this poem?
4. What is the tone of the poem?

Suggestions for Writing

1. Write a description of how you imagine the setting and characters in this poem.
2. What is happening in each stanza of "The Flea"? That is, what are the stages of the speaker's argument?
3. Write an answer to the speaker of the poem from the point of view of the person to whom the poem is addressed.

Critical Resources

1. Carey, John, ed. *John Donne.* Oxford, England: Oxford UP, 1990.
2. Manfred, Malzahn. "The Flea, the Sun and the Critic: A Communicational Approach to John Donne's Poetry." *Symbolism: An International Annual of Critical Aesthetics* 3 (2003): 53–70.
3. Marotti, Arthur, ed. *Critical Essays on John Donne.* New York: G. K. Hall, 1994.
4. Perrine, Laurence. "Explicating Donne: 'The Apparition' and 'The Flea.'" *College Literature* 17 (1990): 1–20.

WILLIAM BLAKE (1757–1827)

William Blake was born in London. Although he didn't receive a formal education, he did study art and drawing as a young boy. At fourteen, he was apprenticed to an engraver and earned a meager living engraving for the rest of his life. Blake self-published his poems, often surrounding the verse with his own elaborate illustrations. For many, understanding a Blake poem in its entirety means

seeing the original combination of words and images. Although Blake lived dur-
ing the same period as such Romantic poets as Wordsworth and Shelly, his dis-
tinctive focus on the inner life of the individual, religious symbolism, and mystical
themes varies greatly from the idealization of nature in Romantic poetry. For this
reason, his visionary poetics were little appreciated during his time. Since his re-
discovery in the 1920s, the work of Blake, like that of John Donne before him, is
considered a cornerstone that defines "metaphysical" poetry. His major works in-
clude Songs of Innocence *(1789),* The Marriage of Heaven and Hell *(1790), and*
Songs of Experience *(1794). In the poem "The Garden of Love," first published*
in Songs of Experience, *a questioning speaker walks into a speculative, gothic-like*
realm where religiosity takes on a darker tint.

The Garden of Love   (1794)

I went to the Garden of Love,
And saw what I never had seen:
A Chapel was built in the midst,
Where I used to play on the green.

And the gates of this Chapel were shut,   5
And "Thou shalt not" writ over the door;
So I turn'd to the Garden of Love
That so many sweet flowers bore;

And I saw it was filled with graves,
And tomb-stones where flowers should be;   10
And Priests in black gowns were walking their rounds,
And binding with briars my joys & desires.

Study and Discussion Questions

1. What contrast runs through the poem?
2. What does "Thou shalt not" allude to?
3. Why a *garden* of love?
4. Why are the gates of the chapel shut?
5. Discuss the importance of the rhythm and internal rhymes of the last two
   lines.

Suggestion for Writing

1. What is the poem saying about organized religion? What do you think of
   what it is saying?

Critical Resources

1. Adams, Hazard, ed. *Critical Essays on William Blake*. Boston: G. K. Hall, 1991.
2. Behrendt, Stephen. *Reading William Blake*. New York: St. Martin's, 1992.
3. Bentley, G. E. *The Stranger from Paradise: a biography of William Blake*. New Haven, CT: Yale UP, 2001.
4. Robertson, Graham W. *The Life of William Blake by Alexander Gilchrist*. Mineola, NY: Dover, 1997.

EDNA ST. VINCENT MILLAY (1892–1950)

Raised in Camden, Maine, Millay published her first poem at the age of fourteen. Under the guidance of a dedicated mother, Millay underwent an intensive study program of music and literature, always encouraged to be strong-willed and independent. Her poem "Renascence," published in Lyric Year *in 1912, was met with critical praise and helped secure a scholarship for Millay at Vasser College. After graduating, she moved to New York's Greenwich Village—a "bohemian" community of actors, painters and writers—and began to write poetry and plays. In 1923, she became the first woman to win the Pulitzer Prize for poetry for her collection* The Ballad of the Harp-Weaver *(1923). Although Millay was an active and popular poet during the modernist movement of the first half of the twentieth century, her conservative and formal techniques (she is best known for her sonnets) set her apart from the free-verse developments of the era. While her form remained traditional, her content did not. Like the work of the Greek poet Sappho, many of Millay's precise and lyric poems explore the physical and mental aspects of female sexuality and sexual autonomy. Select works from her 15 volumes of poetry, several plays, essays, and short fiction include the poetry works* Renascence and Other Poems *(1912),* A Few Figs from Thistles: Poems and Sonnets *(1921),* Fatal Interview *(1931),* Wine from These Grapes *(1934),* Make Bright the Arrows *(1940), and the drama collection* Three Plays *(1926). In "An Ancient Gesture," Millay's distinct lyricism enhances the poem's subtle play of meanings.*

An Ancient Gesture   (1954)

I thought, as I wiped my eyes on the corner of my apron:
Penelope did this too.
And more than once: you can't keep weaving all day

And undoing it all through the night;
Your arms get tired, and the back of your neck gets tight   5
And along towards morning, when you think it will never be light,
And your husband has been gone, and you don't know where, for years,
Suddenly you burst into tears;
There is simply nothing else to do.

And I thought, as I wiped my eyes on the corner of my apron: 10
This is an ancient gesture, authentic, antique,
In the very best tradition, classic, Greek;
Ulysses did this too.
But only as a gesture,—a gesture which implied
To the assembled throng that he was much too moved to speak.   15
He learned it from Penelope . . .
Penelope,[1] who really cried.

Study and Discussion Questions

1. What are the two senses of the word *gesture* which emerge in the poem? Note the references to *gesture.* Look up the word in an unabridged dictionary.
2. Compare/contrast the characters of Penelope and of Ulysses (Odysseus) as they are presented in Millay's poem.
3. Who is the third character in the poem? What does it appear her situation is? How does she feel about it?
4. Trace the rhyme scheme of this poem using the method where each subsequent letter in the alphabet identifies a new rhyme.
5. Look at the first line of each stanza. Why do you think Millay did this? What effect does it have?

Suggestion for Writing

1. Write a paragraph exploring the tone of "An Ancient Gesture." How does the speaker of the poem feel about her own situation and how does this develop through the poem? Why do you think she chose to foreground the story of Penelope while only implying her own? What emotion are you feeling by the end of "An Ancient Gesture" and how might that be connected to choices of word and structure the poet made?

Critical Resources

1. Freedman, Diane, ed. *Millay at 100: A Critical Reappraisal.* Carbondale: Southern Illinois UP, 1995.

---

[1]Penelope: Wife of Odysseus (Ulysses) in Homer's *Odyssey,* who waited years for her husband, thought dead, to return from the Trojan War. She promised to marry one of her numerous suitors when she had finished her weaving, but each night she unwove what she had done that day.

2. Michaildou, Artemis. "Edna St. Vincent Millay and Anne Sexton: The Disruption of Domestic Bliss." *Journal of American Studies* 38.1 (2004): 67–88.
3. Milford, Nancy. *Savage Beauty: The Life of Edna St. Vincent Millay.* New York: Random House, 2001.
4. Miller, Nina. *Making Love Modern: The Intimate Public Worlds of New York Literary Women.* New York: Oxford UP, 1999.

D. H. LAWRENCE (1885–1939)

David Herber Lawrence was born into a lower-middle-class family from Nottinghampshire, England. His father was a coal miner and his mother was a schoolteacher. He attended the University College of Nottingham and then taught school for four years. The publication of his first poems and the short story "The White Peacock" in 1911 convinced him he could pursue writing full-time. Although more known for his novels and short stories, Lawrence's poetry has garnered its own critical recognition. Influenced by Imagism and other modernist forms, Lawrence's poems often utilize images in nature (flowers, the sun, the moon) to symbolize aspects of humanness. And like his prose, many of his poems explore the psychological and erotic undertones of heterosexual desire—motifs that were deemed "indecent" by the reading public of his day but are now seen as pioneering aspects of his work. In addition to his novels and poetry, the prolific Lawrence wrote essays, literary criticism, and travel journals, many of them detailing his expatriate life while living in various countries outside his native England. Such works include the poetry collections Love Poems and Others *(1913),* Look! We Have Come Through! *(1917),* Tortoises *(1921),* Birds, Beasts and Flowers *(1923), and* Pansies *(1929) and the novels* Sons and Lovers *(1913),* The Rainbow *(1915),* Women in Love *(1920),* Kangaroo *(1923), and* Lady Chatterley's Lover *(1928). "Gloire de Dijon" was published in* Look! We Have Come Through!*.*

Gloire de Dijon[1]   (1917)

When she rises in the morning
I linger to watch her;
She spreads the bath-cloth underneath the window
Glistening white on the shoulders,
While down her sides the mellow   5

---

[1]*Gloire de Dijon* ("Glory of Dijon"): a yellow hybrid tea rose.

Golden shadow glows as
She stoops to the sponge, and her swung breasts
Sway like full-blown yellow
Gloire de Dijon roses.

She drips herself with water, and her shoulders   10
Glisten as silver, they crumple up
Like wet and falling roses, and I listen
For the sluicing of their rain-disheveled petals,
In the window full of sunlight
Concentrates her golden shadow   15
Fold on fold, until it glows as
Mellow as the glory roses.

Study and Discussion Questions

1. What is the literal and the implied "story" of this poem? Who is the "I," the
    speaker of the poem? What is his relation to the woman? What is she doing?
2. By the end of the first stanza, we know the woman is being compared to
    a particular kind of rose. Why didn't Lawrence simply call the poem
    "yellow rose"? Why "Gloire de Dijon"?
3. List the images which compare the rose and the woman bathing. List color
    images. List kinetic images (images of movement). Are there images of
    sound, smell, or touch?
4. Note sound patterns in the poem: (a) repeated consonant sounds (conso-
    nance), inside a word as well as at its beginning, and (b) repeated vowel
    sounds (assonance). What effect does each of the patterns you note have?
    What kind of mood do they collectively develop?

Suggestion for Writing

1. Compare/contrast "Gloire de Dijon" with one or more of the following
    love poems: Pablo Neruda, "Every Day You Play," Leopold Sedar
    Senghor, "You Held the Black Face," Edna St. Vincent Millay, "Love is not
    all: It is not meat nor drink."

Critical Resources

1. Beckett, Fiona. *D. H. Lawrence: The Thinker As Poet.* New York: St.
    Martin's, 1997.
2. *The D. H. Lawrence Review.* University of Texas. A quarterly journal.
3. Fernihough, Anne, ed. *Cambridge Companion to D. H. Lawrence.* New
    York: Cambridge UP, 2001.
4. The University of Nottingham. *Manuscripts and Special Collections: D. H.
    Lawrence.* 22 April 2005 <http://mss.library.nottingham.ac.uk/dhl_home
    .html>.

❋ ❋ ❋

ELIZABETH BISHOP (1911–1979)

Elizabeth Bishop was born in Worcester, Massachusetts. Her father died while she was still an infant, and, when Elizabeth was five her mother was hospitalized for mental illness, leaving her to be raised by her grandparents and other relatives. She studied at Vassar College (1930–1934), where she developed a friendship with poet Marianne Moore, who encouraged her to pursue poetry instead of medicine. The two became life-long friends. After graduating, Bishop led a transient, travel- ing life, living in New York City, France, and Key West, and eventually settled in Brazil, though she spent her last few years in Boston. Her experiences traveling and living as an exile would become central themes in her poetry. During her life, Bishop composed only 101 poems. Despite this relatively small number, her work was recognized by her contemporaries (like her good friend Robert Lowell) as some of the most evocative, crafted verse in American poetry, and in 1956 she was awarded the Pulitzer Prize for her collection North and South—A Cold Spring. *Known for her astute observation and subtle irony, Bishop's poetry often details human relationships and human interaction with the natural world in a language noted for its rhythm and meter. Other poetry collections include* Questions of Travel *(1965),* The Complete Poems *(1969), and* Geography III *(1976). "One Art," published in* Geography III, *is written in the form of a villanelle, composed of five tercets and a final quatrain.*

One Art   (1976)

The art of losing isn't hard to master;
so many things seem filled with the intent
to be lost that their loss is no disaster.

Lose something every day. Accept the fluster
of lost door keys, the hour badly spent.   5
The art of losing isn't hard to master.

Then practice losing farther, losing faster:
places, and names, and where it was you meant
to travel. None of these will bring disaster.

I lost my mother's watch. And look! my last, or   10
next-to-last, of three loved houses went.
The art of losing isn't hard to master.

I lost two cities, lovely ones. And, vaster,
some realms I owned, two rivers, a continent.
I miss them, but it wasn't a disaster.   15

—Even losing you (the joking voice, a gesture
I love) I shan't have lied. It's evident
the art of losing's not too hard to master
though it may look like (*Write* it!) like disaster.

Study and Discussion Questions

1. Bishop's "One Art" is a type of poem called a villanelle. Figure out the rhyme scheme of the poem, labeling the first rhyme "A" and marking those throughout the poem and the second rhyme "B" and marking those throughout the poem. Note that the rhymes do not have to be exact.
2. The first line—"The art of losing isn't hard to master"—becomes a refrain, repeated throughout the poem. Does the line change its meaning or carry a different emotional resonance as the poem goes on? Discuss.
3. There is a second and partial refrain in the poem, built on the lines that end with the word *disaster*. How do the two refrains together create a tension in the poem?
3. What are the "things" lost in this poem? How do the losses change as the poem develops?
4. What does the speaker of the poem keep telling herself she feels or should be feeling about these losses?
5. How would you describe the tone of "One Art"? Does it change in the course of the poem?
6. "It's evident" in the last stanza of "One Art" that the poet has been working up to mentioning a very serious loss. What is it? How might a) writing about such a loss, and b) using a very strict form in which to do so, be of help in such a situation?

Suggestion for Writing

1. If you were to write a poem (not necessarily a villanelle) titled "One Art," what would your poem be about? What is the "one art" *you* would write about? Give it a try.

Critical Resources

1. "Elizabeth Bishop." *The Academy of American Poets.* 22 April 2005 <http://www.poets.org/index.cfm>.
2. Miller, Brett Candlish. *Elizabeth Bishop: Life and The Memory of It.* Berkeley: U of California P, 1993 (includes a section on the drafts of "One Art").
3. McCabe, Susan. *Elizabeth Bishop: Her Poetics of Loss.* University Park: Penn State UP, 1994.
4. Schwartz, Lloyd and Sybil Estess, eds. *Elizabeth Bishop and Her Art.* Ann Arbor: U of Michigan P, 1983.

❋ ❋ ❋

ANNE SEXTON (1928–1974)

Anne Sexton was born in Newton, Massachusetts, attended Garland Junior College for a year, and married at twenty. After one of many nervous breakdowns she was to suffer throughout her life, a psychiatrist urged her to try writing, which she did with immediate success. Often labeled as "confessional" poetry, much of Sexton's work explores deep and intimate aspects of her life, especially the torment of her mental illness. Yet to characterize all her work in this way obscures her work as a whole. Similar to the poetry of Sharon Olds, some of Sexton's work embraces physical desire and its ambivalent coupling with love and relationships. In Trans-formations (1971), Sexton again broke from the confessional mode to rewrite in poetry several Brothers Grimm fairy tales—including Sleeping Beauty, Hansel and Gretel, and Snow White—from a feminist perspective. Her poetry collections include To Bedlam and Part Way Back (1960), Live or Die (1966, winner of the Pulitzer Prize), Love Poems (1969), and The Death Notebooks (1974). At the age of forty-five, she took her own life. "Her Kind" is from Sexton's collection To Bedlam and Part Way Back.

Her Kind

(1960)

I have gone out, a possessed witch,
haunting the black air, braver at night;
dreaming evil, I have done my hitch
over the plain houses, light by light:
lonely thing, twelve-fingered, out of mind.   5
A woman like that is not a woman, quite.
I have been her kind.

I have found the warm caves in the woods,
filled them with skillets, carvings, shelves,
closets, silks, innumerable goods;   10
fixed the suppers for the worms and the elves:
whining, rearranging the disaligned.
A woman like that is misunderstood.
I have been her kind.

I have ridden in your cart, driver,   15
waved my nude arms at villages going by,
learning the last bright routes, survivor
where your flames still bite my thigh
and my ribs crack where your wheels wind.
A woman like that is not ashamed to die.   20
I have been her kind.

Study and Discussion Questions

1. List the three different repetitions in the poem. How do these hold the poem together and deepen your understanding of the speaker as the poem goes on?
2. What are the details Sexton's narrator gives you about her witch self in the first stanza?
3. How does the second stanza complicate or make more complex the primary witch image?
4. What is literally happening in stanza three? What historical fact is Sexton evoking?
5. Given what seems to be happening in stanza three, why does the speaker of the poem call herself a "survivor"?
6. Describe the structure of the poem: the rhyme scheme, the number of lines in each stanza, the number of syllables in each line.
7. What do you think the speaker of the poem means by "her kind"?

Suggestion for Writing

1. What *historical* self images are available to women? To men? List as many as you can for each gender. Why might a woman choose a self-image as a witch?
2. Compare/contrast Anne Sexton's "Her Kind" to Sylvia Plath's "Daddy": the use of mythology and history, the relation between men and women in a patriarchal society, the self-image of the speaker of each poem, images in each poem, sound and structure of each poem, the story each poem tells.

Critical Resources

1. Bixler, Francis. *Original Essays on the Poetry of Anne Sexton.* Conway: U of Central Arkansas P, 1988.
2. Gill, Jo. "Anne Sexton and Confessional Poetics." *Review of English Studies* 55.220 (2004): 425–45.
3. Middlebrook, Diane Wood. *Anne Sexton: A Biography.* Boston: Houghton Mifflin, 1991.
4. Wagner-Martin, Linda, ed. *Critical Essays on Anne Sexton.* Boston: G. K. Hall, 1989.

AMIRI BARAKA (b. 1934)

Amiri Baraka was born LeRoi Jones in Newark, New Jersey, into an African-American, middle-class family. After high school, he received an academic scholarship to Rutgers, but he transferred to the all-black Howard University to be in contact with more African Americans. Jones left without a degree, entered the Air Force, but was discharged after three years for possessing communist literature; he moved to New York's bohemian Lower East Side shortly thereafter. It is here that Jones began his artistic career as poet and dramatist at the height of the Beat Movement. His friendship with Beat poet Allen Ginsburg helped him develop his early poetry. By the 1960s, though, Jones became disenchanted with the apolitical nature of this environment and became increasingly involved with black nationalist politics, taking the Muslim name Amiri Baraka. His play Dutchman *(1964), winner of the Obie Award for best American play, with its overt critique of racism and obvious social commentary, marked a new shift in Baraka's writing. He would spend the decade living in Harlem and writing more consciously about black experience in white America. Today, Baraka, a self-proclaimed Marxist and activist, continues to write socially aware but often controversial poetry. His poem "Somebody Blew Up America" (2002), written and recited after September 11, 2001, incurred public criticism for its scathing attack on American history and culture. In almost 50 years of writing, Baraka has composed over twenty plays and screenplays, dozens of poetry collections, and nonfiction essays. Selected works include the plays* The Toilet *(1964),* J-E-L-L-O *(1970), and* Primitive World *(1984) and the poetry collections* April 13 *(1959),* Preface to a Twenty Volume Suicide Note *(1961),* Black Magic *(1969),* Spirit Reach *(1972), and* Funk Lore: New Poems *(1996). His latest nonfiction is* Jesse Jackson & Black People *(2003) and* Jubilee *(2003). "Beautiful Black Women . . . ," published in* Black Magic, *is demonstrative of Baraka's intense focus on black life in the 1960s.*

Beautiful Black Women . . . (1969)

Beautiful black women, fail, they act. Stop them, raining.
They are so beautiful, we want them with us. Stop them, raining.
Beautiful, stop raining, they fail. We fail them and their lips
stick out perpetually, at our weakness. Raining. Stop them. Black
queens. Ruby Dee[1] weeps at the window, raining, being lost in her   5
life, being what we all will be, sentimental bitter frustrated
deprived of her fullest light. Beautiful black women, it is
still raining in this terrible land. We need you. We flex our
muscles, turn to stare at our tormentor, we need you. Raining.
We need you, reigning, black queen. This/terrible black ladies   10
wander, Ruby Dee weeps, the window, raining, she calls, and her voice
is left to hurt us slowly. It hangs against the same wet glass, her
sadness and age, and the trip, and the lost heat, and the gray cold
buildings of our entrapment. Ladies. Women. We need you. We are still
trapped and weak, but we build and grow heavy with our knowledge.   15
    Women.
Come to us. Help us get back what was always ours. Help us. women.
    Where

---

[1]American actor (b. 1924).

are you, women, where, and who, and where, and who, and will you
  help   20
us, will you open your bodysouls, will you lift me up mother, will you
let me help you, daughter, wife/lover, will you

Study and Discussion Questions

1. Line 2 reads, in part, "we want them with us." Who does "we" refer to?
   And where are the black women, if not "with us"?
2. Who is "our tormentor"? Does "our" refer to the same group of people
   as "we"? If so, what does this suggest about the speaker?
3. Why does Baraka repeat "raining" so often?
4. "Help us get back what was always ours." What does this mean?

Suggestions for Writing

1. What does the speaker want black women to be and do?
2. How might a black woman reply to this poem?

Critical Resources

1. *Amiri Baraka*. Director John Dorr and Lewis MacAdams. Sorella Production and The Lannan Foundation: Los Angeles, 1991. 60 minutes.
2. Baraka, Amiri. *The Autobiography of LeRoi Jones*. Chicago: Lawrence
   Hill, 1997.
3. Baraka, Amiri. *The LeRoi Jones/Amiri Baraka Reader*. ed. William Harris in collaborations with Amiri Baraka. NY: Thunder's Mouth, 2000.
4. Salaam, Kalamu Ya. "Amiri Baraka Analyzes How He Writes." *African
   American Review* 37.2 (2003): 211–236 (interview).

KARL SHAPIRO (b. 1913)

*Carl Shapiro was raised in a middle-class Jewish family in Baltimore, Maryland.
He attended the University of Maryland for a short time, but left after feeling alienated by the largely Anglo-Saxon student body and by the German Jewish students
who seemed to look down upon his Russian-Jewish ancestry. This experience
prompted him to change his first name to the German "Karl." His self-published
Poems won him a scholarship to Johns Hopkins University in 1937. In 1941, his
studies were cut short after being drafted to fight in World War II. The war would
be the inspiration for his Pulitzer Prize–winning V-Letter and Other Poems
(1944). Shapiro's work spans 5 decades, and, while it shows considerable variation throughout this time, the satirical and imagistic nature of his verse has remained consistent—moving between formal and free-verse structures, with one eye*

on the local and the other on society at large. He taught at a number of universities and was editor of Poetry *magazine. His other publications include* Essays on Rime *(1945),* Poems of a Jew *(1958),* The Bourgeois Poet *(1964),* Adult Bookstore *(1976), and* New and Selected Poems, 1940–1986 *(1987). "Buick" was published in* Poems: 1940–1953 *(1953).*

Buick   (1953)

As a sloop with a sweep of immaculate wing on her delicate spine
And a keel as steel as a root that holds in the sea as she leans,
Leaning and laughing, my warm-hearted beauty, you ride, you ride,
You tack on the curves with parabola speed and a kiss of goodbye,
Like a thoroughbred sloop, my new high-spirited spirit, my kiss.   5

As my foot suggests that you leap in the air with your hips of a girl,
My finger that praises your wheel and announces your voices of song,
Flouncing your skirts, you blueness of joy, you flirt of politeness,
You leap, you intelligence, essence of wheelness with silvery nose,
And your platinum clocks of excitement stir like the hairs of a fern.   10

But how alien you are from the booming belts of your birth and the smoke
Where you turned on the stinging lathes of Detroit and Lansing at night
And shrieked at the torch in your secret parts and the amorous tests,
But now with your eyes that enter the future of roads you forget;
You are all instinct with your phosphorous glow and your streaking hair. 15

And now when we stop it is not as the bird from the shell that I leave
Or the leathery pilot who steps from his bird with a sneer of delight,
And not as the ignorant beast do you squat and watch me depart,
But with exquisite breathing you smile, with satisfaction of love,
And I touch you again as you tick in the silence and settle in sleep.   20

Study and Discussion Questions

1. Who is speaking in the poem? Why can you assume the speaker is male? What else can you say about him?
2. Go through the poem and list the ways in which the speaker compares his car to a woman. The poem is ostensibly about the speaker's feelings for his car. But what does it suggest about how he perceives women?
3. How do sound and rhythm in the first stanza help convey the speaker's experience as he drives? How and why is the first line of the third stanza different from what comes before? What new emotion does the third stanza reveal?

4. What is the function of the negative comparisons ("it is not as . . .") in the last stanza? How is the speaker feeling at the end of the poem?
5. What is the poet's attitude toward the speaker, towards the *persona* he has created? How can you tell?

Suggestions for Writing

1. To what extent is "Buick" an accurate portrayal of male feelings rather than just a parody of them?
2. Why are cars in our culture usually seen as female? What other kinds of objects or machines are viewed in gendered terms? Why are they so often seen as female?
3. Which line or phrase from the poem stands out most in your mind? Try to explain why.
4. Try writing a poem or prose passage in which the speaker dramatizes his or her intense emotional relationship with an object other than an automobile. Think carefully before ascribing a gender to this object.

Critical Resources

1. Phillips, Robert. "Poetry, Prosody and Meta-Poetics: Karl Shapiro's Self-Reflexive Poetry." *Poetics in the Poem: Critical Essays on American Self-Reflexive Poetry.* Dorothy Baker, ed. New York: Peter Lang, 1997.
2. Phillips, Robert. *The Madness of Art: Interview with Poets and Writers.* Syracuse, NY: Syracuse UP, 2003.
3. Shapiro, Karl. *Poet: An Autobiography In Three Parts.* Chapel Hill, NC: Algonquin, 1988.
4. Walker, Sue. *Seriously Meeting Karl Sharpiro.* Mobile, AL: Negative Capability, 1993.

TED HUGHES (1930–1998)

Ted Hughes was born in Yorkshire, England. He entered college at Cambridge to study English, but eventually graduated with degrees in archeology and anthropology. In 1956 he married American poet Sylvia Plath; they separated shortly before her death in 1963. Hughes's long career as a poet was acknowledged in 1985 when he was appointed England's poet laureate, a position he held until his death in 1998. Throughout his work, nature and myth play central roles. His intense depictions of animals and their surrounding environments often serve as metaphoric commentary on modern humanity's alienation from nature. He wrote radio plays, short stories, and children's literature, but he was best known for his poetry collections The Hawk and the Rain *(1957),* Crow *(1970),* Moortown *(1979),* Flowers and Insects *(1986),* Wolfwataching *(1991),* Tales from Ovid *(1997), and* Birthday Letters *(1998). In "The Lovepet" Hughes utilizes the literary technique of personification to explore the complexities of love.*

The Lovepet (1971)

Was it an animal was it a bird?
She stroked it. He spoke to it softly.
She made her voice its happy forest.
He brought it out with sugarlump smiles.
Soon it was licking their kisses.   5

She gave it the strings of her voice which it swallowed
He gave it the blood of his face it grew eager
She gave it the liquorice of her mouth it began to thrive
He opened the aniseed of his future
And it bit and gulped, grew vicious, snatched   10
The focus of his eyes
She gave it the steadiness of her hand
He gave it the strength of his spine it ate everything

It began to cry what could they give it
They gave it their calendars it bolted their diaries   15
They gave it their sleep it gobbled their dreams
Even while they slept
It ate their bodyskin and the muscle beneath
They gave it vows its teeth clashed its starvation
Through every word they uttered   20

It found snakes under the floor it ate them
It found a spider horror
In their palms and ate it.

They gave it double smiles and blank silence
It chewed holes in their carpets   25
They gave it logic
It ate the colour of their hair
They gave it every argument that would come
They gave it shouting and yelling they meant it
It ate the faces of their children   30
They gave it their photograph albums they gave it their records

It ate the colour of the sun
They gave it a thousand letters they gave it money
It ate their future complete it waited for them
Staring and starving   35
They gave it screams it had gone too far
It ate into their brains
It ate the roof
It ate lonely stone it ate wind crying famine
It went furiously off   40

They wept they called it back it could have everything
It stripped out their nerves chewed chewed flavourless
It bit at their numb bodies they did not resist
It bit into their blank brains they hardly knew

It moved bellowing   45
Through a ruin of starlight and crockery

It drew slowly off they could not move

It went far away they could not speak

Study and Discussion Questions

1. What are the stages this marriage, or love relationship, goes through?
2. Classify the types of "food" the lovepet eats.
3. "They wept they called it back." Why?
4. Discuss Hughes's use of repetition of sounds, words, and phrases in "The Lovepet."

Suggestions for Writing

1. Why is the lovepet so hungry?
2. Choose or invent an animal or plant that represents a relationship in your life (it could be family or work as easily as love). Describe its qualities.

Critical Resources

1. Bell, Charlie. *Ted Hughes: A Beginner's Guide.* London: Hodder and Stoughton, 2002.
2. Bentley, Paul. *The Poetry of Ted Hughes: Language, Illusion and Beyond.* New York: Longman and Harlow, 1998.
3. Scigaj, Leonard. *Critical Essays on Ted Hughes.* New York: G. K. Hall, 1992.

❀ ❀ ❀

OLGA BROUMAS (b. 1949)

Olga Broumas was born in Greece and moved to the United States at age ten. She obtained her B.A. in architecture from the University of Pennsylvania and her M.F.A. at the University of Oregon, where she helped found the women's studies program. Although English is Broumas's second language, her poetic skill won her the Yale Younger Poets Award in 1977 for Beginning with O—*a mixed collection of poems on female relationships and love, erotic desire and myth. While many of these themes surface again and again in her poetry, what makes them uniquely Broumas's is the compact syntax and rhythmic quality of her verse. Other poetry collections include* Soie Sauvage *(1980),* Pastoral Jazz *(1983),* Perpetua *(1989), and* All of the Above *(1991); four works with classical scholar T. Begley (including* Sappho's Gymnasium, *[1994] and* Rave: Poems, 1975–1999 *[1999]). She has also translated the work of Greek poet Odysseus Elytis. Broumas's propensity for feminist revision of myth appears in the poem "Cinderella," first published in* Beginning with O.

Cinderella   (1977)

> *. . . the joy that isn't shared*
> *I heard, dies young.*
>   Anne Sexton, 1928–1974

Apart from my sisters, estranged
from my mother, I am a woman alone
in a house of men
who secretly
call themselves princes, alone   5
with me usually, under cover of dark. I am the one allowed in

to the royal chambers, whose small foot conveniently
fills the slipper of glass. The woman writer, the lady
umpire, the madam chairman, anyone's wife.
I know what I know.   10
And I once was glad

of the chance to use it, even alone
in a strange castle, doing overtime on my own, cracking
the royal code. The princes spoke
in their fathers' language, were eager to praise me   15
my nimble tongue. I am a woman in a state of siege, alone

as one piece of laundry, strung on a windy clothesline a
mile long. A woman co-opted by promises: the lure
of a job, the ruse of a choice, a woman forced
to bear witness, falsely   20
against my kind, as each
other sister was judged inadequate, bitchy, incompetent,
jealous, too thin, too fat. I know what I know.
What sweet bread I make

for myself in this prosperous house   25
is dirty, what good soup I boil turns
in my mouth to mud. Give
me my ashes. A cold stove, a cinder-block pillow, wet
canvas shoes in my sisters', my sisters' hut. Or I swear

I'll die young   30
like those favored before me, hand-picked each one
for her joyful heart.

Study and Discussion Questions

1. What price has the speaker of the poem had to pay for success?
2. List specific images of loneliness in the poem.
3. What is the speaker's relation to other women? What is her relation to men?

Suggestion for Writing

1. How has Broumas rewritten the Cinderella fairy tale for modern readers?
   What changes has she made in the story? (Remember, there is more than
   one version of the fairy tale.) How do the changes serve her purpose?

Critical Resources

1. Carruthers, Mary. "The Re-Vision of the Muse: Adrienne Rich, Audre
   Lorde, Judy Grahn, Olga Broumas." *Hudson Review* 36.2 (1983): 293–322.
2. Hammond, Karla. "An Interview with Olga Broumas." *Northwest Review*
   18.3 (1980): 33–44.
3. Horton, Diane. " 'Scarlet Liturgies': The Poetry of Olga Broumas." *North
   Dakota Quarterly* 55.4 (1987): 322–47.
4. Prins, Yopie. *Dwelling In Possibility: Women Poets and Critics On Poetry.*
   Ithaca, NY: Cornell UP, 1997.

❀ ❀ ❀

LOUISE ERDRICH (b. 1954)

Louise Erdrich grew up in Wahpeton, North Dakota. Her father, a German immigrant, and her mother, an Ojibwa Indian, passed down to her a rich tradition of story telling. She would eventually obtain her B.A. at Dartmouth and her M.A. in writing from Johns Hopkins in 1979. In 1981, she married another writer, Mike Dorris. During the next decade, the two collaborated on several publications, working together and providing feedback for each other. For a short time they published under their penname "Milou North." When her poem "Indian Boarding School" won the 1983 Pushcart Prize, the public began to notice her work—both poetry and prose. Although she has written more prose in her career, her two volumes of poetry, Jacklight *(1984) and* Baptism of Desire *(1989), have been highly acclaimed. In these two volumes, Erdrich uses her imaginative story-telling abilities to write a multifaceted poetry—wandering deftly through themes of family, love, history, Native American mythologizing, and the tension between Ojibwa reservation life and white America. These same story-telling techniques can be found in her prose, such as "The Red Convertible," a short piece included in this anthology, taken from her first novel* Love Medicine *(1984). Among her other novels are* The Beet Queen *(1986),* Tracks *(1988),* A Link With the River *(1989),* The Crown of Columbus *(1991),* The Antelope Wife *(1998),* Four Souls *(2004), and her latest work,* The Painted Drum *(2005). The poem "Jacklight" portrays how one instance of cultural and gender conflict is built upon centuries of history.*

Jacklight[1]   (1984)

> The same Chippewa word is used both for
> flirting and hunting game, while another
> Chippewa word connotes both using force in
> intercourse and also killing a bear with one's
> bare hands.
> —Dunning 1959

We have come to the edge of the woods,
out of brown grass where we slept, unseen,
out of knotted twigs, out of leaves creaked shut,
out of hiding.

At first the light wavered, glancing over us.   5
Then it clenched to a fist of light that pointed,
searched out, divided us.

---

[1]"In the South, the will-o'-the-wisp or swamp gas, the unexpected and haunting flash of light in the dark and deserted place. In the North woods, the word is a verb. People jacklight deer or rabbits, flashing a blinding light in the eyes of the hunted animal." —Rayna Green, *That's What She Said.*

Each took the beams like direct blows the heart answers.
Each of us moved forward alone.

We have come to the edge of the woods,　　　　　　　　　10
drawn out of ourselves by this night sun,
this battery of polarized acids,
that outshines the moon.

We smell them behind it
but they are faceless, invisible.　　　　　　　　　　　15
We smell the raw steel of their gun barrels,
mink oil on leather, their tongues of sour barley.
We smell their mother buried chin-deep in wet dirt.
We smell their fathers with scoured knuckles,
teeth cracked from hot marrow.　　　　　　　　　　20
We smell their sisters of crushed dogwood, bruised apples,
of fractured cups and concussions of burnt hooks.

We smell their breath steaming lightly behind the jacklight.
We smell the itch underneath the caked guts on their clothes.
We smell their minds like silver hammers,　　　　　25
cocked back, held in readiness
for the first of us to step into the open.

We have come to the edge of the woods,
out of brown grass where we slept, unseen,
out of leaves creaked shut, out of our hiding.　　　30
We have come here too long.

It is their turn now,
their turn to follow us. Listen,
they put down their equipment.
It is useless in the tall brush.　　　　　　　　　　　35
And now they take the first steps, not knowing
how deep the woods are and lightless.
How deep the woods are.

Study and Discussion Questions

1. How does the epigraph help you to understand what is going on in the poem?
2. Who are the "we" in this poem?
3. How does the light affect the "we" of the poem?
4. Who are "they"?
5. Where does the poem "turn"? And what does that turn consist of?
6. How does the poem play with the two meanings of "jacklight"?

7. Discuss how images of smell gradually compose a portrait of "them." Why is smell appropriate?

Suggestions for Writing

1. "Each took the beams like direct blows the heart answers. / Each of us moved forward alone." Analyze these lines. How are they significant?
2. Continue the "story" of the poem for a bit, writing (in either prose or poetry) about what happens after "they take the first steps."

Critical Resources

1. Bak, Hans. "Circles Blaze in Ordinary Days: Louise Erdrich's *Jacklight*." *Native American Women in Literature and Culture*. Victor Da Rosa, ed. Porto, Portugal: Fernando Pessoa UP, 1997.
2. Castillo, Susan Perez. *The Construction of Gender and Ethnicity in the Poetry of Leslie Silko and Louise Erdrich*. Earl Miner, ed. Tokyo: International Comparative Literature Association, 1995.
3. Chavkin, Allan and Nancy Chavkin, eds. *Conversations with Louise Erdrich and Michael Dorris*. Jackson: UP of Mississippi, 1994.
4. Hafen, Jane. "Sacramental Language: Ritual in the Poetry of Louise Erdrich." *Great Plains Quarterly* 16.3 (1996): 147–155.
5. Stookey, Lorena L. *Louise Erdrich: A Critical Companion*. Westport, CT: Greenwood, 1999.

TESS GALLAGHER (b. 1943)

Tess Gallagher grew up on the coast of Washington state's Puget Sound in the town of Port Angeles. She received her M.A. at the University of Washington and an M.F.A. at the University of Iowa. She made her first impression on American poetry with her first volume of poetry Stepping Outside, *published in 1974. Her next collection,* Instructions to the Double *(1976), is perhaps her best-known work, featuring poems on loss, birth, family conflict, and the impact of time. Gallagher's use of suggestive metaphor in much of her poetry often creates a world that blurs the distinction between reality and dream: "I have wanted the words to go deep. I have wanted music and passion and tenderness in the poems. Intelligence and loss. Only in the language I have made for myself in the poem am I in touch with all the past, present, and future moments of my consciousness" (*Contemporary Poets, 2001*). *The collections in* Willingly *(1984),* Amplitude *(1987) and* Moon Crossing Bridge *(1992) have several poems written to and about her partner, writer Raymond Carver—intimate poems of love and grief before, during and after his death from cancer. Her other works include the poetry collections* Portable Kisses *(1978) and* My Black Horse: New and Selected Poems *(1995); a screenplay* Dostoevsky *(1985, with Raymond Carver); and the short story collections* The Lover of Horses and Other Stories *(1986) and* At the Owl Woman Saloon *(1997). "I Stop Writing the Poem" was published in* Moon Crossing Bridge.

I Stop Writing the Poem (1992)

to fold the clothes. No matter who lives
or who dies, I'm still a woman.
I'll always have plenty to do.
I bring the arms of his shirt
together. Nothing can stop   5
our tenderness. I'll get back
to the poem. I'll get back to being
a woman. But for now
there's a shirt, a giant shirt
in my hands, and somewhere a small girl   10
standing next to her mother
watching to see how it's done.

Study and Discussion Questions

1. What is the effect of having the title also be the first line of the poem?
2. Locate the exact center of the poem. How is the poem's center in dialogue with the title?
3. What are the components of a woman's life that Gallagher details? Is the speaker of the poem happy or unhappy?
4. List the characters in "I Stop Writing the Poem."
5. Notice the repetitions in the poem. What work are they doing in the poem?
6. What is Gallagher saying about the tensions between being a poet (or creative artist of any kind) and being a woman? Where do these tensions come from? What is the speaker of this poem's solution?

Suggestions for Writing

1. Compare/contrast this poem to two other poems about trying to write: Susan Griffin's "This is the Day in the Life of a Woman Trying . . ." and June Jordan's "Free Flight."
2. Choose some necessary task you do (and perhaps have taken for granted) and write a poem or a prose piece about it—describe it vividly and ponder its individual and social purpose(s) and whatever tensions you uncover as you think about it.

Critical Resources

1. Bourne, Daniel. "A Conversation with Tess Gallagher." *Artful Dodge* (2001): 4–21.
2. Gallagher, Tess. *A Concert of Tenses: Essays On Poetry*. Ann Arbor: U of Michigan P, 1986.
3. Gallagher, Tess. *Soul Barnacles: Ten More Years With Ray*. Ann Arbor: U of Michigan P, 2000.

ALMA LUZ VILLANUEVA (b. 1944)

Alma Villanueva was born in Lopoc, California. As a young Chicana, she was sur-rounded by a close community of resilient women. These women (especially her mother and grandmother, a Yaqui India) influenced her greatly and their strug-gles (as well as other women's) within an oppressive patriarchal culture become a central focus in her poetry. At the age of fourteen, Villanueva was forced to with-draw from high school to give birth to her daughter. Twenty-five years later, she received her M.F.A. from Vermont College. While issues of race surface in her verse, Villanueva is more concerned with gender, womanhood, and her belief in the power of the universal feminine. Since the publication of her first volume of poetry, Bloodroot *(1977), Villanueva's direct and eloquent style has garnered both critical and public awareness. In response to a letter she received from a student who admired her poetry, Villanueva wrote, "I never imagined I'd receive a letter like hers. Which makes me acknowledge the paradox, the mystery of writing: that when we touch the most personal, the most hidden within ourselves, we touch the other, the outer, the universal"* (Contemporary Authors Online, *2004). Her other works include* Mother, May I? *(1978),* Life Span *(1984),* La Chingada *(1985),* The Ultraviolet Sky *(1988),* Naked Ladies *(1994),* Weeping Woman: La Llorona and Other Stories *(1994),* Desire *(1998),* Luna's California Poppies *(2000), and* Vida *(2002). "Crazy Courage" was published in* Desire.

Crazy Courage (1995)

To Michael B.

Why do I think of Michael . . .
He came to my fiction class
as a man (dressed in men's
clothes); then he came

to my poetry class
as a woman (dressed in women's
clothes; but he was still
a man under the clothes).

Was I moved in the face of
such courage (man/woman   10
woman/man) . . .
Was I moved by the gentleness

of his masculinity; the strength
of his femininity . . .
His presence at the class poetry   15
reading, dressed in a miniskirt,

high boots, bright purple tights,
a scooped-neck blouse, carrying
a single, living, red rose, in a
vase, to the podium (the visitors,   20

not from the class, shocked—
the young, seen-it-all MTV[1] crowd—
into silence as he's introduced,
"Michael . . .") And what it was, I think,

was his perfect dignity, the offering   25
of his living, red rose to the perceptive,
to the blind, to the amused, to the impressed,
to those who would kill him, and

to those who would love him.
And of course I remember the surprise   30
of his foamy breasts as we hugged
goodbye, his face blossomed

open, set apart, the pain of it,
the joy of it (the crazy courage
to be whole, as a rose is   35
whole, as a child is

whole before they're
punished for including
everything in their
innocence).   40

---

[1]The Music Television cable channel.

Study and Discussion Questions:

1. Why does the speaker of the poem begin: "Why do I think of Michael . . ."? In what ways is the poem as much about her as it is about Michael, the apparent subject? List the "answers" in "Crazy Courage" to the poem's initial question.
2. "Crazy Courage" could have been written in one long stanza. What effect does breaking the poem into (here, four-line) stanzas have?
3. Keeping in mind that the last word in a line is usually the most important (and the first word in a line usually the next most important), look at the line breaks from line to line and from stanza to stanza in this poem.
4. Why do you think Villaneuva uses so many parenthetical phrases in "Crazy Courage" and in fact ends with one which arguably contains the most important words of the poem? What are parentheses usually used for?

Suggestions for Writing

1. Look up *courage* and *crazy* in an unabridged dictionary. How is Michael's act both crazy and courageous? Think of other acts that the phrase "crazy courage" brings to your mind. Write about one of those.
2. Write a paragraph discussing your personal response to this poem. Were you moved, shocked, elated, pitying, admiring? How did your sense of Michael change through the poem?
3. If you have seen the film *Camp,* about a musical drama summer camp for teenagers, you might compare the film's cross-dressing Michael with Villaneuva's Michael, asking the same question about the film: "What do I think of Michael" and comparing/contrasting the poem and the film.

Critical Resources

1. Corpi, Lucha, ed. *Mascaras.* Berkely, CA: Third Woman, 1997.
2. Herrera-Sobek, Maria, ed. *Beyond Stereotypes: The Critical Analysis of Chicana Literature.* Binghamton, NY: Bilingual, 1985.
3. Sanchez, Marta Ester. *Contemporary Chicana Poetry: A Critical Approach to an Emerging Literature.* U of California P, 1985.

ALBERTA HUNTER (1895–1984) AND LOVIE AUSTIN (1887–1972)

Lovie Austin and Alberta Hunter both grew up in Tennessee. The two did not know each other then, but both would become key figures in the popularization of the blues and jazz in the 1920s and 1930s. Austin was a classically trained pianist, educated at Roger Williams College and Knoxville College. After graduating, she joined the Theater Owners' Booking Association (TOBA)—a group that booked various acts for the circuit of "vaudeville" houses that were springing up throughout the country in the 1910s. She would eventually settle in Chicago's South

*Side, which was becoming recognized as an enclave for some of the era's best blues
and jazz. During the next 20 years, Austin worked as the musical director for the
famous (and dilapidated) Monogram Theater, arranging and performing music,
as well as completing some of the earliest known blues recordings with her own
group, The Blues Serenaders.*

*Unlike Lovie Austin, Alberta Hunter had no formal education, but she did have
a desire to perform and sing. Her difficult childhood became a deep source of inspiration for the blues music she would later make famous: "The blues? Why, the
blues are a part of me . . . When we sing the blues, we're singing out our hearts,
we're singing out our feelings. When I sing . . . what I'm doing is letting my soul
out" (Notable Black American Women, 1992). From her early start singing in a
small Chicago brothel, through her years working vaudeville, singing in Europe
and with the USO during World War II, Hunter's rich vocals and emotive songs
would gain her international fame. In a career that has spanned over six decades,
Hunter is considered a legend and pioneer of blues music.*

*"Down Hearted Blues," coauthored by Hunter and Austin while they worked
together in Chicago during the 1920s, was recorded in 1922 as a "race record."
The song was an immediate success. The two reunited to record the song again
in 1961.*

SONG: *Down-Hearted Blues*   (1922)

Gee, but it's hard to love someone, when that someone don't love you.
I'm so disgusted, heartbroken too. I've got the downhearted blues.
Once I was crazy about a man. He mistreated me all the time.
The next man I get, he's got to promise to be mine, all mine.

'Cause you mistreated me, and you drove me from your door.   5
You mistreated me, and you drove me from your door.
But the Good Book says, "You've got to reap just what you sow."

Trouble, trouble, seems like I've had it all my days.
Trouble, trouble, seems like I've had it all my days.
Sometime I think trouble is gonna follow me to my grave.   10

I ain't never loved but three men in my life.
Lord, I ain't never loved but three men in my life.
One's my father, and my brother, and the man that wrecked my life.

Now it may be a week, and it may be a month or two.
I said, it may be a week, and it may be a month or two.   15
All the dirt you're doing to me is, honey, coming back home to you.

I've got the world in a jug and the stopper in my hand.
I've got the world in a jug and the stopper in my hand.
And if you want me, pretty papa, you've got to come under my command.

Study and Discussion Questions

1. Note the rhyme scheme and stanza structure of "Down-Hearted Blues," which is a classic blues song (1912–1928).*
2. The first, four-line, stanza is a prologue, which sets up the issue of the song and possible solutions. What are these?
3. State the point and the emotion of each stanza. How does the song show the progression of thinking of the "I" narrator?
4. Discuss as many implications as you can of the metaphor of the jug and stopper in the last stanza. How does this image show a change in the speaker's sense of her self?

Suggestions for Writing

1. Listen to some classic or country blues. Write some blues lyrics of your own.
2. Compare "Down-Hearted Blues" to Gladys Bentley's "How Much Can I Stand?"
3. Create a conversation between Hunter/Austin and Tupac Shakur, on the relation between women and men. Does the 70 or so years between the two songs matter? If so, how? If not, why not?

Critical Resources

1. *Alberta Hunter: My Castle's Rocking.* Director Stuart Goldman. The Cinema Guild, 1992 (60 minutes). Documentary on Hunter's career.
2. Alexander, Scott. *The Red Hot Jazz Archive.* March 15, 2000. <http://www.redhotjazz.com/index.htm>. The original audio recording of "Down-Hearted Blues" is available here.
3. Dahl, Linda. *Stormy Weather: The Music and Lives of a Century of Jazz Women.* New York: Pantheon, 1984.
4. Taylor, Frank. *Alberta Hunter: A Celebration in Blues.* New York: McGraw-Hill, 1987.
5. *Wild Women Don't Have The Blues.* Director Christine Dall. 1987 (58 minutes). For more information go to <http://www.newsreel.org/films/wild wome.htm>.

---

*Blues generally uses a 12-bar line, with a three-line stanza in which the first line is repeated (maybe with a small variation) in the second line, while the third line responds to or resolves the issue raised in the first two lines.

TUPAC SHAKUR (1971–1996)

Tupac Amaru Shakur (named after an Incan prince) was born in New York City. His mother, Afeni Shakur, was a well-known activist in the Black Panther move- ment of the late 1960s. Shakur's mother encouraged him artistically, and in high school he studied acting and dance. At 19, he landed a job as a dancer and roadie for the rap group Digital Underground. During this time, he also finished his first album, 2Pacalypse Now, *released in 1991. A year later he starred in the film* Juice. *He released his second album,* Strictly 4 My N.I.G.G.A.Z., *in 1993—an album that went gold within a month. While many have suggested that Shakur's popularity had more to do with his "gangsta" lifestyle than with the music he was writing (throughout this same period, Shakur was arrested and jailed for a va- riety of offenses), others have praised his music and lyrics. Skakur was shot and killed in 1996. Other albums include* Thug Life, Volume One, Out Da Gutta *(1994),* Me Against the World *(1995), and* The Don Killuminati: The 7 Day Theory *(1996, posthumously). "Hold Ya Head Up," recorded on* Strictly 4 My N.I.G.G.A.Z., *diverges from his usual themes of violence to make a tribute to black women.*

SONG: *Keep Ya Head Up* (1993)

Little somethin for my godson Elijah and a little girl named Corinne

Verse One:

Some say the blacker the berry, the sweeter the juice
I say the darker the flesh then the deeper the roots
I give a holler to my sisters on welfare
Tupac cares, and don't nobody else care
And uhh, I know they like to beat ya down a lot   5
When you come around the block brothas clown a lot
But please don't cry, dry your eyes, never let up
Forgive but don't forget, girl keep your head up
And when he tells you you ain't nuttin don't believe him
And if he can't learn to love you you should leave him   10
Cause sista you don't need him
And I ain't tryin to gas ya up, I just call em how I see em
You know it makes me unhappy (what's that)

When brothas make babies, and leave a young mother to be a pappy
And since we all came from a woman   15
Got our name from a woman and our game from a woman
I wonder why we take from our women
Why we rape our women, do we hate our women?
I think it's time to kill for our women
Time to heal our women, be real to our women   20
And if we don't we'll have a race of babies
That will hate the ladies, that make the babies
And since a man can't make one
He has no right to tell a woman when and where to create one
So will the real men get up   25
I know you're fed up ladies, but keep your head up

Chorus

Keep ya head up, oooo child things are gonna get easier
ooooo child things are gonna get brighter (2×)

Verse Two:

Aiyyo, I remember Marvin Gaye, used to sing ta me
He had me feelin like black was tha thing to be
And suddenly tha ghetto didn't seem so tough   30
And though we had it rough, we always had enough
I huffed and puffed about my curfew and broke the rules
Ran with the local crew, and had a smoke or two
And I realize momma really paid the price
She nearly gave her life, to raise me right   35
And all I had ta give her was my pipe dream
Of how I'd rock the mic, and make it to tha bright screen
I'm tryin to make a dollar out of fifteen cents
It's hard to be legit and still pay tha rent
And in the end it seems I'm headin for tha pen   40
I try and find my friends, but they're blowin in the wind
Last night my buddy lost his whole family
It's gonna take the man in me to conquer this insanity
It seems tha rain'll never let up
I try to keep my head up, and still keep from gettin wet up   45
You know it's funny when it rains it pours
They got money for wars, but can't feed the poor
Say there ain't no hope for the youth and the truth is
it ain't no hope for tha future

And then they wonder why we crazy   50
I blame my mother, for turning my brother into a crack baby
We ain't meant to survive, cause it's a setup
And even though you're fed up
Huh, ya got to keep your head up

Chorus

Verse Three:

And uhh   55
To all the ladies havin babies on they own
I know it's kinda rough and you're feelin all alone
Daddy's long gone and he left you by ya lonesome
Thank the Lord for my kids, even if nobody else want em
Cause I think we can make it, in fact, I'm sure   60
And if you fall, stand tall and comeback for more
Cause ain't nuttin worse than when your son
wants to kno why his daddy don't love him no mo'
You can't complain you was dealt this
hell of a hand without a man, feelin helpless   65
Because there's too many things for you to deal with
Dying inside, but outside you're looking fearless
While tears, is rollin down your cheeks
Ya steady hopin things don't all down this week
Cause if it did, you couldn't take it, and don't blame me   70
I was given this world I didn't make it
And now my son's getten older and older and cold
From havin the world on his shoulders
While the rich kids is drivin Benz
I'm still tryin to hold on to my survivin friends   75
And it's crazy, it seems it'll never let up, but
please . . . you got to keep your head up

Study and Discussion Questions

1. This rap song directly takes on the issue of respect for women. List the
   examples of disrespect Tupac Shakur gives in stanza one.
2. Who is each stanza addressed to—notice use of first, second, or third person? Stanza two talks about the artist's own life and the mother/son relationship—what specifically does he say about this?
3. What are the social issues of race and class that 2PAC details in the poem?
   To what extent does the artist suggest the situation of women is a result
   of race and class inequalities?

4. What in particular are the problems Black women face, according to this song? What are the singer's suggestions to the women he's addressing?

5. "So will the real men get up." How does Shakur take on current gender definitions of what a real man is? And where else in the song does he bring this up? List the ways a *real* man would behave toward women, according to the artist.

Suggestions for Writing

1. Compare/contrast "Keep Ya Head Up" to a rap song which expresses a different view of women.

2. Write a short paper discussing the potential of rap for political commentary.

3. Write a verse of rap on some social issue important to you.

Critical Resources

1. Dyson, Michael Eric. *Holler If You Hear Me: Searching for Tupac Shakur.* New York: Basic Civitas Books, 2001.

2. Dimitriada, Greg. *Performing Identity/Performing Culture: Hip Hop As Text, Pedagogy, And Lived Practice.* New York: P. Lang, 2001.

3. Eleveld, Mark, ed. *The Spoken Word Revolution: Slam, Hip-Hop and The Poetry of a New Generation.* Naperville, IL: Sourcebooks Media-Fusion, 2003.

4. *Tupac: Resurrection.* Dir. Lauren Lazin. Paramount Pictures, 2004 (113 minutes). Documentary.

Additional Poems

ANONYMOUS

The Song of Solomon[1]

Behold, thou *art* fair, my love; behold, thou *art* fair; thou *hast* doves' eyes within thy locks: thy hair *is* as a flock of goats, that appear from mount Gĭl'ē-ăd.

2 Thy teeth *are* like a flock *of sheep that are even* shorn, which came up from the washing; whereof every one bear twins, and none *is* barren among them.

3 Thy lips *are* like a thread of scarlet, and thy speech *is* comely: thy temples *are* like a piece of a pomegranate within thy locks.

4 Thy neck *is* like the tower of David builded for an armory, whereon there hang a thousand bucklers, all shields of mighty men.

5 Thy two breasts *are* like two young roes that are twins, which feed among the lilies.

---

[1]King James Bible (1611).

6 Until the day break, and the shadows flee away, I will get me to the mountain of myrrh, and to the hill of frankincense.

7 Thou *art* all fair, my love; *there is* no spot in thee.

8 ¶Come with me from Lebanon, *my* spouse, with me from Lebanon: look from the top of Ăm'å-nå, from the top of She'nir and Hermon, from the lions' dens, on the mountains of the leopards.

9 Thou hast ravished my heart, my sister, *my* spouse; thou hast ravished my heart with one of thine eyes, with one chain of thy neck.

10 How fair is thy love, my sister, *my* spouse! how much better is thy love than wine! and the smell of thine ointments than all spices!

11 Thy lips, O *my* spouse, drop *as* the honeycomb: honey and milk *are* under thy tongue; and the smell of thy garments *is* like the smell of Lebanon.

12 A garden inclosed *is* my sister, *my* spouse; a spring shut up, a fountain sealed.

13 Thy plants *are* an orchard of pomegranates, with pleasant fruits; camphire, with spikenard,

14 Spikenard and saffron; calamus and cinnamon, with all trees of frankincense; myrrh and aloes, with all the chief spices:

15 A fountain of gardens, a well of living waters, and streams from Lebanon.

16 ¶Awake, O north wind; and come, thou south; blow upon my garden *that* the spices thereof may flow out. Let my beloved come into his garden, and eat his pleasant fruits.

❀ ❀ ❀

CHRISTOPHER MARLOWE (1564–1593)

The Passionate Shepherd to His Love   (1600)

Come live with me and be my love,
And we will all the pleasures prove[1]
That valleys, groves, hills, and fields,
Woods, or steepy mountain yields.

And we will sit upon the rocks,   5
Seeing the shepherds feed their flocks,
By shallow rivers to whose falls
Melodious birds sing madrigals.

And I will make thee beds of roses

---

[1]Try out.

And a thousand fragrant posies,   10
A cap of flowers, and a kirtle[2]
Embroidered all with leaves of myrtle;

A gown made of the finest wool
Which from our pretty lambs we pull;
Fair lined slippers for the cold,   15
With buckles of the purest gold;

A belt of straw and ivy buds,
With coral clasps and amber studs:
And if these pleasures may thee move,
Come live with me, and be my love.   20

The shepherds' swains shall dance and sing
For thy delight each May morning:
If these delights thy mind may move,
Then live with me and be my love.

WILLIAM SHAKESPEARE (1564–1616)

When my love swears that she is made of truth   (1609)

CXXXVIII

When my love swears that she is made of truth,
I do believe her, though I know she lies,
That she might think me some untutor'd youth,
Unlearned in the world's false subtleties.
Thus vainly thinking that she thinks me young,   5
Although she knows my days are past the best,
Simply I credit her false-speaking tongue:
On both sides thus is simple truth supprest.
But wherefore says she not she is unjust?
And wherefore say not I that I am old?   10
O! love's best habit is in seeming trust,

---

[2]Dress.

And age in love loves not to have years told:
  Therefore I lie with her, and she with me,
  And in our faults by lies we flatter'd be.

❀ ❀ ❀

JOHN DONNE (1572–1631)

The Sun Rising   (1633)

      Busy old fool, unruly sun,
       Why dost thou thus,
Through windows, and through curtains call on us?
Must to thy motions lovers' seasons run?
        Saucy pedantic wretch, go chide   5
        Late school-boys, and sour prentices,
    Go tell court-huntsmen, that the King will ride,
    Call country ants[1] to harvest offices;
Love, all alike, no season knows, nor clime,
Nor hours, days, months, which are the rags of time.   10

       Thy beams, so reverend, and strong
       Why shouldst thou think?
I could eclipse and cloud them with a wink,
But that I would not lose her sight so long:
        If her eyes have not blinded thine,   15
        Look, and tomorrow late, tell me,
    Whether both the Indias[2] of spice and mine
    Be where thou left'st them, or lie here with me.
Ask for those kings whom thou saw'st yesterday,
And thou shalt hear, All here in one bed lay.   20

       She is all states, and all princes, I,
       Nothing else is.
Princes do but play us; compared to this,
All honour's mimic; all wealth alchemy.
        Thou sun art half as happy as we,   25
        In that the world's contracted thus;
    Thine age asks ease, and since thy duties be

---

[1]Rural workers.
[2]The East and West Indies.

To warm the world, that's done in warming us.
Shine here to us, and thou art everywhere;
This bed thy centre[3] is, these walls, thy sphere.   30

JOHN DONNE (1572–1631)

The Canonization   (1633)

For God's sake hold your tongue, and let me love,
Or chide my palsy, or my gout,
My five grey hairs, or ruined fortune flout,
   With wealth your state, your mind with arts improve,
      Take you a course, get you a place   5
      Observe his Honour, or his Grace,
Or the King's real, or his stamped face
      Contemplate; what you will, approve,[1]
      So you will let me love.

Alas, alas, who's injured by my love?   10
   What merchant's ships have my sighs drowned?
Who says my tears have overflowed his ground?
      When did my colds a forward spring remove?
        When did the heats which my veins fill
        Add one more to the plaguy bill?[2]   15
Soldiers find wars, and lawyers find out still
      Litigious men, which quarrels move,
      Though she and I do love.

Call us what you will, we are made such by love;
   Call her one, me another fly,   20
We are tapers too, and at our own cost die,[3]
      And we in us find the Eagle and the Dove.
        The Phoenix riddle hath more wit
        By us; we two being one, are it.

---

[3]Orbital center.
[1]Try.
[2]List of victims of the plague.
[3]Climax sexually.

So to one neutral thing both sexes fit,   25
    We die and rise the same, and prove
    Mysterious by this love.

We can die by it, if not live by love,
    And if unfit for tombs and hearse
Our legend be, it will be fit for verse;   30
    And if no piece of chronicle we prove,
        We'll build in sonnets pretty rooms;
        As well a well-wrought urn becomes
The greatest ashes, as half-acre tombs,
        And by these hymns, all shall approve   35
        Us canonized for love:

And thus invoke us; 'You whom reverend love
    Made one another's hermitage;
You, to whom love was peace, that now is rage;
    Who did the whole world's soul contract, and drove   40
        Into the glasses of your eyes
        (So made such mirrors, and such spies,
That they did all to you epitomize),
    Countries, towns, courts: beg from above
    A pattern of your love!'   45

❀ ❀ ❀

ANDREW MARVELL (1621–1678)

To His Coy Mistress   (1681)

    Had we but world enough, and time,
This coyness, Lady, were no crime.
We would sit down, and think which way
To walk, and pass our long love's day.
Thou by the Indian Ganges' side   5
Shouldst rubies find; I by the tide
Of Humber would complain. I would
Love you ten years before the Flood,
And you should, if you please, refuse
Till the Conversion of the Jews.   10

My vegetable[1] love should grow
Vaster than empires and more slow;
An hundred years should go to praise
Thine eyes, and on thy forehead gaze;
Two hundred to adore each breast,   15
But thirty thousand to the rest;
An age at least to every part,
And the last age should show your heart.
For, Lady, you deserve this state,
Nor would I love at lower rate.   20
    But at my back I always hear
Time's wingèd chariot hurrying near;
And yonder all before us lie
Deserts of vast eternity.
Thy beauty shall no more be found,   25
Nor, in thy marble vault, shall sound
My echoing song; then worms shall try
That long-preserved virginity,
And your quaint honour turn to dust,
And into ashes all my lust: 30
The grave's a fine and private place,
But none, I think, do there embrace.
    Now therefore, while the youthful hue
Sits on thy skin like morning dew,
And while thy willing soul transpires   35
At every pore with instant fires,
Now let us sport us while we may,
And now, like amorous birds of prey,
Rather at once our time devour
Than languish in his slow chapt[2] power.   40
Let us roll all our strength and all
Our sweetness up into one ball,
And tear our pleasures with rough strife
Thorough[3] the iron gates of life;
Thus, though we cannot make our sun   45
Stand still, yet we will make him run.

[1]Growing on its own.
[2]Slow-jawed.
[3]Through.

WALT WHITMAN (1819–1892)

To a Stranger   (1860)

Passing stranger! you do not know how longingly I look upon you,
You must be he I was seeking, or she I was seeking (it comes to me
     as of a dream,)
I have somewhere surely lived a life of joy with you,
All is recall'd as we flit by each other, fluid, affectionate, chaste,
     matured,   5
You grew up with me, were a boy with me or a girl with me,
I ate with you and slept with you, your body has become not yours
     only nor left my body mine only,
You give me the pleasure of your eyes, face, flesh, as we pass, you   10
     take of my beard, breast, hands, in return,
I am not to speak to you, I am to think of you when I sit alone or
     wake at night alone,
I am to wait, I do not doubt I am to meet you again,
I am to see to it that I do not lose you.   15

WALT WHITMAN (1819–1892)

I Saw in Louisiana a Live-Oak Growing   (1860)

I saw in Louisiana a live-oak growing,
All alone stood it and the moss hung down from the branches,
Without any companion it grew there uttering joyous leaves of dark green,
And its look, rude, unbending, lusty, made me think of myself,   5
But I wonder'd how it could utter joyous leaves standing alone there
     without its friend near, for I knew I could not,
And I broke off a twig with a certain number of leaves upon it, and
     twined around it a little moss,
And brought it away, and I have placed it in sight in my room,   10
It is not needed to remind me as of my own dear friends,
(For I believe lately I think of little else than of them,)
Yet it remains to me a curious token, it makes me think of manly love;
For all that, and though the live-oak glistens there in Louisiana solitary
     in a wide flat space,   15

Uttering joyous leaves all its life without a friend a lover near,
I know very well I could not.

EMILY DICKINSON (1830–1886)

My Life had stood—a Loaded Gun (1863)

My Life had stood—a Loaded Gun—
In Corners—till a Day
The Owner passed—identified—
And carried Me away—

And now We roam in Sovreign Woods— 5
And now We hunt the Doe—
And every time I speak for Him—
The Mountains straight reply—

And do I smile, such cordial light
Upon the Valley glow— 10
It is as a Vesuvian face
Had let it's pleasure through—

And when at Night—Our good Day done—
I guard My Master's Head—
'Tis better than the Eider-Duck's 15
Deep Pillow—to have shared—

To foe of His—I'm deadly foe—
None stir the second time—
On whom I lay a Yellow Eye—
Or an emphatic Thumb— 20

Though I than He—may longer live
He longer must—than I—
For I have but the power to kill,
Without—the power to die—

AMY LOWELL (1874–1925)

A Decade   (1919)

When you came, you were like red wine
   and honey,
And the taste of you burnt my mouth
   with its sweetness.
Now you are like morning bread,   5
Smooth and pleasant.
I hardly taste you at all for I know your
   savour,
But I am completely nourished.

❀ ❀ ❀

CLAUDE MCKAY (1890–1948)

The Harlem Dancer   (1922)

Applauding youths laughed with young prostitutes
And watched her perfect, half-clothed body sway;
Her voice was like the sound of blended flutes
Blown by black players upon a picnic day.
She sang and danced on gracefully and calm,   5
The light gauze hanging loose about her form;
To me she seemed a proudly-swaying palm
Grown lovelier for passing through a storm.
Upon her swarthy neck black shiny curls
Luxuriant fell; and tossing coins in praise,   10
The wine-flushed, bold-eyed boys, and even the girls,
Devoured her shape with eager, passionate gaze;
But looking at her falsely-smiling face,
I knew her self was not in that strange place.

❀ ❀ ❀

WILLIAM BUTLER YEATS (1865–1939)

Leda and the Swan[1] (1923)

A sudden blow: the great wings beating still
Above the staggering girl, her thighs caressed
By the dark webs, her nape caught in his bill,
He holds her helpless breast upon his breast.

How can those terrified vague fingers push   5
The feathered glory from her loosening thighs?
And how can body, laid in that white rush,
But feel the strange heart beating where it lies?

A shudder in the loins engenders there
The broken wall, the burning roof and tower   10
And Agamemnon dead.
Being so caught up,
So mastered by the brute blood of the air,
Did she put on his knowledge with his power
Before the indifferent beak could let her drop?   15

LOUISE BOGAN (1897–1970)

Women (1923)

Women have no wilderness in them,
They are provident instead,
Content in the tight hot cell of their hearts
To eat dusty bread.

They do not see cattle cropping red winter grass,   5
They do not hear
Snow water going down under culverts
Shallow and clear.

---

[1]Greek god Zeus, in the form of a swan, raped Leda, who bore Helen of Troy (whose abduction led to the Trojan War) and Clytemnestra (who murdered her husband Agamemnon upon his return from that war).

They wait, when they should turn to journeys,
They stiffen, when they should bend.   10
They use against themselves that benevolence
To which no man is friend.

They cannot think of so many crops to a field
Or of clean wood cleft by an axe.
Their love is an eager meaninglessness   15
Too tense, or too lax.

They hear in every whisper that speaks to them
A shout and a cry.
As like as not, when they take life over their door-sills
They should let it go by.   20

❋ ❋ ❋

GLADYS BENTLEY (1907–1960)

SONG: *How Much Can I Stand?*   (1928)

I've heard about your lovers
Your pinks and browns
I've heard about your sheiks
And hand me downs

I've got a man   5
I've loved all the while
But now he treats me
Like a darn bad child

One time he said my sugar
Was so sweet   10
But now for his dessert
He goes across the street
How much of that dog can I stand?

My man's love
Has got so cold and dead   15
That now he has to wear
An overcoat to bed
How much of that dog can I stand?

Women selling snakeskins
And alligator tails   20
Tryin to get money
To get my man out of jail
How much of that dog can I stand?

Said I was an angel
He was born to treat me right   25
Who in the devil ever heard of angels
That get beat up every night
How much of that dog can I stand?

Went down to the drug store
Asked the clerk for a dose   30
But when I received the poison
I eyed it very close
Lord, how much of this dog can I stand?

Come home from work
Feelin' tired and sore   35
He makes me shove my money
Underneath my front door
How much of that dog can I stand?

The next man I get
Must be guaranteed   40
When I walk down the aisle
You're gonna hear me scream
How much of this dog can I stand?

❀ ❀ ❀

EDNA ST. VINCENT MILLAY (1892–1950)

Love is not all: it is not meat nor drink   (1931)

Love is not all: it is not meat nor drink
Nor slumber nor a roof against the rain;
Nor yet a floating spar to men that sink
And rise and sink and rise and sink again;
Love can not fill the thickened lung with breath,   5

Nor clean the blood, nor set the fractured bone;
Yet many a man is making friends with death
Even as I speak, for lack of love alone.
It well may be that in a difficult hour,
Pinned down by pain and moaning for release,   10
Or nagged by want past resolution's power,
I might be driven to sell your love for peace,
Or trade the memory of this night for food.
It well may be. I do not think I would.

❀ ❀ ❀

LÉOPOLD SÉDAR SENGHOR (b. 1906)

You Held the Black Face   (1949)

Translated by Gerald Moore and Ulli Beier.

(for Khalam)

You held the black face of the warrior between your hands
Which seemed with fateful twilight luminous.
From the hill I watched the sunset in the bays of your eyes.
When shall I see my land again, the pure horizon of your face?
When shall I sit at the table of your dark breasts?   5
The nest of sweet decisions lies in the shade.
I shall see different skies and different eyes,
And shall drink from the sources of other lips, fresher than lemons,
I shall sleep under the roofs of other hair, protected from storms.
But every year, when the rum of spring kindles the veins afresh, 10
I shall mourn anew my home, and the rain of your eyes over the
        thirsty savannah.

❀ ❀ ❀

LANGSTON HUGHES (1902–1967)

Mellow (1951)

Into the laps
of black celebrities
white girls fall
like pale plums from a tree
beyond a high tension wall   5
wired for killing
which makes it
more thrilling.

❀ ❀ ❀

MARGE PIERCY (b. 1936)

The woman in the ordinary (1970)

The woman in the ordinary pudgy downcast girl
is crouching with eyes and muscles clenched.
Round and pebble smooth she effaces herself
under ripples of conversation and debate.
The woman in the block of ivory soap   5
has massive thighs that neigh,
great breasts that blare and strong arms that trumpet.
The woman of the golden fleece
laughs uproariously from the belly
inside the girl who imitates   10
a Christmas card virgin with glued hands,
who fishes for herself in other's eyes,
who stoops and creeps to make herself smaller.
In her bottled up is a woman peppery as curry,
a yam of a woman of butter and brass,   15
compounded of acid and sweet like a pineapple,
like a handgrenade set to explode,
like goldenrod ready to bloom.

MURIEL RUKEYSER (1913–1980)

Waiting For Icarus[1]   (1973)

He said he would be back and we'd drink wine together
He said we were on the edge of a new relation
He said he would never again cringe before his father
He said that he was going to invent full-time   5
He said he loved me that going into me
He said was going into the world and the sky
He said all the buckles were very firm
He said the wax was the best wax
He said Wait for me here on the beach   10
He said Just don't cry

I remember the gulls and the waves
I remember the islands going dark on the sea
I remember the girls laughing
I remember they said he only wanted to get away from me   15
I remember mother saying: Inventors are like poets,
                              a trashy lot
I remember she told me those who try out inventions are worse
I remember she added: Women who love such are the worst of all   20
I have been waiting all day, or perhaps longer.
I would have liked to try those wings myself.
It would have been better than this.

NTOZAKE SHANGE (b. 1948)

somebody almost walked off wid alla my stuff[1]   (1976)

somebody almost walked off wid alla my stuff
not my poems or a dance i gave up in the street

---

[1]In Greek myth, the son of Daedalus; he tried to escape Crete on wings his father made, but flew too close to the sun, and the wax that held the wings on melted, plunging him into the sea.

[1]From Shange's choreopoem, *for colored girls who have considered suicide / when the rainbow is enuf.*

but somebody almost walked off wid alla my stuff
like a kleptomaniac workin hard & forgettin while stealin
this is mine/ this aint yr stuff/   5
now why dont you put me back & let me hang out in my own self
somebody almost walked off wid alla my stuff
& didnt care enuf to send a note home sayin
i waz late for my solo conversation
or two sizes too small for my own tacky skirts   10
what can anybody do wit somethin of no value on
a open market/ did you getta dime for my things/
hey man/ where are you goin wid alla my stuff/
this is a woman's trip & i need my stuff/
to ohh & ahh abt/ daddy/ i gotta mainline number   15
from my own shit/ now wontchu put me back/ & let
me play this duet/ wit this silver ring in my nose/
honest to god/ somebody almost run off wit alla my stuff/
& i didn't bring anythin but the kick & sway of it
the perfect ass for my man & none of it is theirs   20
this is mine/ ntozake 'her own things'/ that's my name/
now give me my stuff/ i see ya hidin my laugh/ & how i
sit wif my legs open sometimes/ to give my crotch
some sunlight/ & there goes my love my toes my chewed
up finger nails/ niggah/ wif the curls in yr hair/   25
mr. louisiana hot link/ i want my stuff back/
my rhythms & my voice/ open my mouth/ & let me talk ya
outta/ throwin my shit in the sewar/ this is some delicate
leg & whimsical kiss/ i gotta have to give to my choice/
without you runnin off wit alla my shit/   30
now you cant have me less i give me away/ & i waz
doin all that/ til ya run off on a good thing/
who is this you left me wit/ some simple bitch
widda bad attitude/ i wants my things/
i want my arm wit the hot iron scar/ & my leg wit the   35
flea bite/ i want my calloused feet & quik language back
in my mouth/ fried plantains/ pineapple pear juice/
sun-ra[2] & joseph & jules/ i want my own things/ how i lived them/
& give me my memories/ how i waz when i waz there/
you cant have them or do nothin wit them/   40
stealin my shit from me/ dont make it yrs/ makes it stolen/
somebody almost run off wit alla my stuff/ & i waz standin
there/ lookin at myself/ the whole time
& it waznt a spirit took my stuff/ waz a man whose

---

[2]Jazz musician (1914–1993).

ego walked round like Rodan's[3] shadow/ waz a man faster   45
n my innocence/ waz a lover/ i made too much
room for/ almost run off wit alla my stuff/
& i didn't know i'd give it up so quik/ & the one running wit it/
dont know he got it/ & i'm shoutin this is mine/ & he dont
know he got it/ my stuff is the anonymous ripped off treasure   50
of the year/ did you know somebody almost got away with me/
me in a plastic bag under their arm/ me
danglin on a string of personal carelessness/ i'm spattered wit
mud & city rain/ & no i didn't get a chance to take a douche/
hey man/ this is not your perogative/ i gotta have me in my   55
pocket/ to get round like a good woman shd/ & make the poem
in the pot or the chicken in the dance/ what i got to do/
i gotta have my stuff to do it to/
why dont ya find yr own things/ & leave this package
of me for my destiny/ what ya got to get from me/   60
i'll give it to ya/ yeh/ i'll give it to ya/
round 5:00 in the winter/ when the sky is blue-red/
& Dew City is gettin pressed/ if it's really my stuff/
ya gotta give it to me/ if ya really want it/ i'm
the only one/ can handle it   65

ADRIENNE RICH (b. 1929)

FROM *Twenty-one Love Poems*   (1978)

XI

Every peak is a crater. This is the law of volcanoes,
making them eternally and visibly female.
No height without depth, without a burning core,
though our straw soles shred on the hardened lava.
I want to travel with you to every sacred mountain   5
smoking within like the sibyl stooped over her tripod,
I want to reach for your hand as we scale the path,

---

[3]Prehistoric monster in a movie of that title.

to feel your arteries glowing in my clasp,
never failing to note the small, jewel-like flower
unfamiliar to us, nameless till we rename her,　　　　　　10
that clings to the slowly altering rock—
that detail outside ourselves that brings us to ourselves,
was here before us, knew we would come, and sees beyond us.

ALICE BLOCH (b. 1947)

Six Years　　　　　　　　　　　　　　　　　　(1983)

for Nancy

A friend calls us
an old married couple

I flinch
you don't mind
On the way home　　　　　　　　　　　　　　　　5
you ask why I got upset
We are something
like what she said
you say　　I say
No　　　　　　　　　　　　　　　　　　　　　　10

We aren't married
No one has blessed
this union　　no one
gave us kitchen gadgets
We bought our own blender　　　　　　　　　　　　15
We built our common life
in the space between the laws

Six years
What drew us together
a cartographer　　a magnetic force　　　　　　　　20
our bodies　　our speech
the wind　　a hunger
Listeners both
we talked

I wanted: your lean wired energy   25
control   decisiveness
honesty   your past
as an athlete
You wanted:
my 'culture'   30
gentleness   warmth

Of course that was doomed
You brought out
my anger   I resist
your control   your energy   35
exhausts   me my hands
are too hot for you   you gained
the weight I lost   my gentleness
is dishonest   your honesty
is cruel   you hate   40
my reading   I hate
your motorcycle

Yet something has changed
You have become gentler
I more decisive   45
We walk easily
around our house
into each other's language
There is nothing
we cannot say together   50

Solid ground
under our feet
we know this landscape
We have no choice
of destination   only the route   55
is a mystery   every day
a new map of the same terrain

❀ ❀ ❀

MARTHA COLLINS (b. 1940)

Several Things   (1985)

Several things could happen in this poem.
Plums could appear, on a pewter plate.

A dead red hare, hung by one foot.
A vase of flowers. Three shallots.

A man could sing, in a burgundy robe 5
with a gold belt tied in a square knot.
Someone could untie the knot.
A woman could toss a gold coin.

A stranger could say the next line,
I have been waiting for this, 10
and offer a basket piled with apples
picked this morning, before the rain.

It could rain in this poem,
but if it rained, the man would continue
to sing as the burgundy silk fell 15
to the polished parquet floor.

It could snow in this poem:
remember how the hunter stamped his feet
before he leaned his gun in the corner
and hung his cap on the brass hook? 20

Perhaps the woman should open the ebony bench
and find the song her mother used to sing.
Listen: the woman is playing the song.
The man is singing the words.

Meanwhile the hunter is taking a warm bath 25
in the clean white tub with clawed legs.
Or has the hunter left? Are his boots
making tracks in the fallen snow?

When does the woman straighten the flowers?
Is that before the hunter observes 30
the tiny pattern on the vase?
Before the man begins to peel the shallots?

Now it is time for the woman
to slice the apples into a blue bowl.
A child could be watching the unbroken peel 35
spiral below the knife.

Last but not least, you could appear.
You could be the red-cheeked child,

the hunter, or the stranger.
You could stay for a late meal.　　　　　　　　　40

A Provençal recipe.
A bright red hare, shot at dawn.
Shallots. Brandy. Pepper, salt.
An apple in the pan.

❀ ❀ ❀

JUDITH ORTIZ COFER (b. 1952)

Claims　　　　　　　　　　　　　　　　　(1987)

Last time I saw her, Grandmother
had grown seamed as a Bedouin tent.
She had claimed the right
to sleep alone, to own
her nights, to never bear　　　　　　　　　　5
the weight of sex again nor to accept
its gift of comfort, for the luxury
of stretching her bones.
She'd carried eight children,
three had sunk in her belly, *náufragos*[1]　　10
she called them, shipwrecked babies
drowned in her black waters.
Children are made in the night and
steal your days
for the rest of your life, amen. She said this　　15
to each of her daughters in turn. Once she had made a pact
with man and nature and kept it. Now like the sea,
she is claiming back her territory.

❀ ❀ ❀

---

[1]Shipwrecked people.

BARBARA KINGSOLVER (b. 1955)

This House I Cannot Leave (1991)

My friend describes the burglar:
how he touched her clothes, passed through rooms
leaving himself there,
     staining the space
between walls, a thing she can see.   5
She doesn't care what he took, only
that he has driven her out, she can't
stay in this house
she loved, scraped the colors of four families
from the walls and painted with her own,   10
and planted things.
She is leaving fruit trees behind.

She will sell, get out, maybe
another neighborhood.
      People say   15
Get over it. The market isn't good. They advise
that she think about cash to mortgage
and the fruit trees

but the trees have stopped growing for her.

I offer no advice.   20
I tell her I know, she will leave. I am thinking
of the man who broke and entered

me.

 Of the years it took to be home again
in this house I cannot leave.   25

❀ ❀ ❀

STEFANIE MARLIS (b. 1951)

Transsexual Cloud (2003)

all through this metamorphosis we hunt for therapies   burly reasons

ours, a knot that does not slip   thunderclap

yellow basin   settles behind a cloud   lemon blouse   carries the trash
only curly leaves befuddle me and you   were a chiseled man
so long

PABLO NERUDA (1904–1973)

Every Day You Play   (1969)

Translated by W. S. Merwin

Every day you play with the light of the universe.
Subtle visitor, you arrive in the flower and the water.
You are more than this white head that I hold tightly
as a cluster of fruit, every day, between my hands.

You are like nobody since I love you.   5
Let me spread you out among yellow garlands.
Who writes your name in letters of smoke among the stars of the south?
Oh let me remember you as you were before you existed.

Suddenly the wind howls and bangs at my shut window.
The sky is a net crammed with shadowy fish.   10
Here all the winds let go sooner or later, all of them.
The rain takes off her clothes.

The birds go by, fleeing.
The wind. The wind.

I can contend only against the power of men.   15
The storm whirls dark leaves
and turns loose all the boats that were moored last night to the sky.

You are here. Oh, you do not run away. You will answer me to
      the last cry.
Cling to me as though you were frightened.   20
Even so, at one time a strange shadow ran through your eyes.

Now, now too, little one, you bring me honeysuckle,
and even your breasts smell of it.

While the sad wind goes slaughtering butterflies
I love you, and my happiness bites the plum of your mouth.   25

How you must have suffered getting accustomed to me,
my savage, solitary soul, my name that sends them all running.
So many times we have seen the morning star burn, kissing our eyes,
and over our heads the grey light unwind in turning fans.

My words rained over you, stroking you.   30
A long time I have loved the sunned mother-of-pearl of your body.
I go so far as to think that you own the universe.
I will bring you happy flowers from the mountains, bluebells,
dark hazels, and rustic baskets of kisses.
I want   35
to do with you what spring does with the cherry trees.

Drama

JOHN M. SYNGE (1871–1909)

John Millington Synge was born near Dublin and raised in a staunch Protestant family. Coming from moderate wealth, Synge was educated by private tutors until he entered Trinity College, where he studied music. He completed his degree in 1892. A year later he went to Germany to study music, but abandoned the practice, unable to deal with his fear of performing. He then decided to go Paris to study literature at the Sorbonne. It is here that Synge met fellow Irish poet and writer W. B. Yeats, who suggested he take up residence on the Aran Islands (west of mainland Ireland) and write about the ways of life present there. The suggestion turned out to be fortuitous—his experience on the Islands would serve as the inspiration for some of his best work, including three one-act plays: In the Shadow of the Glen, Riders to the Sea, *and* The Tinker's Wedding *(all written in 1902). Using the Aran Islands culture as the setting, these plays dramatize the simple, pastoral life of the island peasants, exploring such themes as isolation, mortality and religion. Synge also used the Gaelic dialect spoken by the people of the island to reproduce more authentic exchanges in the dialogue. His other works include the plays* The Well of the Saints *(1905),* The Playboy of the Western World *(1907), and* Deidre of the Sorrows *(1910, posthumous) and the collection of essays* The Aran Islands *(1907).*

Riders to the Sea (1902)

A Play in One Act

Persons
MAURYA, an old woman
BARTLEY, her son
CATHLEEN, her daughter
NORA, a younger daughter
MEN AND WOMEN

> SCENE *An Island off the West of Ireland°*
> FIRST PRODUCTION *(Dublin, 25 February 1904)*

Scene An Island off the West of Ireland: almost certainly Inishmaan, the middle-sized of the three Aran Islands in Galway Bay, where Synge spent most of his time when visiting Aran. Most of the incidents and details of the play are taken from Synge's observations in *The Aran Islands.*

Maurya	Honor Lavelle
Bartley	W. G. Fay
Cathleen	Sara Allgood
Nora	Emma Vernon
Men and Women	P. J. Kelly, Seamus O'Sullivan,
	George Roberts, Maire Nic
	Shiubhlaigh, Maire Ni
	Gharbhaigh, and Doreen Gunning

Cottage kitchen, with nets, oil-skins, spinning wheel, some new boards stand-
ing by the wall, etc. Cathleen, a girl of about twenty, finishes kneading cake,
and puts it down in the pot-oven° by the fire; then wipes her hands, and be-
gins to spin at the wheel. Nora, a young girl, puts her head in at the door

NORA   [*in a low voice*] Where is she?
CATHLEEN   She's lying down, God help her, and maybe sleeping, if she's able.

[*Nora comes in softly, and takes a bundle from under her shawl*]

CATHLEEN   [*spinning the wheel rapidly*] What is it you have?
NORA   The young priest is after bringing them. It's a shirt and a plain
stocking were got off a drowned man in Donegal.°   5

[*Cathleen stops her wheel with a sudden movement, and leans out° to listen*]

NORA   We're to find out if it's Michael's they are, some time herself will
be down looking by the sea.
CATHLEEN   How would they be Michael's, Nora. How would he go the
length of that way to the far north?
NORA   The young priest says he's known the like of it. 'If it's Michael's   10
they are,' says he, 'you can tell herself he's got a clean burial by the grace
of God, and if they're not his, let no one say a word about them, for she'll
be getting her death,' says he, 'with crying and lamenting.'

[*The door which Nora half closed behind her is blown open by a gust of wind*]

CATHLEEN   [*looking out anxiously*] Did you ask him would he stop Bartley going this day with the horses to the Galway fair?°   15
NORA   'I won't stop him,' says he, 'but let you not be afraid. Herself does
be saying prayers half through the night, and the Almighty God won't
leave her destitute,' says he, 'with no son living.'

Opening S.D.: cake . . . in the pot-oven: the staple soda bread was baked in an iron pot
with embers from the turf fire piled on top of the lid.   5 Donegal: a seaport town in
Donegal Bay, in the furthest north-west county of Ireland.   S.D. leans out: that is, across
the wheel. Synge was insistent that the actress playing Cathleen know how to spin.
15   the Galway fair: the closest market town on the mainland.

(Courtesy of the Library of Congress.)

CATHLEEN   Is the sea bad by the white rocks, Nora?

NORA   Middling bad, God help us. There's a great roaring in the west, and   20
it's worse it'll be getting when the tide's turned to the wind.° [*She goes
over to the table with the bundle*] Shall I open it now?

CATHLEEN   Maybe she'd wake up on us, and come in before we'd done
[*coming to the table*] It's a long time we'll be, and the two of us crying.

NORA   [*goes to the inner door and listens*] She's moving about on the bed.   25
She'll be coming in a minute.

CATHLEEN   Give me the ladder, and I'll put them up in the turf-loft,° the
way° she won't know of them at all, and maybe when the tide turns she'll
be going down to see would he be floating from the east.

---

21 when the tide's turned to the wind: when the tide is against the wind, and the waves
will be higher.   27 turf-loft: an opening for the storage of sods of peat used as fuel.
28 the way: 'so that'; also used by Synge to mean 'so that s/he can or should', 'as' or 'as
if', and (in 'what way') 'how could'.

[*They put the ladder against the gable of the chimney; Cathleen goes up a few steps and hides the bundle in the turf-loft. Maurya comes from the inner room*]

MAURYA [*looking up at Cathleen and speaking querulously*] Isn't it turf 30
enough you have for this day and evening?

CATHLEEN There's a cake baking at the fire for a short space [*throwing down the turf*], and Bartley will want it when the tide turns if he goes to Connemara.

[*Nora picks up the turf and puts it round the pot-oven*]

MAURYA [*sitting down on a stool at the fire*] He won't go this day with 35
the wind rising from the south and west. He won't go this day, for the young priest will stop him surely.

NORA He'll not stop him, mother, and I heard Eamon Simon and Stephen Pheety and Colum Shawn saying he would go.

MAURYA Where is he itself? 40

NORA He went down to see would there be another boat sailing in the week, and I'm thinking it won't be long till he's here now, for the tide's turning at the green head,° and the hooker's tacking from the east.°

CATHLEEN I hear some one passing the big stones.

NORA [*looking out*] He's coming now, and he in a hurry. 45

BARTLEY [*comes in and looks round the room; speaking sadly and quietly*] Where is the bit of new rope, Cathleen, was bought in Connemara?

CATHLEEN [*coming down*] Give it to him, Nora; it's on a nail by the white boards. I hung it up this morning, for the pig with the black feet was eating it.° 50

NORA [*giving him a rope*] Is that is, Bartley?

MAURYA [*as before*] You'd do right to leave that rope, Bartley, hanging by the boards. [*Bartley takes the rope*] It will be wanting in this place, I'm telling you, if Michael is washed up tomorrow morning, or the next morning, or any morning in the week, for it's a deep grave we'll make 55
him by the grace of God.

BARTLEY [*beginning to work with the rope*] I've no halter the way I can ride down on the mare, and I must go now quickly. This is the one boat

---

43 the green head: a grassy headland overlooking the sea; most of the island has steep cliffs of rock. 43 the hooker's tacking from the east: because of the steep cliffs and strong winds on the two smaller islands, even the small sailing cutters (hookers) carrying passengers and produce could not come in to shore, which meant that islanders had to go out to meet them in frail rowing-boats called curaghs, encouraging their tethered (and terrified) animals to swim alongside. 50 the pig with the black feet was eating it: pigs were a valued source of food and commerce on the islands, but the repetition of the familiar description takes on further significance here in that pigs are associated with death in Irish folklore and black with ill luck or even evil.

going for two weeks or beyond it, and the fair will be a good fair for
horses I heard them saying below.   60
MAURYA   It's a hard thing they'll be saying below if the body is washed
up and there's no man in it to make the coffin, and I after giving a big
price for the finest white boards you'd find in Connemara.° [*She looks
round at the boards*]
BARTLEY   How would it be washed up, and we after looking each day for   65
nine days, and a strong wind blowing a while back from the west and
south?
MAURYA   If it isn't found itself, that wind is raising the sea, and there was
a star up against the moon, and it rising in the night. If it was a hundred
horses, or a thousand horses you had itself, what is the price of a thou-   70
sand horses against a son where there is one son only?
BARTLEY   [*working at the halter, to Cathleen*] Let you go down each day,
and see the sheep aren't jumping in on the rye, and if the jobber° comes
you can sell the pig with the black feet if there is a good price going.
MAURYA   How would the like of her get a good price for a pig?   75
BARTLEY   [*to Cathleen*] If the west wind holds with the last bit of the
moon let you and Nora get up weed enough for another cock for the
kelp.° It's hard set we'll be from this day with no one in it but one man
to work.
MAURYA   It's hard set we'll be surely the day you're drown'd with the rest. 80
What way will I live and the girls with me, and I an old woman looking
for the grave?

[*Bartley lays down the halter, takes off his old coat, and puts on a newer
one of the same flannel*]

BARTLEY   [*to Nora*] Is she coming to the pier?
NORA   [*looking out*] She's passing the green head and letting fall her sails.
BARTLEY   [*getting his purse and tobacco*] I'll have half an hour to go   85
down, and you'll see me coming again in two days, or in three days, or
maybe in four days if the wind is bad.
MAURYA   [*turning round to the fire, and putting her shawl over her head*]
Isn't it a hard and cruel man won't hear a word from an old woman,
and she holding him from the sea?   90

---

63 and I after giving . . . in Connemara: trees were almost non-existent on Aran and
boards would also be expensive in rocky Connemara, 10 miles north of Aran on the mainland; Synge recalls the borrowing of some boards 'that a man below has had this two years
to bury his mother' (*Works* ii. 158). 73 jobber: commercial traveller or small tradesman.
78 cock for the kelp: because of the lack of soil on Aran, islanders gathered and burned
seaweed (kelp), then stacked it to dry in conical heaps (cocks) for use as fertilizer.

CATHLEEN   It's the life of a young man to be going on the sea, and who
would listen to an old woman with one thing and she saying it over?

BARTLEY   [*taking the halter*] I must go now quickly. I'll ride down on the
red mare, and the grey pony'll run behind me. . . . The blessing of God
on you. [*He goes out*]   95

MAURYA   [*crying out as he is in the door way*] He's gone now, God spare
us, and we'll not see him again. He's gone now, and when the black night
is falling I'll have no son left me in the world.

CATHLEEN   Why wouldn't you give him your blessing and he looking
round in the door? Isn't it sorrow enough is on every one in this house   100
without your sending him out with an unlucky word behind him, and a
hard word in his ear?°

[*Maurya takes up the tongs and begins raking the fire aimlessly without looking round*]

NORA   [*turning towards her*] You're taking away the turf from the cake.

CATHLEEN   [*crying out*] The Son of God forgive us, Nora, we're after forgetting his bit of bread. [*She comes over to the fire*]   105

NORA   And it's destroyed° he'll be going till dark night, and he after eating nothing since the sun went up.

CATHLEEN   [*turning the cake out of the oven*] It's destroyed he'll be,
surely. There's no sense left on any person in a house where an old
woman will be talking forever.   110

[*Maurya sways herself on her stool*]

CATHLEEN   [*cutting off some of the bread and rolling it in a cloth, to Maurya*] Let you go down now to the spring well and give him this and he
passing. You'll see him then and the dark word will be broken, and you
can say 'God speed you', the way he'll be easy in his mind.

MAURYA   [*taking the bread*] Will I be in it as soon as himself?   115

CATHLEEN   If you go now quickly.

MAURYA   [*standing up unsteadily*] It's hard set I am to walk.

CATHLEEN   [*looking at her anxiously*] Give her the stick, Nora, or maybe
she'll slip on the big stones.

NORA   What stick?   120

CATHLEEN   The stick Michael brought from Connemara.

MAURYA   [*taking a stick Nora gives her*] In the big world° the old people
do be leaving things after them for their sons and children, but in this

---

102 Isn't it sorrow enough . . . word in his ear?: the practical Cathleen is impatient with
her mother's lengthy grieving, but also it was considered unlucky not to return a blessing,
even more dangerous here because Maurya withholds the traditional blessing of the eldest
to someone going on a journey. 106 destroyed: from the Irish meaning injured or harmed,
in this case from hunger, but prophetic in the context of the play; see Glossary for the fre-
quency and range of meanings. 122 the big world: outside the immediate region, beyond
their experience, frequently referring to reports of large cities brought back by travellers.

place it is the young men do be leaving things behind for them that do
be old. [*She goes out slowly*]   125

[*Nora goes over to the ladder*]

CATHLEEN   Wait, Nora, maybe she'd turn back quickly. She's that sorry,
God help her, you wouldn't know the thing she'd do.°
NORA   Is she gone round by the bush?
CATHLEEN   [*looking out*] She's gone now. Throw it down quickly, for the
Lord knows when she'll be out of it again.   130
NORA   [*getting the bundle from the loft*] The young priest said he'd be
passing tomorrow,° and we might go down and speak to him below if
it's Michael's they are surely.
CATHLEEN   [*taking the bundle from Nora*] Did he say what way they were
found?   135
NORA   [*coming down*] 'There were two men,' says he, 'and they rowing
round with poteen° before the cocks crowed, and the oar of one of them
caught the body, and they passing the black cliffs of the north.'
CATHLEEN   [*trying to open the bundle*] Give me a knife, Nora, the string's
perished with the salt water, and there's a black knot on it you wouldn't   140
loosen in a week.°
NORA   [*giving her a knife*] I've heard tell it was a long way to Donegal.
CATHLEEN   [*cutting the string*] It is surely. There was a man in here a while
ago—the man sold us that knife—and he said if you set off walking from
the rocks beyond, it would be in seven days you'd be in Donegal.   145
NORA   And what time would a man take, and he floating?

[*Cathleen opens the bundle and takes out a bit of a shirt and a stocking.
They look at them eagerly*]

CATHLEEN   [*in a low voice*] The Lord spare us, Nora! Isn't it a queer hard
thing° to say if it's his they are surely?
NORA   I'll get his shirt off the hook the way we can put the one flannel
on the other. [*She looks through some clothes hanging in the corner*]   150
It's not with them, Cathleen, and where will it be?

---

127 she's that sorry . . . you wouldn't know the thing she'd do: Maurya is now so distracted with grief that she has lost her strength of will, and may not be able to turn the
tide of ill luck threatening to engulf them all.   132 The young priest said he'd be passing tomorrow: the priest does not live on the smaller island; note the emphasis on his
youth and inexperience.   137 poteen: illicitly distilled whiskey.   141 the string's perished . . . in a week: black is traditionally associated with death; in this case the stiff string
and unyielding knot convey additional poignancy as a reminder of the manner of
Michael's death. The omens have by now accumulated to such an extent that it is impossible to ignore them.   148 a queer hard thing: very difficult.

CATHLEEN   I'm thinking Bartley put it on him in the morning, for his own
shirt was heavy with the salt in it. [*Pointing to the corner*] There's a bit
of a sleeve was of the same stuff. Give me that and it will do.

[*Nora brings it to her and they compare the flannel*]

CATHLEEN   It's the same stuff, Nora; but if it is itself aren't there great   155
rolls of it in the shops of Galway, and isn't it many another man may
have a shirt of it as well as Michael himself?

NORA   [*who has taken up the stocking and counted the stitches, crying out*]
It's Michael, Cathleen, it's Michael; God spare his soul, and what will
herself say when she hears this story, and Bartley on the sea?   160

CATHLEEN   [*taking the stocking*] It's a plain stocking.

NORA   It's the second one of the third pair I knitted, and I put up three
score stitches, and I dropped four of them.

CATHLEEN   [*counts the stitches*] It's that number is in it. [*Crying out*] Ah,
Nora, isn't it a bitter thing to think of him floating that way to the far   165
north, and no one to keen° him but the black hags° that do be flying on
the sea?

NORA   [*swinging herself round and throwing out her arms on the clothes*]
And isn't it a pitiful thing when there is nothing left of a man who was
a great rower and fisher, but a bit of an old shirt and a plain stocking?   170

CATHLEEN   [*after an instant*] Tell me is herself coming, Nora? I hear a little sound on the path.

NORA   [*looking out*] She is, Cathleen. She's coming up to the door.

CATHLEEN   Put these things away before she'll come in. Maybe it's easier she'll be after giving her blessing to Bartley, and we won't let on   175
we've heard anything the time he's on the sea.

NORA   [*helping Cathleen to close the bundle*] We'll put them here in the
corner. [*They put them into a hole in the chimney corner. Cathleen goes
back to the spinning-wheel*]

NORA   Will she see it was crying I was?   180

CATHLEEN   Keep your back to the door the way the light'll not be on you.

[*Nora sits down at the chimney corner, with her back to the door. Maurya comes in very slowly, without looking at the girls, and goes over to
her stool at the other side of the fire. The cloth with the bread is still in her
hand. The girls look at each other, and Nora points to the bundle of bread*]

CATHLEEN   [*after spinning for a moment*] You didn't give him his bit of
bread?

---

166 to keen: the traditional lament for the dead, usually, as later in the play, sung by
a chorus of women.   166 black hags: a direct translation from the Irish for cormorants,
but elsewhere Synge records a flock of black birds encountered by fishermen which were
supernatural (*Works* ii. 181).

[*Maurya begins to keen softly, without turning round*]

CATHLEEN   Did you see him riding down?

[*Maurya goes on keening*]

CATHLEEN   [*a little impatiently*] God forgive you; isn't it a better thing to   185
raise your voice and tell what you seen, than to be making lamentation
for a thing that's done? Did you see Bartley, I'm saying to you.
MAURYA   [*with a weak voice*] My heart's broken from this day.
CATHLEEN   [*as before*] Did you see Bartley?
MAURYA   I seen the fearfullest thing.   190
CATHLEEN   [*leaves her wheel and looks out*] God forgive you; he's riding
the mare now over the green head, and the grey pony behind him.
MAURYA   [*starts, so that her shawl falls back from her head and shows her
white tossed hair. With a frightened voice*] The grey pony behind him . . .
CATHLEEN   [*coming to the fire*] What is it ails you, at all?   195
MAURYA   [*speaking very slowly*] I've seen the fearfullest thing any
person has seen, since the day Bride Dara seen the dead man with the
child in his arms.°
CATHLEEN AND NORA   Uah. [*They crouch down in front of the old
woman at the fire*]   200
NORA   Tell us what it is you seen.
MAURYA   I went down to the spring well, and I stood there saying a
prayer to myself. Then Bartley came along, and he riding on the red
mare with the grey pony behind him [*she puts up her hands, as if to hide
something from her eyes*] The Son of God spare us, Nora!   205
CATHLEEN   What is it you seen?
MAURYA   I seen Michael himself.
CATHLEEN   [*speaking softly*] You did not, mother; it wasn't Michael you
seen, for his body is after being found in the far north, and he's got a
clean burial by the grace of God.   210
MAURYA   [*a little defiantly*] I'm after seeing him this day, and he riding
and galloping. Bartley came first on the red mare; and I tried to say
'God speed you,' but something choked the words in my throat. He
went by quickly; and 'the blessing of God on you,' says he, and I could
say nothing. I looked up then, and I crying, at the grey pony, and there 215

---

198 Bride Dara seen the dead man with the child in his arms: in folklore the dead return when ill at ease or jealous of the living; Synge records a story of a young mother returning to feed her child and promising to be 'on a grey horse, riding behind a young man'
(*Works* ii. 159). Bride, pronounced 'Bride-ee', is short for Bridget.

was Michael upon it°—with fine clothes on him, and new shoes on his
feet.°

CATHLEEN   [*begins to keen*] It's destroyed we are from this day. It's destroyed, surely.°

NORA   Didn't the young priest say the Almighty God won't leave her   220
destitute with no son living?

MAURYA   [*in a low voice, but clearly*] It's little the like of him knows of
the sea.... Bartley will be lost now, and let you call in Eamon and make
me a good coffin out of the white boards, for I won't live after them.
I've had a husband, and a husband's father, and six sons in this house—   225
six fine men, though it was a hard birth I had with every one of them
and they coming to the world—and some of them were found and some
of them were not found, but they're gone now the lot of them....There
were Stephen, and Shawn, were lost in the great wind, and found after
in the Bay of Gregory of the Golden Mouth,° and carried up the two of   230
them on one plank, and in by that door.

[*She pauses for a moment: the girls start as if they heard something
through the door that is half open behind them*]

NORA   [*in a whisper*] Did you hear that, Cathleen? Did you hear a noise
in the north-east?

CATHLEEN   [*in a whisper*] There's some one after crying out by the
seashore.   235

MAURYA   [*continues without hearing anything*] There was Sheamus and
his father, and his own father again, were lost in a dark night, and not a
stick or sign was seen of them when the sun went up. There was Patch
after was drowned out of a curagh° that turned over. I was sitting here
with Bartley, and he a baby, lying on my two knees, and I seen two   240
women, and three women, and four women coming in, and they crossing themselves, and not saying a word. I looked out then, and there were

---

216 *the grey pony, and there was Michael upon it:* the grey horse, its colour ghost-like,
is reminiscent of the Pale Horse in Revelations, but in Irish folklore it is also the *puca,* a
spirit in the form of a horse which lures people to their death; in this case the vision is
compounded because it was believed that the dead can return to claim a companion (see
note to 1. 216 above).   217 *and new shoes on his feet:* further proof that Michael's body
was discovered on the mainland, for as an Irelander he would normally be wearing pam-
pooties, shoes made of uncured skin; again Synge records hearing of a man taken by
the fairies who was seen wearing leather boots and a new suit (*Works* ii. 165).
219 *It's destroyed, surely:* such is the belief in the supernatural that Cathleen readily ac-
cepts the implications of her mother's vision and faces the ruin of the family.   230 *the
Bay of Gregory of the Golden Mouth:* perhaps Gregory Sound, which separates the two
larger Aran islands.   239 *curagh:* a small rowing boat covered in canvas, keel-less with
an upturned bow especially designed for the waves of the bay.

men coming after them, and they holding a thing in the half of a red
sail, and water dripping out of it—it was a dry day, Nora—and leaving
a track to the door.   245

[*She pauses again with her hand stretched out towards the door. It opens softly
and old women begin to come in, crossing themselves on the threshold, and
kneeling down in front of the stage with red petticoats over their heads°*]

MAURYA   [*half in a dream, to Cathleen*] Is it Patch, or Michael, or what is
     it at all?

CATHLEEN   Michael is after being found in the far north, and when he is
     found there how could he be here in this place?

MAURYA   There does be a power of young men floating round in the sea,   250
     and what way would they know if it was Michael they had, or another
     man like him, for when a man is nine days in the sea, and the wind blow-
     ing, it's hard set his own mother would be to say what man was in it.

CATHLEEN   It's Michael, God spare him, for they're after sending us a bit
     of his clothes from the far north.   255

[*She reaches out and hands Maurya the clothes that belonged to Michael.
Maurya stands up slowly, and takes them in her hands. Nora looks out*]

NORA   They're carrying a thing among them and there's water dripping
     out of it and leaving a track by the big stones.

CATHLEEN   [*in a whisper to the women who have come in*] Is it Bartley it
     is?

ONE OF THE WOMEN   It is surely, God rest his soul.   260

[*Two younger women come in and pull out the table. Then men carry in
the body of Bartley, laid on a plank, with a bit of a sail over it, and lay it
on the table*]

CATHLEEN   [*to the women, as they are doing so*] What way was he
     drowned?

ONE OF THE WOMEN   The grey pony knocked him over into the sea, and
     he was washed out where there is a great surf on the white rocks.

[*Maurya has gone over and knelt down at the head of the table. The women
are keening softly and swaying themselves with a slow movement. Cathleen and Nora kneel at the other end of the table. The men kneel near the
door*]

---

s.d. with red petticoats over their heads: the traditional skirt of the island women was
red, a strikingly rare use of colour reflecting the red sail of Maurya's narrative; in this
case their haste in running to the shore is indicated by their reaching for the closest piece
of clothing to use as a shawl.

MAURYA [*raising her head and speaking as if she did not see the peo-*   265
ple around her] They're all gone now, and there isn't anything more
the sea can do to me. . . . I'll have no call now to° be up crying and
praying when the wind breaks from the south, and you can hear the
surf is in the east, and the surf is in the west, making a great stir
with the two noises, and they hitting one on the other. I'll have no   270
call now to be going down and getting Holy Water in the dark
nights after Samhain,° and I won't care what way the sea is when
the other women will be keening. [*To Nora*] Give me the Holy Water, Nora, there's a small sup° still on the dresser. [*Nora gives it to
her. Maurya drops Michael's clothes across Bartley's feet, and sprin-*   275
kles the Holy Water over him] . . . . It isn't that I haven't prayed for
you, Bartley, to the Almighty God. It isn't that I haven't said
prayers in the dark night till you wouldn't know what I'd be saying; but it's a great rest I'll have now, and it's time surely. It's a great
rest I'll have now, and great sleeping in the long nights after   280
Samhain, if it's only a bit of wet flour we do have to eat, and maybe
a fish that would be stinking. [*She kneels down again, crossing her-*
self, and saying prayers under her breath]
CATHLEEN [*to an old man kneeling near her*] Maybe yourself and Eamon
would make a coffin when the sun rises. We have fine white boards her-   285
self bought, God help her, thinking Michael would be found, and I have
a new cake° you can eat while you'll be working.
THE OLD MAN [*looking at the boards*] Are there nails with them?
CATHLEEN There are not, Colum; we didn't think of the nails.
ANOTHER MAN It's a great wonder she wouldn't think of the nails, and   290
all the coffins she's seen made already.
CATHLEEN It's getting old she is, and broken.

[*Maurya stands up again very slowly and spreads out the pieces of
Michael's clothes beside the body, sprinkling them with the last of the
Holy Water*]

---

267 no call . . . to: no need for.   272 getting Holy Water in the dark nights after
Samhain: either water from a holy well or water blessed by the clergy in preparation for
the sacrament she is now performing, more likely during the storms of winter (after
Samhain or 1 November). The double ambiguity reflects Maurya's attitude towards the
young priest: the sea is an older power than his God, and Samhain (pronounced 'sow'in',
as in allow), the feast of the Dead, was originally the Celtic festival when, it was believed,
the spirits of the dead moved freely among the living.   274 a small sup: a small quantity,
a few drops.   287 a new cake: the soda bread baked for Bartley's journey has now come
full circle, even as he and Michael will share a coffin.

NORA   [*in a whisper to Cathleen*] She's quiet now and easy; but the day
Michael was drowned you could hear her crying out from this to the
spring well. It's fonder she was of Michael, and would any one have   295
thought that?

CATHLEEN   [*slowly and clearly*] An old woman will soon be tired with
anything she will do, and isn't it nine days herself is after crying, and
keening, and making great sorrow in the house?

MAURYA   [*puts the empty cup mouth downwards on the table, and lays her*   300
hands together on Bartley's feet°] They're all together this time, and the
end is come. May the Almighty God have mercy on Bartley's soul, and
on Michael's soul, and on the souls of Sheamus and Patch, and Stephen
and Shawn [*bending her head*].... and may He have mercy on my soul,
Nora, and on the soul of everyone is left living in the world. [*She pauses,*   305
and the keen rises a little more loudly from the women, then sinks away.
Continuing] Michael has a clean burial in the far north, by the grace of
the Almighty God. Bartley will have a fine coffin out of the white
boards, and a deep grave surely.... What more can we want than that?
... No man at all can be living for ever, and we must be satisfied.°   310

[*She kneels down again and the curtain falls slowly*]

THE END

Study and Discussion Questions

1. *Riders to the Sea* is set on one of the Aran Islands off the coast of Ireland.
   What does that fact, and the opening set directions, tell us immediately
   about the life of the characters?
2. What do we learn from the opening conversation between the two sisters?
   What are they worried about?
3. Where is Bartley going and why does he feel he must go?

---

301 S.D. puts the empty cup ... on Bartley's feet: the finality of Maurya's gestures not
only reflects her acceptance of the death of her two sons, but becomes symbolic of her
tragic acknowledgement of the power of fate.   310 No man at all can be living for ever,
and we must be satisfied: Declan Kiberd (*Synge and the Irish Language* (1979), 206–7)
has pointed out that this magnificent concluding line to Maurya's internal battle with her
grief is Synge's direct translation from a letter by Martin McDonough, a friend on Inishmaan, reporting of the death of his brother's wife: 'we must be satisfied because nobody
can be living forever', and later in the same letter, 'he must be satisfied'. With these final
words of blessing on both the dead and the living, Maurya comes to terms with her own
earlier weakness, when 'something choked' the words of the blessing in her throat, and
with the grief she bears for all her sons in their hard and losing battle for life.

4. As Bartley is leaving, Maurya, the mother, says: "Isn't it a hard and cruel man won't hear a word from an old woman, and she holding him from the sea?" Her daughter Cathleen replies: "It's the life of a young man to be going on the sea, and who would listen to an old woman with one thing and she saying it over?" (ll. 95–100) What is the conflict being referred to here: between the women and the men, between the older generation and the younger?

5. After the two girls send their mother out to give food and a mother's blessing to Bartley, they try to figure out if the bundle of clothes the priest gave them does in fact belong to their missing brother, Michael. How do they figure this out? Do you think we would be able to do that today? Why or why not?

6. Describe the vision Maurya has when she sees Bartley. What does she think it means? How do the girls react to it?

7. After Maurya tells of her vision, what do we learn about what her life as a mother has been like?

8. What function does the priest have in this play? Note all the places where he is referred to.

9. List the foreshadowings of disaster in the play.

10. What is Maurya left with at the end of the play? How does she feel?

Suggestions for Writing

1. Discuss (a) the lives of men and (b) the lives of women in this island community.

2. At the end of *Riders to the Sea,* Maurya is grieving over the loss of her last two sons, but does she also seem relieved? Analyze the complexity of her emotions in her last two speeches.

3. Discuss the role of religion in *Riders to the Sea*—both organized religion (the priest and the Church) and pagan or pre-Christian religion (for example, the reference to Samhain, All Souls Day, which is celebrated on November 1, the beginning of winter, and from which our Halloween comes. In pre-Christian times, Samhain was the Feast of the Dead) as well as visions and omens.

Critical Resources

1. Fleming, Deborah. *A Man Who Does Not Exist: The Irish Peasant in the Work of W. B. Yeats and J. M. Synge.* Ann Arbor: U of Michigan P, 1995.

2. Kennedy, Joy. "'Sympathy Between Man and Nature': Landscape and Loss in Synge's 'Riders to the Sea.'" *Isle: Interdisciplinary Studies in Literature and Environment,* 11.1 (2004): 15–30.

3. Kopper, Edward A. Jr. *A J. M. Synge Literary Companion.* Westport, CT: Greenwood, 1988.

4. McCormack, W. J. *Fool of the Family: A Life of J. M. Synge.* New York: New York UP, 2000.
5. Synge, John M. *The Aran Islands, with drawings by Jack B. Yeats.* Dublin: Maunsel & Co, 1911.

WILLIAM SHAKESPEARE (1564–1616)

Born in Stratford-on-Avon in England, William Shakespeare attended the free grammar school there, married Anne Hathaway when he was eighteen, and soon after went to live in London. Once there, Shakespeare began working as an actor and playwright, his first plays staged in 1589. As a member of the acting company Lord Chamberlain's Men, Shakespeare established himself as the most popular playwright in London. Eventually the company had the resources to build The Globe Theater and, with Shakespeare as the principal playwright, established themselves as the leading troupe in London. At the time, British culture was moving through a particularly fertile period for artistic achievement—the Elizabethan Era. The theater was becoming the most popular art form for both the aristocracy and peasantry, and Shakespeare's plays deftly incorporated the bawdy language of everyday speech with the more sophisticated use of poetic and dramatic devices. Working effectively in both comedy and tragedy, Shakespeare crafted plays that broadened the implications of many traditional stories and histories through a deeper inquiry into human nature. Today, Shakespeare is considered the most important playwright in the English language. His dramatized explorations into a multitude of universal themes still hold pertinence for modern audiences. Of his 37 plays, Othello *(1604) is considered one of his most distinguished tragedies alongside* Romeo and Juliet *(1595),* Hamlet *(1600),* King Lear *(1605), and* Macbeth *(1606).*

The Tragedy of OTHELLO, The Moor of Venice   (ca. 1604)

Edition and notes by Alvin Kernan.

Dramatis Personae

OTHELLO, *the Moor*
BRABANTIO, *father to Desdemona*
CASSIO, *an honorable lieutenant*
IAGO, *a villain*
RODERIGO, *a gulled gentleman*
DUKE OF VENICE
SENATORS

MONTANO, *Governor of Cyprus*
GENTLEMEN OF CYPRUS
LODOVICO *and* GRATIANO, *two noble Venetians*
SAILORS
CLOWN
DESDEMONA, *wife to Othello*
EMILIA, *wife to Iago*
BIANCA, *a courtesan*
[MESSENGER, HERALD, OFFICERS, GENTLEMEN,
MUSICIANS, ATTENDANTS

Scene: *Venice and Cyprus*]

ACT I

Scene 1. [*Venice. A street.*]

Enter RODERIGO and IAGO.

RODERIGO: Tush! Never tell me? I take it much unkindly
  That thou, Iago, who hast had my purse
  As if the strings were thine, shouldst know of this.
IAGO: 'Sblood,°1 but you'll not hear me! If ever I did dream
  Of such a matter, abhor me.   5
RODERIGO: Thou told'st me
  Thou didst hold him in thy hate.
IAGO: Despise me
  If I do not. Three great ones of the city,
  In personal suit to make me his lieutenant,
  Off-capped° to him; and, by the faith of man,   10
  I know my price; I am worth no worse a place.
  But he, as loving his own pride and purposes,
  Evades them with a bombast circumstance,°
  Horribly stuffed with epithets of war;
  Nonsuits° my mediators. For, "Certes," says he,   15
  "I have already chose my officer." And what was he?

---

[1]The degree sign (°) indicates a footnote, which is keyed to the text by the line number. I.1.4 'Sblood: by God's blood.   11 Off-capped: doffed their caps—as a mark of respect.   14 bombast circumstance: stuffed, roundabout speech.   16 Nonsuits: rejects.

Forsooth, a great arithmetician,°
One Michael Cassio, a Florentine,
(A fellow almost damned in a fair wife)°   20
That never set a squadron in the field,
Nor the division of a battle knows
More than a spinster; unless the bookish theoric,
Wherein the tonguèd° consuls can propose
As masterly as he. Mere prattle without practice   25
Is all his soldiership. But he, sir, had th' election;
And I, of whom his eyes had seen the proof
At Rhodes, at Cyprus, and on other grounds
Christian and heathen, must be belee'd and calmed
By debitor and creditor. This counter-caster,°   30
He, in good time, must his lieutenant be,
And I—God bless the mark!—his Moorship's ancient.°
RODERIGO: By heaven, I rather would have been his hangman.
IAGO: Why, there's no remedy. 'Tis the curse of service:
Preferment goes by letter and affection,°   35
And not by old gradation,° where each second
Stood heir to th' first. Now, sir, be judge yourself,
Whether I in any just term am affined°
To love the Moor.
RODERIGO: I would not follow him then.   40
IAGO: O, sir, content you.
I follow him to serve my turn upon him.
We cannot all be masters, nor all masters
Cannot be truly followed. You shall mark
Many a duteous and knee-crooking° knave   45
That, doting on his own obsequious bondage,
Wears out his time, much like his master's ass,
For naught but provender; and when he's old, cashiered.
Whip me such honest knaves! Others there are
Who, trimmed in forms and visages of duty,   50
Keep yet their hearts attending on themselves,
And, throwing but shows of service on their lords,

---

18 arithmetician: theorist (rather than practical).   20 A . . . wife: (a much-disputed
passage, which is probably best taken as a general sneer at Cassio as a dandy and a ladies'
man. But in the story from which Shakespeare took his plot the counterpart of Cassio is
married, and it may be that at the beginning of the play Shakespeare had decided to keep
him married but later changed his mind).   24 tonguèd: eloquent.   30 counter-caster:
i.e., a bookkeeper who *casts* (reckons up) figures on a *counter* (abacus).   32 ancient:
standard-bearer; an underofficer.   35 letter and affection: recommendations (from men
of power) and personal preference.   36 old gradation: seniority.   38 affined: bound.
45 knee-crooking: bowing.

Do well thrive by them, and when they have lined their coats,
Do themselves homage. These fellows have some soul;
And such a one do I profess myself. For, sir,   55
It is as sure as you are Roderigo,
Were I the Moor, I would not be Iago.
In following him, I follow but myself.
Heaven is my judge, not I for love and duty,
But seeming so, for my peculiar° end;   60
For when my outward action doth demonstrate
The native° act and figure of my heart
In complement extern,° 'tis not long after
But I will wear my heart upon my sleeve
For daws to peck at; I am not what I am.   65
RODERIGO: What a full fortune does the thick-lips owe°
   If he can carry't thus!
IAGO: Call up her father.
   Rouse him. Make after him, poison his delight,
   Proclaim him in the streets, incense her kinsmen,   70
   And though he in a fertile climate dwell,
   Plague him with flies; though that his joy be joy,
   Yet throw such chances of vexation on't
   As it may lose some color.
RODERIGO: Here is her father's house. I'll call aloud.   75
IAGO: Do, with like timorous° accent and dire yell
   As when, by night and negligence, the fire
   Is spied in populous cities.
RODERIGO: What, ho, Brabantio! Signior Brabantio, ho!
IAGO: Awake! What, ho, Brabantio! Thieves! Thieves!   80
   Look to your house, your daughter, and your bags!
   Thieves! Thieves!

BRABANTIO *above*° [at a window].

BRABANTIO: What is the reason of this terrible summons?
   What is the matter there?
RODERIGO: Signior, is all your family within?   85
IAGO: Are your doors locked?
BRABANTIO: Why, wherefore ask you this?
IAGO: Zounds, sir, y'are robbed! For shame. Put on your gown!
   Your heart is burst, you have lost half your soul.

---

60 peculiar: personal. 62 native: natural, innate. 63 complement extern: outward appearances. 66 owe: own. 76 timorous: frightening. 83 s.d. above: (i.e., on the small upper stage above and to the rear of the main platform stage, which resembled the projecting upper story of an Elizabethan house).

Even now, now, very now, an old black ram   90
Is tupping your white ewe. Arise, arise!
Awake the snorting citizens with the bell,
Or else the devil will make a grandsire of you.
Arise, I say!

BRABANTIO: What, have you lost your wits?   95

RODERIGO: Most reverend signior, do you know my voice?

BRABANTIO: Not I. What are you?

RODERIGO: My name is Roderigo.

BRABANTIO: The worser welcome!
I have charged thee not to haunt about my doors.   100
In honest plainness thou hast heard me say
My daughter is not for thee; and now, in madness,
Being full of supper and distemp'ring draughts,°
Upon malicious knavery dost thou come
To start° my quiet.   105

RODERIGO: Sir, sir, sir—

BRABANTIO: But thou must needs be sure
My spirits and my place° have in their power
To make this bitter to thee.

RODERIGO: Patience, good sir.   110

BRABANTIO: What tell'st thou me of robbing? This is Venice;
My house is not a grange.°

RODERIGO: Most grave Brabantio,
In simple and pure soul I come to you.

IAGO: Zounds, sir, you are one of those that will not serve God if the devil   115
bid you. Because we come to do you service and you think we are ruf-
fians, you'll have your daughter covered with a Barbary° horse, you'll
have your nephews° neigh to you, you'll have coursers for cousins,° and
gennets for germans.°

BRABANTIO: What profane wretch art thou?   120

IAGO: I am one, sir, that comes to tell you your daughter and the Moor
are making the beast with two backs.

BRABANTIO: Thou art a villain.

IAGO: You are—a senator.

BRABANTIO: This thou shalt answer. I know thee, Roderigo.   125

RODERIGO: Sir, I will answer anything. But I beseech you,
If't be your pleasure and most wise consent,

---

103 distemp'ring draughts: unsettling drinks.   105 start: disrupt.   108 place: rank,
i.e., of senator.   112 grange: isolated house.   117 Barbary: Arabian, i.e., Moorish.
118 nephews: i.e., grandsons.   118 cousins: relations.   119 gennets for germans:
Spanish horses for blood relatives.

As partly I find it is, that your fair daughter,
At this odd-even° and dull watch o' th' night,
Transported, with no worse nor better guard 　　　　　　　130
But with a knave of common hire, a gondolier,
To the gross clasps of a lascivious Moor—
If this be known to you, and your allowance,
We then have done you bold and saucy wrongs;
But if you know not this, my manners tell me 　　　　　　135
We have your wrong rebuke. Do not believe
That from the sense of all civility°
I thus would play and trifle with your reverence.
Your daughter, if you have not given her leave,
I say again, hath made a gross revolt, 　　　　　　　　　140
Tying her duty, beauty, wit, and fortunes
In an extravagant° and wheeling stranger
Of here and everywhere. Straight satisfy yourself.
If she be in her chamber, or your house,
Let loose on me the justice of the state 　　　　　　　　145
For thus deluding you.

BRABANTIO: 　　　　　　　Strike on the tinder, ho!
Give me a taper! Call up all my people!
This accident° is not unlike my dream.
Belief of it oppresses me already. 　　　　　　　　　　150
Light, I say! Light! 　　　　　　　　　　*Exit [above].*

IAGO: 　　　　　　　Farewell, for I must leave you.
It seems not meet, nor wholesome to my place,
To be produced—as, if I stay, I shall—
Against the Moor. For I do know the State, 　　　　　　155
However this may gall him with some check,°
Cannot with safety cast° him; for he's embarked
With such loud reason to the Cyprus wars,
Which even now stands in act,° that for their souls
Another of his fathom° they have none 　　　　　　　160
To lead their business; in which regard,
Though I do hate him as I do hell-pains,
Yet, for necessity of present life,
I must show out a flag and sign of love,
Which is indeed but sign. That you shall surely find him, 　165

---

129 odd-even: between night and morning. 　137 sense of all civility: feeling of what
is proper. 　142 extravagant: vagrant, wandering (Othello is not Venetian and thus may
be considered a wandering soldier of fortune). 　149 accident: happening. 　156 check:
restraint. 　157 cast: dismiss. 　159 stands in act: takes place. 　160 fathom: ability.

Lead to the Sagittary° the raisèd search;
And there will I be with him. So farewell.   *Exit.*

Enter BRABANTIO [*in his nightgown*], *with Servants and torches.*

BRABANTIO: It is too true an evil. Gone she is;
And what's to come of my despisèd time
Is naught but bitterness. Now, Roderigo,   170
Where didst thou see her?—O unhappy girl!—
With the Moor, say'st thou?—Who would be a father?—
How didst thou know 'twas she?—O, she deceives me
Past thought!—What said she to you? Get moe° tapers!
Raise all my kindred!—Are they married, think you?   175
RODERIGO: Truly I think they are.
BRABANTIO: O heaven! How got she out? O treason of the blood!
Fathers, from hence trust not your daughters' minds
By what you see them act.° Is there not charms
By which the property° of youth and maidhood   180
May be abused? Have you not read, Roderigo,
Of some such thing?
RODERIGO: Yes, sir, I have indeed.
BRABANTIO: Call up my brother.—O, would you had had her!—
Some one way, some another.—Do you know   185
Where we may apprehend her and the Moor?
RODERIGO: I think I can discover him, if you please
To get good guard and go along with me.
BRABANTIO: Pray you lead on. At every house I'll call;
I may command at most.—Get weapons, ho!   190
And raise some special officers of might.—
On, good Roderigo; I will deserve your pains.°

                                                    Exeunt.

Scene 2. [*A street.*]

Enter OTHELLO, IAGO, ATTENDANTS *with torches.*

IAGO: Though in the trade of war I have slain men,
Yet do I hold it very stuff° o' th' conscience
To do no contrived murder. I lack iniquity

---

166 Sagittary: (probably the name of an inn).   174 moe: more.   179 act: do.   180
property: true nature.   192 deserve your pains: be worthy of (and reward) your efforts.
I.2.2 stuff: essence.

Sometime to do me service. Nine or ten times
  I had thought t' have yerked° him here, under the ribs.   5
OTHELLO: 'Tis better as it is.
IAGO: Nay, but he prated,
  And spoke such scurvy and provoking terms
  Against your honor, that with the little godliness I have
  I did full hard forbear him. But I pray you, sir,   10
  Are you fast married? Be assured of this,
  That the magnifico° is much beloved,
  And hath in his effect a voice potential
  As double as the Duke's.° He will divorce you,
  Or put upon you what restraint or grievance   15
  The law, with all his might to enforce it on,
  Will give him cable.°
OTHELLO: Let him do his spite.
  My services which I have done the Signiory°
  Shall out-tongue his complaints. 'Tis yet to know°—   20
  Which when I know that boasting is an honor
  I shall promulgate—I fetch my life and being
  From men of royal siege;° and my demerits°
  May speak unbonneted to as proud a fortune
  As this that I have reached.° For know, Iago,   25
  But that I love the gentle Desdemona,
  I would not my unhousèd° free condition
  Put into circumscription and confine
  For the seas' worth. But look, what lights come yond?

Enter CASSIO, *with* [OFFICERS *and*] *torches.*

IAGO: Those are the raisèd father and his friends.   30
  You were best go in.
OTHELLO: Not I. I must be found.
  My parts, my title, and my perfect soul°
  Shall manifest me rightly. Is it they?
IAGO: By Janus, I think no.   35
OTHELLO: The servants of the Duke? And my lieutenant?
  The goodness of the night upon you, friends.
  What is the news?

---

    5 yerked: stabbed.   12 magnifico: nobleman.   13–14 hath . . . Duke's: i.e., can be as
effective as the Duke.   17 cable: range, scope.   19 Signiory: the rulers of Venice.   20
yet to know: unknown as yet.   23 siege: rank.   23 demerits: deserts.   24–25 May . . .
reached: i.e., are the equal of the family I have married into.   27 unhousèd: unconfined.
33 perfect soul: clear, unflawed conscience.

CASSIO: The Duke does greet you, general;
    And he requires your haste-posthaste appearance   40
    Even on the instant.
OTHELLO: What is the matter, think you?
CASSIO: Something from Cyprus, as I may divine.
    It is a business of some heat. The galleys
    Have sent a dozen sequent° messengers   45
    This very night at one another's heels,
    And many of the consuls, raised and met,
    Are at the Duke's already. You have been hotly called for.
    When, being not at your lodging to be found,
    The Senate hath sent about three several° quests   50
    To search you out.
OTHELLO: 'Tis well I am found by you.
    I will but spend a word here in the house,
    And go with you. [*Exit.*]
CASSIO: Ancient, what makes he here?   55
IAGO: Faith, he tonight hath boarded a land carack.°
    If it prove lawful prize, he's made forever.
CASSIO: I do not understand.
IAGO: He's married.
CASSIO: To who?   60

[*Enter* OTHELLO.]

IAGO: Marry,° to—Come, captain, will you go?
OTHELLO: Have with you.
CASSIO: Here comes another troop to seek for you.

   Enter BRABANTIO, RODERIGO, *with* OFFICERS *and torches.*

IAGO: It is Brabantio. General, be advised.
    He comes to bad intent.   65
OTHELLO: Holla! Stand there!
RODERIGO: Signior, it is the Moor.
BRABANTIO: Down with him, thief!
                     [*They draw swords.*]
IAGO: You, Roderigo? Come, sir, I am for you.
OTHELLO: Keep up your bright swords, for the dew will rust them.   70
    Good signior, you shall more command with years
    Than with your weapons.

---

   45 sequent: successive. 50 several: separate. 56 carack: treasure ship. 61 Marry:
By Mary (an interjection).

BRABANTIO: O thou foul thief, where hast thou stowed my daughter?
    Damned as thou art, thou hast enchanted her!
    For I'll refer me to all things of sense,° 75
    If she in chains of magic were not bound,
    Whether a maid so tender, fair, and happy,
    So opposite to marriage that she shunned
    The wealthy, curlèd darlings of our nation,
    Would ever have, t' incur a general mock,° 80
    Run from her guardage to the sooty bosom
    Of such a thing as thou—to fear, not to delight.
    Judge me the world if 'tis not gross in sense°
    That thou hast practiced° on her with foul charms,
    Abused her delicate youth with drugs or minerals 85
    That weaken motion.° I'll have't disputed on;
    'Tis probable, and palpable to thinking.
    I therefore apprehend and do attach° thee
    For an abuser of the world, a practicer
    Of arts inhibited and out of warrant.° 90
    Lay hold upon him. If he do resist,
    Subdue him at his peril.
OTHELLO: Hold your hands,
    Both you of my inclining and the rest.
    Were it my cue to fight, I should have known it 95
    Without a prompter. Whither will you that I go
    To answer this your charge?
BRABANTIO: To prison, till fit time
    Of law and course of direct session
    Call thee to answer. 100
OTHELLO: What if I do obey?
    How may the Duke be therewith satisfied,
    Whose messengers are here about my side
    Upon some present° business of the state
    To bring me to him? 105
OFFICER: 'Tis true, most worthy signior.
    The Duke's in council, and your noble self
    I am sure is sent for.
BRABANTIO: How? The Duke in council?
    In this time of the night? Bring him away. 110

---

75 refer . . . sense: i.e., base (my argument) on all ordinary understanding of nature.
80 general mock: public shame.   83 gross in sense: obvious.   84 practiced: used tricks.
86 motion: thought, i.e., reason.   88 attach: arrest.   90 inhibited . . . warrant: prohibited
and illegal (black magic).   104 present: immediate.

Mine's not an idle cause. The Duke himself,
Or any of my brothers° of the state,
Cannot but feel this wrong as 'twere their own;
For if such actions may have passage free,
Bondslaves and pagans shall our statesmen be.   115

Exeunt.

Scene 3. [*A council chamber.*]

Enter DUKE, SENATORS, *and* OFFICERS [*set at a table, with lights and* ATTENDANTS].

DUKE: There's no composition° in this news
   That gives them credit.°
FIRST SENATOR: Indeed, they are disproportioned.
   My letters say a hundred and seven galleys.
DUKE: And mine a hundred forty.   5
SECOND SENATOR: And mine two hundred.
   But though they jump° not on a just accompt°—
   As in these cases where the aim° reports
   'Tis oft with difference—yet do they all confirm
   A Turkish fleet, and bearing up to Cyprus.   10
DUKE: Nay, it is possible enough to judgment.°
   I do not so secure me in the error,
   But the main article I do approve
   In fearful sense.°
SAILOR   *(Within):*
   What, ho! What, ho! What, ho!   15

Enter SAILOR.

OFFICER: A messenger from the galleys.
DUKE: Now? What's the business?
SAILOR: The Turkish preparation makes for Rhodes.
   So was I bid report here to the State
   By Signior Angelo.   20

---

112 brothers: i.e., the other senators.   I.3.1 composition: agreement.   2 gives them credit: makes them believable.   7 jump: agree.   7 just accompt: exact counting.   8 aim: approximation.   11 to judgment: when carefully considered.   13–14 I do…sense: i.e., just because the numbers disagree in the reports, I do not doubt that the principal information (that the Turkish fleet is out) is fearfully true.

DUKE: How say you by this change?
FIRST SENATOR: This cannot be
   By no assay of reason. 'Tis a pageant°
   To keep us in false gaze.° When we consider
   Th' importancy of Cyprus to the Turk,   25
   And let ourselves again but understand
   That, as it more concerns the Turk than Rhodes,
   So may he with more facile question° bear it,
   For that it stands not in such warlike brace,°
   But altogether lacks th' abilities   30
   That Rhodes is dressed in. If we make thought of this,
   We must not think the Turk is so unskillful
   To leave that latest which concerns him first,
   Neglecting an attempt of ease and gain
   To wake and wage a danger profitless.   35
DUKE: Nay, in all confidence he's not for Rhodes.
OFFICER: Here is more news.

   Enter a MESSENGER.

MESSENGER: The Ottomites, reverend and gracious,
   Steering with due course toward the isle of Rhodes,
   Have there injointed them with an after° fleet.   40
FIRST SENATOR: Ay, so I thought. How many, as you guess?
MESSENGER: Of thirty sail; and now they do restem
   Their backward course, bearing with frank appearance
   Their purposes toward Cyprus. Signior Montano,
   Your trusty and most valiant servitor,   45
   With his free duty° recommends° you thus,
   And prays you to believe him.
DUKE: 'Tis certain then for Cyprus.
   Marcus Luccicos, is not he in town?
FIRST SENATOR: He's now in Florence.   50
DUKE: Write from us to him; post-posthaste dispatch.
FIRST SENATOR: Here comes Brabantio and the valiant Moor.

   Enter BRABANTIO, OTHELLO, CASSIO, IAGO, RODERIGO, *and* OFFICERS.

DUKE: Valiant Othello, we must straight° employ you
   Against the general° enemy Ottoman.

---

   23 pageant: show, pretense.   24 in false gaze: looking the wrong way.   28 facile
question: easy struggle.   29 warlike brace: "military posture."   40 after: following.
46 free duty: unlimited respect.   46 recommends: informs.   53 straight: at once.   54
general: universal.

[*To* BRABANTIO] I did not see you. Welcome, gentle signior.   55
   We lacked your counsel and your help tonight.
BRABANTIO: So did I yours. Good your grace, pardon me.
   Neither my place, nor aught I heard of business,
   Hath raised me from my bed; nor doth the general care
   Take hold on me; for my particular grief   60
   Is of so floodgate and o'erbearing nature
   That it engluts and swallows other sorrows,
   And it is still itself.
DUKE: Why, what's the matter?
BRABANTIO: My daughter! O, my daughter!   65
SENATORS: Dead?
BRABANTIO: Ay, to me.
   She is abused, stol'n from me, and corrupted
   By spells and medicines bought of mountebanks;
   For nature so prepost'rously to err,   70
   Being not deficient, blind, or lame of sense,
   Sans° witchcraft could not.
DUKE: Whoe'er he be that in this foul proceeding
   Hath thus beguiled your daughter of herself,
   And you of her, the bloody book of law   75
   You shall yourself read in the bitter letter
   After your own sense; yea, though our proper° son
   Stood in your action.°
BRABANTIO: Humbly I thank your Grace.
   Here is the man—this Moor, whom now, it seems,   80
   Your special mandate for the state affairs
   Hath hither brought.
ALL: We are very sorry for't.
DUKE   [*To* OTHELLO]: What in your own part can you say to this?
BRABANTIO: Nothing, but this is so.   85
OTHELLO: Most potent, grave, and reverend signiors,
   My very noble and approved° good masters,
   That I have ta'en away this old man's daughter,
   It is most true; true I have married her.
   The very head and front° of my offending   90
   Hath this extent, no more. Rude am I in my speech,
   And little blessed with the soft phrase of peace,
   For since these arms of mine had seven years' pith°
   Till now some nine moons wasted,° they have used

---

72 Sans: without.   77 proper: own.   78 Stood in your action: were the accused in your suit.   87 approved: tested, proven by past performance.   90 head and front: extreme form (*front* = forehead).   93 pith: strength.   94 wasted: past.

Their dearest° action in the tented field;   95
And little of this great world can I speak
More than pertains to feats of broils and battle;
And therefore little shall I grace my cause
In speaking for myself. Yet, by your gracious patience,
I will a round° unvarnished tale deliver   100
Of my whole course of love—what drugs, what charms,
What conjuration, and what mighty magic,
For such proceeding I am charged withal,
I won his daughter—

BRABANTIO: A maiden never bold,   105
Of spirit so still and quiet that her motion
Blushed at herself;° and she, in spite of nature,
Of years, of country, credit, everything,
To fall in love with what she feared to look on!
It is a judgment maimed and most imperfect   110
That will confess perfection so could err
Against all rules of nature, and must be driven
To find out practices of cunning hell
Why this should be. I therefore vouch again
That with some mixtures pow'rful o'er the blood,   115
Or with some dram, conjured to this effect,
He wrought upon her.

DUKE: To vouch this is no proof,
Without more wider and more overt test
Than these thin habits° and poor likelihoods   120
Of modern° seeming do prefer against him.

FIRST SENATOR: But, Othello, speak.
Did you by indirect and forcèd courses
Subdue and poison this young maid's affections?
Or came it by request, and such fair question°   125
As soul to soul affordeth?

OTHELLO: I do beseech you,
Send for the lady to the Sagittary
And let her speak of me before her father.
If you do find me foul in her report,   130
The trust, the office, I do hold of you
Not only take away, but let your sentence
Even fall upon my life.

DUKE: Fetch Desdemona hither.

---

95 dearest: most important.   100 round: blunt.   107 her motion/Blushed at herself:
i.e., she was so modest that she blushed at every thought (and movement).   120 habits:
clothing.   121 modern: trivial.   125 question: discussion.

OTHELLO: Ancient, conduct them; you best know the place.   135

[*Exit* IAGO, *with two or three* ATTENDANTS.]

And till she come, as truly as to heaven
I do confess the vices of my blood,
So justly to your grave ears I'll present
How I did thrive in this fair lady's love,
And she in mine.   140
DUKE: Say it, Othello.
OTHELLO: Her father loved me; oft invited me;
Still° questioned me the story of my life
From year to year, the battle, sieges, fortune
That I have passed.   145
I ran it through, even from my boyish days
To th' very moment that he bade me tell it.
Wherein I spoke of most disastrous chances,
Of moving accidents by flood and field,
Of hairbreadth scapes i' th' imminent° deadly breach,   150
Of being taken by the insolent foe
And sold to slavery, of my redemption thence
And portance° in my travel's history,
Wherein of anters° vast and deserts idle,°
Rough quarries, rocks, and hills whose heads touch heaven,   155
It was my hint to speak. Such was my process.
And of the Cannibals that each other eat,
The Anthropophagi,° and men whose heads
Grew beneath their shoulders. These things to hear
Would Desdemona seriously incline;   160
But still the house affairs would draw her thence;
Which ever as she could with haste dispatch,
She'd come again, and with a greedy ear
Devour up my discourse. Which I observing,
Took once a pliant hour, and found good means   165
To draw from her a prayer of earnest heart
That I would all my pilgrimage dilate,°
Whereof by parcels she had something heard,
But not intentively.° I did consent,
And often did beguile her of her tears   170
When I did speak of some distressful stroke

---

143 Still: regularly.   150 imminent: threatening.   153 portance: manner of acting.
154 anters: caves.   154 idle: empty, sterile.   158 Anthropophagi: man-eaters.   167 dilate:
relate in full.   169 intentively: at length and in sequence.

That my youth suffered. My story being done,
She gave me for my pains a world of kisses.
She swore in faith 'twas strange, 'twas passing° strange;
'Twas pitiful, 'twas wondrous pitiful.   175
She wished she had not heard it; yet she wished
That heaven had made her such a man. She thanked me,
And bade me, if I had a friend that loved her,
I should but teach him how to tell my story,
And that would woo her. Upon this hint I spake.   180
She loved me for the dangers I had passed,
And I loved her that she did pity them.
This only is the witchcraft I have used.
Here comes the lady. Let her witness it.

Enter DESDEMONA, IAGO, ATTENDANTS.

DUKE: I think this tale would win my daughter too.   185
    Good Brabantio, take up this mangled matter at the best.°
    Men do their broken weapons rather use
    Than their bare hands.
BRABANTIO: I pray you hear her speak.
    If she confess that she was half the wooer,   190
    Destruction on my head if my bad blame
    Light on the man. Come hither, gentle mistress.
    Do you perceive in all this noble company
    Where most you owe obedience?
DESDEMONA: My noble father,   195
    I do perceive here a divided duty.
    To you I am bound for life and education;
    My life and education both do learn me
    How to respect you. You are the lord of duty,
    I am hitherto your daughter. But here's my husband,   200
    And so much duty as my mother showed
    To you, preferring you before her father,
    So much I challenge° that I may profess
    Due to the Moor my lord.
BRABANTIO: God be with you. I have done.   205
    Please it your Grace, on to the state affairs.
    I had rather to adopt a child than get° it.
    Come hither, Moor.
    I here do give thee that with all my heart

---

174 passing: surpassing.   186 Take . . . best: i.e., make the best of this disaster.
203 challenge: claim as right.   207 get: beget.

Which, but thou hast already, with all my heart   210
I would keep from thee. For your sake,° jewel,
I am glad at soul I have no other child,
For thy escape would teach me tyranny,
To hang clogs on them. I have done, my lord.

DUKE: Let me speak like yourself and lay a sentence°   215
Which, as a grise° or step, may help these lovers.
When remedies are past, the griefs are ended
By seeing the worst, which late on hopes depended.°
To mourn a mischief that is past and gone
Is the next° way to draw new mischief on.   220
What cannot be preserved when fortune takes,
Patience her injury a mock'ry makes.
The robbed that smiles, steals something from the thief;
He robs himself that spends a bootless° grief.

BRABANTIO: So let the Turk of Cyprus us beguile: 225
We lose it not so long as we can smile.
He bears the sentence well that nothing bears
But the free comfort which from thence he hears;
But he bears both the sentence and the sorrow
That to pay grief must of poor patience borrow.   230
These sentences, to sugar, or to gall,
Being strong on both sides, are equivocal.
But words are words. I never yet did hear
That the bruisèd heart was piercèd° through the ear.
I humbly beseech you, proceed to th' affairs of state.   235

DUKE: The Turk with a most mighty preparation makes for Cyprus. Othello, the fortitude° of the place is best known to you; and though we have
there a substitute° of most allowed sufficiency,° yet opinion, a more sov-
ereign mistress of effects, throws a more safer voice on you.° You must
therefore be content to slubber° the gloss of your new fortunes with this   240
more stubborn and boisterous° expedition.

OTHELLO: The tyrant Custom, most grave senators,
Hath made the flinty and steel couch of war

---

211 For your sake: because of you.   215 lay a sentence: provide a maxim.
216 grise: step.   218 late on hopes depended: was supported by hope (of a better outcome) until lately.   220 next: closest, surest.   224 bootless: valueless.   234 piercèd:
(some editors emend to *pieced,* i.e., healed." But *pierced* makes good sense: Brabantio is
saying in effect that his heart cannot be further hurt [pierced] by the indignity of the useless, conventional advice the Duke offers him. *Pierced* can also mean, however, "lanced"
in the medical sense, and would then mean "treated").   237 fortitude: fortification.
238 substitute: viceroy.   238 most allowed sufficiency: generally acknowledged capability.   239 opinion . . . you: i.e., the general opinion, which finally controls affairs, is that
you would be the best man in this situation.   240 slubber: besmear.   241 stubborn and
boisterous: rough and violent.

My thrice-driven° bed of down. I do agnize°
A natural and prompt alacrity   245
I find in hardness and do undertake
This present wars against the Ottomites.
Most humbly, therefore, bending to your state,
I crave fit disposition for my wife,
Due reference of place, and exhibition,°   250
With such accommodation and besort
As levels with° her breeding.

DUKE: Why, at her father's.
BRABANTIO: I will not have it so.
OTHELLO: Nor I.   255
DESDEMONA: Nor would I there reside,
To put my father in impatient thoughts
By being in his eye. Most gracious Duke,
To my unfolding° lend your prosperous° ear,
And let me find a charter° in your voice,   260
T' assist my simpleness.

DUKE: What would you, Desdemona?
DESDEMONA: That I love the Moor to live with him,
My downright violence, and storm of fortunes,
May trumpet to the world. My heart's subdued   265
Even to the very quality of my lord.°
I saw Othello's visage in his mind,
And to his honors and his valiant parts
Did I my soul and fortunes consecrate.
So that, dear lords, if I be left behind,   270
A moth of peace, and he go to the war,
The rites° for why I love him are bereft me,
And I a heavy interim shall support
By his dear absence. Let me go with him.

OTHELLO: Let her have your voice.°   275
Vouch with me, heaven, I therefore beg it not
To please the palate of my appetite,
Nor to comply with heat°—the young affects°
In me defunct—and proper satisfaction;°

---

244 thrice-driven: i.e., softest.   244 agnize: know in myself.   250 exhibition: grant of
funds.   252 levels with: is suitable to.   259 unfolding: explanation.   259 prosperous:
favoring.   260 charter: permission.   266 My . . . lord: i.e., I have become one in nature
and being with the man I married (therefore, I too would go to the wars like a soldier).
272 rites: (may refer either to the marriage rites or to the rites, formalities, of war).
275 voice: consent.   278 heat: lust.   278 affects: passions.   279 proper satisfaction: i.e.,
consummation of the marriage.

But to be free and bounteous to her mind;   280
And heaven defend° your good souls that you think
I will your serious and great business scant
When she is with me. No, when light-winged toys
Of feathered Cupid seel° with wanton° dullness
My speculative and officed instrument,°   285
That my disports corrupt and taint my business,
Let housewives make a skillet of my helm,
And all indign° and base adversities
Make head° against my estimation!°—
DUKE: Be it as you shall privately determine,   290
Either for her stay or going. Th' affair cries haste,
And speed must answer it.
FIRST SENATOR: You must away tonight.
OTHELLO: With all my heart.
DUKE: At nine i' th' morning here we'll meet again   295
Othello, leave some officer behind,
And he shall our commission bring to you,
And such things else of quality and respect
As doth import you.
OTHELLO: So please your grace, my ancient;   300
A man he is of honesty and trust.
To his conveyance I assign my wife,
With what else needful your good grace shall think
To be sent after me.
DUKE: Let it be so.   305
Good night to every one. [*To* BRABANTIO] And, noble signior,
If virtue no delighted° beauty lack,
Your son-in-law is far more fair than black.
FIRST SENATOR: Adieu, brave Moor. Use Desdemona well.
BRABANTIO: Look to her, Moor, if thou hast eyes to see: 310
She has deceived her father, and may thee.

[*Exeunt* DUKE, SENATORS, OFFICERS, &c.]

OTHELLO: My life upon her faith! Honest Iago,
My Desdemona must I leave to thee.
I prithee let thy wife attend on her,
And bring them after in the best advantage.°   315

---

281 defend: forbid.   284 seel: sew up.   284 wanton: lascivious.   285 speculative . . . instrument: i.e., sight (and, by extension, the mind).   288 indign: unworthy.
289 Make head: form an army, i.e., attack.   289 estimation: reputation.   307 delighted:
delightful.   315 advantage: opportunity.

Come, Desdemona. I have but an hour
Of love, of worldly matter, and direction
To spend with thee. We must obey the time.

Exit [Moor with DESDEMONA].

RODERIGO: Iago?
IAGO: What say'st thou, noble heart?   320
RODERIGO: What will I do, think'st thou?
IAGO: Why, go to bed and sleep.
RODERIGO: I will incontinently° drown myself.
IAGO: If thou dost, I shall never love thee after. Why, thou silly
gentleman?   325
RODERIGO: It is silliness to live when to live is torment; and then have
we a prescription to die when death is our physician.
IAGO: O villainous! I have looked upon the world for four times seven
years, and since I could distinguish betwixt a benefit and an injury, I
never found man that knew how to love himself. Ere I would say I   330
would drown myself for the love of a guinea hen, I would change my
humanity with a baboon.
RODERIGO: What should I do? I confess it is my shame to be so fond,
but it is not in my virtue° to amend it.
IAGO: Virtue? A fig! 'Tis in ourselves that we are thus, or thus. Our bod-   335
ies are our gardens, to the which our wills are gardeners; so that if we
will plant nettles or sow lettuce, set hyssop and weed up thyme, supply
it with one gender of herbs or distract° it with many—either to have it
sterile with idleness or manured with industry—why, the power and cor-
rigible° authority of this lies in our wills. If the balance of our lives had 340
not one scale of reason to poise another of sensuality, the blood and baseness of our natures would conduct us to most prepost'rous conclusions.°
But we have reason to cool our raging motions, our carnal stings or
unbitted° lusts, whereof I take this that you call love to be a sect or
scion.°   345
RODERIGO: It cannot be.
IAGO: It is merely a lust of the blood and a permission of the will. Come,
be a man! Drown thyself? Drown cats and blind puppies! I have professed
me thy friend, and I confess me knit to thy deserving with cables of per-
durable toughness. I could never better stead° thee than now. Put money   350
in thy purse. Follow thou the wars; defeat thy favor° with an usurped°

---

323 incontinently: at once.   334 virtue: strength (Roderigo is saying that his nature
controls him).   338 distract: vary.   340 corrigible: corrective.   342 conclusions: ends.
344 unbitted: i.e., uncontrolled   345 sect or scion: offshoot.   350 stead: serve.
351 defeat thy favor: disguise your face.   351 usurped: assumed.

beard. I say, put money in thy purse. It cannot be long that Desdemona should continue her love to the Moor. Put money in thy purse. Nor he his to her. It was a violent commencement in her and thou shalt see an answerable° sequestration—put but money in thy purse. These Moors are   355 changeable in their wills—fill thy purse with money. The food that to him now is as luscious as locusts° shall be to him shortly as bitter as coloquin- tida.° She must change for youth; when she is sated with his body, she will find the errors of her choice. Therefore, put money in thy purse. If thou wilt needs damn thyself, do it a more delicate way than drowning. Make   360 all the money thou canst. If sanctimony° and a frail vow betwixt an erring° barbarian and supersubtle Venetian be not too hard for my wits, and all the tribe of hell, thou shalt enjoy her. Therefore, make money. A pox of drowning thyself, it is clean out of the way. Seek thou rather to be hanged in compassing° thy joy than to be drowned and go without her.   365

RODERIGO: Wilt thou be fast to my hopes, if I depend on the issue?

IAGO: Thou art sure of me. Go, make money. I have told thee often, and I retell thee again and again, I hate the Moor. My cause is hearted;° thine hath no less reason. Let us be conjunctive° in our revenge against him. If thou canst cuckold him, thou dost thyself a pleasure, me a sport. There   370 are many events in the womb of time, which will be delivered. Traverse, go, provide thy money! We will have more of this tomorrow. Adieu.

RODERIGO: Where shall we meet i' th' morning?

IAGO: At my lodging.

RODERIGO: I'll be with thee betimes.   375

IAGO: Go to, farewell. Do you hear, Roderigo?

RODERIGO: I'll sell all my land.   *Exit.*

IAGO: Thus do I ever make my fool my purse;
For I mine own gained knowledge° should profane
If I would time expend with such snipe   380
But for my sport and profit. I hate the Moor,
And it is thought abroad that 'twixt my sheets
H'as done my office. I know not if't be true,
But I, for mere suspicion in that kind,
Will do, as if for surety.° He holds me well;   385
The better shall my purpose work on him.
Cassio's a proper° man. Let me see now:
To get his place, and to plume up my will°

---

355 answerable: similar.   357 locusts: (a sweet fruit).   358 coloquintida: (a purgative derived from a bitter apple).   361 sanctimony: sacred bond (of marriage). 361 erring: wandering.   365 compassing: encompassing, achieving.   368 hearted: deep- seated in the heart.   369 conjunctive: joined.   379 gained knowledge: i.e., practical, worldly wisdom.   385 surety: certainty.   387 proper: handsome.   388 plume up my will: (many explanations have been offered for this crucial line, which in Q1 reads "make up my will." The general sense is something like "to make more proud and gratify my ego").

In double knavery. How? How? Let's see.
After some time, to abuse Othello's ears   390
That he is too familiar with his wife.
He hath a person and a smooth dispose°
To be suspected—framed° to make women false.
The Moor is of a free and open nature
That thinks men honest that but seem to be so;   395
And will as tenderly be led by th' nose
As asses are.
I have't! It is engendered! Hell and night
Must bring this monstrous birth to the world's light.

[*Exit.*]

ACT II

Scene 1. [*Cyprus.*]

Enter MONTANO *and two* GENTLEMEN, [*one above*].°

MONTANO: What from the cape can you discern at sea?
FIRST GENTLEMAN: Nothing at all, it is a high-wrought flood.
I cannot 'twixt the heaven and the main
Descry a sail.
MONTANO: Methinks the wind hath spoke aloud at land;   5
A fuller blast ne'er shook our battlements.
If it hath ruffianed so upon the sea,
What ribs of oak, when mountains melt on them,
Can hold the mortise? What shall we hear of this?
SECOND GENTLEMAN: A segregation° of the Turkish fleet.   10
For do but stand upon the foaming shore,
The chidden billow seems to pelt the clouds;
The wind-shaked surge, with high and monstrous main,°
Seems to cast water on the burning Bear
And quench the guards of th' ever-fixèd pole.°   15
I never did like molestation view

---

392 dispose: manner.   393 framed: designed.   I.1.s.d. (the Folio arrangement of this scene requires that the First Gentleman stand above—on the upper stage—and act as a lookout reporting sights which cannot be seen by Montano standing below on the main stage).   10 segregation: separation.   13 main: (both "ocean" and "strength").   14–15 Seems . . . pole: (the constellation Ursa Minor contains two stars which are the *guards,* or companions, of the *pole,* or North Star).

On the enchafèd flood.
MONTANO: If that the Turkish fleet
Be not ensheltered and embayed, they are drowned;
It is impossible to bear it out.   20

Enter a [third] GENTLEMAN.

THIRD GENTLEMAN: News, lads! Our wars are done.
The desperate tempest hath so banged the Turks
That their designment halts. A noble ship of Venice
Hath seen a grievous wrack and sufferance°
On most part of their fleet.   25
MONTANO: How? Is this true?
THIRD GENTLEMAN: The ship is here put in,
A Veronesa; Michael Cassio,
Lieutenant to the warlike Moor Othello,
Is come on shore; the Moor himself at sea,   30
And is in full commission here for Cyprus.
MONTANO: I am glad on't. 'Tis a worthy governor.
THIRD GENTLEMAN: But this same Cassio, though he speak of comfort
Touching the Turkish loss, yet he looks sadly
And prays the Moor be safe, for they were parted   35
With foul and violent tempest.
MONTANO: Pray heavens he be;
For I have served him, and the man commands
Like a full soldier. Let's to the seaside, ho!
As well to see the vessel that's come in   40
As to throw out our eyes for brave Othello,
Even till we make the main and th' aerial blue
An indistinct regard.°
THIRD GENTLEMAN: Come, let's do so;
For every minute is expectancy   45
Of more arrivancie.°

Enter CASSIO.

CASSIO: Thanks, you the valiant of the warlike isle,
That so approve° the Moor. O, let the heavens

---

24 sufferance: damage. 42–43 the main . . . regard: i.e., the sea and sky become indistinguishable. 46 arrivancie: arrivals. 48 approve: ("honor" or, perhaps, "are as warlike and valiant as your governor").

Give him defense against the elements,
For I have lost him on a dangerous sea. 50
MONTANO: Is he well shipped?
CASSIO: His bark is stoutly timbered, and his pilot
Of very expert and approved allowance;°
Therefore my hopes, not surfeited to death,°
Stand in bold cure.° *(Within)* A sail, a sail, a sail! 55
CASSIO: What noise?
FIRST GENTLEMAN: The town is empty; on the brow o' th' sea
Stand ranks of people, and they cry, "A sail!"
CASSIO: My hopes do shape him for the governor.

[*A shot.*]

SECOND GENTLEMAN: They do discharge their shot of courtesy: 60
Our friends at least.
CASSIO: I pray you, sir, go forth
And give us truth who 'tis that is arrived.
SECOND GENTLEMAN: I shall. *Exit.*
MONTANO: But, good lieutenant, is your general wived? 65
CASSIO: Most fortunately. He hath achieved a maid
That paragons° description and wild fame;°
One that excels the quirks of blazoning pens,°
And in th' essential vesture of creation°
Does tire the ingener.° 70

Enter [*Second*] GENTLEMAN.

How now? Who has put in?
SECOND GENTLEMAN: 'Tis one Iago, ancient to the general.
CASSIO: H'as had most favorable and happy speed:
Tempests themselves, high seas, and howling winds,
The guttered° rocks and congregated° sands, 75
Traitors ensteeped° to enclog the guiltless keel,
As having sense° of beauty, do omit
Their mortal° natures, letting go safely by
The divine Desdemona.

---

53 approved allowance: known and tested.   54 not surfeited to death: i.e., not so great as to be in danger.   55 Stand in bold cure: i.e., are likely to be restored. 67 paragons: exceeds.   67 wild fame: extravagant report.   68 quirks of blazoning pens: ingenuities of praising pens.   69 essential vesture of creation: i.e., essential human nature as given by the Creator.   70 tire the ingener: (a difficult line which probably means something like "outdo the human ability to imagine and picture").   75 guttered: jagged. 75 congregated: gathered.   76 ensteeped: submerged.   77 sense: awareness. 78 mortal: deadly.

MONTANO: What is she?   80
CASSIO: She that I spake of, our great captain's captain,
    Left in the conduct of the bold Iago,
    Whose footing° here anticipates our thoughts
    A se'nnight's° speed. Great Jove, Othello guard,
    And swell his sail with thine own pow'rful breath,   85
    That he may bless this bay with his tall° ship,
    Make love's quick pants in Desdemona's arms,
    Give renewed fire to our extincted spirits.

Enter DESDEMONA, IAGO, RODERIGO, *and* EMILIA.

    O, behold! The riches of the ship is come on shore!
    You men of Cyprus, let her have your knees.   90
                                        [*Kneeling.*]
    Hail to thee, lady! and the grace of heaven,
    Before, behind thee, and on every hand,
    Enwheel thee round.
DESDEMONA: I thank you, valiant Cassio.
    What tidings can you tell of my lord?   95
CASSIO: He is not yet arrived, nor know I aught
    But that he's well and will be shortly here.
DESDEMONA: O but I fear. How lost you company?
CASSIO: The great contention of sea and skies
    Parted our fellowship. *(Within)* A sail, a sail!   100
                                        [*A shot.*]
                       But hark. A sail!
SECOND GENTLEMAN: They give this greeting to the citadel;
    This likewise is a friend.
CASSIO: See for the news.
                                        [*Exit* GENTLEMAN.]
    Good ancient, you are welcome. [*To* EMILIA] Welcome, mistress.   105
    Let it not gall your patience, good Iago,
    That I extend° my manners. 'Tis my breeding°
    That gives me this bold show of courtesy. [*Kisses* EMILIA.]

_____

    83 footing: landing.   84 se'nnight's: week's.   86 tall: brave.   107 extend: stretch.
107 breeding: careful training in manners (Cassio is considerably more the polished gentleman than Iago, and aware of it).

IAGO: Sir, would she give you so much of her lips
    As of her tongue she oft bestows on me,   110
    You would have enough.
DESDEMONA: Alas, she has no speech.
IAGO: In faith, too much.
    I find it still when I have leave to sleep.°
    Marry, before your ladyship,° I grant,   115
    She puts her tongue a little in her heart
    And chides with thinking.
EMILIA: You have little cause to say so.
IAGO: Come on, come on! You are pictures° out of door,
    Bells in your parlors, wildcats in your kitchens,   120
    Saints in your injuries,° devils being offended,
    Players in your housewifery,° and housewives in your beds.
DESDEMONA: O, fie upon thee, slanderer!
IAGO: Nay, it is true, or else I am a Turk:
    You rise to play, and go to bed to work.   125
EMILIA: You shall not write my praise.
IAGO: No, let me not.
DESDEMONA: What wouldst write of me, if thou shouldst praise me?
IAGO: O gentle lady, do not put me to't,
    For I am nothing if not critical.   130
DESDEMONA: Come on, assay. There's one gone to the harbor?
IAGO: Ay, madam.
DESDEMONA   [*Aside*]: I am not merry; but I do beguile
    The thing I am by seeming otherwise.—
    Come, how wouldst thou praise me?   135
IAGO: I am about it; but indeed my invention
    Comes from my pate as birdlime° does from frieze°—
    It plucks out brains and all. But my Muse labors,
    And thus she is delivered:
    If she be fair° and wise: fairness and wit,   140
    The one's for use, the other useth it.

---

114 still . . . sleep: i.e., even when she allows me to sleep she continues to scold.
115 before your ladyship: in your presence.   119 pictures: models (of virtue).   121 in
your injuries: when you injure others.   122 housewifery: (this word can mean "careful,
economical household management," and Iago would then be accusing women of only
pretending to be good housekeepers, while in bed they are either [1] economical of their
favors, or more likely [2] serious and dedicated workers).   137 birdlime: a sticky substance put on branches to catch birds.   137 frieze: rough cloth.   140 fair: light-
complexioned.

DESDEMONA: Well praised. How if she be black° and witty?

IAGO: If she be black, and thereto have a wit,
 She'll find a white that shall her blackness fit.

DESDEMONA: Worse and worse!   145

EMILIA: How if fair and foolish?

IAGO: She never yet was foolish that was fair,
 For even her folly helped her to an heir.

DESDEMONA: These are old fond° paradoxes to make fools laugh i' th'
 alehouse. What miserable praise hast thou for her that's foul and 150
 foolish?

IAGO: There's none so foul, and foolish thereunto,
 But does foul pranks which fair and wise ones do.

DESDEMONA: O heavy ignorance. Thou praisest the worst best. But what
 praise couldst thou bestow on a deserving woman indeed—one that in 155
 the authority of her merit did justly put on the vouch of very malice itself?°

IAGO: She that was ever fair, and never proud;
 Had tongue at will, and yet was never loud;
 Never lacked gold, and yet went never gay;   160
 Fled from her wish, and yet said "Now I may";
 She that being angered, her revenge being nigh,
 Bade her wrong stay, and her displeasure fly;
 She that in wisdom never was so frail
 To change the cod's head for the salmon's tail;°   165
 She that could think, and nev'r disclose her mind;
 See suitors following, and not look behind:
 She was a wight° (if ever such wights were)—

DESDEMONA: To do what?

IAGO: To suckle fools and chronicle small beer.°   170

DESDEMONA: O most lame and impotent conclusion. Do not learn of
 him, Emilia, though he be thy husband. How say you, Cassio? Is he not
 a most profane and liberal° counselor?

CASSIO: He speaks home,° madam. You may relish him more in° the soldier than in the scholar. [Takes DESDEMONA's hand.]   175

IAGO [Aside]: He takes her by the palm. Ay, well said, whisper! With as
 little a web as this will I ensnare as great a fly as Cassio. Ay, smile upon

---

 142 black: brunette. 149 fond: foolish. 155–57 one . . . itself: i.e., a woman so honest and deserving that even malice would be forced to approve of her. 165 To . . . tail:
i.e., to exchange something valuable for something useless. 168 wight: person.
170 chronicle small beer: i.e., keep household accounts (the most trivial of occupations
in Iago's opinion). 173 liberal: licentious. 174 speaks home: thrusts deeply with his
speech. 174 relish him more in: enjoy him more as.

her, do! I will gyve° thee in thine own courtship.—You say true; 'tis so,
indeed!—If such tricks as these strip you out of your lieutenantry, it had
been better you had not kissed your three fingers so oft—which now   180
again you are most apt to play the sir° in. Very good! Well kissed! An
excellent curtsy!° 'Tis so, indeed. Yet again your fingers to your lips?
Would they were clyster pipes° for your sake! [*Trumpets within.*] The
Moor! I know his trumpet.°

CASSIO: 'Tis truly so.   185

DESDEMONA: Let's meet him and receive him.

CASSIO: Lo, where he comes.

Enter OTHELLO *and* ATTENDANTS.

OTHELLO: O my fair warrior!

DESDEMONA: My dear Othello.

OTHELLO: It gives me wonder great as my content   190
To see you here before me. O my soul's joy!
If after every tempest come such calms,
May the winds blow till they have wakened death.
And let the laboring bark climb hills of seas
Olympus-high, and duck again as low   195
As hell's from heaven. If it were now to die,
'Twere now to be most happy; for I fear
My soul hath her content so absolute
That not another comfort like to this
Succeeds in unknown fate.   200

DESDEMONA: The heavens forbid
But that our loves and comforts should increase
Even as our days do grow.

OTHELLO: Amen to that, sweet powers!
I cannot speak enough of this content;   205
It stops me here [*touches his heart*]; it is too much of joy.
And this, and this, the greatest discords be

                                                  [*They kiss.*]

That e'er our hearts shall make!

IAGO: [*Aside*] O, you are well tuned now!
But I'll set down the pegs° that make this music,   210
As honest as I am.

_____

178 gyve: bind.   181 the sir: the fashionable gentleman.   182 curtsy: courtesy, i.e.,
bow.   183 clyster pipes: enema tubes.   184 his trumpet: (great men had their own distinctive calls).   210 set down the pegs: loosen the strings (to produce discord).

OTHELLO: Come, let us to the castle.
  News, friends! Our wars are done; the Turks are drowned.
  How does my old acquaintance of this isle?
  Honey, you shall be well desired in Cyprus;   215
  I have found great love amongst them. O my sweet,
  I prattle out of fashion, and I dote
  In mine own comforts. I prithee, good Iago,
  Go to the bay and disembark my coffers.
  Bring thou the master to the citadel;   220
  He is a good one, and his worthiness
  Does challenge° much respect. Come, Desdemona,
  Once more well met at Cyprus.

Exit OTHELLO *and* DESDEMONA [*and all but* IAGO *and* RODERIGO].

IAGO: [*To an* ATTENDANT] Do thou meet me presently at the harbor.
  [*To* RODERIGO] Come hither. If thou be'st valiant (as they say base   225
  men being in love have then a nobility in their natures more than is
  native to them), list me. The lieutenant tonight watches on the court
  of guard.° First, I must tell thee this: Desdemona is directly in love with
  him.
RODERIGO: With him? Why, 'tis not possible.   230
IAGO: Lay thy finger thus [*puts his finger to his lips*], and let thy soul be
  instructed. Mark me with what violence she first loved the Moor but for
  bragging and telling her fantastical lies. To love him still for prating? Let
  not thy discreet heart think it. Her eye must be fed. And what delight
  shall she have to look on the devil? When the blood is made dull with   235
  the act of sport, there should be a game° to inflame it and to give sati-
  ety a fresh appetite, loveliness in favor,° sympathy in years,° manners,
  and beauties; all which the Moor is defective in. Now for want of these
  required conveniences,° her delicate tenderness will find itself abused,
  begin to heave the gorge,° disrelish and abhor the Moor. Very nature   240
  will instruct her in it and compel her to some second choice. Now, sir,
  this granted—as it is a most pregnant° and unforced position—who
  stands so eminent in the degree of this fortune as Cassio does? A knave
  very voluble; no further conscionable° than in putting on the mere form
  of civil and humane° seeming for the better compass of his salt° and   245
  most hidden loose° affection. Why, none! Why, none! A slipper° and sub-

---

222 challenge: require, exact.   227–28 court of guard: guardhouse.   236 game:
sport (with the added sense of "gamey," "rank").   237 favor: countenance, appearance.
237 sympathy in years: sameness of age.   239 conveniences: advantages.   240 heave
the gorge: vomit.   242 pregnant: likely.   244 no further conscionable: having no
more conscience.   245 humane: polite.   245 salt: lecherous.   246 loose: immoral.
246 slipper: slippery.

tle knave, a finder of occasion, that has an eye can stamp and counterfeit advantages, though true advantage never present itself. A devilish
knave. Besides, the knave is handsome, young, and hath all those requi-
sites in him that folly and green minds look after. A pestilent complete   250
knave, and the woman hath found him already.

RODERIGO: I cannot believe that in her; she's full of most blessed condition.

IAGO: Blessed fig's-end! The wine she drinks is made of grapes. If she had
been blessed, she would never have loved the Moor. Blessed pudding!
Didst thou not see her paddle with the palm of his hand? Didst not   255
mark that?

RODERIGO: Yes, that I did; but that was but courtesy.

IAGO: Lechery, by this hand! [*Extends his index finger.*] An index° and obscure prologue to the history of lust and foul thoughts. They met so near
with their lips that their breaths embraced together. Villainous thoughts,   260
Roderigo. When these mutualities so marshal the way, hard at hand
comes the master and main exercise, th' incorporate° conclusion: Pish!
But, sir, be you ruled by me. I have brought you from Venice. Watch you
tonight; for the command, I'll lay't upon you. Cassio knows you not. I'll
not be far from you. Do you find some occasion to anger Cassio, either   265
by speaking too loud, or tainting° his discipline, or from what other
course you please which the time shall more favorably minister.

RODERIGO: Well.

IAGO: Sir, he's rash and very sudden in choler,° and haply may strike at
you. Provoke him that he may; for even out of that will I cause these of   270
Cyprus to mutiny, whose qualification shall come into no true taste°
again but by the displanting of Cassio. So shall you have a shorter journey to your desires by the means I shall then have to prefer them; and
the impediment most profitably removed without the which there were
no expectation of our prosperity.   275

RODERIGO: I will do this if you can bring it to any opportunity.

IAGO: I warrant thee. Meet me by and by at the citadel. I must fetch his
necessaries ashore. Farewell.

RODERIGO: Adieu.   *Exit.*

IAGO: That Cassio loves her, I do well believe 't;   280
That she loves him, 'tis apt and of great credit.
The Moor, howbeit that I endure him not,
Is of a constant, loving, noble nature,
And I dare think he'll prove to Desdemona
A most dear° husband. Now I do love her too;   285
Not out of absolute° lust, though peradventure°

---

258 index: pointer.   262 incorporate: carnal.   266 tainting: discrediting.   269
choler: anger.   271 qualification . . . taste: i.e., appeasement will not be brought about
(wine was "qualified" by adding water).   285 dear: expensive.   286 out of absolute:
absolutely out of.   286 peradventure: perchance.

I stand accountant for as great a sin,
But partly led to diet° my revenge,
For that I do suspect the lusty Moor
Hath leaped into my seat; the thought whereof   290
Doth, like a poisonous mineral, gnaw my inwards;
And nothing can or shall content my soul
Till I am evened with him, wife for wife.
Or failing so, yet that I put the Moor
At least into a jealousy so strong   295
That judgment cannot cure. Which thing to do,
If this poor trash of Venice, whom I trace°
For his quick hunting, stand the putting on,
I'll have our Michael Cassio on the hip,
Abuse him to the Moor in the right garb°   300
(For I fear Cassio with my nightcap too),
Make the Moor thank me, love me, and reward me
For making him egregiously an ass
And practicing upon° his peace and quiet,
Even to madness. 'Tis here, but yet confused: 305
Knavery's plain face is never seen till used.

Exit.

Scene 2. [*A street.*]

Enter OTHELLO'S HERALD, *with a proclamation.*

HERALD: It is Othello's pleasure, our noble and valiant general, that upon
certain tidings now arrived importing the mere perdition° of the Turkish fleet, every man put himself into triumph. Some to dance, some to
make bonfires, each man to what sport and revels his addition° leads   5
him. For, besides these beneficial news, it is the celebration of his nuptial. So much was his pleasure should be proclaimed. All offices° are
open, and there is full liberty of feasting from this present hour of five
till the bell have told eleven. Bless the isle of Cyprus and our noble general Othello!

Exit.

---

288 diet: feed.   297 trace: (most editors emend to "trash," meaning to hang weights
on a dog to slow his hunting; but "trace" clearly means something like "put on the trace"
or "set on the track").   300 right garb: i.e., "proper fashion."   304 practicing upon:
scheming to destroy.   II.2.2 mere perdition: absolute destruction.   4 addition: rank.
6 offices: kitchens and storerooms of food.

Scene 3. [*The citadel of Cyprus.*]

Enter OTHELLO, DESDEMONA, CASSIO, *and* ATTENDANTS.

OTHELLO: Good Michael, look you to the guard tonight.
Let's teach ourselves that honorable stop,
Not to outsport discretion.
CASSIO: Iago hath direction what to do;
But notwithstanding, with my personal eye   5
Will I look to't.
OTHELLO: Iago is most honest.
Michael, good night. Tomorrow with your earliest
Let me have speech with you. [*To* DESDEMONA]
Come, my dear love,   10
The purchase made, the fruits are to ensue,
That profit's yet to come 'tween me and you.
Good night.

Exit [OTHELLO *with* DESDEMONA *and* ATTENDANTS].

Enter IAGO.

CASSIO: Welcome, Iago. We must to the watch.
IAGO: Not this hour, lieutenant; 'tis not yet ten o' th' clock. Our general   15
cast° us thus early for the love of his Desdemona; who let us not there-
fore blame. He hath not yet made wanton the night with her, and she is
sport for Jove.
CASSIO: She's a most exquisite lady.
IAGO: And, I'll warrant her, full of game.   20
CASSIO: Indeed, she's a most fresh and delicate creature.
IAGO: What an eye she has! Methinks it sounds a parley to provocation.
CASSIO: An inviting eye; and yet methinks right modest.
IAGO: And when she speaks, is it not an alarum° to love?
CASSIO: She is indeed perfection.   25
IAGO: Well, happiness to their sheets! Come, lieutenant, I have a stoup°
of wine, and here without are a brace of Cyprus gallants that would fain
have a measure to the health of black Othello.
CASSIO: Not tonight, good Iago. I have very poor and unhappy brains for
drinking; I could well wish courtesy would invent some other custom of   30
entertainment.
IAGO: O, they are our friends. But one cup! I'll drink for you.

II.3.16 cast: dismissed.   24 alarum: the call to action, "general quarters."   26 stoup:
two-quart tankard.

CASSIO: I have drunk but one cup tonight, and that was craftily qualified°
    too; and behold what innovation it makes here. I am unfortunate in the
    infirmity and dare not task my weakness with any more.   35
IAGO: What, man! 'Tis a night of revels, the gallants desire it.
CASSIO: Where are they?
IAGO: Here, at the door. I pray you call them in.
CASSIO: I'll do't, but it dislikes me.   *Exit.*
IAGO: If I can fasten but one cup upon him   40
    With that which he hath drunk tonight already,
    He'll be as full of quarrel and offense
    As my young mistress' dog. Now, my sick fool Roderigo,
    Whom love hath turned almost the wrong side out,
    To Desdemona hath tonight caroused   45
    Potations pottle-deep;° and he's to watch.
    Three else° of Cyprus, noble swelling spirits,
    That hold their honors in a wary distance,°
    The very elements of this warlike isle,
    Have I tonight flustered with flowing cups,   50
    And they watch too. Now, 'mongst this flock of drunkards
    Am I to put our Cassio in some action
    That may offend the isle. But here they come.

    Enter CASSIO, MONTANO, *and* GENTLEMEN.

    If consequence do but approve my dream,
    My boat sails freely, both with wind and stream.   55
CASSIO: 'Fore God, they have given me a rouse° already.
MONTANO: Good faith, a little one; not past a pint, as I am a soldier.
IAGO: Some wine, ho!
    [*Sings*] And let me the canakin clink, clink;
        And let me the canakin clink.   60
        A soldier's a man;
        O man's life's but a span,
        Why then, let a soldier drink.
        Some wine, boys!
CASSIO: 'Fore God, an excellent song!   65
IAGO: I learned it in England, where indeed they are most potent in pot-
    ting. Your Dane, your German, and your swag-bellied° Hollander—
    Drink, ho!—are nothing to your English.

---

33 qualified: diluted.   46 pottle-deep: to the bottom of the cup.   47 else: others.
48 hold . . . distance: are scrupulous in maintaining their honor.   56 rouse: drink.
67 swag-bellied: hanging.

CASSIO: Is your Englishman so exquisite° in his drinking?

IAGO: Why, he drinks you with facility your Dane dead drunk; he sweats 70
not to overthrow your Almain; he gives your Hollander a vomit ere the
next pottle can be filled.

CASSIO: To the health of our general!

MONTANO: I am for it, lieutenant, and I'll do you justice.

IAGO: O sweet England! 75
[*Sings*] King Stephen was and a worthy peer;
His breeches cost him but a crown;
He held them sixpence all too dear,
With that he called the tailor lown.°
He was a wight of high renown, 80
And thou art but of low degree:
'Tis pride that pulls the country down;
And take thine auld cloak about thee.
Some wine, ho!

CASSIO: 'Fore God, this is a more exquisite song than the other. 85

IAGO: Will you hear't again?

CASSIO: No, for I hold him to be unworthy of his place that does those
things. Well, God's above all; and there be souls must be saved, and there
be souls must not be saved.

IAGO: It's true, good lieutenant. 90

CASSIO: For mine own part—no offense to the general, nor any man of
quality—I hope to be saved.

IAGO: And so do I too, lieutenant.

CASSIO: Ay, but, by your leave, not before me. The lieutenant is to be
saved before the ancient. Let's have no more of this; let's to our af- 95
fairs.—God forgive us our sins!—Gentlemen, let's look to our business.
Do not think, gentlemen, I am drunk. This is my ancient; this is my right
hand, and this is my left. I am not drunk now. I can stand well enough,
and I speak well enough.

GENTLEMEN: Excellent well! 100

CASSIO: Why, very well then. You must not think then that I am drunk.
Exit.

MONTANO: To th' platform, masters. Come, let's set the watch.

IAGO: You see this fellow that is gone before.
He's a soldier fit to stand by Caesar
And give direction; and do but see his vice. 105
'Tis to his virtue a just equinox,°
The one as long as th' other. 'Tis pity of him.

_____

69 exquisite: superb.   79 lown: lout.   106 just equinox: exact balance (of dark and
light).

I fear the trust Othello puts him in,
On some odd time of his infirmity,
Will shake this island.   110
MONTANO: But is he often thus?
IAGO: 'Tis evermore his prologue to his sleep:
    He'll watch the horologe a double set°
    If drink rock not his cradle.
MONTANO: It were well   115
    The general were put in mind of it.
    Perhaps he sees it not, or his good nature
    Prizes the virtue that appears in Cassio
    And looks not on his evils. Is not this true?

Enter RODERIGO

IAGO   [*Aside*]: How now, Roderigo?   120
    I pray you after the lieutenant, go!   [*Exit* RODERIGO.]
MONTANO: And 'tis great pity that the noble Moor
    Should hazard such a place as his own second
    With one of an ingraft° infirmity.
    It were an honest action to say so   125
    To the Moor.
IAGO: Not I, for this fair island!
    I do love Cassio well and would do much
    To cure him of this evil.   (Help! Help! *Within.*)
                                                       But hark? What noise?   130

Enter CASSIO, *pursuing* RODERIGO.

CASSIO: Zounds, you rogue! You rascal!
MONTANO: What's the matter, lieutenant?
CASSIO: A knave teach me my duty? I'll beat the knave into a twiggen°
    bottle.
RODERIGO: Beat me?   135
CASSIO: Dost thou prate, rogue?   [*Strikes him.*]
MONTANO: Nay, good lieutenant! I pray you, sir, hold your hand.
                                                                  [*Stays him.*]
CASSIO: Let me go, sir, or I'll knock you o'er the mazzard.°
MONTANO: Come, come, you're drunk!

---

113 watch . . . set: stay awake twice around the clock.   124 ingraft: ingrained.
133 twiggen: wicker-covered.   138 mazzard: head.

CASSIO: Drunk?   [*They fight.*] 140
IAGO   [*Aside to* RODERIGO]: Away, I say! Go out and cry a mutiny!
                                              [*Exit* RODERIGO.]
   Nay, good lieutenant. God's will, gentlemen!
   Help, ho! Lieutenant. Sir. Montano.
   Help, masters! Here's a goodly watch indeed!

                  [*A bell rung.*]

   Who's that which rings the bell? Diablo, ho!   145
   The town will rise. God's will, lieutenant,
   You'll be ashamed forever.

Enter OTHELLO *and* ATTENDANTS.

OTHELLO: What is the matter here?
MONTANO: Zounds, I bleed still. I am hurt to the death.
   He dies.   [*He and* CASSIO *fight again.*]   150
OTHELLO: Hold for your lives!
IAGO: Hold, ho! Lieutenant. Sir. Montano. Gentlemen!
   Have you forgot all place of sense and duty?
   Hold! The general speaks to you. Hold, for shame!
OTHELLO: Why, how now, ho? From whence ariseth this?   155
   Are we turned Turks, and to ourselves do that
   Which heaven hath forbid the Ottomites?°
   For Christian shame put by this barbarous brawl!
   He that stirs next to carve for his own rage
   Holds his soul light;° he dies upon his motion.   160
   Silence that dreadful bell! It frights the isle
   From her propriety.° What is the matter, masters?
   Honest Iago, that looks dead with grieving,
   Speak. Who began this? On thy love, I charge thee.
IAGO: I do not know. Friends all, but now, even now,   165
   In quarter° and in terms like bride and groom
   Devesting them for bed; and then, but now—
   As if some planet had unwitted men—
   Swords out, and tilting one at other's breasts
   In opposition bloody. I cannot speak   170
   Any beginning to this peevish odds,°

---

157 heaven . . . Ottomites: i.e., by sending the storm which dispersed the Turks.
160 Holds his soul light: values his soul lightly.   162 propriety: proper order.   166 In
quarter: on duty.   171 odds: quarrel.

And would in action glorious I had lost
Those legs that brought me to a part of it!
OTHELLO: How comes it, Michael, you are thus forgot?
CASSIO: I pray you pardon me; I cannot speak.   175
OTHELLO: Worthy Montano, you were wont to be civil;
The gravity and stillness of your youth
The world hath noted, and your name is great
In mouths of wisest censure.° What's the matter
That you unlace° your reputation thus   180
And spend your rich opinion° for the name
Of a night-brawler? Give me answer to it.
MONTANO: Worthy Othello, I am hurt to danger.
Your officer, Iago, can inform you,
While I spare speech, which something now offends° me,   185
Of all that I do know; nor know I aught
By me that's said or done amiss this night,
Unless self-charity be sometimes a vice,
And to defend ourselves it be a sin
When violence assails us.   190
OTHELLO: Now, by heaven,
My blood begins my safer guides to rule,
And passion, having my best judgment collied,°
Assays to lead the way. If I once stir
Or do but lift this arm, the best of you   195
Shall sink in my rebuke. Give me to know
How this foul rout began, who set it on;
And he that is approved in this offense,
Though he had twinned with me, both at a birth,
Shall lose me. What? In a town of war   200
Yet wild, the people's hearts brimful of fear,
To manage° private and domestic quarrel?
In night, and on the court and guard of safety?
'Tis monstrous. Iago, who began't?
MONTANO: If partially affined, or leagued in office,°   205
Thou dost deliver more or less than truth,
Thou art no soldier.
IAGO: Touch me not so near.
I had rather have this tongue cut from my mouth

---

179 censure: judgment.   180 unlace: undo (the term refers specifically to the dressing of a wild boar killed in the hunt).   181 opinion: reputation.   185 offends: harms,
hurts.   193 collied: darkened.   202 manage: conduct.   205 If . . . office: if you are partial because you are related ("affined") or the brother officer (of Cassio).

Than it should do offense to Michael Cassio. 210
Yet I persuade myself to speak the truth
Shall nothing wrong him. This it is, general.
Montano and myself being in speech,
There comes a fellow crying out for help,
And Cassio following him with determined sword 215
To execute upon him. Sir, this gentleman
Steps in to Cassio and entreats his pause.
Myself the crying fellow did pursue,
Lest by his clamor—as it so fell out—
The town might fall in fright. He, swift of foot, 220
Outran my purpose; and I returned then rather
For that I heard the clink and fall of swords,
And Cassio high in oath; which till tonight
I ne'er might say before. When I came back—
For this was brief—I found them close together 225
At blow and thrust, even as again they were
When you yourself did part them.
More of this matter cannot I report;
But men are men; the best sometimes forget.
Though Cassio did some little wrong to him, 230
As men in rage strike those that wish them best,
Yet surely Cassio I believe received
From him that fled some strange indignity,
Which patience could not pass.°

OTHELLO: I know, Iago, 235
  Thy honesty and love doth mince° this matter,
Making it light to Cassio. Cassio, I love thee;
But never more be officer of mine.

Enter DESDEMONA, *attended.*

Look if my gentle love be not raised up.
I'll make thee an example. 240
DESDEMONA: What is the matter, dear.
OTHELLO: All's well, sweeting; come away to bed.

[*To* MONTANO] Sir, for your hurts, myself will be your surgeon.

Lead him off.   [MONTANO *led off.*]
Iago, look with care about the town 245

---

234 pass: allow to pass.   236 mince: cut up (i.e., tell only part of).

And silence those whom this vile brawl distracted.
Come, Desdemona: 'tis the soldiers' life
To have their balmy slumbers waked with strife.

Exit [*with all but* IAGO *and* CASSIO].

IAGO: What, are you hurt, lieutenant?
CASSIO: Ay, past all surgery.   250
IAGO: Marry, God forbid!
CASSIO: Reputation, reputation, reputation! O, I have lost my reputation!
   I have lost the immortal part of myself, and what remains is bestial. My
   reputation, Iago, my reputation.
IAGO: As I am an honest man, I had thought you had received some bod-   255
   ily wound. There is more sense° in that than in reputation. Reputation
   is an idle and most false imposition,° oft got without merit and lost without deserving. You have lost no reputation at all unless you repute yourself such a loser. What, man, there are more ways to recover the general
   again. You are but now cast in his mood°—a punishment more in pol-   260
   icy° than in malice—even so as one would beat his offenseless dog to
   affright an imperious lion. Sue to him again, and he's yours.
CASSIO: I will rather sue to be despised than to deceive so good a commander with so slight, so drunken, and so indiscreet an officer. Drunk!
   And speak parrot!° And squabble! Swagger! Swear! and discourse fus-   265
   tian° with one's own shadow! O thou invisible spirit of wine, if thou hast
   no name to be known by, let us call thee devil!
IAGO: What was he that you followed with your sword? What had he
   done to you?
CASSIO: I know not.   270
IAGO: Is't possible?
CASSIO: I remember a mass of things, but nothing distinctly: a quarrel, but
   nothing wherefore. O God, that men should put an enemy in their
   mouths to steal away their brains! that we should with joy, pleasance,
   revel, and applause transform ourselves into beasts!   275
IAGO: Why, but you are now well enough. How came you thus recovered?
CASSIO: It hath pleased the devil drunkenness to give place to the devil
   wrath. One unperfectness shows me another, to make me frankly despise myself.   280
IAGO: Come, you are too severe a moraler. As the time, the place, and
   the condition of this country stands, I could heartily wish this had not
   befall'n; but since it is as it is, mend it for your own good.

---

256 sense: physical feeling.   257 imposition: external thing.   260 cast in his mood:
dismissed because of his anger.   261 in policy: politically necessary.   265 speak parrot:
gabble without sense.   265–66 discourse fustian: speak nonsense ("fustian" was a coarse
cotton cloth used for stuffing).

CASSIO: I will ask him for my place again: he shall tell me I am a drunk-
ard. Had I as many mouths as Hydra, such an answer would stop them   285
all. To be now a sensible man, by and by a fool, and presently a beast!
O strange! Every inordinate cup is unblest, and the ingredient is a devil.
IAGO: Come, come, good wine is a good familiar creature if it be well
used. Exclaim no more against it. And, good lieutenant, I think you think
I love you.   290
CASSIO: I have well approved it, sir. I drunk?
IAGO: You or any man living may be drunk at a time, man. I tell you what
you shall do. Our general's wife is now the general. I may say so in this
respect, for that he hath devoted and given up himself to the contemplation, mark, and devotement of her parts° and graces. Confess your-   295
self freely to her; importune her help to put you in your place again.
She is of so free, so kind, so apt, so blessed a disposition she holds it a
vice in her goodness not to do more than she is requested. This broken
joint between you and her husband entreat her to splinter;° and my fortunes against any lay° worth naming, this crack of your love shall grow   300
stronger than it was before.
CASSIO: You advise me well.
IAGO: I protest, in the sincerity of love and honest kindness.
CASSIO: I think it freely; and betimes in the morning I will beseech the
virtuous Desdemona to undertake for me. I am desperate of my for-   305
tunes if they check° me.
IAGO: You are in the right. Good night, lieutenant; I must to the watch.
CASSIO: Good night, honest Iago.   *Exit* CASSIO.
IAGO: And what's he then that says I play the villain,
When this advice is free° I give, and honest,   310
Probal to° thinking, and indeed the course
To win the Moor again? For 'tis most easy
Th' inclining° Desdemona to subdue
In any honest suit; she's framed as fruitful°
As the free elements.° And then for her   315
To win the Moor—were't to renounce his baptism,
All seals and symbols of redeemèd sin—
His soul is so enfettered to her love
That she may make, unmake, do what she list,
Even as her appetite° shall play the god   320
With his weak function.° How am I then a villain
To counsel Cassio to this parallel course,

---

295 devotement of her parts: devotion to her qualities.   299 splinter: splint.   300
lay: wager.   306 check: repulse.   310 free: generous and open.   311 Probal to:
provable by.   313 inclining: inclined (to be helpful).   314 framed as fruitful: made as
generous.   315 elements: i.e., basic nature.   320 appetite: liking.   321 function:
thought.

Directly to his good? Divinity of hell!
When devils will the blackest sins put on,°
They do suggest at first with heavenly shows,°   325
As I do now. For whiles this honest fool
Plies Desdemona to repair his fortune,
And she for him pleads strongly to the Moor,
I'll pour this pestilence into his ear:
That she repeals him° for her body's lust;   330
And by how much she strives to do him good,
She shall undo her credit with the Moor.
So will I turn her virtue into pitch,
And out of her own goodness make the net
That shall enmesh them all. How now, Roderigo?   335

Enter RODERIGO.

RODERIGO: I do follow here in the chase, not like a hound that hunts,
   but one that fills up the cry.° My money is almost spent; I have been
   tonight exceedingly well cudgeled; and I think the issue will be, I shall
   have so much experience for my pains; and so, with no money at all, and
   a little more wit, return again to Venice.   340
IAGO: How poor are they that have not patience!
   What would did ever heal but by degrees?
   Thou know'st we work by wit, and not by witchcraft;
   And wit depends on dilatory time.
   Does't not go well? Cassio hath beaten thee,   345
   And thou by that small hurt hath cashiered Cassio.
   Though other things grow fair against the sun,
   Yet fruits that blossom first will first be ripe.
   Content thyself awhile. By the mass, 'tis morning!
   Pleasure and action make the hours seem short.   350
   Retire thee; go where thou art billeted.
   Away, I say! Thou shalt know more hereafter.
   Nay, get thee gone!   *Exit* RODERIGO.
               Two things are to be done:
   My wife must move° for Cassio to her mistress;   355
   I'll set her on;
   Myself awhile° to draw the Moor apart

---

324 put on: advance, further.   325 shows: appearances.   330 repeals him: asks for
(Cassio's reinstatement).   337 fills up the cry: makes up one of the hunting pack, adding
to the noise but not actually tracking.   355 move: petition.   357 awhile: at the same
time.

And bring him jump° when he may Cassio find
Soliciting his wife. Ay, that's the way!
Dull not device by coldness and delay.   *Exit.*   360

ACT III

Scene 1. [*A street.*]

Enter CASSIO [*and*] MUSICIANS.

CASSIO: Masters, play here. I will content your pains.° Something that's
brief; and bid "Good morrow, general."   [*They play.*]

[*Enter* CLOWN.°]

CLOWN: Why, masters, have your instruments been in Naples° that they
speak i' th' nose thus?
MUSICIAN: How, sir, how?   5
CLOWN: Are these, I pray you, wind instruments?
MUSICIAN: Ay, marry, are they, sir.
CLOWN: O, thereby hangs a tale.
MUSICIAN: Whereby hangs a tale, sir?
CLOWN: Marry, sir, by many a wind instrument that I know. But, masters,   10
here's money for you; and the general so likes your music that he de-
sires you, for love's sake, to make no more noise with it.
MUSICIAN: Well, sir, we will not.
CLOWN: If you have any music that may not be heard, to't again. But, as
they say, to hear music the general does not greatly care.   15
MUSICIAN: We have none such, sir.
CLOWN: Then put up your pipes in your bag, for I'll away. Go, vanish into
air, away!
                                                           Exit MUSICIANS.
CASSIO: Dost thou hear me, mine honest friend?
CLOWN: No. I hear not your honest friend. I hear you.   20

---

358 jump: at the precise moment and place.   III.1.1 content your pains: reward your
efforts.   s.d. Clown: fool.   3 Naples: (this may refer either to the Neapolitan nasal tone,
or to syphilis—rife in Naples—which breaks down the nose).

CASSIO: Prithee keep up thy quillets.° There's a poor piece of gold for thee.
    If the gentlewoman that attends the general's wife be stirring, tell her
    there's one Cassio entreats her a little favor of speech. Wilt thou do this?
CLOWN: She is stirring, sir. If she will stir hither, I shall seem to notify unto
    her.°   *Exit* CLOWN.   25

Enter IAGO.

CASSIO: In happy time, Iago.
IAGO: You have not been abed then?
CASSIO: Why no, the day had broke before we parted.
    I have made bold, Iago, to send in to your wife;
    My suit to her is that she will to virtuous Desdemona   30
    Procure me some access.
IAGO: I'll send her to you presently,
    And I'll devise a mean to draw the Moor
    Out of the way, that your converse and business
    May be more free.   35
CASSIO: I humbly thank you for 't.   *Exit* [IAGO].
                          I never knew
    A Florentine° more kind and honest.

Enter EMILIA.

EMILIA: Good morrow, good lieutenant. I am sorry
    For your displeasure;° but all will sure be well.   40
    The general and his wife are talking of it,
    And she speaks for you stoutly. The Moor replies
    That he you hurt is of great fame in Cyprus
    And great affinity,° and that in wholesome wisdom
    He might not but refuse you. But he protests he loves you,   45
    And needs no other suitor but his likings
    To bring you in again.
CASSIO: Yet I beseech you,
    If you think fit, or that it may be done,
    Give me advantage of some brief discourse   50
    With Desdemona alone.

---

    21 quillets: puns.   25 seem ... her: (the Clown is mocking Cassio's overly elegant man-
ner of speaking).   38 Florentine: i.e., Iago is as kind as if he were from Cassio's home
town, Florence.   40 displeasure: discomforting.   44 affinity: family.

EMILIA: Pray you come in.
   I will bestow you where you shall have time
   To speak your bosom° freely.
CASSIO: I am much bound to you.   55

                                                      [*Exeunt.*]

Scene 2. [*The citadel.*]

Enter OTHELLO, IAGO, *and* GENTLEMEN.

OTHELLO: These letters give, Iago, to the pilot
   And by him do my duties to the Senate.
   That done, I will be walking on the works;
   Repair° there to me.
IAGO: Well, my good lord, I'll do't.   5
OTHELLO: This fortification, gentlemen, shall we see't?
GENTLEMEN: We'll wait upon your lordship.   *Exeunt.*

Scene 3. [*The citadel.*]

Enter DESDEMONA, CASSIO, *and* EMILIA.

DESDEMONA: Be thou assured, good Cassio, I will do
   All my abilities in thy behalf.
EMILIA: Good madam, do. I warrant it grieves my husband
   As if the cause were his.
DESDEMONA: O, that's an honest fellow. Do not doubt, Cassio,   5
   But I will have my lord and you again
   As friendly as you were.
CASSIO: Bounteous madam,
   Whatever shall become of Michael Cassio,
   He's never anything but your true servant.   10
DESDEMONA: I know't; I thank you. You do love my lord.
   You have known him long, and be you well assured
   He shall in strangeness stand no farther off
   Than in a politic distance.°
CASSIO: Ay, but, lady,   15
   That policy may either last so long,
   Or feed upon such nice° and waterish diet,

---

   54 bosom: inmost thoughts.   III.2.4 Repair: go.   III.3.13–14 He . . . distance: i.e., he
shall act no more distant to you than is necessary for political reasons.   17 nice: trivial.

Or breed itself so out of circumstances,°
That, I being absent, and my place supplied,°
My general will forget my love and service.   20
DESDEMONA: Do not doubt° that; before Emilia here
  I give thee warrant of thy place. Assure thee,
  If I do vow a friendship, I'll perform it
  To the last article. My lord shall never rest;
  I'll watch him tame° and talk him out of patience;   25
  His bed shall seem a school, his board a shrift;°
  I'll intermingle everything he does
  With Cassio's suit. Therefore be merry, Cassio,
  For thy solicitor shall rather die
  Than give thy cause away.   30

Enter OTHELLO *and* IAGO [*at a distance*].

EMILIA: Madam, here comes my lord.
CASSIO: Madam, I'll take my leave.
DESDEMONA: Why, stay, and hear me speak.
CASSIO: Madam, not now. I am very ill at ease,
  Unfit for mine own purposes.   35
DESDEMONA: Well, do your discretion.   *Exit* CASSIO.
IAGO: Ha! I like not that.
OTHELLO: What dost thou say?
IAGO: Nothing, my lord; or if—I know not what.
OTHELLO: Was not that Cassio parted from my wife?   40
IAGO: Cassio, my lord? No, sure, I cannot think it
  That he would steal away so guilty-like,
  Seeing your coming.
OTHELLO: I do believe 'twas he.
DESDEMONA [*Coming to them*]:   How now, my lord?   45
  I have been talking with a suitor here,
  A man that languishes in your displeasure.
OTHELLO: Who is't you mean?
DESDEMONA: Why, your lieutenant, Cassio. Good my lord,
  If I have any grace or power to move you,   50
  His present° reconciliation take.
  For if he be not one that truly loves you,

_____

18 Or . . . circumstances: i.e., or grow so on the basis of accidental happenings and political needs. 19 supplied: filled. 21 doubt: imagine. 25 watch him tame: (animals
were tamed by being kept awake). 26 board a shrift: table (seem) a confessional.
51 present: immediate.

That errs in ignorance, and not in cunning,
I have no judgment in an honest face.
I prithee call him back.   55
OTHELLO: Went he hence now?
DESDEMONA: I' sooth so humbled
That he hath left part of his grief with me
To suffer with him. Good love, call him back.
OTHELLO: Not now, sweet Desdemon; some other time.   60
DESDEMONA: But shall't be shortly?
OTHELLO: The sooner, sweet, for you.
DESDEMONA: Shall't be tonight at supper?
OTHELLO: No, not tonight.
DESDEMONA: Tomorrow dinner then?   65
OTHELLO: I shall not dine at home;
I meet the captains at the citadel.
DESDEMONA: Why then, tomorrow night, on Tuesday morn,
On Tuesday noon, or night, on Wednesday morn.
I prithee name the time, but let it not   70
Exceed three days. In faith, he's penitent;
And yet his trespass, in our common reason
(Save that, they say, the wars must make example
Out of her best), is not almost a fault
T' incur a private check.° When shall he come?   75
Tell me, Othello. I wonder in my soul
What you would ask me that I should deny
Or stand so mamm'ring° on. What? Michael Cassio,
That came awooing with you, and so many a time,
When I have spoke of you dispraisingly,   80
Hath ta'en your part—to have so much to do
To bring him in? By'r Lady, I could do much—
OTHELLO: Prithee no more. Let him come when he will!
I will deny thee nothing.
DESDEMONA: Why, this is not a boon;   85
'Tis as I should entreat you wear your gloves,
Or feed on nourishing dishes, or keep you warm,
Or sue to you to do a peculiar profit°
To your own person. Nay, when I have a suit
Wherein I mean to touch your love indeed,   90
It shall be full of poise° and difficult weight,

74–75 is . . . check: is almost not serious enough for a private rebuke (let alone a public disgrace).   78 mamm'ring: hesitating.   88 peculiar profit: particularly personal
good.   91 poise: weight.

And fearful to be granted.

OTHELLO: I will deny thee nothing!
  Whereon I do beseech thee grant me this,
  To leave me but a little to myself.   95

DESDEMONA: Shall I deny you? No. Farewell, my lord.

OTHELLO: Farewell, my Desdemona: I'll come to thee straight.°

DESDEMONA: Emilia, come. Be as your fancies teach you;
  Whate'er you be, I am obedient.   *Exit* [*with* EMILIA].

OTHELLO: Excellent wretch! Perdition catch my soul   100
  But I do love thee! And when I love thee not,
  Chaos is come again.

IAGO: My noble lord—

OTHELLO: What dost thou say, Iago?

IAGO: Did Michael Cassio, when you wooed my lady,   105
  Know of your love?

OTHELLO: He did, from first to last. Why dost thou ask?

IAGO: But for a satisfaction of my thought,
  No further harm.

OTHELLO: Why of thy thought, Iago?   110

IAGO: I did not think he had been acquainted with her.

OTHELLO: O, yes, and went between us° very oft.

IAGO: Indeed?

OTHELLO: Indeed? Ay, indeed! Discern'st thou aught in that?
  Is he not honest?   115

IAGO: Honest, my lord?

OTHELLO: Honest? Ay, honest.

IAGO: My lord, for aught I know.

OTHELLO: What dost thou think?

IAGO: Think, my lord?   120

OTHELLO: Think, my lord?
  By heaven, thou echoest me,
  As if there were some monster in thy thought
  Too hideous to be shown. Thou dost mean something.
  I heard thee say even now, thou lik'st not that,   125
  When Cassio left my wife. What didst not like?
  And when I told thee he was of my counsel°
  Of my whole course of wooing, thou cried'st "Indeed?"
  And didst contract and purse thy brow together,
  As if thou then hadst shut up in thy brain   130
  Some horrible conceit.° If thou dost love me,
  Show me thy thought.

---

97 straight: at once. 112 between us: i.e., as messenger. 127 of my counsel: in my
confidence. 131 conceit: thought.

IAGO: My lord, you know I love you.
OTHELLO: I think thou dost;
 And, for I know thou'rt full of love and honesty   135
 And weigh'st thy words before thou giv'st them breath,
 Therefore these stops° of thine fright me the more;
 For such things in a false disloyal knave
 Are tricks of custom;° but in a man that's just
 They're close dilations,° working from the heart   140
 That passion cannot rule.
IAGO: For Michael Cassio,
 I dare be sworn, I think that he is honest.
OTHELLO: I think so too.
IAGO: Men should be what they seem; 145
 Or those that be not, would they might seem none!
OTHELLO: Certain, men should be what they seem.
IAGO: Why then, I think Cassio's an honest man.
OTHELLO: Nay, yet there's more in this?
 I prithee speak to me as to thy thinkings,   150
 As thou dost ruminate, and give thy worst of thoughts
 The worst of words.
IAGO: Good my lord, pardon me:
 Though I am bound to every act of duty,
 I am not bound to that all slaves are free to.   155
 Utter my thoughts? Why, say they are vile and false,
 As where's that palace whereinto foul things
 Sometimes intrude not? Who has that breast so pure
 But some uncleanly apprehensions
 Keep leets and law days,° and in sessions sit   160
 With meditations lawful?
OTHELLO: Thou dost conspire against thy friend, Iago,
 If thou but think'st him wronged, and mak'st his ear
 A stranger to thy thoughts.
IAGO: I do beseech you—   165
 Though I perchance am vicious in my guess
 (As I confess it is my nature's plague
 To spy into abuses, and of my jealousy
 Shape faults that are not), that your wisdom
 From one that so imperfectly conceits   170
 Would take no notice, nor build yourself a trouble
 Out of his scattering and unsure observance.
 It were not for your quiet nor your good,

---

  137 stops: interruptions. 139 of custom: customary. 140 close dilations: expressions of hidden thoughts. 160 leets and law days: meetings of local courts.

Nor for my manhood, honesty, and wisdom,
To let you know my thoughts.   175
OTHELLO: What dost thou mean?
IAGO: Good name in man and woman, dear my lord,
   Is the immediate jewel of their souls.
   Who steals my purse steals trash; 'tis something, nothing;
   'Twas mine, 'tis his, and has been slave to thousands;   180
   But he that filches from me my good name
   Robs me of that which not enriches him
   And makes me poor indeed.
OTHELLO: By heaven, I'll know thy thoughts!
IAGO: You cannot, if my heart were in your hand;   185
   Nor shall not whilst 'tis in my custody.
OTHELLO: Ha!
IAGO: O, beware, my lord, of jealousy!
   It is the green-eyed monster, which doth mock
   The meat it feeds on. That cuckold lives in bliss   190
   Who, certain of his fate, loves not his wronger;
   But O, what damnèd minutes tells° he o'er
   Who dotes, yet doubts—suspects, yet fondly° loves!
OTHELLO: O misery.
IAGO: Poor and content is rich, and rich enough;   195
   But riches fineless° is as poor as winter
   To him that ever fears he shall be poor.
   Good God the souls of all my tribe defend
   From jealousy!
OTHELLO: Why? Why is this?   200
   Think'st thou I'd make a life of jealousy,
   To follow still° the changes of the moon
   With fresh suspicions? No! To be once in doubt
   Is to be resolved. Exchange me for a goat
   When I shall turn the business of my soul   205
   To such exsufflicate and blown° surmises,
   Matching thy inference. 'Tis not to make me jealous
   To say my wife is fair, feeds well, loves company,
   Is free of speech, sings, plays, and dances;
   Where virtue is, these are more virtuous.   210
   Nor from mine own weak merits will I draw
   The smallest fear or doubt of her revolt,
   For she had eyes, and chose me. No, Iago;

---

192 tells: counts.   193 fondly: foolishly.   196 fineless: infinite.   202 To follow still:
to change always (as the phases of the moon).   206 exsufflicate and blown: inflated and
flyblown.

I'll see before I doubt; when I doubt, prove;
And on the proof there is no more but this: 215
Away at once with love or jealousy!

IAGO: I am glad of this; for now I shall have reason
To show the love and duty that I bear you
With franker spirit. Therefore, as I am bound,
Receive it from me. I speak not yet of proof. 220
Look to your wife; observe her well with Cassio;
Wear your eyes thus: not jealous nor secure.
I would not have your free and noble nature
Out of self-bounty° be abused. Look to't.
I know our country disposition well 225
In Venice they do let heaven see the pranks
They dare not show their husbands; their best conscience
Is not to leave't undone, but kept unknown.°

OTHELLO: Dost thou say so?

IAGO: She did deceive her father, marrying you; 230
And when she seemed to shake and fear your looks,
She loved them most.

OTHELLO: And so she did.

IAGO: Why, go to then!
She that so young could give out such a seeming 235
To seel° her father's eyes up close as oak°—
He thought 'twas witchcraft. But I am much to blame.
I humbly do beseech you of your pardon
For too much loving you.

OTHELLO: I am bound to thee forever. 240

IAGO: I see this hath a little dashed your spirits.

OTHELLO: Not a jot, not a jot.

IAGO: Trust me, I fear it has.
I hope you will consider what is spoke
Comes from my love. But I do see y' are moved. 245
I am to pray you not to strain° my speech
To grosser issues, nor to larger reach°
Than to suspicion.

OTHELLO: I will not.

IAGO: Should you do so, my lord, 250
My speech should fall into such vile success

---

224 self-bounty: innate kindness (which attributes his own motives to others).
227–28 their . . . unknown: i.e., their morality does not forbid adultery, but it does forbid
being found out.   236 seel: hoodwink.   236 oak: (a close-grained wood).   246 strain:
enlarge the meaning of.   247 reach: meaning.

Which my thoughts aimed not. Cassio's my worthy friend—
My lord, I see y' are moved.
OTHELLO: No, not much moved.
　I do not think but Desdemona's honest.   255
IAGO:　Long live she so. And long live you to think so.
OTHELLO:　And yet, how nature erring from itself—
IAGO:　Ay, there's the point, as (to be bold with you)
　Not to affect many proposèd matches
　Of her own clime, complexion, and degree,°   260
　Whereto we see in all things nature tends°—
　Foh! one may smell in such a will most rank,
　Foul disproportions, thoughts unnatural.
　But, pardon me, I do not in position°
　Distinctly° speak of her; though I may fear   265
　Her will, recoiling to her better judgment,
　May fall to match° you with her country forms,°
　And happily° repent.
OTHELLO: Farewell, farewell!
　If more thou dost perceive, let me know more.   270
　Set on thy wife to observe. Leave me, Iago.
IAGO:　My lord, I take my leave.   [Going.]
OTHELLO:　Why did I marry? This honest creature doubtless
　Sees and knows more, much more, than he unfolds.
IAGO [Returns.]:　My lord, I would I might entreat your honor   275
　To scan this thing no farther. Leave it to time.
　Although 'tis fit that Cassio have his place,
　For sure he fills it up with great ability,
　Yet, if you please to hold him off awhile,
　You shall by that perceive him and his means.   280
　Note if your lady strain his entertainment°
　With any strong or vehement importunity;
　Much will be seen in that. In the meantime
　Let me be thought too busy in my fears
　(As worthy cause I have to fear I am)   285
　And hold her free, I do beseech your honor.
OTHELLO:　Fear not my government.°

---

260 degree: social station.　261 in . . . tends: i.e., all things in nature seek out their
own kind.　264 position: general argument.　265 Distinctly: specifically.　267 fall to
match: happen to compare.　267 country forms: i.e., the familiar appearances of her
countrymen.　268 happily: by chance.　281 strain his entertainment: urge strongly that
he be reinstated.　287 government: self-control.

IAGO: I once more take my leave.   *Exit.*
OTHELLO: This fellow's of exceeding honesty,
    And knows all qualities,° with a learnèd spirit   290
    Of human dealings. If I do prove her haggard,°
    Though that her jesses° were my dear heartstrings,
    I'd whistle her off and let her down the wind°
    To prey at fortune. Haply for° I am black
    And have not those soft parts° of conversation   295
    That chamberers° have, or for I am declined
    Into the vale of years—yet that's not much—
    She's gone. I am abused, and my relief
    Must be to loathe her. O curse of marriage,
    That we can call these delicate creatures ours,   300
    And not their appetites! I had rather be a toad
    And live upon the vapor of a dungeon
    Than keep a corner in the thing I love
    For others' uses. Yet 'tis the plague to great ones;
    Prerogatived are they less than the base.   305
    'Tis destiny unshunnable, like death.
    Even then this forkèd° plague is fated to us
    When we do quicken.° Look where she comes.

Enter DESDEMONA *and* EMILIA.

    If she be false, heaven mocked itself!
    I'll not believe't.   310
DESDEMONA: How now, my dear Othello?
    Your dinner, and the generous islanders
    By you invited, do attend° your presence.
OTHELLO: I am to blame.
DESDEMONA: Why do you speak so faintly?   315
    Are you not well?
OTHELLO: I have a pain upon my forehead, here.°
DESDEMONA: Why, that's with watching; 'twill away again.
    Let me but bind it hard, within this hour

---

290 qualities: natures, types of people.   291 haggard: a partly trained hawk which has gone wild again.   292 jesses: straps which held the hawk's legs to the trainer's wrist. 293 I'd . . . wind: I would release her (like an untamable hawk) and let her fly free. 294 Haply for: it may be because.   295 soft parts: gentle qualities and manners. 296 chamberers: courtiers—or perhaps, accomplished seducers.   307 forkèd: horned (the sign of the cuckold was horns).   308 do quicken: are born.   313 attend: wait. 317 here: (he points to his imaginary horns).

It will be well.   320
OTHELLO: Your napkin° is too little;
       [*He pushes the handkerchief away, and it falls.*]
  Let it° alone. Come, I'll go in with you.
DESDEMONA: I am very sorry that you are not well.

Exit [*with* OTHELLO].

EMILIA: I am glad I have found this napkin;
  This was her first remembrance from the Moor.   325
  My wayward husband hath a hundred times
  Wooed me to steal it; but she so loves the token
  (For he conjured her she should ever keep it)
  That she reserves it evermore about her
  To kiss and talk to. I'll have the work ta'en out°   330
  And give't Iago. What he will do with it,
  Heaven knows, not I; I nothing° but to please his fantasy.°

Enter IAGO.

IAGO: How now? What do you here alone?
EMILIA: Do not you chide; I have a thing for you.
IAGO: You have a thing for me? It is a common thing—   335
EMILIA: Ha?
IAGO: To have a foolish wife.
EMILIA: O, is that all? What will you give me now
  For that same handkerchief?
IAGO: What handkerchief?   340
EMILIA: What handkerchief?
  Why, that the Moor first gave to Desdemona,
  That which so often you did bid me steal.
IAGO: Hast stol'n it from her?
EMILIA: No, but she let it drop by negligence,   345
  And to th' advantage,° I, being here, took't up.
  Look, here 't is.
IAGO: A good wench. Give it me.

---

321 **napkin:** elaborately worked handkerchief.   322 **it:** (it makes a considerable difference in the interpretation of later events whether this "it" refers to Othello's forehead or to the handkerchief; nothing in the text makes the reference clear).   330 **work ta'en out:** needlework copied.   332 **I nothing:** I wish nothing.   332 **fantasy:** fancy, whim. 346 **to th' advantage:** being lucky.

EMILIA: What will you do with't, that you have been so earnest
 To have me filch it?   350

IAGO: Why, what is that to you?

                   [Takes it.]

EMILIA: If it be not for some purpose of import,°
 Give't me again. Poor lady, she'll run mad
 When she shall lack° it.

IAGO: Be not acknown on't.°   355
 I have use for it. Go, leave me.   *Exit* EMILIA.
 I will in Cassio's lodging lose this napkin
 And let him find it. Trifles light as air
 Are to the jealous confirmations strong
 As proofs of Holy Writ. This may do something. 360
 The Moor already changes with my poison:
 Dangerous conceits are in their natures poisons,
 Which at the first are scarce found to distaste,°
 But, with a little,° act upon the blood,
 Burn like the mines of sulfur. I did say so.   365

 Enter OTHELLO.

 Look where he comes! Not poppy nor mandragora,°
 Nor all the drowsy syrups of the world,
 Shall ever medicine thee to that sweet sleep
 Which thou owedst° yesterday.

OTHELLO: Ha! ha! False to me?   370

IAGO: Why, how now, general? No more of that.

OTHELLO: Avaunt! be gone! Thou hast set me on the rack.
 I swear 'tis better to be much abused
 Than but to know't a little.

IAGO: How now, my lord?   375

OTHELLO: What sense had I of her stol'n hours of lust?
 I saw't not, thought it not, it harmed not me;
 I slept the next night well, fed well, was free and merry;
 I found not Cassio's kisses on her lips.
 He that is robbed, not wanting° what is stol'n,   380
 Let him not know't, and he's not robbed at all.

---

 352 import: importance. 354 lack: miss. 355 Be not acknown on't: forget you ever
saw it. 363 are scarce found to distaste: scarcely can be tasted. 364 with a little: in a
short time. 366 poppy nor mandragora: (soporifics). 369 owedst: possessed.
380 wanting: missing.

IAGO: I am sorry to hear this.
OTHELLO: I had been happy if the general camp,
   Pioners° and all, had tasted her sweet body,
   So I had nothing known. O now, forever   385
   Farewell the tranquil mind! Farewell content!
   Farewell the plumèd troops, and the big wars
   That makes ambition virtue! O, farewell!
   Farewell the neighing steed and the shrill trump,
   The spirit-stirring drum, th' ear-piercing fife,   390
   The royal banner, and all quality,
   Pride, pomp, and circumstance° of glorious war!
   And O you mortal engines° whose rude throats
   Th' immortal Jove's dread clamors° counterfeit,
   Farewell! Othello's occupation's gone!   395
IAGO: Is't possible, my lord?
OTHELLO: Villain, be sure thou prove my love a whore!
   Be sure of it; give me the ocular proof;
   Or, by the worth of mine eternal soul,
   Thou hadst been better have been born a dog   400
   Than answer my waked wrath!
IAGO: Is't come to this?
OTHELLO: Make me to see't; or at the least so prove it
   That the probation° bear no hinge nor loop
   To hang a doubt on—or woe upon thy life!   405
IAGO: My noble lord—
OTHELLO: If thou dost slander her and torture me,
   Never pray more; abandon all remorse;
   On horror's head horrors accumulate;
   Do deeds to make heaven weep, all earth amazed;   410
   For nothing canst thou to damnation add
   Greater than that.
IAGO: O grace! O heaven forgive me!
   Are you a man? Have you a soul or sense?
   God b' wi' you! Take mine office. O wretched fool,   415
   That lov'st to make thine honesty a vice!
   O monstrous world! Take note, take note, O world,
   To be direct and honest is not safe.
   I thank you for this profit, and from hence

---

384 Pioners: (the basest manual laborers in the army, who dug trenches and mines).
392 circumstance: pageantry.   393 mortal engines: lethal weapons, i.e., cannon.
394 clamors: i.e., thunder.   404 probation: proof.

I'll love no friend, sith° love breeds such offense.   420
OTHELLO: Nay, stay. Thou shouldst be honest.
IAGO: I should be wise; for honesty's a fool
    And loses that it works for.
OTHELLO: By the world,
    I think my wife be honest, and think she is not;   425
    I think that thou art just, and think thou art not.
    I'll have some proof. My name, that was as fresh
    As Dian's° visage, is now begrimed and black
    As mine own face. If there be cords, or knives,
    Poison, or fire, or suffocating streams,   430
    I'll not endure it. Would I were satisfied!
IAGO: I see you are eaten up with passion.
    I do repent me that I put it to you.
    You would be satisfied?
OTHELLO: Would? Nay, and I will.   435
IAGO: And may; but how? How satisfied, my lord?
    Would you, the supervisor,° grossly gape on?
    Behold her topped?
OTHELLO: Death and damnation! O!
IAGO: It were a tedious° difficulty, I think,   440
    To bring them to that prospect.° Damn them then,
    If ever mortal eyes do see them bolster°
    More than their own! What then? How then?
    What shall I say? Where's satisfaction?
    It is impossible you should see this,   445
    Were they as prime° as goats, as hot as monkeys,
    As salt° as wolves in pride,° and fools as gross
    As ignorance made drunk. But yet, I say,
    If imputation and strong circumstances
    Which lead directly to the door of truth   450
    Will give you satisfaction, you might have't.
OTHELLO: Give me a living reason she's disloyal.
IAGO: I do not like the office.°
    But sith I am entered in this cause so far,
    Pricked° to't by foolish honesty and love,   455
    I will go on. I lay with Cassio lately,

---

420 sith: since.   428 Dian's: Diana's (goddess of the moon and of chastity).
437 supervisor: onlooker.   440 tedious: hard to arrange.   441 prospect: sight (where
they can be seen).   442 bolster: go to bed.   446–47 prime, salt: lustful.   447 pride:
heat.   453 office: duty.   455 Pricked: spurred.

And being troubled with a raging tooth,
I could not sleep.
There are a kind of men so loose of soul
That in their sleeps will mutter their affairs.   460
One of this kind is Cassio.
In sleep I heard him say, "Sweet Desdemona,
Let us be wary, let us hide our loves!"
And then, sir, would he gripe° and wring my hand,
Cry "O sweet creature!" Then kiss me hard,   465
As if he plucked up kisses by the roots
That grew upon my lips; laid his leg o'er my thigh,
And sigh, and kiss, and then cry, "Cursèd fate
That gave thee to the Moor!"

OTHELLO: O monstrous! monstrous!   470
IAGO: Nay, this was but his dream.
OTHELLO: But this denoted a foregone conclusion,°
'Tis a shrewd doubt,° though it be but a dream.
IAGO: And this may help to thicken other proofs
That do demonstrate° thinly.   475
OTHELLO: I'll tear her all to pieces!
IAGO: Nay, yet be wise. Yet we see nothing done;
She may be honest yet. Tell me but this:
Have you not sometimes seen a handkerchief
Spotted with strawberries in your wife's hand?   480
OTHELLO: I gave her such a one; 'twas my first gift.
IAGO: I know not that; but such a handkerchief—
I am sure it was your wife's—did I today
See Cassio wipe his beard with.
OTHELLO: If it be that—   485
IAGO: If it be that, or any that was hers,
It speaks against her with the other proofs.
OTHELLO: O, that the slave had forty thousand lives!
One is too poor, too weak for my revenge.
Now do I see 'tis true. Look here, Iago: 490
All my fond love thus do I blow to heaven.
'Tis gone.
Arise, black vengeance, from the hollow hell!
Yield up, O Love, thy crown and hearted° throne
To tyrannous hate! Swell, bosom, with thy fraught,°   495

---

464 gripe: seize.   472 foregone conclusion: consummated fact.   473 shrewd doubt:
penetrating guess.   475 demonstrate: show, appear.   494 hearted: seated in the heart.
495 fraught: burden.

For 'tis of aspics° tongues.

IAGO: Yet be content.°

OTHELLO: O, blood, blood, blood!

IAGO: Patience, I say. Your mind may change.

OTHELLO: Never, Iago. Like to the Pontic Sea,°   500

Whose icy current and compulsive course

Nev'r keeps retiring ebb, but keeps due on

To the Propontic and the Hellespont,

Even so my bloody thoughts, with violent pace,

Shall nev'r look back, nev'r ebb to humble love,   505

Till that a capable and wide° revenge

Swallow them up. [*He kneels.*] Now, by yond mable heaven,

In the due reverence of a sacred vow

I here engage my words.

IAGO: Do not rise yet.   510

[IAGO *kneels.*]

Witness, you ever-burning lights above,

You elements that clip° us round about,

Witness that here Iago doth give up

The execution° of his wit, hands, heart

To wronged Othello's service! Let him command,   515

And to obey shall be in me remorse,°

What bloody business ever.° [*They rise.*]

OTHELLO: I greet thy love,

Not with vain thanks but with acceptance bounteous,°

And will upon the instant put thee to't.°   520

Within these three days let me hear thee say

That Cassio's not alive.

IAGO: My friend is dead. 'Tis done at your request.

But let her live.

OTHELLO: Damn her, lewd minx! O, damn her! Damn her!   525

Come, go with me apart. I will withdraw

To furnish me with some swift means of death

For the fair devil. Now art thou my lieutenant.

IAGO: I am your own forever.   *Exeunt.*

---

496 aspics': asps'.   497 content: patient, quiet.   500 Pontic Sea: the Black Sea (famous for the strong and constant current with which it flows through the Bosporus into the Mediterranean, where the water level is lower).   506 capable and wide: sufficient and far-reaching.   512 clip: enfold.   514 execution: workings, action.   516 remorse: pity.   517 ever: soever.   519 bounteous: absolute.   520 to't: i.e., to the work you have said you are prepared to do.

Scene 4. [*A street.*]

Enter DESDEMONA, EMILIA, *and* CLOWN.

DESDEMONA: Do you know, sirrah, where Lieutenant Cassio lies?°
CLOWN: I dare not say he lies anywhere.
DESDEMONA: Why, man?
CLOWN: He's a soldier, and for me to say a soldier lies, 'tis stabbing.
DESDEMONA: Go to. Where lodges he?   5
CLOWN: To tell you where he lodges is to tell you where I lie.
DESDEMONA: Can anything be made of this?
CLOWN: I know not where he lodges, and for me to devise a lodging, and
    say he lies here or he lies there, were to lie in mine own throat.°
DESDEMONA: Can you enquire him out, and be edified° by report?   10
CLOWN: I will catechize the world for him; that is, make questions, and
    by them answer.
DESDEMONA: Seek him, bid him come hither. Tell him I have moved° my
    lord on his behalf and hope all will be well.
CLOWN: To do this is within the compass° of man's wit, and therefore I   15
    will attempt the doing it.   *Exit* CLOWN.
DESDEMONA: Where should° I lose the handkerchief, Emilia?
EMILIA: I know not, madam.
DESDEMONA: Believe me, I had rather have lost my purse
    Full of crusadoes.° And but my noble Moor   20
    Is true of mind, and made of no such baseness
    As jealous creatures are, it were enough
    To put him to ill thinking.
EMILIA: Is he not jealous?
DESDEMONA: Who? He? I think the sun where he was born   25
    Drew all such humors° from him.
EMILIA: Look where he comes.

Enter OTHELLO.

DESDEMONA: I will not leave him now till Cassio
    Be called to him. How is't with you, my lord?

III.4.1 lies: lodges.   9 lie in mine own throat: (to lie in the throat is to lie absolutely
and completely).   10 edified: enlightened (Desdemona mocks the Clown's overly elaborate diction).   13 moved: pleaded with.   15 compass: reach.   17 should: might.
20 crusadoes: Portuguese gold coins.   26 humors: characteristics.

OTHELLO: Well, my good lady. [*Aside*] O, hardness to dissemble!°— 30
    How do you, Desdemona?
DESDEMONA: Well, my good lord.
OTHELLO: Give me your hand. This hand is moist,° my lady.
DESDEMONA: It hath felt no age nor known no sorrow.
OTHELLO: This argues° fruitfulness and liberal° heart. 35
    Hot, hot, and moist. This hand of yours requires
    A sequester° from liberty; fasting and prayer;
    Much castigation; exercise devout;
    For here's a young and sweating devil here
    That commonly rebels. 'Tis a good hand, 40
    A frank one.
DESDEMONA: You may, indeed, say so;
    For 'twas that hand that gave away my heart.
OTHELLO: A liberal hand! The hearts of old gave hands,
    But our new heraldry° is hands, not hearts. 45
DESDEMONA: I cannot speak of this. Come now, your promise!
OTHELLO: What promise, chuck?
DESDEMONA: I have sent to bid Cassio come speak with you.
OTHELLO: I have a salt and sorry rheum° offends me.
    Lend me thy handkerchief. 50
DESDEMONA: Here, my lord.
OTHELLO: That which I gave you.
DESDEMONA: I have it not about me.
OTHELLO: Not?
DESDEMONA: No, indeed, my lord. 55
OTHELLO: That's a fault.
    That handkerchief
    Did an Egyptian to my mother give.
    She was a charmer,° and could almost read
    The thoughts of people. She told her, while she kept it 60
    'Twould make her amiable° and subdue my father
    Entirely to her love; but if she lost it
    Or made a gift of it, my father's eye

---

30 hardness to dissemble: (Othello may refer here either to the difficulty he has in maintaining his appearance of composure, or to what he believes to be Desdemona's hardened hypocrisy). 33 moist: (a moist, hot hand was taken as a sign of a lustful nature). 35 argues: suggests. 35 liberal: free, open (but also with a suggestion of "licentious"; from here on in this scene Othello's words bear a double meaning, seeming to be normal but accusing Desdemona of being unfaithful). 37 sequester: separation. 45 heraldry: heraldic symbolism. 49 a salt and sorry rheum: a heavy, running head cold. 59 charmer: magician. 61 amiable: desirable.

Should hold her loathèd, and his spirits should hunt
After new fancies. She, dying, gave it me,   65
And bid me, when my fate would have me wived,
To give it her. I did so; and take heed on't;
Make it a darling like your precious eye.
To lose't or give't away were such perdition
As nothing else could match.   70
DESDEMONA: Is't possible?
OTHELLO: 'Tis true. There's magic in the web° of it.
A sibyl that had numbered in the world
The sun to course two hundred compasses,
In her prophetic fury° sewed the work;   75
The worms were hallowed that did breed the silk,
And it was dyed in mummy° which the skillful
Conserved of maidens' hearts.
DESDEMONA: Indeed? Is't true?
OTHELLO: Most veritable. Therefore look to't well.   80
DESDEMONA: Then would to God that I had never seen't!
OTHELLO: Ha! Wherefore?
DESDEMONA: Why do you speak so startingly and rash?
OTHELLO: Is't lost? Is't gone? Speak, is it out o' th' way?
DESDEMONA: Heaven bless us!   85
OTHELLO: Say you?
DESDEMONA: It is not lost. But what an if it were?
OTHELLO: How?
DESDEMONA: I say it is not lost.
OTHELLO: Fetch't, let me see't!   90
DESDEMONA: Why, so I can; but I will not now.
This is a trick to put me from my suit:
Pray you let Cassio be received again.
OTHELLO: Fetch me the handkerchief! My mind misgives.
DESDEMONA: Come, come!   95
You'll never meet a more sufficient° man—
OTHELLO: The handkerchief!
DESDEMONA: A man that all his time
Hath founded his good fortunes on your love,
Shared dangers with you—   100
OTHELLO: The handkerchief!
DESDEMONA: I'faith, you are to blame.
OTHELLO: Away!   *Exit* OTHELLO.

---

72 web: weaving.   75 prophetic fury: seized by the spirit and able to prophesy.
77 mummy: liquid drained from embalmed bodies.   96 sufficient: complete, with all
proper qualities.

EMILIA: Is not this man jealous?

DESDEMONA: I nev'r saw this before.   105
   Sure there's some wonder in this handkerchief;
   I am most unhappy in the loss of it.

EMILIA: 'Tis not a year or two shows us a man.
   They are all but stomachs, and we all but food;
   They eat us hungerly, and when they are full,   110
   They belch us.

   Enter IAGO *and* CASSIO.

               Look you, Cassio and my husband.

IAGO: There is no other way; 'tis she must do't.
   And lo the happiness! Go and importune her.

DESDEMONA: How now, good Cassio? What's the news with you?   115

CASSIO: Madam, my former suit. I do beseech you
   That by your virtuous means I may again
   Exist, and be a member of his love
   Whom I with all the office° of my heart
   Entirely honor. I would not be delayed.   120
   If my offense be of such mortal kind
   That nor my service past, nor present sorrows,
   Nor purposed merit in futurity,
   Can ransom me into his love again,
   But to know so must be my benefit.°   125
   So shall I clothe me in a forced content,
   And shut myself up in some other course
   To fortune's alms.

DESDEMONA:　　　　　Alas, thrice-gentle Cassio,
   My advocation° is not now in tune.   130
   My lord is not my lord; nor should I know him
   Were he in favor° as in humor altered.
   So help me every spirit sanctified
   As I have spoken for you all my best
   And stood within the blank° of his displeasure   135
   For my free speech. You must awhile be patient.
   What I can do I will; and more I will
   Than for myself I dare. Let that suffice you.

IAGO: Is my lord angry?

EMILIA:　　　　　　　He went hence but now,   140
   And certainly in strange unquietness.

---

119 office: duty.   125 benefit: good.   130 advocation: advocacy.   132 favor:
countenance.   135 blank: bull's-eye of a target.

IAGO: Can he be angry? I have seen the cannon
   When it hath blown his ranks into the air
   And, like the devil, from his very arm
   Puffed his own brother. And is he angry?   145
   Something of moment° then. I will go meet him.
   There's matter in't indeed if he be angry.
DESDEMONA: I prithee do so.   *Exit* [IAGO].
                       Something sure of state,°
   Either from Venice or some unhatched practice°   150
   Made demonstrable here in Cyprus to him,
   Hath puddled° his clear spirit; and in such cases
   Men's natures wrangle with inferior things,
   Though great ones are their object. 'Tis even so.
   For let our finger ache, and it endues°   155
   Our other, healthful members even to a sense
   Of pain. Nay, we must think men are not gods,
   Nor of them look for such observancy
   As fits the bridal. Beshrew me much, Emilia,
   I was, unhandsome warrior as I am,   160
   Arraigning his unkindness with my soul;
   But now I find I had suborned the witness,
   And he's indicted falsely.
EMILIA: Pray heaven it be
   State matters, as you think, and no conception   165
   Nor no jealous toy° concerning you.
DESDEMONA: Alas the day! I never gave him cause.
EMILIA: But jealous souls will not be answered so;
   They are not ever jealous for the cause,
   But jealous for they're jealous. It is a monster   170
   Begot upon itself, born on itself.
DESDEMONA: Heaven keep the monster from Othello's mind!
EMILIA: Lady, amen.
DESDEMONA: I will go seek him. Cassio, walk here about.
   If I do find him fit,° I'll move your suit   175
   And seek to effect it to my uttermost.
CASSIO: I humbly thank your ladyship.
                    Exit [DESDEMONA *with* EMILIA].

Enter BIANCA.

---

  146 moment: importance.   149 of state: state affairs.   150 unhatched practice:
undisclosed plot.   152 puddled: muddied.   155 endues: leads.   166 toy: trifle.   175
fit: receptive.

BIANCA: Save you, friend Cassio!

CASSIO: What make you from home?
How is't with you, my most fair Bianca?   180
I' faith, sweet love, I was coming to your house.

BIANCA: And I was going to your lodging, Cassio.
What, keep a week away? Seven days and nights?
Eightscore eight hours? And lovers' absent hours
More tedious than the dial eightscore times?   185
O weary reck'ning.°

CASSIO: Pardon me, Bianca.
I have this while with leaden thoughts been pressed,
But I shall in a more continuate° time
Strike off this score° of absence. Sweet Bianca,   190

                        [*Gives her* DESDEMONA's *handkerchief.*]

Take me this work out.

BIANCA: O Cassio, whence came this?
This is some token from a newer friend.
To the felt absence now I feel a cause.
Is't come to this? Well, well.   195

CASSIO: Go to, woman!
Throw your vile guesses in the devil's teeth,
From whence you have them. You are jealous now
That this is from some mistress, some remembrance.
No, by my faith, Bianca.   200

BIANCA: Why, whose is it?

CASSIO: I know not neither; I found it in my chamber.
I like the work well; ere it be demanded,°
As like enough it will, I would have it copied.
Take it and do't, and leave me for this time.   205

BIANCA: Leave you? Wherefore?

CASSIO: I do attend here on the general
And think it no addition, nor my wish,
To have him see me womaned.

BIANCA: Why, I pray you?   210

CASSIO: Not that I love you not.

BIANCA: But that you do not love me!
I pray you bring° me on the way a little,

---

186 reck'ning: addition.   189 continuate: uninterrupted.   190 Strike off this score:
i.e., pay this bill (the *score* being the account of drinks kept in a tavern).   203 demanded:
asked for (by the person who lost it).   213 bring: accompany.

And say if I shall see you soon at night.
CASSIO: 'Tis but a little way that I can bring you,   215
    For I attend here; but I'll see you soon.
BIANCA: 'Tis very good. I must be circumstanced.°

                                        Exeunt omnes.

ACT IV

Scene 1. [*A street.*]

Enter OTHELLO *and* IAGO.

IAGO: Will you think so?
OTHELLO: Think so, Iago?
IAGO: What,
    To kiss in private?
OTHELLO: An unauthorized° kiss?   5
IAGO: Or to be naked with her friend in bed
    An hour or more, not meaning any harm?
OTHELLO: Naked in bed, Iago, and not mean harm?
    It is hypocrisy against the devil.
    They that mean virtuously, and yet do so,   10
    The devil their virtue tempts, and they tempt heaven.
IAGO: If they do nothing, 'tis a venial slip.
    But if I give my wife a handkerchief—
OTHELLO: What then?
IAGO: Why, then 'tis hers, my lord; and being hers,   15
    She may, I think, bestow't on any man.
OTHELLO: She is protectress of her honor too.
    May she give that?
IAGO: Her honor is an essence that's not seen;
    They have it very oft that have it not.   20
    But for the handkerchief—
OTHELLO: By heaven, I would most gladly have forgot it!
    Thou said'st—O, it comes o'er my memory
    As doth the raven° o'er the infected house,
    Boding to all—he had my handkerchief.   25

_____

217 circumstanced: accept things as they are. IV.1.5 unauthorized: illicit. 24
raven: (a harbinger of death).

IAGO: Ay, what of that?

OTHELLO: That's not so good now.

IAGO: What if I had said I had seen him do you wrong?
Or heard him say—as knaves be such abroad°
Who having, by their own importunate suit,   30
Or voluntary dotage° of some mistress,
Convincèd or supplied° them, cannot choose
But they must blab—

OTHELLO: Hath he said anything?

IAGO: He hath, my lord; but be you well assured,   35
No more than he'll unswear.

OTHELLO: What hath he said?

IAGO: Why, that he did—I know not what he did.

OTHELLO: What? what?

IAGO: Lie—   40

OTHELLO: With her?

IAGO: With her, on her; what you will.

OTHELLO: Lie with her? Lie on her?—We say lie on her when they belie her.—Lie with her! Zounds, that's fulsome.°— Handkerchief—con-
fessions—handkerchief!—To confess, and be hanged for his labor—first   45
to be hanged, and then to confess! I tremble at it. Nature would not invest herself in such shadowing passion without some instruction.° It is
not words that shakes me thus.—Pish! Noses, ears, and lips? Is't possible?—Confess?—Handkerchief—O devil!   *Falls in a trance.*

IAGO: Work on.   50
My med'cine works! Thus credulous fools are caught,
And many worthy and chaste dames even thus,
All guiltless, meet reproach.° What, ho! My lord!
My lord, I say! Othello!

Enter CASSIO.

How now, Cassio?   55

CASSIO: What's the matter?

---

29 abroad: i.e., in the world. 31 voluntary dotage: weakness of the will.
32 Convinced or supplied: persuaded or gratified (the mistress). 44 fulsome: foul, repulsive. 47–48 Nature . . . instruction: i.e., my mind would not become so darkened
(with anger) unless there were something in this (accusation); (it should be remembered
that Othello believes in the workings of magic and supernatural forces). 53 reproach:
shame.

IAGO: My lord is fall'n into an epilepsy.
   This is his second fit; he had one yesterday.
CASSIO: Rub him about the temples.
IAGO: The lethargy° must have his quiet course.   60
   If not, he foams at mouth, and by and by
   Breaks out to savage madness. Look, he stirs.
   Do you withdraw yourself a little while.
   He will recover straight. When he is gone,
   I would on great occasion° speak with you.   65

                                        [*Exit* CASSIO.]

   How is it, general? Have you not hurt your head?
OTHELLO: Dost thou mock° me?
IAGO: I mock you not, by heaven.
   Would you would bear your fortune like a man.
OTHELLO: A hornèd man's a monster and a beast.   70
IAGO: There's many a beast then in a populous city,
   And many a civil° monster.
OTHELLO: Did he confess it?
IAGO: Good, sir, be a man.
   Think every bearded fellow that's but yoked   75
   May draw° with you. There's millions now alive
   That nightly lie in those unproper° beds
   Which they dare swear peculiar.° Your case is better.
   O, 'tis the spite of hell, the fiend's arch-mock,
   To lip a wanton in a secure couch,   80
   And to suppose her chaste. No, let me know;
   And knowing what I am, I know what she shall be.
OTHELLO: O, thou art wise! 'Tis certain.
IAGO: Stand you awhile apart;
   Confine yourself but in a patient list.°   85
   Whilst you were here, o'erwhelmèd with your grief—
   A passion most unsuiting such a man—
   Cassio came hither. I shifted him away°
   And laid good 'scuses upon your ecstasy;°
   Bade him anon return, and here speak with me;   90

---

60 lethargy: coma.   65 great occasion: very important matter.   67 mock: Othello
takes Iago's comment as a reference to his horns—which it is).   72 civil: city-dwelling.
76 draw: i.e., like the horned ox.   77 unproper: i.e., not exclusively the husband's.   78
peculiar: their own alone.   85 a patient list: the bounds of patience.   88 shifted him
away: got rid of him by a stratagem.   89 ecstasy: trance (the literal meaning, "outside
one-self," bears on the meaning of the change Othello is undergoing).

The which he promised. Do but encave° yourself
And mark the fleers,° the gibes, and notable° scorns
That dwell in every region of his face.
For I will make him tell the tale anew:
Where, how, how oft, how long ago, and when   95
He hath, and is again to cope your wife.
I say, but mark his gesture. Marry patience,
Or I shall say you're all in all in spleen,°
And nothing of a man.

OTHELLO: Dost thou hear, Iago?   100
I will be found most cunning in my patience;
But—dost thou hear?—most bloody.

IAGO: That's not amiss;
But yet keep time in all. Will you withdraw?

[OTHELLO *moves to one side, where his remarks are not audible to*
CASSIO *and* IAGO.]

Now will I question Cassio of Bianca,   105
A huswife° that by selling her desires
Buys herself bread and cloth. It is a creature
That dotes on Cassio, as 'tis the strumpet's plague
To beguile many and be beguiled by one.
He, when he hears of her, cannot restrain   110
From the excess of laughter. Here he comes.

Enter CASSIO.

As he shall smile, Othello shall go mad;
And his unbookish° jealousy must conster°
Poor Cassio's smiles, gestures, and light behaviors
Quite in the wrong. How do you, lieutenant?   115

CASSIO: The worser that you give me the addition°
Whose want even kills me.

IAGO: Ply Desdemona well, and you are sure on't.
Now, if this suit lay in Bianca's power,
How quickly should you speed!   120

CASSIO: Alas, poor caitiff!°

---

91 encave: hide.   92 fleers: mocking looks or speeches.   92 notable: obvious.
98 spleen: passion, particularly anger.   106 huswife: housewife (but with the special
meaning here of "prostitute").   113 unbookish: ignorant.   113 conster: construe.   116
addition: title   121 caitiff: wretch.

OTHELLO: Look how he laughs already!

IAGO: I never knew woman love man so.

CASSIO: Alas, poor rogue! I think, i' faith, she loves me.

OTHELLO: Now he denies it faintly, and laughs it out.   125

IAGO: Do you hear, Cassio?

OTHELLO: Now he importunes him
   To tell it o'er. Go to! Well said, well said!

IAGO: She gives it out that you shall marry her.
   Do you intend it?   130

CASSIO: Ha, ha, ha!

OTHELLO: Do ye triumph, Roman? Do you triumph?

CASSIO: I marry? What, a customer?° Prithee bear some charity to my
   wit; do not think it so unwholesome. Ha, ha, ha!

OTHELLO: So, so, so, so. They laugh that win.   135

IAGO: Why, the cry goes that you marry her.

CASSIO: Prithee, say true.

IAGO: I am a very villain else.

OTHELLO: Have you scored° me? Well.

CASSIO: This is the monkey's own giving out. She is persuaded I will   140
   marry her out of her own love and flattery, not out of my promise.

OTHELLO: Iago beckons me; now he begins the story.

                                    [OTHELLO *moves close enough to hear.*]

CASSIO: She was here even now; she haunts me in every place. I was the
   other day talking on the sea bank with certain Venetians, and thither
   comes the bauble,° and falls me thus about my neck—   145

OTHELLO: Crying "O dear Cassio!" as it were. His gesture imports it.

CASSIO: So hangs, and lolls, and weeps upon me; so shakes and pulls me!
   Ha, ha, ha!

OTHELLO: Now he tells how she plucked him to my chamber. O, I see that
   nose of yours, but not that dog I shall throw it to.   150

CASSIO: Well, I must leave her company.

IAGO: Before me!° Look where she comes.

Enter BIANCA.

CASSIO: 'Tis such another fitchew!° Marry a perfumed one? What do you
   mean by this haunting of me?

BIANCA: Let the devil and his dam haunt you! What did you mean by that   155
   same handkerchief you gave me even now? I was a fine fool to take it.

---

   133 customer: one who sells, a merchant (here, a prostitute).   139 scored: marked,
defaced.   145 bauble: plaything.   152 Before me!: (an exclamation of surprise).
153 fitchew: polecat, i.e., strong-smelling creature.

I must take out the work? A likely piece of work that you should find it in your chamber and know not who left it there! This is some minx's token, and I must take out the work? There! [*She throws down the handkerchief.*] Give it your hobbyhorse.° Wheresoever you had it, I'll take out no work on't. 160

CASSIO: How now, my sweet Bianca? How now? how now?

OTHELLO: By heaven, that should be my handkerchief!

BIANCA: If you'll come to supper tonight, you may; if you will not, come when you are next prepared for.° *Exit.* 165

IAGO: After her, after her!

CASSIO: Faith, I must; she'll rail in the streets else.

IAGO: Will you sup there?

CASSIO: Yes, I intend so.

IAGO: Well, I may chance to see you, for I would very fain speak with you. 170

CASSIO: Prithee come. Will you?

IAGO: Go to, say no more. [*Exit* CASSIO.]

OTHELLO [*Comes forward.*]: How shall I murder him, Iago?

IAGO: Did you perceive how he laughed at his vice? 175

OTHELLO: O Iago!

IAGO: And did you see the handkerchief?

OTHELLO: Was that mine?

IAGO: Yours, by this hand! And to see how he prizes the foolish woman your wife! She gave it him, and he hath giv'n it his whore. 180

OTHELLO: I would have him nine years a-killing!—A fine woman, a fair woman, a sweet woman?

IAGO: Nay, you must forget that.

OTHELLO: Ay, let her rot, and perish, and be damned tonight; for she shall not live. No, my heart is turned to stone; I strike it, and it hurts my hand. 185 O, the world hath not a sweeter creature! She might lie by an emperor's side and command him tasks.

IAGO: Nay, that's not your way.°

OTHELLO: Hang her! I do but say what she is. So delicate with her needle. An admirable musician. O, she will sing the savageness out of a bear! 190 Of so high and plenteous wit and invention°—

IAGO: She's the worse for all this.

OTHELLO: O, a thousand, a thousand times. And then, of so gentle a condition?°

IAGO: Ay, too gentle. 195

---

160 hobbyhorse: prostitute. 165 next prepared for: next expected—i.e., never. 188 way: proper course. 191 invention: imagination. 193–94 gentle a condition: (1) well born (2) of a gentle nature.

OTHELLO: Nay, that's certain. But yet the pity of it, Iago. O Iago, the pity
 of it, Iago.

IAGO: If you are so fond over her iniquity, give her patent to offend; for
 if it touch° not you, it comes near nobody.

OTHELLO: I will chop her into messes!° Cuckold me!   200

IAGO: O, 'tis foul in her.

OTHELLO: With mine officer!

IAGO: That's fouler.

OTHELLO: Get me some poison, Iago, this night. I'll not expostulate with
 her, lest her body and beauty unprovide my mind° again. This night,   205
 Iago!

IAGO: Do it not with poison. Strangle her in her bed, even the bed she
 hath contaminated.

OTHELLO: Good, good! The justice of it pleases. Very good!

IAGO: And for Cassio, let me be his undertaker.° You shall hear more by   210
 midnight.

OTHELLO: Excellent good!   [A trumpet.]
      What trumpet is that same?

IAGO: I warrant something from Venice.

Enter LODOVICO, DESDEMONA, *and* ATTENDANTS.

                'Tis Lodovico.   215
This comes from the Duke. See, your wife's with him.

LODOVICO: God save you, worthy general.

OTHELLO: With° all my heart, sir.

LODOVICO: The Duke and the senators of Venice greet you.
            [*Gives him a letter.*]

OTHELLO: I kiss the instrument of their pleasures.   220
        [*Opens the letter and reads.*]

DESDEMONA: And what's the news, good cousin Lodovico?

IAGO: I am very glad to see you, signior.
 Welcome to Cyprus.

LODOVICO: I thank you. How does Lieutenant Cassio?

IAGO: Lives, sir.   225

DESDEMONA: Cousin, there's fall'n between him and my lord
 An unkind° breach; but you shall make all well.

OTHELLO: Are you sure of that?

DESDEMONA: My lord?

---

 199 touch: affects.   200 messes: bits.   205 unprovide my mind: undo my resolution.
210 undertaker: (not "burier" but "one who undertakes to do something").
218 With: i.e., I greet you with.   227 unkind: unnatural.

OTHELLO [*Reads*]: "This fail you not to do, as you will—" 230
LODOVICO: He did not call; he's busy in the paper.
    Is there division 'twixt my lord and Cassio?
DESDEMONA: A most unhappy one. I would do much
    T' atone° them, for the love I bear to Cassio.
OTHELLO: Fire and brimstone! 235
DESDEMONA: My lord?
OTHELLO: Are you wise?
DESDEMONA: What, is he angry?
LODOVICO: May be th' letter moved him;
    For, as I think, they do command him home, 240
    Deputing Cassio in his government.°
DESDEMONA: Trust me, I am glad on't.
OTHELLO: Indeed?
DESDEMONA: My lord?
OTHELLO: I am glad to see you mad. 245
DESDEMONA: Why, sweet Othello—
OTHELLO: Devil!   [*Strikes her.*]
DESDEMONA: I have not deserved this.
LODOVICO: My lord, this would not be believed in Venice,
    Though I should swear I saw't. 'Tis very much. 250
    Make her amends; she weeps.
OTHELLO: O devil, devil!
    If that the earth could teem° with woman's tears,
    Each drop she falls° would prove a crocodile.°
    Out of my sight! 255
DESDEMONA: I will not stay to offend you.   [*Going.*]
LODOVICO: Truly, an obedient lady.
    I do beseech your lordship call her back.
OTHELLO: Mistress!
DESDEMONA: My lord? 260
OTHELLO: What would you with her, sir?
LODOVICO: Who? I, my lord?
OTHELLO: Ay! You did wish that I would make her turn.
    Sir, she can turn, and turn, and yet go on
    And turn again; and she can weep, sir, weep; 265
    And she's obedient; as you say, obedient.
    Very obedient. Proceed you in your tears.
    Concerning this, sir—O well-painted passion!

---

234 atone: reconcile. 241 government: office. 253 teem: conceive. 254 falls: drops. 254 crocodile: (the crocodile was supposed to shed false tears to lure its victims).

I am commanded home.—Get you away;
I'll send for you anon.—Sir, I obey the mandate   270
And will return to Venice.—Hence, avaunt!

                                        [*Exit* DESDEMONA.]

Cassio shall have my place. And, sir, tonight
I do entreat that we may sup together.
You are welcome, sir, to Cyprus.—Goats and monkeys!

                                                Exit.

LODOVICO: Is this the noble Moor whom our full Senate   275
Call all in all sufficient? Is this the nature
Whom passion could not shake? whose solid virtue
The shot of accident nor dart of chance
Could neither graze nor pierce?
IAGO: He is much changed.   280
LODOVICO: Are his wits safe? Is he not light of brain?
IAGO: He's that he is; I may not breathe my censure.
What he might be (if, what he might, he is not)
I would to heaven he were!
LODOVICO: What, strike his wife?   285
IAGO: Faith, that was not so well; yet would I knew
That stroke would prove the worst.
LODOVICO: Is it his use?°
Or did the letters work upon his blood°
And new-create his fault?   290
IAGO: Alas, alas!
It is not honesty in me to speak
What I have seen and known. You shall observe him,
And his own courses° will denote him so
That I may save my speech. Do but go after   295
And mark how he continues.
LODOVICO: I am sorry that I am deceived in him.

                                                Exeunt.

Scene 2. [*The citadel.*]

Enter OTHELLO *and* EMILIA.

OTHELLO: You have seen nothing then?
EMILIA: Nor ever heard, nor ever did suspect.

---

288 use: habit.   289 blood: passion.   294 courses: actions.

OTHELLO: Yes, you have seen Cassio and she together.
EMILIA: But then I saw no harm, and then I heard
  Each syllable that breath made up° between them.   5
OTHELLO: What, did they never whisper?
EMILIA: Never, my lord.
OTHELLO: Nor send you out o' th' way?
EMILIA: Never.
OTHELLO: To fetch her fan, her gloves, her mask, nor nothing?   10
EMILIA: Never, my lord.
OTHELLO: That's strange.
EMILIA: I durst, my lord, to wager she is honest,
  Lay down my soul at stake.° If you think other,
  Remove your thought. It doth abuse your bosom.   15
  If any wretch have put this in your head,
  Let heaven requite it with the serpent's curse,°
  For if she be not honest,° chaste, and true,
  There's no man happy. The purest of their wives
  Is foul as slander.   20
OTHELLO: Bid her come hither. Go.

                                              Exit EMILIA.

  She says enough; yet she's a simple bawd°
  That cannot say as much. This is a subtle whore,
  A closet lock and key of villainous secrets,
  And yet she'll kneel and pray; I have seen her do 't.   25

  Enter DESDEMONA *and* EMILIA.

DESDEMONA: My lord, what is your will?
OTHELLO: Pray you, chuck, come hither.
DESDEMONA: What is your pleasure?
OTHELLO: Let me see your eyes.
  Look in my face.   30
DESDEMONA: What horrible fancy's this?
OTHELLO [*To* EMILIA]:   Some of your function,° mistress:
  Leave procreants alone and shut the door;
  Cough or cry hem if anybody come.

IV.2.5 that breath made up: spoken.   14 at stake: as the wager.   17 serpent's curse:
(God's curse on the serpent after the fall in Eden).   18 honest: chaste.   22 bawd:
procuress.   32 Some of your function: do your proper work (as the operator of a
brothel).

Your mystery,° your mystery! Nay, dispatch!   35

                                  Exit EMILIA.

DESDEMONA: Upon my knee, what doth your speech import?

  I understand a fury in your words.°

OTHELLO: Why, what art thou?

DESDEMONA: Your wife, my lord; your true

  And loyal wife.   40

OTHELLO: Come, swear it, damn thyself;

  Lest, being like one of heaven, the devils themselves

  Should fear to seize thee. Therefore be doubledamned:

  Swear thou art honest.

DESDEMONA: Heaven doth truly know it.   45

OTHELLO: Heaven truly knows that thou art false as hell.

DESDEMONA: To whom, my lord? With whom? How am I false?

OTHELLO: Ah, Desdemon! Away! Away! Away!

DESDEMONA: Alas the heavy day! Why do you weep?

  Am I the motive° of these tears, my lord?   50

  If haply° you my father do suspect

  An instrument of this your calling back,

  Lay not your blame on me. If you have lost him,

  I have lost him too.

OTHELLO: Had it pleased heaven   55

  To try me with affliction, had they rained

  All kinds of sores and shames on my bare head,

  Steeped° me in poverty to the very lips,

  Given to captivity me and my utmost hopes,

  I should have found in some place of my soul   60

  A drop of patience. But, alas, to make me

  The fixèd figure for the time of scorn°

  To point his slow and moving finger at.

  Yet could I bear that too, well, very well.

  But there where I have garnered up my heart,   65

  Where either I must live or bear no life,

  The fountain from the which my current runs

  Or else dries up—to be discarded thence,

  Or keep it as a cistern for foul toads

  To knot and gender° in—turn thy complexion there,   70

---

  35 mystery: trade.   37 words: (Q1 adds to this line, "But not the words").   50
motive: cause.   51 haply: by chance.   58 Steeped: submerged.   62 The . . . scorn: the
very image of scorn in our time.   70 knot and gender: twist in bunches and procreate.

Patience, thou young and rose-lipped cherubin!
I here look grim as hell!°
DESDEMONA: I hope my noble lord esteems me honest.
OTHELLO: O, ay, as summer flies are in the shambles,°
    That quicken even with blowing.° O thou weed,   75
    Who art so lovely fair, and smell'st so sweet,
    That the sense aches at thee, would thou hadst never been born!
DESDEMONA: Alas, what ignorant° sin have I committed?
OTHELLO: Was this fair paper, this most goodly book,
    Made to write "whore" upon? What committed?   80
    Committed? O thou public commoner,°
    I should make very forges of my cheeks
    That would to cinders burn up modesty,
    Did I but speak thy deeds. What committed?
    Heaven stops the nose at it, and the moon winks;°   85
    The bawdy wind that kisses all it meets
    Is hushed within the hollow mine of earth
    And will not hear 't. What committed?
DESDEMONA: By heaven, you do me wrong!
OTHELLO: Are not you a strumpet?   90
DESDEMONA: No, as I am a Christian!
    If to preserve this vessel for my lord
    From any other foul unlawful touch
    Be not to be a strumpet, I am none.
OTHELLO: What, not a whore?   95
DESDEMONA: No, as I shall be saved!
OTHELLO: Is't possible?
DESDEMONA: O, heaven forgive us!
OTHELLO: I cry you mercy° then.
    I took you for that cunning whore of Venice   100
    That married with Othello. [*Calling*] You, mistress,

Enter EMILIA.

That have the office opposite to Saint Peter
And keep the gate of hell! You, you, ay, you!
We have done our course; there's money for your pains.

70–72 turn ... hell: (the rough sense would seem to be, "even Patience would grow pale turn complexion, at Desdemona's perfidy, but that Othello looks grimly on").   74 shambles: abattoirs.   75 quicken even with blowing: become impregnated as soon as they lay their eggs.   78 ignorant: unknowing.   81 commoner: prostitute.   85 winks: closes its eyes (the moon was the symbol of chastity).   99 cry you mercy: ask your pardon.

[Throws her some coins.]

I pray you turn the key and keep your counsel.   105

                                                                            Exit.

EMILIA: Alas, what does this gentleman conceive?

How do you, madam? How do you, my good lady?

DESDEMONA: Faith, half asleep.

EMILIA: Good madam, what's the matter with my lord?

DESDEMONA: With who?   110

EMILIA: Why, with my lord, madam.

DESDEMONA: Who is thy lord?

EMILIA: He that is yours, sweet lady.

DESDEMONA: I have none. Do not talk to me, Emilia.

I cannot weep, nor answers have I none   115

But what should go by water.° Prithee tonight

Lay on my bed my wedding sheets, remember;

And call thy husband hither.

EMILIA: Here's a change indeed!

                                                                            Exit.

DESDEMONA: 'Tis meet I should be used so, very meet.   120

How have I been behaved, that he might stick

The small'st opinion on my least misuse?°

Enter IAGO *and* EMILIA.

IAGO: What is your pleasure, madam? How is't with you?

DESDEMONA: I cannot tell. Those that do teach young babes

Do it with gentle means and easy tasks.   125

He might have chid me so; for, in good faith,

I am a child to chiding.

IAGO: What is the matter, lady?

EMILIA: Alas, Iago, my lord hath so bewhored her,

Thrown such despite° and heavy terms upon her   130

That true hearts cannot bear it.

DESDEMONA: Am I that name, Iago?

IAGO: What name, fair lady?

DESDEMONA: Such as she said my lord did say I was.

---

116 water: tears.   121–22 stick . . . misuse: base any doubt on my smallest fault.
130 despite: abuse.

EMILIA: He called her whore. A beggar in his drink   135
    Could not have laid such terms upon his callet.°
IAGO: Why did he so?
DESDEMONA: I do not know; I am sure I am none such.
IAGO: Do not weep, do not weep. Alas the day.
EMILIA: Hath she forsook so many noble matches,   140
    Her father and her country, and her friends,
    To be called whore? Would it not make one weep?
DESDEMONA: It is my wretched fortune.
IAGO: Beshrew° him for 't!
    How comes this trick upon him?   145
DESDEMONA: Nay, heaven doth know.
EMILIA: I will be hanged if some eternal villain,
    Some busy and insinuating rogue,
    Some cogging,° cozening slave, to get some office,
    Have not devised this slander. I will be hanged else.   150
IAGO: Fie, there is no such man! It is impossible.
DESDEMONA: If any such there be, heaven pardon him.
EMILIA: A halter pardon him! And hell gnaw his bones!
    Why should he call her whore? Who keeps her company?
    What place? What time? What form? What likelihood?   155
    The Moor's abused by some most villainous knave,
    Some base notorious knave, some scurvy fellow.
    O heavens, that such companions° thou'dst unfold,°
    And put in every honest hand a whip
    To lash the rascals naked through the world   160
    Even from the east to th' west!
IAGO: Speak within door.°
EMILIA: O, fie upon them! Some such squire° he was
    That turned your wit the seamy side without
    And made you to suspect me with the Moor.   165
IAGO: You are a fool. Go to.
DESDEMONA: Alas, Iago,
    What shall I do to win my lord again?
    Good friend, go to him, for, by this light of heaven,
    I know not how I lost him. Here I kneel: 170
    If e'er my will did trespass 'gainst his love

---

136 callet: slut.   144 Beshrew: curse.   149 cogging: cheating.   158 companions: fellows, rogues.   158 unfold: disclose.   162 within door: more quietly and moderately. 163 squire: (a term of contempt).

Either in discourse of thought° or actual deed,
Or that mine eyes, mine ears, or any sense
Delighted them in any other form;
Or that I do not yet, and ever did,   175
And ever will (though he do shake me off
To beggarly divorcement) love him dearly,
Comfort forswear me. Unkindness may do much,
And his unkindness may defeat° my life,
But never taint my love. I cannot say "whore."   180
It does abhor me now I speak the word;
To do the act that might the addition earn
Not the world's mass of vanity could make me.

IAGO: I pray you be content. 'Tis but his humor.°
The business of the state does him offense.   185

DESDEMONA: If 'twere no other.

IAGO: It is but so, I warrant.

                                                   [*Trumpets within.*]

Hark how these instruments summon to supper.
The messengers of Venice stay the meat.°
Go in, and weep not. All things shall be well.   190

                              [*Exeunt* DESDEMONA *and* EMILIA.]

Enter RODERIGO.

How now, Roderigo?

RODERIGO: I do not find that thou deal'st justly with me.

IAGO: What in the contrary?

RODERIGO: Every day thou daff'st° me with some device,° Iago, and
rather, as it seems to me now, keep'st from me all conveniency° than   195
suppliest me with the least advantage of hope. I will indeed no longer
endure it; nor am I yet persuaded to put up° in peace what already I
have foolishly suffered.

IAGO: Will you hear me, Roderigo?

RODERIGO: I have heard too much, and your words and performances   200
are no kin together.

IAGO: You charge me most unjustly.

RODERIGO: With naught but truth. I have wasted myself out of my
means. The jewels you have had from me to deliver Desdemona would

---

172 discourse of thought: thinking.   179 defeat: destroy.   184 humor: mood.
189 stay the meat: await the meal.   194 daff'st: put off.   194 device: scheme.
195 conveniency: what is needful.   197 put up: accept.

half have corrupted a votarist.° You have told me she hath received   205
them, and returned me expectations and comforts of sudden respect°
and acquaintance; but I find none.

IAGO: Well, go to; very well.

RODERIGO: Very well? Go to? I cannot go to, man; nor 'tis not very well.
Nay, I think it is scurvy, and begin to find myself fopped° in it.   210

IAGO: Very well.

RODERIGO: I tell you 'tis not very well. I will make myself known to Desdemona. If she will return me my jewels, I will give over my suit and repent my unlawful solicitation. If not, assure yourself I will seek
satisfaction of you.   215

IAGO: You have said now?

RODERIGO: Ay, and said nothing but what I protest° intendment of doing.

IAGO: Why, now I see there's mettle° in thee, and even from this instant
do build on thee a better opinion than ever before. Give me thy hand,
Roderigo. Thou hast taken against me a most just exception;° but yet I   220
protest I have dealt most directly° in thy affair.

RODERIGO: It hath not appeared.

IAGO: I grant indeed it hath not appeared, and your suspicion is not without wit and judgment. But, Roderigo, if thou hast that in thee indeed
which I have greater reason to believe now than ever—I mean purpose,   225
courage, and valor—this night show it. If thou the next night following
enjoy not Desdemona, take me from this world with treachery and
devise engines for° my life.

RODERIGO: Well, what is it? Is it within reason and compass?°

IAGO: Sir, there is especial commission come from Venice to depute Cas-   230
sio in Othello's place.

RODERIGO: Is that true? Why, then Othello and Desdemona return again
to Venice.

IAGO: O, no; he goes into Mauritania and taketh away with him the fair
Desdemona, unless his abode be lingered here by some accident;   235
wherein none can be so determinate° as the removing of Cassio.

RODERIGO: How do you mean, removing him?

IAGO: Why, by making him uncapable of Othello's place—knocking out
his brains.

RODERIGO: And that you would have me to do?   240

IAGO: Ay, if you dare do yourself a profit and a right. He sups tonight with
a harlotry,° and thither will I go to him. He knows not yet of his

---

205 votarist: nun.   206 sudden   respect: immmediate   consideration.
210 fopped: duped.   217 protest: aver.   218 mettle: spirit.   220 exception: objection.
221 directly: straightforwardly.   228 engines for: schemes against.   229 compass:
possibility.   236 determinate: effective.   242 harlotry: female.

honorable fortune. If you will watch his going thence, which I will
fashion to fall out° between twelve and one, you may take him at your
pleasure. I will be near to second° your attempt, and he shall fall be-   245
tween us. Come, stand not amazed at it, but go along with me. I will show
you such a necessity in his death that you shall think yourself bound to
put it on him. It is now high supper time, and the night grows to waste.
About it.

RODERIGO: I will hear further reason for this.   250

IAGO: And you shall be satisfied.   *Exeunt.*

Scene 3. [*The citadel.*]

Enter OTHELLO, LODOVICO, DESDEMONA, EMILIA, *and* ATTENDANTS.

LODOVICO: I do beseech you, sir, trouble yourself no further.

OTHELLO: O, pardon me; 'twill do me good to walk.

LODOVICO: Madam, good night. I humbly thank your ladyship.

DESDEMONA: Your honor is most welcome.

OTHELLO: Will you walk, sir? O, Desdemona.   5

DESDEMONA: My lord?

OTHELLO: Get you to bed on th' instant; I will be returned forthwith. Dismiss your attendant there. Look't be done.

DESDEMONA: I will, my lord.

Exit [OTHELLO, *with* LODOVICO *and* ATTENDANTS].

EMILIA: How goes it now? He looks gentler than he did.   10

DESDEMONA: He says he will return incontinent,°
And hath commanded me to go to bed,
And bade me to dismiss you.

EMILIA: Dismiss me?

DESDEMONA: It was his bidding; therefore, good Emilia,   15
Give me my nightly wearing, and adieu.
We must not now displease him.

EMILIA: I would you had never seen him!

DESDEMONA: So would not I. My love doth so approve him
That even his stubbornness, his checks,° his frowns—   20
Prithee unpin me—have grace and favor.

EMILIA: I have laid these sheets you bade me on the bed.

---

244 fall out: occur. 245 second: support. IV.3.11 incontinent: at once. 20
checks: rebukes.

DESDEMONA: All's one.° Good Father, how foolish are our minds!
    If I do die before, prithee shroud me
    In one of these same sheets. 25
EMILIA: Come, come! You talk.
DESDEMONA: My mother had a maid called Barbary.
    She was in love; and he she loved proved mad
    And did forsake her. She had a song of "Willow";
    An old thing 'twas, but it expressed her fortune, 30
    And she died singing it. That song tonight
    Will not go from my mind; I have much to do
    But to go hang my head all at one side
    And sing it like poor Barbary. Prithee dispatch.
EMILIA: Shall I go fetch your nightgown? 35
DESDEMONA: No, unpin me here.
    This Lodovico is a proper man.
EMILIA: A very handsome man.
DESDEMONA: He speaks well.
EMILIA: I know a lady in Venice would have walked 40
    barefoot to Palestine for a touch of his nether lip.
DESDEMONA *[Sings]*:
    "The poor soul sat singing by a sycamore tree,
        Sing all a green willow;
    Her hand on her bosom, her head on her knee, 45
        Sing willow, willow, willow.
    The fresh streams ran by her and murmured her moans;
        Sing willow, willow, willow;
    Her salt tears fell from her, and soft'ned the stones—
        Sing willow, willow, willow—" 50
Lay by these.   *[Gives* EMILIA *her clothes.]*
    "Willow, Willow"—
Prithee hie° thee; he'll come anon.°
    "Sing all a green willow must be my garland.
    Let nobody blame him; his scorn I approve"— 55
Nay, that's not next. Hark! Who is't that knocks?
EMILIA: It is the wind.
DESDEMONA *[Sings]*:
    "I called my love false love; but what said he then?
        Sing willow, willow, willow: 60
    If I court moe° women, you'll couch with moe men."
So, get thee gone; good night. Mine eyes do itch.
    Doth that bode weeping?

---

23 All's one: no matter.   53 hie: hurry.   53 anon: at once.   61 moe: more.

EMILIA: 'Tis neither here nor there.
DESDEMONA: I have heard it said so. O, these men, these men.   65
   Dost thou in conscience think, tell me, Emilia,
   That there be women do abuse their husbands
   In such gross kind?
EMILIA: There be some such, no question.
DESDEMONA: Wouldst thou do such a deed for all the world?   70
EMILIA: Why, would not you?
DESDEMONA: No, by this heavenly light!
EMILIA: Nor I neither by this heavenly light.
   I might do't as well i' th' dark.
DESDEMONA: Wouldst thou do such a deed for all the world?   75
EMILIA: The world's a huge thing; it is a great price for a small vice.
DESDEMONA: In troth, I think thou wouldst not.
EMILIA: In troth, I think I should; and undo't when I had done. Marry, I
   would not do such a thing for a joint-ring,° nor for measures of lawn,°
   nor for gowns, petticoats, nor caps, nor any petty exhibition,° but for all   80
   the whole world? Why, who would not make her husband a cuckold to
   make him a monarch? I should venture purgatory for't.
DESDEMONA: Beshrew me if I would do such a wrong for the whole
   world.
EMILIA: Why, the wrong is but a wrong i' th' world; and having the world   85
   for your labor, 'tis a wrong in your own world, and you might quickly
   make it right.
DESDEMONA: I do not think there is any such woman.
EMILIA: Yes, a dozen; and as many to th' vantage as
   would store° the world they played for.   90
   But I do think it is their husbands' faults
   If wives do fall. Say that they slack their duties
   And pour our treasures into foreign° laps;
   Or else break out in peevish jealousies,
   Throwing restraint upon us; or say they strike us,   95
   Or scant our former having in despite°—
   Why, we have galls; and though we have some grace,
   Yet have we some revenge. Let husbands know
   Their wives have sense like them. They see, and smell,
   And have their palates both for sweet and sour,   100
   As husbands have. What is it that they do

---

79 joint-ring: (a ring with two interlocking halves). 79 lawn: fine linen.
80 exhibition: payment.   89–90 to . . . store: in addition as would fill.   93 foreign: alien,
i.e., other than the wife.   96 scant . . . despite: reduce, in spite, our household allowance
(?).

When they change° us for others? Is it sport?
I think it is. And doth affection° breed it?
I think it doth. Is't frailty that thus errs?
It is so too. And have not we affections?   105
Desires for sport? and frailty? as men have?
Then let them use us well; else let them know,
The ills we do, their ills instruct us so.°

DESDEMONA: Good night, good night. Heaven me such uses° send,
  Not to pick bad from bad, but by bad mend.   *Exeunt.*   110

ACT V

Scene 1. [*A street.*]

Enter IAGO *and* RODERIGO.

IAGO: Here, stand behind this bulk;° straight will he come.
  Wear thy good rapier bare, and put it home.
  Quick, quick! Fear nothing; I'll be at thy elbow.
  It makes us, or it mars us, think on that,
  And fix most firm thy resolution.   5

RODERIGO: Be near at hand; I may miscarry in't.

IAGO: Here, at thy hand. Be bold, and take thy stand.
                                 [*Moves to one side.*]

RODERIGO: I have no great devotion to the deed,
  And yet he hath given me satisfying reasons.
  'Tis but a man gone. Forth my sword! He dies!   10

IAGO: I have rubbed this young quat° almost to the sense,°
  And he grows angry. Now, whether he kills Cassio,
  Or Cassio him, or each do kill the other,
  Every way makes my gain. Live Roderigo,
  He calls me to a restitution large   15
  Of gold and jewels that I bobbed° from him
  As gifts to Desdemona.
  It must not be. If Cassio do remain,
  He hath a daily beauty in his life
  That makes me ugly; and besides, the Moor   20
  May unfold me to him; there stand I in much peril.

---

102 change: exchange.   103 affection: strong feeling, desire.   108 instruct us so:
teach us to do likewise.   109 uses: practices.   V.1.1 bulk: projecting stall of a shop.
11 quat: pimple.   11 to the sense: raw.   16 bobbed: swindled.

No, he must die. But so, I hear him coming.

Enter CASSIO.

RODERIGO: I know his gait. 'Tis he. Villain, thou diest!
                                             [*Thrusts at* CASSIO.]
CASSIO: That thrust had been mine enemy indeed
But that my coat° is better than thou know'st.   25
I will make proof of thine.   [*Fights with* RODERIGO.]
RODERIGO: O, I am slain!°
CASSIO: I am maimed forever. Help, ho! Murder! Murder!

Enter OTHELLO [*to one side*].

OTHELLO: The voice of Cassio. Iago keeps his word.
RODERIGO: O, villain that I am!   30
OTHELLO: It is even so.
CASSIO: O help, ho! Light! A surgeon!
OTHELLO: 'Tis he. O brave Iago, honest and just,
That hast such noble sense of thy friend's wrong!
Thou teachest me. Minion,° your dear lies dead,   35
And your unblest° fate hies.° Strumpet, I come.
Forth of my heart those charms, thine eyes, are blotted.
Thy bed, lust-stained, shall with lust's blood be spotted.
                                                      Exit OTHELLO.

Enter LODOVICO *and* GRATIANO.

CASSIO: What, ho? No watch? No passage?° Murder! Murder!
GRATIANO: 'Tis some mischance. The voice is very direful.   40
CASSIO: O, help!
LODOVICO: Hark!
RODERIGO: O wretched villain!
LODOVICO: Two or three groan. 'Tis heavy night.

---

25 coat: i.e., a mail shirt or bulletproof vest.   27 slain: (most editors add here a stage
direction which has Iago wounding Cassio in the leg from behind, but remaining unseen.
However, nothing in the text requires this, and Cassio's wound can be given him in the
fight with Roderigo, for presumably when Cassio attacks Roderigo the latter would not
simply accept the thrust but would parry. Since Iago enters again at line 48, he must exit at
some point after line 22).   35 Minion: hussy, i.e., Desdemona.   36 unblest: unsanctified.
36 hies: approaches swiftly.   39 passage: passersby.

These may be counterfeits. Let's think't unsafe 45
To come into the cry without more help.
RODERIGO: Nobody come? Then shall I bleed to death.
LODOVICO: Hark!

Enter IAGO [*with a light*].

GRATIANO: Here's one comes in his shirt, with light and weapons.
IAGO: Who's there? Whose noise is this that cries on murder? 50
LODOVICO: We do not know.
IAGO: Do not you hear a cry?
CASSIO: Here, here! For heaven's sake, help me!
IAGO: What's the matter?
GRATIANO: This is Othello's ancient, as I take it. 55
LODOVICO: The same indeed, a very valiant fellow.
IAGO: What are you here that cry so grievously?
CASSIO: Iago? O, I am spoiled, undone by villains.
    Give me some help.
IAGO: O me, lieutenant! What villains have done this? 60
CASSIO: I think that one of them is hereabout
    And cannot make away.
IAGO: O treacherous villains!
    [*To* LODOVICO *and* GRATIANO] What are you there?
    Come in, and give some help. 65
RODERIGO: O, help me there!
CASSIO: That's one of them.
IAGO: O murd'rous slave! O villain!
                                [*Stabs* RODERIGO.]
RODERIGO: O damned Iago! O inhuman dog!
IAGO: Kill men i' th' dark?—Where be these bloody thieves?— 70
    How silent is this town!—Ho! Murder! Murder!—
    What may you be? Are you of good or evil?
LODOVICO: As you shall prove us, praise us.
IAGO: Signior Lodovico?
LODOVICO: He, sir. 75
IAGO: I cry you mercy. Here's Cassio hurt by villains.
GRATIANO: Cassio?
IAGO: How is't, brother?
CASSIO: My leg is cut in two.
IAGO: Marry, heaven forbid! 80
    Light, gentlemen. I'll bind it with my shirt.

Enter BIANCA.

BIANCA:　What is the matter, ho? Who is't that cried?
IAGO:　Who is't that cried?
BIANCA:　O my dear Cassio! My sweet Cassio!
　O Cassio, Cassio, Cassio!　　　　　　　　　　　　　85
IAGO:　O notable strumpet!—Cassio, may you suspect
　Who they should be that have thus mangled you?
CASSIO:　No.
GRATIANO:　I am sorry to find you thus. I have been to seek you.
IAGO:　Lend me a garter. So. O for a chair　　　　　90
　To bear him easily hence.
BIANCA:　Alas, he faints! O Cassio, Cassio, Cassio!
IAGO:　Gentlemen all, I do suspect this trash
　To be a party in this injury.—
　Patience awhile, good Cassio.—Come, come.　　　95
　Lend me a light. Know we this face or no?
　Alas, my friend and my dear countryman
Roderigo? No.—Yes, sure.—Yes, 'tis Roderigo!
GRATIANO:　What, of Venice?
IAGO:　Even he, sir. Did you know him?　　　　　　100
GRATIANO:　　　　　　　　　　　Know him? Ay.
IAGO:　Signior Gratiano? I cry your gentle pardon.
　These bloody accidents must excuse my manners
　That so neglected you.
GRATIANO:　　　　　　I am glad to see you.　　　105
IAGO:　How do you, Cassio?—O, a chair, a chair!
GRATIANO:　Roderigo?
IAGO:　He, he, 'tis he! [*A chair brought in.*] O, that's well said;° the chair.
　Some good man bear him carefully from hence.
　I'll fetch the general's surgeon. [*To* BIANCA] For you, mistress,　　110
　Save you your labor. [*To* CASSIO] He that lies slain here, Cassio,
　Was my dear friend. What malice was between you?
CASSIO:　None in the world; nor do I know the man.
IAGO:　What, look you pale?—O, bear him out o' th' air.
　　　　　　　　　　　　　　[CASSIO *is carried off.*]
　Stay you, good gentlemen.—Look you pale, mistress?　　115
　Do you perceive the gastness° of her eye?
　Nay, if you stare, we shall hear more anon.
　Behold her well; I pray you look upon her.
　Do you see, gentlemen? Nay, guiltiness will speak,

---

108 well said: well done.　116 gastness: terror.

Though tongues were out of use.° 120

[*Enter* EMILIA.]

EMILIA: Alas, what is the matter? What is the matter, husband?
IAGO: Cassio hath here been set on in the dark
    By Roderigo and fellows that are scaped.
    He's almost slain, and Roderigo quite dead.
EMILIA: Alas, good gentleman! Alas, good Cassio! 125
IAGO: This is the fruits of whoring. Prithee, Emilia,
    Go know of Cassio where he supped tonight.
    [*To* BIANCA] What, do you shake at that?
BIANCA: He supped at my house; but I therefore shake not.
IAGO: O, did he so? I charge° you go with me. 130
EMILIA: Oh fie upon thee, strumpet!
BIANCA: I am no strumpet, but of life as honest
    As you that thus abuse me.
EMILIA: As I? Fie upon thee!
IAGO: Kind gentlemen, let's go see poor Cassio dressed.° 135
    [*To* BIANCA] Come, mistress, you must tell's another tale.
    Emilia, run you to the citadel
    And tell my lord and lady what hath happed.
                                  [*Exit* EMILIA.]
    Will you go on afore?   *Exeunt* [*all but* IAGO].
               This is the night 140
    That either makes me or fordoes me quite.°   [*Exit.*]

Scene 2. [*Desdemona's chamber.*]

Enter OTHELLO [*with a light*]; *and* DESDEMONA *in her bed.*

OTHELLO: It is the cause, it is the cause, my soul.
    Let me not name it to you, you chaste stars.
    It is the cause. Yet I'll not shed her blood,
    Nor scar that whiter skin of hers than snow,
    And smooth as monumental alabaster. 5
    Yet she must die, else she'll betray more men.
    Put out the light, and then put out the light.

---

120 tongues were out of use: men no longer spoke.   130 charge: command.
135 dressed: bandaged.   141 fordoes me quite: completely ruins me.

If I quench thee, thou flaming minister,°
I can again thy former light restore,
Should I repent me; but once put out thy light,   10
Thou cunning'st° pattern of excelling nature,
I know not where is that Promethean heat°
That can thy light relume.° When I have plucked the rose,
I cannot give it vital° growth again;
It needs must wither. I'll smell thee on the tree.   15

                            [He kisses her.]

O balmy breath, that dost almost persuade
Justice to break her sword. One more, one more!
Be thus when thou art dead, and I will kill thee,
And love thee after. One more, and that's the last!
So sweet was ne'er so fatal. I must weep,   20
But they are cruel tears. This sorrow's heavenly;
It strikes where it doth love. She wakes.
DESDEMONA: Who's there? Othello?
OTHELLO: Ay, Desdemona.
DESDEMONA: Will you come to bed, my lord?   25
OTHELLO: Have you prayed tonight, Desdemon?
DESDEMONA: Ay, my lord.
OTHELLO: If you bethink yourself of any crime
  Unreconciled as yet to heaven and grace,
  Solicit for it straight.   30
DESDEMONA: Alack, my lord, what may you mean by that?
OTHELLO: Well, do it, and be brief; I will walk by.°
  I would not kill thy unprepared spirit.
  No, heavens forfend! I would not kill thy soul.
DESDEMONA: Talk you of killing?   35
OTHELLO: Ay, I do.
DESDEMONA: Then heaven
  Have mercy on me!
OTHELLO: Amen, with all my heart.
DESDEMONA: If you say so, I hope you will not kill me.   40
OTHELLO: Humh.
DESDEMONA: And yet I fear you; for you're fatal then
  When your eyes roll so. Why I should fear I know not,
  Since guiltiness I know not; but yet I feel I fear.

---

8 minister: worker, servant.   11 cunning'st: most intricate and skillfully wrought
(by nature excelling itself).   12 Promethean heat: divine fire (Prometheus is the Titan
who stole fire from heaven and gave it to man).   13 relume: relight.   14 vital: living.
32 by: nearby.

OTHELLO: Think on thy sins.   45
DESDEMONA: They are loves I bear to you.
OTHELLO: Ay, and for that thou diest.
DESDEMONA: That death's unnatural that kills for loving.
    Alas, why gnaw you so your nether lip?
    Some bloody passion shakes your very frame.   50
    These are portents; but yet I hope, I hope,
    They do not point on me.
OTHELLO: Peace and be still.
DESDEMONA: I will so. What's the matter?
OTHELLO: That handkerchief which I so loved and gave thee,   55
    Thou gav'st to Cassio.
DESDEMONA: No, by my life and soul!
    Send for the man and ask him.
OTHELLO: Sweet soul, take heed,
    Take heed of perjury; thou art on thy deathbed.
DESDEMONA: Ay, but not yet to die.   60
OTHELLO: Presently.°
    Therefore confess thee freely of thy sin,
    For to deny each article° with oath
    Cannot remove nor choke the strong conception   65
    That I do groan withal. Thou art to die.
DESDEMONA: Then Lord have mercy on me.
OTHELLO: I say, amen.
DESDEMONA: And have you mercy too. I never did
    Offend you in my life; never loved Cassio   70
    But with such general warranty° of heaven
    As I might love. I never gave him token.
OTHELLO: By heaven, I saw my handkerchief in's hand!
    O perjured woman! thou dost stone° my heart,
    And mak'st me call what I intend to do   75
    A murder, which I thought a sacrifice.
    I saw the handkerchief.
DESDEMONA: He found it then.
    I never gave it him. Send for him hither.
    Let him confess a truth.   80
OTHELLO: He hath confessed.
DESDEMONA: What, my lord?

---

62 Presently: immediately.   64 article: item (of the charge of adultery. Othello makes heavy use of legal terms in this scene).   71 warranty: allowance.   74 stone: turn to stone.

OTHELLO: That he hath used thee.

DESDEMONA: How? Unlawfully?

OTHELLO: Ay.   85

DESDEMONA: He will not say so.

OTHELLO: No, his mouth is stopped.
　Honest Iago hath ta'en order for't.°

DESDEMONA: O, my fear interprets. What, is he dead?

OTHELLO: Had all his hairs been lives, my great revenge   90
　Had stomach° for them all.

DESDEMONA: Alas, he is betrayed, and I undone!

OTHELLO: Out, strumpet! Weep'st thou for him to my face?

DESDEMONA: O, banish me, my lord, but kill me not!

OTHELLO: Down, strumpet!   95

DESDEMONA: Kill me tomorrow; let me live tonight!

OTHELLO: Nay, if you strive—

DESDEMONA: But half an hour!

OTHELLO: Being done, there is no pause.

DESDEMONA: But while I say one prayer!   100

OTHELLO: It is too late.

                                            Smothers her.

EMILIA *at the door.*

EMILIA [*Calls within.*]:   My lord, my lord! What, ho, my lord, my lord!

OTHELLO: What noise is this? Not dead? Not yet quite dead?
　I that am cruel am yet merciful;
　I would not have thee linger in thy pain.   105
　So, so.

EMILIA [*Within*]:   What, ho! My lord, my lord!

OTHELLO: Who's there?

EMILIA [*Within*]:   O, good my lord, I would speak a word with you.

OTHELLO: Yes, 'tis Emilia.—By and by.—She's dead.—   110
　'Tis like she comes to speak of Cassio's death.
　The noise was high.° Ha! No more moving?
　Still as the grave.—Shall she come in? Were't good?—
　I think she stirs again. No.—What's best to do?
　If she come in, she'll sure speak to my wife.   115
　My wife! My wife! What wife? I have no wife.
　O, insupportable! O heavy hour!

---

　88 ta'en order for't: make sure of it.　91 stomach: appetite.　112 high: loud (Q1 reads "here").

Methinks it should be now a huge eclipse
Of sun and moon, and that th' affrighted globe
Should yawn° at alteration.°   120
EMILIA: [*Within*] I do beseech you
   That I may speak with you, O good my lord!
OTHELLO: I had forgot thee. O, come in, Emilia.
   Soft, by and by.—Let me the curtains draw.—
   [*Draws the bed hangings and then opens the door.*]
   Where art thou?   125

Enter EMILIA.

                  What's the matter with thee now?
EMILIA: O my good lord, yonder's foul murders done!
OTHELLO: What? Now?
EMILIA: But now, my lord.
OTHELLO: It is the very error° of the moon.   130
   She comes more nearer earth than she was wont
   And makes men mad.
EMILIA: Cassio, my lord, hath killed a young Venetian
   Called Roderigo.
OTHELLO: Roderigo killed?   135
   And Cassio killed?
EMILIA: No, Cassio is not killed.
OTHELLO: Not Cassio killed? Then murder's out of tune,
   And sweet revenge grows harsh.
DESDEMONA: O, falsely, falsely murdered!   140
EMILIA: O Lord! What cry is that?
OTHELLO: That? What?
EMILIA: Out and alas! that was my lady's voice.
   Help! Help, ho! Help! O lady, speak again!
   Sweet Desdemona! O sweet mistress, speak!   145
DESDEMONA: A guiltless death I die.
EMILIA: O, who hath done this deed?
DESDEMONA: Nobody—I myself. Farewell.
   Commend me to my kind lord. O, farewell!

                                                            [*She dies.*]

_____

118–20 Methinks . . . alteration: (the Elizabethans believed that great changes in human affairs were reflected by disorders in nature).   120 yawn: gape open (as in an earthquake).   130 error: wandering out of regular course (disorders in the heavens were
believed by some to cause disorders on earth, as well as vice versa).

OTHELLO: Why, how should she be murd'red?   150
EMILIA: Alas, who knows?
OTHELLO: You heard her say herself, it was not I.
EMILIA: She said so. I must needs report the truth.
OTHELLO: She's like a liar gone to burning hell!
    'Twas I that killed her.   155
EMILIA: O, the more angel she,
    And you the blacker devil!
OTHELLO: She turned to folly, and she was a whore.
EMILIA: Thou dost belie her, and thou art a devil.
OTHELLO: She was false as water.   160
EMILIA: Thou art rash as fire to say
    That she was false. O, she was heavenly true!
OTHELLO: Cassio did top her. Ask thy husband else.
    O, I were damned beneath all depth in hell
    But that I did proceed upon just grounds   165
    To this extremity. Thy husband knew it all.
EMILIA: My husband?
OTHELLO: Thy husband.
EMILIA: That she was false to wedlock?
OTHELLO: Ay, with Cassio. Had she been true,   170
    If heaven would make me such another world
    Of one entire and perfect chrysolite,°
    I'd not have sold her for it.
EMILIA: My husband?
OTHELLO: Ay, 'twas he that told me on her first.   175
    An honest man he is, and hates the slime
    That sticks on filthy deeds.
EMILIA: My husband?
OTHELLO: What needs this iterance? Woman, I say thy husband.
EMILIA: O mistress, villainy hath made mocks with love!   180
    My husband say she was false?
OTHELLO: He, woman.
    I say, thy husband. Dost understand the word?
    My friend, thy husband; honest, honest Iago.
EMILIA: If he say so, may his pernicious soul   185
    Rot half a grain a day! He lies to th' heart.
    She was too fond of her most filthy bargain.
OTHELLO: Hah?
EMILIA: Do thy worst.
    This deed of thine is no more worthy heaven   190
    Than thou wast worthy her.

---

172 chrysolite: topaz.

OTHELLO: Peace, you were best.°
EMILIA: Thou hast not half that pow'r to do me harm
    As I have to be hurt. O gull! O dolt!
    As ignorant as dirt! Thou hast done a deed—   195
        [OTHELLO *moves to draw his sword.*]
    I care not for thy sword; I'll make thee known,
    Though I lost twenty lives. Help! Help! Ho! Help!
    The Moor hath killed my mistress! Murder! murder!

Enter MONTANO, GRATIANO, *and* IAGO [*and Others*].

MONTANO: What is the matter? How now, general?
EMILIA: O, are you come, Iago? You have done well,   200
    That men must lay their murders on your neck.
GRATIANO: What is the matter?
EMILIA: Disprove this villain, if thou be'st a man.
    He says thou told'st him that his wife was false.
    I know thou didst not; thou'rt not such a villain.   205
    Speak, for my heart is full.
IAGO: I told him what I thought, and told no more
    Than what he found himself was apt and true.
EMILIA: But did you ever tell him she was false?
IAGO: I did.   210
EMILIA: You told a lie, an odious damnèd lie!
    Upon my soul, a lie! A wicked lie!
    She false with Cassio? Did you say with Cassio?
IAGO: With Cassio, mistress. Go to, charm° your tongue.
EMILIA: I will not charm my tongue; I am bound to speak: 215
    My mistress here lies murdered in her bed.
ALL: O heavens forfend!
EMILIA: And your reports have set the murder on.
OTHELLO: Nay, stare not, masters. It is true indeed.
GRATIANO: 'Tis a strange truth.   220
MONTANO: O monstrous act!
EMILIA: Villainy, villainy, villainy!
    I think upon't—I think I smell't!—O villainy!
    I thought so then.—I'll kill myself for grief.—
    O villainy, villainy!   225
IAGO: What, are you mad? I charge you get you home.

---

192 Peace, you were best: i.e., you had better be silent.   214 charm: control.

EMILIA: Good gentlemen, let me have leave to speak.
  'Tis proper I obey him, but not now.
  Perchance, Iago, I will ne'er go home.
OTHELLO: O! O! O!   [*Falls on the bed.*]   230
EMILIA: Nay, lay thee down and roar,
  For thou hast killed the sweetest innocent
  That e'er did lift up eye.
OTHELLO: O, she was foul!   [*Rises.*]
  I scarce did know you, uncle. There lies your niece,   235
  Whose breath, indeed, these hands have newly stopped.
  I know this act shows horrible and grim.
GRATIANO: Poor Desdemon! I am glad thy father's dead.
  Thy match was mortal to him, and pure grief
  Shore his old thread in twain. Did he live now,   240
  This sight would make him do a desperate turn;
  Yea, curse his better angel from his side,
  And fall to reprobation.°
OTHELLO: 'Tis pitiful; but yet Iago knows
  That she with Cassio hath the act of shame   245
  A thousand times committed. Cassio confessed it;
  And she did gratify his amorous works
  With that recognizance and pledge of love,
  Which I first gave her. I saw it in his hand.
  It was a handkerchief, an antique token   250
  My father gave my mother.
EMILIA: O God! O heavenly God!
IAGO: Zounds, hold your peace!
EMILIA: 'Twill out, 'twill out! I peace?
  No, I will speak as liberal as the north.°   255
  Let heaven and men and devils, let them all,
  All, all, cry shame against me, yet I'll speak.
IAGO: Be wise, and get you home.
EMILIA: I will not.
               [IAGO *draws and threatens* EMILIA.]
GRATIANO: Fie! Your sword upon a woman?   260
EMILIA: O thou dull Moor, that handkerchief thou speak'st of
  I found by fortune, and did give my husband;
  For often with a solemn earnestness—
  More than indeed belonged to such a trifle—
  He begged of me to steal't.   265

---

243 reprobation: damnation.   255 liberal as the north: freely (and bitingly) as the north wind blows.

IAGO: Villainous whore!

EMILIA: She give it Cassio? No, alas, I found it,
And I did give't my husband.

IAGO: Filth, thou liest!

EMILIA: By heaven, I do not, I do not, gentlemen.   270
O murd'rous coxcomb! What should such a fool
Do with so good a wife?

OTHELLO: Are there no stones° in heaven
But what serves for the thunder? Precious villain!

> [*The Moor runs at* IAGO, *but is disarmed by* MONTANO.
> IAGO *kills his wife*.]

GRATIANO: The woman falls. Sure he hath killed his wife.   275

EMILIA: Ay, ay. O, lay me by my mistress' side.

> [*Exit* IAGO.]

GRATIANO: He's gone, but his wife's killed.

MONTANO: 'Tis a notorious° villain. Take you this weapon,
Which I have recovered from the Moor.
Come, guard the door without. Let him not pass,   280
But kill him rather. I'll after that same villain,
For 'tis a damnèd slave.

> *Exit* [*with all but* OTHELLO *and* EMILIA].

OTHELLO: I am not valiant neither;
But every puny whipster° gets my sword.
But why should honor outlive honesty?   285
Let it go all.

EMILIA: What did thy song bode, lady?
Hark, canst thou hear me? I will play the swan,
And die in music. [*Sings*] "Willow, willow, willow."
Moor, she was chaste. She loved thee, cruel Moor,   290
So come my soul to bliss as I speak true.
So speaking as I think, alas, I die.   [*She dies*.]

OTHELLO: I have another weapon in this chamber;
It was a sword of Spain, the ice-brook's temper.
O, here it is.—Uncle, I must come forth.   295

GRATIANO   [*Within*]:
If thou attempt it, it will cost thee dear.
Thou hast no weapon, and perforce must suffer.

---

273 stones: thunderbolts.   278 notorious: out-and-out.   284 puny whipster: small
top-whipping boy(?).

OTHELLO: Look in upon me then and speak with me,
Or, naked as I am, I will assault thee.

[*Enter* GRATIANO.]

GRATIANO: What is the matter?   300
OTHELLO: Behold, I have a weapon;
A better never did itself sustain
Upon a soldier's thigh. I have seen the day
That with this little arm and this good sword
I have made my way through more impediments   305
Than twenty times your stop. But O vain boast!
Who can control his fate? 'Tis not so now.
Be not afraid, though you do see me weaponed.
Here is my journey's end, here is my butt,°
And very seamark of my utmost sail.°   310
Do you go back dismayed? 'Tis a lost fear.
Man but a rush° against Othello's breast,
And he retires. Where should Othello go?
Now, how dost thou look now? O ill-starred wench!
Pale as thy smock! When we shall meet at compt,°   315
This look of thine will hurl my soul from heaven,
And fiends will snatch at it. Cold, cold, my girl?
Even like thy chastity.
O cursèd, cursèd slave! Whip me, ye devils,
From the possession of° this heavenly sight!   320
Blow me about in winds! roast me in sulfur!
Wash me in steep-down gulfs of liquid fire!
O Desdemon! Dead Desdemon; dead. O! O!
Enter LODOVICO, CASSIO, MONTANO, *and* IAGO [*as prisoner.*]
with OFFICERS.
LODOVICO: Where is this rash and most unfortunate man?
OTHELLO: That's he that was Othello; Here I am.   325
LODOVICO: Where is that viper? Bring the villain forth.
OTHELLO: I look down towards his feet°—but that's a fable.
If that thou be'st a devil, I cannot kill thee.

[*Wounds* IAGO.]

---

309 butt: target, stopping place.   310 seamark of my utmost sail: marker of my farthest journey.   312 Man but a rush: attack with only a reed.   315 compt: Judgment Day.
320 the possession of: being possessed by.   327 towards his feet: i.e., for his cloven hoofs.

LODOVICO: Wrench his sword from him.

                                        [OTHELLO *is disarmed.*]

IAGO: I bleed, sir, but not killed.   330

OTHELLO: I am not sorry neither. I'd have thee live;
  For in my sense, 'tis happiness to die.

LODOVICO: O thou Othello that was once so good,
  Fall'n in the practice° of a cursèd slave,
  What shall be said to thee?   335

OTHELLO: Why, anything:
  An honorable murderer, if you will;
  For naught I did in hate, but all in honor.

LODOVICO: This wretch hath part confessed his villainy.
  Did you and he consent in Cassio's death?   340

OTHELLO: Ay.

CASSIO: Dear general, I never gave you cause.

OTHELLO: I do believe it, and I ask your pardon.
  Will you, I pray, demand that demi-devil
  Why he hath thus ensnared my soul and body?   345

IAGO: Demand me nothing. What you know, you know.
  From this time forth I never will speak word.

LODOVICO: What, not to pray?

GRATIANO: Torments will ope your lips.

OTHELLO: Well, thou dost best.   350

LODOVICO: Sir, you shall understand what hath befall'n,
  Which, as I think, you know not. Here is a letter
  Found in the pocket of the slain Roderigo;
  And here another. The one of them imports
  The death of Cassio to be undertook   355
  By Roderigo.

OTHELLO: O villain!

CASSIO: Most heathenish and most gross!

LODOVICO: Now here's another discontented paper
  Found in his pocket too; and this, it seems,   360
  Roderigo meant t' have sent this damnèd villain;
  But that, belike, Iago in the interim
  Came in and satisfied him.

OTHELLO: O thou pernicious caitiff!
  How came you, Cassio, by that handkerchief   365
  That was my wife's?

---

334 practice: plotting.

CASSIO: I found it in my chamber;
   And he himself confessed it but even now
   That there he dropped it for a special purpose
   Which wrought to his desire.   370
OTHELLO: O fool! Fool! Fool!
CASSIO: There is besides in Roderigo's letter,
   How he upbraids Iago that he made him
   Brave me upon the watch; whereon it came
   That I was cast; and even but now he spake,   375
   After long seeming dead—Iago hurt him,
   Iago set him on.
LODOVICO: You must forsake this room and go with us.
   Your power and your command is taken off,
   And Cassio rules in Cyprus. For this slave,   380
   If there be any cunning cruelty
   That can torment him much and hold him long,
   It shall be his. You shall close prisoner rest
   Till that the nature of your fault be known
   To the Venetian state. Come, bring away.   385
OTHELLO: Soft you, a word or two before you go.
   I have done the state some service, and they know't.
   No more of that. I pray you, in your letters,
   When you shall these unlucky deeds relate,
   Speak of me as I am. Nothing extenuate,   390
   Nor set down aught in malice. Then must you speak
   Of one that loved not wisely, but too well;
   Of one not easily jealous, but, being wrought,
   Perplexed in the extreme; of one whose hand,
   Like the base Judean,° threw a pearl away   395
   Richer than all his tribe; of one whose subdued eyes,
   Albeit unusèd to the melting mood,
   Drops tears as fast as the Arabian trees
   Their med'cinable gum. Set you down this.
   And say besides that in Aleppo once,   400
   Where a malignant and a turbaned Turk
   Beat a Venetian and traduced the state,
   I took by th' throat the circumcisèd dog
   And smote him—thus.   [*He stabs himself.*]
LODOVICO: O bloody period!°   405
GRATIANO: All that is spoke is marred.

---

   395 Judean: (most editors use the Q1 reading, "Indian," here, but F is clear; both readings point toward the infidel, the unbeliever).   405 period: end.

OTHELLO: I kissed thee ere I killed thee. No way but this,
Killing myself, to die upon a kiss.

                              [*He falls over* DESDEMONA *and dies.*]

CASSIO: This did I fear, but thought he had no weapon;
For he was great of heart.   410
LODOVICO: [*To* IAGO] O Spartan dog,
More fell° than anguish, hunger, or the sea!
Look on the tragic loading of this bed.
This is thy work. The object poisons sight;
Let it be hid.   [*Bed curtains drawn.*]   415
Gratiano, keep° the house,
And seize upon the fortunes of the Moor,
For they succeed on you. To you, lord governor,
Remains the censure of this hellish villain,
The time, the place, the torture. O, enforce it!   420
Myself will straight aboard, and to the state
This heavy act with heavy heart relate.   *Exeunt.*

FINIS

Study and Discussion Questions

1. What sets in motion Iago's plotting against Othello?
2. What arguments does Iago use in Act I to persuade Desdemona's father, the Senator Brabantio, to act against Othello?
3. Discuss Brabantio's accusations of sorcery against Othello and Othello's defense, which is the title character's first extended speech in the play.
4. Name two or three ways in which Othello is an outsider in Venice.
5. a. Draw a chart or diagram of who loves/lusts for whom in this play.
   b. How do these yearnings motivate various characters to act in the ways they do?
   c. How is Iago able to manipulate these characters using such yearnings?
6. Name three or four ways in which Othello is presented as a typical heroic figure in the opening scenes of the play. What character traits of the conventional hero does Othello possess? How do some of these traits get him into trouble?
7. a. Research and record definitions of the following words: envy, jealousy, pride, ambition, love, lust, hate, malice.
   b. What characters in *Othello* seem motivated by each of these emotions?
8. List some of the power struggles in *Othello*.

---

412 fell: cruel.   416 keep: remain in.

9. Do a close analysis of one of Iago's speeches (for example, I, 1, 38–62; I, 3, 330–55; I, 3, 374–95; II, 1, 286–312).

10. Discuss irony and foreshadowing in the following passage in I, 3:

    BRABANTIO: Look to her Moor, if thou hast eyes to see:
                  She has deceived her father, and may thee.
    OTHELLO: My life upon her faith! Honest Iago,
                  My Desdemona must I leave to thee.

11. How does Iago, a superb on-the-spot plotter, discover and use a weakness of Cassio's against him?

12. It is in Act III, scene 3, the center of the play, that Iago's plot moves into action. What arguments does Iago use in this scene to poison Othello's mind against Desdemona?

13. How does Desdemona unknowingly play into Iago's plot?

14. Discuss the character of Emilia, wife to Iago. What are her opinions of marriage and of men and women? How is she a foil to Desdemona?

15. What inclines Othello to believe Iago's tale about Desdemona? You might consider here both the situation that Iago has manipulated into being and what Othello himself brings to the situation.

16. Outline, or make a synopsis of the plot of *Othello* by acts. What happens in Act I, in Act II, and so on through Act V?

17. Trace the journey of the handkerchief through the play.

18. Who has died and who is still alive at the end of *Othello*? Do you feel balance has been restored—or are there still loose ends?

19. What significance might there be in Shakespeare's locating most of the play's action not in Venice but in Cypress, a military outpost far from the European urban setting to which most of the characters are accustomed?

20. How is *Othello* a tragedy?

Suggestions for Writing

1. Write a paper exploring the nature of jealousy and envy in *Othello*. Analyze how these emotions motivate characters in the play and influence action. Based on your reading of the play, which of the two—jealousy or envy—would you say is the more destructive?

2. How is Othello's position as an "outsider" central to the play?

3. Discuss the character of Desdemona. How is she a strong and in some ways unconventional woman for her time and place? How is her position in the situation of *Othello* somewhat vulnerable?

4. Discuss the nature of Iago's villainy. Why do you think his machinations in *Othello* are so effective? Why do you suppose Shakespeare gave him such great lines?

5. Sketch a contemporary version of *Othello*. Where would you set your play? How would you adapt your characters to the contemporary world? What might you use instead of a handkerchief as the device on which the plot turns?

6. Have you ever experienced an episode of jealousy? What do you recognize in Othello's jealous reactions or in Desdemona's reactions as the victim of jealousy? Or have you ever been the victim of a malicious envy

like Iago's? Discuss your sense of the accuracy of Shakespeare's reading of human behavior in the grip of such emotions.

7. How do race, gender, social class, and/or cultural background play a role in the misunderstandings that lead to the tragedy in *Othello?*

8. Write a paper on the function in *Othello* of one of the minor characters, such as Emilia, Cassio, or Roderigo.

9. "He hath a daily beauty in his life
That makes me ugly . . ."
Who speaks these lines? When? Who is being referred to? Discuss how this remark might be central to an understanding of *Othello.*

10. What view of marriage does *Othello* offer? Consider the marriages both of Othello and Desdemona and of Iago and Emilia.

11. After reading the play, view one of the three feature length film adaptations of *Othello* with, respectively, Orson Wells, Lawrence Olivier, and Laurence Fishburne in the title role. Choose one scene from the film and analyze it in depth comparing it with the corresponding scene in the play.

Critical Resource

1. Barthelemy, Anthony, ed. *Critical Essays on Shakespeare's Othello.* New York: G. K. Hall, 1994.

2. Bradley, AC. *Shakespearean Tragedy: Lectures on Hamlet, Othello, King Lear, Macbeth,* New York: St. Martin's, 1959, third edition 1992.

3. Kolin, Philip. *Othello: New Critical Essays.* New York: Routledge, 2002.

4. McEachern, Claire, ed. *The Cambridge Companion to Shakespearean Tragedy.* New York: Cambridge UP, 2002 (see pages 189–96 and 123–41).

5. Synder, Susan. *The Comic Matrix of Shakespeare's Tragedies: Romeo and Juliet, Hamlet, Othello, and King Lear.* Princeton, NJ: Princeton UP, 1979.

SUSAN GLASPELL (1882–1948)

Susan Glaspell was born in Davenport, Iowa. After receiving her Ph.D. from the University of Chicago, she began work as a journalist. During that period she also began publishing her first short stories and novels. In 1913 she married George Cram Cook, and the couple settled in Provincetown, Massachusetts. It was here that the two cofounded the Provincetown Players—an experimental, grass-roots theater group set up to counter Broadway's dominance of contemporary drama by creating a space for new playwrights. Glaspell's work helped establish the group's reputation as avant-garde American theater. Her play Allison's House *(1930), loosely based on the life of poet Emily Dickinson, won the Pulitzer Prize. With simple sets and subtle uses of lighting and sound, Glaspell's plays are often referred* to as "plays of ideas"—philosophical and dramatic works that explore the inner-world of characters through their actions and the symbolic use of setting. Her other plays include Suppressed Desires *(1914),* The Verge *(1921), and* Chains of Dew *(1922). In addition to her plays, she published ten novels and about forty short stories.* Trifles *(1916), an experimental one-act play, problematizes the standard, masculinized mystery plot; she also published it in short story form, as "A Jury of Her Peers."*

Trifles   (1916)

Characters

GEORGE HENDERSON, *County Attorney*
HENRY PETERS, *Sheriff*
LEWIS HALE, *A Neighboring Farmer*
MRS. PETERS
MRS. HALE

Scene: *The kitchen in the now abandoned farmhouse of* John Wright, *a gloomy kitchen, and left without having been put in order—unwashed pans under the sink, a loaf of bread outside the breadbox, a dish-towel on the table—other signs of incompleted work. At the rear the outer door opens and the* SHERIFF *comes in followed by the* COUNTY ATTORNEY *and* HALE. *The* SHERIFF *and* HALE *are men in middle life, the* COUNTY ATTORNEY *is a young man; all are much bundled up and go at once to the stove. They are followed by the two women—the* SHERIFF's *wife first; she is a slight wiry woman, a thin nervous face.* MRS. HALE *is larger and would ordinarily be called more comfortable looking, but she is disturbed now and looks fearfully about as she enters. The women have come in slowly, and stand close together near the door.*

COUNTY ATTORNEY [*Rubbing his hands.*]:   This feels good. Come up to the fire, ladies.

MRS. PETERS [*After taking a step forward.*]:   I'm not—cold.

SHERIFF [*Unbuttoning his overcoat and stepping away from the stove as if to mark the beginning of official business.*]:   Now, Mr. Hale, before we move things about, you explain to Mr. Henderson just what you saw when you came here yesterday morning.

COUNTY ATTORNEY: By the way, has anything been moved? Are things just as you left them yesterday?

SHERIFF [*Looking about.*]:   It's just the same. When it dropped below zero last night I thought I'd better send Frank out this morning to make a fire for us—

no use getting pneumonia with a big case on, but I told him not to touch anything except the stove—and you know Frank.

COUNTY ATTORNEY: Somebody should have been left here yesterday.

SHERIFF: Oh—yesterday. When I had to send Frank to Morris Center for that
man who went crazy—I want you to know I had my hands full yesterday. I
knew you could get back from Omaha by today and as long as I went over
everything here myself—

COUNTY ATTORNEY: Well, Mr. Hale, tell just what happened when you came
here yesterday morning.

HALE: Harry and I had started to town with a load of potatoes. We came along
the road from my place and as I got here I said, "I'm going to see if I can't get
John Wright to go in with me on a party telephone." I spoke to Wright about
it once before and he put me off, saying folks talked too much anyway, and
all he asked was peace and quiet—I guess you know about how much he
talked himself; but I thought maybe if I went to the house and talked about
it before his wife, though I said to Harry that I didn't know as what his wife
wanted made much difference to John—

COUNTY ATTORNEY: Let's talk about that later, Mr. Hale. I do want to talk
about that, but tell now just what happened when you got to the house.

HALE: I didn't hear or see anything; I knocked at the door, and still it was all
quiet inside. I knew they must be up, it was past eight o'clock. So I knocked
again, and I thought I heard somebody, say "Come in." I wasn't sure, I'm not
sure yet, but I opened the door—this door [*Indicating the door by which the
two women are still standing*] and there in that rocker—[*pointing to it*] sat Mrs.
Wright.

They all look at the rocker.

COUNTY ATTORNEY: What—was she doing?

HALE: She was rockin' back and forth. She had her apron in her hand and was
kind of—pleating it.

COUNTY ATTORNEY: And how did she—look?

HALE: Well, she looked queer.

COUNTY ATTORNEY: How do you mean—queer?

HALE: Well, as if she didn't know what she was going to do next. And kind of
done up.

COUNTY ATTORNEY: How did she seem to feel about your coming?

HALE: Why, I don't think she minded—one way or other. She didn't pay much
attention. I said, "How do, Mrs. Wright, it's cold, ain't it?" And she said, "Is
it?"—and went on kind of pleating at her apron. Well, I was surprised; she
didn't ask me to come up to the stove, or to set down, but just sat there, not
even looking at me, so I said, "I want to see John." And then she—laughed. I
guess you would call it a laugh. I thought of Harry and the team outside, so I
said a little sharp: "Can't I see John?" "No," she says, kind o' dull like. "Ain't

he home?" says I. "Yes," says she, "he's home." "Then why can't I see him?" I asked her, out of patience. "Cause he's dead," says she. "*Dead?*" says I. She just nodded her head, not getting a bit excited, but rockin' back and forth. "Why—where is he?" says I, not knowing what to say. She just pointed upstairs—like that [*himself pointing to the room above*]. I got up, with the idea of going up there. I walked from there to here—then I says, "Why, what did he die of?" "He died of a rope round his neck," says she, and just went on pleatin' at her apron. Well, I went out and called Harry. I thought I might—need help. We went upstairs and there he was lyin'—

COUNTY ATTORNEY: I think I'd rather have you go into that upstairs, where you can point it all out. Just go on now with the rest of the story.

HALE: Well, my first thought was to get that rope off. It looked . . . [*Stops, his face twitches*] . . . but Harry, he went up to him, and he said, "No, he's dead all right, and we'd better not touch anything." So we went back down stairs. She was still sitting that same way. "Has anybody been notified?" I asked. "No," says she, unconcerned. "Who did this, Mrs. Wright?" said Harry. He said it business-like—and she stopped pleatin' of her apron. "I don't know," says she. "You don't *know?*" says Harry. "No," says she. "Weren't you sleepin' in the bed with him?" says Harry. "Yes," says she, "but I was on the inside." "Somebody slipped a rope round his neck and strangled him you didn't wake up?" says Harry. "I didn't wake up," she said after him. We must 'a looked as if we didn't see how that could be, for after a minute she said, "I sleep sound." Harry was going to ask her more questions but I said maybe we ought to let her tell her story first to the coroner, or the sheriff, so Harry went fast as he could to Rivers' place, where there's a telephone.

COUNTY ATTORNEY: And what did Mrs. Wright do when she knew that you had gone for the coroner?

HALE: She moved from that chair to this one over here [*Pointing to a small chair in the corner*] and just sat there with her hands held together and looking down. I got a feeling that I ought to make some conversation, so I said I had come in to see if John wanted to put in a telephone, and at that she started to laugh, and then she stopped and looked at me—scared. [*The* COUNTY ATTORNEY, *who has had his notebook out, makes a note.*] I dunno, maybe it wasn't scared. I wouldn't like to say it was. Soon Harry got back, and then Dr. Lloyd came, and you, Mr. Peters, and so I guess that's all I know that you don't.

COUNTY ATTORNEY [*Looking around.*]:   I guess we'll go upstairs first—and then out to the barn and around there. [*To the* SHERIFF.] You're convinced that there was nothing important here—nothing that would point to any motive.

SHERIFF: Nothing here but kitchen things.

The COUNTY ATTORNEY, *after again looking around the kitchen, opens the door of cupboard closet. He gets up on a chair and looks on a shelf. Pulls his hand away, sticky.*

COUNTY ATTORNEY: Here's a nice mess.

The women draw nearer.

MRS. PETERS [*To the other woman.*]:   Oh, her fruit; it did freeze. [*To the* LAWYER.] She worried about that when it turned so cold. She said the fire'd go out and her jars would break.

SHERIFF: Well, can you beat the women! Held for murder and worryin' about her preserves.

COUNTY ATTORNEY: I guess before we're through she may have something more serious than preserves to worry about.

HALE: Well, women are used to worrying over trifles.

The two women move a little closer together.

COUNTY ATTORNEY [*With the gallantry of a young politician.*]:   And yet, for all their worries, what would we do without the ladies? [*The women do not unbend. He goes to the sink, takes a dipperful of water from the pail and pouring it into a basin, washes his hands. Starts to wipe them on the roller-towel, turns it for a cleaner place.*] Dirty towels! [*Kicks his foot against the pans under the sink.*] Not much of a housekeeper, would you say, ladies?

MRS. HALE [*Stiffly.*]:   There's a great deal of work to be done on a farm.

COUNTY ATTORNEY: To be sure. And yet [*With a little bow to her*] I know there are some Dickson county farmhouses which do not have such roller towels.

He gives it a pull to expose its full length again.

MRS. HALE: Those towels get dirty awful quick. Men's hands aren't always as clean as they might be.

COUNTY ATTORNEY: Ah, loyal to your sex, I see. But you and Mrs. Wright were neighbors. I suppose you were friends, too.

MRS. HALE [*Shaking her head.*]:   I've not seen much of her of late years. I've not been in this house—it's more than a year.

COUNTY ATTORNEY: And why was that? You didn't like her?

MRS. HALE: I liked her all well enough. Farmers' wives have their hands full, Mr. Henderson. And then—

COUNTY ATTORNEY: Yes—?

MRS. HALE [*Looking about.*]:   It never seemed a very cheerful place.

COUNTY ATTORNEY: No—it's not cheerful. I shouldn't say she had the home-making instinct.

MRS. HALE: Well, I don't know as Wright had, either.

COUNTY ATTORNEY: You mean that they didn't get on very well?

MRS. HALE: No, I don't mean anything. But I don't think a place'd be any cheerfuller for John Wright's being in it.

COUNTY ATTORNEY: I'd like to talk more of that a little later. I want to get the
lay of things upstairs now.

He goes to the left, where three steps lead to a stair door.

SHERIFF: I suppose anything Mrs. Peters does'll be all right. She was to take in
some clothes for her, you know, and a few little things. We left in such a hurry
yesterday.
COUNTY ATTORNEY: Yes, but I would like to see what you take, Mrs. Peters,
and keep an eye out for anything that might be of use to us.
MRS. PETERS: Yes, Mr. Henderson.

The women listen to the men's steps on the stairs, then look about the kitchen.

MRS. HALE: I'd hate to have men coming into my kitchen, snooping around and
criticising.

She arranges the pans under sink which the LAWYER *had shoved out of place.*

MRS. PETERS: Of course it's no more than their duty.
MRS. HALE: Duty's all right, but I guess that deputy sheriff that came out to
make the fire might have got a little of this on. [*Gives the roller towel a pull.*]
Wish I'd thought of that sooner. Seems mean to talk about her for not having things slicked up when she had to come away in such a hurry.
MRS. PETERS [*Who has gone to a small table in the left rear corner of the room,
and lifted one end of a towel that covers a pan.*]:   She had bread set.

Stands still.

MRS. HALE [*Eyes fixed on a loaf of bread beside the breadbox, which is on a low
shelf at the other side of the room. Moves slowly toward it.*]:   She was going
to put this in there. [*Picks up loaf, then abruptly drops it. In a manner of returning to familiar things.*] It's a shame about her fruit. I wonder if it's all gone.
[*Gets up on the chair and looks.*] I think there's some here that's all right, Mrs.
Peters. Yes—here; [*Holding it toward the window*] this is cherries, too.
[*Looking again.*] I declare I believe that's the only one. [*Gets down, bottle in
her hand. Goes to the sink and wipes it off on the outside.*] She'll feel awful
bad after all her hard work in the hot weather. I remember the afternoon I
put up my cherries last summer.

*She puts the bottle on the big kitchen table, center of the room. With a sigh,
is about to sit down in the rocking-chair. Before she is seated realizes what chair
it is; with a slow look at it, steps back. The chair which she has touched rocks
back and forth.*

MRS. PETERS: Well, I must get those things from the front room closet. [*She goes to the door at the right, but after looking into the other room, steps back.*] You coming with me, Mrs. Hale? You could help me carry them.

They go in the other room; reappear, MRS. PETERS *carrying a dress and skirt,* MRS. HALE *following with a pair of shoes.*

MRS. PETERS: My, it's cold in there.

She puts the clothes on the big table, and hurries to the stove.

MRS. HALE [*Examining the skirt.*]:   Wright was close. I think maybe that's why she kept so much to herself. She didn't even belong to the Ladies Aid. I suppose she felt she couldn't do her part, and then you don't enjoy things when you feel shabby. She used to wear pretty clothes and be lively, when she was Minnie Foster, one of the town girls singing in the choir. But that—oh, that was thirty years ago. This all you was to take in?

MRS. PETERS: She said she wanted an apron. Funny thing to want, for there isn't much to get you dirty in jail, goodness knows. But I suppose just to make her feel more natural. She said they was in the top drawer in this cupboard. Yes, here. And then her little shawl that always hung behind the door. [*Opens stair door and looks.*] Yes, here it is.

Quickly shuts door leading upstairs.

MRS. HALE [*Abruptly moving toward her.*]:   Mrs. Peters?
MRS. PETERS: Yes, Mrs. Hale?
MRS. HALE: Do you think she did it?
MRS. PETERS [*In a frightened voice.*]:   Oh, I don't know.
MRS. HALE: Well, I don't think she did. Asking for an apron and her little shawl. Worrying about her fruit.
MRS. PETERS [*Starts to speak, glances up, where footsteps are heard in the room above. In a low voice.*]:   Mr. Peters says it looks bad for her. Mr. Henderson is awful sarcastic in a speech and he'll make fun of her sayin' she didn't wake up.
MRS. HALE: Well, I guess John Wright didn't wake when they was slipping that rope under his neck.
MRS. PETERS: No, it's strange. It must have been done awful crafty and still. They say it was such a—funny way to kill a man, rigging it all up like that.
MRS. HALE: That's just what Mr. Hale said. There was a gun in the house. He says that's what he can't understand.
MRS. PETERS: Mr. Henderson said coming out that what was needed for the case was a motive; something to show anger, or—sudden feeling.
MRS. HALE [*Who is standing by the table.*]:   Well, I don't see any signs of anger around here. [*She puts her hand on the dish towel which lies on the table, stands*

looking down at table, one half of which is clean, the other half messy.] It's wiped to here. [*Makes a move as if to finish work, then turns and looks at loaf of bread outside the breadbox. Drops towel. In that voice of coming back to familiar things.*] Wonder how they are finding things upstairs. I hope she had it a little more red-up there. You know, it seems kind of *sneaking.* Locking her up in town and then coming out here and trying to get her own house to turn against her!

MRS. PETERS: But Mrs. Hale, the law is the law.

MRS. HALE: I s'pose 'tis. [*Unbuttoning her coat.*] Better loosen up your things, Mrs. Peters. You won't feel them when you go out.

MRS. PETERS *takes off her fur tippet, goes to hang it on hook at back of room, stands looking at the under part of the small corner table.*

MRS. PETERS: She was piecing a quilt.

She brings the large sewing basket and they look at the bright pieces.

MRS. HALE: It's log cabin pattern. Pretty, isn't it? I wonder if she was goin' to quilt it or just knot it?

Footsteps have been heard coming down the stairs. The SHERIFF *enters followed by* HALE *and the* COUNTY ATTORNEY.

SHERIFF: They wonder if she was going to quilt it or just knot it!

The men laugh, the women look abashed.

COUNTY ATTORNEY [*Rubbing his hands over the stove*]:   Frank's fire didn't do much up there, did it? Well, let's go out to the barn and get that cleared up.

The men go outside.

MRS. HALE [*Resentfully.*]:   I don't know as there's anything so strange, our takin' up our time with little things while we're waiting for them to get the evidence. [*She sits down at the big table smoothing out a block with decision.*] I don't see as it's anything to laugh about.

MRS. PETERS [*Apologetically.*]:   Of course they've got awful important things on their minds.

Pulls up a chair and joins MRS. HALE *at the table.*

MRS. HALE [*Examining another block.*]:   Mrs. Peters, look at this one. Here, this is the one she was working on, and look at the sewing! All the rest of it has been so nice and even. And look at this! It's all over the place! Why, it looks as if she didn't know what she was about!

After she has said this they look at each other, then start to glance back at the door. After an instant MRS. HALE *has pulled at a knot and ripped the sewing.*

MRS. PETERS: Oh, what are you doing, Mrs. Hale?

MRS. HALE [*Mildly.*]:   Just pulling out a stitch or two that's not sewed very good. [*Threading a needle.*] Bad sewing always make me fidgety.

MRS. PETERS [*Nervously.*]:   I don't think we ought to touch things.

MRS. HALE: I'll just finish up this end. [*Suddenly stopping and leaning forward.*] Mrs. Peters?

MRS. PETERS: Yes, Mrs. Hale?

MRS. HALE: What do you suppose she was so nervous about?

MRS. PETERS: Oh—I don't know. I don't know as she was nervous. I sometimes sew awful queer when I'm just tired. [MRS. HALE *starts to say something, looks at* MRS. PETERS, *then goes on sewing.*] Well I must get these things wrapped up. They may be through sooner than we think. [*Putting apron and other things together.*] I wonder where I can find a piece of paper, and string.

MRS. HALE: In that cupboard, maybe.

MRS. PETERS [*Looking in cupboard.*]:   Why, here's a bird-cage. [*Holds it up.*] Did she have a bird, Mrs. Hale?

MRS. HALE: Why, I don't know whether she did or not—I've not been here for so long. There was a man around last year selling canaries cheap, but I don't know as she took one; maybe she did. She used to sing real pretty herself.

MRS. PETERS [*Glancing around.*]:   Seems funny to think of a bird here. But she must have had one, or why would she have a cage? I wonder what happened to it.

MRS. HALE: I s'pose maybe the cat got it.

MRS. PETERS: No, she didn't have a cat. She's got that feeling some people have about cats—being afraid of them. My cat got in her room and she was real upset and asked me to take it out.

MRS. HALE: My sister Bessie was like that. Queer, ain't it?

MRS. PETERS [*Examining the cage.*]:   Why, look at this door. It's broke. One hinge is pulled apart.

MRS. HALE [*Looking too.*]:   Looks as if someone must have been rough with it.

MRS. PETERS: Why, yes.

She brings the cage forward and puts it on the table.

MRS. HALE: I wish if they're going to find any evidence they'd be about it. I don't like this place.

MRS. PETERS: But I'm awful glad you came with me, Mrs. Hale. It would be lonesome for me sitting here alone.

MRS. HALE: It would, wouldn't it? [*Dropping her sewing.*] But I tell you what I do wish, Mrs. Peters. I wish I had come over sometimes when *she* was here. I—[*Looking around the room*]—wish I had.

MRS. PETERS: But of course you were awful busy, Mrs. Hale—your house and your children.

MRS. HALE: I could've come. I stayed away because it weren't cheerful—and that's why I ought to have come. I—I've never liked this place. Maybe because it's down in a hollow and you don't see the road. I dunno what it is, but it's a lonesome place and always was. I wish I had come over to see Minnie Foster sometimes. I can see now—

Shakes her head.

MRS. PETERS: Well, you mustn't reproach yourself, Mrs. Hale. Somehow we just don't see how it is with other folks until—something comes up.

MRS. HALE: Not having children makes less work—but it makes a quiet house, and Wright out to work all day, and no company when he did come in. Did you know John Wright, Mrs. Peters?

MRS. PETERS: Not to know him; I've seen him in town. They say he was a good man.

MRS. HALE: Yes—good; he didn't drink, and kept his word as well as most, I guess, and paid his debts. But he was a hard man, Mrs. Peters. Just to pass the time of day with him—[*Shivers.*]   Like a raw wind that gets to the bone. [*Pauses, her eye falling on the cage.*] I should think she would 'a wanted a bird. But what do you suppose went with it?

MRS. PETERS: I don't know, unless it got sick and died.

She reaches over and swings the broken door, swings it again, both women watch it.

MRS. HALE: You weren't raised round here, were you? [MRS. PETERS *shakes her head.*]   You didn't know—her?

MRS. PETERS: Not till they brought her yesterday.

MRS. HALE: She—come to think of it, she was kind of like a bird herself—real sweet and pretty, but kind of timid and—fluttery. How—she—did—change. [*Silence; then as if struck by a happy thought and relieved to get back to every day things.*] Tell you what, Mrs. Peters, why don't you take the quilt in with you? It might take up her mind.

MRS. PETERS: Why, I think that's a real nice idea, Mrs. Hale. There couldn't possibly be any objection to it, could there? Now, just what would I take? I wonder if her patches are in here—and her things.

They look in the sewing basket.

MRS. HALE: Here's some red. I expect this has got sewing things in it. [*Brings out a fancy box.*] What a pretty box. Looks like something somebody would give you. Maybe her scissors are in here. [*Opens box. Suddenly puts her hand to her nose.*] Why—[MRS. PETERS *bends nearer, then turns her face away.*] There's something wrapped up in this piece of silk.

MRS. PETERS: Why, this isn't her scissors.

MRS. HALE [*Lifting the silk.*]:   Oh, Mrs. Peters—its—

MRS. PETERS *bends closer.*

MRS. PETERS: It's the bird.

MRS. HALE [*Jumping up.*]:   But, Mrs. Peters—look at it! It's neck! Look at its neck! It's all—other side *to.*

MRS. PETERS: Somebody—wrung—its—neck.

Their eyes meet. A look of growing comprehension, of horror. Steps are heard outside. MRS. HALE *slips box under quilt pieces, and sinks into her chair. Enter* SHERIFF *and* COUNTY ATTORNEY. MRS. PETERS *rises.*

COUNTY ATTORNEY [*As one turning from serious things to little pleasantries.*]:   Well, ladies, have you decided whether she was going to quilt it or knot it?

MRS. PETERS: We think she was going to—knot it.

COUNTY ATTORNEY: Well, that's interesting, I'm sure. [*Seeing the bird cage.*] Has the bird flown?

MRS. HALE [*Putting more quilt pieces over the box.*]:   We think the—cat got it.

COUNTY ATTORNEY [*Preoccupied.*]:   Is there a cat?

MRS. HALE *glances in a quick covert way at* MRS. PETERS.

MRS. PETERS: Well, not *now.* They're superstitious, you know. They leave.

COUNTY ATTORNEY [*To* SHERIFF PETERS, *continuing an interrupted conversation.*]:   No sign at all of anyone having come from the outside. Their own rope. Now let's go up again and go over it piece by piece. [*They start upstairs.*] It would have to have been someone who knew just the—

MRS. PETERS *sits down. The two women sit there not looking at one another, but as if peering into something and at the same time holding back. When they talk now it is in the manner of feeling their way over strange ground, as if afraid of what they are saying, but as if they can not help saying it.*

MRS. HALE: She liked the bird. She was going to bury it in that pretty box.

MRS. PETERS [*In a whisper.*]:   When I was a girl—my kitten—there was a boy took a hatchet, and before my eyes—and before I could get there—[*Covers her face an instant.*] If they hadn't held me back I would have—[*Catches herself, looks upstairs where steps are heard, falters weakly*]—hurt him.

MRS. HALE [*With a slow look around her.*]:   I wonder how it would seem never to have had any children around. [*Pause.*] No, Wright wouldn't like the bird—a thing that sang. She used to sing. He killed that, too.

MRS. PETERS [*Moving uneasily.*]:   We don't know who killed the bird.

MRS. HALE: I knew John Wright.

MRS. PETERS: It was an awful thing was done in this house that night, Mrs. Hale. Killing a man while he slept, slipping a rope around his neck that choked the life out of him.

MRS. HALE: His neck. Choked the life out of him.

Her hand goes out and rests on the bird-cage.

MRS. PETERS [*With rising voice.*]:   We don't know who killed him. We don't *know.*

MRS. HALE [*Her own feeling not interrupted.*]:   If there'd been years and years of nothing, then a bird to sing to you, it would be awful—still, after the bird was still.

MRS. PETERS [*Something within her speaking.*]:   I know what stillness is. When we homesteaded in Dakota, and my first baby died—after he was two years old, and me with no other then—

MRS. HALE [*Moving.*]:   How soon do you suppose they'll be through, looking for the evidence?

MRS. PETERS: I know what stillness is. [*Pulling herself back.*] The law has got to punish crime, Mrs. Hale.

MRS. HALE [*Not as if answering that.*]:   I wish you'd seen Minnie Foster when she wore a white dress with blue ribbons and stood up there in the choir and sang. [*A look around the room.*] Oh, I *wish* I'd come over here once in a while! That was a crime! That was a crime! Who's going to punish that?

MRS. PETERS [*Looking upstairs.*]:   We mustn't—take on.

MRS. HALE: I might have known she needed help! I know how things can be— for women. I tell you, it's queer, Mrs. Peters. We live close together and we live far apart. We all go through the same things—it's all just a different kind of the same thing. [*Brushes her eyes, noticing the bottle of fruit, reaches out for it.*] If I was you I wouldn't tell her her fruit was gone. Tell her it *ain't.* Tell her it's all right. Take this in to prove it to her. She—she may never know whether it was broke or not.

MRS. PETERS [*takes the bottle, looks about for something to wrap it in; takes petticoat from the clothes brought from the other room, very nervously begins winding this around the bottle. In a false voice.*]:   My, it's a good thing the men couldn't hear us. Wouldn't they just laugh! Getting all stirred up over a little thing like a—dead canary. As if that could have anything to do with— with—wouldn't they *laugh!*

The men are heard coming down stairs.

MRS. HALE [*Under her breath.*]:   Maybe they would—maybe they wouldn't.

COUNTY ATTORNEY: No, Peters, it's all perfectly clear except a reason for doing it. But you know juries when it comes to women. If there was some definite thing. Something to show—something to make a story about—a thing that would connect up with this strange way of doing it—

The women's eyes meet for an instant. Enter HALE *from outer door.*

HALE: Well, I've got the team around. Pretty cold out there.

COUNTY ATTORNEY: I'm going to stay here a while by myself. [*To the* SHERIFF.] You can send Frank out for me, can't you? I want to go over everything. I'm not satisfied that we can't do better.

SHERIFF: Do you want to see what Mrs. Peters is going to take in?

The LAWYER *goes to the table, picks up the apron, laughs.*

COUNTY ATTORNEY: Oh, I guess they're not very dangerous things the ladies have picked out. [*Moves a few things about, disturbing the quilt pieces which cover the box. Steps back.*] No, Mrs. Peters doesn't need supervising. For that matter, a sheriff's wife is married to the law. Ever think of it that way, Mrs. Peters?

MRS. PETERS: Not—just that way.

SHERIFF [*Chuckling.*]:   Married to the law. [*Moves toward the other room.*] I just want you to come in here a minute, George. We ought to take a look at these windows.

COUNTY ATTORNEY [*Scoffingly.*]:   Oh, windows!

SHERIFF: We'll be right out, Mr. Hale.

HALE *goes outside. The* SHERIFF *follows the* COUNTY ATTORNEY *into the other room. Then* MRS. HALE *rises, hands tight together, looking intensely at* MRS. PE-TERS, *whose eyes make a slow turn, finally meeting* MRS. HALE's. *A moment* MRS. HALE *holds her, then her own eyes point the way to where the box is concealed. Suddenly* MRS. PETERS *throws back quilt pieces and tries to put the box in the bag she is wearing. It is too big. She opens box, starts to take bird out, cannot touch it, goes to pieces, stands there helpless. Sound of a knob turning in the other room.* MRS. HALE *snatches the box and puts it in the pocket of her big coat. Enter* COUNTY ATTORNEY *and* SHERIFF.

COUNTY ATTORNEY [*Facetiously.*]:   Well, Henry, at least we found out that she was not going to quilt it. She was going to—what is it you call it, ladies?

MRS. HALE [*Her hand against her pocket.*]:   We call it—knot it, Mr. Henderson.

CURTAIN

Study and Discussion Questions

1. Characterize Minnie Wright and John Wright. What was their marriage like?
2. List the series of clues that lead Mrs. Hale and Mrs. Peters to conclude that Minnie Wright murdered her husband. Do the broken bird cage and the dead canary have any significance in the play beyond their role as clues?
3. Trace the various signs throughout the play that the men and the women see things differently.
4. Early on, Sheriff Peters says, "Nothing here but kitchen things," meaning that the men should look elsewhere for clues. Find other examples of irony in the play. Is there a pattern to the ironies?
5. Compare Mrs. Hale and Mrs. Peters. Which one changes more over the course of the play, and how? Trace the signs and the causes of the growing empathy the two women feel with Minnie Wright.
6. What are some of the conflicts in this drama? Is any one primary?
7. What has Glaspell lost and what has she gained by shaping the play so that we never meet either John or Minnie Wright?

Suggestions for Writing

1. Glaspell rewrote *Trifles* as a short story, which she titled "A Jury of Her Peers." Would that have made a better or worse title for the play? Does it change the emphasis? Explain.
2. Try to imagine a play with the same plot, but with the gender of every character reversed and with male-oriented clues that men see but women don't. Would such a play make sense? Would it have the same impact as *Trifles*?
3. Write an entry or two for the journal you imagine Minnie Wright might have kept.
4. Suppose the canary was found and Minnie Wright was convicted and about to be sentenced. Write a speech she might address to the court explaining why she killed her husband.
5. Were Mrs. Hale and Mrs. Peters justified in covering up the murder of John Wright? Explain.

Critical Resources

1. Ben-Zvi, Linda, ed. *Susan Glaspell: Essays on Theater and Fiction.* Ann Arbor: U of Michigan P, 1995.
2. Gainor, Ellen. *Susan Glaspell in Context: American Theater, Culture and Politics, 1915–1948.* Ann Arbor: U of Michigan P, 2001.
3. Ozieblo, Barbara. *Susan Glaspell: A Critical Biography.* Chapel Hill: U of North Carolina P, 2000.

❈ ❈ ❈

NONFICTION

VIRGINIA WOOLF (1882–1941)

Virginia Woolf was born in London and grew up in an environment of wealth and culture, meeting many of the most distinguished intellectuals of the time. Unlike her brothers, Virginia and her sister were not sent to school or the university, but educated at home. From her mother's death in 1895 to the death of her father, writer Leslie Stephen, in 1904, she was responsible for running the household; after that, she moved to London and became the center of the intellectual and artistic Bloomsbury Group. In 1912, she married Leonard Woolf; a decade later she began a long relationship with the writer Vita Sackville-West. Woolf's experimental fiction helped to define modernism as a literary movement and earned her a reputation as a major English novelist. Her continuing attacks of depression and her fear of a Nazi invasion of England led to her suicide in 1941. Among her works are the novels Mrs. Dalloway *(1925),* To the Lighthouse *(1927),* The Waves *(1931), and* Three Guineas *(1938). In "Shakespeare's Sister," excerpted from the nonfiction* A Room of One's Own *(1929), Woolf asks the rhetorical question, "... what would have happened had Shakespeare had a wonderfully gifted sister ..." as a way to set up a critique of patriarchal notions of genius and the lack of opportunity for talented women.*

Shakespeare's Sister (1929)

It would have been impossible, completely and entirely, for any woman to have written the plays of Shakespeare in the age of Shakespeare. Let me imagine, since facts are so hard to come by, what would have happened had Shakespeare had a wonderfully gifted sister, called Judith, let us say. Shakespeare himself went, very probably—his mother was an heiress—to the grammar school, where he may have learnt Latin—Ovid, Virgil and Horace—and the elements of grammar and logic. He was, it is well known, a wild boy who poached rabbits, perhaps shot a deer, and had, rather sooner than he should have done, to marry a woman in the neighbourhood, who bore him a child rather quicker than was right. That escapade sent him to seek his fortune in London. He had, it seemed, a taste for the theatre; he began by holding horses at the stage door. Very soon he got work in the theatre, became a successful actor, and lived at the hub of the universe, meeting everybody, knowing everybody, practising his art on the boards, exercising his wits in the streets, and even getting access to the palace of the queen. Meanwhile his extraordinarily gifted sister, let us suppose, remained at home. She was as adventurous, as imaginative, as agog to see the world as he was. But she was not sent to school. She had no chance of learning grammar and logic, let alone of reading Horace and Virgil. She picked up a book now and then, one of her brother's perhaps, and read a few pages. But then her parents came in and told her to mend the stockings or mind the stew and not moon about with books and papers. They would have spoken sharply but kindly, for they were substantial people who knew the conditions of life for a woman and loved their daughter—indeed, more likely than not she was the apple of her father's eye. Perhaps she scribbled some pages up in an apple loft on the sly, but was careful to hide them or set fire to them. Soon, however, before she was out of her teens, she was to be betrothed to the son of a neighbouring woolstapler. She cried out that marriage was hateful to her, and for that she was severely beaten by her father. Then he ceased to scold her. He begged her instead not to hurt him, not to shame him in this matter of her marriage. He would give her a chain of beads or a fine petticoat, he said; and there were tears in his eyes. How could she disobey him? How could she break his heart? The force of her own gift alone drove her to it. She made up a small parcel of her belongings, let herself down by a rope one summer's night and took the road to London. She was not seventeen. The birds that sang in the hedge were not more musical than she was. She had the quickest fancy, a gift like her brother's, for the tune of words. Like him, she had a taste for the theatre. She stood at the stage door; she wanted to act, she said. Men laughed in her face. The manager—a fat, loose-lipped man— guffawed. He bellowed something about poodles dancing and women acting— no woman, he said, could possibly be an actress. He hinted—you can imagine what. She could get no training in her craft. Could she even seek her dinner in a tavern or roam the streets at midnight? Yet her genius was for fiction and lusted to feed abundantly upon the lives of men and women and the study of their ways. At last—for she was very young, oddly like Shakespeare the poet in her face, with the same grey eyes and rounded brows—at last Nick Greene the actor-manager took pity on her; she found herself with child by that gentleman and so—who shall measure the heat and violence of the poet's heart when caught and tangled in a woman's body?—killed herself one winter's night and lies buried at some cross-roads where the omnibuses now stop outside the Elephant and Castle.[1]

    That, more or less, is how the story would run, I think, if a woman in Shakespeare's day had had Shakespeare's genius. But for my part, I agree with the deceased bishop, if such he was—it is unthinkable that any woman in Shakespeare's day should have had Shakespeare's genius. For genius like Shakespeare's is not born among labouring, uneducated, servile people. It was not born in England among the Saxons and the Britons. It is not born today among the working classes. How, then, could it have been born among women whose work began, according to Professor Trevelyan, almost before they were out of the nursery, who were forced to it by their parents and held to it by all the power of law and

---

[1] A tavern.

custom? Yet genius of a sort must have existed among women as it must have existed among the working classes. Now and again an Emily Brontë or a Robert Burns[2] blazes out and proves its presence. But certainly it never got itself on to paper. When, however, one reads of a witch being ducked, of a woman possessed by devils, of a wise woman selling herbs, or even of a very remarkable man who had a mother, then I think we are on the track of a lost novelist, a suppressed poet, of some mute and inglorious Jane Austen, some Emily Brontë who dashed her brains out on the moor or mopped and mowed about the highways crazed with the torture that her gift had put her to. Indeed, I would venture to guess that Anon, who wrote so many poems without signing them, was often a woman.

Study and Discussion Questions

1. What kind of education does Woolf say Shakespeare received? What kind would Judith receive?
2. How do Judith's parents demonstrate their love for her?
3. How does Judith's father try to get her to marry?
4. How do theater people respond to her desire to act and to write?
5. Woolf writes that Judith's "genius was for fiction and lusted to feed abundantly upon the lives of men and women and the study of their ways." What kept her from doing this?

Suggestions for Writing

1. What are the dangers of challenging the limits of what you are allowed to do—in this sketch? in your own life?
2. Write a paragraph stating Woolf's thesis. Why is creating Judith as a character an effective way of making this argument?
3. Are there any ways in which women today who want to write are barred from certain kinds of experience?

Critical Resources

1. Barrett, Michele. "Reason and Truth in *A Room of One's Own:* A Master in Lunacy." *Virginia Woolf Out of Bounds: Selected Papers from the Tenth Annual Conference on Virginia Woolf.* New York: Pace UP, 2001. (Also contains a chapter on ways to teach *A Room of One's Own.*)
2. Froula, Christine. "Virginia Woolf as Shakespeare's Sister: Chapters in a Woman Writer's Autobiography." *Women's Re-Visions of Shakespeare On the Responses of Dickinson, Woolf, Rich, H.D., George Eliot and Others.* Marianne Novy, ed. Urbana: U of Illinois P, 1990, 123–42.
3. Roe, Sue, ed. *The Cambridge Companion to Virginia Woolf.* Cambridge: Cambridge UP, 2000.

---

[2]Brontë (1818–1848), English novelist; Burns (1759–1796), Scottish poet.

4. Woolf, Virginia. *The Letters of Virginia Woolf.* Nigel Nicolson, ed. New York: Harcourt Brace Jovanovich, 1975.

SOJOURNER TRUTH (1797?–1883)

Isabella (later Isabella Van Wagener) was born a slave in upstate New York, escaped in 1827, and in 1829 moved to New York City, where she worked as a servant. She developed her speaking talent working with an evangelical preacher. In 1843, she had visions and heard voices that led her to take the name Sojourner Truth, and she began touring the country, preaching religion and the abolition of slavery. Near the end of the Civil War, she helped recruit black troops for the Union army. She was a powerful and a popular speaker, and, at an 1851 women's rights convention in Akron, Ohio, she turned the tide in an angry debate between feminists and conservative ministers with the following speech, recorded by a convention participant. In the sermon-like "Ain't I a Woman?" Truth convincingly exposes the blatant contradictions of white, male, and middle-class hegemony.

Ain't I a Woman?   (1851)

Well, children, where there is so much racket there must be something out of kilter. I think that 'twixt the negroes of the South and the women at the North, all talking about rights, the white men will be in a fix pretty soon. But what's all this here talking about?

That man over there says that women need to be helped into carriages, and lifted over ditches, and to have the best place everywhere. Nobody ever helps me into carriages, or over mud-puddles, or gives me any best place! And ain't I a woman? Look at me! Look at my arm! I have ploughed and planted, and gathered into barns, and no man could head me! And ain't I a woman? I could work as much and eat as much as a man—when I could get it—and bear the lash as well! And ain't I a woman? I have borne thirteen children, and seen them most all sold off to slavery, and when I cried out with my mother's grief, none but Jesus heard me! And ain't I a woman?

Then they talk about this thing in the head; what's this they call it? [Intellect, someone whispers.] That's it, honey. What's that got to do with women's rights or negro's rights? If my cup won't hold but a pint, and yours holds a quart, wouldn't you be mean not to let me have my little half-measure full?

Then that little man in black there, he says women can't have as much rights as men, 'cause Christ wasn't a woman! Where did your Christ come from? Where did your Christ come from? From God and a woman! Man had nothing to do with Him.

If the first woman God ever made was strong enough to turn the world upside down all alone, these women together ought to be able to turn it back, and get it right side up again! And now they is asking to do it, the men better let them.

Obliged to you for hearing me, and now old Sojourner ain't got nothing more to say.

Study and Discussion Questions

1. How does Sojourner Truth use the Bible to argue for women's rights?
2. What is ironic about her argument concerning intellect?
3. List Truth's metaphors and images.
4. Locate some of her rhetorical devices (e.g., repetition). What other effective argumentative strategies does she use?
5. How does she overturn both race and gender stereotypes to make her argument?
6. This is a speech, so read it out loud.

Suggestions for Writing

1. Look at "Ain't I a Woman" as part of a political speech, not to win an election but to promote a cause. Compare this to a political speech in the twenty-first century. How is it similar? How is it different?
2. Compare/contrast Sojourner Truth's "Ain't I a Woman" to another famous speech by an African American, Martin Luther King's "I Have a Dream" (Protest).

Critical Resources:

1. Fitch, Suzanne. *Sojourner Truth as Orator: Wit, Story, and Song.* Westport, CT: Greenwood, 1997.
2. Gilbert, Olive. *Narrative of Sojourner Truth: A Bondswoman of Olden Time; With a History of Her Labors and Correspondence Drawn form her Book Of Life.* New York: Oxford UP, 1991.
3. *The Life and Legend of Sojourner Truth.* Princeton, NJ: Films for the Humanities, 2001, (57 minutes).
4. Painter, Nell. *Sojourner Truth: a life, a symbol.* New York: W.W. Norton. 1996.

JUDY BRADY (b. 1931)

Judy Syfers Brady grew up in the Midwest and studied at the University of Iowa. In the late 1960s she was an ardent activist for women's rights. In 1971, her article "I Want A Wife" appeared in the first edition of Ms. *magazine at a time when the promise of equality for women had lagged in an American culture still holding tight to traditional roles for women. The article has become a key document of that era and is now read in university courses throughout the country. In the piece, Brady deftly uses rhetorical devices (sarcasm, irony, hyperbole) to create a penetrating social satire. Brady currently lives in San Francisco, where she continues her activism, working on environmental issues and with the Women's Cancer Research Center.*

I Want a Wife   (1971)

I belong to that classification of people known as wives. I am A Wife. And, not altogether incidentally, I am a mother.

Not too long ago a male friend of mine appeared on the scene fresh from a recent divorce. He had one child, who is, of course, with his ex-wife. He is obviously looking for another wife. As I thought about him while I was ironing one evening, it suddenly occurred to me that I, too, would like to have a wife. Why do I want a wife?

I would like to go back to school so that I can become economically independent, support myself, and, if need be, support those dependent upon me. I want a wife who will work and send me to school. And while I am going to school I want a wife to take care of my children. I want a wife to keep track of the children's doctor and dentist appointments. And to keep track of mine, too. I want a wife to make sure my children eat properly and are kept clean. I want a wife who will wash the children's clothes and keep them mended. I want a wife who is a good nurturant attendant to my children, who arranges for their schooling, makes sure that they have an adequate social life with their peers, takes them to the park, the zoo, etc. I want a wife who takes care of the children when they are sick, a wife who arranges to be around when the children need special care, because, of course, I cannot miss classes at school. My wife must arrange to lose time at work and not lose the job. It may mean a small cut in my wife's income from time to time, but I guess I can tolerate that. Needless to say, my wife will arrange and pay for the care of the children while my wife is working.

I want a wife who will take care of *my* physical needs. I want a wife who will keep my house clean. A wife who will pick up after me. I want a wife who will keep my clothes clean, ironed, mended, replaced when need be, and who will see to it that my personal things are kept in their proper place so that I can find what I need the minute I need it. I want a wife who cooks the meals, a wife who is a *good* cook. I want a wife who will plan the menus, do the necessary grocery shopping, prepare the meals, serve them pleasantly, and then do the cleaning up while I do my studying. I want a wife who will care for me when I am sick and sympathize with my pain and loss of time from school. I want a wife to go along when our family takes a vacation so that someone can continue to care for me and my children when I need a rest and change of scene.

I want a wife who will not bother me with rambling complaints about a wife's duties. But I want a wife who will listen to me when I feel the need to explain a rather difficult point I have come across in my course of studies. And I want a wife who will type my papers for me when I have written them.

I want a wife who will take care of the details of my social life. When my wife and I are invited out by my friends, I want a wife who will take care of the babysitting arrangements. When I meet people at school that I like and want to entertain, I want a wife who will have the house clean, will prepare a special meal, serve it to me and my friends, and not interrupt when I talk about the things that interest me and my friends. I want a wife who will have arranged that the children are fed and ready for bed before my guests arrive so that the children do not bother us.

And I want a wife who knows that sometimes I need a night out by myself.

I want a wife who is sensitive to my sexual needs, a wife who makes love passionately and eagerly when I feel like it, a wife who makes sure that I am satisfied. And, of course, I want a wife who will not demand sexual attention when I am not in the mood for it. I want a wife who assumes the complete responsibility for birth control, because I do not want more children. I want a wife who will remain sexually faithful to me so that I do not have to clutter up my intellectual life with jealousies. And I want a wife who understands that *my* sexual needs may entail more than strict adherence to monogamy. I must, after all, be able to relate to people as fully as possible.

If, by chance, I find another person more suitable as a wife than the wife I already have, I want the liberty to replace my present wife with another one. Naturally, I will expect a fresh, new life; my wife will take the children and be solely responsible for them so that I am left free.

When I am through with school and have a job, I want my wife to quit working and remain at home so that my wife can more fully and completely take care of a wife's duties.

My god, who *wouldn't* want a wife?

Study and Discussion Questions

1. What is the point of this essay? Is Brady simply trying to explain how hard a wife works?
2. What does Brady achieve by making her point indirectly? Why doesn't she simply *tell* us how she feels about being a wife? How does the choice of form—satire—serve the writer's purposes?
3. How does repetition function in the essay? Why do so many sentences begin with "I want . . ."—in fact with "I want a wife who . . ."? What effect does this have on the reader?
4. Brady names a great many things she wants a wife for. How does she organize them? Is the ordering of the paragraphs in which she lists her wants significant?

5. How does the mention, in the second paragraph, of Brady's divorced male friend serve her purpose in the essay?

Suggestions for Writing

1. Would a parallel essay, "I Want a Husband," have equal force? Explain. Try writing one.
2. Try writing an essay modeled on this one, but protesting some other social role you think unfair, one that you might be or imagine yourself in— "I Want a Secretary," for example.
3. Study a number of television or magazine advertisements that depict housewives. How closely do they correspond to the role of wife as Brady describes it? What attitudes do they express towards the role or roles they depict?

Critical Resources

1. Brady, Judy. "Conflicted Science." *Greenaction.* 22 April 2005. <http://www.greenaction.org/cancer/conflictedscience.shtml>
2. Brady, Judy. "Why I [Still] Want a Wife." *Ms.* July 1990.
3. Linda Morris, *American Women Humanists: Critical Essays.* New York: Garland, 1994.
4. Walker, Nancy. *A Very Serious Thing: Women's Humor and American Culture.* Minneapolis: U of Minnesota P, 1988.

RICHARD RODRIGUEZ (b. 1944)

Richard Rodriguez grew up in San Francisco, one of four children in a Mexican working-class family. In his autobiographical Hunger for Memory *(1981), Rodriguez writes in depth about his experiences as a young Mexican American male—his assimilation into American culture and the tensions it produced. Rodriguez obtained his B.A. in English from Stanford in 1974, his M.A. at Columbia, and was then granted a Fulbright fellowship to do Ph.D. work in England. On track for a life in academia, Rodriguez surprised many by declining teaching positions; he instead decided to write full time. Noted for his synthesis of journalism and personal narrative, Rodriguez's subsequent publications include* Days of Obligation: An Argument with My Mexican American Father *(1992) and* Brown: The Last Discovery of America *(2002). "Huck Finn, Dan Quayle, and The Value of Acceptance" originally appeared in the* Los Angeles Times Magazine *in 1992 and concerns sexual and cultural identity.*

Huck Finn, Dan Quayle and the Value of Acceptance (1992)

I am sitting alone in my car, in front of my parents' house—a middle-aged man with a boy's secret to tell. What words will I use to tell them? I hate the word *gay,* find its little affirming sparkle more pathetic than assertive. I am happier with the less polite *queer.* But to my parents I would say *homosexual,* avoid the Mexican slang *joto* (I had always heard it said in our house with hints of condescension), though *joto* is less mocking than the sissy-boy *maricón.*

The buzz on everyone's lips now: Family values. The other night on TV, the vice president of the United States, his arm around his wife, smiled into the camera and described homosexuality as "mostly a choice." But how would he know? Homosexuality never felt like a choice to me.

A few minutes ago Rush Limbaugh, the radio guy with a voice that reminds me, for some reason, of a butcher's arms, was banging his console and booming a near-reasonable polemic about family values. Limbaugh was not very clear about which values exactly he considers to be family values. A divorced man who lives alone in New York?

My parents live on a gray, treeless street in San Francisco not far from the ocean. Probably more than half of the neighborhood is immigrant. India lives next door to Greece, who lives next door to Russia. I wonder what the Chinese lady next door to my parents makes of the politicians' phrase *family values.*

What immigrants know, what my parents certainly know, is that when you come to this country, you risk losing your children. The assurance of family—continuity, inevitability—is precisely what America encourages its children to overturn. *Become your own man.* We who are native to this country know this too, of course, though we are likely to deny it. Only a society so guilty about its betrayal of family would tolerate the pieties of politicians regarding family values.

On the same summer day that Republicans were swarming in Houston[1] (buzzing about family values), a friend of mine who escaped family values awhile back and who now wears earrings resembling intrauterine devices, was complaining to me over coffee about the Chinese. The Chinese will never take over San Francisco, my friend said, because the Chinese do not want to take over San Francisco. The Chinese do not even *see* San Francisco! All they care about is their damn families. All they care about is double-parking smack in front of the restaurant on Clement Street and pulling granny out of the car—and damn anyone who happens to be in the car behind them or the next or the next.

Politicians would be horrified by such an American opinion, of course. But then, what do politicians, Republicans or Democrats, really know of our family life? Or what are they willing to admit? Even in that area where they could reasonably be expected to have something to say—regarding the relationship of

---

[1]Site of 1992 Republican National Convention.

family life to our economic system—the politicians say nothing. Republicans celebrate American economic freedom, but Republicans don't seem to connect that economic freedom to the social breakdown they find appalling. Democrats, on the other hand, if more tolerant of the drift from familial tradition, are suspicious of the very capitalism that creates social freedom.

How you become free in America: Consider the immigrant. He gets a job. Soon he is earning more money than his father ever made (his father's authority is thereby subtly undermined). The immigrant begins living a life his father never knew. The immigrant moves from one job to another, changes houses. His economic choices determine his home address—not the other way around. The immigrant is on his way to becoming his own man.

When I was broke a few years ago and trying to finish a book, I lived with my parents. What a thing to do! A major theme of America is leaving home. We trust the child who forsakes family connections to make it on his own. We call that the making of a man.

Let's talk about this man stuff for a minute. America's ethos is anti-domestic. We may be intrigued by blood that runs through wealth—the Kennedys or the Rockefellers—but they seem European to us. Which is to say, they are movies. They are Corleones.[2] Our real pledge of allegiance: We say in America that nothing about your family—your class, your race, your pedigree—should be as important as what you yourself achieve. We end up in 1992 introducing ourselves by first names.

What authority can Papa have in a country that formed its identity in an act of Oedipal rebellion against a mad British king? Papa is a joke in America, a stock sitcom figure—Archie Bunker or Homer Simpson. But my Mexican father went to work every morning, and he stood in a white smock, making false teeth, oblivious of the shelves of grinning false teeth mocking his devotion.

The nuns in grammar school—my wonderful Irish nuns—used to push Mark Twain on me. I distrusted Huck Finn,[3] he seemed like a gringo kid I would steer clear of in the schoolyard. (He was too confident.) I realize now, of course, that Huck is the closest we have to a national hero. We trust the story of a boy who has no home and is restless for the river. (Huck's Pap is drunk.) Americans are more forgiving of Huck's wildness than of the sweetness of the Chinese boy who walks to school with his mama or grandma. (There is no worse thing in America than to be a mama's boy, nothing better than to be a real boy—all boy—like Huck, who eludes Aunt Sally, and is eager for the world of men.)

There's a bent old woman coming up the street. She glances nervously as she passes my car. What would you tell us, old lady, of family values in America?

---

[2]Italian crime family in *The Godfather,* novel by Mario Puzo and film by Francis Ford Coppola.

[3]Hero of Mark Twain's novel, *The Adventures of Huckleberry Finn.*

America is an immigrant country, we say. Motherhood—parenthood—is less our point than adoption. If I had to assign gender to America, I would note the consensus of the rest of the world. When America is burned in effigy, a male is burned. Americans themselves speak of Uncle Sam.

Like the Goddess of Liberty, Uncle Sam has no children of his own. He steals children to make men of them, mocks all reticence, all modesty, all memory. Uncle Sam is a hectoring Yankee, a skinflint uncle, gaunt, uncouth, unloved. He is the American Savonarola—hater of moonshine, destroyer of stills, burner of cocaine. Sam has no patience with mamas' boys.

You betray Uncle Sam by favoring private over public life, by seeking to exempt yourself, by cheating on your income taxes, by avoiding jury duty, by trying to keep your boy on the farm.

Mothers are traditionally the guardians of the family—against America—though even Mom may side with America against queers and deserters, at least when the Old Man is around. Premature gray hair. Arthritis in her shoulders. Bowlegged with time, red hands. In their fiercely flowered housedresses, mothers are always smarter than fathers in America. But in reality they are betrayed by their children who leave. In a thousand ways. They end up alone.

We kind of like the daughter who was a tomboy. Remember her? It was always easier to be a tomboy in America than a sissy. Americans admired Annie Oakley more than they admired Liberace[4] (who, nevertheless, always remembered his mother). But today we do not admire Annie Oakley when we see Mom becoming Annie Oakley.

The American household now needs two incomes, everyone says. Meaning: Mom is *forced* to leave home out of economic necessity. But lots of us know lots of moms who are sick and tired of being mom, or only mom. It's like the nuns getting fed up, teaching kids for all those years and having those kids grow up telling stories of how awful Catholic school was! Not every woman in America wants her life's work to be forgiveness. Today there are moms who don't want their husbands' names. And the most disturbing possibility: What happens when Mom doesn't want to be Mom at all? Refuses pregnancy?

Mom is only becoming an American like the rest of us. Certainly, people all over the world are going to describe the influence of feminism on women (all over the world) as their "Americanization." And rightly so.

Nothing of this, of course, will the politician's wife tell you. The politician's wife is careful to follow her husband's sentimental reassurances that nothing has changed about America except perhaps for the sinister influence of deviants. Like myself.

I contain within myself an anomaly at least as interesting as the Republican Party's version of family values. I am a homosexual Catholic, a communicant in a tradition that rejects even as it upholds me.

---

[4]Annie Oakley, sharpshooter; Liberace, pianist and entertainer.

I do not count myself among those Christians who proclaim themselves pro-
tectors of family values. They regard me as no less an enemy of the family than
the "radical feminists." But the joke about families that all homosexuals know is
that we are the ones who stick around and make families possible. Call on us. I
can think of 20 or 30 examples. A gay son or daughter is the only one who is
"free" (married brothers and sisters are too busy). And, indeed, because we have
admitted the inadmissible about ourselves (that we are queer)—we are adepts
at imagination—we can even imagine those who refuse to imagine us. We can
imagine Mom's loneliness, for example. If Mom needs to be taken to church or
to the doctor or ferried between Christmas dinners, depend on the gay son or
lesbian daughter.

I won't deny that the so-called gay liberation movement, along with feminism,
undermined the heterosexual household, if that's what politicians mean when
they say family values. Against churchly reminders that sex was for procreation,
the gay bar as much as the birth-control pill taught Americans not to fear sexual pleasure. In the past two decades—and, not co-incidentally, parallel to the
feminist movement—the gay liberation movement moved a generation of Americans toward the idea of a childless adulthood. If the women's movement was
ultimately more concerned about getting out of the house and into the work-
place, the gay movement was in its way more subversive to Puritan America because it stressed the importance of play.

Several months ago, the society editor of the morning paper in San Francisco
suggested (on a list of "must haves") that every society dame must have at least
one gay male friend. A ballet companion. A lunch date. The remark was glib and
incorrect enough to beg complaints from homosexual readers, but there was a
truth about it as well. Homosexual men have provided women with an alternate
model of masculinity. And the truth: The Old Man, God bless him, is a bore. Thus
are we seen as preserving marriages? Even Republican marriages?

For myself, homosexuality is a deep brotherhood but does not involve domestic life. Which is why, my married sisters will tell you, I can afford the time
to be a writer. And why are so many homosexuals such wonderful teachers and
priests and favorite aunts, if not because we are freed from the house? On the
other hand, I know lots of homosexual couples (male and female) who model
their lives on the traditional heterosexual version of domesticity and marriage.
Republican politicians mock the notion of a homosexual marriage, but ironically
such marriages honor the heterosexual marriage by imitating it.

"The only loving couples I know," a friend of mine recently remarked, "are
all gay couples."

This woman was not saying that she does not love her children or that she is
planning a divorce. But she was saying something about the sadness of American domestic life: the fact that there is so little joy in family intimacy. Which is
perhaps why gossip (public intrusion into the private) has become a national industry. All day long, in forlorn houses, the television lights up a freakish parade
of husbands and mothers-in-law and children upon the stage of Sally or Oprah

or Phil.[5] They tell on each other. The audience ooohhhs. Then a psychiatrist-shaman appears at the end to dispense prescriptions—the importance of family members granting one another more "space."

The question I desperately need to ask you is whether we Americans have ever truly valued the family. We are famous, or our immigrant ancestors were famous, for the willingness to leave home. And it is ironic that a crusade under the banner of family values has been taken up by those who would otherwise pass themselves off as patriots. For they seem not to understand America, nor do I think they love the freedoms America grants. Do they understand why, in a country that prizes individuality and is suspicious of authority, children are disinclined to submit to their parents? You cannot celebrate American values in the public realm without expecting them to touch our private lives. As Barbara Bush remarked recently, family values are also neighborhood values. It may be harmless enough for Barbara Bush to recall a sweeter America—Midland, Texas, in the 1950s. But the question left begging is why we chose to leave Midland, Texas. Americans like to say that we can't go home again. The truth is that we don't want to go home again, don't want to be known, recognized. Don't want to respond in the same old ways. (And you know you will if you go back there.)

Little 10-year-old girls know that there are reasons for getting away from the family. They learn to keep their secrets—under lock and key—addressed to Dear Diary. Growing up queer, you learn to keep secrets as well. In no place are those secrets more firmly held than within the family house. You learn to live in closets. I know a Chinese man who arrived in America about 10 years ago. He got a job and made some money. And during that time he came to confront his homosexuality. And then his family arrived. I do not yet know the end of this story.

The genius of America is that it permits children to leave home, it permits us to become different from our parents. But the sadness, the loneliness of America, is clear too.

Listen to the way Americans talk about immigrants. If, on the one hand, there is impatience when today's immigrants do not seem to give up their family, there is also a fascination with this reluctance. In Los Angeles, Hispanics are considered people of family. Hispanic women are hired to be at the center of the American family—to babysit and diaper, to cook and to clean and to ease the dying. Hispanic attachment to family is seen by many Americans, I think, as the reason why Hispanics don't get ahead. But if Asians privately annoy us for being so family oriented, they are also stereotypically celebrated as the new "whiz kids" in school. Don't Asians go to college, after all, to honor their parents?

More important still is the technological and economic ascendancy of Asia, particularly Japan, on the American imagination. Americans are starting to wonder whether perhaps the family values of Asia put the United States at a disadvantage. The old platitude had it that ours is a vibrant, robust society for

---

[5]Sally Jessy Raphael, Oprah Winfrey, and Phil Donahue, television talk show hosts.

being a society of individuals. Now we look to Asia and see team effort paying off.

In this time of national homesickness, of nostalgia, for how we imagine America used to be, there are obvious dangers. We are going to start blaming each other for the loss. Since we are inclined, as Americans, to think of ourselves individually, we are disinclined to think of ourselves as creating one another or influencing one another.

But it is not the politician or any political debate about family values that has brought me here on a gray morning to my parents' house. It is some payment I owe to my youth and to my parents' youth. I imagine us sitting in the living room, amid my mother's sentimental doilies and the family photographs, trying to take the measure of the people we have turned out to be in America.

A San Francisco poet, when he was in the hospital and dying, called a priest to his bedside. The old poet wanted to make his peace with Mother Church. He wanted baptism. The priest asked why. "Because the Catholic Church has to accept me," said the poet. "Because I am a sinner."

Isn't willy-nilly inclusiveness the point, the only possible point to be derived from the concept of family? Curiously, both President Bush and Vice President Quayle got in trouble with their constituents recently for expressing a real family value. Both men said that they would try to dissuade a daughter or granddaughter from having an abortion. But, finally, they said they would support her decision, continue to love her, never abandon her.

There are families that do not accept. There are children who are forced to leave home because of abortions or homosexuality. There are family secrets that Papa never hears. Which is to say there are families that never learn the point of families.

But there she is at the window. My mother has seen me and she waves me in. Her face asks: Why am I sitting outside? (Have they, after all, known my secret for years and kept it, out of embarrassment, not knowing what to say?) Families accept, often by silence. My father opens the door to welcome me in.

Study and Discussion Questions:

1. Why does Rodriguez open his personal essay with him sitting by himself in his car outside his parents' house? Why does he end it with his father opening the door for him to come in?
2. Discuss Rodriguez's pondering of the names/labels/designations for his sexual identity. What are the connotations for each of these names? Why is finding the right *name* important—not only in this essay: think about instances in your own experience?
3. In his second paragraph, Rodriguez challenges Dan Quayle's assertion that homosexuality is a choice. (Dan Quayle was the first President Bush's choice for vice-presidential running mate in the 1992 election, an election which they lost.) Rodriguez brings up the political buzz phrase "family values", which is still a hotly debated issue. How do various groups in this country define "family values"? What do *you* think consti-

tute family values you would live by? How does Richard Rodriguez define family values?

4. Rodriguez discusses what seem like two very different issues: American attitudes toward (a) immigrants and (b) gays. What connections is he making?
5. "It was always easier to be a tomboy in America than a sissy." Why might that be? Do you find that to be true in your own experience?
6. Why does Rodriguez want to tell his parents that he is gay?

Suggestions for Writing:

1. Narrate the conversation you imagine Rodriguez will have with his parents about his sexual orientation.
2. Compare/contrast Rodriguez's essay with Tommy Avicolli Mecca's essay, "He Defies You Still: The Memoirs of a Sissy." You could discuss their experiences, their attitude toward being gay, their relation to parents, religion, and education, their first-person narrative voice, and the choices each makes in terms of style and form.

Critical Resources

1. Fogelquist, Jim. "Ethnicity, Sexuality and Identity in the Autobiographies of Richard Rodriguez." *Double Crossings/Entre Cruzamientos*. Ario Martin Flores & Carlos von Son, eds. New Jersey: Nuevo Espacio, 2001.
2. Rodriguez, Randy A. "Richard Rodriguez Reconsidered: Queering the Sissy (Ethnic) Subject." *Texas Studies in Literature and Language* 40.4 (1998): 396–423.
3. Torres, Hector. "'I Don't Think I Exist': An Interview with Richard Rodriguez." *MELUS* 28.2 (2003): 164–202.

❀ ❀ ❀

WOMEN AND MEN: PAPER TOPICS

1. Discuss what light the experience of those who don't have or choose traditional gender or sexual identities, as this experience is depicted in one or more works, can shed on traditional gender roles. (Suggestions: Villanueva, "Crazy Courage"; Grahn, "Boys at the Rodeo"; Rodriguez, "Huck Finn, Dan Quayle, and the Value of Acceptance")
2. Pick a poem and a short story that explore similar themes and analyze how the choice of genre shapes meaning. Could each be rewrit-

ten in the other genre? If so, what consequences would the change of form bring? (Suggestions: Yamamoto, "Seventeen Syllables" and Gallagher "I Stop Writing The Poem"; Glaspell, "Trifles" and Hughes, "The Lovepet")

3. Analyze how their social class affects the relations between men and women in one or more works. (Suggestions: Carver, "Signals"; Naqui, "A Man of Integrity"; Bentley, "How Much Can I Stand?")

4. Trace and compare images of entrapment and liberation in two or more poems. (Suggestions: Piercy, "The woman in the ordinary"; Kingsolver, "This House I Cannot Leave"; Yeats, "Leda and the Swan"; Erdrich, "Jacklight")

5. Analyze the critique or rewriting of myths or fairy tales in one or more poems. (Suggestions: Rukeyser, "Waiting For Icarus"; Broumas, "Cinderella"; Sexton, "Her Kind"; Millay, "An Ancient Gesture")

6. Compare any two works as comments on the meaning of "masculinity." (Suggestions: Grahn, "Boys at the Rodeo"; Updike, "A & P"; Marvell, "To His Coy Mistress"; 2Pac, "Keep Ya Head Up")

7. Discuss the significance of the presence or absence of relationships between women in one or more works. (Suggestions: Broumas, "Cinderella"; Bloch, "Six Years"; Rich, Poem XI from *Twenty-One Love Poems*)

8. Discuss how one or more stories and/or plays show the problems men and women have understanding each other. (Suggestions: Toomer, "Fern"; Glaspell, "Trifles"; Gilman, "The Yellow Wallpaper"; Hemingway, "Hills Like White Elephants"; Naqui, "A Man of Integrity")

9. Using one or more works, discuss how race, class, or ethnic identity shapes the experience of being a woman or being a man. (Suggestions: Yamamoto, "Seventeen Syllables"; Shakespeare, *Othello*; Baraka, "Beautiful Black Women"; Garcia, "Ines in the Kitchen"; Sojourner Truth, "Ain't I a Woman?")

10. Explore the use of humor in one or more works. (Suggestions: Marvell, "To His Coy Mistress"; Brady, "I Want a Wife"; Donne, "The Flea")

11. Compare the images of love in two or more poems. (Suggestions: "Song of Solomon"; Blake, "The Garden of Love"; Senghor, "You Held the Black Face"; Whitman, "I Saw in Louisiana a Live-Oak Growing"; Neruda, "Every Day You Play"; Millay, "Love is not all: it is not meat nor drink")

12. Explore the role of irony in one or more works. (Suggestions: Woolf, "Shakespeare's Sister"; Chopin, "The Story of an Hour"; Glaspell, "Trifles"; Shakespeare, *Othello*)

13. Analyze the methods of argument in one or more of the nonfiction selections.
14. Examine how setting significantly contributes to the theme in any one of the stories or plays in this section.
15. Use the explication questions at the end of "How Poetry Works" to explicate any one poem in this section.

Money and Work

"Government Bureau," The Metropolitan Museum of Art, George A. Hearn Fund, 1956.

"Work makes life sweet," declares a woman interviewed in *The Life and Times of Rosie the Riveter,* a documentary film about American women workers during World War II. Between 1941 and 1945, many women had for the first time in their lives real, important, and well-paid work outside the home. It gave them independence, dignity, and pride. When the war ended and the men came back, these women, along with many others who had always had to work, were pushed out of their jobs and back into their kitchens, where they continued to work but now at a job that wasn't valued and for which they received no pay. What does this situation (back in the days when a family could live on one salary) suggest about work and about how work and money are interwoven?

We probably all know the satisfaction of a job well done, whether it's a lawn mowed, a baby bathed and sung to sleep, or an essay you feel good about turning in. Further, there is the joy of the work itself, moment by moment, when you are entirely absorbed in what you are doing. We can see an example of this sort of nonalienated work in Robert Frost's "Two Tramps in Mudtime," wherein the speaker of the poem is enjoying chopping wood and doesn't want to give it up to the tramps who have asked to do it for pay, or in Todd Jailer's poem "Bill Hastings," about an electrical line worker at the moment he's turning on the power for an entire town. Nonalienated work is satisfying, engages us beyond any considerations of pay, and usually involves doing the job from start to finish—that is, we are able to see the result or product of our labor, have a sense of control and completion, and say, "I accomplished that."

The need for satisfying work is probably as basic and central to what it means to be human as is the urge to love: "Work makes life sweet." Though we might fantasize about winning the lottery and never working again, how many of us could actually never work? We might give up our McJobs as waitresses or computer technicians, but we would find something else to do, something satisfying, such as playing drums in a rock band or writing a book or sailing singlehandedly across the Pacific Ocean or doing some kind of political or community work— because without work, most of us would go a little nuts. That making music, writing, or doing "volunteer" work at a homeless shelter are usually seen as hobbies has mostly to do with the fact that people generally are not paid for these activities, but they are work nonetheless. June Jordan's poem "Free Flight" and Susan Griffin's prose poem "This Is the Story of the Day in the Life of a Woman Trying" portray people who struggle through whatever their days are filled with so they can get to their real work, which is writing. Can you imagine a world in which we all were doing the kind of work we most wanted to do?

Why, then, do we generally put money and work together in the same thought? Work may be a basic human need, but what has that to do with money? Money is certainly a need, too, but it is a social or socialized rather than a purely human need. That is to say, we live in a time and in a society in which money is the medium of exchange between work, regardless of our motivation, and food, shelter, and everything else that we need or want. We work, get paid, and use the money to buy what will satisfy our other basic needs. Indeed, for the past 60 years, a lot more political and corporate attention has gone into making us consumers than producers. History, not human nature, has linked work to money. Visionary and utopian thinkers have repeatedly sought ways to free work from the grip of money.

B. Traven, in "Assembly Line," shows us a situation in which one character, a North American investor, attempts to restructure a situation of nonalienated labor in order to maximize profit. The other main character, a Mexican farmer, is an artisan who weaves baskets in his spare time with, as he puts it, "my song in them and with bits of my soul woven into them." The conflict or tension in the story is between work as an expression of human creativity and work as a means of making money. Ultimately, of course, the investor would make most of the money, and the assembly-line process he plans would destroy much of the baskets' beauty and all of their individuality. It would also greatly decrease the artisan's satisfaction in making them. A number of other selections take up the theme of unsatisfying or alienated labor. Judy Grahn's poem "Ella, in a square apron, along Highway 80" gives us a portrait of a tired and angry truck-stop waitress; Theodore Roethke's "Dolor" paints a terrifyingly static and colorless portrait of office work, emblematic of our bureaucratic and paper-choked society. Mafika Mbuli's "The Miners" introduces us to the bitterness and finally numbness of a work life underground, digging up gold for other people. In the screenplay of the 1953 film *Salt of the Earth* (Varieties of Protest), Mexican American zinc miners go on strike in the American Southwest. Here we see the clash, historically often vicious, between management and labor—with the addition of racial and gender struggles.

Richard Wright, in "The Man Who Went to Chicago," surveys bitterly the kind of jobs open to black men in the 1930s and the effect the available work has on their self-esteem. Kate Rushin, in her poem "The Black Back-Ups," writes about the unpraised but necessary labor of women, usually black women like the speaker's mother, who did domestic work in white people's houses. In Pietro Di Donato's *Christ in Concrete,* twelve-year-old Paul, after his father is killed on the job, begins to do a man's work as a bricklayer. As an Italian immigrant in the 1920s and as a child laborer, Paul is doubly exploited. Yet while he finds the long day of work exhausting and the dangers of the work frightening, he also finds the work itself (the craft of masonry) exhilarating, satisfying, and an important part of his identity. The exhilaration comes through in Di Donato's prose style. Paul's relation to Job, as Di Donato calls it, is ambivalent and complex. A different but equally powerful energy and ambivalence can be seen in Mary Fell's poetic sequence "The Triangle Fire," commemorating the almost 150 Italian and Jewish women garment workers who died in a fire due to unsafe working conditions in 1911 at the Triangle Shirtwaist Company in New York City.

And what about when there is no work? In an economy based on labor for wages, those who cannot find work fall between the cracks. Meridel Le Sueur's essay "Women on the Breadlines" and the episode from Tom Kromer's novel *Waiting for Nothing* are both set in the worst years of the Great Depression, 1932 to 1934. "Women on the Breadlines" treats the plight of unemployed women through character portraits of three representative types—an immigrant woman in her thirties, a young woman of eighteen or so, and a woman in her fifties with a number of children. Tom Kromer, who was himself a stiff or hobo during those same years, recounts in the episode from *Waiting for Nothing* an evening in the life of a penniless man we would now call a homeless or street person as he searches for something to eat and a place to sleep. What happens when capitalism breaks down, as it did in a big way during the 1930s?

Money as a force or entity in itself, not in relation to work but to the commodities it can buy, is the subject of Toni Cade Bambara's story "The Lesson," in which a number of poor African American schoolchildren are taken on a window-shopping expedition. Here they begin to learn of the luxuries that some people can afford. The story is told from the point of view of one of the children, and her resistance to this painful lesson is its central tension. William Faulkner's story "Spotted Horses" is also about money rather than work. In some parts of the South and West, until fairly recently, "horse trading" was almost synonymous with sharp practice. Making a good trade on a horse was a measure of someone's shrewdness, and getting conned on a horse deal was a humiliation that a person might have to live down for the rest of his (usually "his") life. "Spotted Horses" tells how a whole town was conned into giving up its money for a dream of pinto ponies and asks where the responsibility falls when people spend their money for an illusion. In this story, we have moved very far from the simple exchange of work for money and money for goods.

What weaves in and through this section on money and work is the concept of social class. What does it mean to be poor, working class, middle class, upper class? What does it mean to be comfortably well off instead of scrambling for a job? What does it mean to have privilege and choice, and what does it mean to do without? What does it mean to own a bank or a factory or, on the other hand, to have to sell your labor for wages? One angry and potentially revolutionary answer emerges in two poems—Bertolt Brecht's "A Worker Reads History" and Nazim Hikmet's "About Your Hands and Lies"—and in a song by an anonymous worker, "Let Them Wear Their Watches Fine." At the other end of the emotional spectrum are Sherman Alexie's poem, "The Reservation Cab Driver" and Harvey Pekar's graphic story "Hypothetical Quandary." For example, in the comic book narrative of Harvey Pekar, "Hypothetical Quandary," Pekar walks to the bakery in his working-class neighborhood thinking about how his life might change if he finally got the call from his agent he's been waiting for. Then he remembers to enjoy the moment he is in.

Work, if one has work, and the social status that work confers do have a tendency to affect one's life outside of work. A number of the selections explore relations between individuals from different social classes. In addition to B. Traven's story "Assembly Line," Jimmy Santiago Baca's angry and ironic poem "So Mexicans Are Taking Jobs from Americans"; Woody Guthrie's song "Plane Wreck at Los Gatos (Deportees)"; and (in Varieties of Protest) the screenplay *Salt of the Earth* look at the situation of Mexican workers in the U.S. economy. Southern working-class writer Dorothy Allison, in her autobiographical essay,

"A Question of Class," describes the rural poverty and the social contempt from other classes she grew up experiencing and grounds her own genesis as a writer in this: "I was born poor into a world that despises the poor. The need to make my world believable to people who have never experienced it is part of why I write fiction." Alice Walker's story "Everyday Use" considers class relations within a family when an upwardly mobile daughter comes home for a visit with her mother and sister. Like "Everyday Use," Tillie Olsen's "I Stand Here Ironing" gives us the perspective of a working-class mother thinking about her daughter. Olsen's character tries to account for the gap between the social definition of what it means to be a good mother and the grim necessities of her life as a woman who had to work outside the home, who had to leave her child so they could have a home and food, and who was often tired, irritable, and not available to her daughter. Again, the question of responsibility comes up. And that of guilt. If our notions of appropriate behavior are based on middle-class privilege, how is a person who struggles to get and keep a job and to put food on the table and a roof over her head to judge herself? Another story from a mother's perspective is the opening chapter of Ann Petry's novel, *The Street*, where we go with Lutie Johnson to look at an apartment in a run down tenement in a dangerous neighborhood—which is all she can afford. Arthur Miller's *Death of a Salesman* explores, from a male perspective, similar stresses concerning money and work and how those affect family life, because Willy Loman has dragged his wife and his sons into his fantasies about making it big. August Wilson's play, *The Piano Lesson*, introduces complex issues of race, social class, economic opportunity, and the legacies of history as a brother and sister struggle over who has control of a carved piano from slavery times that belonged to their grandfather: Should it be sold so the brother can buy land or kept as a family heirloom as the sister wishes? Gwendolyn Brooks's poem "Bronzeville Woman in a Red Hat" is written by a black woman poet but from the point of view of a white upper-middle-class housewife threatened by the power and vitality of the black woman she has just hired as a maid. Reading this poem, we might ask to what extent the *persona* or speaker of the poem is able to come to terms with her class as well as race prejudices.

In this section, we hear about money and work from the perspectives of artisans, waitresses, secretaries, steelworkers, poets, prostitutes, bricklayers, housewives, farmers, factory workers, and people who would like to have a job but don't. Work makes life sweet, but the combination of money and work is more complicated.

FICTION

TILLIE OLSEN (b. 1913)

*Tillie Lerner was born in Omaha, Nebraska, the daughter of social activist
Jewish-Russian immigrants. During the Great Depression she had to quit high
school to work; she also began work as a labor activist and writer. She joined the
Communist Party at the age of seventeen and was arrested and jailed for her part
in several Depression-era strikes. She then married Jack Olsen and raised four
children while continuing to work as a waitress and secretary, writing little until
the 1950s. Those twenty years of raising children and making ends meet have
served as the foundation of much of her writing. Although Olsen hasn't published
much in her lifetime, she has gained acclaim for the emotional intensity of her
prose and her ability to make apparent the heroic in common people. As the title of her book* Silences *(1978) suggests, Olsen's work, steeped in issues of class,
race, and gender, seeks to give an authentic voice to the silent and stifled worlds
of the oppressed. Her other works include the short story collection* Tell Me a
Riddle *(1961) and the novel* Yonnondio *(1974). In "I Stand Here Ironing," first
published in* Tell Me a Riddle, *Olsen shifts narration from present to past as a
mother takes inventory of her daughter's life and her own role as a working-class
parent.*

I Stand Here Ironing   (1954)

I stand here ironing, and what you asked me moves tormented back and forth
with the iron.

"I wish you would manage the time to come in and talk with me about your
daughter. I'm sure you can help me understand her. She's a youngster who needs
help and whom I'm deeply interested in helping."

"Who needs help." . . . Even if I came, what good would it do? You think because I am her mother I have a key, or that in some way you could use me as a
key? She has lived for nineteen years. There is all that life that has happened outside of me, beyond me.

And when is there time to remember, to sift, to weigh, to estimate, to total? I
will start and there will be an interruption and I will have to gather it all together
again. Or I will become engulfed with all I did or did not do, with what should
have been and what cannot be helped.

She was a beautiful baby. The first and only one of our five that was beautiful at birth. You do not guess how new and uneasy her tenancy in her now-

loveliness. You did not know her all those years she was thought homely, or see her poring over her baby pictures, making me tell her over and over how beautiful she had been—and would be, I would tell her—and was now, to the seeing eye. But the seeing eyes were few or nonexistent. Including mine.

I nursed her. They feel that's important nowadays. I nursed all the children, but with her, with all the fierce rigidity of first motherhood, I did like the books then said. Though her cries battered me to trembling and my breasts ached with swollenness, I waited till the clock decreed.

Why do I put that first? I do not even know if it matters, or if it explains anything.

She was a beautiful baby. She blew shining bubbles of sound. She loved motion, loved light, loved color and music and textures. She would lie on the floor in her blue overalls patting the surface so hard in ecstasy her hands and feet would blur. She was a miracle to me, but when she was eight months old I had to leave her daytimes with the woman downstairs to whom she was no miracle at all, for I worked or looked for work and for Emily's father, who "could no longer endure" (he wrote in his good-bye note) "sharing want with us."

I was nineteen. It was the pre-relief, pre-WPA world of the depression. I would start running as soon as I got off the streetcar, running up the stairs, the place smelling sour, and awake or asleep to startle awake, when she saw me she would break into a clogged weeping that could not be comforted, a weeping I can hear yet.

After a while I found a job hashing at night so I could be with her days, and it was better. But it came to where I had to bring her to his family and leave her.

It took a long time to raise the money for her fare back. Then she got chicken pox and I had to wait longer. When she finally came, I hardly knew her, walking quick and nervous like her father, looking like her father, thin, and dressed in a shoddy red that yellowed her skin and glared at the pockmarks. All the baby loveliness gone.

She was two. Old enough for nursery school they said, and I did not know then what I know now—the fatigue of the long day, and the lacerations of group life in the kinds of nurseries that are only parking places for children.

Except that it would have made no difference if I had known. It was the only place there was. It was the only way we could be together, the only way I could hold a job.

And even without knowing, I knew. I knew the teacher that was evil because all these years it has curdled into my memory, the little boy hunched in the corner, her rasp, "why aren't you outside, because Alvin hits you? that's no reason, go out, scaredy." I knew Emily hated it even if she did not clutch and implore "don't go Mommy" like the other children, mornings.

She always had a reason why we should stay home. Momma, you look sick. Momma, I feel sick. Momma, the teachers aren't there today, they're sick. Momma, we can't go, there was a fire there last night. Momma, it's a holiday today, no school, they told me.

But never a direct protest, never rebellion. I think of our others in their three-, four-year-oldness—the explosions, the tempers, the denunciations, the demands—and I feel suddenly ill. I put the iron down. What in me demanded that goodness in her? And what was the cost, the cost to her of such goodness?

The old man living in the back once said in his gentle way: "You should smile at Emily more when you look at her." What *was* in my face when I looked at her? I loved her. There were all the acts of love.

It was only with the others I remembered what he said, and it was the face of joy, and not of care or tightness or worry I turned to them—too late for Emily. She does not smile easily, let alone almost always as her brothers and sisters do. Her face is closed and sombre, but when she wants, how fluid. You must have seen it in her pantomimes, you spoke of her rare gift for comedy on the stage that rouses a laughter out of the audience so dear they applaud and applaud and do not want to let her go.

Where does it come from, that comedy? There was none of it in her when she came back to me that second time, after I had had to send her away again. She had a new daddy now to learn to love, and I think perhaps it was a better time.

Except when we left her alone nights, telling ourselves she was old enough.

"Can't you go some other time, Mommy, like tomorrow?" she would ask. "Will it be just a little while you'll be gone? Do you promise?"

The time we came back, the front door open, the clock on the floor in the hall. She rigid awake. "It wasn't just a little while. I didn't cry. Three times I called you, just three times, and then I ran downstairs to open the door so you could come faster. The clock talked loud. I threw it away, it scared me what it talked."

She said the clock talked loud again that night I went to the hospital to have Susan. She was delirious with the fever that comes before red measles, but she was fully conscious all the week I was gone and the week after we were home when she could not come near the new baby or me.

She did not get well. She stayed skeleton thin, not wanting to eat, and night after night she had nightmares. She would call for me, and I would rouse from exhaustion to sleepily call back: "You're all right, darling, go to sleep, it's just a dream," and if she still called, in a sterner voice, "now go to sleep, Emily, there's nothing to hurt you." Twice, only twice, when I had to get up for Susan anyhow, I went in to sit with her.

Now when it is too late (as if she would let me hold and comfort her like I do the others) I get up and go to her at once at her moan or restless stirring. "Are you awake, Emily? Can I get you something?" And the answer is always the same: "No, I'm all right, go back to sleep, Mother."

They persuaded me at the clinic to send her away to a convalescent home in the country where "she can have the kind of food and care you can't manage for her, and you'll be free to concentrate on the new baby." They still send children to that place. I see pictures on the society page of sleek young women planning affairs to raise money for it, or dancing at the affairs, or decorating Easter eggs or filling Christmas stockings for the children.

They never have a picture of the children so I do not know if the girls still wear those gigantic red bows and the ravaged looks on the every other Sunday when parents can come to visit "unless otherwise notified"—as we were notified the first six weeks.

Oh it is a handsome place, green lawns and tall trees and fluted flower beds. High up on the balconies of each cottage the children stand, the girls in their red bows and white dresses, the boys in white suits and giant red ties. The parents stand below shrieking up to be heard and the children shriek down to be heard, and between them the invisible wall "Not To Be Contaminated by Parental Germs or Physical Affection."

There was a tiny girl who always stood hand in hand with Emily. Her parents never came. One visit she was gone. "They moved her to Rose Cottage" Emily shouted in explanation. "They don't like you to love anybody here."

She wrote once a week, the labored writing of a seven-year-old. "I am fine. How is the baby. If I write my leter nicly I will have a star. Love." There never was a star. We wrote every other day, letters she could never hold or keep but only hear read—once. "We simply do not have room for children to keep any personal possessions," they patiently explained when we pieced one Sunday's shrieking together to plead how much it would mean to Emily, who loved so to keep things, to be allowed to keep her letters and cards.

Each visit she looked frailer. "She isn't eating," they told us.

(They had runny eggs for breakfast or mush with lumps, Emily said later, I'd hold it in my mouth and not swallow. Nothing ever tasted good, just when they had chicken.)

It took us eight months to get her released home, and only the fact that she gained back so little of her seven lost pounds convinced the social worker.

I used to try to hold and love her after she came back, but her body would stay stiff, and after a while she'd push away. She ate little. Food sickened her, and I think much of life too. Oh she had physical lightness and brightness, twinkling by on skates, bouncing like a ball up and down up and down over the jump rope, skimming over the hill; but these were momentary.

She fretted about her appearance, thin and dark and foreign-looking at a time when every little girl was supposed to look or thought she should look a chubby blonde replica of Shirley Temple. The doorbell sometimes rang for her, but no one seemed to come and play in the house or be a best friend. Maybe because we moved so much.

There was a boy she loved painfully through two school semesters. Months later she told me how she had taken pennies from my purse to buy him candy. "Licorice was his favorite and I brought him some every day, but he still liked Jennifer better'n me. Why, Mommy?" The kind of question for which there is no answer.

School was a worry to her. She was not glib or quick in a world where glibness and quickness were easily confused with ability to learn. To her overworked and exasperated teachers she was an overconscientious "slow learner" who kept trying to catch up and was absent entirely too often.

I let her be absent, though sometimes the illness was imaginary. How different from my now-strictness about attendance with the others. I wasn't working. We had a new baby, I was home anyhow. Sometimes, after Susan grew old enough, I would keep her home from school, too, to have them all together.

Mostly Emily had asthma, and her breathing, harsh and labored, would fill the house with a curiously tranquil sound. I would bring the two old dresser mirrors and her boxes of collections to her bed. She would select beads and single earrings, bottle tops and shells, dried flowers and pebbles, old postcards and scraps, all sorts of oddments; then she and Susan would play Kingdom, setting up landscapes and furniture, peopling them with action.

Those were the only times of peaceful companionship between her and Susan. I have edged away from it, that poisonous feeling between them, that terrible balancing of hurts and needs I had to do between the two, and did so badly, those earlier years.

Oh there are conflicts between the others too, each one human, needing, demanding, hurting, taking—but only between Emily and Susan, no, Emily toward Susan that corroding resentment. It seems so obvious on the surface, yet it is not obvious. Susan, the second child, Susan, golden- and curly-haired and chubby, quick and articulate and assured, everything in appearance and manner Emily was not; Susan, not able to resist Emily's precious things, losing or sometimes clumsily breaking them; Susan telling jokes and riddles to company for applause while Emily sat silent (to say to me later: that was *my* riddle, Mother, I told it to Susan); Susan, who for all the five years' difference in age was just a year behind Emily in developing physically.

I am glad for that slow physical development that widened the difference between her and her contemporaries, though she suffered over it. She was too vulnerable for that terrible world of youthful competition, of preening and parading, of constant measuring of yourself against every other, of envy, "If I had that copper hair," "If I had that skin. . . ." She tormented herself enough about not looking like the others, there was enough of the unsureness, the having to be conscious of words before you speak, the constant caring—what are they thinking of me? without having it all magnified by the merciless physical drives.

Ronnie is calling. He is wet and I change him. It is rare there is such a cry now. That time of motherhood is almost behind me when the ear is not one's own but must always be racked and listening for the child cry, the child call. We sit for a while and I hold him, looking out over the city spread in charcoal with its soft aisles of light. "*Shoogily*," he breathes and curls closer. I carry him back to bed, asleep. *Shoogily*. A funny word, a family word, inherited from Emily, invented by her to say: *comfort*.

In this and other ways she leaves her seal, I say aloud. And startle at my saying it. What do I mean? What did I start to gather together, to try and make coherent? I was at the terrible, growing years. War years. I do not remember them well. I was working, there were four smaller ones now, there was not time for her. She had to help be a mother, and housekeeper, and shopper. She had to set her seal. Mornings of crisis and near hysteria trying to get lunches packed, hair combed, coats and shoes found, everyone to school or Child Care on time, the baby ready for transportation. And always the paper scribbled on by a smaller one, the book looked at by Susan then mislaid, the homework not done. Running out to that huge school where she was one, she was lost, she was a drop; suffering over the unpreparedness, stammering and unsure in her classes.

There was so little time left at night after the kids were bedded down. She would struggle over books, always eating (it was in those years she developed her enormous appetite that is legendary in our family) and I would be ironing, or preparing food for the next day, or writing V-mail to Bill, or tending the baby. Sometimes, to make me laugh, or out of her despair, she would imitate happenings or types at school.

I think I said once: "Why don't you do something like this in the school amateur show?" One morning she phoned me at work, hardly understandable through the weeping: "Mother, I did it. I won, I won; they gave me first prize; they clapped and clapped and wouldn't let me go."

Now suddenly she was Somebody, and as imprisoned in her difference as she had been in anonymity.

She began to be asked to perform at other high schools, even in colleges, then at city and statewide affairs. The first one we went to, I only recognized her that first moment when thin, shy, she almost drowned herself into the curtains. Then: Was this Emily? The control, the command, the convulsing and deadly clowning, the spell, then the roaring, stamping audience, unwilling to let this rare and precious laughter out of their lives.

Afterwards: You ought to do something about her with a gift like that—but without money or knowing how, what does one do? We have left it all to her, and the gift has as often eddied inside, clogged and clotted, as been used and growing.

She is coming. She runs up the stairs two at a time with her light graceful step, and I know she is happy tonight. Whatever it was that occasioned your call did not happen today.

"Aren't you ever going to finish the ironing, Mother? Whistler painted his mother in a rocker. I'd have to paint mine standing over an ironing board." This is one of her communicative nights and she tells me everything and nothing as she fixes herself a plate of food out of the icebox.

She is so lovely. Why did you want me to come in at all? Why were you concerned? She will find her way.

She starts up the stairs to bed. "Don't get me up with the rest in the morning." "But I thought you were having midterms." "Oh, those," she comes back in, kisses me, and says quite lightly, "in a couple of years when we'll all be atom-dead they won't matter a bit."

She has said it before. She *believes* it. But because I have been dredging the past, and all that compounds a human being is so heavily and meaningful in me, I cannot endure it tonight.

I will never total it all. I will never come in to say: She was a child seldom smiled at. Her father left me before she was a year old. I had to work her first six years when there was work, or I sent her home and to his relatives. There were years she had care she hated. She was dark and thin and foreign-looking in a world where the prestige went to blondeness and curly hair and dimples, she was slow where glibness was prized. She was a child of anxious, not proud, love. We were poor and could not afford for her the soil of easy growth. I was a young mother, I was a distracted mother. There were the other children pushing up, demanding. Her younger sister seemed all that she was not. There were years she did not want me to touch her. She kept too much in herself, her life was such she had to keep too much in herself. My wisdom came too late. She has much to her and probably little will come of it. She is a child of her age, of depression, of war, of fear.

Let her be. So all that is in her will not bloom—but in how many does it? There is still enough left to live by. Only help her to know—help make it so there is cause for her to know—that she is more than this dress on the ironing board, helpless before the iron.

Study and Discussion Questions

1. How does ironing function as a symbol in this story?
2. How does the narrator feel about herself as a mother?
3. What regrets does the mother have about Emily's childhood?
4. "And when is there time . . . ," the mother says. How does the paragraph that begins this way anticipate what happens in the story?
5. What forms did the narrator's love for her daughter take?
6. What connections can you make between Emily's gift for comedy and her early life?

Suggestions for Writing

1. How did economic factors affect the narrator's relationship with her daughter?
2. Who is the narrator's imagined audience, the "you" of the opening sentence? What is the narrator's tone?
3. If Emily were to write an account of these same years, what might she say?

Critical Resources

1. Coiner, Constance. *Better Red: The Writing and Resistance of Tillie Olsen and Meridel Le Sueur.* New York: Oxford University Press, 1995.
2. Frye, Joanne. *Tillie Olsen: A Study of the Short Fiction.* New York: Twayne, 1995.
3. Nelson, Kay, ed. *The Critical Response to Tillie Olsen.* Westport, CT: Greenwood Press, 1994.
4. Rosenfelt, Deborah. "From the Thirties: Tillie Olsen and the Radical Tradition." *Feminist Studies* 7.3 (1981): 371–406.

❋ ❋ ❋

ANN PETRY (1908–1997)

*Ann Lane Petry was born in Old Saybrook, Connecticut. Her father was a phar-
macist who owned an established drugstore, providing a firm financial environment while Petry grew up. After graduating from high school, Petry entered the
University of Connecticut. Five years later she received her Ph.D. in pharmacy and
began working in the family business. In 1938, she married George Petry and the
couple moved to New York City. She found work as a reporter for several black
newspapers during the time, covering Harlem. This radical change in culture—
from quiet, well-to-do life in Connecticut to fast-paced Harlem—was a revelatory
experience for Petry. For the first time she witnessed the impoverished urban world
which many African Americans endured—and was especially moved by the plight
of struggling African American mothers. Fueled by the poverty and struggle she
was reporting on, Petry published* The Street *in 1946. The book was met with instant popularity, making Petry the first African American woman to write a best-
seller (over 1.5 million copies sold). Petry's style has often been compared with
other black writers of that era (Richard Wright, Ralph Ellison). Petry writes in the
realist/naturalist mode and explores the social implications of the urban, African
American experience. Her other works include the novels* The Country Place
(1947) and The Narrows *(1953) and the short-story collection* Miss Muriel and
Other Stories *(1971). She has also written several books for young readers.*

FROM *The Street* (1946)

There was a cold November wind blowing through 116th Street. It rattled the
tops of garbage cans, sucked window shades out through the top of opened windows and set them flapping back against the windows; and it drove most of the
people off the street in the block between Seventh and Eighth Avenues except
for a few hurried pedestrians who bent double in an effort to offer the least possible exposed surface to its violent assault.

It found every scrap of paper along the street—theater throwaways, an-
nouncements of dances and lodge meetings, the heavy waxed paper that loaves
of bread had been wrapped in, the thinner waxed paper that had enclosed sandwiches, old envelopes, newspapers. Fingering its way along the curb, the wind set
the bits of paper to dancing high in the air, so that a barrage of paper swirled
into the faces of the people on the street. It even took time to rush into doorways and areaways and find chicken bones and pork-chop bones and pushed
them along the curb.

It did everything it could to discourage the people walking along the street.
It found all the dirt and dust and grime on the sidewalk and lifted it up so that
the dirt got into their noses, making it difficult to breathe; the dust got into their
eyes and blinded them; and the grit stung their skins. It wrapped newspaper
around their feet entangling them until the people cursed deep in their throats,

stamped their feet, kicked at the paper. The wind blew it back again and again until they were forced to stoop and dislodge the paper with their hands. And then the wind grabbed their hats, pried their scarves from around their necks, stuck its fingers inside their coat collars, blew their coats away from their bodies.

The wind lifted Lutie Johnson's hair away from the back of her neck so that she felt suddenly naked and bald, for her hair had been resting softly and warmly against her skin. She shivered as the cold fingers of the wind touched the back of her neck, explored the sides of her head. It even blew her eyelashes away from her eyes so that her eyeballs were bathed in a rush of coldness and she had to blink in order to read the words on the sign swaying back and forth over her head.

Each time she thought she had the sign in focus, the wind pushed it away from her so that she wasn't certain whether it said three rooms or two rooms. If it was three, why, she would go in and ask to see it, but if it said two—why, there wasn't any point. Even with the wind twisting the sign away from her, she could see that it had been there for a long time because its original coat of white paint was streaked with rust where years of rain and snow had finally eaten the paint off down to the metal and the metal had slowly rusted, making a dark red stain like blood.

It was three rooms. The wind held it still for an instant in front of her and then swooped it away until it was standing at an impossible angle on the rod that suspended it from the building. She read it rapidly. Three rooms, steam heat, parquet floors, respectable tenants. Reasonable.

She looked at the outside of the building. Parquet floors here meant that the wood was so old and so discolored no amount of varnish or shellac would conceal the scars and the old scraped places, the years of dragging furniture across the floors, the hammer blows of time and children and drunks and dirty, slovenly women. Steam heat meant a rattling, clanging noise in radiators early in the morning and then a hissing that went on all day.

Respectable tenants in these houses where colored people were allowed to live included anyone who could pay the rent, so some of them would be drunk and loud-mouthed and quarrelsome; given to fits of depression when they would curse and cry violently, given to fits of equally violent elation. And, she thought, because the walls would be flimsy, why, the good people, the bad people, the children, the dogs, and the godawful smells would all be wrapped up together in one big package—the package that was called respectable tenants.

The wind pried at the red skullcap on her head, and as though angered because it couldn't tear it loose from its firm anchorage of bobby pins, the wind blew a great cloud of dust and ashes and bits of paper into her face, her eyes, her nose. It smacked against her ears as though it were giving her a final, exasperated blow as proof of its displeasure in not being able to make her move on.

Lutie braced her body against the wind's attack determined to finish thinking about the apartment before she went in to look at it. Reasonable—now that could mean almost anything. On Eighth Avenue it meant tenements—ghastly places not fit for humans. On St. Nicholas Avenue it meant high rents for small apartments; and on Seventh Avenue it meant great big apartments where you had to take in roomers in order to pay the rent. On this street it could mean almost anything.

She turned and faced the wind in order to estimate the street. The buildings were old with small slitlike windows, which meant the rooms were small and dark. In a street running in this direction there wouldn't be any sunlight in the apartments. Not ever. It would be hot as hell in summer and cold in winter. 'Reasonable' here in this dark, crowded street ought to be about twenty-eight dollars, provided it was on a top floor.

The hallways here would be dark and narrow. Then she shrugged her shoulders, for getting an apartment where she and Bub would be alone was more important than dark hallways. The thing that really mattered was getting away from Pop and his raddled women, and anything was better than that. Dark hallways, dirty stairs, even roaches on the walls. Anything. Anything. Anything.

Anything? Well, almost anything. So she turned toward the entrance of the building and as she turned, she heard someone clear his or her throat. It was so distinct—done as it was on two notes, the first one high and then the grunting expiration of breath on a lower note—that it came to her ears quite clearly under the sound of the wind rattling the garbage cans and slapping at the curtains. It was as though someone had said 'hello,' and she looked up at the window over her head.

There was a faint light somewhere in the room she was looking into and the enormous bulk of a woman was silhouetted against the light. She half-closed her eyes in order to see better. The woman was very black, she had a bandanna knotted tightly around her head, and Lutie saw, with some surprise, that the window was open. She began to wonder how the woman could sit by an open window on a cold, windy night like this one. And she didn't have on a coat, but a kind of loose-looking cotton dress—or at least it must be cotton, she thought, for it had a clumsy look—bulky and wrinkled.

'Nice little place, dearie. Just ring the Super's bell and he'll show it to you.'

The woman's voice was rich. Pleasant. Yet the longer Lutie looked at her, the less she liked her. It wasn't that the woman had been sitting there all along staring at her, reading her thoughts, pushing her way into her very mind, for that was merely annoying. But it was understandable. She probably didn't have anything else to do; perhaps she was sick and the only pleasure she got out of life was in watching what went on in the street outside her window. It wasn't that. It was the woman's eyes. They were as still and as malignant as the eyes of a snake. She could see them quite plainly—flat eyes that stared at her—wandering over her body, inspecting and appraising her from head to foot.

'Just ring the Super's bell, dearie,' the woman repeated.

Lutie turned toward the entrance of the building without answering, thinking about the woman's eyes. She pushed the door open and walked inside and stood there nodding her head. The hall was dark. The low-wattage bulb in the ceiling shed just enough light so that you wouldn't actually fall over—well, a piano that someone had carelessly left at the foot of the stairs; so that you could see the outlines of—oh, possibly an elephant if it were dragged in from the street by some enterprising tenant.

However, if you dropped a penny, she thought, you'd have to get down on your hands and knees and scrabble around on the cracked tile floor before you could ever hope to find it. And she was wrong about being able to see an elephant or a piano because the hallway really wasn't wide enough to admit either one. The stairs went up steeply—dark high narrow steps. She stared at them fascinated. Going up stairs like those you ought to find a newer and more intricate—a much-involved and perfected kind of hell at the top—the very top.

She leaned over to look at the names on the mail boxes. Henry Lincoln Johnson lived here, too, just as he did in all the other houses she'd looked at. Either he or his blood brother. The Johnsons and the Jacksons were mighty prolific. Then she grinned, thinking who am I to talk, for I, too, belong to that great tribe, that mighty mighty tribe of Johnsons. The bells revealed that the Johnsons had roomers—Smith, Roach, Anderson—holy smoke! even Rosenberg. Most of the names were inked in over the mail boxes in scrawling handwriting—the letters were big and bold on some of them. Others were written in pencil; some printed in uneven scraggling letters where names had been scratched out and other names substituted.

There were only two apartments on the first floor. And if the Super didn't live in the basement, why, he would live on the first floor. There it was printed over One A. One A must be the darkest apartment, the smallest, most unrentable apartment, and the landlord would feel mighty proud that he'd given the Super a first-floor apartment.

She stood there thinking that it was really a pity they couldn't somehow manage to rent the halls, too. Single beds. No. Old army cots would do. It would bring in so much more money. If she were a landlord, she'd rent out the hallways. It would make it so much more entertaining for the tenants. Mr. Jones and wife could have cots number one and two; Jackson and girl friend could occupy number three. And Rinaldi, who drove a cab nights, could sublet the one occupied by Jackson and girl friend.

She would fill up all the cots—row after row of them. And when the tenants who had apartments came in late at night, they would have the added pleasure of checking up on the occupants. Jackson not home yet but girl friend lying in the cot alone—all curled up. A second look, because the lack of light wouldn't show all the details, would reveal—ye gods, why, what's Rinaldi doing home at night! Doggone if he ain't tucked up cozily in Jackson's cot with Jackson's girl friend. No wonder she looked contented. And the tenants who had apartments would sit on the stairs just as though the hall were a theater and the performance about to start—they'd sit there waiting until Jackson came home to see what he'd do when he found Rinaldi tucked into his cot with his girl friend. Rinaldi might explain that he thought the cot was his for sleeping and if the cot had blankets on it did not he, too, sleep under blankets; and if the cot had girl friend on it, why should not he, too, sleep with girl friend?

Instead of laughing, she found herself sighing. Then it occurred to her that if there were only two apartments on the first floor and the Super occupied one of them, then the occupant of the other apartment would be the lady with the snake's eyes. She looked at the names on the mail boxes. Yes. A Mrs. Hedges lived in One B. The name was printed on the card—a very professional-looking card. Obviously an extraordinary woman with her bandanna on her head and her sweet, sweet voice. Perhaps she was a snake charmer and she sat in her window in order to charm away at the snakes, the wolves, the foxes, the bears that prowled and loped and crawled on their bellies through the jungle of 116th Street.

Lutie reached out and rang the Super's bell. It made a shrill sound that echoed and re-echoed inside the apartment and came back out into the hall. Immediately a dog started a furious barking that came closer and closer as he ran toward the door of the apartment. Then the weight of his body landed against the door and she drew back as he threw himself against the door. Again and again until the door began to shiver from the impact of his weight. There was the horrid sound of his nose snuffing up air, trying to get her scent. And then his weight hurled against the door again. She retreated toward the street door, pausing there with her hand on the knob. Then she heard heavy footsteps, the sound of a man's voice threatening the dog, and she walked back toward the apartment.

She knew instantly by his faded blue overalls that the man who opened the door was the Super. The hot fetid air from the apartment in back of him came out into the hall. She could hear the faint sound of steam hissing in the radiators. Then the dog tried to plunge past the man and the man kicked the dog back into the apartment. Kicked him in the side until the dog cringed away from him with its tail between its legs. She heard the dog whine deep in its throat and then the murmur of a woman's voice—a whispering voice talking to the dog.

'I came to see about the apartment—the three-room apartment that's vacant,' she said.

'It's on the top floor. You wanta look at it?'

The light in the hall was dim. Dim like that light in Mrs. Hedges' apartment. She pulled her coat around her a little tighter. It's this bad light, she thought. Somehow the man's eyes were worse than the eyes of the woman sitting in the window. And she told herself that it was because she was so tired; that was the reason she was seeing things, building up pretty pictures in people's eyes.

He was a tall, gaunt man and he towered in the doorway, looking at her. It isn't the bad light, she thought. It isn't my imagination. For after his first quick furtive glance, his eyes had filled with a hunger so urgent that she was instantly afraid of him and afraid to show her fear.

But the apartment—did she want the apartment? Not in this house where he was super; not in this house where Mrs. Hedges lived. No. She didn't want to see the apartment—the dark, dirty three rooms called an apartment. Then she thought of where she lived now. Those seven rooms where Pop lived with Lil, his girl friend. A place filled with roomers. A place spilling over with Lil.

There seemed to be no part of it that wasn't full of Lil. She was always swallowing coffee in the kitchen; trailing through all seven rooms in housecoats that didn't quite meet across her lush, loose bosom; drinking beer in tall glasses and leaving the glasses in the kitchen sink so the foam dried in a crust around the rim—the dark red of her lipstick like an accent mark on the crust; lounging on the wide bed she shared with Pop and only God knows who else; drinking gin with the roomers until late at night.

And what was far more terrifying giving Bub a drink on the sly; getting Bub to light her cigarettes for her. Bub at eight with smoke curling out of his mouth.

Only last night Lutie slapped him so hard that Lil cringed away from her dismayed; her housecoat slipping even farther away from the fat curve of her breasts. 'Jesus!' she said. 'That's enough to make him deaf. What's the matter with you?'

But did she want to look at the apartment? Night after night she'd come home from work and gone out right after supper to peer up at the signs in front of the apartment houses in the neighborhood, looking for a place just big enough for her and Bub. A place where the rent was low enough so that she wouldn't come home from work some night to find a long sheet of white paper stuck under the door: 'These premises must be vacated by————' better known as an eviction notice. Get out in five days or be tossed out. Stand by and watch your furniture pile up on the sidewalk. If you could call those broken beds, wornout springs, old chairs with the stuffing crawling out from under, chipped porcelain-topped kitchen table, flimsy kitchen chairs with broken rungs—if you could call those things furniture. That was an important point—now could you call fire-cracked china from the five-and-dime, and red-handled knives and forks and spoons that were bent and coming apart, could you really call those things furniture?

'Yes,' she said firmly. 'I want to look at the apartment.'

'I'll get a flashlight,' he said and went back into his apartment, closing the door behind him so that it made a soft, sucking sound. He said something, but she couldn't hear what it was. The whispering voice inside the apartment stopped and the dog was suddenly quiet.

Then he was back at the door, closing it behind him so it made the same soft, sucking sound. He had a long black flashlight in his hand. And she went up the stairs ahead of him thinking that the rod of its length was almost as black as his hands. The flashlight was a shiny black—smooth and gleaming faintly as the light lay along its length. Whereas the hand that held it was flesh—dull, scarred, worn flesh—no smoothness there. The knuckles were knobs that stood out under the skin, pulled out from hauling ashes, shoveling coal.

But not apparently from using a mop or a broom, for, as she went up and up the steep flight of stairs, she saw that they were filthy, with wastepaper, cigarette butts, the discarded wrappings from packages of snuff, pink ticket stubs from the movie houses. On the landings there were empty gin and whiskey bottles.

She stopped looking at the stairs, stopped peering into the corners of the long hallways, for it was cold, and she began walking faster trying to keep warm. As they completed a flight of stairs and turned to walk up another hall, and then started climbing another flight of stairs, she was aware that the cold increased. The farther up they went, the colder it got. And in summer she supposed it would get hotter and hotter as you went up until when you reached the top floor your breath would be cut off completely.

The halls were so narrow that she could reach out and touch them on either side without having to stretch her arms any distance. When they reached the fourth floor, she thought, instead of her reaching out for the walls, the walls were reaching out for her—bending and swaying toward her in an effort to envelop her. The Super's footsteps behind her were slow, even, steady. She walked a little faster and apparently without hurrying, without even increasing his pace, he was exactly the same distance behind her. In fact his heavy footsteps were a little nearer than before.

She began to wonder how it was that she had gone up the stairs first, why was she leading the way? It was all wrong. He was the one who knew the place, the one who lived here. He should have gone up first. How had he got her to go up the stairs in front of him? She wanted to turn around and see the expression on his face, but she knew if she turned on the stairs like this, her face would be on a level with his; and she wouldn't want to be that close to him.

She didn't need to turn around, anyway; he was staring at her back, her legs, her thighs. She could feel his eyes traveling over her—estimating her, summing her up, wondering about her. As she climbed up the last flight of stairs, she was aware that the skin on her back was crawling with fear. Fear of what? she asked herself. Fear of him, fear of the dark, of the smells in the halls, the high steep stairs, of yourself? She didn't know, and even as she admitted that she didn't know, she felt sweat start pouring from her armpits, dampening her forehead, breaking out in beads on her nose.

The apartment was in the back of the house. The Super fished another flashlight from his pocket which he handed to her before he bent over to unlock the door very quietly. And she thought, everything he does, he does quietly.

She played the beam of the flashlight on the walls. The rooms were small. There was no window in the bedroom. At least she supposed it was the bedroom. She walked over to look at it, and then went inside for a better look. There wasn't a window—just an air shaft and a narrow one at that. She looked around the room, thinking that by the time there was a bed and a chest of drawers in it there'd be barely space enough to walk around in. At that she'd probably bump her knees every time she went past the corner of the bed. She tried to visualize how the room would look and began to wonder why she had already decided to take this room for herself.

It might be better to give it to Bub, let him have a real bedroom to himself for once. No, that wouldn't do. He would swelter in this room in summer. It would be better to have him sleep on the couch in the living room, at least he'd get some air, for there was a window out there, though it wasn't a very big one. She looked out into the living room, trying again to see the window, to see just how much air would come through, how much light there would be for Bub to study by when he came home from school, to determine, too, the amount of air that would reach into the room at night when the window was open, and he was sleeping curled up on the studio couch.

The Super was standing in the middle of the living room. Waiting for her. It wasn't anything that she had to wonder about or figure out. It wasn't by any stretch of the imagination something she had conjured up out of thin air. It was a simple fact. He was waiting for her. She knew it just as she knew she was standing there in that small room. He was holding his flashlight so the beam fell down at his feet. It turned him into a figure of never-ending tallness. And his silent waiting and his appearance of incredible height appalled her.

With the light at his feet like that, he looked as though his head must end somewhere in the ceiling. He simply went up and up into darkness. And he radiated such desire for her that she could feel it. She told herself she was a fool, an idiot, drunk on fear, on fatigue and gnawing worry. Even while she thought it, the hot, choking awfulness of his desire for her pinioned her there so that she couldn't move. It was an aching yearning that filled the apartment, pushed against the walls, plucked at her arms.

She forced herself to start walking toward the kitchen. As she went past him, it seemed to her that he actually did reach one long arm out toward her, his body swaying so that its exaggerated length almost brushed against her. She really couldn't be certain of it, she decided, and resolutely turned the beam of her flashlight on the kitchen walls.

It isn't possible to read people's minds, she argued. Now the Super was probably not even thinking about her when he was standing there like that. He probably wanted to get back downstairs to read his paper. Don't kid yourself, she thought, he probably can't read, or if he can, he probably doesn't spend any time at it. Well—listen to the radio. That was it, he probably wanted to hear his favorite program and she had thought he was filled with the desire to leap upon her. She was as bad as Granny. Which just went on to prove you couldn't be brought up by someone like Granny without absorbing a lot of nonsense that would spring at you out of nowhere, so to speak, and when you least expected it. All those tales about things that people sensed before they actually happened. Tales that had been handed down and down and down until, if you tried to trace them back, you'd end up God knows where—probably Africa. And Granny had them all at the tip of her tongue.

Yet would wanting to hear a radio program make a man look quite like that? Impatiently she forced herself to inspect the kitchen; holding the light on first one wall, then another. It was no better and no worse than she had anticipated. The sink was battered; and the gas stove was a little rusted. The faint smell of gas that hovered about it suggested a slow, incurable leak somewhere in its connections.

Peering into the bathroom, she saw that the fixtures were old-fashioned and deeply chipped. She thought Methuselah himself might well have taken baths in the tub. Certainly it looked ancient enough, though he'd have had to stick his beard out in the hall while he washed himself, for the place was far too small for a man with a full-grown beard to turn around in. She presumed because there was no window that the vent pipe would serve as a source of nice, fresh, clean air.

One thing about it the rent wouldn't be very much. It couldn't be for a place like this. Tiny hall. Bathroom on the right, kitchen straight ahead; living room to the left of the hall and you had to go through the living room to get to the bedroom. The whole apartment would fit very neatly into just one good-sized room.

She was conscious that all the little rooms smelt exactly alike. It was a mixture that contained the faint persistent odor of gas, of old walls, dusty plaster, and over it all the heavy, sour smell of garbage—a smell that seeped through the dumb-waiter shaft. She started humming under her breath, not realizing she was doing it. It was an old song that Granny used to sing. 'Ain't no restin' place for a sinner like me. Like me. Like me.' It had a nice recurrent rhythm. 'Like me. Like me.' The humming increased in volume as she stood there thinking about the apartment.

There was a queer, muffled sound from the Super in the living room. It startled her so she nearly dropped the flashlight. 'What was that?' she said sharply, thinking, My God, suppose I'd dropped it, suppose I'd been left standing here in the dark of this little room, and he'd turned out his light. Suppose he'd started walking toward me, nearer and nearer in the dark. And I could only hear his footsteps, couldn't see him, but could hear him coming closer until I started reaching out in the dark trying to keep him away from me, trying to keep him from touching me—and then—then my hands found him right in front of me ———— At the thought she gripped the flashlight so tightly that the long beam of light from it started wavering and dancing over the walls so that the shadows moved—shadow from the light fixture overhead, shadow from the tub, shadow from the very doorway itself—shifting, moving back and forth.

'I cleared my throat,' the Super said. His voice had a choked, unnatural sound as though something had gone wrong with his breathing.

She walked out into the hall, not looking at him; opened the door of the apartment and stepping over the threshold, still not looking at him, said, 'I've finished looking.'

He came out and turned the key in the lock. He kept his back turned toward her so that she couldn't have seen the expression on his face even if she'd looked at him. The lock clicked into place, smoothly. Quietly. She stood there not moving, waiting for him to start down the hall toward the stairs, thinking, Never, so help me, will he walk down those stairs in back of me.

When he didn't move, she said, 'You go first.' Then he made a slight motion toward the stairs with his flashlight indicating that she was to precede him. She shook her head very firmly.

'Think you'll take it?' he asked.

'I don't know yet. I'll think about it going down.'

When he finally started down the hall, it seemed to her that he had stood there beside her for days, weeks, months, willing her to go down the stairs first. She followed him, thinking, It wasn't my imagination when I got that feeling at the sight of him standing there in the living room; otherwise, why did he have to go through all that rigamarole of my going down the stairs ahead of him? Like going through the motions of a dance; you first; no, you first; but you see, you'll spoil the pattern if you don't go first; but I won't go first, you go first; but no, it'll spoil the ———

She was aware that they'd come up the stairs much faster than they were going down. Was she going to take the apartment? The price wouldn't be too high from the looks of it and by being careful she and Bub could manage—by being very, very careful. White paint would fix the inside of it up; not exactly fix it up, but keep it from being too gloomy, shove the darkness back a little.

Then she thought, Layers and layers of paint won't fix that apartment. It would always smell; finger marks and old stains would come through the paint; the very smell of the wood itself would eventually win out over the paint. Scrubbing wouldn't help any. Then there were these dark, narrow halls, the long flights of stairs, the Super himself, that woman on the first floor.

Or she could go on living with Pop. And Lil. Bub would learn to like the taste of gin, would learn to smoke, would learn in fact a lot of other things that Lil could teach him—things that Lil would think it amusing to teach him. Bub at eight could get a liberal education from Lil, for she was home all day and Bub got home from school a little after three.

You've got a choice a yard wide and ten miles long. You can sit down and twiddle your thumbs while your kid gets a free education from your father's blowsy girl friend. Or you can take this apartment. The tall gentleman who is the superintendent is supposed to rent apartments, fire the furnace, sweep the halls, and that's as far as he's supposed to go. If he tries to include making love to the female tenants, why, this is New York City in the year 1944, and as yet there's no grass growing in the streets and the police force still functions. Certainly you can holler loud enough so that if the gentleman has some kind of dark designs on you and tries to carry them out, a cop will eventually rescue you. That's that.

As for the lady with the snake eyes, you're supposed to be renting the top-floor apartment and if she went with the apartment the sign out in front would say so. Three rooms and snake charmer for respectable tenant. No extra charge for the snake charmer. Seeing as the sign didn't say so, it stood to reason if the snake charmer tried to move in, she could take steps—whatever the hell that meant.

Her high-heeled shoes made a clicking noise as she went down the stairs, and she thought, Yes, take steps like these. It was all very well to reason light-heartedly like that; to kid herself along—there was no explaining away the instinctive, immediate fear she had felt when she first saw the Super. Granny would have said, 'Nothin' but evil, child. Some folks so full of it you can feel it comin' at you—oozin' right out of their skins.'

She didn't believe things like that and yet, looking at his tall, gaunt figure going down that last flight of stairs ahead of her, she half-expected to see horns sprouting from behind his ears; she wouldn't have been greatly surprised if, in place of one of the heavy work shoes on his feet, there had been a cloven hoof that twitched and jumped as he walked so slowly down the stairs.

Outside the door of his apartment, he stopped and turned toward her.

'What's the rent?' she asked, not looking at him, but looking past him at the One A printed on the door of his apartment. The gold letters were filled with tiny cracks, and she thought that in a few more years they wouldn't be distinguishable from the dark brown of the door itself. She hoped the rent would be so high she couldn't possibly take it.

'Twenty-nine fifty.'

He wants me to take it, she thought. He wants it so badly that he's bursting with it. She didn't have to look at him to know it; she could feel him willing it. What difference does it make to him? Yet it was of such obvious importance that if she hesitated just a little longer, he'd be trembling. No, she decided, not that apartment. Then she thought Bub would look cute learning to drink gin at eight.

'I'll take it,' she said grimly.

'You wanta leave a deposit?' he asked.

She nodded, and he opened his door, standing aside to let her go past him. There was a dim light burning in the small hall inside and she saw that the hall led into a living room. She didn't wait for an invitation, but walked on into the living room. The dog had been lying near the radio that stood under a window at the far side of the room. He got up when he saw her, walking toward her with his head down, his tail between his legs; walking as though he were drawn toward her irresistibly, even though he knew that at any moment he would be forced to stop. Though he was a police dog, his hair had such a worn, rusty look that he resembled a wolf more than a dog. She saw that he was so thin, his great haunches and the small bones of his ribs were sharply outlined against his skin. As he got nearer to her, he got excited and she could hear his breathing.

'Lie down,' the Super said.

The dog moved back to the window, shrinking and walking in such a way that she thought if he were human he'd walk backward in order to see and be able to dodge any unexpected blow. He lay down calmly enough and looked at her, but he couldn't control the twitching of his nose; he looked, too, at the Super as though he were wondering if he could possibly cross the room and get over to her without being seen.

The Super sat down in front of an old office desk, found a receipt pad, picked up a fountain pen and, carefully placing a blotter in front of him, turned toward her. 'Name?' he asked.

She swallowed an impulse to laugh. There was something so solemn about the way he'd seated himself, grasping the pen firmly, moving the pad in front of him to exactly the right angle, opening a big ledger book whose pages were filled with line after line of heavily inked writing that she thought he's acting like a big businessman about to transact a major deal.

'Mrs. Lutie Johnson. Present address 2370 Seventh Avenue.' Opening her pocketbook she took out a ten-dollar bill and handed it to him. Ten whole dollars that it had taken a good many weeks to save. By the time she had moved in here and paid the balance which would be due on the rent, her savings would have disappeared. But it would be worth it to be living in a place of her own.

He wrote with a painful slowness, concentrating on each letter, having difficulty with the numbers twenty-three seventy. He crossed it out and bit his lip. 'What was that number?' he asked.

'Twenty-three seventy,' she repeated, thinking perhaps it would be simpler to write it down for him. At the rate he was going, it would take him all of fifteen minutes to write ten dollars and then figure out the difference between ten dollars and twenty-nine dollars which would in this case constitute that innocuous looking phrase, 'the balance due.' She shouldn't be making fun of him, very likely he had taught himself to read and write after spending a couple of years in grammar school where he undoubtedly didn't learn anything. He looked to be in his fifties, but it was hard to tell.

It irritated her to stand there and watch him go through the slow, painful process of forming the letters. She wanted to get out of the place, to get back to Pop's house, plan the packing, get hold of a moving man. She looked around the room idly. The floor was uncarpeted—a terrible-looking floor. Rough and splintered. There was a sofa against the long wall; its upholstery marked by a greasy line along the back. All the people who had sat on it from the time it was new until the time it had passed through so many hands it finally ended up here must have ground their heads along the back of it.

Next to the sofa there was an overstuffed chair and she drew her breath in sharply as she looked at it, for there was a woman sitting in it, and she had thought that she and the dog and the Super were the only occupants of the room. How could anyone sit in a chair and melt into it like that? As she looked, the shapeless small dark woman in the chair got up and bowed to her without speaking.

Lutie nodded her head in acknowledgment of the bow, thinking, That must be the woman I heard whispering. The woman sat down in the chair again. Melting into it. Because the dark brown dress she wore was almost the exact shade of the dark brown of the upholstery and because the overstuffed chair swallowed her up until she was scarcely distinguishable from the chair itself. Because, too, of a shrinking withdrawal in her way of sitting as though she were trying to take up the least possible amount of space. So that after bowing to her Lutie completely forgot the woman was in the room, while she went on studying its furnishings.

No pictures, no rugs, no newspapers, no magazines, nothing to suggest anyone had ever tried to make it look homelike. Not quite true, for there was a canary huddled in an ornate birdcage in the corner. Looking at it, she thought, Everything in the room shrinks: the dog, the woman, even the canary, for it had only one eye open as it perched on one leg. Opposite the sofa an overornate table shone with varnish. It was a very large table with intricately carved claw feet and looking at it she thought, That's the kind of big ugly furniture white women love to give to their maids. She turned to look at the shapeless little woman because she was almost certain the table was hers.

The woman must have been looking at her, for when Lutie turned the woman smiled; a toothless smile that lingered while she looked from Lutie to the table.

'When you want to move in?' the Super asked, holding out the receipt.

'This is Tuesday—do you think you could have the place ready by Friday?'

'Easy,' he said. 'Some special color you want it painted?'

'White. Make all the rooms white,' she said, studying the receipt. Yes, he had it figured out correctly—balance due, nineteen fifty. He had crossed out his first attempt at the figures. Evidently nines were hard for him to make. And his name was William Jones. A perfectly ordinary name. A highly suitable name for a superintendent. Nice and normal. Easy to remember. Easy to spell. Only the name didn't fit him. For he was obviously unusual, extraordinary, abnormal. Everything about him was the exact opposite of his name. He was standing up now looking at her, eating her up with his eyes.

She took a final look around the room. The whispering woman seemed to be holding her breath; the dog was dying with the desire to growl or whine, for his throat was working. The canary, too, ought to be animated with some desperate emotion, she thought, but he had gone quietly to sleep. Then she forced herself to look directly at the Super. A long hard look, malignant, steady, continued. Thinking, That'll fix you, Mister William Jones, but, of course, if it was only my imagination upstairs, it isn't fair to look at you like this. But just in case some dark leftover instinct warned me of what was on your mind—just in case it made me know you were snuffing on my trail, slathering, slobbering after me like some dark hound of hell seeking me out, tonguing along in back of me, this look, my fine feathered friend, should give you much food for thought.

She closed her pocketbook with a sharp, clicking final sound that made the Super's eyes shift suddenly to the ceiling as though seeking out some pattern in the cracked plaster. The dog's ears straightened into sharp points; the canary opened one eye and the whispering woman almost showed her gums again, for her mouth curved as though she were about to smile.

Lutie walked quickly out of the apartment, pushed the street door open and shivered as the cold air touched her. It had been hot in the Super's apartment, and she paused a second to push her coat collar tight around her neck in an effort to make a barrier against the wind howling in the street outside. Now that she had this apartment, she was just one step farther up on the ladder of success. With the apartment Bub would be standing a better chance, for he'd be away from Lil.

Inside the building the dog let out a high shrill yelp. Immediately she headed for the street, thinking he must have kicked it again. She paused for a moment at the corner of the building, bracing herself for the full blast of the wind that would hit her head-on when she turned the corner.

'Get fixed up, dearie?' Mrs. Hedges' rich voice asked from the street-floor window.

She nodded at the bandannaed head in the window and flung herself into the wind, welcoming its attack, aware as she walked along that the woman's hard flat eyes were measuring her progress up the street.

Study and Discussion Questions

1. Reread the first three paragraphs which is also the opening of the novel (you have the first chapter of *The Street*). What is Petry doing here to establish an atmosphere or mood through her representation of the setting? Also, how is she describing the relation between the characters and the setting?
2. Discuss the images, the word choices—the nouns, verbs, adjectives, adverbs—and the physical senses (touch, sound, taste, sight, smell, movement) Petry evokes in these opening three paragraphs.
3. Why is Lutie looking for an apartment?
4. Lutie Johnson is a single mother. What do we learn about Lutie's relationship with her eight year old son, Bub? What are her dreams and fears for him?
5. List at least three characteristics of Jones, the superintendent of the apartment building. Give some details that show why Lutie is afraid of him. Would you rent an apartment from this man?
6. Discuss the other characters Lutie meets in this opening chapter of *The Street*. What do they suggest about the environment Lutie is moving into?
7. What factors does Lutie consider in her decision to take the apartment or not? What are the reasons not to take it? What are the reasons to do so?
8. Petry spends some time describing the inside of the apartment building and the apartment itself as Lutie looks it over. What are three or four characteristics of the place?
9. Do you think Lutie made the right decision (to take the apartment)? What do you think might happen, given what you've learned here? What makes you think that?

Suggestions for Writing

1. One of Petry's writing techniques is the "list," where she will give the reader a series of objects or actions one after the other. Find one or two of these lists. Discuss their effectiveness: What do they help the writer do? Now make a list of your own that will evoke an atmosphere or a person or a place.
2. How are Lutie's choices defined and limited by her class, race, and gender? Are there ways in which your own choices are or have been limited because of your gender, race, class, or some other socially defined limitation? How do/did you feel about that limitation? How is/was your situation different from/similar to Lutie Johnson's?
3. Look over a number of apartment ads in your local newspapers. Select one and write a scene or a short short story or a poem based on the ad.

Critical Resources

1. Andrews, Larry. "The Sensory Assault of the City in Ann Petry's *The Street.*" *The City in African-American Literature,* Yoshinobo Hakutani and Robert Butler, eds. Madison, NJ: Fairleigh Dickinson University Press, 1995.
2. Ervin, Hazel Arnett. *Ann Petry: A Bio-Bibliography.* New York: G. K. Hall, 1993.
3. Holladay, Hilary. *Ann Petry.* New York: Twayne, 1996.
4. McBride, Kecia. "Fear, Consumption and Desire: Naturalism and Ann Petry's *The Street.*" *Twisted from the Ordinary: Essays on American Literary Naturalism.* Knoxville: University of Tennessee Press, 2003.

WILLIAM FAULKNER (1897–1962)

William Faulkner grew up in Oxford, Mississippi. His ancestors included a great-grandfather who was a famous Civil War colonel and popular novelist. Little interested in high school, Faulkner dropped out and, because he was too short for the U.S. Army, enlisted in the Canadian Royal Air Force. He studied briefly at the University of Mississippi, held odd jobs in New York City, and in 1924 published a volume of poetry. He then turned to fiction and published the novel Soldier's Pay *in 1926.* Sartoris *(1929) was the first of his many novels set in the fictional Yoknapatawpha County in Mississippi and* The Sound and the Fury *(1929) and* As I Lay Dying *(1930) followed soon after. One distinguishing aspect of much of Faulkner's work is his use of the literary device called "stream of consciousness," where the author attempts to describe the continuous flow of thought as it passes through a character's mind. Among Faulkner's major novels are* Sanctuary *(1931),* Light in August *(1932),* Absalom, Absalom! *(1936), and the three novels that comprise the Snopes Trilogy:* The Hamlet *(1940),* The Town *(1957), and* The Mansion *(1959). He received the Nobel Prize for literature in 1950. The short story "Spotted Horses" was originally published in 1931. Faulkner would later rework the story and incorporate it into* The Hamlet.

Spotted Horses (1931)

I

Yes, sir. Flem Snopes has filled that whole country full of spotted horses. You can hear folks running them all day and all night, whooping and hollering, and the horses running back and forth across them little wooden bridges ever now and then kind of like thunder. Here I was this morning pretty near half way to town, with the team ambling along and me setting in the buckboard about half asleep, when all of a sudden something come swurging up outen the bushes and jumped the road clean, without touching hoof to it. It flew right over my team, big as a billboard and flying through the air like a hawk. It taken me thirty minutes to stop my team and untangle the harness and the buckboard and hitch them up again.

That Flem Snopes. I be dog if he ain't a case, now. One morning about ten years ago, the boys was just getting settled down on Varner's porch for a little talk and tobacco, when here come Flem out from behind the counter, with his coat off and his hair all parted, like he might have been clerking for Varner for ten years already. Folks all knowed him; it was a big family of them about five miles down the bottom. That year, at least. Share-cropping. They never stayed on any place over a year. Then they would move on to another place, with the chap or maybe the twins of that year's litter. It was a regular nest of them. But Flem. The rest of them stayed tenant farmers, moving ever year, but here come Flem one day, walking out from behind Jody Varner's counter like he owned it. And he wasn't there but a year or two before folks knowed that, if him and Jody was both still in that store in ten years more, it would be Jody clerking for Flem Snopes. Why, that fellow could make a nickel where it wasn't but four cents to begin with. He skun me in two trades, myself, and the fellow that can do that, I just hope he'll get rich before I do; that's all.

All right. So here Flem was, clerking at Varner's, making a nickel here and there and not telling nobody about it. No, sir. Folks never knowed when Flem got the better of somebody lessen the fellow he beat told it. He'd just set there in the storechair, chewing his tobacco and keeping his own business to hisself, until about a week later we'd find out it was somebody else's business he was keeping to hisself—provided the fellow he trimmed was mad enough to tell it. That's Flem.

We give him ten years to own ever thing Jody Varner had. But he never waited no ten years. I reckon you-all know that gal of Uncle Billy Varner's, the youngest one; Eula. Jody's sister. Ever Sunday ever yellow-wheeled buggy and curried riding horse in that country would be hitched to Bill Varner's fence, and the young bucks setting on the porch, swarming around Eula like bees around a honey pot. One of these here kind of big, soft-looking gals that could giggle richer than plowed new-ground. Wouldn't none of them leave before the others, and so they would set there on the porch until time to go home, with some of them with nine and ten miles to ride and then get up tomorrow and go back to the field. So they would all leave together and they would ride in a clump down to the creek ford and hitch them curried horses and yellow-wheeled buggies and get out and fight one another. Then they would get in the buggies again and go on home.

Well, one day about a year ago, one of them yellow-wheeled buggies and one of them curried saddle-horses quit this country. We heard they was heading for Texas. The next day Uncle Billy and Eula and Flem come in to town in Uncle Bill's surrey, and when they come back, Flem and Eula was married. And on the next day we heard that two more of them yellow-wheeled buggies had left the country. They mought have gone to Texas, too. It's a big place.

Anyway, about a month after the wedding, Flem and Eula went to Texas, too. They was gone pretty near a year. Then one day last month, Eula come back, with a baby. We figured up, and we decided that it was as well-growed a three-months-old baby as we ever see. It can already pull up on a chair. I reckon Texas makes big men quick, being a big place. Anyway, if it keeps on like it started, it'll be chewing tobacco and voting time it's eight years old.

And so last Friday here come Flem himself. He was on a wagon with another fellow. The other fellow had one of these two-gallon hats and a ivory-handled pistol and a box of gingersnaps sticking out of his hind pocket, and tied to the tail-gate of the wagon was about two dozen of them Texas ponies, hitched to one another with barbed wire. They was colored like parrots and they was quiet as doves, and ere a one of them would kill you quick as a rattlesnake. Nere a one of them had two eyes the same color, and nere a one of them had ever see a bridle, I reckon; and when that Texas man got down offen the wagon and walked up to them to show how gentle they was, one of them cut his vest clean offen him, same as with a razor.

Flem had done already disappeared; he had went on to see his wife, I reckon, and to see if that ere baby had done gone on to the field to help Uncle Billy plow maybe. It was the Texas man that taken the horses on to Mrs. Littlejohn's lot. He had a little trouble at first, when they come to the gate, because they hadn't never see a fence before, and when he finally got them in and taken a pair of wire cutters and unhitched them and got them into the barn and poured some shell corn into the trough, they durn nigh tore down the barn. I reckon they thought that shell corn was bugs, maybe. So he left them in the lot and he announced that the auction would begin at sunup to-morrow.

That night we was setting on Mrs. Littlejohn's porch. You-all mind the moon was nigh full that night, and we could watch them spotted varmints swirling along the fence and back and forth across the lot same as minnows in a pond. And then now and then they would all kind of huddle up against the barn and rest themselves by biting and kicking one another. We would hear a squeal, and then a set of hoofs would go Bam! against the barn, like a pistol. It sounded just like a fellow with a pistol, in a nest of cattymounts,[1] taking his time.

II

It wasn't ere a man knowed yet if Flem owned them things or not. They just knowed one thing: that they wasn't never going to know for sho if Flem did or not, or if maybe he didn't just get on that wagon at the edge of town, for the ride or not. Even Eck Snopes didn't know, Flem's own cousin. But wasn't nobody surprised at that. We knowed that Flem would skin Eck quick as he would ere a one of us.

They was there by sunup next morning, some of them come twelve and sixteen miles, with seed-money tied up in tobacco sacks in their overalls, standing

---

[1]Wildcats.

along the fence, when the Texas man come out of Mrs. Littlejohn's after breakfast and clumb onto the gate post with that ere white pistol butt sticking outen
his hind pocket. He taken a new box of gingersnaps outen his pocket and bit the
end offen it like a cigar and spit out the paper, and said the auction was open. And
still they was coming up in wagons and a horse- and mule-back and hitching the
teams across the road and coming to the fence. Flem wasn't nowhere in sight.

But he couldn't get them started. He begun to work on Eck, because Eck holp
him last night to get them into the barn and feed them that shell corn. Eck got
out just in time. He come outen that barn like a chip on the crest of a busted
dam of water, and clumb into the wagon just in time.

He was working on Eck when Henry Armstid come up in his wagon. Eck was
saying he was skeered to bid on one of them, because he might get it, and the
Texas man says, "Them ponies? Them little horses?" He clumb down offen the
gate post and went toward the horses. They broke and run, and him following
them, kind of chirping to them, with his hand out like he was fixing to catch a
fly, until he got three or four of them cornered. Then he jumped into them, and
then we couldn't see nothing for a while because of the dust. It was a big cloud
of it, and them blare-eyed, spotted things swoaring outen it twenty foot to a jump,
in forty directions without counting up. Then the dust settled and there they was,
that Texas man and the horse. He had its head twisted clean around like a owl's
head. Its legs was braced and it was trembling like a new bride and groaning like
a saw mill, and him holding its head wrung clean around on its neck so it was
snuffing sky. "Look it over," he says, with his heels dug too and that white pistol
sticking outen his pocket and his neck swole up like a spreading adder's until
you could just tell what he was saying, cussing the horse and talking to us all at
once: "Look him over, the fiddle-headed son of fourteen fathers. Try him, buy
him; you will get the best—" Then it was all dust again, and we couldn't see nothing but spotted hide and mane, and that ere Texas man's boot-heels like a couple of walnuts on two strings, and after a while that two-gallon hat come sailing
out like a fat old hen crossing a fence.

When the dust settled again, he was just getting outen the far fence corner,
brushing himself off. He come and got his hat and brushed it off and come and
clumb onto the gate post again. He was breathing hard. He taken the ginger-
snap box outen his pocket and et one, breathing hard. The hammer-head horse
was still running round and round the lot like a merry-go-round at a fair. That
was when Henry Armstid come shoving up to the gate in them patched overalls
and one of them dangle-armed shirts of hisn. Hadn't nobody noticed him until
then. We was all watching the Texas man and the horses. Even Mrs. Littlejohn;
she had done come out and built a fire under the wash-pot in her back yard, and
she would stand at the fence a while and then go back into the house and come
out again with a arm full of wash and stand at the fence again. Well, here come
Henry shoving up, and then we see Mrs. Armstid right behind him, in that ere
faded wrapper and sunbonnet and them tennis shoes. "Git on back to that
wagon," Henry says.

"Henry," she says.

"Here, boys," the Texas man says; "make room for missus to git up and see. Come on, Henry," he says; "here's your chance to buy that saddle-horse missus has been wanting. What about ten dollars, Henry?"

"Henry," Mrs. Armstid says. She put her hand on Henry's arm. Henry knocked her hand down.

"Git on back to that wagon, like I told you," he says.

Mrs. Armstid never moved. She stood behind Henry, with her hands rolled into her dress, not looking at nothing. "He hain't no more despair than to buy one of them things," she says. "And us not five dollars ahead of the pore house, he hain't no more despair." It was the truth, too. They ain't never made more than a bare living offen that place of theirs, and them with four chaps and the very clothes they wears she earns by weaving by the firelight at night while Henry's asleep.

"Shut your mouth and git on back to that wagon," Henry says. "Do you want I taken a wagon stake to you here in the big road?"

Well, that Texas man taken one look at her. Then he begun on Eck again, like Henry wasn't even there. But Eck was skeered. "I can git me a snapping turtle or a water moccasin for nothing. I ain't going to buy none."

So the Texas man said he would give Eck a horse. "To start the auction, and because you help me last night. If you'll start the bidding on the next horse," he says, "I'll give you that fiddle-head horse."

I wish you could have seen them, standing there with their seed-money in their pockets, watching that Texas man give Eck Snopes a live horse, all fixed to call him a fool if he taken it or not. Finally Eck says he'll take it. "Only I just starts the bidding," he says. "I don't have to buy the next one lessen I ain't overtopped." The Texas man said all right, and Eck bid a dollar on the next one, with Henry Armstid standing there with his mouth already open, watching Eck and the Texas man like a mad-dog or something. "A dollar," Eck says.

The Texas man looked at Eck. His mouth was already open too, like he had started to say something and what he was going to say had up and died on him. "A dollar?" he says. "One dollar? You mean, *one* dollar, Eck?"

"Durn it," Eck says; "two dollars, then."

Well, sir, I wish you could a seen that Texas man. He taken out that ginger-snap box and held it up and looked into it, careful, like it might have been a diamond ring in it, or a spider. Then he throwed it away and wiped his face with a bandanna. "Well," he says. "Well, Two dollars. Two dollars. Is your pulse all right, Eck?" he says. "Do you have agersweats[2] at night, maybe?" he says. "Well," he says, "I got to take it. But are you boys going to stand there and see Eck get two horses at a dollar a head?"

That done it. I be dog if he wasn't nigh as smart as Flem Snopes. He hadn't no more than got the words outen his mouth before here was Henry Armstid,

---

[2] Ague, cold sweats.

waving his hand. "Three dollars," Henry says. Mrs. Armstid tried to hold him again. He knocked her hand off, shoving up to the gate post.

"Mister," Mrs. Armstid says, "we got chaps in the house and not corn to feed the stock. We got five dollars I earned my chaps a-weaving after dark, and him snoring in the bed. And he hain't no more despair."

"Henry bids three dollars," the Texas man says. "Raise him a dollar, Eck, and the horse is yours."

"Henry," Mrs. Armstid says.

"Raise him, Eck," the Texas man says.

"Four dollars," Eck says.

"Five dollars," Henry says, shaking his fist. He shoved up right under the gate post. Mrs. Armstid was looking at the Texas man too.

"Mister," she says, "if you take that five dollars I earned my chaps a-weaving for one of them things, it'll be a curse onto you and yourn during all the time of man."

But it wasn't no stopping Henry. He had shoved up, waving his fist at the Texas man. He opened it; the money was in nickels and quarters, and one dollar bill that looked like a cow's cud. "Five dollars," he says. "And the man that raises it'll have to beat my head off, or I'll beat hisn."

"All right," the Texas man says. "Five dollars is bid. But don't you shake your hand at me."

III

It taken till nigh sundown before the last one was sold. He got them hotted up once and the bidding got up to seven dollars and a quarter, but most of them went around three or four dollars, him setting on the gate post and picking the horses out one at a time by mouth-word, and Mrs. Littlejohn pumping up and down at the tub and stopping and coming to the fence for a while and going back to the tub again. She had done got done too, and the wash was hung on the line in the back yard, and we could smell supper cooking. Finally they was all sold; he swapped the last two and the wagon for a buckboard.

We was all kind of tired, but Henry Armstid looked more like a maddog than ever. When he bought, Mrs. Armstid had went back to the wagon, setting in it behind them two rabbit-sized, bone-pore mules, and the wagon itself looking like it would fall all to pieces soon as the mules moved. Henry hadn't even waited to pull it outen the road; it was still in the middle of the road and her setting in it, not looking at nothing, ever since this morning.

Henry was right up against the gate. He went up to the Texas man. "I bought a horse and I paid cash," Henry says. "And yet you expect me to stand around here until they are all sold before I can get my horse. I'm going to take my horse outen that lot."

The Texas man looked at Henry. He talked like he might have been asking for a cup of coffee at the table. "Take your horse," he says.

Then Henry quit looking at the Texas man. He begun to swallow, holding onto the gate. "Ain't you going to help me?" he says.

"It ain't my horse," the Texas man says.

Henry never looked at the Texas man again, he never looked at nobody. "Who'll help me catch my horse?" he says. Never nobody said nothing. "Bring the plowline," Henry says. Mrs. Armstid got outen the wagon and brought the plowline. The Texas man got down offen the post. The woman made to pass him, carrying the rope.

"Don't you go in there, missus," the Texas man says.

Henry opened the gate. He didn't look back. "Come on here," he says.

"Don't you go in there, missus," the Texas man says.

Mrs. Armstid wasn't looking at nobody, neither, with her hands across her middle, holding the rope. "I reckon I better," she says. Her and Henry went into the lot. The horses broke and run. Henry and Mrs. Armstid followed.

"Get him into the corner," Henry says. They got Henry's horse cornered finally, and Henry taken the rope, but Mrs. Armstid let the horse get out. They hemmed it up again, but Mrs. Armstid let it get out again, and Henry turned and hit her with the rope. "Why didn't you head him back?" Henry says. He hit her again. "Why didn't you?" It was about that time I looked around and see Flem Snopes standing there.

It was the Texas man that done something. He moved fast for a big man. He caught the rope before Henry could hit the third time, and Henry whirled and made like he would jump at the Texas man. But he never jumped. The Texas man went and taken Henry's arm and led him outen the lot. Mrs. Armstid come behind them and the Texas man taken some money outen his pocket and he give it into Mrs. Armstid's hand. "Get him into the wagon and take him on home," the Texas man says, like he might have been telling them he enjoyed his supper.

Then here come Flem. "What's that for, Buck?" Flem says.

"Thinks he bought one of them ponies," the Texas man says. "Get him on away, missus."

But Henry wouldn't go. "Give him back that money," he says. "I bought that horse and I aim to have him if I have to shoot him."

And there was Flem, standing there with his hands in his pockets, chewing, like he had just happened to be passing.

"You take your money and I take my horse," Henry says. "Give it back to him," he says to Mrs. Armstid.

"You don't own no horse of mine," the Texas man says. "Get him on home, missus."

Then Henry seen Flem. "You got something to do with these horses," he says. "I bought one. Here's the money for it." He taken the bill outen Mrs. Armstid's hand. He offered it to Flem. "I bought one. Ask him. Here. Here's the money," he says, giving the bill to Flem.

When Flem taken the money, the Texas man dropped the rope he had snatched outen Henry's hand. He had done sent Eck Snopes's boy up to the store for another box of gingersnaps, and he taken the box outen his pocket and looked into it. It was empty and he dropped it on the ground. "Mr. Snopes will have your money for you to-morrow," he says to Mrs. Armstid. "You can get it from him to-morrow. He don't own no horse. You get him into the wagon and get him on home." Mrs. Armstid went back to the wagon and got in. "Where's that ere buckboard I bought?" the Texas man says. It was after sundown then. And then Mrs. Littlejohn come out on the porch and rung the supper bell.

IV

I come on in and et supper. Mrs. Littlejohn would bring in a pan of bread or something, then she would go out to the porch a minute and come back and tell us. The Texas man had hitched his team to the buckboard he had swapped them last two horses for, and him and Flem had gone, and then she told that the rest of them that never had ropes had went back to the store with I.O. Snopes to get some ropes, and wasn't nobody at the gate but Henry Armstid, and Mrs. Armstid setting in the wagon in the road, and Eck Snopes and that boy of hisn. "I don't care how many of them fool men gets killed by them thing," Mrs. Littlejohn says, "but I ain't going to let Eck Snopes take that boy into that lot again." So she went down to the gate, but she come back without the boy or Eck neither.

"It ain't no need to worry about that boy," I says. "He's charmed." He was right behind Eck last night when Eck went to help feed them. The whole drove of them jumped clean over that boy's head and never touched him. It was Eck that touched him. Eck snatched him into the wagon and taken a rope and frailed the tar outen him.

So I had done et and went to my room and was undressing, long as I had a long trip to make next day; I was trying to sell a machine to Mrs. Bundren up past Whiteleaf; when Henry Armstid opened that gate and went in by hisself. They couldn't make him wait for the balance of them to get back with their ropes. Eck Snopes said he tried to make Henry wait, but Henry wouldn't do it. Eck said Henry walked right up to them and that when they broke, they run clean over Henry like a haymow breaking down. Eck said he snatched that boy of hisn out of the way just in time and that them things went through that gate like a creek flood and into the wagons and teams hitched side the road, busting wagon tongues and snapping harness like it was fishing-line, with Mrs. Armstid still setting in their wagon in the middle of it like something carved outen wood. Then they scattered, wild horses and tame mules with pieces of harness and single trees dangling offen them, both ways up and down the road.

"There goes ourn, paw!" Eck says his boy said. "There it goes, into Mrs. Littlejohn's house." Eck says it run right up the steps and into the house like a boarder late for supper. I reckon so. Anyway, I was in my room, in my underclothes, with one sock on and one sock in my hand, leaning out the window when the commotion busted out, when I heard something run into the melodeon in the hall; it sounded like a railroad engine. Then the door to my room come sailing in like when you throw a tin bucket top into the wind and I looked over my shoulder and see something that looked like a fourteen-foot pinwheel a-blaring its eyes at me. It had to blare them fast, because I was already done jumped out the window.

I reckon it was anxious, too. I reckon it hadn't never seen barbed wire or shell corn before, but I know it hadn't never seen underclothes before, or maybe it was a sewing-machine agent it hadn't never seen. Anyway, it swirled and turned to run back up the hall and outen the house, when it met Eck Snopes and that boy just coming in, carrying a rope. It swirled again and run down the hall and out the back door just in time to meet Mrs. Littlejohn. She had just gathered up the clothes she had washed, and she was coming onto the back porch with a armful of washing in one hand and a scrubbing-board in the other, when the horse skidded up to her, trying to stop and swirl again. It never taken Mrs. Littlejohn no time a-tall.

"Git outen here, you son," she says. She hit it across the face with the scrubbing-board; that ere scrubbing-board split as neat as ere a axe could have done it, and when the horse swirled to run back up the hall, she hit it again with what was left of the scrubbing-board, not on the head this time. "And stay out," she says.

Eck and that boy was half-way down the hall by this time. I reckon that horse looked like a pinwheel to Eck too. "Git to hell outen here, Ad!" Eck says. Only there wasn't time. Eck dropped flat on his face, but the boy never moved. The boy was about a yard tall maybe, in overhalls just like Eck's; that horse swoared over his head without touching a hair. I saw that, because I was just coming back up the front steps, still carrying that ere sock and still in my underclothes, when the horse come onto the porch again. It taken one look at me and swirled again and run to the end of the porch and jumped the banisters and the lot fence like a hen-hawk and lit in the lot running and went out the gate again and jumped eight or ten upside-down wagons and went on down the road. It was a full moon then. Mrs. Armstid was still setting in the wagon like she had done been carved outen wood and left there and forgot.

That horse. It ain't never missed a lick. It was going about forty miles a hour when it come to the bridge over the creek. It would have had a clear road, but it so happened that Vernon Tull was already using the bridge when it got there. He was coming back from town; he hadn't heard about the auction; him and his wife and three daughters and Mrs. Tull's aunt, all setting in chairs in the wagon bed, and all asleep, including the mules. They waked up when the horse hit the bridge one time, but Tull said the first he knew was when the mules tried to turn the wagon around in the middle of the bridge and he seen that spotted varmint run right twixt the mules and run up the wagon tongue like a squirrel. He said he just had time to hit it across the face with his whip-stock, because about that time the mules turned the wagon around on that ere one-way bridge and that horse clumb across one of the mules and jumped down onto the bridge again and went on, with Vernon standing up in the wagon and kicking at it.

Tull said the mules turned in the harness and clumb back into the wagon too, with Tull trying to beat them out again, with the reins wrapped around his wrist. After that he says all he seen was overturned chairs and womenfolks' legs and white drawers shining in the moonlight, and his mules and that spotted horse going on up the road like a ghost.

The mules jerked Tull outen the wagon and drug him a spell on the bridge before the reins broke. They thought at first that he was dead, and while they was kneeling around him, picking the bridge splinters outen him, here come Eck and that boy, still carrying the rope. They was running and breathing a little hard. "Where'd he go?" Eck says.

V

I went back and got my pants and shirt and shoes on just in time to go and help get Henry Armstid outen the trash in the lot. I be dog if he didn't look like he was dead, with his head hanging back and his teeth showing in the moonlight, and a little rim of white under his eyelids. We could still hear them horses, here and there; hadn't none of them got more than four-five miles away yet, not knowing the country, I reckon. So we could hear them and folks yelling now and then: "Whooey. Head him!"

We toted Henry into Mrs. Littlejohn's. She was in the hall; she hadn't put down the armful of clothes. She taken one look at us, and she laid down the busted scrubbing-board and taken up the lamp and opened a empty door. "Bring him in here," she says.

We toted him in and laid him on the bed. Mrs. Littlejohn set the lamp on the dresser, still carrying the clothes. "I'll declare, you men," she says. Our shadows was way up the wall, tiptoeing too; we could hear ourselves breathing. "Better get his wife," Mrs. Littlejohn says. She went out, carrying the clothes.

"I reckon we had," Quick says. "Go get her, somebody."

"Whyn't you go?" Winterbottom says.

"Let Ernest git her," Durley says. "He lives neighbors with them."

Ernest went to fetch her. I be dog if Henry didn't look like he was dead. Mrs. Littlejohn come back, with a kettle and some towels. She went to work on Henry, and then Mrs. Armstid and Ernest come in. Mrs. Armstid come to the foot of the bed and stood there, with her hands rolled into her apron, watching what Mrs. Littlejohn was doing, I reckon.

"You men git outen the way," Mrs. Littlejohn says. "Git outside," she says. "See if you can't find something else to play with that will kill some more of you."

"Is he dead?" Winterbottom says.

"It ain't your fault if he ain't," Mrs. Littlejohn says. "Go tell Will Varner to come up here. I reckon a man ain't so different from a mule, come long come short. Except maybe a mule's got more sense."

We went to get Uncle Billy. It was a full moon. We could hear them, now and then, four mile away: "Whooey. Head him." The country was full of them, one on ever wooden bridge in the land, running across it like thunder: "Whooey. There he goes. Head him."

We hadn't got far before Henry begun to scream. I reckon Mrs. Littlejohn's water had brung him to; anyway, he wasn't dead. We went on to Uncle Billy's. The house was dark. We called to him, and after a while the window opened and Uncle Billy put his head out, peart as a peckerwood,[3] listening. "Are they still trying to catch them durn rabbits?" he says.

He come down, with his britches on over his night-shirt and his suspenders dangling, carrying his horse-doctoring grip. "Yes, sir," he says, cocking his head like a woodpecker, "They're still a-trying."

We could hear Henry before we reached Mrs. Littlejohn's. He was going Ah-Ah-Ah. We stopped in the yard. Uncle Billy went on in. We could hear Henry. We stood in the yard, hearing them on the bridges, this-a-way and that: "Whooey. Whooey."

"Eck Snopes ought to caught hisn," Ernest says.

"Looks like he ought," Winterbottom said.

Henry was going Ah-Ah-Ah steady in the house; then he begun to scream. "Uncle Billy's started," Quick says. We looked into the hall. We could see the light where the door was. Then Mrs. Littlejohn come out.

"Will needs some help," she says. "You, Ernest. You'll do." Ernest went into the house.

"Hear them?" Quick said. "That one was on Four Mile bridge." We could hear them; it sounded like thunder a long way off; it didn't last long: "Whooey."

We could hear Henry: "Ah-Ah-Ah-Ah-Ah."

"They are both started now," Winterbottom says. "Ernest too."

That was early in the night. Which was a good thing, because it taken a long night for folks to chase them things right and for Henry to lay there and holler, being as Uncle Billy never had none of this here chloryfoam to set Henry's leg with. So it was considerate of Flem to get them started early. And what do you reckon Flem's com-ment was?

That's right. Nothing. Because he wasn't there. Hadn't nobody see him since that Texas man left.

VI

That was Saturday night. I reckon Mrs. Armstid got home about daylight, to see about the chaps. I don't know where they thought her and Henry was. But lucky the oldest one was a gal, about twelve, big enough to take care of the little ones. Which she did for the next two days. Mrs. Armstid would nurse Henry all night and work in the kitchen for hern and Henry's keep, and in the

---

[3]Woodpecker.

afternoon she would drive home (it was about four miles) to see to the chaps. She would cook up a pot of victuals and leave it on the stove, and the gal would bar the house and keep the little ones quiet. I would hear Mrs. Littlejohn and Mrs. Armstid talking in the kitchen. "How are the chaps making out?" Mrs. Littlejohn says.

"All right," Mrs. Armstid says.

"Don't they git skeered at night?" Mrs. Littlejohn says.

"Ina May bars the door when I leave," Mrs. Armstid says. "She's got the axe in bed with her. I reckon she can make out."

I reckon they did. And I reckon Mrs. Armstid was waiting for Flem to come back to town; hadn't nobody seen him until this morning; to get her money the Texas man said Flem was keeping for her. Sho. I reckon she was.

Anyway, I heard Mrs. Armstid and Mrs. Littlejohn talking in the kitchen this morning while I was eating breakfast. Mrs. Littlejohn had just told Mrs. Armstid that Flem was in town. "You can ask him for that five dollars," Mrs. Littlejohn says.

"You reckon he'll give it to me?" Mrs. Armstid says.

Mrs. Littlejohn was washing dishes, washing them like a man, like they was made out of iron. "No," she says. "But asking him won't do no hurt. It might shame him. I don't reckon it will, but it might."

"If he wouldn't give it back, it ain't no use to ask," Mrs. Armstid says.

"Suit yourself," Mrs. Littlejohn says. "It's your money."

I could hear the dishes.

"Do you reckon he might give it back to me?" Mrs. Armstid says. "That Texas man said he would. He said I could get it from Mr. Snopes later."

"Then go and ask him for it," Mrs. Littlejohn says.

I could hear the dishes.

"He won't give it back to me," Mrs. Armstid says.

"All right," Mrs. Littlejohn says. "Don't ask him for it, then."

I could hear the dishes; Mrs. Armstid was helping. "You don't reckon he would, do you?" she says. Mrs. Littlejohn never said nothing. It sounded like she was throwing the dishes at one another. "Maybe I better go and talk to Henry about it," Mrs. Armstid says.

"I would," Mrs. Littlejohn says. I be dog if it didn't sound like she had two plates in her hands, beating them together. "Then Henry can buy another five-dollar horse with it. Maybe he'll buy one next time that will out and out kill him. If I thought that, I'd give you back the money, myself."

"I reckon I better talk to him first," Mrs. Armstid said. Then it sounded like Mrs. Littlejohn taken up all the dishes and throwed them at the cookstove, and I come away.

That was this morning. I had been up to Bundren's and back, and I thought that things would have kind of settled down. So after breakfast, I went up to the store. And there was Flem, setting in the store-chair and whittling, like he might not have ever moved since he come to clerk for Jody Varner. I. O. was leaning in the door, in his shirt sleeves and with his hair parted too, same as Flem was before he turned the clerking job over to I. O. It's a funny thing about them Snopes: they all looks alike, yet there ain't ere a two of them that claims brothers. They're always just cousins, like Flem and Eck and Flem and I. O. Eck was there too, squatting against the wall, him and that boy, eating cheese and crackers outen a sack; they told me that Eck hadn't been home a-tall. And that Lon Quick hadn't got back to town, even. He followed his horse clean down to Samson's Bridge, with a wagon and a camp outfit. Eck finally caught one of hisn. It run into a blind lane at Freeman's and Eck and the boy taken and tied their rope across the end of the lane, about three foot high. The horse come to the end of the lane and whirled and run back without ever stopping. Eck says it never seen the rope a-tall. He says it looked just like one of these here Christmas pinwheels. "Didn't it try to run again?" I says.

"No," Eck says, eating a bite of cheese offen his knife blade. "Just kicked some."

"Kicked some?" I says.

"It broke its neck," Eck says.

Well, they was squatting there, about six of them, talking, talking at Flem; never nobody knowed yet if Flem had ere a interest in them horses or not. So finally I come right out and asked him. "Flem's done skun all of us so much," I says, "that we're proud of him. Come on, Flem," I says, "how much did you and that Texas man make offen them horses? You can tell us. Ain't nobody here but Eck that bought one of them; the others ain't got back to town yet, and Eck's your own cousin; he'll be proud to hear, too. How much did you-all make?"

They was all whittling, not looking at Flem, making like they was studying. But you could a heard a pin drop. And I. O. He had been rubbing his back up and down on the door, but he stopped now, watching Flem like a pointing dog. Flem finished cutting the sliver offen his stick. He spit across the porch, into the road. "'Twarn't none of my horses," he says.

I. O. cackled, like a hen, slapping his legs with both hands. "You boys might just as well quit trying to get ahead of Flem," he said.

Well, about that time I see Mrs. Armstid come outen Mrs. Littlejohn's gate, coming up the road. I never said nothing. I says, "Well, if a man can't take care of himself in a trade, he can't blame the man that trims him."

Flem never said nothing, trimming at the stick. He hadn't seen Mrs. Armstid. "Yes, sir," I says. "A fellow like Henry Armstid ain't got nobody but hisself to blame."

"Course he ain't," I. O. says. He ain't seen her, neither. "Henry Armstid's a born fool. Always is been. If Flem hadn't a got his money, somebody else would."

We looked at Flem. He never moved. Mrs. Armstid come on up the road.

"That's right," I says. "But, come to think of it, Henry never bought no horse." We looked at Flem; you could a heard a match drop. "That Texas man told her to get that five dollars back from Flem next day. I reckon Flem's done already taken that money to Mrs. Littlejohn's and give it to Mrs. Armstid."

We watched Flem. I. O. quit rubbing his back against the door again. After a while Flem raised his head and spit across the porch, into the dust. I. O. cackled, just like a hen. "Ain't he a beating fellow, now?" I. O. says.

Mrs. Armstid was getting closer, so I kept on talking, watching to see if Flem would look up and see her. But he never looked up. I went on talking about Tull, about how he was going to sue Flem, and Flem setting there, whittling his stick, not saying nothing else after he said they wasn't none of his horses.

Then I. O. happened to look around. He seen Mrs. Armstid. "Psssst!" he says. Flem looked up. "Here she comes!" I. O. says. "Go out the back. I'll tell her you done went in to town to-day."

But Flem never moved. He just set there, whittling, and we watched Mrs. Armstid come up onto the porch, in that ere faded sunbonnet and wrapper and them tennis shoes that made a kind of hissing noise on the porch. She come onto the porch and stopped, her hands rolled into her dress in front, not looking at nothing.

"He said Saturday," she says, "that he wouldn't sell Henry no horse. He said I could get the money from you."

Flem looked up. The knife never stopped. It went on trimming off a sliver same as if he was watching it. "He taken that money off with him when he left," Flem says.

Mrs. Armstid never looked at nothing. We never looked at her, neither, except that boy of Eck's. He had a half-et cracker in his hand, watching her, chewing.

"He said Henry hadn't bought no horse," Mrs. Armstid says. "He said for me to get the money from you today."

"I reckon he forgot about it," Flem said. "He taken that money off with him Saturday." He whittled again. I. O. kept on rubbing his back, slow. He licked his lips. After a while the woman looked up the road, where it went on up the hill, toward the graveyard. She looked up that way for a while, with that boy of Eck's watching her and I. O. rubbing his back slow against the door. Then she turned back toward the steps.

"I reckon it's time to get dinner started," she says.

"How's Henry this morning, Mrs. Armstid?" Winterbottom says.

She looked at Winterbottom; she almost stopped. "He's resting, I thank you kindly," she says.

Flem got up, outen the chair, putting his knife away. He spit across the porch. "Wait a minute, Mrs. Armstid," he says. She stopped again. She didn't look at him. Flem went on into the store, with I. O. done quit rubbing his back now, with his head craned after Flem, and Mrs. Armstid standing there with her hands rolled into her dress, not looking at nothing. A wagon come up the road and passed; it was Freeman, on the way to town. Then Flem come out again, with I. O. still watching him. Flem had one of these little striped sacks of Jody Varner's candy; I bet he still owes Jody that nickel, too. He put the sack into Mrs. Armstid's hand, like he would have put it into a hollow stump. He spit again across the porch. "A little sweetening for the chaps," he says.

"You're right kind," Mrs. Armstid says. She held the sack of candy in her hand, not looking at nothing. Eck's boy was watching the sack, the half-et cracker in his hand; he wasn't chewing now. He watched Mrs. Armstid roll the sack into her apron. "I reckon I better get on back and help with dinner," she says. She turned and went back across the porch. Flem set down in the chair again and opened his knife. He spit across the porch again, past Mrs. Armstid where she hadn't went down the steps yet. Then she went on, in that ere sunbonnet and wrapper all the same color, back down the road toward Mrs. Littlejohn's. You couldn't see her dress move, like a natural woman walking. She looked like a old snag still standing up and moving along on a high water. We watched her turn in at Mrs. Littlejohn's and go outen sight. Flem was whittling. I. O. begun to rub his back on the door. Then he begun to cackle, just like a durn hen.

"You boys might just as well quit trying," I. O. says. "You can't git ahead of Flem. You can't touch him. Ain't he a sight, now?"

I be dog if he ain't. If I had brung a herd of wild cattymounts into town and sold them to my neighbors and kinfolks, they would have lynched me. Yes, sir.

Study and Discussion Questions

1. List or sum up the characteristics of each of the following characters in the story: the Texan, Flem, Mrs. Littlejohn, Mrs. Armstid, Henry Armstid.
2. Who is the narrator of "Spotted Horses"? What is his relation to the events of the story?
3. Who owns the horses?
4. What words are used to describe the horses? What are the horses compared to?
5. What do Flem and the spotted horses have in common?
6. What is Mrs. Littlejohn's opinion of the situation? Give examples of her expressing her opinion.

Suggestions for Writing

1. Find a passage that made you smile or laugh and analyze Faulkner's use of humor.
2. Though he is the focus of much of the story, Flem Snopes rarely speaks and is not even present for much of the action. How is it, then, that Flem has so much power? Why is it, as I. O. says, that "you can't touch him"?
3. What do the horses represent or mean to the community? How do they operate as a symbol in the story? That is, what do they come to mean for the reader?
4. Consider Henry Armstid's purchase of a horse and how the Texas man handles that situation. Can you state the unwritten code of ethics out of which the Texas man is acting? What is Flem Snope's relation to that same code of ethics?

Critical Resources

1. Parini, Jay. *One Matchless Time: A Life of William Faulkner.* New York: HarperCollins, 2004.
2. Holmes, Catherine D., ed. *Annotations to William Faulkner's The Hamlet.* New York: Garland Publishers, 1996.

3. Rankin, Elizabeth D. "Chasing Spotted Horses: The Quest for Human Dignity in Faulkner's Snopes Trilogy." *Faulkner: The Unappeased Imagination: A Collection of Critical Essays.* Ed. Glenn Carey. Troy, NY: Whitston, 1980.
4. Ramsey, Allen. " 'Spotted Horses' and Spotted Pups." *The Faulkner Journal* 5.1 (1990): 35–38.

❁ ❁ ❁

B. TRAVEN (c. 1890–1969)

The facts of B. Traven's life remain a mystery. Many believe that as a young man he lived in Germany, went by the name of Ret Marut, and published an underground anarchist magazine, Der Ziegelbrenner (The Brick Burner). *According to this account, Traven disappeared, spent some time in a British prison, and lived reclusively in Mexico until his death. Much of his fiction was published in German, though it is unclear whether or not German was the original language he wrote in. His work has appeared in thirty-six languages and in more than five hundred editions since the 1920s. It includes* The Cotton Pickers *(1926),* The Treasures of the Sierra Madre *(1927),* Death Ship *(1934), and* The Rebellion of the Hanged *(1936). "Assembly Line," first published in* The Night Visitor and Other Stories *(1966), touches on issues of labor, low wages, and exploitation—themes that run throughout Traven's work.*

Assembly Line   (1966)

Mr. E. L. Winthrop of New York was on vacation in the Republic of Mexico. It wasn't long before he realized that this strange and really wild country had not yet been fully and satisfactorily explored by Rotarians and Lions,[1] who are forever conscious of their glorious mission on earth. Therefore, he considered it his duty as a good American citizen to do his part in correcting this oversight.

In search for opportunities to indulge in his new avocation, he left the beaten track and ventured into regions not especially mentioned, and hence not recommended, by travel agents to foreign tourists. So it happened that one day he found himself in a little, quaint Indian village somewhere in the State of Oaxaca.

Walking along the dusty main street of this pueblecito,[2] which knew nothing of pavements, drainage, plumbing, or of any means of artificial light save candles

---

[1]Members of two business organizations.
[2]Small village.

or pine splinters, he met with an Indian squatting on the earthen-floor front porch of a palm hut, a so-called jacalito.

The Indian was busy making little baskets from bast and from all kinds of fibers gathered by him in the immense tropical bush which surrounded the village on all sides. The material used had not only been well prepared for its purpose but was also richly colored with dyes that the basketmaker himself extracted from various native plants, barks, roots and from certain insects by a process known only to him and the members of his family.

His principal business, however, was not producing baskets. He was a peasant who lived on what the small property he possessed—less than fifteen acres of not too fertile soil—would yield, after much sweat and labor and after constantly worrying over the most wanted and best suited distribution of rain, sunshine, and wind and the changing balance of birds and insects beneficial or harmful to his crops. Baskets he made when there was nothing else for him to do in the fields, because he was unable to dawdle. After all, the sale of his baskets, though to a rather limited degree only, added to the small income he received from his little farm.

In spite of being by profession just a plain peasant, it was clearly seen from the small baskets he made that at heart he was an artist, a true and accomplished artist. Each basket looked as if covered all over with the most beautiful sometimes fantastic ornaments, flowers, butterflies, birds, squirrels, antelope, tigers, and a score of other animals of the wilds. Yet, the most amazing thing was that these decorations, all of them symphonies of color, were not painted on the baskets but were instead actually part of the baskets themselves. Bast and fibers dyed in dozens of different colors were so cleverly—one must actually say intrinsically—interwoven that those attractive designs appeared on the inner part of the basket as well as on the outside. Not by painting but by weaving were those highly artistic effects achieved. This performance he accomplished without ever looking at any sketch or pattern. While working on a basket these designs came to light as if by magic, and as long as a basket was not entirely finished one could not perceive what in this case or that the decoration would be like.

People in the market town who bought these baskets would use them for sewing baskets or to decorate tables with or window sills, or to hold little things to keep them from lying around. Women put their jewelry in them or flowers or little dolls. There were in fact a hundred and two ways they might serve certain purposes in a household or in a lady's own room.

Whenever the Indian had finished about twenty of the baskets he took them to town on market day. Sometimes he would already be on his way shortly after midnight because he owned only a burro to ride on, and if the burro had gone astray the day before, as happened frequently, he would have to walk the whole way to town and back again.

At the market he had to pay twenty centavos in taxes to sell his wares. Each basket cost him between twenty and thirty hours of constant work, not counting the time spent gathering bast and fibers, preparing them, making dyes and coloring the bast. All this meant extra time and work. The price he asked for each basket was fifty centavos, the equivalent of about four cents. It seldom happened, however, that a buyer paid outright the full fifty centavos asked—or four reales[3] as the Indian called that money. The prospective buyer started bargaining, telling the Indian that he ought to be ashamed to ask such a sinful price. "Why, the whole dirty thing is nothing but ordinary petate straw which you find in heaps wherever you may look for it; the jungle is packed full of it," the buyer would argue. "Such a little basket, what's it good for anyhow? If I paid you, you thief, ten centavitos for it you should be grateful and kiss my hand. Well, it's your lucky day, I'll be generous this time, I'll pay you twenty, yet not one green centavo more. Take it or run along."

So he sold finally for twenty-five centavos, but then the buyer would say, "Now, what do you think of that? I've got only twenty centavos change on me. What can we do about that? If you can change me a twenty-peso bill, all right, you shall have your twenty-five fierros." Of course, the Indian could not change a twenty-peso bill and so the basket went for twenty centavos.

He had little if any knowledge of the outside world or he would have known that what happened to him was happening every hour of every day to every artist all over the world. That knowledge would perhaps have made him very proud, because he would have realized that he belonged to the little army which is the salt of the earth and which keeps culture, urbanity and beauty for their own sake from passing away.

Often it was not possible for him to sell all the baskets he had brought to market, for people here as elsewhere in the world preferred things made by the millions and each so much like the other that you were unable, even with the help of a magnifying glass, to tell which was which and where was the difference between two of the same kind.

Yet he, this craftsman, had in his life made several hundreds of those exquisite baskets, but so far no two of them had he ever turned out alike in design. Each was an individual piece of art and as different from the other as was a Murillo from a Velásquez.[4]

Naturally he did not want to take those baskets which he could not sell at the market place home with him again if he could help it. In such a case he went peddling his products from door to door where he was treated partly as a beggar and partly as a vagrant apparently looking for an opportunity to steal, and he frequently had to swallow all sorts of insults and nasty remarks.

Then, after a long run, perhaps a woman would finally stop him, take one of the baskets and offer him ten centavos, which price through talks and talks would perhaps go up to fifteen or even to twenty. Nevertheless, in many instances he would actually get no more than just ten centavos, and the buyer, usually a woman, would grasp that little marvel and right before his eyes throw it carelessly upon the nearest table as if to say, "Well, I take that piece of nonsense only for charity's sake. I know my money is wasted. But then, after all, I'm a Chris-

---

[3]One hundred centavos make one peso; "four reales" is four U.S. cents.
[4]Spanish painters.

tian and I can't see a poor Indian die of hunger since he has come such a long way from his village." This would remind her of something better and she would hold him and say, "Where are you at home anyway, Indito? What's your pueblo?[5] So, from Huehuetonoc? Now, listen here, Indito, can't you bring me next Saturday two or three turkeys from Huehuetonoc? But they must be heavy and fat and very, very cheap or I won't even touch them. If I wish to pay the regular price I don't need you to bring them. Understand? Hop along, now, Indito."

The Indian squatted on the earthen floor in the portico of his hut, attended to his work and showed no special interest in the curiosity of Mr. Winthrop watching him. He acted almost as if he ignored the presence of the American altogether.

"How much that little basket, friend?" Mr. Winthrop asked when he felt that he at least had to say something as not to appear idiotic.

"Fifty centavitos, patroncito;[6] my good little lordy, four reales," the Indian answered politely.

"All right, sold," Mr. Winthrop blurted out in a tone and with a wide gesture as if he had bought a whole railroad. And examining his buy he added, "I know already who I'll give that pretty little thing to. She'll kiss me for it, sure. Wonder what she'll use it for?"

He had expected to hear a price of three or even four pesos. The moment he realized that he had judged the value six times too high, he saw right away what great business possibilities this miserable Indian village might offer to a dynamic promoter like himself. Without further delay he started exploring those possibilities. "Suppose, my good friend, I buy ten of these little baskets of yours which, as I might as well admit right here and now, have practically no real use whatsoever. Well, as I was saying, if I buy ten, how much would you then charge me apiece?"

The Indian hesitated for a few seconds as if making calculations. Finally he said, "If you buy ten I can let you have them for forty-five centavos each, señorito gentleman."

"All right, amigo. And now, let's suppose I buy from you straight away one hundred of these absolutely useless baskets, how much will cost me each?"

The Indian, never fully looking up to the American standing before him and hardly taking his eyes off his work, said politely and without the slightest trace of enthusiasm in his voice, "In such a case I might not be quite unwilling to sell each for forty centavitos."

Mr. Winthrop bought sixteen baskets, which was all the Indian had in stock.

After three weeks' stay in the Republic, Mr. Winthrop was convinced that he knew this country perfectly, that he had seen everything and knew all about the inhabitants, their character and their way of life, and that there was nothing left

---

[5]Indito, little Indian; pueblo, village.
[6]Diminutive form of "patron," boss or patron.

for him to explore. So he returned to good old Nooyorg and felt happy to be once more in a civilized country, as he expressed it to himself.

One day going out for lunch he passed a confectioner's and, looking at the display in the window, he suddenly remembered the little baskets he had bought in that faraway Indian village.

He hurried home and took all the baskets he still had left to one of the best-known candy-makers in the city.

"I can offer you here," Mr. Winthrop said to the confectioner, "one of the most artistic and at the same time the most original of boxes, if you wish to call them that. These little baskets would be just right for the most expensive chocolates meant for elegant and high-priced gifts. Just have a good look at them, sir, and let me listen."

The confectioner examined the baskets and found them extraordinarily well suited for a certain line in his business. Never before had there been anything like them for originality, prettiness and good taste. He, however, avoided most carefully showing any sign of enthusiasm, for which there would be time enough once he knew the price and whether he could get a whole load exclusively.

He shrugged his shoulders and said, "Well, I don't know. If you asked me I'd say it isn't quite what I'm after. However, we might give it a try. It depends, of course, on the price. In our business the package mustn't cost more than what's in it."

"Do I hear an offer?" Mr. Winthrop asked.

"Why don't you tell me in round figures how much you want for them? I'm not good at guessing."

"Well, I'll tell you, Mr. Kemple: since I'm the smart guy who discovered these baskets and since I'm the only Jack who knows where to lay his hands on more, I'm selling to the highest bidder, on an exclusive basis, of course. I'm positive you can see it my way, Mr. Kemple."

"Quite so, and may the best man win," the confectioner said. "I'll talk the matter over with my partners. See me tomorrow same time, please, and I'll let you know how far we might be willing to go."

Next day when both gentlemen met again Mr. Kemple said: "Now, to be frank with you, I know art on seeing it, no getting around that. And these baskets are little works of art, they surely are. However, we are no art dealers, you realize that of course. We've no other use for these pretty little things except as fancy packing for our French pralines made by us. We can't pay for them what we might pay considering them pieces of art. After all to us they're only wrappings. Fine wrappings, perhaps, but nevertheless wrappings. You'll see it our way I hope, Mr.——oh, yes, Mr. Winthrop. So, here is our offer, take it or leave it: a dollar and a quarter apiece and not one cent more."

Mr. Winthrop made a gesture as if he had been struck over the head.

The confectioner, misunderstanding this involuntary gesture of Mr. Winthrop, added quickly, "All right, all right, no reason to get excited, no reason at all. Perhaps we can do a trifle better. Let's say one-fifty."

"Make it one-seventy-five," Mr. Winthrop snapped, swallowing his breath while wiping his forehead.

"Sold. One-seventy-five apiece free at port of New York. We pay the customs and you pay the shipping. Right?"

"Sold," Mr. Winthrop said also and the deal was closed.

"There is, of course, one condition," the confectioner explained just when Mr. Winthrop was to leave. "One or two hundred won't do for us. It wouldn't pay the trouble and the advertising. I won't consider less than ten thousand, or one thousand dozens if that sounds better in your ears. And they must come in no less than twelve different patterns well assorted. How about that?"

"I can make it sixty different patterns or designs."

"So much the better. And you're sure you can deliver ten thousand let's say early October?"

"Absolutely," Mr. Winthrop avowed and signed the contract.

Practically all the way back to Mexico, Mr. Winthrop had a notebook in his left hand and a pencil in his right and he was writing figures, long rows of them, to find out exactly how much richer he would be when this business had been put through.

"Now, let's sum up the whole goddamn thing," he muttered to himself. "Damn it, where is that cursed pencil again? I had it right between my fingers. Ah, there it is. Ten thousand he ordered. Well, well, there we got a clean-cut profit of fifteen thousand four hundred and forty genuine dollars. Sweet smackers. Fifteen grand right into papa's pocket. Come to think of it, that Republic isn't so backward after all."

"Buenas tardes, mi amigo,[7] how are you?" he greeted the Indian whom he found squatting in the porch of his jacalito as if he had never moved from his place since Mr. Winthrop had left for New York.

The Indian rose, took off his hat, bowed politely and said in his soft voice, "Be welcome, patroncito. Thank you, I feel fine, thank you. Muy buenas tardes.[8] This house and all I have is at your kind disposal." He bowed once more, moved his right hand in a gesture of greeting and sat down again. But he excused himself for doing so by saying, "Perdoneme,[9] patroncito, I have to take advantage of the daylight, soon it will be night."

"I've got big business for you, my friend," Mr. Winthrop began.

"Good to hear that, señor."

Mr. Winthrop said to himself, "Now, he'll jump up and go wild when he learns what I've got for him." And aloud he said: "Do you think you can make me one thousand of these little baskets?"

"Why not, patroncito? If I can make sixteen, I can make one thousand also."

---

[7]Good afternoon, my friend.
[8]Good afternoon (emphatically).
[9]Excuse me.

"That's right, my good man. Can you also make five thousand?"

"Of course, señor. I can make five thousand if I can make one thousand."

"Good. Now, if I should ask you to make me ten thousand, what would you say? And what would be the price of each? You can make ten thousand, can't you?"

"Of course, I can, señor. I can make as many as you wish. You see, I am an expert in this sort of work. No one else in the whole state can make them the way I do."

"That's what I thought and that's exactly why I came to you."

"Thank you for the honor, patroncito."

"Suppose I order you to make me ten thousand of these baskets, how much time do you think you would need to deliver them?"

The Indian, without interrupting his work, cocked his head to one side and then to the other as if he were counting the days or weeks it would cost him to make all these baskets.

After a few minutes he said in a slow voice, "It will take a good long time to make so many baskets, patroncito. You see, the bast and the fibers must be very dry before they can be used properly. Then all during the time they are slowly drying, they must be worked and handled in a very special way so that while drying they won't lose their softness and their flexibility and their natural brilliance. Even when dry they must look fresh. They must never lose their natural properties or they will look just as lifeless and dull as straw. Then while they are drying up I got to get the plants and roots and barks and insects from which I brew the dyes. That takes much time also, believe me. The plants must be gathered when the moon is just right or they won't give the right color. The insects I pick from the plants must also be gathered at the right time and under the right conditions or else they produce no rich colors and are just like dust. But, of course, jefecito,[10] I can make as many of these canastitas[11] as you wish, even as many as three dozen if you want them. Only give me time."

"Three dozens? Three dozens?" Mr. Winthrop yelled, and threw up both arms in desperation. "Three dozens!" he repeated as if he had to say it many times in his own voice so as to understand the real meaning of it, because for a while he thought that he was dreaming. He had expected the Indian to go crazy on hearing that he was to sell ten thousand of his baskets without having to peddle them from door to door and be treated like a dog with a skin disease.

So the American took up the question of price again, by which he hoped to activate the Indian's ambition. "You told me that if I take one hundred baskets you will let me have them for forty centavos apiece. Is that right, my friend?"

"Quite right, jefecito."

"Now," Mr. Winthrop took a deep breath, "now, then, if I ask you to make me one thousand, that is, ten times one hundred baskets, how much will they cost me, each basket?"

---

[10]Diminutive form of "jefe," chief or boss.
[11]Little baskets.

That figure was too high for the Indian to grasp. He became slightly confused and for the first time since Mr. Winthrop had arrived he interrupted his work and tried to think it out. Several times he shook his head and looked vaguely around as if for help. Finally he said, "Excuse me, jefecito, little chief, that is by far too much for me to count. Tomorrow, if you will do me the honor, come and see me again and I think I shall have my answer ready for you, patroncito."

When on the next morning Mr. Winthrop came to the hut he found the Indian as usual squatting on the floor under the overhanging palm roof working at his baskets.

"Have you got the price for ten thousand?" he asked the Indian the very moment he saw him, without taking the trouble to say "Good Morning!"

"Si, patroncito, I have the price ready. You may believe me when I say it has cost me much labor and worry to find out the exact price, because, you see, I do not wish to cheat you out of your honest money."

"Skip that, amigo. Come out with the salad. What's the price?" Mr. Winthrop asked nervously.

"The price is well calculated now without any mistake on my side. If I got to make one thousand canastitas each will be three pesos. If I must make five thousand, each will cost nine pesos. And if I have to make ten thousand, in such a case I can't make them for less than fifteen pesos each." Immediately he returned to his work as if he were afraid of losing too much time with such idle talk.

Mr. Winthrop thought that perhaps it was his faulty knowledge of this foreign language that had played a trick on him.

"Did I hear you say fifteen pesos each if I eventually would buy ten thousand?"

"That's exactly and without any mistake what I've said, patroncito," the Indian answered in his soft courteous voice.

"But now, see here, my good man, you can't do this to me. I'm your friend and I want to help you get on your feet."

"Yes, patroncito, I know this and I don't doubt any of your words."

"Now, let's be patient and talk this over quietly as man to man. Didn't you tell me that if I would buy one hundred you would sell each for forty centavos?"

"Si, jefecito, that's what I said. If you buy one hundred you can have them for forty centavos apiece, provided that I have one hundred, which I don't."

"Yes, yes, I see that." Mr. Winthrop felt as if he would go insane any minute now. "Yes, so you said. Only what I can't comprehend is why you cannot sell at the same price if you make me ten thousand. I certainly don't wish to chisel on the price. I am not that kind. Only, well, let's see now, if you can sell for forty centavos at all, be it for twenty or fifty or a hundred, I can't quite get the idea why the price has to jump that high if I buy more than a hundred."

"Bueno, patroncito, what is there so difficult to understand? It's all very simple. One thousand canastitas cost me a hundred times more work than a dozen. Ten thousand cost me so much time and labor that I could never finish them, not even in a hundred years. For a thousand canastitas I need more bast than for a hundred, and I need more little red beetles and more plants and roots and bark for the dyes. It isn't that you just can walk into the bush and pick all the things you need at your heart's desire. One root with the true violet blue may cost me four or five days until I can find one in the jungle. And have you thought how much time it costs and how much hard work to prepare the bast and fibers? What is more, if I must make so many baskets, who then will look after my corn and my beans and my goats and chase for me occasionally a rabbit for meat on Sunday? If I have no corn, then I have no tortillas to eat, and if I grow no beans, where do I get my frijoles[12] from?"

"But since you'll get so much money from me for your baskets you can buy all the corn and beans in the world and more than you need."

"That's what you think, señorito, little lordy. But you see, it is only the corn I grow myself that I am sure of. Of the corn which others may or may not grow, I cannot be sure to feast upon."

"Haven't you got some relatives here in this village who might help you to make baskets for me?" Mr. Winthrop asked hopefully.

"Practically the whole village is related to me somehow or other. Fact is, I got lots of close relatives in this here place."

"Why then can't they cultivate your fields and look after your goats while you make baskets for me? Not only this, they might gather for you the fibers and the colors in the bush and lend you a hand here and there in preparing the material you need for the baskets."

"They might, patroncito, yes, they might. Possible. But then you see who would take care of their fields and cattle if they work for me? And if they help me with the baskets it turns out the same. No one would any longer work his fields properly. In such a case corn and beans would get up so high in price that none of us could buy any and we all would starve to death. Besides, as the price of everything would rise and rise higher still how could I make baskets at forty centavos apiece? A pinch of salt or one green chili would set me back more than I'd collect for one single basket. Now you'll understand, highly estimated caballero[13] and jefecito, why I can't make the baskets any cheaper than fifteen pesos each if I got to make that many."

Mr. Winthrop was hard-boiled, no wonder considering the city he came from. He refused to give up the more than fifteen thousand dollars which at that moment seemed to slip through his fingers like nothing. Being really desperate now, he talked and bargained with the Indian for almost two full hours, trying to make him understand how rich he, the Indian, would become if he would take this greatest opportunity of his life.

The Indian never ceased working on his baskets while he explained his points of view.

"You know, my good man," Mr. Winthrop said, "such a wonderful chance might never again knock on your door, do you realize that? Let me explain to

---

[12]Beans.
[13]Gentleman.

you in ice-cold figures what fortune you might miss if you leave me flat on this deal."

He tore out leaf after leaf from his notebook, covered each with figures and still more figures, and while doing so told the peasant he would be the richest man in the whole district.

The Indian without answering watched with a genuine expression of awe as Mr. Winthrop wrote down these long figures, executing complicated multiplications and divisions and subtractions so rapidly that it seemed to him the greatest miracle he had ever seen.

The American, noting this growing interest in the Indian, misjudged the real significance of it. "There you are, my friend," he said. "That's exactly how rich you're going to be. You'll have a bankroll of exactly four thousand pesos. And to show you that I'm a real friend of yours, I'll throw in a bonus. I'll make it a round five thousand pesos, and all in silver."

The Indian, however, had not for one moment thought of four thousand pesos. Such an amount of money had no meaning to him. He had been interested solely in Mr. Winthrop's ability to write figures so rapidly.

"So, what do you say now? Is it a deal or is it? Say yes and you'll get your advance this very minute."

"As I have explained before, patroncito, the price is fifteen pesos each."

"But, my good man," Mr. Winthrop shouted at the poor Indian in utter despair, "where have you been all this time? On the moon or where? You are still at the same price as before."

"Yes, I know that, jefecito, my little chief," the Indian answered, entirely unconcerned. "It must be the same price because I cannot make any other one. Besides, señor, there's still another thing which perhaps you don't know. You see, my good lordy and caballero, I've to make these canastitas my own way and with my song in them and with bits of my soul woven into them. If I were to make them in great numbers there would no longer be my soul in each, or my songs. Each would look like the other with no difference whatever and such a thing would slowly eat up my heart. Each has to be another song which I hear in the morning when the sun rises and when the birds begin to chirp and the butterflies come and sit down on my baskets so that I may see a new beauty, because, you see, the butterflies like my baskets and the pretty colors on them, that's why they come and sit down, and I can make my canastitas after them. And now, señor jefecito, if you will kindly excuse me, I have wasted much time already, although it was a pleasure and a great honor to hear the talk of such a distinguished caballero like you. But I'm afraid I've to attend to my work now, for day after tomorrow is market day in town and I got to take my baskets there. Thank you, señor, for your visit. Adiós."

And in this way it happened that American garbage cans escaped the fate of being turned into receptacles for empty, torn, and crumpled little multicolored canastitas into which an Indian of Mexico had woven dreams of his soul, throbs of his heart: his unsung poems.

Study and Discussion Questions

1. What is the narrator's tone? Does it change? Is there greater narrative distance from Winthrop or from the Indian?
2. Why does the Indian make baskets? What do they mean to him? To his Mexican customers? To Winthrop? What is the story saying about art and commerce?
3. We witness three kinds of business discussions in the story: between the Indian and other Mexicans, between Winthrop and the candy manufacturer, and between the Indian and Winthrop. What similarities and differences are there?
4. Why does Winthrop think the price per basket should be lower for 10,000 than for a few? What assumptions is he making when he thinks this? What is he blind to?

Suggestions for Writing

1. What would Winthrop say to the charge that, by buying baskets at less than four cents each and selling them for $1.75 each, he would be exploiting the Indian? How might you reply to him?
2. Summarize the Indian's reasons why the price per basket should be higher for thousands than for a few. Suppose the Indian's life (and much of the village) were reorganized, as he suggests it would have to be, for mass production for export. What further consequences might there be? What light might this story shed on Third World poverty and its relation to investment from wealthier countries?
3. Consider a creative hobby or craft you enjoy. What would change if you set up for full-time, large-scale production for profit?

Critical Resources

1. Goldwasser, James. "Ret Marut: The Early B. Traven." *The Germanic Review* 68.3 (1993): 133–42.
2. Schure, Ernst and Philip Jenkins, eds. *B. Traven: Life and Work.* University Park: Penn State Press, 1987.
3. *The Treasure of the Sierra Madre.* Director John Huston. Performer Humphrey Bogart. Warner Brothers, 1948.
4. Wood, Warner. "Stories from the Field, Handicraft Production and Mexican National Patrimony: A Lesson in Translocality from B. Traven." *Ethnology: An International Journal of Cultural and Social Anthropology* 39.3 (2000): 183–203.

PIETRO DI DONATO (1911–1992)

Pietro Di Donato was born in West Hoboken, New Jersey. His autobiographical novel Christ in Concrete *(1939) dramatizes his experience as the son of an Ital-*

ian-American immigrant bricklayer killed in a construction accident. Like the pro-
tagonist in the novel (Paul), Di Donato himself had to take over the responsibil-
ity of providing for his family at the age of twelve. Sixteen years later he published
the book, receiving both critical and public praise for the realism of its plot and
the rhythmic quality of the dialogue. Di Donato would not publish again until
1958, but Christ in Concrete *remains a central novel of the Italian-American ex-*
perience during the Great Depression. His other works include This Woman
(1958, play), Three Circles of Light *(1960), the short story collection* Naked Author *(1970), and two nonfiction works,* Immigrant Saint: The Life of Mother
Cabrini *(1960) and* The Penitent *(1962).*

FROM *Christ in Concrete*   (1939)

Big steel was downtown. It straddled the city block and its metal skeleton shot
up fifty floors to the sky. At street level was a ten-foot wooden fence, and protecting the street people was a thick timbered bridge that reached the first floor.
Trucks pulled in and out of its entrances loaded with sand cement lime bricks
stone lumber pipes and steel. Laborers stood about in groups seeking to enter
and ask for work. High up were ironworkers walking the thin girders ... and Paul
afraid to watch them. At about the twentieth floor were concrete workers pushing the heavy big-wheeled buggies from the hoists and dumping the fresh concrete into the floor forms. Above them the scaffold hangers were fastening the
protruding I-beams from which other scaffolders hung the swinging scaffolds for
the bricklayers. From the very peak the hundred-foot derrick swung its steel lat-
ticed arm out beyond the building and from it descended a cable with an ironworker clinging to it. The man was small-small and grew larger as he came
toward the ground. When he reached the street two other ironworkers fastened
the cable about a five-ton girder. Soon the great steel body and the ironworker
upon it were rising slowly up up; the girder seesawing as a ship on rolling water
and the surefooted ironworker captaining it up through space. Paul's breast
prided for him. Far up in the bone-work of Job he saw the riveting crew. A rickety scaffolding held the little forge where the smith fired his bolts. He drew them
white-hot, passed them to the thrower who sent them bulleting up to the catcher
on his precarious rope-plank scaffold who snared them neatly in his tin cone
and then with pincers inserted them into the bolt holes that matched in the
beams to be mated fast by his partner, who pushed his compressor-gun upon the
hot bolt's unheaded end, and while the sledgeman resisted from the other end
of the bolt the furious ra-tat tat tat—tat-tat smashed the malleable hot pin into
locked steel home.

Skirting the structure at the fourth floor were the swinging cable scaffolds.
The labor-foreman, a big heavy-voiced man, shouted directions. He called for
tubs bricks and mortar, and under his command Irish, Italian, and Negro laborers

swiftly loaded the scaffolds. Soon a gang of bricklayers appeared on the scaffolds and went to work. Hicky Nicky went along the scaffold inspecting their union cards. Paul whistled and called. Nicky leaned over the scaffold-rail and summoned him. He motioned with his hands that it was all fixed. Paul crossed the street excitedly and went into Job through the truck entrance. Inside it was cool and shadowed, and in the half light was an activity that bewildered him. Great concrete and mortar-mixers chugged their huge barrelbellies about with incessant disturbance while ragged laborers made indistinguishable with cement dust fed the maw into the mixers with broken stone, sand, water and cement. Men pushing barrows and buggies from mixer to hoists—at the bell's clanging the hoistmen throwing the cable reels in and out of gear and the hoists shooting up madly through the shafts, to hurtle down again suckingly in a few minutes, pull up short near the bottom and hit the floor to send the barrows clattering—men in overalls begrimed and shouldering heavy steam pipes and tools—watch your head buddy—trucks' bodies racketing up and dumping thousands of bricks and tons and tons of sand and stone and men transferring with human strength the dead weights—men seeming all alike in olympic contest for living with Job.

Nicky met Paul on the fourth floor and sent him to the construction office to sign up. Soon he had a brass check, a number and badge—and then out onto the swinging scaffold with the bricklayers. The swinging scaffold unnerved him. The scaffolds on the flats were all putlog[1] affairs, but these were planks lapped into the steel braces underfoot and overhead that were attached to the suspended cables, and to every brace and pair of cables was a pair of winches that when jacked pulled the scaffold up and wound up cable. As he laid brick along the wall he couldn't believe the thin cables would really hold the gang of men and the piles of brick and mortar, but in the speed of work he forgot about it. No sooner was a setting-up of five courses and header-binder[2] laid than the scaffolders came along with their jack-handles and jacked the scaffolds, keeping the wall always about waist level. Within a few hours Nicky came to Paul and told him that the foreman thought Paul was a "dandy little bricklayer" and wanted him to take his tools and come in and work on the particular walls of the stairwells.

He'll put his tools here—no—put them there . . . workers up and down the stairs—then the battery of riveting guns let loose and reverberating the live metal air of Job—whang! whang! resound the ironworkers' sledges . . . hey buddy dump some mortar here—I can't stretch to the other tub—and get me an armful of damn brick in this corner!—put it up!—what's the bond in this angle?—uorrrrhhhhhh sing the hoists—goddamn-damn sonofabastarddd I said brick on the hoist—not tile! Brick you dago screwball! *brick* . . .

Hey Murrphpheeee . . . !

Ratatatatatat—ratatatatatatatattt

Hal—lloooo?

---

[1]A piece of scaffolding set flush with the beam.
[2]Each course is a layer of brick; the header is the piece that goes over a window or door; the binder is an inset for that piece in the course or layer of bricks.

Send up the fourfoot angleirons!

Noise! noise O noise O noise and sounds swelling in from the sea of city life without of pushing scurrying purring motors and horns and bells and cries and sirens and whistles and padded stream of real feet O noise O noise—O noi—se and through Job mouths stretch wide screaming:

I want brick!

I want tile!

I want the scaffolder!

I want mortar!

I want speed I want rush I want haste I want noise I want action

I want you all of you to throw yourselves into Job!

With the midday sun the close stairwell became a hotbox, and Paul stripped off his shirt. Just before lunch hour, as Paul was working a wall up along the stairs, someone came slowly down. When the man neared him Paul felt drops plash on his sweated back. He wiped his back and saw his hand covered with blood. He was frightened. He turned and looked up. A Swedish carpenter was coming down slowly and holding up his right hand. It looked like a ghastly dripping rose. The four fingers had been shorn off to the palm and the mangled remains ran red faucets. He walked silently with white face down the stairs. Later, Nicky told Paul that the carpenter was greasing the wheel at the top of the hoist when the cable suddenly ran and caught his hand against the wheel rubbing off his fingers.

"Don't let that bother you, kid," said Nicky.

O my Jesus, guard me. I am not afraid—It's that I am needed . . . and I know O Lord that I shall work on Job unharmed . . . in constant prayer and thanksgiving to Thee—our Jesus.

The scaffolds rose a floor a day. With each floor the height and majesty of skyscraper fascinated him, but he never told mother Annunziata about the danger of falling or being pushed from a swinging scaffold forty or fifty floors above the street. Or of a derrick cable snapping and sending a girder crashing the scaffold to earth. It seemed so daring to lay brick at the edge of a wall that ran down hundreds and hundreds of feet to a toy world below, a wall that leaned out and seemed about to fall away.

This was steel Job where danger was ever present with falling planks and beams and bolts and white-hot molten steel from acetylene torch and breaking cable and unexpected drop of hoist—great dangerous Job who thrilled Paul.

Study and Discussion Questions

1. Paul, the Italian-American protagonist of this excerpt from Pietro Di Donato's novel *Christ in Concrete* (set in New York City in the 1920s), is about twelve years old. At the beginning of the novel, Paul's father has been killed when a building he was working on collapsed. So Paul, the oldest of eight children, has had to pick up his father's tools and go to work

to support the family. What details in this excerpt show you that Paul is still fairly young and inexperienced?

2. Why do you think Di Donato capitalizes "Job"? Look at each specific place he does so in this excerpt. What does this stylistic choice say about the workers' (specifically Paul's) relation to their work? What effect does it have on you?

3. Reread the first paragraph. What is Di Donato doing here? What do we learn by the end of the paragraph (a) about Paul and (b) about the work? Comment on Di Donato's style of writing.

4. Look at the opening sentences and then at the closing paragraph, which comes back to "steel Job . . . great dangerous Job." What has Di Donato turned the job into? What does Paul's relation to Job make you think of?

5. How does Di Donato achieve a sense of rush, of power, of noise?

Suggestions for Writing

1. Describe a work experience of your own, using as many specific details and sense impressions as you can, so that your reader can see, hear, smell, taste, touch the experience. Also, decide what your attitude toward the work is and what the mood/tone of your piece will be; try to choose words and details that will maintain a consistent mood.

2. Discuss the various dangers of Job that Paul notices. How does he feel about these? How would you feel about them?

Critical Resources

1. Diomede, Matthew. *Pietro DiDonato, The Master Builder.* Lewisburg, PA: Bucknell University Press, 1995.

2. Napolitano, Louise. *An American Story: Pietro DiDonato's Christ in Concrete.* New York: Peter Lang, 1995.

3. Tamburri, Anthony. "Pietro di Donato's *Christ in Concrete:* An Italian/American Novel Not Set in Stone." *Literature Interpretation Theory* 14.1 (2003): 3–16.

4. Von Huene-Greenberg, Dorothee. "A MELUS Interview: Pietro DiDonato." *Melus* 14.3 (1987): 33–53.

TOM KROMER (1906–1969)

Tom Kromer was born to a working-class family in Huntington, West Virginia. His parents died young, leaving him at twenty to care for a brother and three sisters. He managed to finish three years of college, taught for two years, and when the Great Depression arrived, hopped a freight train to Kansas. Kromer found no work in the wheat fields there, nor anywhere else, and like countless others during the Great Depression, roamed the country looking for work. His largely autobiographical novel Waiting for Nothing *(1935) won critical acclaim when it was pub-*

lished. Often referred to as a "proletarian" novel, Waiting for Nothing *employs narration in the present tense, giving the book an urgent and imploratory tone. Moreover, Kromer's unadorned diction and deliberately unsophisticated style could, in some respects, be seen as antiliterary—his straightforward narrative and plain-spoken protagonist obscure the presence of the author to create a text that appears more documentary than fictional. Tuberculosis caused Kromer to settle in New Mexico where, with his wife, he put out a small magazine for a few years.* Waiting for Nothing *is his only novel.*

FROM *Waiting for Nothing* (1935)

It is night. I am walking along this dark street, when my foot hits a stick. I reach down and pick it up. I finger it. It is a good stick, a heavy stick. One sock from it would lay a man out. It wouldn't kill him, but it would lay him out. I plan. Hit him where the crease is in his hat, hard, I tell myself, but not too hard. I do not want his head to hit the concrete. It might kill him. I do not want to kill him. I will catch him as he falls. I can frisk him in a minute. I will pull him over in the shadows and walk off. I will not run. I will walk.

I turn down a side street. This is a better street. There are fewer houses along this street. There are large trees on both sides of it. I crouch behind one of these. It is dark here. The shadows hide me. I wait. Five, ten minutes, I wait. Then under an arc light a block away a man comes walking. He is a well-dressed man. I can tell even from that distance. I have good eyes. This guy will be in the dough. He walks with his head up and a jaunty step. A stiff does not walk like that. A stiff shuffles with tired feet, his head huddled in his coat collar. This guy is in the dough. I can tell that. I clutch my stick tighter. I notice that I am calm. I am not scared. I am calm. In the crease of his hat, I tell myself. Not too hard. Just hard enough. On he comes. I slink farther back in the shadows. I press closer against this tree. I hear his footsteps thud on the concrete walk. I raise my arm high. I must swing hard. I poise myself. He crosses in front of me. Now is my chance. Bring it down hard, I tell myself, but not too hard. He is under my arm. He is right under my arm, but my stick does not come down. Something has happened to me. I am sick in the stomach. I have lost my nerve. Christ, I have lost my nerve. I am shaking all over. Sweat stands out on my forehead. I can feel the clamminess of it in the cold, damp night. This will not do. This will not do. I've got to get me something to eat. I am starved.

I stagger from the shadows and follow behind this guy. He had a pretty good face. I could tell as he passed beneath my arm. This guy ought to be good for two bits. Maybe he will be good for four bits. I quicken my steps. I will wait until he is under an arc light before I give him my story. I do not have long to wait. He stops under an arc light and fumbles in his pocket for a cigarette. I catch up with him.

"Pardon me, mister, but could you help a hungry man get—"

"You goddamn bums give me a pain in the neck. Get the hell away from me before I call a cop."

He jerks his hand into his overcoat pocket. He wants me to think he has a gun. He has not got a gun. He is bluffing.

I hurry down the street. The bastard. The dirty bastard. I could have laid him out cold with the stick. I could have laid him out cold with the stick, and he calls me a goddamn bum. I had the stick over his head, and I could not bring it down. I am yellow. I can see that I am yellow. If I am not yellow, why am I shaking like a leaf? I am starved, too, and I ought to starve. A guy without enough guts to get himself a feed ought to starve.

I walk on up the street. I pass people, but I let them pass. I do not ding them. I have lost my nerve. I walk until I am on the main stem. Never have I been so hungry. I have got to get me something to eat. I pass a restaurant. In the window is a roast chicken. It is brown and fat. It squats in a silver platter. The platter is filled with gravy. The gravy is thick and brown. It drips over the side, slow. I stand there and watch it drip. Underneath it the sign says: "All you can eat for fifty cents." I lick my lips. My mouth waters. I sure would like to sit down with that before me. I look inside. It is a classy joint. I can see waitresses in blue and white uniforms. They hurry back and forth. They carry heavy trays. The dishes stick over the edge of the trays. There are good meals still left in these trays. They will throw them in the garbage cans. In the center of the floor a water fountain bubbles. It is made of pink marble. The chairs are red leather, bordered in black. The counter is full of men eating. They are eating, and I am hungry. There are long rows of tables. The cloths on them are whiter than white. The glassware sparkles like diamonds on its whiteness. The knives and forks on the table are silver. I can tell that they are pure silver from where I am standing on the street. They shine so bright. I cannot go in there. It is too classy, and besides there are too many people. They will laugh at my seedy clothes, and my shoes without soles.

I stare in at this couple that eat by the window. I pull my coat collar up around my neck. A man will look hungrier with his coat collar up around his neck. These people are in the dough. They are in evening clothes. This woman is sporting a satin dress. The blackness of it shimmers and glows in the light that comes from the chandelier that hangs from the dome. Her fingers are covered with diamonds. There are diamond bracelets on her wrists. She is beautiful. Never have I seen a more beautiful woman. Her lips are red. They are even redder against the whiteness of her teeth when she laughs. She laughs a lot.

I stare in at the window. Maybe they will know a hungry man when they see him. Maybe this guy will be willing to shell out a couple of nickels to a hungry stiff. It is chicken they are eating. A chicken like the one in the window. Brown and fat. They do not eat. They only nibble. They are nibbling at chicken, and they are not even hungry. I am starved. That chicken was meant for a hungry man. I watch them as they cut it into tiny bits. I watch their forks as they carry them to their mouths. The man is facing me. Twice he glances out of the window. I meet his eyes with mine. I wonder if he can tell the eyes of a hungry man. He has never been hungry himself. I can tell that. This one has always nibbled at chicken. I see him speak to the woman. She turns her head and looks at me through the window. I do not look at her. I look at the chicken on the plate. They can see that I am a hungry man. I will stand here until they come out. When they come out, they will maybe slip me a four-bit piece.

A hand slaps down on my shoulder. It is a heavy hand. It spins me around in my tracks.

"What the hell are you doin' here?" It is a cop.

"Me? Nothing," I say. "Nothing, only watching a guy eat chicken. Can't a guy watch another guy eat chicken?"

"Wise guy," he says. "Well, I know what to do with wise guys."

He slaps me across the face with his hand, hard. I fall back against the building. His hands are on the holster by his side. What can I do? Take it is all I can do. He will plug me if I do anything.

"Put up your hands," he says.

I put up my hands.

"Where's your gat?" he says.

"I have no gat," I say. "I never had a gat in my life."

"That's what they all say," he says.

He pats my pockets. He don't find anything. There is a crowd around here now. Everybody wants to see what is going on. They watch him go through my pockets. They think I am a stick-up guy. A hungry stiff stands and watches a guy eat chicken, and they think he is a stick-up guy. That is a hell of a note.

"All right," he says, "get down the street before I run you in. If I ever catch you stemming this beat, I will sap the living hell out of you. Beat it."

I hurry down the street. I know better than not to hurry. The lousy son of a bitch. I had a feed right in my lap, and he makes me beat it. That guy was all right in there. He was a good guy. That guy could see I was a hungry man. He would have fixed me up right when he came out.

I pass a small café. There are no customers in here. There is only a guy sitting by the cash register. This is my place. I go in and walk up to him. He is a fat guy with a double chin. I can see very well that he hasn't missed many meals in his life.

"Mister," I say, "have you got some kind of work like washing dishes I can do for something to eat? I am damn near starved. I'll do anything."

He looks hard at me. I can see right away that this guy is no good.

"Tell me," he says, "in God's name, why do you stiffs always come in here? You're the fourth guy in the last half-hour. I can't even pay my rent. There ain't been a customer in here for an hour. Go to some of the big joints where they do all the business."

"Could you maybe give me a cup of coffee?" I say. "That would hold me over. I've been turned down at about twenty places already."

"I can't give you nothing. Coffee costs money," he says. "Go to one of the chain stores and bum your coffee. When you've got any money, where do you go to spend it? You go to the chains. I can't do nothing for you."

I walk out. Wouldn't even give a hungry man a cup of coffee. Can you imagine a guy like that? The bastard. I'd like to catch him on a dark street. I'd give him a cup of coffee, and a sock on the snout he wouldn't soon forget. I walk. When I pass a place where there are no customers, I go in. They turn me down flat. No business, they say. Why don't I go to the big places? I am getting sick in the stomach. I feel like vomiting. I have to get me something to eat. What the hell? I will hit me one of these classy joints. Pride! What do I care about pride? Who cares about me? Nobody. The bastards don't care if I live or die.

I pass a joint. A ritzy place. It is all white inside. The tables are full. The counters are full. They are eating, and I am hungry. These guys pay good dough for a feed, and they are not even hungry. When they are through, they will maybe tip the waitress four bits. It is going to be cold tonight. Four bits will buy me a flop that will be warm, and not cold.

I go into this joint and walk up to the middle of the counter. I flop down in a seat. These cash customers gape at me. I am clean, but my front is seedy. They know I don't belong in here. I know I don't belong in here, too. But I am hungry. A hungry man belongs where there is food. Let them gape.

This waiter sticks the menu out to me. I do not take it. What do I want with a menu?

"Buddy," I say, "I am broke and hungry. Could you maybe give me something to eat?"

He shakes his head no, he cannot give me anything to eat.

"Busy. Manager's not in. Sorry."

I can feel my face getting red. They are all gaping at me. They crane their necks to gape at me. I get up out of this seat and walk towards the door. I can't get anything to eat anywhere. God damn them, if I could get my fingers on a gat.

"Say, buddy."

I turn around. A guy in a gray suit is motioning to me. He sits at the middle of the counter. I go back.

"You hungry?"

"I'm damn near starved. I have not eat in two days, and that is the God's truth."

"Down on your luck?" he says.

"Down so far I don't know how far," I say.

"Sit down. I've been down on my luck myself. I know how it is."

I sit down beside him.

"What'll it be?" he says.

"You order it," I say. "Anything you say."

"Order up anything you want. Fill up."

"A ham sandwich and a cup of coffee," I tell this waiter.

He is all smiles now, damn him. He sees where he can make a dime. I bet he owns this joint. He said the manager wasn't in, and I bet he's the manager himself.

"Give him a beef-steak dinner with everything that goes with it," says this guy in the gray suit. "This man is hungry."

This is a good guy. He orders my steak dinner in a loud voice so everyone can see how big-hearted he is, but he is a good guy anyway. Any guy is a good guy when he is going to buy me a steak dinner. Let him show off a little bit. He deserves to show off a little bit. I sit here at this counter, and I feel like pinching myself. This is a funny world. Five minutes ago I was down in the dumps. Here I am now waiting on a steak dinner in a classy joint. Let them gape. What do I care? Didn't they ever see a hungry man before?

This waiter shoves my dinner in front of me. Christ, I've never seen anything look so good. This steak with all the trimmings is a picture for sore eyes. Big and thick and brown, it sits there. Around it, all around it, are tomatoes, sliced. I start in. I do not look up from my plate. They are all gaping at me. Fill up and get out of here, I tell myself.

The guy three seats down gets up and calls for his check. He is a little guy with horn-rimmed glasses. The check is thirty cents. I see it before the waiter turns it upside down. Why do they always have to turn a man's check upside down? Afraid the price will turn his stomach? This guy pulls a dollar out of his pocket and walks over to the cashier. I wonder how it feels to have a buck in your jeans. Four bits will set me on top of the world right now. A good warm flop tonight and breakfast in the morning. That's the way to live. Pay for what you get, and look every copper you pass on the street straight in the eye, and say: "You bastard, I don't owe you a cent."

The cashier hands this guy his change. He walks back and lays it down by my plate.

"Flop for tonight," he says.

He speaks low. He is not trying to show off like this guy in the gray suit. Not that I don't think that this guy in the gray suit is not all right. He is a good guy. He bought me a steak dinner when I was damn near starved. No, he is a good guy, but he likes to show off a little bit. I look up at this guy. He is walking out of the door. I do not thank him. He is too far away, and besides, what can I say? I can't believe it. Thirty cents, the check said. Thirty cents from a dollar. That makes seventy cents. I got seventy cents. A good warm flop tonight, breakfast in the morning, and enough left over for cigarettes. No fishing around in the gutters for snipes for me. I will have me a package of tailor-made cigarettes. I pick up this change and stick it in my pocket. That guy is a mindreader. I was sitting here wishing I had four bits, and before I know it, I got seventy cents. That guy is all right. I bet that guy has had troubles of his own some time. I bet he knows how it is to be hungry. I hurry up with my dinner. In here I am only a hungry stiff. Outside with seventy cents in my kick, I am as good as the next one. Say, I'd like to meet that guy, and I had a million dollars.

"Do you remember the time you give me seventy cents in a restaurant? You don't? Well, you give me seventy cents in a restaurant one time. I was damn near starved. I was just about ready to bump myself off, and you give me seventy cents."

I hand him a roll of bills. It is a big roll of bills. I walk off. That guy won't have to worry any more about dough. There was plenty in that roll to keep him in wheatcakes the rest of his life.

I finish my pie and get up.

"Thank you, Jack," I say to this guy in the gray suit. "I certainly appreciate what you done for me. I was damn near starved."

"That's all right, buddy," he says. "Glad to help a hungry man."

He speaks loud. They can hear him to the other end of the counter. He is a good guy, though. He bought me a steak dinner.

I walk outside. I put my hand in my pocket and jingle my money. It feels good to have money to jingle. I am not broke or hungry now. I cannot imagine I was broke and hungry an hour ago. No park for me tonight. No lousy mission flop.

I go down the street and walk through the park. I look at these benches with their iron legs and their wooden slats.

"To hell with you," I say. "I have nothing to do with you. I do not know you. You will leave no grooves in my back tonight. Tonight I will have me a good warm flop. I will have me a flop that will be warm, and not cold."

I look at these stiffs sprawled out on the benches. I like to walk to the time of the jingle in my pocket and think how miserable I was last night.

It is getting late, and I am tired. I head down the skid road and stop in front of my four-bit flop. There is no marquee in front to keep the guests from getting wet. There is no doorman dressed like a major in the Imperial Guards. They do not need these things, because all the suites are on the fourth floor. I am puffing when I get to the top of the rickety stairs. At the landing a guy squats on a stool in a wire cage.

"I want a four-bit flop," I say, "a four-bit flop with a clean bed."

This guy is hunched over a desk with his belly sticking out of a dirty green sweater. He rubs his hands together and shows his yellow teeth in a grin. He winks one of his puffy eyes.

"For a little extra, just a little extra," he says, "I can give you a nice room, a very nice room. But it is too big a room for one. You will be lonely. A little company will not go bad, eh? Especially if the company is very young and very pretty?" He licks his puffy lips. "We have a girl, a new girl. Only tonight she came. Because it is you, and she must learn, only a dollar extra, yes?"

I look at him, and I think of the fish-eyed, pot-bellied frogs I used to gig when I was a kid. I imagine myself sticking a sharp gig into his belly and watching him kick and croak.

"A four-bit flop is what I want," I say. "I do not wish to play nursemaid to your virgins. I am broke, and besides, I am sleepy."

"But you should see her," he says, "so tiny, so beautiful. I will get her. You will change your mind when you see her."

"I do not want to see her," I say.

"So high," he says. "Only so high she is, and so beautiful. I will get her. You will see how beautiful she is."

He climbs off his stool.

"Do I get me a flop or do I have to bury my foot in your dirty belly?" I say.

"Some other time, then," he says, "some other time when you have more money. You will see how very beautiful."

He waddles through the dirty hall. I follow him. His legs are swollen with dropsy. His ankles overflow his ragged houseslippers and hang down in folds over the sides. I can imagine I hear the water gurgling as he walks. He opens the door and holds out his hand for the money.

"How many beds in this room?" I say.

"Forty," he says, "but they are good, clean beds."

I walk into this room. It is a big room. It is filled with these beds. They do not look so hot to me. They are only cots. They look lousy. I bet they are lousy, but a stiff has got to sleep, lousy or not. Most of these beds are already full. I can hear the snores of the stiffs as they sleep. I pick me out a flop at the other end of the room. There is no mattress. Only two dirty blankets. They are smelly. Plenty of stiffs have slept under these blankets.

Four or five stiffs are gathered in a bunch over next to the wall. I watch them. I know very well what they are going to do. They are gas hounds, and they are going to get soused on derail.

"Give me that handkerchief," says this red-headed guy with the wens on his face. "I will squeeze more alky out of a can of heat than any stiff I know."

This little guy with the dirty winged collar examines this can of heat.

"The bastards," he says. "You know what? They're makin' the cans smaller and smaller. This can right here is smaller than they was yestiddy. The dirty crooks. They'd take the bread right out of your mouths, the bastards would."

He jumps up and down as he talks. His red eyes flash. The sweat stands in beads on his forehead. How can a guy get so mad about the size of a can of heat? Well, it does not take much to make you mad when you have been swigging heat for a year.

This red-headed guy takes this can of heat and empties it out in a handkerchief. The handkerchief is filthy, but that don't worry them none. What's a little filth to a gas hound? Pretty soon they will be high and nothing will worry them. Pretty soon they won't have any more troubles. This derail will see to that. They squeeze this stuff out of the handkerchief and let it drip into the glass. They pour water into the glass. The smell of this stuff will turn your stomach, but it don't turn their stomach. They are going to drink it. They take turns about taking a swig. They elbow each other out of the way to get at the glass. When it is all gone, they squeeze out some more. They choke and gag when this stuff goes down, but they drink it. Pretty soon they have guzzled all the heat they have. In a little while they are singing. I do not blame these guys for getting soused on derail. A guy can't always be thinking. If a guy is thinking all the time, pretty soon he will go crazy. A man is bound to land up in the booby-hatch if he stays on the fritz. So these guys make derail and drink it.

This stiff in the bed next to mine turns up his nose at these guys who are soused up on derail.

"I got my opinion of a guy who will drink derail," he says. "A guy who will drink derail is lower down than a skunk."

He pulls a bottle out from under his pillow. It is marked: "Bay Rum." There are directions on the label. It says it will grow new hair. It says it will stop the old from falling out. But this guy does not need this stuff to keep his hair from falling out. This stiff has not had a haircut for a year.

"This is the stuff," he says. "I have been drinkin' this old stuff for a year, and I don't even get a headache afterwards."

He sticks this bottle up to his trap, and he does not take it down until he has emptied it.

"This is good stuff," he says. "It has got derail beat all to a frazzle."

I do not see how it can be such good stuff when he has to gag so much when he downs it. But that is his business. If a guy has been drinking this stuff for a year, he ought to know if it is good stuff or not. Pretty soon this guy is dead to the world. He sprawls out on his bunk and sleeps. He sleeps with his eyes wide open. Christ, he gives me the willies with his eyes wide open like that. He looks like a dead man, but I never see a dead man with his face covered with sweat like his is. It is plenty chilly in this room, but his face is covered with sweat. That is the bay rum coming out of him. A guy that has been drinking this stuff for a year must have plenty inside him. I bet the inside of his gut is covered with hair. That would be a good way to find out if this bay rum is a fake or not. When this stiff croaks from swigging too much bay rum, just cut him open. If his gut is not covered with hair, then this bay rum is a fake.

I watch him. I cannot keep my eyes off him. His legs twitch. He quivers and jerks. He is having a spasm. He almost jumps off the bed. All the time his eyes are wide open, and the sweat pours out of him. But he does not know what it is all about. He is dead to the world. If this is the good stuff, I will take the bad stuff. I will not even put this stuff on my hair. I would be afraid it would sink down into my gut and give me the spasms like this guy has got. The rest of these stiffs do not pay any attention to him. These bay horse fiends are old stuff to them. But they are not old stuff to me. It gets on my nerves. If this guy is going to act like this all night, I am going to walk the streets. It will be cold as hell walking the streets all night, but it will not be as bad as watching this guy jump up and down with his eyes wide open, and him dead to the world.

I cover up my head with this dirty blanket and try not to think about him.

Study and Discussion Questions

1. This selection from *Waiting for Nothing* contains a number of separate episodes. List as many as you can.
2. Characterize the style of Kromer's sentences—their length, verb tense, and so on. How are they unusual?
3. The narrator uses a number of slang words in this story. List them and define them as well as you can from the context.
4. Describe the physical setting, the world the narrator lives in.
5. Discuss the social setting of the story. Can you classify the types of people the narrator encounters?

6. What significance does the title have?
7. The narrator stares into a restaurant window and thinks, "That chicken was meant for a hungry man." What can we infer about his political philosophy from this statement?
8. How does the narrator's attitude change when he has seventy cents in his pocket?
9. What do we learn about the narrator in the flophouse scene?

Suggestions for Writing

1. How does the narrator view himself? Give evidence. Do you agree with his self-assessment?
2. Does the narrator ever get anything for free? Analyze the scene in the restaurant. How does he "pay" for his meal?
3. Has anyone ever asked you for spare change? How did you react? Narrate such an incident.

Critical Resources

1. Casey, Janet, ed. *The Novel and the American Left: Critical Essays on Depression-Era Fiction.* Iowa City: University of Iowa Press, 2004.
2. Crawford, Hugh. "On the Fritz: Tom Kromer's Imaging of the Machine." *South Atlantic Review* 55.2 (1990): 101–116.
3. Kromer, Tom. *Waiting for Nothing and Other Writings.* Arthur Casciato, Ed. Athens: University of Georgia Press, 1986.
4. Solomon, William. "Politics and Rhetoric in the Novel in the 1930s." *American Literature* 68.4 (1996): 799–818.

TONI CADE BAMBARA (1939–1995)

*Toni Cade Bambara was born in New York City. In 1959, she obtained her B.A. in Theater Arts at Queens College and her M.A. from City College of the City University of New York in 1964. During this time, and throughout the 1960s, Bambara worked persistently as a social activist in Harlem and Brooklyn and published a few short stories in magazines. Her experiences as a "cultural worker" (a phrase she often used) inevitably found their way into her stories—stories with radical plots, lively street dialogue, and resilient characters: "I work to celebrate, to applaud the tradition of struggle in our community, to bring together all those characters, just ordinary folks on the block who've been waiting in the wings, characters we thought we had to ignore because they weren't pimp-flashy or hustler-slick . . ." (*Notable Black American Women, 2002). The publication of* The Black Woman: An Anthology *(1970), edited by Bambara, was one of the first anthologies specifically about the black female experience. In 1972, with Toni Morrison as her editor, Bambara published her first collection of short stories,* Gorilla My Love. *In* *addition to her writing, Bambara was also active in the theater and wrote several screenplays. Her other works include* Tales and Stories for Black Folks *(1971, editor and contributor); the short story collection* The Sea Birds Are Still Alive *(1977); and the novels* The Salt Eaters *(1980),* If Blessing Comes *(1987), and* These Bones Are Not My Child *(1999). "The Lesson" first appeared in* Gorilla My Love.

The Lesson   (1972)

Back in the days when everyone was old and stupid or young and foolish and me and Sugar were the only ones just right, this lady moved on our block with nappy hair and proper speech and no makeup. And quite naturally we laughed at her, laughed the way we did at the junk man who went about his business like he was some big-time president and his sorry-ass horse his secretary. And we kinda hated her too, hated the way we did the winos who cluttered up our parks and pissed on our handball walls and stank up our hallways and stairs so you couldn't halfway play hide-and-seek without a goddamn gas mask. Miss Moore was her name. The only woman on the block with no first name. And she was black as hell, cept for her feet, which were fish-white and spooky. And she was always planning these boring-ass things for us to do, us being my cousin, mostly, who lived on the block cause we all moved North the same time and to the same apartment then spread out gradual to breathe. And our parents would yank our heads into some kinda shape and crisp up our clothes so we'd be presentable for travel with Miss Moore, who always looked like she was going to church, though she never did. Which is just one of things the grownups talked about when they talked behind her back like a dog. But when she came calling with some sachet she'd sewed up or some gingerbread she'd made or some book, why then they'd all be too embarrassed to turn her down and we'd get handed over all spruced up. She'd been to college and said it was only right that she should take responsibility for the young ones' education, and she not even related by marriage or blood. So they'd go for it. Specially Aunt Gretchen. She was the main gofer in the family. You got some ole dumb shit foolishness you want somebody to go for, you send for Aunt Gretchen. She been screwed into the go-along for so long, it's a blood-deep natural thing with her. Which is how she got saddled with me and Sugar and Junior in the first place while our mothers were in a la-de-da apartment up the block having a good ole time.

So this one day Miss Moore rounds us all up at the mailbox and it's puredee hot and she's knockin herself out about arithmetic. And school suppose to let up in summer I heard, but she don't never let up. And the starch in my pinafore scratching the shit outta me and I'm really hating this nappy-head bitch and her goddamn college degree. I'd much rather go to the pool or to the show where it's cool. So me and Sugar leaning on the mailbox being surly, which is a Miss Moore word. And Flyboy checking out what everybody brought for lunch. And

Fat Butt already wasting his peanut-butter-and-jelly sandwich like the pig he is. And Junebug punchin on Q.T.'s arm for potato chips. And Rosie Giraffe shifting from one hip to the other waiting for somebody to step on her foot or ask her if she from Georgia so she can kick ass, preferably Mercedes'. And Miss Moore asking us do we know what money is, like we a bunch of retards. I mean real money, she say, like it's only poker chips or monopoly papers we lay on the grocer. So right away I'm tired of this and say so. And would much rather snatch Sugar and go to the Sunset and terrorize the West Indian kids and take their hair ribbons and their money too. And Miss Moore files that remark away for next week's lesson on brotherhood, I can tell. And finally I say we oughta get to the subway cause it's cooler and besides we might meet some cute boys. Sugar done swiped her mama's lipstick, so we ready.

So we heading down the street and she's boring us silly about what things cost and what our parents make and how much goes for rent and how money ain't divided up right in this country. And then she gets to the part about we all poor and live in the slums, which I don't feature. And I'm ready to speak on that, but she steps out in the street and hails two cabs just like that. Then she hustles half the crew in with her and hands me a five-dollar bill and tells me to calculate 10 percent tip for the driver. And we're off. Me and Sugar and Junebug and Flyboy hangin out the window and hollering to everybody, putting lipstick on each other cause Flyboy a faggot anyway, and making farts with our sweaty armpits. But I'm mostly trying to figure how to spend this money. But they all fascinated with the meter ticking and Junebug starts laying bets as to how much it'll read when Flyboy can't hold his breath no more. Then Sugar lays bets as to how much it'll be when we get there. So I'm stuck. Don't nobody want to go for my plan, which is to jump out at the next light and run off to the first bar-b-que we can find. Then the driver tells us to get the hell out cause we there already. And the meter reads eighty-five cents. And I'm stalling to figure out the tip and Sugar say give him a dime. And I decide he don't need it bad as I do, so later for him. But then he tries to take off with Junebug foot still in the door so we talk about his mama something ferocious. Then we check out that we on Fifth Avenue and everybody dressed up in stockings. One lady in a fur coat, hot as it is. White folks crazy.

"This is the place," Miss Moore say, presenting it to us in the voice she uses at the museum. "Let's look in the windows before we go in."

"Can we steal?" Sugar asks very serious like she's getting the ground rules squared away before she plays. "I beg your pardon," say Miss Moore, and we fall out. So she leads us around the windows of the toy store and me and Sugar screamin, "This is mine, that's mine, I gotta have that, that was made for me, I was born for that," till Big Butt drowns us out.

"Hey, I'm goin to buy that there."

"That there? You don't even know what it is, stupid."

"I do so," he say punchin on Rosie Giraffe. "It's a microscope."

"Whatcha gonna do with a microscope, fool?"

"Look at things."

"Like what, Ronald?" ask Miss Moore. And Big Butt ain't got the first notion. So here go Miss Moore gabbing about the thousands of bacteria in a drop of water and the somethinorother in a speck of blood and the million and one living things in the air around us is invisible to the naked eye. And what she say that for? Junebug go to town on that "naked" and we rolling. Then Miss Moore ask what it cost. So we all jam into the window smudgin it up and the price tag say $300. So then she ask how long'd take for Big Butt and Junebug to save up their allowances. "Too long," I say. "Yeh," adds Sugar, "outgrown it by that time." And Miss Moore say no, you never outgrow learning instruments. "Why, even medical students and interns and," blah, blah, blah. And we ready to choke Big Butt for bringing it up in the first damn place.

"This here costs four hundred eighty dollars," say Rosie Giraffe. So we pile up all over her to see what she pointin out. My eyes tell me it's a chunk of glass cracked with something heavy, and different-color inks dripped into the splits, then the whole thing put into a oven or something. But for $480 it don't make sense.

"That's a paperweight made of semi-precious stones fused together under tremendous pressure," she explains slowly, with her hands doing the mining and all the factory work.

"So what's a paperweight?" asks Rosie Giraffe.

"To weigh paper with, dumbbell," say Flyboy, the wise man from the East.

"Not exactly," say Miss Moore, which is what she say when you warm or way off too. "It's to weigh paper down so it won't scatter and make your desk untidy." So right away me and Sugar curtsy to each other and then to Mercedes who is more the tidy type.

"We don't keep paper on top of the desk in my class," say Junebug, figuring Miss Moore crazy or lyin one.

"At home, then," she say. "Don't you have a calendar and a pencil case and a blotter and a letter-opener on your desk at home where you do your homework?" And she know damn well what our homes look like cause she nosys around in them every chance she gets.

"I don't even have a desk," say Junebug. "Do we?"

"No. And I don't get no homework neither," say Big Butt.

"And I don't even have a home," say Flyboy like he do at school to keep the white folks off his back and sorry for him. Send this poor kid to camp posters, is his specialty.

"I do," says Mercedes. "I have a box of stationery on my desk and a picture of my cat. My godmother bought the stationery and the desk. There's a big rose on each sheet and the envelopes smell like roses."

"Who wants to know about your smelly-ass stationery," say Rosie Giraffe fore I can get my two cents in.

"It's important to have a work area all your own so that . . ."

"Will you look at this sailboat, please," say Flyboy, cuttin her off and pointin to the thing like it was his. So once again we tumble all over each other to gaze

at this magnificent thing in the toy store which is just big enough to maybe sail
two kittens across the pond if you strap them to the posts tight. We all start reciting the price tag like we in assembly. "Handcrafted sailboat of fiberglass at one
thousand one hundred ninety-five dollars."

"Unbelievable," I hear myself say and am really stunned. I read it again for
myself just in case the group recitation put me in a trance. Same thing. For some
reason this pisses me off. We look at Miss Moore and she lookin at us, waiting
for I dunno what.

"Who'd pay all that when you can buy a sailboat set for a quarter at Pop's, a
tube of glue for a dime, and a ball of string for eight cents? It must have a motor and a whole lot else besides," I say. "My sailboat cost me about fifty cents."

"But will it take water?" say Mercedes with her smart ass.

"Took mine to Alley Pond Park once," say Flyboy. "String broke, Lost it. Pity."

"Sailed mine in Central Park and it keeled over and sank. Had to ask my father for another dollar."

"And you got the strap," laugh Big Butt. "The jerk didn't even have a string
on it. My old man wailed on his behind."

Little Q.T. was staring hard at the sailboat and you could see he wanted it bad.
But he too little and somebody'd just take it from him. So what the hell. "This
boat for kids, Miss Moore?"

"Parents silly to buy something like that just to get all broke up," say
Rosie Giraffe.

"That much money it should last forever," I figure.

"My father'd buy it for me if I wanted it."

"Your father, my ass," say Rosie Giraffe getting a chance to finally push
Mercedes.

"Must be rich people shop here," say Q.T.

"You are a very bright boy," say Flyboy. "What was your first clue?" And he
rap him on the head with the back of his knuckles, since Q. T. the only one he
could get away with. Though Q. T. liable to come up behind you years later and
get his licks in when you half expect it.

"What I want to know is," I says to Miss Moore though I never talk to her, I
wouldn't give the bitch that satisfaction, "is how much a real boat costs? I figure
a thousand'd get you a yacht any day."

"Why don't you check that out," she says, "and report back to the group?"
Which really pains my ass. If you gonna mess up a perfectly good swim day least
you could do is have some answers. "Let's go in," she say like she got something
up her sleeve. Only she don't lead the way. So me and Sugar turn the corner to
where the entrance is, but when we get there I kinda hang back. Not that I'm
scared, what's there to be afraid of, just a toy store. But I feel funny, shame. But
what I got to be shamed about? Got as much right to go in as anybody. But somehow I can't seem to get hold of the door, so I step away for Sugar to lead. But
she hangs back too. And I look at her and she looks at me and this is ridiculous.
I mean, damn, I have never ever been shy about doing nothing or going nowhere.

But then Mercedes steps up and then Rosie Giraffe and Big Butt crowd in behind and shove, and next thing we all stuffed into the doorway with only Mercedes squeezing past us, smoothing out her jumper and walking right down the
aisle. Then the rest of us tumble in like a glued-together jigsaw done all wrong.
And people lookin at us. And it's like the time me and Sugar crashed into the
Catholic church on a dare. But once we got in there and everything so hushed
and holy and the candles and the bowin and the handkerchiefs on all the drooping heads, I just couldn't go through with the plan. Which was for me to run up
to the altar and do a tap dance while Sugar played the nose flute and messed
around in the holy water. And Sugar kept givin me the elbow. Then later teased
me so bad I tied her up in the shower and turned it on and locked her in. And
she'd be there till this day if Aunt Gretchen hadn't finally figured I was lyin about
the boarder takin a shower.

Same thing in the store. We all walkin on tiptoe and hardly touchin the games
and puzzles and things. And I watched Miss Moore who is steady watchin us
like she waitin for a sign. Like Mama Drewery watches the sky and sniffs the
air and takes note of just how much slant is in the bird formation. Then me and
Sugar bump smack into each other, so busy gazing at the toys, 'specially the sailboat. But we don't laugh and go into our fat-lady bump-stomach routine. We
just stare at that price tag. Then Sugar run a finger over the whole boat. And
I'm jealous and want to hit her. Maybe not her, but I sure want to punch somebody in the mouth.

"Watcha bring us here for, Miss Moore?"

"You sound angry, Sylvia. Are you mad about something?" Givin me one of
them grins like she tellin a grown-up joke that never turns out to be funny. And
she's lookin very closely at me like maybe she plannin to do my portrait from
memory. I'm mad, but I won't give her that satisfaction. So I slouch around the
store bein very bored and say, "Let's go."

Me and Sugar at the back of the train watchin the tracks whizzin by large then
small then gettin gobbled up in the dark. I'm thinkin about this tricky toy I saw
in the store. A clown that somersaults on a bar then does chin-ups just cause you
yank lightly at his leg. Cost $35. I could see me askin my mother for a $35 birthday clown. "You wanna who that costs what?" she'd say, cocking her head to the
side to get a better view of the hole in my head. Thirty-five dollars could buy new
bunk beds for Junior and Gretchen's boy. Thirty-five dollars and the whole
household could go visit Granddaddy Nelson in the country. Thirty-five dollars
would pay for the rent and the piano bill too. Who are these people that spend
that much for performing clowns and $1,000 for toy sailboats? What kinda work
they do and how they live and how come we ain't in on it? Where we are is who
we are, Miss Moore always pointin out. But it don't necessarily have to be that
way, she always adds then waits for somebody to say that poor people have to
wake up and demand their share of the pie and don't none of us know what kind
of pie she talkin about in the first damn place. But she ain't so smart cause I still
got her four dollars from the taxi and she sure ain't gettin it. Messin up my day
with this shit. Sugar nudges me in my pocket and winks.

Miss Moore lines us up in front of the mailbox where we started from, seem like years ago, and I got a headache for thinkin so hard. And we lean all over each other so we can hold up under the draggy-ass lecture she always finishes us off with at the end before we thank her for borin us to tears. But she just looks at us like she readin tea leaves. Finally she say, "Well, what did you think of F. A. O. Schwartz?"

Rosie Giraffe mumbles, "White folks crazy."

"I'd like to go there again when I get my birthday money," says Mercedes, and we shove her out the pack so she has to lean on the mailbox by herself.

"I'd like a shower. Tiring day," say Flyboy.

Then Sugar surprises me by sayin, "You know, Miss Moore, I don't think all of us here put together eat in a year what that sailboat costs." And Miss Moore lights up like somebody goosed her. "And?" she say, urging Sugar on. Only I'm standin on her foot so she don't continue.

"Imagine for a minute what kind of society it is in which some people can spend on a toy what it would cost to feed a family of six or seven. What do you think?"

"I think," say Sugar pushing me off her feet like she never done before, cause I whip her ass in a minute, "that this is not much of a democracy if you ask me. Equal chance to pursue happiness means an equal crack at the dough, don't it?" Miss Moore is besides herself and I am disgusted with Sugar's treachery. So I stand on her foot one more time to see if she'll shove me. She shuts up, and Miss Moore looks at me, sorrowfully I'm thinkin. And somethin weird is goin on, I can feel it in my chest.

"Anybody else learn anything today?" lookin dead at me. I walk away and Sugar has to run to catch up and don't even seem to notice when I shrug her arm off my shoulder.

"Well, we got four dollars anyway," she says.

"Uh hunh."

"We could go to Hascombs and get half a chocolate layer and then go to the Sunset and still have plenty money for potato chips and ice-cream sodas."

"Uh hunh."

"Race you to Hascombs," she say.

We start down the block and she gets ahead which is O.K. by me cause I'm goin to the West End and then over to the Drive to think this day through. She can run if she want to and even run faster. But ain't nobody gonna beat me at nuthin.

Study and Discussion Questions

1. What exactly is the lesson Miss Moore is trying to teach? To what extent does the narrator, Sylvia, learn it? What are the sources of her resistance to it?
2. Why does Sylvia feel ashamed entering the toy store? What does this reveal about her?

3. What is the significance of the last sentence of the story?
4. Why does Miss Moore feel the need to teach Sylvia and her friends a lesson now that they would no doubt eventually learn on their own?
5. What does Bambara gain by using Sylvia as a first-person narrator?
6. Who is Miss Moore? What is her role in the neighborhood? Why is she taking the children on these "field trips"?
7. Discuss the interactions between Miss Moore and the children in the toy store. Discuss the interactions between the children while they are in the store.

Suggestions for Writing

1. What kind of society is it, Miss Moore asks, "in which some people can spend on a toy what it would cost to feed a family of six or seven?" How would you answer?
2. Describe the first time you can remember being aware of social class differences.

Critical Resources

1. Butler-Evans, Elliot. *Race, Gender, and Desire: Narrative Strategies in the Fiction of Bambara, Morrison and Walker.* Philadelphia: Temple, 1989.
2. Heller, Janet Ruth. "Toni Cade Bambara's Use of African American Vernacular English in 'The Lesson'." *Style* 37.3 (2003): 279–293.
3. Tate, Claudia. "Toni Cade Bambara" Interview. *Black Women Writers at Work.* New York: Continuum, 1983.

ALICE WALKER (b. 1944)

Alice Walker was born in Eatonton, Georgia. Her parents were sharecroppers who managed to raise eight children (Walker was the youngest) on minimal wages. At the age of eight, Walker's brother accidentally shot her in the eye with a BB gun, blinding her right eye. Due to the accident, Walker withdrew and became very shy. It was during this time that she began to develop an acute ability to observe people and to write. In 1961, she was awarded a scholarship to Spelman College. After graduating, she moved to Mississippi and became active in the civil rights movement. In 1967, she published her first essay, "The Civil Rights Movement: What Good Was It?" and her professional career as a writer began. While her reputation as a writer grew through the 1970s with the publication of the short story collection In Love and Trouble *(1973) and the novel* Meridian *(1976), it was her novel* The Color Purple *(1983), winner of the Pulitzer Prize, that signaled Walker's recognition by a broader audience. Influenced by Zora Neale Hurston and Jean Toomer, Walker's work is imbued with the concept of the "womanist"—a phrase she penned as an alternative to "feminist." And indeed, Walker is best known for her powerful depictions of black women who persevere despite brutal oppression from men and society. Her other works include the short story collection* You Can't Keep a Good Woman Down *(1981); the novels* The Temple of My Familiar *(1989),* Possessing the Street of Joy *(1992),* By The Light of My Father's Smile *(1998),* The Way Forward Is With a Broken Heart *(2000), and* Now is the Time to Open Your Heart *(2004); the poetry collection* Revolutionary Petunias *(1973); and the essay collections* In Search of Our Mothers' Gardens: Womanist Prose *(1983) and* Anything We Love Can Be Saved: A Writer's Activism *(1997). "Everyday Use" was first published in* In Love and Trouble.

Everyday Use   (1973)

for your grandmama

I will wait for her in the yard that Maggie and I made so clean and wavy yesterday afternoon. A yard like this is more comfortable than most people know. It is not just a yard. It is like an extended living room. When the hard clay is swept clean as a floor and the fine sand around the edges lined with tiny, irregular grooves, anyone can come and sit and look up into the elm tree and wait for the breezes that never come inside the house.

Maggie will be nervous until after her sister goes: she will stand hopelessly in corners, homely and ashamed of the burn scars down her arms and legs, eying her sister with a mixture of envy and awe. She thinks her sister has held life always in the palm of one hand, that "no" is a word the world never learned to say to her.

You've no doubt seen those TV shows where the child who has "made it" is confronted, as a surprise, by her own mother and father, tottering in weakly from backstage. (A pleasant surprise, of course: What would they do if parent and child came on the show only to curse out and insult each other?) On TV mother and child embrace and smile into each other's faces. Sometimes the mother and father weep, the child wraps them in her arms and leans across the table to tell how she would not have made it without their help. I have seen these programs.

Sometimes I dream a dream in which Dee and I are suddenly brought together on a TV program of this sort. Out of a dark and soft-seated limousine I am ushered into a bright room filled with many people. There I meet a smiling, gray, sporty man like Johnny Carson who shakes my hand and tells me what a fine girl I have. Then we are on the stage and Dee is embracing me with tears in her eyes. She pins on my dress a large orchid, even though she has told me once that she thinks orchids are tacky flowers.

In real life I am a large, big-boned woman with rough, man-working hands. In the winter I wear flannel nightgowns to bed and overalls during the day. I can kill and clean a hog as mercilessly as a man. My fat keeps me hot in zero weather.

I can work outside all day, breaking ice to get water for washing; I can eat pork liver cooked over the open fire minutes after it comes steaming from the hog. One winter I knocked a bull calf straight in the brain between the eyes with a sledge hammer and had the meat hung up to chill before nightfall. But of course all this does not show on television. I am the way my daughter would want me to be: a hundred pounds lighter, my skin like an uncooked barley pancake. My hair glistens in the hot bright lights. Johnny Carson has much to do to keep up with my quick and witty tongue.

But that is a mistake. I know even before I wake up. Who ever knew a Johnson with a quick tongue? Who can even imagine me looking a strange white man in the eye? It seems to me I have talked to them always with one foot raised in flight, with my head turned in whichever way is farthest from them. Dee, though. She would always look anyone in the eye. Hesitation was no part of her nature.

"How do I look, Mama?" Maggie says, showing just enough of her thin body enveloped in pink skirt and red blouse for me to know she's there, almost hidden by the door.

"Come out into the yard," I say.

Have you ever seen a lame animal, perhaps a dog run over by some careless person rich enough to own a car, sidle up to someone who is ignorant enough to be kind to him? That is the way my Maggie walks. She has been like this, chin on chest, eyes on ground, feet in shuffle, ever since the fire that burned the other house to the ground.

Dee is lighter than Maggie, with nicer hair and a fuller figure. She's a woman now, though sometimes I forget. How long ago was it that the other house burned? Ten, twelve years? Sometimes I can still hear the flames and feel Maggie's arms sticking to me, her hair smoking and her dress falling off her in little black papery flakes. Her eyes seemed stretched open, blazed open by the flames reflected in them. And Dee. I see her standing off under the sweet gum tree she used to dig gum out of; a look of concentration on her face as she watched the last dingy gray board of the house fall in toward the red-hot brick chimney. Why don't you do a dance around the ashes? I'd wanted to ask her. She had hated the house that much.

I used to think she hated Maggie, too. But that was before we raised the money, the church and me, to send her to Augusta to school. She used to read to us without pity; forcing words, lies, other folks' habits, whole lives upon us two, sitting trapped and ignorant underneath her voice. She washed us in a river of make-believe, burned us with a lot of knowledge we didn't necessarily need to know. Pressed us to her with the serious way she read, to shove us away at just the moment, like dimwits, we seemed about to understand.

Dee wanted nice things. A yellow organdy dress to wear to her graduation from high school; black pumps to match a green suit she'd made from an old suit somebody gave me. She was determined to stare down any disaster in her efforts. Her eyelids would not flicker for minutes at a time. Often I fought off the temptation to shake her. At sixteen she had a style of her own: and knew what style was.

I never had an education myself. After second grade the school was closed down. Don't ask me why: in 1927 colored asked fewer questions than they do now. Sometimes Maggie reads to me. She stumbles along good-naturedly but can't see well. She knows she is not bright. Like good looks and money, quickness passed her by. She will marry John Thomas (who has mossy teeth in an earnest face) and then I'll be free to sit here and I guess just sing church songs to myself. Although I never was a good singer. Never could carry a tune. I was always better at a man's job. I used to love to milk till I was hooked in the side in '49. Cows are soothing and slow and don't bother you, unless you try to milk them the wrong way.

I have deliberately turned my back on the house. It is three rooms, just like the one that burned, except the roof is tin; they don't make shingle roofs any more. There are no real windows, just some holes cut in the sides, like the portholes in a ship, but not round and not square, with rawhide holding the shutters up on the outside. This house is in a pasture, too, like the other one. No doubt when Dee sees it she will want to tear it down. She wrote me once that no matter where we "choose" to live, she will manage to come see us. But she will never bring her friends. Maggie and I thought about this and Maggie asked me, "Mama, when did Dee ever *have* any friends?"

She had a few. Furtive boys in pink shirts hanging about on washday after school. Nervous girls who never laughed. Impressed with her they worshiped the well-turned phrase, the cute shape, the scalding humor that erupted like bubbles in lye. She read to them.

When she was courting Jimmy T she didn't have much time to pay to us, but turned all her faultfinding power on him. He *flew* to marry a cheap city girl from a family of ignorant flashy people. She hardly had time to recompose herself.

When she comes I will meet—but there they are!

Maggie attempts to make a dash for the house, in her shuffling way, but I stay her with my hand. "Come back here," I say. And she stops and tries to dig a well in the sand with her toe.

It is hard to see them clearly through the strong sun. But even the first glimpse of leg out of the car tells me it is Dee. Her feet were always neat-looking, as if God himself had shaped them with a certain style. From the other side of the car comes a short, stocky man. Hair is all over his head a foot long and hanging from his chin like a kinky mule tail. I hear Maggie suck in her breath. "Uhnnnh," is what it sounds like. Like when you see the wriggling end of a snake just in front of your foot on the road. "Uhnnnh."

Dee next. A dress down to the ground, in this hot weather. A dress so loud it hurts my eyes. There are yellows and oranges enough to throw back the light of the sun. I feel my whole face warming from the heat waves it throws out. Earrings gold, too, and hanging down to her shoulders. Bracelets dangling and

making noises when she moves her arm up to shake the folds of the dress out of
her armpits. The dress is loose and flows, and as she walks closer, I like it. I hear
Maggie go "Uhnnnh" again. It is her sister's hair. It stands straight up like the
wool on a sheep. It is black as night and around the edges are two long pigtails
that rope about like small lizards disappearing behind her ears.

"Wa-su-zo-Tean-o!"[1] she says, coming on in that gilding way the dress makes
her move. The short stocky fellow with the hair to his navel is all grinning and
he follows up with "Asalamalakim,[2] my mother and sister!" He moves to hug
Maggie but she falls back, right up against the back of my chair. I feel her trembling there and when I look up I see the perspiration falling off her chin.

"Don't get up," says Dee. Since I am stout it takes something of a push. You
can see me trying to move a second or two before I make it. She turns, showing
white heels through her sandals, and goes back to the car. Out she peeks next
with a Polaroid. She stoops down quickly and lines up picture after picture of
me sitting there in front of the house with Maggie cowering behind me. She
never takes a shot without making sure the house is included. When a cow comes
nibbling around the edge of the yard she snaps it and me and Maggie *and* the
house. Then she puts the Polaroid in the back seat of the car, and comes up and
kisses me on the forehead.

Meanwhile Asalamalakim is going through motions with Maggie's hand. Maggie's hand is as limp as a fish, and probably as cold, despite the sweat, and she
keeps trying to pull it back. It looks like Asalamalakim wants to shake hands
but wants to do it fancy. Or maybe he don't know how people shake hands. Anyhow, he soon gives up on Maggie.

"Well," I say. "Dee."

"No, Mama," she says. "Not 'Dee,' Wangero Leewanika Kemanjo!"

"What happened to 'Dee'?" I wanted to know.

"She's dead," Wangero said. "I couldn't bear it any longer, being named after
the people who oppress me."

"You know as well as me you was named after your aunt Dicie," I said. Dicie
is my sister. She named Dee. We called her "Big Dee" after Dee was born.

"But who was *she* named after?" asked Wangero.

"I guess after Grandma Dee," I said.

"And who was she named after?" asked Wangero.

"Her mother," I said, and saw Wangero was getting tired. "That's about as far
back as I can trace it," I said. Though, in fact, I probably could have carried it
back beyond the Civil War through the branches.

"Well," said Asalamalakim, "there you are."

"Uhnnnh," I heard Maggie say.

"There I was not," I said, "before 'Dicie' cropped up in our family, so why
should I try to trace it that far back?"

---

[1]Swahili greeting.
[2]Arabic greeting.

He just stood there grinning, looking down on me like somebody inspecting a Model A car. Every once in a while he and Wangero sent eye signals over my head.

"How do you pronounce this name?" I asked.

"You don't have to call me by it if you don't want to," said Wangero.

"Why shouldn't I?" I asked. "If that's what you want us to call you, we'll call you."

"I know it might sound awkward at first," said Wangero.

"I'll get used to it," I said. "Ream it out again."

Well, soon we got the name out of the way. Asalamalakim had a name twice as long and three times as hard. After I tripped over it two or three times he told me to just call him Hakim-a-barber. I wanted to ask him was he a barber, but I didn't really think he was, so I didn't ask.

"You must belong to those beef-cattle peoples down the road," I said. They said "Asalamalakim" when they met you, too, but they didn't shake hands. Always too busy: feeding the cattle, fixing the fences, putting up salt-lick shelters, throwing down hay. When the white folks poisoned some of the herd the men stayed all night with rifles in their hands. I walked a mile and a half just to see the sight.

Hakim-a-barber said, "I accept some of their doctrines, but farming and raising cattle is not my style." (They didn't tell me, and I didn't ask, whether Wangero (Dee) had really gone and married him.)

We sat down to eat and right away he said he didn't eat collards and pork was unclean. Wangero, though, went on through the chitlins and corn bread, the greens and everything else. She talked a blue streak over the sweet potatoes. Everything delighted her. Even the fact that we still used the benches her daddy made for the table when we couldn't afford to buy chairs.

"Oh, Mama!" she cried. Then turned to Hakim-a-barber. "I never knew how lovely these benches are. You can feel the rump prints," she said, running her hands underneath her and along the bench. Then she gave a sigh and her hand closed over Grandma Dee's butter dish. "That's it!" she said. "I knew there was something I wanted to ask you if I could have." She jumped up from the table and went over in the corner where the churn stood, the milk in it clabber by now. She looked at the churn and looked at it.

"This churn top is what I need," she said. "Didn't Uncle Buddy whittle it out of a tree you all used to have?"

"Yes," I said.

"Uh huh," she said happily. "And I want the dasher, too."

"Uncle Buddy whittle that, too?" asked the barber.

Dee (Wangero) looked up at me.

"Aunt Dee's first husband whittled the dash," said Maggie so low you almost couldn't hear her. "His name was Henry, but they called him Stash."

"Maggie's brain is like an elephant's," Wangero said, laughing. "I can use the churn top as a centerpiece for the alcove table," she said, sliding a plate over the churn, "and I'll think of something artistic to do with the dasher."

When she finished wrapping the dasher the handle stuck out. I took it for a moment in my hands. You didn't even have to look close to see where hands pushing the dasher up and down to make butter had left a kind of sink in the wood. In fact, there were a lot of small sinks; you could see where thumbs and fingers had sunk into the wood. It was beautiful light yellow wood, from a tree that grew in the yard where Big Dee and Stash had lived.

After dinner Dee (Wangero) went to the trunk at the foot of my bed, and started rifling through it. Maggie hung back in the kitchen over the dishpan. Out came Wangero with two quilts. They had been pieced by Grandma Dee and then Big Dee and me had hung them on the quilt frames on the front porch and quilted them. One was in the Lone Star pattern. The other was Walk Around the Mountain. In both of them were scraps of dresses Grandma Dee had worn fifty and more years ago. Bits and pieces of Grandpa Jarrell's Paisley shirts. And one teeny faded blue piece, about the size of a penny matchbox, that was from Great Grandpa Ezra's uniform that he wore in the Civil War.

"Mama," Wangero said sweet as a bird. "Can I have these old quilts?"

I heard something fall in the kitchen, and a minute later the kitchen door slammed.

"Why don't you take one or two of the others?" I asked. "These old things was just done by me and Big Dee from some tops your grandma pieced before she died."

"No," said Wangero. "I don't want those. They are stitched around the borders by machine."

"That'll make them last better," I said.

"That's not the point," said Wangero. "These are all pieces of dresses Grandma used to wear. She did all this stitching by hand. Imagine!" She held the quilts securely in her arms, stroking them.

"Some of the pieces, like those lavender ones, come from old clothes her mother handed down to her," I said, moving up to touch the quilts. Dee (Wangero) moved back just enough so that I couldn't reach the quilts. They already belonged to her.

"Imagine!" she breathed again, clutching them closely to her bosom.

"The truth is," I said, "I promised to give them quilts to Maggie, for when she marries John Thomas."

She gasped like a bee had stung her.

"Maggie can't appreciate these quilts!" she said. "She'd probably be backward enough to put them to everyday use."

"I reckon she would," I said. "God knows I been saving 'em for long enough with nobody using 'em. I hope she will!" I didn't want to bring up how I had offered Dee (Wangero) a quilt when she went away to college. Then she had told me they were old-fashioned, out of style.

"But they're *priceless!*" she was saying now, furiously; for she has a temper. "Maggie would put them on the bed and in five years they'd be in rags. Less than that!"

"She can always make some more," I said. "Maggie knows how to quilt."

Dee (Wangero) looked at me with hatred. "You just will not understand. The point is these quilts, *these* quilts!"

"Well," I said, stumped. "What would *you* do with them?"

"Hang them," she said. As if that was the only thing you *could* do with quilts.

Maggie by now was standing in the door. I could almost hear the sound her feet made as they scraped over each other.

"She can have them, Mama," she said, like somebody used to never winning anything, or having anything reserved for her. "I can 'member Grandma Dee without the quilts."

I looked at her hard. She had filled her bottom lip with checkerberry snuff and it gave her face a kind of dopey, hangdog look. It was Grandma Dee and Big Dee who taught her how to quilt herself. She stood there with her scarred hands hidden in the folds of her skirt. She looked at her sister with something like fear but she wasn't mad at her. This was Maggie's portion. This was the way she knew God to work.

When I looked at her like that something hit me in the top of my head and ran down to the soles of my feet. Just like when I'm in church and the spirit of God touches me and I get happy and shout. I did something I never had done before: hugged Maggie to me, then dragged her on into the room, snatched the quilts out of Miss Wangero's hands and dumped them into Maggie's lap. Maggie just sat there on my bed with her mouth open.

"Take one or two of the others," I said to Dee.

But she turned without a word and went out to Hakim-a-barber.

"You just don't understand," she said, as Maggie and I came out to the car.

"What don't I understand?" I wanted to know.

"Your heritage," she said. And then she turned to Maggie, kissed her, and said, "You ought to try to make something of yourself, too, Maggie. It's really a new day for us. But from the way you and Mama still live you'd never know it."

She put on some sunglasses that hid everything above the tip of her nose and her chin.

Maggie smiled; maybe at the sunglasses. But a real smile, not scared. After we watched the car dust settle I asked Maggie to bring me a dip of snuff. And then the two of us sat there just enjoying, until it was time to go in the house and go to bed.

Study and Discussion Questions

1. Who is the first-person narrator of this story?
2. Why do you think the mother describes herself in terms of the work she does? What are the differences between the real mother and the TV version she sometimes dreams?
3. What are we told about Dee before we ever meet her?
4. What does the house-burning incident tell us about the three characters and their relation to each other?
5. What does the title of the story refer to?
6. How has Dee changed, according to her mother? What have social class and class mobility to do with this?

7. Why does Dee take pictures of the house and want the churn top and the quilts?
8. What does Dee plan to do with the quilts? What will Maggie do with them?

Suggestions for Writing

1. Contrast Maggie and Dee.
2. Do you have any sympathy for Dee? If so, on what grounds? If not, why not?
3. Discuss the importance in this story of education, what it is, and what one does with it.
4. What is the wealth this family possesses? How do Maggie, Dee, and the mother each see that wealth and themselves in relation to it?
5. What does "Everyday Use" suggest about one's relation to one's past, heritage, and tradition?
6. Discuss the importance of names in the story.
7. Write about an experience you've had going home, either from your own perspective or from the point of view of another family member.

Critical Resources

1. *Alice Walker.* Lannan Foundation (documentary), 1989 (60 minutes). See <http://www.lannan.org/lf/lit/search_detail/alice-walker/> for more information.
2. Christian, Barbara, ed. *Everyday Use: Alice Walker.* New Brunswick, NJ: Rutgers University Press, 1994.
3. Gates, Henry Louis, ed. *Alice Walker: Critical Perspectives Past and Present.* New York: Amistad, 1993.
4. Lauret, Maria. *Alice Walker.* New York: St. Martin's, 2000.

HARVEY PEKAR (b. 1939)

Harvey Pekar was born in Cleveland, Ohio, and has lived there all his life. The town itself has been the setting for Pekar's autobiographical American Splendor— *a literary comic-book series based on his life as a file clerk at a Veteran's Administration hospital. Pekar self-published the comic annually from 1976 to the early 1990s, employing various illustrators (Robert Crumb, Sue Cavey, Frank Stack, and Joe Zabel, among others) to do the drawings. In 1987, it won the American Book Award. A few years later, the comic's popularity caught the attention of Dark Horse Comics, who took over publication. Pekar calls himself a "working-class intellectual," and* American Splendor *focuses on Pekar's introspective and heroic search for meaning amidst the complexity of a modern working-class life. In addition to* American Splendor, *Pekar has written as a music critic and is currently a freelance writer for a radio station in Cleveland. His other works include Our Cancer Year (1994)—a graphic novel about his fight with cancer, and most recently, his book length graphic autobiography,* The Quitter *(2005).*

BUT THEN I'D SORT OF BE OUT OF THE STRUGGLE, SORT OF IN AN IVORY TOWER WATCHING THE MAINSTREAM OF LIFE GO BY RATHER THAN PARTICIPATING IN IT...

I'D BE ALIENATED BUT I WOULDN'T THINK I HAD THE RIGHT TO FEEL BAD ABOUT IT. I MEAN, I'D BE A WELL-PAID, FAMOUS AUTHOR. WHAT RIGHT WOULD I HAVE TO COMPLAIN ABOUT ANYTHING?

MAYBE MY WRITING WOULD SUFFER. I'VE GOT A PRETTY UNIQUE VIEWPOINT NOW... I'M A WRITER BUT IN A LOTTA WAYS I'VE GOT A WORKING MAN'S OUTLOOK ON LIFE. I'D HAVE TO AS LONG AS I'VE WORKED AT REGULAR DAY JOBS.

A COUPLA THOSE, ANNA RYE BREAD...

STILL, MAYBE I'M MAKING TOO MUCH OF THIS. AS LONG AS I'M ALIVE I'LL BE FINDING INTERESTING THINGS TO WRITE ABOUT, MEETING INTERESTING PEOPLE...

IF I LIVED A DIFFERENT LIFE I COULD STILL WRITE ABOUT IT.

Study and Discussion Questions

1. What is a "hypothetical quandary"? Look up the words in a large dictionary. Give an example of a hypothetical quandary in your own life. What is Pekar's hypothetical quandary in this story?
2. Describe the setting of this story.
3. What literally happens in this story? Give a plot summary.
4. Is the ending of "Hypothetical Quandary" a satisfactory answer to the protagonist's dilemma? Say how or how not. Would it be for you?
5. What do we learn about the main character from the way he is presented visually?
6. In the introduction to the collection *American Splendor: The Life and Times of Harvey Pekar,* from which this piece comes, illustrator R. Crumb writes in 1985, "Pekar has proven once and for all that even the most seemingly dreary and monotonous of lives is filled with poignancy and heroic struggle. . . . What Pekar does is certainly new to the comic book medium. There's never been anything even approaching this kind of stark realism." If you have read other comic books or graphic novels, how were they similar to and different from "Hypothetical Quandary"?
7. Harvey Pekar has worked with several artists in the course of his career creating serious comics about his life and times. Characterize R. Crumb's art work in this particular story.
8. Why include a comic strip such as this in a literature anthology?

Suggestions for Writing

1. See the 2003 biographical film about Harvey Pekar, *American Splendor* and write about "Hypothetical Quandary" in the context of what you have learned about Pekar's life.
2. Compare/contrast this example of graphic literature with Marjane Satrapi's "The Dowry" from her graphic memoir *Persepolis* (Peace and War). You might discuss the visual style of each and how it is an essential aspect of this narrative medium. Or you could discuss each protagonist's relation to the world he or she lives in. Or choose your own topic.
3. Select one panel or frame in "Hypothetical Quandary" and analyze it—in terms of mood or atmosphere, presentation of character and setting, relation of words to picture, use of black and white, use of space, and any other aspects you find interesting.

Critical Resources

1. *American Splendor.* Directors Shari Springer Berman and Robert Pulcini. Performers Paul Giamatti, Hope Davis. HBO Films, 2003 (101 minutes).
2. Witek, Joseph. *Comic Books as History: The Narrative Art of Jack Jackson, Art Spiegelman and Harvey Pekar.* Jackson: University Press of Mississippi, 1989.
3. Weiner, Stephen. *Faster Than A Speeding Bullet: The Rise of the Graphic Novel.* New York: NBM Publishers, 2003.

❀ ❀ ❀

POETRY

BERTOLT BRECHT (1898–1956)

Bertolt Brecht was born in Augsburg, Germany, studied medicine at Munich University, and worked as an orderly in a military hospital during World War I. Afterward, Brecht became a radical critic of war and nationalism and began to write. Though he also wrote poetry and prose, Brecht found his strongest artistic outlet in drama. Regardless of genre, as a Marxist, Brecht saw the vocation of writer as socially responsible for social education. His work, through the use of satire and unconventional forms, questioned his era's perceptions of literature and its cultural role. Brecht's "theater of alienation" (Adorno) or "epic theater" sought to dismantle traditional Aristotelian notions of catharsis by staging dramas that didn't allow an audience to escape from reality, but instead presented an unadorned, unsentimental exposition of human crises. His theatrical ideas have heavily influenced modern drama. His work was banned in Germany in the 1930s with the rise of Hitler, forcing Brecht to leave. He would eventually move to California in 1941, where he worked with Charlie Chaplin and others in the film industry. A prolific writer of plays, poetry, and prose, selected works include his major plays The Three-Penny Opera *(1928),* The Life of Galileo *(1939),* Mother Courage and Her Children *(1941),* The Good Woman of Setzuan *(1943), and* The Caucasian Chalk Circle *(1954). The poem "A Worker Reads History" illustrates Brecht's concern for the working class and his techniques of defamiliarization and reframing perspective on a subject.*

A Worker Reads History   (1936)

Translated by H. R. Hays.

Who built the seven gates of Thebes?
The books are filled with names of kings.
Was it kings who hauled the craggy blocks of stone?
And Babylon, so many times destroyed,
Who built the city up each time? In which of Lima's houses,   5
That city glittering with gold, lived those who built it?
In the evening when the Chinese wall was finished
Where did the masons go? Imperial Rome
Is full of arcs of triumph. Who reared them up? Over whom
Did the Caesars triumph? Byzantium lives in song,   10
Were all her dwellings palaces? And even in Atlantis of the legend

The night the sea rushed in,
The drowning men still bellowed for their slaves.

Young Alexander conquered India.
He alone?   15
Caesar beat the Gauls.
Was there not even a cook in his army?
Philip of Spain wept as his fleet
Was sunk and destroyed. Were there no other tears?
Frederick the Great triumphed in the Seven Years War. Who   20
Triumphed with him?

Each page a victory,
At whose expense the victory ball?
Every ten years a great man,
Who paid the piper?   25

So many particulars.
So many questions.

Study and Discussion Questions

1. List the different roles in the poem (invisible in history books) that members of the working classes have played.
2. Why are so many sentences in the poem questions? Is this only a rhetorical device?
3. What are the meanings and the irony of "Each page a victory"?
4. Explain "Every ten years a great man, Who paid the piper?"

Suggestions for Writing

1. Where do women of the working classes appear in the poem? Why doesn't Brecht mention *their* work?
2. To what extent and how were the working classes represented in the history you learned in school?
3. Write a poem or paragraph about a woman or an African American or a member of another historically dispossessed group reading history.

Critical Resources

1. Brooker, Peter. *Bertolt Brecht: Dialectics, Poetry, Politics.* New York: Croom Helm, 1988.
2. Hayman, Ronald. *Brecht: A Biography.* New York: Oxford University Press, 1983.
3. Kuhn, Tom and Karen Leeder, eds. *Empedocles' Shoe: Essays on Brecht's Poetry.* London: Methuen, 2002.

4. Thompson, Phillip. *The Poetry of Brecht: Seven Studies.* Chapel Hill: University of North Carolina, 1989.

JONATHAN SWIFT (1667–1745)

Jonathon Swift was born in Dublin, Ireland and educated at Trinity College there. Throughout a very active and political life, Swift held a variety of positions— secretary for essayist and diplomat Sir Williams Temple; vicar; political pamphleteer; journalist; and Dean of St. Patrick's Cathedral in Dublin. By 1720, he had become a passionate critic of British imperial exploitation of Ireland, writing caustic satire on behalf of Irish national interests. Swift is best known for his prose writings, including Battle of the Books *(1704),* The Tale of a Tub *(1704),* Gulliver's Travels *(1726), and* A Modest Proposal *(1729). "A Description of the Morning," written in rhymed couplets, was first published in the Tory journal* The Tattler.*

Description of the Morning (1709)

Now hardly here and there a hackney-coach
Appearing, showed the ruddy morn's approach.
Now Betty from her master's bed had flown,
And softly stole to discompose her own;
The slip-shod 'prentice from his master's door   5
Had pared the dirt and sprinkled round the floor.
Now Moll had whirled her mop with dext'rous airs,
Prepared to scrub the entry and the stairs.
The youth with broomy stumps began to trace
The kennel-edge, where wheels had worn the place.[1]   10
The small-coal man was heard with cadence deep,
Till drowned in shriller notes of chimney-sweep:
Duns at his lordship's gate began to meet;
And brickdust Moll had screamed through half the street.
The turnkey now his flock returning sees,   15
Duly let out a-nights to steal for fees:[2]
The watchful bailiffs take their silent stands,
And schoolboys lag with satchels in their hands.

---

[1]The youth is scavenging in the gutter.
[2]To pay their jailer.

Study and Discussion Questions

1. Spell out what each person described is doing and why.
2. What is the speaker's attitude toward what is described?
3. What comment is the poem making on differences in social class?
4. What is the significance of the juxtaposition in the last two lines?
5. What is the rhyme scheme of this poem?
6. How does the use of couplets as a structure for Swift's description of a morning work with the content or meaning of the poem? How does what he does with the couplets change as the poem goes on?

Suggestions for Writing

1. There is a long tradition of poems describing the morning's beauty in *pastoral* terms, picturing glorious fields, idle shepherds, and so on. What relation does "A Description of the Morning" have to such poems?
2. Try capturing Swift's tone in a poem or a paragraph describing the morning at a place you are familiar with. Use whatever genre (prose or poetry) and whatever form within the genre (e.g., if poetry, line length, rhyme or not) are appropriate to the place you are describing and your feelings about it.

Critical Resources

1. Fox, Christopher, ed. *The Cambridge Companion to Jonathan Swift.* New York: Cambridge University Press, 2003.
2. Manlove, C. N. "Swift's Structures: A Description of the Morning and Some Others." *Studies in English Literature 1500–1900* 29.3 (1989): 463–72.
3. Rawson, Claude. *Jonathan Swift: A Collection of Critical Essays.* Englewood Cliffs, NJ: Prentice Hall, 1995.
4. Vieth, David. *Essential Articles for the Study of Jonathan Swift's Poetry.* Hamden: Archon Books, 1984.

THEODORE ROETHKE (1908–1963)

Theodore Roethke was born in Saginaw, Michigan, where his German immigrant father owned greenhouses. This controlled, verdant world of his childhood surfaces repeatedly and in various forms throughout his poetry, often as a metaphor for the "inner world" of a person in contrast to the chaos of the world outside. While attending Michigan State University, Roethke developed an interest in teaching and resolved to become a poet. He was known as a dedicated and energetic teacher of literature and writing, first at the University of Michigan and then at the University of Washington. In addition to teaching, Roethke was also dedicated to his poetry. Influenced by Wordsworth, T. S. Eliot, and W. B. Yeats, Roethke's met-

*rical verse is deeply introspective and often erratic—moving from high moments
of revelation to low moments of despondency. Such emotional differences are a
product of Roethke's exploration of his subconscious world for meaning and his
effort to reconcile this with external reality. The pressure of both teaching and writing caused him to suffer several nervous breakdowns throughout his life. His poetry collections include* Open House *(1941),* The Lost Son *(1948),* Praise the End!
(1951), The Waking *(1953, Pulitzer Prize winner), and* The Far Field *(1964,
posthumously). "Dolor," first published in* The Lost Son, *is suggestive of the pensive tone found in much of his poetry and remains one of the most vivid evocations of bureaucratic work.*

Dolor   (1948)

I have known the inexorable sadness of pencils,
Neat in their boxes, dolor of pad and paper-weight,
All the misery of manila folders and mucilage,
Desolation in immaculate public places,
Lonely reception room, lavatory, switchboard,   5
The unalterable pathos of basin and pitcher,
Ritual of multigraph, paper-clip, comma,
Endless duplication of lives and objects.
And I have seen dust from the walls of institutions,
Finer than flour, alive, more dangerous than silica,   10
Sift, almost invisible, through long afternoons of tedium,
Dropping a fine film on nails and delicate eyebrows,
Glazing the pale hair, the duplicate grey standard faces.

Study and Discussion Questions

1. Look up *dolor* in the dictionary. How does the poem convey the various
   aspects of the definition of that word? (And of course, look up any other
   word you don't know all the meanings of.)
2. What does Roethke suggest is the effect of office work on office workers?
3. What specific kinds of office work does Roethke have in mind? It can be
   said that the boss also works in an office. Do you think Roethke's poem
   refers to that person?
4. Many of the words in "Dolor," like the title itself, are abstract rather than
   concrete. List some of those words. How does the extensive use of ab-
   stractions add to the effect of the poem?
5. What has power and life in this poem? What is powerless and lifeless?
   How does Roethke achieve this transformation?

Suggestion for Writing

1. Gather the materials to write a comparable poem about some kind of work you have done. What objects would you select? What are their qualities? What is the relation between the workers and those objects? What kind of mood would you want to convey? What would you title your poem?

Critical Resources

1. Allan, Seager. *The Glass House: The Life of Theodore Roethke.* Introduction by Donald Hall. Ann Arbor: University of Michigan Press, 1991.
2. Bogen, Don. *Theodore Roethke and the Writing Process.* Athens: Ohio University Press, 1991.
3. Kalaidjian, Walter. *Understanding Theodore Roethke.* Columbia: University of South Carolina Press 1987.
4. Malkoff, Karl. *Theodore Roethke: An Introduction to the Poetry.* New York: Columbia University Press, 1971.

JUDY GRAHN (b. 1940)

Judy Grahn grew up in New Mexico and has worked as a waitress, typist, sandwich maker, and meat wrapper. She has also taught in women's writing programs in New York and Berkeley, and she cofounded the Gay and Lesbian Studies Program at the New College of California in San Francisco. Grahn was a cofounder of the Women's Press Collective in 1970 in northern California. Her writings include The Work of a Common Woman *(1978) and* The Queen of Wands *(1982), poetry;* Another Mother Tongue: Gay Words, Gay Worlds *(1984) and* Blood and Bread and Roses *(1986), nonfiction;* Mundane's World *(1988) a novel; and* Really Reading Gertrude Stein *(1989). She has also edited two volumes of* True to Life Adventure Stories *(1978, 1980). Grahn has consistently brought a working-class perspective into feminist poetry. "Ella, in a square apron, along Highway 80," is one of seven portraits of working-class women in the sequence,* The Common Woman Poems *(1969). See also Grahn's "A Woman is Talking to Death" in Varieties of Protest.*

Ella, in a square apron, along Highway 80   (1969)

She's a copperheaded waitress,
tired and sharp-worded, she hides
her bad brown tooth behind a wicked
smile, and flicks her ass

out of habit, to fend off the pass 　　　　　　　　　　5
that passes for affection.
She keeps her mind the way men
keep a knife—keen to strip the game
down to her size. She has a thin spine,
swallows her eggs cold, and tells lies. 　　　　　　　10
She slaps a wet rag at the truck drivers
if they should complain. She understands
the necessity for pain, turns away
the smaller tips, out of pride, and
keeps a flask under the counter. Once, 　　　　　　15
she shot a lover who misused her child.
Before she got out of jail, the courts had pounced
and given the child away. Like some isolated lake,
her flat blue eyes take care of their own stark
bottoms. Her hands are nervous, curled, ready 　　20
to scrape.
The common woman is as common
as a rattlesnake.

Study and Discussion Questions

1. Describe Ella's character. What kind of person is she? What outside forces have helped shape who she is?
2. Would you call Ella a survivor? What are the means she uses to survive, psychologically and spiritually as well as physically?
3. The last line of this poem is "The common woman is as common/as a rattlesnake." How is Ella like a rattlesnake? List words and phrases in the poem that contribute to the rattlesnake image.
4. Grahn said in her preface to *The Common Woman Poems,* of which "Ella, in a square apron, along Highway 80" is the second in the sequence, that one of her goals in writing these poems was to change the stereotypes of the work that women do. How has your sense of the person who brings your coffee changed now that you've read Grahn's poem?
5. Read the poem out loud. Locate and list some of the sound patterns in the poem. These may include end rhyme, internal rhyme, off rhyme, consonance, assonance. (See "How Poetry Works" for explanations of these terms.)

Suggestions for Writing

1. "Ella, in a square apron, along Highway 80" is the second in a sequence of seven poems Judy Grahn wrote about women and their lives. She called this sequence *The Common Woman Poems.* Freewrite for five or ten minutes on the word *common,* writing down all the meanings and associations of "common" that come to mind and any words you can think of that are related to the word "common." In what ways is Ella a "common woman"? How is Grahn redefining the concept of "common"?

2. Write a poetic portrait of a woman or man: (a) about their relation to their work and (b) using a controlling metaphor or image as Grahn does in "Ella . . ." with the rattlesnake image.

Critical Resources

1. Carruthers, Mary S. "The Re-Vision of the Muse: Adrienne Rich, Audre Lorde, Judy Grahn, Olga Broumas." *The Hudson Review,* Summer 1983, 36:2.
2. Felstiner, John. "Judy Grahn." *Women Writers of the West-Coast: Speaking of Their Lives and Careers.* Santa Barbara: Capra Press, 1983.
3. Ostriker, Alicia. *Stealing the Language: The Emergence of Women's Poetry in America.* Boston: Beacon Press, 1986.
4. Whitehead, Kim. *The Feminist Poetry Movement.* Jackson: University Press of Mississippi, 1996.

CARL SANDBURG (1878–1967)

Born to Swedish immigrants in Galesburg, Illinois, Sandburg's imagistic poetry celebrated the vibrant and continuous flow of Midwestern America. Sandburg left school at thirteen to work odd jobs and to travel (sometimes in freight trains), experiencing first hand working-class life. He served as a war correspondent during the Spanish-American War and afterward enrolled in college in Galesburg, but left to continue his travels. Although he never obtained his degree, it was here that Sandburg began to write poetry. In addition to his vagabond lifestyle, Sandburg's participation in socialist politics in Milwaukee (1908–1914) and his subsequent job as a private secretary for the town's socialist mayor helped shape his humanistic view of the world. In 1916 he published his first book of poetry, Chicago Poems, *establishing himself as an important figure in the literary scene of the Chicago Renaissance. Sandburg's rhythmic free verse is often compared to Walt Whitman's (whom he read in college), characterized by the colloquial patterns of everyday speech and a profound belief in the essential goodness of the common American. His* Complete Poems *was awarded the Pulitzer Prize for poetry in 1950. Other poetic works include* Cornhuskers *(1918),* Smoke and Steel *(1920), and* The People, Yes *(1936). Sandburg also won a Pulitzer for his six-volume biography of Abraham Lincoln, a work that took 15 years to complete. "Chicago" was first published in* Chicago Poems.

Chicago   (1916)

Hog Butcher for the World,
Tool Maker, Stacker of Wheat,

Player with Railroads and the Nation's Freight Handler;
    Stormy, husky, brawling,
    City of the Big Shoulders: 5
They tell me you are wicked and I believe them, for I have seen your
    painted women under the gas lamps luring the farm boys.
And they tell me you are crooked and I answer: Yes, it is true I have
    seen the gunman kill and go free to kill again.
And they tell me you are brutal and my reply is: On the faces of   10
    women and children I have seen the marks of wanton hunger.
And having answered so I turn once more to those who sneer at this
    my city, and I give them back the sneer and say to them:
Come and show me another city with lifted head singing so proud
    to be alive and coarse and strong and cunning.   15
Flinging magnetic curses amid the toil of piling job on job, here is a tall
    bold slugger set vivid against the little soft cities;
Fierce as a dog with tongue lapping for action, cunning as a savage
    pitted against the wilderness,
            Bareheaded,   20
            Shoveling,
            Wrecking,
            Planning,
            Building, breaking, rebuilding,
Under the smoke, dust all over his mouth, laughing with white teeth,   25
Under the terrible burden of destiny laughing as a young man laughs,
Laughing even as an ignorant fighter laughs who has never lost a battle,
Bragging and laughing that under his wrist is the pulse,
    and under his ribs the heart of the people,
            Laughing!   30
Laughing the stormy, husky, brawling laughter of Youth, half-naked,
    sweating, proud to be Hog Butcher, Tool Maker, Stacker of Wheat,
    Player with Railroads and Freight Handler to the Nation.

Study and Discussion Questions

1. What criticisms of the city does the speaker accept? What is it about the city that the speaker celebrates nonetheless?
2. How does the style of the poem match the speaker's feelings about Chicago?
3. What do the way the city is personified and the dismissal of "the soft little cities" tell us about the speaker's values?

Suggestions for Writing

1. What do the treatment of the city's problems and the way physical labor is portrayed in the poem suggest about the social class of the speaker?

2. Write a poem or an image-filled prose piece about the city or town you live in. Like "Chicago," it might be a poem of praise. If you don't like where you live, you might consider writing a parody of Sandburg's style.

Critical Resources

1. Callahan, North. *Carl Sandburg: His Life and Works.* University Park, PA: Pennsylvania State University Press, 1987.
2. Niven, Penelope. *Carl Sandburg: A Biography.* New York: Charles Scribner's & Sons, 1991.
3. Salwak, Dale. *Carl Sandburg: A Reference Guide.* Boston: G. K. Hall, 1988.
4. Van Wienen, Mark. "Taming the Socialist: Carl Sandburg's *Chicago Poems* and Its Critics." *American Literature* 63.1 (1991): 89–103.

JIMMY SANTIAGO BACA (b. 1952)

Of Chicano and Apache heritage, Jimmy Santiago Baca was born in Santa Fe, New Mexico, and spent much of his childhood in an orphanage, until he ran away at age eleven. He lived on the street and at twenty was convicted of drug possession and sentenced to a maximum security prison for 10 years, experiencing prison brutality (solitary confinement, shock treatments). During this time, Baca taught himself to read and began studying and writing poetry. Encouraged by another inmate, Baca sent a poem to Mother Jones *magazine and the poem was published. In 1979, Baca published his first collection of poems (while still in prison)* Immigrants in Our Own Land, *which took a hard look at prison life and the individual's courage to persevere in such conditions. In a mixed and varied verse, Baca's poems at times utilize long, proselike lines, then abruptly shift to short, staccato rhythms. His other poetry collections include* Swords of Darkness *(1981),* Black Mesa Poems *(1989),* In The Way of the Sun *(1997),* Set This Book on Fire *(1999),* C-Train (Dream Boy's Story), *and* Thirteen Mexicans *(2002); the memoir* A Place to Stand: The Making of a Poet *(2002); the essay collection* Working in the Dark: Reflections of a Poet of the Barrio *(1992); and his latest work, the short story collection* The Importance of a Piece of Paper *(2002). "So Mexicans are Taking Jobs From Americans" was published in* Immigrants in Our Own Land.

So Mexicans Are Taking Jobs From Americans   (1979)

O Yes? Do they come on horses
with rifles, and say,

Ese gringo,[1] gimmee your job?
And do you, gringo, take off your ring,
drop your wallet into a blanket   5
spread over the ground, and walk away?

I hear Mexicans are taking your jobs away.
Do they sneak into town at night,
and as you're walking home with a whore,
do they mug you, a knife at your throat,   10
saying, I want your job?

Even on TV, an asthmatic leader
crawls turtle heavy, leaning on an assistant,
and from a nest of wrinkles on his face,
a tongue paddles through flashing waves   15
of lightbulbs, of cameramen, rasping
"They're taking our jobs away."

Well, I've gone about trying to find them,
asking just where the hell are these fighters.

The rifles I hear sound in the night   20
are white farmers shooting blacks and browns
whose ribs I see jutting out
and starving children,
I see the poor marching for a little work,
I see small white farmers selling out   25
to clean-suited farmers living in New York,
who've never been on a farm,
don't know the look of a hoof or the smell
of a woman's body bending all day long in fields.

I see this, and I hear only a few people   30
got all the money in this world, the rest
count their pennies to buy bread and butter.

Below that cool green sea of money,
millions and millions of people fight to live,
search for pearls in the darkest depths   35
of their dreams, hold their breath for years
trying to cross poverty to just having something.

---

[1]Hey, whitey.

The children are dead already. We are killing them,
that is what America should be saying;
on TV, in the streets, in offices, should be saying,   40
    "We aren't giving the children a chance to live."

Mexicans are taking our jobs, they say instead.
What they really say is, let them die,
and the children too.

Study and Discussion Questions

1. To whom is the poem addressed; who is Baca's imagined reader? How
   does Baca's portrait of the reader and the reader's culture make you feel?
2. How would you characterize Baca's tone in this poem? Does the tone
   change as the poem goes on?
3. How, according to the poem, do Americans characterize Mexicans? What
   emotions motivate these characterizations?
4. What, instead, does Baca say is the true picture of these Mexicans?
5. What does the situation Baca writes about in this poem have to do with
   money and social class? Give examples from the poem of behavior motivated by people wanting to hold on to their money or property and of
   people wanting to make a living.
6. The starving children appear in the middle of the poem and their image
   dominates by the poem's end. How does this image change the argument
   and the tone of the poem? Do you find it effective?

Suggestions for Writing

1. Analyze the extended image in the five-line stanza that begins, "Below
   that cool green sea of money."
2. Take a position on immigration into the United States. You might look up
   statistics on immigration patterns over the past hundred years. Does immigration help, hurt, or have little effect on the quality of life and the
   availability of work for most Americans? Has the rise of the global economy over the past twenty or so years changed the immigration issue in
   any significant way? Baca's poem raises ethical as well as economic concerns; how in fact do we respond to the world's starving children?
3. Compare/contrast Baca's poem with two other selections in *Literature and
   Society* that depict the situation of immigrant and/or migrant workers and
   the response to them from people already in place: the chapter from John
   Steinbeck's *The Grapes of Wrath* and Woody Guthrie's song: "Plane
   Wreck at Los Gatos (Deportees)."

Critical Resources

1. Franklin, Bruce, ed. *Prison Writing in 20th Century America*. New York:
   Penguin, 1998.

2. Gish, Robert. *Beyond Bounds: Cross-Cultural Essays on Anglo, American Indian and Chicano Literature.* Albuquerque: University of New Mexico Press, 1996.
3. Keene, John. "Poetry is What We Speak to Each Other: An Interview with Jimmy Santiago Baca." *Callaloo* 17.1 (1994): 33–51.
4. *Palabra: A Sampling of Contemporary Latino Writers* (documentary). The Poetry Center and American Poetry Archives, 1993 (60 minutes).

JULIA ALVAREZ (b. 1950)

Julia Alvarez was born in the Dominican Republic and emigrated to the United States in 1960. In 1971 she received her B.A. in English from Middlebury College. She obtained her M.A. in Creative Writing from Syracuse University. After a decade of teaching and writing, Alvarez published her first collection of poetry, Homecoming *(1984). Although* Homecoming *is dominated by the layered sonnets of "33," other poems explore Alvarez's experience as a "hyphenated American." Through vivid lyricism, Alvarez's poetry attempts to reconcile the alienation and cultural duality that many immigrant Americans experience—especially that of Hispanic women who must negotiate two cultures and two languages. Her novel* How the Garcia Girls Lost Their Accents *(1991) has found its place in the growing canon of multiethnic literature. Other works include the poetry compilations* The Other Side/El Otro Lado *(1995),* Seven Trees *(1999),* The Woman I Kept to Myself *(2004); the novels* In the Time of Butterflies *(1994),* Yo! *(1997),* In the Name of Salome *(2001); and the essay collection* Something to Declare *(1998). She has also written several books for young adults. "Homecoming," the title poem from her first collection, juxtaposes issues of cultural duality and the tensions of social class.*

Homecoming (1984)

When my cousin Carmen married, the guards
at her father's *finca*[1] took the guests' bracelets
and wedding rings and put them in an armored truck
for safekeeping while wealthy, dark-skinned men,
their plump, white women and spoiled children   5
bathed in a river whose bottom had been cleaned
for the occasion. She was Uncle's only daughter,

---

[1] Country house.

and he wanted to show her husband's family,
a bewildered group of sunburnt Minnesotans,
that she was valued. He sat me at their table   10
to show off my English, and when he danced with me,
fondling my shoulder blades beneath my bridesmaid's gown
as if they were breasts, he found me skinny
but pretty at seventeen, and clever.
Come back from that cold place, Vermont, he said,   15
all this is yours! Over his shoulder
a dozen workmen hauled in blocks of ice
to keep the champagne lukewarm and stole
glances at the wedding cake, a dollhouse duplicate
of the family *rancho,* the shutters marzipan,   20
the cobbles almonds. A maiden aunt housekept,
touching up whipped cream roses with a syringe
of eggwhites, rescuing the groom when the heat
melted his chocolate shoes into the frosting.
On too much rum Uncle led me across the dance floor,   25
dusted with talcum for easy gliding, a smell
of babies underfoot. He twirled me often,
excited by my pleas of dizziness, teasing me,
saying that my merengue had lost its Caribbean.
Above us, Chinese lanterns strung between posts   30
came on and one snapped off and rose
into a purple postcard sky.
A grandmother cried: *The children all grow up too fast.*
The Minnesotans finally broke loose and danced a Charleston
and were pronounced good gringos with latino hearts.   35
The little sister, freckled with a week of beach,
her hair as blonde as movie stars, was asked
by maids if they could touch her hair or skin,
and she backed off, until it was explained to her,
they meant no harm. *This is all yours,*   40
Uncle whispered, pressing himself into my dress.
The workmen costumed in their workclothes danced
a workman's jig. The maids went by with trays
of wedding bells and matchbooks monogrammed
with Dick's and Carmen's names. It would be years   45
before I took the courses that would change my mind
in schools paid for by sugar from the fields around us,
years before I could begin to comprehend
how one does not see the maids when they pass by . . .
—It was too late, or early, to be wise—   50
The sun was coming up beyond the amber waves
of cane, the roosters crowed, the band struck up

Las Mañanitas,[2] a morning serenade. I had a vision
that I blamed on the champagne:
the fields around us were burning. At last   55
a yawning bride and groom got up and cut
the wedding cake, but everyone was full
of drink and eggs, roast pig, and rice and beans.
Except the maids and workmen,
sitting on stoops behind the sugar house,   60
ate with their fingers from their open palms
windows, shutters, walls, pillars, doors,
made from the cane they had cut in the fields.

Study and Discussion Questions

1. List what has been done to prepare for the wedding.
2. What do we know about the speaker of the poem?
3. Why does she repeat her uncle's words about all of this being hers?
4. Characterize the uncle.
5. What vision does the speaker of the poem have? Why is it significant?
6. Discuss the irony of the poem's last five lines, when the maids and workmen eat the wedding cake. Also, what famous quote does this scene
   bring to mind?
7. Discuss the line: "how one does not see the maids when they pass by . . ."

Suggestions for Writing

1. Who are the different groups of people who inhabit this poem? Describe
   each group.
2. Write a paragraph looking at this wedding from the perspective of one of
   the maids or workmen.

Critical Resources

1. Alvarez, Julia. "On Finding a Latino Voice." *The Writing Life: Writers on
   How They Think and Work.* New York: Public Affairs, 2003.
2. Henao, Eda. *The Colonial Subject's Search for Nation, Culture, and Identity in the Works of Julia Alvarez, Rosario Ferre and Ana Lydia Vega.*
   Lewiston: Edwin Mellen Press, 2003.
3. Varnes, Katherine. "Practicing for the Real Me: Form and Authenticity in
   the Poetry of Julia Alvarez." *Antipodas: Journal of Hispanic and Galician
   Studies* 10 (1998): 67–77.
4. *Women of Hope: Latinas Abriendo Camino: Twelve Ground Breaking
   Latina Women.* Princeton: Films for the Humanities, 1996 (29 minutes).

---

[2]Popular song sung early in the morning to celebrate a birthday, a saint's day, or a
wedding.

GWENDOLYN BROOKS (1917–2000)

Gwendolyn Brooks grew up in Chicago. She began writing poetry at an early age, publishing her first poem at age thirteen. After receiving her BA in English from Wilson Junior College in 1936, Brooks worked for the NAACP Youth Council. During this time, Brooks was greatly influenced by poet Langston Hughes and other writers from the Harlem Renaissance who encouraged her to study the modernist poetry of Eliot and Pound. As is evident in much of her early work, Brooks combines the technical skill and form of modernist poetry with the imagery and rhythms of African American life and language. In 1950, she became the first African American to win the Pulitzer Prize for her poetry collection Annie Allen *(1950). In 1967, Brook's visit to Fisk University was a transformative moment for her as a poet and African American. Impressed by the energy of young black poets like Leroi Jones, Brooks' penchant for formal structures (she was a master of the sonnet) and themes loosened. While her devotion to the African American experience remained, her poetry increasingly became more political, more contentious, as she became aware of her role as a black feminist in the Civil Rights Movement. In 1985, she was appointed poetry consultant to the Library of Congress (Poet Laureate). She has written several poetry collections, including* A Street in Bronzeville *(1945),* Annie Allen *(1950),* The Bean Eaters *(1960),* In the Mecca *(1968),* Beckonings *(1975),* Black Love *(1982), and* In Montgomery *(2001, posthumously); the novel* Maud Martha *(1953); and the autobiography* Report from Part One *(1972). "Bronzeville Woman in a Red Hat" appeared in Brooks's collection* The Bean Eaters.*

Bronzeville[1] *Woman in a Red Hat*   (1960)

hires out to Mrs. Miles

I

They had never had one in the house before.
      The strangeness of it all. Like unleashing
A lion, really. Poised
To pounce. A puma. A panther. A black
Bear.   5
There it stood in the door,
Under a red hat that was rash, but refreshing—
In a tasteless way, of course—across the dull dare,
The semi-assault of that extraordinary blackness.
The slackness   10

---

[1] African American neighborhood in Chicago.

Of that light pink mouth told little. The eyes told of heavy care . . .
But that was neither here nor there,
And nothing to a wage-paying mistress as should
Be getting her due whether life had been good
For her slave, or bad.   15
There it stood
in the door. They had never had
One in the house before.

But the Irishwoman had left!
A message had come.   20
Something about a murder at home.
A daughter's husband—"berserk," that was the phrase:
The dear man had "gone berserk"
And short work—
With a hammer—had been made   25
Of this daughter and her nights and days.
The Irishwoman (underpaid,
Mrs. Miles remembered with smiles),
Who was a perfect jewel, a red-faced trump,
A good old sort, a baker   30
Of rum cake, a maker
Of Mustard, would never return.
Mrs. Miles had begged the bewitched woman
To finish, at least, the biscuit blending,
To tarry till the curry was done,   35
To show some concern
For the burning soup, to attend to the tending
Of the tossed salad. "Inhuman,"
Pasty Houlihan had called Mrs. Miles.
"Inhuman." And "a fool."   40
And "a cool
One."

The Alert Agency had leafed through its files—
On short notice could offer
Only this dusky duffer   45
That now made its way to her kitchen and sat on her kitchen stool.

II

Her creamy child kissed by the black maid! square on the mouth!
World yelled, world writhed, world turned to light and rolled
Into her kitchen, nearly knocked her down.

Quotations, of course, from baby books were great   50
Ready armor; (but her animal distress
Wore, too and under, a subtler metal dress,
Inheritance of approximately hate).
Say baby shrieked to see his finger bleed,
Wished human humoring—there was a kind   55
Of unintimate love, a love more of the mind
To order the nebulousness of that need.
—This was the way to put it, this the relief.
This sprayed a honey upon marvelous grime.
This told it possible to postpone the reef.   60
Fashioned a huggable darling out of crime.
Made monster personable in personal sight
By cracking mirrors down the personal night.

Disgust crawled through her as she chased the theme.
She, quite supposing purity despoiled,   65
Committed to sourness, disordered, soiled,
Went in to pry the ordure from the cream.
Cooing, "Come." (Come out of the cannibal wilderness,
Dirt, dark, into the sun and bloomful air.
Return to freshness of your right world, wear   70
Sweetness again. Be done with beast, duress.)

Child with continuing cling issued his No in final fire,
                Kissed back the colored maid,
                Not wise enough to freeze or be afraid.
                Conscious of kindness, easy creature bond.   75
                Love had been handy and rapid to respond.

Heat at the hairline, heat between the bowels,
Examining seeming coarse unnatural scene,
She saw all things except herself serene:
Child, big black woman, pretty kitchen towels.   80

Study and Discussion Questions

1. Who is the speaker of this poem?
2. How is the Bronzeville woman described in part I? What is she compared to?
3. Why does Mrs. Miles refer to her as "it"?
4. What does the stanza about her previous domestic worker, the Irish woman, tell us about Mrs. Miles?
5. What is the crisis described in part II? Why is it a crisis for Mrs. Miles?

Suggestions for Writing

1. Gwendolyn Brooks, who is black, has created a white upper-middle-class persona, Mrs. Miles, through whose eyes we see the black woman who comes to work for her. How does this situation create intentional irony in the poem?
2. Are there any places where human sympathy and identification begin to break through the wall of Mrs. Miles's racism? What does she do when that happens?
3. What does Mrs. Miles's racism consist of? Give examples.

Critical Resources

1. Mootry, Maria and Gary Smith, eds. *A Life Distilled: Gwendolyn Brooks, Her Poetry and Fiction.* Urbana: University of Illinois Press, 1987.
2. Smith, Gary. "Gwendolyn Brooks's A Street in Bronzeville, the Harlem Renaissance and the Mythologies of Black Women." *Melus* 10.3 (1983): 33–46.
3. Upton, Lee. "Language in a Red Hat." *Field: Contemporary Poetry and Poetics* 61 (1999): 48–54.

❁ ❁ ❁

LANGSTON HUGHES (1902–1967)

Langston Hughes was born in Joplin, Missouri and raised primarily by his maternal grandmother in Lawrence, Kansas. He entered Columbia University in 1920, but left a year later, working odd jobs and traveling throughout Europe and Africa. During this time Hughes would publish his first poems and novels and establish himself as a central figure in the literary and artistic movement known as the Harlem Renaissance. Influenced by such writers as W.E.B. Dubois and the poet Walt Whitman, Hughes' work often expresses subtle political meaning in a style influenced by the rhythms of African American music (the blues) and language. Intentionally eschewing traditional poetic form, his poetry aspired to reach ordinary people, both black and white, by writing in an accessible way that spoke to and acknowledged their experiences. For this he became know as a "the bard of Harlem." His works include the poetry collections The Weary Blues *(1926),* Fine Clothes to the Jew *(1927),* The Dream Keeper and Other Poems *(1932),* Freedom's Plow *(1943),* Fields of Wonder *(1947),* Montage of a Dream Deferred *(1951),* Ask Your Mama: Twelve Moods for Jazz *(1961) and* The Panther and the Lash *(1967); the novels* Not Without Laughter *(1930) and* Tambourines of Glory *(1958); the short story collections* The Ways of White Folks *(1934),* Simple Speaks His Mind *(1950),* Simple Takes a Wife *(1953) and* Something in Common and Other Stories *(1963); and the autobiography* I Wonder as I Wander *(1956). Hughes also published essays and children's books. "Ballad of the Landlord" comes from his book-length sequence* Montage of a Dream Deferred, *set in post World War II Harlem.*

Ballad of the Landlord   (1951)

Landlord, landlord,
My roof has sprung a leak.
Don't you 'member I told you about it
Way last week?

Landlord, landlord,   5
These steps is broken down.
When you come up yourself
It's a wonder you don't fall down.

Ten Bucks you say I owe you?
Ten Bucks you say is due?   10
Well, that's Ten Bucks more'n I'll pay you
Till you fix this house up new.

What? You gonna get eviction orders?
You gonna cut off my heat?
You gonna take my furniture and   15
Throw it in the street?

Um-huh! You talking high and mighty.
Talk on—till you get through.
You ain't gonna be able to say a word
If I land my fist on you.   20

Police! Police!
Come and get this man!
He's trying to ruin the government
And overturn the land!

Copper's whistle!   25
Patrol bell!
Arrest.

Precinct Station.
Iron cell.
Headlines in press: 30

MAN THREATENS LANDLORD

TENANT HELD NO BAIL

. . .

JUDGE GIVES NEGRO 90 DAYS IN COUNTY JAIL

Study and Discussion Questions

1. Who is speaking in the first five stanzas? Who is speaking in stanza six?
2. Describe what is happening in the last 10 lines of the poem.
3. Why does Hughes call this poem a "ballad"? Look up the word, consider its form and themes, and discuss how this might be a ballad.
4. What happens in the opening five stanzas? What we hear is a monologue, yet we get the sense of a drama. How does Hughes accomplish this?
5. Make an outline of the events described in the poem from the opening stanza to the final line. How do events escalate?
6. What do race and social class have to do with the dynamics and the outcome of this ballad/story?

Suggestions for Writing

1. Compare/contrast "Ballad of the Landlord" with one of the other Langston Hughes poems included in *Literature and Society.*
2. Write a ballad poem of your own about trying to ask for something reasonable from someone higher in the power structure than yourself (a teacher, a boss, a parent, a landlord) and what might happen.

Critical Resources

1. Alston, Francis. "Harlem: A Major Motif in the Poetry of Langston Hughes from the 1920's to the 1950's." *MAWA Review* 10.2 (1995): 77–85.
2. Gates, Henry Louis and K. A. Appiah, eds. *Langston Hughes: Critical Perspectives Past and Present.* New York: Amistad, 1993.
3. Hughes, Langston. "The Negro Artist and the Racial Mountain," in *Langston Hughes,* James C. Hall, ed. New York: Harcourt Brace, 1998.
4. Jarroway, David R. "Montage of an Otherness Deferred: Dreaming Subjectivity in Langston Hughes." *American Literature* 68.4 (December 1996): 819–41.
5. Tracy, Steven C. *A Historical Guide to Langston Hughes.* New York: Oxford University Press, 2004.

❀ ❀ ❀

LAUREEN MAR (b. 1953)

Laureen Mar was born and raised in Seattle, Washington. Whether poetry or prose, Mar's work, often set in her native Seattle, chronicles various aspects of Asian-American life. In addition to her writing, Mar has been a teacher of literature and writing at Washington State University and at Pacific Lutheran University in Tacoma, Washington. Her work has been anthologized in various publications, including a selection of her prose entitled "Resistance" in Charlie Chan Is Dead: An Anthology of Contemporary Asian American Fiction *(1993). Her poem "My Mother Who Came From China, Where She Never Saw Snow" stitches images together in the same way the speaker's mother deftly stitches coat sleeves.*

My Mother, Who Came From China, Where She Never Saw Snow   (1977)

In the huge, rectangular room, the ceiling
a machinery of pipes and fluorescent lights,
ten rows of women hunch over machines,
their knees pressing against pedals
and hands pushing the shiny fabric thick as tongues   5
through metal and thread.
My mother bends her head to one of these machines.
Her hair is coarse and wiry, black as burnt scrub.
She wears glasses to shield her intense eyes.
A cone of orange thread spins. Around her,   10
talk flutters harshly in Toisan wah.[1]
Chemical stings. She pushes cloth
through a pounding needle, under, around, and out,
breaks thread with a snap against fingerbone, tooth.
Sleeve after sleeve, sleeve.   15
It is easy. The same piece.
For eight or nine hours, sixteen bundles maybe,
250 sleeves to ski coats, all the same.
It is easy, only once she's run the needle
through her hand. She earns money   20
by each piece, on a good day,
thirty dollars. Twenty-four years.
It is frightening how fast she works.
She and the women who were taught sewing
terms in English as Second Language.   25
Dull thunder passes through their fingers.

----

[1]Chinese dialect.

Study and Discussion Questions

1. Consider the title of the poem, which is unusually long and packed with information. Why does Mar want us to know all this before we read the poem? Why in particular do you think she mentions "snow" in the title?
2. This poem has a lot of literal imagery, realistic description, in it. It is startling then when Mar shifts into figurative imagery, for example "shiny fabric thick as tongues." Find some other examples of metaphor or simile. What is Mar doing with these moves into the realm of imagination?
3. The reference to the danger of the work her mother does is minimal, slipped in almost as an afterthought. Why does Mar minimize this? Why does she mention it at all?
4. Near the end of the poem, Mar writes: "She and the women who were taught sewing/terms in English as Second Language." What information does this give you about the situation of working class women who emigrate from China?
5. What portrait of the speaker's mother do you come away with? List several words in the poem that characterize her.
6. We get a vivid description in this poem of textile factory (perhaps sweatshop) work. List some characteristics of this work.
7. Discuss the irony of the particular product the women in the poem are making.

Suggestions for Writing

1. Despite being illegal, sweatshops still exist in the United States and, whether legal or not, exist in many other countries where clothes we wear are made. Look at the labels in several items of clothing you own and make a list of those. Do some research to find out under what conditions the clothes you wear are made and write down your findings.
2. Look through the selections in "Money and Work" for other poems about a type of work. Compare/contrast one or two of those poems with "My Mother, Who Came From China, Where She Never Saw Snow."

Critical Resources

1. Hagedorn, Jessica, ed. *Charlie Chan Is Dead: An Anthology of Contemporary Asian American Fiction.* New York: Penguin, 1993.
2. ———. *Charlie Chan Is Dead 2: An Anthology of Contemporary Asian American Fiction.* New York: Penguin, 2004.
3. Mar, Laureen. "Leaping Beyond the Woman Warrior: The Myths and Realities of a Culture." Paper presented at the MLA Convention, 1979.

PHILIP LEVINE (b. 1928)

Philip Levine was born the son of Russian-Jewish immigrants in Detroit, Michigan, and grew up in the industrial world of the auto factories. From the time he was 14 and on through his twenties, Levine worked on the assembly lines as he made his way through college. It was during this time that he began reading poetry and aspired to give a poetic voice to the blue-collar experience. In 1957, he received his M.F.A. from the University of Iowa and began a teaching career. Six years later he published his first volume of poetry On the Edge *and has since published over 20 collections in 4 decades. Levine has forged his own style of freeverse poetry—a sometimes imaged, sometimes narrative poetry that attempts to tell the stories of working people and to render this experience in a vernacular that is both accessible and vivid. He was awarded the Pulitzer Prize for* The Simple Truth *in 1994. Other notable poetry collections include* Not This Pig *(1968),* 5 Detroits *(1970),* They Feed They Lion *(1972),* 7 Years From Somewhere *(1979),* Sweet Will *(1985),* A Walk With Tom Jefferson *(1988),* What Work Is *(1991, winner National Book Award),* Mercy *(2001), and his latest collection* Breath *(2004). He has also written a memoir,* The Bread of Time *(2001), and a nonfiction collection,* So Ask: Essays, Conversations, and Interviews *(2002).*

You Can Have It (1979)

My brother comes home from work
and climbs the stairs to our room.
I can hear the bed groan and his shoes drop
one by one. You can have it, he says.

The moonlight streams in the window 5
and his unshaven face is whitened
like the face of the moon. He will sleep
long after noon and waken to find me gone.

Thirty years will pass before I remember
that moment when suddenly I knew each man 10
has one brother who dies when he sleeps
and sleeps when he rises to face this life,

and that together they are only one man
sharing a heart that always labors, hands
yellowed and cracked, a mouth that gasps 15
for breath and asks, Am I gonna make it?

All night at the ice plant he had fed
the chute its silvery blocks, and then I

stacked cases of orange soda for the children
of Kentucky, one gray boxcar at a time   20

with always two more waiting. We were twenty
for such a short time and always in
the wrong clothes, crusted with dirt
and sweat. I think now we were never twenty.

In 1948 in the city of Detroit, founded   25
by de la Mothe Cadillac for the distant purposes
of Henry Ford, no one wakened or died,
no one walked the streets or stoked a furnace,

for there was no such year, and now
that year has fallen off all the old newspapers,   30
calendars, doctors' appointments, bonds,
wedding certificates, drivers licenses.

The city slept. The snow turned to ice.
The ice to standing pools or rivers
racing in the gutters. Then bright grass rose   35
between the thousands of cracked squares,

and that grass died. I give you back 1948.
I give you all the years from then
to the coming one. Give me back the moon
with its frail light falling across a face.   40

Give me back my young brother, hard
and furious, with wide shoulders and a curse
for God and burning eyes that look upon
all creation and say, You can have it.

Study and Discussion Questions

1. "You Can Have It" begins with a portrait of the speaker's brother. What
   do we learn about the brother in the first half of the poem?
2. Discuss the images of moon and water in the poem.
3. What is the work situation of the two brothers? How is that important to
   the tension between duality and identity in the poem? And, by the way,
   Philip Levine actually has a twin brother.
4. Discuss stanzas three and four where the poem metamorphoses from biography into philosophy. What is Levine saying here? And what is the
   effect of his using a working-class situation as the basis of this philosophical statement?
5. Why 1948? Why does Levine say, in stanza eight, that "there was no such
   year as 1948"?

6. Discuss Levine's images in stanzas seven to the end of the poem.
7. The poem ends as it began (in the title) with the words "You can have it." What does this sentence mean to you by the time you've reached the end of the poem?
8. What is Levine's attitude toward memory in this poem?
9. How does Levine use sound in "You Can Have It"? Look at any one stanza closely, read it aloud, and listen for sound patterns.

Suggestions for Writing

1. Choose a passage from the poem that you especially liked and discuss the images and word choices. Look up any words that you don't know, or that seem important, to check for fuller definitions.
2. Write a poem or a prose paragraph vividly capturing a memory at least 10 years in your past.
3. Compare "You Can Have It" with "They Feed They Lion" and/or "Among Children," other Philip Levine poems in *Literature and Society*.

Critical Resources

1. Buckley, Christopher, ed. *On the Poetry of Philip Levine: Stranger to Nothing.* Ann Arbor: University of Michigan Press, 1991.
2. Levine, Philip. *The Bread of Time: Toward an Autobiography.* Ann Arbor: University of Michigan Press, 2001.
3. Levine, Philip. *So Ask: Essays, Conversations, and Interviews.* Ann Arbor: University of Michigan Press, 2002.
4. Hirsch, Edward. "The Visionary Poetics of Philip Levine and Charles Wright." *The Columbia History of American Poetry.* Ed. Jay Parini, New York: Columbia Press, 1993.
5. Jacobsen, Sally. "Philip Levine on Teaching Poetry: An Interview." *Life and The Poem.* Ed. Terrence Des Pres. Chicago: University of Illinois, 1992.

MARY FELL (b. 1947)

Mary Fell was born to working-class parents in Worcester, Massachusetts. In 1964, she enrolled at Worcester State College as an English major. It is here that Fell began writing poetry amidst the volatile political movements of the 1960s. After graduating, Fell did social work for the City of Worcester until returning to school to obtain her M.F.A. at the University of Massachusetts Amherst in 1981. She currently teaches at Indiana University. Much of Fell's work centers on how our lives relate to the human experiences of others. Fell's poetry endeavors to present working-class experience in very real, unsentimental ways through earthy, precise imagery. Her poetry collections include Triangle Fire *(1983),* The Persistence of

Memory *(1984), and* Worcester in Sunlight and Darkness *(1991). "Triangle Fire" is a sequence of poems that revisit the tragic 1911 factory fire that took the lives of 146 immigrant women workers.*

The Triangle Fire[1] (1983)

1. Havdallah[2]

This is the great divide
by which God split
the world:
on the Sabbath side
he granted rest,
eternal toiling
on the workday side.

But even one
revolution of the world
is an empty promise   10
where bosses
where bills to pay
respect no heavenly bargains.
Until each day is ours

let us pour   15
darkness in a dish
and set it on fire,
bless those who labor
as we pray, praise God
his holy name,   20
strike for the rest.

2. Among the Dead

First a lace of smoke
decorated the air of the workroom,
the far wall unfolded
into fire. The elevator shaft   25

---

[1]On March 25, 1911, a fire started at the Triangle Shirtwaist Company, on the ninth floor of the Asch building. Hundreds of women workers, mostly Italian and Russian Jewish immigrants, had been locked in to keep out union organizers and therefore could not escape. Nearly one hundred fifty women, some as young as fourteen, died in the fire.
[2]Ceremony marking the end of the Jewish Sabbath.

spun out flames like a bobbin,
the last car sank.
I leaped for the cable,
my only chance. Woven steel
burned my hands as I wound   30
to the bottom.

I opened my eyes. I was lying
in the street. Water and blood
washed the cobbles, the sky
rained ash. A pair of shoes   35
lay beside me, in them
two blistered feet.
I saw the weave in the fabric
of a girl's good coat,
the wilted nosegay pinned to her collar.   40
Not flowers, what I breathed then,
awake among the dead.

3. Asch Building

In a window,
lovers embrace
haloed by light.
He kisses her, holds her
gently, lets her go
nine stories to the street.

Even the small ones
put on weight
as they fall:
eleven thousand pounds split
the fireman's net,
implode the deadlights

on the Greene Street side,   55
until the basement catches them
and holds. Here
two faceless ones are found
folded neatly over the steam pipes
like dropped rags.   60

I like the one
on that smoky ledge, taking stock
in the sky's deliberate mirror.

She gives her hat
to wind, noting its style,
spills her week's pay

from its envelope, a joke
on those who pretend
heaven provides, and chooses
where there is no choice
to marry air, to make
a disposition of her life.

4. Personal Effects

One lady's
handbag, containing
rosary beads, elevated
railroad ticket, small pin
with picture, pocket knife,
one small purse containing
$1.68 in cash,
handkerchiefs,
a small mirror, a pair of gloves,
two thimbles, a Spanish
comb, one yellow metal ring,
five keys, one
fancy glove button,
one lady's handbag containing
one gent's watch case
number of movement 6418593
and a $1 bill,
one half dozen postal cards,
a buttonhook, a man's photo,
a man's garter,
a razor strap,
one portion of limb and hair
of human being.

5. Industrialist's Dream

This one's
dependable won't
fall apart
under pressure doesn't
lie down on the job
doesn't leave early

come late
won't join unions
strike
ask for a raise   105
unlike one hundred
forty six
others I could name
who couldn't
take the heat this one's   110
still at her machine
and doubtless
of spotless moral
character you
can tell by the bones   115
pure white
this one
does what she's told
and you don't hear
her complaining.   120

6. The Witness

Woman, I might have watched you
sashay down Washington Street
some warm spring evening
when work let out,
your one thin dress   125
finally right for the weather,
an ankle pretty
as any flower's stem, full
breasts the moon's envy, eyes bold
or modest as you passed me by.   130

I might have thought, as heat
climbed from the pavement,
what soft work you'd make
for a man like me:
even the time clock, thief of hours,   135
kinder, and the long day
passing in a dream.
Cradled in that dream
I might have slept
forever, but today's nightmare   140
vision woke me:

your arms aflame, wings
of fire, and you a falling star,
a terrible lump of coal
in the burning street.   145
No dream, your hair of smoke,
your blackened face.
No dream the fist I make,
taking your hand
of ashes in my own.   150

7. Cortege

A cold rain comforts the sky.
Everything ash-colored under clouds.
I take my place in the crowd,

move without will as the procession moves,
a gray wave breaking against the street.   155
Up ahead, one hundred and forty seven

coffins float, wreckage of lives. I follow
the box without a name. In it
whose hand encloses whose heart? Whose mouth

presses the air toward a scream?   160
She is no one, the one I claim
as sister. When the familiar is tagged

and taken away, she remains.
I do not mourn her. I mourn no one.
I do not praise her. No one   165

is left to praise. Seventy years after
her death, I walk in March rain behind her.
She travels before me into the dark.

Study and Discussion Questions

1. "The Triangle Fire" is a poetic sequence of seven connected poems. Let's
   look first at the poems one by one. To understand the first poem, "Havdallah," you need to know that havdallah is from a word meaning "to separate." It is the ritual at the end of the Jewish Sabbath to mark the
   separation of the Sabbath from the days of work. A special candle, made
   out of three separate candles, is lighted at the moment you see three stars
   in the sky on Saturday evening. How does understanding this ritual help
   you decode the imagery of this opening poem in the sequence?

2. Given the meaning of "havdallah," how does the poem become ironic in stanza two?

3. In stanza three of "Havdallah," how does the speaker of the poem suggest how the secular and the sacred in our lives are separate but intertwined?

4. Read the footnote and any other research you've done about the Triangle Shirtwaist Company Fire in 1911. Poem 2, "Among the Dead," takes us into that event. Who is speaking here? What happens in this poem?

5. Poem 3, "Asch Building," is based on eyewitness accounts of workers trapped on the eighth and ninth floors who had to make the decision to jump or burn. (Think for a moment about having to make that decision.) List the separate stories in "Asch Building" about some of these people.

6. Discuss the irony in the story told in the last two stanzas of "Asch Building." How does it connect to the irony in "Havdallah"?

7. Who is speaking in "Asch Building"?

8. Poem 4, "Personal Effects," is in a new style. Describe how it differs from the first three poems. How is this style effective at this point in the poem?

9. Who is speaking in poem 5, "Industrialist's Dream"? What point of view is being represented here? Discuss the irony in the extended visual image of "this one."

10. Poem 6, "The Witness," shifts point of view again. Who is speaking here? Who is he speaking to?

11. Does the witness in poem 6 develop or change during the poem? What is his attitude toward the woman at the beginning? How does it change? Discuss the last three lines of the poem.

12. In the seventh and final poem of the sequence, "Cortege," the point of view shifts again. (Look up *cortege* in a dictionary.) Look at the last three lines of the poem. Who do you think is speaking here?

13. "She is no one, the one I claim/as sister." What is the speaker's relation to this woman and all the rest who died that day? The Triangle Fire is from Mary Fell's collection titled *The Persistence of Memory*. What does memory have to do with this poem?

Suggestions for Writing

1. Write a paper about how the seven poems in this poetic sequence work off of each other and work together. What does each of the poems provide for us as readers? How do our understanding of and feelings about this workers' tragedy develop through the seven poems? What is Fell doing through the style and structure of her sequence to make this happen?

2. Research the Triangle Shirtwaist Company Fire of March 25, 1911: the fire itself, the events leading up to it, and the political and social aftermath. Make a poster, a visual and graphic representation, that illuminates the event and provides context for Mary Fell's poetic sequence.

3. How is Fell's "The Triangle Fire" a poem of witness? Look up the several meanings of "witness" in the dictionary. In addition, what does the word "witness" suggest to you? Why might contemporary working-class poets write some 70 years later about an historical event like this one?

4. Lest you think that what happened to the workers at the Triangle Shirtwaist Company in 1911 could not happen today, do some research on cur-

rent conditions in sweatshops and factories around the world and in the United States—places where a lot of the clothes we wear and the toys we played with as children or buy for our own children are made.

Critical Resources

1. Between a Rock and a Hard Place: A History of American Sweatshops, 1820–present Smithsonian Institute. National Museum of American History, virtual exhibit. http://Americanhistory.si.edu/sweatshops
2. The Catherwood Library, Cornell University. *The Triangle Factory Fire.* 1998–2003. May 2, 2005. <http://www.ilr.cornell.edu/trianglefire/>
3. United Students Against Swetshops (USAS). Founded 1998, international student movement. www.usasnet.org
4. Worcester Polytechnical Institute. *Worcester Area Writers—Mary Fell.* May 2, 2005 <http://www.wpi.edu/Academics/Library/Archives/WAuthors/fell/>
5. Zandy, Janet. "Fire Poetry: On the Triangle Shirtwaist Company Fire of March 25, 1911." *College Literature* 24.3 (1997): 33–54.

Additional Poems

WILLIAM BLAKE (1757–1827)

The Chimney Sweeper (1789)

When my mother died I was very young,
And my father sold me while yet my tongue,
Could scarcely cry weep weep weep weep.
So your chimneys I sweep & in soot I sleep.

Theres little Tom Dacre, who cried when his head   5
That curl'd like a lambs back, was shav'd, so I said.
Hush Tom never mind it, for when your head's bare,
You know that the soot cannot spoil your white hair.

And so he was quiet, & that very night,
As Tom was a sleeping he had such a sight,   10
That thousands of sweepers Dick, Joe Ned & Jack
Were all of them lock'd up in coffins of black

And by came an Angel who had a bright key,
And he open'd the coffins & set them all free.

Then down a green plain leaping laughing they run   15
And wash in a river and shine in the Sun.

Then naked & white, all their bags left behind,
They rise upon clouds, and sport in the wind.
And the Angel told Tom if he'd be a good boy,
He'd have God for his father & never want joy.   20

And so Tom awoke and we rose in the dark
And got with our bags & our brushes to work.
Tho' the morning was cold, Tom was happy & warm,
So if all do their duty, they need not fear harm.

WILLIAM WORDSWORTH (1770–1850)

The World Is Too Much With Us   (1807)

The world is too much with us; late and soon,
Getting and spending, we lay waste our powers:
Little we see in Nature that is ours;
We have given our hearts away, a sordid boon!
This Sea that bares her bosom to the moon;   5
The winds that will be howling at all hours,
And are up-gathered now like sleeping flowers;
For this, for everything, we are out of tune;
It moves us not—Great God! I'd rather be
A Pagan suckled in a creed outworn;   10
So might I, standing on this pleasant lea,
Have glimpses that would make me less forlorn;
Have sight of Proteus rising from the sea;
Or hear old Triton blow his wreathèd horn.

ANONYMOUS

SONG: *We raise de wheat*[1]

We raise de wheat,
Dey gib us de corn;

---

[1]Printed in *My Bondage and My Freedom* (1855), by Frederick Douglass.

We bake de bread,
Dey gib us de cruss;
We sif de meal,   5
Dey gib us de huss;
We peal de meat,
Dey gib us de skin,
And dat's de way
Dey takes us in.   10
We skim de pot,
Dey gib us the liquor,
And say dat's good enough for nigger.

    Walk over! walk over!
    Tom butter and de fat;   15
    Poor nigger you can't get over dat;
        Walk over!

THOMAS HARDY (1840–1928)

The Ruined Maid   (1866)

'O 'Melia, my dear, this does everything crown!
Who could have supposed I should meet you in Town?
And whence such fair garments, such prosperi-ty?'—
'O didn't you know I'd been ruined?' said she.

—'You left us in tatters, without shoes or socks,   5
Tired of digging potatoes, and spudding up docks;[1]
And now you've gay bracelets and bright feathers three!'—
'Yes: that's how we dress when we're ruined,' said she.

—'At home in the barton[2] you said "thee" and "thou",
And "thik oon", and "theäs oon", and "t'other"; but now   10
Your talking quite fits 'ee for high compa-ny!'—
'A polish is gained with one's ruin,' said she.

—'Your hands were like paws then, your face blue and bleak,
But now I'm bewitched by your delicate cheek,
And your little gloves fit as on any la-dy!'—   15
'We never do work when we're ruined,' said she.

---

[1]Digging weeds.
[2]Farm yard.

—'You used to call home-life a hag-ridden dream,
And you'd sigh, and you'd sock[3]; but at present you seem
To know not of megrims[4] or melancho-ly!'—   20
'True. One's pretty lively when ruined,' said she.

—'I wish I had feathers, a fine sweeping gown,
And a delicate face, and could strut about Town!'—
'My dear—a raw country girl, such as you be,
Cannot quite expect that. You ain't ruined,' said she.

MATTHEW ARNOLD (1822–1888)

West London   (1867)

Crouch'd on the pavement, close by Belgrave Square,
A tramp I saw, ill, moody, and tongue-tied.
A babe was in her arms, and at her side
A girl; their clothes were rags, their feet were bare.

Some labouring men, whose work lay somewhere there,   5
Pass'd opposite; she touch'd her girl, who hied
Across, and begg'd, and came back satisfied.
The rich she had let pass with frozen stare.

Thought I: 'Above her state this spirit towers;
She will not ask of aliens, but of friends,   10
Of sharers in a common human fate.

'She turns from the cold succour, which attends
The unknown little from the unknowing great,
And points us to a better time than ours.'

WILLIAM CARLOS WILLIAMS (1883–1963)

The Young Housewife   (1917)

At ten A.M. the young housewife
moves about in negligee behind

---

[3]Sigh.
[4]Severe headaches.

the wooden walls of her husband's house.
I pass solitary in my car.

Then again she comes to the curb 5
to call the ice-man, fish-man, and stands
shy, uncorseted, tucking in
stray ends of hair, and I compare her
to a fallen leaf.

The noiseless wheels of my car 10
rush with a crackling sound over
dried leaves as I bow and pass smiling.

SARAH CLEGHORN (1876–1959)

The golf links lie so near the mill (1917)

The golf links lie so near the mill
   That almost every day
The laboring children can look out
   And see the men at play.

FENTON JOHNSON (1888–1958)

Tired (1922)

I am tired of work; I am tired of building up somebody
    else's civilization.
Let us take a rest, M'Lissy Jane.
I will go down to the Last Chance Saloon, drink a gallon
    or two of gin, shoot a game or two of dice and 5
    sleep the rest of the night on one of Mike's barrels.
You will let the old shanty go to rot, the white people's
    clothes turn to dust, and the Calvary Baptist Church
    sink to the bottomless pit.
You will spend your days forgetting you married me and 10
    your nights hunting the warm gin Mike serves the
    ladies in the rear of the Last Chance Saloon.
Throw the children into the river; civilization has given
    us too many. It is better to die than it is to grow up
    and find out that you are colored.

15

Pluck the stars out of the heavens. The stars mark our
    destiny. The stars marked my destiny.
I am tired of civilization.

COUNTEE CULLEN (1903–1946)

For a Lady I Know (1925)

She even thinks that up in heaven
    Her class lies late and snores,
While poor black cherubs rise at seven
    To celestial chores.

ANONYMOUS

Transcribed by Will Geer from singing by a West Virginian woman who said she had
composed the lyrics.

SONG: *Let Them Wear Their Watches Fine* (ca. 1925)

I lived in a town away down south
By the name of Buffalo;
And worked in the mill with the rest of the trash
As we're often called, you know.

You factory folks who sing this rime,   5
Will surely understand
The reason why I love you so
Is I'm a factory hand.

While standing here between my looms
You know I lose no time   10
To keep my shuttles in a whiz
And write this little rime.

We rise up early in the morn
And work all day real hard;
To buy our little meat and bread   15
And sugar, tea, and lard.

We work from week end to week end
And never lose a day;
And when that awful payday comes
We draw our little pay.   20

We then go home on payday night
And sit down in a chair;
The merchant raps upon the door—
He's come to get his share.

When all our little debts are paid   25
And nothing left behind,
We turn our pocket wrong side out
But not a cent can we find.

We rise up early in the morn
And toil from soon to late;   30
We have no time to primp or fix
And dress right up to date.

Our children they grow up unlearned
No time to go to school;
Almost before they've learned to walk   35
They learn to spin or spool.

The boss man jerks them round and round
And whistles very keen;
I'll tell you what, the factory kids
Are really treated mean.   40

The folks in town who dress so fine
And spend their money free
Will hardly look at a factory hand
Who dresses like you and me.

As we go walking down the street   45
All wrapped in lint and strings,
They call us fools and factory trash
And other low-down things.

Well, let them wear their watches fine,
Their rings and pearly strings;   50
When the day of judgment comes
We'll make them shed their pretty things.

EASY PAPA JOHNSON (ROOSEVELT SYKES) (1906–1983)

SONG: *Cotton Seed Blues* (1930)

When the sun goes down, mama, lord, the whole round world turns red
When the sun goes down, mama, lord, the whole round world turns red
Lord, my mind falls on things that my dear old mother have said

Lord, I ain't gonna make no more cotton, mama, lord, I'll tell you the
    reason that I say so   5
Lord, I ain't gonna make no more cotton, mama, lord, I'll tell you the
    reason that I say so
I don't get nothin' out of my seed and the cotton price is so doggone
    low

The boss man told me go to the commissary, I could get anything   10
    that I need
The boss man told me go to the commissary, I could get anything
    that I need
He said I didn't have to have no money right away, lord, he said he
    would take it out of my seed   15

Lord make a cotton crop, mama, lord it's just the same as shootin' dice
Lord make a cotton crop, mama, lord it's just the same as shootin' dice
Lord, you work the whole year 'round, and then cotton won't be no
    price

Lord, I plowed all this summer long and the sun would burn my skin   20
Lord, I plowed all this summer long and the sun would burn my skin
And then the cotton sold for twelve and a half cents, you know no way
    that I could win

D. H. LAWRENCE (1885–1930)

City-Life (1930)

When I see the great cities—

When I am in a great city, I know that I despair.
I know there is no hope for us, death waits, it is useless to care.

For oh the poor people, that are flesh of my flesh,
I, that am flesh of their flesh,   5

when I see the iron hooked into their faces
their poor, their fearful faces
I scream in my soul, for I know I cannot
take the iron hook out of their faces, that makes them so drawn,
nor cut the invisible wires of steel that pull them   10
back and forth, to work,
back and forth, to work,
like fearful and corpse-like fishes hooked and being played
by some malignant fisherman on an unseen shore
where he does not choose to land them yet, hooked fishes of the   15
     factory world.

BERTOLT BRECHT (1898–1956)

Song of the Invigorating Effect of Money   (1933)

Translated by H. R. Hays.

Upon this earth we hear dispraise of money
Yet, without it, earth is very cold
And it can be warm and friendly
Suddenly through the power of gold.
Everything that seemed so hard to bear   5
In a gleaming golden glow is cloaked.
Sun is melting what was frozen.
Every man fulfills his hopes!
Rosy beams light the horizon,
Look on high: the chimney smokes!   10
Yes, all at once this world seems quite a different one.
Higher beats the heart, the glance sweeps wider.
Richer are the meals and clothes are finer.
Man himself becomes another man.

Ah, how very sorely they're mistaken   15
They who think that money doesn't count.
Fruitfulness turns into famine
When the kindly stream gives out.
Each one starts to yell and grabs it where he can.
Even were it not so hard to live   20
He who doesn't hunger yet is fearful.
Every heart is empty now of love.
Father, Mother, Brother—cross and tearful!
See, the chimney smokes no more above!

Thick displeasing fog about us furled,   25
All is filled with hatred now and striving.
None will be the horse, all would be riding
And the world becomes an icy world.

So it goes with all that's great and worthy.
In this world it's quickly spoiled indeed,   30
For when feet are bare and bellies empty
Love of virtue always turns to greed.
Gold, not greatness, is what people need.
Poverty of soul puts out our hopes.
Good plus money, too, is what it takes   35
To keep man virtuous without a slip.
He whom crime's already given breaks
Looks up on high: the chimney smokes!
Faith in the human race again grows bright.
Man is noble, good, so on and so forth.   40
Sentiment awakes. Need dimmed its light.
Faster beats the heart. The glance sweeps wider.
We know who the horse is, who the rider.
And once more it's clear that right is right.

C. DAY LEWIS (1904–1972)

Come, live with me and be my love   (1935)

Come, live with me and be my love,
And we will all the pleasures prove
Of peace and plenty, bed and board,
That chance employment may afford.

I'll handle dainties on the docks   5
And thou shalt read of summer frocks:
At evening by the sour canals
We'll hope to hear some madrigals.

Care on thy maiden brow shall put
A wreath of wrinkles, and thy foot   10
Be shod with pain: not silken dress
But toil shall tire thy loveliness.

Hunger shall make thy modest zone
And cheat fond death of all but bone—

If these delights thy mind may move,   15
Then live with me and be my love.

ROBERT FROST (1874–1963)

Two Tramps in Mud Time   (1936)

Out of the mud two strangers came
And caught me splitting wood in the yard.
And one of them put me off my aim
By hailing cheerily "Hit them hard!"
I knew pretty well why he dropped behind   5
And let the other go on a way.
I knew pretty well what he had in mind:
He wanted to take my job for pay.

Good blocks of oak it was I split,
As large around as the chopping block;   10
And every piece I squarely hit
Fell splinterless as a cloven rock.
The blows that a life of self-control
Spares to strike for the common good,
That day, giving a loose to my soul,   15
I spent on the unimportant wood.

The sun was warm but the wind was chill.
You know how it is with an April day
When the sun is out and the wind is still,
You're one month on in the middle of May.   20
But if you so much as dare to speak,
A cloud comes over the sunlit arch,
A wind comes off a frozen peak,
And you're two months back in the middle of March.

A bluebird comes tenderly up to alight   25
And turns to the wind to unruffle a plume,
His song so pitched as not to excite
A single flower as yet to bloom.
It is snowing a flake: and he half knew
Winter was only playing possum.   30
Except in color he isn't blue,
But he wouldn't advise a thing to blossom.

The water for which we may have to look
In summertime with a witching wand,
In every wheelrut's now a brook,   35
In every print of a hoof a pond.
Be glad of water, but don't forget
The lurking frost in the earth beneath
That will steal forth after the sun is set
And show on the water its crystal teeth.   40

The time when most I loved my task
These two must make me love it more
By coming with what they came to ask.
You'd think I never had felt before
The weight of an ax-head poised aloft,   45
The grip on earth of outspread feet,
The life of muscles rocking soft
And smooth and moist in vernal heat.

Out of the woods two hulking tramps
(From sleeping God knows where last night,   50
But not long since in the lumber camps.)
They thought all chopping was theirs of right.
Men of the woods and lumberjacks,
They judged me by their appropriate tool.
Except as a fellow handled an ax   55
They had no way of knowing a fool.

Nothing on either side was said.
They knew they had but to stay their stay
And all their logic would fill my head:
As that I had no right to play   60
With what was another man's work for gain.
My right might be love but theirs was need.
And where the two exist in twain
Theirs was the better right—agreed.

But yield who will to their separation,   65
My object in living is to unite
My avocation and my vocation
As my two eyes make one in sight.
Only where love and need are one,
And the work is play for mortal stakes,   70
Is the deed ever really done
For Heaven and the future's sakes.

MURIEL RUKEYSER (1913–1980)

Boy with His Hair Cut Short (1938)

Sunday shuts down on this twentieth-century evening.
The El passes. Twilight and bulb define
the brown room, the overstuffed plum sofa,
the boy, and the girl's thin hands above his head.
A neighbor radio sings stocks, news, serenade.   5

He sits at the table, head down, the young clear neck exposed,
watching the drugstore sign from the tail of his eye;
tattoo, neon, until the eye blears, while his
solicitous tall sister, simple in blue, bending
behind him, cuts his hair with her cheap shears.   10

The arrow's electric red always reaches its mark,
successful neon! He coughs, impressed by that precision.
His child's forehead, forever protected by his cap,
is bleached against the lamplight as he turns head
and steadies to let the snippets drop.   15

Erasing the failure of weeks with level fingers,
she sleeks the fine hair, combing: "You'll look fine tomorrow!
You'll surely find something, they can't keep turning you down;
the finest gentleman's not so trim as you!" Smiling, he raises
the adolescent forehead wrinkling ironic now.   20

He sees his decent suit laid out, new-pressed,
his carfare on the shelf. He lets his head fall, meeting
her earnest hopeless look, seeing the sharp blades splitting,
the darkened room, the impersonal sign, her motion,
the blue vein, bright on her temple, pitifully beating.   25

WOODY GUTHRIE (1912–1967)

SONG: Plane Wreck at Los Gatos[1] (Deportees) (1948)

The crops are all in and the peaches are rotting,
The oranges are piled in their creosote dumps;

---

[1]Town in western California.

You're flying them back to the Mexican border
To pay all their money to wade back again.

Refrain:
Goodbye to my Juan, Goodbye Rosalita;   5
Adios mis amigos, Jesús and Marie,
You won't have a name when you ride the big airplane:
All they will call you will be deportee.

My father's own father he waded that river,
They took all the money he made in his life;   10
My brothers and sisters come working the fruit trees
And they rode the truck till they took down and died.

Some of us are illegal and some are not wanted,
Our work contract's out and we have to move on;
Six hundred miles to that Mexico border,   15
They chase us like outlaws, like rustlers, like thieves.

We died in your hills, we died in your deserts,
We died in your valleys and died on your plains;
We died neath your trees and we died in your bushes,
Both sides of this river we died just the same.   20

The sky plane caught fire over Los Gatos Canyon,
A fireball of lightning and shook all our hills.
Who are all these friends all scattered like dry leaves?
The radio says they are just deportees.

Is this the best way we can grow our big orchards?   25
Is this the best way we can grow our good fruit?
To fall like dry leaves to rot on my top soil
And be called by no name except deportees?

NAZIM HIKMET   (1902–1963)

About Your Hands and Lies   (1949)

Translated by Randy Blasing and Mutlu Konuk.

Your hands grave like all stones,
sad like all songs sung in prison,

clumsy and heavy like all beasts of burden,
your hands that are like the sullen faces of hungry children.
Your hands nimble and light like bees,   5
full like breasts with milk,
brave like nature,
your hands that hide their friendly softness under their rough
                                                                    skin.

This world doesn't rest on the horns of a bull,   10
            this world rests on your hands.
People, oh my people,
they feed you with lies.
But you're hungry,
you need to be fed with meat and bread.   15
And never once eating a full meal at a white table,
you leave this world where every branch is loaded with fruit.
Oh my people,
especially those in Asia, Africa,
            the Near East, Middle East, Pacific islands   20
                and my countrymen—
I mean, more than seventy percent of all people—
you are old and absent-minded like your hands,
you are curious, amazed, and young like your hands.
Oh my people,   25
my European, my American,
you are awake, bold, and forgetful like your hands,
like your hands you're quick to seduce,
                easy to deceive . . .

People, oh my people,   30
if the antennas are lying,
if the presses are lying,
if the books lie,
if the poster on the wall and the ad in the column lie,
if the naked thighs of girls on the white screen lie,   35
if the prayer lies,
if the lullaby lies,
if the dream is lying,
if the violin player at the tavern is lying,
if the moonlight on the nights of hopeless days lies,   40
if the voice lies,
if the word lies,
if everything but your hands,
        if everyone, is lying,
it's so your hands will be obedient like clay,   45

blind like darkness,
stupid like sheep dogs,
          it's so your hands won't rebel.
And it's so that in this mortal, this livable world
          —where we are guests so briefly anyway—   50
          this merchant's empire, this cruelty, won't end.

MAFIKA MBULI

The Miners   (1973)

This dungeon
Makes the mind weary
Kneaded with the sight of
A million stones
Passing through my hands   5
I see the flesh sticking like hair
On thorns
Against the grating rocks
Of these hills dug for gold,
And life is bitter here.   10
Crawling through the day
In a sleepwalker's dream,
Frightening the night away with my snores,
I dream of the diminished breath
Of miners planted in the stones—   15
The world is not at ease
But quakes under the march of our boots
Tramping the dust under our feet....
Click, clack, our picks knock for life
Until the eyes are dazed   20
Counting the rubble of scattered stones.

Day and night are one,
but I know each day dawns
And the heated sun licks every shrub dry
While we who burrow the earth   25
Tame the dust with our lungs.
Click, clack we knock with picks
And our minds
Drone with the voices of women

Harassing our loins   30
To force courage into the heart.
Wherefore might we scorn their sacrifice
Made in blood,
Greater that the blood of men
Sacrificed to the earth   35
For its possession!
And so
Clap, scrape
With our hands manacled
With weariness   40
We mine
All our lives
Till the mind is numb
And ceases to ask. . . .

SUSAN GRIFFIN (b. 1943)

This Is the Story of the Day in the Life of a Woman Trying

(1976)

This is the story of the day in the life of a woman trying
to be a writer and her child got sick. And in the midst of
writing this story someone called her on the telephone.
And, of course, despite her original hostile reaction to the
ring of the telephone, she got interested in the conversation   5
which was about teaching writing in a women's prison,
for no pay of course, and she would have done it if it
weren't for the babysitting and the lack of money for the
plane fare, and then she hung up the phone and looked
at her typewriter, and for an instant swore her original   10
sentence was not there. But after a while she found it. Then
she began again, but in the midst of the second sentence,
a man telephoned wanting to speak to the woman she
shares her house with, who was not available to speak on
the telephone, and by the time she got back to her typewriter   15
she began to worry about her sick daughter downstairs.
And why hadn't the agency for babysitters called back
and why hadn't the department for health called back
because she was looking for a day sitter and a night sitter,
one so she could teach the next day and one so she could   20
read her poetry. And she was hoping that the people who

had asked her to read poetry would pay for the babysitter
since the next evening after that would be a meeting of
teachers whom she wanted to meet and she could not afford
two nights of babysitters let alone one, actually. This was   25
the second day her child was sick and the second day she
tried to write (she had been trying to be a writer for years)
but she failed entirely the first day because of going to the
market to buy Vitamin C and to the toy store to buy cutouts
and crayons, and making soup from the chicken carcass that   30
had been picked nearly clean to make sandwiches for
lunch, and watering the plants, sending in the mortgage
check and other checks to cover that check to the bank,
and feeling tired, wishing she had a job, talking on the telephone,
and putting out newspaper and glue and scissors   35
on the kitchen table for her tired, bored child and squinting
her eyes at the clock waiting for *Sesame Street*[1] to begin
again. Suddenly, after she went upstairs to her bedroom
with a book, having given up writing as impossible, it was
time to cook dinner. But she woke up on the second day   40
with the day before as a lesson in her mind. Then an old
friend called who had come to town whom she was eager
to see and she said, "Yes, I'm home with a sick child," and
they spent the morning talking. She was writing poetry and
teaching she said. He had written four books he   45
said. Her daughter showed him her red and blue and
orange colored pictures. She wished he didn't have to leave
so early, she thought but didn't say, and went back to pick
up tissue paper off the floor and fix lunch for her and her
child and begin telephoning for babysitters because she   50
knew she had to teach the next day. And the truth was,
if she did not have a sick child to care for, she was
not sure she could write anyway because the kitchen was
still there needing cleaning, the garden there needing
weeding and watering, the living room needing curtains,   55
the couch needing pillows, a stack of mail needing answers
(for instance if she didn't call the woman who had lived
in her house the month before about the phone bill soon,
she would lose a lot of money). All besides, she had
nothing to write. She had had fine thoughts for writing the   60
night before but in the morning they took on a sickly
complexion. And anyway, she had begun to think her life

---

[1]Television program for children.

trivial and so it was, and she was tired writing the same
words, or different words about the same situation, the
situation or situations being that she was tired, tired of trying 65
to write, tired of poverty or almost poverty or fear of
poverty, tired of the kitchen being dirty, tired of having
no lover. She was amazed that she had gotten herself
dressed, actually, with thoughts like these, and caught herself
saying maybe I should take a trip when she realized she 70
had just come back from a trip and had wanted to be
home so much she came back early. And even in the writing
of this she thought I have written all this before and
went downstairs to find her daughter had still not eaten a
peanut butter sandwich and she wondered to herself what 75
keeps that child alive?

MARGE PIERCY (b. 1936)

The market economy (1977)

Suppose some peddler offered
you can have a color TV
but your baby will be
born with a crooked spine;
you can have polyvinyl cups 5
and wash and wear
suits but it will cost
you your left lung
rotted with cancer; suppose
somebody offered you 10
a frozen precooked dinner
every night for ten years
but at the end
your colon dies
and then you do, 15
slowly and with much pain.
You get a house in the suburbs
but you work in a new plastics
factory and die at fifty-one
when your kidneys turn off. 20

But where else will you
work? where else can

you rent but Smog City?
The only houses for sale
are under the yellow sky.   25
You've been out of work for
a year and they're hiring
at the plastics factory.
Don't read the fine
print, there isn't any.   30

JUNE JORDAN (b. 1936)

Free Flight   (1980)

Nothing fills me up at night
I fall asleep for one or two hours then
up again my gut
alarms
I must arise   5
and wandering into the refrigerator
think about evaporated milk homemade vanilla ice cream
cherry pie hot from the oven with Something Like Vermont
Cheddar Cheese disintegrating luscious
on the top while   10
mildly
I devour almonds and raisins mixed to mathematical
criteria or celery or my very own sweet and sour snack
composed of brie peanut butter honey and
a minuscule slice of party size salami   15
on a single whole wheat cracker *no salt added*
or I read Cesar Vallejo[1]/Gabriela Mistral[2]/last year's
complete anthology or
I might begin another list of things to do
that starts with toilet paper and   20
I notice that I never jot down fresh
strawberry shortcake: never
even though fresh strawberry shortcake shoots down
raisins and almonds 6 to nothing
effortlessly   25
effortlessly

---

[1]Peruvian poet and novelist (1895–1938).
[2]Chilean poet (1889–1957).

is this poem on my list?
light bulbs lemons envelopes ballpoint refill
post office and zucchini
oranges no   30
it's not
I guess that means I just forgot
walking my dog around the block leads
to a space in my mind where
during the newspaper strike questions   35
sizzle through suddenly like
Is there an earthquake down in Ecuador?
Did a TWA supersaver flight to San Francisco
land in Philadelphia instead
or   40
whatever happened to human rights
in Washington D.C.? Or what about downward destabilization
of the consumer price index
and I was in this school P. S. Tum-Ta-Tum and time came
for me to leave but   45
No! I couldn't leave: The Rule was anybody leaving
the premises without having taught somebody something
valuable would be henceforth proscribed from the
premises would be forever null and void/dull and
vilified well   50
I had stood in front of 40 to 50 students running my
mouth and I had been generous with deceitful smiles/softspoken
and pseudo-gentle wiles if and when forced
into discourse amongst such adults as constitutes
the regular treacheries of On The Job Behavior   55
ON THE JOB BEHAVIOR
is this poem on that list
polish shoes file nails coordinate tops and bottoms
lipstick control no
screaming I'm bored because   60
this is whoring away the hours of god's creation
pay attention to your eyes your hands the twilight
sky in the institutional big windows
no
I did not presume I was not so bold as to put this   65
poem on that list
then at the end of the class this boy gives me Mahler's 9th
symphony the double album listen
to it let it seep into you he
says transcendental love   70
he says

I think naw
I been angry all day long/nobody did the assignment
I am not prepared
I am not prepared for so much grace   75
the catapulting music of surprise that makes me
hideaway my face
nothing fills me up at night
yesterday the houseguest left a brown
towel in the bathroom for tonight   80
I set out a blue one and
an off-white washcloth seriously
I don't need no houseguest
I don't need no towels/lovers
I just need a dog   85

Maybe I'm kidding

Maybe I need a woman
a woman be so well you know so wifelike
so more or less motherly so listening so much
the universal skin you love to touch and who the   90
closer she gets to you the better she looks to me/somebody
say yes and make me laugh and tell me she know she
been there she spit bullets at my enemies she say you
need to sail around Alaska fuck it all try this new
cerebral tea and take a long bath   95

Maybe I need a man
a man be so well you know so manly so lifelike
so more or less virile so sure so much the deep
voice of opinion and the shoulders like a window
seat and cheeks so closely shaven by a twin-edged   100
razor blade no oily hair and no dandruff besides/
somebody say yes and make
me laugh and tell me he know he been there he spit
bullets at my enemies he say you need to sail around
Alaska fuck it all and take a long bath   105

lah-ti-dah and lah-ti-dum
what's this socialized obsession with the bathtub

Maybe I just need to love myself myself
(anyhow I'm more familiar with the subject)
Maybe when my cousin tells me you remind me   110
of a woman past her prime maybe I need

to hustle my cousin into a hammerlock
position make her cry out uncle and
I'm sorry
Maybe when I feel this horrible   115
inclination to kiss folks I despise
because the party's like that
an occasion to be kissing people
you despise maybe I should tell them kindly
kiss my   120

Maybe when I wake up in the middle of the night
I should go downstairs
dump the refrigerator contents on the floor
and stand there in the middle of the spilled milk
and the wasted butter spread beneath my dirty feet   125
writing poems
writing poems
maybe I just need to love myself myself and
anyway
I'm working on it   130

LORNA DEE CERVANTES (b. 1954)

Cannery Town in August   (1981)

All night it humps the air.
Speechless, the steam rises
from the cannery columns. I hear
the night bird rave about work
or lunch, or sing the swing shift   5
home. I listen, while bodyless
uniforms and spinach specked shoes
drift in monochrome down the dark
moon-possessed streets. Women
who smell of whiskey and tomatoes,   10
peach fuzz reddening their lips and eyes—
I imagine them not speaking, dumbed
by the can's clamor and drop
to the trucks that wait, grunting
in their headlights below.   15
They spotlight those who walk
like a dream, with no one
waiting in the shadows
to palm them back to living.

KATE RUSHIN (b. 1951)

The Black Back-Ups   (1983)

This is dedicated to Merry Clayton, Cissy Houston, Vonetta
Washington, Dawn, Carrietta McClellen, Rosie Farmer, Marsha
Jenkins and Carolyn Williams. This is for all of the Black
women who sang back-up for Elvis Presley, John Denver, James
Taylor, Lou Reed, Etc. Etc. Etc.   5

I said Hey Babe
Take a Walk on the Wild Side
I said Hey Babe
Take a Walk on the Wild Side

And the colored girls say   10

Do dodo do do dodododo
Do dodo do do dodododo
Do dodo do do dodododo ooooo

This is for my Great Grandmother Esther, my Grandmother
Addie, my Grandmother called Sister, my Great Aunt Rachel,   15
my Aunt Hilda, my Aunt Tine, my Aunt Breda, my Aunt
Gladys, my Aunt Helen, my Aunt Ellie, my Cousin Barbara, my
Cousin Dottie and my Great Great Aunt Vene

This is dedicated to all of the Black women riding on buses
and subways Back and forth to the Main Line, Haddonfield,   20
N.J., Cherry Hill and Chevy Chase. This is for those women who
spend their summers in Rockport, Newport, Cape Cod and
Camden, Maine. This is for the women who open bundles of
dirty laundry sent home from ivy-covered campuses

And the colored girls say   25

Do dodo do do dodododo
Do dodo do do dodododo
Do dodo do do dodododo ooooo

Jane Fox Jane Fox
Calling Jane Fox   30
Where are you Jane?

My Great Aunt Rachel worked for the Foxes
Ever since I can remember
There was The Boy
Whose name I never knew   35
And there was The Girl
Whose name was Jane

My Aunt Rachel brought Jane's dresses for me to wear
Perfectly Good Clothes
And I should've been glad to get them   40
Perfectly Good Clothes
No matter they didn't fit quite right
Perfectly Good Clothes Jane
Brought home in a brown paper bag with an air of
Accomplishment and excitement   45
Perfectly Good Clothes
Which I hated
It's not that I have anything *personal* against *you* Jane

It's just that I felt guilty
For hating those clothes   50

I mean
Can you get to the irony of it Jane?

And the colored girls say

Do dodo do do dodododo
Do dodo do do dodododo   55
Do dodo do do dodododo ooooo

At school
In Ohio
I swear to Gawd
There was always somebody   60
Telling me that the only person
In their whole house
Who listened and understood them
Despite the money and the lessons
Was the housekeeper   65
And I knew it was true
But what was I supposed to say?

I know it's true
I watch them getting off the train

And moving slowly toward the Country Squire   70
With their uniform in their shopping bag
And the closer they get to the car
The more the two little kids jump and laugh
And even the dog is about to
Turn inside out   75
Because they just can't wait until she gets there
Edna Edna Wonderful Edna
(But Aunt Edna to me, or Gram, or Miz Johnson, or Sister
Johnson on Sundays)

And the colored girls say   80

Do dodo do do dodododo
Do dodo do do dodododo
Do dodo do do dodododo ooooo

This is for Hattie McDaniel, Butterfly McQueen, Ethel Waters[1]
Saphire[2]   85
Saphronia
Ruby Begonia
Aunt Jemima
Aunt Jemima on the Pancake Box
Aunt Jemima on the Pancake Box?   90
AuntJemimaonthepancakebox?
auntjemimaonthepancakebox?
Ainchamamaonthepancakebox?
Ain't chure Mama on the pancake box?

Mama Mama   95
Get offa that damn box
And come home to me

And my Mama leaps offa that box
She swoops down in her nurse's cape
Which she wears on Sunday   100
And on Wednesday night prayer meeting
And she wipes my forehead
And she fans my face for me
And she makes me a cup o' tea
And it don't do a thing for my real pain   105
Except she is my Mama

---

[1]The first two are actors, the third a jazz and blues singer.
[2]Black character on a popular radio and television show.

Mama Mommy Mommy Mammy Mammy
Mam-mee Mam-mee
I'd Walk a mill-yon miles
For one o' your smiles   110

This is for the Black Back-ups
This is for my mama and your mama
My grandma and your grandma
This is for the thousand thousand Black Back-Ups

And the colored girls say   115

Do dodo do do dodododo
Dododododo
Dodo
do
Do   120
do

BRUCE SPRINGSTEEN (b. 1949)

SONG: *My Hometown*   (1984)

I was eight years old and running with a dime in my hand
Into the bus stop to pick up a paper for my old man
I'd sit on his lap in that big old Buick and steer as we drove through
   town
He'd tousle my hair and say son take a good look around
This is your hometown   5
This is your hometown
This is your hometown
This is your hometown

In '65 tension was running high at my high school
There was a lot of fights between the black and white   10
There was nothing you could do
Two cars at a light on a Saturday night in the back seat there was a gun
Words were passed in a shotgun blast
Troubled times had come to my hometown
My hometown   15
My hometown
My hometown

Now Main Street's whitewashed windows and vacant stores
Seems like there ain't nobody wants to come down here no more

They're closing down the textile mill across the railroad tracks   20
Foreman says these jobs are going boys and they ain't coming back to
    your hometown
Your hometown
Your hometown
Your hometown

Last night me and Kate we laid in bed talking about getting out   25
Packing up our bags maybe heading south
I'm thirty-five we got a boy of our own now
Last night I sat him up behind the wheel and said son take a good look
    around this is your hometown

PATRICIA DOBLER   (b. 1939)

Uncles' Advice, 1957   (1986)

My handsome uncles like dark birds
flew away to war. They all flew back
glossier and darker than before, but willing
to be clipped to the mill for reasons
of their own—a pregnant girl,   5
a business failed, the seductive sound
of accents they'd grown up with—
so they settled, breaking promises to themselves.
This was the time when, moping in my room
while the aunts' voices rose through the floorboards   10
prophesying my life—stews and babushkas—
the uncles' advice also filtered up
like the smoky, persistent 5-note song
of the mourning dove: get out, don't come back.

MAGGIE ANDERSON   (b. 1948)

Mining Camp Residents West Virginia, July, 1935   (1986)

They had to seize something in the face of the camera.
The woman's hand touches her throat as if feeling
for a necklace that isn't there. The man buries one hand

in his overall pocket, loops the other through a strap,
and the child twirls a strand of her hair as she hunkers   5
in the dirt at their feet. Maybe Evans[1] asked them to stand
in that little group in the doorway, a perfect triangle
of people in the morning sun. Perhaps he asked them
to hold their arms that way, or bend their heads. It was
his composition after all. And they did what he said.   10

TODD JAILER (b. 1956)

Bill Hastings

(1990)

Listen to me, college boy, you can
keep your museums and poetry and string quartets
'cause there's nothing more beautiful than
line work. Clamp your jaws together
and listen: 5
      It's a windy night, you're freezing the teeth out
of your zipper in the ten below, working stiff
jointed and dreaming of Acapulco, the truck cab.
Can't keep your footing for the ice, and
even the geese who died to fill your vest   10
are sorry you answered the call-out tonight.
You drop a connector and curses
take to the air like sparrows who freeze
and fall back dead at your feet.
Finally you slam the SMD fuse[1] home.   15
Bang! The whole valley lights up below you
where before was unbreathing darkness.
In one of those houses a little girl
stops shivering. Now that's beautiful,
and it's all because of you.   20

---

[1]Walker Evans (1903–1975), photographer known especially for his portrayal of the
Great Depression in rural America.
[1]Fuse in an electrical substation.

SHERMAN ALEXIE (b. 1966)

The Reservation Cab Driver   (1991)

waits outside the Breakaway Bar
in the '65 Malibu with no windshield.

It's a beer a mile. No exceptions.

He picks up Lester FallsApart
who lives in the West End   5
twelve miles away, good for a half-rack.

When congress raised the minimum wage
the reservation cab driver upped his rates
made it a beer and a cigarette each mile.

HUD[1] evicted him   10
so he wrapped himself in old blankets
and slept in the front seat of his cab.

When the BIA[2] rescinded his benefits
he added a can of commodities for every mile.

Seymour climbed in the cab   15
said, this is a hell of a pony.
Ain't no pony, the reservation cab driver
said, it's a car.

During the powwow, he works 24 hours a day
gets paid in quilts, beads, fry bread, firewood.   20
3 a.m., he picks up Crazy Horse hitchhiking.
Where are you going, asks the reservation cab driver.
Same place you are, Crazy Horse answers
somewhere way up the goddamn road.

---

[1]Department of Housing and Urban Development.
[2]Bureau of Indian Affairs.

RUTH STONE (b. 1915)

Eden, Then and Now   (2002)

In '29 before the dust storms
sandblasted Indianapolis,
we believed in the milk company.
Milk came in glass bottles.
We spread dye-colored butter,   5
now connected to cancer.
We worked seven to seven
with no overtime pay;
pledged allegiance every day,
pitied the starving Armenians.   10
One morning in the midst of plenty,
there were folks out of context,
who were living on nothing.
Some slept in shacks
on the banks of the river.   15
This phenomenon investors said
would pass away.
My father worked for the daily paper.
He was a union printer;
lead slugs and blue smoke.   20
He worked with hot lead
at a two-ton machine,
in a low-slung seat;
a green-billed cap
pulled low on his forehead.   25
He gave my mother a dollar a day.
You could say we were rich.
This was the Jazz Age.
All over the country
the dispossessed wandered   30
with their hungry children,
harassed by the law.
When the market broke, bad losers
jumped out of windows.
It was time to lay an elegant table,   35
as it is now; corporate paradise;
the apple before the rot caved in.
It was the same worm
eating the same fruit.
In fact, the same Eden.   40

DRAMA

ARTHUR MILLER (1915–2005)

Born and raised in Brooklyn, New York, Arthur Miller worked for two years af-
ter high school in an auto parts warehouse until he enrolled at the University of
Michigan, where he began writing plays. In 1938 he returned to New York and con-
tinued writing while working in the Brooklyn Navy Yard. Miller's career took off
with the Broadway production of All My Sons *(1947) and of the immensely suc-*
cessful Death of a Salesman *(1949). His 1953 play* The Crucible, *a dramatization*
of the seventeenth-century witch trials in Salem, Massachusetts, was also an attack
on the government's anticommunist "witch-hunts" of the early 1950s. The play
caught the attention of the House of Un-American Activities Committee in 1956,
and Miller's subsequent questioning led to his blacklisting in Hollywood. His pro-
lific output as a writer includes dozens of plays, screenplays, novels, and essays.
Selected works include the plays A View from the Bridge *(1955),* After the Fall
(1964); the screenplay The Misfits *(1961)—a movie that starred his wife Marilyn*
Monroe; and the autobiography Timebends: A Life *(1987). His most recent plays*
include The Ride Down Mt. Morgan *(1991),* The Last Yankee *(1993),* Broken
Glass *(1994), and* Resurrection Blues *(2002). Still performed regularly, the*
tragedy Death of a Salesman *blurs reality and illusion, probing the psychological*
and dehumanizing struggle of protagonist Willy Loman and his search for the
"American dream."

Death of a Salesman   (1949)

Certain private conversations in two acts and a requiem

Characters

WILLY LOMAN	UNCLE BEN
LINDA	HOWARD WAGNER
BIFF	JENNY
HAPPY	STANLEY
BERNARD	MISS FORSYTHE
THE WOMAN	LETTA
CHARLEY	

The action takes place in WILLY LOMAN's *house and yard and in various places*
he visits in the New York and Boston of today.

Throughout the play, in the stage directions, left and right mean stage left and stage
right.

ACT I

A melody is heard, played upon a flute. It is small and fine, telling of grass and trees and the horizon. The curtain rises.

Before us is the Salesman's house. We are aware of towering, angular shapes behind it, surrounding it on all sides. Only the blue light of the sky falls upon the house and forestage; the surrounding area shows an angry glow of orange. As more light appears, we see a solid vault of apartment houses around the small, fragile-seeming home. An air of the dream clings to the place, a dream rising out of reality. The kitchen at center seems actual enough, for there is a kitchen table with three chairs, and a refrigerator. But no other fixtures are seen. At the back of the kitchen there is a draped entrance, which leads to the living-room. To the right of the kitchen, on a level raised two feet, is a bedroom furnished only with a brass bedstead and a straight chair. On a shelf over the bed a silver athletic trophy stands. A window opens onto the apartment house at the side.

Behind the kitchen, on a level raised six and a half feet, is the boys' bedroom, at present barely visible. Two beds are dimly seen, and at the back of the room a dormer window. (This bedroom is above the unseen living-room.) At the left a stairway curves up to it from the kitchen.

The entire setting is wholly or, in some places, partially transparent. The roof-line of the house is one-dimensional; under and over it we see the apartment buildings. Before the house lies an apron, curving beyond the forestage into the orchestra. This forward area serves as the back yard as well as the locale of all WILLY's *imaginings and of his city scenes. Whenever the action is in the present the actors observe the imaginary wall-lines, entering the house only through its door at the left. But in the scenes of the past these boundaries are broken, and characters enter or leave a room by stepping "through" a wall onto the forestage.*

From the right, WILLY LOMAN, *the Salesman, enters, carrying two large sample cases. The flute plays on. He hears but is not aware of it. He is past sixty years of age, dressed quietly. Even as he crosses the stage to the doorway of the house, his exhaustion is apparent. He unlocks the door, comes into the kitchen, and thankfully lets his burden down, feeling the soreness of his palms. A word-sigh escapes his lips—it might be "Oh, boy, oh, boy." He closes the door, then carries his cases out into the living-room, through the draped kitchen doorway.*

LINDA, *his wife, has stirred in her bed at the right. She gets out and puts on a robe, listening. Most often jovial, she has developed an iron repression of her exceptions to* WILLY's *behavior—she more than loves him, she admires him, as though his mercurial nature, his temper, his massive dreams and little cruelties, served her only as sharp reminders of the turbulent longings within him, longings which she shares but lacks the temperament to utter and follow to their end.*

LINDA: *hearing* WILLY *outside the bedroom, calls with some trepidation.* Willy!

WILLY: It's all right. I came back.

LINDA: Why? What happened? *Slight pause.* Did something happen, Willy?

WILLY: No, nothing happened.

LINDA: You didn't smash the car, did you?

WILLY: *with casual irritation.* I said nothing happened. Didn't you hear me?

LINDA: Don't you feel well?

WILLY: I'm tired to the death. *The flute has faded away. He sits on the bed beside her, a little numb.* I couldn't make it. I just couldn't make it, Linda.

LINDA: *very carefully, delicately.* Where were you all day? You look terrible.

WILLY: I got as far as a little above Yonkers. I stopped for a cup of coffee. Maybe it was the coffee.

LINDA: What?

WILLY: *after a pause.* I suddenly couldn't drive any more. The car kept going off onto the shoulder, y'know?

LINDA: *helpfully.* Oh. Maybe it was the steering again. I don't think Angelo knows the Studebaker.

WILLY: No, it's me, it's me. Suddenly I realize I'm goin' sixty miles an hour and I don't remember the last five minutes. I'm—I can't seem to—keep my mind to it.

LINDA: Maybe it's your glasses. You never went for your new glasses.

WILLY: No, I see everything. I came back ten miles an hour. It took me nearly four hours from Yonkers.

LINDA: *resigned.* Well, you'll just have to take a rest, Willy, you can't continue this way.

WILLY: I just got back from Florida.

LINDA: But you didn't rest your mind. Your mind is overactive, and the mind is what counts, dear.

WILLY: I'll start out in the morning. Maybe I'll feel better in the morning. *She is taking off his shoes.* These goddam arch supports are killing me.

LINDA: Take an aspirin. Should I get you an aspirin? It'll soothe you.

WILLY: *with wonder.* I was driving along, you understand? And I was fine. I was even observing the scenery. You can imagine, me looking at scenery, on the road every week of my life. But it's so beautiful up there, Linda, the trees are so thick, and the sun is warm. I opened the windshield and just let the warm air bathe over me. And then all of a sudden I'm goin' off the road! I'm tellin' ya, I absolutely forgot I was driving. If I'd've gone the other way over the white line I might've killed somebody. So I went on again—and five minutes later I'm dreamin' again, and I nearly—*He presses two fingers against his eyes.* I have such thoughts, I have such strange thoughts.

LINDA: Willy, dear. Talk to them again. There's no reason why you can't work in New York.

WILLY: They don't need me in New York. I'm the New England man. I'm vital in New England.

LINDA: But you're sixty years old. They can't expect you to keep traveling every week.

WILLY: I'll have to send a wire to Portland. I'm supposed to see Brown and Morrison tomorrow morning at ten o'clock to show the line. Goddammit, I could sell them!

He starts putting on his jacket.

LINDA: *taking the jacket from him.* Why don't you go down to the place tomorrow and tell Howard you've simply got to work in New York? You're too accommodating, dear.

WILLY: If old man Wagner was alive I'd a been in charge of New York now! That man was a prince, he was a masterful man. But that boy of his, that Howard, he don't appreciate. When I went north the first time, the Wagner Company didn't know where New England was!

LINDA: Why don't you tell those things to Howard, dear?

WILLY: *encouraged.* I will, I definitely will. Is there any cheese?

LINDA: I'll make you a sandwich.

WILLY: No, go to sleep. I'll take some milk. I'll be up right away. The boys in?

LINDA: They're sleeping. Happy took Biff on a date tonight.

WILLY: *interested.* That so?

LINDA: It was so nice to see them shaving together, one behind the other, in the bathroom. And going out together. You notice? The whole house smells of shaving lotion.

WILLY: Figure it out. Work a lifetime to pay off a house. You finally own it, and there's nobody to live in it.

LINDA: Well, dear, life is a casting off. It's always that way.

WILLY: No, no, some people—some people accomplish something. Did Biff say anything after I went this morning?

LINDA: You shouldn't have criticized him, Willy, especially after he just got off the train. You mustn't lose your temper with him.

WILLY: When the hell did I lose my temper? I simply asked him if he was making any money. Is that a criticism?

LINDA: But, dear, how could he make any money?

WILLY: *worried and angered.* There's such an undercurrent in him. He became a moody man. Did he apologize when I left this morning?

LINDA: He was crestfallen, Willy. You know how he admires you. I think if he finds himself, then you'll both be happier and not fight any more.

WILLY: How can he find himself on a farm? Is that a life? A farmhand? In the beginning, when he was young, I thought, well, a young man, it's good for him to tramp around, take a lot of different jobs. But it's more than ten years now and he has yet to make thirty-five dollars a week!

LINDA: He's finding himself, Willy.

WILLY: Not finding yourself at the age of thirty-four is a disgrace!

LINDA: Shh!

WILLY: The trouble is he's lazy, goddammit!

LINDA: Willy, please!

WILLY: Biff is a lazy bum!

LINDA: They're sleeping. Get something to eat. Go on down.

WILLY: Why did he come home? I would like to know what brought him home.

LINDA: I don't know. I think he's still lost, Willy. I think he's very lost.

WILLY: Biff Loman is lost. In the greatest country in the world a young man with such—personal attractiveness, gets lost. And such a hard worker. There's one thing about Biff—he's not lazy.

LINDA: Never.

WILLY: *with pity and resolve.* I'll see him in the morning; I'll have a nice talk with him. I'll get him a job selling. He could be big in no time. My God! Remember how they used to follow him around in high school? When he smiled at one of them their faces lit up. When he walked down the street . . .

He loses himself in reminiscences.

LINDA: *trying to bring him out of it.* Willy, dear, I got a new kind of American-type cheese today. It's whipped.

WILLY: Why do you get American when I like Swiss?

LINDA: I just thought you'd like a change—

WILLY: I don't want a change! I want Swiss cheese. Why am I always being contradicted?

LINDA: *with a covering laugh.* I thought it would be a surprise.

WILLY: Why don't you open a window in here, for God's sake?

LINDA: *with infinite patience.* They're all open, dear.

WILLY: The way they boxed us in here. Bricks and windows, windows and bricks.

LINDA: We should've bought the land next door.

WILLY: The street is lined with cars. There's not a breath of fresh air in the neighborhood. The grass don't grow any more, you can't raise a carrot in the back yard. They should've had a law against apartment houses. Remember those two beautiful elm trees out there? When I and Biff hung the swing between them?

LINDA: Yeah, like being a million miles from the city.

WILLY: They should've arrested the builder for cutting those down. They massacred the neighborhood. *Lost:* More and more I think of those days, Linda. This time of year it was lilac and wisteria. And then the peonies would come out, and the daffodils. What fragrance in this room!

LINDA: Well, after all, people had to move somewhere.

WILLY: No, there's more people now.

LINDA: I don't think there's more people. I think—

WILLY: There's more people! That's what's ruining this country! Population is getting out of control. The competition is maddening! Smell the stink from that apartment house! And another one on the other side . . . How can they whip cheese?

On WILLY's *last line,* BIFF *and* HAPPY *raise themselves up in their beds, listening.*

LINDA: Go down, try it. And be quiet.

WILLY: *turning to* LINDA, *guiltily.* You're not worried about me, are you, sweet-heart?

BIFF: What's the matter?

HAPPY: Listen!

LINDA: You've got too much on the ball to worry about.

WILLY: You're my foundation and my support, Linda.

LINDA: Just try to relax, dear. You make mountains out of molehills.

WILLY: I won't fight with him any more. If he wants to go back to Texas, let him go.

LINDA: He'll find his way.

WILLY: Sure. Certain men just don't get started till later in life. Like Thomas Edison, I think. Or B.F. Goodrich. One of them was deaf. *He starts for the bed-room doorway.* I'll put my money on Biff.

LINDA: And Willy—if it's warm Sunday we'll drive in the country. And we'll open the windshield, and take lunch.

WILLY: No, the windshields don't open on the new cars.

LINDA: But you opened it today.

WILLY: Me? I didn't. *He stops.* Now isn't that peculiar! Isn't that a remark-able—

He breaks off in amazement and fright as the flute is heard distantly.

LINDA: What, darling?

WILLY: That is the most remarkable thing.

LINDA: What, dear?

WILLY: I was thinking of the Chevvy. *Slight pause.* Nineteen twenty-eight . . . when I had that red Chevvy—*Breaks off.* That funny? I coulda sworn I was driving that Chevvy today.

LINDA: Well, that's nothing. Something must've reminded you.

WILLY: Remarkable. Ts. Remember those days? The way Biff used to simonize that car? The dealer refused to believe there was eighty thousand miles on it. *He shakes his head.* Heh! *To* LINDA: Close your eyes, I'll be right up.

He walks out of the bedroom.

HAPPY: *to* BIFF. Jesus, maybe he smashed up the car again!

LINDA: *calling after* WILLY. Be careful on the stairs, dear! The cheese is on the middle shelf!

She turns, goes over to the bed, takes his jacket, and goes out of the bedroom.

Light has risen on the boys' room. Unseen, WILLY *is heard talking to himself, "Eighty thousand miles," and a little laugh.* BIFF *gets out of bed, comes down-stage a bit, and stands attentively.* BIFF *is two years older than his brother* HAPPY, *well built, but in these days bears a worn air and seems less self-assured.*

He has succeeded less, and his dreams are stronger and less acceptable than HAPPY's. HAPPY *is tall, powerfully made. Sexuality is like a visible color on him, or a scent that many women have discovered. He, like his brother, is lost, but in a different way, for he has never allowed himself to turn his face toward defeat and is thus more confused and hard-skinned, although seemingly more content.*

HAPPY: *getting out of bed.* He's going to get his license taken away if he keeps that up. I'm getting nervous about him, y'know, Biff?

BIFF: His eyes are going.

HAPPY: No, I've driven with him. He sees all right. He just doesn't keep his mind on it. I drove into the city with him last week. He stops at a green light and then it turns red and he goes.

He laughs.

BIFF: Maybe he's color-blind.

HAPPY: Pop? Why he's got the finest eye for color in the business. You know that.

BIFF: *sitting down on his bed.* I'm going to sleep.

HAPPY: You're not still sour on Dad, are you, Biff?

BIFF: He's all right, I guess.

WILLY: *underneath them, in the living-room.* Yes, sir, eighty thousand miles— eighty-two thousand!

BIFF: You smoking?

HAPPY: *holding out a pack of cigarettes.* Want one?

BIFF: *taking a cigarette.* I can never sleep when I smell it.

WILLY: What a simonizing job, heh!

HAPPY: *with deep sentiment.* Funny, Biff, y'know? Us sleeping in here again? The old beds. *He pats his bed affectionately.* All the talk that went across those two beds, huh? Our whole lives.

BIFF: Yeah. Lotta dreams and plans.

HAPPY: *with a deep and masculine laugh.* About five hundred women would like to know what was said in this room.

They share a soft laugh.

BIFF: Remember that big Betsy something—what the hell was her name—over on Bushwick Avenue?

HAPPY: *combing his hair.* With the collie dog!

BIFF: That's the one. I got you in there, remember?

HAPPY: Yeah, that was my first time—I think. Boy, there was a pig! *They laugh, almost crudely.* You taught me everything I know about women. Don't forget that.

BIFF: I bet you forgot how bashful you used to be. Especially with girls.

HAPPY: Oh, I still am, Biff.

BIFF: Oh, go on.

HAPPY: I just control it, that's all. I think I got less bashful and you got more so. What happened, Biff? Where's the old humor, the old confidence? *He shakes* BIFF's *knee.* BIFF *gets up and moves restlessly about the room.* What's the matter?

BIFF: Why does Dad mock me all the time?

HAPPY: He's not mocking you, he—

BIFF: Everything I say there's a twist of mockery on his face. I can't get near him.

HAPPY: He just wants you to make good, that's all. I wanted to talk to you about Dad for a long time, Biff. Something's—happening to him. He—talks to himself.

BIFF: I noticed that this morning. But he always mumbled.

HAPPY: But not so noticeable. It got so embarrassing I sent him to Florida. And you know something? Most of the time he's talking to you.

BIFF: What's he say about me?

HAPPY: I can't make it out.

BIFF: What's he say about me?

HAPPY: I think the fact that you're not settled, that you're still kind of up in the air . . .

BIFF: There's one or two other things depressing him, Happy.

HAPPY: What do you mean?

BIFF: Never mind. Just don't lay it all to me.

HAPPY: But I think if you just got started—I mean—is there any future for you out there?

BIFF: I tell ya, Hap, I don't know what the future is. I don't know—what I'm supposed to want.

HAPPY: What do you mean?

BIFF: Well, I spent six or seven years after high school trying to work myself up. Shipping clerk, salesman, business of one kind or another. And it's a measly manner of existence. To get on that subway on the hot mornings in summer. To devote your whole life to keeping stock, or making phone calls, or selling or buying. To suffer fifty weeks of the year for the sake of a two-week vacation, when all you really desire is to be outdoors, with your shirt off. And always to have to get ahead of the next fella. And still—that's how you build a future.

HAPPY: Well, you really enjoy it on a farm? Are you content out there?

BIFF: *with rising agitation.* Hap, I've had twenty or thirty different kinds of jobs since I left home before the war, and it always turns out the same. I just realized it lately. In Nebraska when I herded cattle, and the Dakotas, and Arizona, and now in Texas. It's why I came home now, I guess, because I realized it. This farm I work on, it's spring there now, see? And they've got about fifteen new colts. There's nothing more inspiring or—beautiful than the sight of a mare and a new colt. And it's cool there now, see? Texas is cool now, and it's spring.

And whenever spring comes to where I am, I suddenly get the feeling, my God, I'm not gettin' anywhere! What the hell am I doing, playing around with horses, twenty-eight dollars a week! I'm thirty-four years old, I oughta be makin' my future. That's when I come running home. And now, I get here, and I don't know what to do with myself. *After a pause:* I've always made a point of not wasting my life, and everytime I come back here I know that all I've done is to waste my life.

HAPPY: You're a poet, you know that, Biff? You're a—you're an idealist!

BIFF: No, I'm mixed up very bad. Maybe I oughta get married. Maybe I oughta get stuck into something. Maybe that's my trouble. I'm like a boy. I'm not married, I'm not in business, I just—I'm like a boy. Are you content, Hap? You're a success, aren't you? Are you content?

HAPPY: Hell, no!

BIFF: Why? You're making money, aren't you?

HAPPY: *moving about with energy, expressiveness.* All I can do now is wait for the merchandise manager to die. And suppose I get to be merchandise manager? He's a good friend of mine, and he just built a terrific estate on Long Island. And he lived there about two months and sold it, and now he's building another one. He can't enjoy it once it's finished. And I know that's just what I would do. I don't know what the hell I'm workin' for. Sometimes I sit in my apartment—all alone. And I think of the rent I'm paying. And it's crazy. But then, it's what I always wanted. My own apartment, a car, and plenty of women. And still, goddammit, I'm lonely.

BIFF: *with enthusiasm.* Listen, why don't you come out West with me?

HAPPY: You and I, heh?

BIFF: Sure, maybe we could buy a ranch. Raise cattle, use our muscles. Men built like we are should be working out in the open.

HAPPY: *avidly.* The Loman Brothers, heh?

BIFF: *with vast affection.* Sure, we'd be known all over the counties!

HAPPY: *enthralled.* That's what I dream about, Biff. Sometimes I want to just rip my clothes off in the middle of the store and outbox that goddam merchandise manager. I mean I can outbox, outrun, and outlift anybody in that store, and I have to take orders from those common, petty sons-of-bitches till I can't stand it any more.

BIFF: I'm tellin' you, kid, if you were with me I'd be happy out there.

HAPPY: *enthused.* See, Biff, everybody around me is so false that I'm constantly lowering my ideals ...

BIFF: Baby, together we'd stand up for one another, we'd have someone to trust.

HAPPY: If I were around you—

BIFF: Hap, the trouble is we weren't brought up to grub for money. I don't know how to do it.

HAPPY: Neither can I!

BIFF: Then let's go!

HAPPY: The only thing is—what can you make out there?

BIFF: But look at your friend. Builds an estate and then hasn't the peace of mind to live in it.

HAPPY: Yeah, but when he walks into the store the waves part in front of him. That's fifty-two thousand dollars a year coming through the revolving door, and I got more in my pinky finger than he's got in his head.

BIFF: Yeah, but you just said—

HAPPY: I gotta show some of those pompous, self-important executives over there that Hap Loman can make the grade. I want to walk into the store the way he walks in. Then I'll go with you, Biff. We'll be together yet, I swear. But take those two we had tonight. Now weren't they gorgeous creatures?

BIFF: Yeah, yeah, most gorgeous I've had in years.

HAPPY: I get that any time I want, Biff. Whenever I feel disgusted. The only trouble is, it gets like bowling or something. I just keep knockin' them over and it doesn't mean anything. You still run around a lot?

BIFF: Naa. I'd like to find a girl—steady, somebody with substance.

HAPPY: That's what I long for.

BIFF: Go on! You'd never come home.

HAPPY: I would! Somebody with character, with resistance! Like Mom, y'know? You're gonna call me a bastard when I tell you this. That girl Charlotte I was with tonight is engaged to be married in five weeks.

He tries on his new hat.

BIFF: No kiddin'!

HAPPY: Sure, the guy's in line for the vice-presidency of the store. I don't know what gets into me, maybe I just have an overdeveloped sense of competition or something, but I went and ruined her, and furthermore I can't get rid of her. And he's the third executive I've done that to. Isn't that a crummy characteristic? And to top it all, I go to their weddings! *Indignantly, but laughing:* Like I'm not supposed to take bribes. Manufacturers offer me a hundred-dollar bill now and then to throw an order their way. You know how honest I am, but it's like this girl, see. I hate myself for it. Because I don't want the girl, and, still, I take it and—I love it!

BIFF: Let's go to sleep.

HAPPY: I guess we didn't settle anything, heh?

BIFF: I just got one idea that I think I'm going to try.

HAPPY: What's that?

BIFF: Remember Bill Oliver?

HAPPY: Sure, Oliver is very big now. You want to work for him again?

BIFF: No, but when I quit he said something to me. He put his arm on my shoulder, and he said, "Biff, if you ever need anything, come to me."

HAPPY: I remember that. That sounds good.

BIFF: I think I'll go to see him. If I could get ten thousand or even seven or eight thousand dollars I could buy a beautiful ranch.

HAPPY: I bet he'd back you. 'Cause he thought highly of you, Biff. I mean, they all do. You're well liked, Biff. That's why I say to come back here, and we both have the apartment. And I'm tellin' you, Biff, any babe you want . . .

BIFF: No, with a ranch I could do the work I like and still be something. I just wonder though. I wonder if Oliver still thinks I stole that carton of basketballs.

HAPPY: Oh, he probably forgot that long ago. It's almost ten years. You're too sensitive. Anyway, he didn't really fire you.

BIFF: Well, I think he was going to. I think that's why I quit. I was never sure whether he knew or not. I know he thought the world of me, though. I was the only one he'd let lock up the place.

WILLY: *below.* You gonna wash the engine, Biff?

HAPPY: Shh!

BIFF *looks at* HAPPY, *who is gazing down, listening.* WILLY *is mumbling in the parlor.*

HAPPY: You hear that?

They listen. WILLY *laughs warmly.*

BIFF: *growing angry.* Doesn't he know Mom can hear that?

WILLY: Don't get your sweater dirty, Biff!

A look of pain crosses BIFF's *face.*

HAPPY: Isn't that terrible? Don't leave again, will you? You'll find a job here. You gotta stick around. I don't know what to do about him, it's getting embarrassing.

WILLY: What a simonizing job!

BIFF: Mom's hearing that!

WILLY: No kiddin', Biff, you got a date? Wonderful!

HAPPY: Go on to sleep. But talk to him in the morning, will you?

BIFF: *reluctantly getting into bed.* With her in the house. Brother!

HAPPY: *getting into bed.* I wish you'd have a good talk with him.

The light on their room begins to fade.

BIFF: *to himself in bed.* That selfish, stupid . . .

HAPPY: Sh . . . Sleep, Biff.

Their light is out. Well before they have finished speaking, WILLY's *form is dimly seen below in the darkened kitchen. He opens the refrigerator, searches in there, and takes out a bottle of milk. The apartment houses are fading out, and the*

*entire house and surroundings become covered with leaves. Music insinuates it-
self as the leaves appear.*

WILLY: Just wanna be careful with those girls, Biff, that's all. Don't make any
promises. No promises of any kind. Because a girl, y'know, they always believe what you tell 'em, and you're very young, Biff, you're too young to be
talking seriously to girls.

Light rises on the kitchen. WILLY, *talking, shuts the refrigerator door and comes
downstage to the kitchen table. He pours milk into a glass. He is totally immersed in himself, smiling faintly.*

WILLY: Too young entirely, Biff. You want to watch your schooling first. Then
when you're all set, there'll be plenty of girls for a boy like you. *He smiles
broadly at a kitchen chair.* That so? The girls pay for you? *He laughs.* Boy, you
must really be makin' a hit.

WILLY *is gradually addressing—physically—a point offstage, speaking through the
wall of the kitchen, and his voice has been rising in volume to that of a normal
conversation.*

WILLY: I been wondering why you polish the car so careful. Ha! Don't leave
the hubcaps, boys. Get the chamois to the hubcaps. Happy, use newspaper on
the windows, it's the easiest thing. Show him how to do it, Biff! You see,
Happy? Pad it up, use it like a pad. That's it, that's it, good work. You're doin'
all right, Hap. *He pauses, then nods in approbation for a few seconds, then
looks upward.* Biff, first thing we gotta do when we get time is clip that big
branch over the house. Afraid it's gonna fall in a storm and hit the roof. Tell
you what. We get a rope and sling her around, and then we climb up there
with a couple of saws and take her down. Soon as you finish the car, boys, I
wanna see ya. I got a surprise for you, boys.
BIFF: *offstage.* Whatta ya got, Dad?
WILLY: No, you finish first. Never leave a job till you're finished—remember
that. *Looking toward the "big trees":* Biff, up in Albany I saw a beautiful ham-
mock. I think I'll buy it next trip, and we'll hang it right between those two
elms. Wouldn't that be something? Just swingin' there under those branches.
Boy, that would be . . .

Young BIFF *and Young* HAPPY *appear from the direction* WILLY *was addressing.*
HAPPY *carries rags and a pail of water.* BIFF, *wearing a sweater with a block
"S," carries a football.*

BIFF: *pointing in the direction of the car offstage,* How's that, Pop, professional?
WILLY: Terrific. Terrific job, boys. Good work, Biff.
HAPPY: Where's the surprise, Pop?

WILLY: In the back seat of the car.

HAPPY: Boy! *He runs off.*

BIFF: What is it, Dad? Tell me, what'd you buy?

WILLY: *laughing, cuffs him.* Never mind, something I want you to have.

BIFF: *turns and starts off.* What is it, Hap?

HAPPY: *offstage.* It's a punching bag!

BIFF: Oh, Pop!

WILLY: It's got Gene Tunney's[1] signature on it!

HAPPY *runs onstage with a punching bag.*

BIFF: Gee, how'd you know we wanted a punching bag?

WILLY: Well, it's the finest thing for the timing.

HAPPY: *lies down on his back and pedals with his feet.* I'm losing weight, you notice, Pop?

WILLY: *to* HAPPY. Jumping rope is good too.

BIFF: Did you see the new football I got?

WILLY: *examining the ball.* Where'd you get a new ball?

BIFF: The coach told me to practice my passing.

WILLY: That so? And he gave you the ball, heh?

BIFF: Well, I borrowed it from the locker room.

He laughs confidentially.

WILLY: *laughing with him at the theft.* I want you to return that.

HAPPY: I told you he wouldn't like it!

BIFF: *angrily.* Well, I'm bringing it back!

WILLY: *stopping the incipient argument, to* HAPPY. Sure, he's gotta practice with a regulation football, doesn't he? *To* BIFF: Coach'll probably congratulate you on your initiative!

BIFF: Oh, he keeps congratulating my initiative all the time, Pop.

WILLY: That's because he likes you. If somebody else took that ball there'd be an uproar. So what's the report, boys, what's the report?

BIFF: Where'd you go this time, Dad? Gee we were lonesome for you.

WILLY: *pleased, puts an arm around each boy and they come down to the apron.* Lonesome, heh?

BIFF: Missed you every minute.

WILLY: Don't say? Tell you a secret, boys. Don't breathe it to a soul. Someday I'll have my own business, and I'll never have to leave home any more.

HAPPY: Like Uncle Charley, heh?

WILLY: Bigger than Uncle Charley! Because Charley is not—liked. He's liked, but he's not—well liked.

------

[1]Heavy-weight boxer (1898–1978).

BIFF: Where'd you go this time, Dad?

WILLY: Well, I got on the road, and I went north to Providence. Met the Mayor.

BIFF: The Mayor of Providence!

WILLY: He was sitting in the hotel lobby.

BIFF: What'd he say?

WILLY: He said, "Morning!" And I said, "You got a fine city here, Mayor." And then he had coffee with me. And then I went to Waterbury. Waterbury is a fine city. Big clock city, the famous Waterbury clock. Sold a nice bill there. And then Boston—Boston is the cradle of the Revolution. A fine city. And a couple of other towns in Mass., and on to Portland and Bangor and straight home!

BIFF: Gee, I'd love to go with you sometime, Dad.

WILLY: Soon as summer comes.

HAPPY: Promise?

WILLY: You and Hap and I, and I'll show you all the towns. America is full of beautiful towns and fine, upstanding people. And they know me, boys, they know me up and down New England. The finest people. And when I bring you fellas up, there'll be open sesame for all of us, 'cause one thing, boys: I have friends. I can park my car in any street in New England, and the cops protect it like their own. This summer, heh?

BIFF AND HAPPY: *together.* Yeah! You bet!

WILLY: We'll take our bathing suits.

HAPPY: We'll carry your bags, Pop!

WILLY: Oh, won't that be something! Me comin' into the Boston stores with you boys carryin' my bags. What a sensation!

BIFF *is prancing around, practicing passing the ball.*

WILLY: You nervous, Biff, about the game?

BIFF: Not if you're gonna be there.

WILLY: What do they say about you in school, now that they made you captain?

HAPPY: There's a crowd of girls behind him every time the classes change.

BIFF: *taking* WILLY's *hand.* This Saturday, Pop, this Saturday—just for you, I'm going to break through for a touchdown.

HAPPY: You're supposed to pass.

BIFF: I'm takin' one play for Pop. You watch me, Pop, and when I take off my helmet, that means I'm breakin' out. Then you watch me crash through that line!

WILLY: *kisses* BIFF. Oh, wait'll I tell this in Boston!

BERNARD *enters in knickers. He is younger than* BIFF, *earnest and loyal, a worried boy.*

BERNARD: Biff, where are you? You're supposed to study with me today.

WILLY: Hey, looka Bernard. What're you lookin' so anemic about, Bernard?

BERNARD: He's gotta study, Uncle Willy. He's got Regents[2] next week.

HAPPY: *tauntingly, spinning* BERNARD *around.* Let's box, Bernard!

BERNARD: Biff! *He gets away from* HAPPY. Listen, Biff, I heard Mr. Birnbaum say that if you don't start studyin' math he's gonna flunk you, and you won't graduate. I heard him!

WILLY: You better study with him, Biff. Go ahead now.

BERNARD: I heard him!

BIFF: Oh, Pop, you didn't see my sneakers!

He holds up a foot for WILLY *to look at.*

WILLY: Hey, that's a beautiful job of printing!

BERNARD: *wiping his glasses.* Just because he printed University of Virginia on his sneakers doesn't mean they've got to graduate him, Uncle Willy!

WILLY: *angrily.* What're you talking about? With scholarships to three universities they're gonna flunk him?

BERNARD: But I heard Mr. Birnbaum say—

WILLY: Don't be a pest, Bernard! *To his boys:* What an anemic!

BERNARD: Okay, I'm waiting for you in my house, Biff.

BERNARD *goes off. The Lomans laugh.*

WILLY: Bernard is not well liked, is he?

BIFF: He's liked, but he's not well liked.

HAPPY: That's right, Pop.

WILLY: That's just what I mean. Bernard can get the best marks in school, y'understand, but when he gets out in the business world, y'understand, you are going to be five times ahead of him. That's why I thank Almighty God you're both built like Adonises. Because the man who makes an appearance in the business world, the man who creates personal interest, is the man who gets ahead. Be liked and you will never want. You take me, for instance. I never have to wait in line to see a buyer. "Willy Loman is here!" That's all they have to know, and I go right through.

BIFF: Did you knock them dead, Pop?

WILLY: Knocked 'em cold in Providence, slaughtered 'em in Boston.

HAPPY: *on his back, pedaling again.* I'm losing weight, you notice, Pop?

LINDA *enters, as of old, a ribbon in her hair, carrying a basket of washing.*

LINDA: *with youthful energy.* Hello, dear!

WILLY: Sweetheart!

LINDA: How'd the Chevvy run?

---

[2]Standardized examinations for high school students in New York State.

WILLY: Chevrolet, Linda, is the greatest car ever built. *To the boys:* Since when do you let your mother carry wash up the stairs?

BIFF: Grab hold there, boy!

HAPPY: Where to, Mom?

LINDA: Hang them up on the line. And you better go down to your friends, Biff. The cellar is full of boys. They don't know what to do with themselves.

BIFF: Ah, when Pop comes home they can wait!

WILLY: *laughs appreciatively.* You better go down and tell them what to do, Biff.

BIFF: I think I'll have them sweep out the furnace room.

WILLY: Good work, Biff.

BIFF: *goes through wall-line of kitchen to doorway at back and calls down.* Fellas! Everybody sweep out the furnace room! I'll be right down!

VOICES: All right! Okay, Biff.

BIFF: George and Sam and Frank, come out back! We're hangin' up the wash! Come on, Hap, on the double!

He and HAPPY *carry out the basket.*

LINDA: The way they obey him!

WILLY: Well, that's training, the training. I'm tellin' you, I was sellin' thousands and thousands, but I had to come home.

LINDA: Oh, the whole block'll be at that game. Did you sell anything?

WILLY: I did five hundred gross in Providence and seven hundred gross in Boston.

LINDA: No! Wait a minute, I've got a pencil. *She pulls pencil and paper out of her apron pocket.* That makes your commission . . . Two hundred—my God! Two hundred and twelve dollars!

WILLY: Well, I didn't figure it yet, but . . .

LINDA: How much did you do?

WILLY: Well, I—I did—about a hundred and eighty gross in Providence. Well, no—it came to—roughly two hundred gross on the whole trip.

LINDA: *without hesitation.* Two hundred gross. That's . . .

She figures.

WILLY: The trouble was that three of the stores were half closed for inventory in Boston. Otherwise I woulda broke records.

LINDA: Well, it makes seventy dollars and some pennies. That's very good.

WILLY: What do we owe?

LINDA: Well, on the first there's sixteen dollars on the refrigerator—

WILLY: Why sixteen?

LINDA: Well, the fan belt broke, so it was a dollar eighty.

WILLY: But it's brand new.

LINDA: Well, the man said that's the way it is. Till they work themselves in, y'know.

They move through the wall-line into the kitchen.

WILLY: I hope we didn't get stuck on that machine.

LINDA: They got the biggest ads of any of them!

WILLY: I know, it's a fine machine. What else?

LINDA: Well, there's nine-sixty for the washing machine. And for the vacuum cleaner there's three and a half due on the fifteenth. Then the roof, you got twenty-one dollars remaining.

WILLY: It don't leak, does it?

LINDA: No, they did a wonderful job. Then you owe Frank for the carburetor.

WILLY: I'm not going to pay that man! That goddam Chevrolet, they ought to prohibit the manufacture of that car!

LINDA: Well, you owe him three and a half. And odds and ends, comes to around a hundred and twenty dollars by the fifteenth.

WILLY: A hundred and twenty dollars! My God, if business don't pick up I don't know what I'm gonna do!

LINDA: Well, next week you'll do better.

WILLY: Oh, I'll knock 'em dead next week. I'll go to Hartford. I'm very well liked in Hartford. You know, the trouble is, Linda, people don't seem to take to me.

They move onto the forestage.

LINDA: Oh, don't be foolish.

WILLY: I know it when I walk in. They seem to laugh at me.

LINDA: Why? Why would they laugh at you? Don't talk that way, Willy.

WILLY *moves to the edge of the stage,* LINDA *goes into the kitchen and starts to darn stockings.*

WILLY: I don't know the reason for it, but they just pass me by. I'm not noticed.

LINDA: But you're doing wonderful, dear. You're making seventy to a hundred dollars a week.

WILLY: But I gotta be at it ten, twelve hours a day. Other men—I don't know—they do it easier. I don't know why—I can't stop myself—I talk too much. A man oughta come in with a few words. One thing about Charley. He's a man of few words, and they respect him.

LINDA: You don't talk too much, you're just lively.

WILLY: *smiling.* Well, I figure, what the hell, life is short, a couple of jokes. *To himself:* I joke too much! *The smile goes.*

LINDA: Why? You're—

WILLY: I'm fat. I'm very—foolish to look at, Linda. I didn't tell you, but Christmas time I happened to be calling on F. H. Stewarts, and a salesman I know, as I was going in to see the buyer I heard him say something about—walrus.

And I—I cracked him right across the face. I won't take that. I simply will not take that. But they do laugh at me. I know that.

LINDA: Darling ...

WILLY: I gotta overcome it. I know I gotta overcome it. I'm not dressing to advantage, maybe.

LINDA: Willy, darling, you're the handsomest man in the world—

WILLY: Oh, no, Linda.

LINDA: To me you are. *Slight pause.* The handsomest.

From the darkness is heard the laughter of a woman. WILLY *doesn't turn to it, but it continues through* LINDA's *lines.*

LINDA: And the boys, Willy. Few men are idolized by their children the way you are.

Music is heard as behind a scrim, to the left of the house, THE WOMAN, *dimly seen, is dressing.*

WILLY: *with great feeling.* You're the best there is, Linda, you're a pal, you know that? On the road—on the road I want to grab you sometimes and just kiss the life outa you.

The laughter is loud now, and he moves into a brightening area at the left, where THE WOMAN *has come from behind the scrim and is standing, putting on her hat, looking into a "mirror" and laughing.*

WILLY: 'Cause I get so lonely—especially when business is bad and there's nobody to talk to. I get the feeling that I'll never sell anything again, that I won't make a living for you, or a business, a business for the boys. *He talks through* THE WOMAN's *subsiding laughter;* THE WOMAN *primps at the "mirror."* There's so much I want to make for—

THE WOMAN: Me? You didn't make me, Willy. I picked you.

WILLY: *pleased.* You picked me?

THE WOMAN: *who is quite proper-looking,* WILLY's *age.* I did. I've been sitting at that desk watching all the salesmen go by, day in, day out. But you've got such a sense of humor, and we do have such a good time together, don't we?

WILLY: Sure, sure. *He takes her in his arms.* Why do you have to go now?

THE WOMAN: It's two o'clock ...

WILLY: No, come on in! *He pulls her.*

THE WOMAN: ... my sisters'll be scandalized. When'll you be back?

WILLY: Oh, two weeks about. Will you come up again?

THE WOMAN: Sure thing. You do make me laugh. It's good for me. *She squeezes his arm, kisses him.* And I think you're a wonderful man.

WILLY: You picked me, heh?

THE WOMAN: Sure. Because you're so sweet. And such a kidder.

WILLY: Well, I'll see you next time I'm in Boston.

THE WOMAN: I'll put you right through to the buyers.

WILLY: *slapping her bottom.* Right. Well, bottoms up!

THE WOMAN: *slaps him gently and laughs.* You just kill me, Willy. *He suddenly grabs her and kisses her roughly.* You kill me. And thanks for the stockings. I love a lot of stockings. Well, good night.

WILLY: Good night. And keep your pores open!

THE WOMAN: Oh, Willy!

THE WOMAN *bursts out laughing, and* LINDA'*s laughter blends in.* THE WOMAN *disappears into the dark. Now the area at the kitchen table brightens.* LINDA *is sitting where she was at the kitchen table, but now is mending a pair of her silk stockings.*

LINDA: You are, Willy. The handsomest man. You've got no reason to feel that—

WILLY: *coming out of* THE WOMAN'*s dimming area and going over to* LINDA. I'll make it all up to you, Linda, I'll—

LINDA: There's nothing to make up, dear. You're doing fine, better than—

WILLY: *noticing her mending.* What's that?

LINDA: Just mending my stockings. They're so expensive—

WILLY: *angrily, taking them from her.* I won't have you mending stockings in this house! Now throw them out!

LINDA *puts the stockings in her pocket.*

BERNARD: *entering on the run.* Where is he? If he doesn't study!

WILLY: *moving to the forestage, with great agitation.* You'll give him the answers!

BERNARD: I do, but I can't on a Regents! That's a state exam! They're liable to arrest me!

WILLY: Where is he? I'll whip him, I'll whip him!

LINDA: And he'd better give back that football, Willy, it's not nice.

WILLY: Biff! Where is he? Why is he taking everything?

LINDA: He's too rough with the girls, Willy. All the mothers are afraid of him!

WILLY: I'll whip him!

BERNARD: He's driving the car without a license!

THE WOMAN'*s laugh is heard.*

WILLY: Shut up!

LINDA: All the mothers—

WILLY: Shut up!

BERNARD: *backing quietly away and out.* Mr. Birnbaum says he's stuck up.

WILLY: Get outa here!

BERNARD: If he doesn't buckle down he'll flunk math!

He goes off.

LINDA: He's right, Willy, you've gotta—

WILLY: *exploding at her.* There's nothing the matter with him! You want him to be a worm like Bernard? He's got spirit, personality . . .

As he speaks, LINDA, *almost in tears, exits into the living-room.* WILLY *is alone in the kitchen, wilting and staring. The leaves are gone. It is night again, and the apartment houses look down from behind.*

WILLY: Loaded with it. Loaded! What is he stealing? He's giving it back, isn't he? Why is he stealing? What did I tell him? I never in my life told him anything but decent things.

HAPPY *in pajamas has come down the stairs;* WILLY *suddenly becomes aware of* HAPPY's *presence.*

HAPPY: Let's go now, come on.

WILLY: *sitting down at the kitchen table.* Huh! Why did she have to wax the floors herself? Everytime she waxes the floors she keels over. She knows that!

HAPPY: Shh! Take it easy. What brought you back tonight?

WILLY: I got an awful scare. Nearly hit a kid in Yonkers. God! Why didn't I go to Alaska with my brother Ben that time! Ben! That man was a genius, that man was success incarnate! What a mistake! He begged me to go.

HAPPY: Well, there's no use in—

WILLY: You guys! There was a man started with the clothes on his back and ended up with diamond mines!

HAPPY: Boy, someday I'd like to know how he did it.

WILLY: What's the mystery? The man knew what he wanted and went out and got it! Walked into a jungle, and comes out, the age of twenty-one, and he's rich! The world is an oyster, but you don't crack it open on a mattress!

HAPPY: Pop, I told you I'm gonna retire you for life.

WILLY: You'll retire me for life on seventy goddam dollars a week? And your women and your car and your apartment, and you'll retire me for life! Christ's sake, I couldn't get past Yonkers today! Where are you guys, where are you? The woods are burning! I can't drive a car!

CHARLEY *has appeared in the doorway. He is a large man, slow of speech, laconic, immovable. In all he says, despite what he says, there is pity, and, now, trepidation. He has a robe over pajamas, slippers on his feet. He enters the kitchen.*

CHARLEY: Everything all right?

HAPPY: Yeah, Charley, everything's . . .

WILLY: What's the matter?

CHARLEY: I heard some noise. I thought something happened. Can't we do something about the walls? You sneeze in here, and in my house hats blow off.

HAPPY: Let's go to bed, Dad. Come on.

CHARLEY *signals to* HAPPY *to go.*

WILLY: You go ahead, I'm not tired at the moment.

HAPPY: *to* WILLY. Take it easy, huh? *He exits.*

WILLY: What're you doin' up?

CHARLEY: *sitting down at the kitchen table opposite* WILLY. Couldn't sleep good. I had a heartburn.

WILLY: Well, you don't know how to eat.

CHARLEY: I eat with my mouth.

WILLY: No, you're ignorant. You gotta know about vitamins and things like that.

CHARLEY: Come on, let's shoot. Tire you out a little.

WILLY: *hesitantly.* All right. You got cards?

CHARLEY: *taking a deck from his pocket.* Yeah, I got them. Someplace. What is it with those vitamins?

WILLY: *dealing.* They build up your bones. Chemistry.

CHARLEY: Yeah, but there's no bones in a heartburn.

WILLY: What are you talkin' about? Do you know the first thing about it?

CHARLEY: Don't get insulted.

WILLY: Don't talk about something you don't know anything about.

They are playing. Pause.

CHARLEY: What're you doin' home?

WILLY: A little trouble with the car.

CHARLEY: Oh. *Pause.* I'd like to take a trip to California.

WILLY: Don't say.

CHARLEY: You want a job?

WILLY: I got a job, I told you that. *After a slight pause:* What the hell are you offering me a job for?

CHARLEY: Don't get insulted.

WILLY: Don't insult me.

CHARLEY: I don't see no sense in it. You don't have to go on this way.

WILLY: I got a good job. *Slight pause.* What do you keep comin' in here for?

CHARLEY: You want me to go?

WILLY: *after a pause, withering.* I can't understand it. He's going back to Texas again. What the hell is that?

CHARLEY: Let him go.

WILLY: I got nothin' to give him, Charley, I'm clean, I'm clean.

CHARLEY: He won't starve. None a them starve. Forget about him.

WILLY: Then what have I got to remember?

CHARLEY: You take it too hard. To hell with it. When a deposit bottle is broken you don't get your nickel back.

WILLY: That's easy enough for you to say.

CHARLEY: That ain't easy for me to say.

WILLY: Did you see the ceiling I put up in the living-room?

CHARLEY: Yeah, that's a piece of work. To put up a ceiling is a mystery to me. How do you do it?

WILLY: What's the difference?

CHARLEY: Well, talk about it.

WILLY: You gonna put up a ceiling?

CHARLEY: How could I put up a ceiling?

WILLY: Then what the hell are you bothering me for?

CHARLEY: You're insulted again.

WILLY: A man who can't handle tools is not a man. You're disgusting.

CHARLEY: Don't call me disgusting, Willy.

UNCLE BEN, *carrying a valise and an umbrella, enters the forestage from around the right corner of the house. He is a stolid man, in his sixties, with a mustache and an authoritative air. He is utterly certain of his destiny, and there is an aura of far places about him. He enters exactly as* WILLY *speaks.*

WILLY: I'm getting awfully tired, Ben.

BEN's *music is heard.* BEN *looks around at everything.*

CHARLEY: Good, keep playing; you'll sleep better. Did you call me Ben?

BEN *looks at his watch.*

WILLY: That's funny. For a second there you reminded me of my brother Ben.

BEN: I only have a few minutes. *He strolls, inspecting the place.* WILLY *and* CHARLEY *continue playing.*

CHARLEY: You never heard from him again, heh? Since that time?

WILLY: Didn't Linda tell you? Couple of weeks ago we got a letter from his wife in Africa. He died.

CHARLEY: That so.

BEN: *chuckling.* So this is Brooklyn, eh?

CHARLEY: Maybe you're in for some of his money.

WILLY: Naa, he had seven sons. There's just one opportunity I had with that man ...

BEN: I must make a train, William. There are several properties I'm looking at in Alaska.

WILLY: Sure, sure! If I'd gone with him to Alaska that time, everything would've been totally different.

CHARLEY: Go on, you'd froze to death up there.

WILLY: What're you talking about?

BEN: Opportunity is tremendous in Alaska, William. Surprised you're not up there.

WILLY: Sure, tremendous.

CHARLEY: Heh?

WILLY: There was the only man I ever met who knew the answers.

CHARLEY: Who?

BEN: How are you all?

WILLY: *taking a pot, smiling.* Fine, fine.

CHARLEY: Pretty sharp tonight.

BEN: Is Mother living with you?

WILLY: No, she died a long time ago.

CHARLEY: Who?

BEN: That's too bad. Fine specimen of a lady, Mother.

WILLY: to CHARLEY. Heh?

BEN: I'd hoped to see the old girl.

CHARLEY: Who died?

BEN: Heard anything from Father, have you?

WILLY: *unnerved.* What do you mean, who died?

CHARLEY: *taking a pot.* What're you talkin' about?

BEN: *looking at his watch.* William, it's half-past eight!

WILLY: *as though to dispel his confusion he angrily stops* CHARLEY's *hand.* That's my build!

CHARLEY: I put the ace—

WILLY: If you don't know how to play the game I'm not gonna throw my money away on you!

CHARLEY: *rising.* It was my ace, for God's sake!

WILLY: I'm through, I'm through!

BEN: When did Mother die?

WILLY: Long ago. Since the beginning you never knew how to play cards.

CHARLEY: *picks up the cards and goes to the door.* All right! Next time I'll bring a deck with five aces.

WILLY: I don't play that kind of game!

CHARLEY: *turning to him.* You ought to be ashamed of yourself!

WILLY: Yeah?

CHARLEY: Yeah! *He goes out.*

WILLY: *slamming the door after him.* Ignoramus!

BEN: *as* WILLY *comes toward him through the wall-line of the kitchen.* So you're William.

WILLY: *shaking* BEN's *hand.* Ben! I've been waiting for you so long! What's the answer? How did you do it?

BEN: Oh, there's a story in that.

LINDA *enters the forestage, as of old, carrying the wash basket.*

LINDA: Is this Ben?

BEN: *gallantly.* How do you do, my dear.

LINDA: Where've you been all these years? Willy's always wondered why you—

WILLY: *pulling* BEN *away from her impatiently.* Where is Dad? Didn't you follow him? How did you get started?

BEN: Well, I don't know how much you remember.

WILLY: Well, I was just a baby, of course, only three or four years old—

BEN: Three years and eleven months.

WILLY: What a memory, Ben!

BEN: I have many enterprises, William, and I have never kept books.

WILLY: I remember I was sitting under the wagon in—was it Nebraska?

BEN: It was South Dakota, and I gave you a bunch of wild flowers.

WILLY: I remember you walking away down some open road.

BEN: *laughing.* I was going to find Father in Alaska.

WILLY: Where is he?

BEN: At that age I had a very faulty view of geography, William. I discovered after a few days that I was heading due south, so instead of Alaska, I ended up in Africa.

LINDA: Africa!

WILLY: The Gold Coast!

BEN: Principally diamond mines.

LINDA: Diamond mines!

BEN: Yes, my dear. But I've only a few minutes—

WILLY: No! Boys! Boys! *Young* BIFF *and* HAPPY *appear.* Listen to this. This is your Uncle Ben, a great man! Tell my boys, Ben!

BEN: Why, boys, when I was seventeen I walked into the jungle, and when I was twenty-one I walked out. *He laughs.* And by God I was rich.

WILLY: *to the boys.* You see what I been talking about? The greatest things can happen!

BEN: *glancing at his watch.* I have an appointment in Ketchikan Tuesday week.

WILLY: No, Ben! Please tell about Dad. I want my boys to hear. I want them to know the kind of stock they spring from. All I remember is a man with a big beard, and I was in Mamma's lap, sitting around a fire, and some kind of high music.

BEN: His flute. He played the flute.

WILLY: Sure, the flute, that's right!

New music is heard, a high, rollicking tune.

BEN: Father was a very great and a very wild-hearted man. We would start in Boston, and he'd toss the whole family into the wagon, and then he'd drive the team right across the country; through Ohio, and Indiana, Michigan, Illinois, and all the Western states. And we'd stop in the towns and sell the flutes that he'd made on the way. Great inventor, Father. With one gadget he made more in a week than a man like you could make in a lifetime.

WILLY: That's just the way I'm bringing them up, Ben—rugged, well liked, all-around.

BEN: Yeah? *To* BIFF: Hit that, boy—hard as you can. *He pounds his stomach.*

BIFF: Oh, no, sir!

BEN: *taking boxing stance.* Come on, get to me! *He laughs.*

WILLY: Go to it, Biff! Go ahead, show him!

BIFF: Okay! *He cocks his fists and starts in.*

LINDA: *to* WILLY. Why must he fight, dear?

BEN: *sparring with* BIFF. Good boy! Good boy!

WILLY: How's that, Ben, heh?

HAPPY: Give him the left, Biff!

LINDA: Why are you fighting?

BEN: Good boy! *Suddenly comes in, trips* BIFF, *and stands over him, the point of his umbrella poised over* BIFF's *eye.*

LINDA: Look out, Biff!

BIFF: Gee!

BEN: *patting* BIFF's *knee.* Never fight fair with a stranger, boy. You'll never get out of the jungle that way. *Taking* LINDA's *hand and bowing.* It was an honor and a pleasure to meet you, Linda.

LINDA: *withdrawing her hand coldly, frightened.* Have a nice—trip.

BEN: *to* WILLY. And good luck with your—what do you do?

WILLY: Selling.

BEN: Yes. Well . . . *He raises his hand in farewell to all.*

WILLY: No, Ben, I don't want you to think . . . *He takes* BEN's *arm to show him.* It's Brooklyn, I know, but we hunt too.

BEN: Really, now.

WILLY: Oh, sure, there's snakes and rabbits and—that's why I moved out here. Why, Biff can fell any one of these trees in no time! Boys! Go right over to where they're building the apartment house and get some sand. We're gonna rebuild the entire front stoop right now! Watch this, Ben!

BIFF: Yes, sir! On the double, Hap!

HAPPY: *as he and* BIFF *run off.* I lost weight, Pop, you notice?

CHARLEY *enters in knickers, even before the boys are gone.*

CHARLEY: Listen, if they steal any more from that building the watchman'll put the cops on them!

LINDA: *to* WILLY. Don't let Biff . . .

BEN *laughs lustily.*

WILLY: You shoulda seen the lumber they brought home last week. At least a dozen six-by-tens worth all kinds a money.

CHARLEY: Listen, if that watchman—

WILLY: I gave them hell, understand. But I got a couple of fearless characters there.

CHARLEY: Willy, the jails are full of fearless characters.

BEN: *clapping* WILLY *on the back, with a laugh at* CHARLEY. And the stock exchange, friend!

WILLY: *joining in* BEN's *laughter.* Where are the rest of your pants?

CHARLEY: My wife bought them.

WILLY: Now all you need is a golf club and you can go upstairs and go to sleep. *To* BEN: Great athlete! Between him and his son Bernard they can't hammer a nail!

BERNARD: *rushing in.* The watchman's chasing Biff!

WILLY: *angrily.* Shut up! He's not stealing anything!

LINDA: *alarmed, hurrying off left.* Where is he? Biff, dear! *She exits.*

WILLY: *moving toward the left, away from* BEN. There's nothing wrong. What's the matter with you?

BEN: Nervy boy. Good!

WILLY: *laughing.* Oh, nerves of iron, that Biff!

CHARLEY: Don't know that it is. My New England man comes back and he's bleedin', they murdered him up there.

WILLY: It's contacts, Charley, I got important contacts!

CHARLEY: *sarcastically.* Glad to hear it, Willy. Come in later, we'll shoot a little casino. I'll take some of your Portland money. *He laughs at* WILLY *and exits.*

WILLY: *turning to* BEN. Business is bad, it's murderous. But not for me, of course.

BEN: I'll stop by on my way back to Africa.

WILLY: *longingly.* Can't you stay a few days? You're just what I need, Ben, because I—I have a fine position here, but I—well, Dad left when I was such a baby and I never had a chance to talk to him and I still feel—kind of temporary about myself.

BEN: I'll be late for my train.

They are at opposite ends of the stage.

WILLY: Ben, my boys—can't we talk? They'd go into the jaws of hell for me, see, but I—

BEN: William, you're being first-rate with your boys. Outstanding, manly chaps!

WILLY: *hanging on to his words.* Oh, Ben, that's good to hear! Because sometimes I'm afraid that I'm not teaching them the right kind of—Ben, how should I teach them?

BEN: *giving great weight to each word, and with a certain vicious audacity.* William, when I walked into the jungle, I was seventeen. When I walked out I was twenty-one. And, by God, I was rich! *He goes off into darkness around the right corner of the house.*

WILLY: . . . was rich! That's just the spirit I want to imbue them with! To walk
into a jungle! I was right! I was right! I was right!

BEN *is gone, but* WILLY *is still speaking to him as* LINDA, *in nightgown and robe,
enters the kitchen, glances around for* WILLY, *then goes to the door of the house,
looks out and sees him. Comes down to his left. He looks at her.*

LINDA: Willy, dear? Willy?
WILLY: I was right!
LINDA: Did you have some cheese? *He can't answer.* It's very late, darling.
Come to bed, heh?
WILLY: *looking straight up.* Gotta break your neck to see a star in this yard.
LINDA: You coming in?
WILLY: Whatever happened to that diamond watch fob? Remember? When
Ben came from Africa that time? Didn't he give me a watch fob with a dia-
mond in it?
LINDA: You pawned it, dear. Twelve, thirteen years ago. For Biff's radio corre-
spondence course.
WILLY: Gee, that was a beautiful thing. I'll take a walk.
LINDA: But you're in your slippers.
WILLY: *starting to go around the house at the left.* I was right! I was! *Half to*
LINDA, *as he goes, shaking his head:* What a man! There was a man worth talk-
ing to. I was right!
LINDA: *calling after* WILLY. But in your slippers, Willy!

WILLY *is almost gone when* BIFF, *in his pajamas, comes down the stairs and
enters the kitchen.*

BIFF: What is he doing out there?
LINDA: Sh!
BIFF: God Almighty, Mom, how long has he been doing this?
LINDA: Don't, he'll hear you.
BIFF: What the hell is the matter with him?
LINDA: It'll pass by morning.
BIFF: Shouldn't we do anything?
LINDA: Oh, my dear, you should do a lot of things, but there's nothing to do, so
go to sleep.

HAPPY *comes down the stair and sits on the steps.*

HAPPY: I never heard him so loud, Mom.
LINDA: Well, come around more often; you'll hear him. *She sits down at the
table and mends the lining of* WILLY's *jacket.*
BIFF: Why didn't you ever write me about this, Mom?

LINDA: How would I write to you? For over three months you had no address.

BIFF: I was on the move. But you know I thought of you all the time. You know that, don't you, pal?

LINDA: I know, dear, I know. But he likes to have a letter. Just to know that there's still a possibility for better things.

BIFF: He's not like this all the time, is he?

LINDA: It's when you come home he's always the worst.

BIFF: When I come home?

LINDA: When you write you're coming, he's all smiles, and talks about the future, and—he's just wonderful. And then the closer you seem to come, the more shaky he gets, and then, by the time you get here, he's arguing, and he seems angry at you. I think it's just that maybe he can't bring himself to—to open up to you. Why are you so hateful to each other? Why is that?

BIFF: *evasively.* I'm not hateful, Mom.

LINDA: But you no sooner come in the door than you're fighting!

BIFF: I don't know why. I mean to change. I'm tryin', Mom, you understand?

LINDA: Are you home to stay now?

BIFF: I don't know. I want to look around, see what's doin'.

LINDA: Biff, you can't look around all your life, can you?

BIFF: I just can't take hold, Mom. I can't take hold of some kind of a life.

LINDA: Biff, a man is not a bird, to come and go with the springtime.

BIFF: Your hair ... *He touches her hair.* Your hair got so gray.

LINDA: Oh, it's been gray since you were in high school. I just stopped dyeing it, that's all.

BIFF: Dye it again, will ya? I don't want my pal looking old. *He smiles.*

LINDA: You're such a boy! You think you can go away for a year and ... You've got to get it into your head now that one day you'll knock on this door and there'll be strange people here—

BIFF: What are you talking about? You're not even sixty, Mom.

LINDA: But what about your father?

BIFF: *lamely.* Well, I meant him too.

HAPPY: He admires Pop.

LINDA: Biff, dear, if you don't have any feeling for him, then you can't have any feeling for me.

BIFF: Sure I can, Mom.

LINDA: No. You can't just come to see me, because I love him. *With a threat, but only a threat, of tears.* He's the dearest man in the world to me, and I won't have anyone making him feel unwanted and low and blue. You've got to make up your mind now, darling, there's no leeway any more. Either he's your father and you pay him that respect, or else you're not to come here. I know he's not easy to get along with—nobody knows that better than me—but ...

WILLY: *from the left, with a laugh.* Hey, hey, Biffo!

BIFF: *starting to go out after* WILLY. What the hell is the matter with him? HAPPY *stops him.*

LINDA: Don't—don't go near him!

BIFF: Stop making excuses for him! He always, always wiped the floor with you. Never had an ounce of respect for you.

HAPPY: He's always had respect for—

BIFF: What the hell do you know about it?

HAPPY: *surlily.* Just don't call him crazy!

BIFF: He's got no character—Charley wouldn't do this. Not in his own house— spewing out that vomit from his mind.

HAPPY: Charley never had to cope with what he's got to.

BIFF: People are worse off than Willy Loman. Believe me, I've seen them!

LINDA: Then make Charley your father, Biff. You can't do that, can you? I don't say he's a great man. Willy Loman never made a lot of money. His name was never in the paper. He's not the finest character that ever lived. But he's a human being, and a terrible thing is happening to him. So attention must be paid. He's not to be allowed to fall into his grave like an old dog. Attention, attention must be finally paid to such a person. You called him crazy—

BIFF: I didn't mean—

LINDA: No, a lot of people think he's lost his—balance. But you don't have to be very smart to know what his trouble is. The man is exhausted.

HAPPY: Sure!

LINDA: A small man can be just as exhausted as a great man. He works for a company thirty-six years this March, opens up unheard-of territories to their trademark, and now in his old age they take his salary away.

HAPPY: *indignantly.* I didn't know that, Mom.

LINDA: You never asked, my dear! Now that you get your spending money someplace else you don't trouble your mind with him.

HAPPY: But I gave you money last—

LINDA: Christmas time, fifty dollars! To fix the hot water it cost ninety-seven fifty! For five weeks he's been on straight commission, like a beginner, an un-known!

BIFF: Those ungrateful bastards!

LINDA: Are they any worse than his sons? When he brought them business, when he was young, they were glad to see him. But now his old friends, the old buyers that loved him so and always found some order to hand him in a pinch—they're all dead, retired. He used to be able to make six, seven calls a day in Boston. Now he takes his valises out of the car and puts them back and takes them out again and he's exhausted. Instead of walking he talks now. He drives seven hundred miles, and when he gets there no one knows him any more, no one welcomes him. And what goes through a man's mind, driving seven hundred miles home without having earned a cent? Why shouldn't he talk to himself. Why? When he has to go to Charley and borrow fifty dollars a week and pretend to me that it's his pay? How long can that go on? How long? You see what I'm sitting here and waiting for? And you tell me he has no character? The man who never worked a day but for your benefit? When does he get the medal for that? Is this his reward—to turn around at the age

of sixty-three and find his sons, who he loved better than his life, one a phi-
landering bum—

HAPPY: Mom!

LINDA: That's all you are, my baby! *To* BIFF: And you! What happened to the
love you had for him? You were such pals! How you used to talk to him on
the phone every night! How lonely he was till he could come home to you!

BIFF: All right, Mom. I'll live here in my room, and I'll get a job. I'll keep away
from him, that's all.

LINDA: No, Biff. You can't stay here and fight all the time.

BIFF: He threw me out of this house, remember that.

LINDA: Why did he do that? I never knew why.

BIFF: Because I know he's a fake and he doesn't like anybody around who
knows!

LINDA: Why a fake? In what way? What do you mean?

BIFF: Just don't lay it all at my feet. It's between me and him—that's all I have
to say. I'll chip in from now on. He'll settle for half my pay check. He'll be all
right. I'm going to bed. *He starts for the stairs.*

LINDA: He won't be all right.

BIFF: *turning on the stairs, furiously.* I hate this city and I'll stay here. Now what
do you want?

LINDA: He's dying, Biff.

HAPPY *turns quickly to her, shocked.*

BIFF: *after a pause.* Why is he dying?

LINDA: He's been trying to kill himself.

BIFF: *with great horror.* How?

LINDA: I live from day to day.

BIFF: What're you talking about?

LINDA: Remember I wrote you that he smashed up the car again? In February?

BIFF: Well?

LINDA: The insurance inspector came. He said that they have evidence. That all
these accidents in the last year—weren't—weren't—accidents.

HAPPY: How can they tell that? That's a lie.

LINDA: It seems there's a woman . . . *She takes a breath as*

BIFF: *sharply but contained.* What woman?

LINDA: *simultaneously.* . . . and this woman . . .

LINDA: What?

BIFF: Nothing. Go ahead.

LINDA: What did you say?

BIFF: Nothing. I just said what woman?

HAPPY: What about her?

LINDA: Well, it seems she was walking down the road and saw his car. She says that he wasn't driving fast at all, and that he didn't skid. She says he came to that little bridge, and then deliberately smashed into the railing, and it was only the shallowness of the water that saved him.

BIFF: Oh, no, he probably just fell asleep again.

LINDA: I don't think he fell asleep.

BIFF: Why not?

LINDA: Last month ... *With great difficulty.* Oh, boys, it's so hard to say a thing like this! He's just a big stupid man to you, but I tell you there's more good in him than in many other people. *She chokes, wipes her eyes.* I was looking for a fuse. The lights blew out, and I went down the cellar. And behind the fuse box—it happened to fall out—was a length of rubber pipe—just short.

HAPPY: No kidding?

LINDA: There's a little attachment on the end of it. I knew right away. And sure enough, on the bottom of the water heater there's a new little nipple on the gas pipe.

HAPPY: *angrily.* That—jerk.

BIFF: Did you have it taken off?

LINDA: I'm—I'm ashamed to. How can I mention it to him? Every day I go down and take away that little rubber pipe. But, when he comes home, I put it back where it was. How can I insult him that way? I don't know what to do. I live from day to day, boys. I tell you, I know every thought in his mind. It sounds so old-fashioned and silly, but I tell you he put his whole life into you and you've turned your backs on him. *She is bent over in the chair, weeping, her face in her hands.* Biff, I swear to God! Biff, his life is in your hands!

HAPPY: *to* BIFF. How do you like that damned fool!

BIFF: *kissing her.* All right, pal, all right. It's all settled now. I've been remiss. I know that, Mom. But now I'll stay, and I swear to you, I'll apply myself. *Kneeling in front of her, in a fever of self-reproach.* It's just—you see, Mom, I don't fit in business. Not that I won't try. I'll try, and I'll make good.

HAPPY: Sure you will. The trouble with you in business was you never tried to please people.

BIFF: I know, I—

HAPPY: Like when you worked for Harrison's. Bob Harrison said you were tops, and then you go and do some damn fool thing like whistling whole songs in the elevator like a comedian.

BIFF: *against* HAPPY. So what? I like to whistle sometimes.

HAPPY: You don't raise a guy to a responsible job who whistles in the elevator!

LINDA: Well, don't argue about it now.

HAPPY: Like when you'd go off and swim in the middle of the day instead of taking the line around.

BIFF: *his resentment rising.* Well, don't you run off? You take off sometimes, don't you? On a nice summer day?

HAPPY: Yeah, but I cover myself!

LINDA: Boys!

HAPPY: If I'm going to take a fade the boss can call any number where I'm supposed to be and they'll swear to him that I just left. I'll tell something that I hate to say, Biff, but in the business world some of them think you're crazy.

BIFF: *angered.* Screw the business world!

HAPPY: All right, screw it! Great, but cover yourself!

LINDA: Hap, Hap!

BIFF: I don't care what they think! They've laughed at Dad for years, and you know why? Because we don't belong in this nuthouse of a city! We should be mixing cement on some open plain, or—or carpenters. A carpenter is allowed to whistle!

WILLY *walks in from the entrance of the house, at left.*

WILLY: Even your grandfather was better than a carpenter. *Pause. They watch him.* You never grew up. Bernard does not whistle in the elevator, I assure you.

BIFF: *as though to laugh* WILLY *out of it.* Yeah, but you do, Pop.

WILLY: I never in my life whistled in an elevator! And who in the business world thinks I'm crazy?

BIFF: I didn't mean it like that, Pop. Now don't make a whole thing out of it, will ya?

WILLY: Go back to the West! Be a carpenter, a cowboy, enjoy yourself!

LINDA: Willy, he was just saying—

WILLY: I heard what he said!

HAPPY: *trying to quiet* WILLY. Hey, Pop, come on now . . .

WILLY: *continuing over* HAPPY's *line.* They laugh at me, heh? Go to Filene's, go to the Hub, go to Slattery's, Boston. Call out the name Willy Loman and see what happens! Big shot!

BIFF: All right, Pop.

WILLY: Big!

BIFF: All right!

WILLY: Why do you always insult me?

BIFF: I didn't say a word. *To* LINDA: Did I say a word?

LINDA: He didn't say anything, Willy.

WILLY: *going to the doorway of the living-room.* All right, good night, good night.

LINDA: Willy, dear, he just decided . . .

WILLY: to BIFF. If you get tired hanging around tomorrow, paint the ceiling I put up in the living-room.

BIFF: I'm leaving early tomorrow.

HAPPY: He's going to see Bill Oliver, Pop.

WILLY: *interestedly.* Oliver? For what?

BIFF: *with reserve, but trying, trying.* He always said he'd stake me. I'd like to go into business, so maybe I can take him up on it.

LINDA: Isn't that wonderful?

WILLY: Don't interrupt. What's wonderful about it? There's fifty men in the City of New York who'd stake him. *To* BIFF: Sporting goods?

BIFF: I guess so. I know something about it and—

WILLY: He knows something about it! You know sporting goods better than Spalding, for God's sake! How much is he giving you?

BIFF: I don't know, I didn't even see him yet, but—

WILLY: Then what're you talkin' about?

BIFF: *getting angry.* Well, all I said was I'm gonna see him, that's all!

WILLY: *turning away.* Ah, you're counting your chickens again.

BIFF: *starting left for the stairs.* Oh, Jesus, I'm going to sleep!

WILLY: *calling after him.* Don't curse in this house!

BIFF: *turning.* Since when did you get so clean?

HAPPY: *trying to stop them.* Wait a . . .

WILLY: Don't use that language to me! I won't have it!

HAPPY: *grabbing* BIFF, *shouts.* Wait a minute! I got an idea. I got a feasible idea. Come here, Biff, let's talk this over now, let's talk some sense here. When I was down in Florida last time, I thought of a great idea to sell sporting goods. It just came back to me. You and I, Biff—we have a line, the Loman Line. We train a couple of weeks, and put on a couple of exhibitions, see?

WILLY: That's an idea!

HAPPY: Wait! We form two basketball teams, see? Two waterpolo teams. We play each other. It's a million dollars' worth of publicity. Two brothers, see? The Loman Brothers. Displays in the Royal Palms—all the hotels. And banners over the ring and the basketball court: "Loman Brothers." Baby, we could sell sporting goods!

WILLY: That is a one-million-dollar idea!

LINDA: Marvelous!

BIFF: I'm in great shape as far as that's concerned.

HAPPY: And the beauty of it is, Biff, it wouldn't be like a business. We'd be out playin' ball again . . .

BIFF: *enthused.* Yeah, that's . . .

WILLY: Million-dollar . . .

HAPPY: And you wouldn't get fed up with it, Biff. It'd be the family again. There'd be the old honor, and comradeship, and if you wanted to go off for a swim or somethin'—well, you'd do it! Without some smart cooky gettin' up ahead of you!

WILLY: Lick the world! You guys together could absolutely lick the civilized world.

BIFF: I'll see Oliver tomorrow. Hap, if we could work that out . . .

LINDA: Maybe things are beginning to—

WILLY: *wildly enthused, to* LINDA. Stop interrupting! *To* BIFF: But don't wear sport jacket and slacks when you see Oliver.

BIFF: No, I'll—

WILLY: A business suit, and talk as little as possible, and don't crack any jokes.

BIFF: He did like me. Always liked me.

LINDA: He loved you!

WILLY: *to* LINDA. Will you stop! *To* BIFF: Walk in very serious. You are not applying for a boy's job. Money is to pass. Be quiet, fine, and serious. Everybody likes a kidder, but nobody lends him money.

HAPPY: I'll try to get some myself, Biff. I'm sure I can.

WILLY: I see great things for you kids, I think your troubles are over. But remember, start big and you'll end big. Ask for fifteen. How much you gonna ask for?

BIFF: Gee, I don't know—

WILLY: And don't say "Gee." "Gee" is a boy's word. A man walking in for fifteen thousand dollars does not say "Gee!"

BIFF: Ten, I think, would be top though.

WILLY: Don't be so modest. You always started too low. Walk in with a big laugh. Don't look worried. Start off with a couple of your good stories to lighten things up. It's not what you say, it's how you say it—because personality always wins the day.

LINDA: Oliver always thought the highest of him—

WILLY: Will you let me talk?

BIFF: Don't yell at her, Pop, will ya?

WILLY: *angrily.* I was talking, wasn't I?

BIFF: I don't like you yelling at her all the time, and I'm tellin' you, that's all.

WILLY: What're you, takin' over this house?

LINDA: Willy—

WILLY: *turning on her.* Don't take his side all the time, goddammit!

BIFF: *furiously.* Stop yelling at her!

WILLY: *suddenly pulling on his cheek, beaten down, guilt ridden.* Give my best to Bill Oliver—he may remember me. *He exits through the living-room doorway.*

LINDA: *her voice subdued.* What'd you have to start that for? BIFF *turns away.* You see how sweet he was as soon as you talked hopefully? *She goes over to* BIFF. Come up and say good night to him. Don't let him go to bed that way.

HAPPY: Come on, Biff, let's buck him up.

LINDA: Please, dear. Just say good night. It takes so little to make him happy. Come. *She goes through the living-room doorway, calling upstairs from within the living-room:* Your pajamas are hanging in the bathroom, Willy!

HAPPY: *looking toward where* LINDA *went out.* What a woman! They broke the mold when they made her. You know that, Biff?

BIFF: He's off salary. My God, working on commission!

HAPPY: Well, let's face it: he's no hot-shot selling man. Except that sometimes, you have to admit, he's a sweet personality.

BIFF: *deciding.* Lend me ten bucks, will ya? I want to buy some new ties.

HAPPY: I'll take you to a place I know. Beautiful stuff. Wear one of my striped shirts tomorrow.

BIFF: She got gray. Mom got awful old. Gee, I'm gonna go in to Oliver tomorrow and knock him for a—

HAPPY: Come on up. Tell that to Dad. Let's give him a whirl. Come on.

BIFF: *steamed up.* You know, with ten thousand bucks, boy!

HAPPY: *as they go into the living-room.* That's the talk, Biff, that's the first time I've heard the old confidence out of you! *From within the living-room, fading off:* You're gonna live with me, kid, and any babe you want just say the word . . . *The last lines are hardly heard. They are mounting the stairs to their parents' bedroom.*

LINDA: *entering her bedroom and addressing* WILLY, *who is in the bathroom. She is straightening the bed for him.* Can you do anything about the shower? It drips.

WILLY: *from the bathroom.* All of a sudden everything falls to pieces! Goddam plumbing, oughta be sued, those people. I hardly finished putting it in and the thing . . . *His words rumble off.*

LINDA: I'm just wondering if Oliver will remember him. You think he might?

WILLY: *coming out of the bathroom in his pajamas.* Remember him? What's the matter with you, you crazy? If he'd've stayed with Oliver he'd be on top by now! Wait'll Oliver gets a look at him. You don't know the average caliber any more. The average young man today—*he is getting into bed*—is got a caliber of zero. Greatest thing in the world for him was to bum around.

BIFF *and* HAPPY *enter the bedroom. Slight pause.*

WILLY: *stops short, looking at* BIFF. Glad to hear it, boy.

HAPPY: He wanted to say good night to you, sport.

WILLY: *to* BIFF. Yeah. Knock him dead, boy. What'd you want to tell me?

BIFF: Just take it easy, Pop. Good night. *He turns to go.*

WILLY: *unable to resist.* And if anything falls off the desk while you're talking to him—like a package or something—don't you pick it up. They have office boys for that.

LINDA: I'll make a big breakfast—

WILLY: Will you let me finish? *To* BIFF: Tell him you were in the business in the West. Not farm work.

BIFF: All right, Dad.

LINDA: I think everything—

WILLY: *going right through her speech.* And don't undersell yourself. No less than fifteen thousand dollars.

BIFF: *unable to bear him.* Okay. Good night, Mom. *He starts moving.*

WILLY: Because you got a greatness in you, Biff, remember that. You got all kinds of greatness . . . *He lies back, exhausted.* BIFF *walks out.*

LINDA: *calling after* BIFF. Sleep well, darling!

HAPPY: I'm gonna get married, Mom. I wanted to tell you.

LINDA: Go to sleep, dear.

HAPPY: *going.* I just wanted to tell you.

WILLY: Keep up the good work. HAPPY *exits.* God . . . remember that Ebbets Field[3] game? The championship of the city?

LINDA: Just rest. Should I sing to you?

WILLY: Yeah. Sing to me. LINDA *hums a soft lullaby.* When that team came out—he was the tallest, remember?

LINDA: Oh, yes. And in gold.

BIFF *enters the darkened kitchen, takes a cigarette, and leaves the house. He comes downstage into a golden pool of light. He smokes, staring at the night.*

WILLY: Like a young god. Hercules—something like that. And the sun, the sun all around him. Remember how he waved to me? Right up from the field, with the representatives of three colleges standing by? And the buyers I brought, and the cheers when he came out—Loman, Loman, Loman! God Almighty, he'll be great yet. A star like that, magnificent, can never really fade away!

The light on WILLY *is fading. The gas heater begins to glow through the kitchen wall, near the stairs, a blue flame beneath red coils.*

LINDA: *timidly.* WILLY dear, what has he got against you?

WILLY: I'm so tired. Don't talk any more.

BIFF *slowly returns to the kitchen. He stops, stares toward the heater.*

LINDA: Will you ask Howard to let you work in New York?

WILLY: First thing in the morning. Everything'll be all right.

BIFF *reaches behind the heater and draws out a length of rubber tubing. He is horrified and turns his head toward* WILLY*'s room, still dimly lit, from which the strains of* LINDA*'s desperate but monotonous humming rise.*

WILLY: *staring through the window into the moonlight.* Gee, look at the moon moving between the buildings!

---

[3]Sports stadium in Brooklyn, New York.

BIFF *wraps the tubing around his hand and quickly goes up the stairs.*

CURTAIN

ACT II

Music is heard, gay and bright. The curtain rises as the music fades away. WILLY, *in shirt sleeves, is sitting at the kitchen table, sipping coffee, his hat in his lap,* LINDA *is filling his cup when she can.*

WILLY: Wonderful coffee. Meal in itself.

LINDA: Can I make you some eggs?

WILLY: No. Take a breath.

LINDA: You look so rested, dear.

WILLY: I slept like a dead one. First time in months. Imagine, sleeping till ten on a Tuesday morning. Boys left nice and early, heh?

LINDA: They were out of here by eight o'clock.

WILLY: Good work!

LINDA: It was so thrilling to see them leaving together. I can't get over the shaving lotion in this house!

WILLY: *smiling.* Mmm—

LINDA: Biff was very changed this morning. His whole attitude seemed to be hopeful. He couldn't wait to get downtown to see Oliver.

WILLY: He's heading for a change. There's no question, there simply are certain men that take longer to get—solidified. How did he dress?

LINDA: His blue suit. He's so handsome in that suit. He could be a—anything in that suit!

WILLY *gets up from the table.* LINDA *holds his jacket for him.*

WILLY: There's no question, no question at all. Gee, on the way home tonight I'd like to buy some seeds.

LINDA: *laughing.* That'd be wonderful. But not enough sun gets back there. Nothing'll grow any more.

WILLY: You wait, kid, before it's all over we're gonna get a little place out in the country, and I'll raise some vegetables, a couple of chickens . . .

LINDA: You'll do it yet, dear.

WILLY *walks out of his jacket.* LINDA *follows him.*

WILLY: And they'll get married, and come for a weekend. I'd build a little guest house. 'Cause I got so many fine tools, all I'd need would be a little lumber and some peace of mind.

LINDA: *joyfully.* I sewed the lining . . .

WILLY: I could build two guest houses, so they'd both come. Did he decide how much he's going to ask Oliver for?

LINDA: *getting him into the jacket.* He didn't mention it, but I imagine ten or fifteen thousand. You going to talk to Howard today?

WILLY: Yeah. I'll put it to him straight and simple. He'll just have to take me off the road.

LINDA: And Willy, don't forget to ask for a little advance, because we've got the insurance premium. It's the grace period now.

WILLY: That's a hundred . . .?

LINDA: A hundred and eight, sixty-eight. Because we're a little short again.

WILLY: Why are we short?

LINDA: Well, you had the motor job on the car . . .

WILLY: That goddam Studebaker!

LINDA: And you got one more payment on the refrigerator . . .

WILLY: But it just broke again!

LINDA: Well, it's old, dear.

WILLY: I told you we should've bought a well-advertised machine. Charley bought a General Electric and it's twenty years old and it's still good, that son-of-a-bitch.

LINDA: But, Willy—

WILLY: Whoever heard of a Hastings refrigerator? Once in my life I would like to own something outright before it's broken! I'm always in a race with the junkyard! I just finished paying for the car and it's on its last legs. The refrigerator consumes belts like a goddam maniac. They time those things. They time them so when you finally paid for them, they're used up.

LINDA: *buttoning up his jacket as he unbuttons it.* All told, about two hundred dollars would carry us, dear. But that includes the last payment on the mortgage. After this payment, Willy, the house belongs to us.

WILLY: It's twenty-five years!

LINDA: Biff was nine years old when we bought it.

WILLY: Well, that's a great thing. To weather a twenty-five year mortgage is—

LINDA: It's an accomplishment.

WILLY: All the cement, the lumber, the reconstruction I put in this house! There ain't a crack to be found in it any more.

LINDA: Well, it served its purpose.

WILLY: What purpose? Some stranger'll come along, move in, and that's that. If only Biff would take this house, and raise a family . . . *He starts to go.* Goodby, I'm late.

LINDA: *suddenly remembering.* Oh, I forgot! You're supposed to meet them for dinner.

WILLY: Me?

LINDA: At Frank's Chop House on Forty-eighth near Sixth Avenue.

WILLY: Is that so! How about you?

LINDA: No, just the three of you. They're gonna blow you to a big meal!

WILLY: Don't say! Who thought of that?

LINDA: Biff came to me this morning, Willy, and he said, "Tell Dad, we want to blow him to a big meal." Be there six o'clock. You and your two boys are going to have dinner.

WILLY: Gee whiz! That's really somethin'. I'm gonna knock Howard for a loop, kid. I'll get an advance, and I'll come home with a New York job. Goddammit, now I'm gonna do it!

LINDA: Oh, that's the spirit, Willy!

WILLY: I will never get behind a wheel the rest of my life!

LINDA: It's changing, Willy, I can feel it changing!

WILLY: Beyond a question. G'by, I'm late. *He starts to go again.*

LINDA: *calling after him as she runs to the kitchen table for a handkerchief.* You got your glasses?

WILLY: *feels for them, then comes back in.* Yeah, yeah, got my glasses.

LINDA: *giving him the handkerchief.* And a handkerchief.

WILLY: Yeah, handkerchief.

LINDA: And your saccharine?

WILLY: Yeah, my saccharine.

LINDA: Be careful on the subway stairs.

She kisses him, and a silk stocking is seen hanging from her hand. WILLY *notices it.*

WILLY: Will you stop mending stockings? At least while I'm in the house. It gets me nervous. I can't tell you. Please.

LINDA *hides the stocking in her hand as she follows* WILLY *across the forestage in front of the house.*

LINDA: Remember, Frank's Chop House.

WILLY: *passing the apron.* Maybe beets would grow out there.

LINDA: *laughing.* But you tried so many times.

WILLY: Yeah. Well, don't work hard today. *He disappears around the right corner of the house.*

LINDA: Be careful!

As WILLY *vanishes,* LINDA *waves to him. Suddenly the phone rings. She runs across the stage and into the kitchen and lifts it.*

LINDA: Hello? Oh, Biff I'm so glad you called, I just . . . Yes, sure, I just told him. Yes, he'll be there for dinner at six o'clock, I didn't forget. Listen, I was just dying to tell you. You know that little rubber pipe I told you about? That he connected to the gas heater? I finally decided to go down the cellar this morning and take it away and destroy it. But it's gone! Imagine? He took it away himself, it isn't there! *She listens.* When? Oh, then you took it. Oh—nothing, it's just that I'd hoped he'd taken it away himself. Oh, I'm not worried, darling, because this morning he left in such high spirits, it was like the old days! I'm not afraid any more. Did Mr. Oliver see you? . . . Well, you wait there then. And make a nice impression on him, darling. Just don't perspire too much before you see him. And have a nice time with Dad. He may have big news too! . . . That's right, a New York job. And be sweet to him tonight, dear. Be loving to him. Because he's only a little boat looking for a harbor. *She is trembling with sorrow and joy.* Oh, that's wonderful, Biff, you'll save his life. Thanks, darling. Just put your arm around him when he comes into the restaurant. Give him a smile. That's the boy . . . Good-by, dear . . . You got your comb? . . . That's fine. Good-by, Biff dear.

In the middle of her speech, HOWARD WAGNER, *thirty-six, wheels on a small typewriter table on which is a wire-recording machine and proceeds to plug it in. This is on the left forestage. Light slowly fades on* LINDA *as it rises on* HOWARD. HOWARD *is intent on threading the machine and only glances over his shoulder as* WILLY *appears.*

WILLY: Pst! Pst!

HOWARD: Hello, Willy, come in.

WILLY: Like to have a little talk with you, Howard.

HOWARD: Sorry to keep you waiting. I'll be with you in a minute.

WILLY: What's that, Howard?

HOWARD: Didn't you ever see one of these? Wire recorder.

WILLY: Oh. Can we talk a minute?

HOWARD: Records things. Just got delivery yesterday. Been driving me crazy, the most terrific machine I ever saw in my life. I was up all night with it.

WILLY: What do you do with it?

HOWARD: I bought it for dictation, but you can do anything with it. Listen to this. I had it home last night. Listen to what I picked up. The first one is my daughter. Get this. *He flicks the switch and "Roll out the Barrel" is heard being whistled.* Listen to that kid whistle.

WILLY: That is lifelike, isn't it?

HOWARD: Seven years old. Get that tone.

WILLY: Ts, ts. Like to ask a little favor if you . . .

The whistling breaks off, and the voice of HOWARD's *daughter is heard.*

HIS DAUGHTER: "Now you, Daddy."

HOWARD: She's crazy for me! *Again the same song is whistled.* That's me! Ha! *He winks.*

WILLY: You're very good!

The whistling breaks off again. The machine runs silent for a moment.

HOWARD: Sh! Get this now, this is my son.

HIS SON: "The capital of Alabama is Montgomery; the capital of Arizona is
   Phoenix; the capital of Arkansas is Little Rock; the capital of California is
   Sacramento ..." *and on, and on.*
HOWARD: *holding up five fingers.* Five years old, Willy!
WILLY: He'll make an announcer some day!
HIS SON: *continuing.* "The capital ..."
HOWARD: Get that—alphabetical order! *The machine breaks off suddenly.*
   Wait a minute. The maid kicked the plug out.
WILLY: It certainly is a—
HOWARD: Sh, for God's sake!
HIS SON: "It's nine o'clock, Bulova watch time. So I have to go to sleep."
WILLY: That really is—
HOWARD: Wait a minute! The next is my wife.

They wait.

HOWARD'S VOICE: "Go on, say something." *Pause.* "Well, you gonna talk?"
HIS WIFE: "I can't think of anything."
HOWARD'S VOICE: "Well, talk—it's turning."
HIS WIFE: *shyly, beaten.* "Hello." *Silence.* "Oh, Howard, I can't talk into
   this ..."
HOWARD: *snapping the machine off.* That was my wife.
WILLY: That is a wonderful machine. Can we—
HOWARD: I tell you, Willy, I'm gonna take my camera, and my bandsaw, and
   all my hobbies, and out they go. This is the most fascinating relaxation I ever
   found.
WILLY: I think I'll get one myself.
HOWARD: Sure, they're only a hundred and a half. You can't do without it. Sup-
   posing you wanna hear Jack Benny,[4] see? But you can't be at home at that
   hour. So you tell the maid to turn the radio on when Jack Benny comes on,
   and this automatically goes on with the radio ...
WILLY: And when you come home you ...
HOWARD: You can come home twelve o'clock, one o'clock, any time you like,
   and you get yourself a Coke and sit yourself down, throw the switch, and
   there's Jack Benny's program in the middle of the night!
WILLY: I'm definitely going to get one. Because lots of time I'm on the road,
   and I think to myself, what I must be missing on the radio!
HOWARD: Don't you have a radio in the car?
WILLY: Well, yeah, but who ever thinks of turning it on?
HOWARD: Say, aren't you supposed to be in Boston?
WILLY: That's what I want to talk to you about, Howard. You got a minute? *He
   draws a chair in from the wing.*

---

[4](1894–1974), comedian.

GROWING UP AND GROWING OLDER

The gorgeous primary colors of this painting evoke the vivid sense-based memories of childhood. Describe in similar lush detail an image from your own childhood. Or find a passage in one of the poems or prose pieces in "Growing Up and Growing Older" that creates a comparably vibrant image and discuss.

"Colored Clothes," 1988, by Jonathan Green, Oil on Masonite 23.5" × 23.5".
From a private collection. Photography by Tim Stamm.

The "Venus of Willendorf" dates from Paleolithic times and the stone carving is Native American, probably Inuit, both fairly distant from contemporary 21st century culture. What qualities about women and about men do these two

Dave King © Dorling Kindersley,
Courtesy of the Natural History Museum, London.

separate images evoke for you? To what extent do you think these qualities are still perceived as essential to what it means to be a woman or what it means to be a man? How do various stories, poems, plays, and nonfiction in "Women and Men" work off of these perceptions?

Neg./Transparency no. K9859. Courtesy Dept. of Library Services, American Museum of Natural History.

MONEY AND WORK

"Construction Work" is one of many kinds of work portrayed in the literature of "Money and Work." Compare this picture, for example, to the excerpt from Pietro di Donato's novel *Christ in Concrete*. How are the workers in Leger's painting relating to each other and to their setting? How do the shapes and colors of the painting create a mood and an attitude toward work? Compare this to the way in which image and word choice create mood and an attitude toward work in any one of the poems in "Money and Work."

Fernand Leger (1881–1955) French, "Construction Workers." SuperStock, Inc./© 2004 Artist Rights Society (ARS), New York/ADAGP, Paris.

PEACE AND WAR

Consider Thomas McGrath's poem, "Reading the Names of the Vietnam War Dead" along with Lee Teter's *Reflections*. How do poem and painting each evoke a mood and a stance toward the Vietnam War? Find other selections in "Peace and War" specifically about the Vietnam War. Or write a short story about the man in this picture—why is he here?

Courtesy of VVA Chapter 172, www.vietnamreflections.com.

VARIETIES OF PROTEST

Why is the man on horseback carrying a gun? Why are most of the workers'
faces hidden? Describe the tension you see in this painting. Is this a situation
ripe for protest? Are there any signs some kind of protest might occur?
Consider this painting by Jose Clemente Orozco alongside the screenplay of
the film *Salt of the Earth* or any other selection from "Varieties of Protest"
that seems to you to evoke a parallel situation.

Art Museum of the Americas.

HOWARD: What happened? What're you doing here?

WILLY: Well . . .

HOWARD: You didn't crack up again, did you?

WILLY: Oh, no. No . . .

HOWARD: Geez, you had me worried there for a minute. What's the trouble?

WILLY: Well, tell you the truth, Howard. I've come to the decision that I'd rather not travel any more.

HOWARD: Not travel! Well, what'll you do?

WILLY: Remember, Christmas time, when you had the party here? You said you'd try to think of some spot for me here in town.

HOWARD: With us?

WILLY: Well, sure.

HOWARD: Oh, yeah, yeah. I remember. Well, I couldn't think of anything for you, Willy.

WILLY: I tell ya, Howard. The kids are all grown up, y'know. I don't need much any more. If I could take home—well, sixty-five dollars a week, I could swing it.

HOWARD: Yeah, but Willy, see I—

WILLY: I tell ya why, Howard. Speaking frankly and between the two of us, y'know—I'm just a little tired.

HOWARD: Oh, I could understand that, Willy. But you're a road man, Willy, and we do a road business. We've only got a half-dozen salesmen on the floor here.

WILLY: God knows, Howard, I never asked a favor of any man. But I was with the firm when your father used to carry you in here in his arms.

HOWARD: I know that, Willy, but—

WILLY: Your father came to me the day you were born and asked me what I thought of the name of Howard, may he rest in peace.

HOWARD: I appreciate that, Willy, but there just is no spot here for you. If I had a spot I'd slam you right in, but I just don't have a single solitary spot.

He looks for his lighter. WILLY *has picked it up and gives it to him. Pause.*

WILLY: *with increasing anger.* Howard, all I need to set my table is fifty dollars a week.

HOWARD: But where am I going to put you, kid?

WILLY: Look, it isn't a question of whether I can sell merchandise, is it?

HOWARD: No, but it's a business, kid, and everybody's gotta pull his own weight.

WILLY: *desperately.* Just let me tell you a story, Howard—

HOWARD: 'Cause you gotta admit, business is business.

WILLY: *angrily.* Business is definitely business, but just listen for a minute. You don't understand this. When I was a boy—eighteen, nineteen—I was already on the road. And there was a question in my mind as to whether selling had a future for me. Because in those days I had a yearning to go to Alaska. See, there were three gold strikes in one month in Alaska, and I felt like going out. Just for the ride, you might say.

HOWARD: *barely interested.* Don't say.

WILLY: Oh, yeah, my father lived many years in Alaska. He was an adventurous man. We've got quite a little streak of self-reliance in our family. I thought I'd go out with my older brother and try to locate him, and maybe settle in the North with the old man. And I was almost decided to go, when I met a salesman in the Parker House. His name was Dave Singleman. And he was eighty-four years old, and he'd drummed merchandise in thirty-one states. And old Dave, he'd go up to his room, y'understand, put on his green velvet slippers—I'll never forget—and pick up his phone and call the buyers, and without ever leaving his room, at the age of eighty-four, he made his living. And when I saw that, I realized that selling was the greatest career a man could want. 'Cause what could be more satisfying than to be able to go, at the age of eighty-four, into twenty or thirty different cities, and pick up a phone, and be remembered and loved and helped by so many different people? Do you know? when he died—and by the way he died the death of a salesman, in his green velvet slippers in the smoker of the New York, New Haven and Hartford, going into Boston—when he died, hundreds of salesmen and buyers were at his funeral. Things were sad on a lotta trains for months after that. *He stands up.* HOWARD *has not looked at him.* In those days there was personality in it, Howard. There was respect, and comradeship, and gratitude in it. Today, it's all cut and dried, and there's no chance for bringing friendship to bear—or personality. You see what I mean? They don't know me any more.

HOWARD: *moving away, to the right.* That's just the thing, Willy.

WILLY: If I had forty dollars a week—that's all I'd need. Forty dollars, Howard.

HOWARD: Kid, I can't take blood from a stone, I—

WILLY: *desperation is on him now.* Howard, the year Al Smith[5] was nominated, your father came to me and—

HOWARD: *starting to go off.* I've got to see some people, kid.

WILLY: *stopping him.* I'm talking about your father! There were promises made across this desk! You mustn't tell me you've got people to see—I put thirty-four years into this firm, Howard, and now I can't pay my insurance! You can't eat the orange and throw the peel away—a man is not a piece of fruit! *After a pause:* Now pay attention. Your father—in 1928 I had a big year. I averaged a hundred and seventy dollars a week in commissions.

HOWARD: *impatiently.* Now, Willy, you never averaged—

WILLY: *banging his hand on the desk.* I averaged a hundred and seventy dollars a week in the year of 1928! And your father came to me—or rather, I was in the office here—it was right over this desk—and he put his hand on my shoulder—

---

[5]Democratic candidate for president in 1928.

HOWARD: *getting up.* You'll have to excuse me, Willy, I gotta see some people. Pull yourself together. *Going out:* I'll be back in a little while.

On HOWARD's *exit, the light on his chair grows very bright and strange.*

WILLY: Pull myself together! What the hell did I say to him? My God, I was yelling at him! How could I! WILLY *breaks off, staring at the light, which occupies the chair, animating it. He approaches this chair, standing across the desk from it.* Frank, Frank, don't you remember what you told me that time? How you put your hand on my shoulder, and Frank . . . *He leans on the desk and as he speaks the dead man's name he accidentally switches on the recorder, and instantly*

HOWARD'S SON: ". . . of New York is Albany. The capital of Ohio is Cincinnati, the capital of Rhode Island is . . ." *The recitation continues.*

WILLY: *leaping away with fright, shouting.* Ha! Howard! Howard! Howard!

HOWARD: *rushing in.* What happened?

WILLY: *pointing at the machine, which continues nasally, childishly, with the capital cities.* Shut it off! Shut it off!

HOWARD: *pulling the plug out.* Look, Willy . . .

WILLY: *pressing his hands to his eyes.* I gotta get myself some coffee. I'll get some coffee . . .

WILLY *starts to walk out.* HOWARD *stops him.*

HOWARD: *rolling up the cord.* Willy, look . . .

WILLY: I'll go to Boston.

HOWARD: Willy, you can't go to Boston for us.

WILLY: Why can't I go?

HOWARD: I don't want you to represent us. I've been meaning to tell you for a long time now.

WILLY: Howard, are you firing me?

HOWARD: I think you need a good long rest, Willy.

WILLY: Howard—

HOWARD: And when you feel better, come back, and we'll see if we can work something out.

WILLY: But I gotta earn money, Howard. I'm in no position to—

HOWARD: Where are your sons? Why don't your sons give you a hand?

WILLY: They're working on a very big deal.

HOWARD: This is no time for false pride, Willy. You go to your sons and you tell them that you're tired. You've got two great boys, haven't you?

WILLY: Oh, no question, no question, but in the meantime . . .

HOWARD: Then that's that, heh?

WILLY: All right, I'll go to Boston tomorrow.

HOWARD: No, no.

WILLY: I can't throw myself on my sons. I'm not a cripple!

HOWARD: Look, kid, I'm busy this morning.

WILLY: *grasping* HOWARD*'s arm.* Howard, you've got to let me go to Boston!

HOWARD: *hardly keeping himself under control.* I've got a line of people to see this morning. Sit down, take five minutes, and pull yourself together, and then go home, will ya? I need the office, Willy. *He starts to go, turns, remembering the recorder, starts to push off the table holding the recorder.* Oh, yeah. Whenever you can this week, stop by and drop off the samples. You'll feel better, Willy, and then come back and we'll talk. Pull yourself together, kid, there's people outside.

HOWARD *exits, pushing the table off left,* WILLY *stares into space, exhausted. Now the music is heard—*BEN*'s music—first distantly, then closer, closer. As* WILLY *speaks,* BEN *enters from the right. He carries valise and umbrella.*

WILLY: Oh, Ben, how did you do it? What is the answer? Did you wind up the Alaska deal already?

BEN: Doesn't take much time if you know what you're doing. Just a short business trip. Boarding ship in an hour. Wanted to say good-by.

WILLY: Ben, I've got to talk to you.

BEN: *glancing at his watch.* Haven't the time, William.

WILLY: *crossing the apron to* BEN. Ben, nothing's working out. I don't know what to do.

BEN: Now, look here, William. I've bought timberland in Alaska and I need a man to look after things for me.

WILLY: God, timberland! Me and my boys in those grand outdoors!

BEN: You've a new continent at your doorstep, William. Get out of these cities, they're full of talk and time payments and courts of law. Screw on your fists and you can fight for a fortune up there.

WILLY: Yes, yes! Linda, Linda!

LINDA *enters as of old, with the wash.*

LINDA: Oh, you're back?

BEN: I haven't much time.

WILLY: No, wait! Linda, he's got a proposition for me in Alaska.

LINDA: But you've got— *To* BEN: He's got a beautiful job here.

WILLY: But in Alaska, kid, I could—

LINDA: You're doing well enough, Willy!

BEN: *to* LINDA. Enough for what, my dear?

LINDA: *frightened of* BEN *and angry at him.* Don't say those things to him! Enough to be happy right here, right now. *To* WILLY, *while* BEN *laughs:* Why must everybody conquer the world? You're well liked, and the boys love you, and someday—*to* BEN—why, old man Wagner told him just the other day that if he keeps it up he'll be a member of the firm, didn't he, Willy?

WILLY: Sure, sure. I am building something with this firm, Ben, and if a man is
    building something he must be on the right track, mustn't he?

BEN: What are you building? Lay your hand on it. Where is it?

WILLY: *hesitantly.* That's true, Linda, there's nothing.

LINDA: Why? *To* BEN: There's a man eighty-four years old—

WILLY: That's right, Ben, that's right. When I look at that man I say, what is
    there to worry about?

BEN: Bah!

WILLY: It's true, Ben. All he has to do is go into any city, pick up the phone, and
    he's making his living and you know why?

BEN: *picking up his valise.* I've got to go.

WILLY: *holding* BEN *back.* Look at this boy!

BIFF, *in his high school sweater, enters carrying suitcase.* HAPPY *carries* BIFF's
shoulder guards, gold helmet, and football pants.

WILLY: Without a penny to his name, three great universities are begging for
    him, and from there the sky's the limit, because it's not what you do, Ben. It's
    who you know and the smile on your face! It's contacts, Ben, contacts! The
    whole wealth of Alaska passes over the lunch table at the Commodore Ho-
    tel, and that's the wonder, the wonder of this country, that a man can end with
    diamonds here on the basis of being liked! *He turns to* BIFF. And that's why
    when you get out on that field today it's important. Because thousands of peo-
    ple will be rooting for you and loving you. *To* BEN, *who has again begun to
    leave:* And Ben! when he walks into a business office his name will sound out
    like a bell and all the doors will open to him! I've seen it, Ben, I've seen it a
    thousand times! You can't feel it with your hand like timber, but it's there!

BEN: Good-by, William.

WILLY: Ben, am I right? Don't you think I'm right? I value your advice.

BEN: There's a new continent at your doorstep, William. You could walk out
    rich. Rich! *He is gone.*

WILLY: We'll do it here, Ben! You hear me? We're gonna do it here!

Young BERNARD *rushes in. The gay music of the Boys is heard.*

BERNARD: Oh, gee, I was afraid you left already!

WILLY: Why? What time is it?

BERNARD: It's half-past one!

WILLY: Well, come on, everybody! Ebbets Field next stop! Where's the pen-
    nants? *He rushes through the wall-line of the kitchen and out into the living-
    room.*

LINDA: *to* BIFF. Did you pack fresh underwear?

BIFF: *who has been limbering up.* I want to go!

BERNARD: Biff, I'm carrying your helmet, ain't I?

HAPPY: No, I'm carrying the helmet.

BERNARD: Oh, Biff, you promised me.

HAPPY: I'm carrying the helmet.

BERNARD: How am I going to get in the locker room?

LINDA: Let him carry the shoulder guards. *She puts her coat and hat on in the kitchen.*

BERNARD: Can I, Biff? 'Cause I told everybody I'm going to be in the locker room.

HAPPY: In Ebbets Field it's the clubhouse.

BERNARD: I meant the clubhouse. Biff!

HAPPY: Biff!

BIFF: *grandly, after a slight pause.* Let him carry the shoulder guards.

HAPPY: *as he gives* BERNARD *the shoulder guards.* Stay close to us now.

WILLY *rushes in with the pennants.*

WILLY: *handing them out.* Everybody wave when Biff comes out on the field. HAPPY *and* BERNARD *run off.* You set now, boy?

The music has died away.

BIFF: Ready to go, Pop. Every muscle is ready.

WILLY: *at the edge of the apron.* You realize what this means?

BIFF: That's right, Pop.

WILLY: *feeling* BIFF's *muscles.* You're comin' home this afternoon captain of the All-Scholastic Championship Team of the City of New York.

BIFF: I got it, Pop. And remember, pal, when I take off my helmet, that touchdown is for you.

WILLY: Let's go! *He is starting out, with his arm around* BIFF, *when* CHARLEY *enters, as of old, in knickers.* I got no room for you, Charley.

CHARLEY: Room? For what?

WILLY: In the car.

CHARLEY: You goin' for a ride? I wanted to shoot some casino.

WILLY: *furiously.* Casino! *Incredulously:* Don't you realize what today is?

LINDA: Oh, he knows, Willy. He's just kidding you.

WILLY: That's nothing to kid about!

CHARLEY: No, Linda, what's goin' on?

LINDA: He's playing in Ebbets Field.

CHARLEY: Baseball in this weather?

WILLY: Don't talk to him. Come on, come on! *He is pushing them out.*

CHARLEY: Wait a minute, didn't you hear the news?

WILLY: What?

CHARLEY: Don't you listen to the radio? Ebbets Field just blew up.

WILLY: You go to hell! CHARLEY *laughs. Pushing them out:* Come on, come on! We're late.

CHARLEY: *as they go.* Knock a homer, Biff, knock a homer!

WILLY: *the last to leave, turning to* CHARLEY. I don't think that was funny, Charley. This is the greatest day of his life.

CHARLEY: Willy, when are you going to grow up?

WILLY: Yeah, heh? When this game is over, Charley, you'll be laughing out of the other side of your face. They'll be calling him another Red Grange.[6] Twenty-five thousand a year.

CHARLEY: *kidding.* Is that so?

WILLY: Yeah, that's so.

CHARLEY: Well, then, I'm sorry, Willy. But tell me something.

WILLY: What?

CHARLEY: Who is Red Grange?

WILLY: Put up your hands. Goddam you, put up your hands!

CHARLEY, *chuckling, shakes his head and walks away, around the left corner of the stage.* WILLY *follows him. The music rises to a mocking frenzy.*

WILLY: Who the hell do you think you are, better than everybody else? You don't know everything, you big, ignorant, stupid. . . . Put up your hands!

Light rises, on the right side of the forestage, on a small table in the reception room of CHARLEY'*s office. Traffic sounds are heard.* BERNARD, *now mature, sits whistling to himself. A pair of tennis rackets and an overnight bag are on the floor beside him.*

WILLY: *offstage.* What are you walking away for? Don't walk away! If you're going to say something say it to my face! I know you laugh at me behind my back. You'll laugh out of the other side of your goddam face after this game. Touchdown! Touchdown! Eighty thousand people! Touchdown! Right between the goal posts.

BERNARD *is a quiet, earnest, but self-assured young man.* WILLY'*s voice is coming from right upstage now.* BERNARD *lowers his feet off the table and listens.* JENNY, *his father's secretary, enters.*

JENNY: *distressed.* Say, Bernard, will you go out in the hall?

BERNARD: What is that noise? Who is it?

JENNY: Mr. Loman. He just got off the elevator.

BERNARD: *getting up.* Who's he arguing with?

JENNY: Nobody. There's nobody with him. I can't deal with him any more, and your father gets all upset everytime he comes. I've got a lot of typing to do, and your father's waiting to sign it. Will you see him?

---

[6]College, then professional football player.

WILLY: *entering.* Touchdown! Touch—*He sees* JENNY. Jenny, Jenny, good to see you. How're ya? Workin'? Or still honest?

JENNY: Fine. How've you been feeling?

WILLY: Not much anymore, Jenny. Ha, ha! *He is surprised to see the rackets.*

BERNARD: Hello, Uncle Willy.

WILLY: *almost shocked.* Bernard! Well, look who's here! *He comes quickly, guiltily, to* BERNARD *and warmly shakes his hand.*

BERNARD: How are you? Good to see you.

WILLY: What are you doing here?

BERNARD: Oh, just stopped by to see Pop. Get off my feet till my train leaves. I'm going to Washington in a few minutes.

WILLY: Is he in?

BERNARD: Yes, he's in his office with the accountant. Sit down.

WILLY: *Sitting down.* What're you going to do in Washington?

BERNARD: Oh, just a case I've got there, Willy.

WILLY: That so? *Indicating the rackets:* You going to play tennis there?

BERNARD: I'm staying with a friend who's got a court.

WILLY: Don't say. His own tennis court. Must be fine people, I bet.

BERNARD: They are, very nice. Dad tells me Biff's in town.

WILLY: *with a big smile.* Yeah, Biff's in. Working on a very big deal, Bernard.

BERNARD: What's Biff doing?

WILLY: Well, he's been doing very big things in the West. But he decided to establish himself here. Very big. We're having dinner. Did I hear your wife had a boy?

BERNARD: That's right. Our second.

WILLY: Two boys! What do you know!

BERNARD: What kind of a deal has Biff got?

WILLY: Well, Bill Oliver—very big sporting-goods man—he wants Biff very badly. Called him in from the West. Long distance, carte blanche, special deliveries. Your friends have their own private tennis court?

BERNARD: You still with the old firm, Willy?

WILLY: *after a pause.* I'm—I'm overjoyed to see how you made the grade, Bernard, overjoyed. It's an encouraging thing to see a young man really—really—Looks very good for Biff—very—*He breaks off, then:* Bernard—*He is so full of emotion, he breaks off again.*

BERNARD: What is it, Willy?

WILLY: *small and alone.* What—what's the secret?

BERNARD: What secret?

WILLY: How—how did you? Why didn't he ever catch on?

BERNARD: I wouldn't know that, Willy.

WILLY: *confidentially, desperately.* You were his friend, his boyhood friend. There's something I don't understand about it. His life ended after that Ebbets Field game. From the age of seventeen nothing good ever happened to him.

BERNARD: He never trained himself for anything.

WILLY: But he did, he did. After high school he took so many correspondence
    courses. Radio mechanics; television; God knows what, and never made the
    slightest mark.

BERNARD: *taking off his glasses.* Willy, do you want to talk candidly?

WILLY: *rising, faces* BERNARD. I regard you as a very brilliant man, Bernard. I
    value your advice.

BERNARD: Oh, the hell with the advice, Willy. I couldn't advise you. There's just
    one thing I've always wanted to ask you. When he was supposed to graduate,
    and the math teacher flunked him—

WILLY: Oh, that son-of-a-bitch ruined his life.

BERNARD: Yeah, but, Willy, all he had to do was go to summer school and make
    up that subject.

WILLY: That's right, that's right.

BERNARD: Did you tell him not to go to summer school?

WILLY: Me? I begged him to go. I ordered him to go!

BERNARD: Then why wouldn't he go?

WILLY: Why? Why! Bernard, that question has been trailing me like a ghost
    for the last fifteen years. He flunked the subject, and laid down and died like
    a hammer hit him!

BERNARD: Take it easy, kid.

WILLY: Let me talk to you—I got nobody to talk to. Bernard, Bernard, was it
    my fault? Y'see? It keeps going around in my mind, maybe I did something
    to him. I got nothing to give him.

BERNARD: Don't take it so hard.

WILLY: Why did he lay down? What is the story there? You were his friend!

BERNARD: Willy, I remember, it was June, and our grades came out. And he'd
    flunked math.

WILLY: That son-of-a-bitch!

BERNARD: No, it wasn't right then. Biff just got very angry, I remember, and
    he was ready to enroll in summer school.

WILLY: *surprised.* He was?

BERNARD: He wasn't beaten by it at all. But then, Willy, he disappeared from
    the block for almost a month. And I got the idea that he'd gone up to New
    England to see you. Did he have a talk with you then?

WILLY *stares in silence.*

BERNARD: Willy?

WILLY: *with a strong edge of resentment in his voice.* Yeah, he came to Boston.
    What about it?

BERNARD: Well, just that when he came back—I'll never forget this, it always
    mystifies me. Because I'd thought so well of Biff, even though he'd always
    taken advantage of me. I loved him, Willy, y'know? And he came back after
    that month and took his sneakers—remember those sneakers with "Univer-
    sity of Virginia" printed on them? He was so proud of those, wore them every

day. And he took them down in the cellar, and burned them up in the furnace. We had a fist fight. It lasted at least half an hour. Just the two of us, punching each other down the cellar, and crying right through it. I've often thought of how strange it was that I knew he'd given up his life. What happened in Boston, Willy?

WILLY *looks at him as at an intruder.*

BERNARD: I just bring it up because you asked me.

WILLY: *angrily.* Nothing. What do you mean, "What happened?" What's that got to do with anything?

BERNARD: Well, don't get sore.

WILLY: What are you trying to do, blame it on me? If a boy lays down is that my fault?

BERNARD: Now, Willy, don't get—

WILLY: Well, don't—don't talk to me that way! What does that mean, "What happened?"

CHARLEY *enters. He is in his vest, and he carries a bottle of bourbon.*

CHARLEY: Hey, you're going to miss that train. *He waves the bottle.*

BERNARD: Yeah, I'm going. *He takes the bottle.* Thanks, Pop. *He picks up his rackets and bag.* Good-by, Willy, and don't worry about it. You know, "If at first you don't succeed . . ."

WILLY: Yes, I believe in that.

BERNARD: But sometimes, Willy, it's better for a man just to walk away.

WILLY: Walk away?

BERNARD: That's right.

WILLY: But if you can't walk away?

BERNARD: *after a slight pause.* I guess that's when it's tough. *Extending his hand:* Good-by, Willy.

WILLY: *shaking BERNARD's hand.* Good-by, boy.

CHARLEY: *an arm on BERNARD's shoulder.* How do you like this kid? Gonna argue a case in front of the Supreme Court.

BERNARD: *protesting.* Pop!

WILLY: *genuinely shocked, pained, and happy.* No! The Supreme Court!

BERNARD: I gotta run. 'By, Dad!

CHARLEY: Knock 'em dead, Bernard!

BERNARD *goes off.*

WILLY: *as CHARLEY takes out his wallet.* The Supreme Court! And he didn't even mention it!

CHARLEY: *counting out money on the desk.* He don't have to—he's gonna do it.

WILLY: And you never told him what to do, did you? You never took any interest in him.

CHARLEY: My salvation is that I never took any interest in anything. There's some money—fifty dollars. I got an accountant inside.

WILLY: Charley, look . . . *With difficulty:* I got my insurance to pay. If you can manage it—I need a hundred and ten dollars.

CHARLEY *doesn't reply for a moment; merely stops moving.*

WILLY: I'd draw it from my bank but Linda would know, and I . . .

CHARLEY: Sit down, Willy.

WILLY: *moving toward the chair.* I'm keeping an account of everything, remember. I'll pay every penny back. *He sits.*

CHARLEY: Now listen to me, Willy.

WILLY: I want you to know I appreciate . . .

CHARLEY: *sitting down on the table.* Willy, what're you doin'? What the hell is goin' on in your head?

WILLY: Why? I'm simply . . .

CHARLEY: I offered you a job. You can make fifty dollars a week. And I won't send you on the road.

WILLY: I've got a job.

CHARLEY: Without pay? What kind of a job is a job without pay? *He rises.* Now, look, kid, enough is enough. I'm no genius but I know when I'm being insulted.

WILLY: Insulted!

CHARLEY: Why don't you want to work for me?

WILLY: What's the matter with you? I've got a job.

CHARLEY: Then what're you walkin' in here every week for?

WILLY: *getting up.* Well, if you don't want me to walk in here—

CHARLEY: I am offering you a job.

WILLY: I don't want your goddam job!

CHARLEY: When the hell are you going to grow up?

WILLY: *furiously.* You big ignoramus, if you say that to me again I'll rap you one! I don't care how big you are! *He's ready to fight.*

Pause.

CHARLEY: *kindly, going to him.* How much do you need, Willy?

WILLY: Charley, I'm strapped. I'm strapped. I don't know what to do. I was just fired.

CHARLEY: Howard fired you?

WILLY: That snotnose. Imagine that? I named him. I named him Howard.

CHARLEY: Willy, when're you gonna realize that them things don't mean anything? You named him Howard, but you can't sell that. The only thing you got in this world is what you can sell. And the funny thing is that you're a salesman, and you don't know that.

WILLY: I've always tried to think otherwise, I guess. I always felt that if a man was impressive, and well liked, that nothing—

CHARLEY: Why must everybody like you? Who liked J. P. Morgan? Was he impressive? In a Turkish bath he'd look like a butcher. But with his pockets on he was very well liked. Now listen, Willy, I know you don't like me, and nobody can say I'm in love with you, but I'll give you a job because—just for the hell of it, put it that way. Now what do you say?

WILLY: I—I just can't work for you, Charley.

CHARLEY: What're you, jealous of me?

WILLY: I can't work for you, that's all, don't ask me why.

CHARLEY: *angered, takes out more bills.* You been jealous of me all your life, you damned fool! Here, pay your insurance. *He puts the money in* WILLY's *hand.*

WILLY: I'm keeping strict accounts.

CHARLEY: I've got some work to do. Take care of yourself. And pay your insurance.

WILLY: *Moving to the right.* Funny, y'know? After all the highways, and the trains, and the appointments, and the years, you end up worth more dead than alive.

CHARLEY: Willy, nobody's worth nothin' dead. *After a slight pause:* Did you hear what I said?

WILLY *stands still, dreaming.*

CHARLEY: Willy!

WILLY: Apologize to Bernard for me when you see him. I didn't mean to argue with him. He's a fine boy. They're all fine boys, and they'll end up big— all of them. Someday they'll all play tennis together. Wish me luck, Charley. He saw Bill Oliver today.

CHARLEY: Good luck.

WILLY: *on the verge of tears.* Charley, you're the only friend I got. Isn't that a remarkable thing? *He goes out.*

CHARLEY: Jesus!

CHARLEY *stares after him a moment and follows. All light blacks out. Suddenly raucous music is heard, and a red glow rises behind the screen at right.* STANLEY, *a young waiter, appears, carrying a table, followed by* HAPPY, *who is carrying two chairs.*

STANLEY: *putting the table down.* That's all right, Mr. Loman, I can handle it myself. *He turns and takes the chairs from* HAPPY *and places them at the table.*

HAPPY: *glancing around.* Oh, this is better.

STANLEY: Sure, in the front there you're in the middle of all kinds a noise. Whenever you got a party, Mr. Loman, you just tell me and I'll put you back here. Y'know, there's a lotta people they don't like it private, because when they go out they like to see a lotta action around them because they're sick and tired to stay in the house by theirself. But I know you, you ain't from Hackensack. You know what I mean?

HAPPY: *sitting down.* So how's it coming, Stanley?

STANLEY: Ah, it's a dog's life. I only wish during the war they'd a took me in the Army. I coulda been dead by now.

HAPPY: My brother's back, Stanley.

STANLEY: Oh, he come back, heh? From the Far West.

HAPPY: Yeah, big cattle man, my brother, so treat him right. And my father's coming too.

STANLEY: Oh, your father too!

HAPPY: You got a couple of nice lobsters?

STANLEY: Hundred per cent, big.

HAPPY: I want them with the claws.

STANLEY: Don't worry, I don't give you no mice. HAPPY *laughs.* How about some wine? It'll put a head on the meal.

HAPPY: No. You remember, Stanley, that recipe I brought you from overseas? With the champagne in it?

STANLEY: Oh, yeah, sure. I still got it tacked up yet in the kitchen. But that'll have to cost a buck apiece anyways.

HAPPY: That's all right.

STANLEY: What'd you, hit a number or somethin'?

HAPPY: No, it's a little celebration. My brother is—I think he pulled off a big deal today. I think we're going into business together.

STANLEY: Great! That's the best for you. Because a family business, you know what I mean?—that's the best.

HAPPY: That's what I think.

STANLEY: 'Cause what's the difference? Somebody steals? It's in the family. Know what I mean? *Sotto voce:* Like this bartender here. The boss is goin' crazy what kinda leak he's got in the cash register. You put it in but it don't come out.

HAPPY: *raising his head.* Sh!

STANLEY: What?

HAPPY: You notice I wasn't lookin' right or left, was I?

STANLEY: No.

HAPPY: And my eyes are closed.

STANLEY: So what's the—?

HAPPY: Strudel's comin'.

STANLEY: *catching on, looks around.* Ah, no, there's no—

He breaks off as a furred, lavishly dressed girl enters and sits at the next table. Both follow her with their eyes.

STANLEY: Geez, how'd ya know?

HAPPY: I got radar or something. *Staring directly at her profile:* Oooooooo . . .
Stanley.

STANLEY: I think that's for you, Mr. Loman.

HAPPY: Look at that mouth. Oh, God. And the binoculars.

STANLEY: Geez, you got a life, Mr. Loman.

HAPPY: Wait on her.

STANLEY: *going to the girl's table.* Would you like a menu, ma'am?

GIRL: I'm expecting someone, but I'd like a—

HAPPY: Why don't you bring her—excuse me, miss, do you mind? I sell champagne, and I'd like you to try my brand. Bring her a champagne, Stanley.

GIRL: That's awfully nice of you.

HAPPY: Don't mention it. It's all company money. *He laughs.*

GIRL: That's a charming product to be selling, isn't it?

HAPPY: Oh, gets to be like everything else. Selling is selling, y'know.

GIRL: I suppose.

HAPPY: You don't happen to sell, do you?

GIRL: No, I don't sell.

HAPPY: Would you object to a compliment from a stranger? You ought to be
on a magazine cover.

GIRL: *looking at him a little archly.* I have been.

STANLEY *comes in with a glass of champagne.*

HAPPY: What'd I say before, Stanley? You see? She's a cover girl.

STANLEY: Oh, I could see, I could see.

HAPPY: *to the* GIRL. What magazine?

GIRL: Oh, a lot of them. *She takes the drink.* Thank you.

HAPPY: You know what they say in France, don't you? "Champagne is the
drink of the complexion"—Hya, Biff!

BIFF *has entered and sits with* HAPPY.

BIFF: Hello, kid. Sorry I'm late.

HAPPY: I just got here. Uh, Miss—?

GIRL: Forsythe.

HAPPY: Miss Forsythe, this is my brother.

BIFF: Is Dad here?

HAPPY: His name is Biff. You might've heard of him. Great football player.

GIRL: Really? What team?

HAPPY: Are you familiar with football?

GIRL: No, I'm afraid I'm not.

HAPPY: Biff is quarterback with the New York Giants.

GIRL: Well, that is nice, isn't it? *She drinks.*

HAPPY: Good health.

GIRL: I'm happy to meet you.

HAPPY: That's my name. Hap. It's really Harold, but at West Point they called me Happy.

GIRL: *now really impressed.* Oh, I see. How do you do? *She turns her profile.*

BIFF: Isn't Dad coming?

HAPPY: You want her?

BIFF: Oh, I could never make that.

HAPPY: I remember the time that idea would never come into your head. Where's the old confidence, Biff?

BIFF: I just saw Oliver—

HAPPY: Wait a minute. I've got to see that old confidence again. Do you want her? She's on call.

BIFF: Oh, no. *He turns to look at the* GIRL.

HAPPY: I'm telling you. Watch this. *Turning to the* GIRL: Honey? *She turns to him.* Are you busy?

GIRL: Well, I am . . . but I could make a phone call.

HAPPY: Do that, will you, honey? And see if you can get a friend. We'll be here for a while. Biff is one of the greatest football players in the country.

GIRL: *standing up.* Well, I'm certainly happy to meet you.

HAPPY: Come back soon.

GIRL: I'll try.

HAPPY: Don't try, honey, try hard.

The GIRL, *exits.* STANLEY *follows, shaking his head in bewildered admiration.*

HAPPY: Isn't that a shame now? A beautiful girl like that? That's why I can't get married. There's not a good woman in a thousand. New York is loaded with them, kid!

BIFF: Hap, look—

HAPPY: I told you she was on call!

BIFF: *strangely unnerved.* Cut it out, will ya? I want to say something to you.

HAPPY: Did you see Oliver?

BIFF: I saw him all right. Now look, I want to tell Dad a couple of things and I want you to help me.

HAPPY: What? Is he going to back you?

BIFF: Are you crazy? You're out of your goddam head, you know that?

HAPPY: Why? What happened?

BIFF: *breathlessly.* I did a terrible thing today, Hap. It's been the strangest day I ever went through. I'm all numb, I swear.

HAPPY: You mean he wouldn't see you?

BIFF: Well, I waited six hours for him, see? All day. Kept sending my name in. Even tried to date his secretary so she'd get me to him, but no soap.

HAPPY: Because you're not showin' the old confidence, Biff. He remembered you, didn't he?

BIFF: *stopping* HAPPY *with a gesture.* Finally, about five o'clock, he comes out. Didn't remember who I was or anything. I felt like such an idiot, Hap.

HAPPY: Did you tell him my Florida idea?

BIFF: He walked away. I saw him for one minute. I got so mad I could've torn the walls down! How the hell did I ever get the idea I was a salesman there? I even believed myself that I'd been a salesman for him! And then he gave me one look and— I realized what a ridiculous lie my whole life has been! We've been talking in a dream for fifteen years. I was a shipping clerk.

HAPPY: What'd you do?

BIFF: *with great tension and wonder.* Well, he left, see. And the secretary went out. I was all alone in the waiting-room. I don't know what came over me, Hap. The next thing I know I'm in his office—paneled walls, everything. I can't explain it. I—Hap, I took his fountain pen.

HAPPY: Geez, did he catch you?

BIFF: I ran out. I ran down all eleven flights. I ran and ran and ran.

HAPPY: That was an awful dumb—what'd you do that for?

BIFF: *agonized.* I don't know, I just—wanted to take something, I don't know. You gotta help me, Hap, I'm gonna tell Pop.

HAPPY: You crazy? What for?

BIFF: Hap, he's got to understand that I'm not the man somebody lends that kind of money to. He thinks I've been spiting him all these years and it's eating him up.

HAPPY: That's just it. You tell him something nice.

BIFF: I can't.

HAPPY: Say you got a lunch date with Oliver tomorrow.

BIFF: So what do I do tomorrow?

HAPPY: You leave the house tomorrow and come back at night and say Oliver is thinking it over. And he thinks it over for a couple of weeks, and gradually it fades away and nobody's the worse.

BIFF: But it'll go on forever!

HAPPY: Dad is never so happy as when he's looking forward to something!

WILLY *enters.*

HAPPY: Hello, scout!

WILLY: Gee, I haven't been here in years!

STANLEY *has followed* WILLY *in and sets a chair for him.* STANLEY *starts off but* HAPPY *stops him.*

HAPPY: Stanley!

STANLEY *stands by, waiting for an order.*

BIFF: *going to* WILLY *with guilt, as to an invalid.* Sit down, Pop. You want a drink?

WILLY: Sure, I don't mind.

BIFF: Let's get a load on.

WILLY: You look worried.

BIFF: N-no. *To* STANLEY: Scotch all around. Make it doubles.

STANLEY: Doubles, right. *He goes.*

WILLY: You had a couple already, didn't you?

BIFF: Just a couple, yeah.

WILLY: Well, what happened, boy? *Nodding affirmatively, with a smile:* Everything go all right?

BIFF: *takes a breath, then reaches out and grasps* WILLY's *hand. Pa . . . He is smiling bravely, and* WILLY *is smiling too.* I had an experience today.

HAPPY: Terrific, Pop.

WILLY: That so? What happened?

BIFF: *high, slightly alcoholic, above the earth.* I'm going to tell you everything from first to last. It's been a strange day. *Silence. He looks around, composes himself as best he can, but his breath keeps breaking the rhythm of his voice.* I had to wait quite a while for him, and—

WILLY: Oliver?

BIFF: Yeah, Oliver. All day, as a matter of cold fact. And a lot of—instances—facts, Pop, facts about my life came back to me. Who was it, Pop? Who ever said I was a salesman with Oliver?

WILLY: Well, you were.

BIFF: No, Dad, I was a shipping clerk.

WILLY: But you were practically—

BIFF: *with determination.* Dad, I don't know who said it first, but I was never a salesman for Bill Oliver.

WILLY: What're you talking about?

BIFF: Let's hold on to the facts tonight, Pop. We're not going to get anywhere bullin' around. I was a shipping clerk.

WILLY: *angrily.* All right, now listen to me—

BIFF: Why don't you let me finish?

WILLY: I'm not interested in stories about the past or any crap of that kind because the woods are burning, boys, you understand? There's a big blaze going on all around. I was fired today.

BIFF: *shocked.* How could you be?

WILLY: I was fired, and I'm looking for a little good news to tell your mother, because the woman has waited and the woman has suffered. The gist of it is that I haven't got a story left in my head, Biff. So don't give me a lecture about facts and aspects. I am not interested. Now what've you got to say to me?

STANLEY *enters with three drinks. They wait until he leaves.*

WILLY: Did you see Oliver?

BIFF: Jesus, Dad!

WILLY: You mean you didn't go up there?

HAPPY: Sure he went up there.

BIFF: I did. I—saw him. How could they fire you?

WILLY: *on the edge of his chair.* What kind of a welcome did he give you?

BIFF: He won't even let you work on commission?

WILLY: I'm out! *Driving:* So tell me, he gave you a warm welcome?

HAPPY: Sure, Pop, sure!

BIFF: *driven.* Well, it was kind of—

WILLY: I was wondering if he'd remember you. *To* HAPPY: Imagine, man doesn't see him for ten, twelve years and gives him that kind of a welcome!

HAPPY: Damn right!

BIFF: *trying to return to the offensive.* Pop, look—

WILLY: You know why he remembered you, don't you? Because you impressed him in those days.

BIFF: Let's talk quietly and get this down to the facts, huh?

WILLY: *as though* BIFF *had been interrupting.* Well, what happened? It's great news, Biff. Did he take you into his office or'd you talk in the waiting-room?

BIFF: Well, he came in, see, and—

WILLY: *with a big smile.* What'd he say? Betcha he threw his arm around you.

BIFF: Well, he kinda—

WILLY: He's a fine man. *To* HAPPY: Very hard man to see, y'know.

HAPPY: *agreeing.* Oh, I know.

WILLY: *to* BIFF. Is that where you had the drinks?

BIFF: Yeah, he gave me a couple of—no, no!

HAPPY: *cutting in.* He told him my Florida idea.

WILLY: Don't interrupt. *To* BIFF. How'd he react to the Florida idea?

BIFF: Dad, will you give me a minute to explain?

WILLY: I've been waiting for you to explain since I sat down here! What happened? He took you into his office and what?

BIFF: Well—I talked. And—and he listened, see.

WILLY: Famous for the way he listens, y'know. What was his answer?

BIFF: His answer was—*He breaks off, suddenly angry.* Dad, you're not letting me tell you what I want to tell you!

WILLY: *accusing, angered.* You didn't see him, did you?

BIFF: I did see him!

WILLY: What'd you insult him or something? You insulted him, didn't you?

BIFF: Listen, will you let me out of it, will you just let me out of it!

HAPPY: What the hell!

WILLY: Tell me what happened!

BIFF: *to* HAPPY. I can't talk to him!

A single trumpet note jars the ear. The light of green leaves stains the house, which holds the air of night and a dream. YOUNG BERNARD *enters and knocks on the door of the house.*

YOUNG BERNARD: *frantically.* Mrs. Loman, Mrs. Loman!

HAPPY: Tell him what happened!

BIFF: *to* HAPPY. Shut up and leave me alone!

WILLY: No, no! You had to go and flunk math!

BIFF: What math? What're you talking about?

YOUNG BERNARD: Mrs. Loman, Mrs. Loman!

LINDA *appears in the house, as of old.*

WILLY: *wildly.* Math, math, math!

BIFF: Take it easy, Pop!

YOUNG BERNARD: Mrs. Loman!

WILLY: *furiously.* If you hadn't flunked you'd've been set by now!

BIFF: Now, look, I'm gonna tell you what happened, and you're going to listen to me.

YOUNG BERNARD: Mrs. Loman!

BIFF: I waited six hours—

HAPPY: What the hell are you saying?

BIFF: I kept sending in my name but he wouldn't see me. So finally he ... *He continues unheard as light fades low on the restaurant.*

YOUNG BERNARD: Biff flunked math!

LINDA: No!

YOUNG BERNARD: Birnbaum flunked him! They won't graduate him!

LINDA: But they have to. He's gotta go to the university. Where is he? Biff! Biff!

YOUNG BERNARD: No, he left. He went to Grand Central.

LINDA: Grand—You mean he went to Boston!

YOUNG BERNARD: Is Uncle Willy in Boston?

LINDA: Oh, maybe Willy can talk to the teacher. Oh, the poor, poor boy!

Light on house area snaps out.

BIFF: *at the table, now audible, holding up a gold fountain pen ...* so I'm washed up with Oliver, you understand? Are you listening to me?

WILLY: *at a loss.* Yeah, sure. If you hadn't flunked—

BIFF: Flunked what? What're you talking about?

WILLY: Don't blame everything on me! I didn't flunk math—you did! What pen?

HAPPY: That was awful dumb, Biff, a pen like that is worth—

WILLY: *seeing the pen for the first time.* You took Oliver's pen?

BIFF: *weakening.* Dad, I just explained it to you.

WILLY: You stole Bill Oliver's fountain pen!

BIFF: I didn't exactly steal it! That's just what I've been explaining to you!

HAPPY: He had it in his hand and just then Oliver walked in, so he got nervous and stuck it in his pocket!

WILLY: My God, Biff!

BIFF: I never intended to do it, Dad!

OPERATOR'S VOICE: Standish Arms, good evening!

WILLY: *shouting.* I'm not in my room!

BIFF: *frightened.* Dad, what's the matter? *He and* HAPPY *stand up.*

OPERATOR: Ringing Mr. Loman for you!

WILLY: I'm not there, stop it!

BIFF: *horrified, gets down on one knee before* WILLY. Dad, I'll make good, I'll make good. WILLY *tries to get to his feet.* BIFF *holds him down.* Sit down now.

WILLY: No, you're no good, you're no good for anything.

BIFF: I am, Dad, I'll find something else, you understand? Now don't worry about anything. *He holds up* WILLY's *face:* Talk to me, Dad.

OPERATOR: Mr. Loman does not answer. Shall I page him?

WILLY: *attempting to stand, as though to rush and silence the Operator.* No, no, no!

HAPPY: He'll strike something, Pop.

WILLY: No, no . . .

BIFF: *desperately, standing over* WILLY. Pop, listen! Listen to me! I'm telling you something good. Oliver talked to his partner about the Florida idea. You listening? He—he talked to his partner, and he came to me . . . I'm going to be all right, you hear? Dad, listen to me, he said it was just a question of the amount!

WILLY: Then you . . . got it?

HAPPY: He's gonna be terrific, Pop!

WILLY: *trying to stand.* Then you got it, haven't you? You got it! You got it!

BIFF: *agonized, holds* WILLY *down.* No, no. Look, Pop. I'm supposed to have lunch with them tomorrow. I'm just telling you this so you'll know that I can still make an impression, Pop. And I'll make good somewhere, but I can't go tomorrow, see?

WILLY: Why not? You simply—

BIFF: But the pen, Pop!

WILLY: You give it to him and tell him it was an oversight!

HAPPY: Sure, have lunch tomorrow!

BIFF: I can't say that—

WILLY: You were doing a crossword puzzle and accidentally used his pen!

BIFF: Listen, kid, I took those balls years ago, now I walk in with his fountain pen? That clinches it, don't you see? I can't face him like that! I'll try elsewhere.

PAGE'S VOICE: Paging Mr. Loman!

WILLY: Don't you want to be anything?

BIFF: Pop, how can I go back?

WILLY: You don't want to be anything, is that what's behind it?

BIFF: *now angry at* WILLY *for not crediting his sympathy.* Don't take it that way! You think it was easy walking into that office after what I'd done to him? A team of horses couldn't have dragged me back to Bill Oliver!

WILLY: Then why'd you go?

BIFF: Why did I go? Why did I go! Look at you! Look at what's become of you!

Off left, THE WOMAN *laughs.*

WILLY: Biff, you're going to go to that lunch tomorrow, or—

BIFF: I can't go. I've got no appointment!

HAPPY: Biff, for . . .!

WILLY: Are you spiting me?

BIFF: Don't take it that way! Goddammit!

WILLY: *strikes* BIFF *and falters away from the table.* You rotten little louse! Are
   you spiting me?

THE WOMAN: Someone's at the door, Willy!

BIFF: I'm no good, can't you see what I am?

HAPPY: *separating them.* Hey, you're in a restaurant! Now cut it out, both of
   you! *The girls enter.* Hello, girls, sit down.

THE WOMAN *laughs, off left.*

MISS FORSYTHE: I guess we might as well. This is Letta.

THE WOMAN: Willy, are you going to wake up?

BIFF: *ignoring* WILLY. How're ya, miss, sit down. What do you drink?

MISS FORSYTHE: Letta might not be able to stay long.

LETTA: I gotta get up very early tomorrow. I got jury duty. I'm so excited! Were
   you fellows ever on a jury?

BIFF: No, but I been in front of them! *The girls laugh.* This is my father.

LETTA: Isn't he cute? Sit down with us, Pop.

HAPPY: Sit him down, Biff!

BIFF: *going to him.* Come on, slugger, drink us under the table. To hell with it!
   Come on, sit down, pal.

On BIFF's *last insistence,* WILLY *is about to sit.*

THE WOMAN: *now urgently.* Willy, are you going to answer the door!

THE WOMAN's *call pulls* WILLY *back. He starts right, befuddled.*

BIFF: Hey, where are you going?

WILLY: Open the door.

BIFF: The door?

WILLY: The washroom . . . the door . . . where's the door?

BIFF: *leading* WILLY *to the left.* Just go straight down.

WILLY *moves left.*

THE WOMAN: Willy, Willy, are you going to get up, get up, get up, get up?

WILLY *exits left.*

LETTA: I think it's sweet you bring your daddy along.

MISS FORSYTHE: Oh, he isn't really your father!

BIFF: *at left, turning to her resentfully.* Miss Forsythe, you've just seen a prince walk by. A fine, troubled prince. A hardworking, unappreciated prince. A pal, you understand? A good companion. Always for his boys.

LETTA: That's so sweet.

HAPPY: Well, girls, what's the program? We're wasting time. Come on, Biff. Gather round. Where would you like to go?

BIFF: Why don't you do something for him?

HAPPY: Me!

BIFF: Don't you give a damn for him, Hap?

HAPPY: What're you talking about? I'm the one who—

BIFF: I sense it, you don't give a good goddam about him. *He takes the rolled-up hose from his pocket and puts it on the table in front of* HAPPY. Look what I found in the cellar, for Christ's sake. How can you bear to let it go on?

HAPPY: Me? Who goes away? Who runs off and—

BIFF: Yeah, but he doesn't mean anything to you. You could help him—I can't! Don't you understand what I'm talking about? He's going to kill himself, don't you know that?

HAPPY: Don't I know it! Me!

BIFF: Hap, help him! Jesus . . . help him . . . Help me, help me, I can't bear to look at his face! *Ready to weep, he hurries out, up right.*

HAPPY: *starting after him.* Where are you going?

MISS FORSYTHE: What's he so mad about?

HAPPY: Come on, girls, we'll catch up with him.

MISS FORSYTHE: *as* HAPPY *pushes her out.* Say, I don't like that temper of his!

HAPPY: He's just a little overstrung, he'll be all right!

WILLY: *off left, as* THE WOMAN *laughs.* Don't answer! Don't answer!

LETTA: Don't you want to tell your father—

HAPPY: No, that's not my father. He's just a guy. Come on, we'll catch Biff, and, honey, we're going to paint this town! Stanley, where's the check! Hey, Stanley!

They exit. STANLEY *looks toward left.*

STANLEY: *calling to* HAPPY *indignantly.* Mr. Loman! Mr. Loman!

STANLEY *picks up a chair and follows them off. Knocking is heard off left.* THE WOMAN *enters, laughing.* WILLY *follows her. She is in a black slip; he is buttoning his shirt. Raw, sensuous music accompanies their speech.*

WILLY: Will you stop laughing? Will you stop?

THE WOMAN: Aren't you going to answer the door? He'll wake the whole hotel.

WILLY: I'm not expecting anybody.

THE WOMAN: Whyn't you have another drink, honey, and stop being so damn
  self-centered?

WILLY: I'm so lonely.

THE WOMAN: You know you ruined me, Willy? From now on, whenever you
  come to the office, I'll see that you go right through to the buyers. No waiting at my desk any more, Willy. You ruined me.

WILLY: That's nice of you to say that.

THE WOMAN: Gee, you are self-centered! Why so sad? You are the saddest, self-
  centeredest soul I ever did see-saw. *She laughs. He kisses her.* Come on inside,
  drummer boy. It's silly to be dressing in the middle of the night. *As knocking
  is heard:* Aren't you going to answer the door?

WILLY: They're knocking on the wrong door.

THE WOMAN: But I felt the knocking. And he heard us talking in here. Maybe
  the hotel's on fire!

WILLY: *his terror rising.* It's a mistake.

THE WOMAN: Then tell him to go away!

WILLY: There's nobody there.

THE WOMAN: It's getting on my nerves, Willy. There's somebody standing out
  there and it's getting on my nerves!

WILLY: *pushing her away from him.* All right, stay in the bathroom here, and
  don't come out. I think there's a law in Massachusetts about it, so don't come
  out. It may be that new room clerk. He looked very mean. So don't come out.
  It's a mistake, there's no fire.

*The knocking is heard again. He takes a few steps away from her, and she van-
ishes into the wing. The light follows him, and now he is facing* YOUNG BIFF,
who carries a suitcase. BIFF *steps toward him. The music is gone.*

BIFF: Why didn't you answer?

WILLY: Biff. What are you doing in Boston?

BIFF: Why didn't you answer? I've been knocking for five minutes, I called you
  on the phone—

WILLY: I just heard you. I was in the bathroom and had the door shut. Did anything happen home?

BIFF: Dad—I let you down.

WILLY: What do you mean?

BIFF: Dad . . .

WILLY: Biffo, what's this about? *Putting his arm around* BIFF: Come on, let's
  go downstairs and get you a malted.

BIFF: Dad, I flunked math.

WILLY: Not for the term?

BIFF: The term. I haven't got enough credits to graduate.

WILLY: You mean to say Bernard wouldn't give you the answers?

BIFF: He did, he tried, but I only got a sixty-one.

WILLY: And they wouldn't give you four points?

BIFF: Birnbaum refused absolutely. I begged him, Pop, but he won't give me those points. You gotta talk to him before they close the school. Because if he saw the kind of man you are, and you just talked to him in your way, I'm sure he'd come through for me. The class came right before practice, see, and I didn't go enough. Would you talk to him? He'd like you, Pop. You know the way you could talk.

WILLY: You're on. We'll drive right back.

BIFF: Oh, Dad, good work! I'm sure he'll change it for you!

WILLY: Go downstairs and tell the clerk I'm checkin' out. Go right down.

BIFF: Yes, sir! See, the reason he hates me, Pop—one day he was late for class so I got up at the blackboard and imitated him. I crossed my eyes and talked with a lithp.

WILLY: *laughing.* You did? The kids like it?

BIFF: They nearly died laughing!

WILLY: Yeah? What'd you do?

BIFF: The thquare root of thixthy twee is ... WILLY *bursts out laughing;* BIFF *joins him.* And in the middle of it he walked in!

WILLY *laughs and* THE WOMAN *joins in offstage.*

WILLY: *without hesitation.* Hurry downstairs and—

BIFF: Somebody in there?

WILLY: No, that was next door.

THE WOMAN *laughs offstage.*

BIFF: Somebody got in your bathroom!

WILLY: No, it's the next room, there's a party—

THE WOMAN: *enters, laughing. She lisps this.* Can I come in? There's something in the bathtub, Willy, and it's moving!

WILLY *looks at* BIFF, *who is staring open-mouthed and horrified at* THE WOMAN.

WILLY: Ah—you better go back to your room. They must be finished painting by now. They're painting her room so I let her take a shower here. Go back, go back ... *He pushes her.*

THE WOMAN: *resisting.* But I've got to get dressed, Willy, I can't—

WILLY: Get out of here! Go back, go back ... *Suddenly striving for the ordinary:* This is Miss Francis, Biff, she's a buyer. They're painting her room. Go back, Miss Francis, go back ...

THE WOMAN: But my clothes, I can't go out naked in the hall!

WILLY: *pushing her offstage.* Get outa here! Go back, go back!

BIFF *slowly sits down on his suitcase as the argument continues off stage.*

THE WOMAN: Where's my stockings? You promised me stockings, Willy!

WILLY: I have no stockings here!

THE WOMAN: You had two boxes of size nine sheers for me, and I want them!

WILLY: Here, for God's sake, will you get outa here!

THE WOMAN: *enters holding a box of stockings.* I just hope there's nobody in the hall. That's all I hope. *To* BIFF. Are you football or baseball?

BIFF: Football.

THE WOMAN: *angry, humiliated.* That's me too. G'night. *She snatches her clothes from* WILLY, *and walks out.*

WILLY: *after a pause.* Well, better get going. I want to get to the school first thing in the morning. Get my suits out of the closet. I'll get my valise. BIFF *doesn't move.* What's the matter? BIFF *remains motionless, tears falling.* She's a buyer. Buys for J. H. Simmons. She lives down the hall—they're painting. You don't imagine—*He breaks off. After a pause:* Now listen, pal, she's just a buyer. She sees merchandise in her room and they have to keep it looking just so . . . *Pause. Assuming command:* All right, get my suits. BIFF *doesn't move.* Now stop crying and do as I say. I gave you an order. Biff, I gave you an order! Is that what you do when I give you an order? How dare you cry! *Putting his arm around* BIFF. Now look, Biff, when you grow up you'll understand about these things. You mustn't—you mustn't overemphasize a thing like this. I'll see Birnbaum first thing in the morning.

BIFF: Never mind.

WILLY: *getting down beside* BIFF. Never mind! He's going to give you those points. I'll see to it.

BIFF: He wouldn't listen to you.

WILLY: He certainly will listen to me. You need those points for the U. of Virginia.

BIFF: I'm not going there.

WILLY: Heh? If I can't get him to change that mark you'll make it up in summer school. You've got all summer to—

BIFF: *his weeping breaking from him.* Dad . . .

WILLY: *infected by it.* Oh, my boy . . .

BIFF: Dad . . .

WILLY: She's nothing to me, Biff. I was lonely, I was terribly lonely.

BIFF: You—you gave her Mama's stockings! *His tears break through and he rises to go.*

WILLY: *grabbing for* BIFF. I gave you an order!

BIFF: Don't touch me, you—liar!

WILLY: Apologize for that!

BIFF: You fake! You phony little fake! You fake! *Overcome, he turns quickly and weeping fully goes out with his suitcase.* WILLY *is left on the floor on his knees.*

WILLY: I gave you an order! Biff, come back here or I'll beat you! Come back here! I'll whip you!

STANLEY *comes quickly in from the right and stands in front of* WILLY.

WILLY: *shouts at* STANLEY. I gave you an order . . .
STANLEY: Hey, let's pick it up, pick it up, Mr. Loman. *He helps* WILLY *to his feet.*
  Your boys left with the chippies. They said they'll see you home.

A second waiter watches some distance away.

WILLY: But we were supposed to have dinner together.

Music is heard, WILLY*'s theme.*

STANLEY: Can you make it?
WILLY: I'll—sure, I can make it. *Suddenly concerned about his clothes:* Do I—
  I look all right?
STANLEY: Sure, you look all right. *He flicks a speck off* WILLY*'s lapel.*
WILLY: Here—here's a dollar.
STANLEY: Oh, your son paid me. It's all right.
WILLY: *putting it in* STANLEY*'s hand.* No, take it. You're a good boy.
STANLEY: Oh, no, you don't have to . . .
WILLY: Here—here's some more, I don't need it any more. *After a slight pause:*
  Tell me—is there a seed store in the neighborhood?
STANLEY: Seeds? You mean like to plant?

As WILLY *turns,* STANLEY *slips the money back into his jacket pocket.*

WILLY: Yes. Carrots, peas . . .
STANLEY: Well, there's hardware stores on Sixth Avenue, but it may be too late
  now.
WILLY: *anxiously.* Oh, I'd better hurry. I've got to get some seeds. *He starts off
  to the right.* I've got to get some seeds, right away. Nothing's planted. I don't
  have a thing in the ground.

WILLY *hurries out as the light goes down.* STANLEY *moves over to the right after
  him, watches him off. The other waiter has been staring at* WILLY.

STANLEY: *to the waiter.* Well, whatta you looking at?

The waiter picks up the chairs and moves off right. STANLEY *takes the table and
  follows him. The light fades on this area. There is a long pause, the sound of the
  flute coming over. The light gradually rises on the kitchen, which is empty.*
  HAPPY *appears at the door of the house, followed by* BIFF. HAPPY *is carrying
  a large bunch of long-stemmed roses. He enters the kitchen, looks around for*
  LINDA. *Not seeing her, he turns to* BIFF, *who is just outside the house door, and
  makes a gesture with his hands, indicating "Not here, I guess." He looks into*

the living room and freezes. Inside, LINDA, *unseen, is seated,* WILLY's *coat on her lap. She rises ominously and quietly and moves toward* HAPPY, *who backs up into the kitchen, afraid.*

HAPPY: Hey, what're you doing up? LINDA *says nothing but moves toward him implacably.* Where's Pop? *He keeps backing to the right, and now* LINDA *is in full view in the doorway to the living-room.* Is he sleeping?

LINDA: Where were you?

HAPPY: *trying to laugh it off.* We met two girls, Mom, very fine types. Here, we brought you some flowers. *Offering them to her:* Put them in your room, Ma.

She knocks them to the floor at BIFF's *feet. He has now come inside and closed the door behind him. She stares at* BIFF, *silent.*

HAPPY: Now what'd you do that for? Mom, I want you to have some flowers—

LINDA: *cutting* HAPPY *off, violently to* BIFF. Don't you care whether he lives or dies?

HAPPY: *going to the stairs.* Come upstairs, Biff.

BIFF: *with a flare of disgust, to* HAPPY. Go away from me! *To* LINDA: What do you mean, lives or dies? Nobody's dying around here, pal.

LINDA: Get out of my sight! Get out of here!

BIFF: I wanna see the boss.

LINDA: You're not going near him!

BIFF: Where is he? *He moves into the living-room and* LINDA *follows.*

LINDA: *Shouting after* BIFF. You invite him for dinner. He looks forward to it all day—BIFF *appears in his parents' bedroom, looks around, and exits* —and then you desert him there. There's no stranger you'd do that to!

HAPPY: Why? He had a swell time with us. Listen, when I—LINDA *comes back into the kitchen* —desert him I hope I don't outlive the day!

LINDA: Get out of here!

HAPPY: Now look, Mom . . .

LINDA: Did you have to go to women tonight? You and your lousy rotten whores!

BIFF *re-enters the kitchen.*

HAPPY: Mom, all we did was follow Biff around trying to cheer him up! *To* BIFF: Boy, what a night you gave me!

LINDA: Get out of here, both of you, and don't come back! I don't want you tormenting him any more. Go on now, get your things together! *To* BIFF: You can sleep in his apartment. *She starts to pick up the flowers and stops herself.* Pick up this stuff, I'm not your maid any more. Pick it up, you bum, you!

HAPPY *turns his back to her in refusal.* BIFF *slowly moves over and gets down on his knees, picking up the flowers.*

LINDA: You're a pair of animals! Not one, not another living soul would have
   had the cruelty to walk out on that man in a restaurant!
BIFF: *not looking at her.* Is that what he said?
LINDA: He didn't have to say anything. He was so humiliated he nearly limped
   when he came in.
HAPPY: But, Mom, he had a great time with us—
BIFF: *cutting him off violently.* Shut up!

Without another word, HAPPY *goes upstairs.*

LINDA: You! You didn't even go in to see if he was all right!
BIFF: *still on the floor in front of* LINDA, *the flowers in his hand; with self-
   loathing.* No. Didn't. Didn't do a damned thing. How do you like that, heh?
   Left him babbling in a toilet.
LINDA: You louse. You . . .
BIFF: Now you hit it on the nose! *He gets up, throws the flowers in the waste-
   basket.* The scum of the earth, and you're looking at him!
LINDA: Get out of here!
BIFF: I gotta talk to the boss, Mom. Where is he?
LINDA: You're not going near him. Get out of this house!
BIFF: *with absolute assurance, determination.* No. We're gonna have an abrupt
   conversation, him and me.
LINDA: You're not talking to him!

Hammering is heard from outside the house, off right. BIFF *turns toward the noise.*

LINDA: *suddenly pleading.* Will you please leave him alone?
BIFF: What's he doing out there?
LINDA: He's planting the garden!
BIFF: *quietly.* Now? Oh, my God!

BIFF *moves outside,* LINDA *following. The light dies down on them and comes up
   on the center of the apron as* WILLY *walks into it. He is carrying a flashlight, a
   hoe, and a handful of seed packets. He raps the top of the hoe sharply to fix it
   firmly, and then moves to the left, measuring off the distance with his foot. He
   holds the flashlight to look at the seed packets, reading off the instructions. He
   is in the blue of night.*

WILLY: Carrots . . . quarter-inch apart. Rows . . . one-foot rows. *He measures it
   off.* One foot. *He puts down a package and measures off.* Beets. *He puts down
   another package and measures again.* Lettuce. *He reads the package, puts it
   down.* One foot—*He breaks off as* BEN *appears at the right and moves slowly
   down to him.* What a proposition, ts, ts. Terrific, terrific. 'Cause she's suffered,
   Ben, the woman has suffered. You understand me? A man can't go out the
   way he came in, Ben, a man has got to add up to something. You can't, you

can't—BEN *moves toward him as though to interrupt.* You gotta consider, now. Don't answer so quick. Remember, it's a guaranteed twenty-thousand-dollar proposition. Now look, Ben, I want you to go through the ins and outs of this thing with me. I've got nobody to talk to, Ben, and the woman has suffered, you hear me?

BEN: *standing still, considering.* What's the proposition?

WILLY: It's twenty thousand dollars on the barrelhead. Guaranteed, gilt-edged, you understand?

BEN: You don't want to make a fool of yourself. They might not honor the policy.

WILLY: How can they dare refuse? Didn't I work like a coolie to meet every premium on the nose? And now they don't pay off? Impossible!

BEN: It's called a cowardly thing, William.

WILLY: Why? Does it take more guts to stand here the rest of my life ringing up a zero?

BEN: *yielding.* That's a point, William. *He moves, thinking, turns.* And twenty thousand—that *is* something one can feel with the hand, it is there.

WILLY: *now assured, with rising power.* Oh, Ben, that's the whole beauty of it! I see it like a diamond, shining in the dark, hard and rough, that I can pick up and touch in my hand. Not like—like an appointment! This would not be another damned-fool appointment, Ben, and it changes all the aspects. Because he thinks I'm nothing, see, and so he spites me. But the funeral—*Straightening up:* Ben, that funeral will be massive! They'll come from Maine, Massachusetts, Vermont, New Hampshire! All the old-timers with the strange license plates—that boy will be thunderstruck, Ben, because he never realized—I am known! Rhode Island, New York, New Jersey—I am known, Ben, and he'll see it with his eyes once and for all. He'll see what I am, Ben! He's in for a shock, that boy!

BEN: *coming down to the edge of the garden.* He'll call you a coward.

WILLY: *suddenly fearful.* No, that would be terrible.

BEN: Yes. And a damned fool.

WILLY: No, no, he mustn't, I won't have that! *He is broken and desperate.*

BEN: He'll hate you, William.

The gay music of the Boys is heard.

WILLY: Oh, Ben, how do we get back to all the great times? Used to be so full of light, and comradeship, the sleigh-riding in winter, and the ruddiness on his cheeks. And always some kind of good news coming up, always something nice coming up ahead. And never even let me carry the valises in the house, and simonizing, simonizing that little red car! Why, why can't I give him something and not have him hate me?

BEN: Let me think about it. *He glances at his watch.* I still have a little time. Remarkable proposition, but you've got to be sure you're not making a fool of yourself.

BEN *drifts off upstage and goes out of sight.* BIFF *comes down from the left.*

WILLY: *suddenly conscious of* BIFF, *turns and looks up at him, then begins picking up the packages of seeds in confusion.* Where the hell is that seed? *Indignantly:* You can't see nothing out here! They boxed in the whole goddam neighborhood!

BIFF: There are people all around here. Don't you realize that?

WILLY: I'm busy. Don't bother me.

BIFF: *taking the hoe from* WILLY. I'm saying good-by to you, Pop. WILLY *looks at him, silent, unable to move.* I'm not coming back any more.

WILLY: You're not going to see Oliver tomorrow?

BIFF: I've got no appointment, Dad.

WILLY: He put his arm around you, and you've got no appointment?

BIFF: Pop, get this now, will you? Everytime I've left it's been a fight that sent me out of here. Today I realized something about myself and I tried to explain it to you and I—I think I'm just not smart enough to make any sense out of it for you. To hell with whose fault it is or anything like that. *He takes* WILLY'*s arm.* Let's just wrap it up, heh? Come on in, we'll tell Mom. *He gently tries to pull* WILLY *to left.*

WILLY: *frozen, immobile, with guilt in his voice.* No, I don't want to see her.

BIFF: Come on! *He pulls again, and* WILLY *tries to pull away.*

WILLY: *highly nervous.* No, no, I don't want to see her.

BIFF: *tries to look into* WILLY'*s face, as if to find the answer there.* Why don't you want to see her?

WILLY: *more harshly now.* Don't bother me, will you?

BIFF: What do you mean, you don't want to see her? You don't want them calling you yellow, do you? This isn't your fault; it's me, I'm a bum. Now come inside! WILLY *strains to get away.* Did you hear what I said to you?

WILLY *pulls away and quickly goes by himself into the house.* BIFF *follows.*

LINDA: *to* WILLY. Did you plant, dear?

BIFF: *at the door, to* LINDA. All right, we had it out. I'm going and I'm not writing any more.

LINDA: *going to* WILLY *in the kitchen.* I think that's the best way, dear. 'Cause there's no use drawing it out, you'll just never get along.

WILLY *doesn't respond.*

BIFF: People ask where I am and what I'm doing, you don't know, and you don't care. That way it'll be off your mind and you can start brightening up again. All right? That clears it, doesn't it? WILLY *is silent, and* BIFF *goes to him.* You gonna wish me luck, scout? *He extends his hand.* What do you say?

LINDA: Shake his hand, Willy.

WILLY: *turning to her, seething with hurt.* There's no necessity to mention the pen at all, y'know.

BIFF: *gently.* I've got no appointment, Dad.

WILLY: *erupting fiercely.* He put his arm around . . .?

BIFF: Dad, you're never going to see what I am, so what's the use of arguing? If I strike oil I'll send you a check. Meantime forget I'm alive.

WILLY: *to* LINDA. Spite, see?

BIFF: Shake hands, Dad.

WILLY: Not my hand.

BIFF: I was hoping not to go this way.

WILLY: Well, this is the way you're going. Good-by.

BIFF *looks at him a moment, then turns sharply and goes to the stairs.*

WILLY: *stops him with.* May you rot in hell if you leave this house!

BIFF: *turning.* Exactly what is it that you want from me?

WILLY: I want you to know, on the train, in the mountains, in the valleys, wherever you go, that you cut down your life for spite!

BIFF: No, no.

WILLY: Spite, spite, is the word of your undoing! And when you're down and out, remember what did it. When you're rotting somewhere beside the railroad tracks, remember, and don't you dare blame it on me!

BIFF: I'm not blaming it on you!

WILLY: I won't take the rap for this, you hear?

HAPPY *comes down the stairs and stands on the bottom step, watching.*

BIFF: That's just what I'm telling you!

WILLY: *sinking into a chair at the table, with full accusation.* You're trying to put a knife in me—don't think I don't know what you're doing!

BIFF: All right, phony! Then let's lay it on the line. *He whips the rubber tube out of his pocket and puts it on the table.*

HAPPY: You crazy—

LINDA: Biff! *She moves to grab the hose, but* BIFF *holds it down with his hand.*

BIFF: Leave it there! Don't move it!

WILLY: *not looking at it.* What is that?

BIFF: You know goddam well what that is.

WILLY: *caged, wanting to escape.* I never saw that.

BIFF: You saw it. The mice didn't bring it into the cellar! What is this supposed to do, make a hero out of you? This supposed to make me sorry for you?

WILLY: Never heard of it.

BIFF: There'll be no pity for you, you hear it? No pity!

WILLY: *to* LINDA. You hear the spite!

BIFF: No, you're going to hear the truth—what you are and what I am!

LINDA: Stop it!

WILLY: Spite!

HAPPY: *coming down toward* BIFF. You cut it now!

BIFF: *to* HAPPY. The man don't know who we are! The man is gonna know! *To* WILLY: We never told the truth for ten minutes in this house!

HAPPY: We always told the truth!

BIFF: *turning on him.* You big blow, are you the assistant buyer? You're one of the two assistants to the assistant, aren't you?

HAPPY: Well, I'm practically—

BIFF: You're practically full of it! We all are! And I'm through with it. *To* WILLY: Now hear this, Willy, this is me.

WILLY: I know you!

BIFF: You know why I had no address for three months? I stole a suit in Kansas City and I was in jail. *To* LINDA, *who is sobbing:* Stop crying. I'm through with it.

LINDA *turns away from them, her hands covering her face.*

WILLY: I suppose that's my fault!

BIFF: I stole myself out of every good job since high school!

WILLY: And whose fault is that?

BIFF: And I never got anywhere because you blew me so full of hot air I could never stand taking orders from anybody! That's whose fault it is!

WILLY: I hear that!

LINDA: Don't, Biff!

BIFF: It's goddam time you heard that! I had to be boss big shot in two weeks, and I'm through with it!

WILLY: Then hang yourself! For spite, hang yourself!

BIFF: No! Nobody's hanging himself, Willy! I ran down eleven flights with a pen in my hand today. And suddenly I stopped, you hear me? And in the middle of that office building, do you hear this? I stopped in the middle of that building and I saw—the sky. I saw the things that I love in this world. The work and the food and time to sit and smoke. And I looked at the pen and said to myself, what the hell am I grabbing this for? Why am I trying to become what I don't want to be? What am I doing in an office, making a contemptuous, begging fool of myself, when all I want is out there, waiting for me the minute I say I know who I am! Why can't I say that, Willy? *He tries to make* WILLY *face him, but* WILLY *pulls away and moves to the left.*

WILLY: *with hatred, threateningly.* The door of your life is wide open!

BIFF: Pop! I'm a dime a dozen, and so are you!

WILLY: *turning on him now in an uncontrolled outburst.* I am not a dime a dozen! I am Willy Loman, and you are Biff Loman!

BIFF *starts for* WILLY, *but is blocked by* HAPPY. *In his fury,* BIFF *seems on the verge of attacking his father.*

BIFF: I am not a leader of men, Willy, and neither are you. You were never anything but a hard-working drummer who landed in the ash can like all the rest of them! I'm one dollar an hour, Willy! I tried seven states and couldn't raise it. A buck an hour! Do you gather my meaning? I'm not bringing home any prizes any more, and you're going to stop waiting for me to bring them home!

WILLY: *directly to* BIFF. You vengeful, spiteful mut!

BIFF *breaks from* HAPPY. WILLY, *in fright, starts up the stairs.* BIFF *grabs him.*

BIFF: *at the peak of his fury.* Pop, I'm nothing! I'm nothing, Pop. Can't you understand that? There's no spite in it any more. I'm just what I am, that's all.

BIFF's *fury has spent itself, and he breaks down, sobbing, holding on to* WILLY, *who dumbly fumbles for* BIFF's *face.*

WILLY: *astonished.* What're you doing? What're you doing? *To* LINDA: Why is he crying?

BIFF: *crying, broken.* Will you let me go, for Christ's sake? Will you take that phony dream and burn it before something happens? *Struggling to contain himself, he pulls away and moves to the stairs.* I'll go in the morning. Put him—put him to bed. *Exhausted,* BIFF *moves up the stairs to his room.*

WILLY: *after a long pause, astonished, elevated.* Isn't that—isn't that remarkable? Biff—he likes me!

LINDA: He loves you, Willy!

HAPPY: *deeply moved.* Always did, Pop.

WILLY: Oh, Biff! *Staring wildly:* He cried! Cried to me. *He is choking with his love, and now cries out his promise:* That boy—that boy is going to be magnificent!

BEN *appears in the light just outside the kitchen.*

BEN: Yes, outstanding, with twenty thousand behind him.

LINDA: *sensing the racing of his mind, fearfully, carefully.* Now come to bed, Willy. It's all settled now.

WILLY: *finding it difficult not to rush out of the house.* Yes, we'll sleep. Come on. Go to sleep, Hap.

BEN: And it does take a great kind of a man to crack the jungle.

In accents of dread, BEN's *idyllic music starts up.*

HAPPY: *his arm around* LINDA. I'm getting married, Pop, don't forget it. I'm changing everything. I'm gonna run that department before the year is up. You'll see, Mom. *He kisses her.*

BEN: The jungle is dark but full of diamonds, Willy.

WILLY *turns, moves, listening to* BEN.

LINDA: Be good. You're both good boys, just act that way, that's all.
HAPPY: 'Night, Pop. *He goes upstairs.*
LINDA: *to* WILLY. Come, dear.
BEN: *with greater force.* One must go in to fetch a diamond out.
WILLY: *to* LINDA, *as he moves slowly along the edge of the kitchen, toward the door.* I just want to get settled down, Linda. Let me sit alone for a little.
LINDA: *almost uttering her fear.* I want you upstairs.
WILLY: *taking her in his arms.* In a few minutes, Linda. I couldn't sleep right now. Go on, you look awful tired. *He kisses her.*
BEN: Not like an appointment at all. A diamond is rough and hard to the touch.
WILLY: Go on now. I'll be right up.
LINDA: I think this is the only way, Willy.
WILLY: Sure, it's the best thing.
BEN: Best thing!
WILLY: The only way. Everything is gonna be—go on, kid, get to bed. You look so tired.
LINDA: Come right up.
WILLY: Two minutes.

LINDA *goes into the living-room, then reappears in her bedroom.* WILLY *moves just outside the kitchen door.*

WILLY: Loves me. *Wonderingly:* Always loved me. Isn't that a remarkable thing? Ben, he'll worship me for it!
BEN: *with promise.* It's dark there, but full of diamonds.
WILLY: Can you imagine that magnificence with twenty thousand dollars in his pocket?
LINDA: *calling from her room.* Willy! Come up!
WILLY: *calling into the kitchen.* Yes! Yes. Coming! It's very smart, you realize that, don't you, sweetheart? Even Ben sees it. I gotta go, baby. 'By! 'By! *Going over to* BEN, *almost dancing:* Imagine? When the mail comes he'll be ahead of Bernard again!
BEN: A perfect proposition all around.
WILLY: Did you see how he cried to me? Oh, if I could kiss him, Ben!
BEN: Time, William, time!
WILLY: Oh, Ben, I always knew one way or another we were gonna make it, Biff and I!
BEN: *looking at his watch.* The boat. We'll be late. *He moves slowly off into the darkness.*
WILLY: *elegiacally, turning to the house.* Now when you kick off, boy, I want a seventy-yard boot, and get right down the field under the ball, and when you hit, hit low and hit hard, because it's important, boy. *He swings around and faces the audience.* There's all kinds of important people in the stands, and the

first thing you know . . . *Suddenly realizing he is alone:* Ben! Ben, where do I . . .? *He makes a sudden movement of search.* Ben, how do I . . .?

LINDA: *calling.* Willy, you coming up?

WILLY: *uttering a gasp of fear, whirling about as if to quiet her.* Sh! *He turns around as if to find his way; sounds, faces, voices, seem to be swarming in upon him and he flicks at them, crying.* Sh! Sh! *Suddenly music, faint and high, stops him. It rises in intensity, almost to an unbearable scream. He goes up and down on his toes, and rushes off around the house.* Shhh!

LINDA: Willy?

There is no answer. LINDA *waits.* BIFF *gets up off his bed. He is still in his clothes.* HAPPY *sits up.* BIFF *stands listening.*

LINDA: *with real fear.* Willy, answer me! Willy!

There is the sound of a car starting and moving away at full speed.

LINDA: No!

BIFF: *rushing down the stairs.* Pop!

As the car speeds off, the music crashes down in a frenzy of sound, which becomes the soft pulsation of a single cello string. BIFF *slowly returns to his bedroom. He and* HAPPY *gravely don their jackets.* LINDA *slowly walks out of her room. The music has developed into a dead march. The leaves of day are appearing over everything.* CHARLEY *and* BERNARD, *somberly dressed, appear and knock on the kitchen door.* BIFF *and* HAPPY *slowly descend the stairs to the kitchen as* CHARLEY *and* BERNARD *enter. All stop a moment when* LINDA, *in clothes of mourning, bearing a little bunch of roses, comes through the draped doorway into the kitchen. She goes to* CHARLEY *and takes his arm. Now all move toward the audience, through the wall-line of the kitchen. At the limit of the apron,* LINDA *lays down the flowers, kneels, and sits back on her heels. All stare down at the grave.*

REQUIEM

CHARLEY: It's getting dark, Linda.

LINDA *doesn't react. She stares at the grave.*

BIFF: How about it, Mom? Better get some rest, heh? They'll be closing the gate soon.

LINDA *makes no move. Pause.*

HAPPY: *deeply angered.* He had no right to do that. There was no necessity for it. We would've helped him.

CHARLEY: *grunting.* Hmmm.

BIFF: Come along, Mom.

LINDA: Why didn't anybody come?

CHARLEY: It was a very nice funeral.

LINDA: But where are all the people he knew? Maybe they blame him.

CHARLEY: Naa. It's a rough world, Linda. They wouldn't blame him.

LINDA: I can't understand it. At this time especially. First time in thirty-five years we were just about free and clear. He only needed a little salary. He was even finished with the dentist.

CHARLEY: No man only needs a little salary.

LINDA: I can't understand it.

BIFF: There were a lot of nice days. When he'd come home from a trip; or on Sundays, making the stoop; finishing the cellar; putting on the new porch; when he built the extra bathroom; and put up the garage. You know something, Charley, there's more of him in that front stoop than in all the sales he ever made.

CHARLEY: Yeah. He was a happy man with a batch of cement.

LINDA: He was so wonderful with his hands.

BIFF: He had the wrong dreams. All, all, wrong.

HAPPY: *almost ready to fight* BIFF. Don't say that!

BIFF: He never knew who he was.

CHARLEY: *stopping* HAPPY's *movement and reply. To* BIFF. Nobody dast blame this man. You don't understand: Willy was a salesman. And for a salesman, there is no rock bottom to the life. He don't put a bolt to a nut, he don't tell you the law or give you medicine. He's a man way out there in the blue, riding on a smile and a shoeshine. And when they start not smiling back—that's an earthquake. And then you get yourself a couple of spots on your hat, and you're finished. Nobody dast blame this man. A salesman is got to dream, boy. It comes with the territory.

BIFF: Charley, the man didn't know who he was.

HAPPY: *infuriated.* Don't say that!

BIFF: Why don't you come with me, Happy?

HAPPY: I'm not licked that easily. I'm staying right in this city, and I'm gonna beat this racket! *He looks at* BIFF, *his chin set.* The Loman Brothers!

BIFF: I know who I am, kid.

HAPPY: All right, boy. I'm gonna show you and everybody else that Willy Loman did not die in vain. He had a good dream. It's the only dream you can have—to come out number-one man. He fought it out here, and this is where I'm gonna win it for him.

BIFF: *with a hopeless glance at* HAPPY, *bends toward his mother.* Let's go, Mom.

LINDA: I'll be with you in a minute. Go on, Charley. *He hesitates.* I want to, just for a minute. I never had a chance to say good-by.

CHARLEY *moves away, followed by* HAPPY. BIFF *remains a slight distance up and left of* LINDA. *She sits there, summoning herself. The flute begins, not far away, playing behind her speech.*

LINDA: Forgive me, dear. I can't cry. I don't know what it is, but I can't cry. I
don't understand it. Why did you ever do that? Help me, Willy, I can't cry. It
seems to me that you're just on another trip. I keep expecting you. Willy, dear,
I can't cry. Why did you do it? I search and search and I search, and I can't
understand it, Willy. I made the last payment on the house today. Today, dear.
And there'll be nobody home. *A sob rises in her throat.* We're free and clear.
Sobbing more fully, released: We're free. BIFF *comes slowly toward her.* We're
free ... We're free ...

BIFF *lifts her to her feet and moves out up right with her in his arms.* LINDA *sobs
quietly.* BERNARD *and* CHARLEY *come together and follow them, followed by*
HAPPY. *Only the music of the flute is left on the darkening stage as over the
house the hard towers of the apartment buildings rise into sharp focus, and*

THE CURTAIN FALLS

Study and Discussion Questions

1. Characterize Happy and Biff. How is each like and unlike his father?
2. What is Linda's relationship to Willy like? How does she help him? Is
    there any way in which she hurts him? Who suffers more, Linda or Willy?
3. What does Willy feel is the key to getting ahead? Is he right?
4. What is the significance of Ben in the play? Of Charley? Of Bernard?
5. When Willy comes to Howard to ask for a desk job, Howard refuses, say-
    ing "business is business." What is Willy trying to say to *him?* What clash
    of values does this scene dramatize?
6. What is the significance of Willy's occupation? What would be lost if the
    play were rewritten as, say, *Death of a Plumber?*
7. How does Happy try to compensate for the powerlessness and lack of sta-
    tus he feels at work?
8. What kind of work did Willy's father do? What kind of work does Biff
    describe so lyrically to Happy early in Act I? How do these kinds of work
    differ from Willy's? At the funeral, why does Biff say "there's more of him
    in that front stoop [he built] than in all the sales he ever made"?

Suggestions for Writing

1. The family is often viewed as a refuge from the harsh reality of the com-
    petitive business world. What comment is the play making on that notion?
2. Willy Loman is not an appealing fellow. He is a tiresome blowhard. He is
    rude and insulting to his wife, his sons, and his very generous friend
    Charley. He snivels shamelessly before his boss, Howard. Why, then, does
    he get our sympathy (if he does)?
3. Characterize Linda as fully as possible. How would the play be different
    if she, rather than Willy, were the central character?

4. Take one section of the play and analyze the logic of Willy's drifting into and out of the past.
5. If the surviving Lomans did get $20,000 from Willy's life insurance, what do you think they would do with it?
6. To a great extent, the plot of the play hinges on the fact, fully revealed only near the end, that Biff found his father with a woman in a hotel room. Some critics have seen this as a weakness, since (a) the incident cannot carry the weight it is meant to in explaining Biff's failure; and (b) it distracts from the social criticism of the play by pointing to Willy himself as the cause of his and Biff's problems. Do you agree or disagree?

Critical Resources:

1. Abbotson, Susan. *Student Companion to Arthur Miller.* Westport, CT: Greenwood Press, 2000.
2. Gottfried, Martin. *Arthur Miller, His Life and Work.* Cambridge, MA: Da Capo Press, 2003.
3. Gussow, Mel. *Conversations with Arthur Miller.* New York: Applause, 2002.
4. Koorey, Stefani. *Arthur Miller's Life and Literature: An Annotated and Comprehensive Guide.* Lanham, MD: Scarecrow Press, 2000.
5. The University of Michigan. *Arthur Miller Files.* 2001. April 29, 2005. <http://www.umich.edu/~amfiles/>

AUGUST WILSON (1945–2005)

August Wilson grew up in an impoverished neighborhood of Pittsburgh, Pennsylvania; his mother was a cleaning woman and his German immigrant father a baker. As a mulatto, Wilson's early education was marked by racial insults and harassment, driving Wilson to drop out of school at the age of 15. Nonetheless, Wilson continued to read voraciously at local libraries and became intimately acquainted with the works of black authors such as Ralph Ellison, Richard Wright, and Langston Hughes. By 20, Wilson was determined to become a writer and would spend the next decade working low-paying jobs and writing. In 1979, his play, Jitney! *was produced in Pittsburgh, but it wasn't until the production of* Ma Rainey's Black Bottom, *which opened on Broadway in 1984, that Wilson was recognized as an important contemporary dramatist. Three years later,* Fences *opened on Broadway, winning the New York Drama Critics Award as well as the Pulitzer Prize. Wilson's plays, each set in a particular decade of the twentieth century, attempt to historicize the black experience through the medium of drama and, taken as whole, seek to uncover a unique black cultural identity within mainstream American culture and history. For this project, as well as his keen sense for the poignant and poetic (as well as for his humor), Wilson has become one of America's most celebrated playwrights. Other plays include* Recycle (1973), Fullerton

Street *(1980)*, Joe Turner's Come and Gone *(1986)*. The Piano Lesson *(1987)*, Two Trains Running *(1990)*, King Hedley II *(2000)*, Gem of the Ocean *(2003)*, *and his last production,* Radio Golf *(2005) which completes his planned cycle of ten plays. August Wilson died in October 2005, his place in American Theater secure.* The Piano Lesson *was awarded the Pulitzer Prize in 1990.*

The Piano Lesson (1987)

> Gin my cotton
> Sell my seed
> Buy my baby
> Everything she need
> —Skip James

THE SETTING

The action of the play takes place in the kitchen and parlor of the house where DOAKER CHARLES *lives with his niece,* BERNIECE, *and her eleven-year-old daughter,* MARETHA. *The house is sparsely furnished, and although there is evidence of a woman's touch, there is a lack of warmth and vigor.* BERNIECE *and* MARETHA *occupy the upstairs rooms.* DOAKER's *room is prominent and opens onto the kitchen. Dominating the parlor is an old upright piano. On the legs of the piano, carved in the manner of African sculpture, are mask-like figures resembling totems. The carvings are rendered with a grace and power of invention that lifts them out of the realm of craftsmanship and into the realm of art. At left is a staircase leading to the upstairs.*

ACT ONE

Scene 1

(The lights come up on the Charles household. It is five o'clock in the morning. The dawn is beginning to announce itself, but there is something in the air that belongs to the night. A stillness that is a portent, a gathering, a coming together of something akin to a storm. There is a loud knock at the door.)

BOY WILLIE: *(Off stage, calling.)* Hey, Doaker . . . Doaker! *(He knocks again and calls.)* Hey, Doaker! Hey, Berniece! Berniece!

(DOAKER enters from his room. He is a tall, thin man of forty-seven, with severe features, who has for all intents and purposes retired from the world though he works full-time as a railroad cook.)

DOAKER: Who is it?

BOY WILLIE: Open the door, nigger! It's me . . . Boy Willie!

DOAKER: Who?

BOY WILLIE: Boy Willie! Open the door!

(DOAKER *opens the door and* BOY WILLIE *and* LYMON *enter.* BOY WILLIE *is thirty years old. He has an infectious grin and a boyishness that is apt for his name. He is brash and impulsive, talkative and somewhat crude in speech and manner.* LYMON *is twenty-nine.* BOY WILLIE's *partner, he talks little, and then with a straightforwardness that is often disarming.)*

DOAKER: What you doing up here?

BOY WILLIE: I told you, Lymon. Lymon talking about you might be sleep. This is Lymon. You remember Lymon Jackson from down home? This my Uncle Doaker.

DOAKER: What you doing up here? I couldn't figure out who that was. I thought you was still down in Mississippi.

BOY WILLIE: Me and Lymon selling watermelons. We got a truck out there. Got a whole truckload of watermelons. We brought them up here to sell. Where's Berniece?

(Calls.)

Hey, Berniece!

DOAKER: Berniece up there sleep.

BOY WILLIE: Well, let her get up.

(Calls.)

Hey, Berniece!

DOAKER: She got to go to work in the morning.

BOY WILLIE: Well she can get up and say hi. It's been three years since I seen her.

(Calls.)

Hey, Berniece! It's me . . . Boy Willie.

DOAKER: Berniece don't like all that hollering now. She got to work in the morning.

BOY WILLIE: She can go on back to bed. Me and Lymon been riding two days in that truck . . . the least she can do is get up and say hi.

DOAKER: *(Looking out the window.)* Where you all get that truck from?

BOY WILLIE: It's Lymon's. I told him let's get a load of watermelons and bring them up here.

LYMON: Boy Willie say he going back, but I'm gonna stay. See what it's like up here.

BOY WILLIE: You gonna carry me down there first.

LYMON: I told you I ain't going back down there and take a chance on that truck breaking down again. You can take the train. Hey, tell him Doaker, he can take the train back. After we sell them watermelons he have enough money he can buy him a whole railroad car.

DOAKER: You got all them watermelons stacked up there no wonder the truck broke down. I'm surprised you made it this far with a load like that. Where you break down at?

BOY WILLIE: We broke down three times! It took us two and a half days to get here. It's a good thing we picked them watermelons fresh.

LYMON: We broke down twice in West Virginia. The first time was just as soon as we got out of Sunflower. About forty miles out she broke down. We got it going and got all the way to West Virginia before she broke down again.

BOY WILLIE: We had to walk about five miles for some water.

LYMON: It got a hole in the radiator but it runs pretty good. You have to pump the brakes sometime before they catch. Boy Willie have his door open and be ready to jump when that happens.

BOY WILLIE: Lymon think that's funny. I told the nigger I give him ten dollars to get the brakes fixed. But he thinks that funny.

LYMON: They don't need fixing. All you got to do is pump them till they catch.

(BERNIECE enters on the stairs. Thirty-five years old, with an eleven-year-old daughter, she is still in mourning for her husband after three years.)

BERNIECE: What you doing all that hollering for?

BOY WILLIE: Hey, Berniece. Doaker said you was sleep. I said at least you could get up and say hi.

BERNIECE: It's five o'clock in the morning and you come in here with all this noise. You can't come like normal folks. You got to bring all that noise with you.

BOY WILLIE: Hell, I ain't done nothing but come in and say hi. I ain't got in the house good.

BERNIECE: That's what I'm talking about. You start all that hollering and carry on as soon as you hit the door.

BOY WILLIE: Aw hell, woman, I was glad to see Doaker. You ain't had to come down if you didn't want to. I come eighteen hundred miles to see my sister I figure she might want to get up and say hi. Other than that you can go back upstairs. What you got, Doaker? Where your bottle? Me and Lymon want a drink.

(To BERNIECE.*)*

This is Lymon. You remember Lymon Jackson from down home.

LYMON: How you doing, Berniece. You look just like I thought you looked.

BERNIECE: Why you all got to come in hollering and carrying on? Waking the neighbors with all that noise.

BOY WILLIE: They can come over and join the party. We fixing to have a party. Doaker, where your bottle? Me and Lymon celebrating. The Ghosts of the Yellow Dog got Sutter.

BERNIECE: Say what?

BOY WILLIE: Ask Lymon, they found him the next morning. Say he drowned in his well.

DOAKER: When this happen, Boy Willie?

BOY WILLIE: About three weeks ago. Me and Lymon was over in Stoner County when we heard about it. We laughed. We thought it was funny. A great big old three-hundred-and-forty-pound man gonna fall down his well.

LYMON: It remind me of Humpty Dumpty.

BOY WILLIE: Everybody say the Ghosts of the Yellow Dog pushed him.

BERNIECE: I don't want to hear that nonsense. Somebody down there pushing them people in their wells.

DOAKER: What was you and Lymon doing over in Stoner County?

BOY WILLIE: We was down there working. Lymon got some people down there.

LYMON: My cousin got some land down there. We was helping him.

BOY WILLIE: Got near about a hundred acres. He got it set up real nice. Me and Lymon was down there chopping down trees. We was using Lymon's truck to haul the wood. Me and Lymon used to haul wood all around them parts.

(To BERNIECE.*)*

Me and Lymon got a truckload of watermelons out there.

*(*BERNIECE *crosses to the window to the parlor.)*

Doaker, where your bottle? I know you got a bottle stuck up in your room. Come on, me and Lymon want a drink.

*(*DOAKER *exits into his room.)*

BERNIECE: Where you all get that truck from?

BOY WILLIE: I told you it's Lymon's.

BERNIECE: Where you get the truck from, Lymon?

LYMON: I bought it.

BERNIECE: Where he get that truck from, Boy Willie?

BOY WILLIE: He told you he bought it. Bought it for a hundred and twenty dollars. I can't say where he got that hundred and twenty dollars from . . . but he bought that old piece of truck from Henry Porter. *(To* LYMON.*)* Where you get that hundred and twenty dollars from, nigger?

LYMON: I got it like you get yours. I know how to take care of money.

(DOAKER *brings a bottle and sets it on the table.*)

BOY WILLIE: Aw hell, Doaker got some of that good whiskey. Don't give Lymon none of that. He ain't used to good whiskey. He liable to get sick.

LYMON: I done had good whiskey before.

BOY WILLIE: Lymon bought that truck so he have him a place to sleep. He down there wasn't doing no work or nothing. Sheriff looking for him. He bought that truck to keep away from the sheriff. Got Stovall looking for him too. He down there sleeping in that truck ducking and dodging both of them. I told him come on let's go up and see my sister.

BERNIECE: What the sheriff looking for you for, Lymon?

BOY WILLIE: The man don't want you to know all his business. He's my company. He ain't asking you no questions.

LYMON: It wasn't nothing. It was just a misunderstanding.

BERNIECE: He in my house. You say the sheriff looking for him, I wanna know what he looking for him for. Otherwise you all can go back out there and be where nobody don't have to ask you nothing.

LYMON: It was just a misunderstanding. Sometimes me and the sheriff we don't think alike. So we just got crossed on each other.

BERNIECE: Might be looking for him about that truck. He might have stole that truck.

BOY WILLIE: We ain't stole no truck, woman. I told you Lymon bought it.

DOAKER: Boy Willie and Lymon got more sense than to ride all the way up here in a stolen truck with a load of watermelons. Now they might have stole them watermelons, but I don't believe they stole that truck.

BOY WILLIE: You don't even know the man good and you calling him a thief. And we ain't stole them watermelons either. Them old man Pitterford's watermelons. He give me and Lymon all we could load for ten dollars.

DOAKER: No wonder you got them stacked up out there. You must have five hundred watermelons stacked up out there.

BERNIECE: Boy Willie, when you and Lymon planning on going back?

BOY WILLIE: Lymon say he staying. As soon as we sell them watermelons I'm going on back.

BERNIECE: (*Starts to exit up the stairs.*) That's what you need to do. And you need to do it quick. Come in here disrupting the house. I don't want all that loud carrying on around here. I'm surprised you ain't woke Maretha up.

BOY WILLIE: I was fixing to get her now.

(*Calls.*)

Hey, Maretha!

DOAKER: Berniece don't like all that hollering now.

BERNIECE: Don't you wake that child up!

BOY WILLIE: You going up there . . . wake her up and tell her her uncle's here. I ain't seen her in three years. Wake her up and send her down here. She can go back to bed.

BERNIECE: I ain't waking that child up . . . and don't you be making all that noise. You and Lymon need to sell them watermelons and go on back.

(BERNIECE *exits up the stairs.*)

BOY WILLIE: I see Berniece still try to be stuck up.

DOAKER: Berniece alright. She don't want you making all that noise. Maretha up there sleep. Let her sleep until she get up. She can see you then.

BOY WILLIE: I ain't thinking about Berniece. You hear from Wining Boy? You know Cleotha died?

DOAKER: Yeah, I heard that. He come by here about a year ago. Had a whole sack of money. He stayed here about two weeks. Ain't offered nothing. Berniece asked him for three dollars to buy some food and he got mad and left.

LYMON: Who's Wining Boy?

BOY WILLIE: That's my uncle. That's Doaker's brother. You heard me talk about Wining Boy. He play piano. He done made some records and everything. He still doing that, Doaker?

DOAKER: He made one or two records a long time ago. That's the only ones I ever known him to make. If you let him tell it he a big recording star.

BOY WILLIE: He stopped down home about two years ago. That's what I hear. I don't know. Me and Lymon was up on Parchman Farm doing them three years.

DOAKER: He don't never stay in one place. Now, he been here about eight months ago. Back in the winter. Now, you subject not to see him for another two years. It's liable to be that long before he stop by.

BOY WILLIE: If he had a whole sack of money you liable never to see him. You ain't gonna see him until he get broke. Just as soon as that sack of money is gone you look up and he be on your doorstep.

LYMON: (*Noticing the piano.*) Is that the piano?

BOY WILLIE: Yeah . . . look here, Lymon. See how it got all those carvings on it. See, that's what I was talking about. See how it's carved up real nice and polished and everything? You never find you another piano like that.

LYMON: Yeah, that look real nice.

BOY WILLIE: I told you. See how it's polished? My mama used to polish it every day. See all them pictures carved on it? That's what I was talking about. You can get a nice price for that piano.

LYMON: That's all Boy Willie talked about the whole trip up here. I got tired of hearing him talk about the piano.

BOY WILLIE: All you want to talk about is women. You ought to hear this nig-ger, Doaker. Talking about all the women he gonna get when he get up here. He ain't had none down there but he gonna get a hundred when he get up here.

DOAKER: How your people doing down there, Lymon?

LYMON: They alright. They still there. I come up here to see what it's like up here. Boy Willie trying to get me to go back and farm with him.

BOY WILLIE: Sutter's brother selling the land. He say he gonna sell it to me. That's why I come up here. I got one part of it. Sell them watermelons and get me another part. Get Berniece to sell that piano and I'll have the third part.

DOAKER: Berniece ain't gonna sell that piano.

BOY WILLIE: I'm gonna talk to her. When she see I got a chance to get Sutter's land she'll come around.

DOAKER: You can put that thought out your mind. Berniece ain't gonna sell that piano.

BOY WILLIE: I'm gonna talk to her. She been playing on it?

DOAKER: You know she won't touch that piano. I ain't never known her to touch it since Mama Ola died. That's over seven years now. She say it got blood on it. She got Maretha playing on it though. Say Maretha can go on and do everything she can't do. Got her in an extra school down at the Irene Kaufman Settlement House. She want Maretha to grow up and be a school-teacher. Say she good enough she can teach on the piano.

BOY WILLIE: Maretha don't need to be playing on no piano. She can play on the guitar.

DOAKER: How much land Sutter got left?

BOY WILLIE: Got a hundred acres. Good land. He done sold it piece by piece, he kept the good part for himself. Now he got to give that up. His brother come down from Chicago for the funeral . . . he up there in Chicago got some kind of business with soda fountain equipment. He anxious to sell the land, Doaker. He don't want to be bothered with it. He called me to him and said cause of how long our families done known each other and how we been good friends and all, say he wanted to sell the land to me. Say he'd rather see me with it than Jim Stovall. Told me he'd let me have it for two thousand dollars cash money. He don't know I found out the most Stovall would give him for it was fifteen hundred dollars. He trying to get that extra five hundred out of me telling me he doing me a favor. I thanked him just as nice. Told him what a good man Sutter was and how he had my sympathy and all. Told him to give me two weeks. He said he'd wait on me. That's why I come up here. Sell them watermelons. Get Berniece to sell that piano. Put them two parts with the part I done saved. Walk in there. Tip my hat. Lay my money down on the table. Get my deed and walk on out. This time I get to keep all the cotton. Hire me some men to work it for me. Gin my cotton. Get my seed. And I'll see you again next year. Might even plant some tobacco or some oats.

DOAKER: You gonna have a hard time trying to get Berniece to sell that piano. You know Avery Brown from down there don't you? He up here now. He followed Berniece up here trying to get her to marry him after Crawley got killed. He been up here about two years. He call himself a preacher now.

BOY WILLIE: I know Avery. I know him from when he used to work on the Willshaw place. Lymon know him too.

DOAKER: He after Berniece to marry him. She keep telling him no but he won't give up. He keep pressing her on it.

BOY WILLIE: Avery think all white men is bigshots. He don't know there some white men ain't got as much as he got.

DOAKER: He supposed to come past here this morning. Berniece going down to the bank with him to see if he can get a loan to start his church. That's why I know Berniece ain't gonna sell that piano. He tried to get her to sell it to help him start his church. Sent the man around and everything.

BOY WILLIE: What man?

DOAKER: Some white fellow was going around to all the colored people's houses looking to buy up musical instruments. He'd buy anything. Drums. Guitars. Harmonicas. Pianos. Avery sent him past here. He looked at the piano and got excited. Offered her a nice price. She turned him down and got on Avery for sending him past. The man kept on her about two weeks. He seen where she wasn't gonna sell it, he gave her his number and told her if she ever wanted to sell it to call him first. Say he'd go one better than what anybody else would give her for it.

BOY WILLIE: How much he offer her for it?

DOAKER: Now you know me. She didn't say and I didn't ask. I just know it was a nice price.

LYMON: All you got to do is find out who he is and tell him somebody else wanna buy it from you. Tell him you can't make up your mind who to sell it to, and if he like Doaker say, he'll give you anything you want for it.

BOY WILLIE: That's what I'm gonna do. I'm gonna find out who he is from Avery.

DOAKER: It ain't gonna do you no good. Berniece ain't gonna sell that piano.

BOY WILLIE: She ain't got to sell it. I'm gonna sell it. I own just as much of it as she does.

BERNIECE: (Offstage, hollers.) Doaker! Go on get away. Doaker!

DOAKER: (Calling.) Berniece?

(DOAKER and BOY WILLIE rush to the stairs, BOY WILLIE runs up the stairs, passing BERNIECE as she enters, running.)

DOAKER: Berniece, what's the matter? You alright? What's the matter?

(BERNIECE tries to catch her breath. She is unable to speak.)

DOAKER: That's alright. Take your time. You alright. What's the matter?

(He calls.)

Hey, Boy Willie?

BOY WILLIE: *(Offstage.)* Ain't nobody up here.

BERNIECE: Sutter . . . Sutter's standing at the top of the steps.

DOAKER: *(Calls.)* Boy Willie!

(LYMON crosses to the stairs and looks up. BOY WILLIE *enters from the stairs.)*

BOY WILLIE: Hey Doaker, what's wrong with her? Berniece, what's wrong? Who was you talking to?

DOAKER: She say she seen Sutter's ghost standing at the top of the stairs.

BOY WILLIE: Seen what? Sutter? She ain't seen no Sutter.

BERNIECE: He was standing right up there.

BOY WILLIE: *(Entering on the stairs.)* That's all in Berniece's head. Ain't nobody up there. Go on up there, Doaker.

DOAKER: I'll take your word for it. Berniece talking about what she seen. She say Sutter's ghost standing at the top of the steps. She ain't just make all that up.

BOY WILLIE: She up there dreaming. She ain't seen no ghost.

LYMON: You want a glass of water, Berniece? Get her a glass of water, Boy Willie.

BOY WILLIE: She don't need no water. She ain't seen nothing. Go on up there and look. Ain't nobody up there but Maretha.

DOAKER: Let Berniece tell it.

BOY WILLIE: I ain't stopping her from telling it.

DOAKER: What happened, Berniece?

BERNIECE: I come out my room to come back down here and Sutter was standing there in the hall.

BOY WILLIE: What he look like?

BERNIECE: He look like Sutter. He look like he always look.

BOY WILLIE: Sutter couldn't find his way from Big Sandy to Little Sandy. How he gonna find his way all the way up here to Pittsburgh? Sutter ain't never even heard of Pittsburgh.

DOAKER: Go on, Berniece.

BERNIECE: Just standing there with the blue suit on.

BOY WILLIE: The man ain't never left Marlin County when he was living . . . and he's gonna come all the way up here now that he's dead?

DOAKER: Let her finish. I want to hear what she got to say.

BOY WILLIE: I'll tell you this. If Berniece had seen him like she think she seen him she'd still be running.

DOAKER: Go on, Berniece. Don't pay Boy Willie no mind.

BERNIECE: He was standing there . . . had his hand on top of his head. Look like he might have thought if he took his hand down his head might have fallen off.

LYMON: Did he have on a hat?

BERNIECE: Just had on that blue suit . . . I told him to go away and he just stood there looking at me . . . calling Boy Willie's name.

BOY WILLIE: What he calling my name for?

BERNIECE: I believe you pushed him in the well.

BOY WILLIE: Now what kind of sense that make? You telling me I'm gonna go out there and hide in the weeds with all them dogs and things he got around there . . . I'm gonna hide and wait till I catch him looking down his well just right . . . then I'm gonna run over and push him in. A great big old three-hundred-and-forty-pound man.

BERNIECE: Well, what he calling your name for?

BOY WILLIE: He bending over looking down his well, woman . . . how he know who pushed him? It could have been anybody. Where was you when Sutter fell in his well? Where was Doaker? Me and Lymon was over in Stoner County. Tell her, Lymon. The Ghosts of the Yellow Dog got Sutter. That's what happened to him.

BERNIECE: You can talk all that Ghosts of the Yellow Dog stuff if you want. I know better.

LYMON: The Ghosts of the Yellow Dog pushed him. That's what the people say. They found him in his well and all the people say it must be the Ghosts of the Yellow Dog. Just like all them other men.

BOY WILLIE: Come talking about he looking for me. What he come all the way up here for? If he looking for me all he got to do is wait. He could have saved himself a trip if he looking for me. That ain't nothing but in Berniece's head. Ain't no telling what she liable to come up with next.

BERNIECE: Boy Willie, I want you and Lymon to go ahead and leave my house. Just go on somewhere. You don't do nothing but bring trouble with you everywhere you go. If it wasn't for you Crawley would still be alive.

BOY WILLIE: Crawley what? I ain't had nothing to do with Crawley getting killed. Crawley three time seven. He had his own mind.

BERNIECE: Just go on and leave. Let Sutter go somewhere else looking for you.

BOY WILLIE: I'm leaving. Soon as we sell them watermelons. Other than that I ain't going nowhere. Hell, I just got here. Talking about Sutter looking for me. Sutter was looking for that piano. That's what he was looking for. He had to die to find out where that piano was at . . . If I was you I'd get rid of it. That's the way to get rid of Sutter's ghost. Get rid of that piano.

BERNIECE: I want you and Lymon to go on and take all this confusion out of my house!

BOY WILLIE: Hey, tell her, Doaker. What kind of sense that make? I told you, Lymon, as soon as Berniece see me she was gonna start something. Didn't I tell you that? Now she done made up that story about Sutter just so she could tell me to leave her house. Well, hell, I ain't going nowhere till I sell them watermelons.

BERNIECE: Well why don't you go out there and sell them! Sell them and go on back!

BOY WILLIE: We waiting till the people get up.

LYMON: Boy Willie say if you get out there too early and wake the people up they get mad at you and won't buy nothing from you.

DOAKER: You won't be waiting long. You done let the sun catch up with you. This the time everybody be getting up around here.

BERNIECE: Come on, Doaker, walk up here with me. Let me get Maretha up and get her started. I got to get ready myself. Boy Willie, just go on out there and sell them watermelons and you and Lymon leave my house.

(BERNIECE and DOAKER exit up the stairs.)

BOY WILLIE: *(Calling after them.)* If you see Sutter up there . . . tell him I'm down here waiting on him.

LYMON: What if she see him again?

BOY WILLIE: That's all in her head. There ain't no ghost up there.

(Calls.)

Hey, Doaker . . . I told you ain't nothing up there.

LYMON: I'm glad he didn't say he was looking for me.

BOY WILLIE: I wish I would see Sutter's ghost. Give me a chance to put a whupping on him.

LYMON: You ought to stay up here with me. You be down there working his land . . . he might come looking for you all the time.

BOY WILLIE: I ain't thinking about Sutter. And I ain't thinking about staying up here. You stay up here. I'm going back and get Sutter's land. You think you ain't got to work up here. You think this the land of milk and honey. But I ain't scared of work. I'm going back and farm every acre of that land.

(DOAKER enters from the stairs.)

I told you there ain't nothing up there, Doaker. Berniece dreaming all that.

DOAKER: I believe Berniece seen something. Berniece level-headed. She ain't just made all that up. She say Sutter had on a suit. I don't believe she ever seen Sutter in a suit. I believe that's what he was buried in, and that's what Berniece saw.

BOY WILLIE: Well, let her keep on seeing him then. As long as he don't mess with me.

(DOAKER starts to cook his breakfast.)

I heard about you, Doaker. They say you got all the women looking out for you down home. They be looking to see you coming. Say you got a different one every two weeks. Say they be fighting one another for you to stay with them.

(To LYMON.*)*

Look at him, Lymon. He know it's true.

DOAKER: I ain't thinking about no women. They never get me tied up with them. After Coreen I ain't got no use for them. I stay up on Jack Slattery's place when I be down there. All them women want is somebody with a steady payday.

BOY WILLIE: That ain't what I hear. I hear every two weeks the women all put on their dresses and line up at the railroad station.

DOAKER: I don't get down there but once a month. I used to go down there every two weeks but they keep switching me around. They keep switching all the fellows around.

BOY WILLIE: Doaker can't turn that railroad loose. He was working the railroad when I was walking around crying for sugartit. My mama used to brag on him.

DOAKER: I'm cooking now, but I used to line track. I pieced together the Yellow Dog stitch by stitch. Rail by rail. Line track all up around there. I lined track all up around Sunflower and Clarksdale. Wining Boy worked with me. He helped put in some of that track. He'd work it for six months and quit. Go back to playing piano and gambling.

BOY WILLIE: How long you been with the railroad now?

DOAKER: Twenty-seven years. Now, I'll tell you something about the railroad. What I done learned after twenty-seven years. See, you got North. You got West. You look over here you got South. Over there you got East. Now, you can start from anywhere. Don't care where you at. You got to go one of them four ways. And whichever way you decide to go they got a railroad that will take you there. Now, that's something simple. You think anybody would be able to understand that. But you'd be surprised how many people trying to go North get on a train going West. They think the train's supposed to go where they going rather than where it's going.

Now, why people going? Their sister's sick. They leaving before they kill somebody . . . and they sitting across from somebody who's leaving to keep from getting killed. They leaving cause they can't get satisfied. They going to meet someone. I wish I had a dollar for every time that someone wasn't at the station to meet them. I done seen that a lot. In between the time they sent the telegram and the time the person get there . . . they done forgot all about them.

They got so many trains out there they have a hard time keeping them from running into each other. Got trains going every whichaway. Got people on all of them. Somebody going where somebody just left. If everybody stay in one place I believe this would be a better world. Now what I done learned after twenty-seven years of railroading is this . . . if the train stays on the track . . . it's going to get where it's going. It might not be where you going. If it ain't, then all you got to do is sit and wait cause the train's coming back to get you. The train don't never stop. It'll come back every time. Now I'll tell you another thing . . .

BOY WILLIE: What you cooking over there, Doaker? Me and Lymon's hungry.

DOAKER: Go on down there to Wylie and Kirkpatrick to Eddie's restaurant. Coffee cost a nickel and you can get two eggs, sausage, and grits for fifteen cents. He even give you a biscuit with it.

BOY WILLIE: That look good what you got. Give me a little piece of that grilled bread.

DOAKER: Here . . . go on take the whole piece.

BOY WILLIE: Here you go, Lymon . . . you want a piece?

(He gives LYMON *a piece of toast.* MARETHA *enters from the stairs.)*

BOY WILLIE: Hey, sugar. Come here and give me a hug. Come on give Uncle Boy Willie a hug. Don't be shy. Look at her, Doaker. She done got bigger. Ain't she got big?

DOAKER: Yeah, she getting up there.

BOY WILLIE: How you doing, sugar?

MARETHA: Fine.

BOY WILLIE: You was just a little old thing last time I seen you. You remember me, don't you? This your Uncle Boy Willie from down South. That there's Lymon. He my friend. We come up here to sell watermelons. You like watermelons?

*(*MARETHA *nods.)*

We got a whole truckload out front. You can have as many as you want. What you been doing?

MARETHA: Nothing.

BOY WILLIE: Don't be shy now. Look at you getting all big. How old is you?

MARETHA: Eleven. I'm gonna be twelve soon.

BOY WILLIE: You like it up here? You like the North?

MARETHA: It's alright.

BOY WILLIE: That there's Lymon. Did you say hi to Lymon?

MARETHA: Hi.

LYMON: How you doing? You look just like your mama. I remember you when you was wearing diapers.

BOY WILLIE: You gonna come down South and see me? Uncle Boy Willie gonna get him a farm. Gonna get a great big old farm. Come down there and I'll teach you how to ride a mule. Teach you how to kill a chicken, too.

MARETHA: I seen my mama do that.

BOY WILLIE: Ain't nothing to it. You just grab him by his neck and twist it. Get
   you a real good grip and then you just wring his neck and throw him in the
   pot. Cook him up. Then you got some good eating. What you like to eat? What
   kind of food you like?
MARETHA: I like everything . . . except I don't like no black-eyed peas.
BOY WILLIE: Uncle Doaker tell me your mama got you playing that piano.
   Come on play something for me.

   (BOY WILLIE crosses over to the piano followed by MARETHA.)

   Show me what you can do. Come on now. Here . . . Uncle Boy Willie give you
   a dime . . . show me what you can do. Don't be bashful now. That dime say
   you can't be bashful.

   (MARETHA plays. It is something any beginner first learns.)

   Here, let me show you something.

   (BOY WILLIE sits and plays a simple boogie-woogie.)

   See that? See what I'm doing? That's what you call the boogie-woogie. See
   now . . . you can get up and dance to that. That's how good it sound. It sound
   like you wanna dance. You can dance to that. It'll hold you up. Whatever kind
   of dance you wanna do you can dance to that right there. See that? See how
   it go? Ain't nothing to it. Go on you do it.
MARETHA: I got to read it on the paper.
BOY WILLIE: You don't need no paper. Go on. Do just like that there.
BERNIECE: Maretha! You get up here and get ready to go so you be on time.
   Ain't no need you trying to take advantage of company.
MARETHA: I got to go.
BOY WILLIE: Uncle Boy Willie gonna get you a guitar. Let Uncle Doaker teach
   you how to play that. You don't need to read no paper to play the guitar. Your
   mama told you about that piano? You know how them pictures got on there?
MARETHA: She say it just always been like that since she got it.
BOY WILLIE: You hear that, Doaker? And you sitting up here in the house with
   Berniece.
DOAKER: I ain't got nothing to do with that. I don't get in the way of Berniece's
   raising her.
BOY WILLIE: You tell your mama to tell you about that piano. You ask her how
   them pictures got on there. If she don't tell you I'll tell you.
BERNIECE: Maretha!
MARETHA: I got to get ready to go.
BOY WILLIE: She getting big, Doaker. You remember her, Lymon?
LYMON: She used to be real little.

(There is a knock on the door. DOAKER *goes to answer it.* AVERY *enters. Thirty-eight years old, honest and ambitious, he has taken to the city like a fish to water, finding in it opportunities for growth and advancement that did not exist for him in the rural South. He is dressed in a suit and tie with a gold cross around his neck. He carries a small Bible.)*

DOAKER: Hey, Avery, come on in. Berniece upstairs.

BOY WILLIE: Look at him . . . look at him . . . he don't know what to say. He wasn't expecting to see me.

AVERY: Hey, Boy Willie. What you doing up here?

BOY WILLIE: Look at him, Lymon.

AVERY: Is that Lymon? Lymon Jackson?

BOY WILLIE: Yeah, you know Lymon.

DOAKER: Berniece be ready in a minute, Avery.

BOY WILLIE: Doaker say you a preacher now. What . . . we supposed to call you Reverend? You used to be plain old Avery. When you get to be a preacher, nigger?

LYMON: Avery say he gonna be a preacher so he don't have to work.

BOY WILLIE: I remember when you was down there on the Willshaw place planting cotton. You wasn't thinking about no Reverend then.

AVERY: That must be your truck out there. I saw that truck with them watermelons, I was trying to figure out what it was doing in front of the house.

BOY WILLIE: Yeah, me and Lymon selling watermelons. That's Lymon's truck.

DOAKER: Berniece say you all going down to the bank.

AVERY: Yeah, they give me a half day off work. I got an appointment to talk to the bank about getting a loan to start my church.

BOY WILLIE: Lymon say preachers don't have to work. Where you working at, nigger?

DOAKER: Avery got him one of them good jobs. He working at one of them skyscrapers downtown.

AVERY: I'm working down there at the Gulf Building running an elevator. Got a pension and everything. They even give you a turkey on Thanksgiving.

LYMON: How you know the rope ain't gonna break? Ain't you scared the rope's gonna break?

AVERY: That's steel. They got steel cables hold it up. It take a whole lot of breaking to break that steel. Naw, I ain't worried about nothing like that. It ain't nothing but a little old elevator. Now, I wouldn't get in none of them airplanes. You couldn't pay me to do nothing like that.

LYMON: That be fun. I'd rather do that than ride in one of them elevators.

BOY WILLIE: How many of them watermelons you wanna buy?

AVERY: I thought you was gonna give me one seeing as how you got a whole truck full.

BOY WILLIE: You can get one, get two. I'll give you two for a dollar.

AVERY: I can't eat but one. How much are they?

BOY WILLIE: Aw, nigger, you know I'll give you a watermelon. Go on, take as many as you want. Just leave some for me and Lymon to sell.

AVERY: I don't want but one.

BOY WILLIE: How you get to be a preacher, Avery? I might want to be a preacher one day. Have everybody call me Reverend Boy Willie.

AVERY: It come to me in a dream. God called me and told me he wanted me to be a shepherd for his flock. That's what I'm gonna call my church . . . The Good Shepherd Church of God in Christ.

DOAKER: Tell him what you told me. Tell him about the three hobos.

AVERY: Boy Willie don't want to hear all that.

LYMON: I do. Lots a people say your dreams can come true.

AVERY: Naw. You don't want to hear all that.

DOAKER: Go on. I told him you was a preacher. He didn't want to believe me. Tell him about the three hobos.

AVERY: Well, it come to me in a dream. See . . . I was sitting out in this railroad yard watching the trains go by. The train stopped and these three hobos got off. They told me they had come from Nazareth and was on their way to Jerusalem. They had three candles. They gave me one and told me to light it . . . but to be careful that it didn't go out. Next thing I knew I was standing in front of this house. Something told me to go knock on the door. This old woman opened the door and said they had been waiting on me. Then she led me into this room. It was a big room and it was full of all kinds of different people. They looked like anybody else except they all had sheep heads and was making noise like sheep make. I heard somebody call my name. I looked around and there was these same three hobos. They told me to take off my clothes and they give me a blue robe with gold thread. They washed my feet and combed my hair. Then they showed me these three doors and told me to pick one.

   I went through one of them doors and that flame leapt off that candle and it seemed like my whole head caught fire. I looked around and there was four or five other men standing there with these same blue robes on. Then we heard a voice tell us to look out across this valley. We looked out and saw the valley was full of wolves. The voice told us that these sheep people that I had seen in the other room had to go over to the other side of this valley and somebody had to take them. Then I heard another voice say, "Who shall I send?" Next thing I knew I said, "Here I am. Send me." That's when I met Jesus. He say, "If you go, I'll go with you." Something told me to say, "Come on. Let's go." That's when I woke up. My head still felt like it was on fire . . . but I had a peace about myself that was hard to explain. I knew right then that I had been filled with the Holy Ghost and called to be a servant of the Lord. It took me a while before I could accept that. But then a lot of little ways God showed me that it was true. So I became a preacher.

LYMON: I see why you gonna call it the Good Shepherd Church. You dreaming about them sheep people. I can see that easy.

BOY WILLIE: Doaker say you sent some white man past the house to look at that piano. Say he was going around to all the colored people's houses looking to buy up musical instruments.

AVERY: Yeah, but Berniece didn't want to sell that piano. After she told me about it . . . I could see why she didn't want to sell it.

BOY WILLIE: What's this man's name?

AVERY: Oh, that's a while back now. I done forgot his name. He give Berniece a card with his name and telephone number on it, but I believe she throwed it away.

(BERNIECE and MARETHA enter from the stairs.)

BERNIECE: Maretha, run back upstairs and get my pocket-book. And wipe that hair grease off your forehead. Go ahead, hurry up.

(MARETHA exits up the stairs.)

How you doing, Avery? You done got all dressed up. You look nice. Boy Willie, I thought you and Lymon was going to sell them watermelons.

BOY WILLIE: Lymon done got sleepy. We liable to get some sleep first.

LYMON: I ain't sleepy.

DOAKER: As many watermelons as you got stacked up on that truck out there, you ought to have been gone.

BOY WILLIE: We gonna go in a minute. We going.

BERNIECE: Doaker. I'm gonna stop down there on Logan Street. You want anything?

DOAKER: You can pick up some ham hocks if you going down there. See if you can get the smoked ones. If they ain't got that get the fresh ones. Don't get the ones that got all that fat under the skin. Look for the long ones. They nice and lean.

(He gives her a dollar.)

Don't get the short ones lessen they smoked. If you got to get the fresh ones make sure that they the long ones. If they ain't got them smoked then go ahead and get the short ones.

(Pause.)

You may as well get some turnip greens while you down there. I got some buttermilk . . . if you pick up some cornmeal I'll make me some cornbread and cook up them turnip greens.

(MARETHA enters from the stairs.)

MARETHA: We gonna take the streetcar?

BERNIECE: Me and Avery gonna drop you off at the settlement house. You mind them people down there. Don't be going down there showing your color. Boy Willie, I done told you what to do. I'll see you later, Doaker.

AVERY: I'll be seeing you again, Boy Willie.

BOY WILLIE: Hey, Berniece . . . what's the name of that man Avery sent past say he want to buy the piano?

BERNIECE: I knew it. I knew it when I first seen you. I knew you was up to something.

BOY WILLIE: Sutter's brother say he selling the land to me. He waiting on me now. Told me he'd give me two weeks. I got one part. Sell them watermelons get me another part. Then we can sell that piano and I'll have the third part.

BERNIECE: I ain't selling that piano, Boy Willie. If that's why you come up here you can just forget about it.

(To DOAKER.*)*

Doaker, I'll see you later. Boy Willie ain't nothing but a whole lot of mouth. I ain't paying him no mind. If he come up here thinking he gonna sell that piano then he done come up here for nothing.

*(*BERNIECE, AVERY, *and* MARETHA *exit the front door.)*

BOY WILLIE: Hey, Lymon! You ready to go sell these watermelons.

*(*BOY WILLIE *and* LYMON *start to exit. At the door* BOY WILLIE *turns to* DOAKER.*)*

Hey, Doaker . . . if Berniece don't want to sell that piano . . . I'm gonna cut it in half and go on and sell my half.

*(*BOY WILLIE *and* LYMON *exit.)*

(The lights go down on the scene.)

SCENE 2

(The lights come up on the kitchen. It is three days later. WINING BOY *sits at the kitchen table. There is a half-empty pint bottle on the table.* DOAKER *busies himself washing pots.* WINING BOY *is fifty-six years old.* DOAKER's *older brother, he tries to present the image of a successful musician and gambler, but his music, his clothes, and even his manner of presentation are old. He is a man who looking back over his life continues to live it with an odd mixture of zest and sorrow.)*

WINING BOY: So the Ghosts of the Yellow Dog got Sutter. That just go to show you I believe I always lived right. They say every dog gonna have his day and time it go around it sure come back to you. I done seen that a thousand times. I know the truth of that. But I'll tell you outright . . . if I see Sutter's ghost I'll be on the first thing I find that got wheels on it.

(DOAKER *enters from his room.*)

DOAKER: Wining Boy!

WINING BOY: And I'll tell you another thing . . . Berniece ain't gonna sell that piano.

DOAKER: That's what she told him. He say he gonna cut it in half and go on and sell his half. They been around here three days trying to sell them watermelons. They trying to get out to where the white folks live but the truck keep breaking down. They go a block or two and it break down again. They trying to get out to Squirrel Hill and can't get around the corner. He say soon as he can get that truck empty to where he can set the piano up in there he gonna take it out of here and go sell it.

WINING BOY: What about them boys Sutter got? How come they ain't farming that land?

DOAKER: One of them going to school. He left down there and come North to school. The other one ain't got as much sense as that frying pan over yonder. That is the dumbest white man I ever seen. He'd stand in the river and watch it rise till it drown him.

WINING BOY: Other than seeing Sutter's ghost how's Berniece doing?

DOAKER: She doing alright. She still got Crawley on her mind. He been dead three years but she still holding on to him. She need to go out here and let one of these fellows grab a whole handful of whatever she got. She act like it done got precious.

WINING BOY: They always told me any fish will bite if you got good bait.

DOAKER: She stuck up on it. She think it's better than she is. I believe she messing around with Avery. They got something going. He a preacher now. If you let him tell it the Holy Ghost sat on his head and heaven opened up with thunder and lightning and God was calling his name. Told him to go out and preach and tend to his flock. That's what he gonna call his church. The Good Shepherd Church.

WINING BOY: They had that joker down in Spear walking around talking about he Jesus Christ. He gonna live the life of Christ. Went through the Last Supper and everything. Rented him a mule on Palm Sunday and rode through the town. Did everything . . . talking about he Christ. He did everything until they got up to that crucifixion part. Got up to that part and told everybody to go home and quit pretending. He got up to the crucifixion part and changed his mind. Had a whole bunch of folks come down there to see him get nailed to the cross. I don't know who's the worse fool. Him or them. Had all them folks come down there . . . even carried the cross up this little hill. People

standing around waiting to see him get nailed to the cross and he stop everything and preach a little sermon and told everybody to go home. Had enough
nerve to tell them to come to church on Easter Sunday to celebrate his resurrection.

DOAKER: I'm surprised Avery ain't thought about that. He trying every little
thing to get him a congregation together. They meeting over at his house till
he get him a church.

WINING BOY: Ain't nothing wrong with being a preacher. You got the preacher
on one hand and the gambler on the other. Sometimes there ain't too much
difference in them.

DOAKER: How long you been in Kansas City?

WINING BOY: Since I left here. I got tied up with some old gal down there.

(Pause.)

You know Cleotha died.

DOAKER: Yeah, I heard that last time I was down there. I was sorry to hear that.

WINING BOY: One of her friends wrote and told me. I got the letter right here.

(He takes the letter out of his pocket.)

I was down in Kansas City and she wrote and told me Cleotha had died.
Name of Willa Bryant. She say she know cousin Rupert.

(He opens the letter and reads.)

Dear Wining Boy: I am writing this letter to let you know Miss Cleotha Holman passed on Saturday the first of May she departed this world in the loving arms of her sister Miss Alberta Samuels. I know you would want to know
this and am writing as a friend of Cleotha. There have been many hardships
since last you seen her but she survived them all and to the end was a good
woman whom I hope have God's grace and is in His Paradise. Your cousin
Rupert Bates is my friend also and he give me your address and I pray this
reaches you about Cleotha. Miss Willa Bryant. A friend.

(He folds the letter and returns it to his pocket.)

They was nailing her coffin shut by the time I heard about it. I never knew
she was sick. I believe it was that yellow jaundice. That's what killed her
mama.

DOAKER: Cleotha wasn't but forty-some.

WINING BOY: She was forty-six. I got ten years on her. I met her when she was
sixteen. You remember I used to run around there. Couldn't nothing keep me
still. Much as I loved Cleotha I loved to ramble. Couldn't nothing keep me
still. We got married and we used to fight about it all the time. Then one day

she asked me to leave. Told me she loved me before I left. Told me, Wining
Boy, you got a home as long as I got mine. And I believe in my heart I always
felt that and that kept me safe.

DOAKER: Cleotha always did have a nice way about her.

WINING BOY: Man that woman was something. I used to thank the Lord. Many
a night I sat up and looked out over my life. Said, well, I had Cleotha. When
it didn't look like there was nothing else for me, I said, thank God, at least I
had that. If ever I go anywhere in this life I done known a good woman. And
that used to hold me till the next morning.

(Pause.)

What you got? Give me a little nip. I know you got something stuck up in your
room.

DOAKER: I ain't seen you walk in here and put nothing on the table. You done
sat there and drank up your whiskey. Now you talking about what you got.

WINING BOY: I got plenty money. Give me a little nip.

*(DOAKER carries a glass into his room and returns with it half-filled. He sets it
on the table in front of WINING BOY.)*

WINING BOY: You hear from Coreen?

DOAKER: She up in New York. I let her go from my mind.

WINING BOY: She was something back then. She wasn't too pretty but she had
a way of looking at you made you know there was a whole lot of woman there.
You got married and snatched her out from under us and we all got mad at
you.

DOAKER: She up in New York City. That's what I hear.

(The door opens and BOY WILLIE and LYMON enter.)

BOY WILLIE: Aw hell . . . look here! We was just talking about you. Doaker say
you left out of here with a whole sack of money. I told him we wasn't going
see you till you got broke.

WINING BOY: What you mean broke? I got a whole pocketful of money.

DOAKER: Did you all get that truck fixed?

BOY WILLIE: We got it running and got halfway out there on Centre and it
broke down again. Lymon went out there and messed it up some more. Fellow told us we got to wait till tomorrow to get it fixed. Say he have it running
like new. Lymon going back down there and sleep in the truck so the people
don't take the watermelons.

LYMON: Lymon nothing. You go down there and sleep in it.

BOY WILLIE: You was sleeping in it down home, nigger! I don't know nothing
about sleeping in no truck.

LYMON: I ain't sleeping in no truck.

BOY WILLIE: They can take all the watermelons. I don't care. Wining Boy, where you coming from? Where you been?

WINING BOY: I been down in Kansas City.

BOY WILLIE: You remember Lymon? Lymon Jackson.

WINING BOY: Yeah, I used to know his daddy.

BOY WILLIE: Doaker say you don't never leave no address with nobody. Say he got to depend on your whim. See when it strike you to pay a visit.

WINING BOY: I got four or five addresses.

BOY WILLIE: Doaker say Berniece asked you for three dollars and you got mad and left.

WINING BOY: Berniece try and rule over you too much for me. That's why I left. It wasn't about no three dollars.

BOY WILLIE: Where you getting all these sacks of money from? I need to be with you. Doaker say you had a whole sack of money ... turn some of it loose.

WINING BOY: I was just fixing to ask you for five dollars.

BOY WILLIE: I ain't got no money. I'm trying to get some. Doaker tell you about Sutter? The Ghosts of the Yellow Dog got him about three weeks ago. Berniece done seen his ghost and everything. He right upstairs.

(Calls.)

Hey Sutter! Wining Boy's here. Come on, get a drink!

WINING BOY: How many that make the Ghosts of the Yellow Dog done got?

BOY WILLIE: Must be about nine or ten, eleven or twelve. I don't know.

DOAKER: You got Ed Saunders. Howard Peterson. Charlie Webb.

WINING BOY: Robert Smith. That fellow that shot Becky's boy ... say he was stealing peaches ...

DOAKER: You talking about Bob Mallory.

BOY WILLIE: Berniece say she don't believe all that about the Ghosts of the Yellow Dog.

WINING BOY: She ain't got to believe. You go ask them white folks in Sunflower County if they believe. You go ask Sutter if he believe. I don't care if Berniece believe or not. I done been to where the Southern cross the Yellow Dog and called out their names. They talk back to you, too.

LYMON: What they sound like? The wind or something?

BOY WILLIE: You done been there for real, Wining Boy?

WINING BOY: Nineteen thirty. July of nineteen thirty I stood right there on that spot. It didn't look like nothing was going right in my life. I said everything can't go wrong all the time ... let me go down there and call on the Ghosts of the Yellow Dog, see if they can help me. I went down there and right there where them two railroads cross each other ... I stood right there on that spot and called out their names. They talk back to you, too.

LYMON: People say you can ask them questions. They talk to you like that?

WINING BOY: A lot of things you got to find out on your own. I can't say how they talked to nobody else. But to me it just filled me up in a strange sort of way to be standing there on that spot. I didn't want to leave. It felt like the longer I stood there the bigger I got. I seen the train coming and it seem like I was bigger than the train. I started not to move. But something told me to go ahead and get on out the way. The train passed and I started to go back up there and stand some more. But something told me not to do it. I walked away from there feeling like a king. Went on and had a stroke of luck that run on for three years. So I don't care if Berniece believe or not. Berniece ain't got to believe. I know cause I been there. Now Doaker'll tell you about the Ghosts of the Yellow Dog.

DOAKER: I don't try and talk that stuff with Berniece. Avery got her all tied up in that church. She just think it's a whole lot of nonsense.

BOY WILLIE: Berniece don't believe in nothing. She just think she believe. She believe in anything if it's convenient for her to believe. But when that convenience run out then she ain't got nothing to stand on.

WINING BOY: Let's not get on Berniece now. Doaker tell me you talking about selling that piano.

BOY WILLIE: Yeah ... hey, Doaker, I got the name of that man Avery was talking about. The man what's fixing the truck gave me his name. Everybody know him. Say he buy up anything you can make music with. I got his name and his telephone number. Hey, Wining Boy, Sutter's brother say he selling the land to me. I got one part. Sell them watermelons get me the second part. Then ... soon as I get them watermelons out that truck I'm gonna take and sell that piano and get the third part.

DOAKER: That land ain't worth nothing no more. The smart white man's up here in these cities. He cut the land loose and step back and watch you and the dumb white man argue over it.

WINING BOY: How you know Sutter's brother ain't sold it already? You talking about selling the piano and the man's liable to sold the land two or three times.

BOY WILLIE: He say he waiting on me. He say he give me two weeks. That's two weeks from Friday. Say if I ain't back by then he might gonna sell it to somebody else. He say he wanna see me with it.

WINING BOY: You know as well as I know the man gonna sell the land to the first one walk up and hand him the money.

BOY WILLIE: That's just who I'm gonna be. Look, you ain't gotta know he waiting on me. I know. Okay. I know what the man told me. Stoval already done tried to buy the land from him and he told him no. The man say he waiting on me ... he waiting on me. Hey, Doaker ... give me a drink. I see Wining Boy got his glass.

(DOAKER *exits into his room.*)

Wining Boy, what you doing in Kansas City? What they got down there?

LYMON: I hear they got some nice-looking women in Kansas City. I sure like to go down there and find out.

WINING BOY: Man, the women down there is something else.

(DOAKER enters with a bottle of whiskey. He sets it on the table with some glasses.)

DOAKER: You wanna sit up here and drink up my whiskey, leave a dollar on the table when you get up.

BOY WILLIE: You ain't doing nothing but showing your hospitality. I know we ain't got to pay for your hospitality.

WINING BOY: Doaker say they had you and Lymon down on the Parchman Farm. Had you on my old stomping grounds.

BOY WILLIE: Me and Lymon was down there hauling wood for Jim Miller and keeping us a little bit to sell. Some white fellows tried to run us off of it. That's when Crawley got killed. They put me and Lymon in the penitentiary.

LYMON: They ambushed us right there where that road dip down and around that bend in the creek. Crawley tried to fight them. Me and Boy Willie got away but the sheriff got us. Say we was stealing wood. They shot me in my stomach.

BOY WILLIE: They looking for Lymon down there now. They rounded him up and put him in jail for not working.

LYMON: Fined me a hundred dollars. Mr. Stovall come and paid my hundred dollars and the judge say I got to work for him to pay him back his hundred dollars. I told them I'd rather take my thirty days but they wouldn't let me do that.

BOY WILLIE: As soon as Stovall turned his back, Lymon was gone. He down there living in that truck dodging the sheriff and Stovall. He got both of them looking for him. So I brought him up here.

LYMON: I told Boy Willie I'm gonna stay up here. I ain't going back with him.

BOY WILLIE: Ain't nobody twisting your arm to make you go back. You can do what you want to do.

WINING BOY: I'll go back with you. I'm on my way down there. You gonna take the train? I'm gonna take the train.

LYMON: They treat you better up here.

BOY WILLIE: I ain't worried about nobody mistreating me. They treat you like you let them treat you. They mistreat me I mistreat them right back. Ain't no difference in me and the white man.

WINING BOY: Ain't no difference as far as how somebody supposed to treat you. I agree with that. But I'll tell you the difference between the colored man and the white man. Alright. Now you take and eat some berries. They taste real good to you. So you say I'm gonna go out and get me a whole pot of these berries and cook them up to make a pie or whatever. But you ain't looked to see them berries is sitting in the white fellow's yard. Ain't got no fence around them. You figure anybody want something they'd fence it in. Alright. Now the white man come along and say that's my land. Therefore everything that grow on it belong to me. He tell the sheriff, "I want you to put this nigger in jail as a warning to all the other niggers. Otherwise first thing you know these niggers have everything that belong to us."

BOY WILLIE: I'd come back at night and haul off his whole patch while he was sleep.

WINING BOY: Alright. Now Mr. So and So, he sell the land to you. And he come to you and say, "John, you own the land. It's all yours now. But them is my berries. And come time to pick them I'm gonna send my boys over. You got the land . . . but them berries, I'm gonna keep them. They mine." And he go and fix it with the law that them is his berries. Now that's the difference between the colored man and the white man. The colored man can't fix nothing with the law.

BOY WILLIE: I don't go by what the law say. The law's liable to say anything. I go by if it's right or not. It don't matter to me what the law say. I take and look at it for myself.

LYMON: That's why you gonna end up back down there on the Parchman Farm.

BOY WILLIE: I ain't thinking about no Parchman Farm. You liable to go back before me.

LYMON: They work you too hard down there. All that weeding and hoeing and chopping down trees. I didn't like all that.

WINING BOY: You ain't got to like your job on Parchman. Hey, tell him, Doaker, the only one got to like his job is the waterboy.

DOAKER: If he don't like his job he need to set that bucket down.

BOY WILLIE: That's what they told Lymon. They had Lymon on water and everybody got mad at him cause he was lazy.

LYMON: That water was heavy.

BOY WILLIE: They had Lymon down there singing:

(Sings.)

O Lord Berta Berta O Lord gal oh-ah
O Lord Berta Berta O Lord gal well

(LYMON and WINING BOY join in.)

Go 'head marry don't you wait on me oh-ah
Go 'head marry don't you wait on me well
Might not want you when I go free oh-ah
Might not want you when I go free well

BOY WILLIE: Come on, Doaker. Doaker know this one.

(As DOAKER joins in the men stamp and clap to keep time. They sing in harmony with great fervor and style.)

O Lord Berta Berta O Lord gal oh-ah
O Lord Berta Berta O Lord gal well

Raise them up higher, let them drop on down oh-ah
Raise them up higher, let them drop on down well
Don't know the difference when the sun go down oh-ah
Don't know the difference when the sun go down well

Berta in Meridan and she living at ease oh-ah
Berta in Meridan and she living at ease well
I'm on old Parchman, got to work or leave oh-ah
I'm on old Parchman, got to work or leave well

O Alberta, Berta, O Lord gal oh-ah
O Alberta, Berta, O Lord gal well

When you marry, don't marry no farming man oh-ah
When you marry, don't marry no farming man well
Everyday Monday, hoe handle in your hand oh-ah
Everyday Monday, hoe handle in your hand well

When you marry, marry a railroad man, oh-ah
When you marry, marry a railroad man, well
Everyday Sunday, dollar in your hand oh-ah
Everyday Sunday, dollar in your hand well

O Alberta, Berta, O Lord gal oh-ah
O Alberta, Berta, O Lord gal well

BOY WILLIE: Doaker like that part. He like that railroad part.

LYMON: Doaker sound like Tangleye. He can't sing a lick.

BOY WILLIE: Hey, Doaker, they still talk about you down on Parchman. They ask me, "You Doaker Boy's nephew?" I say, "Yeah, me and him is family." They treated me alright soon as I told them that. Say, "Yeah, he my uncle."

DOAKER: I don't never want to see none of them niggers no more.

BOY WILLIE: I don't want to see them either. Hey, Wining Boy, come on play some piano. You a piano player, play some piano. Lymon wanna hear you.

WINING BOY: I give that piano up. That was the best thing that ever happened to me, getting rid of that piano. That piano got so big and I'm carrying it around on my back. I don't wish that on nobody. See, you think it's all fun being a recording star. Got to carrying that piano around and man did I get slow. Got just like molasses. The world just slipping by me and I'm walking around with that piano. Alright. Now, there ain't but so many places you can go. Only so many road wide enough for you and that piano. And that piano get heavier and heavier. Go to a place and they find out you play piano, the first thing they want to do is give you a drink, find you a piano, and sit you right down. And that's where you gonna be for the next eight hours. They ain't gonna let you get up! Now, the first three or four years of that is fun. You can't get enough whiskey and you can't get enough women and you don't never get tired of playing that piano. But that only last so long. You look up one day and you hate the whiskey, and you hate the women, and you hate the piano. But that's all you got. You can't do nothing else. All you know how to do is play that piano. Now, who am I? Am I me? Or am I the piano player? Sometime it seem like the only thing to do is shoot the piano player cause he the cause of all the trouble I'm having.

DOAKER: What you gonna do when your troubles get like mine?

LYMON: If I knew how to play it, I'd play it. That's a nice piano.

BOY WILLIE: Whoever playing better play quick. Sutter's brother say he waiting on me. I sell them watermelons. Get Berniece to sell that piano. Put them two parts with the part I done saved . . .

WINING BOY: Berniece ain't gonna sell that piano. I don't see why you don't know that.

BOY WILLIE: What she gonna do with it? She ain't doing nothing but letting it sit up there and rot. That piano ain't doing nobody no good.

LYMON: That's a nice piano. If I had it I'd sell it. Unless I knew how to play like Wining Boy. You can get a nice price for that piano.

DOAKER: Now I'm gonna tell you something, Lymon don't know this . . . but I'm gonna tell you why me and Wining Boy say Berniece ain't gonna sell that piano.

BOY WILLIE: She ain't got to sell it! I'm gonna sell it! Berniece ain't got no more rights to that piano than I do.

DOAKER: I'm talking to the man . . . let me talk to the man. See, now . . . to understand why we say that . . . to understand about that piano . . . you got to go back to slavery time. See, our family was owned by a fellow named Robert Sutter. That was Sutter's grandfather. Alright. The piano was owned by a fellow named Joel Nolander. He was one of the Nolander brothers from down in Georgia. It was coming up on Sutter's wedding anniversary and he was looking to buy his wife . . . Miss Ophelia was her name . . . he was looking to buy her an anniversary present. Only thing with him . . . he ain't had no money. But he had some niggers. So he asked Mr. Nolander to see if maybe he could trade off some of his niggers for that piano. Told him he would give him one and a half niggers for it. That's the way he told him. Say he could have one full grown and one half grown. Mr. Nolander agreed only he say he had to pick them. He didn't want Sutter to give him just any old nigger. He say he wanted to have the pick of the litter. So Sutter lined up his niggers and Mr. Nolander looked them over and out of the whole bunch he picked my grandmother . . . her name was Berniece . . . same like Berniece . . . and he picked my daddy when he wasn't nothing but a little boy nine years old. They made the trade off and Miss Ophelia was so happy with that piano that it got to be just about all she would do was play on that piano.

WINING BOY: Just get up in the morning, get all dressed up and sit down and play on that piano.

DOAKER: Alright. Time go along. Time go along. Miss Ophelia got to missing my grandmother . . . the way she would cook and clean the house and talk to her and what not. And she missed having my daddy around the house to fetch things for her. So she asked to see if maybe she could trade back that piano and get her niggers back. Mr. Nolander said no. Said a deal was a deal. Him and Sutter had a big falling out about it and Miss Ophelia took sick to the bed. Wouldn't get out of the bed in the morning. She just lay there. The doctor said she was wasting away.

WINING BOY: That's when Sutter called our granddaddy up to the house.

DOAKER: Now, our granddaddy's name was Boy Willie. That's who Boy Willie's named after . . . only they called him Willie Boy. Now, he was a worker of wood. He could make you anything you wanted out of wood. He'd make you a desk. A table. A lamp. Anything you wanted. Them white fellows around there used to come up to Mr. Sutter and get him to make all kinds of things for them. Then they'd pay Mr. Sutter a nice price. See, everything my granddaddy made Mr. Sutter owned cause he owned him. That's why when Mr. Nolander offered to buy him to keep the family together Mr. Sutter wouldn't sell him. Told Mr. Nolander he didn't have enough money to buy him. Now . . . am I telling it right, Wining Boy?

WINING BOY: You telling it.

DOAKER: Sutter called him up to the house and told him to carve my grandmother and my daddy's picture on the piano for Miss Ophelia. And he took and carved this . . .

(DOAKER *crosses over to the piano.*)

See that right there? That's my grandmother, Berniece. She looked just like that. And he put a picture of my daddy when he wasn't nothing but a little boy the way he remembered him. He made them up out of his memory. Only thing . . . he didn't stop there. He carved all this. He got a picture of his mama . . . Mama Esther . . . and his daddy, Boy Charles.

WINING BOY: That was the first Boy Charles.

DOAKER: Then he put on the side here all kinds of things. See that? That's when him and Mama Berniece got married. They called it jumping the broom. That's how you got married in them days. Then he got here when my daddy was born . . . and here he got Mama Esther's funeral . . . and down here he got Mr. Nolander taking Mama Berniece and my daddy away down to his place in Georgia. He got all kinds of things what happened with our family. When Mr. Sutter seen the piano with all them carvings on it he got mad. He didn't ask for all that. But see . . . there wasn't nothing he could do about it. When Miss Ophelia seen it . . . she got excited. Now she had her piano and her niggers too. She took back to playing it and played on it right up till the day she died. Alright . . . now see, our brother Boy Charles . . . that's Berniece and Boy Willie's daddy . . . he was the oldest of us three boys. He's dead now. But he would have been fifty-seven if he had lived. He died in 1911 when he was thirty-one years old. Boy Charles used to talk about that piano all the time. He never could get it off his mind. Two or three months go by and he be talking about it again. He be talking about taking it out of Sutter's house. Say it was the story of our whole family and as long as Sutter had it . . . he had us. Say we was still in slavery. Me and Wining Boy tried to talk him out of it but it wouldn't do any good. Soon as he quiet down about it he'd start up again. We seen where he wasn't gonna get it off his mind . . . so, on the Fourth of July, 1911 . . . when Sutter was at the picnic what the county give every year . . . me and Wining Boy went on down there with him and took that piano out of Sutter's house. We put it on a wagon and me and Wining Boy carried it over into the next county with Mama Ola's people. Boy Charles decided to stay around there and wait until Sutter got home to make it look like business as usual.

Now, I don't know what happened when Sutter came home and found that piano gone. But somebody went up to Boy Charles's house and set it on fire. But he wasn't in there. He must have seen them coming cause he went down and caught the 3:57 Yellow Dog. He didn't know they was gonna come down and stop the train. Stopped the train and found Boy Charles in the boxcar with four of them hobos. Must have got mad when they couldn't find the piano cause they set the boxcar afire and killed everybody. Now, nobody know who done that. Some people say it was Sutter cause it was his piano. Some people say it was Sheriff Carter. Some people say it was Robert Smith and Ed Saunders. But don't nobody know for sure. It was about two months after that that Ed Saunders fell down his well. Just upped and fell down his well for no reason. People say it was the ghost of them men who burned up in the boxcar that pushed him in his well. They started calling them the Ghosts of the Yellow Dog. Now, that's how all that got started and that why we say Berniece ain't gonna sell that piano. Cause her daddy died over it.

BOY WILLIE: All that's in the past. If my daddy had seen where he could have traded that piano in for some land of his own, it wouldn't be sitting up here now. He spent his whole life farming on somebody else's land. I ain't gonna do that. See, he couldn't do no better. When he come along he ain't had nothing he could build on. His daddy ain't had nothing to give him. The only thing my daddy had to give me was that piano. And he died over giving me that. I ain't gonna let it sit up there and rot without trying to do something with it. If Berniece can't see that, then I'm gonna go ahead and sell my half. And you and Wining Boy know I'm right.

DOAKER: Ain't nobody said nothing about who's right and who's wrong. I was just telling the man about the piano. I was telling him why we say Berniece ain't gonna sell it.

LYMON: Yeah, I can see why you say that now. I told Boy Willie he ought to stay up here with me.

BOY WILLIE: You stay! I'm going back! That's what I'm gonna do with my life! Why I got to come up here and learn to do something I don't know how to do when I already know how to farm? You stay up here and make your own way if that's what you want to do. I'm going back and live my life the way I want to live it.

(WINING BOY gets up and crosses to the piano.)

WINING BOY: Let's see what we got here. I ain't played on this thing for a while.

DOAKER: You can stop telling that. You was playing on it the last time you was through here. We couldn't get you off of it. Go on and play something.

(WINING BOY sits down at the piano and plays and sings. The song is one which has put many dimes and quarters in his pocket, long ago, in dimly remembered towns and way stations. He plays badly, without hesitation, and sings in a forceful voice.)

WINING BOY: *(Singing.)*

I am a rambling gambling man
I gambled in many towns
I rambled this wide world over
I rambled this world around
I had my ups and downs in life
And bitter times I saw
But I never knew what misery was
Till I lit on old Arkansas.

I started out one morning
to meet that early train
He said, "You better work for me
I have some land to drain.
I'll give you fifty cents a day,
Your washing, board and all
And you shall be a different man
In the state of Arkansas."

I worked six months for the rascal
Joe Herrin was his name
He fed me old corn dodgers
They was hard as any rock
My tooth is all got loosened
And my knees begin to knock
That was the kind of hash I got
In the state of Arkansas.

Traveling man
I've traveled all around this world
Traveling man
I've traveled from land to land
Traveling man
I've traveled all around this world
Well it ain't no use
writing no news
I'm a traveling man.

(The door opens and BERNIECE *enters with* MARETHA.)

BERNIECE: Is that . . . Lord, I know that ain't Wining Boy sitting there.

WINING BOY: Hey, Berniece.

BERNIECE: You all had this planned. You and Boy Willie had this planned.

WINING BOY: I didn't know he was gonna be here. I'm on my way down home. I stopped by to see you and Doaker first.

DOAKER: I told the nigger he left out of here with that sack of money, we thought we might never see him again. Boy Willie say he wasn't gonna see him till he got broke. I looked up and seen him sitting on the doorstep asking for two dollars. Look at him laughing. He know it's the truth.

BERNIECE: Boy Willie, I didn't see that truck out there. I thought you was out selling watermelons.

BOY WILLIE: We done sold them all. Sold the truck too.

BERNIECE: I don't want to go through none of your stuff. I done told you to go back where you belong.

BOY WILLIE: I was just teasing you, woman. You can't take no teasing?

BERNIECE: Wining Boy, when you get here?

WINING BOY: A little while ago. I took the train from Kansas City.

BERNIECE: Let me go upstairs and change and then I'll cook you something to eat.

BOY WILLIE: You ain't cooked me nothing when I come.

BERNIECE: Boy Willie, go on and leave me alone. Come on, Maretha, get up here and change your clothes before you get them dirty.

(BERNIECE exits up the stairs, followed by MARETHA.)

WINING BOY: Maretha sure getting big, ain't she, Doaker. And just as pretty as she want to be. I didn't know Crawley had it in him.

(BOY WILLIE crosses to the piano.)

BOY WILLIE: Hey, Lymon . . . get up on the other side of this piano and let me see something.

WINING BOY: Boy Willie, what is you doing?

BOY WILLIE: I'm seeing how heavy this piano is. Get up over there, Lymon.

WINING BOY: Go on and leave that piano alone. You ain't taking that piano out of here and selling it.

BOY WILLIE: Just as soon as I get them watermelons out that truck.

WINING BOY: Well, I got something to say about that.

BOY WILLIE: This my daddy's piano.

WINING BOY: He ain't took it by himself. Me and Doaker helped him.

BOY WILLIE: He died by himself. Where was you and Doaker at then? Don't come telling me nothing about this piano. This is me and Berniece's piano. Am I right, Doaker?

DOAKER: Yeah, you right.

BOY WILLIE: Let's see if we can lift it up, Lymon. Get a good grip on it and pick it up on your end. Ready? Lift!

(As they start to move the piano, the sound of SUTTER'S GHOST *is heard.* DOAKER *is the only one to hear it. With difficulty they move the piano a little bit so it is out of place.)*

BOY WILLIE: What you think?

LYMON: It's heavy . . . but you can move it. Only it ain't gonna be easy.

BOY WILLIE: It wasn't that heavy to me. Okay, let's put it back.

(The sound of SUTTER'S GHOST *is heard again. They all hear it as* BERNIECE *enters on the stairs.)*

BERNIECE: Boy Willie . . . you gonna play around with me one too many times. And then God's gonna bless you and West is gonna dress you. Now set that piano back over there. I done told you a hundred times I ain't selling that piano.

BOY WILLIE: I'm trying to get me some land, woman. I need that piano to get me some money so I can buy Sutter's land.

BERNIECE: Money can't buy what that piano cost. You can't sell your soul for money. It won't go with the buyer. It'll shrivel and shrink to know that you ain't taken on to it. But it won't go with the buyer.

BOY WILLIE: I ain't talking about all that, woman. I ain't talking about selling my soul. I'm talking about trading that piece of wood for some land. Get something under your feet. Land the only thing God ain't making no more of. You can always get you another piano. I'm talking about some land. What you get something out the ground from. That's what I'm talking about. You can't do nothing with that piano but sit up there and look at it.

BERNIECE: That's just what I'm gonna do. Wining Boy, you want me to fry you some pork chops?

BOY WILLIE: Now, I'm gonna tell you the way I see it. The only thing that make that piano worth something is them carvings Papa Willie Boy put on there.

That's what make it worth something. That was my great-grandaddy. Papa Boy Charles brought that piano into the house. Now, I'm supposed to build on what they left me. You can't do nothing with that piano sitting up here in the house. That's just like if I let them watermelons sit out there and rot. I'd be a fool. Alright now, if you say to me, Boy Willie, I'm using that piano. I give out lessons on it and that help me make my rent or whatever. Then that be something else. I'd have to go on and say, well, Berniece using that piano. She building on it. Let her go on and use it. I got to find another way to get Sutter's land. But Doaker say you ain't touched that piano the whole time it's been up here. So why you wanna stand in my way? See, you just looking at the sentimental value. See, that's good. That's alright. I take my hat off whenever somebody say my daddy's name. But I ain't gonna be no fool about no sentimental value. You can sit up here and look at the piano for the next hundred years and it's just gonna be a piano. You can't make more than that. Now I want to get Sutter's land with that piano. I get Sutter's land and I can go down and cash in the crop and get my seed. As long as I got the land and the seed then I'm alright. I can always get me a little something else. Cause that land give back to you. I can make me another crop and cash that in. I still got the land and the seed. But that piano don't put out nothing else. You ain't got nothing working for you. Now, the kind of man my daddy was he would have understood that. I'm sorry you can't see it that way. But that's why I'm gonna take that piano out of here and sell it.

BERNIECE: You ain't taking that piano out of my house.

(She crosses to the piano.)

Look at this piano. Look at it. Mama Ola polished this piano with her tears for seventeen years. For seventeen years she rubbed on it till her hands bled. Then she rubbed the blood in . . . mixed it up with the rest of the blood on it. Every day that God breathed life into her body she rubbed and cleaned and polished and prayed over it. "Play something for me, Berniece. Play something for me, Berniece." Every day. "I cleaned it up for you, play something for me, Berniece." You always talking about your daddy but you ain't never stopped to look at what his foolishness cost your mama. Seventeen years' worth of cold nights and an empty bed. For what? For a piano? For a piece of wood? To get even with somebody? I look at you and you're all the same. You, Papa Boy Charles, Wining Boy, Doaker, Crawley . . . you're all alike. All this thieving and killing and thieving and killing. And what it ever lead to? More killing and more thieving. I ain't never seen it come to nothing. People getting burned up. People getting shot. People falling down their wells. It don't never stop.

DOAKER: Come on now, Berniece, ain't no need in getting upset.

BOY WILLIE: I done a little bit of stealing here and there, but I ain't never killed nobody. I can't be speaking for nobody else. You all got to speak for yourself, but I ain't never killed nobody.

BERNIECE: You killed Crawley just as sure as if you pulled the trigger.

BOY WILLIE: See, that's ignorant. That's downright foolish for you to say something like that. You ain't doing nothing but showing your ignorance. If the nigger was here I'd whup his ass for getting me and Lymon shot at.

BERNIECE: Crawley ain't knew about the wood.

BOY WILLIE: We told the man about the wood. Ask Lymon. He knew all about the wood. He seen we was sneaking it. Why else we gonna be out there at night? Don't come telling me Crawley ain't knew about the wood. Them fellows come up on us and Crawley tried to bully them. Me and Lymon seen the sheriff with them and give in. Wasn't no sense in getting killed over fifty dollars' worth of wood.

BERNIECE: Crawley ain't knew you stole that wood.

BOY WILLIE: We ain't stole no wood. Me and Lymon was hauling wood for Jim Miller and keeping us a little bit on the side. We dumped our little bit down there by the creek till we had enough to make a load. Some fellows seen us and we figured we better get it before they did. We come up there and got Crawley to help us load it. Figured we'd cut him in. Crawley trying to keep the wolf from his door ... we was trying to help him.

LYMON: Me and Boy Willie told him about the wood. We told him some fellows might be trying to beat us to it. He say let me go back and get my thirty-eight. That's what caused all the trouble.

BOY WILLIE: If Crawley ain't had the gun he'd be alive today.

LYMON: We had it about half loaded when they come up on us. We seen the sheriff with them and we tried to get away. We ducked around near the bend in the creek ... but they was down there too. Boy Willie say let's give in. But Crawley pulled out his gun and started shooting. That's when they started shooting back.

BERNIECE: All I know is Crawley would be alive if you hadn't come up there and got him.

BOY WILLIE: I ain't had nothing to do with Crawley getting killed. That was his own fault.

BERNIECE: Crawley's dead and in the ground and you still walking around here eating. That's all I know. He went off to load some wood with you and ain't never come back.

BOY WILLIE: I told you, woman ... I ain't had nothing to do with ...

BERNIECE: He ain't here, is he? He ain't here!

(BERNIECE *hits* BOY WILLIE.)

I said he ain't here. Is he?

(BERNIECE *continues to hit* BOY WILLIE, *who doesn't move to defend himself, other than back up and turning his head so that most of the blows fall on his chest and arms.*)

DOAKER: *(Grabbing* BERNIECE.*)* Come on, Berniece . . . let it go, it ain't his fault.

BERNIECE: He ain't here, is he? Is he?

BOY WILLIE: I told you I ain't responsible for Crawley.

BERNIECE: He ain't here.

BOY WILLIE: Come on now, Berniece . . . don't do this now. Doaker get her. I ain't had nothing to do with Crawley . . .

BERNIECE: You come up there and got him!

BOY WILLIE: I done told you now. Doaker, get her. I ain't playing.

DOAKER: Come on. Berniece.

*(*MARETHA *is heard screaming upstairs. It is a scream of stark terror.)*

MARETHA: Mama! . . . Mama!

(The lights go down to black. End of Act One.)

ACT TWO

Scene One

(The lights come up on the kitchen. It is the following morning. DOAKER *is ironing the pants to his uniform. He has a pot cooking on the stove at the same time. He is singing a song. The song provides him with the rhythm for his work and he moves about the kitchen with the ease born of many years as a railroad cook)*

DOAKER:

> Gonna leave Jackson Mississippi
> and go to Memphis
> and double back to Jackson
> Come on down to Hattiesburg
> Change cars on the Y.D.
> coming through the territory to
> Meridian
> and Meridian to Greenville
> and Greenville to Memphis
> I'm on my way and I know where
>
> Change cars on the Katy
> Leaving Jackson

and going through Clarksdale
Hello Winona!
Courtland!
Bateville!
Como!
Senitobia!
Lewisberg!
Sunflower!
Glendora!
Sharkey!
And double back to Jackson
Hello Greenwood
I'm on my way Memphis
Clarksdale
Moorhead
Indianola
Can a highball pass through?
Highball on through sir
Grand Carson!
Thirty First Street Depot
Fourth Street Depot
Memphis!

(WINING BOY *enters carrying a suit of clothes.*)

DOAKER: I thought you took that suit to the pawnshop?

WINING BOY: I went down there and the man tell me the suit is too old. Look at this suit. This is one hundred percent silk! How a silk suit gonna get too old? I know what it was he just didn't want to give me five dollars for it. Best he wanna give me is three dollars. I figure a silk suit is worth five dollars all over the world. I wasn't gonna part with it for no three dollars so I brought it back.

DOAKER: They got another pawnshop up on Wylie.

WINING BOY: I carried it up there. He say he don't take no clothes. Only thing he take is guns and radios. Maybe a guitar or two. Where's Berniece?

DOAKER: Berniece still at work. Boy Willie went down there to meet Lymon this morning. I guess they got that truck fixed, they been out there all day and ain't come back yet. Maretha scared to sleep up there now. Berniece don't know, but I seen Sutter before she did.

WINING BOY: Say what?

DOAKER: About three weeks ago. I had just come back from down there. Sutter couldn't have been dead more than three days. He was sitting over there at the piano. I come out to go to work . . . and he was sitting right there. Had his hand on top of his head just like Berniece said. I believe he broke his neck when he fell in the well. I kept quiet about it. I didn't see no reason to upset Berniece.

WINING BOY: Did he say anything? Did he say he was looking for Boy Willie?

DOAKER: He was just sitting there. He ain't said nothing. I went on out the door and left him sitting there. I figure as long as he was on the other side of the room everything be alright. I don't know what I would have done if he had started walking toward me.

WINING BOY: Berniece say he was calling Boy Willie's name.

DOAKER: I ain't heard him say nothing. He was just sitting there when I seen him. But I don't believe Boy Willie pushed him in the well. Sutter here cause of that piano. I heard him playing on it one time. I thought it was Berniece but then she don't play that kind of music. I come out here and ain't seen nobody, but them piano keys was moving a mile a minute. Berniece need to go on and get rid of it. It ain't done nothing but cause trouble.

WINING BOY: I agree with Berniece. Boy Charles ain't took it to give it back. He took it cause he figure he had more right to it than Sutter did. If Sutter can't understand that . . . then that's just the way that go. Sutter dead and in the ground . . . don't care where his ghost is. He can hover around and play on the piano all he want. I want to see him carry it out the house. That's what I want to see. What time Berniece get home? I don't see how I let her get away from me this morning.

DOAKER: You up there sleep. Berniece leave out of here early in the morning. She out there in Squirrel Hill cleaning house for some bigshot down there at the steel mill. They don't like you to come late. You come late they won't give you your carfare. What kind of business you got with Berniece?

WINING BOY: My business. I ain't asked you what kind of business you got.

DOAKER: Berniece ain't got no money. If that's why you was trying to catch her. She having a hard enough time trying to get by as it is. If she go ahead and marry Avery . . . he working every day . . . she go ahead and marry him they could do alright for themselves. But as it stands she ain't got no money.

WINING BOY: Well, let me have five dollars.

DOAKER: I just give you a dollar before you left out of here. You ain't gonna take my five dollars out there and gamble and drink it up.

WINING BOY: Aw, nigger, give me five dollars. I'll give it back to you.

DOAKER: You wasn't looking to give me five dollars when you had that sack of money. You wasn't looking to throw nothing my way. Now you wanna come in here and borrow five dollars. If you going back with Boy Willie you need to be trying to figure out how you gonna get train fare.

WINING BOY: That's why I need the five dollars. If I had five dollars I could get me some money.

(DOAKER goes into his pocket.)

Make it seven.

DOAKER: You take this five dollars . . . and you bring my money back here too.

(BOY WILLIE and LYMON *enter. They are happy and excited. They have money in all of their pockets and are anxious to count it.)*

DOAKER: How'd you do out there?

BOY WILLIE: They was lining up for them.

LYMON: Me and Boy Willie couldn't sell them fast enough. Time we got one sold we'd sell another.

BOY WILLIE: I seen what was happening and told Lymon to up the price on them.

LYMON: Boy Willie say charge them a quarter more. They didn't care. A couple of people give me a dollar and told me to keep the change.

BOY WILLIE: One fellow bought five. I say now what he gonna do with five watermelons? He can't eat them all. I sold him the five and asked him did he want to buy five more.

LYMON: I ain't never seen nobody snatch a dollar fast as Boy Willie.

BOY WILLIE: One lady asked me say, "Is they sweet?" I told her say, "Lady, where we grow these watermelons we put sugar in the ground." You know, she believed me. Talking about she had never heard of that before. Lymon was laughing his head off. I told her, "Oh, yeah, we put the sugar right in the ground with the seed." She say, "Well, give me another one." Them white folks is something else . . . ain't they, Lymon?

LYMON: Soon as you holler watermelons they come right out their door. Then they go and get their neighbors. Look like they having a contest to see who can buy the most.

WINING BOY: I got something for Lymon.

(WINING BOY goes to get his suit. BOY WILLIE *and* LYMON *continue to count their money.)*

BOY WILLIE: I know you got more than that. You ain't sold all them watermelons for that little bit of money.

LYMON: I'm still looking. That ain't all you got either. Where's all them quarters?

BOY WILLIE: You let me worry about the quarters. Just put the money on the table.

WINING BOY: *(Entering with his suit.)* Look here, Lymon . . . see this? Look at his eyes getting big. He ain't never seen a suit like this. This is one hundred percent silk. Go ahead . . . put it on. See if it fit you.

(LYMON tries the suit coat on.)

Look at that. Feel it. That's one hundred percent genuine silk. I got that in Chicago. You can't get clothes like that nowhere but New York and Chicago. You can't get clothes like that in Pittsburgh. These folks in Pittsburgh ain't never seen clothes like that.

LYMON: This is nice, feel real nice and smooth.

WINING BOY: That's a fifty-five-dollar suit. That's the kind of suit the bigshots wear. You need a pistol and a pocketful of money to wear that suit. I'll let you have it for three dollars. The women will fall out their windows they see you in a suit like that. Give me three dollars and go on and wear it down the street and get you a woman.

BOY WILLIE: That looks nice, Lymon. Put the pants on. Let me see it with the pants.

(LYMON begins to try on the pants.)

WINING BOY: Look at that . . . see how it fits you? Give me three dollars and go on and take it. Look at that, Doaker . . . don't he look nice?

DOAKER: Yeah . . . that's a nice suit.

WINING BOY: Got a shirt to go with it. Cost you an extra dollar. Four dollars you got the whole deal.

LYMON: How this look, Boy Willie?

BOY WILLIE: That look nice . . . if you like that kind of thing. I don't like them dress-up kind of clothes. If you like it, look real nice.

WINING BOY: That's the kind of suit you need for up here in the North.

LYMON: Four dollars for everything? The suit and the shirt?

WINING BOY: That's cheap. I should be charging you twenty dollars. I give you a break cause you a homeboy. That's the only way I let you have it for four dollars.

LYMON: *(Going into his pocket.)* Okay . . . here go the four dollars.

WINING BOY: You got some shoes? What size you wear?

LYMON: Size nine.

WINING BOY: That's what size I got! Size nine. I let you have them for three dollars.

LYMON: Where they at? Let me see them.

WINING BOY: They real nice shoes, too. Got a nice tip to them. Got pointy toe just like you want.

(WINING BOY goes to get his shoes.)

LYMON: Come on, Boy Willie, let's go out tonight. I wanna see what it looks like up here. Maybe we go to a picture show. Hey, Doaker, they got picture shows up here?

DOAKER: The Rhumba Theater. Right down there on Fullerton Street. Can't miss it. Got the speakers outside on the sidewalk. You can hear it a block away. Boy Willie know where it's at.

(DOAKER exits into his room.)

LYMON: Let's go to the picture show, Boy Willie. Let's go find some women.

BOY WILLIE: Hey, Lymon, how many of them watermelons would you say we got left? We got just under a half a load . . . right?

LYMON: About that much. Maybe a little more.

BOY WILLIE: You think that piano will fit up in there?

LYMON: If we stack them watermelons you can sit it up in the front there.

BOY WILLIE: I'm gonna call that man tomorrow.

WINING BOY: *(Returns with his shoes.)* Here you go . . . size nine. Put them on. Cost you three dollars. That's a Florsheim shoe. That's the kind Staggerlee wore.

LYMON: *(Trying on the shoes.)* You sure these size nine?

WINING BOY: You can look at my feet and see we wear the same size. Man, you put on that suit and them shoes and you got something there. You ready for whatever's out there. But is they ready for you? With them shoes on you be the King of the Walk. Have everybody stop to look at your shoes. Wishing they had a pair. I'll give you a break. Go on and take them for two dollars.

(LYMON pays WINING BOY two dollars.)

LYMON: Come on, Boy Willie . . . let's go find some women. I'm gonna go upstairs and get ready. I'll be ready to go in a minute. Ain't you gonna get dressed?

BOY WILLIE: I'm gonna wear what I got on. I ain't dressing up for these city niggers.

(LYMON exits up the stairs.)

That's all Lymon think about is women.

WINING BOY: His daddy was the same way. I used to run around with him. I know his mama too. Two strokes back and I would have been his daddy! His daddy's dead now . . . but I got the nigger out of jail one time. They was fixing to name him Daniel and walk him through the Lion's Den. He got in a tussle with one of them white fellows and the sheriff lit on him like white on rice. That's how the whole thing come about between me and Lymon's mama. She knew me and his daddy used to run together and he got in jail and she went down there and took the sheriff a hundred dollars. Don't get me to lying about where she got it from. I don't know. The sheriff *looked at that hundred dollars and turned his nose up* Told her, say, "That ain't gonna do him no good. You got to put another hundred on top of that." She come up *there and got me where I was playing at this saloon* . . . said she had all but fifty dollars and asked me if I could help. Now the way I figured it . . . without that fifty dollars the sheriff was gonna turn him over to Parchman. The sheriff turn him over to Parchman it be three years before anybody see him again. Now I'm gonna say it right . . . I will give anybody fifty dollars to keep them out of jail for three years. I give her the fifty dollars and she told me to come over to the house. I ain't asked her. I figure if she was nice enough to invite me I ought to go. I ain't had to say a word. She invited me over just as nice. Say, "Why don't you come over to the house?" She ain't had to say nothing else. Them words rolled off her tongue just as nice. I went on down there and sat about three hours. Started to leave and changed my mind. She grabbed hold to me and say, "Baby, it's all night long." That was one of the shortest nights I have ever spent on this earth! I could have used another eight hours. Lymon's daddy didn't even say nothing to me when he got out. He just looked at me funny. He had a good notion something had happened between me an' her. L. D. Jackson. That was one bad-luck nigger. Got killed at some dance. Fellow walked in and shot him thinking he was somebody else.

(DOAKER enters from his room.)

Hey, Doaker, you remember L. D. Jackson?
DOAKER: That's Lymon's daddy. That was one bad-luck nigger.
BOY WILLIE: Look like you ready to railroad some.
DOAKER: Yeah, I got to make that run.

(LYMON enters from the stairs. He is dressed in his new suit and shoes, to which he has added a cheap straw hat.)

LYMON: How I look?
WINING BOY: You look like a million dollars. Don't he look good, Doaker? Come on, let's play some cards. You wanna play some cards?
BOY WILLIE: We ain't gonna play no cards with you. Me and Lymon gonna find some women. Hey, Lymon, don't play no cards with Wining Boy. He'll take all your money.
WINING BOY: *(To* LYMON.) You got a magic suit there. You can get you a woman easy with that suit . . . but you got to know the magic words. You know the magic words to get you a woman?
LYMON: I just talk to them to see if I like them and they like me.
WINING BOY: You just walk right up to them and say, "If you got the harbor I got the ship." If that don't work ask them if you can put them in your pocket. The first thing they gonna say is, "It's too small." That's when you look them dead in the eye and say, "Baby, ain't nothing small about me." If that don't work then you move on to another one. Am I telling him right, Doaker?
DOAKER: That man don't need you to tell him nothing about no women. These women these days ain't gonna fall for that kind of stuff. You got to buy them a present. That's what they looking for these days.
BOY WILLIE: Come on, I'm ready. You ready, Lymon? Come on, let's go find some women.

WINING BOY: Here, let me walk out with you. I wanna see the women fall out
    their window when they see Lymon.

(They all exit and the lights go down on the scene.)

Scene 2

(The lights come up on the kitchen. It is late evening of the same day. BERNIECE
*has set a tub for her bath in the kitchen. She is heating up water on the stove. There
is a knock at the door.)*

BERNIECE: Who is it?
AVERY: It's me, Avery.

*(*BERNIECE *opens the door and lets him in.)*

BERNIECE: Avery, come on in. I was just fixing to take my bath.
AVERY: Where Boy Willie? I see that truck out there almost empty. They done
    sold almost all them watermelons.
BERNIECE: They was gone when I come home. I don't know where they went
    off to. Boy Willie around here about to drive me crazy.
AVERY: They sell them watermelons . . . he'll be gone soon.
BERNIECE: What Mr. Cohen say about letting you have the place?
AVERY: He say he'll let me have it for thirty dollars a month. I talked him out
    of thirty-five and he say he'll let me have it for thirty.
BERNIECE: That's a nice spot next to Benny Diamond's store.
AVERY: Berniece . . . I be at home and I get to thinking you up here an' I'm
    down there. I get to thinking how that look to have a preacher that ain't mar-
    ried. It makes for a better congregation if the preacher was settled down and
    married.
BERNIECE: Avery . . . not now. I was fixing to take my bath.
AVERY: You know how I feel about you, Berniece. Now . . . I done got the place
    from Mr. Cohen. I get the money from the bank and I can fix it up real nice.
    They give me a ten cents a hour raise down there on the job . . . now Berniece,
    I ain't got much in the way of comforts. I got a hole in my pockets near about
    as far as money is concerned. I ain't never found no way through life to a
    woman I care about like I care about you. I need that. I need somebody on
    my bond side. I need a woman that fits in my hand.
BERNIECE: Avery, I ain't ready to get married now.
AVERY: You too young a woman to close up, Berniece.
BERNIECE: I ain't said nothing about closing up. I got a lot of woman left in me.

AVERY: Where's it at? When's the last time you looked at it?

BERNIECE: *(Stunned by his remark.)* That's a nasty thing to say. And you call yourself a preacher.

AVERY: Anytime I get anywhere near you . . . you push me away.

BERNIECE: I got enough on my hands with Maretha. I got enough people to love and take care of.

AVERY: Who you got to love you? Can't nobody get close enough to you. Doaker can't half say nothing to you. You jump all over Boy Willie. Who you got to love you, Berniece?

BERNIECE: You trying to tell me a woman can't be nothing without a man. But you alright, huh? You can just walk out of here without me—without a woman—and still be a man. That's alright. Ain't nobody gonna ask you, "Avery, who you got to love you?" That's alright for you. But everybody gonna be worried about Berniece. "How Berniece gonna take care of herself? How she gonna raise that child without a man? Wonder what she do with herself. How she gonna live like that?" Everybody got all kinds of questions for Berniece. Everybody telling me I can't be a woman unless I got a man. Well, you tell me, Avery—you know—how much woman am I?

AVERY: It wasn't me, Berniece. You can't blame me for nobody else. I'll own up to my own shortcomings. But you can't blame me for Crawley or nobody else.

BERNIECE: I ain't blaming nobody for nothing. I'm just stating the facts.

AVERY: How long you gonna carry Crawley with you, Berniece? It's been over three years. At some point you got to let go and go on. Life's got all kinds of twists and turns. That don't mean you stop living. That don't mean you cut yourself off from life. You can't go through life carrying Crawley's ghost with you. Crawley's been dead three years. Three years, Berniece.

BERNIECE: I know how long Crawley's been dead. You ain't got to tell me that. I just ain't ready to get married right now.

AVERY: What is you ready for, Berniece? You just gonna drift along from day to day. Life is more than making it from one day to another. You gonna look up one day and it's all gonna be past you. Life's gonna be gone out of your hands—there won't be enough to make nothing with. I'm standing here now, Berniece—but I don't know how much longer I'm gonna be standing here waiting on you.

BERNIECE: Avery, I told you . . . when you get your church we'll sit down and talk about this. I got too many other things to deal with right now. Boy Willie and the piano . . . and Sutter's ghost. I thought I might have been seeing things, but Maretha done seen Sutter's ghost, too.

AVERY: When this happen, Berniece?

BERNIECE: Right after I came home yesterday. Me and Boy Willie was arguing about the piano and Sutter's ghost was standing at the top of the stairs. Maretha scared to sleep up there now. Maybe if you bless the house he'll go away.

AVERY: I don't know, Berniece. I don't know if I should fool around with something like that.

BERNIECE: I can't have Maretha scared to go to sleep up there. Seem like if you bless the house he would go away.

AVERY: You might have to be a special kind of preacher to do something like that.

BERNIECE: I keep telling myself when Boy Willie leave he'll go on and leave with him. I believe Boy Willie pushed him in the well.

AVERY: That's been going on down there a long time. The Ghosts of the Yellow Dog been pushing people in their wells long before Boy Willie got grown.

BERNIECE: Somebody down there pushing them people in their wells. They ain't just upped and fell. Ain't no wind pushed nobody in their well.

AVERY: Oh, I don't know. God works in mysterious ways.

BERNIECE: He ain't pushed nobody in their wells.

AVERY: He caused it to happen. God is the Great Causer. He can do anything. He parted the Red Sea. He say I will smite my enemies. Reverend Thompson used to preach on the Ghosts of the Yellow Dog as the hand of God.

BERNIECE: I don't care who preached what. Somebody down there pushing them people in their wells. Somebody like Boy Willie. I can see him doing something like that. You ain't gonna tell me that Sutter just upped and fell in his well. I believe Boy Willie pushed him so he could get his land.

AVERY: What Doaker say about Boy Willie selling the piano?

BERNIECE: Doaker don't want no part of that piano. He ain't never wanted no part of it. He blames himself for not staying behind with Papa Boy Charles. He washed his hands of that piano a long time ago. He didn't want me to bring it up here—but I wasn't gonna leave it down there.

AVERY: Well, it seems to me somebody ought to be able to talk to Boy Willie.

BERNIECE: You can't talk to Boy Willie. He been that way all his life. Mama Ola had her hands full trying to talk to him. He don't listen to nobody. He just like my daddy. He get his mind fixed on something and can't nobody turn him from it.

AVERY: You ought to start a choir at the church. Maybe if he seen you was doing something with it—if you told him you was gonna put it in my church—maybe he'd see it different. You ought to put it down in the church and start a choir. The Bible say "Make a joyful noise unto the Lord." Maybe if Boy Willie see you was doing something with it he'd see it different.

BERNIECE: I done told you I don't play on that piano. Ain't no need in you to keep talking this choir stuff. When my mama died I shut the top on that piano and I ain't never opened it since. I was only playing it for her. When my daddy died seem like all her life went into that piano. She used to have me playing on it . . . had Miss Eula come in and teach me . . . say when I played it she could hear my daddy talking to her. I used to think them pictures came alive and walked through the house. Sometime late at night I could hear my mama talking to them. I said that wasn't gonna happen to me. I don't play that piano cause I don't want to wake them spirits. They never be walking around in this house.

AVERY: You got to put all that behind you, Berniece.

BERNIECE: I got Maretha playing on it. She don't know nothing about it. Let her go on and be a schoolteacher or something. She don't have to carry all of that with her. She got a chance I didn't have. I ain't gonna burden her with that piano.

AVERY: You got to put all of that behind you, Berniece. That's the same thing like Crawley. Everybody got stones in their passway. You got to step over them or walk around them. You picking them up and carrying them with you. All you got to do is set them down by the side of the road. You ain't got to carry them with you. You can walk over there right now and play that piano. You can walk over there right now and God will walk over there with you. Right now you can set that sack of stones down by the side of the road and walk away from it. You don't have to carry it with you. You can do it right now.

(AVERY crosses over to the piano and raises the lid.)

Come on, Berniece . . . set it down and walk away from it. Come on, play "Old Ship of Zion." Walk over here and claim it as an instrument of the Lord. You can walk over here right now and make it into a celebration.

(BERNIECE moves toward the piano.)

BERNIECE: Avery . . . I done told you I don't want to play that piano. Now or no other time.

AVERY: The Bible say, "The Lord is my refuge . . . and my strength!" With the strength of God you can put the past behind you, Berniece. With the strength of God you can do anything! God got a bright tomorrow. God don't ask what you done . . . God ask what you gonna do. The strength of God can move mountains! God's got a bright tomorrow for you . . . all you got to do is walk over here and claim it.

BERNIECE: Avery, just go on and let me finish my bath. I'll see you tomorrow.

AVERY: Okay, Berniece. I'm gonna go home. I'm gonna go home and read up on my Bible. And tomorrow . . . if the good Lord give me strength tomorrow . . . I'm gonna come by and bless the house . . . and show you the power of the Lord.

(AVERY crosses to the door.)

It's gonna be alright, Berniece. God say he will soothe the troubled waters. I'll come by tomorrow and bless the house.

(The lights go down to black.)

Scene 3

(Several hours later. The house is dark. BERNIECE *has retired for the night.* BOY WILLIE *enters the darkened house with* GRACE.*)*

BOY WILLIE: Come on in. This my sister's house. My sister live here. Come on, I ain't gonna bite you.

GRACE: Put some light on. I can't see.

BOY WILLIE: You don't need to see nothing, baby. This here is all you need to see. All you need to do is see me. If you can't see me you can feel me in the dark. How's that, sugar?

(He attempts to kiss her.)

GRACE: Go on now . . . wait!

BOY WILLIE: Just give me one little old kiss.

GRACE: *(Pushing him away.)* Come on, now. Where I'm gonna sleep at?

BOY WILLIE: We got to sleep out here on the couch. Come on, my sister don't mind. Lymon come back he just got to sleep on the floor. He run off with Dolly somewhere he better stay there. Come on, sugar.

GRACE: Wait now . . . you ain't told me nothing about no couch. I thought you had a bed. Both of us can't sleep on that little old couch.

BOY WILLIE: It don't make no difference. We can sleep on the floor. Let Lymon sleep on the couch.

GRACE: You ain't told me nothing about no couch.

BOY WILLIE: What difference it make? You just wanna be with me.

GRACE: I don't want to be with you on no couch. Ain't you got no bed?

BOY WILLIE: You don't need no bed, woman. My grand-daddy used to take women on the backs of horses. What you need a bed for? You just want to be with me.

GRACE: You sure is country. I didn't know you was this country.

BOY WILLIE: There's a lot of things you don't know about me. Come on, let me show you what this country boy can do.

GRACE: Let's go to my place. I got a room with a bed if Leroy don't come back there.

BOY WILLIE: Who's Leroy? You ain't said nothing about no Leroy.

GRACE: He used to be my man. He ain't coming back. He gone off with some other gal.

BOY WILLIE: You let him have your key?

GRACE: He ain't coming back.

BOY WILLIE: Did you let him have your key?

GRACE: He got a key but he ain't coming back. He took off with some other gal.

BOY WILLIE: I don't wanna go nowhere he might come. Let's stay here. Come on, sugar.

(He pulls her over to the couch.)

Let me heist your hood and check your oil. See if your battery needs charged.

(He pulls her to him. They kiss and tug at each other's clothing. In their anxiety they knock over a lamp.)

BERNIECE: Who's that . . . Wining Boy?

BOY WILLIE: It's me . . . Boy Willie. Go on back to sleep. Everything's alright.

(To GRACE.*)*

That's my sister. Everything's alright, Berniece. Go on back to sleep.

BERNIECE: What you doing down there? What you done knocked over?

BOY WILLIE: It wasn't nothing. Everything's alright. Go on back to sleep.

(To GRACE.*)*

That's my sister. We alright. She gone back to sleep.

(They begin to kiss. BERNIECE *enters from the stairs dressed in a nightgown. She cuts on the light.)*

BERNIECE: Boy Willie, what you doing down here?

BOY WILLIE: It was just that there lamp. It ain't broke. It's okay. Everything's alright. Go on back to bed.

BERNIECE: Boy Willie, I don't allow that in my house. You gonna have to take your company someplace else.

BOY WILLIE: It's alright. We ain't doing nothing. We just sitting here talking. This here is Grace. That's my sister Berniece.

BERNIECE: You know I don't allow that kind of stuff in my house.

BOY WILLIE: Allow what? We just sitting here talking.

BERNIECE: Well, your company gonna have to leave. Come back and talk in the morning.

BOY WILLIE: Go on back upstairs now.

BERNIECE: I got an eleven-year-old girl upstairs. I can't allow that around here.

BOY WILLIE: Ain't nobody said nothing about that. I told you we just talking.

GRACE: Come on . . . let's go to my place. Ain't nobody got to tell me to leave but once.

BOY WILLIE: You ain't got to be like that, Berniece.

BERNIECE: I'm sorry, Miss. But he know I don't allow that in here.

GRACE: You ain't got to tell me but once. I don't stay nowhere I ain't wanted.

BOY WILLIE: I don't know why you want to embarrass me in front of my company.

GRACE: Come on, take me home.

BERNIECE: Go on, Boy Willie. Just go on with your company.

(BOY WILLIE *and* GRACE *exit.* BERNIECE *puts the light on in the kitchen and puts on the teakettle. Presently there is a knock at the door.* BERNIECE *goes to answer it.* BERNIECE *opens the door.* LYMON *enters.*)

LYMON: How you doing, Berniece? I thought you'd be asleep. Boy Willie been back here?
BERNIECE: He just left out of here a minute ago.
LYMON: I went out to see a picture show and never got there. We always end up doing something else. I was with this woman she just wanted to drink up all my money. So I left her there and came back looking for Boy Willie.
BERNIECE: You just missed him. He just left out of here.
LYMON: They got some nice-looking women in this city. I'm gonna like it up here real good. I like seeing them with their dresses on. Got them high heels. I like that. Make them look like they real precious. Boy Willie met a real nice one today. I wish I had met her before he did.
BERNIECE: He come by here with some woman a little while ago. I told him to go on and take all that out of my house.
LYMON: What she look like, the woman he was with? Was she a brown-skinned woman about this high? Nice and healthy? Got nice hips on her?
BERNIECE: She had on a red dress.
LYMON: That's her! That's Grace. She real nice. Laugh a lot. Lot of fun to be with. She don't be trying to put on. Some of these woman act like they the Queen of Sheba. I don't like them kind. Grace ain't like that. She real nice with herself.
BERNIECE: I don't know what she was like. He come in here all drunk knocking over the lamp, and making all kind of noise. I told them to take that somewhere else. I can't really say what she was like.
LYMON: She real nice. I seen her before he did. I was trying not to act like I seen her. I wanted to look at her a while before I said something. She seen me when I come into the saloon. I tried to act like I didn't see her. Time I looked around Boy Willie was talking to her. She was talking to him kept looking at me. That's when her friend Dolly came. I asked her if she wanted to go to the picture show. She told me to buy her a drink while she thought about it. Next thing I knew she done had three drinks talking about she too tired to go. I bought her another drink, then I left. Boy Willie was gone and I thought he might have come back here. Doaker gone, huh? He say he had to make a trip.
BERNIECE: Yeah, he gone on his trip. This is when I can usually get me some peace and quiet, Maretha asleep.
LYMON: She look just like you. Got them big eyes. I remember her when she was in diapers.

BERNIECE: Time just keep on. It go on with or without you. She going on twelve.

LYMON: She sure is pretty. I like kids.

BERNIECE: Boy Willie say you staying . . . what you gonna do up here in this big city? You thought about that?

LYMON: They never get me back down there. The sheriff looking for me. All because they gonna try and make me work for somebody when I don't want to. They gonna try and make me work for Stovall when he don't pay nothing. It ain't like that up here. Up here you more or less do what you want to. I figure I find me a job and try to get set up and then see what the year brings. I tried to do that two or three times down there . . . but it never would work out. I was always in the wrong place.

BERNIECE: This ain't a bad city once you get to know your way around.

LYMON: Up here is different. I'm gonna get me a job unloading boxcars or something. One fellow told me say he know a place. I'm gonna go over there with him next week. Me and Boy Willie finish selling them watermelons I'll have enough money to hold me for a while. But I'm gonna go over there and see what kind of jobs they have.

BERNIECE: You shouldn't have too much trouble finding a job. It's all in how you present yourself. See now, Boy Willie couldn't get no job up here. Somebody hire him they got a pack of trouble on their hands. Soon as they find that out they fire him. He don't want to do nothing unless he do it his way.

LYMON: I know. I told him let's go to the picture show first and see if there was any women down there. They might get tired of sitting at home and walk down to the picture show. He say he wanna look around first. We never did get down there. We tried a couple of places and then we went to this saloon where he met Grace. I tried to meet her before he did but he beat me to her. We left Wining Boy sitting down there running his mouth. He told me if I wear this suit I'd find me a woman. He was almost right.

BERNIECE: You don't need to be out there in them saloons. Ain't no telling what you liable to run into out there. This one liable to cut you as quick as that one shoot you. You don't need to be out there. You start out that fast life you can't keep it up. It makes you old quick. I don't know what them women out there be thinking about.

LYMON: Mostly they be lonely and looking for somebody to spend the night with them. Sometimes it matters who it is and sometimes it don't. I used to be the same way. Now it got to matter. That's why I'm here now. Dolly liable not to even recognize me if she sees me again. I don't like women like that. I like my women to be with me in a nice and easy way. That way we can both enjoy ourselves. The way I see it we the only two people like us in the world. We got to see how we fit together. A woman that don't want to take the time to do that I don't bother with. Used to. Used to bother with all of them. Then I woke up one time with this woman and I didn't know who she was. She was the prettiest woman I had ever seen in my life. I spent the whole night with her and didn't even know it. I had never taken the time to look at her. I guess she kinda knew I ain't never really looked at her. She must have known that cause she ain't wanted to see me no more. If she had wanted to see me I believe we might have got married. How come you ain't married? It seem like to me you would be married. I remember Avery from down home. I used to call him plain old Avery. Now he Reverend Avery. That's kinda funny about him becoming a preacher. I like when he told about how that come to him in a dream about them sheep people and them hobos. Nothing ever come to me in a dream like that. I just dream about women. Can't never seem to find the right one.

BERNIECE: She out there somewhere. You just got to get yourself ready to meet her. That's what I'm trying to do. Avery's alright. I ain't really got nobody in mind.

LYMON: I get me a job and a little place and get set up to where I can make a woman comfortable I might get married. Avery's nice. You ought to go ahead and get married. You be a preacher's wife you won't have to work. I hate living by myself. I didn't want to be no strain on my mama so I left home when I was about sixteen. Everything I tried seem like it just didn't work out. Now I'm trying this.

BERNIECE: You keep trying it'll work out for you.

LYMON: You ever go down there to the picture show?

BERNIECE: I don't go in for all that.

LYMON: Ain't nothing wrong with it. It ain't like gambling and sinning. I went to one down in Jackson once. It was fun.

BERNIECE: I just stay home most of the time. Take care of Maretha.

LYMON: It's getting kind of late. I don't know where Boy Willie went off to. He's liable not to come back. I'm gonna take off these shoes. My feet hurt. Was you in bed? I don't mean to be keeping you up.

BERNIECE: You ain't keeping me up. I couldn't sleep after that Boy Willie woke me up.

LYMON: You got on that nightgown. I likes women when they wear them fancy nightclothes and all. It makes their skin look real pretty.

BERNIECE: I got this at the five-and-ten-cents store. It ain't so fancy.

LYMON: I don't too often get to see a woman dressed like that.

(There is a long pause. LYMON *takes off his suit coat.)*

Well, I'm gonna sleep here on the couch. I'm supposed to sleep on the floor but I don't reckon Boy Willie's coming back tonight. Wining Boy sold me this suit. Told me it was a magic suit. I'm gonna put it on again tomorrow. Maybe it bring me a woman like he say.

(He goes into his coat pocket and takes out a small bottle of perfume.)

I almost forgot I had this. Some man sold me this for a dollar. Say it come from Paris. This is the same kind of perfume the Queen of France wear. That's what he told me. I don't know if it's true or not. I smelled it. It smelled good to me. Here . . . smell it see if you like it. I was gonna give it to Dolly. But I didn't like her too much.

BERNIECE: *(Takes the bottle.)* It smells nice.

LYMON: I was gonna give it to Dolly if she had went to the picture with me. Go on, you take it.

BERNIECE: I can't take it. Here . . . go on you keep it. You'll find somebody to give it to.

LYMON: I wanna give it to you. Make you smell nice.

(He takes the bottle and puts perfume behind BERNIECE's *ear.)*

They tell me you supposed to put it right here behind your ear. Say if you put it there you smell nice all day.

*(*BERNIECE *stiffens at his touch.* LYMON *bends down to smell her.)*

There . . . you smell real good now.

(He kisses her neck.)

You smell real good for Lymon.

(He kisses her again. BERNIECE *returns the kiss, then breaks the embrace and crosses to the stairs. She turns and they look silently at each other.* LYMON *hands her the bottle of perfume.* BERNIECE *exits up the stairs.* LYMON *picks up his suit coat and strokes it lovingly with the full knowledge that it is indeed a magic suit. The lights go down on the scene.)*

Scene 4

(It is late the next morning. The lights come up on the parlor. LYMON *is asleep on the sofa.* BOY WILLIE *enters the front door.)*

BOY WILLIE: Hey, Lymon! Lymon, come on get up.

LYMON: Leave me alone.

BOY WILLIE: Come on, get up, nigger! Wake up, Lymon.

LYMON: What you want?

BOY WILLIE: Come on, let's go. I done called the man about the piano.

LYMON: What piano?

BOY WILLIE: *(Dumps* LYMON *on the floor.)* Come on, get up!

LYMON: Why you leave, I looked around and you was gone.

BOY WILLIE: I come back here with Grace, then I went looking for you. I figured you'd be with Dolly.

LYMON: She just want to drink and spend up your money. I come on back here looking for you to see if you wanted to go to the picture show.

BOY WILLIE: I been up at Grace's house. Some nigger named Leroy come by but I had a chair up against the door. He got mad when he couldn't get in. He went off somewhere and I got out of there before he could come back. Berniece got mad when we came here.

LYMON: She say you was knocking over the lamp busting up the place.

BOY WILLIE: That was Grace doing all that.

LYMON: Wining Boy seen Sutter's ghost last night.

BOY WILLIE: Wining Boy's liable to see anything. I'm surprised he found the right house. Come on, I done called the man about the piano.

LYMON: What he say?

BOY WILLIE: He say to bring it on out. I told him I was calling for my sister, Miss Berniece Charles. I told him some man wanted to buy it for eleven hundred dollars and asked him if he would go any better. He said yeah, he would give me eleven hundred and fifty dollars for it if it was the same piano. I described it to him again and he told me to bring it out.

LYMON: Why didn't you tell him to come and pick it up?

BOY WILLIE: I didn't want to have no problem with Berniece. This way we just take it on out there and it be out the way. He want to charge twenty-five dollars to pick it up.

LYMON: You should have told him the man was gonna give you twelve hundred for it.

BOY WILLIE: I figure I was taking a chance with that eleven hundred. If I had told him twelve hundred he might have run off. Now I wish I had told him twelve-fifty. It's hard to figure out white folks sometimes.

LYMON: You might have been able to tell him anything. White folks got a lot of money.

BOY WILLIE: Come on, let's get it loaded before Berniece come back. Get that end over there. All you got to do is pick it up on that side. Don't worry about this side. You wanna stretch you' back for a minute?

LYMON: I'm ready.

BOY WILLIE: Get a real good grip on it now.

(The sound of SUTTER'S GHOST *is heard. They do not hear it.)*

LYMON: I got this end. You get that end.

BOY WILLIE: Wait till I say ready now. Alright. You got it good? You got a grip on it?

LYMON: Yeah, I got it. You lift up on that end.

BOY WILLIE: Ready? Lift!

(The piano will not budge.)

LYMON: Man, this piano is heavy! It's gonna take more than me and you to move this piano.

BOY WILLIE: We can do it. Come on—we did it before.

LYMON: Nigger—you crazy! That piano weighs five hundred pounds!

BOY WILLIE: I got three hundred pounds of it! I know you can carry two hundred pounds! You be lifting them cotton sacks! Come on lift this piano!

(They try to move the piano again without success.)

LYMON: It's stuck. Something holding it.

BOY WILLIE: How the piano gonna be stuck? We just moved it. Slide you' end out.

LYMON: Naw—we gonna need two or three more people. How this big old piano get in the house?

BOY WILLIE: I don't know how it got in the house. I know how it's going out though! You get on this end. I'll carry three hundred and fifty pounds of it. All you got to do is slide your end out. Ready?

(They switch sides and try again without success. DOAKER *enters from his room as they try to push and shove it.)*

LYMON: Hey, Doaker . . . how this piano get in the house?

DOAKER: Boy Willie, what you doing?

BOY WILLIE: I'm carrying this piano out the house. What it look like I'm doing? Come on, Lymon, let's try again.

DOAKER: Go on let the piano sit there till Berniece come home.

BOY WILLIE: You ain't got nothing to do with this, Doaker. This my business.

DOAKER: This is my house, nigger! I ain't gonna let you or nobody else carry nothing out of it. You ain't gonna carry nothing out of here without my permission!

BOY WILLIE: This is my piano. I don't need your permission to carry my belongings out of your house. This is mine. This ain't got nothing to do with you.

DOAKER: I say leave it over there till Berniece come home. She got part of it too. Leave it set there till you see what she say.

BOY WILLIE: I don't care what Berniece say. Come on, Lymon. I got this side.

DOAKER: Go on and cut it half in two if you want to. Just leave Berniece's half sitting over there. I can't tell you what to do with your piano. But I can't let you take her half out of here.

BOY WILLIE: Go on, Doaker. You ain't got nothing to do with this. I don't want you starting nothing now. Just go on and leave me alone. Come on, Lymon. I got this end.

*(*DOAKER *goes into his room.* BOY WILLIE *and* LYMON *prepare to move the piano.)*

LYMON: How we gonna get it in the truck?

BOY WILLIE: Don't worry about how we gonna get it on the truck. You got to get it out the house first.

LYMON: It's gonna take more than me and you to move this piano.

BOY WILLIE: Just lift up on that end, nigger!

(DOAKER *comes to the doorway of his room and stands.*)

DOAKER: *(Quietly with authority.)* Leave that piano set over there till Berniece come back. I don't care what you do with it then. But you gonna leave it sit over there right now.

BOY WILLIE: Alright . . . I'm gonna tell you this, Doaker. I'm going out of here . . . I'm gonna get me some rope . . . find me a plank and some wheels . . . and I'm coming back. Then I'm gonna carry that piano out of here . . . sell it and give Berniece half the money. See . . . now that's what I'm gonna do. And you . . . or nobody else is gonna stop me. Come on, Lymon . . . let's go get some rope and stuff. I'll be back, Doaker.

(BOY WILLIE *and* LYMON *exit. The lights go down on the scene.*)

Scene 5

(The lights come up. BOY WILLIE *sits on the sofa, screwing casters on a wooden plank.* MARETHA *is sitting on the piano stool.* DOAKER *sits at the table playing solitaire.)*

BOY WILLIE: *(To* MARETHA.) Then after that them white folks down around there started falling down their wells. You ever seen a well? A well got a wall around it. It's hard to fall down a well. You got to be leaning way over. Couldn't nobody figure out too much what was making these fellows fall down their well . . . so everybody says the Ghosts of the Yellow Dog must have pushed them. That's what everybody called them four men what got burned up in the boxcar.

MARETHA: Why they call them that?

BOY WILLIE: Cause the Yazoo Delta railroad got yellow boxcars. Sometime the way the whistle blow sound like an old dog howling so the people call it the Yellow Dog.

MARETHA: Anybody ever see the Ghosts?

BOY WILLIE: I told you they like the wind. Can you see the wind?

MARETHA: No.

BOY WILLIE: They like the wind you can't see them. But sometimes you be in trouble they might be around to help you. They say if you go where the Southern cross the Yellow Dog . . . you go to where them two railroads cross each other . . . and call out their names . . . they say they talk back to you. I don't know, I ain't never done that. But Uncle Wining Boy he say he been down there and talked to them. You have to ask him about that part.

(BERNIECE has entered from the front door.)

BERNIECE: Maretha, you go on and get ready for me to do your hair.

(MARETHA crosses to the steps.)

Boy Willie, I done told you to leave my house.

(To MARETHA.)

Go on, Maretha.

(MARETHA is hesitant about going up the stairs.)

BOY WILLIE: Don't be scared. Here, I'll go up there with you. If we see Sutter's ghost I'll put a whupping on him. Come on, Uncle Boy Willie going with you.

(BOY WILLIE and MARETHA exit up the stairs.)

BERNIECE: Doaker—what is going on here?
DOAKER: I come home and him and Lymon was moving the piano. I told them to leave it over there till you got home. He went out and got that board and them wheels. He say he gonna take that piano out of here and ain't nobody gonna stop him.
BERNIECE: I ain't playing with Boy Willie. I got Crawley's gun upstairs. He don't know but I'm through with it. Where Lymon go?
DOAKER: Boy Willie sent him for some rope just before you come in.
BERNIECE: I ain't studying Boy Willie or Lymon—or the rope. Boy Willie ain't taking that piano out this house. That's all there is to it.

(BOY WILLIE and MARETHA enter on the stairs. MARETHA carries a hot comb and a can of hair grease. BOY WILLIE crosses over and continues to screw the wheels on the board.)

MARETHA: Mama, all the hair grease is gone. There ain't but this little bit left.
BERNIECE: *(Gives her a dollar.)* Here . . . run across the street and get another can. You come straight back, too. Don't you be playing around out there. And watch the cars. Be careful when you cross the street.

(MARETHA exits out the front door.)

Boy Willie, I done told you to leave my house.

BOY WILLIE: I ain't in you' house. I'm in Doaker's house. If he ask me to leave
then I'll go on and leave. But consider me done left your part.

BERNIECE: Doaker, tell him to leave. Tell him to go on.

DOAKER: Boy Willie ain't done nothing for me to put him out of the house. I
told you if you can't get along just go on and don't have nothing to do with
each other.

BOY WILLIE: I ain't thinking about Berniece.

(He gets up and draws a line across the floor with his foot.)

There! Now I'm out of your part of the house. Consider me done left your
part. Soon as Lymon come back with that rope. I'm gonna take that piano
out of here and sell it.

BERNIECE: You ain't gonna touch that piano.

BOY WILLIE: Carry it out of here just as big and bold. Do like my daddy would
have done come time to get Sutter's land.

BERNIECE: I got something to make you leave it over there.

BOY WILLIE: It's got to come better than this thirty-two-twenty.

DOAKER: Why don't you stop all that! Boy Willie, go on and leave her alone.
You know how Berniece get. Why you wanna sit there and pick with her?

BOY WILLIE: I ain't picking with her. I told her the truth. She the one talking
about what she got. I just told her what she better have.

BERNIECE: That's alright, Doaker. Leave him alone.

BOY WILLIE: She trying to scare me. Hell, I ain't scared of dying. I look around
and see people dying every day. You got to die to make room for somebody
else. I had a dog that died. Wasn't nothing but a puppy. I picked it up and put
it in a bag and carried it up there to Reverend C. L. Thompson's church. I carried it up there and prayed and asked Jesus to make it live like he did the
man in the Bible. I prayed real hard. Knelt down and everything. Say ask in
Jesus' name. Well, I must have called Jesus' name two hundred times. I called
his name till my mouth got sore. I got up and looked in the bag and the dog
still dead. It ain't moved a muscle! I say, "Well, ain't nothing precious." And
then I went out and killed me a cat. That's when I discovered the power of
death. See, a nigger that ain't afraid to die is the worse kind of nigger for the
white man. He can't hold that power over you. That's what I learned when I
killed that cat. I got the power of death too. I can command him. I can call
him up. The white man don't like to see that. He don't like for you to stand
up and look him square in the eye and say, "I got it too." Then he got to deal
with you square up.

BERNIECE: That's why I don't talk to him, Doaker. You try and talk to him and
that's the only kind of stuff that comes out his mouth.

DOAKER: You say Avery went home to get his Bible?

BOY WILLIE: What Avery gonna do? Avery can't do nothing with me. I wish Avery would say something to me about this piano.

DOAKER: Berniece ain't said about that. Avery went home to get his Bible. He coming by to bless the house see if he can get rid of Sutter's ghost.

BOY WILLIE: Ain't nothing but a house full of ghosts down there at the church. What Avery look like chasing away somebody's ghost?

(MARETHA enters the front door.)

BERNIECE: Light that stove and set that comb over there to get hot. Get something to put around your shoulders.

BOY WILLIE: The Bible say an eye for an eye, a tooth for a tooth, and a life for a life. Tit for tat. But you and Avery don't want to believe that. You gonna pass up that part and pretend it ain't in there. Everything else you gonna agree with. But if you gonna agree with part of it you got to agree with all of it. You can't do nothing halfway. You gonna go at the Bible halfway. You gonna act like that part ain't in there. But you pull out the Bible and open it and see what it say. Ask Avery. He a preacher. He'll tell you it's in there. He the Good Shepherd. Unless he gonna shepherd you to heaven with half the Bible.

BERNIECE: Maretha, bring me that comb. Make sure it's hot.

(MARETHA brings the comb. BERNIECE begins to do her hair.)

BOY WILLIE: I will say this for Avery. He done figured out a path to go through life. I don't agree with it. But he done fixed it so he can go right through it real smooth. Hell, he liable to end up with a million dollars that he done got from selling bread and wine.

MARETHA: OWWWWWW!

BERNIECE: Be still, Maretha. If you was a boy I wouldn't be going through this.

BOY WILLIE: Don't you tell that girl that. Why you wanna tell her that?

BERNIECE: You ain't got nothing to do with this child.

BOY WILLIE: Telling her you wished she was a boy. How's that gonna make her feel?

BERNIECE: Boy Willie, go on and leave me alone.

DOAKER: Why don't you leave her alone? What you got to pick with her for? Why don't you go on out and see what's out there in the streets? Have something to tell the fellows down home.

BOY WILLIE: I'm waiting on Lymon to get back with that truck. Why don't you go on out and see what's out there in the streets? You ain't got to work tomorrow. Talking about me . . . why don't you go out there? It's Friday night.

DOAKER: I got to stay around here and keep you all from killing one another.

BOY WILLIE: You ain't got to worry about me. I'm gonna be here just as long as it takes Lymon to get back here with that truck. You ought to be talking to Berniece. Sitting up there telling Maretha she wished she was a boy. What kind of thing is that to tell a child? If you want to tell her something tell her about that piano. You ain't even told her about that piano. Like that's something to be ashamed of. Like she supposed to go off and hide somewhere about that piano. You ought to mark down on the calendar the day that Papa Boy Charles brought that piano into the house. You ought to mark that day down and draw a circle around it . . . and every year when it come up throw a party. Have a celebration. If you did that she wouldn't have no problem in life. She could walk around here with her head held high. I'm talking about a big party!

Invite everybody! Mark that day down with a special meaning. That way she know where she at in the world. You got her going out here thinking she wrong in the world. Like there ain't no part of it belong to her.

BERNIECE: Let me take care of my child. When you get one of your own then you can teach it what you want to teach it.

(DOAKER exits into his room.)

BOY WILLIE: What I want to bring a child into this world for? Why I wanna bring somebody else into all this for? I'll tell you this . . . If I was Rockefeller I'd have forty or fifty. I'd make one every day. Cause they gonna start out in life with all the advantages. I ain't got no advantages to offer nobody. Many is the time I looked at my daddy and seen him staring off at his hands. I got a little older I know what he was thinking. He sitting there saying, "I got these big old hands but what I'm gonna do with them? Best I can do is make a fifty-acre crop for Mr. Stovall. Got these big old hands capable of doing anything. I can take and build something with these hands. But where's the tools? All I got is these hands. Unless I go out here and kill me somebody and take what they got . . . it's a long row to hoe for me to get something of my own. So what I'm gonna do with these big old hands? What would you do?"

See now . . . if he had his own land he wouldn't have felt that way. If he had something under his feet that belonged to him he could stand up taller. That's what I'm talking about. Hell, the land is there for everybody. All you got to do is figure out how to get you a piece. Ain't no mystery to life. You just got to go out and meet it square on. If you got a piece of land you'll find everything else fall right into place. You can stand right up next to the white man and talk about the price of cotton . . . the weather, and anything else you want to talk about. If you teach that girl that she living at the bottom of life, she's gonna grow up and hate you.

BERNIECE: I'm gonna teach her the truth. That's just where she living. Only she ain't got to stay there.

(To MARETHA.)

Turn you' head over to the other side.

BOY WILLIE: This might be your bottom but it ain't mine. I'm living at the top of life. I ain't gonna just take my life and throw it away at the bottom. I'm in the world like everybody else. They way I see it everybody else got to come up a little taste to be where I am.

BERNIECE: You right at the bottom with the rest of us.

BOY WILLIE: I'll tell you this . . . and ain't a living soul can put a come back on it. If you believe that's where you at then you gonna act that way. If you act that way then that's where you gonna be. It's as simple as that. Ain't no mystery to life. I don't know how you come to believe that stuff. Crawley didn't think like that. He wasn't living at the bottom of life. Papa Boy Charles and Mama Ola wasn't living at the bottom of life. You ain't never heard them say nothing like that. They would have taken a strap to you if they heard you say something like that.

(DOAKER enters from his room.)

Hey, Doaker . . . Berniece say the colored folks is living at the bottom of life. I tried to tell her if she think that . . . that's where she gonna be. You think you living at the bottom of life? Is that how you see yourself?

DOAKER: I'm just living the best way I know how. I ain't thinking about no top or no bottom.

BOY WILLIE: That's what I tried to tell Berniece. I don't know where she got that from. That sound like something Avery would say. Avery think cause the white man give him a turkey for Thanksgiving that makes him better than everybody else. That's gonna raise him out of the bottom of life. I don't need nobody to give me a turkey. I can get my own turkey. All you have to do is get out my way. I'll get me two or three turkeys.

BERNIECE: You can't even get a chicken let alone two or three turkeys. Talking about get out your way. Ain't nobody in your way.

(To MARETHA.*)*

Straighten your head, Maretha! Don't be bending down like that. Hold your head up!

(To BOY WILLIE.*)*

All you got going for you is talk. You' whole life that's all you ever had going for you.

BOY WILLIE: See now . . . I'll tell you something about me. I done strung along and strung along. Going this way and that. Whatever way would lead me to a moment of peace. That's all I want. To be as easy with everything. But I wasn't born to that. I was born to a time of fire.

The world ain't wanted no part of me. I could see that since I was about seven. The world say it's better off without me. See, Berniece accept that. She trying to come up to where she can prove something to the world. Hell, the world a better place cause of me. I don't see it like Berniece. I got a heart that beats here and it beats just as loud as the next fellow's. Don't care if he black or white. Sometime it beats louder. When it beats louder, then everybody can hear it. Some people get scared of that. Like Berniece. Some people get scared to hear a nigger's heart beating. They think you ought to lay low with that heart. Make it beat quiet and go along with everything the way it is. But my mama ain't birthed me for nothing. So what I got to do? I got to mark my passing on the road. Just like you write on a tree, "Boy Willie was here."

That's all I'm trying to do with that piano. Trying to put my mark on the road. Like my daddy done. My heart say for me to sell that piano and get me some land so I can make a life for myself to live in my own way. Other than that I ain't thinking about nothing Berniece got to say.

(There is a knock at the door. BOY WILLIE *crosses to it and yanks it open thinking it is* LYMON. AVERY *enters. He carries a Bible.)*

BOY WILLIE: Where you been, nigger? Aw . . . I thought you was Lymon. Hey, Berniece, look who's here.

BERNIECE: Come on in, Avery. Don't you pay Boy Willie no mind.

BOY WILLIE: Hey . . . Hey, Avery . . . tell me this . . . can you get to heaven with half the Bible?

BERNIECE: Boy Willie . . . I done told you to leave me alone.

BOY WILLIE: I just ask the man a question. He can answer. He don't need you to speak for him. Avery . . . if you only believe on half the Bible and don't want to accept the other half . . . you think God let you in heaven? Or do you got to have the whole Bible? Tell Berniece . . . if you only believe in part of it . . . when you see God he gonna ask you why you ain't believed in the other part . . . then he gonna send you straight to Hell.

AVERY: You got to be born again. Jesus say unless a man be born again he cannot come unto the Father and who so ever heareth my words and believeth them not shall be cast into a fiery pit.

BOY WILLIE: That's what I was trying to tell Berniece. You got to believe in it all. You can't go at nothing halfway. She think she going to heaven with half the Bible.

(To BERNIECE.*)*

You hear that . . . Jesus say you got to believe in it all.

BERNIECE: You keep messing with me.

BOY WILLIE: I ain't thinking about you.

DOAKER: Come on in, Avery, and have a seat. Don't pay neither one of them no mind. They been arguing all day.

BERNIECE: Come on in, Avery.

AVERY: How's everybody in here?

BERNIECE: Here, set this comb back over there on that stove.

(To AVERY.*)*

Don't pay Boy Willie no mind. He been around here bothering me since I come home from work.

BOY WILLIE: Boy Willie ain't bothering you. Boy Willie ain't bothering nobody. I'm just waiting on Lymon to get back. I ain't thinking about you. You heard the man say I was right and you still don't want to believe it. You just wanna go and make up anythin'. Well there's Avery . . . there's the preacher . . . go on and ask him.

AVERY: Berniece believe in the Bible. She been baptized.

BOY WILLIE: What about that part that say an eye for an eye a tooth for a tooth and a life for a life? Ain't that in there?

DOAKER: What they say down there at the bank, Avery?

AVERY: Oh, they talked to me real nice. I told Berniece . . . they say maybe they let me borrow the money. They done talked to my boss down at work and everything.

DOAKER: That's what I told Berniece. You working every day you ought to be able to borrow some money.

AVERY: I'm getting more people in my congregation every day. Berniece says she gonna be the Deaconess. I get me my church I can get married and settled down. That's what I told Berniece.

DOAKER: That be nice. You all ought to go ahead and get married. Berniece don't need to be by herself. I tell her that all the time.

BERNIECE: I ain't said nothing about getting married. I said I was thinking about it.

DOAKER: Avery get him his church you all can make it nice.

(To AVERY.*)*

Berniece said you was coming by to bless the house.

AVERY: Yeah, I done read up on my Bible. She asked me to come by and see if I can get rid of Sutter's ghost.

BOY WILLIE: Ain't no ghost in this house. That's all in Berniece's head. Go on up there and see if you see him. I'll give you a hundred dollars if you see him. That's all in her imagination.

DOAKER: Well, let her find that out then. If Avery blessing the house is gonna make her feel better . . . what you got to do with it?

AVERY: Berniece say Maretha seen him too. I don't know, but I found a part in the Bible to bless the house. If he is here then that ought to make him go.

BOY WILLIE: You worse than Berniece believing all that stuff. Talking about . . . if he here. Go on up there and find out. I been up there I ain't seen him. If you reading from that Bible gonna make him leave out of Berniece imagination, well, you might be right. But if you talking about . . .

DOAKER: Boy Willie, why don't you just be quiet? Getting all up in the man's business. This ain't got nothing to do with you. Let him go ahead and do what he gonna do.

BOY WILLIE: I ain't stopping him. Avery ain't got no power to do nothing.

AVERY: Oh, I ain't got no power. God got the power! God got power over
   everything in His creation. God can do anything. God say, "As I commandeth
   so it shall be." God said, "Let there be light," and there was light. He made
   the world in six days and rested on the seventh. God's got a wonderful power.
   He got power over life and death. Jesus raised Lazareth from the dead. They
   was getting ready to bury him and Jesus told him say, "Rise up and walk." He
   got up and walked and the people made great rejoicing at the power of God.
   I ain't worried about him chasing away a little old ghost!

(There is a knock at the door. BOY WILLIE *goes to answer it.* LYMON *enters carrying a coil of rope.)*

BOY WILLIE: Where you been? I been waiting on you and you run off some-
   where.
LYMON: I ran into Grace. I stopped and bought her drink. She say she gonna
   go to the picture show with me.
BOY WILLIE: I ain't thinking about no Grace nothing.
LYMON: Hi, Berniece.
BOY WILLIE: Give me that rope and get up on this side of the piano.
DOAKER: Boy Willie, don't start nothing now. Leave the piano alone.
BOY WILLIE: Get that board there, Lymon. Stay out of this, Doaker.

*(*BERNIECE *exits up the stairs.)*

DOAKER: You just can't take the piano. How you gonna take the piano?
   Berniece ain't said nothing about selling that piano.
BOY WILLIE: She ain't got to say nothing. Come on, Lymon. We got to lift one
   end at a time up on the board. You got to watch so that the board don't slide
   up under there.
LYMON: What we gonna do with the rope?
BOY WILLIE: Let me worry about the rope. You just get up on this side over
   here with me.

*(*BERNIECE *enters from the stairs. She has her hand in her pocket where she
has Crawley's gun.)*

AVERY: Boy Willie ... Berniece ... why don't you all sit down and talk this out
   now?
BERNIECE: Ain't nothing to talk out.
BOY WILLIE: I'm through talking to Berniece. You can talk to Berniece till you
   get blue in the face, and it don't make no difference. Get up on that side, Ly-
   mon. Throw that rope around there and tie it to the leg.
LYMON: Wait a minute ... wait a minute, Boy Willie. Berniece got to say. Hey,
   Berniece ... did you tell Boy Willie he could take this piano?

BERNIECE: Boy Willie ain't taking nothing out of my house but himself. Now you let him go ahead and try.

BOY WILLIE: Come on, Lymon, get up on this side with me.

(LYMON stands undecided.)

Come on, nigger! What you standing there for?

LYMON: Maybe Berniece is right, Boy Willie. Maybe you shouldn't sell it.

AVERY: You all ought to sit down and talk it out. See if you can come to an agreement.

DOAKER: That's what I been trying to tell them. Seem like one of them ought to respect the other one's wishes.

BERNIECE: I wish Boy Willie would go on and leave my house. That's what I wish. Now, he can respect that. Cause he's leaving here one way or another.

BOY WILLIE: What you mean one way or another? What's that supposed to mean? I ain't scared of no gun.

DOAKER: Come on, Berniece, leave him alone with that.

BOY WILLIE: I don't care what Berniece say. I'm selling my half. I can't help it if her half got to go along with it. It ain't like I'm trying to cheat her out of her half. Come on, Lymon.

LYMON: Berniece . . . I got to do this . . . Boy Willie say he gonna give you half of the money . . . say he want to get Sutter's land.

BERNIECE: Go on, Lymon. Just go on . . . I done told Boy Willie what to do.

BOY WILLIE: Here, Lymon . . . put that rope up over there.

LYMON: Boy Willie, you sure you want to do this? The way I figure it . . . I might be wrong . . . but I figure she gonna shoot you first.

BOY WILLIE: She just gonna have to shoot me.

BERNIECE: Maretha, get on out the way. Get her out the way, Doaker.

DOAKER: Go on, do what your mama told you.

BERNIECE: Put her in your room.

(MARETHA exits to Doaker's room. BOY WILLIE and LYMON try to lift the piano. The door opens and WINING BOY enters. He has been drinking.)

WINING BOY: Man, these niggers around here! I stopped down there at Seefus. . . . These folks standing around talking about Patchneck Red's coming. They jumping back and getting off the sidewalk talking about Patchneck Red this and Patchneck Red that. Come to find out . . . you know who they was talking about? Old John D. from up around Tyler! Used to run around with Otis Smith. He got everybody scared of him. Calling him Patchneck Red. They don't know I whupped the nigger's head in one time.

BOY WILLIE: Just make sure that board don't slide, Lymon.

LYMON: I got this side. You watch that side.

WINING BOY: Hey, Boy Willie, what you got? I know you got a pint stuck up in your coat.

BOY WILLIE: Wining Boy, get out the way!

WINING BOY: Hey, Doaker. What you got? Gimme a drink. I want a drink.

DOAKER: It look like you had enough of whatever it was. Come talking about
"What you got?" You ought to be trying to find somewhere to lay down.

WINING BOY: I ain't worried about no place to lay down. I can always find me
a place to lay down in Berniece's house. Ain't that right, Berniece?

BERNIECE: Wining Boy, sit down somewhere. You been out there drinking all
day. Come in here smelling like an old polecat. Sit on down there, you don't
need nothing to drink.

DOAKER: You know Berniece don't like all that drinking.

WINING BOY: I ain't disrespecting Berniece. Berniece, am I disrespecting you?
I'm just trying to be nice. I been with strangers all day and they treated me
like family. I come in here to family and you treat me like a stranger. I don't
need your whiskey. I can buy my own. I wanted your company, not your
whiskey.

DOAKER: Nigger, why don't you go upstairs and lay down? You don't need
nothing to drink.

WINING BOY: I ain't thinking about no laying down. Me and Boy Willie fixing
to party. Ain't that right, Boy Willie? Tell him. I'm fixing to play me some piano. Watch this.

(WINING BOY *sits down at the piano.*)

BOY WILLIE: Come on, Wining Boy! Me and Lymon fixing to move the piano.

WINING BOY: Wait a minute . . . wait a minute. This a song I wrote for Cleotha.
I wrote this song in memory of Cleotha.

(*He begins to play and sing.*)

Hey little woman what's the matter with you now
Had a storm last night and blowed the line all down

Tell me how long
Is I got to wait
Can I get it now
Or must I hesitate

It takes a hesitating stocking in her hesitating shoe
It takes a hesitating woman wanna sing the blues

Tell me how long
Is I got to wait
Can I kiss you now
Or must I hesitate.

BOY WILLIE: Come on, Wining Boy, get up! Get up, Wining Boy! Me and Lymon's fixing to move the piano.

WINING BOY: Naw . . . Naw . . . you ain't gonna move this piano!

BOY WILLIE: Get out the way, Wining Boy.

(WINING BOY, *his back to the piano, spreads his arms out over the piano.*)

WINING BOY: You ain't taking this piano out the house. You got to take me with it!

BOY WILLIE: Get on out the way, Wining Boy! Doaker get him!

(*There is a knock on the door.*)

BERNIECE: I got him, Doaker. Come on, Wining Boy. I done told Boy Willie he ain't taking the piano.

(BERNIECE *tries to take* WINING BOY *away from the piano.*)

WINING BOY: He got to take me with it!

(DOAKER *goes to answer the door.* GRACE *enters.*)

GRACE: Is Lymon here?

DOAKER: Lymon.

WINING BOY: He ain't gonna let him take it.

BERNIECE: I ain't gonna let him take it.

GRACE: I thought you was coming back. I ain't gonna sit in that truck all day.

LYMON: I told you I was coming back.

GRACE: (*Sees* BOY WILLIE.) Oh, hi, Boy Willie. Lymon told me you was gone back down South.

LYMON: I said he was going back. I didn't say he had left already.

GRACE: That's what you told me.

BERNIECE: Lymon, you got to take your company someplace else.

LYMON: Berniece, this is Grace. That there is Berniece. That's Boy Willie's sister.

GRACE: Nice to meet you.

(*To* LYMON.)

I ain't gonna sit out in that truck all day. You told me you was gonna take me to the movie.

LYMON: I told you I had something to do first. You supposed to wait on me.

BERNIECE: Lymon, just go on and leave. Take Grace or whoever with you. Just go on get out my house.

BOY WILLIE: You gonna help me move this piano first, nigger!

LYMON: *(To* GRACE.*)* I got to help Boy Willie move the piano first.

(Everybody but GRACE *suddenly senses* SUTTER*'s presence.)*

GRACE: I ain't waiting on you. Told me you was coming right back. Now you got to move a piano. You just like all the other men.

*(*GRACE *now senses something.)*

Something ain't right here. I knew I shouldn't have come back up in this house.

*(*GRACE *exits.)*

LYMON: Hey, Grace! I'll be right back, Boy Willie.
BOY WILLIE: Where you going, nigger?
LYMON: I'll be back. I got to take Grace home.
BOY WILLIE: Come on, let's move the piano first!
LYMON: I got to take Grace home. I told you I'll be back.

*(*LYMON *exits.* BOY WILLIE *exits and calls after him.)*

BOY WILLIE: Come on, Lymon! Hey . . . Lymon! Lymon . . . come on!

(Again, the presence of SUTTER *is felt.)*

WINING BOY: Hey, Doaker, did you feel that? Hey, Berniece . . . did you get cold? Hey, Doaker . . .
DOAKER: What you calling me for?
WINING BOY: I believe that's Sutter.
DOAKER: Well, let him stay up there. As long as he don't mess with me.
BERNIECE: Avery, go on and bless the house.
DOAKER: You need to bless that piano. That's what you need to bless. It ain't done nothing but cause trouble. If you gonna bless anything go on and bless that.
WINING BOY: Hey, Doaker, if he gonna bless something let him bless everything. The kitchen . . . the upstairs. Go on and bless it all.
BOY WILLIE: Ain't no ghost in this house. He need to bless Berniece's head. That's what he need to bless.
AVERY: Seem like that piano's causing all the trouble. I can bless that. Berniece, put me some water in that bottle.

*(*AVERY *takes a small bottle from his pocket and hands it to* BERNIECE, *who goes into the kitchen to get water.* AVERY *takes a candle from his pocket and lights it. He gives it to* BERNIECE *as she gives him the water.)*

Hold this candle. Whatever you do make sure it don't go out.

O Holy Father we gather here this evening in the Holy Name to cast out the spirit of one James Sutter. May this vial of water be empowered with thy spirit. May each drop of it be a weapon and a shield against the presence of all evil and may it be a cleansing and blessing of this humble abode.

Just as Our Father taught us how to pray so He say, "I will prepare a table for you in the midst of mine enemies," and in His hands we place ourselves to come unto his presence. Where there is Good so shall it cause Evil to scatter to the Four Winds.

(He throws water at the piano at each commandment.)

AVERY: Get thee behind me, Satan! Get thee behind the face of Righteousness as we Glorify His Holy Name! Get thee behind the Hammer of Truth that breaketh down the Wall of Falsehood! Father. Father. Praise. Praise. We ask in Jesus' name and call forth the power of the Holy Spirit as it is written. . . .

(He opens the Bible and reads from it.)

I will sprinkle clean water upon thee and ye shall be clean.

BOY WILLIE: All this old preaching stuff. Hell, just tell him to leave.

(AVERY continues reading throughout BOY WILLIE's outburst.)

AVERY: I will sprinkle clean water upon you and you shall be clean: from all your uncleanliness, and from all your idols, will I cleanse you. A new heart also will I give you, and a new spirit will I put within you: and I will take out of your flesh the heart of stone, and I will give you a heart of flesh. And I will put my spirit within you, and cause you to walk in my statutes, and ye shall keep my judgments, and do them.

(BOY WILLIE grabs a pot of water from the stove and begins to fling it around the room.)

BOY WILLIE: Hey Sutter! Sutter! Get your ass out this house! Sutter! Come on and get some of this water! You done drowned in the well, come on and get some more of this water!

(BOY WILLIE is working himself into a frenzy as he runs around the room throwing water and calling SUTTER's name. AVERY continues reading.)

BOY WILLIE: Come on, Sutter!

(He starts up the stairs.)

Come on, get some water! Come on, Sutter!

(The sound of SUTTER'S GHOST *is heard. As* BOY WILLIE *approaches the steps he is suddenly thrown back by the unseen force, which is choking him. As he struggles he frees himself, then dashes up the stairs.)*

BOY WILLIE: Come on, Sutter!
AVERY: *(Continuing.)* A new heart also will I give you and a new spirit will I put within you: and I will take out of your flesh the heart of stone, and I will give you a heart of flesh. And I will put my spirit within you, and cause you to walk in my statutes, and ye shall keep my judgments, and do them.

(There are loud sounds heard from upstairs as BOY WILLIE *begins to wrestle with* SUTTER'S GHOST. *It is a life-and-death struggle fraught with perils and faultless terror.* BOY WILLIE *is thrown down the stairs.* AVERY *is stunned into silence.* BOY WILLIE *picks himself up and dashes back upstairs.)*

AVERY: Berniece, I can't do it.

(There are more sounds heard from upstairs. DOAKER *and* WINING BOY *stare at one another in stunned disbelief. It is in this moment, from somewhere old, that* BERNIECE *realizes what she must do. She crosses to the piano. She begins to play. The song is found piece by piece. It is an old urge to song that is both a commandment and a plea. With each repetition it gains in strength. It is intended as an exorcism and a dressing for battle. A rustle of wind blowing across two continents.)*

BERNIECE: *(Singing.)*
I want you to help me
I want you to help me
I want you to help me
I want you to help me
I want you to help me
I want you to help me
Mama Berniece
I want you to help me
Mama Esther
I want you to help me
Papa Boy Charles
I want you to help me
Mama Ola
I want you to help me

I want you to help me
I want you to help me

I want you to help me
I want you to help me
I want you to help me
I want you to help me
I want you to help me
I want you to help me

(The sound of a train approaching is heard. The noise upstairs subsides.)

BOY WILLIE: Come on, Sutter! Come back, Sutter!

(BERNIECE begins to chant:)

BERNIECE: Thank you.
   Thank you.
   Thank you.

(A calm comes over the house. MARETHA enters from DOAKER's room. BOY WILLIE enters on the stairs. He pauses a moment to watch BERNIECE at the piano.)

BERNIECE: Thank you.
   Thank you.
BOY WILLIE: Wining Boy, you ready to go back down home? Hey, Doaker, what time the train leave?
DOAKER: You still got time to make it.

(MARETHA crosses and embraces BOY WILLIE.)

BOY WILLIE: Hey Berniece . . . if you and Maretha don't keep playing on that piano . . . ain't no telling . . . me and Sutter both liable to be back.

(He exits.)

BERNIECE: Thank you.

(The lights go down to black.)

Study and Discussion Questions

1. What clues from the play help you to situate it in a time period? Why do you think the historical period is not specified in the stage directions, or at the beginning of the play, even though we know that August Wilson has been creating a cycle of plays that would represent the African American experience for each decade of the twentieth century?

2. If it is a stereotype that black people like watermelons, why do you think Wilson turns this stereotype around, and makes white people clamor for watermelons in Act II, scene 1? Think about how the characters describe the people buying watermelons.

3. How does Avery's dream (in Act I, scene 1) connect to the rest of the play?

4. How would you characterize the differences between Boy Willie and Berniece? Think about Berniece in relation to W. E. B. Du Bois's idea of the "talented tenth" and the class differences between blacks in the early twentieth century.

5. After slavery was legally abolished, the economic oppression of African-Americans took new forms in the United States. How are these forms illustrated in *The Piano Lesson?*

6. Why does Boy Willie want Sutter's land? Why does Berniece want the piano? How are their desires similar, and how are they different?

7. Discuss the piano as a central image in the play. What are the carvings on the piano? Why are they there? How are they a kind of history and/or record of Berneice and Boy Willie's family? How is their family history also connected to the Sutter land?

8. What is the relationship in *The Piano Lesson* between history and memory?

9. Ownership is an important concept in this play. What are the different kinds of ownership represented? What does ownership mean to the different characters?

9. *The Piano Lesson,* like most of August Wilson's plays, is as much about gender as it is about race and social class. What is Wilson saying about men and women in this play?

10. Discuss the issues of blame and responsibility brought up by Crawley's death, especially at the end of Act I, scene 2.

11. How do the different characters' relationships to money reflect their personalities?

12. How does *The Piano Lesson* present both the North and the South for African-Americans?

13. The stage directions repeatedly say, "The sound of Sutter's ghost is heard." What do you think this sound is? Why is sound the only physical representation of Sutter on stage?

14. Many of the stage directions describe intangible elements of setting and character. List several of these elements. If you were directing the play, how would you incorporate them into the production?

Writing Suggestions

1. Boy Willie and Berniece have different ideas about what the piano symbolizes and what its purpose should be. Examine these different opinions, and write an essay about the piano as a symbol of the past. What kinds of relationships to the past are represented? How does the meaning of the piano change during the course of the play?

2. Doaker gives a speech in Act I, scene 1 about rail travel; it contains various ideas about mobility and human nature. Summarize his speech, and talk about the undertones of his words. How does this speech connect to the rest of the play?

3. Music plays an important role in *The Piano Lesson*. Research some of the songs in this play in the context of music popular in black communities at the time and write a paper about what you find.
4. Wilson's play contains a lot of magical and/or mystical elements, and some critics have suggested it fits into the tradition of magical realism. Research magical realism, and argue for or against this designation for *The Piano Lesson*.

Critical Resources

1. Bogumil, Mary. *Understanding August Wilson*. Columbia: University of South Carolina Press, 1998.
2. Nadel, Alan, ed. *May All Your Fences Have Gates: Essays on the Drama of August Wilson*. Iowa City: University of Iowa Press, 1994.
3. Shager, Yvonne. *August Wilson: A Research and Production Sourcebook*. Westport, CT: Greenwood Press, 1998.
4. Shannon, Sandra. *The Dramatic Vision of August Wilson*. Washington, DC: Howard University Press, 1995.
5. Snodgrass, Mary. *August Wilson, a Literary Companion*. Jefferson, NC: McFarland, 2004.

Nonfiction

MERIDEL LE SUEUR (1899–1996)

Meridel Le Sueur was born in Iowa and attended high school in Kansas but did not finish. She lived in an anarchist commune in New York City, worked briefly as an actress in Hollywood, and in the late 1920s began publishing journalism and fiction. Her political activism led in the 1950s to her blacklisting, and the FBI intimidated publishers into rejecting her work. She was rediscovered by feminists in the 1970s and a number of her earlier works were reprinted. Much of Le Sueur's writing is set in the American Midwest, from frontier times to urban life in the twentieth century yet rather than reproducing typical stereotypes, Le Sueur sought to dismantle any simple notions about Midwestern life. Permeated with working-class experience, Le Sueur's vision of this landscape and its democratic possibilities is less about romanticized individualism and more about the contradictions inherent in social and class struggle. Among her writings are a novel, The Girl *(1939; first published in 1978) and the collections* Annunciation *(1935),* Salute to Spring *(1940),* Harvest: Collected Stories *(1977),* I Hear Men Talking and Other Stories *(1984), and* Ripening: Selected Work 1927–1980 *(1986). In "Women on the Breadlines," originally published in 1932, Le Sueur meditates on the neglect of unemployed and sometimes homeless women during the pre–New Deal years of the Great Depression.*

Women on the Breadlines (1932)

I am sitting in the city free employment bureau. It's the women's section. We have been sitting here now for four hours. We sit here every day, waiting for a job. There are no jobs. Most of us have had no breakfast. Some have had scant rations for over a year. Hunger makes a human being lapse into a state of lethargy, especially city hunger. Is there any place else in the world where a human being is supposed to go hungry amidst plenty without an outcry, without protest, where only the boldest steal or kill for bread, and the timid crawl the streets, hunger like the beak of a terrible bird at the vitals?

We sit looking at the floor. No one dares think of the coming winter. There are only a few more days of summer. Everyone is anxious to get work to lay up something for that long siege of bitter cold. But there is no work. Sitting in the room we all know it. That is why we don't talk much. We look at the floor dreading to see that knowledge in each other's eyes. There is a kind of humiliation in it. We look away from each other. We look at the floor. It's too terrible to see this animal terror in each other's eyes.

So we sit hour after hour, day after day, waiting for a job to come in. There are many women for a single job. A thin sharp woman sits inside a wire cage looking at a book. For four hours we have watched her looking at that book. She has a hard little eye. In the small bare room there are half a dozen women sitting on the benches waiting. Many come and go. Our faces are all familiar to each other, for we wait here every day.

This is a domestic employment bureau. Most of the women who come here are middle-aged, some have families, some have raised their families and are now alone, some have men who are out of work. Hard times and the man leaves to hunt for work. He doesn't find it. He drifts on. The woman probably doesn't hear from him for a long time. She expects it. She isn't surprised. She struggles alone to feed the many mouths. Sometimes she gets help from the charities. If she's clever she can get herself a good living from the charities, if she's naturally a lick spittle, naturally a little docile and cunning. If she's proud then she starves silently, leaving her children to find work, coming home after a day's searching to wrestle with her house, her children.

Some such story is written on the faces of all these women. There are young girls too, fresh from the country. Some are made brazen too soon by the city. There is a great exodus of girls from the farms into the city now. Thousands of farms have been vacated completely in Minnesota. The girls are trying to get work. The prettier ones can get jobs in the stores when there are any, or waiting on table, but these jobs are only for the attractive and the adroit. The others, the real peasants, have a more difficult time.

Bernice sits next to me. She is a Polish woman of thirty-five. She has been working in people's kitchens for fifteen years or more. She is large, her great body in mounds, her face brightly scrubbed. She has a peasant mind and finds it hard even yet to understand the maze of the city where trickery is worth more than brawn. Her blue eyes are not clever but slow and trusting. She suffers from loneliness and lack of talk. When you speak to her, her face lifts and brightens as if you had spoken through a great darkness, and she talks magically of little things as if the weather were magic, or tells some crazy tale of her adventures on the city streets, embellishing them in bright colors until they hang heavy and thick like embroidery. She loves the city anyhow. It's exciting to her, like a bazaar. She loves to go shopping and get a bargain, hunting out the places where stale bread and cakes can be had for a few cents. She likes walking the streets looking for men to take her to a picture show. Sometimes she goes to five picture shows in one day, or she sits through one the entire day until she knows all the dialog by heart.

She came to the city a young girl from a Wisconsin farm. The first thing that happened to her, a charlatan dentist took out all her good shining teeth and the fifty dollars she had saved working in a canning factory. After that she met men in the park who told her how to look out for herself, corrupting her peasant mind, teaching her to mistrust everyone. Sometimes now she forgets to mistrust everyone and gets taken in. They taught her to get what she could for nothing, to count her change, to go back if she found herself cheated, to demand her rights.

She lives alone in little rooms. She bought seven dollars' worth of second-hand furniture eight years ago. She rents a room for perhaps three dollars a month in an attic, sometimes in a cold house. Once the house where she stayed was condemned and everyone else moved out and she lived there all winter alone on the top floor. She spent only twenty-five dollars all winter.

She wants to get married but she sees what happens to her married friends, left with children to support, worn out before their time. So she stays single. She is virtuous. She is slightly deaf from hanging out clothes in winter. She had done people's washing and cooking for fifteen years and in that time saved thirty dollars. Now she hasn't worked steady for a year and she has spent the thirty dollars. She had dreamed of having a little house or a houseboat perhaps with a spot of ground for a few chickens. This dream she will never realize.

She has lost all her furniture now along with the dream. A married friend whose husband is gone gives her a bed for which she pays by doing a great deal of work for the woman. She comes here every day now sitting bewildered, her pudgy hands folded in her lap. She is hungry. Her great flesh has begun to hang in folds. She has been living on crackers. Sometimes a box of crackers lasts a week. She has a friend who's a baker and he sometimes steals the stale loaves and brings them to her.

A girl we have seen every day all summer went crazy yesterday at the YW. She went into hysterics, stamping her feet and screaming.

She hadn't had work for eight months. "You've got to give me something," she kept saying. The woman in charge flew into a rage that probably came from days and days of suffering on her part, because she is unable to give jobs, having none. She flew into a rage at the girl and there they were facing each other in a rage both helpless, helpless. This woman told me once that she could hardly bear the suffering she saw, hardly hear it, that she couldn't eat sometimes and had nightmares at night.

So they stood there, the two women, in a rage, the girl weeping and the woman shouting at her. In the eight months of unemployment she had gotten ragged, and the woman was shouting that she would not send her out like that. "Why don't you shine your shoes?" she kept scolding the girl, and the girl kept sobbing and sobbing because she was starving.

"We can't recommend you like that," the harassed YWCA woman said, knowing she was starving, unable to do anything. And the girls and the women sat docilely, their eyes on the ground, ashamed to look at each other, ashamed of something.

Sitting here waiting for a job, the women have been talking in low voices about the girl Ellen. They talk in low voices with not too much pity for her, unable to see through the mist of their own torment. "What happened to Ellen?" one of them asks. She knows the answer already. We all know it.

A young girl who went around with Ellen tells about seeing her last evening back of a cafe downtown, outside the kitchen door, kicking, showing her legs so that the cook came out and gave her some food and some men gathered in the alley and threw small coin on the ground for a look at her legs. And the girl says enviously that Ellen had a swell breakfast and treated her to one too, that cost two dollars.

A scrub woman whose hips are bent forward from stooping with hands gnarled like watersoaked branches clicks her tongue in disgust. No one saves their money, she says, a little money and these foolish young things buy a hat, a dollar for breakfast, a bright scarf. And they do. If you've ever been without money, or food, something very strange happens when you get a bit of money, a kind of madness. You don't care. You can't remember that you had no money before, that the money will be gone. You can remember nothing but that there is the money for which you have been suffering. Now here it is. A lust takes hold of you. You see food in the windows. In imagination you eat hugely; you taste a thousand meals. You look in windows. Colors are brighter; you buy something to dress up in. An excitement takes hold of you. You know it is suicide but you can't help it. You must have food, dainty, splendid food, and a bright hat so once again you feel blithe, rid of that ratty gnawing shame.

"I guess she'll go on the street now," a thin woman says faintly, and no one takes the trouble to comment further. Like every commodity now the body is difficult to sell and the girls say you're lucky if you get fifty cents.

It's very difficult and humiliating to sell one's body.

Perhaps it would make it clear if one were to imagine having to go out on the street to sell, say, one's overcoat. Suppose you have to sell your coat so you can have breakfast and a place to sleep, say, for fifty cents. You decide to sell your only coat. You take it off and put it on your arm. The street, that has before been just a street, now becomes a mart, something entirely different. You must approach someone now and admit you are destitute and are now selling your clothes, your most intimate possessions. Everyone will watch you talking to the stranger showing him your overcoat, what a good coat it is. People will stop and watch curiously. You will be quite naked on the street. It is even harder to try to sell one's self, more humiliating. It is even humiliating to try to sell one's labor. When there is no buyer.

The thin woman opens the wire cage. There's a job for a nursemaid, she says. The old gnarled women, like old horses, know that no one will have them walk the streets with the young so they don't move. Ellen's friend gets up and goes to the window. She is unbelievably jaunty. I know she hasn't had work since last January. But she has a flare of life in her that glows like a tiny red flame and some tenacious thing, perhaps only youth, keeps it burning bright. Her legs are thin but the runs in her old stockings are neatly mended clear down her flat shank. Two bright spots of rouge conceal her pallor. A narrow belt is drawn tightly around her thin waist, her long shoulders stoop and the blades show. She runs wild as a colt hunting pleasure, hunting sustenance.

It's one of the great mysteries of the city where women go when they are out of work and hungry. There are not many women in the bread line. There are no flop houses for women as there are for men, where a bed can be had for a quarter or less. You don't see women lying on the floor at the mission in the free flops. They obviously don't sleep in the jungle or under newspapers in the park. There is no law I suppose against their being in these places but the fact is they rarely are.

Yet there must be as many women out of jobs in cities and suffering extreme poverty as there are men. What happens to them? Where do they go? Try to get into the YW without any money or looking down at heel. Charities take care of very few and only those that are called "deserving." The lone girl is under suspicion by the virgin women who dispense charity.

I've lived in cities for many months broke, without help, too timid to get in bread lines. I've known many women to live like this until they simply faint on the street from privations, without saying a word to anyone. A woman will shut herself up in a room until it is taken away from her, and eat a cracker a day and be as quiet as a mouse so there are no social statistics concerning her.

I don't know why it is, but a woman will do this unless she has dependents, will go for weeks verging on starvation, crawling in some hole, going through the streets ashamed, sitting in libraries, parks, going for days without speaking to a living soul like some exiled beast, keeping the runs mended in her stockings, shut up in terror in her own misery, until she becomes too super-sensitive and timid to even ask for a job.

Bernice says even strange men she has met in the park have sometimes, that is in better days, given her a loan to pay her room rent. She has always paid them back.

In the afternoon the young girls, to forget the hunger and the deathly torture and fear of being jobless, try to pick up a man to take them to a ten-cent show. They never go to more expensive ones, but they can always find a man willing to spend a dime to have the company of a girl for the afternoon.

Sometimes a girl facing the night without shelter will approach a man for lodging. A woman always asks a man for help. Rarely another woman. I have known girls to sleep in men's rooms for the night on a pallet without molestation and be given breakfast in the morning.

It's no wonder these young girls refuse to marry, refuse to rear children. They are like certain savage tribes, who, when they have been conquered, refuse to breed.

Not one of them but looks forward to starvation for the coming winter. We are in a jungle and know it. We are beaten, entrapped. There is no way out. Even if there were a job, even if that thin acrid woman came and gave everyone in the room a job for a few days, a few hours, at thirty cents an hour, this would all be repeated tomorrow, the next day and the next.

Not one of these women but knows that despite years of labor there is only starvation, humiliation in front of them.

Mrs. Gray, sitting across from me, is a living spokesman for the futility of labor. She is a warning. Her hands are scarred with labor. Her body is a great puckered scar. She has given birth to six children, buried three, supported them all alive and dead, bearing them, burying them, feeding them. Bred in hunger they have been spare, susceptible to disease. For seven years she tried to save her boy's arm from amputation, diseased from tuberculosis of the bone. It is almost too suffocating to think of that long close horror of years of child-bearing, child-feeding, rearing, with the bare suffering of providing a meal and shelter.

Now she is fifty. Her children, economically insecure, are drifters. She never hears of them. She doesn't know if they are alive. She doesn't know if she is alive. Such subtleties of suffering are not for her. For her the brutality of hunger and cold. Not until these are done away with can those subtle feelings that make a human being be indulged.

She is lucky to have five dollars ahead of her. That is her security. She has a tumor that she will die of. She is thin as a worn dime with her tumor sticking out of her side. She is brittle and bitter. Her face is not the face of a human being. She has borne more than it is possible for a human being to bear. She is reduced to the least possible denominator of human feelings.

It is terrible to see her little bloodshot eyes like a beaten hound's fearful in terror.

We cannot meet her eyes. When she looks at any of us we look away. She is like a woman drowning and we turn away. We must ignore those eyes that are surely the eyes of a person drowning, doomed. She doesn't cry out. She goes down decently. And we all look away.

The young ones know though. I don't want to marry. I don't want any children. So they all say. No children. No marriage. They arm themselves alone, keep up alone. The man is helpless now. He cannot provide. If he propagates he cannot take care of his young. The means are not in his hands. So they live alone. Get what fun they can. The life risk is too horrible now. Defeat is too clearly written on it.

So we sit in this room like cattle, waiting for a nonexistent job, willing to work to the farthest atom of energy, unable to work, unable to get food and lodging, unable to bear children—here we must sit in this shame looking at the floor, worse than beasts at a slaughter.

It is appalling to think that these women sitting so listless in the room may work as hard as it is possible for a human being to work, may labor night and day, like Mrs. Gray wash streetcars from midnight to dawn and offices in the early evening, scrub for fourteen and fifteen hours a day, sleep only five hours or so, do this their whole lives, and never earn one day of security, having always before them the pit of the future. The endless labor, the bending back, the water-soaked hands, earning never more than a week's wages, never having in their hands more life than that.

It's not the suffering of birth, death, love that the young reject, but the suffering of endless labor without dream, eating the spare bread in bitterness, being a slave without the security of a slave.

Study and Discussion Questions

1. What does Le Sueur suggest is specific to *women's* experience during the Great Depression?
2. What is the narrator's relation to the scene she describes?
3. List the characteristics of each of the following women: Bernice, Ellen, Mrs. Gray.
4. List examples of metaphor and simile in this essay. How do they contribute to the mood and the argument Le Sueur is creating?
5. What is Le Sueur's thesis in this essay?
6. Where are the men?
7. Characterize the relation of these women to each other.

Suggestions for Writing

1. Analyze the passage that begins "It is very difficult and humiliating to sell one's body" and ends "When there is no buyer." What series of analogies is Le Sueur making in this passage?
2. To what extent has the situation of unemployed and poor women changed or not changed in the United States since Le Sueur published this essay in 1932? What factors can you advance to account for this?
3. What emotional response did you have to "Women on the Breadlines"? What in particular evoked that response?

Critical Resources

1. Coiner, Constance. "Literature of Resistance: The Intersection of Feminism and the Communist Left in Meridel Le Sueur and Tillie Olsen." *Radical Revisions: Rereading 1930s Culture.* Urbana: University of Illinois Press, 1996.
2. Roberts, Nora Ruth. "Meridel Le Sueur: An Interview Conducted in the Home of Le Sueur's Daughter Rachel Tilsen, in St. Paul, MN., Summer 1994." *Xcp: Cross-Cultural Poetics* 11 (2002): 84–99.
3. ———. *Three Radical Women Writers: Class and Gender in Meridel Le Sueur, Tillie Olsen and Josephine Herbst.* New York: Garland, 1996.
4. Sipple, Susan. "Witness/to/the Suffering of Women: Poverty and Sexual Transgression in Meridel Le Sueur's Women on the Breadlines." *Feminism, Bakhtin, and the Dialogic.* Ed. Susan Jaret McKinstry. Albany: SUNY Press, 1991.

RICHARD WRIGHT (1908–1960)

Richard Wright was born in Natchez, Mississippi. Despite a tumultuous childhood of poverty, Wright managed to graduate from his high school as valedictorian. Afterward, he moved to Memphis and, working odd jobs to support himself, began reading and writing prolifically. In 1927 he moved to Chicago and joined the Federal Writer's Project a few years later. Like many writers and intellectuals disillusioned with the breakdown of capitalism during the Great Depression, Wright joined the Communist Party during the 1930s in response to social inequities. Although Wright left the party years later, Marxist thought would inevitably influence his writing. The publication of Native Son *(1940) brought Wright national recognition, selling 200,000 copies within 30 days. Native Son, like much of Wright's early work, is written in the naturalistic mode, exploring the pathology of racism and its determining effects on both the individual and society. A prolific writer of novels, essays, poetry, and short stories, selected works include the story collections* Uncle Tom's Children *(1938) and* Eight Men *(1945); the novels* Native Son *(1940), the autobiographical* Black Boy *(1945),* The Outsider *(1953), and* The Long Dream *(1958). Several of his works have been published posthumously, including* American Hunger *(1977). "The Man Who Went to Chicago" is included in* Eight Men. *A larger version of the essay was included as part of* American Hunger.

The Man Who Went to Chicago (1945)

When I rose in the morning the temperature had dropped below zero. The house was as cold to me as the Southern streets had been in winter. I dressed, doubling my clothing. I ate in a restaurant, caught a streetcar, and rode south, rode until I could see no more black faces on the sidewalks. I had now crossed the boundary line of the Black Belt and had entered the territory where jobs were perhaps to be had from white folks. I walked the streets and looked into shop windows until I saw a sign in a delicatessen: PORTER WANTED.

I went in and a stout white woman came to me.

"Vat do you vant?" she asked.

The voice jarred me. She's Jewish, I thought, remembering with shame the obscenities I used to shout at Jewish storekeepers in Arkansas.

"I thought maybe you needed a porter," I said.

"Meester 'Offman, he eesn't here yet," she said. "Vill you vait?"

"Yes, ma'am."

"Seet down."

"No, ma'am, I'll wait outside."

"But eet's cold out zhere," she said.

"That's all right," I said.

She shrugged. I went to the sidewalk. I waited for half an hour in the bitter cold, regretting that I had not remained in the warm store, but unable to go back inside. A bald, stoutish white man went into the store and pulled off his coat. Yes, he was the boss man . . .

"Zo you vant a job?" he asked.

"Yes, sir," I answered, guessing at the meaning of his words.

"Vhere you vork before?"

"In Memphis, Tennessee."

"My brudder-in-law vorked in Tennessee vonce," he said.

I was hired. The work was easy, but I found to my dismay that I could not understand a third of what was said to me. My slow Southern ears were baffled by their clouded, thick accents. One morning Mrs. Hoffman asked me to go to a neighboring store—it was owned by a cousin of hers—and get a can of chicken *à la* king. I had never heard the phrase before and I asked her to repeat it.

"Don't you know nosing?" she demanded of me.

"If you would write it down for me, I'd know what to get," I ventured timidly.

"I can't vite!" she shouted in a sudden fury. "Vat kinda boy iss you?"

I memorized the separate sounds that she had uttered and went to the neighboring store.

"Mrs. Hoffman wants a can Cheek Keeng Awr Lar Keeng," I said slowly, hoping he would not think I was being offensive.

"All vite," he said, after staring at me a moment.

He put a can into a paper bag and gave it to me; outside in the street I opened the bag and read the label: Chicken *à la* King. I cursed, disgusted with myself. I knew those words. It had been her thick accent that had thrown me off. Yet I was not angry with her for speaking broken English; my English, too, was broken. But why could she not have taken more patience? Only one answer came to my mind. I was black and she did not care. Or so I thought . . . I was persisting in reading my present environment in the light of my old one. I reasoned thus: though English was my native tongue and America my native land, she, an alien, could operate a store and earn a living in a neighborhood where I could not even live. I reasoned further that she was aware of this and was trying to protect her position against me.

It was not until I had left the delicatessen job that I saw how grossly I had-misread the motives and attitudes of Mr. Hoffman and his wife. I had not yet learned anything that would have helped me to thread my way through these perplexing racial relations. Accepting my environment at its face value, trapped by my own emotions, I kept asking myself what had black people done to bring this crazy world upon them?

The fact of the separation of white and black was clear to me; it was its effect upon the personalities of people that stumped and dismayed me. I did not feel that I was a threat to anybody; yet, as soon as I had grown old enough to think, I had learned that my entire personality, my aspirations, had long ago been discounted; that, in a measure, the very meaning of the words I spoke could not be fully understood.

And when I contemplated the area of No Man's Land into which the Negro mind in America had been shunted I wondered if there had ever been in all human history a more corroding and devastating attack upon the personalities of men than the idea of racial discrimination. In order to escape the racial attack that went to the roots of my life, I would have gladly accepted any way of life but the one in which I found myself. I would have agreed to live under a system of feudal oppression, not because I preferred feudalism but because I felt that feudalism made use of a limited part of a man, defined man, his rank, his function in society. I would have consented to live under the most rigid type of dictatorship, for I felt that dictatorships, too, defined the use of men, however degrading that use might be.

While working as a porter in Memphis I had often stood aghast as a friend of mine had offered himself to be kicked by the white men; but now, while working in Chicago, I was learning that perhaps even a kick was better than uncertainty . . . I had elected, in my fevered search for honorable adjustment to the American scene, not to submit and in doing so I had embraced the daily horror of anxiety, of tension, of eternal disquiet. I could now sympathize with—though I could never bring myself to approve—those tortured blacks who had given up and had gone to their white tormentors and had said: "Kick me, if that's all there is for me; kick me and let me feel at home, let me have peace!"

Color-hate defined the place of black life as below that of white life; and the black man, responding to the same dreams as the white man, strove to bury within his heart his awareness of this difference because it made him lonely and afraid. Hated by whites and being an organic part of the culture that hated him, the black man grew in turn to hate in himself that which others hated in him. But pride would make him hate his self-hate, for he would not want whites to know that he was so thoroughly conquered by them that his total life was conditioned by their attitude; but in the act of hiding his self-hate, he could not help but hate those who evoked his self-hate in him. So each part of his day would be consumed in a war with himself, a good part of his energy would be spent in keeping control of his unruly emotions, emotions which he had not wished to have, but could not help having. Held at bay by the hate of others, preoccupied with his own feelings, he was continuously at war with reality. He became inefficient, less able to see and judge the objective world. And when he reached that state, the white people looked at him and laughed and said:

"Look, didn't I tell you niggers were that way?"

To solve this tangle of balked emotion, I loaded the empty part of the ship of my personality with fantasies of ambition to keep it from toppling over into the sea of senselessness. Like any other American, I dreamed of going into business and making money; I dreamed of working for a firm that would allow me to advance until I reached an important position; I even dreamed of organizing secret groups of blacks to fight all whites . . . And if the blacks would not agree to organize, then they would have to be fought. I would end up again with self-hate, but it was now a self-hate that was projected outward upon other blacks. Yet I knew—with that part of my mind that the whites had given me—that none of my dreams were possible. Then I would hate myself for allowing my mind to dwell upon the unattainable. Thus the circle would complete itself.

Slowly I began to forge in the depths of my mind a mechanism that repressed all the dreams and desires that the Chicago streets, the newspapers, the movies were evoking in me. I was going through a second childhood; a new sense of the limit of the possible was being born in me. What could I dream of that had the barest possibility of coming true? I could think of nothing. And, slowly, it was upon exactly that nothingness that my mind began to dwell, that constant sense of wanting without having, of being hated without reason. A dim notion of what life meant to a Negro in America was coming to consciousness in me, not in terms of external events, lynchings, Jim Crowism, and the endless brutalities, but in terms of crossed-up feeling, of emotional tension. I sensed that Negro life was a sprawling land of unconscious suffering, and there were but few Negroes who knew the meaning of their lives, who could tell their story.

Word reached me that an examination for postal clerk was impending and at once I filed an application and waited. As the date for the examination drew near, I was faced with another problem. How could I get a free day without losing my job? In the South it would have been an unwise policy for a Negro to have gone to his white boss and asked for time to take an examination for another job. It would have implied that the Negro did not like to work for the white boss, that he felt he was not receiving just consideration and, inasmuch as most jobs that Negroes held in the South involved a personal, paternalistic relationship, he would have been risking an argument that might have led to violence.

I now began to speculate about what kind of man Mr. Hoffman was, and I found that I did not know him; that is, I did not know his basic attitude toward Negroes. If I asked him, would he be sympathetic enough to allow me time off with pay? I needed the money. Perhaps he would say: "Go home and stay home if you don't like this job!" I was not sure of him. I decided, therefore, that I had better not risk it. I would forfeit the money and stay away without telling him.

The examination was scheduled to take place on a Monday; I had been working steadily and I would be too tired to do my best if I took the examination without benefit of rest. I decided to stay away from the shop Saturday, Sunday, and Monday. But what could I tell Mr. Hoffman? Yes, I would tell him that I had been ill. No, that was too thin. I would tell him that my mother had died in Memphis and that I had gone down to bury her. That lie might work.

I took the examination and when I came to the store on Tuesday, Mr. Hoffman was astonished, of course.

"I didn't sink you vould ever come back," he said.

"I'm awfully sorry, Mr. Hoffman."

"Vat happened?"

"My mother died in Memphis and I had to go down and bury her," I lied. He looked at me, then shook his head.

"Rich, you lie," he said.

"I'm not lying," I lied stoutly.

"You vanted to do somesink, zo you zayed ervay," he said shrugging.

"No, sir. I'm telling you the truth," I piled another lie upon the first one.

"No. You lie. You disappoint me," he said.

"Well, all I can do is tell you the truth," I lied indignantly.

"Vy didn't you use the phone?"

"I didn't think of it," I told a fresh lie.

"Rich, if your mudder die, you vould tell me," he said.

"I didn't have time. Had to catch the train," I lied yet again.

"Vhere did you get the money?"

"My aunt gave to me," I said, disgusted that I had to lie and lie again.

"I don't vant a boy vat tells lies," he said.

"I don't lie," I lied passionately to protect my lies.

Mrs. Hoffman joined in and both of them hammered at me.

"Ve know. You come from ze Zouth. You feel you can't tell us ze truth. But ve don't bother you. Ve don't feel like people in ze Zouth. Ve treat you nice, don't ve?" they asked.

"Yes, ma'am," I mumbled.

"Zen vy lie?"

"I'm not lying," I lied with all my strength.

I became angry because I knew that they knew that I was lying. I had lied to protect myself, and then I had to lie to protect my lie. I had met so many white faces that would have violently disapproved of my taking the examination that I could not have risked telling Mr. Hoffman the truth. But how could I tell him that I had lied because I was so unsure of myself? Lying was bad, but revealing my own sense of insecurity would have been worse. It would have been shameful, and I did not like to feel ashamed.

Their attitudes had proved utterly amazing. They were taking time out from their duties in the store to talk to me, and I had never encountered anything like that from whites before. A Southern white man would have said: "Get to hell out of here!" or "All right, nigger. Get to work." But no white people had ever stood their ground and probed at me, questioned me at such length. It dawned upon me that they were trying to treat me as an equal, which made it even more impossible for me ever to tell them that I had lied, why I had lied. I felt that if I confessed I would be giving them a moral advantage over me that would have been unbearable.

"All vight, zay and vork," Mr. Hoffman said. "I know you're lying, but I don't care, Rich."

I wanted to quit. He had insulted me. But I liked him in spite of myself. Yes, I had done wrong; but how on earth could I have known the kind of people I was working for? Perhaps Mr. Hoffman would have gladly consented for me to take the examination; but my hopes had been far weaker than my powerful fears.

Working with them from day to day and knowing that they knew I had lied from fear crushed me. I knew that they pitied me and pitied the fear in me. I resolved to quit and risk hunger rather than stay with them. I left the job that following Saturday, not telling them that I would not be back, not possessing the heart to say good-by. I just wanted to go quickly and have them forget that I had ever worked for them.

After an idle week, I got a job as a dishwasher in a North Side café that had just opened. My boss, a white woman, directed me in unpacking barrels of dishes, setting up new tables, painting, and so on. I had charge of serving breakfast; in the late afternoon I carted trays of food to patrons in the hotel who did not want to come down to eat. My wages were fifteen dollars a week; the hours were long, but I ate my meals on the job.

The cook was an elderly Finnish woman with a sharp, bony face. There were several white waitresses. I was the only Negro in the café. The waitresses were a hard, brisk lot, and I was keenly aware of how their attitudes contrasted with those of Southern white girls. They had not been taught to keep a gulf between me and themselves; they were relatively free of the heritage of racial hate.

One morning as I was making coffee, Cora came forward with a tray loaded with food and squeezed against me to draw a cup of coffee.

"Pardon me, Richard," she said.

"Oh, that's all right," I said in an even tone.

But I was aware that she was a white girl and that her body was pressed closely against mine, an incident that had never happened to me before in my life, an incident charged with the memory of dread. But she was not conscious of my blackness or of what her actions would have meant in the South. And had I not been born in the South, her trivial act would have been as unnoticed by me as it was by her. As she stood close to me, I could not help thinking that if a Southern white girl had wanted to draw a cup of coffee, she would have commanded me to step aside so that she might not come in contact with me. The work of the hot and busy kitchen would have had to cease for the moment so that I could have taken my tainted body far enough away to allow the Southern white girl a chance to get a cup of coffee. There lay a deep, emotional safety in knowing that the white girl who was now leaning carelessly against me was not thinking of me, had no deep, vague, irrational fright that made her feel that I was a creature to be avoided at all costs.

One summer morning a white girl came late to work and rushed into the pantry where I was busy. She went into the women's room and changed her clothes; I heard the door open and a second later I was surprised to hear her voice:

"Richard, quick! Tie my apron!"

She was standing with her back to me and the strings of her apron dangled loose. There was a moment of indecision on my part, then I took the two loose strings and carried them around her body and brought them again to her back and tied them in a clumsy knot.

"Thanks a million," she said, grasping my hand for a split second, and was gone.

I continued my work, filled with all the possible meanings that the tiny, simple, human event could have meant to any Negro in the South where I had spent most of my hungry days.

I did not feel any admiration or any hate for the girls. My attitude was one of abiding and friendly wonder. For the most part I was silent with them, though I knew that I had a firmer grasp of life than most of them. As I worked I listened to their talk and perceived its puzzled, wandering, superficial fumbling with the problems and facts of life. There were many things they wondered about that I could have explained to them, but I never dared.

During my lunch hour, which I spent on a bench in a near-by park, the waitresses would come and sit beside me, talking at random, laughing, joking, smoking cigarettes. I learned about their tawdry dreams, their simple hopes, their home lives, their fear of feeling anything deeply, their sex problems, their husbands. They were an eager, restless, talkative, ignorant bunch, but casually kind and impersonal for all that. They knew nothing of hate and fear, and strove instinctively to avoid all passion.

I often wondered what they were trying to get out of life, but I never stumbled upon a clue, and I doubt if they themselves had any notion. They lived on the surface of their days; their smiles were surface smiles, and their tears were surface tears. Negroes lived a truer and deeper life than they, but I wished that Negroes, too, could live as thoughtlessly, serenely, as they. The girls never talked of their feelings; none of them possessed the insight or the emotional equipment to understand themselves or others. How far apart in culture we stood! All my life I had done nothing but feel and cultivate my feelings; all their lives they had done nothing but strive for petty goals, the trivial material prizes of American life. We shared a common tongue, but my language was a different language from theirs.

It was in the psychological distance that separated the races that the deepest meaning of the problem of the Negro lay for me. For these poor, ignorant white girls to have understood my life would have meant nothing short of a vast revolution in theirs. And I was convinced that what they needed to make them complete and grown-up in their living was the inclusion in their personalities of a knowledge of lives such as I lived and suffered containedly.

As I, in memory, think back now upon those girls and their lives I feel that for white America to understand the significance of the problem of the Negro will take a bigger and tougher America than any we have yet known. I feel that America's past is too shallow, her national character too superficially optimistic, her very morality too suffused with color hate for her to accomplish so vast and complex a task. Culturally the Negro represents a paradox: Though he is an organic part of the nation, he is excluded by the entire tide and direction of American culture. Frankly, it is felt to be right to exclude him, and it is felt to be wrong to admit him freely. Therefore if, within the confines of its present culture, the nation ever seeks to purge itself of its color hate, it will find itself at war with itself, convulsed by a spasm of emotional and moral confusion. If the nation ever finds itself examining its real relation to the Negro, it will find itself doing infinitely more than that; for the anti-Negro attitude of whites represents but a tiny part—though a symbolically significant one—of the moral attitude of the nation. Our too-young and too-new America, lusty because it is lonely, aggressive because it is afraid, insists upon seeing the world in terms of good and bad, the holy and the evil, the high and the low, the white and the black; our America is frightened by fact, by history, by processes, by necessity. It hugs the easy way of damning those whom it cannot understand, of excluding those who look different; and it salves its conscience with a self-draped cloak of righteousness. Am I damning my native land? No; for I, too, share these faults of character! And I really do not think that America, adolescent and cocksure, a stranger to suffering and travail, an enemy of passion and sacrifice, is ready to probe into its most fundamental beliefs.

I knew that not race alone, not color alone, but the daily values that gave meaning to life stood between me and those white girls with whom I worked. Their constant outwardlooking, their mania for radios, cars, and a thousand other trinkets, made them dream and fix their eyes upon the trash of life, made it impossible for them to learn a language that could have taught them to speak of what was in theirs or others' hearts. The words of their souls were the syllables of popular songs.

The essence of the irony of the plight of the Negro in America, to me, is that he is doomed to live in isolation, while those who condemn him seek the basest goals of any people on the face of the earth. Perhaps it would be possible for the Negro to become reconciled to his plight if he could be made to believe that his sufferings were for some remote, high, sacrificial end; but sharing the culture that condemns him, and seeing that a lust for trash is what blinds the nation to his claims, is what sets storms to rolling in his soul.

Though I had fled the pressure of the South, my outward conduct had not changed. I had been schooled to present an unalteringly smiling face and I continued to do so despite the fact that my environment allowed more open expression. I hid my feelings and avoided all relationships with whites that might cause me to reveal them.

Tillie, the Finnish cook, was a tall, ageless, red-faced, raw-boned woman with long snow-white hair, which she balled in a knot at the nape of her neck. She cooked expertly and was superbly efficient. One morning as I passed the sizzling stove, I thought I heard Tillie cough and spit, but I saw nothing; her face, obscured by steam, was bent over a big pot. My senses told me that Tillie had coughed and spat into that pot, but my heart told me that no human being could possibly be so filthy. I decided to watch her. An hour or so later I heard Tillie clear her throat with a grunt, saw her cough and spit into the boiling soup. I held my breath; I did not want to believe what I had seen.

Should I tell the boss lady? Would she believe me? I watched Tillie for another day to make sure that she was spitting into the food. She was; there was no doubt of it. But who would believe me if I told them what was happening? I was the only black person in the café. Perhaps they would think that I hated the cook. I stopped eating my meals there and bided my time.

The business of the café was growing rapidly and a Negro girl was hired to make salads. I went to her at once.

"Look, can I trust you?" I asked.

"What are you talking about?" she asked.

"I want you to say nothing, but watch that cook."

"For what?"

"Now, don't get scared. Just watch the cook."

She looked at me as though she thought I was crazy; and frankly, I felt that perhaps I ought not say anything to anybody.

"What do you mean?" she demanded.

"All right," I said. "I'll tell you. That cook spits in the food."

"What are you saying?" she asked aloud.

"Keep quiet," I said.

"Spitting?" she asked me in a whisper. "Why would she do that?"

"I don't know. But watch her."

She walked away from me with a funny look in her eyes. But half a hour later she came rushing to me, looking ill, sinking into a chair.

"Oh, God, I feel awful!"

"Did you see it?"

"She *is* spitting in the food!"

"What ought we do?" I asked.

"Tell the lady," she said.

"She wouldn't believe me," I said.

She widened her eyes as she understood. We were black and the cook was white.

"But I can't work here if she's going to do that," she said.

"Then you tell her," I said.

"She wouldn't believe me either," she said.

She rose and ran to the women's room. When she returned she stared at me. We were two Negroes and we were silently asking ourselves if the white boss lady would believe us if we told her that her expert white cook was spitting in the food all day long as it cooked on the stove.

"I don't know," she wailed, in a whisper, and walked away.

I thought of telling the waitresses about the cook, but I could not get up enough nerve. Many of the girls were friendly with Tillie. Yet I could not let the cook spit in the food all day. That was wrong by any human standard of conduct. I washed dishes, thinking, wondering; I served breakfast, thinking, wondering; I served meals in the apartments of patrons upstairs, thinking, wondering. Each time I picked up a tray of food I felt like retching. Finally the Negro salad girl came to me and handed me her purse and hat.

"I'm going to tell her and quit, goddamn," she said.

"I'll quit too, if she doesn't fire her," I said.

"Oh, she won't believe me," she wailed, in agony.

"You tell her. You're a woman. She might believe you."

Her eyes welled with tears and she sat for a long time; then she rose and went abruptly into the dining room. I went to the door and peered. Yes, she was at the desk, talking to the boss lady. She returned to the kitchen and went into the pantry; I followed her.

"Did you tell her?" I asked.

"Yes."

"What did she say?"

"She said I was crazy."

"Oh, God!" I said.

"She just looked at me with those gray eyes of hers," the girl said. "Why would Tillie do that?"

"I don't know," I said.

The boss lady came to the door and called the girl; both of them went into the dining room. Tillie came over to me; a hard cold look was in her eyes.

"What's happening here?" she asked.

"I don't know," I said, wanting to slap her across the mouth.

She muttered something and went back to the stove, coughed, and spat into a bubbling pot. I left the kitchen and went into the back areaway to breathe. The boss lady came out.

"Richard," she said.

Her face was pale. I was smoking a cigarette and I did not look at her.

"Is this true?"

"Yes, ma'am."

"It couldn't be. Do you know what you're saying?"

"Just watch her," I said.

"I don't know," she moaned.

She looked crushed. She went back into the dining room, but I saw her watching the cook through the doors. I watched both of them, the boss lady and the cook, praying that the cook would spit again. She did. The boss lady came into the kitchen and stared at Tillie, but she did not utter a word. She burst into tears and ran back into the dining room.

"What's happening here?" Tillie demanded.

No one answered. The boss lady came out and tossed Tillie her hat, coat, and money.

"Now, get out of here, you dirty dog!" she said.

Tillie stared, then slowly picked up her hat, coat, and the money; she stood a moment, wiped sweat from her forehead with her hand, then spat—this time on the floor. She left.

Nobody was ever able to fathom why Tillie liked to spit into the food.

Brooding over Tillie, I recalled the time when the boss man in Mississippi had come to me and had tossed my wages to me and said:

"Get out, nigger! I don't like your looks."

And I wondered if a Negro who did not smile and grin was as morally loathsome to whites as a cook who spat into the food.

The following summer I was called for temporary duty in the post office, and the work lasted into the winter. Aunt Cleo succumbed to a severe cardiac condition and, hard on the heels of her illness, my brother developed stomach ulcers. To rush my worries to a climax, my mother also became ill. I felt that I was maintaining a private hospital. Finally, the postoffice work ceased altogether and I haunted the city for jobs. But when I went into the streets in the morning I saw sights that killed my hope for the rest of the day. Unemployed men loitered in doorways with blank looks in their eyes, sat dejectedly on front steps in shabby clothing, congregated in sullen groups on street corners, and filled all the empty benches in the parks of Chicago's South Side.

Luck of a sort came when a distant cousin of mine, who was a superintendent for a Negro burial society, offered me a position on his staff as an agent. The thought of selling insurance policies to ignorant Negroes disgusted me.

"Well, if you don't sell them, somebody else will," my cousin told me "You've got to eat, haven't you?"

During that year I worked for several burial and insurance societies that operated among Negroes, and I received a new kind of education. I found that the burial societies, with some exceptions, were mostly "rackets." Some of them conducted their business legitimately, but there were many that exploited the ignorance of their black customers.

I was paid under a system that netted me fifteen dollars for every dollar's worth of new premiums that I placed upon the company's books, and for every dollar's worth of old premiums that lapsed I was penalized fifteen dollars. In addition, I was paid a commission of ten per cent on total premiums collected, but during the Depression it was extremely difficult to persuade a black family to buy a policy carrying even a dime premium. I considered myself lucky if, after subtracting lapses from new business, there remained fifteen dollars that I could call my own.

This "gambling" method of remuneration was practiced by some of the burial companies because of the tremendous "turnover" in policyholders, and the companies had to have a constant stream of new business to keep afloat. Whenever a black family moved or suffered a slight reverse in fortune, it usually let its policy lapse and later bought another policy from some other company.

Each day now I saw how the Negro in Chicago lived, for I visited hundreds of dingy flats filled with rickety furniture and ill-clad children. Most of the policyholders were illiterate and did not know that their policies carried clauses severely restricting their benefit payments, and, as an insurance agent, it was not my duty to tell them.

After tramping the streets and pounding on doors to collect premiums, I was dry, strained, too tired to read or write. I hungered for relief and, as a salesman of insurance to many young black girls, I found it. There were many comely black housewives who, trying desperately to keep up their insurance payments, were willing to make bargains to escape paying a ten-cent premium. I had a long, tortured affair with one girl by paying her ten-cent premium each week. She was an illiterate black child with a baby whose father she did not know. During the entire period of my relationship with her, she had but one demand to make of me: she wanted me to take her to a circus. Just what significance circuses had for her, I was never able to learn.

After I had been with her one morning—in exchange for the dime premium—I sat on the sofa in the front room and began to read a book I had with me. She came over shyly.

"Lemme see that," she said.

"What?" I asked.

"That book," she said.

I gave her the book; she looked at it intently. I saw that she was holding it upside down.

"What's in here you keep reading?" she asked.

"Can't you really read?" I asked.

"Naw," she giggled. "You know I can't read."

"You can read *some*," I said.

"Naw," she said.

I stared at her and wondered just what a life like hers meant in the scheme of things, and I came to the conclusion that it meant absolutely nothing. And neither did my life mean anything.

"How come you looking at me that way for?"

"Nothing."

"You don't talk much."

"There isn't much to say."

"I wished Jim was here," she sighed.

"Who's Jim?" I asked, jealous. I knew that she had other men, but I resented her mentioning them in my presence.

"Just a friend," she said.

I hated her then, then hated myself for coming to her.

"Do you like Jim better than you like me?" I asked.

"Naw. Jim just likes to talk."

"Then why do you be with me, if you like Jim better?" I asked, trying to make an issue and feeling a wave of disgust because I wanted to.

"You all right," she said, giggling. "I like you."

"I could kill you," I said.

"What?" she exclaimed.

"Nothing," I said, ashamed.

"Kill me, you said? You crazy, man," she said.

"Maybe I am," I muttered, angry that I was sitting beside a human being to whom I could not talk, angry with myself for coming to her, hating my wild and restless loneliness.

"You oughta go home and sleep," she said. "You tired."

"What do you ever think about?" I demanded harshly.

"Lotta things."

"What, for example?"

"You," she said, smiling.

"You know I mean just one dime to you each week," I said.

"Naw, I thinka lotta you."

"Then what do you think?"

"Bout how you talk when you talk. I wished I could talk like you," she said seriously.

"Why?" I taunted her.

"When you gonna take me to a circus?" she demanded suddenly.

"You ought to be in a circus," I said.

"I'd like it," she said, her eyes shining.

I wanted to laugh, but her words sounded so sincere that I could not.

"There's no circus in town," I said.

"I bet there is and you won't tell me 'cause you don't wanna take me," she said, pouting.

"But there's no circus in town, I tell you!"

"When will one come?"

"I don't know."

"Can't you read it in the papers?" she asked.

"There's nothing in the papers about a circus."

"There is," she said. "If I could read, I'd find it."

I laughed, and she was hurt.

"There *is* a circus in town," she said stoutly.

"There's no circus in town," I said. "But if you want to learn to read, then I'll teach you."

She nestled at my side, giggling.

"See that word?" I said, pointing.

"Yeah."

"That's an 'and,'" I said.

She doubled, giggling.

"What's the matter?" I asked.

She rolled on the floor, giggling.

"What's so funny?" I demanded.

"You," she giggled. "You so funny."

I rose.

"The hell with you," I said.

"Don't you go and cuss me now," she said. "I don't cuss you."

"I'm sorry," I said.

I got my hat and went to the door.

"I'll see you next week?" she asked.

"Maybe," I said.

When I was on the sidewalk, she called to me from a window.

"You promised to take me to a circus, remember?"

"Yes." I walked close to the window. "What is it you like about a circus?"

"The animals," she said simply.

I felt that there was a hidden meaning, perhaps, in what she had said, but I could not find it. She laughed and slammed the window shut.

Each time I left her I resolved not to visit her again. I could not talk to her, I merely listened to her passionate desire to see a circus. She was not calculating; if she liked a man, she just liked him. Sex relations were the only relations she had ever had; no others were possible with her, so limited was her intelligence.

Most of the other agents also had their bought girls and they were extremely anxious to keep other agents from tampering with them. One day a new section of the South Side was given to me as a part of my collection area, and the agent from whom the territory had been taken suddenly became very friendly with me.

"Say, Wright," he asked, "did you collect from Ewing on Champlain Avenue yet?"

"Yes," I answered, after consulting my book.

"How did you like her?" he asked, staring at me.

"She's a good-looking number," I said.

"You had anything to do with her yet?" he asked.

"No, but I'd like to," I said laughing.

"Look," he said. "I'm a friend of yours."

"Since when?" I countered.

"No, I'm really a friend," he said.

"What's on your mind?"

"Listen, that gal's sick," he said seriously.

"What do you mean?"

"She's got the clap," he said. "Keep away from her. She'll lay with anybody."

"Gee, I'm glad you told me," I said.

"You had your eye on her, didn't you?" he asked.

"Yes, I did," I said.

"Leave her alone," he said. "She'll get you down."

That night I told my cousin what the agent had said about Miss Ewing. My cousin laughed.

"That gal's all right," he said. "That agent's been fooling around with her. He told you she had a disease so that you'd be scared to bother her. He was protecting her from you."

That was the way the black women were regarded by the black agents. Some of the agents were vicious; if they had claims to pay to a sick black woman and if the woman was able to have sex relations with them, they would insist upon it, using the claims money as a bribe. If the woman refused, they would report to the office that the woman was a malingerer. The average black woman would submit because she needed the money badly.

As an insurance agent it was necessary for me to take part in one swindle. It appears that the burial society had originally issued a policy that was—from their point of view—too liberal in its provisions, and the officials decided to exchange the policies then in the hands of their clients for other policies carrying stricter clauses. Of course, this had to be done in a manner that would not allow the policyholder to know that his policy was being switched—that he was being swindled. I did not like it, but there was only one thing I could do to keep from being a party to it: I could quit and starve. But I did not feel that being honest was worth the price of starvation.

The swindle worked in this way. In my visits to the homes of the policyholders to collect premiums, I was accompanied by the superintendent who claimed to the policyholder that he was making a routine inspection. The policyholder, usually an illiterate black woman, would dig up her policy from the bottom of a trunk or chest and hand it to the superintendent. Meanwhile I would be marking the woman's premium book, an act which would distract her from what the superintendent was doing. The superintendent would exchange the old policy for a new one which was identical in color, serial number, and beneficiary, but which carried smaller payments. It was dirty work and I wondered how I could stop it. And when I could think of no safe way I would curse myself and the victims and forget about it. (The black owners of the burial societies were leaders in the Negro communities and were respected by whites.)

When I reached the relief station, I felt that I was making a public confession of my hunger. I sat waiting for hours, resentful of the mass of hungry people about me. My turn finally came and I was questioned by a middle-class Negro woman who asked me for a short history of my life. As I waited, I became aware of something happening in the room. The black men and women were mumbling quietly among themselves; they had not known one another before they had come here, but now their timidity and shame were wearing off and they were exchanging experiences. Before this they had lived as individuals, each somewhat afraid of the other, each seeking his own pleasure, each stanch in that degree of Americanism that had been allowed him. But now life had tossed them together, and they were learning to know the sentiments of their neighbors for the first time; their talking was enabling them to sense the collectivity of their lives, and some of their fear was passing.

Did the relief officials realize what was happening? No. If they had, they would have stopped it. But they saw their "clients" through the eyes of their profession, saw only what their "science" allowed them to see. As I listened to the talk, I could see black minds shedding many illusions. These people now knew that the past had betrayed them, had cast them out; but they did not know what the future would be like, did not know what they wanted. Yes, some of the things that the Communists said were true; they maintained that there came times in history when a ruling class could no longer rule. And now I sat looking at the beginnings of anarchy. To permit the birth of this new consciousness in these people was proof that those who ruled did not quite know what they were doing, assuming that they were trying to save themselves and their class. Had they understood what was happening, they would never have allowed millions of perplexed and defeated people to sit together for long hours and talk, for out of their talk was rising a new realization of life. And once this new conception of themselves had formed, no power on earth could alter it.

I left the relief station with the promise that food would be sent to me, but I also left with a knowledge that the relief officials had not wanted to give to me. I had felt the possibility of creating a new understanding of life in the minds of people rejected by the society in which they lived, people to whom the Chicago *Tribune* referred contemptuously as the "idle" ones, as though these people had deliberately sought their present state of helplessness.

Who would give these people a meaningful way of life? Communist theory defined these people as the molders of the future of mankind, but the Communist speeches I had heard in the park had mocked that definition. These people, of course, were not ready for a revolution; they had not abandoned their past lives by choice, but because they simply could not live the old way any longer. Now, what new faith would they embrace? The day I begged bread from the city officials was the day that showed me I was not alone in my loneliness; society had cast millions of others with me. But how could I be with them? How many understood what was happening? My mind swam with questions that I could not answer.

I was slowly beginning to comprehend the meaning of my environment; a sense of direction was beginning to emerge from the conditions of my life. I began to feel something more powerful than I could express. My speech and manner changed. My cynicism slid from me. I grew open and questioning. I wanted to know.

If I were a member of the class that rules, I would post men in all the neighborhoods of the nation, not to spy upon or club rebellious workers, not to break strikes or disrupt unions, but to ferret out those who no longer respond to the system under which they live. I would make it known that the real danger does not stem from those who seek to grab their share of wealth through force, or from those who try to defend their property through violence, for both of these groups, by their affirmative acts, support the values of the system under which they live. The millions that I would fear are those who do not dream of the prizes that the nation holds forth, for it is in them, though they may not know it, that a revolution has taken place and is biding its time to translate itself into a new and strange way of life.

I feel that the Negroes' relation to America is symbolically peculiar, and from the Negroes' ultimate reactions to their trapped state a lesson can be learned about America's future. Negroes are told in a language they cannot possibly misunderstand that their native land is not their own; and when, acting upon impulses which they share with whites, they try to assert a claim to their birthright, whites retaliate with terror, never pausing to consider the consequences should the Negroes give up completely. The whites never dream that they would face a situation far more terrifying if they were confronted by Negroes who made no claims at all than by those who are buoyed up by social aggressiveness. My knowledge of how Negroes react to their plight makes me declare that no man can possibly be individually guilty of treason, that an insurgent act is but a man's desperate answer to those who twist his environment so that he cannot fully share the spirit of his native land. Treason is a crime of the State.

Christmas came and I was once more called to the post office for temporary work. This time I met many young white men and we discussed world happenings, the vast armies of unemployed, the rising tide of radical action. I now detected a change in the attitudes of the whites I met; their privations were making them regard Negroes with new eyes, and, for the first time, I was invited to their homes.

When the work in the post office ended, I was assigned by the relief system as an orderly to a medical research institute in one of the largest and wealthiest hospitals in Chicago. I cleaned operating rooms, dog, rat, mice, cat, and rabbit pans, and fed guinea pigs. Four of us Negroes worked there and we occupied an underworld position, remembering that we must restrict ourselves—when not engaged upon some task—to the basement corridors, so that we would not mingle with white nurses, doctors, or visitors.

The sharp line of racial division drawn by the hospital authorities came to me the first morning when I walked along an underground corridor and saw two long lines of women coming toward me. A line of white girls marched past, clad in starched uniforms that gleamed white; their faces were alert, their step quick, their bodies lean and shapely, their shoulders erect, their faces lit with the light of purpose. And after them came a line of black girls, old, fat, dressed in ragged gingham, walking loosely, carrying tin cans of soap powder, rags, mops, brooms . . . I wondered what law of the universe kept them from being mixed? The sun would not have stopped shining had there been a few black girls in the first line, and the earth would not have stopped whirling on its axis had there been a few white girls in the second line. But the two lines I saw graded social status in purely racial terms.

Of the three Negroes who worked with me, one was a boy about my own age, Bill, who was either sleepy or drunk most of the time. Bill straightened his hair and I suspected that he kept a bottle hidden somewhere in the piles of hay which we fed to the guinea pigs. He did not like me and I did not like him, though I tried harder than he to conceal my dislike. We had nothing in common except that we were both black and lost. While I contained my frustration, he drank to drown his. Often I tried to talk to him, tried in simple words to convey to him some of my ideas, and he would listen in sullen silence. Then one day he came to me with an angry look on his face.

"I got it," he said.

"You've got what?" I asked.

"This old race problem you keep talking about," he said.

"What about it?"

"Well, it's this way," he explained seriously. "Let the government give every man a gun and five bullets, then let us all start over again. Make it like it was in the beginning. The ones who come out on top, white or black, let them rule."

His simplicity terrified me. I had never met a Negro who was so irredeemably brutalized. I stopped pumping my ideas into Bill's brain for fear that the fumes of alcohol might send him reeling toward some fantastic fate.

The two other Negroes were elderly and had been employed in the institute for fifteen years or more. One was Brand, a short, black, morose bachelor; the other was Cooke, a tall, yellow, spectacled fellow who spent his spare time keeping track of world events through the Chicago *Tribune*. Brand and Cooke hated each other for a reason that I was never able to determine, and they spent a good part of each day quarreling.

When I began working at the institute, I recalled my adolescent dream of wanting to be a medical research worker. Daily I saw young Jewish boys and girls receiving instruction in chemistry and medicine that the average black boy or girl could never receive. When I was alone, I wandered and poked my fingers into strange chemicals, watched intricate machines trace red and black lines on ruled paper. At times I paused and stared at the walls of the rooms, at the floors, at the wide desks at which the white doctors sat; and I realized—with a feeling that I could never quite get used to—that I was looking at the world of another race.

My interest in what was happening in the institute amused the three other Negroes with whom I worked. They had no curiosity about "white folks' things," while I wanted to know if the dogs being treated for diabetes were getting well; if the rats and mice in which cancer had been induced showed any signs of responding to treatment. I wanted to know the principle that lay behind the Aschheim-Zondek tests that were made with rabbits, the Wassermann tests that were made with guinea pigs. But when I asked a timid question I found that even Jewish doctors had learned to imitate the sadistic method of humbling a Negro that the others had cultivated.

"If you know too much, boy, your brains might explode," a doctor said one day.

Each Saturday morning I assisted a young Jewish doctor in slitting the vocal cords of a fresh batch of dogs from the city pound. The object was to devocalize the dogs so that their howls would not disturb the patients in the other parts of the hospital. I held each dog as the doctor injected Nembutal into its veins to make it unconscious; then I held the dog's jaws open as the doctor inserted the scalpel and severed the vocal cords. Later, when the dogs came to, they would lift their heads to the ceiling and gape in a soundless wail. The sight became lodged in my imagination as a symbol of silent suffering.

To me Nembutal was a powerful and mysterious liquid, but when I asked questions about its properties I could not obtain a single intelligent answer. The doctor simply ignored me with:

"Come on. Bring me the next dog. I haven't got all day."

One Saturday morning, after I had held the dogs for their vocal cords to be slit, the doctor left the Nembutal on a bench. I picked it up, uncorked it, and smelled it. It was odorless. Suddenly Brand ran to me with a stricken face.

"What're you doing?" he asked.

"I was smelling this stuff to see if it had any odor," I said.

"Did you really smell it?" he asked me.

"Yes."

"Oh, God!" he exclaimed.

"What's the matter?" I asked.

"You shouldn't've done that!" he shouted.

"Why?"

He grabbed my arm and jerked me across the room.

"Come on!" he yelled, snatching open the door.

"What's the matter?" I asked.

"I gotta get you to a doctor 'fore it's too late," he gasped.

Had my foolish curiosity made me inhale something dangerous?

"But—Is it poisonous?"

"Run, boy!" he said, pulling me. "You'll fall dead."

Filled with fear, with Brand pulling my arm, I rushed out of the room, raced across a rear areaway, into another room, then down a long corridor. I wanted to ask Brand what symptoms I must expect, but we were running too fast. Brand finally stopped, gasping for breath. My heart beat wildly and my blood pounded in my head. Brand then dropped to the concrete floor, stretched out on his back, and yelled with laughter, shaking all over. He beat his fists against the concrete; he moaned, giggled, he kicked.

I tried to master my outrage, wondering if some of the white doctors had told him to play the joke. He rose and wiped tears from his eyes, still laughing. I walked away from him. He knew that I was angry and he followed me.

"Don't get mad," he gasped through his laughter.

"Go to hell," I said.

"I couldn't help it," he giggled. "You looked at me like you'd believe anything I said. Man, you was scared."

He leaned against the wall, laughing again, stomping his feet. I was angry, for I felt that he would spread the story. I knew that Bill and Cooke never ventured beyond the safe bounds of Negro living, and they would never blunder into anything like this. And if they heard about this, they would laugh for months.

"Brand, if you mention this, I'll kill you," I swore.

"You ain't mad?" he asked, laughing, staring at me through tears.

Sniffing, Brand walked ahead of me. I followed him back into the room that housed the dogs. All day, while at some task, he would pause and giggle, then smother the giggling with his hand, looking at me out of the corner of his eyes, shaking his head. He laughed at me for a week. I kept my temper and let him amuse himself. I finally found out the properties of Nembutal by consulting medical books; but I never told Brand.

One summer morning, just as I began work, a young Jewish boy came to me with a stop watch in his hand.

"Dr.——wants me to time you when you clean a room," he said. "We're trying to make the institute more efficient."

"I'm doing my work, and getting through on time," I said.

"This is the boss's order," he said.

"Why don't you work for a change?" I blurted, angry.

"Now, look," he said. "*This* is my work. Now *you* work."

I got a mop and pail, sprayed a room with disinfectant, and scrubbed at coagulated blood and hardened dog, rat, and rabbit feces. The normal temperature of a room was ninety, but, as the sun beat down upon the skylights, the temperature rose above a hundred. Stripped to my waist, I slung the mop, moving steadily like a machine, hearing the boy press the button on the stop watch as I finished cleaning a room.

"Well, how is it?" I asked.

"It took you seventeen minutes to clean that last room," he said. "That ought to be the time for each room."

"But that room was not very dirty," I said.

"You have seventeen rooms to clean," he went on as though I had not spoken. "Seventeen times seventeen make four hours and forty-nine minutes." He wrote upon a little pad. "After lunch, clean the five flights of stone stairs. I timed a boy who scrubbed one step and multiplied that time by the number of steps. You ought to be through by six."

"Suppose I want relief?" I asked.

"You'll manage," he said and left.

Never had I felt so much the slave as when I scoured those stone steps each afternoon. Working against time, I would wet five steps, sprinkle soap powder, and then a white doctor or a nurse would come along and, instead of avoiding the soapy steps, would walk on them and track the dirty water onto the steps that I had already cleaned. To obviate this, I cleaned but two steps at a time, a distance over which a ten-year-old child could step. But it did no good. The white people still plopped their feet down into the dirty water and muddied the other clean steps. If I ever really hotly hated unthinking whites, it was then. Not once during my entire stay at the institute did a single white person show enough courtesy to avoid a wet step. I would be on my knees, scrubbing, sweating, pouring out what limited energy my body could wring from my meager diet, and I would hear feet approaching. I would pause and curse with tense lips:

"These sonofabitches are going to dirty these steps again, goddamn their souls to hell!"

Sometimes a sadistically observant white man would notice that he had tracked dirty water up the steps, and he would look back down at me and smile and say:

"Boy, we sure keep you busy, don't we?"

And I would not be able to answer.

The feud that went on between Brand and Cooke continued. Although they were working daily in a building where scientific history was being made, the light of curiosity was never in their eyes. They were conditioned to their racial "place," had learned to see only a part of the whites and the white world; and the whites, too, had learned to see only a part of the lives of the blacks and their world.

Perhaps Brand and Cooke, lacking interests that could absorb them, fuming like children over trifles, simply invented their hate of each other in order to have something to feel deeply about. Or perhaps there was in them a vague tension stemming from their chronically frustrating way of life, a pain whose cause they did not know; and, like those devocalized dogs, they would whirl and snap at the air when their old pain struck them. Anyway, they argued about the weather, sports, sex, war, race, politics, and religion; neither of them knew much about the subjects they debated, but it seemed that the less they knew the better they could argue.

The tug of war between the two elderly men reached a climax one winter day at noon. It was incredibly cold and an icy gale swept up and down the Chicago streets with blizzard force. The door of the animal-filled room was locked, for we always insisted that we be allowed one hour in which to eat and rest. Bill and I were sitting on wooden boxes, eating our lunches out of paper bags. Brand was washing his hands at the sink. Cooke was sitting on a rickety stool, munching an apple and reading the Chicago *Tribune*.

Now and then a devocalized dog lifted his nose to the ceiling and howled soundlessly. The room was filled with many rows of high steel tiers. Perched upon each of these tiers were layers of steel cages containing the dogs, rats, mice, rabbits, and guinea pigs. Each cage was labeled in some indecipherable scientific jargon. Along the walls of the room were long charts with zigzagging red and black lines that traced the success or failure of some experiment. The lonely piping of guinea pigs floated unheeded about us. Hay rustled as a rabbit leaped restlessly about in its pen. A rat scampered around in its steel prison. Cooke tapped the newspaper for attention.

"It says here," Cooke mumbled through a mouthful of apple, "that this is the coldest day since 1888."

Bill and I sat unconcerned. Brand chuckled softly.

"What in hell you laughing about?" Cooke demanded of Brand.

"You can't believe what that damn *Tribune* says," Brand said.

"How come I can't?" Cooke demanded. "It's the world's greatest newspaper."

Brand did not reply; he shook his head pityingly and chuckled again.

"Stop that damn laughing at me!" Cooke said angrily.

"I laugh as much as I wanna," Brand said. "You don't know what you talking about. The *Herald-Examiner* says it's the coldest day since 1873."

"But the *Trib* oughta know," Cooke countered. "It's older'n that *Examiner*."

"That damn *Trib* don't know nothing!" Brand drowned out Cooke's voice.

"How in hell you know?" Cooke asked with rising anger.

The argument waxed until Cooke shouted that if Brand did not shut up he was going to "cut his black throat."

Brand whirled from the sink, his hands dripping soapy water, his eye blazing.

"Take that back," Brand said.

"I take nothing back! What you wanna do about it?" Cooke taunted.

The two elderly Negroes glared at each other. I wondered if the quarrel was really serious, or if it would turn out harmlessly as so many others had done.

Suddenly Cooke dropped the Chicago *Tribune* and pulled a long knife from his pocket; his thumb pressed a button and a gleaming steel blade leaped out. Brand stepped back quickly and seized an ice pick that was stuck in a wooden board above the sink.

"Put that knife down," Brand said.

"Stay 'way from me, or I'll cut your throat," Cooke warned.

Brand lunged with the ice pick. Cooke dodged out of range. They circled each other like fighters in a prize ring. The cancerous and tubercular rats and mice leaped about in their cages. The guinea pigs whistled in fright. The diabetic dogs bared their teeth and barked soundlessly in our direction. The Aschheim-Zondek rabbits flopped their ears and tried to hide in the corners of their pens. Cooke now crouched and sprang forward with the knife. Bill and I jumped to our feet, speechless with surprise. Brand retreated. The eyes of both men were hard and unblinking; they were breathing deeply.

"Say, cut it out!" I called in alarm.

"Them damn fools is really fighting," Bill said in amazement.

Slashing at each other, Brand and Cooke surged up and down the aisles of steel tiers. Suddenly Brand uttered a bellow and charged into Cooke and swept him violently backward. Cooke grasped Brand's hand to keep the ice pick from sinking into his chest. Brand broke free and charged Cooke again, sweeping him into an animal-filled steel tier. The tier balanced itself on its edge for an indecisive moment, then toppled.

Like kingpins, one steel tier lammed into another, then they all crashed to the floor with a sound as of the roof falling. The whole aspect of the room altered quicker than the eye could follow. Brand and Cooke stood stock-still, their eyes fastened upon each other, their pointed weapons raised; but they were dimly aware of the havoc that churned about them.

The steel tiers lay jumbled; the doors of the cages swung open. Rats and mice and dogs and rabbits moved over the floor in wild panic. The Wassermann guinea pigs were squealing as though judgment day had come. Here and there an animal had been crushed beneath a cage.

All four of us looked at one another. We knew what this meant. We might lose our jobs. We were already regarded as black dunces; and if the doctors saw this mess they would take it as final proof. Bill rushed to the door to make sure that it was locked. I glanced at the clock and saw that it was 12:30. We had one half-hour of grace.

"Come on," Bill said uneasily. "We got to get this place cleaned."

Brand and Cooke stared at each other, both doubting.

"Give me your knife, Cooke," I said.

"Naw! Take Brand's ice pick *first*," Cooke said.

"The hell you say!" Brand said. "Take his knife *first!*"

A knock sounded at the door.

"Sssssh," Bill said.

We waited. We heard footsteps going away. We'll all lose our jobs, I thought.

Persuading the fighters to surrender their weapons was a difficult task, but at last it was done and we could begin to set things right. Slowly Brand stooped and tugged at one end of a steel tier. Cooke stooped to help him. Both men seemed to be acting in a dream. Soon, however, all four of us were working frantically, watching the clock.

As we labored we conspired to keep the fight a secret; we agreed to tell the doctors—if any should ask—that we had not been in the room during our lunch hour; we felt that that lie would explain why no one had unlocked the door when the knock had come.

We righted the tiers and replaced the cages; then we were faced with the impossible task of sorting the cancerous rats and mice, the diabetic dogs, the Aschheim-Zondek rabbits, and the Wassermann guinea pigs. Whether we kept our jobs or not depended upon how shrewdly we could cover up all evidence of the fight. It was pure guesswork, but we had to try to put the animals back into the correct cages. We knew that certain rats or mice went into certain cages, but we did not know *what* rat or mouse went into *what* cage. We did not know a tubercular mouse from a cancerous mouse—the white doctors had made sure that we would not know. They had never taken time to answer a single question; though we worked in the institute, we were as remote from the meaning of the experiments as if we lived in the moon. The doctors had laughed at what they felt was our childlike interest in the fate of the animals.

First we sorted the dogs; that was fairly easy, for we could remember the size and color of most of them. But the rats and mice and guinea pigs baffled us completely.

We put our heads together and pondered, down in the underworld of the great scientific institute. It was a strange scientific conference; the fate of the entire medical research institute rested in our ignorant, black hands.

We remembered the number of rats, mice, or guinea pigs—we had to handle them several times a day—that went into a given cage, and we supplied the number helter-skelter from those animals that we could catch running loose on the floor. We discovered that many rats, mice, and guinea pigs were missing—they had been killed in the scuffle. We solved that problem by taking healthy stock from other cages and putting them into cages with sick animals. We repeated this process until we were certain that, numerically at least, all the animals with which the doctors were experimenting were accounted for.

The rabbits came last. We broke the rabbits down into two general groups; those that had fur on their bellies and those that did not. We knew that all those rabbits that had shaven bellies—our scientific knowledge adequately covered this point because it was our job to shave the rabbits—were undergoing the Aschheim-Zondek tests. But in what pen did a given rabbit belong? We did not know. I solved the problem very simply. I counted the shaven rabbits; they numbered seventeen. I counted the pens labeled "Aschheim-Zondek," then proceeded to drop a shaven rabbit into each pen at random. And again we were numerically successful. At least white America had taught us how to count....

Lastly we carefully wrapped all the dead animals in newspapers and hid their bodies in a garbage can.

At a few minutes to one the room was in order; that is, the kind of order that we four Negroes could figure out. I unlocked the door and we sat waiting, whispering, vowing secrecy, wondering what the reaction of the doctors would be.

Finally a doctor came, gray-haired, white-coated, spectacled, efficient, serious, taciturn, bearing a tray upon which sat a bottle of mysterious fluid and a hypodermic needle.

"My rats, please."

Cooke shuffled forward to serve him. We held our breath. Cooke got the cage which he knew the doctor always called for at that hour and brought it forward. One by one, Cooke took out the rats and held them as the doctor solemnly injected the mysterious fluid under their skins.

"Thank you, Cooke," the doctor murmured.

"Not at all, sir," Cooke mumbled with a suppressed gasp.

When the doctor had gone we looked at one another, hardly daring to believe that our secret would be kept. We were so anxious that we did not know whether to curse or laugh. Another doctor came.

"Give me A-Z rabbit number 14."

"Yes, sir," I said.

I brought him the rabbit and he took it upstairs to the operating room. We waited for repercussions. None came.

All that afternoon the doctors came and went. I would run into the room—stealing a few seconds from my step-scrubbing—and ask what progress was being made and would learn that the doctors had detected nothing. At quitting time we felt triumphant.

"They won't ever know," Cooke boasted in a whisper.

I saw Brand stiffen. I knew that he was aching to dispute Cooke's optimism, but the memory of the fight he had just had was so fresh in his mind that he could not speak.

Another day went by and nothing happened. Then another day. The doctors examined the animals and wrote in their little black books, in their big black books, and continued to trace red and black lines upon the charts.

A week passed and we felt out of danger. Not one question had been asked.

Of course, we four black men were much too modest to make our contribution known, but we often wondered what went on in the laboratories after that secret disaster. Was some scientific hypothesis, well on its way to validation and ultimate public use, discarded because of unexpected findings on that cold winter day? Was some tested principle given a new and strange refinement because of fresh, remarkable evidence? Did some brooding research worker—those who held stop watches and slopped their feet carelessly in the water of the steps I tried so hard to keep clean—get a wild, if brief, glimpse of a new scientific truth? Well, we never heard. . . .

I brooded upon whether I should have gone to the director's office and told him what had happened, but each time I thought of it I remembered that the director had been the man who had ordered the boy to stand over me while I was working and time my movements with a stop watch. He did not regard me as a human being. I did not share his world. I earned thirteen dollars a week and I had to support four people with it, and should I risk that thirteen dollars by acting idealistically? Brand and Cooke would have hated me and would have eventually driven me from the job had I "told" on them. The hospital kept us four Negroes as though we were close kin to the animals we tended, huddled together down in the underworld corridors of the hospital, separated by a vast psychological distance from the significant processes of the rest of the hospital—just as America had kept us locked in the dark underworld of American life for three hundred years—and we had made our own code of ethics, values, loyalty.

Study and Discussion Questions

1. How many jobs does the narrator tell us about in "The Man Who Went to Chicago"? List and briefly describe each one.
2. What does the narrator learn (a) about himself and (b) about the world he lives in from each job experience?
3. One of the more insidious consequences of oppression is the way it affects the behavior and self-image of those who are oppressed. List examples Wright gives us of this phenomenon in "The Man Who Went To Chicago."
4. What insight does the narrator come to in the relief station?
5. What motivates the narrator in each case to (a) quit Hoffman's, (b) work as an insurance agent, and (c) keep quiet about the laboratory mishap?
6. What do the dogs without vocal cords symbolize?
7. Wright moves between narration and argument in this essay. Note in the text where he is musing/philosophizing/making an argument and where he is narrating/telling a story.
8. Is this combination of narration and reflection/argument effective? What would he gain or lose by only telling the story? What would he gain or lose by only writing the argument?

Suggestions for Writing

1. How do you think a white person's work experiences would have been similar to and different from those of Wright's narrator?
2. List at least three aspects of Wright's criticism of white Americans' treatment of black Americans. Find evidence from "The Man Who Went To Chicago" to support each of your points.
3. Write about a job experience of your own in which you felt exploited, frustrated, and/or misunderstood.

Critical Resources

1. Baldwin, James. *Notes on a Native Son.* New York: Beacon Press, 1955.
2. Butler, Robert, ed. *The Critical Response to Richard Wright.* Westport, CT: Greenwood, 1995.
3. Gates, Henry Louis, ed. *Richard Wright: Critical Perspectives Past and Present.* New York: Amistad, 1993.
4. Kinnamon, Keneth and Michel Fabre, eds. *Conversations with Richard Wright.* Jackson, MS: University of Mississippi Press, 1993.

❋ ❋ ❋

DOROTHY ALLISON (b. 1949)

Dorothy Allison was born in Greenville, South Carolina, and was the first person from her family to finish high school. She studied at Florida Presbyterian College (now Eckerd College) and the New School for Social Research in New York City. Working in the tradition of other Southern writers such as Flannery O'Connor and William Faulkner, Allison's writings offer a more contemporary and complex picture of southern, working-class culture. In both her poetry and fiction, Allison's working class, female characters struggle to find understanding as they grapple with issues of class, gender and sexuality. Her work includes The Women Who Hate Me: Poetry 1980–1990 *(1991); the novels* Bastard Out of Carolina *(1992) and* Cavedweller *(1998); a collection of short stories,* Trash *(1988); an essay collection,* Skin: Talking About Sex, Class and Literature *(1993); and the memoir,* One or Two Things I Know for Sure *(1995). She is currently working on a science fiction trilogy. "Gun Crazy", first printed in* Skin, *tells the story of one girl's experience learning to shoot a real gun. In her eloquent personal essay, "A Question of Class," Allison tells the story of her working-class/poor/white trash background and of her development as a writer, while at the same time debunking American myths about social class.*

A Question of Class   (1993)

The first time I heard, "They're different than us, don't value human life the way we do," I was in high school in Central Florida. The man speaking was an army recruiter talking to a bunch of boys, telling them what the army was really like, what they could expect overseas. A cold angry feeling swept over me. I had heard the word *they* pronounced in that same callous tone before. *They,* those people over there, those people who are not us, they die so easily, kill each other so casually. They are different. *We,* I thought. *Me.*

When I was six or eight back in Greenville, South Carolina, I had heard that same matter-of-fact tone of dismissal applied to me. "Don't you play with her. I don't want you talking to them." Me and my family, we had always been *they.* Who am I? I wondered, listening to that recruiter. Who are my people? We die so easily, disappear so completely—we/they, the poor and the queer. I pressed my bony white trash fists to my stubborn lesbian mouth. The rage was a good feeling, stronger and purer than the shame that followed it, the fear and the sudden urge to run and hide, to deny, to pretend I did not know who I was and what the world would do to me.

My people were not remarkable. We were ordinary, but even so we were mythical. We were the *they* everyone talks about—the ungrateful poor. I grew up trying to run away from the fate that destroyed so many of the people I loved, and having learned the habit of hiding, I found I had also learned to hide from myself. I did not know who I was, only that I did not want to be *they,* the ones who are destroyed or dismissed to make the "real" people, the important people, feel safer. By the time I understood that I was queer, that habit of hiding was deeply set in me, so deeply that it was not a choice but an instinct. Hide, hide to survive, I thought, knowing that if I told the truth about my life, my family, my sexual desire, my history, I would move over into that unknown territory, the land of they, would never have the chance to name my own life, to understand it or claim it.

Why are you so afraid? my lovers and friends have asked me the many times I have suddenly seemed a stranger, someone who would not speak to them, would not do the things they believed I should do, simple things like applying for a job, or a grant, or some award they were sure I could acquire easily. Entitlement, I have told them, is a matter of feeling like we rather than they. You think you have a right to things, a place in the world, and it is so intrinsically a part of you that you cannot imagine people like me, people who seem to live in your world, who don't have it. I have explained what I know over and over, in every way I can, but I have never been able to make clear the degree of my fear, the extent to which I feel myself denied: not only that I am queer in a world that hates queers, but that I was born poor into a world that despises the poor. The need to make my world believable to people who have never experienced it is part of why I write fiction. I know that some things must be felt to be understood, that despair, for example, can never be adequately analyzed; it must be lived. But if I can write a story that so draws the reader in that she imagines herself like my characters, feels their sense of fear and uncertainty, their hopes and terrors, then I have come closer to knowing myself as real, important as the very people I have always watched with awe.

I have known I was a lesbian since I was a teenager, and I have spent a good twenty years making peace with the effects of incest and physical abuse. But what may be the central fact of my life is that I was born in 1949 in Greenville, South Carolina, the bastard daughter of a white woman from a desperately poor family, a girl who had left the seventh grade the year before, worked as a waitress, and was just a month past fifteen when she had me. That fact, the inescapable impact of being born in a condition of poverty that this society finds shameful, contemptible, and somehow deserved, has had dominion over me to such an extent that I have spent my life trying to overcome or deny it. I have learned with great difficulty that the vast majority of people believe that poverty is a voluntary condition.

I have loved my family so stubbornly that every impulse to hold them in contempt has sparked in me a countersurge of pride—complicated and undercut by an urge to fit us into the acceptable myths and theories of both mainstream society and a lesbian-feminist reinterpretation. The choice becomes Steven Spielberg movies or Erskine Caldwell[1] novels, the one valorizing and the other

---

[1] American novelist (1903–1987).

caricaturing, or the patriarchy as villain, trivializing the choices the men and women of my family have made. I have had to fight broad generalizations from every theoretical viewpoint.

Traditional feminist theory has had a limited understanding of class differences and of how sexuality and self are shaped by both desire and denial. The ideology implies that we are all sisters who should only turn our anger and suspicion on the world outside the lesbian community. It is easy to say that the patriarchy did it, that poverty and social contempt are products of the world of the fathers, and often I felt a need to collapse my sexual history into what I was willing to share of my class background, to pretend that my life both as a lesbian and as a working-class escapee was constructed by the patriarchy. Or conversely, to ignore how much my life was shaped by growing up poor and talk only about what incest did to my identity as a woman and as a lesbian. The difficulty is that I can't ascribe everything that has been problematic about my life simply and easily to the patriarchy, or to incest, or even to the invisible and much-denied class structure of our society.

In my lesbian-feminist collective we had long conversations about the mind/body split, the way we compartmentalize our lives to survive. For years I thought that that concept referred to the way I had separated my activist life from the passionate secret life in which I acted on my sexual desires. I was convinced that the fracture was fairly simple, that it would be healed when there was time and clarity to do so—at about the same point when I might begin to understand sex. I never imagined that it was not a split but a splintering, and I passed whole portions of my life—days, months, years—in pure directed progress, getting up every morning and setting to work, working so hard and so continually that I avoided examining in any way what I knew about my life. Busywork became a trance state. I ignored who I really was and how I became that person, continued in that daily progress, became an automaton who was what she did.

I tried to become one with the lesbian-feminist community so as to feel real and valuable. I did not know that I was hiding, blending in for safety just as I had done in high school, in college. I did not recognize the impulse to forget. I believed that all those things I did not talk about, or even let myself think too much about, were not important, that none of them defined me. I had constructed a life, an identity in which I took pride, an alternative lesbian family in which I felt safe, and I did not realize that the fundamental me had almost disappeared.

It is surprising how easy it was to live that life. Everyone and everything cooperated with the process. Everything in our culture—books, television, movies, school, fashion—is presented as if it is being seen by one pair of eyes, shaped by one set of hands, heard by one pair of ears. Even if you know you are not part of that imaginary creature—if you like country music not symphonies, read books cynically, listen to the news unbelievingly, are lesbian not heterosexual, and surround yourself with your own small deviant community—you are still shaped by that hegemony, or your resistance to it. The only way I found to resist that homogenized view of the world was to make myself part of something larger than myself. As a feminist and a radical lesbian organizer, and later as a sex radical (which eventually became the term, along with pro-sex feminist, for those who were not anti-pornography but anti-censorship, those of us arguing for sexual diversity), the need to belong, to feel safe, was just as important for me as for any heterosexual, nonpolitical citizen, and sometimes even more important because the rest of my life was so embattled.

The first time I read the Jewish lesbian Irena Klepfisz's poems,[2] I experienced a frisson of recognition. It was not that my people had been "burned off the map" or murdered as hers had. No, we had been encouraged to destroy ourselves, made invisible because we did not fit the myths of the noble poor generated by the middle class. Even now, past forty and stubbornly proud of my family, I feel the draw of that mythology, that romanticized, edited version of the poor. I find myself looking back and wondering what was real, what was true. Within my family, so much was lied about, joked about, denied, or told with deliberate indirection, an undercurrent of humiliation or a brief pursed grimace that belied everything that had been said. What was real? The poverty depicted in books and movies was romantic, a backdrop for the story of how it was escaped.

The poverty portrayed by left-wing intellectuals was just as romantic, a platform for assailing the upper and middle classes, and from their perspective, the working-class hero was invariably male, righteously indignant, and inhumanly noble. The reality of self-hatred and violence was either absent or caricatured. The poverty I knew was dreary, deadening, shameful, the women powerful in ways not generally seen as heroic by the world outside the family.

My family's lives were not on television, not in books, not even comic books. There was a myth of the poor in this country, but it did not include us, no matter how hard I tried to squeeze us in. There was an idea of the good poor—hardworking, ragged but clean, and intrinsically honorable. I understood that we were the bad poor: men who drank and couldn't keep a job; women, invariably pregnant before marriage, who quickly became worn, fat, and old from working too many hours and bearing too many children; and children with runny noses, watery eyes, and the wrong attitudes. My cousins quit school, stole cars, used drugs, and took dead-end jobs pumping gas or waiting tables. We were not noble, not grateful, not even hopeful. We knew ourselves despised. My family was ashamed of being poor, of feeling hopeless. What was there to work for, to save money for, to fight for or struggle against? We had generations before us to teach us that nothing ever changed, and that those who did try to escape failed.

My mama had eleven brothers and sisters, of whom I can name only six. No one is left alive to tell me the names of the others. It was my grandmother who

---

[2]*A Few Words in the Mother Tongue: Poems, Selected and New* (Eighth Mountain Press: Portland, Oregon, 1990) [Allison's note].

told me about my real daddy, a shiftless pretty man who was supposed to have married, had six children, and sold cut-rate life insurance to poor Black people. My mama married when I was a year old, but her husband died just after my little sister was born a year later.

When I was five, Mama married the man she lived with until she died. Within the first year of their marriage Mama miscarried, and while we waited out in the hospital parking lot, my stepfather molested me for the first time, something he continued to do until I was past thirteen. When I was eight or so, Mama took us away to a motel after my stepfather beat me so badly it caused a family scandal, but we returned after two weeks. Mama told me that she really had no choice: she could not support us alone. When I was eleven I told one of my cousins that my stepfather was molesting me. Mama packed up my sisters and me and took us away for a few days, but again, my stepfather swore he would stop, and again we went back after a few weeks. I stopped talking for a while, and I have only vague memories of the next two years.

My stepfather worked as a route salesman, my mama as a waitress, laundry worker, cook, or fruit packer. I could never understand, since they both worked so hard and such long hours, how we never had enough money, but it was also true of my mama's brothers and sisters who worked hard in the mills or the furnace industry. In fact, my parents did better than anyone else in the family. But eventually my stepfather was fired and we hit bottom—nightmarish months of marshals at the door, repossessed furniture, and rubber checks. My parents worked out a scheme so that it appeared my stepfather had abandoned us, but instead he went down to Florida, got a new job, and rented us a house. He returned with a U-Haul trailer in the dead of night, packed us up, and moved us south.

The night we left South Carolina for Florida, my mama leaned over the backseat of her old Pontiac and promised us girls, "It'll be better there." I don't know if we believed her, but I remember crossing Georgia in the early morning, watching the red clay hills and swaying grey blankets of moss recede through the back window. I kept looking at the trailer behind us, ridiculously small to contain everything we owned. Mama had packed nothing that wasn't fully paid off, which meant she had only two things of worth: her washing and sewing machines, both of them tied securely to the trailer walls. Throughout the trip I fantasized an accident that would burst that trailer, scattering old clothes and cracked dishes on the tarmac.

I was only thirteen. I wanted us to start over completely, to begin again as new people with nothing of the past left over. I wanted to run away from who we had been seen to be, who we had been. That desire is one I have seen in other members of my family. It is the first thing I think of when trouble comes—the geographic solution. Change your name, leave town, disappear, make yourself over. What hides behind that impulse is the conviction that the life you have lived, the person you are, is valueless, better off abandoned, that running away is easier than trying to change things, that change itself is not possible. Sometimes I think it is this conviction—more seductive than alcohol or violence, more subtle than sexual hatred or gender injustice—that has dominated my life and made real change so painful and difficult.

Moving to Central Florida did not fix our lives. It did not stop my stepfather's violence, heal my shame, or make my mother happy. Once there, our lives became controlled by my mother's illness and medical bills. She had a hysterectomy when I was about eight and endured a series of hospitalizations for ulcers and a chronic back problem. Through most of my adolescence she superstitiously refused to allow anyone to mention the word *cancer*. When she was not sick, Mama and my stepfather went on working, struggling to pay off what seemed an insurmountable load of debts.

By the time I was fourteen, my sisters and I had found ways to discourage most of our stepfather's sexual advances. We were not close, but we united against him. Our efforts were helped along when he was referred to a psychotherapist after he lost his temper at work, and was prescribed drugs that made him sullen but less violent. We were growing up quickly, my sisters moving toward dropping out of school while I got good grades and took every scholarship exam I could find. I was the first person in my family to graduate from high school, and the fact that I went on to college was nothing short of astonishing.

We all imagine our lives are normal, and I did not know my life was not everyone's. It was in Central Florida that I began to realize just how different we were. The people we met there had not been shaped by the rigid class structure that dominated the South Carolina Piedmont. The first time I looked around my junior high classroom and realized I did not know who those people were—not only as individuals but as categories, who their people were and how they saw themselves—I also realized that they did not know me. In Greenville, everyone knew my family, knew we were trash, and that meant we were supposed to be poor, supposed to have grim low-paid jobs, have babies in our teens, and never finish school. But Central Florida in the 1960s was full of runaways and immigrants, and our mostly white working-class suburban school sorted us out not by income and family background but by intelligence and aptitude tests. Suddenly I was boosted into the college-bound track, and while there was plenty of contempt for my inept social skills, pitiful wardrobe, and slow drawling accent, there was also something I had never experienced before: a protective anonymity, and a kind of grudging respect and curiosity about who I might become. Because they did not see poverty and hopelessness as a foregone conclusion for my life, I could begin to imagine other futures for myself.

In that new country, we were unknown. The myth of the poor settled over us and glamorized us. I saw it in the eyes of my teachers, the Lion's Club representative who paid for my new glasses, and the lady from the Junior League[3] who told me about the scholarship I had won. Better, far better, to be one of the mythical poor than to be part of the *they* I had known before. I also experienced a

---

[3]Lion's Club, a social organization for businesspeople; Junior League, an upper-class women's organization that does charitable and volunteer work.

new level of fear, a fear of losing what had never before been imaginable. Don't let me lose this chance, I prayed, and lived in terror that I might suddenly be seen again as what I knew myself to be.

As an adolescent I thought that my family's escape from South Carolina played like a bad movie. We fled the way runaway serfs might have done, with the sheriff who would have arrested my stepfather the imagined border guard. I am certain that if we had remained in South Carolina, I would have been trapped by my family's heritage of poverty, jail, and illegitimate children—that even being smart, stubborn, and a lesbian would have made no difference.

My grandmother died when I was twenty, and after Mama went home for the funeral, I had a series of dreams in which we still lived up in Greenville, just down the road from where Granny died. In the dreams I had two children and only one eye, lived in a trailer, and worked at the textile mill. Most of my time was taken up with deciding when I would finally kill my children and myself. The dreams were so vivid, I became convinced they were about the life I was meant to have had, and I began to work even harder to put as much distance as I could between my family and me. I copied the dress, mannerisms, attitudes, and ambitions of the girls I met in college, changing or hiding my own tastes, interests, and desires. I kept my lesbianism a secret, forming a relationship with an effeminate male friend that served to shelter and disguise us both. I explained to friends that I went home so rarely because my stepfather and I fought too much for me to be comfortable in his house. But that was only part of the reason I avoided home, the easiest reason. The truth was that I feared the person I might become in my mama's house, the woman of my dreams—hateful, violent, and hopeless.

It is hard to explain how deliberately and thoroughly I ran away from my own life. I did not forget where I came from, but I gritted my teeth and hid it. When I could not get enough scholarship money to pay for graduate school, I spent a year of rage working as a salad girl, substitute teacher, and maid. I finally managed to find a job by agreeing to take any city assignment where the Social Security Administration needed a clerk. Once I had a job and my own place far away from anyone in my family, I became sexually and politically active, joining the Women's Center support staff and falling in love with a series of middle-class women who thought my accent and stories thoroughly charming. The stories I told about my family, about South Carolina, about being poor itself, were all lies, carefully edited to seem droll or funny. I knew damn well that no one would want to hear the truth about poverty, the hopelessness and fear, the feeling that nothing I did would ever make any difference and the raging resentment that burned beneath my jokes. Even when my lovers and I formed an alternative lesbian family, sharing what we could of our resources, I kept the truth about my background and who I knew myself to be a carefully obscured mystery. I worked as hard as I could to make myself a new person, an emotionally healthy radical lesbian activist, and I believed completely that by remaking myself I was helping to remake the world.

For a decade, I did not go home for more than a few days at a time.

When in the 1980s I ran into the concept of feminist sexuality, I genuinely did not know what it meant. Though I was, and am, a feminist, and committed to claiming the right to act on my sexual desires without tailoring my lust to a sex-fearing society, demands that I explain or justify my sexual fantasies have left me at a loss. How does anyone explain sexual need?

The Sex Wars are over, I've been told, and it always makes me want to ask who won. But my sense of humor may be a little obscure to women who have never felt threatened by the way most lesbians use and mean the words *pervert* and *queer.* I use the word queer to mean more than lesbian. Since I first used it in 1980 I have always meant it to imply that I am not only a lesbian but a transgressive lesbian—femme, masochistic, as sexually aggressive as the women I seek out, and as pornographic in my imagination and sexual activities as the heterosexual hegemony has ever believed.

My aunt Dot used to joke, "There are two or three things I know for sure, but never the same things and I'm never as sure as I'd like." What I know for sure is that class, gender, sexual preference, and prejudice—racial, ethnic, and religious—form an intricate lattice that restricts and shapes our lives, and that resistance to hatred is not a simple act. Claiming your identity in the cauldron of hatred and resistance to hatred is infinitely complicated, and worse, almost unexplainable.

I know that I have been hated as a lesbian both by "society" and by the intimate world of my extended family, but I have also been hated or held in contempt (which is in some ways more debilitating and slippery than hatred) by lesbians for behavior and sexual practices shaped in large part by class. My sexual identity is intimately constructed by my class and regional background, and much of the hatred directed at my sexual preferences is class hatred—however much people, feminists in particular, like to pretend this is not a factor. The kind of woman I am attracted to is invariably the kind of woman who embarrasses respectably middle-class, politically aware lesbian feminists. My sexual ideal is butch, exhibitionistic, physically aggressive, smarter than she wants you to know, and proud of being called a pervert. Most often she is working class, with an aura of danger and an ironic sense of humor. There is a lot of contemporary lip service paid to sexual tolerance, but the fact that my sexuality is constructed within, and by, a butch/femme and leather fetishism is widely viewed with distaste or outright hatred.

For most of my life I have been presumed to be misguided, damaged by incest and childhood physical abuse, or deliberately indulging in hateful and retrograde sexual practices out of a selfish concentration on my own sexual satisfaction. I have been expected to abandon my desires, to become the normalized woman who flirts with fetishization, who plays with gender roles and treats the historical categories of deviant desire with humor or gentle contempt but never takes any of it so seriously as to claim a sexual identity based on these categories. It was hard enough for me to shake off demands when they were made by straight society. It was appalling when I found the same demands made by other lesbians.

One of the strengths I derive from my class background is that I am accustomed to contempt. I know that I have no chance of becoming what my detractors expect of me, and I believe that even the attempt to please them will only further engage their contempt, and my own self-contempt as well. Nonetheless, the relationship between the life I have lived and the way that life is seen by strangers has constantly invited a kind of self-mythologizing fantasy. It has always been tempting for me to play off of the stereotypes and misconceptions of mainstream culture, rather than describe a difficult and sometimes painful reality.

I am trying to understand how we internalize the myths of our society even as we resist them. I have felt a powerful temptation to write about my family as a kind of morality tale, with us as the heroes and middle and upper classes as the villains. It would be within the romantic myth, for example, to pretend that we were the kind of noble Southern whites portrayed in the movies, mill workers for generations until driven out by alcoholism and a family propensity for rebellion and union talk. But that would be a lie. The truth is that no one in my family ever joined a union.

Taken to its limits, the myth of the poor would make my family over into union organizers or people broken by the failure of the unions. As far as my family was concerned union organizers, like preachers, were of a different class, suspect and hated however much they might be admired for what they were supposed to be trying to achieve. Nominally Southern Baptist, no one in my family actually paid much attention to preachers, and only little children went to Sunday school. Serious belief in anything—any political ideology, any religious system, or any theory of life's meaning and purpose—was seen as unrealistic. It was an attitude that bothered me a lot when I started reading the socially conscious novels I found in the paperback racks when I was eleven or so. I particularly loved Sinclair Lewis's[4] novels and wanted to imagine my own family as part of the working man's struggle.

"We were not joiners," my aunt Dot told me with a grin when I asked her about the union. My cousin Butch laughed at that, told me the union charged dues, and said, "Hell, we can't even be persuaded to toss money in the collection plate. An't gonna give it to no union man." It shamed me that the only thing my family wholeheartedly believed in was luck and the waywardness of fate. They held the dogged conviction that the admirable and wise thing to do was keep a sense of humor, never whine or cower, and trust that luck might someday turn as good as it had been bad—and with just as much reason. Becoming a political activist with an almost religious fervor was the thing I did that most outraged my family and the Southern working-class community they were part of.

---

[4]American novelist (1885–1951).

Similarly, it was not my sexuality, my lesbianism, that my family saw as most rebellious; for most of my life, no one but my mama took my sexual preference very seriously. It was the way I thought about work, ambition, and self-respect. They were waitresses, laundry workers, counter girls. I was the one who went to work as a maid, something I never told any of them. They would have been angry if they had known. Work was just work for them, necessary. You did what you had to do to survive. They did not so much believe in taking pride in doing your job as in stubbornly enduring hard work and hard times. At the same time, they held that there were some forms of work, including maid's work, that were only for Black people, not white, and while I did not share that belief, I knew how intrinsic it was to the way my family saw the world. Sometimes I felt as if I straddled cultures and belonged on neither side. I would grind my teeth at what I knew was my family's unquestioning racism while continuing to respect their pragmatic endurance. But more and more as I grew older, what I felt was a deep estrangement from their view of the world, and gradually a sense of shame that would have been completely incomprehensible to them.

"Long as there's lunch counters, you can always find work," I was told by my mother and my aunts. Then they'd add, "I can get me a little extra with a smile." It was obvious there was supposed to be nothing shameful about it, that needy smile across a lunch counter, that rueful grin when you didn't have rent, or the half-provocative, half-pleading way my mama could cajole the man at the store to give her a little credit. But I hated it, hated the need for it and the shame that would follow every time I did it myself. It was begging, as far as I was concerned, a quasi-prostitution that I despised even while I continued to rely on it. After all, I needed the money.

"Just use that smile," my girl cousins used to joke, and I hated what I knew they meant. After college, when I began to support myself and study feminist theory, I became more contemptuous rather than more understanding of the women in my family. I told myself that prostitution is a skilled profession and my cousins were never more than amateurs. There was a certain truth in this, though like all cruel judgments rendered from the outside, it ignored the conditions that made it true. The women in my family, my mother included, had sugar daddies, not johns, men who slipped them money because they needed it so badly. From their point of view they were nice to those men because the men were nice to them, and it was never so direct or crass an arrangement that they would set a price on their favors. Nor would they have described what they did as prostitution. Nothing made them angrier than the suggestion that the men who helped them out did it just for their favors. They worked for a living, they swore, but this was different.

I always wondered if my mother hated her sugar daddy, or if not him then her need for what he offered her, but it did not seem to me in memory that she had. He was an old man, half-crippled, hesitant and needy, and he treated my mama with enormous consideration and, yes, respect. The relationship between them was painful, and since she and my stepfather could not earn enough to support the family, Mama could not refuse her sugar daddy's money. At the same time the man made no assumptions about that money buying anything Mama was not already offering. The truth was, I think, that she genuinely liked him, and only partly because he treated her so well.

Even now, I am not sure whether there was a sexual exchange between them. Mama was a pretty woman, and she was kind to him, a kindness he obviously did not get from anyone else in his life. Moreover, he took extreme care not to cause her any problems with my stepfather. As a teenager, with a teenager's contempt for moral failings and sexual complexity of any kind, I had been convinced that Mama's relationship with that old man was contemptible. Also, that I would never do such a thing. But the first time a lover of mine gave me money and I took it, everything in my head shifted. The amount was not much to her, but it was a lot to me and I needed it. While I could not refuse it, I hated myself for taking it and I hated her for giving it. Worse, she had much less grace about my need than my mama's sugar daddy had displayed toward her. All that bitter contempt I felt for my needy cousins and aunts raged through me and burned out the love. I ended the relationship quickly, unable to forgive myself for selling what I believed should only be offered freely—not sex but love itself.

When the women in my family talked about how hard they worked, the men would spit to the side and shake their heads. Men took real jobs—harsh, dangerous, physically daunting work. They went to jail, not just the cold-eyed, careless boys who scared me with their brutal hands, but their gentler, softer brothers. It was another family thing, what people expected of my mama's people, mine. "His daddy's that one was sent off to jail in Georgia, and his uncle's another. Like as not, he's just the same," you'd hear people say of boys so young they still had their milk teeth. We were always driving down to the county farm to see somebody, some uncle, cousin, or nameless male relation. Shaven-headed, sullen, and stunned, they wept on Mama's shoulder or begged my aunts to help. "I didn't do nothing, Mama," they'd say, and it might have been true, but if even we didn't believe them, who would? No one told the truth, not even about how their lives were destroyed.

One of my favorite cousins went to jail when I was eight years old, for breaking into pay phones with another boy. The other boy was returned to the custody of his parents. My cousin was sent to the boys' facility at the county farm. After three months, my mama took us down there to visit, carrying a big basket of fried chicken, cold cornbread, and potato salad. Along with a hundred others we sat out on the lawn with my cousin and watched him eat like he hadn't had a full meal in the whole three months. I stared at his near-bald head and his ears marked with fine blue scars from the carelessly handled razor. People were laughing, music was playing, and a tall, lazy, uniformed man walked past us chewing on toothpicks and watching us all closely. My cousin kept his head down, his face hard with hatred, only looking back at the guard when he turned away.

"Sons-a-bitches," he whispered, and my mama shushed him. We all sat still when the guard turned back to us. There was a long moment of quiet, and then that man let his face relax into a big wide grin.

"Uh-huh," he said. That was all he said. Then he turned and walked away. None of us spoke. None of us ate. He went back inside soon after, and we left. When we got back to the car, my mama sat there for a while crying quietly. The next week my cousin was reported for fighting and had his stay extended by six months.

My cousin was fifteen. He never went back to school, and after jail he couldn't join the army. When he finally did come home we never talked, never had to. I knew without asking that the guard had had his little revenge, knew too that my cousin would break into another phone booth as soon as he could, but do it sober and not get caught. I knew without asking the source of his rage, the way he felt about clean, well-dressed, contemptuous people who looked at him like his life wasn't as important as a dog's. I knew because I felt it too. That guard had looked at me and Mama with the same expression he used on my cousin. We were trash. We were the ones they built the county farm to house and break. The boy who was sent home was the son of a deacon in the church, the man who managed the hardware store.

As much as I hated that man, and his boy, there was a way in which I also hated my cousin. He should have known better, I told myself, should have known the risk he ran. He should have been more careful. As I grew older and started living on my own, it was a litany I used against myself even more angrily than I used it against my cousin. I knew who I was, knew that the most important thing I had to do was protect myself and hide my despised identity, blend into the myth of both the good poor and the reasonable lesbian. When I became a feminist activist, that litany went on reverberating in my head, but by then it had become a groundnote, something so deep and omnipresent I no longer heard it, even when everything I did was set to its cadence.

By 1975 I was earning a meager living as a photographer's assistant in Tallahassee, Florida. But the real work of my life was my lesbian-feminist activism, the work I did with the local women's center and the committee to found a women's studies program at Florida State University. Part of my role, as I saw it, was to be a kind of evangelical lesbian feminist, and to help develop a political analysis of this woman-hating society. I did not talk about class, except to give lip service to how we all needed to think about it, the same way I thought we all needed to think about racism. I was a determined person, living in a lesbian collective—all of us young and white and serious—studying each new book that purported to address feminist issues, driven by what I saw as a need to revolutionize the world.

Years later it's difficult to convey just how reasonable my life seemed to me at that time. I was not flippant, not consciously condescending, not casual about how tough a struggle remaking social relations would be, but like so many women of my generation, I believed absolutely that I could make a difference with my life, and I was willing to give my life for the chance to make that difference. I expected hard times, long slow periods of self-sacrifice and grinding work, expected to be hated and attacked in public, to have to set aside personal desire, lovers, and family in order to be part of something greater and more important than my individual concerns. At the same time, I was working ferociously to take my desires, my sexuality, my needs as a woman and a lesbian more seriously. I believed I was making the personal political revolution with my life every moment, whether I was scrubbing the floor of the childcare center, setting up a new budget for the women's lecture series at the university, editing the local feminist magazine, or starting a women's bookstore. That I was constantly exhausted and had no health insurance, did hours of dreary unpaid work and still sneaked out of the collective to date butch women my housemates thought retrograde and sexist never interfered with my sense of total commitment to the feminist revolution. I was not living in a closet: I had compartmentalized my own mind to such an extent that I never questioned why I did what I did. And I never admitted what lay behind all my feminist convictions—a class-constructed distrust of change, a secret fear that someday I would be found out for who I really was, found out and thrown out. If I had not been raised to give my life away, would I have made such an effective, self-sacrificing revolutionary?

The narrowly focused concentration of a revolutionary shifted only when I began to write again. The idea of writing stories seemed frivolous when there was so much work to be done, but everything changed when I found myself confronting emotions and ideas that could not be explained away or postponed until after the revolution. The way it happened was simple and unexpected. One week I was asked to speak to two completely different groups: an Episcopalian Sunday school class and a juvenile detention center. The Episcopalians were all white, well-dressed, highly articulate, nominally polite, and obsessed with getting me to tell them (without their having to ask directly) just what it was that two women did together in bed. The delinquents were all women, 80 percent Black and Hispanic, wearing green uniform dresses or blue jeans and workshirts, profane, rude, fearless, witty, and just as determined to get me to talk about what it was that two women did together in bed.

I tried to have fun with the Episcopalians, teasing them about their fears and insecurities, and being as bluntly honest as I could about my sexual practices. The Sunday school teacher, a man who had assured me of his liberal inclinations, kept blushing and stammering as the questions about my growing up and coming out became more detailed. I stepped out into the sunshine when the meeting was over, angry at the contemptuous attitude implied by all their questioning, and though I did not know why, so deeply depressed I couldn't even cry.

The delinquents were another story. Shameless, they had me blushing within the first few minutes, yelling out questions that were part curiosity and partly a way of boasting about what they already knew. "You butch or femme?" "You ever fuck boys?" "You ever want to?" "You want to have children?" "What's your girlfriend like?" I finally broke up when one very tall, confident girl leaned way over and called out, "Hey, girlfriend! I'm getting out of here next weekend. What you doing that night?" I laughed so hard I almost choked. I laughed until we were all howling and giggling together. Even getting frisked as I left didn't ruin my mood. I was still grinning when I climbed into the waterbed with my lover that night, grinning right up to the moment when she wrapped her arms around me and I burst into tears.

That night I understood, suddenly, everything that had happened to my cousins and me, understood it from a wholly new and agonizing perspective, one that made clear how brutal I had been to both my family and myself. I grasped all over again how we had been robbed and dismissed, and why I had worked so hard not to think about it. I had learned as a child that what could not be changed had to go unspoken, and worse, that those who cannot change their own lives have every reason to be ashamed of that fact and to hide it. I had accepted that shame and believed in it, but why? What had I or my cousins done to deserve the contempt directed at us? Why had I always believed us contemptible by nature? I wanted to talk to someone about all the things I was thinking that night, but I could not. Among the women I knew there was no one who would have understood what I was thinking, no other working-class woman in the women's collective where I was living. I began to suspect that we shared no common language to speak those bitter truths.

In the days that followed I found myself remembering that afternoon long ago at the county farm, that feeling of being the animal in the zoo, the thing looked at and laughed at and used by the real people who watched us. For all his liberal convictions, that Sunday school teacher had looked at me with the eyes of my cousin's long-ago guard. I felt thrown back into my childhood, into all the fears I had tried to escape. Once again I felt myself at the mercy of the important people who knew how to dress and talk, and would always be given the benefit of the doubt, while my family and I would not.

I experienced an outrage so old I could not have traced all the ways it shaped my life. I realized again that some are given no quarter, no chance, that all their courage, humor, and love for each other is just a joke to the ones who make the rules, and I hated the rule-makers. Finally, I recognized that part of my grief came from the fact that I no longer knew who I was or where I belonged. I had run away from my family, refused to go home to visit, and tried in every way to make myself a new person. How could I be working class with a college degree? As a lesbian activist? I thought about the guards at the detention center. They had not stared at me with the same picture-window emptiness they turned on the girls who came to hear me, girls who were closer to the life I had been meant to live than I could bear to examine. The contempt in their eyes was contempt for me as a lesbian, different and the same, but still contempt.

While I raged, my girlfriend held me and comforted me and tried to get me to explain what was hurting me so bad, but I could not. She had told me so often about her awkward relationship with her own family, the father who ran his own business and still sent her checks every other month. She knew almost nothing about my family, only the jokes and careful stories I had given her. I felt so alone and at risk lying in her arms that I could not have explained anything at all. I thought about those girls in the detention center and the stories they told in brutal shorthand about their sisters, brothers, cousins, and lovers. I thought about their one-note references to those they had lost, never mentioning the loss of their own hopes, their own futures, the bent and painful shape of their lives when they would finally get free. Cried-out and dry-eyed, I lay watching my sleeping girlfriend and thinking about what I had not been able to say to her. After a few hours I got up and made some notes for a poem I wanted to write, a bare, painful litany of loss shaped as a conversation between two women, one who cannot understand the other, and one who cannot tell all she knows.

It took me a long time to take that poem from a raw lyric of outrage and grief to a piece of fiction that explained to me something I had never let myself see up close before—the whole process of running away, of closing up inside your-self, of hiding. It has taken me most of my life to understand that, to see how and why those of us who are born poor and different are so driven to give our-selves away or lose ourselves, but most of all, simply to disappear as the people we really are. By the time that poem became the story "River of Names,"[5] I had made the decision to reverse that process: to claim my family, my true history, and to tell the truth not only about who I was but about the temptation to lie.

By the time I taught myself the basics of storytelling on the page, I knew there was only one story that would haunt me until I understood how to tell it—the complicated, painful story of how my mama had, and had not, saved me as a girl. Writing *Bastard Out of Carolina*[6] became, ultimately, the way to claim my fam-ily's pride and tragedy, and the embattled sexuality I had fashioned on a base of violence and abuse.

The compartmentalized life I had created burst open in the late 1970s after I began to write what I really thought about my family. I lost patience with my fear of what the women I worked with, mostly lesbians, thought of who I slept with and what we did together. When schisms developed within my community; when I was no longer able to hide within the regular dyke network; when I could not continue to justify my life by constant political activism or distract myself by sleeping around; when my sexual promiscuity, butch/femme orientation, and ex-ploration of sadomasochistic sex became part of what was driving me out of my community of choice—I went home again. I went home to my mother and my sisters, to visit, talk, argue, and begin to understand.

Once home I saw that as far as my family was concerned, lesbians were les-bians whether they wore suitcoats or leather jackets. Moreover, in all that time when I had not made peace with myself, my family had managed to make a kind of peace with me. My girlfriends were treated like slightly odd versions of my sisters' husbands, while I was simply the daughter who had always been difficult but was still a part of their lives. The result was that I started trying to confront what had made me unable really to talk to my sisters for so many years. I dis-covered that they no longer knew who I was either, and it took time and lots of listening to each other to rediscover my sense of family, and my love for them.

---

[5]*Trash* (Firebrand Books: Ithaca, New York, 1988) [Allison's note].
[6]Dutton: New York, 1992 [Allison's note].

It is only as the child of my class and my unique family background that I have been able to put together what is for me a meaningful politics, to regain a sense of why I believe in activism, why self-revelation is so important for lesbians. There is no all-purpose feminist analysis that explains the complicated ways our sexuality and core identity are shaped, the way we see ourselves as parts of both our birth families and the extended family of friends and lovers we invariably create within the lesbian community. For me, the bottom line has simply become the need to resist that omnipresent fear, that urge to hide and disappear, to disguise my life, my desires, and the truth about how little any of us understand—even as we try to make the world a more just and human place. Most of all, I have tried to understand the politics of *they*, why human beings fear and stigmatize the different while secretly dreading that they might be one of the different themselves. Class, race, sexuality, gender—and all the other categories by which we categorize and dismiss each other—need to be excavated from the inside.

The horror of class stratification, racism, and prejudice is that some people begin to believe that the security of their families and communities depends on the oppression of others, that for some to have good lives there must be others whose lives are truncated and brutal. It is a belief that dominates this culture. It is what makes the poor whites of the South so determinedly racist and the middle class so contemptuous of the poor. It is a myth that allows some to imagine that they build their lives on the ruin of others, a secret core of shame for the middle class, a goad and a spur to the marginal working class, and cause enough for the homeless and poor to feel no constraints on hatred or violence. The power of the myth is made even more apparent when we examine how, within the lesbian and feminist communities where we have addressed considerable attention to the politics of marginalization, there is still so much exclusion and fear, so many of us who do not feel safe.

I grew up poor, hated, the victim of physical, emotional, and sexual violence, and I know that suffering does not ennoble. It destroys. To resist destruction, self-hatred, or lifelong hopelessness, we have to throw off the conditioning of being despised, the fear of becoming the *they* that is talked about so dismissively, to refuse lying myths and easy moralities, to see ourselves as human, flawed, and extraordinary. All of us—extraordinary.

Study and Discussion Questions

1. "Entitlement . . . is a matter of feeling like we rather than they," writes Allison in the beginning paragraphs of this essay. What does Allison mean here by "we" and "they"? Give examples of when you have felt either like "we" or like "they."
2. Look up and write definitions for: entitlement, hegemony, frisson, patriarchy, lesbian-feminist, ideology, trash.

3. What is the myth of the poor in the United States: the good noble poor? the bad poor? What does Allison's essay suggest is limiting about both of these categories?
4. Find places in "A Question of Class" where Allison discusses or gives examples of "shame." What does the experience of shame have to do with her arguments about the effects of social class?
5. What does Allison say about anger and related emotions? Find examples in the essay.
6. Discuss "the geographic solution." What does Allison mean by it? Have you ever been tempted by or had experience with this phenomenon? What are its benefits and its limitations?
7. How does Allison say she denied or distorted her background as she moved away from it, went to college on scholarship, moved into middle-class circles and into political activism? Give examples.
8. Discuss the relation to work and to money of (a) the women and (b) the men in Allison's family.
9. Discuss the mixture of grief and outrage that started Allison writing poetry and fiction. What incidents precipitated this reaction? How and why was this an important transition for her? Why is writing, in particular, important for Allison?
10. Discuss the incident when Allison visits her fifteen-year-old cousin in jail. How does this episode become symbolic?
11. Allison talks about her years as a lesbian feminist. How did her social class background affect the way she felt among (and perhaps the way she was seen by) her comrades—other activists, housemates, lovers?

Suggestions for Writing

1. What are the costs for individuals personally and for our society of going along with (a) the myths and (b) the silences and denials around social class in the United States? What does Allison say in this essay? What do you think?
2. Write an account of your own social class background incorporating four or five factors that you believe identify your social class and providing examples from your life to illustrate each factor. How do you think your social class has influenced who you are today?
3. Read another piece of writing by Allison. See "Gun Crazy" in the Growing Up and Growing Older section or read one of Allison's short stories, novels, poems, or essays. Discuss how the two works illuminate each other.
4. What do hopes and expectations (our own, our family's, our society's) have to do with who we become?

Critical Resources

1. Allison, Dorothy. *Skin: Talking About Sex, Class, and Literature.* Ithaca, NY: Firebrand Books, 1994.
2. Irving, Katrina. "Writing It Down So That It Would Be Real: Narrative Strategies in Dorothy Allison's *Bastard Out of Carolina.*" *College Literature,* v25, n2 (Spring 1998).

3. McDonald, Kathlene. "Talking Trash, Talking Back: Resistance to Stereo-types in Dorothy Allison's *Bastard Out of Carolina.*" *Women's Studies Quarterly,* XXVI (1&2) 1998.
4. Rosenbaum, Lew, "What Is Working-Class Literature?" (July 2002) on e.poets.network: Plain Text. http://www.e-poets.net/PlainText/page 02-001 b.shtml

STUDS TERKEL, (b. 1912)

Louis "Studs" Terkel was born in New York City, the son of Russian-Jewish im-migrants. At the age of ten, his family moved to Chicago and opened a rooming house for immigrants. After graduating from high school in 1928, Terkel went on to obtain his law degree from the University of Chicago. Instead of pursuing a ca-reer in law though, Terkel found his way into the television industry. Like other politically left-minded entertainers, Terkel was "blacklisted" in the late 1940s by the House of Un-American Activities Committee, which forced producers to cancel his show "Studs' Place." Terkel would eventually end up in radio and the host of "The Studs Terkel Program," which aired from 1952 to 1997. One of the main fea-tures of the show was Terkel's interviews with people, common and famous alike. Terkel's penchant for interviewing would become the material for his award-win-ning collections of oral history. Referring to himself as a "guerilla journalist with a tape recorder," Terkel's work takes on issues of race, poverty, labor, and war, as seen from a broad spectrum of personal narratives across America. His books in-clude Hard Times: An Oral History of the Great Depression *(1970),* Working: People Talk About What They Do All Day and How They Feel About It What They Do *(1974),* American Dreams: Lost and Found *(1980),* The Good War: An Oral History of World War II *(1988, Pulitzer Prize),* Race: How Blacks and Whites Think and Feel About the American Obsession *(1992), and his latest work* Hope Dies Last: Keeping the Faith in Difficult Times *(2003). "Who Built the Pyramids?", the preface to* Working, *is the oral history of Mike Lefevre, a Chicago steelworker.*

MIKE LEFEVRE: Who Built the Pyramids?   (1974)

Who built the seven towers of Thebes?
The books are filled with the names of kings.
Was it kings, who hauled the craggy blocks of stone? . . .
In the evening when the Chinese wall was finished
Where did the masons go? . . .
                              —Bertolt Brecht

It is a two-flat dwelling, somewhere in Cicero, on the outskirts of Chicago. He is thirty-seven. He works in a steel mill. On occasion, his wife Carol works as a waitress in a neighborhood restaurant; otherwise, she is at home, caring for their two small children, a girl and a boy.

At the time of my first visit, a sculpted statuette of Mother and Child was on the floor, head severed from body. He laughed softly as he indicated his three-year-old daughter: "She Doctor Spock'd it."

I'm a dying breed. A laborer. Strictly muscle work . . . pick it up, put it down, pick it up, put it down. We handle between forty and fifty thousand pounds of steel a day. (Laughs) I know this is hard to believe—from four hundred pounds to three- and four-pound pieces. It's dying.

You can't take pride any more. You remember when a guy could point to a house he built, how many logs he stacked. He built it and he was proud of it. I don't really think I could be proud if a contractor built a home for me. I would be tempted to get in there and kick the carpenter in the ass (laughs), and take the saw away from him. 'Cause I would have to be part of it, you know.

It's hard to take pride in a bridge you're never gonna cross, in a door you're never gonna open. You're mass-producing things and you never see the end result of it. (Muses) I worked for a trucker one time. And I got this tiny satisfaction when I loaded a truck. At least I could see the truck depart loaded. In a steel mill, forget it. You don't see where nothing goes.

I got chewed out by my foreman once. He said, "Mike, you're a good worker but you have a bad attitude." My attitude is that I don't get excited about my job. I do my work but I don't say whoopee-doo. The day I get excited about my job is the day I go to a head shrinker. How are you gonna get excited about pullin' steel? How are you gonna get excited when you're tired and want to sit down?

It's not just the work. Somebody built the pyramids. Somebody's going to build something. Pyramids, Empire State Building—these things just don't happen. There's hard work behind it. I would like to see a building, say, the Empire State, I would like to see on one side of it a foot-wide strip from top to bottom with the name of every bricklayer, the name of every electrician, with all the names. So when a guy walked by, he could take his son and say, "See, that's me over there on the forty-fifth floor. I put the steel beam in." Picasso can point to a painting. What can I point to? A writer can point to a book. Everybody should have something to point to.

It's the not-recognition by other people. To say a woman is *just* a housewife is degrading, right? Okay. *Just* a housewife. It's also degrading to say *just* a laborer. The difference is that a man goes out and maybe gets smashed.

When I was single, I could quit, just split. I wandered all over the country. You worked just enough to get a poke, money in your pocket. Now I'm married and I got two kids . . . (trails off). I worked on a truck dock one time and I was single. The foreman came over and he grabbed my shoulder, kind of gave me a shove. I punched him and knocked him off the dock. I said, "Leave me alone. I'm doing my work, just stay away from me, just don't give me the with-the-hands business."

Hell, if you whip a damn mule he might kick you. Stay out of my way, that's all. Working is bad enough, don't bug me. I would rather work my ass off for eight hours a day with nobody watching me than five minutes with a guy watching me. Who you gonna sock? You can't sock General Motors, you can't sock anybody in Washington, you can't sock a system.

A mule, an old mule, that's the way I feel. Oh yeah. See, (Shows black and blue marks on arms and legs, burns.) You know what I heard from more than one guy at work? "If my kid wants to work in a factory, I am going to kick the hell out of him." I want my kid to be an effete snob. Yeah, mm-hmm. (Laughs.) I want him to be able to quote Walt Whitman, to be proud of it.

If you can't improve yourself, you improve your posterity. Otherwise life isn't worth nothing. You might as well go back to the cave and stay there. I'm sure the first caveman who went over the hill to see what was on the other side—I don't think he went there wholly out of curiosity. He went there because he wanted to get his son out of the cave. Just the same way I want to send my kid to college.

I work so damn hard and want to come home and sit down and lay around. *But I gotta get it out.* I want to be able to turn around to somebody and say, "Hey fuck you." You know? (Laughs.) The guy sitting next to me on the bus too. 'Cause all day I wanted to tell my foreman to go fuck himself, but I can't.

So I find a guy in a tavern. To tell him that. And he tells me too. I've been in brawls. He's punching me and I'm punching him, because we actually want to punch somebody else. The most that'll happen is the bartender will bar us from the tavern. But at work, you lose your job.

This one foreman I've got, he's a kid. He's a college graduate. He thinks he's better than everybody else. He was chewing me out and I was saying, "Yeah, yeah, yeah." He said, "What do you mean, yeah, yeah, yeah. Yes, *sir.*" I told him, "Who the hell are you, Hitler? What is this "*Yes, sir*" bullshit? I came here to work, I didn't come here to crawl. There's a fuckin' difference." One word led to another and I lost.

I got broke down to a lower grade and lost twenty-five cents an hour, which is a hell of a lot. It amounts to about ten dollars a week. He came over—after breaking me down. The guy comes over and smiles at me. I blew up. He didn't know it, but he was about two seconds and two feet away from a hospital. I said, "Stay the fuck away from me." He was just about to say something and was pointing his finger. I just reached my hand up and just grabbed his finger and I just put it back in his pocket. He walked away. I grabbed his finger because I'm married. If I'd a been single, I'd a grabbed his head. That's the difference.

You're doing this manual labor and you know that technology can do it. (Laughs.) Let's face it, a machine can do the work of a man; otherwise they wouldn't have space probes. Why can we send a rocket ship that's unmanned and yet send a man in a steel mill to do a mule's work?

Automation? Depends how it's applied. It frightens me if it puts me out on the street. It doesn't frighten me if it shortens my work week. You read that little thing: what are you going to do when this computer replaces you? Blow up computers. (Laughs.) Really. Blow up computers. I'll be goddamned if a computer is gonna eat before I do! I want milk for my kids and beer for me. Machines can either liberate man or enslave 'im, because they're pretty neutral. It's man who has the bias to put the thing one place or another.

If I had a twenty-hour workweek, I'd get to know my kids better, my wife better. Some kid invited me to go on a college campus. On a Saturday. It was summertime. Hell, if I have a choice of taking my wife and kids to a picnic or going to a college campus, it's gonna be the picnic. But if I worked a twenty-hour week, I could go do both. Don't you think with that extra twenty hours people could really expand? Who's to say? There are some people in factories just by force of circumstance. I'm just like the colored people. Potential Einsteins don't have to be white. They could be in cotton fields, they could be in factories.

The twenty-hour week is a possibility today. The intellectuals, they always say there are potential Lord Byrons, Walt Whitmans, Roosevelts, Picassos working in construction or steel mills or factories. But I don't think they believe it. I think what they're afraid of is the potential Hitlers and Stalins that are there too. The people in power fear the leisure man. Not just the United States. Russia's the same way.

What do you think would happen in this country if, for one year, they experimented and gave everybody a twenty-hour week? How do they know that the guy who digs Wallace[1] today doesn't try to resurrect Hitler tomorrow? Or the guy who is mildly disturbed at pollution doesn't decide to go to General Motors and shit on the guy's desk? You can become a fanatic if you had the time. The whole thing is time. That is, I think, one reason rich kids tend to be fanatic about politics: they have time. Time, that's the important thing.

It isn't that the average working guy is dumb. He's tired, that's all. I picked up a book on chess one time. That thing laid in the drawer for two or three weeks, you're too tired. During the weekends you want to take your kids out. You don't want to sit there and the kid comes up: "Daddy, can I go to the park?" You got your nose in a book? Forget it.

I know a guy fifty-seven years old. Know what he tells me? "Mike, I'm old and tired *all* the time." The first thing happens at work: when the arms start moving, the brain stops. I punch in about ten minutes to seven in the morning. I say hello to a couple of guys I like, I kid around with them. One guy says good morning to you and you say good morning. To another guy you say fuck you. The guy you say fuck you to is your friend.

I put on my hard hat, change into my safety shoes, put on my safety glasses, go to the bonderizer. It's the thing I work on. They rake the metal, they wash it,

---

[1]George Wallace, militantly segregationist governor of Alabama.

they dip it in a paint solution, and we take if off. Put it on, take it off, put it on, take it off, put it on, take it off . . .

I say hello to everybody but my boss. At seven it starts. My arms get tired about the first half-hour. After that, they don't get tired any more until maybe the last half-hour at the end of the day. I work from seven to three thirty. My arms are tired at seven thirty and they're tired at three o'clock. I hope to God I never get broke in, because I always want my arms to be tired at seven thirty and three o'clock. (Laughs.) 'Cause that's when I know that there's a beginning and there's an end. That I'm not brainwashed. In between, I don't even try to think.

If I were to put you in front of a dock and I pulled up a skid in front of you with fifty hundred-pound sacks of potatoes and there are fifty more skids just like it, and this is what you're gonna do all day, what would you think about—potatoes? Unless a guy's a nut, he never thinks about work or talks about it. Maybe about baseball or about getting drunk the other night or he got laid or he didn't get laid. I'd say one out of a hundred will actually get excited about work.

Why is it that the communists always say they're for the workingman, and as soon as they set up a country, you got guys singing to tractors? They're singing about how they love the factory. That's where I couldn't buy communism. It's the intellectuals' utopia, not mine. I cannot picture myself singing to a tractor, I just can't. (Laughs.) Or singing to steel. (Singsongs.) Oh whoop-dee-doo, I'm at the bonderizer, oh how I love this heavy steel. No thanks. Never happen.

Oh yeah, I daydeam. I fantasize about a sexy blonde in Miami who's got my union dues. (Laughs.) I think of the head of the union the way I think of the head of my company. Living it up. I think of February in Miami. Warm weather, a place to lay in. When I hear a college kid say, "I'm oppressed," I don't believe him. You know what I'd like to do for one year? Live like a college kid. Just for one year. I'd love to. Wow! (Whispers) Wow! Sports car! Marijuana! (Laughs.) Wild, sexy broads. I'd love that, hell yes, I would.

Somebody has to do this work. If my kid ever goes to college, I just want him to have a little respect, to realize that his dad is one of those somebodies. This is why even on—(muses) yeah, I guess, sure—on the black thing . . . (Sighs heavily.) I can't really hate the colored fella that's working with me all day. The black intellectual I got no respect for. The white intellectual I got no use for. I got no use for the black militant who's gonna scream three hundred years of slavery to me while I'm busting my ass. You know what I mean? (Laughs.) I have one answer for that guy: go see Rockefeller. See Harriman.[2] Don't bother me. We're in the same cotton field. So just don't bug me. (Laughs.)

After work I usually stop off at a tavern. Cold beer. Cold beer right away. When I was single, I used to go into hillbilly bars, get in a lot of brawls. Just to explode. I got a thing on my arm here (indicates scar). I got slapped with a bicycle chain. Oh, wow! (Softly) Mmm. I'm getting older. (Laughs.) I don't explode

---

[2]Nelson Rockefeller, governor of New York and then vice president of the United States; Averill Harriman, diplomat and U.S. Undersecretary of State.

as much. You might say I'm broken in. (Quickly) No, I'll never be broken in. (Sighs.) When you get a little older, you exchange the words. When you're younger, you exchange the blows.

When I get home, I argue with my wife a little bit. Turn on TV, get mad at the news. (Laughs.) I don't even watch the news that much. I watch Jackie Gleason.[3] I look for any alternative to the ten o'clock news. I don't want to go to bed angry. Don't hit a man with anything heavy at five o'clock. He just can't be bothered. This is his time to relax. The heaviest thing he wants is what his wife has to tell him.

When I come home, know what I do for the first twenty minutes? Fake it. I put on a smile. I got a kid three years old. Sometimes she says, "Daddy, where've you been?" I say, "Work." I could have told her I'd been in Disneyland. What's work to a three-year-old kid? If I feel bad, I can't take it out on the kids. Kids are born innocent of everything but birth. You can't take it out on your wife either. This is why you go to a tavern. You want to release it there rather than do it at home. What does an actor do when he's got a bad movie? I got a bad movie every day.

I don't even need the alarm clock to get up in the morning. I can go out drinking all night, fall asleep at four, and bam! I'm up at six—no matter what I do. (Laughs.) It's a pseudo-death, more or less. Your whole system is paralyzed and you give all the appearance of death. It's an in-grown clock. It's a thing you just get used to. The hours differ. It depends. Sometimes my wife wants to do something crazy like play five hundred rummy or put a puzzle together. It could be midnight, could be ten o'clock, could be nine thirty.

What do you do weekends?

Drink beer, read a book. See that one? *Violence in America.* It's one of them studies from Washington. One of them committees they're always appointing. A thing like that I read on a weekend. But during the weekdays, gee . . . I just thought about it. I don't do that much reading from Monday through Friday. Unless it's a horny book. I'll read it at work and go home and do my homework. (Laughs.) That's what the guys at the plant call it—homework. (Laughs.) Sometimes my wife works on Saturday and I drink beer at the tavern.

I went out drinking with one guy, oh, a long time ago. A college boy. He was working where I work now. Always preaching to me about how you need violence to change the system and all that garbage. We went into a hillbilly joint. Some guy there, I didn't know him from Adam, he said, "You think you're smart." I said, "What's your pleasure?" (Laughs.) He said, "My pleasure's to kick your ass." I told him I really can't be bothered. He said, "What're you, chicken?" I said, "No, I just don't want to be bothered." He came over and said something to me again. I said, "I don't beat women, drunks, or fools. Now leave me alone."

The guy called his brother over. This college boy that was with me, he came nudging my arm, "Mike, let's get out of here." I said, "What are you worried

---

[3]Comedian and actor, best known for the long running comedy TV series *The Honeymooners.*

about?" (Laughs.) This isn't unusual. People will bug you. You fend it off as much as you can with your mouth and when you can't, you punch the guy out.

It was close to closing time and we stayed. We could have left, but when you go into a place to have a beer and a guy challenges you—if you expect to go in that place again, you don't leave. If you have to fight the guy, you fight.

I got just outside the door and one of these guys jumped on me and grabbed me around the neck. I grabbed his arm and flung him against the wall. I grabbed him here (indicates throat), and jiggled his head against the wall quite a few times. He kind of slid down a little bit. This guy who said he was his brother took a swing at me with a garrison belt. He just missed and hit the wall. I'm looking around for my junior Stalin (laughs), who loves violence and everything. He's gone. Split. (Laughs.) Next day I see him at work. I couldn't get mad at him, he's a baby.

He saw a book in my back pocket one time and he was amazed. He walked up to me and he said, "You read?" I said, "What do you mean, I read?" He said, "All these dummies read the sports pages around here. What are you doing with a book?" I got pissed off at the kid right away. I said, "What do you mean, all these dummies? Don't knock a man who's paying somebody else's way through college." He was a nineteen-year-old effete snob.

Yet you want your kid to be an effete snob?

Yes. I want my kid to look at me and say, "Dad you're a nice guy, but you're a fuckin' dummy." Hell yes, I want my kid to tell me that he's not gonna be like me . . .

If I were hiring people to work, I'd try naturally to pay them a decent wage. I'd try to find out their first names, their last names, keep the company as small as possible, so I could personalize the whole thing. All I would ask a man is a handshake, see you in the morning. No applications, nothing. I wouldn't be interested in the guy's past. Nobody ever checks on the pedigree on a mule, do they? But they do on a man. Can you picture walking up to a mule and saying, "I'd like to know who his granddaddy was?"

I'd like to run a combination bookstore and tavern. (Laughs.) I would like to have a place where college kids came and a steelworker could sit down and talk. Where a workingman could not be ashamed of Walt Whitman and where a college professor could not be ashamed that he painted his house over the weekend.

If a carpenter built a cabin for poets, I think the least the poets owe the carpenter is just three or four one-liners on the wall. A little plaque: Though we labor with our minds, this place we can relax in was built by someone who can work with his hands. And his work is as noble as ours. I think the poet owes something to the guy who builds the cabin for him.

I don't think of Monday. You know what I'm thinking about on Sunday night? Next Sunday. If you work real hard, you think of a perpetual vacation. Not perpetual sleep . . . What do I think of on a Sunday night? Lord, I wish the fuck I could do something else for a living.

I don't know who the guy is who said there is nothing sweeter than an unfinished symphony. Like an unfinished painting and an unfinished poem. If he creates this thing one day—let's say, Michelangelo's Sistine Chapel. It took him a long time to do this, this beautiful work of art. But what if he had to create this Sistine Chapel a thousand times a year? Don't you think that would even dull Michelangelo's mind? Or if da Vinci had to draw his anatomical charts thirty, forty, fifty, sixty, eighty, ninety, a hundred times a day? Don't you think that would even bore da Vinci?

Way back, you spoke of the guys who built the pyramids, not the pharaohs, the unknowns. You put yourself in their category?

Yes. I want my signature on 'em, too. Sometimes, out of pure meanness, when I make something, I put a little dent in it. I like to do something to make it really unique. Hit it with a hammer. I deliberately fuck it up to see if it'll get by, just so I can say I did it. It could be anything. Let me put it this way: I think God invented the dodo bird so when we get up there we could tell Him, "Don't you ever make mistakes?" and He'd say, "Sure, look." (Laughs.) I'd like to make my imprint. My dodo bird. A mistake, *mine.* Let's say the whole building is nothing but red bricks. I'd like to have just the black one or the white one or the purple one. Deliberately fuck up.

This is gonna sound square, but my kid is my imprint. He's my freedom. There's a line in one of Hemingway's books. I think it's from *For Whom the Bell Tolls.* They're behind the enemy lines, somewhere in Spain, and she's pregnant. She wants to stay with him. He tells her no. He says, "if you die, I die," knowing he's gonna die. But if you go, I go. Know what I mean? The mystics call it the brass bowl. Continuum. You know what I mean? This is why I work. Every time I see a young guy walk by with a shirt and tie and dressed up real sharp, I'm lookin' at my kid, you know? That's it.

Study and Discussion Questions

1. What are some of LeFevre's main complaints about his job?
2. What is the impact of reading the words of the worker himself? Does it surprise you that LeFevre alludes to Whitman and Hemingway?
3. What are LeFevre's feelings about the value of education? What does he want for his children? (And, by the way, does he have the same educational goals in mind for his daughter and for his son?)
4. What's the difference between being a single worker and a married worker, according to LeFevre?
5. What's LeFevre's attitude toward race and social class?
6. Describe a typical work day for LeFevre, from the time he wakes up until the time he goes to bed that night.
7. What are some of LeFevre's hopes and fantasies: (1) about work and (2) about himself and his family?

8. What is the tone of LeFevre's piece? Point to specific words, phrases, images, incidents that support your assessment.

Suggestions for Writing

1. "What's work to a three year old kid"? LeFevre asks this question half jokingly, but consider it seriously as the beginning of a definition of "work."
2. LeFevre has had the experience of being underestimated because of the work he does. Have you ever had this experience? Have you ever been on the other side and judged someone because of what they do for a living? Describe and discuss.
3. What would happen if there were a twenty-hour work week as LeFevre suggests? If they had the time, would people try to change society as LeFevre imagines, or would they just go to bars and start fights more often? What would you do with the time?

Critical Resources

1. Chicago Historical Society. *Studs Terkel: Conversations with America.* 2002. May 1, 2005. <http://www.studsterkel.org/>
2. De Graaf, John. "The Guerilla Journalist as Oral Historian: An Interview with Louis 'Studs' Terkel." *Oral History Review: Journal of the Oral History Association* 29.1 (2002): 87–107.
3. Parker, Tony. *Studs Terkel: A Life in Words.* New York: Holt, 1996.
4. Terkel, Studs. *Talking to Myself: A Memoir of My Times.* New York: Pantheon, 1977.

MONEY AND WORK: PAPER TOPICS

1. Discuss one or more works that deal with the experience of unemployment. Take into account and discuss the significance of social factors such as gender and historical context such as the Great Depression. (Suggestions: Kromer, *Waiting For Nothing;* Le Sueur, "Women on the Breadlines"; Rukeyser, "Boy With His Hair Cut Short")
2. Discuss one or more works that depict work as a positive experience. What does the work pictured in them have in common? (Suggestions: Traven, "Assembly Line"; Frost, "Two Tramps in Mud Time"; Jailer, "Bill Hastings")
3. Discuss one or more works that depict work as a problematic experience. What does the work depicted have in common? (Suggestions: Lawrence, "City-Life"; Wright, "The Man Who Went to

Chicago"; Roethke, "Dolor"; Terkel, "Mike Lefevre: Who Built the
Pyramids?"; Cervantes, "Connery Town in August")

4. Discuss one or more works that depict work as an ambivalent experience. What, in each case, are the positive and negative factors
about the work? (Suggestions: Di Donato, *Christ in Concrete;* Alexie,
"The Reservation Cab Driver; Stone, "Eden, Then and Now")

5. Discuss one or more works that explore the impact on the family of
the need to make money. (Suggestions: Miller, *Death of a Salesman;*
Olsen, "I Stand Here Ironing"; Wilson, *The Piano Lesson*)

6. Discuss one or more works that explore the relationship between
having money (and what money can buy) and individual self-image.
(Suggestions: Bambara, "The Lesson"; Pekar, "Hypothetical
Quandary"; Hardy, "The Ruined Maid")

7. Discuss social class and its impact on one's sense of possibility in one
or more works. (Suggestions: Dobler, "Uncles' Advice, 1957"; Allison, "A Question of Class"; Olsen, "I Stand Here Ironing"; Petry,
The Street)

8. Discuss one or more works that dramatize encounters between different social classes. (Suggestions: Brooks, "Bronzeville Woman in a
Red Hat"; Walker, "Everyday Use"; Anderson, "Mining Camp Residents West Virginia, July 1935"; Bambara, "The Lesson")

9. There are many familiar sayings about work: "Many hands make
light work"; "Man may work from sun to sun, but woman's work is
never done"; "Work builds character"; and so on. Choose any such
saying about work and show how a piece of writing in this section
illustrates or disputes it.

10. How do gender, race, and ethnicity affect the kind of work available? (Suggestions: Wright, "The Man Who Went to Chicago"; Baca,
"So Mexicans Are Taking Jobs From Americans"; Mbuli, "The Miners"; Rushin, "The Black Back-Ups"; Di Donato, *Christ in Concrete*)

11. Discuss the relation between money and work in one or more writings. (Suggestions: Faulkner, "Spotted Horses"; Frost, "Two Tramps
in Mud Time"; Traven, "Assembly Line")

12. What images are used to present work, or workers, or the relation
between them? Select one poem, story, play, or nonfictional piece
of writing and analyze it in detail, or compare two or more works.
(Suggestions: Grahn, "Ella, in a square apron, along Highway 80";
Di Donato, *Christ in Concrete;* Brecht, "A Worker Reads History";
Levine, "You Can Have It")

13. Describe a day at work at either a job you liked or one you disliked. Write your description so that your overall attitude toward the job is clear in the descriptive details themselves.

14. How does creative work differ from work one has to do to earn a living? (The two may be the same but often are not.) Think about the relation of the worker to the work and about the attitude of the rest of the world toward both worker and work. (Suggestions: Jordan, "Free Flight"; Traven, "Assembly Line"; Griffin, "This is the Story of the Day in the Life of a Woman Trying")

15. Discuss the economic situation and social status of the immigrant in two or more works. (Suggestions: Guthrie, "Plane Wreck at Los Gatos [Deportees]"; Baca, "So Mexicans Are Taking Jobs from Americans"; Mar, "My Mother, Who Came From China, Where She Never Saw Snow"; Fell, "The Triangle Fire")

16. Select a type of work presented in the literature in this section and analyze how effectively a particular piece of literature conveys the experience of that work. For domestic work, for example, you might look at selections by Brooks and Ruskin; for factory work, Fell, Cervantes, Mar; for construction work, Di Donato; for waitressing, Grahn; for office work, Roethke—and so on.

17. Compare Arthur Miller's *Death of a Salesman* and the screenplay of *Salt of the Earth* (Varieties of Protest) in terms of their portrayal of family relations (keeping in mind that both were first produced before 1960). What motivates the characters and how do money, work (or the lack of it), and the nature of work affect the life of the family as well as individual family members?

18. How is social class, work, and the recognition of one's work experienced differently by women and by men? (Suggestions: Petry, *The Street;* Faulkner, "Spotted Horses"; Dobler, "Uncles' Advice"; Le Sueur, "Women on the Breadlines")

PEACE AND WAR

Pablo Picasso, "Guernica" 1937, Oil on canvas. 11'5½ × 25'5¾. Museo Nacional Centro de Arte Reina Sofia/© 2005 Estate of Pablo Picasso/Artists Rights Society (ARS), New York.

The *Oxford English Dictionary* defines war as "hostile contention by means of armed forces, carried on between nations, states, or rulers, or between parties in the same nation or state." It defines peace as "freedom from, or cessation of, war or hostilities; that condition of a nation or community in which it is not at war with another."

It says something about the way we perceive the world and its possibilities that we define peace as the absence of war rather than war as the absence of peace. Do we think of war and conflict as more normal, or more interesting, than peace? Similarly, we often view narrative forms of literature such as fiction and drama in terms of the initiation, acting out, and resolution of conflict. It appears that we are more interested in and at home with conflict, stress, and tension than with stability and tranquility. The literature about peace and war in this section reflects the fact that war as a subject has been written about far more often than peace. Peace appears to be a condition we take for granted or see, as dictionary definitions of the word suggest, as an absence of activity, or at the very least, as a rare condition, the exception rather than the rule. As Margaret Atwood's military historian notes, "for every year of peace there have been four hundred/ years of war."

"Nothing we do has the quickness, the sureness,/ the deep intelligence living at peace would have," writes Denise Levertov in her poem "Life at War." Certainly war is a breakdown of community and communication. Can we go so far as to say it is a form of social insanity? Many of the writers included in this section focus on the chaos of war, some portraying the nightmare of battle itself, as Black Elk does in "The Butchering at Wounded Knee" and as Tim O'Brien does in "The Man I Killed." Others look at the cost of war, at the wreckage of human lives in the aftermath of war. Siegfried Sassoon's poem "Does It Matter?" is concerned with people coming home from war, many of whom are wounded not only physically but also psychologically and spiritually, while Ghassan Kanafani in his story "Letter from Gaza" and Adrienne Rich, in her poem, "The School Among the Ruins" are about the trauma of war for noncombatants in contemporary war zones, Palestine and Iraq respectively. Bruce Weigl gives us a vivid example of the memories combatants often have to live with in his poem "Song of Napalm." Louise Erdrich's story "The Red Convertible" offers an example of the potential consequences in one man's life of what used to be called "shell shock" and has come to be known, since the Vietnam War, as "post-traumatic stress disorder." An interesting discovery of the research into this condition has shown that post-traumatic stress disorder is also exactly what victims of rape and child abuse suffer. Is family life for a child or an ordinary city street for a woman potentially a war zone? Though the literature in this section does not take it up directly (see poems by Kingsolver in "Women and Men" and Carson in "Protest"), this connection with child abuse, battering, and rape suggests that war is one end of a spectrum of institutionalized and sanctioned violence that has devastating consequences.

The drama, prose, and poetry in this section do address very directly the effect of war (and other organized forms of violence backed by political purpose) on civilian populations, as in Marc Kaminsky's play "In the Traffic of a Targeted

City," which is in part about the consequences of the atomic bombing of Hiroshima and Nagasaki, and Dwight Okita's "In Response to Executive Order 9066: ALL AMERICANS OF JAPANESE DESCENT MUST REPORT TO RELOCATION CENTERS." Unlike most of the world, the U.S.A. as a nation has had to cope with war on its own ground only three times in its history so far: the Revolutionary War, the Civil War, and the September 11, 2001, attack on the World Trade Center towers in New York City with its loss of more than three thousand civilian lives. Though this assessment is more complicated than it may seem, since the United States did pursue war—some might say genocide—against the indigenous peoples of North America and fought for territory not only in the Revolutionary War but in areas that are now Texas and California. The Civil War, mostly fought on Southern land, is represented in Ambrose Bierce's story "An Occurrence at Owl Creek Bridge" and poems by Walt Whitman, Emily Dickinson, and Robert Lowell. Brian Doyle's personal narrative essay, "Leap," is a powerful evocation of the World Trade Center tragedy and Martin Espada's poem, "Alabanza: In Praise of Local 100," memorializes restaurant workers who died when the towers were destroyed. Jay Parini's villanelle "After the Terror" comments on the psychological and political fallout after 9/11. Though first performed in 1986, Kaminsky's "In the Traffic of a Targeted City' is eerily prescient of the events in 2001. And Ray Bradbury's 1950s science fiction story "2026: There Will Come Soft Rains" imagines a nuclear attack on the United States.

How do people deal with the memory of war and make the transition from war to peace? Toni Morrison's World War I veteran Shadrack institutes National Suicide Day in his hometown in order to make "a place for fear as a way of controlling it." Lyman Lamartine, in "The Red Convertible," frantically tries to give his Vietnam veteran brother Henry some postwar purpose by providing him with an old car to restore. Rudyard Kipling points out in his 1890 poem "Tommy" that people often don't treat a soldier very well once the war is over. And Robert Lowell, remembering the Union soldiers who died in the Civil War in "For the Union Dead," wonders about what seemingly heroic actions of the past mean in the present, where "a savage servility/ slides by on grease." The juxtapositions of past and present, philosophy and need, suggest that there is no easy answer to the questions of what war means, whether it was worth it, or how to live a life free from the idea of war. A range of responses to the reality of living in an ongoing war zone appear in the poems by Iraqi poets Yousif al-Sa'igh, Bekes Jr. (Sherko Faiq), Fadhil al-Azzawi, and Ahmed Herdi.

Even in the midst of the inhumanity and insanity of war, there are moments of human contact, peace, security, and beauty. Yevgeny Yevtushenko's poem "The Companion" tells how two children in the Soviet Union join together in 1941 to escape the German bombs. Though war is the setting of this poem, the subject is what the children learn from and about each other, about being male and female, about themselves, and about the strength of the human spirit. Babette Deutsch's poem "Dawn in Wartime" contrasts the speaker's memory of the day before, the "burned sore scabby face of the world," with what he now sees, the immense marvel of morning "rolling toward him all its uncreated hours."

Who suffers the most from war? In his 1967 speech "A Time to Break Silence," Martin Luther King, Jr. observes that the United States has sent its poor, both black and white, to fight the poor in Southeast Asia. He speaks of "the cruel irony of watching Negro and white boys on TV screens as they kill and die together for a nation that has been unable to seat them together in the same schools. So we watch them in brutal solidarity burning the huts of a poor village." Do people from different social classes see war differently? How have African Americans seen U.S. war involvement? Look at works by Gwendolyn Brooks, Claude McKay, Owen Dodson, and Martin Luther King, Jr. (who intersects race and class) in this section. How people are positioned in a culture, their access to power and privilege, has an effect on the way they think about and experience war and peace. Regardless of race and class, who suffers the most from war? Adrienne Rich's poem "The School Among the Ruins," Marjane Satrapi's "The Dowry," and Ghassan Kanafani's "Letter from Gaza" remind us that ultimately it is the children, the next generation, who suffer the consequences of their parents' wars.

Do women and men see war differently? Yes, though the range of responses is subtle and sometimes surprising. Alice Dunbar-Nelson, writing in the early years of this century, pictures a woman's role as sitting and waiting, however uncomfortably, while the men fight. Margaret Atwood's poem "At first I was given centuries" views this traditional role ironically, and her poem "The Loneliness of the Military Historian" gives us a woman *persona* in an unusual job. Sappho's "To an army wife, in Sardis" makes a very different distinction between love and glory than Richard Lovelace's "To Lucasta, Going to the Wars." Dwight Okita writes his poem in an adolescent girl's voice. Yousif al-Sai'igh gives us the perspective of an Iraqi mother listening to news clips from a battlefield.

Why do nations and the individuals in them go to war? Is it for patriotism, glory, and a dream of heroism, as in Tennyson's "The Charge of the Light Brigade"? Is it, as Yeats suggests in "An Irish Airman Foresees His Death," neither hate of the enemy nor love of country but a "lonely impulse of delight/ Drove to this tumult in the skies"? Or is it, writes Nguyen Lam Son, a Vietnamese soldier captured in 1967, "to keep our honor,/ Already muddied by the enemy"? Wilfred Owen in his World War I poem "Dulce et Decorum Est" contrasts a vivid description of the actual horror of war to the dreams of "desperate glory" on which children, especially young boys, are raised. Not only the history books but much of our popular culture has presented war as a glorious adventure justified by love of God and country.

The drama, prose, and poetry of "Peace and War" is set mostly in the twentieth century though it begins, historically, with a poem by Sappho composed more than 2000 years ago. World Wars I and II and their aftermath from British, American, Russian, Japanese, and German perspectives are considered, along with portrayals of the Vietnam War and its repercussions, from both American and Vietnamese perspectives, through armed and terrorist conflicts in South America, the Middle East, and the beginnings of literary response to the attacks of September 11, 2001. The perspectives on war that this literature offers range from glorification of wars past, through realistic accounts of the actual devastating experience of war for both soldiers and civilians, to antiwar protest literature. The mood ranges from nostalgia through horror and grief to very dark humor.

Reading about war can provoke an intense longing for peace. How can we think and live peace actively, learn to work at peace day by day? How can we learn to see peace as a presence, not an absence? "I want strong peace, and delight,/ the wild good," writes Muriel Rukeyser in "Waking This Morning":

> today once more
> I will try to be non-violent
> one more day
> this morning, waking the world away
> in the violent day.

Perhaps if we changed our definitions of peace and war, conceptualized them and spoke about them differently, we might also begin to live those states of being in a new way.

FICTION

RAY BRADBURY (b. 1920)

Born in Waukegan, Illinois, Ray Bradbury grew up reading the "pulp" fiction of his era and began writing at an early age. During high school, his family moved to Los Angeles, where he further worked on his writing, publishing his first story in 1938 at the age of 18. He would begin his reputation as an author writing science fiction and fantasy stories for the same pulp magazines he read growing up. The publication of The Martian Chronicles *in 1950 brought him new literary fame. While he is usually thought of as a science fiction writer, Bradbury's work cannot be classified into one genre. Often allegorical in nature, much of Bradbury's work serves as a warning to humanity about the ills and moral deprivations that may come from technological advance. He has published novels, essays, poetry, screenplays, and plays, including the novels* Fahrenheit 451 *(1953, which was made into a film),* Dandelion Wine *(1957), and* Something Wicked This Way Comes *(1962); and the story collections* The Illustrated Man *(1951) and* I Sing The Body Electric *(1969). His most recent work is* One For the Road: A New Story Collection *(2002). "August 2026: There Will Come Soft Rains" is a story from* The Martian Chronicles.

August 2026: There Will Come Soft Rains (1950)

In the living room the voice-clock sang, *Tick-tock, seven o'clock, time to get up, time to get up, seven o'clock!* as if it were afraid that nobody would. The morning house lay empty. The clock ticked on, repeating and repeating its sounds into the emptiness. *Seven-nine, breakfast time, seven-nine!*

In the kitchen the breakfast stove gave a hissing sigh and ejected from its warm interior eight pieces of perfectly browned toast, eight eggs sunnyside up, sixteen slices of bacon, two coffees, and two cool glasses of milk.

"Today is August 4, 2026," said a second voice from the kitchen ceiling, "in the city of Allendale, California." It repeated the date three times for memory's sake. "Today is Mr. Featherstone's birthday. Today is the anniversary of Tilita's marriage. Insurance is payable, as are the water, gas, and light bills."

Somewhere in the walls, relays clicked, memory tapes glided under electric eyes.

Eight-one, tick-tock, eight-one o'clock, off to school, off to work, run, run, eight-one! But no doors slammed, no carpets took the soft tread of rubber heels. It was raining outside. The weather box on the front door sang quietly: "Rain, rain, go away; rubbers, raincoats for today . . ." And the rain tapped on the empty house, echoing.

Outside, the garage chimed and lifted its door to reveal the waiting car. After a long wait the door swung down again.

At eight-thirty the eggs were shriveled and the toast was like stone. An aluminum wedge scraped them into the sink, where hot water whirled them down a metal throat which digested and flushed them away to the distant sea. The dirty dishes were dropped into a hot washer and emerged twinkling dry.

Nine-fifteen, sang the clock, *time to clean.*

Out of warrens in the wall, tiny robot mice darted. The rooms were acrawl with the small cleaning animals, all rubber and metal. They thudded against chairs, whirling their mustached runners, kneading the rug nap, sucking gently at hidden dust. Then, like mysterious invaders, they popped into their burrows. Their pink electric eyes faded. The house was clean.

Ten o'clock. The sun came out from behind the rain. The house stood alone in a city of rubble and ashes. This was the one house left standing. At night the ruined city gave off a radioactive glow which could be seen for miles.

Ten-fifteen. The garden sprinklers whirled up in golden founts, filling the soft morning air with scatterings of brightness. The water pelted window-panes, running down the charred west side where the house had been burned evenly free of its white paint. The entire west face of the house was black, save for five places. Here the silhouette in paint of a man mowing a lawn. Here, as in a photograph, a woman bent to pick flowers. Still farther over, their images burned on wood in one titanic instant, a small boy, hands flung into the air; higher up, the image of a thrown ball, and opposite him a girl, hands raised to catch a ball which never came down.

The five spots of paint—the man, the woman, the children, the ball—remained. The rest was a thin charcoaled layer.

The gentle sprinkler rain filled the garden with falling light.

Until this day, how well the house had kept its peace. How carefully it had inquired, "Who goes there? What's the password?" and, getting no answer from lonely foxes and whining cats, it had shut up its windows and drawn shades in an old-maidenly preoccupation with self-protection which bordered on a mechanical paranoia.

It quivered at each sound, the house did. If a sparrow brushed a window, the shade snapped up. The bird, startled, flew off! No, not even a bird must touch the house!

The house was an altar with ten thousand attendants, big, small, servicing, attending, in choirs. But the gods had gone away, and the ritual of the religion continued senselessly, uselessly.

Twelve noon.

A dog whined, shivering, on the front porch.

The front door recognized the dog voice and opened. The dog, once huge and fleshy, but now gone to bone and covered with sores, moved in and through the house, tracking mud. Behind it whirred angry mice, angry at having to pick up mud, angry at inconvenience.

For not a leaf fragment blew under the door but what the wall panels flipped open and the copper scrap rats flashed swiftly out. The offending dust, hair, or paper, seized in miniature steel jaws, was raced back to the burrows. There, down tubes which fed into the cellar, it was dropped into the sighing vent of an incinerator which sat like evil Baal in a dark corner.

The dog ran upstairs, hysterically yelping to each door, at last realizing, as the house realized, that only silence was here.

It sniffed the air and scratched the kitchen door. Behind the door, the stove was making pancakes which filled the house with a rich baked odor and the scent of maple syrup.

The dog frothed at the mouth, lying at the door, sniffing, its eyes turned to fire. It ran wildly in circles, biting at its tail, spun in a frenzy, and died. It lay in the parlor for an hour.

Two o'clock, sang a voice.

Delicately sensing decay at last, the regiments of mice hummed out as softly as blown gray leaves in an electrical wind.

Two-fifteen.

The dog was gone.

In the cellar, the incinerator glowed suddenly and a whirl of sparks leaped up the chimney.

Two thirty-five.

Bridge tables sprouted from patio walls. Playing cards fluttered onto pads in a shower of pips. Martinis manifested on an oaken bench with egg-salad sandwiches. Music played.

But the tables were silent and the cards untouched.

At four o'clock the tables folded like great butterflies back through the paneled walls.

Four-thirty.

The nursery walls glowed.

Animals took shape: yellow giraffes, blue lions, pink antelopes, lilac panthers cavorting in crystal substance. The walls were glass. They looked out upon color and fantasy. Hidden films clocked through well-oiled sprockets, and the walls lived. The nursery floor was woven to resemble a crisp, cereal meadow. Over this ran aluminum roaches and iron crickets, and in the hot still air butterflies of delicate red tissue wavered among the sharp aroma of animal spoors! There was the sound like a great matted yellow hive of bees within a dark bellows, the lazy bumble of a purring lion. And there was the patter of okapi feet and the murmur of a fresh jungle rain, like other hoofs, falling upon the summer-starched grass. Now the walls dissolved into distances of parched weed, mile on mile, and warm endless sky. The animals drew away into thorn brakes and water holes.

It was the children's hour.

Five o'clock. The bath filled with clear hot water.

Six, seven, eight o'clock. The dinner dishes manipulated like magic tricks, and in the study a click. In the metal stand opposite the hearth where a fire now blazed up warmly, a cigar popped out, half an inch of soft gray ash on it, smoking, waiting.

Nine o'clock. The beds warmed their hidden circuits, for nights were cool here.

Nine-five. A voice spoke from the study ceiling:

"Mrs. McClellan, which poem would you like this evening?"

The house was silent.

The voice said at last, "Since you express no preference, I shall select a poem at random." Quiet music rose to back the voice. "Sara Teasdale.[1] As I recall, your favorite. . . .

> "There will come soft rains and the smell of the ground,
> And swallows circling with their shimmering sound;
>
> And frogs in the pools singing at night,
> And wild plum trees in tremulous white;
>
> Robins will wear their feathery fire,
> Whistling their whims on a low fence-wire;
>
> And not one will know of the war, not one
> Will care at last when it is done.
>
> Not one would mind, neither bird nor tree,
> If mankind perished utterly;
>
> And Spring herself, when she woke at dawn
> Would scarcely know that we were gone."

The fire burned on the stone hearth and the cigar fell away into a mound of quiet ash on its tray. The empty chairs faced each other between the silent walls, and the music played.

At ten o'clock the house began to die.

The wind blew. A falling tree bough crashed through the kitchen window. Cleaning solvent, bottled, shattered over the stove. The room was ablaze in an instant!

"Fire!" screamed a voice. The house lights flashed, water pumps shot water from the ceilings. But the solvent spread on the linoleum, licking, eating, under the kitchen door, while the voices took it up in chorus: "Fire, fire, fire!"

The house tried to save itself. Doors sprang tightly shut, but the windows were broken by the heat and the wind blew and sucked upon the fire.

The house gave ground as the fire in ten billion angry sparks moved with flaming ease from room to room and then up the stairs. While scurrying water

---

[1]American poet (1884–1933).

rats squeaked from the walls, pistoled their water, and ran for more. And the wall sprays let down showers of mechanical rain.

But too late. Somewhere, sighing, a pump shrugged to a stop. The quenching rain ceased. The reserve water supply which had filled baths and washed dishes for many quiet days was gone.

The fire crackled up the stairs. It fed upon Picassos and Matisses in the upper halls, like delicacies, baking off the oily flesh, tenderly crisping the canvases into black shavings.

Now the fire lay in beds, stood in windows, changed the colors of drapes!

And then, reinforcements.

From attic trapdoors, blind robot faces peered down with faucet mouths gushing green chemical.

The fire backed off, as even an elephant must at the sight of a dead snake. Now there were twenty snakes whipping over the floor, killing the fire with a clear cold venom of green froth.

But the fire was clever. It had sent flame outside the house, up through the attic to the pumps there. An explosion! The attic brain which directed the pumps was shattered into bronze shrapnel on the beams.

The fire rushed back into every closet and felt of the clothes hung there.

The house shuddered, oak bone on bone, its bared skeleton cringing from the heat, its wire, its nerves revealed as if a surgeon had torn the skin off to let the red veins and capillaries quiver in the scalded air. Help, help! Fire! Run, run! Heat snapped mirrors like the first brittle winter ice. And the voices wailed Fire, fire, run, run, like a tragic nursery rhyme, a dozen voices, high, low, like children dying in a forest, alone, alone. And the voices fading as the wires popped their sheatings like hot chestnuts. One, two, three, four, five voices died.

In the nursery the jungle burned. Blue lions roared, purple giraffes bounded off. The panthers ran in circles, changing color, and ten million animals, running before the fire, vanished off toward a distant steaming river. . . .

Ten more voices died. In the last instant under the fire avalanche, other choruses, oblivious, could be heard announcing the time, playing music, cutting the lawn by remote-control mower, or setting an umbrella frantically out and in the slamming and opening front door, a thousand things happening, like a clock shop when each clock strikes the hour insanely before or after the other, a scene of maniac confusion, yet unity; singing, screaming, a few last cleaning mice darting bravely out to carry the horrid ashes away! And one voice, with sublime disregard for the situation, read poetry aloud in the fiery study, until all the film spools burned, until all the wires withered and the circuits cracked.

The fire burst the house and let it slam flat down, puffing out skirts of spark and smoke.

In the kitchen, an instant before the rain of fire and timber, the stove could be seen making breakfasts at a psychopathic rate, ten dozen eggs, six loaves of toast, twenty dozen bacon strips, which, eaten by fire, started the stove working again, hysterically hissing!

The crash. The attic smashing into kitchen and parlor. The parlor into cellar, cellar into sub-cellar. Deep freeze, armchair, film tapes, circuits, beds, and all like skeletons thrown in a cluttered mound deep under.

Smoke and silence. A great quantity of smoke.

Dawn showed faintly in the east. Among the ruins, one wall stood alone. Within the wall, a last voice said, over and over again and again, even as the sun rose to shine upon the heaped rubble and steam:

"Today is August 5, 2026, today is August 5, 2026, today is. . . ."

Study and Discussion Questions

1. Think about the Sara Teasdale poem that gives the story its title. How does it apply to the situation the story narrates?
2. Who is the main character of this story?
3. Summarize the story's plot. What does Bradbury use to move you from one event to the next?
4. Though there are no actual human beings in this story, list some of the traces or evidence of people.
5. What can this house do? What can't it do?
6. What is the mood or atmosphere of "August 2026: There Will Come Soft Rains"? What words and images create this mood?
7. Discuss the significance and the use of time in this story.

Suggestions for Writing

1. This is a rare example of a story without any human beings in it. How is that absence necessary to the meaning of this story?
2. Compare/contrast this science fiction story with Pamela Zoline's "The Heat Death of the Universe" (Varieties of Protest).
3. Bradbury writes, "The house was an altar with ten thousand attendants, big, small, servicing, attending, in choirs. But the gods had gone away, and the ritual of the religion continued senselessly, uselessly." Discuss this passage as a comment on our current relation to science and technology.

Critical Resources

1. Aggelis, Steven. *Conversations with Ray Bradbury.* Jackson: University of Mississippi Press, 2004.
2. Eller, Jonathon and William Touponce, eds. *Ray Bradbury: The Life of Fiction.* Kent, OH.: Kent State Press, 2004.
3. Gallagher, Edward. "The Thematic Structure of The Martian Chronicles." *Ray Bradbury.* Joseph Olander, Ed. New York: Taplinger, 1980.
4. Reid, Robin. *Ray Bradbury: A Critical Companion.* Westport, CT: Greenwood Press, 2000.

❋ ❋ ❋

AMBROSE BIERCE (1842–1914?)

Born in rural Meigs County, Ohio, Ambrose Bierce grew up working on the family farm. Despite not having any formal education, his father's library exposed him to a wide range of books. At 19, he joined the Union Army at the beginning of the Civil War and served four years. The experience of war would make a deep imprint on his view of the world. When the war ended, Bierce went to San Francisco and began to forge his reputation as "The Wickedest Man in San Francisco"—a title earned for his scathing and often misanthropic satires of people and human nature. His fiction carries a similar tone, cynical and full of dark humor. Following in the American gothic tradition of Edgar Allen Poe, Bierce's stories hover between reality and the supernatural where characters are faced with morbid twists of fate, vengeful ghosts, and irrationality. In 1913 he went to Mexico to cover the Mexican Civil War and disappeared; his death remains a mystery. Selected works include Tales of Soldiers and Civilians *(1891),* Can Such Things Be? *(1893),* Fantastic Fables *(1899), and* The Cynic's Word Book *(1906), later retitled* The Devils Dictionary *(1911). "An Occurrence at Owl Creek Bridge," first published in* Tales of Soldiers and Civilians, *is one of Bierce's most famous stories.*

An Occurrence at Owl Creek Bridge   (1892)

I

A man stood upon a railroad bridge in northern Alabama, looking down into the swift water twenty feet below. The man's hands were behind his back, the wrists bound with a cord. A rope closely encircled his neck. It was attached to a stout cross-timber above his head and the slack fell to the level of his knees. Some loose boards laid upon the sleepers supporting the metals of the railway supplied a footing for him and his executioners—two private soldiers of the Federal army, directed by a sergeant who in civil life may have been a deputy sheriff. At a short remove upon the same temporary platform was an officer in the uniform of his rank, armed. He was a captain. A sentinel at each end of the bridge stood with his rifle in the position known as "support," that is to say, vertical in front of the left shoulder, the hammer resting on the forearm thrown straight across the chest—a formal and unnatural position, enforcing an erect carriage of the body. It did not appear to be the duty of these two men to know what was occurring at the centre of the bridge; they merely blockaded the two ends of the foot planking that traversed it.

Beyond one of the sentinels nobody was in sight; the railroad ran straight away into a forest for a hundred yards, then, curving, was lost to view. Doubtless there was an outpost farther along. The other bank of the stream was open

ground—a gentle acclivity topped with a stockade of vertical tree trunks, loop-
holed for rifles, with a single embrasure through which protruded the muzzle of
a brass cannon commanding the bridge. Midway of the slope between bridge and
fort were the spectators—a single company of infantry in line, at "parade rest,"
the butts of the rifles on the ground, the barrels inclining slightly backward
against the right shoulder, the hands crossed upon the stock. A lieutenant stood
at the right of the line, the point of his sword upon the ground, his left hand resting upon his right. Excepting the group of four at the centre of the bridge, not a
man moved. The company faced the bridge, staring stonily, motionless. The sentinels, facing the banks of the stream, might have been statues to adorn the
bridge. The captain stood with folded arms, silent, observing the work of his sub-
ordinates, but making no sign. Death is a dignitary who when he comes announced is to be received with formal manifestations of respect, even by those
most familiar with him. In the code of military etiquette silence and fixity are
forms of deference.

The man who was engaged in being hanged was apparently about thirty-five
years of age. He was a civilian, if one might judge from his habit, which was that
of a planter. His features were good—a straight nose, firm mouth, broad forehead, from which his long, dark hair was combed straight back, falling behind his
ears to the collar of his well-fitting frock-coat. He wore a mustache and pointed
beard, but no whiskers; his eyes were large and dark gray, and had a kindly expression which one would hardly have expected in one whose neck was in the
hemp. Evidently this was no vulgar assassin. The liberal military code makes pro-
vision for hanging many kinds of persons, and gentlemen are not excluded.

The preparations being complete, the two private soldiers stepped aside and
each drew away the plank upon which he had been standing. The sergeant turned
to the captain, saluted and placed himself immediately behind that officer, who
in turn moved apart one pace. These movements left the condemned man and
the sergeant standing on the two ends of the same plank, which spanned three
of the cross-ties of the bridge. The end upon which the civilian stood almost, but
not quite, reached a fourth. This plank had been held in place by the weight of
the captain; it was now held by that of the sergeant. At a signal from the former
the latter would step aside, the plank would tilt and the condemned man go
down between two ties. The arrangement commended itself to his judgment as
simple and effective. His face had not been covered nor his eyes bandaged. He
looked a moment at his "unsteadfast footing," then let his gaze wander to the
swirling water of the stream racing madly beneath his feet. A piece of dancing
driftwood caught his attention and his eyes followed it down the current. How
slowly it appeared to move! What a sluggish stream!

He closed his eyes in order to fix his last thoughts upon his wife and children.
The water, touched to gold by the early sun, the brooding mists under the banks
at some distance down the stream, the fort, the soldiers, the piece of drift—all
had distracted him. And now he became conscious of a new disturbance. Striking through the thought of his dear ones was a sound which he could neither ignore nor understand, a sharp, distinct, metallic percussion like the stroke of a

blacksmith's hammer upon the anvil; it had the same ringing quality. He wondered what it was, and whether immeasurably distant or near by—it seemed
both. Its recurrence was regular, but as slow as the tolling of a death knell. He
awaited each stroke with impatience and—he knew not why—apprehension.
The intervals of silence grew progressively longer; the delays became maddening. With their greater infrequency the sounds increased in strength and sharp-
ness. They hurt his ear like the thrust of a knife; he feared he would shriek. What
he heard was the ticking of his watch.

He unclosed his eyes and saw again the water below him. "If I could free my
hands," he thought, "I might throw off the noose and spring into the stream. By
diving I could evade the bullets and, swimming vigorously, reach the bank, take
to the woods and get away home. My home, thank God, is as yet outside their
lines; my wife and little ones are still beyond the invader's farthest advance."

As these thoughts, which have here to be set down in words, were flashed into
the doomed man's brain rather than evolved from it, the captain nodded to the
sergeant. The sergeant stepped aside.

II

Peyton Farquhar was a well-to-do planter, of an old and highly respected Alabama family. Being a slave owner and like other slave owners a politician he
was naturally an original secessionist and ardently devoted to the Southern
cause. Circumstances of an imperious nature, which it is unnecessary to relate
here, had prevented him from taking service with the gallant army that had
fought the disastrous campaigns ending with the fall of Corinth, and he chafed
under the inglorious restraint, longing for the release of his energies, the larger
life of the soldier, the opportunity for distinction. That opportunity, he felt,
would come, as it comes to all in war time. Meanwhile he did what he could. No
service was too humble for him to perform in aid of the South, no adventure
too perilous for him to undertake if consistent with the character of a civilian
who was at heart a soldier, and who in good faith and without too much qualification assented to at least a part of the frankly villainous dictum that all is fair
in love and war.

One evening while Farquhar and his wife were sitting on a rustic bench near
the entrance to his grounds, a gray-clad soldier rode up to the gate and asked
for a drink of water. Mrs. Farquhar was only too happy to serve him with her
own white hands. While she was fetching the water her husband approached the
dusty horseman and inquired eagerly for news from the front.

"The Yanks are repairing the railroads," said the man, "and are getting
ready for another advance. They have reached the Owl Creek bridge, put it in
order and built a stockade on the north bank. The commandant has issued an
order, which is posted everywhere, declaring that any civilian caught interfering with the railroad, its bridges, tunnels or trains will be summarily hanged. I
saw the order."

"How far is it to the Owl Creek bridge?" Farquhar asked.

"About thirty miles."

"Is there no force on this side the creek?"

"Only a picket post half a mile out, on the railroad, and a single sentinel at this end of the bridge."

"Suppose a man—a civilian and student of hanging—should elude the picket post and perhaps get the better of the sentinel," said Farquhar, smiling, "what could he accomplish?"

The soldier reflected. "I was there a month ago," he replied. "I observed that the flood of last winter had lodged a great quantity of driftwood against the wooden pier at this end of the bridge. It is now dry and would burn like tow."

The lady had now brought the water, which the soldier drank. He thanked her ceremoniously, bowed to her husband and rode away. An hour later, after nightfall, he repassed the plantation, going northward in the direction from which he had come. He was a Federal scout.

III

As Peyton Farquhar fell straight downward through the bridge he lost consciousness and was as one already dead. From this state he was awakened—ages later, it seemed to him—by the pain of a sharp pressure upon his throat, followed by a sense of suffocation. Keen, poignant agonies seemed to shoot from his neck downward through every fibre of his body and limbs. These pains appeared to flash along well-defined lines of ramification and to beat with an inconceivably rapid periodicity. They seemed like streams of pulsating fire heating him to an intolerable temperature. As to his head, he was conscious of nothing but a feeling of fullness—of congestion. These sensations were unaccompanied by thought. The intellectual part of his nature was already effaced; he had power only to feel, and feeling was torment. He was conscious of motion. Encompassed in a luminous cloud, of which he was now merely the fiery heart, without material substance, he swung through unthinkable arcs of oscillation, like a vast pendulum. Then all at once, with terrible suddenness, the light about him shot upward with the noise of a loud plash; a frightful roaring was in his ears, and all was cold and dark. The power of thought was restored; he knew that the rope had broken and he had fallen into the stream. There was no additional strangulation; the noose about his neck was already suffocating him and kept the water from his lungs. To die of hanging at the bottom of a river!—the idea seemed to him ludicrous. He opened his eyes in the darkness and saw above him a gleam of light, but how distant, how inaccessible! He was still sinking, for the light became fainter and fainter until it was a mere glimmer. Then it began to grow and brighten, and he knew that he was rising toward the surface—knew it with reluctance, for he was now very comfortable. "To be hanged and drowned," he thought, "that is not so bad; but I do not wish to be shot. No; I will not be shot; that is not fair."

He was not conscious of an effort, but a sharp pain in his wrist apprised him that he was trying to free his hands. He gave the struggle his attention, as an idler might observe the feat of a juggler, without interest in the outcome. What splendid effort!—what magnificent, what superhuman strength! Ah, that was a fine endeavor! Bravo! The cord fell away; his arms parted and floated upward, the hands dimly seen on each side in the growing light. He watched them with a new interest as first one and then the other pounced upon the noose at his neck. They tore it away and thrust it fiercely aside, its undulations resembling those of a water-snake. "Put it back, put it back!" He thought he shouted these words to his hands, for the undoing of the noose had been succeeded by the direst pang that he had yet experienced. His neck ached horribly; his brain was on fire; his heart, which had been fluttering faintly, gave a great leap, trying to force itself out at his mouth. His whole body was racked and wrenched with an insupportable anguish! But his disobedient hands gave no heed to the command. They beat the water vigorously with quick, downward strokes, forcing him to the surface. He felt his head emerge; his eyes were blinded by the sunlight; his chest expanded convulsively, and with a supreme and crowning agony his lungs engulfed a great draught of air, which instantly he expelled in a shriek!

He was now in full possession of his physical senses. They were, indeed, preternaturally keen and alert. Something in the awful disturbance of his organic system had so exalted and refined them that they made record of things never before perceived. He felt the ripples upon his face and heard their separate sounds as they struck. He looked at the forest on the bank of the stream, saw the individual trees, the leaves and the veining of each leaf—saw the very insects upon them: the locusts, the brilliant-bodied flies, the gray spiders stretching their webs from twig to twig. He noted the prismatic colors in all the dewdrops upon a million blades of grass. The humming of the gnats that danced above the eddies of the stream, the beating of the dragon-flies' wings, the strokes of the water-spiders' legs, like oars which had lifted their boat—all these made audible music. A fish slid along beneath his eyes and he heard the rush of its body parting the water.

He had come to the surface facing down the stream; in a moment the visible world seemed to wheel slowly round, himself the pivotal point, and he saw the bridge, the fort, the soldiers upon the bridge, the captain, the sergeant, the two privates, his executioners. They were in silhouette against the blue sky. They shouted and gesticulated, pointing at him. The captain had drawn his pistol, but did not fire; the others were unarmed. Their movements were grotesque and horrible, their forms gigantic.

Suddenly he heard a sharp report and something struck the water smartly within a few inches of his head, spattering his face with spray. He heard a second report, and saw one of the sentinels with his rifle at his shoulder, a light cloud of blue smoke rising from the muzzle. The man in the water saw the eye of the man on the bridge gazing into his own through the sights of the rifle. He observed that it was a gray eye and remembered having read that gray eyes were keenest, and that all famous marksmen had them. Nevertheless, this one had missed.

A counter-swirl had caught Farquhar and turned him half round; he was again looking into the forest on the bank opposite the fort. The sound of a clear, high voice in a monotonous singsong now rang out behind him and came across the water with a distinctness that pierced and subdued all other sounds, even the beating of the ripples in his ears. Although no soldier, he had frequented camps enough to know the dread significance of that deliberate, drawling, aspirated chant; the lieutenant on shore was taking a part in the morning's work. How coldly and pitilessly—with what an even, calm intonation, presaging, and enforcing tranquility in the men—with what accurately measured intervals fell those cruel words:

"Attention, company! ... Shoulder arms! ... Ready! ... Aim! ... Fire!"

Farquhar dived—dived as deeply as he could. The water roared in his ears like the voice of Niagara, yet he heard the dulled thunder of the volley and, rising again toward the surface, met shining bits of metal, singularly flattened, oscillating slowly downward. Some of them touched him on the face and hands, then fell away, continuing their descent. One lodged between his collar and neck; it was uncomfortably warm and he snatched it out.

As he rose to the surface, gasping for breath, he saw that he had been a long time under water; he was perceptibly farther down stream—nearer to safety. The soldiers had almost finished reloading; the metal ramrods flashed all at once in the sunshine as they were drawn from the barrels, turned in the air, and thrust into their sockets. The two sentinels fired again, independently and ineffectually.

The hunted man saw all this over his shoulder; he was now swimming vigorously with the current. His brain was as energetic as his arms and legs; he thought with the rapidity of lightning.

"The officer," he reasoned, "will not make that martinet's error a second time. It is as easy to dodge a volley as a single shot. He has probably already given the command to fire at will. God help me, I cannot dodge them all!"

An appalling plash within two yards of him was followed by a loud, rushing sound, *diminuendo,* which seemed to travel back through the air to the fort and died in an explosion which stirred the very river to its deeps! A rising sheet of water curved over him, fell down upon him, blinded him, strangled him! The cannon had taken a hand in the game. As he shook his head free from the commotion of the smitten water he heard the deflected shot humming through the air ahead, and in an instant it was cracking and smashing the branches in the forest beyond.

"They will not do that again," he thought; "the next time they will use a charge of grape. I must keep my eye upon the gun; the smoke will apprise me—the report arrives too late; it lags behind the missile. That is a good gun."

Suddenly he felt himself whirled round and round—spinning like a top. The water, the banks, the forests, the now distant bridge, fort and men—all were commingled and blurred. Objects were represented by their colors only; circular horizontal streaks of color—that was all he saw. He had been caught in a vortex and was being whirled on with a velocity of advance and gyration that made him giddy and sick. In a few moments he was flung upon the gravel at the foot of the left bank of the stream—the southern bank—and behind a projecting point which concealed him from his enemies. The sudden arrest of his motion, the abrasion of one of his hands on the gravel, restored him, and he wept with delight. He dug his fingers into the sand, threw it over himself in handfuls and audibly blessed it. It looked like diamonds, rubies, emeralds; he could think of nothing beautiful which it did not resemble. The trees upon the bank were giant garden plants; he noted a definite order in their arrangement, inhaled the fragrance of their blooms. A strange, roseate light shone through the spaces among their trunks and the wind made in their branches the music of æolian harps. He had no wish to perfect his escape—was content to remain in that enchanting spot until retaken.

A whiz and rattle of grapeshot among the branches high above his head roused him from his dream. The baffled cannoneer had fired him a random farewell. He sprang to his feet, rushed up the sloping bank, and plunged into the forest.

All that day he traveled, laying his course by the rounding sun. The forest seemed interminable; nowhere did he discover a break in it, not even a woodman's road. He had not known that he lived in so wild a region. There was something uncanny in the revelation.

By nightfall he was fatigued, footsore, famishing. The thought of his wife and children urged him on. At last he found a road which led him in what he knew to be the right direction. It was as wide and straight as a city street, yet it seemed untraveled. No fields bordered it, no dwelling anywhere. Not so much as the barking of a dog suggested human habitation. The black bodies of the trees formed a straight wall on both sides, terminating on the horizon in a point, like a diagram in a lesson in perspective. Overhead, as he looked up through this rift in the wood, shone great golden stars looking unfamiliar and grouped in strange constellations. He was sure they were arranged in some order which had a secret and malign significance. The wood on either side was full of singular noises, among which—once, twice, and again—he distinctly heard whispers in an unknown tongue.

His neck was in pain and lifting his hand to it he found it horribly swollen. He knew that it had a circle of black where the rope had bruised it. His eyes felt congested; he could no longer close them. His tongue was swollen with thirst; he relieved its fever by thrusting it forward from between his teeth into the cold air. How softly the turf had carpeted the untraveled avenue—he could no longer feel the roadway beneath his feet!

Doubtless, despite his suffering, he had fallen asleep while walking, for now he sees another scene—perhaps he has merely recovered from a delirium. He stands at the gate of his own home. All is as he left it, and all bright and beautiful in the morning sunshine. He must have traveled the entire night. As he pushes open the gate and passes up the wide white walk, he sees a flutter of female garments; his wife, looking fresh and cool and sweet, steps down from the veranda to meet him. At the bottom of the steps she stands waiting, with a smile of ineffable joy, an attitude of matchless grace and dignity. Ah, how beautiful she is! He springs forward with extended arms. As he is about to clasp her he feels a stunning blow upon the back of the neck; a blinding white light blazes all about him with a sound like the shock of a cannon—then all is darkness and silence!

Peyton Farquhar was dead; his body, with a broken neck, swung gently from side to side beneath the timbers of the Owl Creek bridge.

Study and Discussion Questions

1. How does Bierce work to make us think Farquhar's imagined escape is real? What hints are there along the way that it is in fact imaginary?
2. Trace Bierce's manipulation of point of view throughout the story. What does it accomplish? Why does Bierce narrate the events leading up to the hanging in a flashback in Part II rather than at the beginning of the story?
3. Characterize the way Bierce describes the hanging proceedings in the first two paragraphs. Compare it to the way he describes Farquhar's imaginary escape. What does this contrast in style suggest?
4. Why do you think Bierce, who himself volunteered to fight on the Union side in the Civil War, makes his hero a Southern planter, a slave owner, a supporter of the Confederates? How does this choice shape the kind of statement the story makes about war?

Suggestions for Writing

1. One critic has argued that the story makes fun of "the orthodox war yarn in which the hero's death or survival is noble and significant." Interpret the story taking this statement as your thesis. (You might begin by reexamining the characterization of Farquhar in Part II.)
2. How would you go about making a film of this story? How would you handle the shifts in point of view, the flashback, and the imaginary nature of Farquhar's escape? (If you've seen and remember a film version, discuss how well you think it does the job.)

Critical Resources

1. *An Occurrence at Owl Creek Bridge.* Director Brian James Egen. Performers Bradley M. Egen, Jody Chansuolme. Owl Creek Productions, 2003. For more information see <http://www.owlcreekproductions.com/>. This is most recent film adaptation. Robert Enrico's 1962 (28-minute) version is another notable interpretation of Bierce's story.
2. Blume, Donald. *Ambrose Bierce's Civilians and Soldiers in Context: A Critical Study.* Kent, OH: Kent State Press, 2004.

3. Evans, Robert, ed. *Ambrose Bierce's An Occurrence at Owl Creek Bridge: An Annotated Critical Edition.* West Cornwall CT: Locust Hill, 2003.
4. Gale, Robert. *An Ambrose Bierce Companion.* Westport, CI: Greenwood Press, 2001.
5. Stoicheff, Peter. "Something Uncanny: The Dream Structure in Ambrose Bierce's An Occurrence at Owl Creek Bridge." *Studies in Short Fiction* 30.3 (1993): 349–58.

TONI MORRISON (b. 1931)

*Born in Lorain, Ohio, Toni Morrison received a BA in English from Howard University and her MA in English at Cornell. Yet, it was her early life experiences in Ohio that would become a cornerstone of her writing: "No matter what I write, I begin there . . . Ohio offers an escape from the stereotyped black settings. It is neither plantation or ghetto" (*Black Women Writers at Work, *1986*). From such a vantage point, Morrison has sought to offer a more complicated version of the African American experience—one infused with myth and folklore, race and identity. After teaching for a few years, Morrison accepted a position as a book editor at Random House in New York in 1964. In 1969, Morrison published her first book, *The Bluest Eye, *at the age of 38. She spent the next 25 years at Random House, helping raise public awareness of other black writers as well as publishing her own work: *Sula *(1973), *Song of Solomon *(1977), *Tar Baby *(1981), *Beloved (1987), which won the Pulitzer Prize for Fiction, *Jazz *(1992), *Paradise *(1998), and her most recent novel *Love *(2003). In addition to her novels, Morrison has also written and edited several critical works, including *Playing in the Dark: Whiteness and the Literary Imagination *(1992), and co-authored several children's books with her son Slade Morrison. In 1993, Morrison became the first African American to win the Nobel Prize for literature. "1919," excerpted from Morrison's novel *Sula, *tells the story of a young man's mental transformation when he comes back to his community after fighting in World War I.*

1919   (1973)

Except for World War II, nothing ever interfered with the celebration of National Suicide Day. It had taken place every January third since 1920, although Shadrack, its founder, was for many years the only celebrant. Blasted and permanently astonished by the events of 1917, he had returned to Medallion handsome but ravaged, and even the most fastidious people in the town sometimes caught themselves dreaming of what he must have been like a few years back before he went off to war. A young man of hardly twenty, his head full of nothing and his mouth recalling the taste of lipstick, Shadrack had found himself in December, 1917, running with his comrades across a field in France. It was his first encounter with the enemy and he didn't know whether his company was running toward them or away. For several days they had been marching, keeping close to a stream that was frozen at its edges. At one point they crossed it, and no sooner had he stepped foot on the other side than the day was adangle with shouts and explosions. Shellfire was all around him, and though he knew that this was something called *it,* he could not muster up the proper feeling—the feeling that would accommodate *it.* He expected to be terrified or exhilarated—to feel *something* very strong. In fact, he felt only the bite of a nail in his boot, which pierced the ball of his foot whenever he came down on it. The day was cold enough to make his breath visible, and he wondered for a moment at the purity and whiteness of his own breath among the dim, gray explosions surrounding him. He ran, bayonet fixed, deep in the great sweep of men flying across this field. Wincing at the pain in his foot, he turned his head a little to the right and saw the face of a soldier near him fly off. Before he could register shock, the rest of the soldier's head disappeared under the inverted soup bowl of his helmet. But stubbornly, taking no direction from the brain, the body of the headless soldier ran on, with energy and grace, ignoring altogether the drip and slide of brain tissue down its back.

When Shadrack opened his eyes he was propped up in a small bed. Before him on a tray was a large tin plate divided into three triangles. In one triangle was rice, in another meat, and in the third stewed tomatoes. A small round depression held a cup of whitish liquid. Shadrack stared at the soft colors that filled these triangles: the lumpy whiteness of rice, the quivering blood tomatoes, the grayish-brown meat. All their repugnance was contained in the neat balance of the triangles—a balance that soothed him, transferred some of its equilibrium to him. Thus reassured that the white, the red and the brown would stay where they were—would not explode or burst forth from their restricted zones—he suddenly felt hungry and looked around for his hands. His glance was cautious at first, for he had to be very careful—anything could be anywhere. Then he noticed two lumps beneath the beige blanket on either side of his hips. With extreme care he lifted one arm and was relieved to find his hand attached to his wrist. He tried the other and found it also. Slowly he directed one hand toward the cup and, just as he was about to spread his fingers, they began to grow in higgledy-piggledy fashion like Jack's beanstalk all over the tray and the bed. With a shriek he closed his eyes and thrust his huge growing hands under the covers. Once out of sight they seemed to shrink back to their normal size. But the yell had brought a male nurse.

"Private? We're not going to have any trouble today, are we? Are we, Private?'

Shadrack looked up at a balding man dressed in a green-cotton jacket and trousers. His hair was parted low on the right side so that some twenty or thirty yellow hairs could discreetly cover the nakedness of his head.

"Come on. Pick up that spoon. Pick it up, Private. Nobody is going to feed you forever."

Sweat slid from Shadrack's armpits down his sides. He could not bear to see his hands grow again and he was frightened of the voice in the apple-green suit.

"Pick it up, I said. There's no point to this . . ." The nurse reached under the cover for Shadrack's wrist to pull out the monstrous hand. Shadrack jerked it back and overturned the tray. In panic he raised himself to his knees and tried to fling off and away his terrible fingers, but succeeded only in knocking the nurse into the next bed.

When they bound Shadrack into a straitjacket, he was both relieved and grateful, for his hands were at last hidden and confined to whatever size they had attained.

Laced and silent in his small bed, he tried to tie the loose cords in his mind. He wanted desperately to see his own face and connect it with the word "private"—the word the nurse (and the others who helped bind him) had called him. "Private" he thought was something secret, and he wondered why they looked at him and called him a secret. Still, if his hands behaved as they had done, what might he expect from his face? The fear and longing were too much for him, so he began to think of other things. That is, he let his mind slip into whatever cave mouths of memory it chose.

He saw a window that looked out on a river which he knew was full of fish. Someone was speaking softly just outside the door . . .

Shadrack's earlier violence had coincided with a memorandum from the hospital executive staff in reference to the distribution of patients in high-risk areas. There was clearly a demand for space. The priority or the violence earned Shadrack his release, $217 in cash, a full suit of clothes and copies of very official-looking papers.

When he stepped out of the hospital door the grounds overwhelmed him: the cropped shrubbery, the edged lawns, the undeviating walks. Shadrack looked at the cement stretches: each one leading clearheadedly to some presumably desirable destination. There were no fences, no warnings, no obstacles at all between concrete and green grass, so one could easily ignore the tidy sweep of stone and cut out in another direction—a direction of one's own.

Shadrack stood at the foot of the hospital steps watching the heads of trees tossing ruefully but harmlessly, since their trunks were rooted too deeply in the earth to threaten him. Only the walks made him uneasy. He shifted his weight, wondering how he could get to the gate without stepping on the concrete. While plotting his course—where he would have to leap, where to skirt a clump of bushes—a loud guffaw startled him. Two men were going up the steps. Then he noticed that there were many people about, and that he was just now seeing them, or else they had just materialized. They were thin slips, like paper dolls floating down the walks. Some were seated in chairs with wheels, propelled by other paper figures from behind. All seemed to be smoking, and their arms and legs curved in the breeze. A good high wind would pull them up and away and they would land perhaps among the tops of the trees.

Shadrack took the plunge. Four steps and he was on the grass heading for the gate. He kept his head down to avoid seeing the paper people swerving and bending here and there, and he lost his way. When he looked up, he was standing by a low red building separated from the main building by a covered walkway. From somewhere came a sweetish smell which reminded him of something painful. He looked around for the gate and saw that he had gone directly away from it in his complicated journey over the grass. Just to the left of the low building was a graveled driveway that appeared to lead outside the grounds. He trotted quickly to it and left, at last, a haven of more than a year, only eight days of which he fully recollected.

Once on the road, he headed west. The long stay in the hospital had left him weak—too weak to walk steadily on the gravel shoulders of the road. He shuffled, grew dizzy, stopped for breath, started again, stumbling and sweating but refusing to wipe his temples, still afraid to look at his hands. Passengers in dark, square cars shuttered their eyes at what they took to be a drunken man.

The sun was already directly over his head when he came to a town. A few blocks of shaded streets and he was already at its heart—a pretty, quietly regulated downtown.

Exhausted, his feet clotted with pain, he sat down at the curbside to take off his shoes. He closed his eyes to avoid seeing his hands and fumbled with the laces of the heavy high-topped shoes. The nurse had tied them into a double knot, the way one does for children, and Shadrack, long unaccustomed to the manipulation of intricate things, could not get them loose. Uncoordinated, his fingernails tore away at the knots. He fought a rising hysteria that was not merely anxiety to free his aching feet; his very life depended on the release of the knots. Suddenly without raising his eyelids, he began to cry. Twenty-two years old, weak, hot, frightened, not daring to acknowledge the fact that he didn't even know who or what he was ... with no past, no language, no tribe, no source, no address book, no comb, no pencil, no clock, no pocket handkerchief, no rug, no bed, no can opener, no faded postcard, no soap, no key, no tobacco pouch, no soiled underwear and nothing nothing nothing to do ... he was sure of one thing only: the unchecked monstrosity of his hands. He cried soundlessly at the curbside of a small Midwestern town wondering where the window was, and the river, and the soft voices just outside the door ...

Through his tears he saw the fingers joining the laces, tentatively at first, then rapidly. The four fingers of each hand fused into the fabric, knotted themselves and zigzagged in and out of the tiny eyeholes.

By the time the police drove up, Shadrack was suffering from a blinding headache, which was not abated by the comfort he felt when the policemen pulled his hands away from what he thought was a permanent entanglement with his shoelaces. They took him to jail, booked him for vagrancy and intoxication, and locked him in a cell. Lying on a cot, Shadrack could only stare helplessly at the wall, so paralyzing was the pain in his head. He lay in this agony for a long while and then realized he was staring at the painted-over letters of a command to fuck himself. He studied the phrase as the pain in his head subsided.

Like moonlight stealing under a window shade an idea insinuated itself: his earlier desire to see his own face. He looked for a mirror; there was none. Finally, keeping his hands carefully behind his back he made his way to the toilet bowl and peeped in. The water was unevenly lit by the sun so he could make nothing out. Returning to his cot he took the blanket and covered his head, rendering the water dark enough to see his reflection. There in the toilet water he saw a grave black face. A black so definite, so unequivocal, it astonished him. He had been harboring a skittish apprehension that he was not real—that he didn't exist at all. But when the blackness greeted him with its indisputable presence, he wanted nothing more. In his joy he took the risk of letting one edge of the blanket drop and glanced at his hands. They were still. Courteously still.

Shadrack rose and returned to the cot, where he fell into the first sleep of his new life. A sleep deeper than the hospital drugs; deeper than the pits of plums, steadier than the condor's wing; more tranquil than the curve of eggs.

The sheriff looked through the bars at the young man with the matted hair. He had read through his prisoner's papers and hailed a farmer. When Shadrack awoke, the sheriff handed him back his papers and escorted him to the back of a wagon. Shadrack got in and in less than three hours he was back in Medallion, for he had been only twenty-two miles from his window, his river, and his soft voices just outside the door.

In the back of the wagon, supported by sacks of squash and hills of pumpkins, Shadrack began a struggle that was to last for twelve days, a struggle to order and focus experience. It had to do with making a place for fear as a way of controlling it. He knew the smell of death and was terrified of it, for he could not anticipate it. It was not death or dying that frightened him, but the unexpectedness of both. In sorting it all out, he hit on the notion that if one day a year were devoted to it, everybody could get it out of the way and the rest of the year would be safe and free. In this manner he instituted National Suicide Day.

On the third day of the new year, he walked through the Bottom down Carpenter's Road with a cowbell and a hangman's rope calling the people together. Telling them that this was their only chance to kill themselves or each other.

At first the people in the town were frightened; they knew Shadrack was crazy but that did not mean that he didn't have any sense or, even more important, that he had no power. His eyes were so wild, his hair so long and matted, his voice was so full of authority and thunder that he caused panic on the first, or Charter, National Suicide Day in 1920. The next one, in 1921, was less frightening but still worrisome. The people had seen him a year now in between. He lived in a shack on the riverbank that had once belonged to his grandfather long time dead. On Tuesday and Friday he sold the fish he had caught that morning, the rest of the week he was drunk, loud, obscene, funny and outrageous. But he never touched anybody, never fought, never caressed. Once the people understood the boundaries and nature of his madness, they could fit him, so to speak, into the scheme of things.

Then, on subsequent National Suicide Days, the grown people looked out from behind curtains as he rang his bell; a few stragglers increased their speed, and little children screamed and ran. The tetter heads tried goading him (although he was only four or five years older than they) but not for long, for his curses were stingingly personal.

As time went along, the people took less notice of these January thirds, or rather they thought they did, thought they had no attitudes or feelings one way or another about Shadrack's annual solitary parade. In fact they had simply stopped remarking on the holiday because they had absorbed it into their thoughts, into their language, into their lives.

Someone said to a friend, "You sure was a long time delivering that baby. How long was you in labor?"

And the friend answered, "'Bout three days. The pains started on Suicide Day and kept up till the following Sunday. Was borned on Sunday. All my boys is Sunday boys."

Some lover said to his bride-to-be, "Let's do it after New Years, 'stead of before. I get paid New Year's Eve."

And his sweetheart answered, "OK, but make sure it ain't on Suicide Day. I ain't 'bout to be listening to no cowbells whilst the weddin's going on."

Somebody's grandmother said her hens always started a laying of double yolks right after Suicide Day.

Then Reverend Deal took it up, saying the same folks who had sense enough to avoid Shadrack's call were the ones who insisted on drinking themselves to death or womanizing themselves to death. "May's well go on with Shad and save the Lamb the trouble of redemption."

Easily, quietly, Suicide Day became a part of the fabric of life up in the Bottom of Medallion, Ohio.

Study and Discussion Questions

1. What is Shadrack's problem with his hands? When, how, and why does this problem end?
2. The first paragraph of "1919" describes Shadrack's experience of battle. What are the elements of this experience?
3. What is National Suicide Day? Why does Shadrack create it?
4. How do National Suicide Day and Shadrack himself become "part of the fabric of life" in the community?

Suggestions for Writing

1. Is Shadrack crazy? Make a brief argument either way. Give evidence from the story.

2. Imagine that you have awakened with "no past, no language, no tribe, no source, no address book, no comb, no pencil, no clock, no pocket hand-kerchief, no rug, no bed, no can opener, no faded postcard, no soap, no key, no tobacco pouch, no soiled underwear, and nothing nothing nothing to do . . ." What would you do?

3. What are the essentials out of which you construct your own identity? That is, what are the things which, if taken away, would leave you wondering who you are?

Critical Resources

1. Barrett, Eileen. "Septimus and Shadrack: Woolf and Morrison Envision the Madness of War." *Virginia Woolf: Emerging Perspectives.* Vara Neverow, Ed. New York: Pace University Press, 1994.

2. Hunt, Patricia. "War and Peace: Transfigured Categories and the Politics of *Sula.*" *African American Review* 27.3 (1993): 443–459.

3. Ryan, Katy. "Revolutionary Suicide in Toni Morrison's Fiction." *African American Review* 34.3 (2000): 389–412.

LOUISE ERDRICH (b. 1954)

Louise Erdrich grew up in Wahpeton, North Dakota. Her father, a German immigrant, and her mother, an Ojibwa Indian, passed down to her a rich tradition of story telling. She would eventually obtain her B.A. at Dartmouth and her M.A. in writing from John Hopkins in 1979. In 1981, she married another writer, Mike Dorris. During the next decade, the two collaborated on several publications, working together and providing feedback for each other. For a short time they published under their penname "Milou North." When her poem "Indian Boarding School" won the 1983 Pushcart Prize, the public began to notice her work—both poetry and prose. Although she has written more prose in her career, her two volumes of poetry, Jacklight *(1984) and* Baptism of Desire *(1989), have been highly acclaimed. In these two volumes, Erdrich uses her imaginative story-telling abilities to write a multifaceted poetry—wandering deftly through themes of family, love, history, Native American mythologizing, and the tension between Ojibwa reservation life and white America. These same story-telling techniques can be found in her prose. Among her novels are* The Beet Queen *(1986),* Tracks *(1988),* A Link With the River *(1989),* The Crown of Columbus *(1991),* The Antelope Wife *(1998), and her latest work* Four Souls *(2004). "The Red Convertible" is one of fourteen stories that comprise her first novel,* Love Medicine *(1984).*

The Red Convertible   (1984)

I was the first one to drive a convertible on my reservation. And of course it was red, a red Olds. I owned that car along with my brother Henry Junior. We owned it together until his boots filled with water on a windy night and he bought out my share. Now Henry owns the whole car, and his younger brother Lyman (that's myself), Lyman walks everywhere he goes.

How did I earn enough money to buy my share in the first place? My one talent was I could always make money. I had a touch for it, unusual in a Chippewa. From the first I was different that way, and everyone recognized it. I was the only kid they let in the American Legion Hall to shine shoes, for example, and one Christmas I sold spiritual bouquets for the mission door to door. The nuns let me keep a percentage. Once I started, it seemed the more money I made the easier the money came. Everyone encouraged it. When I was fifteen I got a job washing dishes at the Joliet Café, and that was where my first big break happened.

It wasn't long before I was promoted to bussing tables, and then the short-order cook quit and I was hired to take her place. No sooner than you know it I was managing the Joliet. The rest is history. I went on managing. I soon become part owner, and of course there was no stopping me then. It wasn't long before the whole thing was mine.

After I'd owned the Joliet for one year, it blew over in the worst tornado ever seen around here. The whole operation was smashed to bits. A total loss. The fryalator was up in a tree, the grill torn in half like it was paper. I was only sixteen. I had it all in my mother's name, and I lost it quick, but before I lost it I had every one of my relatives, and their relatives, to dinner, and I also bought that red Olds I mentioned, along with Henry.

The first time we saw it! I'll tell you when we first saw it. We had gotten a ride up to Winnipeg, and both of us had money. Don't ask me why, because we never mentioned a car or anything, we just had all our money. Mine was cash, a big bankroll from the Joliet's insurance. Henry had two checks—a week's extra pay for being laid off, and his regular check from the Jewel Bearing Plant.

We were walking down Portage anyway, seeing the sights, when we saw it. There it was, parked, large as life. Really as *if* it was alive. I thought of the word *repose,* because the car wasn't simply stopped, parked, or whatever. That car reposed, calm and gleaming, a FOR SALE sign in its left front window. Then, before we had thought it over at all, the car belonged to us and our pockets were empty. We had just enough money for gas back home.

We went places in that car, me and Henry. We took off driving all one whole summer. We started off toward the Little Knife River and Mandaree in Fort Berthold and then we found ourselves down in Wakpala somehow, and then suddenly we were over in Montana on the Rocky Boys, and yet the summer was not even half over. Some people hang on to details when they travel, but we didn't let them bother us and just lived our everyday lives here to there.

I do remember this one place with willows. I remember I laid under those trees and it was comfortable. So comfortable. The branches bent down all around me like a tent or a stable. And quiet, it was quiet, even though there was a pow-wow close enough so I could see it going on. The air was not too still, not too windy either. When the dust rises up and hangs in the air around the dancers like that, I feel good. Henry was asleep with his arms thrown wide. Later on, he woke up and we started driving again. We were somewhere in Montana, or maybe on the Blood Reserve—it could have been anywhere. Anyway it was where we met the girl.

All her hair was in buns around her ears, that's the first thing I noticed about her. She was posed alongside the road with her arm out, so we stopped. That girl was short, so short her lumber shirt looked comical on her, like a nightgown. She had jeans on and fancy moccasins and she carried a little suitcase.

"Hop on in," says Henry. So she climbs in between us.

"We'll take you home," I says. "Where do you live?"

"Chicken," she says.

"Where the hell's that?" I ask her.

"Alaska."

"Okay," says Henry, and we drive.

We got up there and never wanted to leave. The sun doesn't truly set there in summer, and the night is more a soft dusk. You might doze off, sometimes, but before you know it you're up again, like an animal in nature. You never feel like you have to sleep hard or put away the world. And things would grow up there. One day just dirt or moss, the next day flowers and long grass. The girl's name was Susy. Her family really took to us. They fed us and put us up. We had our own tent to live in by their house, and the kids would be in and out of there all day and night. They couldn't get over me and Henry being brothers, we looked so different. We told them we knew we had the same mother, anyway.

One night Susy came in to visit us. We sat around in the tent talking of this thing and that. The season was changing. It was getting darker by that time, and the cold was even getting just a little mean. I told her it was time for us to go. She stood up on a chair.

"You never seen my hair," Susy said.

That was true. She was standing on a chair, but still, when she unclipped her buns the hair reached all the way to the ground. Our eyes opened. You couldn't tell how much hair she had when it was rolled up so neatly. Then my brother Henry did something funny. He went up to the chair and said, "Jump on my shoulders." So she did that, and her hair reached down past his waist, and he started twirling, this way and that, so her hair was flung out from side to side.

"I always wondered what it was like to have long pretty hair," Henry says. Well we laughed. It was a funny sight, the way he did it. The next morning we got up and took leave of those people.

On to greener pastures, as they say. It was down through Spokane and across Idaho then Montana and very soon we were racing the weather right along under the Canadian border through Columbus, Des Lacs, and then we were in Bottineau County and soon home. We'd made most of the trip, that summer, without putting up the car hood at all. We got home just in time, it turned out, for the army to remember Henry had signed up to join it.

I don't wonder that the army was so glad to get my brother that they turned him into a Marine. He was built like a brick outhouse anyway. We liked to tease him that they really wanted him for his Indian nose. He had a nose big and sharp as a hatchet, like the nose on Red Tomahawk, the Indian who killed Sitting Bull, whose profile is on signs all along the North Dakota highways. Henry went off to training camp, came home once during Christmas, then the next thing you know we got an overseas letter from him. It was 1970, and he said he was stationed up in the northern hill country. Whereabouts I did not know. He wasn't such a hot letter writer, and only got off two before the enemy caught him. I could never keep it straight, which direction those good Vietnam soldiers were from.

I wrote him back several times, even though I didn't know if those letters would get through. I kept him informed all about the car. Most of the time I had it up on blocks in the yard or half taken apart, because that long trip did a hard job on it under the hood.

I always had good luck with numbers, and never worried about the draft myself. I never even had to think about what my number was. But Henry was never lucky in the same way as me. It was at least three years before Henry came home. By then I guess the whole war was solved in the government's mind, but for him it would keep on going. In those years I'd put his car into almost perfect shape. I always thought of it as his car while he was gone, even though when he left he said, "Now it's yours," and threw me his key.

"Thanks for the extra key," I'd said. "I'll put it up in your drawer just in case I need it." He laughed.

When he came home, though, Henry was very different, and I'll say this: the change was no good. You could hardly expect him to change for the better, I know. But he was quiet, so quiet, and never comfortable sitting still anywhere but always up and moving around. I thought back to times we'd sat still for whole afternoons, never moving a muscle, just shifting our weight along the ground, talking to whoever sat with us, watching things. He'd always had a joke, then, too, and now you couldn't get him to laugh, or when he did it was more the sound of a man choking, a sound that stopped up the throats of other people around him.

They got to leaving him alone most of the time, and I didn't blame them. It was a fact: Henry was jumpy and mean.

I'd bought a color TV set for my mom and the rest of us while Henry was away. Money still came very easy. I was sorry I'd ever bought it though, because of Henry. I was also sorry I'd bought color, because with black-and-white the pictures seem older and farther away. But what are you going to do? He sat in front of it, watching it, and that was the only time he was completely still. But it was the kind of stillness that you see in a rabbit when it freezes and before it will bolt. He was not easy. He sat in his chair gripping the armrests with all his might, as if the chair itself was moving at a high speed and if he let go at all he would rocket forward and maybe crash right through the set.

Once I was in the room watching TV with Henry and I heard his teeth click at something. I looked over, and he'd bitten through his lip. Blood was going down his chin. I tell you right then I wanted to smash that tube to pieces. I went over to it but Henry must have known what I was up to. He rushed from his chair and shoved me out of the way, against the wall. I told myself he didn't know what he was doing.

My mom came in, turned the set off real quiet, and told us she had made something for supper. So we went and sat down. There was still blood going down Henry's chin, but he didn't notice it and no one said anything, even though every time he took a bite of his bread his blood fell onto it until he was eating his own blood mixed in with the food.

While Henry was not around we talked about what was going to happen to him. There were no Indian doctors on the reservation, and my mom was afraid of trusting Old Man Pillager because he courted her long ago and was jealous of her husbands. He might take revenge through her son. We were afraid that if we brought Henry to a regular hospital they would keep him.

"They don't fix them in those places," Mom said; "they just give them drugs."

"We wouldn't get him there in the first place," I agreed, "so let's just forget about it."

Then I thought about the car.

Henry had not even looked at the car since he'd gotten home, though like I said, it was in tip-top condition and ready to drive. I thought the car might bring the old Henry back somehow. So I bided my time and waited for my chance to interest him in the vehicle.

One night Henry was off somewhere. I took myself a hammer. I went out to that car and I did a number on its underside. Whacked it up. Bent the tail pipe double. Ripped the muffler loose. By the time I was done with the car it looked worse than any typical Indian car that has been driven all its life on reservation roads, which they always say are like government promises—full of holes. It just about hurt me, I'll tell you that! I threw dirt in the carburetor and I ripped all the electric tape off the seats. I made it look just as beat up as I could. Then I sat back and waited for Henry to find it.

Still, it took him over a month. That was all right, because it was just getting
warm enough, not melting, but warm enough to work outside.

"Lyman," he says, walking in one day, "that red car looks like shit."

'Well it's old," I says. "You got to expect that."

"No way!" says Henry. "That car's a classic! But you went and ran the piss
right out of it, Lyman, and you know it don't deserve that. I kept that car in A-
one shape. You don't remember. You're too young. But when I left, that car was
running like a watch. Now I don't even know if I can get it to start again, let alone
get it anywhere near its old condition."

"Well you try," I said, like I was getting mad, "but I say it's a piece of junk."

Then I walked out before he could realize I knew he'd strung together more
than six words at once.

After that I thought he'd freeze himself to death working on that car. He was
out there all day, and at night he rigged up a little lamp, ran a cord out the window, and had himself some light to see by while he worked. He was better than
he had been before, but that's still not saying much. It was easier for him to do
the things the rest of us did. He ate more slowly and didn't jump up and down
during the meal to get this or that or look out the window. I put my hand in the
back of the TV set, I admit, and fiddled around with it good, so that it was almost impossible now to get a clear picture. He didn't look at it very often anyway. He was always out with that car or going off to get parts for it. By the time
it was really melting outside, he had it fixed.

I had been feeling down in the dumps about Henry around this time. We had
always been together before. Henry and Lyman. But he was such a loner now
that I didn't know how to take it. So I jumped at the chance one day when Henry
seemed friendly. It's not that he smiled or anything. He just said, "Let's take that
old shitbox for a spin." Just the way he said it made me think he could be coming around.

We went out to the car. It was spring. The sun was shining very bright. My only
sister, Bonita, who was just eleven years old, came out and made us stand together for a picture. Henry leaned his elbow on the red car's windshield, and he
took his other arm and put it over my shoulder, very carefully, as though it was
heavy for him to lift and he didn't want to bring the weight down all at once.

"Smile," Bonita said, and he did.

That picture. I never look at it anymore. A few months ago, I don't know why, I
got his picture out and tacked it on the wall. I felt good about Henry at the time,
close to him. I felt good having his picture on the wall, until one night when I
was looking at television. I was a little drunk and stoned. I looked up at the wall
and Henry was staring at me. I don't know what it was, but his smile had changed,
or maybe it was gone. All I know is I couldn't stay in the same room with that
picture. I was shaking. I got up, closed the door, and went into the kitchen. A little later my friend Ray came over and we both went back into that room. We

put the picture in a brown bag, folded the bag over and over tightly, then put it way back in a closet.

I still see that picture now, as if it tugs at me, whenever I pass that closet door. The picture is very clear in my mind. It was so sunny that day Henry had to squint against the glare. Or maybe the camera Bonita held flashed like a mirror, blinding him, before she snapped the picture. My face is right out in the sun, big and round. But he might have drawn back, because the shadows on his face are deep as holes. There are two shadows curved like little hooks around the ends of his smile, as if to frame it and try to keep it there—that one, first smile that looked like it might have hurt his face. He has his field jacket on and the worn-in clothes he'd come back in and kept wearing ever since. After Bonita took the picture, she went into the house and we got into the car. There was a full cooler in the trunk. We started off, east, toward Pembina and the Red River because Henry said he wanted to see the high water.

The trip over there was beautiful. When everything starts changing, drying up, clearing off, you feel like your whole life is starting. Henry felt it, too. The top was down and the car hummed like a top. He'd really put it back in shape, even the tape on the seats was very carefully put down and glued back in layers. It's not that he smiled again or even joked, but his face looked to me as if it was clear, more peaceful. It looked as though he wasn't thinking of anything in particular except the bare fields and windbreaks and houses we were passing.

The river was high and full of winter trash when we got there. The sun was still out, but it was colder by the river. There were still little clumps of dirty snow here and there on the banks. The water hadn't gone over the banks yet, but it would, you could tell. It was just at its limit, hard swollen, glossy like an old gray scar. We made ourselves a fire, and we sat down and watched the current go. As I watched it I felt something squeezing inside me and tightening and trying to let go all at the same time. I knew I was not just feeling it myself; I knew I was feeling what Henry was going through at that moment. Except that I couldn't stand it, the closing and opening. I jumped to my feet. I took Henry by the shoulders and I started shaking him. "Wake up," I says, "wake up, wake up, wake up!" I didn't know what had come over me. I sat down beside him again.

His face was totally white and hard. Then it broke, like stones break all of a sudden when water boils up inside them.

"I know it," he says. "I know it. I can't help it. It's no use."

We start talking. He said he knew what I'd done with the car. It was obvious it had been whacked out of shape and not just neglected. He said he wanted to give the car to me for good now, it was no use. He said he'd fixed it just to give it back and I should take it.

"No way," I says, "I don't want it."

"That's okay," he says, "you take it."

"I don't want it, though," I says back to him, and then to emphasize, just to emphasize, you understand, I touch his shoulder. He slaps my hand off.

"Take that car," he says.

"No," I say, "make me," I say, and then he grabs my jacket and rips the arm loose. That jacket is a class act, suede with tags and zippers. I push Henry backwards, off the log. He jumps up and bowls me over. We go down in a clinch and come up swinging hard, for all we're worth, with our fists. He socks my jaw so hard I feel like it swings loose. Then I'm at his ribcage and land a good one under his chin so his head snaps back. He's dazzled. He looks at me and I look at him and then his eyes are full of tears and blood and at first I think he's crying. But no, he's laughing. "Ha! Ha!" he says. "Ha! Ha! Take good care of it."

"Okay," I says, "okay, no problem. Ha! Ha!"

I can't help it, and I start laughing, too. My face feels fat and strange, and after a while I get a beer from the cooler in the trunk, and when I hand it to Henry he takes his shirt and wipes my germs off. "Hoof-and-mouth disease," he says. For some reason this cracks me up, and so we're really laughing for a while, and then we drink all the rest of the beers one by one and throw them in the river and see how far, how fast, the current takes them before they fill up and sink.

"You want to go on back?" I ask after a while. "Maybe we could snag a couple nice Kashpaw girls."

He says nothing. But I can tell his mood is turning again.

"They're all crazy, the girls up here, every damn one of them."

"You're crazy too," I say, to jolly him up. "Crazy Lamartine boys!"

He looks as though he will take this wrong at first. His face twists, then clears, and he jumps up on his feet. "That's right!" he says. "Crazier 'n hell. Crazy Indians!"

I think it's the old Henry again. He throws off his jacket and starts swinging his legs out from the knees like a fancy dancer. He's down doing something between a grouse dance and a bunny hop, no kind of dance I ever saw before, but neither has anyone else on all this green growing earth. He's wild. He wants to pitch whoopee! He's up and at me and all over. All this time I'm laughing so hard, so hard my belly is getting tied up in a knot.

"Got to cool me off!" he shouts all of a sudden. Then he runs over to the river and jumps in.

There's boards and other things in the current. It's so high. No sound comes from the river after the splash he makes, so I run right over. I look around. It's getting dark. I see he's halfway across the water already, and I know he didn't swim there but the current took him. It's far. I hear his voice, though, very clearly across it.

"My boots are filling," he says.

He says this in a normal voice, like he just noticed and he doesn't know what to think of it. Then he's gone. A branch comes by. Another branch. And I go in.

By the time I get out of the river, off the snag I pulled myself onto, the sun is down. I walk back to the car, turn on the high beams, and drive it up the bank. I put it in first gear and then I take my foot off the clutch. I get out, close the door, and watch it plow softly into the water. The headlights reach in as they go down, searching, still lighted even after the water swirls over the back end. I wait.

The wires short out. It is all finally dark. And then there is only the water, the sound of it going and running and going and running and running.

Study and Discussion Questions

1. How does the tone of the story shift when Henry returns from Vietnam?
2. How has Henry changed now that he's back from Vietnam?
3. List the various ways that Erdrich gives us clues throughout "The Red Convertible" about how it will end.
4. What are the phases the car goes through? How do these stand for what Lyman and Henry are going through?
5. What does the description of Henry's picture tell us about Henry? About the narrator Lyman? Why is the picture incident placed where it is in the story?
6. Why do Henry and Lyman fight down by the river?
7. How does the first paragraph of the story manage to tell us exactly what the end of the story will be and yet not give that ending away?

Suggestions for Writing

1. Discuss the image of the red convertible's "drowning." Why does Lyman send the car into the water? Why do you think the car's lights are left on?
2. Are there any ways in which Erdrich suggests that being Native Americans shapes Henry's and Lyman's experience?
3. Pick one incident in the story (e.g., the visit to long-haired Susy in Alaska, or Henry's watching TV and biting through his lip) and discuss why you think Erdrich included it.

Critical Resources

1. Chavkin, Allan, ed. *The Chippewa Landscape of Louise Erdrich.* Tuscaloosa: University of Alabama Press, 1999.
2. Stookey, Lorena. *Louise Erdrich: A Critical Companion.* Westport, CT: Greenwood Press, 1999.
3. Wong, Hertha. *Louise Erdrich's Love Medicine: A Casebook.* New York: Oxford University Press, 2000.

❁ ❁ ❁

DONALD BARTHELME (1931–1989)

Donald Barthelme was born in Philadelphia but grew up in Houston, Texas. As a college student at the University of Houston, Barthelme was active as an editor and reporter for the school newspaper. After serving in the army for a couple of years, Barthelme returned to Houston and began writing in a variety of contexts, as well as taking a job as the director of the Contemporary Arts Mu-

seum. In 1962, he moved to New York and began writing short stories for The New Yorker *magazine. His work was instantly recognized for its radical, unconventional uses of language—intentional misspellings, ambiguous meanings, and unusual form. Indeed, one of Barthelme's goals was to draw attention to the complexities of language while at the same maintaining the semblance of a narrative structure that supported his satirical critique of modern life. Yet his work tends to defy easy categorization into one set genre. Like Franz Kafka, Barthelme works in the world of the absurd and bizarre. Selected works include the short story collections* Unspeakable Practices, Unnatural Acts *(1968),* City Life *(1970),* Sadness *(1972),* Guilty Pleasures *(1974), and* Sixty Stories *(1981); and the novels* Snow White *(1967),* The Dead Father *(1975),* Paradise *(1986), and* The King *(1990, published posthumously). "Report" was first published in* Unspeakable Practices, Unnatural Acts.

Report

(1968)

Our group is against the war. But the war goes on. I was sent to Cleveland to talk to the engineers. The engineers were meeting in Cleveland. I was supposed to persuade them not to do what they are going to do. I took United's 4:45 from LaGuardia arriving in Cleveland at 6:13. Cleveland is dark blue at that hour. I went directly to the motel, where the engineers were meeting. Hundreds of engineers attended the Cleveland meeting. I noticed many fractures among the engineers, bandages, traction. I noticed what appeared to be fracture of the carpal scaphoid in six examples. I notice numerous fractures of the humeral shaft, of the os calcis, of the pelvic girdle. I noticed a high incidence of clay-shoveller's fracture. I could not account for these fractures. The engineers were making calculations, taking measurements, sketching on the black board, drinking beer, throwing bread, buttonholing employers, hurling glasses into the fireplace. They were friendly.

They were friendly. They were full of love and information. The chief engineer wore shades. Patella in Monk's traction, clamshell fracture by the look of it. He was standing in a slum of beer bottles and microphone cable. "Have some of this chicken à la Isambard Kingdom Brunel[1] the Great Ingineer," he said. "And declare who you are and what we can do for you. What is your line, distinguished guest?"

"Software," I said. "In every sense. I am here representing a small group of interested parties. We are interested in your thing, which seems to be functioning in the midst of so much dysfunction, function is interesting. Other people's things don't seem to be working. The State Department's thing doesn't seem to

---

[1] Nineteenth-century British engineer.

be working. The U.N.'s thing doesn't seem to be working. The democratic left's thing doesn't seem to be working. Buddha's thing—"

"Ask us anything about our thing, which seems to be working," the chief engineer said. "We will open our hearts and heads to you, Software Man, because we want to be understood and loved by the great lay public, and have our marvels appreciated by that public, for which we daily unsung produce tons of new marvels each more life-enhancing than the last. Ask us anything. Do you want to know about evaporated thin-film metallurgy? Monolithic and hybrid integrated-circuit processes? The algebra of inequalities? Optimization theory? Complex high-speed micro-miniature closed and open loop systems? Fixed variable mathematical cost searches? Epitaxial deposition of semi-conductor materials? Gross interfaced space gropes? We also have specialists in the cuckooflower, the doctorfish, and the dumdum bullet as these relate to aspects of today's expanding technology, and they do in the damnedest ways."

I spoke to him then about the war. I said the same things people always say when they speak against the war. I said that the war was wrong. I said that large countries should not burn down small countries. I said that the government had made a series of errors. I said that these errors once small and forgivable were now immense and unforgivable. I said that the government was attempting to conceal its original errors under layers of new errors. I said that the government was sick with error, giddy with it. I said that ten thousand of our soldiers had already been killed in pursuit of the government's errors. I said that tens of thousands of the enemy's soldiers and civilians had been killed because of various errors, ours and theirs. I said that we are responsible for errors made in our name. I said that the government should not be allowed to make additional errors.

"Yes, yes," the chief engineer said, "there is doubtless much truth in what you say, but we can't possibly *lose* the war, can we? And stopping is losing, isn't it? The war regarded as a process, stopping regarded as an abort? We don't know *how* to lose a war. That skill is not among our skills. Our array smashes their array, that is what we know. That is the process. That is what is.

"But let's not have any more of this dispiriting downbeat counterproductive talk. I have a few new marvels here I'd like to discuss with you just briefly. A few new marvels that are just about ready to be gaped at by the admiring layman. Consider for instance the area of realtime online computer-controlled wish evaporation. Wish evaporation is going to be crucial in meeting the rising expectations of the world's peoples, which are as you know rising entirely too fast."

I noticed then distributed about the room a great many transverse fractures of the ulna. "The development of the pseudo-ruminant stomach for underdeveloped peoples," he went on, "is one of our interesting things you should be interested in. With the pseudo-ruminant stomach they can chew cuds, that is to say, eat grass. Blue is the most popular color worldwide and for that reason we are working with certain strains of your native Kentucky *Poa pratensis,* or bluegrass, as the staple input for the p/r stomach cycle, which would also give a shot in the arm to our balance-of-payments thing don't you know...." I noticed about me then a great number of metatarsal fractures in banjo splints. "The kangaroo initiative . . . eight hundred thousand harvested last year . . . highest percentage of edible protein of any herbivore yet studied . . ."

"Have new kangaroos been planted?"

The engineer looked at me.

"I intuit your hatred and jealousy of our thing," he said. "The ineffectual always hate our thing and speak of it as anti-human, which is not at all a meaningful way to speak of our thing. Nothing mechanical is alien to me," he said (amber spots making bursts of light in his shades), "because I am human, in a sense, and if I think it up, then 'it' is human too, whatever 'it' may be. Let me tell you, Software Man, we have been damned forbearing in the matter of this little war you declare yourself to be interested in. Function is the cry, and our thing is functioning like crazy. There are things we could do that we have not done. Steps we could take that we have not taken. These steps are, regarded in a certain light, the light of our enlightened self-interest, quite justifiable steps. We could, of course, get irritated. We could, of course, *lose patience.*

"We could, of course, release thousands upon thousands of self-powered crawling-along-the-ground lengths of titanium wire eighteen inches long with a diameter of .0005 centimetres (that is to say, invisible) which, scenting an enemy, climb up his trouser leg and wrap themselves around his neck. We have developed those. They are within our capabilities. We could, of course, release in the arena of the upper air our new improved pufferfish toxin which precipitates an identity crisis. No special technical problems there. That is almost laughably easy. We could, of course, place up to two million maggots in their rice within twenty-four hours. The maggots are ready, massed in secret staging areas in Alabama. We have hypodermic darts capable of piebalding the enemy's pigmentation. We have rots, blights, and rusts capable of attacking his alphabet. Those are dandies. We have a hut-shrinking chemical which penetrates the fibres of the bamboo, causing it, the hut, to strangle its occupants. This operates only after 10 P.M., when people are sleeping. Their mathematics are at the mercy of a suppurating surd we have invented. We have a family of fishes trained to attack their fishes. We have the deadly testicle-destroying telegram. The cable companies are coöperating. We have a green substance that, well, I'd rather not talk about. We have a secret word that, if pronounced, produces multiple fractures in all living things in an area the size of four football fields."

"That's why—"

"Yes. Some damned fool couldn't keep his mouth shut. The point is that the whole structure of enemy life is within our power to *rend, vitiate, devour,* and *crush.* But that's not the interesting thing."

"You recount these possibilities with uncommon relish."

"Yes I realize that there is too much relish here. But *you* must realize that these capabilities represent in and of themselves highly technical and complex and interesting problems and hurdles on which our boys have expended many thousands of hours of hard work and brilliance. And that the effects are often grossly exaggerated by irresponsible victims. And that the whole thing represents a fantastic series of triumphs for the multidisciplined problem-solving team concept."

"I appreciate that."

"We *could* unleash all this technology at once. You can imagine what would happen then. But that's not the interesting thing."

"What is the interesting thing?"

"The interesting thing is that we have a *moral sense*. It is on punched cards, perhaps the most advanced and sensitive moral sense the world has ever known."

"Because it is on punched cards?"

"It considers all considerations in endless and subtle detail," he said. "It even quibbles. With this great new moral tool, how can we go wrong? I confidently predict that, although we *could* employ all this splendid new weaponry I've been telling you about, *we're not going to do it*."

"We're not going to do it?"

I took United's 5:44 from Cleveland arriving at Newark at 7:19. New Jersey is bright pink at that hour. Living things move about the surface of New Jersey at that hour molesting each other only in traditional ways. I made my report to the group. I stressed the friendliness of the engineers. I said, It's all right. I said, We have a moral sense. I said, *We're not going to do it*. They didn't believe me.

Study and Discussion Questions

1. Describe the chief engineer's attitude toward the war, toward technology, toward social problems, and toward morality.
2. What do the chief engineer's discussions of "wish evaporation" and the "pseudo-ruminant stomach" suggest about how he views the people of poor nations?
3. What kind of person is Software Man? What does he represent? What effect does his talk with the chief engineer have on him?
4. Reread the long paragraph in which the chief engineer describes the new weapons available. How are we supposed to react? What is the effect of the matter-of-fact tone in which these bizarre horrors are described?
5. "Report" was first published during the Vietnam War. What in the story points to that war in particular?
6. Compare/contrast the attitude toward weapons technology in this story with actual attitudes toward weapons technology in the military and government today.

Suggestions for Writing

1. Discuss a product of modern technology that you find frightening.
2. Speculate on how high-technology weaponry changes the nature of war.

Critical Resources

1. Barthelme, Donald. *Not-Knowing: The Essays and Interviews of Donald Barthelme*. Ed. Kim Herzinger. New York: Random House, 1997.

2. Barthelme, Helen. *Donald Barthelme: The Genesis of a Cool Sound.* College Station, TX: Texas A&M University Press, 2001.
3. Roe, Barbara. *Donald Barthelme: A Study of the Short Fiction.* New York: Twayne Publishers, 1992.
4. Trachtenberg, Stanley. *Understanding Donald Barthelme.* Columbia: University of South Carolina Press, 1990.

TIM O'BRIEN (b. 1946)

Tim O'Brien was born in Austin, Minnesota. After high school, he entered Macalester College in St. Paul to study political science. He graduated in 1968 summa cum laude. Any intentions of studying further, however, were dashed after being drafted into the army to fight in Vietnam. The traumatic experience of Vietnam had a deep impact on his life, and, after returning to the United States, he turned to writing as a way to cope with the insanity of war. In 1973, while studying at Harvard, O'Brien published If I Die in a Combat Zone, Box Me Up and Ship Me Home, *a memoir of his experience in Vietnam—a work that compelled American culture to rethink the human costs of war and established him as the writerly conscience of Vietnam. In a terse, compact prose style (he is often compared to Ernest Hemingway in both theme and technique) O'Brien often disrupts standard narrative sequence by rearranging linear plot schemes through the blurring of reality and imagination. Within this mode, his protagonists grapple with false and romantic notions of courage, integrity, wisdom, and fear. While Vietnam serves as the backdrop for many of his works, O'Brien has explored other themes in more recent books yet still maintains a commitment to the human desire to find understanding in a chaotic world. Selected works include* Northern Lights *(1975),* Going After Cacciato *(1978, National Book Award),* The Nuclear Age *(1985),* The Things They Carried *(1990),* In the Lake of the Woods *(1994),* Tomcat in Love *(1998) and his latest novel* July, July, *(2002). "The Man I Killed" comes from* The Things They Carried.

The Man I Killed (1990)

His jaw was in his throat, his upper lip and teeth were gone, his one eye was shut, his other eye was a star-shaped hole, his eyebrows were thin and arched like a woman's, his nose was undamaged, there was a slight tear at the lobe of one ear, his clean black hair was swept upward into a cowlick at the rear of the skull, his forehead was lightly freckled, his fingernails were clean, the skin at his left cheek was peeled back in three ragged strips, his right cheek was smooth and hairless, there was a butterfly on his chin, his neck was open to the spinal cord and the blood there was thick and shiny and it was this wound that had killed him. He lay face-up in the center of the trail, a slim, dead, almost dainty young man. He had bony legs, a narrow waist, long shapely fingers. His chest was sunken and poorly muscled—a scholar, maybe. His wrists were the wrists of a child. He wore a black shirt, black pajama pants, a gray ammunition belt, a gold ring on the third finger of his right hand. His rubber sandals had been blown off. One lay beside him, the other a few meters up the trail. He had been born, maybe, in 1946 in the village of My Khe near the central coastline of Quang Ngai Province,[1] where his parents farmed, and where his family had lived for several centuries, and where, during the time of the French, his father and two uncles and many neighbors had joined in the struggle for independence. He was not a Communist. He was a citizen and a soldier. In the village of My Khe, as in all of Quang Ngai, patriotic resistance had the force of tradition, which was partly the force of legend, and from his earliest boyhood the man I killed would have listened to stories about the heroic Trung sisters and Tran Hung Dao's famous rout of the Mongols and Le Loi's final victory against the Chinese at Tot Dong.[2] He would have been taught that to defend the land was a man's highest duty and highest privilege. He had accepted this. It was never open to question. Secretly, though, it also frightened him. He was not a fighter. His health was poor, his body small and frail. He liked books. He wanted someday to be a teacher of mathematics. At night, lying on his mat, he could not picture himself doing the brave things his father had done, or his uncles, or the heroes of the stories. He hoped in his heart that he would never be tested. He hoped the Americans would go away. Soon, he hoped. He kept hoping and hoping, always, even when he was asleep.

"Oh, man, you fuckin' trashed the fucker," Azar said. "You scrambled his sorry self, look at that, you *did,* you laid him out like Shredded fuckin' Wheat."

"Go away," Kiowa said.

"I'm just saying the truth. Like oatmeal."

"Go," Kiowa said.

"Okay, then, I take it back," Azar said. He started to move away, then stopped and said, "Rice Krispies, you know? On the dead test, this particular individual gets A-Plus."

Smiling at this, he shrugged and walked up the trail toward the village behind the trees.

Kiowa kneeled down.

"Just forget that crud," he said. He opened up his canteen and held it out for a while and then sighed and pulled it away. "No sweat, man. What else could you do?"

---

[1]Province in central South Vietnam.

[2]The Trung sisters led a Vietnamese rebellion against Chinese rule in A.D. 40; Tran Hung Dao repelled a Mongol attack in 1287; Le Loi defeated the Chinese in 1426.

Later, Kiowa said, "I'm serious. Nothing *anybody* could do. Come on, stop staring."

The trail junction was shaded by a row of trees and tall brush. The slim young man lay with his legs in the shade. His jaw was in his throat. His one eye was shut and the other was a star-shaped hole.

Kiowa glanced at the body.

"All right, let me ask a question," he said. "You want to trade places with him? Turn it all upside down—you *want* that? I mean, be honest."

The star-shaped hole was red and yellow. The yellow part seemed to be getting wider, spreading out at the center of the star. The upper lip and gum and teeth were gone. The man's head was cocked at a wrong angle, as if loose at the neck, and the neck was wet with blood.

"Think it over," Kiowa said.

Then later he said, "Tim, it's a *war*. The guy wasn't Heidi—he had a weapon, right? It's a tough thing, for sure, but you got to cut out that staring."

Then he said, "Maybe you better lie down a minute."

Then after a long empty time he said, "Take it slow. Just go wherever the spirit takes you."

The butterfly was making its way along the young man's forehead, which was spotted with small dark freckles. The nose was undamaged. The skin on the right cheek was smooth and fine-grained and hairless. Frail-looking, delicately boned, the young man would not have wanted to be a soldier and in his heart would have feared performing badly in battle. Even as a boy growing up in the village of My Khe, he had often worried about this. He imagined covering his head and lying in a deep hole and closing his eyes and not moving until the war was over. He had no stomach for violence. He loved mathematics. His eyebrows were thin and arched like a woman's, and at school the boys sometimes teased him about how pretty he was, the arched eyebrows and long shapely fingers, and on the playground they mimicked a woman's walk and made fun of his smooth skin and his love for mathematics. The young man could not make himself fight them. He often wanted to, but he was afraid, and this increased his shame. If he could not fight little boys, he thought, how could he ever become a soldier and fight the Americans with their airplanes and helicopters and bombs? It did not seem possible. In the presence of his father and uncles, he pretended to look forward to doing his patriotic duty, which was also a privilege, but at night he prayed with his mother that the war might end soon. Beyond anything else, he was afraid of disgracing himself, and therefore his family and village. But all he could do, he thought, was wait and pray and try not to grow up too fast.

"Listen to me," Kiowa said. "You feel terrible, I know that."

Then he said, "Okay, maybe I *don't* know."

Along the trail there were small blue flowers shaped like bells. The young man's head was wrenched sideways, not quite facing the flowers, and even in the shade a single blade of sunlight sparkled against the buckle of his ammunition belt. The left cheek was peeled back in three ragged strips. The wounds at his neck had not yet clotted, which made him seem animate even in death, the blood still spreading out across his shirt.

Kiowa shook his head.

There was some silence before he said, "Stop *staring*."

The young man's fingernails were clean. There was a slight tear at the lobe of one ear, a sprinkling of blood on the forearm. He wore a gold ring on the third finger of his right hand. His chest was sunken and poorly muscled—a scholar, maybe. His life was now a constellation of possibilities. So, yes, maybe a scholar. And for years, despite his family's poverty, the man I killed would have been determined to continue his education in mathematics. The means for this were arranged, perhaps, through the village liberation cadres, and in 1964 the young man began attending classes at the university in Saigon, where he avoided politics and paid attention to the problems of calculus. He devoted himself to his studies. He spent his nights alone, wrote romantic poems in his journal, took pleasure in the grace and beauty of differential equations. The war, he knew, would finally take him, but for the time being he would not let himself think about it. He had stopped praying; instead, now, he waited. And as he waited, in his final year at the university, he fell in love with a classmate, a girl of seventeen, who one day told him that his wrists were like the wrists of a child, so small and delicate, and who admired his narrow waist and the cowlick that rose up like a bird's tail at the back of his head. She liked his quiet manner; she laughed at his freckles and bony legs. One evening, perhaps, they exchanged gold rings.

Now one eye was a star.

"You okay?" Kiowa said.

The body lay almost entirely in shade. There were gnats at the mouth, little flecks of pollen drifting above the nose. The butterfly was gone. The bleeding had stopped except for the neck wounds.

Kiowa picked up the rubber sandals, clapping off the dirt, then bent down to search the body. He found a pouch of rice, a comb, a fingernail clipper, a few soiled piasters, a snapshot of a young woman standing in front of a parked motorcycle. Kiowa placed these items in his rucksack along with the gray ammunition belt and rubber sandals.

Then he squatted down.

"I'll tell you the straight truth," he said. "The guy was dead the second he stepped on the trail. Understand me? We all had him zeroed. A good kill—weapon, ammunition, everything." Tiny beads of sweat glistened at Kiowa's forehead. His eyes moved from the sky to the dead man's body to the knuckles of his own hands. "So listen, you best pull your shit together. Can't just sit here all day."

Later he said, "Understand?"

Then he said, "Five minutes, Tim. Five more minutes and we're moving out."

The one eye did a funny twinkling trick, red to yellow. His head was wrenched sideways, as if loose at the neck, and the dead young man seemed to be staring at some distant object beyond the bell-shaped flowers along the trail. The blood at the neck had gone to a deep purplish black. Clean fingernails, clean hair—he had been a soldier for only a single day. After his years at the university, the man I killed returned with his new wife to the village of My Khe, where he enlisted as a common rifleman with the 48th Vietcong Battalion. He knew he would die quickly. He knew he would see a flash of light. He knew he would fall dead and wake up in the stories of his village and people.

Kiowa covered the body with a poncho.

"Hey, you're looking better," he said. "No doubt about it. All you needed was time—some mental R&R."

Then he said, "Man, I'm sorry."

Then later he said, "Why not talk about it?"

Then he said, "Come on, man, talk."

He was a slim, dead, almost dainty young man of about twenty. He lay with one leg bent beneath him, his jaw in his throat, his face neither expressive nor inexpressive. One eye was shut. The other was a star-shaped hole.

"Talk," Kiowa said.

Study and Discussion Questions

1. Why do you think the narrator describes the dead man's body in such detail?
2. Why does the narrator persist in imagining the life of the man he killed?
3. What's the significance of the narrator's guess that the dead man was born in a place "where his family had lived for several centuries"?
4. Why do you think the narrator imagines that the man he killed was a fearful and reluctant soldier?
5. Why does the narrator assert that the dead man "was not a Communist"?
6. What role does Azar play in the story? What do his reactions add to the story's condemnation of war? And what is Kiowa's role?

Suggestions for Writing

1. What can we infer about the narrator of "The Man I Killed"? Write a sketch of what you imagine him to be like.
2. In an effort to ease the narrator's guilt, Kiowa says: "Tim, it's a *war*. The guy wasn't Heidi—he had a weapon, right?" How might Tim reply? How might you?

Critical Resources

1. Heberle, Mark. *A Trauma Artist: Tim O'Brien and the Fiction of Vietnam.* Iowa City: University of Iowa Press, 2001.
2. Heroz, Tobey. *Tim O'Brien.* New York: Twayne, 1997.
3. Kaplan Steven. *Understanding Tim O'Brien.* Columbia: University of South Carolina Press, 1995.
4. Robinson, Daniel. "Getting it Right: The Short Fiction of Tim O'Brien." *Critique: Studies in Contemporary Fiction* 40.3 (1999): 257–64.

5. Wharton, Lynn. "Journeying from Life to Literature: An Interview with American Novelist Tim O'Brien." *Interdisciplinary Studies: A Journal of Criticism and Theory* 1.2 (2000): 229–47.

GHASSAN KANAFANI (1936–1972)

Ghassan Kanafani was born a middle-class Sunni Muslim in Acre, Palestine. His family was forced to leave in 1948 due to persecution during the establishment of the nation of Israel. They would eventually settle in Damascus, where Kanafani studied Arabic literature at the University of Damascus. After working as a teacher and journalist in Syria and Kuwait, Kanafani went to Beirut and founded the political magazine Al-Hadaf *(The Target) in 1969—a weekly journal for the PFLP—Popular Front for the Liberation of Palestine. In addition to his journalistic writing, Kanafani's short fiction established him as an important voice for the Palestinian struggle. Often experimenting with narrative form, Kanafani's fiction is marked by an economy of language. Unlike his journalism, though, Kanafani's fiction is less obviously political. Through the exploration of more universal themes of poverty, victimization, love, and death, Kanafani's work often demonstrates that the Palestinian struggle is really the struggle of all oppressed peoples in the world. Kanafani was killed by a car bomb in 1972 at the age of 36. His works include the short stories "The Land of Sad Oranges" (1958), "If You Were a Horse" (1961), "The Falcon" (1961), and "A Hand in the Grave" (1962); and the novellas* Men in the Sun *(1962),* All That's Left to You *(1966), and* Umm Saad *(1969). "Letter from Gaza" was written in 1956.*

Letter from Gaza   (1956)

DEAR MUSTAFA,

I have now received your letter, in which you tell me that you've done everything necessary to enable me to stay with you in Sacramento. I've also received news that I have been accepted in the department of Civil Engineering in the University of California. I must thank you for everything, my friend. But it'll strike you as rather odd when I proclaim this news to you—and make no doubt about it, I feel no hesitation at all, in fact I am pretty well positive that I have never seen things so clearly as I do now. No, my friend, I have changed my mind. I won't follow you to "the land where there is greenery, water, and lovely faces," as you wrote. No, I'll stay here, and I won't ever leave.

I am really upset that our lives won't continue to follow the same course, Mustafa. For I can almost hear you reminding me of our vow to go on together, and of the way we used to shout: "We'll get rich!" But there's nothing I can do, my friend. Yes, I still remember the day when I stood in the hall of Cairo airport, pressing your hand and staring at the frenzied motor. At that moment everything was rotating in time with the ear-splitting motor, and you stood in front of me, your round face silent.

Your face hadn't changed from the way it used to be when you were growing up in the Shajiya quarter of Gaza, apart from those slight wrinkles. We grew up together, understanding each other completely, and we promised to go on together till the end. But . . .

"There's a quarter of an hour left before the plane takes off. Don't look into space like that. Listen! You'll go to Kuwait next year, and you'll save enough from your salary to uproot you from Gaza and transplant you to California. We started off together and we must carry on. . . ."

At that moment I was watching your rapidly moving lips. That was always your manner of speaking, without commas or full stops. But in an obscure way I felt that you were not completely happy with your flight. You couldn't give three good reasons for it. I too suffered from this wrench, but the clearest thought was: why don't we abandon this Gaza and flee? Why don't we? Your situation had begun to improve, however. The Ministry of Education in Kuwait had given you a contract, though it hadn't given me one. In the trough of misery where I existed, you sent me small sums of money. You wanted me to consider them as loans, because you feared that I would feel slighted. You knew my family circumstances in and out; you knew that my meagre salary in the UN-RWA schools was inadequate to support my mother, my brother's widow, and her four children.

"Listen carefully. Write to me every day . . . every hour . . . every minute! The plane's just leaving. Farewell! Or rather, till we meet again!"

Your cold lips brushed my cheek, you turned your face away from me towards the plane, and when you looked at me again I could see your tears.

Later the Ministry of Education in Kuwait gave me a contract. There's no need to repeat to you how my life there went in detail. I always wrote to you about everything. My life there had a gluey, vacuous quality as though I were a small oyster, lost in oppressive loneliness, slowly struggling with a future as dark as the beginning of the night, caught in a rotten routine, a spewed-out combat with time. Everything was hot and sticky. There was a slipperiness to my whole life, it was all a hankering for the end of the month.

In the middle of the year, that year, the Jews bombarded the central district of Sabha and attacked Gaza, our Gaza, with bombs and flamethrowers. That event might have made some change in my routine, but there was nothing for me to take much notice of; I was going to leave this Gaza behind me and go to California where I would live for myself, my own self which had suffered so long. I hated Gaza and its inhabitants. Everything in the amputated town reminded me of failed pictures painted in gray by a sick man. Yes, I would send my mother and my brother's widow and her children a meagre sum to help them to live, but I would liberate myself from this last tie too, there in green California, far from the reek of defeat that for seven years had filled my nostrils. The sympathy that bound me to my brother's children, their mother, and mine would never be enough to justify my tragedy in taking this perpendicular dive. It mustn't drag me any farther down than it already had. I must flee!

You know these feelings, Mustafa, because you've really experienced them. What is this ill-defined tie we had with Gaza that blunted our enthusiasm for flight? Why didn't we analyze the matter in such a way as to give it a clear meaning? Why didn't we leave this defeat with its wounds behind us and move on to a brighter future that would give us deeper consolation! Why? We didn't exactly know.

When I went on holiday in June and assembled all my possessions, longing for the sweet departure, the start towards those little things which give life a nice, bright meaning, I found Gaza just as I had known it, closed like the introverted lining of a rusted snail-shell thrown up by the waves on the sticky, sandy shore by the slaughterhouse. This Gaza was more cramped than the mind of a sleeper in the throes of a fearful nightmare, with its narrow streets that had their peculiar smell, the smell of defeat and poverty, its houses with their bulging balconies . . . this Gaza! But what are the obscure causes that draw a man to his family, his house, his memories, as a spring draws a small flock of mountain goats? I don't know. All I know is that I went to my mother in our house that morning. When I arrived my late brother's wife met me there and asked me, weeping, if I would do as her wounded daughter, Nadia, in Gaza hospital wished and visit her that evening. Do you know Nadia, my brother's beautiful thirteen-year-old daughter?

That evening I bought a pound of apples and set out for the hospital to visit Nadia. I knew that there was something about it that my mother and my sister-in-law were hiding from me, something that their tongues could not utter, something strange that I could not put my finger on. I loved Nadia from habit, the same habit that made me love all that generation which had been so brought up on defeat and displacement that it had come to think that a happy life was a kind of social deviation.

What happened at that moment? I don't know. I entered the white room very calm. Ill children have something of saintliness, and how much more so if the child is ill as a result of cruel, painful wounds. Nadia was lying on her bed, her back propped up on a big pillow over which her hair was spread like a thick pelt. There was a profound silence in her wide eyes and a tear always shining in the depths of her black pupils. Her face was calm and still but eloquent as the face of a tortured prophet might be. Nadia was still a child, but she seemed more than a child, much more, and older than a child, much older.

"Nadia!"

I've no idea whether I was the one who said it, or whether it was someone else behind me. But she raised her eyes to me and I felt them dissolve me like a piece of sugar that had fallen into a hot cup of tea. Together with her slight smile I heard her voice.

"Uncle! Have you just come from Kuwait?"

Her voice broke in her throat, and she raised herself with the help of her hands and stretched out her neck towards me. I patted her back and sat down near her.

"Nadia! I've brought you presents from Kuwait, lots of presents. I'll wait till you can leave your bed, completely well and healed, and you'll come to my house and I'll give them to you. I've bought you the red trousers you wrote and asked me for. Yes, I've bought them."

It was a lie, born of the tense situation, but as I uttered it I felt that I was speaking the truth for the first time. Nadia trembled as though she had had an electric shock, and lowered her head in a terrible silence. I felt her tears wetting the back of my hand.

"Say something, Nadia! Don't you want the red trousers?"

She lifted her gaze to me and made as if to speak, but then she stopped, gritted her teeth, and I heard her voice again, coming from far away.

"Uncle!"

She stretched out her hand, lifted the white coverlet with her fingers, and pointed to her leg, amputated from the top of the thigh.

My friend. . . . Never shall I forget Nadia's leg, amputated from the top of the thigh. No! Nor shall I forget the grief which had molded her face and merged into its traits forever. I went out of the hospital in Gaza that day, my hand clutched in silent derision on the two pounds I had brought with me to give Nadia. The blazing sun filled the streets with the color of blood. And Gaza was brand new, Mustafa! You and I never saw it like this. The stone piled up at the beginning of the Shajiya quarter where we lived had a meaning, and they seemed to have been put there for no other reason but to explain it. This Gaza in which we had lived and with whose good people we had spent seven years of defeat was something new. It seemed to me just a beginning. I don't know why I thought it was just a beginning. I imagined that the main street that I walked along on the way back home was only the beginning of a long, long road leading to Safad. Everything in this Gaza throbbed with sadness, which was not confined to weeping. It was a challenge; more than that, it was something like reclamation of the amputated leg!

I went out into the streets of Gaza, streets filled with blinding sunlight. They told me that Nadia had lost her leg when she threw herself on top of her little brothers and sisters to protect them from the bombs and flames that had fastened their claws into the house. Nadia could have saved herself, she could have run away, rescued her leg. But she didn't.

Why?

No, my friend, I won't come to Sacramento, and I've no regrets. No, and nor will I finish what we began together in childhood. This obscure feeling that you had as you left Gaza, this small feeling must grow into a giant deep within you. It must expand, you must seek it in order to find yourself, here among the ugly debris of defeat.

I won't come to you. But you, return to us! Come back, to learn from Nadia's leg, amputated from the top of the thigh, what life is and what existence is worth.

Come back, my friend! We are all waiting for you.

Study and Discussion Questions

1. What metaphors and images does Kanafani use to describe Gaza? What do these suggest about Gaza and about the narrator?
2. Why does the narrator change his mind about emigrating to California? What did California mean to him and to Mustafa, and how does that meaning change for the narrator?
3. What kind of relationship do the narrator and Mustafa have? How does the language in the story describe this relationship?
4. Kanafani writes, "Ill children have something of saintliness." What role do children play in this story? How is the fate of children a part of the narrator's decision?
5. Why do you think Kanafani chose to tell this story in the form of a letter? What effect does this have on the reader? What does Kanafani gain by using the epistolary (letter) form? Does he lose anything?
6. "Letter from Gaza" was first published around 50 years ago. Does it, however, seem contemporary? And does that surprise you, as you consider the situation in the Middle East today? Discuss.

Suggestions for Writing

1. Gaza has been a contested territory and the scene of long-standing tension and warfare. Research the history of Gaza, and write about how "Letter from Gaza" fits into and relates to the political and social events that have taken and are taking place there.
2. "Letter from Gaza" describes the conflict between leaving a difficult homeland in order to make a better life for yourself, or staying to try to make that country better for yourself and others. Do you know anyone personally who has had to make that kind of choice? Write about the different aspects of this conflict and the implications of the narrator's choice in this story.

Critical Resources

1. Abdel-Malek, Kamel. "Living on Borderlines: War and Exile in Selected Works by Ghassan Kanafani, Fawaz Turki and Mahmud Darwish." *Israeli and Palestinian Identities in History and Literature.* Ed. David Jacobson. New York: St. Martin's, 1999.
2. Harlow, Barbara. *After Lives: Legacies of Revolutionary Writing.* London: Verso, 1996.
3. Kanafani, Ghassan. *Men in the Sun and Other Palestinian Stories.* Trans. Hilary Kilpatrick. London: Lynne Rienner Publishers, 1999.
4. Siddiq, Muhammad. *Man is a Cause: Political Consciousness and the Fiction of Ghassan Kanafani.* Seattle: University of Washington Press, 1984.

✸ ✸ ✸

Poetry

WILFRED OWEN (1893–1918)

Wilfred Owen was born in Oswestry, England, and raised in a strict Calvinist home. His interest in poetry began at an early age, in particular the poetry of John Keats. Hoping to enroll at the University of London, Owen was unable to secure a scholarship that would have enabled him to pay the tuition. In 1913, he left to teach English in France, returning two years later to enlist in the British Army at the height of World War I. After many months fighting on the Western Front, Owen suffered shell shock and was hospitalized. It was during this convalescence that Owen met Siegfried Sassoon, another injured soldier and poet who encouraged and worked with Owen on his poetry. At the time, Owen had already published a few poems, but Sassoon's influence impelled Owen to develop the innovative poetry he would become known for. His brutal depictions of the realities of war helped to dismantle the era's popular and romanticized versions of valor and heroism. Owen's verse stood as the voice of the silent and unknown soldier. He was killed at the front in 1918, a week before the Armistice that ended World War I. His Poems *appeared in 1920. "Dulce Et Decorum Est" is one of Owen's best-known poems.*

Dulce Et Decorum Est[1]   (1920)

Bent double, like old beggars under sacks,
Knock-kneed, coughing like hags, we cursed through sludge,
Till on the haunting flares we turned our backs
And towards our distant rest began to trudge.
Men marched asleep. Many had lost their boots   5
But limped on, blood-shod. All went lame; all blind;
Drunk with fatigue; deaf even to the hoots
Of tired, outstripped Five-Nines[2] that dropped behind.

Gas! Gas! Quick boys!—An ecstasy of fumbling,
Fitting the clumsy helmets just in time;   10
But someone still was yelling out and stumbling

---

[1]See the last two lines for full quotation from Horace: "It is sweet and proper to die for one's country."
[2]Gas shells.

And flound'ring like a man in fire or lime . . .
Dim, through the misty panes and thick green light,
As under a green sea, I saw him drowning.

In all my dreams, before my helpless sight,   15
He plunges at me, guttering, choking, drowning.

If in some smothering dreams you too could pace
Behind the wagon that we flung him in,
And watch the white eyes writhing in his face,
His hanging face, like a devil's sick of sin;   20
If you could hear, at every jolt, the blood
Come gargling from the froth-corrupted lungs,
Obscene as cancer, bitter as the cud
Of vile, incurable sores on innocent tongues,—
My friend, you would not tell with such high zest   25
To children ardent for some desperate glory,
The old Lie: Dulce et decorum est
Pro patria mori.

Study and Discussion Questions

1. Who is speaking in the poem? Where is he? What does he list in the first
   stanza about the conditions of himself and the other soldiers?
2. In terms of the "plot" of this poem, what happens, suddenly, in the second stanza?
3. Where is the speaker of the poem in the third, two-line, stanza?
4. Note the change in verb tense in the final stanza. How is this prepared for
   in the previous couplet?
5. To whom is the poem addressed? How does Owens involve the reader before the poem is done? And why does he want to do so?
6. Look at the images: What are the soldiers in general and the dying soldier
   in particular compared to?
7. Do some research on World War I weapons and modes of warfare. How
   does Owen's use of metaphor and simile capture the experience?

Suggestions for Writing

1. Which image in the poem strikes you most forcefully? Why?
2. Write your own critique (or defense) of the quote from Horace.
3. Compare World War I warfare and weapons with contemporary warfare
   and weapons.

4. Write a contemporary poem on the actual experience of battle. What is your theme? Choose the words and the images to convey that theme and mood.

Critical Resources

1. Fussell, Paul. *The Great War and Modern Memory.* London: Oxford University Press, 1975.
2. Hibberd, Dominic. *Wilfred Owen: A New Biography.* Chicago: Ivan R. Dee, 2003.
3. Hipp, Daniel. "By Degrees Regain[ing] Cool Peaceful Air in Wonder: Wilfred Owen's War Poetry as Psychological Therapy." *Journal of the Midwest Modern Language Association* 35.1 (2002) 25–49.
4. Purkis, John. *A Preface to Wilfred Owen.* London: Longman, 1999.

EMILY DICKINSON (1830–1886)

Emily Dickinson was born in Amherst, Massachusetts in 1830. Raised in an intellectual and religious environment, Dickinson's exposure to both literature and Calvinism would play central roles in her poetry. While the common assumption has been that Dickinson made few attempts to publish her poetry in her lifetime, it is clear now, by evidence of the hundreds of letters she wrote, that she made an earnest effort to be recognized, submitting poetry quite often throughout the 1850s and 1860s. It was after these decades of rejection that Dickinson assumed the reclusive lifestyle she is now famous for. At the time of her death in 1886, Dickinson had written over 1500 poems, the majority of them found bundled in her dresser drawer. Due to her sister Lavinia's dedication and work, Dickinson's first volume of poems (titled Poems*) was published in 1890. Even at this time, publishers were reluctant to publish Dickinson's verse, claiming it was unorthodox and amateur. But the public thought differently.* Poems *was an instant success and went through 16 editions in the next eight years. As is the case with many artists, Dickinson was an innovator ahead of her time. Her radical verse, eschewing traditional forms and meter, experimented with what was later called "slant" and internal rhymes—rhymes that did not necessarily fall at the end of a line, but were often embedded within lines. Moreover, her uneven line breaks, abrupt dashes, and terse, lyrical metaphors were techniques that wouldn't be accepted as valid poetic forms until the Imagist Movement of the early twentieth-century. Dickinson was a constant revisionist, reworking and polishing her poems and their meanings. Thus, when you read a Dickinson poem, you are presented with rich allegories, irony, and symbolism packed tightly in precise language. The 770-page* The Complete Poems of Emily Dickinson, *edited by Thomas Johnson, was published in 1970.*

Flags vex a dying face   (1890)

The world feels dusty
When we stop to die;
We want the dew then,
Honors taste dry.

Flags vex a dying face,   5
But the least fan
Stirred by a friend's hand
Cools like the rain. . . .

Study and Discussion Questions

1. Since Emily Dickinson did not generally give her poems titles, "flags vex
   a dying face" was chosen by an editor. Usually when a poem is without
   a title, the first line of the poem serves that function. Why do you think
   whoever chose this title used the fifth line of the poem rather than the
   first?
2. This poem was written in the nineteenth century, after the Civil War, and
   though it can apply to any kind of death, what makes it pertinent to war-
   related deaths?
3. Discuss Dickinson's imagery in this poem. What are the two groups of images in tension here?
4. Look at Dickinson's end rhymes in this eight-line, two-stanza poem. Chart
   the rhyme pattern. Emily Dickinson uses slant rhyme frequently; which
   are the slant rhymes in this poem?

Suggestions for Writing

1. In Dickinson's view, what are the priorities when someone is close to death?
   Do you agree or disagree? How does she make her case in this poem?
2. Write about Emily Dickinson's word choices, especially her verbs, adjectives, and adverbs, in this poem. Try substituting another word for one of
   hers in several places and see whether it works and how it changes the
   meaning and the mood.

Critical Resources

1. Grabher, Gudrun et al., eds. *The Emily Dickinson Handbook*. Amherst:
   University of Massachusetts Press, 1998.
2. Martin, Wendy. *The Cambridge Companion to Emily Dickinson*. New
   York: Cambridge University Press, 2002.

3. Mitchell, Domhnall. *Emily Dickinson: Monarch of Perception*. Amherst: University of Massachusetts Press, 2000.
4. Pollak, Vivan, ed. *A Historical Guide to Emily Dickinson*. New York: Oxford Press, 2004.

H. D. (1886–1961)

Hilda Doolittle was born in Bethlehem, Pennsylvania, the only daughter in a family of six children. At the age of fifteen she met the poet Ezra Pound. Together, along with other poets such as William Carlos Williams, Richard Aldington, and F. S. Flint, the group created a kind of poetry known as Imagism—short lived as a movement, Imagism would have a large impact on twentieth-century poetry. In 1913 she published her first three poems under the name of "H. D. Imagiste," a title invented by Ezra Pound. Doolittle would continue to use the initials H. D. as her authorial name for the rest of her life. As is seen in her early work, H. D.'s economical use of words, direct and vivid treatment of the object, and abandonment of traditional meter and rhyme are often considered quintessential features of Imagist poetry. By the early 1920s, the Imagists disbanded and H. D. continued to evolve as a writer, experimenting with both drama and prose. H. D.'s later work can be seen as proto-feminist, exploring issues of female identity and sexuality; questioning masculine constructions of history; and rewriting several Greek myths from a woman's perspective. Recent scholarship has brought a reevaluation of the large body of work she completed after her early recognition as an Imagist poet. Selected writings include the poetry collections Hymnen *(1921),* Heliodora and Other Poems *(1924),* Red Roses for Bronze *(1929),* Helen in Egypt *(1961), and* Trilogy *(1973), and the novels* Palimsest *(1926),* Hedylus *(1928),* Kora and Ka *(1934),* Bid Me to Live: A Madrigal *(1960), and the posthumous* Pilate's Wife *(2000). In "Helen," written in 1924, H. D. employs concise imagery in an exploration of an ancient Greek myth.*

Helen[1] (1924)

All Greece hates
the still eyes in the white face,
the lustre as of olives

---

[1]Helen of Troy, daughter of Zeus and Leda, whose abduction led to the Trojan War.

where she stands,
and the white hands.   5

All Greece reviles
the wan face when she smiles,
hating it deeper still
when it grows wan and white,
remembering past enchantments   10
and past ills.

Greece sees unmoved,
God's daughter, born of love,
the beauty of cool feet
and slenderest knees,   15
could love indeed the maid,
only if she were laid,
white ash amid funereal cypresses.

Study and Discussion Questions

1. Discuss the opening lines of each stanza. How do they each work in tension with the rest of that stanza? How do they work together in the poem
   as a whole?
2. List the physical characteristics of Helen in this poem.
3. Note the rhyme scheme, keeping in mind that rhymes may be slant or off
   rhymes as well as true rhymes.
4. What is the mood or atmosphere of this poem? What words establish that
   mood?
5. How does the speaker of the poem feel about Helen?
6. This is an imagist poem (see "How Poetry Works" for a discussion of the
   Imagist Movement). Discuss how the poem is constructed of a single image. How is an imagist poem like "Helen" like and unlike an image in a
   photograph, a painting, or a film?

Suggestions for Writing

1. List the sources for your own image of "Helen of Troy." How is H. D.'s image of Helen similar to and different from the image you brought to the
   poem?
2. Compare/contrast H. D.'s "Helen" with another portrait of a woman from
   the same historical/legendary period, Penelope, in Edna St. Vincent Millay's poem "An Ancient Gesture" (Women and Men).

Critical Resources

1. Copeland, Donna. "Doolittle's Helen." *Explicator* 46.4 (1988): 33–35.
2. Hollenberg, Donna, ed. *H.D. and Poets After.* Iowa City: University of Iowa Press, 2000.
3. Lowell, Amy. *Tendencies in Modern American Poetry.* Boston: Houghton-Mifflin, 1926.
4. Robinson, Janice. *H.D., The Life and Work of an American Poet.* Boston: Houghton-Mifflin, 1982.

MARGARET ATWOOD (b. 1939)

Margaret Atwood was born in Ottawa, Canada, and spent her early childhood in the rugged wilderness of northern Quebec until her family moved to Toronto in 1946. While attending the University of Toronto, Atwood took classes with the literary critic and scholar Northrop Frye and was introduced to the thought of Carl Jung and archetypal theory—ideas that would later have an impact on her writing. In 1962, she obtained her M.A. from Radcliffe College and continued on to do Ph.D. work at Harvard. The political ferment of the 1960s, and especially the rise of feminism (and her own active role in the movement), set the backdrop for her early poetry and fiction. In 1969 she published her first novel, The Edible Woman—*a book that explores representations of women and female identity in a patriarchal society—themes that surface again and again in Atwood's work. While feminist concerns are at the base of Atwood's writing, it is her literary technique and experimentation that force readers to reassess the social implications of power. Through satire and the use of dystopian settings, Atwood "creates unease" in the reader, thus (ideally) instigating awareness. Selected works include the poetry collections* Double Persephone *(1961),* Power Politics *(1973),* True Stories *(1981), and* The Journals of Susanna Moodie *(1997); the short story collections* Wilderness Tips *(1991),* Good Bones and Simple Murders *(1992); and the novels* Surfacing *(1972),* The Handmaid's Tale *(1985),* The Robber Bride *(1993),* Alias Grace *(1996),* The Blind Assassin *(2000), and* Oryx and Crack *(2003). In her poem "At first I was given centuries," Atwood moves through a history seen by women who, for centuries, have endured the loss of their lovers to war.*

At first I was given centuries (1971)

At first I was given centuries
to wait in caves, in leather
tents, knowing you would never come back

Then it speeded up: only
several years between   5
the day you jangled off
into the mountains, and the day (it was
spring again) I rose from the embroidery
frame at the messenger's entrance.

That happened twice, or was it   10
more; and there was once, not so
long ago, you failed,
and came back in a wheelchair
with a moustache and a sunburn
and were insufferable.   15

Time before last though, I remember
I had a good eight months between
running alongside the train, skirts hitched, handing
you violets in at the window
and opening the letter; I watched   20
your snapshot fade for twenty years.

And last time (I drove to the airport
still dressed in my factory
overalls, the wrench
I had forgotten sticking out of the back   25
pocket; there you were,
zippered and helmeted, it was zero
hour, you said Be
Brave) it was at least three weeks before
I got the telegram and could start regretting.   30

But recently, the bad evenings
there are only seconds
between the warning on the radio and the
explosion; my hands
don't reach you   35

and on quieter nights
you jump up from
your chair without even touching your dinner
and I can scarcely kiss you goodbye
before you run out into the street and they shoot   40

Study and Discussion Questions

1. Who is speaking; who is the "I" of the poem? Who is the "you" of the poem?
2. In what ways does the speaker change and in what ways remain the same?
3. Describe the progression of situations from stanza to stanza.
4. Discuss how time is used in this poem.
4. Who are "they" in the last line?
5. Why do you think there is no period at the end of the poem?
6. Discuss the gender roles described in the poem.

Suggestions for Writing

1. Can you identify any particular wars the speaker has lived through? What are the clues?
2. What is the mood of the poem? What feelings does it evoke as you read it?
3. Compare/contrast "At first I was given centuries" to another Margaret Atwood poem about war, "The Loneliness of the Miliary Historian," on the issues of both war and gender.

Critical Resources

1. Cooke, Natalie. *Margaret Atwood: A Biography.* Toronto: ECW Press, 1998.
2. Nischik, Reingard, ed. *Margaret Atwood: Works and Impact.* Rochester, NY: Camden House, 2000.
3. Wilson, Sharon, ed. *Margaret Atwood's Textual Assassinations: Recent Poetry and Fiction.* Columbus: Ohio State University Press, 2003.
4. York, Lorraine, ed. *Various Atwoods: Essays on the Later Poems, Short Fiction and Novels.* Toronto: Anansi, 1995.

e. e. cummings (1894–1962)

Edward Estlin Cummings was born in Cambridge, Massachusetts, the son of a well-known Harvard professor and congregational minister. After receiving his M.A. at Harvard in 1916, Cummings left for France to become a volunteer ambulance driver during World War I. His rebellious attitudes led to his internment for several months in a French prison camp as a suspected spy—an experience he described in his first published work The Enormous Room *(1922). Although this was a prose work, its experimental style (blending autobiography with symbolic poetry) was a precursor to the particular style of poetry cummings would subsequently develop. Infused with the transcendental thinking of Ralph Waldo Emerson and influenced by the English Romantic poets, cummings's work unsettles traditional poetic themes such as love and beauty through the intentional use of jumbled words, improper grammar, dislocated syntax, and a lack of capitalization (he wrote his name as* e. e. cummings*). While some critics have suggested such techniques are simple tricks and gimmicks, others contend that cummings's disregard for language conventions created original work that celebrates the importance and energy of play in poetry. His poetry includes* Tulips and Chimneys *(1923),* XLI Poems *(1925),* is 5 *(1926),* ViVa *(1931),* 1 × 1 *(1944), and* Ninety-Five Poems *(1958). In "next to of course god america i," first published in 1926, cummings uses his brand of wordplay for a serious critique of American society.*

"next to of course god america i   (1926)

"next to of course god america i
love you land of the pilgrims' and so forth oh
say can you see by the dawn's early my
country 'tis of centuries come and go
and are no more what of it we should worry   5
in every language even deafanddumb
thy sons acclaim your glorious name by gorry
by jingo by gee by gosh by gum
why talk of beauty what could be more beaut-
iful than these heroic happy dead   10
who rushed like lions to the roaring slaughter
they did not stop to think they died instead
then shall the voice of liberty be mute?"

He spoke. And drank rapidly a glass of water

Study and Discussion Questions

1. Who is speaking in lines 1 to 13? What is the setting?
2. Identify the original sources of as many of the familiar phrases used as you can. Why does Cummings run them together?
3. Why has Cummings written this as a (Petrarchan) sonnet? What is the function of the last line?
4. Discuss the phrase "these heroic happy dead." What is the poem saying about war?

Suggestions for Writing

1. Restate as an argument the point the poem is making.
2. Compare/contrast e. e. cummings's "next to of course god america i" with another post–World War I poem, Wilfred Owen's "Dulce Et Decorum Est." Look both at the rhetorical point each is making and at the poetic strategies each uses.

Critical Resources

1. Bloom, Harold. *E. E. Cummings: Comprehensive Research and Study Guide.* Philadelphia: Chelsea House Publishers, 2003.
2. *ee cummings: An American Original.* The Master Poet's Series (video), 1979 (30 min.).
3. Friedman, Norman. *Revaluing Cummings: Further Essays on the Poet, 1962–1993.* Gainsville: University Press of Florida, 1996.
4. Sawyer-Luacanno, Christopher. *E. E. Cummings: A Biography.* Naperville, IL: Sourcebooks, 2004.

DWIGHT OKITA (b. 1958)

Born in Chicago, Illinois, Okita took to writing early. He received a degree in creative writing from the University of Illinois, Chicago, and shortly thereafter published his first and only book of poetry, Crossing the Light *(1992). Okita's work is strikingly contemporary and immediate—an open verse that employs introspective speakers and their attempts to make sense of the world (both objects and people) around them. One aspect that is often overlooked about Okita's work is his poems are not only on Asian-American subjects but also about male homosexuality. Yet unlike much gay and lesbian literature, Okita's "refreshing lack of anger and alienation" (*Asian American Drama, *1997) offers a different vision of gay experience. In addition to his poetry, Okita has also written the plays* The Rainy Season *(1993) and* My Last Week on Earth *(1993). He is currently working on a novel entitled* The Prospect of My Arrival. *The poem "In Response to Executive Order 9066: All Americans of Japanese Descent Must Report to Relocation Centers" is arguably Okita's most known work. It was published in* Crossing the Light.

In Response to Executive Order 9066:
ALL AMERICANS OF JAPANESE DESCENT
MUST REPORT TO RELOCATION CENTERS[1]   (1989)

Dear Sirs:
Of course I'll come. I've packed my galoshes
and three packets of tomato seeds. Janet calls them
"love apples." My father says where we're going
they won't grow.   5

---

[1]More than 100,000 Japanese-Americans were sent to "relocation centers," or internment camps, in the United States during World War II.

I am a fourteen-year-old girl with bad spelling
and a messy room. If it helps any, I will tell you
I have always felt funny using chopsticks
and my favorite food is hot dogs.
My best friend is a white girl named Denise—   10
we look at boys together. She sat in front of me
all through grade school because of our names:
O'Connor, Ozawa. I know the back of Denise's head very well.
I tell her she's going bald. She tells me I copy on tests.
We're best friends.   15

I saw Denise today in Geography class.
She was sitting on the other side of the room.
"You're trying to start a war," she said, "giving secrets away
to the Enemy, Why can't you keep your big mouth shut?"
I didn't know what to say.   20
I gave her a packet of tomato seeds
and asked her to plant them for me, told her
when the first tomato ripens
to miss me

Study and Discussion Questions

1. Okita structures this poem as though it were a letter. Why do you think
   he does this?
2. To whom is the letter written? What is the tone of the letter, and of course
   the poem? How is the tone created?
3. What is the significance of the tomatoes in this poem? Where do they appear in the poem? Why tomatoes?
4. In the second stanza the speaker of the poem says: "I have always felt
   funny using chopsticks/ and my favorite food is hot dogs." What kind of
   details does she give in this stanza about herself? Why?
5. The relationship between the 14-year-old speaker of the poem and her friend
   Denise is central and takes up most of the poem. Why is it so important?

Suggestions for Writing

1. Research a copy of Executive Order 9066, which sent Japanese-Americans to "relocation camps" for the duration of World War II. Write about
   the language of the order and what actions, specifically, the order allows.
2. Research other poems and prose about the experience of Japanese and
   Japanese-Americans in relocation camps and write a paper on what you find.
3. Compare/contrast this epistolary poem with Kanafani's story "Letter from
   Gaza" and discuss what the epistolary form allows each writer to do.
4. Write an epistolary poem of your own. Whom you choose as recipient of
   the "letter" may have a considerable effect on subsequent choices, such
   as language and voice.

Critical Resources

1. "Dwight Okita." *Pride of Voice, Voice of Pride.* May 8, 2005. <http://voices.epoets.net/Pride2K/index.html>. Audio recording of Okita reading his work.
2. Ling, Amy, ed. *Yellow Light: The Flowering of Asian American Arts.* Philadelphia: Temple Press, 1999.
3. Liu, Miles, ed. *Asian-American Playwrights: A Bio-Bibliographical Critical Sourcebook.* Westport, CT: Greenwood, 2002.
4. Rustomji-Kerns, Roshni, ed. *Encounters: People of Asian Descent in the Americas.* Lanham, MD: Rowman and Littlefield, 1999.

CAROLYN FORCHÉ (b. 1950)

Forché's poetic skill was recognized early when she was awarded the Yale Younger Poets Award in 1975 for her collection Gathering the Tribes. *That same year she received her M.F.A. from Bowling Green State University. Two years later she began working as a journalist for Amnesty International in El Salvador and lived there for several years. Forché was deeply affected by the human rights violations in the poverty-stricken country—disproportionate wealth, martial law, and inadequate health care. Her second volume of poetry,* The Country Between Us *(1981), published after her time in El Salvador, is marked by a change in tone and greater political awareness. While* Gathering the Tribes *explored Forché's girlhood growing up in the Midwestern city of Detroit, Michigan,* The Country Between Us *engages head-on with the atrocities Forché witnessed while living in El Salvador. Stylistically, Forché has been noted for the narrative quality or her poetry, her work in the prose poem form, and for her ability to blend the personal and the political to make larger claims about humanity. Like another Detroit poet, Philip Levine, Forché's poetry is built around the juxtaposition of precisely rendered images, weaving place, the senses, and language to create a verse that succeeds both lyrically and thematically. Her other works include the poetry collection* The Angel of History *(1994) and* Blue Hour *(2003). She has also published translations of Salvadorian poet Claribel Alegria and French poet Robert Desnos and edited the anthology* Against Forgetting: Twentieth-Century Poetry of Witness *(1993). "The Colonel," taken from* The Country Between Us, *is a prose poem.*

The Colonel   (1978)

What you have heard is true. I was in his house. His wife carried a tray of coffee and sugar. His daughter filed her nails, his son went out for the night. There were daily papers, pet dogs, a pistol on the cushion beside him. The moon swung bare on its black cord over the house. On the television was a cop show. It was in English. Broken bottles were embedded in the walls around the house to scoop the kneecaps from a man's legs or cut his hands to lace. On the windows there were gratings like those in liquor stores. We had dinner, rack of lamb, good wine, a gold bell was on the table for calling the maid. The maid brought green mangoes, salt, a type of bread. I was asked how I enjoyed the country. There was a brief commercial in Spanish. His wife took everything away. There was some talk then of how difficult it had become to govern. The parrot said hello on the terrace. The colonel told it to shut up, and pushed himself from the table. My friend said to me with his eyes: say nothing. The colonel returned with a sack used to bring groceries home. He spilled many human ears on the table. They were like dried peach halves. There is no other way to say this. He took one of them in his hands, shook it in our faces, dropped it into a water glass. It came alive there. I am tired of fooling around he said. As for the rights of anyone, tell your people they can go fuck themselves. He swept the ears to the floor with his arm and held the last of his wine in the air. Something for your poetry, no? he said. Some of the ears on the floor caught this scrap of his voice. Some of the ears on the floor were pressed to the ground.

Study and Discussion Questions

1. What is going on in the poem? Who is the colonel? Why is the speaker visiting him?
2. Characterize the speaker's tone. What does it suggest?
3. Why does Forché mention such commonplace details as the daily papers, the pet dogs, the colonel's daughter's filing her nails?
4. Choose a section of this prose poem and look at and listen to the sound of the poem. How is Forché using assonance and consonance, repetition, and rhyme/slant rhyme? How does this create a mood and pull the observations together?
5. Why does the colonel have a sack of human ears? Why does he show them to the speaker?
6. What is the symbolic significance of the poem's final image?
7. Forché edited a large international collection of poetry entitled *Against Forgetting: The Poetry of Witness*. Look up the word *witness* for its various meanings. What do you think a "poetry of witness" is? How is "The Colonel" a poem of witness?

Suggestions for Writing

1. How is this "prose poem" like poetry and how is it like prose? Why do you think Forché chose this form instead of writing the poem in lines?
2. "On the television was a cop show. It was in English." What is the significance of this detail? Look into the history of El Salvador in the last few decades (Forché's subject) and discuss the poem in that context.

Critical Resources

1. *Carolyn Forché.* The Lannan Foundation (video), 1990 (65 minutes).
2. Gass, William, ed. *The Writer in Politics.* Carbondale: Southern Illinois University, 1996.
3. Goett, Lise. "A Conversation with Carolyn Forché." *Image: A Journal of the Arts and Religion* 39 (2003): 53–69.
4. Lehman, David. *Great American Prose Poems: From Poe to Present.* New York: Scribner, 2003.
5. Moyers, Bill, ed. *The Language of Life: Bill Moyers.* New York: Random House Audible, 2000. An audio series of poets reading their work.

DENISE LEVERTOV (1923–1997)

Denise Levertov was born at Ilford, England. Her mother was Welsh and her father a Russian Jew who became an Anglican priest. After serving as a nurse during World War II, Levertov moved to the United States in 1948 and began establishing herself as a serious poet. While many critics associate her early work with the Black Mountain College poets of the 1950s such as Charles Olson and Robert Creeley, Levertov's work more precisely follows in the Imagist tradition of H. D. and William Carlos Williams. Her poetry is often noted for its balance between the material and spiritual worlds of existence. For Levertov, poetry was a mystical act: "To believe, as an artist, in inspiration or the intuitive, to know that without imagination . . . no amount of acquired scholarship or brilliant reasoning will suffice, is to live with the door of one's life open to the transcendent, the numinous" (241, Levertov, New and Selected Essays, *1992). Her writings include the poetry collections* The Jacob's Ladder *(1961),* The Sorrow Dance *(1968),* Relearning the Alphabet *(1970),* Freeing the Dust *(1975),* Candles in Babylon *(1982),* Breathing the Water *(1987),* A Door in the Hive *(1989), and* Sands of the Well *(1996); and several essay collections, including* The Poet in the World *(1973) and* Light Up the Cave *(1981). The poem "Life at War," written in 1968, is an example of Levertov's increasing preoccupation with the impact of the Vietnam War.*

Life at War (1968)

The disasters numb within us
caught in the chest, rolling
in the brain like pebbles. The feeling

resembles lumps of raw dough

weighing down a child's stomach on baking day.   5
Or Rilke said it, 'My heart . . .
Could I say of it, it overflows
with bitterness . . . but no, as though

its contents were simply balled into
formless lumps, thus   10
do I carry it about.'
The same war
continues.
We have breathed the grits of it in, all our lives,
our lungs are pocked with it,   15
the mucous membrane of our dreams
coated with it, the imagination
filmed over with the gray filth of it:

the knowledge that humankind,

delicate Man, whose flesh   20
responds to a caress, whose eyes
are flowers that perceive the stars,
whose music excels the music of birds,
whose laughter matches the laughter of dogs,
whose understanding manifests designs   25
fairer than the spider's most intricate web,

still turns without surprise, with mere regret
to the scheduled breaking open of breasts whose milk
runs out over the entrails of still-alive babies,
transformation of witnessing eyes to pulp-fragments,   30
implosion of skinned penises into carcass-gulleys.

We are the humans, men who can make;
whose language imagines *mercy,*
lovingkindness; we have believed one another
mirrored forms of a God we felt as good—   35

who do these acts, who convince ourselves
it is necessary; these acts are done
to our own flesh; burned human flesh
is smelling in Viet Nam as I write.

Yes, this is the knowledge that jostles for space   40

in our bodies along with all we
go on knowing of joy, of love;

our nerve filaments twitch with its presence
day and night,
nothing we say has not the husky phlegm of it in the saying,   45
nothing we do has the quickness, the sureness,
the deep intelligence living at peace would have.

Study and Discussion Questions

1. What images does Levertov use to describe what war does?
2. What images does she use to describe what human beings are and can be?
3. What does Levertov mean when she writes: "these acts are done/to our own flesh"?

Suggestions for Writing

1. Which one or more of the following best describes your initial response to this poem: despair, joy, nausea, pain, hope, disgust, shock, indifference? Why?
2. What does "living at peace" mean to you?
3. In a short paragraph, write what you see as the argument Levertov is making in this poem. That is, attempt to translate the poem into a brief, reasoned essay.

Critical Resources

1. Colclough Little, Anne and Susie Paul, eds. *Denise Levertov: New Perspectives*. West Cornwall, CT: Locust Hill Press, 2000.
2. *Denise Levertov*. Dir. Dan Giggs. The Lannan Foundation, 1994 (60min).
3. Gelpi, Albert, ed. *Denise Levertov: Selected Criticism*. Ann Arbor: University of Mich Press, 1993.
4. Levetov, Denise. "A Poet's View." *New and Selected Essays*. New York: Doubleday, 1992.

MURIEL RUKEYSER (1913–1980)

Muriel Rukeyser was born in New York City and attended Vassar College and Columbia University. Known as a "poet of social protest," Rukeyser spent much of her life as an activist against oppression and inequality, including some time as president of the American Center for PEN (Poets/Playwrights, Essayists, Editors, Novelists), *an organization that supports the rights of writers around the world. Through five decades of writing, Rukeyser's eclectic approach to writing drew on history, biography, current events, and feminist revisions of mythology. Always concerned with*

*bridging the personal and political, her poetry often mingles themes such as moth-
erhood, female sexuality, or death with the larger social concerns of racism and war.
While some critics suggest there is a streak of sentimentality in Rukeyser's work, most
agree that her vigorous stance on social issues has served to influence a generation
of female poets, including Adrienne Rich, Sharon Olds, and Erica Jong. Her poetry
includes* Theory of Flight *(1935), for which she won the Yale Younger Poet's Award,*
The Green Wave *(1948),* The Body of Waking *(1958),* The Speed of Darkness
(1968), and Breaking Open *(1973); and the nonfiction* The Life of Poetry *(1949).
"Waking This Morning," published in* Breaking Open, *shows the speaker of the
poem contemplating the complexity of the violence that permeates our lives and
committing herself to "strong peace, and/delight,/the wild good."*

Waking This Morning   (1973)

Waking this morning,
a violent woman in the violent day
Laughing.
               Past the line of memory
along the long body of your life   5
in which move childhood, youth, your lifetime of touch,
eyes, lips, chest, belly, sex, legs, to the waves of the sheet.
I look past the little plant
on the city windowsill
to the tall towers bookshaped, crushed together in greed,   10
the river flashing flowing corroded,
the intricate harbor and the sea, the wars, the moon, the
    planets, all who people space
in the sun visible invisible.
African violets in the light   15
breathing, in a breathing universe. I want strong peace, and
delight,
the wild good.
I want to make my touch poems:
to find my morning, to find you entire   20
alive moving among the anti-touch people.

            I say across the waves of the air to you:
today once more
I will try to be non-violent
one more day   25
this morning, waking the world away
in the violent day.

Study and Discussion Questions

1. Why does the speaker call herself "a violent woman"?
2. What does she remember and see when she wakes up? Why those particular things?
3. To whom is the poem addressed?
4. Discuss phrases like "strong peace" and "wild good."
4. What are "touch poems"?
5. Who are the "anti-touch people"?
6. What does the speaker of the poem want for herself?

Suggestion for Writing

1. Analyze Rukeyser's use of the word *violent* in this poem. Begin by looking up *violent* in a big dictionary. How does Rukeyser play with the word, extend it, redefine it? What other words/concepts is she redefining in this poem? Why might it be necessary to redefine such words and concepts in order to change the way people think about war and peace and violence?

Critical Resources

1. Clunas, Alex. "Rukeyser's "Waking This Morning." *Explicator* 54.4 (1994): 237–39.
2. Dayton, Tim. *Muriel Rukeyser's The Book of the Dead.* Columbia: University of Missouri Press, 2003.
3. Herzog, Anne and Janet Kaufman, eds. *How Shall We Teach Each Other of the Poet?: The Life and Writing of Muriel Rukeyser.* New York: St. Martin's, 1999.
4. Rukeyser, Muriel et al. *Five American Women.* New York: Random House Audio Publications, 2001 (57 minutes). Audio recording of poems read by Rukeyser, H. D., Millay, and Gertrude Stein.

CARMEN TAFOLLA (b. 1951)

Carmen Tafolla was born and raised in the west-side barrio of San Antonio, Texas. She gained recognition as a poet during the post-1960s Chicano Movement, a nationwide struggle by Mexican-Americans for greater political representation and recognition of their cultural heritage. Tafolla's poetry reflects the turbulence of these times, writing in the voices of working-class Chicanos with a focus on maintaining human dignity and Chicano values. Perhaps the strongest voices found in her poetry are those of her female speakers—Chicana women, historically and today, who persevere despite the injustices of a sexist, patriarchal system. She has been a lifelong educator, teaching at both the high-school and university level, including teaching as a professor of Women's Studies at the University of California, Fresno. In addition to her poetry, Tafolla also writes short

stories, screenplays, and children's books. Her poetry includes the coauthored Get
Your Tortillas Out *(1976),* Curandera *(1983), and the recently expanded* Sonnets
and Salsa *(2004). She has also written a prose work,* To Split a Human: Mitos,
Machos y la Mujer Chicana *(1985). The poem "How Shall I Tell You?" looks
beyond Tafolla's earlier focus on Chicano identity to speculate on the human
costs of war and nuclear fallout.*

How Shall I Tell You?   (1989)

> *listening to the news, the U.S. attack on Libya, the Soviet nuclear accident at
> Chernobyl . . .*

When no soul walks the softened green
and no foot beats the pulse on crumbling brown
and no one lives to sing to rain
or soak to sun the spirit of its golden gown
to weave the many colors of the after-arch   5
from sky to human skin to wooded wealth
in fiber fabrics beads and tusks and seeds
all leading up in rows of beauty drumbeat
to black neck, like venison in stealth

When no one lulls the child to sleep   10
or takes the wrinkled story's hand
or listens to the news—a wired sound
of tribe on tribe—stet now—man on man
How shall I tell you that I love you then?
How shall I touch your fingers tip to tip   15
and say that we were blood and human voice and friend?

Study and Discussion Questions

1. To whom is the poem addressed?
2. "Stet" is a printer's term indicating that material previously marked for
   deletion or change is to remain. What does the speaker of the poem mean
   by using "stet" in line 13?
3. What is the emotion that best describes this poem?
4. What will the speaker of the poem miss if war or nuclear accident destroys
   the world as we know it?

5. What are the poem's rhyme scheme and meter? What is the combined effect of the sound of the poem and the subject of the poem?

Suggestion for Writing

1. Imagine the end of the world. What would you miss most? Make a list of detailed images.

Critical Resources

1. Perez-Torres, Rafael. *Movements in Chicano Poetry: Against Myths, Against Margins.* New York: Cambridge University Press, 1995.
2. Tafolla, Carmen. *Carmen Tafolla.* 2003. April 3, 2005. <http://www.carmentafolla.com/>
3. The University of Minnesota. *Voices from the Gaps: Women Writers of Color—Carmen Tafolla.* 2003. May 1, 2005. <http://voices.cla.umn.edu/newsite/authors/TAFOLLAcarmen.htm>

❋ ❋ ❋

JAY PARINI (b. 1948)

Jay Parini grew up in Scranton, Pennsylvania, attended Lafayette College, and received his Ph.D. from the University of St. Andrews in Scotland in 1975. Parini is known for his diverse choice of genre, moving fluidly among poetry, prose, and biography. As he states in Contemporary Authors Online (2005), "Although my primary interest is writing poetry, I am now doing a lot of fiction and criticism . . . In a sense I use writing to pay attention to the world, to explain it to myself. The poems arise out of a strong wish to embody things: objects, emotions, ideas." Parini's poetry is often compared to that of Robert Frost's—introspective and searching, seeking to understand humankind's relationship to nature and the cosmos. Coincidentally, in 1999, Parini published the biography Robert Frost: A Life, *a contemporary and sympathetic portrait of Frost and his complicated legacy. But Parini has created his own poetic style, one marked by craft and emotion and an innate sense of the malleability of language. He currently teaches at Middlebury College in Vermont. His writings include the poetry collections* Singing in Time *(1972),* Anthracite Country *(1982),* Town Life *(1988), and* House of Days *(1998); the novels* The Love Run *(1980),* The Patch Boys *(1986),* The Last Station *(1990), and* The Apprentice Lover *(2002); and the biographies* John Steinbeck: A Biography *(1995) and* One Matchless Time: The Life of William Faulkner *(2004). The poem "After the Terror" was written in response to the terrorist attacks of September 11, 2001.*

After the Terror   (2003)

Everything has changed, though nothing has.
They've changed the locks on almost every door,
and windows have been bolted just in case:

It's business as usual, someone says.
Is anybody left to mind the store?   5
Everything has changed, though nothing has.

The same old buildings huddle in the haze,
with faces at the windows, floor by floor,
the windows they have bolted just in case.

No cause for panic, they maintain, because   10
the streets go places they have been before.
Everything has changed, though nothing has.

We're still a country that is ruled by laws.
The system's working, and it's quite a bore
that windows have been bolted just in case.   15

Believe in victory and all that jazz.
Believe we're better off, that less is more.
Everything has changed, though nothing has.
The windows have been bolted just in case.

Study and Discussion Questions

1. "After the Terror" is a villanelle, a type of poem which has a fixed form:
    five tercets, or three-line stanzas, plus one quatrain. What do you notice
    about the rhyme scheme of this poem and the use of repetition?
2. What does the title tell you about the subject of the poem?
3. The opening stanza sets the proposition for the poem; what is that
    proposition?
4. What kind of changes have been instituted, according to Parini? What
    hasn't changed?
5. What are the two images in the opening stanza?
6. Stanzas two, three, four, and five could be seen as stages in an argument
    Parini is making. What point does each stanza make? Through what im-
    age is each point made?
7. If we accept that Parini is making an argument here (and you may not),
    then the final quatrain is his conclusion. What is it?

Suggestions for Writing

1. Do you see "After the Terror" as a poem about fear and what we do with it? About the futility of changing the locks and bolting the windows after the disaster? About the political decisions that September 11, 2001, put in motion and their effect on the country? About . . . (add your own interpretation here)? Write a paper in dialogue with Parini's poem.
2. Compare/contrast "After the Terror" with two other examples of the villanelle form included in *Literature and Society:* "Do Not Go Gentle Into that Good Night" by Dylan Thomas and "One Art" by Elizabeth Bishop.

Critical Resources

1. Alvarez, Julia, et al. *Cry Out: Poets Protest the War.* New York: G. Braziller in collaboration with Northshire Bookstore, 2003.
2. Pack, Robert and Jay Parini. *Touchstones: American Poets on a Favorite Poem.* Hanover: Middlebury College Press, 1996. Includes a chapter by Parini explicating a favorite poem.
3. ———*Writers on Writing.* Hanover, NH: University Press of New England, 1991.
4. Stefanile, Felix. "Poets of Emulation: Dana Giola and Jay Parini." *VIA: Voices in Italian Americana* 1.1 (1990): 35–50.

ADRIENNE RICH (b. 1929)

Born in Baltimore, Maryland, Adrienne Rich grew up in an intellectual and artistic environment—her mother was a musician, her father a professor at Johns Hopkins University. Her poetic ability was first recognized by W. H. Auden when he selected A Change of World *for the Yale Younger Poets Award in 1951 while Rich was attending Radcliffe College. Rich would marry two years later and have three children. The experience of motherhood would have a large impact on her perception of women in society (a topic she explores in* Of Woman Born: Motherhood as Experience and Institution, *1976). While family responsibilities slowed her artistic output amidst the arrival of the 1960s, the Vietnam War, and the rise of feminism, Rich's work moved from its early formal structure to a more radical and political style, experimenting with line length, unorthodox spacing, dialogue, and longer sequencing. By the end of the 1960s, and into the 1970s, Rich produced some of her best-known work (poetry as well as essays)—writing that centers on acts of "transformation." For Rich, change is inevitable, but change and transformation are not synonymous: ". . . if the imagination is to transcend and transform experience, it has to question, to challenge, to conceive of alternatives, perhaps to the very life you are living at that moment" (from her essay, "When We Dead Awaken: Writing as Re-Vision"). This process often centers on questions of sexuality and what Rich sees as a patriarchal culture that has degraded the value of women. As exemplified throughout her career, Rich continues to assert the need for writers to participate actively in both the private and public well-being of a culture. Her other works include the poetry collections* Snapshots of a Daughter-in-Law: Poems 1954–1962 *(1963),* Leaflets: Poems *(1969),* The Will to Change: Poems, 1968–1970 *(1971),* Diving into the Wreck: Poems, 1971–1972 *(1973),* Twenty-One Love Poems *(1977),* The Fact of a Doorframe: Poems Selected and New, 1950–1984 *(1984),* Dark Fields of the Republic, 1991–1995 *(1995); and the essay collections* On Lies, Secrets, and Silence: Selected Prose, 1966–1978 *(1979) and* What is Found There: Notebooks on Poetry and Politics *(1993). Her latest work of poetry is entitled* The School Among Ruins: Poems 2000–2004. *The following poem, the title poem of the collection, takes a critical look at the civilian consequences of war.*

The School Among the Ruins   (2004)

    Beirut. Baghdad. Sarajevo. Bethlehem. Kabul. Not of course here.

1.

Teaching the first lesson and the last
—great falling light of summer will you last
longer than schooltime?

When children flow
in columns at the doors   5
BOYS GIRLS and the busy teachers

open or close high windows
with hooked poles drawing darkgreen shades

closets unlocked, locked
questions unasked, asked, when   10

love of the fresh impeccable
sharp-pencilled yes
order without cruelty

a street on earth neither heaven nor hell
busy with commerce and worship   15
young teachers walking to school

fresh bread and early-open foodstalls

2.

When the offensive rocks the sky when nightglare
misconstrues day and night when lived-in

rooms from the upper city   20
tumble cratering lower streets

cornices of olden ornament human debris
when fear vacuums out the streets

When the whole town flinches
blood on the undersole thickening to glass   25

Whoever crosses hunched knees bent a contested zone
knows why she does this suicidal thing

School's now in session day and night
children sleep
in the classrooms teachers rolled close   30

3.

How the good teacher loved
his school the students
the lunchroom with fresh sandwiches

lemonade and milk
the classroom glass cages   35
of moss and turtles
teaching responsibility

A morning breaks without bread or fresh-poured milk
parents or lesson-plans
diarrhea first question of the day   40
children shivering it's September
Second question: where is my mother?

4.

One: I don't know where your mother
is Two: I don't know
why they are trying to hurt us   45

Three: or the latitude and longitude
of their hatred Four: I don't know if we
hate them as much I think there's more toilet paper
in the supply closet I'm going to break it open

Today this is your lesson: 50
write as clearly as you can
your name home street and number
down on this page
No you can't go home yet
but you aren't lost   55
this is our school

I'm not sure what we'll eat
we'll look for healthy roots and greens
searching for water though the pipes are broken

5.

There's a young cat sticking   60
her head through window bars
she's hungry like us
but can feed on mice
her bronze erupting fur
speaks of a life already wild   65

her golden eyes
don't give quarter She'll teach us Let's call her
Sister
when we get milk we'll give her some

6.

I've told you, let's try to sleep in this funny camp   70
All night pitiless pilotless things go shrieking
above us to somewhere

Don't let your faces turn to stone
Don't stop asking me why
Let's pay attention to our cat she needs us   75

Maybe tomorrow the bakers can fix their ovens

7.

"We sang them to naps told stories made
shadow-animals with our hands

washed human debris off boots and coats
sat learning by heart the names   80
some were too young to write
some had forgotten how"

Study and Discussion Questions

1. What function does the preface to the poem—"Beruit. Baghdad. Sarajevo. Bethlehem. Kabul. Not of course here."—serve?
2. There are seven sections to "The School Among the Ruins." What purpose does each section have? How does each section develop the overall image of the school among the ruins? As well as an image, is there a story being told here? What is it?
3. List at least four things that have changed for the students and teachers now that the school is in a war zone.
4. Discuss the images and the importance of food in the poem.
5. Discuss the appearance of the cat in section 5. How does the teacher turn this into a lesson? How is this lesson a measure of their changed circumstances?
6. In section 6 the teacher says to the students: "Don't let your faces turn to stone/ Don't stop asking me why." Discuss.
7. Section seven is in quotation marks. Who is speaking here and to whom? Identify the point of view in each of the seven sections of "The School Among the Ruins."
8. "The School Among the Ruins" gives us a vivid image of the situation of children in a time of war. Why do you think Adrienne Rich set this poem in a school instead of, say, in a refugee camp or some other location?

Suggestions for Writing

1. Do some research on the situation of children in a contemporary war zone. Unfortunately, you have quite a few to choose from.
2. Write a short poem or vivid prose piece from the point of view of one of the boys or girls in Rich's "The School Among the Ruins."

Critical Resources

1. *Adrienne Rich.* The Lannen Foundation, 1992 (60 minutes). For more information go to <http://www.lannan.org>. This is one film of several on Adrienne Rich's work.
2. Birkle, Carmen. *Women's Stories of the Looking Glass: Autobiographical Reflections and Self-Representations in the Poetry of Sylvia Plath, Adrienne Rich, and Audre Lorde.* Munich, Germany: Fink, 1996.

3. Charlesworth, Barbara and Albert Gelpi, eds. *Adrienne Rich's Poetry and Prose: Poems, Prose, Reviews and Criticism.* New York: Norton, 1993.

4. Rich, Adrienne. *Arts of the Possible: Essays and Conversations.* New York: Norton, 2001.

5. Sielke, Sabine. *Fashioning the Female Subject: The Intertextual Networking of Dickinson, Moore, and Rich.* Ann Arbor: University of Michigan Press, 1997.

Additional Poems

SAPPHO (ca. 630–ca. 580 B.C.)

To an army wife, in Sardis:[1]

(ca. 600 B.C.)

Translated by Mary Barnard

Some say a cavalry corps,
some infantry, some, again,
will maintain that the swift oars

of our fleet are the finest
sight on dark earth; but I say   5
that whatever one loves, is.

This is easily proved: did
not Helen—she who had scanned
the flower of the world's manhood—

choose as first among men one   10
who laid Troy's honor in ruin?
warped to his will, forgetting

love due her own blood, her own
child, she wandered far with him.
So Anactoria, although you   15

being far away forget us,
the dear sound of your footstep
and light glancing in your eyes

---

[1]Ancient city in West Africa Minor, the capital of Lydia.

would move me more than glitter
of Lydian[2] horse or armored   20
tread of mainland infantry

RICHARD LOVELACE (1618–1658)

To Lucasta, Going to the Wars   (1649)

Tell me not, sweet, I am unkind
That from the nunnery
Of thy chaste breast and quiet mind,
To war and arms I fly.

True, a new mistress now I chase,   5
The first foe in the field;
And with a stronger faith embrace
A sword, a horse, a shield.

Yet this inconstancy is such
As you too shall adore;   10
I could not love thee, dear, so much,
Loved I not honor more.

JOHN MILTON (1608–1674)

On the Late Massacre at Piemont[1]   (1655)

Avenge, O Lord, thy slaughtered saints, whose bones
    Lie scattered on the Alpine mountains cold,
    Ev'n them who kept thy truth so pure of old
    When all our fathers worshiped stocks and stones,
Forget not; in thy book record their groans   5

---

[2]Ancient Kingdom in West Asia Minor; under Croesus, a wealthy empire including most of Asia Minor.

[1]In 1655, the Roman Catholic Duke of Savoy sent troops to massacre members of a Protestant religious community in northwestern Italy.

Who were thy sheep, and in their ancient fold
   Slain by the bloody Piemontese that rolled
   Mother with infant down the rocks. Their moans
The vales redoubled to the hills, and they
   To heav'n. Their martyred blood and ashes sow   10
   O'er all th' Italian fields, where still doth sway
The triple tyrant,[2] that from these may grow
   A hundredfold, who, having learnt thy way,
   Early may fly the Babylonian[3] woe.

ALFRED, LORD TENNYSON (1809–1892)

The Charge of the Light Brigade[1]   (1854)

I

Half a league, half a league,
Half a league onward,
All in the valley of Death
   Rode the six hundred.
"Forward, the Light Brigade!
Charge for the guns!" he said.   5
Into the valley of Death
   Rode the six hundred.

II

"Forward, the Light Brigade!"
Was there a man dismay'd?   10
Not tho' the soldier knew
   Some one had blunder'd.
Theirs not to make reply,
Theirs not to reason why,
Theirs but to do and die.   15

---

[2]The Pope.
[3]Protestants associated the Catholic Church with the corrupt city of Babylon, the destruction of which the Bible prophesies.
[1]Reconnaissance cavalry.

Into the valley of Death
 Rode the six hundred.

III

Cannon to right of them,
Cannon to left of them,
Cannon in front of them   20
 Volley'd and thunder'd;
Storm'd at with shot and shell,
Boldly they rode and well,
Into the jaws of Death,
Into the mouth of hell   25
 Rode the six hundred.

IV

Flash'd all their sabres bare,
Flash'd as they turn'd in air
Sabring the gunners there,
Charging an army, while   30
 All the world wonder'd.
Plunged in the battery-smoke
Right thro' the line they broke;
Cossack and Russian
Reel'd from the sabre-stroke   35
 Shatter'd and sunder'd.
Then they rode back, but not,
 Not the six hundred.

V

Cannon to right of them,
 Cannon to left of them,   40
Cannon behind them
 Volley'd and thunder'd;
Storm'd at with shot and shell,
While horse and hero fell,
They that had fought so well   45
Came thro' the jaws of Death,

Back from the mouth of hell,
All that was left of them,
 Left of six hundred.

VI

When can their glory fade?   50
O the wild charge they made!
 All the world wonder'd.
Honour the charge they made!
Honour the Light Brigade,
 Noble six hundred!   55

RUDYARD KIPLING (1865–1936)

Tommy   (1890)

I went into a public 'ouse to get a pint o' beer,
The publican 'e up an' sez, "We serve no red-coats here."
The girls be'ind the bar they laughed an' giggled fit to die,
I outs into the street again an' to myself sez I:
  O it's Tommy this, an' Tommy that, an' "Tommy, go away";   5
  But it's "Thank you, Mister Atkins,"[1] when the band begins to play—
  The band begins to play, my boys, the band begins to play,
  O it's "Thank you, Mister Atkins," when the band begins to play.

I went into a theatre as sober as could be,
They gave a drunk civilian room, but 'adn't none for me;   10
They sent me to the gallery or round the music-'alls,
But when it comes to fightin', Lord! they'll shove me in the stalls![2]
  For it's Tommy this, an' Tommy that, an' "Tommy, wait outside";
  But it's "Special train for Atkins" when the trooper's on the tide—
  The troopship's on the tide, my boys, the troopship's on the tide, 15
  O it's "Special train for Atkins" when the trooper's on the tide.

Yes, makin' mock o' uniforms that guard you while you sleep
Is cheaper than them uniforms, an' they're starvation cheap;

---

[1]Thomas Atkins, generic name for a British soldier.
[2]Cheap seats.

An' hustlin' drunken soldiers when they're goin' large a bit
Is five times better business than paradin' in full kit.   20
    Then it's Tommy this, an' Tommy that, an' "Tommy, 'ow's yer soul?"
    But it's "Thin red line of 'eroes" when the drums begin to roll—
    The drums begin to roll, my boys, the drums begin to roll,
    O it's "Thin red line of 'eroes" when the drums begin to roll.

We aren't no thin red 'eroes, nor we aren't no blackguards too,   25
But single men in barricks, most remarkable like you;
An' if sometimes our conduck isn't all your fancy paints,
Why, single men in barricks don't grow into plaster saints;
    While it's Tommy this, an' Tommy that, an' "Tommy, fall be'ind,"
    But it's "Please to walk in front, sir," when there's trouble
        in the wind—   30
    There's trouble in the wind, my boys, there's trouble in the wind,
    O it's "Please to walk in front, sir," when there's trouble in the wind.

You talk o'better food for us, an' schools, an' fires, an' all:
We'll wait for extry rations if you treat us rational.
Don't mess about the cook-room slops, but prove it to our face   35
The Widow's[3] Uniform is not the soldier-man's disgrace.
    For it's Tommy this, an' Tommy that, an' "Chuck him out, the brute!"
    But it's "Saviour of 'is country" when the guns begin to shoot;
    An' it's Tommy this, an' Tommy that, an' anything you please;
    An' Tommy ain't a bloomin' fool—you bet that Tommy sees!   40

JOHN MCCRAE (1878–1918)

In Flanders Fields   (1915)

In Flanders fields the poppies blow
Between the crosses, row on row
That mark our place; and in the sky
The larks, still bravely singing, fly
Scarce heard amid the guns below.   5

We are the Dead. Short days ago
We lived, felt dawn, saw sunset glow,

---

[3]Queen's.

Loved and were loved, and now we lie
In Flanders fields.

Take up our quarrel with the foe: 10
To you from failing hands we throw
The torch; be yours to hold it high.
If ye break faith with us who die
We shall not sleep, though poppies grow
In Flanders fields.   15

WALT WHITMAN (1819–1892)

The Dying Veteran   (1892)

(A Long Island incident—early part of the nineteenth century)

Amid these days of order, ease, prosperity,
Amid the current songs of beauty, peace, decorum,
I cast a reminiscence—(likely 'twill offend you,
I heard it in my boyhood;)—More than a generation since,
A queer old savage man, a fighter under Washington himself,   5
(Large, brave, cleanly, hot-blooded, no talker, rather spiritualistic,
Had fought in the ranks—fought well—had been all through the
          Revolutionary war,)
Lay dying—sons, daughters, church-deacons, lovingly tending him,
Sharping their sense, their ears, towards his murmuring, half-caught 10
          words:
"Let me return again to my war-days,
To the sights and scenes—to forming the line of battle,
To the scouts ahead reconnoitering,
To the cannons, the grim artillery,   15
To the galloping aids, carrying orders,
To the wounded, the fallen, the heat, the suspense,
The perfume strong, the smoke, the deafening noise;
Away with your life of peace!—your joys of peace!
Give me my old wild battle-life again!"   20

MARGARET SACKVILLE (1881–1963)

Nostra Culpa[1]   (1916)

We knew, this thing at least we knew,—the worth
Of life: this was our secret learned at birth.
We knew that Force the world has deified,
How weak it is. We spoke not, so men died.
Upon a world down-trampled, blood-defiled,   5
Fearing that men should praise us less, we smiled.

We knew the sword accursed, yet with the strong
Proclaimed the sword triumphant. Yea, this wrong
Unto our children, unto those unborn
We did, blaspheming God. We feared the scorn   10
Of men; men worshipped pride; so were they led,
We followed. Dare we now lament our dead?

Shadows and echoes, harlots! We betrayed
Our sons; because men laughed we were afraid.
That silent wisdom which was ours we kept   15
Deep-buried; thousands perished; still we slept.
Children were slaughtered, women raped, the weak
Down-trodden. Very quiet was our sleep.

Ours was the vision, but the vision lay
Too far, too strange; we chose an easier way.   20
The light, the unknown light, dazzled our eyes.—
Oh! sisters in our choice were we not wise?
When all men hated, could we pity or plead
For love with those who taught the Devil's creed?

Reap we with pride the harvest! it was sown   25
By our own toil. Rejoice! it is our own.
This is the flesh we might have saved—our hands,
Our hands prepared these blood-drenched, dreadful lands.
What shall we plead? That we were deaf and blind?
We mothers and we murderers of mankind.   30

---

[1]Our blame (Latin).

MARINA TSVETAYEVA (1892–1941)

'*A white low sun*'   (1917)

Translated by David McDuff and Jon Silken.

A white low sun, low thunderclouds; and back
behind the kitchen-garden's white wall, graves.
On the sand, serried ranks of straw-stuffed forms
as large as men, hang from some cross-beam.

Through the staked fence, moving about, I see   5
a scattering: of soldiers, trees, and roads;
and an old woman standing by her gate
who chews on a black hunk of bread with salt.

What have these grey huts done to anger you,
my God? and why must so many be killed?   10
A train passed, wailing, and the soldiers wailed
as its retreating path got trailed with dust.

Better to die, or not to have been born,
than hear that plaining, piteous convict wail
about these beautiful dark eyebrowed women.   15
It's soldiers who sing these days. O Lord God.

SIEGFRIED SASSOON (1886–1967)

Does it Matter?   (1918)

Does it matter?—losing your legs? . . .
For people will always be kind,
And you need not show that you mind
When the others come in after hunting
To gobble their muffins and eggs.   5

Does it matter?—losing your sight? . . .
There's such splendid work for the blind;
And people will always be kind,
As you sit on the terrace remembering
And turning your face to the light.   10

Do they matter?—those dreams from the pit? . . .
You can drink and forget and be glad,
And people won't say that you're mad;
For they'll know you've fought for your country
And no one will worry a bit.   15

WILLIAM BUTLER YEATS (1865–1939)

An Irish Airman Foresees His Death   (1919)

I know that I shall meet my fate
Somewhere among the clouds above;
Those that I fight I do not hate,
Those that I guard I do not love;
My country is Kiltartan Cross,   5
My countrymen Kiltartan's poor,
No likely end could bring them loss
Or leave them happier than before.
Nor law, nor duty bade me fight,
Nor public men, nor cheering crowds,   10
A lonely impulse of delight
Drove to this tumult in the clouds;
I balanced all, brought all to mind,
The years to come seemed waste of breath,
A waste of breath the years behind   15
In balance with this life, this death.

ALICE DUNBAR-NELSON (1875–1935)

I Sit and Sew   (1920)

I sit and sew—a useless task it seems,
My hands grown tired, my head weighed down with dreams—
The panoply of war, the martial tread of men,
Grim-faced, stern-eyed, gazing beyond the ken
Of lesser souls, whose eyes have not seen Death   5
Nor learned to hold their lives but as a breath—
But—I must sit and sew.

I sit and sew—my heart aches with desire—
That pageant terrible, that fiercely pouring fire
On wasted fields, and writhing grotesque things   10
Once men. My soul in pity flings
Appealing cries, yearning only to go
There in that holocaust of hell, those fields of woe—
But—I must sit and sew.

The little useless seam, the idle patch;   15
Why dream I here beneath my homely thatch,
When there they lie in sodden mud and rain,
Pitifully calling me, the quick ones and the slain?
You need me, Christ! It is no roseate dream
That beckons me—this pretty futile seam,   20
It stifles me—God, must I sit and sew?

WILLIAM BUTLER YEATS (1865–1939)

The Second Coming   (1921)

Turning and turning in the widening gyre
The falcon cannot hear the falconer;
Things fall apart; the centre cannot hold;
Mere anarchy is loosed upon the world,
The blood-dimmed tide is loosed, and everywhere   5
The ceremony of innocence is drowned;
The best lack all conviction, while the worst
Are full of passionate intensity.

Surely some revelation is at hand;
Surely the Second Coming is at hand.   10
The Second Coming! Hardly are those words out
When a vast image out of *Spiritus Mundi*[1]
Troubles my sight: somewhere in sands of the desert
A shape with lion body and the head of a man
A gaze blank and pitiless as the sun,   15
Is moving its slow thighs, while all about it
Reel shadows of the indignant desert birds.

---

[1]Spirit of the world [Latin]; to Yeats a collective source of images and inspiration for poets.

The darkness drops again; but now I know
That twenty centuries of stony sleep
Were vexed to nightmare by a rocking cradle,   20
And what rough beast, its hour come round at last,
Slouches towards Bethlehem to be born?

e. e. cummings (1894–1962)

my sweet old etcetera

(1926)

my sweet old etcetera
aunt lucy during the recent

war could and what
is more did tell you just
what everybody was fighting   5

for,
my sister

isabel created hundreds
(and
hundreds) of socks not to   10
mention shirts fleaproof earwarmers

etcetera wristers etcetera, my
mother hoped that

i would die etcetera
bravely of course my father used   15
to become hoarse talking about how it was
a privilege and if only he
could meanwhile my

self etcetera lay quietly
in the deep mud et   20

cetera
(dreaming,
et
    cetera, of
Your smile   25
eyes knees and of your Etcetera)

FEDERICO GARCÍA LORCA (1898–1936)

Ballad of the Spanish Civil Guard[1]   (1927)

Translated by Langston Hughes

Their horses are black.
Black are their iron shoes.
On their capes shimmer stains
of ink and wax.
They have, and so they never weep,   5
skulls of lead.
With patent-leather souls
they come down the road.
Wherever they pass they spread
silences of thick rubber   10
and rears of fine sand.
They go by, if they wish to go,
concealing in their heads
a vague astronomy
of abstract pistols.   15

Oh, city of the gypsies!
On the corners, banners,
The moon and pumpkins
preserved with gooseberries.
Oh, city of the gypsies!   20
Who could see you and not remember you?
City of grief and of musk
with towers of cinnamon.
When the night that came
nightly came nightly,   25
the gypsies in their forges
made suns and arrows.
A horse with a mortal wound
went from one door to another.
Glass roosters crowed   30

---

[1]National police force, organized along military lines and frequently used for political repression.

toward Jerez de la Frontera.[2]
The naked wind turns
the corner in surprise
in the night-silver night
that nightly comes nightly.   35

San José and the Virgin
loose their castanets
and come looking for the gypsies
to see if they can find them.
The Virgin comes dressed   40
in her village finery
of chocolate paper
and necklaces of almonds.
San José swings his arms
under a silken cape.   45
Behind comes Pedro Domecq
With three sultans of Persia.

The half moon dreams
an ecstasy of cranes.
Banners and torches   50
invade the roof-tops.
In the looking glasses sob
dancers who have no hips.
Water and shadow, shadow and water
toward Jerez de la Frontera.   55
Oh, city of the gypsies!
On the corners, banners.
Put out your green lights
for the Civil Guards are coming.
Oh, city of the gypsies!   60
Who could see you and not remember you?
Leave her far off from the sea
with no combs for her hair.

Two by two they come
to the city of fiesta.   65
A rustle of *siemprevivas*[3]
invades their cartridge belts.

---

[2]City in Southwest Spain known for its sherry and cognac.
[3]Everlastings or immortellers, flowers that keep their shape and color when dried.

Two by two they come.
A night of double thickness.
To them the sky is nothing   70
but a window full of spurs.
Fear ran wild in a city
that multiplied its door.
Through them came forty Civil Guards
bent on pillage.   75
The clocks all stopped
and the cognac in the bottles
put on their November mask
to invite no suspicions.
A flight of screams unending   80
rose among the weather-vanes.
Sabers cut the air
that the horses trampled.

Through the dusky streets
old gypsy women   85
flew with drowsy nags
and crocks of money.
Up the steep streets
the sinister capes mount,
followed by fugitive   90
whirlwinds of scissors.

At the Gate of Belen
the gypsies gather.
San José, full of wounds,
shrouds a young maiden.   95
All through the night
stubborn guns sound sharply.
The Virgin treats the children
with drops of small saliva.

But the Civil Guard   100
advances sowing fires
where imagination burns
young and naked.
Rosa de los Camborios
sobs on her doorstep   105
with two breasts cut away
and put on a platter.
And other girls flee

pursued by their tresses
through the air where the roses   110
of black dust explode.
When the roof-tops are no more
than furrows on the earth,
dawn rocks her shoulders
in a long profile of stone.   115
Oh, city of the gypsies!
As the flames draw near
the Civil Guard goes off
down a tunnel full of silence.
Oh, city of the gypsies!   120
Who could see you and not remember you?
Let them look for you on my forehead,
game of the sand and the moon.

BABETTE DEUTSCH (1895–1982)

Dawn in Wartime   (1943)

Sunrise tumbling in like a surf,
A foam of petals, curling thousands, lightly crumbling
Away in light.
Waking to this, how could the eyes hold
The shape of night's barren island, the cold cliffs   5
Climbed in sleep, how
Recall the burned sore scabby
Face of the world?
Into that sea of light the spirit waded
Like a young child at morning on the beach,   10
Saw only those giant combers, soft as roses,
That mothy spume unfeathering into air.
Lingered there, as a child lingers
To smooth bastions of whitest sand,
To finger shells brighter than dogwood flowers,   15
To stand, quietly,
Watching the immense marvel of morning
Rolling toward him all its uncreated hours.

GWENDOLYN BROOKS (1917–2000)

the white troops had their orders but the Negroes looked like men[1]

(1945)

They had supposed their formula was fixed.
They had obeyed instructions to devise
A type of cold, a type of hooded gaze.
But when the Negroes came they were perplexed.
These Negroes looked like men. Besides, it taxed   5
Time and the temper to remember those
Congenital iniquities that cause
Disfavor of the darkness. Such as boxed
Their feelings properly, complete to tags—
A box for dark men and a box for Other—   10
Would often find the contents had been scrambled.
Or even switched. Who really gave two figs?
Neither the earth nor heaven ever trembled.
And there was nothing startling in the weather.

CLAUDE MCKAY (1890–1948)

Look Within

(1945)

Lord, let me not be silent while we fight
    In Europe Germans, Asia Japanese
For setting up a Fascist way of might
    While fifteen million Negroes on their knees
Pray for salvation from the Fascist yoke   5
    Of these United States. Remove the beam
(Nearly two thousand years since Jesus spoke)
    From your own eyes before the mote you deem
It proper from your neighbor's to extract!
    We bathe our lies in vapors of sweet myrrh,   10

---

[1]Brooks points out (in 1988) that the poem was published in 1945; she writes that the word "Negro" is "no longer used by self-respecting blacks."

And close our eyes not to perceive the fact!
  But Jesus said: You whited sepulchre,
Pretending to be uncorrupt of sin,
  While worm-infested, rotten through within!

HENRY REED (1914–1986)

Naming of Parts   (1946)

To-day we have naming of parts. Yesterday,
We had daily cleaning. And to-morrow morning,
We shall have what to do after firing. But to-day,
To-day we have naming of parts. Japonica
Glistens like coral in all of the neighbouring gardens,   5
  And to-day we have naming of parts.

This is the lower sling swivel. And this
Is the upper sling swivel, whose use you will see,
When you are given your slings. And this is the piling swivel,
Which in your case you have not got. The branches   10
Hold in the gardens their silent, eloquent gestures,
  Which in our case we have not got.

This is the safety-catch, which is always released
With an easy flick of the thumb. And please do not let me
See anyone using his finger. You can do it quite easy   15
If you have any strength in your thumb. The blossoms
Are fragile and motionless, never letting anyone see
  Any of them using their finger.

And this you can see is the bolt. The purpose of this
Is to open the breech, as you see. We can slide it   20
Rapidly backwards and forwards: we call this
Easing the spring. And rapidly backwards and forwards
The early bees are assaulting and fumbling the flowers:
  They call it easing the Spring.

They call it easing the Spring: it is perfectly easy   25
If you have any strength in your thumb: like the bolt,
And the breech, and the cocking-piece, and the point of
balance,

Which in our case we have not got; and the almond-blossom
Silent in all of the gardens and the bees going backwards and forwards,　　30
　　For to-day we have naming of parts.

YEVGENY YEVTUSHENKO　(b. 1933)

The Companion　　　　　　　　　　　　　　　　　　(1954)

Translated by Robin Milner-Gulland and Peter Levi, S. J.

She was sitting on the rough embankment,
her cape too big for her tied on slapdash
over an odd little hat with a bobble on it,
her eyes brimming with tears of hopelessness.
An occasional butterfly floated down　　　　　　　　　　　　5
fluttering warm wings onto the rails.
The clinkers underfoot were deep lilac.
We got cut off from our grandmothers
while the Germans were dive-bombing the train.
Katya was her name. She was nine.　　　　　　　　　　　　10
I'd no idea what I could do about her,
but doubt quickly dissolved to certainty:
I'd have to take this thing under my wing;
—girls were in some sense of the word human,
a human being couldn't just be left.　　　　　　　　　　　　15
The droning in the air and the explosions
receded farther into the distance,
I touched the little girl on her elbow.
'Come on. Do you hear? What are you waiting for?'
The world was big and we were not big,　　　　　　　　　　20
and it was tough for us to walk across it.
She had galoshes on and felt boots,
I had a pair of second-hand boots.
We forded streams and tramped across the forest;
each of my feet at every step it took　　　　　　　　　　　25
taking a smaller step inside the boot.
The child was feeble, I was certain of it.
'Boo-hoo,' she'd say. 'I'm tired,' she'd say.
She'd tire in no time I was certain of it,
but as things turned out it was me who tired.　　　　　　　30
I growled I wasn't going any further
and sat down suddenly beside the fence.
'What's the matter with you?' she said.

'Don't be so stupid! Put grass in your boots.
Do you want to eat something? Why won't you talk? 35
Hold this tin, this is crab.
We'll have refreshments. You small boys,
you're always pretending to be brave.'
Then out I went across the prickly stubble
marching beside her in a few minutes. 40
Masculine pride was muttering in my mind:
I scraped together strength and I held out
for fear of what she'd say. I even whistled.
Grass was sticking out from my tattered boots.
So on and on 45
we walked without thinking of rest
passing craters, passing fire,
under the rocking sky of '41
tottering crazy on its smoking columns.

ROBERT LOWELL (1917–1977)

For the Union Dead (1964)

"Relinquunt Omnia Servare Rem Publicam."[1]

The old South Boston Aquarium stands
in a Sahara of snow now. Its broken windows are boarded.
The bronze weathervane cod has lost half its scales.
The airy tanks are dry.

Once my nose crawled like a snail on the glass; 5
my hand tingled
to burst the bubbles
drifting from the noses of the cowed, compliant fish.

My hand draws back. I often sigh still
for the dark downward and vegetating kingdom 10
of the fish and reptile. One morning last March,
I pressed against the new barbed and galvanized

fence on the Boston Common. Behind their cage,
yellow dinosaur steamshovels were grunting

---

[1]"They give up everything to serve the republic."

as they cropped up tons of mush and grass   15
to gouge their underworld garage.

Parking spaces luxuriate like civic
sandpiles in the heart of Boston.
A girdle of orange, Puritan-pumpkin colored girders
braces the tingling Statehouse,   20

shaking over the excavations, as it faces Colonel Shaw[2]
and his bell-cheeked Negro infantry
on St. Gaudens' shaking Civil War relief,
propped by a plank splint against the garage's earthquake.

Two months after marching through Boston,   25
half the regiment was dead;
at the dedication,
William James could almost hear the bronze Negroes breathe.

Their monument sticks like a fishbone
in the city's throat.   30
Its Colonel is as lean
as a compass-needle.

He has an angry wrenlike vigilance,
a greyhound's gentle tautness;
he seems to wince at pleasure,   35
and suffocate for privacy.

He is out of bounds now. He rejoices in man's lovely,
peculiar power to choose life and die—
when he leads his black soldiers to death,
he cannot bend his back.   40

On a thousand small town New England greens,
the old white churches hold their air
of sparse, sincere rebellion; frayed flags
quilt the graveyards of the Grand Army of the Republic.

The stone statues of the abstract Union Soldier   45
grow slimmer and younger each year—
wasp-waisted, they doze over muskets
and muse through their sideburns . . .

---

[2]Robert Gould Shaw, white, led a black regiment.

Shaw's father wanted no monument
except the ditch,   50
where his son's body was thrown
and lost with his "niggers."

The ditch is nearer.
There are no statues for the last war here;
on Boylston Street, a commercial photograph   55
shows Hiroshima boiling

over a Mosler Safe, the "Rock of Ages"
that survived the blast. Space is nearer.
When I crouch to my television set,
the drained faces of Negro school-children rise like balloons.   60

Colonel Shaw
is riding on his bubble,
he waits
for the blessèd break.

The Aquarium is gone. Everywhere,   65
giant finned cars nose forward like fish;
a savage servility
slides by on grease.

NGUYEN LAM SON (unknown)

Can Tho[1]   (1967)

*Translated by Bruce Weigl and Thanh Nguyen, from North Vietnamese documents
captured September 27, 1967.*

Can Tho, country of my heart,
Country of the whitest rice, clearest water
And most beautiful sunshine.
Country of the green banana,
The betal palm and coconut tree,   5
Who forces me to walk away from this country?
With a strong will I journey,
Determined to cross all oceans

---

[1]Can Tho is in the Mekong Delta in South Vietnam.

To join the revolution at Ca Mau.
But fighting, even hand and hand   10
With my countrymen in another village
Is like fighting in another country.
I cannot return home.
Step by step we march forward to keep our honor,
Already muddied by the enemy.   15
Please do not let our country be defeated.
Use all of your strength and all of your life
So that Ca Rang City and Phung Hiep
Will be remembered forever and the Hoa Vu forests
Will still shine bright as fire.   20
With hope that you will keep your will,
I write this poem for you, my friends.

LANGSTON HUGHES (1902–1967)

Without Benefit of Declaration   (1967)

Listen here, Joe,
Don't you know
That tomorrow
You got to go
Out yonder where   5
The steel winds blow?

Listen here, kid,
It's been said
Tomorrow you'll be dead
Out there where   10
The rain is lead.

Don't ask me why.
Just go ahead and die.
Hidden from the sky
Out yonder you'll lie: 15
A medal to your family—
In exchange for
A guy.

Mama, don't cry.

OTTO ORBAN (b. 1936)

Chile (1987)

Translated by Jascha Kessler and Maria Korosy.

The MP tramps empty-handed down the stairs.—This is the third time you've been here, the woman says, and you've found nothing.—See you around some-time, the Lieutenant says to the kid, we're not coming back.—Then you saw Daddy in the attic? the child asks.—So we did, says the Lieutenant, going into the house, bringing the man down, and shooting him in the yard, right before the mother and child. Pupils the size of the world: Earth, its seas and springtime, green-gowned amongst the burning stars.

BRUCE WEIGL (b. 1949)

Song of Napalm (1988)

for my wife

After the storm, after the rain stopped pounding,
we stood in the doorway watching horses
walk off lazily across the pasture's hill.
We stared through the black screen,
our vision altered by the distance   5
so I thought I saw a mist
kicked up around their hooves when they faded
like cut-out horses
away from us.
The grass was never more blue in that light, more   10
scarlet; beyond the pasture
trees scraped their voices into the wind, branches
crisscrossed the sky like barbed wire
but you said they were only branches.

Okay. The storm stopped pounding.   15
I am trying to say this straight: for once
I was sane enough to pause and breathe
outside my wild plans and after the hard rain
I turned my back on the old curses. I believed
they swung finally away from me . . .   20

But still the branches are wire
and thunder is the pounding mortar,

still I close my eyes and see the girl
running from her village, napalm
stuck to her dress like jelly,   25
her hands reaching for the no one
who waits in waves of heat before her.

So I can keep on living,
so I can stay here beside you,
I try to imagine she runs down the road and wings   30
beat inside her until she rises
above the stinking jungle and her pain
eases, and your pain, and mine.
But the lie swings back again.
The lie works only as long as it takes to speak   35
and the girl runs only as far
as the napalm allows

until her burning tendons and crackling
muscles draw her up
into that final position   40
burning bodies so perfectly assume. Nothing
can change that, she is burned behind my eyes
and not your good love and not the rain-swept air
and not the jungle-green
pasture unfolding before us can deny it.   45

THOMAS MCGRATH (1916–1990)

Reading the Names of the Vietnam War Dead   (1973)

For a long day and a night we read the names:
Many thousand brothers fallen in the green and distant land . . .

Sun going south after the autumn equinox.
By night the vast moon: "Moon of the Falling Leaves";

Our voices hoarse in the cold of the first October rains.   5
And the long winds of the season to carry our words away.

The citizens go on about their business.
By night sleepers condense in the houses grown cloudy with dreams.

By day a few come to hear us and leave, shaking their heads
Or cursing. On Sunday the moral animal prays in his church.   10

It is Fall; but a host of dark birds flies toward the cold North.
Thousands of dense black stones fall forever through the
          darkness under the earth.

MARGARET ATWOOD (b. 1939)

The Loneliness of the Military Historian   (1990)

Confess: it's my profession
that alarms you.
This is why few people ask me to dinner,
though Lord knows I don't go out of my way to be scary.
I wear dresses of sensible cut   5
and unalarming shades of beige,
I smell of lavender and go to the hairdresser's:
no prophetess mane of mine
complete with snakes, will frighten the youngsters.
If my eyes roll and I mutter,   10
if my arms are gloved in blood right up to the elbow,
if I clutch at my heart and scream in horror
like a third-rate actress chewing up a mad scene,
I do it in private and nobody sees
but the bathroom mirror.   15

In general I might agree with you:
women should not contemplate war,
should not weigh tactics impartially,
or evade the word *enemy*,
or view both sides and denounce nothing.   20
Women should march for peace,
or hand out white feathers to inspire bravery,
spit themselves on bayonets
to protect their babies,
whose skulls will be split anyway,   25
or, having been raped repeatedly,
hang themselves with their own hair.
These are the functions that inspire general comfort.

That, and the knitting of socks for the troops
and a sort of moral cheerleading.   30
Also: mourning the dead.
Sons, lovers, and so forth.
All the killed children.

Instead of this, I tell
what I hope will pass as truth.   35
A blunt thing, not lovely.
The truth is seldom welcome,
especially at dinner,
though I am good at what I do.
My trade is in courage and atrocities.   40
I look at them and do not condemn.
I write things down the way they happened,
as near as can be remembered.
I don't ask *why* because it is mostly the same.
Wars happen because the ones who start them   45
think they can win.

In my dreams there is glamour.
The Vikings leave their fields
each year for a few months of killing and plunder,
much as the boys go hunting.   50
In real life they were farmers.
They come back loaded with splendor.
The Arabs ride against Crusaders
with scimitars that could sever
silk in the air.   55
A swift cut to the horse's neck
and a hunk of armor crashes down
like a tower. Fire against metal.
A poet might say: romance against banality.
When awake, I know better.   60

Despite the propaganda, there are no monsters,
or none that can be finally buried.
Finish one off and circumstances
and the radio create another.
Believe me: whole armies have prayed fervently   65
to God all night and meant it,
and been slaughtered anyway.
Brutality wins frequently,

and large outcomes have turned on the invention
of a mechanical device, viz. radar.   70

True, sometimes valor counts for something,
as at Thermopylae. Sometimes being right,
though ultimate virtue by agreed tradition
is decided by the winner.
Sometimes men throw themselves on grenades   75
and burst like paper bags of guts
to save their comrades.
I can admire that.
But rats and cholera have won many wars.
Those, and potatoes   80
or the absence of them.
It's no use pinning all those medals
across the chests of the dead.
Impressive, but I know too much.
Grand exploits merely depress me.   85

In the interests of research
I have walked on many battlefields
that once were liquid with pulped
men's bodies and spangled with burst
shells and splayed bone.   90
All of them have been green again
by the time I got there.
Each has inspired a few good quotes in its day.
Sad marble angels brood like hens
over the grassy nests where nothing hatches.   95
(The angels could just as well be described as *vulgar,*
or *pitiless,* depending on camera angle.)
The word *glory* figures a lot on gateways.
Of course I pick a flower or two
from each, and press it in the hotel   100
Bible, for a souvenir.
I'm just as human as you.

But it's no use asking me for a final statement.
As I say, I deal in tactics.
Also statistics: 105
for every year of peace there have been four hundred
years of war.

BARBARA KINGSOLVER (b. 1955)

Deadline (1991)

January 15, 1991[1]

The night before war begins, and you are still here.
You can stand in a breathless cold
ocean of candles, a thousand issues of your same face
rubbed white from below by clear waxed light.
A vigil. You are wondering what it is   5
you can hold a candle to.

You have a daughter. Her cheeks curve
like aspects of the Mohammed's perfect pear.
She is three. Too young for candles but
you are here, this is war.   10
Flames covet the gold-sparked ends of her hair,
her nylon parka laughing in color,
inflammable. It has taken your whole self
to bring her undamaged to this moment,
and waiting in the desert at this moment   15
is a bomb that flings gasoline in a liquid sheet,
a laundress's snap overhead, wide as the ancient Tigris,
and ignites as it descends.

The polls have sung their opera of assent: the land
wants war. But here is another America,   20
candle-throated, sure as tide.
Whoever you are, you are also this granite anger.
In history you will be the vigilant dead
who stood in front of every war with old hearts
in your pockets, stood on the carcass of hope   25
listening for the thunder of its feathers.

The desert is diamond ice and only stars above us here
and elsewhere, a thousand issues of a clear waxed star,
a holocaust of heaven
and somewhere, a way out.   30

---

[1]Under U.S. pressure, the United Nations Security Council authorized the use of force against Iraq if it did not withdraw from Kuwait by January 15, 1991. Iraq did not withdraw, and the United States and its allies attacked immediately.

BEKES JR (SHERKO FAIQ) (b. 1940)

Picture   (1979)

Iraqi Kurdish; Translated by Muhamad Tawfiq Ali.

Four children
a Turk, a Persian
an Arab and a Kurd
were collectively drawing the picture of a man.
The first drew his head   5
The second drew his hands and upper limbs
The third drew his legs and torso
The fourth drew a gun on his shoulder

YOUSIF AL-SA'IGH (b. 1932)

An Iraqi Evening   (1986)

Translated by Saadi A Simawe, Ralph Savarese and Chuck Miller.

Clips from the battlefield
in an Iraqi evening:
a peaceable home
two boys
preparing their homework   5
a little girl
absentmindedly drawing on scrap paper
funny pictures.
—breaking news coming shortly.
The entire house becomes ears   10
ten Iraqi eyes glued to the screen in frightened silence.
Smells mingle:
the smell of war
and the smell of just baked bread.
The mother raises her eyes to a photo on the wall   15
whispering
— May God protect you
and she begins preparing supper
quietly
and in her mind   20
clips float past of the battlefield
carefully selected for hope.

AHMED HERDI (b. 1922)

God's freedom lovers (1957)

Iraqi Kurdish; Translated by Muhamad Tawfiq Ali.

We Kurds are God's freedom lovers,
We are walls of masonry and steel,
We are the defenders of servile peasants,
We are the flag of unity hoisted high
We are the swords in the hands of the broken   5
We have risen against tyranny.
Aghas and Begs are feudal lords,
Tormentors of the poor people's soul.
They are blood suckers of this homeland,
They are tools in the hands of foreign powers,   10
One day we will kick the living hell out of them,
One day we will avenge the people's suffering.
Not even the shackles of a hundred prisons,
Not even the torture tools in the hands of foreign rulers
Not even the gunpowder, lead and steel bullets   15
Not even the live ammunition of the despised tyrants,
Will affect us an iota or stop us from marching on.
Even if we die on these highways and byways,
We refuse to become lackeys of foreign masters.

FADHIL AL-AZZAWI (b. 1940)

The Last Iraq (1987)

Translated by Salaam Yousif.

Every night I place this creature on my table
And pull its ears,
Till tears of joy come to its eyes.
Another cold winter, penetrated by airplanes
And soldiers sitting on the edge of a hillock,   5
Waiting for history
To rise up from the darkness of the marshes

With a gun in its hand,
To shoot angels
Training for the revolution.   10
Every night I put my hand on this country,
It slips away from my fingers,
Like a soldier running from the front.

JENNIFER COMPTON

The Soldier Born in 1983   (2004)

Before he could walk he crawled
for all the world the way a soldier
slithered through New Guinea
or Vietnam.

I could almost see the rifle   5
in his crooked arms
as he went elbows and knees
across the kitchen floor.

He searched the house through
but could not find his gun.   10
Rose up on his hind legs
found the wood basket and

something comfortable like a weapon.
He turned with a happy grin
slew his family with a practised sweep   15
and exactly the right sound.

MARTIN ESPADA (b. 1957)

Alabanza: In Praise of Local 100   (2002)

*for the 43 members of Hotel Employees and Restaurant Employees Local 100, working
at the Windows on the World restaurant, who lost their lives in the attack on the World
Trade Center*

Alabanza.[1] Praise the cook with a shaven head
and a tattoo on his shoulder that said *Oye,*[2]
a blue-eyed Puerto Rican with people from Fajardo,
the harbor of pirates centuries ago.
Praise the lighthouse in Fajardo, candle   5
glimmering white to worship the dark saint of the sea.
Alabanza. Praise the cook's yellow Pirates cap
worn in the name of Roberto Clemente, his plane
that flamed into the ocean loaded with cans for Nicaragua,
for all the mouths chewing the ash of earthquakes.   10
Alabanza. Praise the kitchen radio, dial clicked
even before the dial on the oven, so that music and Spanish
rose before bread. Praise the bread. *Alabanza.*

Praise Manhattan from a hundred and seven flights up,
like Atlantis glimpsed through the windows of an ancient aquarium.   15
Praise the great windows where immigrants from the kitchen
could squint and almost see their world, hear the chant of nations:
Ecuador, México, Republica Dominicana,
Haiti, Yemen, Ghana, Bangladesh.
Alabanza. Praise the kitchen in the morning,   20
where the gas burned blue on every stove
and exhaust fans fired their diminutive propellers,
hands cracked eggs with quick thumbs
or sliced open cartons to build an altar of cans.
Alabanza. Praise the busboy's music, the *chime-chime*   25
of his dishes and silverware in the tub.
Alabanza. Praise the dish-dog, the dishwasher
who worked that morning because another dishwasher
could not stop coughing, or because he needed overtime
to pile the sacks of rice and beans for a family   30
floating away on some Caribbean island plagued by frogs.
Alabanza. Praise the waitress who heard the radio in the kitchen
and sang to herself about a man gone. *Alabanza.*

After the thunder wilder than thunder,
after the shudder deep in the glass of the great windows,   35
after the radio stopped singing like a tree full of terrified frogs,
after night burst the dam of day and flooded the kitchen,
for a time the stoves glowed in darkness like the lighthouse in Fajardo,
like a cook's soul. Soul I say, even if the dead cannot tell us

[1]*Alabanza:* Praise. From *alabar,* "to celebrate with words."
[2]*Oye:* "listen" or "hey."

about the bristles of God's beard because God has no face,　　40
soul I say, to name the smoke-beings flung in constellations
across the night sky of this city and cities to come.
Alabanza I say, even if God has no face.

Alabanza. When the war began, from Manhattan and Kabul
two constellations of smoke rose and drifted to each other,　　45
mingling in icy air, and one said with an Afghan tongue:
Teach me to dance. We have no music here.
And the other said with a Spanish tongue:
I will teach you. Music is all we have.

DRAMA

MARC KAMINSKY (b. 1943)

Marc Kaminsky was born in New York City and educated at Columbia University. He has taught English at the City University of New York, worked at a senior citizens center, run writing workshops, and been co-director of the Brookdale Institute for the Humanities, Arts, and Aging. He has written poetry, nonfiction, and drama. His book The Road From Hiroshima *(1984) includes accounts by Hiroshima survivors.* In the Traffic of a Targeted City *premiered at the Theater for the New City in 1986.*

In the Traffic of a Targeted City   (1986)

CHARACTERS

New York:
JONAH, *a sculptor*
WALKMAN, *a teenager*
JOANNA, *a political activist*
UNCLE MAX, *a Holocaust survivor*

Hiroshima:
MOTHER
WOMAN IN WHITE KIMONO
SET-CHAN
NAKAJIMA HIROSHI, *a poet*
TOWNSWOMAN
NAKAJIMA'S WIFE
MISAO, *Nakajima's sister*
OLD WOMAN

Characters are played by two actors. Character definition is made by costume and lighting changes, as well as by changes in the actors' physical and vocal life.

Setting

Japanese-like screens define the space of a New York studio, subway, office, cocktail party, bedroom and also several locations in Hiroshima. The screens have windows that can be opened and closed, a sliding door and one other entrance.

The set pieces consist of a bench and a stool; they are used to suggest a subway, an artist's stool and a Japanese desk. Shifts in lighting and music help to create the various locations.

The play takes place in New York today and Hiroshima, 1945.

As the audience enters, saxophone and piano music play over speakers. Jonah sits SR weaving together a network of wood slats with copper wire. He rolls up the slats, puts them aside, moves the ladder from UR to extreme DR (with slats) and exits. Lights to black. Music plays in darkness, finishes.

Music changes to saxophone clacks. Lights up DL on Walkman bopping on the subway. Sound changes to subway noise, then screech. Jonah enters DR and dresses hurriedly as:

SUBWAY ANNOUNCEMENT: Attention! Attention! We are holding this train due to a delay behind us! This is an express train making local stops. I repeat, this is a local train making express stops only. It is imperative that all passengers immediately proceed to . . . (words become unintelligible). . . . Please follow these instructions exactly. Thank you for your co-operation and patience.

JONAH: *(has finished dressing and rushed to subway entrance).* What did he say? *(Walkman doesn't answer. Jonah sits, subway starts. Jonah looks at date-book.)*

It's amazing how little time there is in New York City! Men with brief-cases on their laps do paperwork in the subway, thinking the whole time: In Tucson, maybe there there is time.

Women with ladles in their hands and telephones in their necks are talk-ing to Kansas: In Grandmother's time there was time, but in these reno-vated brownstones there isn't any left.

I'm no different from anybody else. I run across a lot of women in the course of a week. In offices, in parties, in bed, they are all depressed.

(They lean as subway stops, Walkman exits.)

There's no time for supper. The men are grabbing a slice of pizza on Forty-Second Street.

The women are making up before a make-up exam at the New School.[1]

There is no time to transplant the bride's veil.

There is no time because there are dirty socks in the hamper.

There are 10,000 mile tune-ups, there are friends from Boston, there is snow, there are innuendos, there are taxes, dentists, dissertations, parking meters, bonuses, transfers, cousins and ice cream or fortune cookies.

---

[1]The New School for Social Research, a university in New York City.

(Subway stops. Joanna enters, sits.)

There are three important relationships.

(They lean as subway starts.)

There are twenty-five people ahead of you waiting to be tested for herpes.

There are children fracturing common daylight in prism studies, they all want to do well on the rainbow exam.

There is software and geology, there is the shortage of French brie, there are stamps, there is fluorescent lighting, there is the bartender who takes forever to serve you.

There are people who push six when you are trying to get to the ground floor.

There is the subway conductor who presides over husbands who are getting left behind.

There are usually benefits, there are often stop signs, there are long lines at the teller's window every Friday, there is Susan Sontag's[2] new book on authenticity, and this week there are dress rehearsals and tomatoes on sale.

There is no time because there is Marlon Brando[3] at the Trans Lux East and the general disposition of everything to run down, be reviewed, or require sleep.

(They lean as subway stops.)

There is no time because it takes so much time to think of all this and to feel depressed about it and to go through with it.

(They lean as subway starts.)

Datebooks don't seem to help.

No matter how ingeniously the men and women of New York fold and pack their hours, they can't take everything with them in a seven-day week.

They spread out their calendars before them like generals. They move love into the position occupied by the Soho opening to make room for the piano.

They drop pottery, juggle basketball, cancel dance, advance Spanish, they wake up, they go to sleep, they miss appointments with their therapists, forty-five minutes does not leave them enough time for breakfast. They get finished with sex in time to walk the dog.

(They lean as subway stops.)

I would like to open my closets and show you what lack of time has done to my shoes and make you see what happens when there is no time in the courtrooms and in the heads of households.

---

[2](1933–2004), American critic.
[3](1924–2004), American movie actor.

(He turns to her and speaks. She doesn't hear him.)

I would like to touch the back of your head with a strong pair of feelings.
I would like to massage your eyes, neck and temples until the tension
leaves you and you start to cry.
But I know you don't have time for this, and I too have to be getting on.

(They lean as subway starts.)

*(Joanna has been reading a book. Jonah looks over her shoulder. She catches him;
he goes back to his datebook. She looks over to see what he is reading and becomes very interested. He catches her; she goes back to her book. They both lean
over and read the other's book. They catch each other and laugh. As the train
comes to a stop, she gives him her book, and then, as she goes off, she swipes his
datebook. The door shuts before he can catch her. He starts to read the book she
gave him. A very long screech is heard. There is a blackout. The lights come back
up in silence. Jonah goes back to the book. Live chords are heard, and a woman
in a kimono appears behind a screen. She speaks what Jonah is reading. She is carrying a blanket that appears to have a baby inside it.)*

MOTHER: It happened something like an electric short
     a bluish-white light
     blanked out everything
     there was noise more than the ground beneath me
     could take I felt great heat
     even inside the house
     I was underneath the destroyed house
     I thought: a bomb
     has fallen directly upon me our house
     has been directly hit I became furious
     roof tiles and walls everything black covering me
     I screamed from all around I heard screaming
     then I felt a kind of danger
     unable to do anything by my own power
     I didn't know where I was or what I was under
     I thought: I'm going to die.

*(The woman disappears. Jonah slams the book shut. Blackout, music and lights
up on Uncle Max in hat, overcoat, with cane.)*

UNCLE MAX: I alone survived:

       my wife
       couldn't abandon
       her furniture

my son was
determined to finish his book
on Wagner[4]

Father couldn't believe
the ministers in black leather
were death

my friend
buried his circumcised dread
in the little hours you rent in hotel rooms

but I
who found the consolations of daily life
insufficient, I alone

survived.

(Uncle Max removes his hat and straightens up to reveal Jonah, who removes and hangs up his coat and hat as he speaks.)

JONAH: That's what my Great Uncle Max told me last Friday. Every other Friday we meet in the park and we talk. He makes me ask myself—and I hate the question—"What can I be in this wretched time?"

(Jonah crosses DR to his "studio" and examines his ladder sculpture until there is a beep of a phone answering-machine. Joanna's voice as phone message comes over speaker.)

JOANNA: Hi. My name is Joanna Green. I'm the one who stole your datebook this morning on the subway. You certainly are a busy fellow. But your datebook says you're free tonight. I'm going to be at a meeting of Artists for a Nuclear Free Harbor at 7:30, 225 Lafayette Street. You could meet me there, and I can give you the book back, and we could use your help. I hope to see you there. Oh—I hope you read the book I gave you. I'd like to know what you think of it.

(Jonah puts sculpture away and picks up book. As he reads, a woman in a long white kimono enters behind him, carrying a lantern. She speaks what he is reading.)

_____

[4]Richard Wagner (1813–1883), German composer.

WOMAN: A great river runs through Hiroshima
and every year
we bring lanterns
inscribed with the names of the family dead

and light them and set them afloat—
lanterns
that carry the dead
vows of the living who will never forget

them and the way they died—
and for miles
the full breadth of the river is one
mass of flames.

(She hangs the lantern UC. It will remain there throughout the play. She turns her back to the audience.)

JONAH *(reading):*   August 10, 1945.

Along the main road out
of Hiroshima
all the shutters were closed.
So the wounded walked on

or lay down in front of the houses
that no cry
would open.
But at a dry-goods store

on this side of Mitaki Station
they found
a woman who had managed to sneak inside
and die in one of their closets.

The owner, annoyed
at this disagreeable consequence,
dragged the body out by its feet
which were bare

and filthy
And his wife was distraught
and he was scandalized
when they saw

the corpse dressed in their
daughter's best
summer kimono—a wonderful
piece of work

which they instantly tore
off the dead body,
only to find
that it had no underwear on.

And they could feel only
how unlucky they were
till the priest came
and explained what had probably happened.

She must have been burnt out
of her home—a girl
of no more than sixteen years—
who fled

all the way from the city,
looking for something
to hide her nakedness
even before she sought water.

(Woman tears off her kimono slowly, turns downstage and walks as she describes):

There was no light at all every time
an oil drum exploded
the ground shook huge pillars
of smoke went up they broke

into a run they ran
a few feet then went back
to their dead walk
their eyes closed

they swayed to and fro pushed
they staggered in any direction
they were carried by the long lines leaving
Hiroshima

covered with black rain
with chalky ash there wasn't one
who wasn't bleeding the hands
the face the feet the anus

from any place it is possible
to bleed they bled
their mouths their eyes I am
still with them I see them

like walking ghosts their arms
bent forward like this
they had a special way of walking—
very slowly—like this—

if only
there were one or two of them!
but wherever I walked
I met these people

many of them
died along the road—
I myself
was one of them.

(Music and ghost walk continue until phone rings. Blackout. Music. Lights up on Jonah UC with the book.)

JONAH: What is to be done?
The time given to me on earth
is already half gone

I have little to waste
on public causes
and I dislike the righteous ones
who wave aside my nuances.

(Joanna enters with datebook, shakes hands with Jonah.)

JOANNA: I don't know how many nights
I lay awake with an aching conscience—like you
I wasted days, months, asking:
what is to be done?

(She hands him datebook, he hands her Hiroshima book; during the following they pass the two books back and forth. Jonah ends up with both.)

JONAH: Look, I am
an artist. I mean:
my days are eaten up
with putting bread on the table

my nights with putting on paper
what my life has given me
to make known, my friends
complain they don't see me

enough, and I also yearn
for them, and a few hours
of ceasing to drop
through these bottomless weeks

in this speeded-up, well-planned
rampantly efficient absence
of time—

JOANNA: We have a hall to rent. Posters
                   to print. Money to raise.

JONAH: Where will I fit
                   more tasks? how can I commit
                   more hours—

JOANNA: Come back when you are tired
                   of being agitated. And don't think
                   I'm promising you peace
                   of mind. The exhilaration

                   of working to save the planet
                   will pass quickly enough.
                   Immersed in routine tasks, you
                   won't feel particularly ennobled.

                   Nor will you feel despairing.
                   You will simply know: you
                   are doing what must be done.
                   But this will be enough

                   to allow you to remain fully conscious—
                   even of the anguish at the bottom
                   of oceans
                   in these deadening times.

JONAH: But this will be enough.

                   to allow me to remain fully conscious—
                   even of the anguish at the bottom

> of oceans
> in these deadening times.

(She exits. Jonah opens Hiroshima book. Voice of Nakajima is heard over speakers.)

> Yoshiko! Nanae! Misa!
> If you are here among this pile of bones,
> move your fingers a little,
> so that I can tell it is you—
> I will take you home for proper burial.

(Lights down on Jonah. Up on Walkman UC.)

WALKMAN: In History
the teacher asked us:
How do you prepare
for nuclear war?
Can it be done?
He divided the class

into two teams
and had us debate
the issue.
At the end we voted.
Mostly everyone
voted no.

And my heart
was racing
so fast I didn't think
I'd be able to
talk
maybe what I wanted

to say
was stupid
but how could they
raise their arms
and vote no
so calmly?

Listen, I said,
I made a tape

exactly 26 minutes long
it took me weeks
to pick out the top 8 songs
of my life.

I'll tell you something
I cried
when I had to leave out
"Like a Virgin."
But there just wasn't time
for everything.

And I carry this
tape with me everywhere I go.
So people can prepare
and they do, everyone
does in his own way.

When the warning comes
I'll put on my headphones
and turn on
my tape
and let the music blast off

let it take my mind
off the earth
and go to my feet
and I'll just start walking on air
till I meet the bomb.

(Walkman dances to the music on her headphones, exits as lights fade on her and come up on Jonah. Nakajima's voice comes over speakers.)

Even those
who looked like they were going to be spared
were not spared.

One by one
those who escaped with light injuries
began to sicken.

Nosebleeds, bloody vomit, bleeding
from the vagina,
bloodspots under the skin—

with these signs

the bomb took up its second life
among us. Without privacy

we open every fold
of our bodies to anyone
who happens to be looking,

hundreds of times a day, looking
for the hidden spot that tells
how soon

each of us is going to turn the mulberry
color of worms
and die.

JONAH *(interrupts voice):* There are taxes, dentists, dissertations, parking meters, bonuses, transfers, cousins, and ice cream or fortune cookies. There are three important relationships. . . .

(Woman in long dark kimono appears upstage, speaks)

SET-CHAN: Her voice under the burning house
saying:

Mother will come after you, Set-Chan,
so you go away first.
Now quickly. Quickly.

Forty-one years have passed
walking
   and lying down

alone
or in the arms of any man
I hear my mother shouting at me:

you go away
quickly!

(Blackout. Lights up on Jonah pacing and Joanna sitting on stool DR.)

JOANNA: Tell!

JONAH: I was born in 1943

JOANNA: Grew up in the traffic
of a targeted city.

JONAH: With chalk. And asphalt.
                    Home and second
                    base were manhole
                    covers. I played
                    in the intervals
                    between oncoming cars.

JOANNA: At school?

JONAH: Acquired
                    the basic skills.

JOANNA: And a stainless steel
                    chain around the neck.

JONAH: I learned: this
                    was a first acquisition
                    of status.

JOANNA: And it is the necklace
                    that soldiers wear
                    into battle.

JONAH: I loved
                    its silveriness

                    and the clattering
                    sound of running
                    the name plate

                    along its string
                    of tiny
                    ball bearings. I

                    put them into my mouth
                    and pulled them taut
                    like a horse's bit.

JOANNA: A nervous habit.

JONAH: My teachers
                    tried to break me

                    of this. So I started
                    to finger my chain
                    as if it were both

                    my rosary
                    and my worry beads

JOANNA: No one explained it
to you.

JONAH: But I knew:
my name
and my charred remains

could be separated
and thanks
to the dog tag

I would be sent
to the correct parents
for burial.

(Fifties-style rock and roll music begins. Jonah speaks, then sings as Joanna joins him singing in the style of a 50's doo-wop song.)

JONAH: Oh air raid drills of the early fifties!
sublime minutes
when Linda Brandon and I
huddled under our desk chairs—
my first taste of romantic love!

JONAH:	JOANNA:
I remember how hushed the room was	The grotto of love
we were taken by surprise	The grotto of love
every time the teacher	The grotto of love
whispered it breathlessly—	
"Take cover!"	cover cover cover
	cover cover cover ...
and we dove into a cave	
a cave of arms, our own	
and those of our desk chairs—	
two virginal bodies in the fifth grade	two virginal bodies in the fifth grade
I knew you had nothing on	The grotto of love
under your dress	The grotto of love
when you brushed against me	
and your straight black hair	
fell across my arm	
and a sheet of flame ran across my skin	and a sheet of flame ran across my skin

Oooooo . . .
The grotto—   The grotto . . .
Room 417! What a place
for a love-grotto!
            —of love.   . . . of love.

(The music continues; Jonah and Joanna dance a slow jitterbug.)

JOANNA   *(while dancing):*
                    Under every highway
                    At the mouth

                    Of every tunnel
                    We drive into the dark

                    Half-believing
                    We'll never get out of it

                    We grew up knowing
                    What no generation before us

                    Could know: the planet
                    Is now as difficult

                    To maintain as an intimate
                    Relationship.

JONAH: Are you always this serious?

JOANNA: You want fun? Go bowling. Don't get your hopes up on me.

JONAH: I only meant—it must be hell for you, living in some imagi-
                    nary Hiroshima.

JOANNA: It isn't imaginary. It happened. It could happen again.
                    Hiroshima—New York. We're commuters.

(Blackout. Lights up on Uncle Max UC.)

UNCLE MAX: There were heroes: first
                    and foremost were those with the courage
                    to see in time.

                    I was not with them. Blinded
                    by humility. Or what I once called humility.
                    And by love. Or what passed

in our world for love. My attachment
to those who looked at the mask of evil
and called it a human face.

I thought: Who are you
to move against the weight
of their judgement?

And I thought: You will be crushed.
I thought: Who
will listen to you?

And even if
your nightmares are the real
news

who
will repair the damage if you
awaken the sleepwalkers?

So when the officials told us
to pack our bags
and come to the terminal

I, too,
took my place
quietly, in line.

(Blackout. Jonah and Joanna appear DR with cocktails. Music as at a party.)

JOANNA: Everyone's running around
         Hungry to be saved

         Vitamin C, Jesus, jogging

JONAH: Oral worship of the foot

JOANNA: Each day we commit ourselves
         To another regimen

JONAH: Muktananda[5]

---

[5]Swami Paramhamsa Muktananda (1908–1982), guru popular in the United States.

JOANNA: juice fasts

JONAH: changing
                    Apartments

JOANNA: partners

JONAH: or genders

JOANNA: We go geneological and hunt
                    For roots

JONAH: Make a latter-day communion
                    With ethnic food

JOANNA: Or return to librium

JONAH: Or the Ph.D. program
                    In industrial psychology

JOANNA: With a little cocaine, a little
                    Real estate speculation

JONAH: Or the Lubavitcher Rebbe[6]
                    The Moonie[7] kids
                    Greet us with roses
                    Under every highway
                    At the mouth

                    Of every tunnel

JOANNA: We drive into the dark

                    Half-believing
                    We'll never get out of it.

                    We grew up knowing
                    What no generation before us

---

[6]Leader of Jewish sect.
[7]Member of cult led by Sun Myung Moon.

                    Could know: the planet
                    Is now as difficult

                    To maintain as an intimate
                    Relationship

JOANNA: And we go through
                    One enlightening experience

                    After another, hoping
                    Each time

                    To take final vows—
                    We, who are no good

                    At long-term affairs

(They kiss. Joanna exits. Jonah crosses DR. Nakajima's voice is heard over the speakers.)

NAKAJIMA *(over speakers)*:   Yoshiko! Nanae! Misa!
YOSHIKO *(over speakers)*:   Where are your daughters? In good health?
JONAH: Joanna, do you ever think about having children?

(The Hibakusha Mother enters in short kimono, carrying blanket/baby.)

MOTHER: I am still on the road to the doctor's house
                    carrying my baby
                    in my arms
                    thinking: he is going to survive

                    He was five months old
                    and all I could give him was gruel—
                    thin gruel
                    there were no spots on his body

                    A week after the bomb fell
                    he began to look better
                    I was pleased—
                    he was the only one I had left

                    and while we were on the road
                    to the doctor's house

he died
I found two big spots on his bottom

I am always on the road to the doctor.

(She crosses to Jonah and hands him the folded blanket. He begins to unfold it.)

JOANNA *(over speakers)*:   Something meant for use. A shadow passport.
                              This is your chance.

(Jonah unfolds the blanket completely to reveal a kimono jacket and the Hi-roshima book. Jonah hesitates, then puts on kimono, kneels Japanese-style and picks up the book—the same one Joanna gave him on the subway. As he does this, the Mother folds the blanket and set it DL with a pair of Japanese sandals. An air raid siren is heard; Jonah, as Nakajima Hiroshi, runs DL to his desk.)

NAKAJIMA: The screeching alarm bells
                   and rattle
                   of antiaircraft fire

                   woke me at three this morning.
                   The enemy planes
                   had already passed over

                   our house and were dropping
                   incendiary bombs
                   in the distance.

                   At my desk, my hands
                   tremble. I can do nothing
                   but helplessly record

                   these events
                   in a journal I have to keep
                   hidden.

                   If I live
                   to have grandchildren
                   ask me about the war

                   I will tell them:
                   it wasn't possible to write
                   let alone publish

the truth. To speak
sometimes meant
never to speak again.

Hiroshima, New Year's Day, 1945.

After the all clear
my daughters went up to Gobenden shrine
to pray.

Today the temple bells
that signal the end of the year
did not sound.

And it began to snow
just before dawn.
Bit by bit, in unison, the sky

and the earth became one
color, and the seven rivers froze
From the hills at Futaba-no-sato

I looked down at Hiroshima
and I saw the many
bridges of the city

bleed
into the white
rivers

and the rivers meld
with the unaccustomed whiteness
of the streets

and the sun breaks
through
onto this field of lost edges

turning it
into a blinding
sheet of light.

*(A Woman in a short kimono appears behind a window. She appears at doors
and windows during the next section.)*

WOMAN: What can this mean, snowfall
                    in January?

NAKAJIMA: They walked side by side
                    with their heads bowed, speaking
                    in whispers:
                    old and young, walking
                    home from the factories, across
                    Aioi Bridge.

WOMAN: When was the last time
                    this happened?

NAKAJIMA: *(in the voice of a naive young man):*
                                    Snow
                    on the Inland Sea?

WOMAN: In
                        the warmth of our winter?

NAKAJIMA: The old ones tried to remember
                    details of the storm
                    that befell their grandparents—

                    The young ones insisted:

WOMAN: It is not a sign
                    that some catastrophe will come
                    before the year is out.

NAKAJIMA: In whispers, the questions.
                    In whispers, the answers
                    the repetitions. . . .

WOMAN: It is an omen
                    that the B-29's will continue
                    to pass

                    over Hiroshima without dropping
                    their load.

BOTH: Our luck will hold good.

NAKAJIMA: Listening
                    as always to the conversations

among which I walk

I measure the intervals
between these exchanges of
the correct views.

Each day they get longer.
The list
Of things we dare not say

has gotten so huge
it blots out nearly all discussion.
Once we had victories

of the Imperial Army
to talk about.
Then there was rationing

then factory work
then the black market
then the air raids

but all that is used up.
Today we have snow in January.

BOTH: *(singing):*   the war has gone on too long
our luck can't hold

holidays can't be told
apart from days of hunger
and every day beaten

into nightmare by the erratic
air-raid warnings and lack
of sleep

the endless drills and hours
of "volunteer labor"—nothing exists now
but the war.

(She exits. Nakajima folds blanket and lays it out as a tablecloth.)

NAKAJIMA: May 7, 1945.

This morning—six small clams.

I dug them
out of the sand under Miyuki Bridge.

My daughters
foraged for wild plants
near the banks of the Ota
but even their secret place
was picked clean.

So my wife set out
with our youngest one's
best summer kimono—
the last fine piece of
anything we had to trade.

NAKAJIMA'S WIFE: *(enters with a tray of dishes to be used later for dinner):*

I sold it
for a cake of bean curd
two Chinese cabbages
six carrots, a bunch of spinach
and four eggplants—

all this
because my sister Misao arrived
from Tokyo today

and we didn't want her
coming under our roof
without a proper welcome.

(He crosses UC. Misao, dressed in short kimono, enters. They bow.)

NAKAJIMA: Three steps
out of the train
as she embraced me
Misao whispered:

MISAO: Do you still eat here
in Hiroshima?

(They cross DR, Misao kneels.)

NAKAJIMA: We walked
for miles beyond the city

and in a scorched field

where only the crows
could overhear us
I answered, "No."   *(Nakajima kneels, they lean to-*
                                     ward each other.)

MISAO: My husband   *(Misao pulls back, looks around*
                was not captured   *to see if they are being watched,*
                he is dead   *and leans back to Nakajima. She*
                                     speak-sings this section.)

                and our house
                destroyed
                after the latest raid

                Tokyo
                is a plain of broken objects
                I have nothing

                not even a photograph
                to place on a family altar
                nothing

                remains of my life
                in Tokyo
                my daughter was seized

                by the Kempei-tai[8]
                for making defeatist remarks
                marched into a meadow

                made to sit down
                and pummeled
                from early morning

                until late at night.
                Don't think I believe   *(Her tone of voice changes.)*
                that Japan will lose the war.

NAKAJIMA: Misao! I'm your brother! *(He reaches to comfort her.)*

(They rise and move to the blanket.)

---

[8]Secret Police.

NAKAJIMA: I ushered her into *(They remove shoes.)*
our house
ceremoniously

MISAO: We sat down formally *(She begins to set places at the table.)*
on our heels.

NAKAJIMA: My sister Misao, my brother Kyoji, *(He walks around*
my daughters Yoshiko, Nanae, Misa, *the table indicating*
my wife and I. *the places where*
each will sit, then
kneels.)

Our daughters served the meal:

MISAO: A tempura *(She lays out serving dishes.)*
of eggplant and cabbage,
a bit of bean curd, broiled
with salt, two
raw slices of carrot—

NAKAJIMA: a great luxury—

MISAO: and a bowl of barley.

NAKAJIMA: The clams—

MISAO: six
little reminders
of days of peace—

NAKAJIMA: were beautifully displayed—

MISAO: three apiece—

NAKAJIMA: on the plates
of my sister and brother.

And so we entered the circle
of the comfort of food. *(They reach for chopsticks.)*
But Yoshiko could not
contain herself! She asked:

MISAO: Where is your daughter?
In good health?

(Her chopstick drops.)

NAKAJIMA: Misao answered:

MISAO: In Tokyo.

NAKAJIMA: For one night let us forget
                  the war:

                  I have something
                  which can draw
                  out forgotten feelings

and give us a taste of
                  how we will live
                  when it ends.   *(He exits, returns with tray of
                                             sake and two cups.)*

NAKAJIMA: Sake!—homemade—
                  that I managed to lay my hands on.
                  To our health   *(He pours glass for
                                                  Misao, she pours
                  and to the health of everyone here.   one for him.)*
                  Two glasses of this
                  will get you quite happy   *(They clink glasses,
                                                  drink.)*
                  and if you think you are happy—   *(She pours him an-
                  then you are—in a way—   other glass, they
                  happy. One by one   clink again, drink.)*

                  we drank to each other's health:
                  sister and brother and brother
                  and sister-in-law and wife

                  and daughters and aunt and nieces
                  and uncle and parents—
                  all gathered at one table.

                  That night
                  while we were together
                  again

                  it seemed as though a line
                  had been drawn
                  around my house

                  and for as long as we sat there
                  banqueting
                  the war couldn't come in.

July 1st, 1945.   *(Shift in music.)*

MISAO: Used up the last of our salt   *(She hurriedly puts dishes*
                with tonight's meal.   *back on tray.)*

NAKAJIMA: At sundown we crawled
                into our bedrolls, hoping
                to get some rest   *(He extinguishes the*
                before the air raid sirens . . . *lantern and unfolds*
                                                  the blanket to a bed.)

                our fatigue   *(Air siren is heard.)*
                is so vast
                it has gotten the better of

                our fears. We yearn
                for one thing only: a night
                of sleep.   *(She exits with tray,*
                                                  comes back and gets
MISAO: Let them   *under blanket.)*
                get it over with!
                We've been at it so long—

                let it come! tonight!
                let the worst of it
                be finished!

(Nakajima embraces her as light fades slowly to black and then comes up on
Jonah and Joanna in a similar embrace.)

JOANNA: If I shriek
                who will hear me
                if I don't
                break the silence
                          who will
                hear me
                if I speak normal
                words in the normal
                order
                who will hear me

                if I tell
                what they saw and heard on the road
                from Hiroshima

> will I disturb
> the dead
>
> will I
> be a merchant of their disaster
>
> if I fail
> who will forgive me

(Lights down to black and then up on Nakajima and Misao in original embrace.)

NAKAJIMA: August 6th, 1945.

(They get up as in morning. He kneels at his desk. As she hands him a cup of tea, there is a blinding flash and a blackout. During the following poem, which is heard in the voice of Nakajima over the speakers, there is a series of "tableaux vivants." In each one, the lights come up slowly on the image and then there is a blinding flash and a blackout:

> **Set-Chan at the window.*
> **Nakajima, reaching through the door to light the lantern.*
> **Misao, offering a bowl of rice.*
> **Uncle Max and Joanna, arm-in-arm.*
> **Walkman, dancing.*

NAKAJIMA: *(over speakers):*
> A terrible flash
> rushed from east to west
> and became everywhere
> at once
>
> there was a wave
> of heat
> that reached under my clothes
> and scorched my skin
>
> it passed
> the sky held its breath
> trees broke
> into flame
>
> there was a blank
> in time
> then a huge boom
> came thundering

toward the mountain
a violent rush of air
took my body
and flung it against the ground

my hair tangled in branches
a wall of wind
pressed my being
into the earth

there was a silence
then a series
of shattering sounds
a mass of clouds

rose
and climbed rapidly into the sky
a column of boiling
clouds

spread and climbed, erupted
unfolded sideways, constantly
changing shape and color
climbed higher and wider

then burst
at the summit
and put out a monstrous head
that loomed over everything

I looked out
over a ledge of rock
and what I felt then
and what I feel now

I can't explain
it was not shock
or horror
I became mute with

I could see streets
in the distance
a few buildings
standing

here and there
but Hiroshima didn't exist
I saw
Hiroshima did not exist.

(Lights up on Jonah and Joanna in bed. Joanna wakes as from a nightmare. She speaks the following, initially as a nightmare, then more and more as a young Japanese girl. Jonah puts on Nakajima's kimono and listens.)

JOANNA: Not aware
of what I was doing
I jumped
down to the train track and braced
myself against it

somebody fell on top of me, screaming
a stream of pebbles lashed my face
trying to scream
my tongue fought an eerie
weight and I couldn't
hear me

though I lay there shrieking with all
my strength

I found
I had stuffed a handkerchief into my mouth
and covered my eyes and ears
with my hands

I tried to open
my eyes
I thought: Lord
why have you blinded me?
I thought: this is happening
in a dream

there wasn't a soul on the platform

but their shoes! hundreds
of shoes, left
and right separated, confused

with clogs, strewn
among sandals and slippers

half buried
under hoods and parasols—
only the shoes and hats, shorn
of their people!

like headstones and footstones

and I
the only one left?

leaving Yokogawa Station
I couldn't make out the road.

I walked through what had once been
a house

shreds of someone's daily routine—
a clock, an ironing board, a photograph
Of a sailor carrying a boy on his back—

pieces of white blouse and mattress
hanging
from telegraph poles

Anyone here?

I realized I
was together with the dead
woman in her bedroom

only we weren't really inside the house

all the walls between outside
and inside missing

fire beginning to fan out before me
around me

everywhere was out-of-doors
and cemetery.

One thing consoled me: my watch
was still ticking

it was 8:31! Only sixteen minutes
since the blast

I began counting my footsteps
timing my progress.

8:50 A.M. near Yokogawa Station:

Again
it came back to me: the sensation
this is happening in a dream—

the thatched roof on fire
the peasant and his wife
were carrying
a great laquered chest of drawers
they got stuck
in the doorway

no matter how they turned
and angled it
they couldn't come through

so they stood facing each other

the man taking a half-step to the left, slowly
the woman to the right
then back again
as if in a trance

a slow, solemn, mesmerizing dance
in the open doorway
as the cottage burned

nobody stopped to help them.

9:15 A.M., crossing Misasa Bridge:

From a distance
I could see only the woman, lying
on her side
half-blocking
the other end of the bridge

and the refugees, as they approached
her, hesitated

one turned back
and ran toward the burning city

"What is it?" I cried
but she didn't answer

"You'll get past this," I told myself
"if you don't look!"

but after counting a hundred steps
afraid
something bad was about to happen
I dropped my hands

and a baby girl
was undoing the buttons
of her mother's blouse

I drew close
and I saw
her clutch at the breasts of a corpse
she looked up at me
terrified

What could I possibly do for her?

"Go on," I said to my legs
"step over the body
and go on."

9:20 A.M., on the other side:

A girl my age
was standing with vacant eyes in the middle
of the road
the great wound in her forehead
like a pomegranate
cracked open

instinctively
I ran
my fingers across the skin
of my face

when I looked

down at my hands
there was blood on them

so I got the mirror
out of my emergency kit
and located
a small cut on my eyebrow

which I washed with spittle

then I
did up my hair
in a handkerchief
neatly
and went on.

9:40 A.M. at the bank of the Nagatsuka:

I was wearing a white blouse
with a blue pattern
miraculously it was free
of dirt
and it
didn't get torn

everyone else
was in rags and hurt
a woman
with the flesh of her side scooped out
and her ribs exposed
seeing me thread my way through the crowd
in my nice clothes
asked, "Can you help me?"

but a man came between us
and admonished her, saying, "Everyone
has the same pain as you.
Endure it
and we will find shelter."

4:30 P.M.

I reached my aunt's village

and I went to the river

to wash my clothes

the moment
I dipped my blouse in the water
it fell apart.

(She weeps. Jonah/Nakajima embraces her, as before.)

JONAH: Are you always this serious?

JOANNA: You want fun? Go bowling.
JONAH: If I shriek
who will hear me
if I don't
break the silence
          who will
hear me
if I speak normal
words in the normal
order

who will hear me

if I put myself on the road
from Hiroshima
and tell what I hear and see

will I disturb
the dead

will I
be a merchant of our disaster

if I fail
who will forgive me

(Blackout. Lights up on Nakajima DC. Boogie woogie piano plays underneath.)

NAKAJIMA: Instead of the usual rations
each of us was given seven cartons of
Wrigley's Spearmint Gum

we chewed
until the sugar was out of it
then spit it out

unfolding and working through
new sticks
at the rate of fifty an hour

I watched refugees
walk along, dropping
rubbery pellets

and silver
gum wrappers, ceaselessly
chewing.

When would they give us rice?
No one asked.
But how hopefully we greeted

each convoy of jeeps! the GIs beeped
in their good-natured way

there was a chorus of
"Hi!
How are you?"

and lines of frightened
beggars
immediately formed—

they were barraged with
Wrigley's
with a shower of

thousands of packs
of spearmint chewing
gum.

Already
the American century was carpeting Japan
with peculiar abundance

the road to the A-bomb ward
was now paved
with silver.

(Nakajima has picked up Jonah's shoes, and dances with them to the music.)

NAKAJIMA: *(over speakers):*
                   When the moment came
                   I bent down
                   and removed the shoes from the feet
                   of a woman not yet

                   dead.
                   Glass scattered on the road—
                   in bare feet
                   I would never have escaped

                   On the day I forget her
                   eyes
                   and begin to live
                   at peace with my memories

                   I will not recognize what
                   I am, pure
                   as a bone, and all my words
                   lies.

NAKAJIMA: And I ask myself:
                   will I ever again find anything
                   to celebrate?

                   Then I remember:

                   on the outskirts of the ruined city
                   all the houses collapsed
                   suddenly I was greeted by
                   dragonflies
                   flitting this way and that, so quickly, above
                   emerald fields
                   of rice

                   And I hated myself, realizing
                   that even on the day of horrors
                   I rejoiced!

(Old Woman appears at door in long white kimono. She sings.)

OLD WOMAN: I still keep two pillows
                   on your side of the bed
                   but instead of puffing them up every morning
                   my hands sink into them

                   and put back the impression

your head left
when you slipped noiselessly into the day
I was still asleep

when the bomb fell
and all that remained
of your body
was this hollow place.

Anyone who might have seen you die
also evaporated
I have no thought
of anything now but you.

You must have gone
from driving full speed across Aioi Bridge
to death
in an instant.

My hands sink into them
and put back the impression
your head left
when you slipped noiselessly into the day.

*(Lights out on Old Woman. During next poem, Nakajima removes kimono, puts
on Jonah's shirt. Joanna enters and sits, peeling an orange into a bowl.)*

NAKAJIMA: I had a visitor.
He told me
he was a scrivener
he told me
he was sorry for talking too much
and he told me
this story:

In Danbara Shin-machi
he came
upon four women at the side of the road
and he wouldn't have stopped
but

they were sitting in a circle
they were sitting and facing each other
in a circle
and this
struck him as a remarkable thing

more than that—
an act of resistance
something
like meditation
like women
in a temple courtyard

so he was drawn to them
and their eyes
unlike the eyes of other victims
their eyes were open
they were

looking into each other's eyes

and this
more than anything else he saw that day
kept death from ascendancy
everywhere

He asked one of them where her home was

she said, "This is my home.
I am Yoshiko, oldest daughter
of the poet
Nakajima Hiroshi. If you meet my father
tell him not to waste time
looking for me
or Nanae or Misa or Aunt Misao.
We are all going to die
right here."

The others nodded in agreement

then the tears came
and he was helpless before them

Yoshiko said, "If you would shield us   *(He builds a lean-*
from the sun   *to with the ladder,*
if you would find a way to shield us   *the slats and a piece*
from the wind   *of the bench left*
it would make us quite happy."   *on-stage from the*
                                                bombing section.)
So he built them a lean-to
of straw mats
and a few sheets of corrugated steel

and he went inside
and sat with them for a while

in his lunch box—three ripe tomatoes
which he sliced into halves
and he squeezed the juice onto the lips
and into the mouths
of my daughters   *(He hangs Naka-*
                                                             jima's kimono
and though they could barely swallow   *over the lean-to.)*
each one mumbled
"*Oishii!* delicious!"

(Joanna crosses to Jonah and embraces him. The voice of Nakajima comes over
speakers with other voices, singing.)

Rains will fall on the ruins
of the castle
as before

and trees will respond
each with its own kind of leaves
applauding the sun.

(While the song is playing, Joanna brings Jonah a slice of orange. He eats it as
they look at lean-to.)

JONAH: *(as song finishes)* Delicious! *(They look at each other. Blackout.)*

(Uncle Max enters UC.)

UNCLE MAX: No one told us: no

not the shoes you wore
to the state opera house

but the old boots
in the back of the closet—

and even then
you probably won't survive.

Here, retired admirals
speak against the arms race.

Scientists proclaim their warnings

on television.

You ask: How could we
go to our deaths like sleepwalkers?

But you of all people
should not ask.

(Jonah removes Uncle Max's hat and coat, takes down lantern. Joanna enters with
the blanket and lays it out like the table near the lean-to.)

JONAH: A great river runs through Hiroshima

BOTH: and every year
                    we bring lanterns
                    inscribed with the names of the family dead

(He places lantern on blanket and they kneel.)

                    and light them and set them afloat.

(He lights lantern.)

JOANNA: In Danbara Shin-machi
                    he came
                    upon four women by the side of the road
                    and he wouldn't have stopped
                    but
                    they were sitting in a circle

JONAH: they were sitting and facing each other
                    in a circle

JOANNA: and this
                    struck him as a remarkable thing

JONAH: more than that—
                    an act of resistance

JOANNA: And their eyes

JONAH: unlike the eyes of other victims

BOTH: their eyes were open

JONAH: they were sitting and
                  looking into each other's eyes

JOANNA: and this
                  more than anything else he saw that day

BOTH: kept death from ascendancy
                  everywhere.

Study and Discussion Questions

1. What are the two settings of *In the Traffic of a Targeted City*? What point is Kaminsky making by intersecting and juxtaposing these places and times?
2. *In the Traffic of a Targeted City* was first performed in 1986. How do the layers of meaning in the play deepen and expand when read today, in the wake of September 11, 2001?
3. How and why is there little or no time in New York City?
4. Who is Uncle Max? What does he add to the play?
5. Discuss the situation of Jonah and Joanna in New York City. What emotions do they experience? How do they cope with these? What is their sense of the future?
6. In Walkman's history class the teacher asks, "How do you prepare for nuclear war? Can it be done?" Discuss.
7. Are there elements of humor in this play? Give two or three examples. How does the humor function in the play?
8. What does the title of the play, *In the Traffic of a Targeted City*, mean to you?
9. Choose a story/poem from the Hiroshima sequences in the play and discuss.
10. Why do you think Kaminsky calls for all the parts to be played by only two actors?
11. Why do Jonah and Joanna put on kimonos halfway through the play?
12. Why are the four women sitting at the side of the road toward the end of the play seen as engaging in "an act of resistance"?
13. What parallels are there between atomic bombs dropping on Hiroshima and Nagasaki in 1945 and planes destroying the twin towers in New York City in 2001?
14. "The planet/ is now as difficult/ to maintain as an intimate/ relationship." What does this comment mean in the context of the play? Do you agree or disagree?

Suggestions for Writing

1. Select one of the following and write about its significance in the play: the subway in New York City, the river in Hiroshima, Nakajima's family dinner, the road from Hiroshima, Wrigley's spearmint chewing gum, shoes.

2. Select a pair of juxtaposed speeches and discuss how their placement next to each other heightens meaning. Example: Walkman's speech about preparing for nuclear war by making a tape of favorite songs and the speech soon after by Nakajima which begins, "even those/ who looked like they were going to be spared/ were not spared."

Critical Resources

1. In The Traffic of a Targeted City. Radio broadcast of the play, on Pacifica Radio. <http://www.pacifica.org/programs/flashpoints/flashpoints_050808.htm/#>
2. Kaminsky, Marc. *The Road from Hiroshima.* New York: Simon and Schuster, 1984.
3. Kaminsky, Marc. "Voicing Voicelessness: On the Poetics of Faith." *American Journal of Psychoanalysis* 58.4 (1998). 405–416.
4. Seldon, Mark & Kyoko Selden. *The Atomic Bomb: Voices from Hiroshima and Nagasaki.* Armonk, NY: M.E. Sharpe, 1989

NONFICTION

BLACK ELK (1863–1950)

Black Elk was born in what is now Wyoming, a Lakota Sioux of the Ogala tribe. The son of an Ogala medicine man, Black Elk would live through the final transition of an autonomous Sioux way of life to the reservation system of the United States government. At the age of nine, he had a "great vision"—a vivid, spiritual "calling" that advised him to follow in the ways of his shaman father in order to lead the Sioux to an era of peace. The experience would have a profound effect on his life and came to be known publicly decades later (1930) when John G. Neihardt, then the poet laureate of Nebraska and a student of Native American history, sought out the elderly Black Elk (now named "Nicholas" Black Elk after his conversion to Catholicism) to record an oral history of his life and the disappearing traditions of the Sioux. The transcripts of Neidhardt's meetings with Black Elk over the following year, in which Black Elk spoke of his life and the great vision, would be pieced together into a chronological narrative and published as Black Elk Speaks *in 1932. Although not recognized immediately by the public, since the publication of its second edition in 1961,* Black Elk Speaks *has become a key text in the canon of Native American literature. The excerpt presented here is the chapter entitled "The Butchering at Wounded Knee," Black Elk's account of the 1890 massacre of over 300 Native Americans by U.S. soldiers.*

The Butchering at Wounded Knee[1]   (1932)

That evening before it happened, I went in to Pine Ridge and heard these things, and while I was there, soldiers started for where the Big Foots were. These made about five hundred soldiers that were there next morning. When I saw them starting I felt that something terrible was going to happen. That night I could hardly sleep at all. I walked around most of the night.

In the morning I went out after my horses, and while I was out I heard shooting off toward the east, and I knew from the sound that it must be wagon-guns (cannon) going off. The sounds went right through my body, and I felt that something terrible would happen.

When I reached camp with the horses, a man rode up to me and said: "Hey-hey-hey! The people that are coming are fired on! I know it!"

I saddled up my buckskin and put on my sacred shirt. It was one I had made to be worn by no one but myself. It had a spotted eagle outstretched on the back

---

[1]South Dakota scene of the 1890 massacre described here.

of it, and the daybreak star was on the left shoulder, because when facing south that shoulder is toward the east. Across the breast, from the left shoulder to the right hip, was the flaming rainbow, and there was another rainbow around the neck, like a necklace, with a star at the bottom. At each shoulder, elbow, and wrist was an eagle feather, and over the whole shirt were red streaks of lightning. You will see that this was from my great vision, and you will know how it protected me that day.

I painted my face all red, and in my hair I put one eagle feather for the One Above.

It did not take me long to get ready, for I could still hear the shooting over there.

I started out alone on the old road that ran across the hills to Wounded Knee. I had no gun. I carried only the sacred bow of the west that I had seen in my great vision. I had gone only a little way when a band of young men came galloping after me. The first two who came up were Loves War and Iron Wasichu. I asked what they were going to do, and they said they were just going to see where the shooting was. Then others were coming up, and some older men.

We rode fast, and there were about twenty of us now. The shooting was getting louder. A horseback from over there came galloping very fast toward us, and he said: "Hey-hey-hey! They have murdered them!" Then he whipped his horse and rode away faster toward Pine Ridge.

In a little while we had come to the top of the ridge where, looking to the east, you can see for the first time the monument and the burying ground on the little hill where the church is. That is where the terrible thing started. Just south of the burying ground on the little hill a deep dry gulch runs about east and west, very crooked, and it rises westward to nearly the top of the ridge where we were. It had no name, but the Wasichus sometimes call it Battle Creek now. We stopped on the ridge not far from the head of the dry gulch. Wagon-guns were still going off over there on the little hill, and they were going off again where they hit along the gulch. There was much shooting down yonder, and there were many cries, and we could see cavalrymen scattered over the hills ahead of us. Cavalrymen were riding along the gulch and shooting into it, where the women and children were running away and trying to hide in the gullies and the stunted pines.

A little way ahead of us, just below the head of the dry gulch, there were some women and children who were huddled under a clay bank, and some cavalrymen were there pointing guns at them.

We stopped back behind the ridge, and I said to the others: "Take courage. These are our relatives. We will try to get them back." Then we all sang a song which went like this:

A thunder being nation I am, I have said.
A thunder being nation I am, I have said.
You shall live.
You shall live.
You shall live.
You shall live.

Then I rode over the ridge and the others after me, and we were crying: "Take courage! It is time to fight!" The soldiers who were guarding our relatives shot at us and then ran away fast, and some more cavalrymen on the other side of the gulch did too. We got our relatives and sent them across the ridge to the northwest where they would be safe.

I had no gun, and when we were charging, I just held the sacred bow out in front of me with my right hand. The bullets did not hit us at all.

We found a little baby lying all alone near the head of the gulch. I could not pick her up just then, but I got her later and some of my people adopted her. I just wrapped her up tighter in a shawl that was around her and left her there. It was a safe place, and I had other work to do.

The soldiers had run eastward over the hills where there were some more soldiers, and they were off their horses and lying down. I told the others to stay back, and I charged upon them holding the sacred bow out toward them with my right hand. They all shot at me, and I could hear bullets all around me, but I ran my horse right close to them, and then swung around. Some soldiers across the gulch began shooting at me too, but I got back to the others and was not hurt at all.

By now many other Lakotas, who had heard the shooting, were coming up from Pine Ridge, and we all charged on the soldiers. They ran eastward toward where the trouble began. We followed down along the dry gulch, and what we saw was terrible. Dead and wounded women and children and little babies were scattered all along there where they had been trying to run away. The soldiers had followed along the gulch, as they ran, and murdered them in there. Sometimes they were in heaps because they had huddled together, and some were scattered all along. Sometimes bunches of them had been killed and torn to pieces where the wagon-guns hit them. I saw a little baby trying to suck its mother, but she was bloody and dead.

There were two little boys at one place in this gulch. They had guns and they had been killing soldiers all by themselves. We could see the soldiers they had killed. The boys were all alone there, and they were not hurt. These were very brave little boys.

When we drove the soldiers back, they dug themselves in, and we were not enough people to drive them out from there. In the evening they marched off up Wounded Knee Creek, and then we saw all that they had done there.

Men and women and children were heaped and scattered all over the flat at the bottom of the little hill where the soldiers had their wagon-guns, and westward up the dry gulch all the way to the high ridge, the dead women and children and babies were scattered.

When I saw this I wished that I had died too, but I was not sorry for the women and children. It was better for them to be happy in the other world, and I wanted to be there too. But before I went there I wanted to have revenge. I thought there might be a day, and we should have revenge.

After the soldiers marched away, I heard from my friend, Dog Chief, how the trouble started, and he was right there by Yellow Bird when it happened. This is the way it was:

In the morning the soldiers began to take all the guns away from the Big Foots, who were camped in the flat below the little hill where the monument and burying ground are now. The people had stacked most of their guns, and even their knives, by the tepee where Big Foot was lying sick. Soldiers were on the little hill and all around, and there were soldiers across the dry gulch to the south and over east along Wounded Knee Creek too. The people were nearly surrounded, and the wagon-guns were pointing at them.

Some had not yet given up their guns, and so the soldiers were searching all the tepees, throwing things around and poking into everything. There was a man called Yellow Bird, and he and another man were standing in front of the tepee where Big Foot was lying sick. They had white sheets around and over them, with eyeholes to look through, and they had guns under these. An officer came to search them. He took the other man's gun, and then started to take Yellow Bird's. But Yellow Bird would not let go. He wrestled with the officer, and while they were wrestling, the gun went off and killed the officer. Wasichus and some others have said he meant to do this, but Dog Chief was standing right there, and he told me it was not so. As soon as the gun went off, Dog Chief told me, an officer shot and killed Big Foot who was lying sick inside the tepee.

Then suddenly nobody knew what was happening, except that the soldiers were all shooting and the wagon-guns began going off right in among the people.

Many were shot down right there. The women and children ran into the gulch and up west, dropping all the time, for the soldiers shot them as they ran. There were only about a hundred warriors and there were nearly five hundred soldiers. The warriors rushed to where they had piled their guns and knives. They fought soldiers with only their hands until they got their guns.

Dog Chief saw Yellow Bird run into a tepee with his gun, and from there he killed soldiers until the tepee caught fire. Then he died full of bullets.

It was a good winter day when all this happened. The sun was shining. But after the soldiers marched away from their dirty work, a heavy snow began to fall. The wind came up in the night. There was a big blizzard, and it grew very cold. The snow drifted deep in the crooked gulch, and it was one long grave of butchered women and children and babies, who had never done any harm and were only trying to run away.

Study and Discussion Questions

1. What is the narrator's tone? Does it change?
2. How is the narrative structured?
3. In the narrative, what is the significance of ritual? Of the natural environment?

Suggestions for Writing

1. What can we infer from "The Butchering at Wounded Knee" about the Native Americans' way of life?

2. Do some research on the history of Native Americans in the United States. What light does it shed on the narrative?
3. Though different in subject, "Mike Lefevre: Who Built the Pyramids?" (Money and Work) is also an oral history. Compare/contrast the two. Collect an oral history from a family member or person in your neighborhood.

Critical Resources

1. DeMallie, Raymond, ed. *The Sixth Grandfather: Black Elk's Teachings Given to John G. Neihardt.* Lincoln: University of Nebraska Press, 1984.
2. Holler, Clyde. *The Black Elk Reader.* Syracuse, NY: Syracuse University Press, 2000.
3. Holloway, Brian. *Interpreting the Legacy: John Neihardt and Black Elk Speaks.* Boulder: University of Colorado Press, 2003.

MARTIN LUTHER KING, JR. (1929–1968)

Martin Luther King, Jr. was born in Atlanta, Georgia, attended segregated schools, and enrolled at Morehouse College at age fifteen. Despite his religious upbringing (his father was a Baptist minister), King questioned the over-zealous Christianity of his father, developed his own brand of Christian belief and earned a Ph.D. in theology at Boston University. In 1954, King was appointed pastor of a church in Montgomery, Alabama and the next year, spurred by Rosa Parks's refusal to give up her bus seat to a white man, he led a boycott by African Americans of segregated buses. Two years later he became president of the new civil rights organization, the Southern Christian Leadership Conference, which would be instrumental in the Civil Rights Movement of the 1960s and the end of legal segregation. In 1963 he led a massive march (250,000 people) on Washington, D.C., where he delivered his speech, "I Have a Dream." The following year, at the age of 35, he was awarded the Nobel Prize for Peace for his commitment to non-violent protest. In both his passionate speeches and his writing, King's style appealed to the conscience of various classes of people through the crafting of rational arguments supported by potent metaphors: "If America's soul becomes totally poisoned, part of the autopsy must read Vietnam." King was assassinated in Memphis, Tennessee, in 1968 after giving a speech in support of striking sanitation workers. His books include Stride Toward Freedom *(1958),* Why We Can't Wait *(1964), and* Trumpet of Conscience *(1968). The preceding quote was taken from* A Time to Break Silence *(1967), in which King explains the connection between war and poverty.*

A Time to Break Silence[1]   (1967)

IMPORTANCE OF VIETNAM

Since I am a preacher by trade, I suppose it is not surprising that I have seven major reasons for bringing Vietnam into the field of my moral vision. There is at the outset a very obvious and almost facile connection between the war in Vietnam and the struggle I, and others, have been waging in America. A few years ago there was a shining moment in that struggle. It seemed as if there was a real promise of hope for the poor—both black and white—through the poverty program. There were experiments, hopes, new beginnings. Then came the buildup in Vietnam and I watched the program broken and eviscerated as if it were some idle political plaything of a society gone mad on war, and I knew that America would never invest the necessary funds or energies in rehabilitation of its poor so long as adventures like Vietnam continued to draw men and skills and money like some demonic destructive suction tube. So I was increasingly compelled to see the war as an enemy of the poor and to attack it as such.

Perhaps the more tragic recognition of reality took place when it became clear to me that the war was doing far more than devastating the hopes of the poor at home. It was sending their sons and their brothers and their husbands to fight and to die in extraordinarily high proportions relative to the rest of the population. We were taking the black young men who had been crippled by our society and sending them eight thousand miles away to guarantee liberties in Southeast Asia which they had not found in southwest Georgia and East Harlem. So we have been repeatedly faced with the cruel irony of watching Negro and white boys on TV screens as they kill and die together for a nation that has been unable to seat them together in the same schools. So we watch them in brutal solidarity burning the huts of a poor village, but we realize that they would never live on the same block in Detroit. I could not be silent in the face of such cruel manipulation of the poor.

My third reason moves to an even deeper level of awareness, for it grows out of my experience in the ghettos of the North over the last three years—especially the last three summers. As I have walked among the desperate, rejected and angry young men I have told them that Molotov cocktails and rifles would not solve their problems. I have tried to offer them my deepest compassion while maintaining my conviction that social change comes most meaningfully through nonviolent action. But they asked—and rightly so—what about Vietnam? They asked if our own nation wasn't using massive doses of violence to solve its problems, to bring about the changes it wanted. Their questions hit home, and I knew

---

[1]Speech delivered April 4, 1967, at the Riverside Church in New York City to Clergy and Laity Concerned, a group opposing the war in Vietnam.

that I could never again raise my voice against the violence of the oppressed in the ghettos without having first spoken clearly to the greatest purveyor of violence in the world today—my own government. For the sake of those boys, for the sake of this government, for the sake of the hundreds of thousands trembling under our violence, I cannot be silent.

For those who ask the question, "Aren't you a civil rights leader?" and thereby mean to exclude me from the movement for peace, I have this further answer. In 1957 when a group of us formed the Southern Christian Leadership Conference, we chose as our motto: "To save the soul of America." We were convinced that we could not limit our vision to certain rights for black people, but instead affirmed the conviction that America would never be free or saved from itself unless the descendants of its slaves were loosed completely from the shackles they still wear. In a way we were agreeing with Langston Hughes,[2] that black bard of Harlem, who had written earlier:

O, yes,
I say it plain,
America never was America to me,
And yet I swear this oath—
America will be!

Now, it should be incandescently clear that no one who has any concern for the integrity and life of America today can ignore the present war. If America's soul becomes totally poisoned, part of the autopsy must read Vietnam. It can never be saved so long as it destroys the deepest hopes of men the world over. So it is that those of us who are yet determined that America *will* be are led down the path of protest and dissent, working for the health of our land.

As if the weight of such a commitment to the life and health of America were not enough, another burden of responsibility was placed upon me in 1964; and I cannot forget that the Nobel Prize for Peace was also a commission—a commission to work harder than I had ever worked before for "the brotherhood of man." This is a calling that takes me beyond national allegiances, but even if it were not present I would yet have to live with the meaning of my commitment to the ministry of Jesus Christ. To me the relationship of this ministry to the making of peace is so obvious that I sometimes marvel at those who ask me why I am speaking against the war. Could it be that they do not know that the good news was meant for all men—for Communist and capitalist, for their children and ours, for black and for white, for revolutionary and conservative? Have they forgotten that my ministry is in obedience to the one who loved his enemies so fully that he died for them? What then can I say to the "Vietcong" or to Castro or to Mao as a faithful minister of this one? Can I threaten them with death or must I not share with them my life?

---

[2]American writer (1902–1967).

Finally, as I try to delineate for you and for myself the road that leads from Montgomery[3] to this place I would have offered all that was most valid if I simply said that I must be true to my conviction that I share with all men the calling to be a son of the living God. Beyond the calling of race or nation or creed is this vocation of sonship and brotherhood, and because I believe that the Father is deeply concerned especially for his suffering and helpless and outcast children, I come tonight to speak for them.

This I believe to be the privilege and the burden of all of us who deem ourselves bound by allegiances and loyalties which are broader and deeper than nationalism and which go beyond our nation's self-defined goals and positions. We are called to speak for the weak, for the voiceless, for victims of our nation and for those it calls enemy, for no document from human hands can make these humans any less our brothers.

STRANGE LIBERATORS

And as I ponder the madness of Vietnam and search within myself for ways to understand and respond to compassion my mind goes constantly to the people of that peninsula. I speak now not of the soldiers of each side, not of the junta in Saigon, but simply of the people who have been living under the curse of war for almost three continuous decades now. I think of them too because it is clear to me that there will be no meaningful solution there until some attempt is made to know them and hear their broken cries.

They must see Americans as strange liberators. The Vietnamese people proclaimed their own independence in 1945 after a combined French and Japanese occupation, and before the Communist revolution in China. They were led by Ho Chi Minh. Even though they quoted the American Declaration of Independence in their own document of freedom, we refused to recognize them. Instead, we decided to support France in its reconquest of her former colony.

Our government felt then that the Vietnamese people were not "ready" for independence, and we again fell victim to the deadly Western arrogance that has poisoned the international atmosphere for so long. With that tragic decision we rejected a revolutionary government seeking self-determination, and a government that had been established not by China (for whom the Vietnamese have no great love) but by clearly indigenous forces that included some Communists. For the peasants this new government meant real land reform, one of the most important needs in their lives.

For nine years following 1945 we denied the people of Vietnam the right of independence. For nine years we vigorously supported the French in their abortive effort to recolonize Vietnam.

---

[3]Alabama city where King led 1955 boycott to integrate city buses.

Before the end of the war we were meeting eighty per cent of the French war costs. Even before the French were defeated at Dien Bien Phu, they began to despair of the reckless action, but we did not. We encouraged them with our huge financial and military supplies to continue the war even after they had lost the will. Soon we would be paying almost the full costs of this tragic attempt at recolonization.

After the French were defeated it looked as if independence and land reform would come again through the Geneva agreements. But instead there came the United States, determined that Ho should not unify the temporarily divided nation, and the peasants watched again as we supported one of the most vicious modern dictators—our chosen man, Premier Diem. The peasants watched and cringed as Diem ruthlessly routed out all opposition, supported their extortionist landlords and refused even to discuss reunification with the north. The peasants watched as all this was presided over by U.S. influence and then by increasing numbers of U.S. troops who came to help quell the insurgency that Diem's methods had aroused. When Diem was overthrown they may have been happy, but the long line of military dictatorships seemed to offer no real change—especially in terms of their need for land and peace.

The only change came from America as we increased our troop commitments in support of governments which were singularly corrupt, inept and without popular support. All the while the people read our leaflets and received regular promises of peace and democracy—and land reform. Now they languish under our bombs and consider us—not their fellow Vietnamese—the real enemy. They move sadly and apathetically as we herd them off the land of their fathers into concentration camps where minimal social needs are rarely met. They know they must move or be destroyed by our bombs. So they go—primarily women and children and the aged.

They watch as we poison their water, as we kill a million acres of their crops. They must weep as the bulldozers roar through their areas preparing to destroy the precious trees. They wander into the hospitals, with at least twenty casualties from American firepower for one "Vietcong"-inflicted injury. So far we may have killed a million of them—mostly children. They wander into the towns and see thousands of the children, homeless, without clothes, running in packs on the streets like animals. They see the children degraded by our soldiers as they beg for food. They see the children selling their sisters to our soldiers, soliciting for their mothers.

What do the peasants think as we ally ourselves with the landlords and as we refuse to put any action into our many words concerning land reform? What do they think as we test out our latest weapons on them, just as the Germans tested out new medicine and new tortures in the concentration camps of Europe? Where are the roots of the independent Vietnam we claim to be building? Is it among these voiceless ones?

We have destroyed their two most cherished institutions: the family and the village. We have destroyed their land and their crops. We have cooperated in the crushing of the nation's only non-Communist revolutionary political force—

the unified Buddhist church. We have supported the enemies of the peasants of Saigon. We have corrupted their women and children and killed their men. What liberators!

Now there is little left to build on—save bitterness. Soon the only solid physical foundations remaining will be found at our military bases and in the concrete of the concentration camps we call fortified hamlets. The peasants may well wonder if we plan to build our new Vietnam on such grounds as these? Could we blame them for such thoughts? We must speak for them and raise the questions they cannot raise. These too are our brothers.

Perhaps the more difficult but no less necessary task is to speak for those who have been designated as our enemies. What of the National Liberation Front— that strangely anonymous group we call VC or Communists? What must they think of us in America when they realize that we permitted the repression and cruelty of Diem which helped to bring them into being as a resistance group in the south? What do they think of our condoning the violence which led to their own taking up of arms? How can they believe in our integrity when now we speak of "aggression from the north" as if there were nothing more essential to the war? How can they trust us when now we charge them with violence after the murderous reign of Diem and charge them with violence while we pour every new weapon of death into their land? Surely we must understand their feelings even if we do not condone their actions. Surely we must see that the men we supported pressed them to their violence. Surely we must see that our own computerized plans of destruction simply dwarf their greatest acts.

How do they judge us when our officials know that their membership is less than twenty-five percent Communist and yet insist on giving them the blanket name? What must they be thinking when they know that we are aware of their control of major sections of Vietnam and yet we appear ready to allow national elections in which this highly organized political parallel government will have no part? They ask how we can speak of free elections when the Saigon press is censored and controlled by the military junta. And they are surely right to wonder what kind of new government we plan to help form without them—the only party in real touch with the peasants. They question our political goals and they deny the reality of a peace settlement from which they will be excluded. Their questions are frighteningly relevant. Is our nation planning to build on political myth again and then shore it up with the power of new violence?

Here is the true meaning and value of compassion and nonviolence when it helps us to see the enemy's point of view, to hear his questions, to know his assessment of ourselves. For from his view we may indeed see the basic weaknesses of our own condition, and if we are mature, we may learn and grow and profit from the wisdom of the brothers who are called the opposition.

So, too, with Hanoi. In the north, where our bombs now pummel the land, and our mines endanger the waterways, we are met by a deep but understandable mistrust. To speak for them is to explain this lack of confidence in Western words, and especially their distrust of American intentions now. In Hanoi are the men who led the nation to independence against the Japanese and the French, the men who sought membership in the French commonwealth and were betrayed by the weakness of Paris and the willfulness of the colonial armies. It was they who led a second struggle against French domination at tremendous costs, and then were persuaded to give up the land they controlled between the thirteenth and seventeenth parallels as a temporary measure at Geneva. After 1954 they watched us conspire with Diem to prevent elections which would have surely brought Ho Chi Minh to power over a united Vietnam, and they realized they had been betrayed again.

When we ask why they do not leap to negotiate, these things must be remembered. Also it must be clear that the leaders of Hanoi considered the presence of American troops in support of the Diem regime to have been the initial military breach of the Geneva agreements concerning foreign troops, and they remind us that they did not begin to send in any large number of supplies or men until American forces had moved into the tens of thousands.

Hanoi remembers how our leaders refused to tell us the truth about the earlier North Vietnamese overtures for peace, how the president claimed that none existed when they had clearly been made. Ho Chi Minh has watched as America has spoken of peace and built up its forces, and now he has surely heard of the increasing international rumors of American plans for an invasion of the north. He knows the bombing and shelling and mining we are doing are part of traditional pre-invasion strategy. Perhaps only his sense of humor and of irony can save him when he hears the most powerful nation of the world speaking of aggression as it drops thousands of bombs on a poor weak nation more than eight thousand miles away from its shores.

At this point I should make it clear that while I have tried in these last few minutes to give a voice to the voiceless on Vietnam and to understand the arguments of those who are called enemy, I am as deeply concerned about our troops there as anything else. For it occurs to me that what we are submitting them to in Vietnam is not simply the brutalizing process that goes on in any war where armies face each other and seek to destroy. We are adding to the process of death, for they must know after a short period there that none of the things we claim to be fighting for are really involved. Before long they must know that their government has sent them into a struggle among Vietnamese, and the more sophisticated surely realize that we are on the side of the wealthy and the secure while we create a hell for the poor.

Somehow this madness must cease. We must stop now. I speak as a child of God and brother to the suffering poor of Vietnam. I speak for those whose land is being laid waste, whose homes are being destroyed, whose culture is being subverted. I speak for the poor of America who are paying the double price of smashed hopes at home and death and corruption in Vietnam. I speak as a citizen of the world, for the world as it stands aghast at the path we have taken. I speak as an American to the leaders of my own nation. The great initiative in this war is ours. The initiative to stop it must be ours.

Study and Discussion Questions

1. What are King's "seven major reasons for bringing Vietnam into the field of [his] moral vision"?
2. What does he mean when he calls Americans the "strange liberators"?
3. Why does King have a number of paragraphs composed entirely or mostly of questions? From whose perspective are these questions asked? Is there an ethical or moral purpose behind this rhetorical device? Is it effective?
4. What are the assumptions underlying his argument that the United States must stop military involvement in Vietnam?

Suggestions for Writing

1. Select one paragraph in this speech and analyze it in detail. What is the main point or thesis of the paragraph? What are the supporting evidence and secondary points?
2. Choose a contemporary war or armed conflict the United States is engaged in and apply King's argument to it.
3. If you were to construct an argument against King's position in "A Time to Break Silence," what would your major points be? Come up with at least five.

Critical Resources

1. Bogumil, Mary. "Pretext, Context, Subtext: Textual Power in the Writing of Langston Hughes, Richard Wright and MLK Jr." *College English* 52.7 (1990): 800–11.
2. Ling, Peter. *Martin Luther King Jr.* London: Routledge, 2002.
3. Sharman, Nick. "Remaining Awake Through a Great Revolution: The Rhetorical Strategies of Martin Luther King Jr." *Social Semiotics* 9.1 (1999): 85–105.
4. Stull, Bradford. *Amid the Fall, Dreaming of Eden: Du Bois, Malcolm X and Emancipatory Composition.* Carbondale: Southern Illinois University Press, 1999.
5. Warren, Mervyn. *King Came Preaching: The Pulpit Power of Martin Luther King Jr.* Downers Grove, IL: Inter Varsity Press, 2001.

MARJANE SATRAPI (b. 1969)

Marjane Satrapi was born in Iran. After living through the fall of the Shah and the rise of fundamentalist Islam in Iran, her family moved her to Vienna when Marjane was 14 years old to protect her from Iran's newly oppressive government. After studying illustration in Strasbourg, France, she moved to Paris, where she published her acclaimed graphic novel Persepolis: The Story of a Childhood *in 2003.* Persepolis *is autobiographical in nature, told from the point of view of*

Satrapi as a child in the turbulent Iran of the 1970s. As she has noted in several in-
terviews, her goal was to tell (and show) a more complex version of Iranian life
that was largely neglected by the European media. When asked by the Seattle Post-
Intelligencer *why she chose to write her story in the form of a graphic novel,*
Satrapi replied, "That is my way of expressing myself, and I think the pictures, they
say always more than the words can say. Also, in pictures, they help me to have the
distance without becoming cynical, and be able to describe a part of the story with
humor—which I couldn't do otherwise" (2003). Satrapi's distinct black and white
illustrations (in the style of the woodcut) starkly shift from frame to frame, ex-
ploring the confusion of the 10- to 14-year-old narrator as she and her family grap-
ple with the impact of the Iranian Revolution. Often compared to Art Speigleman's
award winning graphic novel Maus *(first published in book form in 1986),*
Persepolis *has met with both public and critical success. Satrapi followed with*
Persepolis 2: The Story of a Return *in 2004. Her latest work,* Embroideries, *was*
published in 2005.

FROM *Persepolis*   (2003)

Introduction

In the second millennium B.C., while the Elam nation was developing a civilization alongside Babylon, Indo-European invaders gave their name to the immense Iranian plateau where they settled. The word "Iran" was derived from
"Ayryana Vaejo," which means "the origin of the Aryans." These people were
semi-nomads whose descendants were the Medes and the Persians. The Medes
founded the first Iranian nation in the seventh century B.C.; it was later destroyed by Cyrus the Great. He established what became one of the largest empires of the ancient world, the Persian Empire, in the sixth century B.C. Iran was
referred to as Persia—its Greek name—until 1935 when Reza Shah, the father
of the last Shah of Iran, asked everyone to call the country Iran.

Iran was rich. Because of its wealth and its geographic location, it invited attacks: From Alexander the Great, from its Arab neighbors to the west, from
Turkish and Mongolian conquerors, Iran was often subject to foreign domination. Yet the Persian language and culture withstood these invasions. The invaders assimilated into this strong culture, and in some ways they became
Iranians themselves.

In the twentieth century, Iran entered a new phase. Reza Shah decided to
modernize and westernize the country, but meanwhile a fresh source of wealth
was discovered: oil. And with the oil came another invasion. The West, particularly Great Britain, wielded a strong influence on the Iranian economy. During
the Second World War, the British, Soviets, and Americans asked Reza Shah to
ally himself with them against Germany. But Reza Shah, who sympathized with

the Germans, declared Iran a neutral zone. So the Allies invaded and occupied Iran. Reza Shah was sent into exile and was succeeded by his son, Mohammad Reza Pahlavi, who was known simply as the Shah.

In 1951, Mohammed Mossadeq, then prime minister of Iran, nationalized the oil industry. In retaliation, Great Britain organized an embargo on all exports of oil from Iran. In 1953, the CIA, with the help of British intelligence, organized a coup against him. Mossadeq was overthrown and the Shah, who had earlier escaped from the country, returned to power. The Shah stayed on the throne until 1979, when he fled Iran to escape the Islamic revolution.

Since then, this old and great civilization has been discussed mostly in connection with fundamentalism, fanaticism, and terrorism. As an Iranian who has lived more than half of my life in Iran, I know that this image is far from the truth. This is why writing *Persepolis* was so important to me. I believe that an entire nation should not be judged by the wrongdoings of a few extremists. I also don't want those Iranians who lost their lives in prisons defending freedom, who died in the war against Iraq, who suffered under various repressive regimes, or who were forced to leave their families and flee their homeland to be forgotten.

One can forgive but one should never forget.

Marjane Satrapi
Paris, September 2002

THE DOWRY

AFTER THE DEATH OF NEDA BABA-LEVY, MY LIFE TOOK A NEW TURN. IN 1984, I WAS FOURTEEN AND A REBEL. NOTHING SCARED ME ANYMORE.

I'VE TOLD YOU A HUNDRED TIMES THAT IT IS STRICTLY FORBIDDEN TO WEAR JEWELRY AND JEANS!

WHAT ARE YOU DOING WITH THAT BRACELET? GIVE IT TO ME RIGHT NOW!

OVER MY DEAD BODY! IT WAS A GIFT FROM MY MOM.

I HAD LEARNED THAT YOU SHOULD ALWAYS SHOUT LOUDER THAN YOUR AGGRESSOR.

IF YOU'RE STILL WEARING JEWELRY TOMORROW...

YEAH, I KNOW!

AND THE NEXT DAY...

LET ME SEE YOUR WRIST.

WHAT FOR?

LET ME SEE IT, I'M TELLING YOU.

WITH ALL THE JEWELRY YOU STEAL FROM US, YOU MUST BE MAKING A PILE OF MONEY.

WHAT HAPPENED?

MARJI HIT THE PRINCIPAL

SHE'S FINISHED!

EXCUSE ME! I DIDN'T MEAN IT!

SATRAPI, YOU'RE EXPELLED!

OBVIOUSLY, THAT EVENING MY FATHER GOT A PHONE CALL.

YES. OF COURSE...YES...

WHO IS IT?

IT WAS THE PRINCIPAL OF MARJI'S SCHOOL. APPARENTLY SHE TOLD OFF THE RELIGION TEACHER. SHE GETS THAT FROM HER UNCLE.

MAYBE YOU'D LIKE HER TO END UP LIKE HIM TOO? EXECUTED?

YOU KNOW WHAT THEY DO TO THE YOUNG GIRLS THEY ARREST?

YOU KNOW WHAT HAPPENED TO NILOUFAR? THE GIRL YOU MET AT KHOSRO'S HOUSE? THE MAN WHO MADE PASSPORTS?

YOU KNOW THAT IT'S AGAINST THE LAW TO KILL A VIRGIN...

SO A GUARDIAN OF THE REVOLUTION MARRIES HER...

...AND TAKES HER VIRGINITY BEFORE EXECUTING HER. DO YOU UNDERSTAND WHAT THAT MEANS???

IF SOMEONE SO MUCH AS TOUCHES A HAIR ON YOUR HEAD, I'LL KILL HIM!

BUT HOW DO YOU KNOW THAT FOR SURE? MAYBE THEY JUST EXECUTED HER!

NO. YOUR MOTHER'S RIGHT. TRADITIONALLY, WHEN A GIRL GETS MARRIED, THE HUSBAND IS SUPPOSED TO PAY HER A DOWRY.

IF THE GIRL DIES, THE HUSBAND HAS TO GIVE THE DOWRY TO HER FAMILY.

THAT'S WHAT HAPPENED WITH NILOUFAR. AFTER SHE WAS EXECUTED, TO MAKE SURE HER AWFUL FATE WAS UNDERSTOOD, THEY SENT 500 TUMANS* TO HER PARENTS.

500 TUMANS FOR THE LIFE AND VIRGINITY OF AN INNOCENT GIRL.

I HAD NO IDEA.

*EQUIVALENT TO $5.00

ALL NIGHT LONG, I THOUGHT OF THAT PHRASE: "TO DIE A MARTYR IS TO INJECT BLOOD INTO THE VEINS OF SOCIETY." NILOUFAR WAS A REAL MARTYR, AND HER BLOOD CERTAINLY DID NOT FEED OUR SOCIETY'S VEINS.

ONE WEEK LATER...

MARJI, CAN YOU COME HERE FOR A FEW MINUTES? WE WANT TO TALK TO YOU.

I WENT TO SEE THE PRINCIPAL TODAY. SHE ASSURED ME THAT SHE HAD NOT SENT A REPORT THIS TIME. BUT CONSIDERING THE PERSON YOU ARE AND THE EDUCATION YOU'VE RECEIVED, WE THOUGHT THAT IT WOULD BE BETTER IF YOU LEFT IRAN.

WHAT?

YOUR MOTHER AND I HAVE DECIDED TO SEND YOU TO AUSTRIA.

WHY AUSTRIA?

FIRST OF ALL, BECAUSE IT'S EASIER TO GET AN AUSTRIAN VISA, AND SECOND BECAUSE MY BEST FRIEND LIVES IN VIENNA. DO YOU REMEMBER HER? ZOZO? SHERINE'S MOM?

YEAH, YEAH, BUT I DON'T SPEAK GERMAN!

THERE'S A FRENCH SCHOOL IN VIENNA. ONE OF THE BEST IN EUROPE!

AND WHAT ARE YOU GOING TO DO THERE?

YOU'RE GOING ON AHEAD OF US. WE HAVE SOME BUSINESS TO TAKE CARE OF. WE'LL JOIN YOU A FEW MONTHS FROM NOW!

BUT I'M ONLY FOURTEEN! YOU TRUST ME?

YOU'RE FOURTEEN AND I KNOW HOW I BROUGHT YOU UP. ABOVE ALL, TRUST YOUR EDUCATION.

YOU'RE THE SAME PERSON WHO WENT ON VACA-
TION TO FRANCE ALL BY YOURSELF, REMEMBER?

BEFORE THE REVOLUTION, MY PARENTS SENT ME
TO SUMMER CAMP IN FRANCE. MY MOTHER DIDN'T
WANT ME TO GROW UP LIKE AN ONLY CHILD.

IT'S TRUE, THAT WAS
GREAT...REAL INDEPENDENCE.

WE LOVE YOU SO MUCH THAT
WE WANT YOU TO GO.

WE FEEL IT'S BETTER FOR
YOU TO BE FAR AWAY AND
HAPPY THAN CLOSE BY AND
MISERABLE. JUDGING BY THE
SITUATION HERE, YOU'LL BE
BETTER OFF SOMEWHERE ELSE.

AT THAT POINT, I STARTED TO HAVE MY DOUBTS.
WHY SAY THOSE THINGS IF THEY WERE COMING TOO?

WE ADORE YOU!

DON'T EVER FORGET
WHO YOU ARE!

NO. I WON'T EVER FORGET.

I REPEATED WHAT THEY HAD TOLD ME OVER AND OVER IN MY HEAD. I WAS PRETTY SURE THEY WEREN'T COMING TO VIENNA.

I STAYED UP ALL NIGHT AND WONDERED IF THE MOON SHONE AS BRIGHTLY IN VIENNA.

THE NEXT DAY I FILLED A JAR WITH SOIL FROM OUR GARDEN. IRANIAN SOIL.

I TOOK DOWN ALL OF MY POSTERS.

KIM WI

I INVITED MY GIRLFRIENDS OVER TO SAY GOODBYE.

HERE. I'M GIVING YOU MY MOST PRECIOUS THINGS, SO THAT YOU WON'T FORGET ME.

I NEVER REALIZED HOW MUCH THEY LOVED ME.

AND I UNDERSTOOD HOW IMPORTANT THEY WERE TO ME.

ON THE EVE OF MY DEPARTURE, MY GRANDMOTHER CAME TO SPEND THE NIGHT AT OUR HOUSE.

CAN I SLEEP WITH YOU?

THAT'S WHY I'M HERE!

I WATCHED MY GRANDMA UNDRESS. EACH MORNING, SHE PICKED JASMINE FLOWERS TO PUT IN HER BRA SO THAT SHE WOULD SMELL NICE. WHEN SHE UNDRESSED, YOU COULD SEE THE FLOWERS FALL FROM HER BREASTS.

IT WAS SOMETHING TO SEE

GRANDMA, HOW DO YOU HAVE SUCH ROUND BREASTS AT YOUR AGE?

EVERY MORNING AND NIGHT, I SOAK THEM IN A BOWL OF ICE WATER FOR TEN MINUTES.

SHE ACTUALLY DID, AND I KNEW IT. I JUST WANTED TO HEAR HER SAY IT.

I'LL MISS YOU.

OH, I'LL COME SEE YOU.

SHE TOO WAS LYING TO ME.

LISTEN, I DON'T WANT TO PREACH, BUT LET ME GIVE YOU SOME ADVICE THAT WILL ALWAYS HELP YOU.

IN LIFE YOU'LL MEET A LOT OF JERKS. IF THEY HURT YOU, TELL YOURSELF THAT IT'S BECAUSE THEY'RE STUPID. THAT WILL HELP KEEP YOU FROM REACTING TO THEIR CRUELTY. BECAUSE THERE IS NOTHING WORSE THAN BITTERNESS AND VENGEANCE... ALWAYS KEEP YOUR DIGNITY AND BE TRUE TO YOURSELF.

I SMELLED MY GRANDMA'S BOSOM. IT SMELLED GOOD. I'LL NEVER FORGET THAT SMELL.

Study and Discussion Questions

1. Why is this story (a chapter from Satrapi's graphic memoir *Persepolis*) called "The Dowry"? Look up the word in a large dictionary. Discuss the specific part of the story where "dowry" comes up. How is the dowry both horrible and ironic? How does it precipitate the decision of Marjane's parents?

2. Why is Marjane being sent to Austria? Why are so many young boys also leaving Iran at this time?

3. What do you learn about the situation in Iran during this period? How do the 13- or so year-old Marjane and her friends want to live? What are they forbidden to do? Locate specific visual images that convey this.

4. What do you learn about the political and the social class position of Marjane's family? Beyond Marjane's own behavior, how does the situation of her family make her unsafe?

5. Why does Marjane think Niloufar is "a real martyr"? What is the difference between Niloufar's martyrdom and that of the other martyrs Marjane is thinking of?

6. Describe and discuss Marjane's farewell night with her grandmother, both the visual images and the verbal text. What does Marjane gain from this time with her grandmother?

7. Why do you think Marjane's parents tell her they will be coming to Austria a few months after her? What makes it clear to her that they will not?

8. Why do Marjane's parents repeatedly tell her not to forget who she is and where she comes from?

9. Describe and discuss Satrapi's drawings and the predominant graphic elements in "The Dowry": line, color, perspective, shading, placement of words on the page, the way the characters are drawn.

10. Which panels stand out the most for you? Why do you think these are significant? What elements of the drawings and text make these panels memorable?

11. "The Dowry," which is the last chapter and therefore the conclusion of *Persepolis,* ends with a visual image and little written text. What elements does Satrapi utilize in the final panel? What is the most striking visual element for you? What does this convey that Satrapi could not write? Is the issue that Satrapi could not write it, or that the visual element conveys it better? Could someone else have *written* it better? *Drawn* it better? Does it matter? Why do these questions come up around the graphic novel/memoir?

Suggestions for Writing

1. Choose one panel from "The Dowry" and analyze the way the visual and verbal elements work together. Look at her use of line, color, perspective, shading, placement of words on the page. How does the panel you have chosen advance the narrative?

2. Read another graphic novel or memoir (Spiegelman's *Maus* (1986) is a good choice, since it is also a graphic memoir) and compare/contrast the visual and verbal style. Or compare with Harvey Pekar's "Hypothetical

Quandary" (Money and Work). You could choose one panel from each artist/writer to analyze.

3. Read the rest of Satrapi's book length *Persepolis;* write a paper about how "The Dowry" concludes this first volume of her memoir. Satrapi published the second volume, *Persepolis 2,* in 2004, if you want to go on with her story.

4. Research the Islamic Revolution and the overthrow of the Shah in Iran and write about the experiences of girls like Marjane during and after the revolution.

Critical Resources

1. Hadju, David. "Persian Miniatures." *The Review for Art, Fiction and Culture* 11.3 (2004): 32–35.

2. "Illustrator Marjane Satrapi." *NPR.* <http://www.npr.org/templates/story/story.php?storyId=128352>. A 20-minute audio interview from the radio show "Fresh Air."

3. Satrapi, Marjane. "Why I Wrote Persepolis." *Writing* 26.3 (2003): 9–12.

4. Storace, Patricia. "A Double Life in Black and White." *New York Review of Books* 52.6 (4/7/05), 40–43.

5. Tabachnick, Steven. "A Course in the Graphic Novel." *Readerly/Writerly Texts; Essays on Literature, Literary/Textual Criticism, and Pedagogy* 1.2 (1994): 141–55.

BRIAN DOYLE (b. 1956)

Born in New York, Brian Doyle graduated from the University of Notre Dame and worked on magazines and newspapers in Boston and Chicago before becoming editor of Portland Magazine *at the University of Portland, in Oregon. He writes on a variety of topics, including literature, music, and Catholic spirituality. Through a personal style of writing, Doyle's perceptive eye and hold on the language seeks to discover the beauty present in even the simplest of human acts. He is the author of five collections of essays, including* Leaping: Revelations and Epiphanies *(2003),* Spirited Men: Story, Soul and Substance *(2004), and his latest collection* Wet Engine *(2005), a book about the "muddle & mangle & murk & music & miracle" of hearts. His poetry and essays have also appeared in such publications as* American Scholar, U.S. Catholic, Atlantic Monthly, *and* The Best American Essays *(1998, 1999, 2003, and 2005). In addition to his work at* Portland Magazine, *Doyle is also a columnist for* Eureka Street *magazine in Melbourne, Australia. In regards to "Leap," written about the September 11, 2001 destruction of the World Trade Center towers, Doyle writes, "I knew three of the men roasted in the towers and 'Leap' is a continuing prayer for them and all of us, including the haunted murderers and those who love them."*

Leap   (2002)

A couple leaped from the south tower, hand in hand. They reached for each other and their hands met and they jumped.

Jennifer Brickhouse saw them falling, hand in hand.

Many people jumped. Perhaps hundreds. No one knows. They struck the pavement with such force that there was a pink mist in the air.

The mayor reported the mist.

A kindergarten boy who saw people falling in flames told his teacher that the birds were on fire. She ran with him on her shoulders out of the ashes.

Tiffany Keeling saw fireballs falling that she later realized were people. Jennifer Griffin saw people falling and wept as she told the story. Niko Winstral saw people free-falling backwards with their hands out, like they were parachuting. Joe Duncan on his roof on Duane Street looked up and saw people jumping. Henry Weintraub saw people "leaping as they flew out." John Carson saw six people fall, "falling over themselves, falling, they were somersaulting." Steve Miller saw people jumping from a thousand feet in the air. Kirk Kjeldsen saw people flailing on the way down, people lining up and jumping, "too many people falling." Jane Tedder saw people leaping and the sight haunts her at night. Steve Tamas counted fourteen people jumping and then he stopped counting. Stuart DeHann saw one woman's dress billowing as she fell, and he saw a shirtless man falling end over end, and he too saw the couple leaping hand in hand.

Several pedestrians were killed by people falling from the sky. A fireman was killed by a body falling from the sky.

But he reached for her hand and she reached for his hand and they leaped out the window holding hands.

I try to whisper prayers for the sudden dead and the harrowed families of the dead and the screaming souls of the murderers but I keep coming back to his hand and her hand nestled in each other with such extraordinary ordinary succinct ancient naked stunning perfect simple ferocious love.

Their hands reaching and joining are the most powerful prayer I can imagine, the most eloquent, the most graceful. It is everything that we are capable of against horror and loss and death. It is what makes me believe that we are not craven fools and charlatans to believe in God, to believe that human beings have greatness and holiness within them like seeds that open only under great fires, to believe that some unimaginable essence of who we are persists past the dissolution of what we were, to believe against such evil hourly evidence that love is why we are here.

No one knows who they were: husband and wife, lovers, dear friends, colleagues, strangers thrown together at the window there at the lip of hell. Maybe they didn't even reach for each other consciously, maybe it was instinctive, a reflex, as they both decided at the same time to take two running steps and jump out the shattered window, but they *did* reach for each other, and they held on tight, and leaped, and fell endlessly into the smoking canyon, at two hundred miles an hour, falling so far and so fast that they would have blacked out before they hit the pavement near Liberty Street so hard that there was a pink mist in the air.

Jennifer Brickhouse saw them holding hands, and Stuart DeHann saw them holding hands, and I hold onto that.

Study and Discussion Questions

1. What is the tone of this essay? How does Doyle use pacing, syntax, repetition, and other elements of form and language to create this tone? Does the tone change?
2. Doyle repeats the words *fall, leap,* and *jump* many times throughout "Leap." What effect does this particular repetition have?
3. Why does Doyle keep coming back to the two people holding hands? What do they represent for him? Why does he speculate on their relationship to each other?
4. How do the experiences recounted here reinforce the narrator's faith in God? What other kinds of faith does it reinforce for him?
5. What is the effect of the author's use of eyewitness accounts? Why does Doyle choose to open and close the piece this way?

Suggestions for Writing

1. Write about your own recollections of September 11, 2001. You could discuss your own emotional response to the images of people jumping from the World Trade Center towers. Or you could choose an image from that day that stays in your memory and somehow symbolizes the event for you. Try to use word choices and an overall structure for your writing that conveys the complexity and depth of your response.
2. Compare/contrast "Leap" with Mary Fell's poetic sequence, "The Triangle Fire," in which 146 workers had to make a similar choice about whether to jump from a lethal height to escape a burning factory. How are both "Leap" and "The Triangle Fire" writings of "witness"?

Critical Resources

1. Cohen, Allen and Clive Matson, eds. *An Eye for an Eye Makes the Whole World Blind: Poets on 9/11.* Oakland, CA: Regent Press, 2002.
2. "Frontline: Faith and Doubt at Ground Zero." *PBS.org.* May 1, 2005. <http://www.pbs.org/wgbh/pages/frontline/shows/faith/questions/leap .html>. Online text of poem.

3. Heyen, William, ed. *September 11, 2001: American Writers Respond.* Silver Springs, MD: Etruscan Press, 2002. Includes poetry and essays by Lucille Clifton, Joy Harjo, John Updike, and others.
4. Rothberg, Michael. "There is no Poetry in This: Writing, Trauma, and Home." *Trauma At Home: After 9/11.* Ed. Judith Greenberg. Lincoln: University of Nebraska Press, 2003.
5. Stern, Rebecca. " 'A Use in Measured Language': Poetry and Poetic Criticism after September 11." *Victorian Poetry* 41.4 (2003): 636–42.

Peace and War: Paper Topics

1. Analyze in detail the way one work conveys the fragility of peace. (Suggestions: Rukeyser, "Waking This Morning"; Atwood, "At first I was given centuries"; Yousif al-sa'igh, "An Iraqi Evening")
2. Compare the descriptions of battle in two or more works. (Suggestions: Owen, "Dulce et Decorum Est"; Black Elk, "The Butchering at Wounded Knee"; Tennyson, "The Charge of the Light Brigade")
3. Pick two works, one supporting and one opposing war, that seem to be in dialogue with each other; analyze the argument implicit (or explicit) in each and the literary devices used to persuade the reader. (Suggestions: Lovelace, "To Lucasta, Going to the Wars" and cummings, "next to of course god America i")
4. Discuss the ways people cope with the memory of war. (Suggestions: Erdrich, "The Red Convertible"; Whitman, "The Dying Veteran"; Morrison, "1919"; Doyle, "Leap")
5. Discuss the consequences of war for individuals or communities in one or more works. (Suggestions: Kaminsky, "In the Traffic of a Targeted City"; O'Brien, "The Man I Killed"; Karafani, "Letter from Gaza")
6. Discuss in one or more works the various strategies for survival used by the people involved, either willingly or unwillingly, in war. (Suggestions: Kaminsky, "In the Traffic of a Targeted City"; Yevtushenko, "The Companion"; Rich, "The School Among the Ruins")
7. Discuss the relationship between those who kill and those who are killed in one or more works. (Suggestions: O'Brien, "The Man I Killed"; Weigl, "Song of Napalm"; Forche, "The Colonel")

8. Analyze one or more works that explore why people go to war. (Suggestions: Lovelace, "For Lucasta, Going to the Wars"; Yeats, "An Irish Airman Foresees His Death"; Son, "Can Tho"; Atwood, "The Loneliness of the Military Historian"; Herdi, "God's Freedom Fighters")

9. Choose two or more works whose subject is the same war and compare their perspectives on that war.

10. Is there a difference between male and female perspectives on war? Support your argument with reference to at least two works by men and at least two by women.

11. Discuss the way an individual's race or social class affects his or her relation to war in one or more works. (Suggestions: Okita, "In Response to Executive Order 9066 . . ."; King, "A Time to Break Silence"; Brecht, "From a German War Primer"; Dodson, "Black Mother Praying"; Satrapi, "The Dowry")

12. Discuss the psychology of those who make war, as depicted in one or more works. (Suggestions: Barthelme, "Report"; Reed, "Naming of Parts")

13. Analyze how formal elements such as character, setting, point of view, and sequencing of events make meaning in one or more stories. (Suggestions: Bradbury, "August 2026: There Will Come Soft Rains"; Bierce, "An Occurrence at Owl Creek Bridge"; Erdrich, "The Red Convertible")

14. Explicate one poem about war that particularly moves you. How does the poet use imagery, sound, and perhaps perspective to convey an experience, create a mood, and/or argue a position?

15. Compare two works that are about different wars (either the experience of war itself or the aftermath of that war). What is similar and what is different about the experience of war for the inhabitants of those works? (Suggestions: Weigl, "Song of Napalm" and Owens, "Dulce et Decorum Est"; Sassoon, "Does It Matter?" and McGrath, "Reading The Names of the Vietnam War Dead")

16. Compare the experience of children in wartime in two or more works. (Suggestions: Yevtushenko, "The Companion"; Satrapi, "The Dowry"; Rich, "The School Among the Ruins"; Bekes Jr, "Picture")

VARIETIES OF PROTEST

Fundamentally, to protest means to say "no." The stories, essays, speeches, poems, plays, and songs in this section present a vivid and extensive variety of ways to say no to injustice, oppression, and lack of choice. Some of the protests written about here succeed; some don't. In some cases we don't know the outcome. Some are protests by groups of people; some come from individuals. Many concern issues touched upon throughout this anthology: slavery and its legacy of racism; poor working conditions, low pay, job discrimination, and other forms of economic oppression; sexism and heterosexism; war. What characterizes the selections here is that they are as much about the act of protest as they are about the issues protested.

With a few exceptions (Sophocles, Yeats, Soyinka, Neruda) the literary works in this section are from the United States. The fact that our national history began in protest and that the United States was founded in revolution with proclamations of equality and justice for all is the irony at the center of several of the selections included here. In his famous speech, "I Have a Dream," delivered at the 1963 March on Washington for Jobs and Freedom, Martin Luther King, Jr., sees the Constitution and the Declaration of Independence as promissory notes that America has defaulted on where black Americans are concerned. (See a photo of this protest at the beginning of this section.) More than a century earlier, John Greenleaf Whittier, in his abolitionist poem "For Righteousness' Sake," writes that "The brave old strife the fathers saw/ For Freedom calls for men again" and worries that his own era has become complacent and indifferent to injustice, "dull and mean."

Because slavery and racism have been our most glaring national shame, much American protest literature has been concerned with these issues. In an excerpt from one of the few slave narratives written by a woman, *Incidents in the Life of a Slave Girl*, Harriet Jacobs writes about some of the suffering she endured to escape from slavery. Margaret Walker's prose poem "For My People," written almost a hundred years after Jacobs's narrative, details Walker's love for her people, her sense of their suffering, America's continuing history of racism, and how far we have yet to go. Equally barbaric in American history has been the destruction of Native American cultures; a powerful literature of self-assertion and protest by Native American poets, storytellers and fiction writers, essayists, and filmmakers has at last begun to be available. Sherman Alexie's poem "The Powwow at the End of the World" imagines a restitution of nature and spirit after which he might be able to, as his white friends have suggested, forgive. Joy Harjo, Linda Hogan, Black Elk, Thomas S. Whitecloud, Louise Erdrich, and Sherman Alexie, in poems, stories, and memoirs, consider matters of gender, social class, the Vietnam War, poverty, American history, birth and parenting, spirituality, and the tension for American Indians between their own and contemporary white culture.

Many of the protested issues overlap. Though we are often conscious of a weary yearning to reduce their complexity to manageable proportions, life and literature are rarely simple or one dimensional. Harriet Jacobs is oppressed both because she is a woman and because she is black. Thoreau is protesting war as well as slavery in "Civil Disobedience." In Sophocles' play, Antigone's protest against King Creon occurs on at least four fronts: female against male, youth against age, the rights of the individual against the power of the state, and religious against secular priorities. Judy Grahn's long and complex poem "A Woman Is Talking to Death" touches upon war and violence, and also upon race, class, and gender oppression as well as the protest against homophobia that is at its center. For Grahn in this poem, protest takes the form of commitment and engagement rather than a turning away from those who are oppressed; she redefines heroism as involvement, cowardice as detachment. Love in all its forms—physical, emotional, spiritual, and political—is, she concludes, "the resistance that tells death he will starve for lack of the fat of us."

The forms the protests take, from individual acts of conscience to demonstrations, strikes, and riots, are as various as the issues protested. In Joy Harjo's poem, "The Woman Hanging from the Thirteenth Floor Window" may or may not be committing suicide. The title character of Herman Melville's short story "Bartleby, the Scrivener" engages in passive resistance throughout that fable, his verbal leitmotif a polite "I would prefer not to." Though what exactly Bartleby is protesting is only hinted at in the story, we can clearly see the impact of the tactic of passive resistance on the people around him, particularly on the narrator. Thoreau, in his essay "Civil Disobedience," similarly writes about an individual act of resistance. Thoreau would undoubtedly agree with an earlier American, the Quaker John Woolman, who argued in his *Journal* (1774) that people must act out of conscience whether or not current law and custom support them: "It is the duty of all to be firm in that which they certainly know is right for them." Thoreau spends a night in jail for refusing to pay taxes to a government that supports slavery and the Mexican-American War, though he does tell us he is released the next morning when someone pays his taxes for him. That, however, is not his concern. In Essex Hemphill's "Baby Can You Love Me?", the speaker of the poem, who is dying from AIDS, asks his partner if he loves him enough to help him kill himself when the indignity and the pain become too much to bear.

Sometimes to protest means to pack up and leave, to realize that you are in a situation that is oppressive to you even if most other people think it's not so bad, to overcome the inertia that has kept you there and, simply, to get out. The speaker of Jo Carson's poem "I Cannot Remember All the Times . . ." details years of physical abuse and urges battered women like herself to be alert for the early signs that they've married an abuser and to get out while they can. Also making a choice to leave is the narrator of Thomas S. Whitecloud's "Blue Winds Dancing," who abandons the rat race of white civilization ("Being civilized means trying to do everything you don't want to, never doing anything you want to") to go home to his own Chippewa people. W. B. Yeats's early poem "The Lake Isle of Innisfree" begins "I will arise and go now . . ." as he imagines retreating from the frenzy and responsibility of urban revolutionary Ireland to a contemplative life on an island. And in Martín Espada's "Jorge the Church Janitor Finally Quits," the janitor walks away from his job, leaving his mop to carry on.

More indirect forms of protest occur in Pamela Zoline's short story "The Heat Death of the Universe" and Adrienne Rich's poem "The Trees." Both focus on a crisis for the female protagonist or *persona,* where either a breakdown or a breakthrough is possible. In each case, the image of suddenly mobile or out-of-control vegetation becomes a metaphor for the changes going on inside the main character or speaker. Both of these pieces were written by married American women in the years immediately preceding the contemporary wave of feminism. How angry are these women, we might ask, and how come they are displacing their anger onto plants?

Speaking of anger, Alan Sillitoe's "The Loneliness of the Long-distance Runner" gives us an unabashed, undiluted, angry, working-class view of the British class system. For the first-person narrator of this piece, a Borstal (reform school) boy, the world is divided into "us" and "them." Because he is a good runner, "they" try to bribe him to win a race for them with the carrot of class mobility. He muses,

> I realized it might be possible to do such a thing, run for money, trot for wages on piece work at a bob a puff rising bit by bit to a guinea a gasp and retiring through old age at thirty-two because of lace-curtain lungs, a football heart, and legs like varicose beanstalks. But I'd have a wife and car and get my grinning long-distance clock in the papers and have a smashing secretary to answer piles of letters sent by tarts who'd mob me when they saw who I was as I pushed my way into Woolworth's for a packet of razor blades and a cup of tea.

His ultimate protest against his situation is clever, cynical, and effective—and it costs him. It is an individual protest, but made in the context of his self-definition as a member of the working class.

The contrasts between individual and collective protest, between working within the system and changing it, between charitable and political action, inform Dorothy Canfield Fisher's 1913 short story "A Drop in the Bucket." A New England spinster rescues a single mother and her children from the city tenements and is seen as crazy by her conservative small-town community and as misguided—a provider of Band-Aids for a case of social gangrene—by the revolutionary who has unwittingly provoked her into action. Her particular form of protest is to give up her own middle-class comfort and solitude in order to share what she has with a family that has less. An important question is where in this story the writer's sympathy lies and whether the story's title is ironic.

Collective protest is represented in the complete screenplay of *Salt of the Earth,* a film made in the early 1950s about a zinc miners' strike by Local 890 of the Mine, Mill and Smelter Workers Union against New Jersey Zinc in Bayard, New Mexico. The workers were mostly Mexican-American and a number of the actors were local strikers. *Salt of the Earth* tells the story of the strike, treating with passion and humor male/female tensions, ethnic and racial tensions, and issues of social class. The film itself was banned in the United States, its director blacklisted and hauled in front of Senator McCarthy's Commission on Un-American Activities. The story the film tells and the film itself are both acts of protest.

A few of the selections memorialize people who spent their lives, and sometimes died, trying to make the world a better place. Robert Hayden's poem "Frederick Douglass" eulogizes a black leader who worked for his people's rights. So does Susan Griffin's poem "I Like to Think of Harriet Tubman," but specifically in the context of Tubman's relevance as a hero for the contemporary women's movement. "At That Moment," by Raymond Patterson, memorializes the assassination of Malcolm X. Pablo Neruda's "Ode to Federico García Lorca" is a tribute to a Spanish poet who used his art to protest injustice in the years leading up to the Spanish Civil War; Lorca was executed barely a year after Neruda's ode to him was written. We might compare Neruda's poem with Lorca's own "Ballad of the Spanish Civil Guard" in the "Peace and War" section. Even in translation, we can see how Neruda's poem evokes Lorca's language and imagery, his "black-draped orange-tree voice."

What is the role of writers and artists in working for social justice and freedom of speech? A recent action by American poets protesting the United States entry into war on Iraq is represented both here and in the "Peace and War" section by several poems from the poetsagainstthewar.org Web site. In February 2003, the Bush administration cancelled a poetry reading at the White House organized by Laura Bush when it learned that some of the poets would be reading poems protesting the invasion of Iraq. In response, Sam Hammil created poetsagainstthewar.org and invited everyone to send in a poem. In less than six weeks he received more than 13,000 poems by 11,000 poets, including some people who had never before written a poem, indicating the extent of opposition to the war and incidentally proving the power of the Internet as a new and democratic technique for protest. Julia Alvarez's" poem "The White House Has Disinvited the Poets" vividly moves the situation into the White House itself in the aftermath of the poetry reading's cancellation.

The question of violent versus nonviolent means of protest is raised in several of these selections. Langston Hughes, in "Harlem," suggests through a brilliant series of images that a community too long oppressed is bound eventually to explode. James Alan McPherson's story "A Loaf of Bread" traces the consequences and suggests the power of an organized nonviolent protest, and Martin Luther King, Jr.'s eloquent speech, "I Have a Dream," urges black Americans, despite their impatience and despite the violence that has been directed against them, to follow the path of nonviolent civil disobedience. If riots are one form of collectivity, union activism is another and usually gentler form, though the resistance to union organizing has sometimes been violently confrontational. The union song "Solidarity Forever" urges workers toward a consciousness of economic injustice and of their potential strength in acting together.

Protest is the crossroads of conviction and action, and so the theme of this group of readings is about choice. The characters and personae choose individual or collective paths of action that are based on both ethical and practical considerations and grounded in need and belief.

FICTION

HERMAN MELVILLE (1819–1891)

It is now common practice to place Herman Melville as one of America's great writers. But this was not always the case, and at the time of his death in 1891, Melville and his work were virtually unknown to the public. He grew up in various parts of New York, moving from New York City to Albany as his father struggled to meet the family's economic needs. By the time Melville was twelve, he would be in and out of school, taking on various jobs to help support his family. At the age of 21, in urgent need of work, Melville signed on as a sailor for a whaling ship headed for the Pacific Ocean. Four years later Melville would arrive back in Massachusetts, full of the stories and experiences that would make up his first novels Typee *(1846) and* Omoo *(1947). Both were met with popular success as exciting sea adventures and appealed to a public that was curious about distant and exotic lands. As Melville matured, so did his literacy aspirations. His new acquaintance with fellow writer Nathanial Hawthorne and a deep study of the works of Shakespeare would have a profound impact on the writing of* Moby Dick, *which was published in 1851. Unlike his previous novels,* Moby Dick *was filled with complicated symbolism and allegory in a structure that combined satire, nonfiction, autobiography, and even elements of drama. Moreover, Melville openly questioned taboo topics such as Christian hypocrisy, racism, and homosexuality. Despite Melville's personal sense of accomplishment, most critics wrote the novel off as the work of a madman. It wasn't until 1919, the year of Melville's centennial, that his work would be reassessed and* Moby Dick, *along with the rest of Melville's oeuvre, took its place in the canon of American literature. Other works include the novels* Mardi: And a Voyage Thither *(1849),* Redburn: His First Voyage *(1849),* White Jacket: or, The World in a Man-o-War *(1850),* Pierre; or The Ambiguities *(1852), and* The Confidence Man: His Masquerade *(1857); the collection of short stories* The Piazza Tales *(1856); and the posthumously published* Billy Budd and Other Prose Pieces *(1924). "Bartleby the Scrivner," first published in* The Piazza Tales, *demonstrates Melville's use of allegory to create multiple meanings.*

Bartleby, The Scrivener   (1853)

A Story of Wall Street

I am a rather elderly man. The nature of my avocations, for the last thirty years, has brought me into more than ordinary contact with what would seem an interesting and somewhat singular set of men, of whom, as yet, nothing, that

I know of, has ever been written—I mean, the law-copyists, or scriveners. I have known very many of them, professionally and privately, and, if I pleased, could relate divers histories, at which good-natured gentlemen might smile, and sentimental souls might weep. But I waive the biographies of all other scriveners, for a few passages in the life of Bartleby, who was a scrivener, the strangest I ever saw, or heard of. While, of other law-copyists, I might write the complete life, of Bartleby nothing of that sort can be done. I believe that no materials exist, for a full and satisfactory biography of this man. It is an irreparable loss to literature. Bartleby was one of those beings of whom nothing is ascertainable, except from the original sources, and, in his case, those are very small. What my own astonished eyes saw of Bartleby, *that* is all I know of him, except, indeed, one vague report, which will appear in the sequel.

Ere introducing the scrivener, as he first appeared to me, it is fit I make some mention of myself, my employés, my business, my chambers, and general surroundings; because some such description is indispensable to an adequate understanding of the chief character about to be presented. Imprimis: I am a man who, from his youth upward, has been filled with a profound conviction that the easiest way of life is the best. Hence, though I belong to a profession proverbially energetic and nervous, even to turbulence, at times, yet nothing of that sort have I ever suffered to invade my peace. I am one of those unambitious lawyers who never addresses a jury, or in any way draws down public applause; but, in the cool tranquillity of a snug retreat, do a snug business among rich men's bonds, and mortgages, and title-deeds. All who know me, consider me an eminently *safe* man. The late John Jacob Astor, a personage little given to poetic enthusiasm, had no hesitation in pronouncing my first grand point to be prudence; my next, method. I do not speak it in vanity, but simply record the fact, that I was not unemployed in my profession by the late John Jacob Astor; a name which, I admit, I love to repeat; for it hath a rounded and orbicular sound to it, and rings like unto bullion. I will freely add, that I was not insensible to the late John Jacob Astor's good opinion.

Some time prior to the period at which this little history begins, my avocations had been largely increased. The good old office, now extinct in the State of New York, of a Master in Chancery, had been conferred upon me. It was not a very arduous office, but very pleasantly remunerative. I seldom lose my temper; much more seldom indulge in dangerous indignation at wrongs and outrages; but, I must be permitted to be rash here, and declare, that I consider the sudden and violent abrogation of the office of Master in Chancery, by the new Constitution, as a—premature act; inasmuch as I had counted upon a life-lease of the profits, whereas I only received those of a few short years. But this is by the way.

My chambers were upstairs, at No.—Wall Street. At one end, they looked upon the white wall of the interior of a spacious skylight shaft, penetrating the building from top to bottom.

This view might have been considered rather tame than otherwise, deficient in what landscape painters call 'life.' But, if so, the view from the other end of my chambers offered, at least, a contrast, if nothing more. In that direction, my windows commanded an unobstructed view of a lofty brick wall, black by age and everlasting shade; which wall required no spy-glass to bring out its lurking beauties, but, for the benefit of all near-sighted spectators, was pushed up to within ten feet of my window panes. Owing to the great height of the surrounding buildings, and my chambers being on the second floor, the interval between this wall and mine not a little resembled a huge square cistern.

At the period just preceding the advent of Bartleby, I had two persons as copyists in my employment, and a promising lad as an office-boy. First, Turkey; second, Nippers; third, Ginger Nut. These may seem names, the like of which are not usually found in the Directory. In truth, they were nicknames, mutually conferred upon each other by my three clerks, and were deemed expressive of their respective persons or characters. Turkey was a short, pursy[1] Englishman, of about my own age—that is, somewhere not far from sixty. In the morning, one might say, his face was of a fine florid hue, but after twelve o'clock, meridian—his dinner hour—it blazed like a grate full of Christmas coals; and continued blazing—but, as it were, with a gradual wane—till six o'clock, P.M., or thereabouts; after which, I saw no more of the proprietor of the face, which, gaining its meridian with the sun, seemed to set with it, to rise, culminate, and decline the following day, with the like regularity and undiminished glory. There are many singular coincidences I have known in the course of my life, not the least among which was the fact, that, exactly when Turkey displayed his fullest beams from his red and radiant countenance, just then, too, at that critical moment, began the daily period when I considered his business capacities as seriously disturbed for the remainder of the twenty-four hours. Not that he was absolutely idle, or averse to business, then; far from it. The difficulty was, he was apt to be altogether too energetic. There was a strange, inflamed, flurried, flighty recklessness of activity about him. He would be incautious in dipping his pen into his inkstand. All his blots upon my documents were dropped there after twelve o'clock, meridian. Indeed, not only would he be reckless, and sadly given to making blots in the afternoon, but, some days, he went further, and was rather noisy. At such times, too, his face flamed with augmented blazonry, as if cannel coal had been heaped on anthracite. He made an unpleasant racket with his chair; spilled his sand-box; in mending his pens, impatiently split them all to pieces, and threw them on the floor in a sudden passion; stood up, and leaned over his table, boxing his papers about in a most indecorous manner, very sad to behold in an elderly man like him. Nevertheless, as he was in many ways a most valuable person to me, and all the time before twelve o'clock, meridian, was the quickest, steadiest creature, too, accomplishing a great deal of work in a style not easily to be matched—for these reasons, I was willing to overlook his eccentricities, though, indeed, occasionally, I remonstrated with him. I did this very gently, however, because, though the civilest, nay, the blandest and most reverential of men in the morning, yet, in

---

[1]Short-winded; fat.

the afternoon, he was disposed, upon provocation, to be slightly rash with his tongue—in fact, insolent. Now, valuing his morning services as I did, and resolved not to lose them—yet, at the same time, made uncomfortable by his inflamed ways after twelve o'clock—and being a man of peace, unwilling by my admonitions to call forth unseemly retorts from him, I took upon me, one Saturday noon (he was always worse on Saturdays) to hint to him, very kindly, that, perhaps, now that he was growing old, it might be well to abridge his labours; in short, he need not come to my chambers after twelve o'clock, but, dinner over, had best go home to his lodgings, and rest himself till tea-time. But no; he insisted upon his afternoon devotions. His countenance became intolerably fervid, as he oratorically assured me—gesticulating with a long ruler at the other end of the room—that if his services in the morning were useful, how indispensable, then, in the afternoon?

'With submission, sir,' said Turkey, on this occasion, 'I consider myself your right-hand man. In the morning I but marshal and deploy my columns; but in the afternoon I put myself at their head, and gallantly charge the foe, thus'—and he made a violent thrust with the ruler.

'But the blots, Turkey,' intimated I.

'True; but, with submission, sir, behold these hairs! I am getting old. Surely, sir, a blot or two of a warm afternoon is not to be severely urged against gray hairs. Old age—even if it blot the page—is honourable. With submission, sir, we *both* are getting old.'

This appeal to my fellow-feeling was hardly to be resisted. At all events, I saw that go he would not. So, I made up my mind to let him stay, resolving, nevertheless, to see to it that, during the afternoon, he had to do with my less important papers.

Nippers, the second on my list, was a whiskered, sallow, and, upon the whole, rather piratical-looking young man, of about five-and-twenty. I always deemed him the victim of two evil powers—ambition and indigestion. The ambition was evinced by a certain impatience of the duties of a mere copyist, an unwarrantable usurpation of strictly professional affairs, such as the original drawing up of legal documents. The indigestion seemed betokened in an occasional nervous testiness and grinning irritability, causing the teeth to audibly grind together over mistakes committed in copying; unnecessary maledictions, hissed, rather than spoken, in the heat of business; and especially by a continual discontent with the height of the table where he worked. Though of a very ingenious mechanical turn, Nippers could never get this table to suit him. He put chips under it, blocks of various sorts, bits of pasteboard, and at last went so far as to attempt an exquisite adjustment, by final pieces of folded blotting-paper. But no invention would answer. If, for the sake of easing his back, he brought the table lid at a sharp angle well up toward his chin, and wrote there like a man using the steep roof of a Dutch house for his desk, then he declared that it stopped the circulation in his arms. If now he lowered the table to his waistbands, and stooped over it in writing, then there was a sore aching in his back.

In short, the truth of the matter was, Nippers knew not what he wanted. Or, if he wanted anything, it was to be rid of a scrivener's table altogether. Among the manifestations of his diseased ambition was a fondness he had for receiving visits from certain ambiguous-looking fellows in seedy coats, whom he called his clients. Indeed, I was aware that not only was he, at times, considerable of a ward-politician, but he occasionally did a little business at the Justices' courts, and was not unknown on the steps of the Tombs.[2] I have good reason to believe, however, that one individual who called upon him at my chambers, and who, with a grand air, he insisted was his client, was no other than a dun, and the alleged title-deed, a bill. But, with all his failings, and the annoyances he caused me, Nippers, like his compatriot Turkey, was a very useful man to me; wrote a neat, swift hand; and, when he chose, was not deficient in a gentlemanly sort of deportment. Added to this, he always dressed in a gentlemanly sort of way; and so, incidentally, reflected credit upon my chambers. Whereas, with respect to Turkey, I had much ado to keep him from being a reproach to me. His clothes were apt to look oily, and smell of eating-houses. He wore his pantaloons very loose and baggy in summer. His coats were execrable; his hat not to be handled. But while the hat was a thing of indifference to me, inasmuch as his natural civility and deference, as a dependent Englishman, always led him to doff it the moment he entered the room, yet his coat was another matter. Concerning his coats, I reasoned with him; but with no effect. The truth was, I suppose, that a man with so small an income could not afford to sport such a lustrous face and a lustrous coat at one and the same time. As Nippers once observed, Turkey's money went chiefly for red ink. One winter day, I presented Turkey with a highly respectable-looking coat of my own—a padded gray coat, of a most comfortable warmth, and which buttoned straight up from the knee to the neck. I thought Turkey would appreciate the favour, and abate his rashness and obstreperousness of afternoons. But no; I verily believe that buttoning himself up in so downy and blanket-like a coat had a pernicious effect upon him—upon the same principle that too much oats are bad for horses. In fact, precisely as a rash, restive horse is said to feel his oats, so Turkey felt his coat. It made him insolent. He was a man whom prosperity harmed.

Though, concerning the self-indulgent habits of Turkey, I had my own private surmises, yet, touching Nippers, I was well persuaded that, whatever might be his faults in other respects, he was, at least, a temperate young man. But, indeed, nature herself seemed to have been his vintner, and, at his birth, charged him so thoroughly with an irritable, brandy-like disposition, that all subsequent potations were needless. When I consider how, amid the stillness of my chambers, Nippers would sometimes impatiently rise from his seat, and stooping over his table, spread his arms wide apart, seize the whole desk, and move it, and jerk it, with a grim, grinding motion on the floor, as if the table were a perverse volun-

---

[2]New York City prison.

tary agent, intent on thwarting and vexing him, I plainly perceive that, for Nippers, brandy-and-water were altogether superfluous.

It was fortunate for me that, owing to its peculiar cause—indigestion—the irritability and consequent nervousness of Nippers were mainly observable in the morning, while in the afternoon he was comparatively mild. So that, Turkey's paroxysms only coming on about twelve o'clock, I never had to do with their eccentricities at one time. Their fits relieved each other, like guards. When Nipper's was on, Turkey's was off; and *vice versa*. This was a good natural arrangement, under the circumstances.

Ginger Nut, the third on my list, was a lad, some twelve years old. His father was a carman, ambitious of seeing his son on the bench instead of a cart, before he died. So he sent him to my office, as student at law, errand-boy, cleaner and sweeper, at the rate of one dollar a week. He had a little desk to himself, but he did not use it much. Upon inspection, the drawer exhibited a great array of the shells of various sorts of nuts. Indeed, to this quick-witted youth, the whole noble science of the law was contained in a nut-shell. Not the least among the employments of Ginger Nut, as well as one which he discharged with the most alacrity, was his duty as cake and apple purveyor for Turkey and Nippers. Copying law-papers being proverbially a dry, husky sort of business, my two scriveners were fain to moisten their mouths very often with Spitzenbergs, to be had at the numerous stalls nigh the Custom House and Post Office. Also, they sent Ginger Nut very frequently for that peculiar cake—small, flat, round, and very spicy—after which he had been named by them. Of a cold morning, when business was but dull, Turkey would gobble up scores of these cakes, as if they were mere wafers—indeed, they sell them at the rate of six or eight for a penny—the scrape of his pen blending with the crunching of the crisp particles in his mouth. Of all the fiery afternoon blunders and flurried rashness of Turkey, was his once moistening a ginger-cake between his lips, and clapping it on to a mortgage, for a seal. I came within an ace of dismissing him then. But he mollified me by making an oriental bow, and saying—'With submission, sir, it was generous of me to find you in[3] stationery on my own account.'

Now my original business—that of a conveyancer and title-hunter, and drawer-up of recondite documents of all sorts—was considerably increased by receiving the master's office. There was now great work for scriveners. Not only must I push the clerks already with me, but I must have additional help.

In answer to my advertisement, a motionless young man one morning stood upon my office threshold, the door being open, for it was summer. I can see that figure now—pallidly neat, pitiably respectable, incurably forlorn! It was Bartleby.

After a few words touching his qualifications, I engaged him, glad to have among my corps of copyists a man of so singularly sedate an aspect, which I thought might operate beneficially upon the flighty temper of Turkey, and the fiery one of Nippers.

---

[3]To supply you with.

I should have stated before that ground-glass folding-doors divided my premises into two parts, one of which was occupied by my scriveners, the other by myself. According to my humour, I threw open these doors, or closed them. I resolved to assign Bartleby a corner by the folding-doors, but on my side of them, so as to have this quiet man within easy call, in case any trifling thing was to be done. I placed his desk close up to a small side-window in that part of the room, a window which originally had afforded a lateral view of certain grimy back-yards and bricks, but which, owing to subsequent erections, commanded at present no view at all, though it gave some light. Within three feet of the panes was a wall, and the light came down from far above, between two lofty build-ings, as from a very small opening in a dome. Still further to a satisfactory arrangement, I procured a high green folding-screen, which might entirely iso-late Bartleby from my sight, though not remove him from my voice. And thus, in a manner, privacy and society were conjoined.

At first, Bartleby did an extraordinary quantity of writing. As if long famish-ing for something to copy, he seemed to gorge himself on my documents. There was no pause for digestion. He ran a day and night line, copying by sun-light and by candle-light. I should have been quite delighted with his application, had he been cheerfully industrious. But he wrote on silently, palely, mechanically.

It is, of course, an indispensable part of a scrivener's business to verify the ac-curacy of his copy, word by word. Where there are two or more scriveners in an office, they assist each other in this examination, one reading from the copy, the other holding the original. It is a very dull, wearisome, and lethargic affair. I can readily imagine that, to some sanguine temperaments, it would be altogether in-tolerable. For example, I cannot credit that the mettlesome poet, Byron, would have contentedly sat down with Bartleby to examine a law document of, say, five hundred pages, closely written in a crimpy hand.

Now and then, in the haste of business, it had been my habit to assist in com-paring some brief document myself, calling Turkey or Nippers for this purpose. One object I had, in placing Bartleby so handy to me behind the screen, was, to avail myself of his services on such trivial occasions. It was on the third day, I think, of his being with me, and before any necessity had arisen for having his own writing examined, that, being much hurried to complete a small affair I had in hand, I abruptly called to Bartleby. In my haste and natural expectancy of in-stant compliance, I sat with my head bent over the original on my desk, and my right hand sideways, and somewhat nervously extended with the copy, so that, immediately upon emerging from his retreat, Bartleby might snatch it and pro-ceed to business without the least delay.

In this very attitude did I sit when I called to him, rapidly stating what it was I wanted him to do—namely, to examine a small paper with me. Imagine my sur-prise, nay, my consternation, when, without moving from his privacy, Bartleby, in a singularly mild, firm voice, replied, 'I would prefer not to.'

I sat a while in perfect silence, rallying my stunned faculties. Immediately it occurred to me that my ears had deceived me, or Bartleby had entirely misunderstood my meaning. I repeated my request in the clearest tone I could assume; but in quite as clear a one came the previous reply, 'I would prefer not to.'

'Prefer not to,' echoed I, rising in high excitement, and crossing the room with a stride. 'What do you mean? Are you moon-struck? I want you to help me compare this sheet here—take it,' and I thrust it toward him.

'I would prefer not to,' said he.

I looked at him steadfastly. His face was leanly composed; his gray eye dimly calm. Not a wrinkle of agitation rippled him. Had there been the least uneasiness, anger, impatience, or impertinence in his manner; in other words, had there been anything ordinarily human about him, doubtless I should have violently dismissed him from the premises. But as it was, I should have as soon thought of turning my pale plaster-of-paris bust of Cicero out of doors. I stood gazing at him a while, as he went on with his own writing, and then reseated myself at my desk. This is very strange, thought I. What had one best do? But my business hurried me. I concluded to forget the matter for the present, reserving it for my future leisure. So calling Nippers from the other room, the paper was speedily examined.

A few days after this, Bartleby concluded four lengthy documents, being quadruplicates of a week's testimony taken before me in my High Court of Chancery. It became necessary to examine them. It was an important suit, and great accuracy was imperative. Having all things arranged, I called Turkey, Nippers, and Ginger Nut, from the next room, meaning to place the four copies in the hands of my four clerks, while I should read from the original. Accordingly, Turkey, Nippers, and Ginger Nut had taken their seats in a row, each with his document in his hand, when I called to Bartleby to join this interesting group.

'Bartleby! quick, I am waiting.'

I heard a slow scrape of his chair legs on the uncarpeted floor, and soon he appeared standing at the entrance of this hermitage.

'What is wanted?' said he mildly.

'The copies, the copies,' said I hurriedly. 'We are going to examine them. There'—and I held toward him the fourth quadruplicate.

'I would prefer not to,' he said, and gently disappeared behind the screen.

For a few moments I was turned into a pillar of salt, standing at the head of my seated column of clerks. Recovering myself, I advanced toward the screen, and demanded the reason for such extraordinary conduct.

'*Why* do you refuse?'

'I would prefer not to.'

With any other man I should have flown outright into a dreadful passion, scorned all further words, and thrust him ignominiously from my presence. But there was something about Bartleby that not only strangely disarmed me, but, in a wonderful manner, touched and disconcerted me. I began to reason with him.

'These are your own copies we are about to examine. It is labour saving to you, because one examination will answer for your four papers. It is common usage. Every copyist is bound to help examine his copy. Is it not so? Will you not speak? Answer!'

'I prefer not to,' he replied in a flute-like tone. It seemed to me that, while I had been addressing him, he carefully revolved every statement that I made; fully comprehended the meaning; could not gainsay the irresistible conclusion; but, at the same time, some paramount consideration prevailed with him to reply as he did.

'You are decided, then, not to comply with my request—a request made according to common usage and common sense?'

He briefly gave me to understand, that on that point my judgment was sound. Yes: his decision was irreversible.

It is not seldom the case that, when a man is browbeaten in some unprecedented and violently unreasonable way, he begins to stagger in his own plainest faith. He begins, as it were, vaguely to surmise that, wonderful as it may be, all the justice and all the reason is on the other side. Accordingly, if any disinterested persons are present, he turns to them for some reinforcement for his own faltering mind.

'Turkey,' said I, 'what do you think of this? Am I not right?'

'With submission, sir,' said Turkey, in his blandest tone, 'I think that you are.'

'Nippers,' said I, 'what do *you* think of it?'

'I think I should kick him out of the office.'

(The reader, of nice perceptions, will here perceive that, it being morning, Turkey's answer is couched in polite and tranquil terms, but Nipper's replies in ill-tempered ones. Or, to repeat a previous sentence, Nipper's ugly mood was on duty, and Turkey's off.)

'Ginger Nut,' said I, willing to enlist the smallest suffrage in my behalf, 'what do *you* think of it?'

'I think, sir, he's a little *luny*,' replied Ginger Nut, with a grin.

'You hear what they say,' said I, turning toward the screen, 'come forth and do your duty.'

But he vouchsafed no reply. I pondered a moment in sore perplexity. But once more business hurried me. I determined again to postpone the consideration of this dilemma to my future leisure. With a little trouble we made out to examine the papers without Bartleby, though at every page or two Turkey deferentially dropped his opinion, that this proceeding was quite out of the common; while Nippers, twitching in his chair with a dyspeptic nervousness, ground out, between his set teeth, occasional hissing maledictions against the stubborn oaf behind the screen. And for his (Nippers's) part, this was the first and the last time he would do another man's business without pay.

Meanwhile Bartleby sat in his hermitage, oblivious to everything but his own peculiar business there.

Some days passed, the scrivener being employed upon another lengthy work. His late remarkable conduct led me to regard his ways narrowly. I observed that he never went to dinner; indeed, that he never went anywhere. As yet I had never, of my personal knowledge, known him to be outside of my office. He was a perpetual sentry in the corner. At about eleven o'clock though, in the morning, I noticed that Ginger Nut would advance toward the opening in Bartleby's screen, as if silently beckoned thither by a gesture invisible to me where I sat. The boy would then leave the office, jingling a new pence, and reappear with a handful of ginger-nuts, which he delivered in the hermitage, receiving two of the cakes for his trouble.

He lives, then, on ginger-nuts, thought I; never eats a dinner, properly speaking; he must be a vegetarian, then; but no; he never eats even vegetables, he eats nothing but ginger-nuts. My mind then ran on in reveries concerning the probable effects upon the human constitution of living entirely on ginger-nuts. Ginger-nuts are so called, because they contain ginger as one of their peculiar constituents, and the final flavouring one. Now, what was ginger? A hot, spicy thing. Was Bartleby hot and spicy? Not at all. Ginger, then, had no effect upon Bartleby. Probably he preferred it should have none.

Nothing so aggravates an earnest person as a passive resistance. If the individual so resisted be of a not inhumane temper, and the resisting one perfectly harmless in his passivity, then, in the better moods of the former, he will endeavour charitably to construe to his imagination what proves impossible to be solved by his judgment. Even so, for the most part, I regarded Bartleby and his ways. Poor fellow! thought I, he means no mischief; it is plain he intends no insolence; his aspect sufficiently evinces that his eccentricities are involuntary. He is useful to me. I can get along with him. If I turn him away, the chances are he will fall in with some less-indulgent employer, and then he will be rudely treated, and perhaps driven forth miserably to starve. Yes. Here I can cheaply purchase a delicious self-approval. To befriend Bartleby; to humour him in his strange wilfulness, will cost me little or nothing, while I lay up in my soul what will eventually prove a sweet morsel for my conscience. But this mood was not invariable with me. The passiveness of Bartleby sometimes irritated me. I felt strangely goaded on to encounter him in new opposition—to elicit some angry spark from him answerable to my own But, indeed, I might as well have essayed to strike fire with my knuckles against a bit of Windsor soap. But one afternoon the evil impulse in me mastered me, and the following little scene ensued:—

'Bartleby,' said I, 'when those papers are all copied, I will compare them with you.'

'I would prefer not to.'

'How? Surely you do not mean to persist in that mulish vagary?'

No answer.

I threw open the folding-doors near by, and, turning upon Turkey and Nippers, exclaimed:

'Bartleby a second time says, he won't examine his papers. What do you think of it, Turkey?'

It was afternoon, be it remembered. Turkey sat glowing like a brass boiler; his bald head steaming; his hands reeling among his blotted papers.

'Think of it?' roared Turkey; 'I think I'll just step behind his screen, and black his eyes for him!'

So saying, Turkey rose to his feet and threw his arms into a pugilistic position. He was hurrying away to make good his promise, when I detained him, alarmed at the effect of incautiously rousing Turkey's combativeness after dinner.

'Sit down, Turkey,' said I, 'and hear what Nippers has to say. What do you think of it, Nippers? Would I not be justified in immediately dismissing Bartleby?'

'Excuse me, that is for you to decide, sir. I think his conduct quite unusual, and, indeed, unjust, as regards Turkey and myself. But it may only be a passing whim.'

'Ah,' exclaimed I, 'you have strangely changed your mind, then—you speak very gently of him now.'

'All beer,' cried Turkey; 'gentleness is effects of beer—Nippers and I dined together to-day. You see how gentle *I* am, sir. Shall I go and black his eyes?'

'You refer to Bartleby, I suppose. No, not to-day, Turkey,' I replied; 'pray, put up your fists.'

I closed the doors, and again advanced toward Bartleby. I felt additional incentives tempting me to my fate. I burned to be rebelled against again. I remembered that Bartleby never left the office.

'Bartleby,' said I, 'Ginger Nut is away; just step around to the Post Office, won't you? (it was but a three minutes' walk), and see if there is anything for me.'

'I would prefer not to.'

'You *will* not?'

'I *prefer* not.'

I staggered to my desk, and sat there in a deep study. My blind inveteracy returned. Was there any other thing in which I could procure myself to be ignominiously repulsed by this lean, penniless wight?—my hired clerk? What added thing is there, perfectly reasonable, that he will be sure to refuse to do?

'Bartleby!'

No answer.

'Bartleby,' in a louder tone.

No answer.

'Bartleby,' I roared.

Like a very ghost, agreeably to the laws of magical invocation, at the third summons, he appeared at the entrance of his hermitage.

'Go to the next room, and tell Nippers to come to me.'

'I prefer not to,' he respectfully and slowly said, and mildly disappeared.

'Very good, Bartleby,' said I, in a quiet sort of serenely-severe self-possessed tone, intimating the unalterable purpose of some terrible retribution very close at hand. At the moment I half intended something of the kind. But upon the whole, as it was drawing toward my dinner-hour, I thought it best to put on my hat and walk home for the day, suffering much from perplexity and distress of mind.

Shall I acknowledge it? The conclusion of this whole business was, that it soon became a fixed fact of my chambers, that a pale young scrivener, by the name of Bartleby, had a desk there; that he copied for me at the usual rate of four cents a folio (one hundred words); but he was permanently exempt from examining the work done by him, that duty being transferred to Turkey and Nippers, out of compliment, doubtless, to their superior acuteness; moreover, said Bartleby was never, on any account, to be dispatched on the most trivial errand of any sort; and that even if entreated to take upon him such a matter, it was generally understood that he would 'prefer not to'—in other words, that he would refuse point-blank.

As days passed on, I became considerably reconciled to Bartleby. His steadiness, his freedom from all dissipation, his incessant industry (except when he chose to throw himself into a standing revery behind his screen), his great stillness, his unalterableness of demeanour under all circumstances, made him a valuable acquisition. One prime thing was this—*he was always there*—first in the morning, continually through the day, and the last at night. I had a singular confidence in his honesty. I felt my most precious papers perfectly safe in his hands. Sometimes, to be sure, I could not, for the very soul of me, avoid falling into sudden spasmodic passions with him. For it was exceeding difficult to bear in mind all the time those strange peculiarities, privileges, and unheard-of exemptions, forming the tacit stipulations on Bartleby's part under which he remained in my office. Now and then, in the eagerness of dispatching pressing business, I would inadvertently summon Bartleby, in a short, rapid tone, to put his finger, say, on the incipient tie of a bit of red tape with which I was about compressing some papers. Of course, from behind the screen the usual answer, 'I prefer not to,' was sure to come; and then, how could a human creature, with the common infirmities of our nature, refrain from bitterly exclaiming upon such perverseness—such unreasonableness. However, every added repulse of this sort which I received only tended to lessen the probability of my repeating the inadvertence.

Here it must be said, that according to the custom of most legal gentlemen occupying chambers in densely populated law-buildings, there were several keys to my door. One was kept by a woman residing in the attic, which person weekly scrubbed and daily swept and dusted my apartments. Another was kept by Turkey for convenience sake. The third I sometimes carried in my own pocket. The fourth I knew not who had.

Now, one Sunday morning I happened to go to Trinity Church, to hear a celebrated preacher, and finding myself rather early on the ground I thought I would walk round to my chambers for a while. Luckily I had my key with me; but upon applying it to the lock, I found it resisted by something inserted from the inside. Quite surprised, I called out; when to my consternation a key was turned from within; and thrusting his lean visage at me, and holding the door ajar, the apparition of Bartleby appeared, in his shirt-sleeves, and otherwise in a strangely tattered dishabille, saying quietly that he was sorry, but he was deeply engaged just then, and—preferred not admitting me at present. In a brief word or two, he moreover added, that perhaps I had better walk round the block two or three times, and by that time he would probably have concluded his affairs.

Now, the utterly unsurmised appearance of Bartleby, tenanting my lawchambers of a Sunday morning, with his cadaverously gentlemanly nonchalance, yet withal firm and self-possessed, had such a strange effect upon me, that incontinently I slunk away from my own door, and did as desired. But not without sundry twinges of impotent rebellion against the mild effrontery of this unaccountable scrivener. Indeed, it was his wonderful mildness chiefly, which not only disarmed me, but unmanned me as it were. For I consider that one, for the time, is a sort of unmanned when he tranquilly permits his hired clerk to dictate to him, and order him away from his own premises. Furthermore, I was full of uneasiness as to what Bartleby could possibly be doing in my office in his shirtsleeves, and in an otherwise dismantled condition of a Sunday morning. Was anything amiss going on? Nay, that was out of the question. It was not to be thought of for a moment that Bartleby was an immoral person. But what could he be doing there?—copying? Nay again, whatever might be his eccentricities, Bartleby was an eminently decorous person. He would be the last man to sit down to his desk in any state approaching to nudity. Besides, it was Sunday; and there was something about Bartleby that forbade the supposition that he would by any secular occupation violate the proprieties of the day.

Nevertheless, my mind was not pacified; and full of a restless curiosity, at last I returned to the door. Without hindrance I inserted my key, opened it, and entered. Bartleby was not to be seen. I looked round anxiously, peeped behind his screen; but it was very plain that he was gone. Upon more closely examining the place, I surmised that for an indefinite period Bartleby must have ate, dressed, and slept in my office, and that, too, without plate, mirror, or bed. The cushioned seat of a rickety old sofa in one corner bore the faint impress of a lean, reclining form. Rolled away under his desk, I found a blanket; under the empty grate a blacking box and brush; on a chair, a tin basin, with soap and a ragged towel; in a newspaper a few crumbs of ginger-nuts and a morsel of cheese. Yes, thought I, it is evident enough that Bartleby has been making his home here, keeping bachelor's hall all by himself. Immediately then the thought came sweeping across me, what miserable friendlessness and loneliness are here revealed! His poverty is great; but his solitude, how horrible! Think of it. Of a Sunday, Wall Street is deserted as Petra; and every night of every day it is an emptiness. This building, too, which of week-days hums with industry and life, at nightfall echoes with sheer vacancy, and all through Sunday is forlorn. And here Bartleby makes his home; sole spectator of a solitude which he has seen all-populous—a sort of innocent and transformed Marius brooding among the ruins of Carthage!

For the first time in my life a feeling of overpowering stinging melancholy seized me. Before, I had never experienced aught but a not unpleasing sadness. The bond of a common humanity now drew me irresistibly to gloom. A fraternal melancholy! For both I and Bartleby were sons of Adam. I remembered the bright silks and sparkling faces I had seen that day, in gala trim, swan-like sailing down the Mississippi of Broadway; and I contrasted them with the pallid copyist, and thought to myself, Ah, happiness courts the light, so we deem the world is gay; but misery hides aloof, so we deem that misery there is none. These sad fancyings—chimeras, doubtless, of a sick and silly brain—led on to other and more special thoughts, concerning the eccentricities of Bartleby. Presentiments of strange discoveries hovered round me. The scrivener's pale form appeared to me laid out, among uncaring strangers, in its shivering winding-sheet.

Suddenly I was attracted by Bartleby's closed desk, the key in open sight left in the lock.

I mean no mischief, seek the gratification of no heartless curiosity, thought I; besides, the desk is mine, and its contents, too, so I will make bold to look within. Everything was methodically arranged, the papers smoothly placed. The pigeon-holes were deep, and removing the files of documents, I groped into their recesses. Presently I felt something there, and dragged it out. It was an old bandanna handkerchief, heavy and knotted. I opened it, and saw it was a savings-bank.

I now recalled all the quiet mysteries which I had noted in the man. I remembered that he never spoke but to answer; that, though at intervals he had considerable time to himself, yet I had never seen him reading—no, not even a newspaper; that for long periods he would stand looking out, at his pale window behind the screen, upon the dead brick wall; I was quite sure he never visited any refectory or eating-house; while his pale face clearly indicated that he never drank beer like Turkey, or tea and coffee even, like other men; that he never went anywhere in particular that I could learn; never went out for a walk, unless, indeed, that was the case at present; that he had declined telling who he was, or whence he came, or whether he had any relatives in the world; that though so thin and pale, he never complained of ill health. And more than all, I remembered a certain unconscious air of pallid—how shall I call it?—of pallid haughtiness, say, or rather an austere reserve about him, which had positively awed me into my tame compliance with his eccentricities, when I had feared to ask him to do the slightest incidental thing for me, even though I might know, from his long-continued motionlessness, that behind his screen he must be standing in one of those dead-wall reveries of his.

Revolving all these things, and coupling them with the recently discovered fact, that he made my office his constant abiding-place and home, and not forgetful of his morbid moodiness; revolving all these things, a prudential feeling began to steal over me. My first emotions had been those of pure melancholy and sincerest pity; but just in proportion as the forlornness of Bartleby grew and grew to my imagination, did that same melancholy merge into fear, that pity into repulsion. So true it is, and so terrible, too, that up to a certain point the thought or sight of misery enlists our best affections; but, in certain special cases, beyond that point it does not. They err who would assert that invariably this is owing to the inherent selfishness of the human heart. It rather proceeds from a certain hopelessness of remedying excessive and organic ill. To a sensitive being, pity is not seldom pain. And when at last it is perceived that such pity cannot lead to effectual succour, common-sense bids the soul be rid of it. What I saw that morning persuaded me that the scrivener was the victim of innate and incurable disorder. I might give alms to his body; but his body did not pain him; it was his soul that suffered, and his soul I could not reach.

I did not accomplish the purpose of going to Trinity Church that morning. Somehow, the things I had seen disqualified me for the time from church-going. I walked homeward thinking what I would do with Bartleby. Finally, I resolved upon this—I would put certain calm questions to him the next morning, touching his history, etc., and if he declined to answer them openly and unreservedly (and I supposed he would prefer not), then to give him a twenty-dollar bill over and above whatever I might owe him, and tell him his services were no longer required; but that if in any other way I could assist him, I would be happy to do so, especially if he desired to return to his native place, wherever that might be, I would willingly help to defray the expenses. Moreover, if, after reaching home, he found himself at any time in want of aid, a letter from him would be sure of a reply.

The next morning came.

'Bartleby,' said I, gently calling to him behind his screen.

No reply.

'Bartleby,' said I, in a still gentler tone, 'come here; I am not going to ask you to do anything you would prefer not to do—I simply wish to speak to you.'

Upon this he noiselessly slid into view.

'Will you tell me, Bartleby, where you were born?'

'I would prefer not to.'

'Will you tell me *anything* about yourself?'

'I would prefer not to.'

'But what reasonable objection can you have to speak to me? I feel friendly toward you.'

He did not look at me while I spoke, but kept his glance fixed upon my bust of Cicero, which, as I then sat, was directly behind me, some six inches above my head.

'What is your answer, Bartleby?' said I, after waiting a considerable time for a reply, during which his countenance remained immovable, only there was the faintest conceivable tremor of the white attenuated mouth.

'At present I prefer to give no answer,' he said, and retired into his hermitage.

It was rather weak in me, I confess, but his manner, on this occasion, nettled me. Not only did there seem to lurk in it a certain calm disdain, but his perverseness seemed ungrateful, considering the undeniable good usage and indulgence he had received from me.

Again I sat ruminating what I should do. Mortified as I was at his behaviour, and resolved as I had been to dismiss him when I entered my office, nevertheless I strangely felt something superstitious knocking at my heart, and forbidding me to carry out my purpose, and denouncing me for a villain if I dared to breathe one bitter word against this forlornest of mankind. At last, familiarly drawing my chair behind his screen, I sat down and said: 'Bartleby, never mind, then, about revealing your history; but let me entreat you, as a friend, to comply as far as may be with the usages of this office. Say now, you will help to examine papers tomorrow or next day: in short, say now, that in a day or two you will begin to be a little reasonable:—say so, Bartleby.'

'At present I would prefer not to be a little reasonable,' was his mildly cadaverous reply.

Just then the folding-doors opened, and Nippers approached. He seemed suffering from an unusually bad night's rest, induced by severer indigestion than common. He overheard those final words of Bartleby.

'*Prefer not*, eh?' gritted Nippers—'I'd *prefer* him, if I were you, sir,' addressing me—'I'd *prefer* him; I'd give him preferences, the stubborn mule! What is it, sir, pray, that he *prefers* not to do now?'

Bartleby moved not a limb.

'Mr. Nippers,' said I, 'I'd prefer that you would withdraw for the present.'

Somehow, of late, I had got into the way of involuntarily using this word 'prefer' upon all sorts of not exactly suitable occasions. And I trembled to think that my contact with the scrivener had already and seriously affected me in a mental way. And what further and deeper aberration might it not yet produce? This apprehension had not been without efficacy in determining me to summary measures.

As Nippers, looking very sour and sulky, was departing, Turkey blandly and deferentially approached.

'With submission, sir,' said he, 'yesterday I was thinking about Bartleby here, and I think that if he would but prefer to take a quart of good ale every day, it would do much toward mending him, and enabling him to assist in examining his papers.'

'So you have got the word too,' said I, slightly excited.

'With submission, what word, sir,' asked Turkey, respectfully crowding himself into the contracted space behind the screen, and by so doing, making me jostle the scrivener. 'What word, sir?'

'I would prefer to be left alone here,' said Bartleby, as if offended at being mobbed in his privacy.

'*That's* the word, Turkey,' said I—'*that's* it.'

'Oh, *prefer?* oh yes—queer word. I never use it myself. But, sir, as I was saying, if he would but prefer—'

'Turkey,' interrupted I, 'you will please withdraw.'

'Oh certainly, sir, if you prefer that I should.'

As he opened the folding-door to retire, Nippers at his desk caught a glimpse of me, and asked whether I would prefer to have a certain paper copied on blue paper or white. He did not in the least roguishly accent the word prefer. It was plain that it involuntarily rolled from his tongue. I thought to myself, surely I must get rid of a demented man, who already has in some degree turned the tongues, if not the heads of myself and clerks. But I thought it prudent not to break the dismission at once.

The next day I noticed that Bartleby did nothing but stand at his window in his dead-wall revery. Upon asking him why he did not write, he said that he had decided upon doing no more writing.

'Why, how now? what next?' exclaimed I, 'do no more writing?'

'No more.'

'And what is the reason?'

'Do you not see the reason for yourself?' he indifferently replied.

I looked steadfastly at him, and perceived that his eyes looked dull and glazed. Instantly it occurred to me, that his unexampled diligence in copying by his dim window for the first few weeks of his stay with me might have temporarily impaired his vision.

I was touched. I said something in condolence with him. I hinted that of course he did wisely in abstaining from writing for a while; and urged him to embrace that opportunity of taking wholesome exercise in the open air. This, however, he did not do. A few days after this, my other clerks being absent, and being in a great hurry to dispatch certain letters by the mail, I thought that having nothing else earthly to do, Bartleby would surely be less inflexible than usual, and carry these letters to the Post Office. But he blankly declined. So, much to my inconvenience, I went myself.

Still added days went by. Whether Bartleby's eyes improved or not, I could not say. To all appearance, I thought they did. But when I asked him if they did, he vouchsafed no answer. At all events, he would do no copying. At last, in replying to my urgings, he informed me that he had permanently given up copying.

'What!' exclaimed I; 'suppose your eyes should get entirely well—better than ever before—would you not copy then?'

'I have given up copying,' he answered, and slid aside.

He remained as ever, a fixture in my chamber. Nay—if that were possible— he became still more of a fixture than before. What was to be done? He would do nothing in the office; why should he stay there? In plain fact, he had now become a millstone to me, not only useless as a necklace, but afflictive to bear. Yet I was sorry for him. I speak less than truth when I say that, on his own account, he occasioned me uneasiness. If he would but have named a single relative or friend, I would instantly have written, and urged their taking the poor fellow away to some convenient retreat. But he seemed alone, absolutely alone in the universe. A bit of wreck in the mid-Atlantic. At length, necessities connected with my business tyrannised over all other considerations. Decently as I could, I told Bartleby that in six days' time he must unconditionally leave the office. I warned him to take measures, in the interval, for procuring some other abode. I offered to assist him in this endeavour, if he himself would but take the first step toward a removal. 'And when you finally quit me, Bartleby,' added I, 'I shall see that you go not away entirely unprovided. Six days from this hour, remember.'

At the expiration of that period, I peeped behind the screen, and lo! Bartleby was there.

I buttoned up my coat, balanced myself; advanced slowly toward him, touched his shoulder, and said, 'The time has come; you must quit this place; I am sorry for you; here is money; but you must go.'

'I would prefer not,' he replied, with his back still toward me.

'You *must*.'

He remained silent.

Now I had an unbounded confidence in this man's common honesty. He had frequently restored to me sixpences and shillings carelessly dropped upon the floor, for I am apt to be very reckless in such shirt-button affairs. The proceeding, then, which followed will not be deemed extraordinary.

'Bartleby,' said I, 'I owe you twelve dollars on account; here are thirty-two; the odd twenty are yours—Will you take it?' and I handed the bills toward him.

But he made no motion.

'I will leave them here, then,' putting them under a weight on the table. Then taking my hat and cane and going to the door, I tranquilly turned and added— 'After you have removed your things from these offices, Bartleby, you will of course lock the door—since everyone is now gone for the day but you—and if you please, slip your key underneath the mat, so that I may have it in the morning. I shall not see you again; so good-bye to you. If, hereafter, in your new place of abode, I can be of any service to you, do not fail to advise me by letter. Good-bye, Bartleby, and fare you well.'

But he answered not a word; like the last column of some ruined temple, he remained standing mute and solitary in the middle of the otherwise deserted room.

As I walked home in a pensive mood, my vanity got the better of my pity. I could not but highly plume myself on my masterly management in getting rid of Bartleby. Masterly I call it, and such it must appear to any dispassionate thinker. The beauty of my procedure seemed to consist in its perfect quietness. There was no vulgar bullying, no bravado of any sort, no choleric hectoring, and striding to and fro across the apartment, jerking out vehement commands for Bartleby to bundle himself off with his beggarly traps. Nothing of the kind. Without loudly bidding Bartleby depart—as an inferior genius might have done—I *assumed* the ground that depart he must; and upon that assumption built all I had to say. The more I thought over my procedure, the more I was charmed with it. Nevertheless, next morning, upon awakening, I had my doubts—I had somehow slept off the fumes of vanity. One of the coolest and wisest hours a man has, is just after he awakes in the morning. My procedure seemed as sagacious as ever—but only in theory. How it would prove in practice—there was the rub. It was truly a beautiful thought to have assumed Bartleby's departure; but, after all, that assumption was simply my own, and none of Bartleby's. The great point was, not whether I had assumed that he would quit me, but whether he would prefer so to do. He was more a man of preferences than assumptions.

After breakfast, I walked down town, arguing the probabilities *pro* and *con*. One moment I thought it would prove a miserable failure, and Bartleby would be found all alive at my office as usual; the next moment it seemed certain that I should find his chair empty. And so I kept veering about. At the corner of Broadway and Canal Street, I saw quite an excited group of people standing in earnest conversation.

'I'll take odds he doesn't,' said a voice as I passed.

'Doesn't go?—done!' said I; 'put up your money.'

I was instinctively putting my hand in my pocket to produce my own, when I remembered that this was an election day. The words I had overheard bore no reference to Bartleby, but to the success or non-success of some candidate for the mayoralty. In my intent frame of mind, I had, as it were, imagined that all Broadway shared in my excitement, and were debating the same question with me. I passed on, very thankful that the uproar of the street screened my momentary absentmindedness.

As I had intended, I was earlier than usual at my office door. I stood listening for a moment. All was still. He must be gone. I tried the knob. The door was locked. Yes, my procedure had worked to a charm; he indeed must be vanished. Yet a certain melancholy mixed with this: I was almost sorry for my brilliant success. I was fumbling under the doormat for the key, which Bartleby was to have left there for me, when accidentally my knee knocked against a panel, producing a summoning sound, and in response a voice came to me from within—'Not yet; I am occupied.'

It was Bartleby.

I was thunderstruck. For an instant I stood like the man who, pipe in mouth, was killed one cloudless afternoon long ago in Virginia, by summer lightning; at his own warm open window he was killed, and remained leaning out there upon the dreamy afternoon, till someone touched him, when he fell.

'Not gone!' I murmured at last. But again obeying that wondrous ascendency which the inscrutable scrivener had over me, and from which ascendency, for all my chafing, I could not completely escape, I slowly went downstairs and out into the street, and while walking round the block, considered what I should next do in this unheard-of perplexity. Turn the man out by an actual thrusting I could not; to drive him away by calling him hard names would not do; calling in the police was an unpleasant idea; and yet, permit him to enjoy his cadaverous triumph over me—this, too, I could not think of. What was to be done? or, if nothing could be done, was there anything further that I could *assume* in the matter? Yes, as before I had prospectively assumed that Bartleby would depart, so now I might retrospectively assume that departed he was. In the legitimate carrying out of this assumption, I might enter my office in a great hurry, and pretending not to see Bartleby at all, walk straight against him as if he were air. Such a proceeding would in a singular degree have the appearance of a homethrust. It was hardly possible that Bartleby could withstand such an application of the doctrine of assumptions. But upon second thoughts the success of the plan seemed rather dubious. I resolved to argue the matter over with him again.

'Bartleby,' said I, entering the office, with a quietly severe expression, 'I am seriously displeased. I am pained, Bartleby. I had thought better of you. I had imagined you of such a gentlemanly organisation, that in any delicate dilemma a slight hint would suffice—in short, an assumption. But it appears I am deceived. Why,' I added, unaffectedly starting, 'you have not even touched that money yet,' pointing to it, just where I had left it the evening previous.

He answered nothing.

'Will you, or will you not, quit me?' I now demanded in a sudden passion, advancing close to him.

'I would prefer *not* to quit you,' he replied, gently emphasizing the *not*.

'What earthly right have you to stay here? Do you pay any rent? Do you pay my taxes? Or is this property yours?'

He answered nothing.

'Are you ready to go on and write now? Are your eyes recovered? Could you copy a small paper for me this morning? or help examine a few lines? or step round to the Post Office? In a word, will you do anything at all, to give a colouring to your refusal to depart the premises?'

He silently retired into his hermitage.

I was now in such a state of nervous resentment that I thought it but prudent to check myself at present from further demonstrations. Bartleby and I were alone. I remembered the tragedy of the unfortunate Adams and the still more unfortunate Colt[4] in the solitary office of the latter; and how poor Colt, being dreadfully incensed by Adams, and imprudently permitting himself to get wildly excited, was at unawares hurried into his fatal act—an act which certainly no man could possibly deplore more than the actor himself. Often it had occurred to me in my ponderings upon the subject, that had that altercation taken place in the public street, or at a private residence, it would not have terminated as it did. It was the circumstance of being alone in a solitary office, upstairs, of a building entirely unhallowed by humanising domestic associations—an uncarpeted office, doubtless, of a dusty, haggard sort of appearance—this it must have been, which greatly helped to enhance the irritable desperation of the hapless Colt.

But when this old Adam of resentment rose in me and tempted me concerning Bartleby, I grappled him and threw him. How? Why, simply by recalling the divine injunction: 'A new commandment give I unto you, that ye love one another.' Yes, this it was that saved me. Aside from higher considerations, charity often operates as a vastly wise and prudent principle—a great safeguard to its possessor. Men have committed murder for jealousy's sake, and anger's sake, and hatred's sake, and selfishness' sake, and spiritual pride's sake; but no man, that ever I heard of, ever committed a diabolical murder for sweet charity's sake. Mere self-interest, then, if no better motive can be enlisted, should, especially with high-tempered men, prompt all beings to charity and philanthropy. At any rate, upon the occasion in question, I strove to drown my exasperated feelings toward the scrivener by benevolently construing his conduct. Poor fellow, poor fellow! thought I, he don't mean anything; and besides, he has seen hard times, and ought to be indulged.

I endeavoured, also, immediately to occupy myself, and at the same time to comfort my despondency. I tried to fancy, that in the course of the morning, at such time as might prove agreeable to him, Bartleby, of his own free accord, would emerge from his heritage and take up some decided line of march in the direction of the door. But no. Half-past twelve o'clock came; Turkey began to

---

[4]In 1841, John C. Colt struck and killed Samuel Adams in a fight.

glow in the face, overturn his inkstand, and become generally obstreperous; Nippers abated down into quietude and courtesy; Ginger Nut munched his noon apple; and Bartleby remained standing at his window in one of his profoundest dead-wall reveries. Will it be credited? Ought I to acknowledge it? That afternoon I left the office without saying one further word to him.

Some days now passed, during which, at leisure intervals, I looked a little into 'Edwards on the Will,' and 'Priestley on Necessity.'[5] Under the circumstances, those books induced a salutary feeling. Gradually I slid into the persuasion that these troubles of mine, touching the scrivener, had been all predestinated from eternity, and Bartleby was billeted upon me for some mysterious purpose of an all-wise Providence, which it was not for a mere mortal like me to fathom. Yes, Bartleby, stay there behind your screen, thought I; I shall persecute you no more; you are harmless and noiseless as any of these old chairs; in short, I never feel so private as when I know you are here. At last I see it, I feel it; I penetrate to the predestinated purpose of my life. I am content. Others may have loftier parts to enact; but my mission in this world, Bartleby, is to furnish you with office-room for such period as you may see fit to remain.

I believe that this wise and blessed frame of mind would have continued with me, had it not been for the unsolicited and uncharitable remarks obtruded upon me by my professional friends who visited the rooms. But thus it often is, that the constant friction of illiberal minds wears out at last the best resolves of the more generous. Though to be sure, when I reflected upon it, it was not strange that people entering my office should be struck by the peculiar aspect of the unaccountable Bartleby, and so be tempted to throw out some sinister observations concerning him. Sometimes an attorney, having business with me, and calling at my office, and finding no one but the scrivener there, would undertake to obtain some sort of precise information from him touching my whereabouts; but without heeding his idle talk, Bartleby would remain standing immovable in the middle of the room. So after contemplating him in that position for a time, the attorney would depart, no wiser than he came.

Also, when a reference was going on, and the room full of lawyers and witnesses, and business driving fast, some deeply occupied legal gentleman present, seeing Bartleby wholly unemployed, would request him to run round to his (the legal gentleman's) office and fetch some papers for him. Thereupon, Bartleby would tranquilly decline, and yet remain idle as before. Then the lawyer would give a great stare, and turn to me. And what could I say? At last I was made aware that all through the circle of my professional acquaintance, a whisper of wonder was running round, having reference to the strange creature I kept at my office. This worried me very much. And as the idea came upon me of his possibly turning out a long-lived man, and keep occupying my chambers, and denying my authority; and perplexing my visitors; and scandalising my professional

---

[5]American theologian Jonathan Edwards (1703–1758) and English scientist Joseph Priestley (1733–1804) both argued against the existence of free will.

reputation; and casting a general gloom over the premises; keeping soul and body together to the last upon his savings (for doubtless he spent but half a dime a day), and in the end perhaps outlive me, and claim possession of my office by right of his perpetual occupancy: as all these dark anticipations crowded upon me more and more, and my friends continually intruded their relentless remarks upon the apparition in my room; a great change was wrought in me. I resolved to gather all my faculties together, and forever rid me of this intolerable incubus.

Ere revolving any complicated project, however, adapted to this end, I first simply suggested to Bartleby the propriety of his permanent departure. In a calm and serious tone, I commended the idea to his careful and mature consideration. But, having taken three days to meditate upon it, he appraised me, that his original determination remained the same; in short, that he still preferred to abide with me.

What shall I do? I now said to myself, buttoning up my coat to the last button. What shall I do? what ought I to do? what does conscience say I *should* do with this man, or, rather, ghost. Rid myself of him, I must; go, he shall. But how? You will not thrust him, the poor, pale, passive mortal—you will not thrust such a helpless creature out of your door? you will not dishonour yourself by such cruelty? No, I will not, I cannot do that. Rather would I let him live and die here, and then mason up his remains in the wall. What, then, will you do? For all your coaxing, he will not budge. Bribes he leaves under your own paperweight on your table; in short, it is quite plain that he prefers to cling to you.

Then something severe, something unusual must be done. What! surely you will not have him collared by a constable, and commit his innocent pallor to the common jail? And upon what ground could you procure such a thing to be done?—a vagrant, is he? What! he a vagrant, a wanderer, who refuses to budge? It is because he will *not* be a vagrant, then, that you seek to count him *as* a vagrant. That is too absurd. No visible means of support; there I have him. Wrong again: for indubitably he *does* support himself, and that is the only unanswerable proof that any man can show of his possessing the means so to do. No more, then. Since he will not quit me, I must quit him. I will change my offices; I will move elsewhere, and give him fair notice, that if I find him on my new premises I will then proceed against him as a common trespasser.

Acting accordingly, next day I thus addressed him: 'I find these chambers too far from the City Hall; the air is unwholesome. In a word, I propose to remove my offices next week, and shall no longer require your services. I tell you this now, in order that you may seek another place.'

He made no reply, and nothing more was said.

On the appointed day I engaged carts and men, proceeded to my chambers, and, having but little furniture, everything was removed in a few hours. Throughout, the scrivener remained standing behind the screen, which I directed to be removed the last thing. It was withdrawn; and, being folded up like a huge folio, left him the motionless occupant of a naked room. I stood in the entry watching him a moment, while something from within me upbraided me.

I re-entered, with my hand in my pocket—and—and my heart in my mouth.

'Good-bye, Bartleby; I am going—good-bye, and God some way bless you; and take that,' slipping something in his hand. But it dropped upon the floor, and then—strange to say—I tore myself from him whom I had so longed to be rid of.

Established in my new quarters, for a day or two I kept the door locked, and started at every footfall in the passages. When I returned to my rooms, after any little absence, I would pause at the threshold for an instant, and attentively listen ere applying my key. But these fears were needless. Bartleby never came nigh me.

I thought all was going well, when a perturbed-looking stranger visited me, inquiring whether I was the person who had recently occupied rooms at No.— Wall Street.

Full of forebodings, I replied that I was.

'Then, sir,' said the stranger, who proved a lawyer, 'you are responsible for the man you left there. He refuses to do any copying; he refuses to do anything; he says he prefers not to; and he refuses to quit the premises.'

'I am very sorry, sir,' said I, with assumed tranquillity, but an inward tremor, 'but, really, the man you allude to is nothing to me—he is no relation or apprentice of mine, that you should hold me responsible for him.'

'In mercy's name, who is he?'

'I certainly cannot inform you. I know nothing about him. Formerly I employed him as a copyist, but he has done nothing for me now for some time past.'

'I shall settle him, then—good morning, sir.'

Several days passed, and I heard nothing more; and, though I often felt a charitable prompting to call at the place and see poor Bartleby, yet a certain squeamishness, of I know not what, withheld me.

All is over with him, by this time, thought I, at last, when, through another week, no further intelligence reached me. But, coming to my room the day after, I found several persons waiting at my door in a high state of nervous excitement.

'That's the man—here he comes,' cried the foremost one, whom I recognized as the lawyer who had previously called upon me alone.

'You must take him away, sir, at once,' cried a portly person among them, advancing upon me, and whom I knew to be the landlord of No.—Wall Street. 'These gentlemen, my tenants, cannot stand it any longer; Mr. B—,' pointing to the lawyer, 'has turned him out of his room, and he now persists in haunting the building generally, sitting upon the banisters of the stairs by day, and sleeping in the entry by night. Everybody is concerned; clients are leaving the offices; some fears are entertained of a mob; something you must do, and that without delay.'

Aghast at this torrent, I fell back before it, and would fain have locked myself in my new quarters. In vain I persisted that Bartleby was nothing to me— no more than to anyone else. In vain—I was the last person known to have anything to do with him, and they held me to the terrible account. Fearful, then, of being exposed in the papers (as one person present obscurely threatened), I considered the matter, and, at length, said, that if the lawyer would give me a confidential interview with the scrivener, in his (the lawyer's) own room, I would, that afternoon, strive my best to rid them of the nuisance they complained of.

Going upstairs to my old haunt, there was Bartleby silently sitting upon the banister at the landing.

'What are you doing here, Bartleby?' said I.

'Sitting upon the banister,' he mildly replied.

I motioned him into the lawyer's room, who then left us.

'Bartleby,' said I, 'are you aware that you are the cause of great tribulation to me, by persisting in occupying the entry after being dismissed from the office?' No answer.

'Now one of two things must take place. Either you must do something, or something must be done to you. Now what sort of business would you like to engage in? Would you like to re-engage in copying for someone?'

'No; I would prefer not to make any change.'

'Would you like a clerkship in a dry-goods store?'

'There is too much confinement about that. No, I would not like a clerkship; but I am not particular.'

'Too much confinement,' I cried, 'why, you keep yourself confined all the time!'

'I would prefer not to take a clerkship,' he rejoined, as if to settle that little item at once.

'How would a bar-tender's business suit you? There is no trying of the eyesight in that.'

'I would not like it at all; though, as I said before, I am not particular.'

His unwonted wordiness inspirited me. I returned to the charge.

'Well, then, would you like to travel through the country collecting bills for the merchants? That would improve your health.'

'No, I would prefer to be doing something else.'

'How, then, would going as a companion to Europe, to entertain some young gentleman with your conversation—how would that suit you?'

'Not at all. It does not strike me that there is anything definite about that. I like to be stationary. But I am not particular.'

'Stationary you shall be, then,' I cried, now losing all patience, and, for the first time in all my exasperating connection with him, fairly flying into a passion. 'If you do not go away from these premises before night, I shall feel bound—indeed, I *am* bound—to—to quit the premises myself!' I rather absurdly concluded, knowing not with what possible threat to try to frighten his immobility into compliance. Despairing of all further efforts, I was precipitately leaving him, when a final thought occurred to me—one which had not been wholly unindulged before.

'Bartleby,' said I, in the kindest tone I could assume under such exciting circumstances, 'will you go home with me now—not to my office, but my dwelling—and remain there till we can conclude upon some convenient arrangement for you at our leisure? Come, let us start now, right away.'

'No; at present I would prefer not to make any change at all.'

I answered nothing; but, effectually dodging everyone by the suddenness and rapidity of my flight, rushed from the building, ran up Wall Street toward Broadway, and, jumping into the first omnibus, was soon removed from pursuit. As soon as tranquillity returned, I distinctly perceived that I had now done all that I possibly could, both in respect to the demands of the landlord and his tenants, and with regard to my own desire and sense of duty, to benefit Bartleby, and shield him from rude persecution. I now strove to be entirely carefree and quiescent; and my conscience justified me in the attempt; though, indeed, it was not so successful as I could have wished. So fearful was I of being again hunted out by the incensed landlord and his exasperated tenants, that, surrendering my business to Nippers, for a few days, I drove about the upper part of the town and through the suburbs, in my rockaway; crossed over to Jersey City and Hoboken, and paid fugitive visits to Manhattanville and Astoria. In fact, I almost lived in my rockaway for the time.

When again I entered my office, lo, a note from the landlord lay upon the desk. I opened it with trembling hands. It informed me that the writer had sent to the police, and had Bartleby removed to the Tombs as a vagrant. Moreover, since I knew more about him than anyone else, he wished me to appear at that place, and make a suitable statement of the facts. These tidings had a conflicting effect upon me. At first I was indignant; but, at last, almost approved. The landlord's energetic, summary disposition had led him to adopt a procedure which I do not think I would have decided upon myself; and yet, as a last resort, under such peculiar circumstances, it seemed the only plan.

As I afterward learned, the poor scrivener, when told that he must be conducted to the Tombs, offered not the slightest obstacle, but, in his pale, unmoving way, silently acquiesced.

Some of the compassionate and curious bystanders joined the party; and headed by one of the constables arm in arm with Bartleby, the silent procession filed its way through all the noise, and heat, and joy of the roaring thoroughfares at noon.

The same day I received the note, I went to the Tombs, or, to speak more properly, the Halls of Justice. Seeking the right officer, I stated the purpose of my call, and was informed that the individual I described was, indeed, within. I then assured the functionary that Bartleby was a perfectly honest man, and greatly to be compassionated, however unaccountably eccentric. I narrated all I knew, and closed by suggesting the idea of letting him remain in as indulgent confinement as possible, till something less harsh might be done—though, indeed, I hardly knew what. At all events, if nothing else could be decided upon, the almshouse must receive him. I then begged to have an interview.

Being under no disgraceful charge, and quite serene and harmless in all his ways, they had permitted him freely to wander about the prison, and, especially, in the enclosed grass-platted yards thereof. And so I found him there, standing all alone in the quietest of the yards, his face toward a high wall, while all around, from the narrow slits of the jail windows, I thought I saw peering out upon him the eyes of murderers and thieves.

'Bartleby!'

'I know you,' he said, without looking round—'and I want nothing to say to you.'

'It was not I that brought you here, Bartleby,' said I, keenly pained at his implied suspicion. 'And to you, this should not be so vile a place. Nothing reproachful attaches to you by being here. And see, it is not so sad a place as one might think. Look, there is the sky, and here is the grass.'

'I know where I am,' he replied, but would say nothing more, and so I left him.

As I entered the corridor again, a broad meat-like man, in an apron, accosted me, and, jerking his thumb over his shoulder, said, 'Is that your friend?'

'Yes.'

'Does he want to starve? If he does, let him live on the prison fare, that's all.'

'Who are you?' asked I, not knowing what to make of such an unofficially speaking person in such a place.

'I am the grub-man. Such gentlemen as have friends here, hire me to provide them with something good to eat.'

'Is this so?' said I, turning to the turnkey.

He said it was.

'Well, then,' said I, slipping some silver into the grub-man's hands (for so they called him), 'I want you to give particular attention to my friend there; let him have the best dinner you can get. And you must be as polite to him as possible.'

'Introduce me, will you?' said the grub-man, looking at me with an expression which seemed to say he was all impatience for an opportunity to give a specimen of his breeding.

Thinking it would prove of benefit to the scrivener, I acquiesced; and, asking the grub-man his name, went up with him to Bartleby.

'Bartleby, this is a friend; you will find him very useful to you.'

'Your sarvant, sir, your sarvant,' said the grub-man, making a low salutation behind his apron. 'Hope you find it pleasant here, sir; nice grounds—cool apartments—hope you'll stay with us some time—try to make it agreeable. What will you have for dinner to-day?'

'I prefer not to dine to-day,' said Bartleby, turning away. 'It would disagree with me; I am unused to dinners.' So saying, he slowly moved to the other side of the enclosure, and took up a position fronting the dead-wall.

'How's this?' said the grub-man, addressing me with a stare of astonishment. 'He's odd, ain't he?'

'I think he is a little deranged,' said I sadly.

'Deranged? deranged is it? Well, now, upon my word, I thought that friend of yourn was a gentleman forger; they are always pale and genteellike, them forgers. I can't help pity 'em—can't help it, sir. Did you know Monroe Edwards?' he added touchingly, and paused. Then, laying his hand piteously on my shoulder, sighed, 'he died of consumption at Sing-Sing. So you weren't acquainted with Monroe?'

'No, I was never socially acquainted with any forgers. But I cannot stop longer. Look to my friend yonder. You will not lose by it. I will see you again.'

Some few days after this, I again obtained admission to the Tombs, and went through the corridors in quest of Bartleby; but without finding him.

'I saw him coming from his cell not long ago,' said a turnkey, 'maybe he's gone to loiter in the yards.'

So I went in that direction.

'Are you looking for the silent man?' said another turnkey, passing me. 'Yonder he lies—sleeping in the yard there. 'Tis not twenty minutes since I saw him lie down.'

The yard was entirely quiet. It was not accessible to the common prisoners. The surrounding walls, of amazing thickness, kept off all sounds behind them. The Egyptian character of the masonry weighed upon me with its gloom. But a soft imprisoned turf grew under foot. The heart of the eternal pyramids, it seemed, wherein, by some strange magic, through the clefts, grass-seed, dropped by birds, had sprung.

Strangely huddled at the base of the wall, his knees drawn up, and lying on his side, his head touching the cold stones, I saw the wasted Bartleby. But nothing stirred. I paused; then went close up to him; stooped over, and saw that his dim eyes were open; otherwise he seemed profoundly sleeping. Something prompted me to touch him. I felt his hand, when a tingling shiver ran up my arm and down my spine to my feet.

The round face of the grub-man peered upon me now. 'His dinner is ready. Won't he dine to-day, either? Or does he live without dining?'

'Lives without dining,' said I, and closed the eyes.

'Eh!—He's asleep, ain't he?'

'With kings and counsellors,' murmured I.

There would seem little need for proceeding further in this history. Imagination will readily supply the meagre recital of poor Bartleby's interment. But, ere parting with the reader, let me say, that if this little narrative has sufficiently interested him, to awaken curiosity as to who Bartleby was, and what manner of life he led prior to the present narrator's making his acquaintance, I can only reply, that in such curiosity I fully share, but am wholly unable to gratify it. Yet here I hardly know whether I should divulge one little item of rumour, which came to my ear a few months after the scrivener's decease. Upon what basis it rested I could never ascertain; and hence, how true it is I cannot now tell. But, inasmuch as this vague report has not been without a certain suggestive interest to me, however sad, it may prove the same with some others; and so I will briefly mention it. The report was this: that Bartleby had been a subordinate clerk in the Dead Letter Office at Washington, from which he had been suddenly removed by a change in the administration. When I think over this rumour, hardly can I express the emotions which seize me. Dead letters! does it not sound like dead men? Conceive a man by nature and misfortune prone to a pallid hopelessness, can any business seem more fitted to heighten it than that of continually handling these dead letters, and assorting them for the flames? For by the cartload they are annually burned. Sometimes from out the folded paper the pale clerk takes a ring—the finger it was meant for, perhaps, moulders in the grave; a bank-note sent in swiftest charity—he whom it would relieve, nor eats nor hungers any more; pardon for those who died despairing; hope for those who died unhoping; good tidings for those who died stifled by unrelieved calamities. On errands of life, these letters speed to death.

Ah, Bartleby! Ah, humanity!

Study and Discussion Questions

1. Why do you think the narrator says that knowing something about himself, his employees, his business, and his physical setting "is indispensible to an adequate understanding" of Bartleby?
2. What does the narrator say about himself? Do his encounters with Bartleby change him? How?
3. What words does the narrator use to introduce Bartleby?
4. What does Bartleby actually say in the course of this story?
5. Chart the stages of Bartleby's withdrawal.
6. Where did Bartleby work, according to rumor, before he came to work for the narrator? Does that sufficiently explain his attitude?
7. What purpose do Nippers, Ginger Nut, and Turkey serve in the story?
8. Is this simply a story about an elaborate suicide?

Suggestions for Writing

1. "Nothing so aggravates an earnest person as passive resistance." Imagine that someone you work with or live with suddenly began to say nothing but, "I would prefer not to." How would you respond? Try narrating the story of a day (or part of a day) with this person.
2. What does the narrator give as his motives for his treatment of Bartleby? Do you agree, or do you think there are other things going on?
3. How strange a creature is Bartleby? Make a case that his behavior makes more sense than anyone else's in the story.
4. Act a bit like Bartleby. (Maybe you already do.) Try mild, yet steadfast passive resistance for part of a day and take note of people's reactions, including your own reaction to behaving unconventionally. Write about what you discover.

Critical Resources

1. Eastwood, D. R. "Melville's 'Bartleby' (An Essay in Old Criticism). *Hypothesis: Neo-Aristotelian Analysis* 17 (1996): 21–30.
2. McCall, Dan, ed. *Melville's Short Novels: Authoritative Texts, Contexts, Criticism.* New York: Norton, 2002.
3. Norberg, Peter. "On Teaching *Bartleby.*" *Leviathan: A Journal of Melville Studies* 2.2 (2000): 87–99.
4. Parker, Hershel. *Herman Melville: A Biography.* Baltimore, MD: Johns Hopkins University Press, 1997.

❀ ❀ ❀

PAMELA ZOLINE (b. 1941)

Pamela Zoline was born in Chicago and educated at the Slade School of Fine Arts in London. With the publication of "The Heat Death of the Universe" in 1967, Zoline was seen as a brilliant new female voice in the male dominated genre of science fiction. Yet the label of science fiction does not adequately describe Zoline's work. Other critics have suggested that Zoline's use of diverging realities and simultaneous dimensions of time, along with the use of lists and her unconventional mixing of literary forms, suggest not simply science fiction, but rather a postmodern form of the genre that seeks to convey the irrational nature of modern life. Nevertheless, Zoline has never chosen to write full time so her literary output has been minimal. Her other artistic pursuits include painting and sculpting and working to build a progressive and environmentally conscious community in her home town of Telluride, Colorado: "After years of effort I can report that yes, in fact, the work of sustainability—building community and supporting the natural environment—is clearly open to a radicalizing modality" (scifi.com). Her collected short stories were published in 1988 as The Heat Death of the Universe and Other Stories. *She has also written the children's story* Annika and the Wolves: A Fairy Tale *(1985).*

The Heat Death of the Universe (1967)

1. ONTOLOGY: That branch of metaphysics which concerns itself with the problems of the nature of existence or being.

2. Imagine a pale blue morning sky, almost green, with clouds only at the rims. The earth rolls and the sun appears to mount, mountains erode, fruits decay, the Foraminifera adds another chamber to its shell, babies' fingernails grow as does the hair of the dead in their graves, and in egg timers the sands fall and the eggs cook on.

3. Sarah Boyle thinks of her nose as too large, though several men have cherished it. The nose is generous and performs a well-calculated geometric curve, at the arch of which the skin is drawn very tight and a faint whiteness of bone can be seen showing through, it has much the same architectural tension and sense of mathematical calculation as the day after Thanksgiving breastbone on the carcass of turkey; her maiden name was Sloss, mixed German, English and Irish descent; in grade school she was very bad at playing softball and, besides being chosen last for the team, was always made to play center field, no one could ever hit to center field; she loves music best of all the arts, and of music, Bach, J.S.; she lives in California, though she grew up in Boston and Toledo.

4. Breakfast time at the Boyles' House on La Florida Street, Alameda, California, The children demand sugar Frosted Flakes.

With some reluctance Sarah Boyle dishes out Sugar Frosted Flakes to her children, already hearing the decay set in upon the little milk-white teeth, the bony whine of the dentist's drill. The dentist is a short, gentle man with a moustache who sometimes reminds Sarah of an uncle who lives in Ohio. One bowl per child.

5. If one can imagine it considered as an abstract object, by members of a totally separate culture, one can see that the cereal box might seem a beautiful thing. The solid rectangle is neatly joined and classical in proportions, on it are squandered wealths of richest colors, virgin blues, crimsons, dense ochres, precious pigments once reserved for sacred paintings and as cosmetics for the blind faces of marble gods. Giant size. Net Weight 16 ounces, 250 grams. "They're tigeriffic!" says Tony the Tiger. The box blatts promises: Energy, Nature's Own Goodness, an endless pubescence. On its back is a mask of William Shakespeare to be cut out, folded, worn by thousands of tiny Shakespeares in Kansas City, Detroit, Tucson, San Diego, Tampa. He appears at once more kindly and somewhat more vacant than we are used to seeing him. Two or more of the children lay claim to the mask, but Sarah puts off that Solomon's decision until such time as the box is empty.

6. A notice in orange flourishes states that a Surprise Gift is to be found somewhere in the package, nestled amongst the golden flakes. So far it has not been unearthed, and the children request more cereal than they wish to eat, great yellow heaps of it, to hurry the discovery. Even so, at the end of the meal, some layers of flakes remain in the box and the Gift must still be among them.

7. There is even a Special Offer of a secret membership, code and magic ring; these to be obtained by sending in the box top with 50¢.

8. Three offers on one cereal box. To Sarah Boyle this seems to be oversell. Perhaps something is terribly wrong with the cereal and it must be sold quickly, got off the shelves before the news breaks. Perhaps it causes a special, cruel Cancer in little children. As Sarah Boyle collects the bowls printed with bunnies and baseball statistics, still slopping half full of milk and wilted flakes, she imagines *in her mind's eye* the headlines, "Nation's Small Fry Stricken, Fate's Finger Sugar Coated, Lethal Sweetness Socks Tots."

9. Sarah Boyle is a vivacious and intelligent young wife and mother, educated at a fine Eastern college, proud of her growing family which keeps her busy and happy around the house.

10. Birthday.

Today is the birthday of one of the children. There will be a party in the late afternoon.

11. CLEANING UP THE HOUSE. ONE.

Cleaning up the kitchen. Sarah Boyle puts the bowls, plates, glasses and silverware into the sink. She scrubs at the stickiness on the yellow-marbled formica table with a blue synthetic sponge, a special blue which we shall see again. There are marks of children's hands in various sizes printed with sugar and grime on all the table's surfaces. The marks catch the light, they appear and disappear according to the position of the observing eye. The floor sweepings include a triangular half of toast spread with grape jelly, bobby pins, a green band-aid, flakes, a doll's eye, dust, dog's hair and a button.

12. Until we reach the statistically likely planet and begin to converse with whatever green-faced, teleporting denizens thereof—considering only this shrunk and communication-ravaged world—can we any more postulate a separate culture? Viewing the metastasis of Western Culture, it seems progressively less likely. Sarah Boyle imagines a whole world which has become like California, all topographical imperfections sanded away with the sweet-smelling burr of the plastic surgeon's cosmetic polisher; a world populace dieting, leisured, similar in pink and mauve hair and rhinestone shades. A land Cunt Pink and Avocado Green, brassiered and girdled by monstrous complexities of Super Highways, a California endless and unceasing, embracing and transforming the entire globe, California, California!

13. INSERT ONE. ON ENTROPY.

ENTROPY: A quantity introduced in the first place to facilitate the calculations, and to give clear expressions to the results of thermodynamics. Changes of entropy can be calculated only for a reversible process, and may then be defined as the ratio of the amount of heat taken up to the absolute temperature at which the heat is absorbed. Entropy changes for actual irreversible processes are calculated by postulating equivalent theoretical reversible changes. The entropy of a system is a measure of its degree of disorder. The total entropy of any isolated system can never decrease in any change; it must either increase (irreversible process) or remain constant (reversible process). The total entropy of the Universe therefore is increasing, tending toward a maximum, corresponding to complete disorder of the particles in it (assuming that it may be regarded as an isolated system). See *Heat Death of the Universe.*

14. CLEANING UP THE HOUSE. TWO.

Washing the baby's diapers. Sarah Boyle writes notes to herself all over the house; a mazed wild script larded with arrows, diagrams, pictures; graffiti on every available surface in a desperate/heroic attempt to index, record, bluff, invoke, order and placate. On the fluted and flowered white plastic lid of the diaper bin she has written in Blushing Pink Nitetime lipstick a phrase to ward off fumey ammoniac despair: "The nitrogen cycle is the vital round of organic and inorganic exchange on earth. The sweet breath of the Universe." On the wall by the washing machine are Yin and Yang signs, mandalas and the words, "Many young wives feel trapped. It is a contemporary sociological phenomenon which may be explained in part by a gap between changing living patterns and the accommodation of social services to these patterns." Over the stove she had written "Help, Help, Help, Help, Help."

15. Sometimes she numbers or letters the things in a room, writing the assigned character on each object. There are 819 separate moveable objects in the living room, counting books. Sometimes she labels objects with their names, or with false names, thus on her bureau the hair brush is labeled HAIR BRUSH, the cologne, COLOGNE, the hand cream, CAT. She is passionately fond of children's dictionaries, encyclopedias, ABCs and all reference books, transfixed and comforted at their simulacra of a complete listing and ordering.

16. On the door of a bedroom are written two definitions from reference books, "GOD: An object of worship"; "HOMEOSTASIS: Maintenance of constancy of internal environment."

17. Sarah Boyle washes the diapers, washes the linen, Oh Saint Veronica, changes the sheets on the baby's crib. She begins to put away some of the toys, stepping over and around the organizations of playthings which still seem inhabited. There are various vehicles, and articles of medicine, domesticity and war; whole zoos of stuffed animals, bruised and odorous with years of love; hundreds of small figures, plastic animals, cowboys, cars, spacemen, with which the children make sub and supra worlds in their play. One of Sarah's favorite toys is the Baba, the wooden Russian doll which, opened, reveals a smaller but otherwise identical doll which opens to reveal, etc., a lesson in infinity at least to the number of seven dolls.

18. Sarah Boyle's mother has been dead for two years. Sarah Boyle thinks of music as the formal articulation of the passage of time, and of Bach as the most poignant rendering of this. Her eyes are sometimes the color of the aforementioned kitchen sponge. Her hair is natural spaniel brown; months ago on an hysterical day she dyed it red, so now it is two-toned with a stripe in the middle, like the painted walls of slum buildings or old schools.

19. INSERT TWO. HEAT DEATH OF THE UNIVERSE.
The second law of thermodynamics can be interpreted to mean that the ENTROPY of a closed system tends toward a maximum and that its available ENERGY tends toward a minimum. It has been held that the Universe constitutes a thermodynamically closed system, and if this were true it would mean that a time must finally come when the Universe "unwinds" itself, no energy being available for use. This state is referred to as the "heat death of the Universe." It is by no means certain, however, that the Universe can be considered as a closed system in this sense.

20. Sarah Boyle pours out a Coke from the refrigerator and lights a cigarette. The coldness and sweetness of the thick brown liquid make her throat ache and her teeth sting briefly, sweet juice of my youth, her eyes glass with the carbonation, she thinks of the Heat Death of the Universe. A logarithmic of those late summer days, endless as the Irish serpent twisting through jeweled manuscripts forever, tail in mouth, the heat pressing, bloating, doing violence. The Los Angeles sky becomes so filled and bleached with detritus that it loses all color and silvers like a mirror, reflecting back the fricasseeing earth. Everything becoming warmer and warmer, each particle of matter becoming more agitated, more excited until the bonds shatter, the glues fail, the deodorants lose their seals. She imagines the whole of New York City melting like a Dali into a great chocolate mass, a great soup, the Great Soup of New York.

21. CLEANING UP THE HOUSE. THREE.

Beds made. Vacuuming the hall, a carpet of faded flowers, vines and leaves which endlessly wind and twist into each other in a fevered and permanent ecstasy. Suddenly the vacuum blows instead of sucks, spewing marbles, dolls' eyes, dust, crackers. An old trick. "Oh my god," says Sarah. The baby yells on cue for attention/changing/food. Sarah kicks the vacuum cleaner and it retches and begins working again.

22. AT LUNCH ONLY ONE GLASS OF MILK IS SPILLED.

At lunch only one glass of milk is spilled.

23. The plants need watering, Geranium, Hyacinth, Lavender, Avocado, Cyclamen. Feed the fish, happy fish with china castles and mermaids in the bowl. The turtle looks more and more unwell and is probably dying.

24. Sarah Boyle's blue eyes, how blue? Bluer far and of a different quality than the Nature metaphors which were both engine and fuel to so much of precedent literature. A fine, modern, acid, synthetic blue; the shiny cerulean of the skies on postcards sent from lush subtropics, the natives grinning ivory ambivalent grins in their dark faces; the promising, fat, unnatural blue of the heavy tranquilizer capsule; the cool, mean blue of that fake kitchen sponge; the deepest, most unbelievable azure of the tiled and mossless interiors of California swimming pools. The chemists in their kitchens cooked, cooled and distilled this blue from thousands of colorless and wonderfully constructed crystals, each one unique and nonpareil; and now that color hisses, bubbles, burns in Sarah's eyes.

25. INSERT THREE. ON LIGHT.

LIGHT: Name given to the agency by means of which a viewed object influences the observer's eyes. Consists of electromagnetic radiation within the wavelength range 4×10^{25} cm. to 7×10^{25} cm. approximately; variations in the wavelength produce different sensations in the eye, corresponding to different colors. See color vision.

26. LIGHT AND CLEANING THE LIVING ROOM.

All the objects (819) and surfaces in the living room are dusty, gray common dust as though this were the den of a giant, molting mouse. Suddenly quantities of waves or particles of very strong sunlight speed in through the window, and everything incandesces, multiple rainbows. Poised in what has become a solid cube of light, like an ancient insect trapped in amber, Sarah Boyle realizes that the dust is indeed the most beautiful stuff in the room, a manna for the eyes. Duchamp, that father of thought, has set with fixative some dust which fell on one of his sculptures, counting it as part of the work. "That way madness lies, says Sarah," says Sarah. The thought of ordering a household on Dada principles balloons again. All the rooms would fill up with objects, newspapers and magazines would compost, the potatoes in the rack, the canned green beans in the garbage can would take new heart and come to life again, reaching out green shoots toward the sun. The plants would grow wild and wind into a jungle around the house, splitting plaster, tearing shingles, the garden would enter in at the door. The goldfish would die, the birds would die, we'd have them stuffed; the dog would die from lack of care, and probably the children—all stuffed and sitting around the house, covered with dust.

27. INSERT FOUR. DADA.

DADA (Fr., hobby-horse) was a nihilistic precursor of Surrealism, invented in Zurich during World War I, a product of hysteria and shock lasting from about 1915 to 1922. It was deliberately anti-art and anti-sense, intended to outrage and scandalize, and its most characteristic production was the reproduction of the *Mona Lisa* decorated with a moustache and the obscene caption LHOOQ (read: *elle a chaud au cul*) "by" Duchamp. Other manifestations included Arp's collages of colored paper cut out at random and shuffled, ready-made objects such as the bottle drier and the bicycle wheel "signed" by Duchamp, Picabia's drawings of bits of machinery with incongruous titles, incoherent poetry, a lecture given by 38 lecturers in unison, and an exhibition in Cologne in 1920, held in an annex to a café lavatory, at which a chopper was provided for spectators to smash the exhibits with—which they did.

28. TIME PIECES AND OTHER MEASURING DEVICES.

In the Boyle house there are four clocks; three watches (one a Mickey Mouse watch which does not work); two calendars and two engagement books; three rulers; a yard stick; a measuring cup; a set of red plastic measuring spoons which includes a tablespoon, a teaspoon, a one-half teaspoon, one-fourth teaspoon and one-eighth teaspoon; an egg timer; an oral thermometer and a rectal thermometer; a Boy Scout compass; a barometer in the shape of a house, in and out of which an old woman and an old man chase each other forever without fulfilment; a bathroom scale; an infant scale; a tape measure which can be pulled out of a stuffed felt strawberry; a wall on which the children's heights are marked; a metronome.

29. Sarah Boyle finds a new line in her face after lunch while cleaning the bathroom. It is as yet hardly visible, running from the midpoint of her forehead to the bridge of her nose. By inward curling of her eyebrows she can etch it clearly as it will come to appear in the future. She marks another mark on the wall where she has drawn out a scoring area. Face Lines and Other Limitations of Mortality, the heading says. There are thirty-two marks, counting this latest one.

30. Sarah Boyle is a vivacious and witty young wife and mother, educated at a fine Eastern college, proud of her growing family which keeps her happy and busy around the house, involved in many hobbies and community activities, and only occasionally given to obsessions concerning Time/Entropy/Chaos and Death.

31. Sarah Boyle is never quite sure how many children she has.

32. Sarah thinks from time to time; Sarah is occasionally visited with this thought; at times this thought comes upon Sarah, that there are things to be hoped for, accomplishments to be desired beyond the mere reproductions, mirror reproduction of one's kind. The babies. Lying in bed at night sometimes the memory of the act of birth, always the hue and texture of red plush theater seats, washes up; the rending which always, at a certain intensity of pain, slipped into landscapes, the sweet breath of the sweating nurse. The wooden Russian doll has bright, perfectly round red spots on her cheeks, she splits in the center to reveal a doll smaller but in all other respects identical with round bright red spots on her cheeks, etc.

33. How fortunate for the species, Sarah muses or is mused, that children are as ingratiating as we know them. Otherwise they would soon be salted off for the leeches they are, and the race would extinguish itself in a fair sweet flowering, the last generations, massive achievement in the arts and pursuits of high civilization. The finest women would have their tubes tied off at the age of twelve, or perhaps refrain altogether from the Act of Love? All interests would be bent to a refining and perfecting of each febrile sense, each fluid hour, with no more cowardly investment in immortality via the patchy and too often disappointing vegetables of one's own womb.

34. INSERT FIVE. LOVE.
LOVE: a typical sentiment involving fondness for, or attachment to, an object, the idea of which is emotionally colored whenever it arises in the mind, and capable, as Shand has pointed out, of evoking any one of a whole gamut of primary emotions, according to the situation in which the object is placed, or represented; often, and by psychoanalysts always, used in the sense of *sex-love* or even *lust* (q.v.).

35. Sarah Boyle has at times felt a unity with her body, at other times a complete separation. The mind/body duality considered. The time/space duality con-

sidered. The male/female duality considered. The matter/energy duality considered. Sometimes, at extremes, her Body seems to her an animal on a leash, taken for walks in the park by her Mind. The lamp posts of experience. Her arms are lightly freckled, and when she gets very tired the places under her eyes become violet.

36. Housework is never completed, the chaos always lurks ready to encroach on any area left unweeded, a jungle filled with dirty pans and the roaring of giant stuffed toy animals suddenly turned savage. Terrible glass eyes.

37. SHOPPING FOR THE BIRTHDAY CAKE.

Shopping in the supermarket with the baby in front of the cart and a larger child holding on. The light from the ice-cube-tray-shaped fluorescent lights is mixed blue and pink and brighter, colder, and cheaper than daylight. The doors swing open just as you reach out your hand for them, Tantalus, moving with a ghastly quiet swing. Hot dogs for the party. Potato chips, gum drops, a paper table cloth with birthday designs, hot dog buns, catsup, mustard, picalilli, balloons, instant coffee Continental style, dog food, frozen peas, ice cream, frozen lima beans, frozen broccoli in butter sauce, paper birthday hats, paper napkins in three colors, a box of Sugar Frosted Flakes with a Wolfgang Amadeus Mozart mask on the back, bread, pizza mix. The notes of a just graspable music filter through the giant store, for the most part bypassing the brain and acting directly on the liver, blood and lymph. The air is delicately scented with aluminum. Half and half cream, tea bags, bacon, sandwich meat, strawberry jam. Sarah is in front of the shelves of cleaning products now, and the baby is beginning to whine. Around her are whole libraries of objects, offering themselves. Some of that same old hysteria that had incarnadined her hair rises up again, and she does not refuse it. There is one moment when she can choose direction, like standing on a chalk drawn X, a hot cross bun, and she does not choose calm and measure. Sarah Boyle begins to pick out, methodically, deliberately and with a careful ecstasy, one of every cleaning product which the store sells. Window Cleaner, Glass Cleaner, Brass Polish, Silver Polish, Steel Wool, eighteen different brands of Detergent, Disinfectant, Toilet Cleanser, Water Softener, Fabric Softener, Drain Cleanser, Spot Remover, Floor Wax, Furniture Wax, Car Wax, Carpet Shampoo, Dog Shampoo, Shampoo for people with dry, oily and normal hair, for people with dandruff, for people with gray hair. Tooth Paste, Tooth Powder, Denture Cleaner, Deodorants, Antiperspirants, Antiseptics, Soaps, Cleansers, Abrasives, Oven Cleansers, Makeup Removers. When the same products appear in different sizes Sarah takes one of each size. For some products she accumulates whole little families of containers: a giant Father bottle of shampoo, a Mother bottle, an Older Sister bottle just smaller than the Mother bottle, and a very tiny Baby Brother bottle. Sarah fills three shopping carts and has to have help wheeling them all down the aisles. At the check-out counter her laughter and hysteria keep threatening to overflow as the pale blonde clerk with no eyebrows like the *Mona Lisa* pretends normality and disinterest. The bill comes to $57.53 and Sarah has to write a check. Driving home, the baby strapped in the drive-a-cot and the paper bags bulging in the back seat, she cries.

38. BEFORE THE PARTY.

Mrs. David Boyle, mother-in-law of Sarah Boyle, is coming to the party of her grandchild. She brings a toy, a yellow wooden duck on a string, made in Austria; the duck quacks as it is pulled along the floor. Sarah is filling paper cups with gum drop and chocolates, and Mrs. David Boyle sits at the kitchen table and talks to her. She is talking about several things, she is talking about her garden which is flourishing except for a plague of rare black beetles, thought to have come from Hong Kong, which are undermining some of the most delicate growths at the roots, and feasting on the leaves of other plants. She is talking about a sale of household linens which she plans to attend on the following Tuesday. She is talking about her neighbor who has cancer and is wasting away. The neighbor is a Catholic woman who had never had a day's illness in her life until the cancer struck, and now she is, apparently, failing with dizzying speed. The doctor says her body's chaos, chaos, cells running wild all over, says Mrs. David Boyle. When I visited her she hardly *knew* me, can hardly *speak,* can't keep herself *clean,* says Mrs. David Boyle.

39. Sometimes Sarah can hardly remember how many cute, chubby little children she has.

40. When she used to stand out in center field far away from the other players, she used to make up songs and sing them to herself.

41. She thinks of the end of the world by ice.

42. She thinks of the end of the world by water.

43 She thinks of the end of the world by nuclear war.

44. There must be more than this, Sarah Boyle thinks, from time to time. What could one do to justify one's passage? Or less ambitiously, to change, even in the motion of the smallest mote, the course and circulation of the world? Sometimes Sarah's dreams are of heroic girth, a new symphony using laboratories of machinery and all invented instruments, at once giant in scope and intelligible to all, to heal the bloody breach; a series of paintings which would transfigure and astonish and calm the frenzied art world in its panting race; a new novel that would refurbish language. Sometimes she considered the mystical, the streaky and random, and it seems that one change, no matter how small, would be enough. Turtles are supposed to live for many years. To carve a name, date and perhaps a word of hope upon a turtle's shell, then set him free to wend the world, surely this one act might cancel out absurdity?

45. Mrs. David Boyle has a faint moustache, like Duchamp's *Mona Lisa*.

46. THE BIRTHDAY PARTY.

Many children, dressed in pastels, sit around the long table. They are exhausted and overexcited from games fiercely played, some are flushed and wet, others unnaturally pale. This general agitation, and the paper party hats they wear, combine to make them appear a dinner party of debauched midgets. It is time for the cake. A huge chocolate cake in the shape of a rocket and launching pad and covered with blue and pink icing is carried in. In the hush the birthday child begins to cry. He stops crying, makes a wish and blows out the candles.

47. One child will not eat hot dogs, ice cream or cake, and asks for cereal. Sarah pours him out a bowl of Sugar Frosted Flakes, and a moment later he chokes. Sarah pounds him on the back and out spits a tiny green plastic snake with red glass eyes, the Surprise Gift. All the children want it.

48. AFTER THE PARTY THE CHILDREN ARE PUT TO BED.

Bath time. Observing the nakedness of children, pink and slippery as seals, squealing as seals, now the splashing, grunting and smacking of cherry flesh on raspberry flesh reverberate in the pearl tiled steamy cubicle. The nakedness of children is so much more absolute than that of the mature. No musky curling hair to indicate the target points, no knobbly clutch of plane and fat and curvature to ennoble this prince of beasts. All well-fed naked children appear edible, Sarah's teeth hum in her head with memory of bloody feastings, prehistory. Young humans appear too like the young of other species for smugness, and the comparison is not even in their favor, they are much the most peeled and unsupple of those young. Such pinkness, such utter nuded pinkness; the orifices neatly incised, rimmed with a slightly deeper rose, the incessant demands for breast time milks of many sorts.

49. INSERT SIX. WEINER ON ENTROPY.

In Gibbs' Universe order is least probable, chaos most probable. But while the Universe as a whole, if indeed there is a whole Universe, tends to run down, there are local enclaves whose direction seems opposed to that of the Universe at large and in which there is a limited and temporary tendency for organization to increase. Life finds its home in some of these enclaves.

50. Sarah Boyle imagines, in her mind's eye, cleaning and ordering the whole world, even the Universe. Filling the great spaces of Space with a marvelous sweet smelling, deep cleansing foam. Deodorizing rank caves and volcanoes. Scrubbing rocks.

51. INSERT SEVEN. TURTLES.

Many different species of carnivorous Turtles live in the fresh waters of the tropical and temperate zones of various continents. Most Northerly of the

European Turtles (extending as far as Holland and Lithuania) is the European Pond Turtle *(Emys orbicularis).* It is from 8 to 10 inches long and may live a hundred years.

52. CLEANING UP AFTER THE PARTY.

Sarah is cleaning up after the party. Gum drops and melted ice cream surge off paper plates, making holes in the paper tablecloth through the printed roses. A fly has died a splendid death in a pool of strawberry ice cream. Wet jelly beans stain all they touch, finally becoming themselves colorless, opaque white like flocks of tamed or sleeping maggots. Plastic favors mount half-eaten pieces of blue cake. Strewn about are thin strips of fortune papers from the Japanese poppers. Upon them are printed strangely assorted phrases selected by apparently unilingual Japanese. Crowds of delicate yellow people spending great chunks of their lives in producing these most ephemeral of objects, and inscribing thousands of fine papers with absurd and incomprehensible messages. "The very hairs of your head are all numbered," reads one. Most of the balloons have popped. Someone has planted a hot dog in the daffodil pot. A few of the helium balloons have escaped their owners and now ride the ceiling. Another fortune paper reads, "Emperor's horses meet death worse, numbers, numbers."

53. She is very tired, violet under the eyes, mauve beneath the eyes. Her uncle in Ohio used to get the same marks under his eyes. She goes to the kitchen to lay the table for tomorrow's breakfast, then she sees that in the turtle's bowl the turtle is floating, still, on the surface of the water. Sarah Boyle pokes at it with a pencil but it does not move. She stands for several minutes looking at the dead turtle on the surface of the water. She is crying again.

54. She begins to cry. She goes to the refrigerator and takes out a carton of eggs, white eggs, extra large. She throws them one by one onto the kitchen floor which is patterned with strawberries in squares. They break beautifully. There is a Secret Society of Dentists, all moustached, with Special Code and Magic Rings. She begins to cry. She takes up three bunny dishes and throws them against the refrigerator, they shatter, and then the floor is covered with shards, chunks of partial bunnies, an ear, an eye here, a paw; Stockton, California, Acton, California, Chico, California, Redding, California, Glen Ellen, California, Cadix, California, Angels Camps, California, Half Moon Bay. The total ENTROPY of the Universe therefore is increasing, tending toward a maximum, corresponding to complete disorder of the particles in it. She is crying, her mouth is open. She throws a jar of grape jelly and it smashes the window over the sink. Her eyes are blue. She begins to open her mouth. It has been held that the Universe constitutes a thermodynamically closed system, and if this were true it would mean that a time must finally come when the Universe "unwinds" itself, no energy being available for use. This state is referred to as the "Heat Death of the Universe." Sarah Boyle begins to cry. She throws a jar of strawberry jam against the stove, enamel chips off and the stove begins to bleed. Bach had twenty children,

how many children has Sarah Boyle? Her mouth is open. Her mouth is opening. She turns on the water and fills the sinks with detergent. She writes on the kitchen wall, "William Shakespeare has Cancer and lives in California." She writes, "Sugar Frosted Flakes are the Food of the Gods." The water foams up in the sink, overflowing, bubbling onto the strawberry floor. She is about to begin to cry. Her mouth is opening. She is crying. She cries. How can one ever tell whether there are one or many fish? She begins to break glasses and dishes, she throws cups and cooking pots and jars of food which shatter and break and spread over the kitchen. The sand keeps falling, very quietly, in the egg timer. The old man and woman in the barometer never catch each other. She picks up eggs and throws them into the air. She begins to cry. She opens her mouth. The eggs arch slowly through the kitchen, like a baseball, hit high against the spring sky, seen from far away. They go higher and higher in the stillness, hesitate at the zenith, then begin to fall away slowly, slowly, through the fine, clear air.

Study and Discussion Questions

1. How does Sarah Boyle spend her day?
2. What function do the "Inserts" have in the story?
3. How many children does Sarah Boyle have?
4. Find examples of irony in the story.
5. List instances in the story of the passing of time.
6. Why do you think one of Sarah's favorite toys is the Russian Baba doll?
7. How does Zoline use color in this story? Find some examples.
8. What happens to Sarah Boyle in the supermarket?
9. In the last paragraph, Sarah Boyle "begins to cry." What else does she do and where do you think it is leading?
10. Discuss turtles, plants, dust, and cleansers.

Suggestions for Writing

1. Why do you think Zoline tells this story in numbered paragraphs?
2. Write a short character sketch of Sarah Boyle.
3. Choose any one of the paragraphs, analyze it, and discuss its function in the development of the story.
4. Is Sarah Boyle's life a "closed system"? (See paragraph 19.) If so, how? If not, where are the potential or actual openings?
5. Is Sarah Boyle crazy or has she just become sane?
6. Write a postscript to this story. What is Sarah Boyle going to do next? You might set your postscript immediately after the time of the story or you might set it a few years later.

Critical Resources

1. Hewitt, Elizabeth. "Generic Exhaustion and the 'Heat Death' of Science Fiction." *Science-Fiction Studies* 21.3 (1994): 289–301.

2. Papke, Mary. "Context: 'What Do Women Want?' " *Center for Book Culture.org.* May 15; 2005. <http://www.centerforbookculture.org/context/no11/Papke.html>

3. Sargent, Pamela, ed. *Women of Wonder: The Classic Years: Science Fiction by Women From the 1940s to the 1970s.* San Diego, CA: Harcourt, 1995.

4. "SciFiction: Pamela Zoline." *SciFi.com.* May 15, 2005. <http://www.scifi .com/scifiction/classics/classics_archive/zoline/zoline1.html>

JAMES ALAN MCPHERSON (b. 1943)

Despite attending segregated schools as a youth growing up in Savanna, Georgia, James Alan McPherson's exposure to the diverse cultures of the city would inevitably influence his thematic concerns as a writer. McPherson would eventually receive a law degree from Harvard University (1968) and his M.F.A. from the University of Iowa in 1969. His first published work, the short story collection Hue and Cry, *published in 1969, was met with both critical and public approval. While much was expected from him as a promising young African-American writer, it would be eight years until McPherson would publish his second collection of short stories,* Elbow Room *(1977), a book demonstrative of his maturation and one that would be awarded the Pulitzer Prize. Working within an acute realism, McPherson's stories often center around the issue of race and the relationships between blacks and whites. Yet McPherson resists easy racial stereotypes by creating characters that are unique—individuals, both black and white, who must grapple not only with the complex problems of racism, but racism as it collides with poverty and violence. His latest works include* Crabcakes: A Memoir *(1998) and* A Region Not Home: Reflections from Exile *(2000). In "A Loaf of Bread," first published in* Elbow Room, *McPherson uses an omniscient narrator to show how the conflict between Nelson Reed and Harold Green is much more than a simple black/white issue.*

A Loaf of Bread   (1977)

It was one of those obscene situations, pedestrian to most people, but invested with meaning for a few poor folk whose lives are usually spent outside the imaginations of their fellow citizens. A grocer named Harold Green was caught red-handed selling to one group of people the very same goods he sold at lower prices at similar outlets in better neighborhoods. He had been doing this for many years, and at first he could not understand the outrage heaped upon him. He acted only from habit, he insisted, and had nothing personal against the people whom he served. They were his neighbors. Many of them he had carried on the cuff during hard times. Yet, through some mysterious access to a television station, the poor folk were now empowered to make grand denunciations of the grocer. Green's children now saw their father's business being picketed on the Monday evening news.

No one could question the fact that the grocer had been overcharging the people. On the news even the reporter grimaced distastefully while reading the statistics. His expression said, "It is my job to report the news, but sometimes even I must disassociate myself from it to protect my honor." This, at least, was the impression the grocer's children seemed to bring away from the television. Their father's name had not been mentioned, but there was a close-up of his store with angry black people, and a few outraged whites, marching in groups of three in front of it. There was also a close-up of his name. After seeing this, they were in no mood to watch cartoons. At the dinner table, disturbed by his children's silence, Harold Green felt compelled to say, "I am not a dishonest man." Then he felt ashamed. The children, a boy and his older sister, immediately left the table, leaving Green alone with his wife. "Ruth, I am not dishonest," he repeated to her.

Ruth Green did not say anything. She knew, and her husband did not, that the outraged people had also picketed the school attended by their children. They had threatened to return each day until Green lowered his prices. When they called her at home to report this, she had promised she would talk with him. Since she could not tell him this, she waited for an opening. She looked at her husband across the table.

"I did not make the world," Green began, recognizing at once the seriousness in her stare. "My father came to this country with nothing but his shirt. He was exploited for as long as he couldn't help himself. He did not protest or picket. He put himself in a position to play by the rules he had learned." He waited for his wife to answer, and when she did not, he tried again. "I did not make this world," he repeated. "I only make my way in it. Such people as these, they do not know enough to not be exploited. If not me, there would be a Greek, a Chinaman, maybe an Arab or a smart one of their own kind. Believe me, I deal with them. There is something in their style that lacks the patience to run a concern such as mine. If I closed down, take my word on it, someone else would do what has to be done."

But Ruth Green was not thinking of his leaving. Her mind was on other matters. Her children had cried when they came home early from school. She had no special feeling for the people who picketed, but she did not like to see her children cry. She had kissed them generously, then sworn them to silence. "One day this week," she told her husband, "you will give free, for eight hours, anything your customers come in to buy. There will be no publicity, except what they spread by word of mouth. No matter what they say to you, no matter what they take, you will remain silent." She stared deeply into him for what she knew was there. "If you refuse, you have seen the last of your children and myself."

Her husband grunted. Then he leaned toward her. "I will not knuckle under," he said. "I will *not* give!"

"We shall see," his wife told him.

The black pickets, for the most part, had at first been frightened by the audacity of their undertaking. They were peasants whose minds had long before become resigned to their fate as victims. None of them, before now, had thought to challenge this. But now, when they watched themselves on television, they hardly recognized the faces they saw beneath the hoisted banners and placards. Instead of reflecting the meekness they all felt, the faces looked angry. The close-ups looked especially intimidating. Several of the first pickets, maids who worked in the suburbs, reported that their employers, seeing the activity on the afternoon news, had begun treating them with new respect. One woman, midway through the weather report, called around the neighborhood to disclose that her employer had that very day given her a new china plate for her meals. The paper plates, on which all previous meals had been served, had been thrown into the wastebasket. One recipient of this call, a middle-aged woman known for her bashfulness and humility, rejoined that her husband, a sheet-metal worker, had only a few hours before been called "Mister" by his supervisor, a white man with a passionate hatred of color. She added the tale of a neighbor down the street, a widow-woman named Murphy, who had at first been reluctant to join the picket; this woman now was insisting it should be made a daily event. Such talk as this circulated among the people who had been instrumental in raising the issue. As news of their victory leaked into the ears of others who had not participated, they received all through the night calls from strangers requesting verification, offering advice, and vowing support. Such strangers listened, and then volunteered stories about indignities inflicted on them by city officials, policemen, other grocers. In this way, over a period of hours, the community became even more incensed and restless than it had been at the time of the initial picket.

Soon, the man who had set events in motion found himself a hero. His name was Nelson Reed, and all his adult life he had been employed as an assembly-line worker. He was a steady husband, the father of three children, and a deacon in the Baptist church. All his life he had trusted in God and gotten along. But now something in him capitulated to the reality that came suddenly into focus. "I was wrong," he told people who called him. "The onliest thing that matters in this world is *money*. And when was the last time you seen a picture of Jesus on a dollar bill?" This line, which he repeated over and over, caused a few callers to laugh nervously, but not without some affirmation that this was indeed the way things were. Many said they had known it all along. Others argued that although it was certainly true, it was one thing to live without money and quite another to live without faith. But still most callers laughed and said, "You right. You *know* I know you right. Ain't it the truth, though?" Only a few people, among them Nelson Reed's wife, said nothing and looked very sad.

Why they looked sad, however, they would not communicate. And anyone observing their troubled faces would have to trust his own intuition. It is known that Reed's wife, Betty, measured all events against the fullness of her own experience. She was skeptical of everything. Brought to the church after a number of years of living openly with a jazz musician, she had embraced religion when she married Nelson Reed. But though she no longer believed completely in the world, she nonetheless had not fully embraced God. There was something in the nature of Christ's swift rise that had always bothered her, and something in the blood and vengeance of the Old Testament that was mellowing and refreshing. But she had never communicated these thoughts to anyone, especially her husband. Instead, she smiled vacantly while others professed leaps of faith, remained silent when friends spoke fiercely of their convictions. The presence of this vacuum in her contributed to her personal mystery; people said she was beautiful, although she was not outwardly so. Perhaps it was because she wished to protect this inner beauty that she did not smile now, and looked extremely sad, listening to her husband on the telephone.

Nelson Reed had no reason to be sad. He seemed to grow more energized and talkative as the days passed. He was invited by an alderman, on the Tuesday after the initial picket, to tell his story on a local television talk show. He sweated heavily under the hot white lights and attempted to be philosophical. "I notice," the host said to him, "that you are not angry at this exploitative treatment. What, Mr. Reed, is the source of your calm?" The assembly-line worker looked unabashedly into the camera and said, "I have always believed in *Justice* with a capital *J.* I was raised up from a baby believin' that God ain't gonna let nobody go *too* far. See, in *my* mind God is in charge of *all* the capital letters in the alphabet of this world. It say in the Scripture He is Alpha and Omega, the first and the last. He is just about the *onliest* capitalizer they is." Both Reed and the alderman laughed. "Now, when *men* start to capitalize, they gets *greedy.* They put a little *j* in *joy* and a littler one in *justice.* They raise up a big *G* in *Greed* and a big *E* in *Evil.* Well, soon as they commence to put a little *g* in *God,* you can expect some kind of reaction. The Savior will just raise up the *H* in *Hell* and go on from there. And that's just what I'm doin', giving these sharpies *HELL* with a big *H.*" The talk show host laughed along with Nelson Reed and the alderman. After the taping they drank coffee in the back room of the studio and talked about the sad shape of the world.

Three days before he was to comply with his wife's request, Green, the grocer, saw this talk show on television while at home. The words of Nelson Reed sent a chill through him. Though Reed had attempted to be philosophical, Green did not perceive the statement in this light. Instead, he saw a vindictive-looking black man seated between an ambitious alderman and a smug talk-show host. He saw them chatting comfortably about the nature of evil. The cameraman had shot mostly close-ups, and Green could see the set in Nelson Reed's jaw. The color of Reed's face was maddening. When his children came into the den, the grocer was in a sweat. Before he could think, he had shouted at them and struck the button turning off the set. The two children rushed from the room screaming. Ruth Green ran in from the kitchen. She knew why he was upset because she had received a call about the show; but she said nothing and pretended ignorance. Her children's school had been picketed that day, as it had the day before. But both children were still forbidden to speak of this to their father.

"Where do they get so much power?" Green said to his wife. "Two days ago, nobody would have cared. Now, everywhere, even in my home, I am condemned as a rascal. And what do I own? An airline? A multi-national? Half of South America? *No!* I own three stores, one of which happens to be run in a certain neighborhood inhabited by people who cost me money to run it." He sighed and sat upright on the sofa, his chubby legs spread wide. "A cab driver has a meter that clicks as he goes along. I pay extra for insurance, iron bars, pilfering by customers and employees. Nothing clicks. But when I add a little overhead to my prices, suddenly everything clicks. But for someone else. When was there last such a world?" He pressed the palms of both hands to his temples, suggesting a bombardment of brain-stinging sounds.

This gesture evoked no response from Ruth Green. She remained standing by the door, looking steadily at him. She said, "To protect yourself, I would not stock any more fresh cuts of meat in the store until after the giveaway on Saturday. Also, I would not tell it to the employees until after the first customer of the day has begun to check out. But I would urge you to hire several security guards to close the door promptly at seven-thirty, as is usual." She wanted to say much more than this, but did not. Instead she watched him. He was looking at the blank gray television screen, his palms still pressed against his ears. "In case you need to hear again," she continued in a weighty tone of voice, "I said two days ago, and I say again now, that if you fail to do this you will not see your children again for many years."

He twisted his head and looked up at her. "What is the color of these people?" he asked.

"Black," his wife said.

"And what is the name of my children?"

"Green."

The grocer smiled. "There is your answer," he told his wife. "Green is the only color I am interested in."

His wife did not smile. "Insufficient," she said.

"The world is mad!" he moaned. "But it is a point of sanity with me to not bend. I will not bend." He crossed his legs and pressed one hand firmly atop his knee. "*I will not bend,*" he said.

"We will see," his wife said.

Nelson Reed, after the television interview, became the acknowledged leader of the disgruntled neighbors. At first a number of them met in the kitchen at his house; then, as space was lacking for curious newcomers, a mass meeting was held on Thursday in an abandoned theater. His wife and three children sat in the front row. Behind them sat the widow Murphy, Lloyd Dukes, Tyrone Brown, Les Jones—those who had joined him on the first picket line. Behind these sat people who bought occasionally at the store, people who lived on the fringes of the neighborhood, people from other neighborhoods come to investigate the problem, and the merely curious. The middle rows were occupied by a few people from the suburbs, those who had seen the talk show and whose outrage at the grocer proved much more powerful than their fear of black people. In the rear of the theater crowded aging, old-style leftists, somber students, cynical young black men with angry grudges to explain with inarticulate gestures. Leaning against the walls, and huddled near the doors at the rear, tape-recorder-bearing social scientists looked as detached and serene as bookies at the track. Here and there, in this diverse crowd, a politician stationed himself, pumping hands vigorously and pressing his palms gently against the shoulders of elderly people. Other visitors passed out leaflets, buttons, glossy color prints of men who promoted causes, the familiar and obscure. There was a hubbub of voices, a blend of the strident and the playful, the outraged and the reverent, lending an undercurrent of ominous energy to the assembly.

Nelson Reed spoke from a platform on the stage, standing before a yellowed, shredded screen that had once reflected the images of matinee idols. "I don't mind sayin' that I have always been a sucker," he told the crowd. "All my life I have been a sucker for the words of Jesus. Being a natural-born fool, I just ain't never had the *sense* to learn no better. Even right today, while the whole world is sayin' wrong is right and up is down, I'm so dumb I'm *still* steady believin' what is wrote in the Good Book. . . ."

From the audience, especially the front rows, came a chorus singing, "Preach!"

"I have no doubt," he continued in a low baritone, "that it's true what is writ in the Good Book: 'The last shall be first and the first shall be last.' I don't know about y'all, but I have *always* been the last. I never wanted to be the first, but sometimes it look like the world get so bad that them that's holdin' onto the tree of life is the onliest ones left when God commence to blowin' dead leafs off the branches."

"Now you preaching," someone called.

In the rear of the theater a white student shouted an awkward "Amen."

Nelson Reed began walking across the stage to occupy the major part of his nervous energy. But to those in the audience, who now hung on his every word, it looked as though he strutted. "All my life," he said, "I have claimed to be a man without earnin' the right to call myself that. You know, the *average* man ain't really a man. The average man is a *boot-licker.* In fact, the *average* man would *run away* if he found hisself standing alone facin' down a adversary. I have done that *too many a time* in my life! But *not no more.* Better to be *once* was than *never* was a man. I will tell you tonight, there is somethin' *wrong* in being average. *I intend to stand up!* Now, if your average man that ain't really a man stand up, two things gonna happen: *One,* he g'on bust through all the weights that been place on his head, and, *two,* he g'on feel a lot of pain. But that same hurt is what make things fall in place. That, and gettin' your hands on one of these slick four-flushers tight enough so's you can squeeze him and say, '*No more!*' You do that, you g'on hurt some, but *you won't be average no more . . .*"

"*No more!*" a few people in the front rows repeated.

"I say *no more!*" Nelson Reed shouted.

"*No more! No more! No more!*" The chant rustled through the crowd like the rhythm of an autumn wind against a shedding tree.

Then people laughed and chattered in celebration.

As for the grocer, from the evening of the television interview he had begun to make plans. Unknown to his wife, he cloistered himself several times with his brother-in-law, an insurance salesman, and plotted a course. He had no intention of tossing steaks to the crowd. "And why should I, Tommy?" he asked his wife's brother, a lean, bald-headed man named Thomas. "I don't cheat anyone. I have never cheated anyone. The businesses I run are always on the up-and-up. So why should I pay?"

"Quite so," the brother-in-law said, chewing an unlit cigarillo. "The world has gone crazy. Next they will say that people in my business are responsible for prolonging life. I have found that people who refuse to believe in death refuse also to believe in the harshness of life. I sell well by saying that death is a long happiness. I show people the realities of life and compare this to a funeral with dignity, *and* the promise of a bundle for every loved one salted away. When they look around hard at life, they usually buy."

"So?" asked Green. Thomas was a college graduate with a penchant for philosophy.

"So," Thomas answered. "You must fight to show these people the reality of both your situation and theirs. How would it be if you visited one of their meetings and chalked out, on a blackboard, the dollars and cents of your operation? Explain your overhead, your security fees, all the additional expenses. If you treat them with respect, they might understand."

Green frowned. "That I would never do," he said. "It would be admission of a certain guilt."

The brother-in-law smiled, but only with one corner of his mouth. "Then you have something to feel guilty about?" he asked.

The grocer frowned at him. "*Nothing!*" he said with great emphasis.

"So?" Thomas said.

This first meeting between the grocer and his brother-in-law took place on Thursday, in a crowded barroom.

At the second meeting, in a luncheonette, it was agreed that the grocer should speak privately with the leader of the group, Nelson Reed. The meeting at which this was agreed took place on Friday afternoon. After accepting this advice from Thomas, the grocer resigned himself to explain to Reed, in as finite detail as possible, the economic structure of his operation. He vowed to suppress no information. He would explain everything: inventories, markups, sale items, inflation, balance sheets, specialty items, overhead, and that mysterious item called profit. This last item, promising to be the most difficult to explain,

Green and his brother-in-law debated over for several hours. They agreed first of all that a man should not work for free, then they agreed that it was unethical to ruthlessly exploit. From these parameters, they staked out an area between fifteen and forty percent, and agreed that someplace between these two borders lay an amount of return that could be called fair. This was easy, but then Thomas introduced the factor of circumstance. He questioned whether the fact that one serviced a risky area justified the earning of profits closer to the forty-percent edge of the scale. Green was unsure. Thomas smiled. "Here is a case that will point out an analogy," he said, licking a cigarillo. "I read in the papers that a family wants to sell an electric stove. I call the home and the man says fifty dollars. I ask to come out and inspect the merchandise. When I arrive I see they are poor, have already bought a new stove that is connected, and are selling the old one for fifty dollars because they want it out of the place. The electric stove is in good condition, worth much more than fifty. But because I see what I see I offer forty-five."

Green, for some reason, wrote down this figure on the back of the sales slip for the coffee they were drinking.

The brother-in-law smiled. He chewed his cigarillo. "The man agrees to take forty-five dollars, saying he has had no other calls. I look at the stove again and see a spot of rust. I say I will give him forty dollars. He agrees to this, on condition that I myself haul it away. I say I will haul it away if he comes down to thirty. You, of course, see where I am going."

The grocer nodded. "The circumstances of his situation, his need to get rid of the stove quickly, placed him in a position where he has little room to bargain?"

"Yes," Thomas answered. "So? Is it ethical, Harry?"

Harold Green frowned. He had never liked his brother-in-law, and now he thought the insurance agent was being crafty. "But," he answered, "this man does not *have* to sell! It is his choice whether to wait for other calls. It is not the fault of the buyer that the seller is in a hurry. It is the right of the buyer to get what he wants at the lowest price possible. That is the rule. That has *always* been the rule. And the reverse of it applies to the seller as well."

"Yes," Thomas said, sipping coffee from the Styrofoam cup. "But suppose that in addition to his hurry to sell, the owner was also of a weak soul. There are, after all, many such people." He smiled. "Suppose he placed no value on the money?"

"Then," Green answered, "your example is academic. Here we are not talking about real life. One man lives by the code, one man does not. Who is there free enough to make a judgment?" He laughed. "Now you see," he told his brother-in-law. "Much more than a few dollars are at stake. If this one buyer is to be condemned, then so are most people in the history of the world. An examination of history provides the only answer to your question. This code will be here tomorrow, long after the ones who do not honor it are not."

They argued fiercely late into the afternoon, the brother-in-law leaning heavily on his readings. When they parted, a little before 5:00 P.M., nothing had been resolved.

Neither was much resolved during the meeting between Green and Nelson Reed. Reached at home by the grocer in the early evening, the leader of the group spoke coldly at first, but consented finally to meet his adversary at a nearby drugstore for coffee and a talk. They met at the lunch counter, shook hands awkwardly, and sat for a few minutes discussing the weather. Then the grocer pulled two gray ledgers from his briefcase. "You have for years come into my place," he told the man. "In my memory I have always treated you well. Now our relationship has come to this." He slid the books along the counter until they touched Nelson Reed's arm.

Reed opened the top book and flipped the thick green pages with his thumb. He did not examine the figures. "All I know," he said, "is over at your place a can of soup cost me fifty-five cents, and two miles away at your other store for white folks you chargin' thirty-nine cents." He said this with the calm authority of an outraged soul. A quality of condescension tinged with pity crept into his gaze.

The grocer drummed his fingers on the counter top. He twisted his head and looked away, toward shelves containing cosmetics, laxatives, toothpaste. His eyes lingered on a poster of a woman's apple red lips and milk white teeth. The rest of the face was missing.

"Ain't no use to hide," Nelson Reed said, as to a child. "*I* know you wrong, *you* know you wrong, and before I finish, *everybody in this city* g'on know you wrong. God don't *like* ugly." He closed his eyes and gripped the cup of coffee. Then he swung his head suddenly and faced the grocer again. "Man, why you want to *do* people that way?" he asked. "We human, same as you."

"Before *God!*" Green exclaimed, looking squarely into the face of Nelson Reed. "Before God!" he said again. "*I am not an evil man!*" These last words sounded more like a moan as he tightened the muscles in his throat to lower the sound of his voice. He tossed his left shoulder as if adjusting the sleeve of his coat, or as if throwing off some unwanted weight. Then he peered along the countertop. No one was watching. At the end of the counter the waitress was scrubbing the coffee urn. "Look at these figures, please," he said to Reed.

The man did not drop his gaze. His eyes remained fixed on the grocer's face.

"All right," Green said. "Don't look. I'll tell you what is in these books, believe me if you want. I work twelve hours a day, one day off per week, running my business in three stores. I am not a wealthy person. In one place, in the area you call white, I get by barely by smiling lustily at old ladies, stocking gourmet stuff on the chance I will build a reputation as a quality store. The two clerks there cheat me; there is nothing I can do. In this business you must be friendly with everybody. The second place is on the other side of town, in a neighborhood as poor as this one. I get out there seldom. The profits are not worth the gas. I use the loss there as a write-off against some other properties." He paused. "Do you understand write-off?" he asked Nelson Reed.

"Naw," the man said.

Harold Green laughed. "What does it matter?" he said in a tone of voice intended for himself alone. "In this area I will admit I make a profit, but it is not so much as you think. But I do not make a profit here because the people are black. I make a profit because a profit is here to be made. I invest more here in window bars, theft losses, insurance, spoilage; I deserve to make more here than at the other places." He looked, almost imploringly, at the man seated next to him. "You don't accept this as the right of a man in business?"

Reed grunted. "Did the bear shit in the woods?" he said.

Again Green laughed. He gulped his coffee awkwardly, as if eager to go. Yet his motions slowed once he had set the coffee cup down on the blue plastic saucer. "Place yourself in *my* situation," he said, his voice high and tentative. "If *you* were running my store in this neighborhood, what would be *your* position? Say on a profit scale of fifteen to forty percent, at what point in between would you draw the line?"

Nelson Reed thought. He sipped his coffee and seemed to chew the liquid. "Fifteen to forty?" he repeated.

"Yes."

"I'm a churchgoin' man," he said. "Closer to fifteen than to forty."

"How close?"

Nelson Reed thought. "In church you tithe ten percent."

"In restaurants you tip fifteen," the grocer said quickly.

"All right," Reed said. "Over fifteen."

"How much over?"

Nelson Reed thought.

"Twenty, thirty, thirty-five?" Green chanted, leaning closer to Reed. Still the man thought.

"Forty? Maybe even forty-five or fifty?" the grocer breathed in Reed's ear. "In the supermarkets, you know, they have more subtle ways of accomplishing such feats."

Reed slapped his coffee cup with the back of his right hand. The brown liquid swirled across the counter top, wetting the books. "*Damn this!*" he shouted.

Startled, Green rose from his stool.

Nelson Reed was trembling. "I ain't *you*," he said in a deep baritone. "I ain't the *supermarket* neither. All I is is a poor man that works *too* hard to see his pay slip through his fingers like rainwater. All I know is you done *cheat* me, you done *cheat* everybody in the neighborhood, and we organized now to get some of it *back!*" Then he stood and faced the grocer. "My daddy sharecropped down in Mississippi and bought in the company store. He owed them twenty-three years when he died. I paid off five of them years and then run away to up here. Now, I'm a deacon in the Baptist church. I raised my kids the way my daddy raise me and don't bother nobody. Now come to find out, after all my runnin', they done lift that *same company store* up out of Mississippi and slip it down on us here! Well, my daddy was a *fighter,* and if he hadn't owed all them years he would of raise him some hell. Me, I'm steady my daddy's child, plus I got seniority in my union. I'm a free man. Buddy, don't you know *I'm gonna raise me some hell!*"

Harold Green reached for a paper napkin to sop the coffee soaking into his books.

Nelson Reed threw a dollar on top of the books and walked away.

"I *will not* do it!" Harold Green said to his wife that same evening. They were in the bathroom of their home. Bending over the face bowl, she was washing her hair with a towel draped around her neck. The grocer stood by the door, looking in at her. "I will not bankrupt myself tomorrow," he said.

"I've been thinking about it, too," Ruth Green said, shaking her wet hair. "You'll do it, Harry."

"Why should I?" he asked. "You won't leave. You know it was a bluff. I've waited this long for you to calm down. Tomorrow is Saturday. This week has been a hard one. Tonight let's be realistic."

"Of course you'll do it," Ruth Green said. She said it the way she would say "Have some toast." She said, "You'll do it because you want to see your children grow up."

"And for what other reason?" he asked.

She pulled the towel tighter around her neck. "Because you are at heart a moral man."

He grinned painfully. "If I am, why should I have to prove it to *them?*"

"Not them," Ruth Green said, freezing her movements and looking in the mirror. "Certainly not them. By no means them. They have absolutely nothing to do with this."

"Who, then?" he asked, moving from the door into the room. "Who else should I prove something to?"

His wife was crying. But her entire face was wet. The tears moved secretly down her face.

"Who else?" Harold Green asked.

It was almost 11:00 P.M. and the children were in bed. They had also cried when they came home from school. Ruth Green said, "For yourself, Harry. For the love that lives inside your heart."

All night the grocer thought about this.

Nelson Reed also slept little that Friday night. When he returned home from the drugstore, he reported to his wife as much of the conversation as he could remember. At first he had joked about the exchange between himself and the grocer, but as more details returned to his conscious mind he grew solemn and then bitter. "He ask me to put myself in *his* place," Reed told his wife. "Can you imagine that kind of gumption? I never cheated nobody in my life. All my life I have lived on Bible principles. I am a deacon in the church. I have work all my life for other folks and I don't even own the house I live in." He paced up and down the kitchen, his big arms flapping loosely at his sides. Betty Reed sat at the table, watching. "This here's a low-down, ass-kicking world," he said. "I swear to God it is! All my life I have lived on principle and I ain't got a dime in the bank. Betty," he turned suddenly toward her, "don't you think I'm a fool?"

"Mr. Reed," she said. "Let's go on to bed."

But he would not go to bed. Instead, he took the fifth of bourbon from the cabinet under the sink and poured himself a shot. His wife refused to join him.

Reed drained the glass of whiskey, and then another, while he resumed pacing the kitchen floor. He slapped his hands against his sides. "I think I'm a fool," he said. "Ain't got a dime in the bank, ain't got a pot to *pee* in or a wall to pitch it over, and that there *cheat* ask me to put myself inside *his* shoes. Hell, I can't even *afford* the kind of shoes he wears." He stopped pacing and looked at his wife.

"Mr. Reed," she whispered, "tomorrow ain't a work day. Let's go to bed."

Nelson Reed laughed, the bitterness in his voice rattling his wife. "The *hell* I will!" he said.

He strode to the yellow telephone on the wall beside the sink and began to dial. The first call was to Lloyd Dukes, a neighbor two blocks away and a lieutenant in the organization. Dukes was not at home. The second call was to McElroy's Bar on the corner of 65th and Carroll, where Stanley Harper, another of the lieutenants, worked as a bartender. It was Harper who spread the word, among those men at the bar, that the organization would picket the grocer's store the following morning. And all through the night, in the bedroom of their house, Betty Reed was awakened by telephone calls coming from Lester Jones, Nat Lucas, Mrs. Tyrone Brown, the widow-woman named Murphy, all coordinating the time when they would march in a group against the store owned by Harold Green. Betty Reed's heart beat loudly beneath the covers as she listened to the bitterness and rage in her husband's voice. On several occasions, hearing him declare himself a fool, she pressed the pillow against her eyes and cried.

* * *

The grocer opened later than usual this Saturday morning, but still it was early enough to make him one of the first walkers in the neighborhood. He parked his car one block from the store and strolled to work. There were no birds singing. The sky in this area was not blue. It was smog-smutted and gray, seeming on the verge of a light rain. The street, as always, was littered with cans, papers, bits of broken glass. As always the garbage cans overflowed. The morning breeze plastered a sheet of newspaper playfully around the sides of a rusted garbage can. For some reason, using his right foot, he loosened the paper and stood watching it slide into the street and down the block. The movement made him feel good. He whistled while unlocking the bars shielding the windows and door of his store. When he had unlocked the main door he stepped in quickly and threw a switch to the right of the jamb, before the shrill sound of the alarm could shatter his mood. Then he switched on the lights. Everything was as it had been the night before. He had already telephoned his two employees and given them the day off. He busied himself doing the usual things—hauling milk and vegetables from the cooler, putting cash in the till—not thinking about the silence of his wife, or the look in her eyes, only an hour before when he left home. He had determined, at some point while driving through the city, that today it would be business as usual. But he expected very few customers.

The first customer of the day was Mrs. Nelson Reed. She came in around 9:30 A.M. and wandered about the store. He watched her from the checkout counter. She seemed uncertain of what she wanted to buy. She kept glancing at him down the center aisle. His suspicions aroused, he said finally, "Yes, may I help you, Mrs. Reed?" His words caused her to jerk, as if some devious thought had been perceived going through her mind. She reached over quickly and lifted a loaf of whole wheat bread from the rack and walked with it to the counter. She looked at him and smiled. The smile was a broad, shy one, that rare kind of smile one sees on virgin girls when they first confess love to themselves. Betty Reed was a woman of about forty-five. For some reason he could not comprehend, this gesture touched him. When she pulled a dollar from her purse and laid it on the counter, an impulse, from no place he could locate with his mind, seized control of his tongue. "Free," he told Betty Reed. She paused, then pushed the dollar toward him with a firm and determined thrust of her arm. "Free," he heard himself saying strongly, his right palm spread and meeting her thrust with absolute force. She clutched the loaf of bread and walked out of his store.

The next customer, a little girl, arriving well after 10:30 A.M., selected a candy bar from the rack beside the counter. "Free," Green said cheerfully. The little girl left the candy on the counter and ran out of the store.

At 11:15 A.M. a wino came in looking desperate enough to sell his soul. The grocer watched him only for an instant. Then he went to the wine counter and selected a half-gallon of medium-grade red wine. He shoved the jug into the belly of the wino, the man's sour breath bathing his face. "Free," the grocer said. "But you must not drink it in here."

He felt good about the entire world, watching the wino through the window gulping the wine and looking guiltily around.

At 11:25 A.M. the pickets arrived.

Two dozen people, men and women, young and old, crowded the pavement in front of his store. Their signs, placards, and voices denounced him as a parasite. The grocer laughed inside himself. He felt lighthearted and wild, like a man drugged. He rushed to the meat counter and pulled a long roll of brown wrapping paper from the rack, tearing it neatly with a quick shift of his body resembling a dance step practiced fervently in his youth. He laid the paper on the chopping block and with the black-inked, felt-tipped marker scrawled, in giant letters, the word Free. This he took to the window and pasted in place with many strands of Scotch tape. He was laughing wildly. "Free!" he shouted from behind the brown paper. "Free! Free! Free! Free! Free! Free!" He rushed to the door, pushed his head out, and screamed to the confused crowd, "*Free!*" Then he ran back to the counter and stood behind it, like a soldier at attention.

They came in slowly.

Nelson Reed entered first, working his right foot across the dirty tile as if tracking a squiggling worm. The others followed: Lloyd Dukes dragging a placard, Mr. and Mrs. Tyrone Brown, Stanley Harper walking with his fists clenched, Lester Jones with three of his children, Nat Lucas looking sheepish and detached, a clutch of winos, several bashful nuns, ironic-smiling teenagers and a few students. Bringing up the rear was a bearded social scientist holding a tape recorder to his chest. "Free!" the grocer screamed. He threw up his arms in a gesture that embraced, or dismissed, the entire store. "*All free!*" he shouted. He was grinning with the grace of a madman.

The winos began grabbing first. They stripped the shelf of wine in a matter of seconds. Then they fled, dropping bottles on the tile in their wake. The others, stepping quickly through this liquid, soon congealed it into a sticky, blood-like consistency. The young men went for the cigarettes and luncheon meats and beer. One of them had the prescience to grab a sack from the counter, while the others loaded their arms swiftly, hugging cartons and packages of cold cuts like long-lost friends. The students joined them, less for greed than for the thrill of the experience. The two nuns backed toward the door. As for the older people, men and women, they stood at first as if stuck to the wine-smeared floor. Then Stanley Harper, the bartender, shouted, "The man said *free,* y'all heard him." He paused. "Didn't you say *free* now?" he called to the grocer.

"I said free," Harold Green answered, his temples pounding.

A cheer went up. The older people began grabbing, as if the secret lusts of a lifetime had suddenly seized command of their arms and eyes. They grabbed toilet tissue, cold cuts, pickles, sardines, boxes of raisins, boxes of starch, cans of soup, tins of tuna fish and salmon, bottles of spices, cans of boned chicken, slippery cans of olive oil. Here a man, Lester Jones, burdened himself with several heads of lettuce, while his wife, in another aisle, shouted for him to drop those small items and concentrate on the gourmet section. She herself took imported sardines, wheat crackers, bottles of candied pickles, herring, anchovies, imported olives, French wafers, an ancient, half-rusted can of paté, stocked, by mistake, from the inventory of another store. Others packed their arms with detergents, hams, chocolate-coated cereal, whole chickens with hanging asses, wedges of bologna and salami like squashed footballs, chunks of cheeses, yellow and white, shriveled onions, and green peppers. Mrs. Tyrone Brown hung a curve of pepperoni around her neck and seemed to take on instant dignity, much like a person of noble birth in possession now of a long sought-after gem. Another woman, the widow Murphy, stuffed tomatoes into her bosom, holding a half-chewed lemon in her mouth. The more enterprising fought desperately over the three rusted shopping carts, and the victors wheeled these along the narrow aisles, sweeping into them bulk items—beer in six-packs, sacks of sugar, flour, glass bottles of syrup, toilet cleanser, sugar cookies, prune, apple and tomato juices—while others endeavored to snatch the carts from them. There were several fistfights and much cursing. The grocer, standing behind the counter, hummed and rang his cash register like a madman.

Nelson Reed, the first into the store, followed the nuns out, empty-handed.

In less than half an hour the others had stripped the store and vanished in many directions up and down the block. But still more people came, those late in hearing the news. And when they saw the shelves were bare, they cursed soberly and chased those few stragglers still bearing away goods. Soon only the grocer and the social scientist remained, the latter stationed at the door with his tape recorder sucking in leftover sounds. Then he too slipped away up the block.

By 12:10 P.M. the grocer was leaning against the counter, trying to make his mind slow down. Not a man given to drink during work hours, he nonetheless took a swallow from a bottle of wine, a dusty bottle from beneath the wine shelf, somehow overlooked by the winos. Somewhat recovered, he was preparing to remember what he should do next when he glanced toward a figure at the door. Nelson Reed was standing there, watching him.

"All gone," Harold Green said. "My friend, Mr. Reed, there is no more." Still the man stood in the doorway, peering into the store.

The grocer waved his arms about the empty room. Not a display case had a single item standing. "All gone," he said again, as if addressing a stupid child. "There is nothing left to get. You, my friend, have come back too late for a second load. I am cleaned out."

Nelson Reed stepped into the store and strode toward the counter. He moved through wine-stained flour, lettuce leaves, red, green, and blue labels, bits and pieces of broken glass. He walked toward the counter.

"All day," the grocer laughed, not quite hysterically now, "all day long I have not made a single cent of profit. The entire day was a loss. This store, like the others, is *bleeding* me." He waved his arms about the room in a magnificent gesture of uncaring loss. "Now do you understand?" he said. "Now will you put yourself in my shoes? I have nothing here. Come, now, Mr. Reed, would it not be so bad a thing to walk in my shoes?"

"Mr. Green," Nelson Reed said coldly. "My wife bought a loaf of bread in here this mornin'. She forgot to pay you. I, myself, have come here to pay you your money."

"Oh," the grocer said.

"I think it was brown bread. Don't that cost more than white?"

The two men looked away from each other, but not at anything in the store.

"In my store, yes," Harold Green said. He rang the register with the most casual movement of his finger. The register read fifty-five cents.

Nelson Reed held out a dollar.

"And two cents tax," the grocer said.

The man held out the dollar.

"After all," Harold Green said. "We are all, after all, Mr. Reed, in debt to the government."

He rang the register again. It read fifty-seven cents.

Nelson Reed held out a dollar.

Study and Discussion Questions

1. What kind of person is Harold Green? Why does he refuse for so long to "bend"? When he finally gives his groceries away, why does he keep shouting "free"?
2. What kind of person is Nelson Reed? Why does he emerge as a leader of the protest? Why does he persist?

3. How do the attitudes of Ruth Green and Betty Reed toward the conflict differ from those of their husbands? Why?
4. Characterize the narrator's attitude towards the events narrated.
5. What is the significance of Green and his brother-in-law's discussion of business ethics? What does it reveal about Green?
6. At the end, why does Reed insist on paying for the loaf of bread? Why doesn't Green refuse the money? What does the ending mean?

Suggestions for Writing

1. At their meeting, Green tells Reed, "I do not make a profit here because the people are black. I make a profit because a profit is here to be made." Explain the distinction Green is trying to make. Does it make sense? What does Green's statement suggest about the society he lives in?
2. What do you think of Green's method (forced on him by his wife) of making amends? Can you think of a better way? Can amends be made?

Critical Resources

1. Beavers, Herman. *Wrestling Angels into Song: The Fictions of Ernest J. Gaines and James Alan McPherson*, Philadelphia: University of Pennsylvania Press, 1995.
2. Kurtzleben, James. "James Alan McPherson." *A Readers Companion to the Short Story in English*. Westport, CT: Greenwood Press, 2001.
3. Macpherson, James Alan. "On Becoming an American Writer." *Topic* 126 (1980): 39–43.
4. Shacochis, Bob. "Interview with James Alan McPherson." *Iowa Journal of Literature Studies* 4 (1983): 6–33.

JOHN STEINBECK (1902–1968)

John Steinbeck grew up in the fertile Salinas Valley in northern California. The people and the terrain of this region would become central components in much of his writing. Although Steinbeck attended college at Stanford University, he left without a degree in 1925 and spent the following five years traveling around the country, taking odd jobs and writing. During this transitory time, Steinbeck's contact with struggling workers would have a profound effect on his perception of the world. These experiences, along with the onslaught of the Great Depression, would produce Steinbeck's three most acclaimed novels: In Dubious Battle *(1936),* Of Mice and Men *(1937), and* The Grapes of Wrath *(1939). In one way or another, each novel is concerned with the plight of migrant workers and farmers exploited by large agricultural monopolies paying low wages. These novels of "social protest" and their focus on class conflict were both praised and condemned. Despite being labeled a "communist tract" and denounced in Congress,* The Grapes of Wrath *would win the Pulitzer Prize in 1940. While the themes Steinbeck was exploring were timely, it was also his ability to craft compelling and layered narratives with an economy of language that distinguished him as a writer. He was awarded the Nobel Prize for Literature in 1962. Other notable works include* Tortilla Flat *(1935),* The Red Pony *(1937),* Cannery Row *(1945),* The Pearl *(1947),* East of Eden *(1952),* Sweet Thursday *(1954), and* The Winter of Our Discontent *(1961). The following excerpt is taken from* The Grapes of Wrath.

FROM *The Grapes of Wrath*   (1939)

Chapter Twenty-One

The moving, questing people were migrants now. Those families which had lived on a little piece of land, who had lived and died on forty acres, had eaten or starved on the produce of forty acres, had now the whole West to rove in. And they scampered about, looking for work; and the highways were streams of people, and the ditch banks were lines of people. Behind them more were coming. The great highways streamed with moving people. There in the Middle- and Southwest had lived a simple agrarian folk who had not changed with industry, who had not formed with machines or known the power and danger of machines in private hands. They had not grown up in the paradoxes of industry. Their senses were still sharp to the ridiculousness of the industrial life.

And then suddenly the machines pushed them out and they swarmed on the highways. The movement changed them; the highways, the camps along the road, the fear of hunger and the hunger itself, changed them. The children without dinner changed them, the endless moving changed them. They were migrants. And the hostility changed them, welded them, united them—hostility that made the little towns group and arm as though to repel an invader, squads with pick handles, clerks and storekeepers with shotguns, guarding the world against their own people.

In the West there was panic when the migrants multiplied on the highways. Men of property were terrified for their property. Men who had never been hungry saw the eyes of the hungry. Men who had never wanted anything very much saw the flare of want in the eyes of the migrants. And the men of the towns and of the soft suburban country gathered to defend themselves; and they reassured themselves that they were good and the invaders bad, as a man must do before he fights. They said, These goddamned Okies are dirty and ignorant. They're degenerate, sexual maniacs. These goddamned Okies are thieves. They'll steal anything. They've got no sense of property rights.

And the latter was true, for how can a man without property know the ache of ownership? And the defending people said, They bring disease, they're filthy. We can't have them in the schools. They're strangers. How'd you like to have your sister go out with one of 'em?

The local people whipped themselves into a mold of cruelty. Then they formed units, squads, and armed them—armed them with clubs, with gas, with guns. We own the country. We can't let these Okies get out of hand. And the men who were armed did not own the land, but they thought they did. And the clerks who drilled at night owned nothing, and the little storekeepers possessed only a drawerful of debts. But even a debt is something, even a job is something. The clerk thought, I get fifteen dollars a week. S'pose a goddamn Okie would work for twelve? And the little store-keeper thought, How could I compete with a debtless man?

And the migrants streamed in on the highways and their hunger was in their eyes, and their need was in their eyes. They had no argument, no system, nothing but their numbers and their needs. When there was work for a man, ten men fought for it—fought with a low wage. If that fella'll work for thirty cents, I'll work for twenty-five.

If he'll take twenty-five, I'll do it for twenty.

No, me, I'm hungry. I'll work for fifteen. I'll work for food. The kids. You ought to see them. Little boils, like, comin' out, an' they can't run aroun'. Give 'em some windfall fruit, an' they bloated up. Me. I'll work for a little piece of meat.

And this was good, for wages went down and prices stayed up. The great owners were glad and they sent out more handbills to bring more people in. And wages went down and prices stayed up. And pretty soon now we'll have serfs again.

And now the great owners and the companies invented a new method. A great owner bought a cannery. And when the peaches and the pears were ripe he cut the price of fruit below the cost of raising it. And as cannery owner he paid himself a low price for the fruit and kept the price of canned goods up and took his profit. And the little farmers who owned no canneries lost their farms, and they were taken by the great owners, the banks, and the companies who also owned the canneries. As time went on, there were fewer farms. The little farmers moved into town for a while and exhausted their credit, exhausted their friends, their relatives. And then they too went on the highways. And the roads were crowded with men ravenous for work, murderous for work.

And the companies, the banks worked at their own doom and they did not know it. The fields were fruitful, and starving men moved on the roads. The granaries were full and the children of the poor grew up rachitic, and the pustules of pellagra swelled on their sides. The great companies did not know that the line between hunger and anger is a thin line. And money that might have gone to wages went for gas, for guns, for agents and spies, for blacklists, for drilling. On the highways the people moved like ants and searched for work, for food. And the anger began to ferment.

Study and Discussion Questions

1. In *The Grapes of Wrath*, Steinbeck interpolated essayistic style chapters like this one into his narrative about the southern and midwestern

dustbowl migrants of the 1930s who lost their land and became agricultural migrant workers in the orchards and vegetable farms of California. What does Steinbeck say were the factors that changed the lives of these people?

2. How did the local people in California react to this sudden influx of workers desperate for a job?
3. What two moves did the owners and companies make that worsened the situation for the migrant workers?
4. Discuss what happens in a capitalist economy when there are too few jobs and too many workers.
5. Why do the workers have nothing to lose, according to Steinbeck?
6. Read the information about a migrant worker's yearly job cycle in the accompanying document, "The Wandering Wage Earner." (a Works Project Administration Research monograph, 1937) How does the work history outlined here provide support for what Steinbeck is saying?

Suggestions for Writing

1. Discuss the process of demonizing a group of people, as Steinbeck outlines it here. Can you think of any other historical or contemporary examples? Compare one of these to the situation of Steinbeck's migrant workers.
2. Discuss the economics of making a profit in a capitalist economy. Who gains? Who loses? Refer to Steinbeck's example and others that come to mind.
3. Write a short story (or poem) based on any of the information in "The Wandering Wage Earner." Who will be your main character(s)? What point of view will you choose? What images will you highlight?
4. "The line between hunger and anger is a thin line." Write a paper exploring this statement. There have been and currently are plenty of people in poverty in this country. Why then doesn't hunger translate into organized or collective anger more often? Can you think of instances in which it has?

THE WANDERING WAGE EARNER

This selection provides information on the wages and jobs of migratory workers. John N. Webb, The Migratory-Casual Worker [WPA Research Monograph VII] *(Washington: Government Printing Office, 1937), pp. xvii, 3–4.*

IT IS A COMMON PRACTICE among migratory-casual workers to spend part of each year on the road, working or seeking work, and then to withdraw from the labor market during the period, usually in the winter months, when the chances of finding work are small. This practice was followed by a majority of the 500 workers in the study. The median length of the migratory period was 41 weeks. Workers in agriculture had the longest off-season period—averaging 13 weeks; and the combination workers, the shortest—averaging 7 weeks in 1933, and only 4 weeks in 1934.

Necessarily, the migratory-casual worker wastes much time and motion during his migratory period both because of a scarcity of jobs and also because of the lack of proper direction to such jobs as are available. Among the 500 workers, the portion of the migratory period spent in employment averaged 24 weeks in 1933 and 21 weeks in 1934.

In exchange for his labor the migratory-casual worker obtains a meager income at best. When the earnings of the 500 workers were reduced to net yearly income to exclude the uncertain value of perquisites, it was found that although the range was from maintenance to $1,350 a year the most frequent earning was between maintenance and $250 yearly. The agricultural worker had the lowest yearly net earning, averaging $110 in 1933 and $124 in 1934. Industrial workers averaged $257 in 1933 and $272 in 1934. Workers combining agricultural and industrial employment earned on the average $223 net in 1933 and $203 in 1934. . . .

The migratory-casual worker in agriculture, the largest employer of mobile labor, is clearly defined in the following work history:

July-October 1932. Picked figs at Fresno, Calif., and vicinity. Wages, 10 cents a box, average 50-pound box. Picked about 15 boxes a day to earn $1.50; about $40 a month.

October-December 1932. Cut Malaga and muscat (table and wine) grapes near Fresno. Wages, 25 cents an hour. Average 6-hour day, earning $1.50; about $40 a month.

December 1932. Left for Imperial Valley, Calif.

February 1933. Picked peas, Imperial Valley. Wages, 1 cent a pound. Average 125 pounds a day. Earned $30 for season. Also worked as wagon-man in lettuce field on contract. Contract price, 5 cents a crate repack out of packing house; not field pack. This work paid 60 cents to $1 a day. On account of weather, was fortunate to break even at finish of season. Was paying 50 cents a day room and board.

March-April 1933. Left for Chicago. Stayed a couple of weeks. Returned to California 2 months later.

May 1933. Odd-jobs on lawns, radios, and victrolas at Fresno. Also worked as porter and handy man.

June 1933. Returned to picking figs near Fresno. Wages, 10 cents a box. Averaged $1.50 a day, and earned $50 in 2 months.

August 1933. Cut Thompson's seedless grapes near Fresno for 7 days at 1¼ cents a tray. Earned $11. Picked cotton 1 day, 115 pounds; earned $1.

September-November 1933. Cut Malaga and muscat grapes near Fresno. Wages, 25 cents an hour. Made $30 for season.

December 1933. Picked oranges and lemons in Tulare County, Calif. (Earnings not reported.)

January 1934. Picked oranges at 5 cents per box for small jobs and 25 cents per box for large jobs, Redlands, Calif. Earned $30. Picked lemons at 25 cents an hour.

January 1934. Went to Brawley, Calif. Picked peas at 1 cent a pound. Picked 125–150 pounds a day for 15-day season.

February 1934. Picked grapefruit at 25 cents an hour, Koehler, Calif. Worked 8 hours a day on three jobs for a total of 22 days. Also hauled fertilizer at 25 cents an hour.

March 1934. Worked as helper on fertilizer truck at $2 a day for 20 days, Brawley, Calif.

June 1934. Worked as circus hand with Al G. Barnes Circus for 4 weeks at $4.60 a week and board, Seattle to Wallace, Idaho.

July 1934. Tree shaker at 25 cents an hour, averaged $2 a day for 25 days, near Fresno.

August-October 1934. Picked oranges and lemons at 25 cents an hour, working an average of 6 hours a day, for 60 days, near Fresno.

December 1934. Houseman in hotel, Fresno. Received 50 cents a day and board for 1 month, and 25 cents a day and board for 2 months.

The migratory-casual worker following industrial, as distinct from agricultural, employment is equally well defined by the work history presented below:

June-August 1932. Jackhammer operator, railroad construction, Liberty, Mo. Wages $4.80 a day.

September 1932. Extra gang laborer, railroad, Hays, Kans. Wages $3.20 a day.

October 1932. Extra gang laborer, railroad, Cheyenne, Wyo. Wages $4.50 a day.

February-March 1933. Laborer, pipe-line construction, Topeka, Kans. Wages $3 a day.

April-October 1933. Watchman, building construction, Kansas City, Mo. Wages $1.25 a day.

February-May 1934. Extra gang laborer, railroad, Wamsutter, Wyo. Wages $2 a day.

June-September 1934. Extra gang laborer, railroad, Topeka, Kans. Wages $2.80 a day.

Critical Resources

1. Burkhead, Cynthia. *Student Companion to John Steinbeck.* Westport, CT: Greenwood, 2002.
2. *The Grapes of Wrath.* Director John Ford. Performer Henry Fonda. Twentieth Century Fox Productions, 1940 (128 minutes).
3. *The Grapes of Wrath.* Narrated by Donald Sutherland. Discovery University Productions, 2000 (51 minutes). For more information go to <http://www.films.com/>.
4. Kim, Kil-Joong. "The Symbolic Imagination as Narrative Strategies: Steinbeck's The Grapes of Wrath." *Studies in Modern Fiction* 9.1 (2002): 29–47.
5. Lisca, Peter, ed. *The Grapes of Wrath: Text and Criticism.* New York: Penguin, 1997.
6. Parini, Jay. *John Steinbeck: A Biography.* New York: Holt, 1995.

❀ ❀ ❀

DOROTHY CANFIELD FISHER (1879–1958)

Dorothy Canfield Fisher was born in Lawrence, Kansas, and studied at Ohio State University and at the Sorbonne in Paris. In 1904 she received a Ph.D. in comparative literature from Columbia University, becoming one of the first women to be awarded such a degree. She moved with her new husband John Fisher to Vermont in 1907—a region that would later become the setting for many of her most popular works. While traveling in Rome in 1912, Fisher witnessed the innovative teaching methods of Maria Montessori and was a leader in establishing the Montessori system in the United States. After volunteering as a relief worker in France during World War I, Fisher returned to Vermont and continued writing novels, books on educational reform (including adult education), and children's stories. During her life, Fisher's work was well received both critically and by the public. Today, although some modern scholars claim that Fisher's work is often overly didactic and sentimental, there is general agreement that Fisher was a skilled story-teller and observer of human nature with a gift for characterization. Among her works, some published under the name of Dorothy Canfield, are the novels The Squirrel Cage *(1912),* The Bent Twig *(1915), and* The Deepening Stream *(1930); the story collections* Hillsboro People *(1915) and* The Real Motive *(1916); two books on the Montessori method; and the widely read children's book* Understood Betsy *(1917). In the short story "A Drop in the Bucket," first printed in* Hillsboro People, *Fisher utilizes the characterization of Jombatiste as a foil for a larger social message.*

A Drop in the Bucket

(1913)

There is no need to describe in detail the heroine of this tale, because she represents a type familiar to all readers of the conventional New-England-village dialect story. She was for a long time the sole inhabitant of Hillsboro, who came up to the expectations of our visiting friends from the city, on the lookout for Mary Wilkins[1] characters. We always used to take such people directly to see Cousin Tryphena, as dwellers in an Italian city always take their foreign friends to see their one bit of ruined city wall or the heap of stones which was once an Inquisitorial torture chamber, never to see the new water-works or the modern, sanitary hospital.

On the way to the other end of the street, where Cousin Tryphena's tiny, two-roomed house stood, we always laid bare the secrets of her somnolent, respectable, unprofitable life; we always informed our visitors that she lived and kept up a social position on two hundred and fifteen dollars a year, and that she had never been further from home than to the next village. We always drew attention to her one treasure, the fine Sheraton sideboard that had belonged to her great-grandfather, old Priest Perkins; and, when we walked away from the orderly and empty house, we were sure that our friends from the city would always exclaim with great insight into character, "What a charmingly picturesque life! Isn't she perfectly delicious!"

---

[1]Mary E. Wilkins Freeman (1852–1930). See "A Mistaken Charity."

Next door to Cousin Tryphena's minute, snow-white house is a forlorn old building, one of the few places for rent in our village, where nearly everyone owns his own shelter. It stood desolately idle for some time, tumbling to pieces almost visibly, until, one day, two years ago, a burly, white-bearded tramp stopped in front of it, laid down his stick and bundle, and went to inquire at the neighbor's if the place were for rent, then moved in with his stick and bundle and sent away for the rest of his belongings, that is to say, an outfit for cobbling shoes. He cut a big wooden boot out of the side of an empty box, painted it black with axle-grease and soot, hung it up over the door, and announced himself as ready to do all the cobbling and harness-repairing he could get . . . and a fine workman he showed himself to be.

We were all rather glad to have this odd new member of our community settle down among us . . . all, that is, except Cousin Tryphena, who was sure, for months afterward, that he would cut her throat some night and steal away her Sheraton sideboard. It was an open secret that Putnam, the antique-furniture dealer in Troy, had offered her two hundred and fifty dollars for it. The other women of the village, however, not living alone in such dangerous proximity to the formidable stranger, felt reassured by his long, white beard, and by his great liking for little children.

Although, from his name, as from his strong accent, it was evident that old Jombatiste belonged, by birth, to our French-Canadian colony, he never associated himself with that easy-going, devoutly Catholic, law-abiding, and rather unlettered group of our citizens. He allied himself with quite another class, making no secret of the fact that he was an out-and-out Socialist, Anti-clerical, Syndicalist, Anarchist, Nihilist. . . . We in Hillsboro are not acute in distinguishing between the different shades of radicalism, and never have been able exactly to place him, except that, beside his smashing, loudly-voiced theories, young Arthur Robbins' Progressivism sounds like old Martin Pelham's continued jubilation over the Hayes campaign.[2]

The central article of Jombatiste's passionately held creed seemed to be that everything was exactly wrong, and that, while the Socialist party was not nearly sweeping enough in its ideas, it was, as yet, the best means for accomplishing the inevitable, righteous overturning of society. Accordingly, he worked incessantly, not only at his cobbling, but at any odd job he could find to do, lived the life of an anchorite, went in rags, ate mainly crackers and milk, and sent every penny he could save to the Socialist Headquarters. We knew about this not only through his own trumpeting of the programme of his life, but because Phil Latimer, the postmaster, is cousin to us all and often told us about the money-orders, so large that they must have represented almost all the earnings of the fanatical old shoemaker.

---

[2]Probably a reference to Rutherford B. Hayes (1822–1893), who was elected president in 1876 even though his opponent had the greater popular vote.

And yet he was never willing to join in any of our charitable enterprises, although his ardent old heart was evidently as tender as it was hot. Nothing threw him into such bellowing fury as cruelty. He became the terror of all our boys who trapped rabbits, and, indeed, by the sole influence of his whirlwind descents upon them, and his highly illegal destruction of their traps, he practically made that boyish pastime a thing of the past in Hillsboro. Somehow, though the boys talked mightily about how they'd have the law of dirty, hot-tempered old Jombatiste, nobody cared really to face him. He had on tap a stream of red-hot vituperation astonishingly varied for a man of his evident lack of early education. Perhaps it came from his incessant reading and absorption of Socialist and incendiary literature.

He took two Socialist newspapers, and nobody knows how many queer little inflammatory magazines from which he read aloud selections to anyone who did not run away.

Naturally enough, from his point of view, he began with his neighbor, fastidious Cousin Tryphena.

What Cousin Tryphena did not know about the way the world outside of Hillsboro was run would have made a complete treatise on modern civilization. She never took a newspaper, only borrowing, once in a while, the local sheet to read the news items from Greenford, where she had some distant cousins; and, though she occasionally looked at one of the illustrated magazines, it was only at the pictures.

It is therefore plain that old Jombatiste could not have found a worse listener for his bellowed statements that ninety per cent. of the money of this country was in the hands of two per cent. of the population; that the franchise was a farce because the government was controlled by a Wall Street clique; and that any man who could not earn a good living for his family had a moral right to shoot a millionaire. For the most part, Cousin Tryphena counted her tatting stitches and paid not the least attention to her malcontent neighbor. When she did listen, she did not believe a word he said. She had lived in Hillsboro for fifty-five years and she knew what made people poor. It was shiftlessness. There was always plenty of work to be had at the brush-back factory for any man who had the sense and backbone to keep at it. If they *would* stop work in deer-week to go hunting, or go on a spree Town-meeting day, or run away to fish, she'd like to know what business they had blaming millionaires because they lost their jobs. She did not expound her opinions of these points to Jombatiste because, in the first place, she despised him for a dirty Canuck, and, secondly, because opinions seemed shadowy and unsubstantial things to her. The important matters were to make your starch clear and not to be late to church.

It is proverbial that people who are mostly silent often keep for some time a reputation for more wisdom than is theirs. Cousin Tryphena unconsciously profited in the estimation of her neighbor by this fact of psychology. Old Jombatiste had thundered his per cents. of the distribution of capital for many months before he discovered that he was on the wrong track.

Then, one winter day, as Cousin Tryphena was hanging out her washing, he ran over to her, waving his favorite magazine. He read her a paragraph from it, striking the paper occasionally for emphasis with his horny, blackened, shoe-maker's hand, and following her as she moved along the clothes-lines—

"And it is thus definitely *proved*," he shouted in conclusion, "that Senator Burlingame was in the pay of J. D. Darby, when he held up the Rouse Working-man's Bill in the Senate Committee...." He stopped and glared triumphantly at his neighbor. A rare impulse of perversity rose in Cousin Tryphena's unawak-ened heart. She took a clothes-pin out of her mouth and asked with some exas-peration, "Well, what *of* it!" a comment on his information which sent the old man reeling back as though she had struck him.

In the conversation which followed, old Jombatiste, exploring at last Cousin Tryphena's mind, leaned giddily over the abyss of her ignorance of political econ-omy and sociology, dropping one exploring plummet after another into its depths, only to find them fathomless. He went shakily back to his own house, si-lenced for once.

But, although for the first time he neglected work to do it, he returned to the attack the next day with a new weapon. He made no more remarks about in-dustrial slavery, nor did he begin, as was his wont, with the solemnly enunciated axiom, "Wealth comes from labor alone!" He laid down, on the Sheraton side-board, an armful of his little magazines, and settled himself in a chair, observing with a new comprehension how instinctively Cousin Tryphena reached for her tatting as he began to read aloud. He read the story of a man who was burned to death in molten steel because his employers did not install a rather expensive safety device, and who left a young widow and three children. These tried to earn their livings by making artificial flowers. They could earn, all of them working together, three cents an hour. When the last dollar of the dead father's savings was used up, and there was talk of separating the family so that the children could be put in an asylum, the mother drowned the three little ones and herself after them. Cousin Tryphena dropped her tatting, her country-bred mind reel-ing. "Didn't she have any *folks* to help her out?"

Jombatiste explained that she came from East Poland, so that her folks, if in-deed she had any, were too far away to be of use. He struck one fist inside his palm with a fierce gesture, such as he used when he caught a boy trapping, and cried, "... and that in a country that produces three times the food it consumes." For the first time, a statistical statement awoke an echo in Cousin Tryphena's at-rophied brain.

Old Jombatiste read on, this time about a girl of seventeen, left by her par-ents' death in charge of a small brother. She had been paid twenty cents for mak-ing crocheted lace which sold for a dollar and a half. By working twelve hours a day, she had been able to make forty-seven cents. Seeing her little brother grow pale from lack of food, she had, in desperation, taken the first, the awfully deci-sive first step downward, and had almost at once thereafter vanished, drawn down by the maelstrom of vice. The little brother, wild with grief over his sister's disappearance, had been taken to an orphan asylum where he had since twice tried to commit suicide.

Cousin Tryphena sat rigid, her tatting fallen to the floor, her breath coming with difficulty. It is impossible for the average modern mind, calloused by promiscuous reading, to conceive the effect upon her primitive organism of this attack from the printed page. She not only did not dream that these stories might not be true, they seemed as real to her as though she had seen the people. There was not a particle of blood in her haggard face.

Jombatiste read on . . . the story of a decent, ambitious man, employed in a sweatshop tailoring establishment, who contracted tuberculosis from the foul air, and who dragged down with him, in his agonizing descent to the very depths of misery, a wife and two children. He was now dead, and his wife was living in a corner of a moldy, damp basement, a pile of rags the only bed for her and her children, their only heat what fire the mother could make out of paper and rubbish picked up on the streets.

Cousin Tryphena's horrified eyes fell on her well-blacked stove, sending out the aromatic breath of burning white-birch sticks. She recoiled from it with a shudder.

Jombatiste read on, the story of the woman who, when her three sons died in an accident due to negligence on their employer's part . . . he read no more that day, for Cousin Tryphena put her gray head down on the center-table and wept as she never had done in her life. Jombatiste rose softly and tiptoed out of the room.

The tap-tap-tap of his hammer rang loud and fast the rest of that day. He was exulting over having aroused another bourgeois from the sleep of greasy complacency. He had made a convert. To his dire and utter pennilessness, Cousin Tryphena's tiny income seemed a fortune. He had a happy dream of persuading her to join him in his weekly contributions to the sacred funds! As he stood at midnight, in the open door, for the long draught of fresh air he always took before turning in on his pile of hay, he heard in the wood on the hill back of the house the shrill shriek of a trapped rabbit. He plowed furiously out through the deep snow to find it, gave the tortured animal a merciful death, carried the trap back to the river and threw it in with a furious splash. He strode home under the frosty stars, his dirty shirt open over his corded, old neck, his burning heart almost content. He had done a good day's work.

Early the next morning, his neighbor came to his door, very white, very hollow-eyed, evidently with a sleepless night back of her, and asked him for the papers he had read from. Jombatiste gave them to her in a tactful silence. She took them in one shaking hand, drawing her shawl around her wrinkled face with the other, and went back through the snow to her own house.

By noon that day, everyone in the village was thrilling with wild surmise. Cousin Tryphena had gone over to Graham and Sanders', asked to use their long-distance telephone and had telephoned to Putnam to come and get her sideboard. After this strange act, she had passed Albert Graham, then by chance alone in the store, with so wild a mien that he had not ventured to make any inquiries. But he took pains to mention the matter to everyone who happened to come in, that morning; and, by dinner-time, every family in Hillsboro was discussing over its pie the possibility that the well-known *queer streak,* which had sent several of Cousin Tryphena's ancestors to the asylum, was suddenly making its appearance in her.

I was detained, that afternoon, and did not reach her house until nearly four; and I was almost the last to arrive. I found Cousin Tryphena very silent, her usually pale face very red, the center of a group of neighbors who all at once began to tell me what had happened. I could make nothing out of their incoherent explanations. ... "Trypheny was crazy ... she'd ought to have a guardeen ... that Canuck shoemaker had addled her brains ... there'd ought to be a law against that kind of newspaper. ... Trypheny was goin' like her great-aunt, Lucilly, that died in the asylum. ..." I appealed directly to Cousin Tryphena for information as to what the trouble was.

"There ain't any trouble's I know of," she answered in a shaking voice. "I've just heard of a widow-woman, down in the city, who's bringin' up her two children in the corner of a basement where the green mold stands out on the wall, and I'm goin' down to fetch her an' the children up here to live with me ... them an' a little orphan boy as don't like the 'sylum where they've put him—"

Somebody broke in on her to cry, "Why, Trypheny, you simple old critter, that's four people! Where you goin' to put 'em in this little tucked-up place?"

Cousin Tryphena answered doggedly and pointedly, "Your own grandmother, Rebecca Mason, brought up a family of seven in a house no bigger than this, and no cellar."

"But how, ..." another voice exclaimed, "air you goin' to get enough for 'em to eat? You ain't got but barely enough for yourself!"

Cousin Tryphena paled a little, "I'm a good sewer, I could make money sewing ... and I could do washings for city-folks, summer-times. ..." Her set mouth told what a price she paid for this voluntary abandonment of the social standing that had been hers by virtue of her idleness. She went on with sudden spirit, "You all act as though I was doin' it to spite you and to amuse myself! I don't *want* to! When I think of my things I've kept so nice always, I'm *wild* ... but how can I help it, now I know about 'em! I didn't sleep a wink last night. I'll go clean crazy if I don't do something! I saw those three children strugglin' in the water and their mother a-holdin' on 'em down, and then jumpin' in herself—Why, I give enough milk to the *cat* to keep a baby ... what else can I do?"

I was touched, as I think we all were, by her helpless simplicity and ignorance, and by her defenselessness against this first vision of life, the vision which had been spared her so long, only to burst upon her like a forest-fire. I had an odd fancy that she had just awakened after a sleep of half a century.

"Dear Cousin Tryphena," I said as gently as I could, "you haven't had a very wide experience of modern industrial or city conditions and there are some phases of this matter which you don't take into consideration." Then I brought out the old, wordy, eminently reasonable arguments we all use to stifle the thrust of self-questioning: I told her that it was very likely that the editor of that newspaper had invented, or at least greatly exaggerated those stories, and that she would find on investigation that no such family existed.

"I don't see how that lets me out of *lookin'* for them," said Cousin Tryphena.

"Well, at least," I urged, "don't be in such a hurry about it. Take time to think it over! Wait till—"

"Wait!" cried Cousin Tryphena. "Why, another one may be jumpin' in the river this minute! If I'd ha' had the money, I'd ha' gone on the noon train!"

At this point, the man from Putnam's came with a team from our livery to carry away the Sheraton sideboard. Cousin Tryphena bore herself like a martyr at the stake, watching, with dry eyes, the departure of her one certificate to dear gentility and receiving with proud indifference the crisp bills of a denomination most of us had never seen before.

"You won't need all that just to go down to the city," I remonstrated.

She stopped watching the men load her shining old treasure into the wagon and turned her anguished eyes to me. "They'll likely be needing clothes and things."

I gave up. She had indeed thought it all out.

It was time for us to go home to prepare our several suppers and we went our different ways, shaking our heads over Tryphena's queerness. I stopped a moment before the cobbler's open door, watched him briskly sewing a broken halter and telling a folk-tale to some children by his knee. When he finished, I said with some acerbity, "Well, Jombatiste, I hope you're satisfied with what you've done to poor old Miss Tryphena . . . spoiling the rest of her life for her!"

"Such a life, Madame," said Jombatiste dryly, "ought to be spoiled, the sooner the better."

"She's going to start for the city to-morrow," I said, supposing of course that he had heard the news.

Jombatiste looked up very quickly. "For what goes she to the city?"

"Why . . . she's gone daft over those bogie-stories of yours . . . she's looked the list over and picked out the survivors, the widow of the man who died of tuberculosis, and so on, and she's going to bring them back here to share her luxurious life."

Jombatiste bounded into the air as if a bomb had exploded under him, scattering his tools and the children, rushing past me out of the house and toward Cousin Tryphena's. . . . As he ran, he did what I have never seen anyone do, out of a book; he tore at his bushy hair and scattered handfuls in the air. It seemed to me that some sudden madness had struck our dull little village, and I hastened after him to protect Cousin Tryphena.

She opened the door in answer to his battering knocks, frowned, and began to say something to him, but was fairly swept off her feet by the torrent of his reproaches. . . . "How dare you take the information I give you and use it to betray your fellow-man! How do you *dare* stand there, so mealy-mouthed, and face me, when you are planning a cowardly attack on the liberty of your country! You call yourself a nurse . . . what would you think of a mother who hid an ulcer in her child's side from the doctor because it did not look pretty! What *else* are you planning to do? What would you think of a nurse who put paint and powder on her patient's face, to cover up a filthy skin disease? What else are you planning to do . . . you with your plan to put court-plaster over one pustule in ten million and thinking you are helping cure the patient! You are planning simply to please yourself, you cowardly . . . and you are an idiot too. . . ." He beat his hands on the door-jambs, ". . . if you had the money of forty millionaires, you couldn't do anything in that way . . . how many people are you thinking to help . . . two, three . . . maybe four! But there are hundreds of others . . . why, I could read you a thousand stories of worse—"

Cousin Tryphena's limit had been reached. She advanced upon the intruder with a face as excited as his own. . . . "Jombatiste Ramotte, if you ever dare to read me another such story, I'll go right out and jump in the Necronsett River!"

The mania which had haunted earlier generations of her family looked out luridly from her eyes.

I felt the goose-flesh stand out on my arms, and even Jombatiste's hot blood was cooled. He stood silent an instant.

Cousin Tryphena slammed the door in his face.

He turned to me with a bewilderment almost pathetic, so tremendous was it. . . . "Did you hear that . . . what sort of logic do you call—"

"Jombatiste," I counseled him, "if you take my advice, you'll leave Miss Tryphena alone after this."

Cousin Tryphena started off on her crack-brained expedition, the very next morning, on the six-thirty train. I happened to be looking out sleepily and saw her trudging wearily past our house in the bleak gray of our mountain dawn, the inadequate little, yellow flame of her old-fashioned lantern like a glowworm at her side. It seemed somehow symbolical of something, I did not know what.

It was a full week before we heard from her, and we had begun really to fear that we would never see her again, thinking that perhaps, while she was among strangers, her unsettled mind might have taken some new fancy which would be her destruction.

That week Jombatiste shut the door to his house. The children reported that he would not even let them in, and that they could see him through the window stitching away in ominous silence, muttering to himself.

Eight days after Cousin Tryphena had gone away, I had a telegram from her, which read, "Build fires in both my stoves tomorrow afternoon."

The dark comes early in the mountains, and so, although I dare say there was not a house in the village without a face at the pane after the late evening train came up, none of us saw anything but our usual impenetrable December darkness. That, too, seemed, to my perhaps overwrought consciousness of the problem, highly suggestive of the usual course of our lives. At least, I told myself, Cousin Tryphena had taken her absurd little lantern and gone forth.

The next morning, soon after breakfast, I set off for the other end of the street. Cousin Tryphena saw me coming and opened the door. She did not smile, and she was still very pale, but I saw that she had regained her self-control. "Come right in," she said, in rather a tense voice, and, as I entered she added, in our rustic phrase for introduction, "Make you 'quainted with my friend, Mrs. Lindstrom. She's come up from the city to stay with me. And this is her little boy, Sigurd, and this is the baby."

Blinking somewhat, I shook hands with a small, stoop-shouldered woman, in a new, ready-made dress, with abundant yellow hair drawn back from the thinnest, palest, saddest little face I had ever seen. She was holding an immaculately clean baby, asleep, its long golden lashes lying on cheeks as white and sunken as her own. A sturdily built boy of about six scrambled up from where he lay on the floor, playing with the cat, and gave me a hand shyly, hanging down his head. His mother had glanced up at me with a quick, shrinking look of fright, the tears starting to her eyes.

Cousin Tryphena was evidently afraid that I would not take her cue and sound the right note, for she went on hastily, "Mrs. Lindstrom has been real sick and kind o' worried over the baby, so's she's some nervous. I tell her Hillsboro air is thought very good for people's nerves. Lots of city folks come here in summer time, just for that. Don't you think Sigurd is a real big boy for only six and a half? He knows his letters too! He's goin' to school as soon as we get settled down. I want you should bring over those alphabet blocks that your Peggy doesn't use any more—"

The other woman was openly crying now, clinging to her benefactress' hand and holding it against her cheek as she sobbed.

My heroic old cousin patted her hair awkwardly, but kept on talking in her matter-of-fact manner, looking at me sternly as though defying me to show, by look or word, any consciousness of anything unusual in the situation; and we fell at once, she and I, into a commonplace conversation about the incidents of the trip up.

When I came away, half an hour later, Cousin Tryphena slipped a shawl over her head and came down the walk with me to the gate. I was much affected by what seemed to me the dramatically fitting outcome of my old kinswoman's Quixotism. I saw Cousin Tryphena picturesquely as the Happy Fool of old folklore, the character who, through his very lack of worldly wisdom, attains without effort all that self-seeking folks try for in vain. The happy ending of her adventure filled me with a cheerful wonder at the ways of Providence, which I tried to pass on to her in the exclamation, "Why, Cousin Tryphena, it's like a story-book! You're going to *enjoy* having those people. The woman is as nice as she can be, and that's the brightest little boy! He's as smart as a whip!"

I was aware that the oddness of Cousin Tryphena's manner still persisted even now that we were alone. She sighed heavily and said, "I don't sleep much better nights now I've done it!" Then facing me, "I hadn't ought to have brought them up here! I just did it to please myself! Once I saw 'em . . . I wanted 'em!"

This seemed to me the wildest possible perversion of the Puritan instinct for self-condemnation and, half-vexed, I attempted some expostulation.

She stopped me with a look and gesture Dante might have had, "You ain't seen what I've seen."

I was half-frightened by her expression but tried to speak coolly. "Why, was it as bad as that paper said?" I asked.

She laid her hand on my arm, "Child, it was nothing like what the paper said . . . it was so much worse!"

"Oh . . ." I commented inadequately.

"I was five days looking for her . . . they'd moved from the address the paper give. And, in those five days, I saw so many others . . . *so many others* . . ." her face twitched. She put one lean old hand before her eyes. Then, quite unexpectedly, she cast out at me an exclamation which made my notion of the pretty picturesqueness of her adventure seem cheap and trivial and superficial. "Jombatiste is right!" she cried to me with a bitter fierceness: "Everything is wrong! Everything is wrong! If I can do anything, I'd ought to do it to help them as want to smash everything up and start over! What good does it do for me to bring up here just these three out of all I saw . . ." Her voice broke into pitiful, self-excusing quavers, "but when I saw them . . . the baby was so sick . . . and little Sigurd is so cunning . . . he took to me right away, came to me the first thing . . . this morning he wouldn't pick up his new rubbers off the floor for his mother, but, when I asked him, he did, right off . . . you ought to have seen what he had on . . . such rags . . . such dirt . . . and 'twan't her fault either! She's . . . why she's like *any*body . . . like a person's cousin they never happened to see before . . . why, they were all *folks!*" she cried out, her tired old mind wandering fitfully from one thing to another.

"You didn't find the little boy in the asylum?" I asked.

"He was dead before I got there," she answered.

"Oh . . .!" I said again, shocked, and then tentatively, "Had he . . .?"

"I don't know whether he had or not," said Cousin Tryphena, "I didn't ask. I didn't want to know. I know too much now!" She looked up fixedly at the mountain line, high and keen against the winter sky, "Jombatiste is right," she said again unsparingly, "I hadn't ought to be enjoying them . . . their father ought to be alive and with them. He was willing to work all he could, and yet he . . . here I've lived for fifty-five years and never airned my salt a single day. What was I livin' on? The stuff these folks ought to ha' had to eat . . . them and the Lord only knows how many more besides! Jombatiste is right . . . what I'm doin' now is only a drop in the bucket!"

She started from her somber reverie at the sound of a childish wail from the house. . . . "That's Sigurd . . . I *knew* that cat would scratch him!" she told me with instant, breathless agitation, as though the skies were falling, and darted back. After a moment's hesitation I, too, went back and watched her bind up with stiff, unaccustomed old fingers the little scratched hand, watched the frightened little boy sob himself quiet on her old knees that had never before known a child's soft weight, saw the expression in her eyes as she looked down at the sleeping baby and gazed about the untidy room so full of life, which had always been so orderly and so empty.

She lifted the little boy up higher so that his tousled yellow hair rested against her bosom. He put an arm around her neck and she flushed with pleasure like a girl; but, although she held him close to her with a sudden wistful tenderness, there was in her eyes a gloomy austerity which forbade me to sentimentalize over the picture she made.

"But, Cousin Tryphena," I urged, "it *is* a drop in the bucket, you know, and that's something!"

She looked down at the child on her knee, she laid her cheek against his bright hair, but she told me with harsh, self-accusing rigor, "Tain't right for me to be here alive enjoying that dead man's little boy."

That was eighteen months ago. Mrs. Lindstrom is dead of consumption; but the two children are rosy and hearty and not to be distinguished from the other little Yankees of the village. They are devotedly attached to their Aunt Tryphena and rule her despotically.

And so we live along, like a symbol of the great world, bewildered Cousin Tryphena toiling lovingly for her adopted children, with the memory of her descent into hell still darkening and confusing her kind eyes; Jombatiste clothing his old body in rags and his soul in flaming indignation as he batters hopefully at the ramparts of intrenched unrighteousness . . . and the rest of us doing nothing at all.

Study and Discussion Questions

1. How are Cousin Tryphena and Jombatiste different and how are they alike?
2. What is the narrator's attitude toward Tryphena and toward Jombatiste? How does it change?
3. Tryphena's family insanity is frequently cited to explain her behavior. What does this suggest about those who offer such explanations?
4. On several occasions, the narrator compares Tryphena and Jombatiste to characters in fiction. How do such comparisons function in the story?
5. What are the sources of comedy in the story? Why does Fisher take a comic approach with this rather serious material?

Suggestions for Writing

1. Why does Tryphena's planned act of charity so enrage Jombatiste? What do you think of his argument against charity?
2. Discuss your own responses to human suffering due to social injustice when you see or learn about it. You might describe and analyze a particular instance.

Critical Resources

1. "Canfield, Dorothy Fisher, 1879–1958." *The University of Vermont: UVM Libraries.* May 15, 2005. <http://bailey.uvm.edu:6336/dynaweb/finding aids/fisherdc>
2. Champion, Laurie, ed. *American Women Writers, 1900–1945: A Bio-Bibliographical Critical Sourcebook.* Westport, CT: Greenwood Press, 2000.
3. Washington, Ida. *Dorothy Canfield Fisher: A Biography.* Shelburne, VT: New England Press, 1982.

ALAN SILLITOE (b. 1928)

*Alan Sillitoe once stated in an interview that ". . . In [England], as in any other country, a writer is liked if he is loyal to the system. But it is the writer's duty in a sense to be disloyal . . . He can speak up in many ways; the best way is to write a book" (*The Nation, *1969). Sillitoe has spent the past forty years being "disloyal," writing provocative novels and short stories that candidly explore working-class experience. Raised in the northern industrial town of Nottingham, England and largely self-taught, Sillitoe's first publications, the novel* Saturday Night and Sunday Morning *(1958) and the short story collection* The Loneliness of the Long-distance Runner *(1960, title piece presented here), brought the author notoriety as another representative of the "Angry Young Men"—the generation of post–World War II British writers who caustically attacked Britain's middle-class complacency and privilege. Yet it is a label that doesn't quite fit Sillitoe's writing. While elements of his work are often rancorous and "angry," Sillitoe's focus on alienation, brought to life by a mix of perceptive description, Nottingham dialect, and unconventional narrative, presents a more complex version of working-class life than the sometimes romanticized works of other Angry Young Men. In addition to the works already mentioned, Sillitoe has written in various genres. His other works include the novels* Key to the Door *(1962),* The Death of William Posters *(1965),* A Start in Life *(1970),* The Storyteller *(1980), and* Last Loves *(1990); and the plays* All Citizens are Soldiers *(1967),* The Slot Machine *(1970),* Pit Strike *(1977), and* The Interview *(1978). His latest publication is the novel* Birthday *(2001). He wrote his autobiography* Life Without Armor *in 1995.*

The Loneliness of the Long-distance Runner   (1959)

As soon as I got to Borstal[1] they made me a long-distance cross-country runner. I suppose they thought I was just the build for it because I was long and

---

[1]Reform school.

skinny for my age (and still am) and in any case I didn't mind it much, to tell you the truth, because running had always been made much of in our family, especially running away from the police. I've always been a good runner, quick and with a big stride as well, the only trouble being that no matter how fast I run, and I did a very fair lick even though I do say so myself, it didn't stop me getting caught by the cops after that bakery job.

You might think it a bit rare, having long-distance cross-country runners in Borstal, thinking that the first thing a long-distance cross-country runner would do when they set him loose at them fields and woods would be to run as far away from the place as he could get on a bellyful of Borstal slumgullion—but you're wrong, and I'll tell you why. The first thing is that them bastards over us aren't as daft as they most of the time look, and for another thing I'm not so daft as I would look if I tried to make a break for it on my long-distance running, because to abscond and then get caught is nothing but a mug's game, and I'm not falling for it. Cunning is what counts in this life, and even that you've got to use in the slyest way you can; I'm telling you straight: they're cunning, and I'm cunning. If only 'them' and 'us' had the same ideas we'd get on like a house on fire, but they don't see eye to eye with us and we don't see eye to eye with them, so that's how it stands and how it will always stand. The one fact is that all of us are cunning, and because of this there's no love lost between us. So the thing is that they know I won't try to get away from them: they sit there like spiders in that crumbly manor house, perched like jumped-up jackdaws on the roof, watching out over the drives and fields like German generals from the tops of tanks. And even when I jog-trot on behind a wood and they can't see me anymore they know my sweeping-brush head will bob along that hedge-top in an hour's time and that I'll report to the bloke on the gate. Because when on a raw and frosty morning I get up at five o'clock and stand shivering my belly off on the stone floor and all the rest still have another hour to snooze before the bells go, I slink downstairs through all the corridors to the big outside door with a permit running-card in my fist, I feel like the first and last man on the world, both at once, if you can believe what I'm trying to say. I feel like the first man because I've hardly got a stitch on and am sent against the frozen fields in a shimmy and shorts—even the first poor bastard dropped on to the earth in midwinter knew how to make a suit of leaves, or how to skin a pterodactyl for a topcoat. But there I am, frozen stiff, with nothing to get me warm except a couple of hours' long-distance running before breakfast, not even a slice of bread-and-sheepdip. They're training me up fine for the big sports day when all the pig-faced snotty-nosed dukes and ladies—who can't add two and two together and would mess themselves like loonies if they didn't have slavies to beck-and-call—come and make speeches to us about sports being just the thing to get us leading an honest life and keep our itching finger-ends off them shop locks and safe handles and hairgrips to open gas meters. They give us a bit of blue ribbon and a cup for a prize after we've shagged ourselves out running or jumping, like race horses, only we don't get so well looked-after as race horses, that's the only thing.

So there I am, standing in the doorway in shimmy and shorts, not even a dry crust in my guts, looking out at frosty flowers on the ground. I suppose you think this is enough to make me cry? Not likely. Just because I feel like the first bloke in the world wouldn't make me bawl. It makes me feel fifty times better than when I'm cooped up in that dormitory with three hundred others. No, it's sometimes when I stand there feeling like the *last* man in the world that I don't feel so good. I feel like the last man in the world because I think that all those three hundred sleepers behind me are dead. They sleep so well I think that every scruffy head's kicked the bucket in the night and I'm the only one left, and when I look out into the bushes and frozen ponds I have the feeling that it's going to get colder and colder until everything I can see, meaning my red arms as well, is going to be covered with a thousand miles of ice, all the earth, right up to the sky and over every bit of land and sea. So I try to kick this feeling out and act like I'm the first man on earth. And that makes me feel good, so as soon as I'm steamed up enough to get this feeling in me, I take a flying leap out of the doorway, and off I trot.

I'm in Essex. It's supposed to be a good Borstal, at least that's what the governor said to me when I got here from Nottingham. "We want to trust you while you are in this establishment," he said, smoothing out his newspaper with lily-white workless hands, while I read the big words upside down: *Daily Telegraph.* "If you play ball with us, we'll play ball with you." (Honest to God, you'd have thought it was going to be one long tennis match.) "We want hard honest work and we want good athletics," he said as well. "And if you give us both these things you can be sure we'll do right by you and send you back into the world an honest man." Well, I could have died laughing, especially when straight after this I hear the barking sergeant-major's voice calling me and two others to attention and marching us off like we was Grenadier Guards. And when the governor kept saying how 'we' wanted you to do this, and 'we' wanted you to do that, I kept looking round for the other blokes, wondering how many of them there was. Of course, I knew there were thousands of them, but as far as I knew only one was in the room. And there *are* thousands of them, all over the poxeaten country, in shops, offices, railway stations, cars, houses, pubs—In-law blokes like you and them, all on the watch for Out-law blokes like me and us—and waiting to 'phone for the coppers as soon as we make a false move. And it'll always be there, I'll tell you that now, because I haven't finished making all my false moves yet, and I dare say I won't until I kick the bucket. If the In-laws are hoping to stop me making false moves they're wasting their time. They might as well stand me up against a wall and let fly with a dozen rifles. That's the only way they'll stop me, and a few million others. Because I've been doing a lot of thinking since coming here. They can spy on us all day to see if we're pulling our puddings and if we're working good or doing our 'athletics' but they can't make an X-ray of our guts to find out what we're telling ourselves. I've been asking myself all sorts of questions, and thinking about my life up to now. And I like doing all this. It's a treat. It passes the time away and don't make Borstal seem half so bad as the boys in our street used to say it was. And this long-distance running lark is the best of all, because it makes me think so good that I learn things even better than when I'm on my bed at night. And apart from that, what with thinking so much while I'm running I'm getting to be one of the best runners in the Borstal. I can go my five miles round better than anybody else I know.

So as soon as I tell myself I'm the first man ever to be dropped into the world, and as soon as I take that first flying leap out into the frosty grass of an early morning when even birds haven't the heart to whistle, I get to thinking, and that's what I like. I go my rounds in a dream, turning at lane or footpath corners without knowing I'm turning, leaping brooks without knowing they're there, and shouting good morning to the early cow-milker without seeing him. It's a treat, being a long-distance runner, out in the world by yourself with not a soul to make you bad-tempered or tell you what to do or that there's a shop to break and enter a bit back from the next street. Sometimes I think that I've never been so free as during that couple of hours when I'm trotting up the path out of the gates and turning by that bare-faced, big-bellied oak tree at the lane end. Everything's dead, but good, because it's dead before coming alive, not dead after being alive. That's how I look at it. Mind you, I often feel frozen stiff at first. I can't feel my hands or feet or flesh at all, like I'm a ghost who wouldn't know the earth was under him if he didn't see it now and again through the mist. But even though some people would call this frost-pain suffering if they wrote about it to their mams in a letter, I don't, because I know that in half an hour I'm going to be warm, that by the time I get to the main road and am turning on to the wheat-field footpath by the bus stop I'm going to feel as hot as a potbellied stove and as happy as a dog with a tin tail.

It's a good life, I'm saying to myself, if you don't give in to coppers and Borstal-bosses and the rest of them bastard-faced In-laws. Trot-trot-trot. Puff-puff-puff. Slap-slap-slap go my feet on the hard soil. Swish-swish-swish as my arms and side catch the bare branches of a bush. For I'm seventeen now, and when they let me out of this—if I don't make a break and see that things turn out otherwise—they'll try to get me in the army, and what's the difference between the army and this place I'm in now? They can't kid me, the bastards. I've seen the barracks near where I live, and if there weren't swaddies on guard outside with rifles you wouldn't know the difference between their high walls and the place I'm in now. Even though the swaddies come out at odd times a week for a pint of ale, so what? Don't I come out three mornings a week on my long-distance running, which is fifty times better than boozing. When they first said that I was to do my long-distance running without a guard pedalling beside me on a bike I couldn't believe it; but they called it a progressive and modern place, though they can't kid me because I know it's just like any other Borstal, going by the stories I've heard, except that they let me trot about like this. Borstal's Borstal no matter what they do; but anyway I moaned about it being a bit thick sending me out so early to run five miles on an empty stomach, until they talked me round to thinking it wasn't so bad—which I knew all the time—until they called me a good sport and patted me on the back when I said I'd do it and that I'd try to win them the Borstal Blue Ribbon Prize Cup For Long Distance Cross Country Running (All England). And now the governor talks to me when he comes on his rounds, almost as he'd talk to his prize race horse, if he had one.

"All right, Smith?" he asks.

"Yes, sir," I answer.

He flicks his grey moustache: "How's the running coming along?"

"I've set myself to trot round the grounds after dinner just to keep my hand in, sir," I tell him.

The pot-bellied pop-eyed bastard gets pleased at this: "Good show. I know you'll get us that cup," he says.

And I swear under my breath: "Like boggery, I will." No, I won't get them that cup, even though the stupid tash-twitching bastard has all his hopes in me. Because what does his barmy hope mean? I ask myself. Trot-trot-trot, slap-slap-slap, over the stream and into the wood where it's almost dark and frosty-dew twigs sting my legs. It don't mean a bloody thing to me, only to him, and it means as much to him as it would mean to me if I picked up the racing paper and put my bet on a hoss I didn't know, had never seen, and didn't care a sod if I ever did see. That's what it means to him. And I'll lose that race, because I'm not a race horse at all, and I'll let him know it when I'm about to get out—if I don't sling my hook even before the race. By Christ I will. I'm a human being and I've got thoughts and secrets and bloody life inside me that he doesn't know is there, and he'll never know what's there because he's stupid. I suppose you'll laugh at this, me saying the governor's a stupid bastard when I know hardly how to write and he can read and write and add-up like a professor. But what I say is true right enough. He's stupid, and I'm not, because I can see further into the likes of him than he can see into the likes of me. Admitted, we're both cunning, but I'm more cunning and I'll win in the end even if I die in gaol at eighty-two, because I'll have more fun and fire out of my life than he'll ever get out of his. He's read a thousand books I suppose, and for all I know he might even have written a few, but I know for a dead cert, as sure as I'm sitting here, that what I'm scribbling down is worth a million to what he could ever scribble down. I don't care what anybody says, but that's the truth and can't be denied. I know when he talks to me and I look into his army mug that I'm alive and he's dead. He's as dead as a doornail. If he ran ten yards he'd drop dead. If he got ten yards into what goes on in my guts he'd drop dead as well—with surprise. At the moment it's dead blokes like him as have the whip-hand over blokes like me, and I'm almost dead sure it'll always be like that, but even so, by Christ, I'd rather be like I am—always on the run and breaking into shops for a packet of fags and a jar of jam—than have the whip-hand over somebody else and be dead from the toe nails up. Maybe as soon as you get the whip-hand over somebody you do go dead. By God, to say that last sentence has needed a few hundred miles of long-distance running. I could no more have said that at first than I could have took a million-pound note from my back pocket. But it's true, you know, now I think of it again, and has always been true, and always will be true, and I'm surer of it every time I see the governor open that door and say Goodmorning lads.

As I run and see my smoky breath going out into the air as if I had ten cigars stuck in different parts of my body I think more on the little speech the governor made when I first came. Honesty. Be honest. I laughed so much one morning I went ten minutes down in my timing because I had to stop and get rid of the stitch in my side. The governor was so worried when I got back late that he sent me to the doctor's for an X-ray and heart check. Be honest. It's like saying: Be dead, like me, and then you'll have no more pain of leaving your nice slummy house for Borstal or prison. Be honest and settle down in a cosy six pounds a week job. Well, even with all this long-distance running I haven't yet been able to decide what he means by this, although I'm just about beginning to—and I don't like what it means. Because after all my thinking I found that it adds up to something that can't be true about me, being born and brought up as I was. Because another thing people like the governor will never understand is that I *am* honest, that I've never been anything else but honest, and that I'll always be honest. Sounds funny. But it's true because I know what honest means according to me and he only knows what it means according to him. I think my honesty is the only sort in the world, and he thinks his is the only sort in the world as well. That's why this dirty great walled-up and fenced-up manor house in the middle of nowhere has been used to coop-up blokes like me. And if I had the whip-hand I wouldn't even bother to build a place like this to put all the cops, governors, posh whores, penpushers, army officers, Members of Parliament in; no, I'd stick them up against a wall and let them have it, like they'd have done with blokes like us years ago, that is, if they'd ever known what it means to be honest, which they don't and never will so help me God Almighty.

I was nearly eighteen months in Borstal before I thought about getting out. I can't tell you much about what it was like there because I haven't got the hang of describing buildings or saying how many crumby chairs and slatted windows make a room. Neither can I do much complaining, because to tell you the truth I didn't suffer in Borstal at all. I gave the same answer a pal of mine gave when someone asked him how much he hated it in the army. "I didn't hate it," he said. "They fed me, gave me a suit, and pocket-money, which was a bloody sight more than I ever got before, unless I worked myself to death for it, and most of the time they wouldn't let me work but sent me to the dole office twice a week." Well, that's more or less what I say. Borstal didn't hurt me in that respect, so since I've got no complaints I don't have to describe what they gave us to eat, what the dorms were like, or how they treated us. But in another way Borstal does something to me. No, it doesn't get my back up, because it's always been up, right from when I was born. What it does do is show me what they've been trying to frighten me with. They've got other things as well, like prison and, in the end, the rope. It's like me rushing up to thump a man and snatch the coat off his back when, suddenly, I pull up because he whips out a knife and lifts it to stick me like a pig if I come too close. That knife is Borstal, clink, the rope. But once you've seen the knife you learn a bit of unarmed combat. You have to, because you'll never get that sort of knife in your own hands, and this unarmed combat doesn't amount to much. Still, there it is, and you keep on rushing up to this man, knife or not, hoping to get one of your hands on his wrist and the other on his elbow both at the same time, and press back until he drops the knife.

You see, by sending me to Borstal they've shown me the knife, and from now on I know something I didn't know before: that it's war between me and them. I always knew this, naturally, because I was in Remand Homes as well and the boys there told me a lot about their brothers in Borstal, but it was only touch and go then, like kittens, like boxing-gloves, like dobbie. But now that they've shown me the knife, whether I ever pinch another thing in my life again or not, I know who my enemies are and what war is. They can drop all the atom bombs they like for all I care: I'll never call it war and wear a soldier's uniform, because I'm in a different sort of war, that they think is child's play. The war they think is war is suicide, and those that go and get killed in war should be put in clink for attempted suicide because that's the feeling in blokes' minds when they rush to join up or let themselves be called up. I know, because I've thought how good it would be sometimes to do myself in and the easiest way to do it, it occurred to me, was to hope for a big war so's I could join up and get killed. But I got past that when I knew I already was in a war of my own, that I was born into one, that I grew up hearing the sound of 'old soldiers' who'd been over the top at Dartmoor, half-killed at Lincoln, trapped in no-man's-land at Borstal, that sounded louder than any Jerry bombs. Government wars aren't my wars; they've got nowt to do with me, because my own war's all that I'll ever be bothered about. I remember when I was fourteen and I went out into the country with three of my cousins, all about the same age, who later went to different Borstals, and then to different regiments, from which they soon deserted, and then to different gaols where they still are as far as I know. But anyway, we were all kids then, and wanted to go out to the woods for a change, to get away from the roads of stinking hot tar one summer. We climbed over fences and went through fields, scrumping a few sour apples on our way, until we saw the wood about a mile off. Up Colliers' Pad we heard another lot of kids talking in high-school voices behind a hedge. We crept up on them and peeped through the brambles, and saw they were eating a picnic, a real posh spread out of baskets and flasks and towels. There must have been about seven of them, lads and girls sent out by their mams and dads for the afternoon. So we went on our bellies through the hedge like crocodiles and surrounded them, and then dashed into the middle, scattering the fire and batting their tabs and snatching up all there was to eat, then running off over Cherry Orchard fields into the wood, with a man chasing us who'd come up while we were ransacking their picnic. We got away all right, and had a good feed into the bargain, because we'd been clambed to death and couldn't wait long enough to get our chops ripping into them thin lettuce and ham sandwiches and creamy cakes.

Well, I'll always feel during every bit of my life like those daft kids should have felt before we broke them up. But they never dreamed that what happened was going to happen, just like the governor of this Borstal who spouts to us about honesty and all that wappy stuff don't know a bloody thing, while I know every minute of my life that a big boot is always likely to smash any nice picnic I might be barmy and dishonest enough to make for myself. I admit that there've been times when I've thought of telling the governor all this so as to put him on his guard, but when I've got as close as seeing him I've changed my mind, thinking to let him either find out for himself or go through the same mill as I've gone through. I'm not hard-hearted (in fact I've helped a few blokes in my time with the odd quid, lie, fag, or shelter from the rain when they've been on the run) but I'm boggered if I'm going to risk being put in the cells just for trying to give the governor a bit of advice he don't deserve. If my heart's soft I know the sort of people I'm going to save it for. And any advice I'd give the governor wouldn't do him the least bit of good; it'd only trip him up sooner than if he wasn't told at all, which I suppose is what I want to happen. But for the time being I'll let things go on as they are, which is something else I've learned in the last year or two. (It's a good job I can only think of these things as fast as I can write with this stub of pencil that's clutched in my paw, otherwise I'd have dropped the whole thing weeks ago.)

By the time I'm half-way through my morning course, when after a frost-bitten dawn I can see a phlegmy bit of sunlight hanging from the bare twigs of beech and sycamore, and when I've measured my half-way mark by the short-cut scrimmage down the steep bush-covered bank and into the sunken lane, when still there's not a soul in sight and not a sound except the neighing of a piebald foal in a cottage stable that I can't see, I get to thinking the deepest and daftest of all. The governor would have a fit if he could see me sliding down the bank because I could break my neck or ankle, but I can't not do it because it's the only risk I take and the only excitement I ever get, flying flat-out like one of them pterodactyls from the 'Lost World' I once heard on the wireless, crazy like a cut-balled cockerel, scratching myself to bits and almost letting myself go but not quite. It's the most wonderful minute because there's not one thought or word or picture of anything in my head while I'm going down. I'm empty, as empty as I was before I was born, and I don't let myself go, I suppose, because whatever it is that's farthest down inside me don't want me to die or hurt myself bad. And it's daft to think deep, you know, because it gets you nowhere, though deep is what I am when I've passed this half-way mark because the long-distance run of an early morning makes me think that every run like this is a life—a little life, I know—but a life as full of misery and happiness and things happening as you can ever get really around yourself—and I remember that after a lot of these runs I thought that it didn't need much know-how to tell how a life was going to end once it had got well started. But as usual I was wrong, caught first by the cops and then by my own bad brain, I could never trust myself to fly scot-free over these traps, was always tripped up sooner or later no matter how many I got over to the good without even knowing it. Looking back I suppose them big trees put their branches to their snouts and gave each other the wink, and there I was whizzing down the bank and not seeing a bloody thing.

II

I don't say to myself: "You shouldn't have done the job and then you'd have stayed away from Borstal"; no, what I ram into my runner-brain is that my luck had no right to scram just when I was on my way to making the coppers think I hadn't done the job after all. The time was autumn and the night foggy enough to set me and my mate Mike roaming the streets when we should have been rooted in front of the telly or stuck into a plush posh seat at the pictures, but I was restless after six weeks away from any sort of work, and well you might ask me why I'd been bone-idle for so long because normally I sweated my thin guts out on a milling-machine with the rest of them, but you see, my dad died from cancer of the throat, and mam collected a cool five hundred in insurance and benefits from the factory where he'd worked, "for your bereavement," they said, or words like that.

Now I believe, and my mam must have thought the same, that a wad of crisp blue-back fivers ain't a sight of good to a living soul unless they're flying out of your hand into some shopkeeper's till, and the shopkeeper is passing you tip-top things in exchange over the counter, so as soon as she got the money, mam took me and my five brothers and sisters out to town and got us dolled-up in new clothes. Then she ordered a twenty-one-inch telly, a new carpet because the old one was covered with blood from dad's dying and wouldn't wash out, and took a taxi home with bags of grub and a new fur coat. And do you know—you wain't believe me when I tell you—she'd still near three hundred left in her bulging handbag the next day, so how could any of us go to work after that? Poor old dad, he didn't get a look in, and he was the one who'd done the suffering and dying for such a lot of lolly.

Night after night we sat in front of the telly with a ham sandwich in one hand, a bar of chocolate in the other, and a bottle of lemonade between our boots, while mam was with some fancy-man upstairs on the new bed she'd ordered, and I'd never known a family as happy as ours was in that couple of months when we'd got all the money we needed. And when the dough ran out I didn't think about anything much, but just roamed the streets—looking for another job, I told mam—hoping I suppose to get my hands on another five hundred nicker so's the nice life we'd got used to could go on and on for ever. Because it's surprising how quick you can get used to a different life. To begin with, the adverts on the telly had shown us how much more there was in the world to buy than we'd ever dreamed of when we'd looked into shop windows but hadn't seen all there was to see because we didn't have the money to buy it with anyway. And the telly made all these things seem twenty times better than we'd ever thought they were. Even adverts at the cinema were cool and tame, because now we were seeing them in private at home. We used to cock our noses up at things in shops that didn't move, but suddenly we saw their real value because they jumped and glittered around the screen and had some pasty-faced tart going head over heels to get her nail-polished grabbers on to them or her lipstick lips over them, not like the crumby adverts you saw on posters or in newspapers as dead as doornails; these were flickering around loose, half-open packets and tins, making you think that all you had to do was finish opening them before they were yours, like seeing an unlocked safe through a shop window with the man gone away for a cup of tea without thinking to guard his lolly. The films they showed were good as well, in that way, because we couldn't get our eyes unglued from the cops chasing the robbers who had satchel-bags crammed with cash and looked like getting away to spent it—until the last moment. I always hoped they would end up free to blow the lot, and could never stop wanting to put my hand out, smash into the screen (it only looked a bit of rag-screen like at the pictures) and get the copper in a half-nelson so's he'd stop following the bloke with the money-bags. Even when he'd knocked off a couple of bank clerks I hoped he wouldn't get nabbed. In fact I wished more than ever he wouldn't because it meant the hot-chair if he did, and I wouldn't wish that on anybody no matter what they'd done, because I'd read in a book where the hot-chair won't a quick death at all, but that you just sat there scorching to death until you were dead. And it was when these cops were chasing the crooks that we played some good tricks with the telly, because when one of them opened his big gob to spout about getting their man I'd turn the sound down and see his mouth move like a goldfish or mackerel or a minnow mimicking what they were supposed to be acting—it was so funny the whole family nearly went into fits on the brand-new carpet that hadn't yet found its way to the bedroom. It was the best of all though when we did it to some Tory telling us about how good his government was going to be if we kept on voting for them—their slack chops rolling, opening and bumbling, hands lifting to twitch moustaches and touching their buttonholes to make sure the flower hadn't wilted, so that you could see they didn't mean a word they said, especially with not a murmur coming out because we'd cut off the sound. When the governor of the Borstal first talked to me I was reminded of those times so much that I nearly killed myself trying not to laugh. Yes, we played so many good stunts on the box of tricks that mam used to call us the Telly Boys, we got so clever at it.

My pal Mike got let off with probation because it was his first job—anyway the first they ever knew about—and because they said he would never have done it if it hadn't been for me talking him into it. They said I was a menace to honest lads like Mike—hands in his pockets so that they looked stone-empty, head bent forward as if looking for half-crowns to fill 'em with, a ripped jersey on and his hair falling into his eyes so that he could go up to women and ask them for a shilling because he was hungry—and that I was the brains behind the job, the guiding light when it came to making up anybody's mind, but I swear to God I won't owt like that because really I ain't got no more brains than a gnat after hiding the money in the place I did. And I—being cranky like I am—got sent to Borstal because to tell you the honest truth I'd been to Remand Homes before— though that's another story and I suppose if ever I tell it it'll be just as boring as this one is. I was glad though that Mike got away with it, and I only hope he always will, not like silly bastard me.

So on this foggy night we tore ourselves away from the telly and slammed the front door behind us, setting off up our wide street like slow tugs on a river that'd broken their hooters, for we didn't know where the housefronts began what with the perishing cold mist all around. I was snatched to death without an overcoat: mam had forgotten to buy me one in the scrummage of shopping, and by the time I thought to remind her of it the dough was all gone. So we whistled 'The Teddy Boys Picnic' to keep us warm, and I told myself that I'd get a coat soon if it was the last thing I did. Mike said he thought the same about himself, adding that he'd also get some brand-new glasses with gold rims, to wear instead of the wire frames they'd given him at the school clinic years ago. He didn't twig it was foggy at first and cleaned his glasses every time I pulled him back from a lamp-post or car, but when he saw the lights on Alfreton Road looking like octopus eyes he put them in his pocket and didn't wear them again until we did the job. We hadn't got two ha-pennies between us, and though we weren't hungry we wished we'd got a bob or two when we passed the fish and chip shops because the delicious sniffs of salt and vinegar and frying fat made our mouths water. I don't mind telling you we walked the town from one end to the other and if our eyes worn't glued to the ground looking for lost wallets and watches they was swivelling around house windows and shop doors in case we saw something easy and worth nipping into.

Neither of us said as much as this to each other, but I know for a fact that that was what we was thinking. What I don't know—and as sure as I sit here I know I'll never know—is which of us was the first bastard to latch his peepers on to that baker's backyard. Oh yes, it's all right me telling myself it was me, but the truth is that I've never known whether it was Mike or not, because I do know that I didn't see the open window until he stabbed me in the ribs and pointed it out. "See it?" he said.

"Yes," I told him, "so let's get cracking."

"But what about the wall though?" he whispered, looking a bit closer.

"On your shoulders," I chipped in.

His eyes were already up there: "Will you be able to reach?" It was the only time he ever showed any life.

"Leave it to me," I said, ever-ready. "I can reach anywhere from your hamhock shoulders."

Mike was a nipper compared to me, but underneath the scruffy draughtboard jersey he wore were muscles as hard as iron, and you wouldn't think to see him walking down the street with glasses on and hands in pockets that he'd harm a fly, but I never liked to get on the wrong side of him in a fight because he's the sort that don't say a word for weeks on end—sits plugged in front of the telly, or reads a cowboy book, or just sleeps—when suddenly BIFF—half kills somebody for almost nothing at all, such as beating him in a race for the last Football Post on a Saturday night, pushing in before him at a bus stop, or bumping into him when he was day-dreaming about Dolly-on-the-Tub next door. I saw him set on a bloke once for no more than fixing him in a funny way with his eyes, and it turned out that the bloke was cockeyed but nobody knew it because he'd just that day come to live in our street. At other times none of these things would matter a bit, and I suppose the only reason why I was pals with him was because I didn't say much from one month's end to another either.

He puts his hands up in the air like he was being covered with a Gatling-Gun, and moved to the wall like he was going to be mowed down, and I climbed up him like he was a stile or step-ladder, and there he stood, the palms of his up-shot maulers flat and turned out so's I could step on 'em like they was the adjustable jack-spanner under a car, not a sound of a breath nor a shiver of a flinch coming from him. I lost no time in any case, took my coat from between my teeth, chucked it up to the glass-topped wall (where the glass worn't too sharp because the jags had been worn down by years of accidental stones) and was sitting astraddle before I knew where I was. Then down the other side, with my legs rammed up into my throat when I hit the ground, the crack coming about as hard as when you fall after a high parachute drop, that one of my mates told me was like jumping off a twelve-foot wall, which this must have been. Then I picked up my bits and pieces and opened the gate for Mike, who was still grinning and full of life because the hardest part of the job was already done. "I came, I broke, I entered," like that clever-dick Borstal song.

I didn't think about anything at all, as usual, because I never do when I'm busy, when I'm draining pipes, looting sacks, yaling locks, lifting latches, forcing my bony hands and lanky legs into making something move, hardly feeling my lungs going in-whiff and out-whaff, not realizing whether my mouth is clamped tight or gaping, whether I'm hungry, itching from scabies, or whether my flies are open and flashing dirty words like muck and spit into the late-night final fog. And when I don't know anything about all this then how can I honest-to-God say I think of anything at such times? When I'm wondering what's the best way to get a window open or how to force a door, how can I be thinking or have anything on my mind? That's what the four-eyed white-smocked bloke with the note-book couldn't understand when he asked me questions for days and days after I got to Borstal; and I couldn't explain it to him then like I'm writing it down now; and even if I'd been able to maybe he still wouldn't have caught on because I don't know whether I can understand it myself even at this moment, though I'm doing my best you can bet.

So before I knew where I was I was inside the baker's office watching Mike picking up that cash box after he'd struck a match to see where it was, wearing a tailor-made fifty-shilling grin on his square crew-cut nut as his paws closed over the box like he'd squash it to nothing. "Out," he suddenly said, shaking it so's it rattled. "Let's scram."

"Maybe there's some more," I said, pulling half a dozen drawers out of a rollertop desk.

"No," he said, like he'd already been twenty years in the game, "this is the lot," patting his tin box, "this is it."

I pulled out another few drawers, full of bills, books and letters. "How do you know, you loony sod?"

He barged past me like a bull at a gate. "Because I do."

Right or wrong, we'd both got to stick together and do the same thing. I looked at an ever-loving babe of a brand-new typewriter, but knew it was too traceable, so blew it a kiss, and went out after him. "Hang on," I said, pulling the door to, "we're in no hurry."

"Not much we aren't," he says over his shoulder.

"We've got months to splash the lolly," I whispered as we crossed the yard, "only don't let that gate creak too much or you'll have the narks tuning-in."

"You think I'm barmy?" he said, creaking the gate so that the whole street heard.

I don't know about Mike, but now I started to think, of how we'd get back safe through the streets with that money-box up my jumper. Because he'd clapped it into my hand as soon as we'd got to the main road, which might have meant that he'd started thinking as well, which only goes to show how you don't know what's in anybody else's mind unless you think about things yourself. But as far as my thinking went at that moment it wasn't up to much, only a bit of fright that wouldn't budge not even with a hot blow-lamp, about what we'd say if a copper asked us where we were off to with that hump in my guts.

"What is it?" he'd ask, and I'd say: "A growth." "What do you mean, a growth, my lad?" he'd say back, narky like. I'd cough and clutch myself like I was in the most tripe-twisting pain in the world, and screw my eyes up like I was on my way to the hospital, and Mike would take my arm like he was the best pal I'd got. "Cancer," I'd manage to say to Narker, which would make his slow punch-drunk brain suspect a thing or two. "A lad of your age?" So I'd groan again, and hope to make him feel a real bully of a bastard, which would be impossible, but anyway: "It's in the family. Dad died of it last month, and I'll die of it next month by the feel of it." "What, did he have it in the guts?" "No, in the throat. But it's got me in the stomach." Groan and cough. "Well, you shouldn't be out like this if you've got cancer, you should be in the hospital." I'd get ratty now: "That's where I'm trying to go if only you'd let me and stop asking so many questions. Aren't I, Mike?" Grunt from Mike as he unslung his cosh. Then just in time the copper would tell us to get on our way, kind and considerate all of a sudden, saying that the outpatient department of the hospital closes at twelve, so hadn't he better call us a taxi? He would if we liked, he says, and he'd pay for it as well. But we tell him not to bother, that he's a good bloke even if he is a copper, that we know a short cut anyway. Then just as we're turning a corner he gets it into his big batchy head that we're going the opposite way to the hospital, and calls us back. So we'd start to run . . . if you can call all that thinking.

Up in my room Mike rips open that money-box with a hammer and chisel, and before we know where we are we've got seventy-eight pounds fifteen and fourpence ha'penny *each* lying all over my bed like tea spread out on Christmas Day: cake and trifle, salad and sandwiches, jam tarts and bars of chocolate: all shared and shared alike between Mike and me because we believed in equal work and equal pay, just like the comrades my dad was in until he couldn't do a stroke anymore and had no breath left to argue with. I thought how good it was that blokes like that poor baker didn't stash all his cash in one of the big marble-fronted banks that take up every corner of the town, how lucky for us that he didn't trust them no matter how many millions of tons of concrete or how many iron bars and boxes they were made of, or how many coppers kept their blue pop-eyed peepers glued on to them, how smashing it was that he believed in money-boxes when so many shopkeepers thought it oldfashioned and tried to be modern by using a bank, which wouldn't give a couple of sincere, honest, hardworking, conscientious blokes like Mike and me a chance.

Now you'd think, and I'd think, and anybody with a bit of imagination would think, that we'd done as clean a job as could ever be done, that, with the baker's shop being at least a mile from where we lived, and with not a soul having seen us, and what with the fog and the fact that we weren't more than five minutes in the place, that the coppers should never have been able to trace us. But then, you'd be wrong, I'd be wrong, and everybody else would be wrong, no matter how much imagination was diced out between us.

Even so, Mike and I didn't splash the money about, because that would have made people think straightaway that we'd latched on to something that didn't belong to us. Which wouldn't do at all, because even in a street like ours there are people who love to do a good turn for the coppers, though I never know why they do. Some people are so mean-gutted that even if they've only got tuppence more than you and they think you're the sort that would take it if you have half the chance, they'd get you put inside if they saw you ripping lead out of a lavatory, even if it weren't their lavatory—just to keep their tuppence out of your reach. And so we didn't do anything to let on about how rich we were, nothing like going down town and coming back dressed in brand-new Teddy boy suits and carrying a set of skiffle-drums like another pal of ours who'd done a factory office about six months before. No, we took the odd bobs and pennies out and folded the notes into bundles and stuffed them up the drainpipe outside the door in the backyard. "Nobody'll ever think of looking for it there," I said to Mike. "We'll keep it doggo for a week or two, then take a few quid a week out till it's all gone. We might be thieving bastards, but we're not green."

Some days later a plain-clothes dick knocked at the door. And asked for me. I was still in bed, at eleven o'clock, and had to unroll myself from the comfortable black sheets when I heard mam calling me. "A man to see you," she said. "Hurry up, or he'll be gone."

I could hear her keeping him at the back door, nattering about how fine it had been but how it looked like rain since early this morning—and he didn't answer her except to snap out a snotty yes or no. I scrambled into my trousers and wondered why he'd come—knowing it was a copper because 'a man to see you' always meant just that in our house—and if I'd had any idea that one had gone to Mike's house as well at the same time I'd have twigged it to be because of that hundred and fifty quid's worth of paper stuffed up the drainpipe outside the back door about ten inches away from that plain-clothed copper's boot, where mam still talked to him thinking she was doing me a favour, and I wishing to God she'd ask him in, though on second thoughts realizing that that would seem more suspicious than keeping him outside, because they know we hate their guts and smell a rat if they think we're trying to be nice to them. Mam wasn't born yesterday, I thought, thumping my way down the creaking stairs.

I'd seen him before: Borstal Bernard in nicky-hat, Remand Home Ronald in rowing-boat boots, Probation Pete in a pit-prop mackintosh, three-months clink in collar and tie (all this out of a Borstal skiffle-ballad that my new mate made up, and I'd tell you it in full but it doesn't belong in this story), a 'tec who'd never had as much in his pockets as that drainpipe had up its jackses. He was like Hitler in the face, right down to the paint-brush tash, except that being six-foot tall made him seem worse. But I straightened my shoulders to look into his illiterate blue eyes—like I always do with any copper.

Then he started asking me questions, and my mother from behind said: "He's never left that television set for the last three months, so you've got nowt on him, mate. You might as well look for somebody else, because you're wasting the rates you get out of my rent and the income-tax that comes out of my pay-packet standing there like that"—which was a laugh because she'd never paid either to my knowledge, and never would, I hoped.

"Well, you know where Papplewick Street is, don't you?" the copper asked me, taking no notice of mam.

"Ain't it off Alfreton Road?" I asked him back, helpful and bright.

"You know there's a baker's half-way down on the left-hand side, don't you?"

"Ain't it next door to a pub, then?" I wanted to know.

He answered me sharp: "No, it bloody well ain't." Coppers always lose their tempers as quick as this, and more often than not they gain nothing by it. "Then I don't know it," I told him, saved by the bell.

He slid his big boot round and round on the doorstep. "Where were you last Friday night?" Back in the ring, but this was worse than a boxing match.

I didn't like him trying to accuse me of something he wasn't sure I'd done. "Was I at that baker's you mentioned? Or in the pub next door?"

"You'll get five years in Borstal if you don't give me a straight answer," he said, unbuttoning his mac even though it was cold where he was standing.

"I was glued to the telly, like mam says," I swore blind. But he went on and on with his looney questions: "Have you got a television?"

The things he asked wouldn't have taken in a kid of two, and what else could I say to the last one except: "Has the aerial fell down? Or would you like to come in and see it?"

He was liking me even less for saying that. "We know you weren't listening to the television set last Friday, and so do you, don't you?"

"P'raps not, but I was *looking* at it, because sometimes we turn the sound down for a bit of fun." I could hear mam laughing from the kitchen, and I hoped Mike's mam was doing the same if the cops had gone to him as well.

"We know you weren't in the house," he said, starting up again, cranking himself with the handle. They always say 'We' 'We', never 'I' 'I'—as if they feel braver and righter knowing there's a lot of them against only one.

"I've got witnesses," I said to him. "Mam for one. Her fancy-man, for two. Ain't that enough? I can get you a dozen more, or thirteen altogether, if it was a baker's that got robbed."

"I don't want no lies," he said, not catching on about the baker's dozen. Where do they scrape cops up from anyway? "All I want is to get from you where you put that money."

Don't get mad, I kept saying to myself, don't get mad—hearing mam setting out cups and saucers and putting the pan on the stove for bacon. I stood back and waved him inside like I was a butler. "Come and search the house. If you've got a warrant."

"Listen, my lad," he said, like the dirty bullying jumped-up bastard he was, "I don't want too much of your lip, because if we get you down to the Guildhall you'll get a few bruises and black-eyes for your trouble." And I knew he wasn't kidding either, because I'd heard about all them sort of tricks. I hoped one day though that him and all his pals would be the ones to get the black-eyes and kicks; you never knew. It might come sooner than anybody thinks, like in Hungary. "Tell me where the money is, and I'll get you off with probation."

"What money?" I asked him, because I'd heard that one before as well.

"You know what money."

"Do I look as though I'd know owt about money?" I said, pushing my fist through a hole in my shirt.

"The money that was pinched, that you know all about," he said. "You can't trick me, so it's no use trying."

"Was it three-and-eightpence ha'penny?" I asked.

"You thieving young bastard. We'll teach you to steal money that doesn't belong to you."

I turned my head around: "Mam," I called out, "get my lawyer on the blower, will you?"

"Clever, aren't you?" he said in a very unfriendly way, "but we won't rest until we clear all this up."

"Look," I pleaded, as if about to sob my socks off because he'd got me wrong, "it's all very well us talking like this, it's like a game almost, but I wish you'd tell me what it's all about, because honest-to-God I've just got out of bed and here you are at the door talking about me having pinched a lot of money, money that I don't know anything about."

He swung around now as if he'd trapped me, though I couldn't see why he might think so. "Who said anything about money? I didn't. What made you bring money into this little talk we're having?"

"It's you," I answered, thinking he was going barmy, and about to start foaming at the chops, "you've got money on the brain, like all policemen. Baker's shops as well."

He screwed his face up. "I want an answer from you: where's that money?"

But I was getting fed-up with all this. "I'll do a deal."

Judging by his flash-bulb face he thought he was suddenly on to a good thing. "What sort of a deal?"

So I told him: "I'll give you all the money I've got, one and fourpence ha'penny, if you stop this third-degree and let me go in and get my breakfast. Honest, I'm clambed to death. I ain't had a bite since yesterday. Can't you hear my guts rollin'?"

His jaw dropped, but on he went, pumping me for another half hour. A routine check-up, as they say on the pictures. But I knew I was winning on points.

Then he left, but came back in the afternoon to search the house. He didn't find a thing, not a French farthing. He asked me questions again and I didn't tell him anything except lies, lies, lies, because I can go on doing that forever without batting an eyelid. He'd got nothing on me and we both of us knew it, otherwise I'd have been down at the Guildhall in no time, but he kept on keeping on because I'd been in a Remand Home for a high-wall job before; and Mike was put through the same mill because all the local cops knew he was my best pal.

When it got dark me and Mike were in our parlour with a low light on and the telly off, Mike taking it easy in the rocking chair and me slouched out on the settee, both of us puffing a packet of Woods. With the door bolted and curtains drawn we talked about the dough we'd crammed up the drainpipe. Mike thought we should take it out and both of us do a bunk to Skegness or Cleethorpes for a good time in the arcades, living like lords in a boarding house near the pier, then at least we'd both have had a big beano before getting sent down.

"Listen, you daft bleeder," I said, "we aren't going to get caught at all, *and* we'll have a good time, later." We were so clever we didn't even go out to the pictures, though we wanted to.

In the morning old Hitler-face questioned me again, with one of his pals this time, and the next day they came, trying as hard as they could to get something out of me, but I didn't budge an inch. I know I'm showing off when I say this, but in me he'd met his match, and I'd never give in to questions no matter how long it was kept up. They searched the house a couple of times as well, which made me think they thought they really had something to go by, but I know now that they hadn't, and that it was all buckshee speculation. They turned the house upside down and inside out like an old sock, went from top to bottom and front to back but naturally didn't find a thing. The copper even poked his face up the front-room chimney (that hadn't been used or swept for years) and came down looking like Al Jolson so that he had to swill himself clean at the scullery sink. They kept tapping and pottering around the big aspidistra plant that grandma had left to mam, lifting it up from the table to look under the cloth, putting it aside so's they could move the table and get at the boards under the rug—but the big headed stupid ignorant bastards never once thought of emptying the soil out of the plant pot, where they'd have found the crumpled-up money-box that we'd buried the night we did the job. I suppose it's still there, now I think about it, and I suppose mam wonders now and again why the plant don't prosper like it used to—as if it could with a fistful of thick black tin lapped around its guts.

The last time he knocked at our door was one wet morning at five minutes to nine and I was sleep-logged in my crumby bed as usual. Mam had gone to work that day so I shouted for him to hold on a bit, and then went down to see who it was. There he stood, six-feet tall and sopping wet, and for the first time in my life I did a spiteful thing I'll never forgive myself for: I didn't ask him to come in out of the rain, because I wanted him to get double pneumonia and die. I suppose he could have pushed by me and come in if he'd wanted, but maybe he'd got used to asking questions on the doorstep and didn't want to be put off by changing his ground even though it was raining. Not that I don't like being spiteful because of any barmy principle I've got, but this bit of spite, as it turned out, did me no good at all. I should have treated him as a brother I hadn't seen for twenty years and dragged him in for a cup of tea and a fag, told him about the picture I hadn't seen the night before, asked him how his wife was after her operation and whether they'd shaved her moustache off to make it, and then sent him happy and satisfied out by the front door. But no, I thought, let's see what he's got to say for himself now.

He stood a little to the side of the door, either because it was less wet there, or because he wanted to see me from a different angle, perhaps having found it monotonous to watch a bloke's face always telling lies from the same side. "You've been identified," he said, twitching raindrops from his tash. "A woman saw you and your mate yesterday and she swears blind you are the same chaps she saw going into that bakery."

I was dead sure he was still bluffing, because Mike and I hadn't even seen each other the day before, but I looked worried. "She's a menace then to innocent people, whoever she is, because the only bakery I've been in lately is the one up our street to get some cut-bread on tick for mam."

He didn't bite on this. "So now I want to know where the money is"—as if I hadn't answered him at all.

"I think mam took it to work this morning to get herself some tea in the canteen." Rain was splashing down so hard I thought he'd get washed away if he didn't come inside. But I wasn't much bothered, and went on: "I remember I put it in the telly-vase last night—it was only one-and-three and I was saving it for a packet of tips this morning—and I nearly had a jibbering black fit just now when I saw it had gone. I was reckoning on it for getting me through today because I don't think life's worth living without a fag, do you?"

I was getting into my stride and began to feel good, twigging that this would be my last pack of lies, and that if I kept it up for long enough this time I'd have the bastards beat: Mike and me would be off to the coast in a few weeks time having the fun of our lives, playing at penny football and latching on to a couple of tarts that would give us all they were good for. "And this weather's no good for picking-up fag-ends in the street," I said, "because they'd be sopping wet. Course, I know you could dry 'em out near the fire, but it don't taste the same you know, all said and done. Rainwater does summat to 'em that don't bear thinkin' about: it turns 'em back into hoss-tods without the taste though."

I began to wonder, at the back of my brainless eyes, why old copperlugs didn't pull me up sharp and say he hadn't got time to listen to all this, but he wasn't looking at me anymore, and all my thoughts about Skegness went bursting to smithereens in my sludgy loaf. I could have dropped into the earth when I saw what he'd fixed his eyes on.

He was looking at *it,* an ever-loving fiver, and I could only jabber: "The one thing is to have some real fags because new hoss-tods is always better than stuff that's been rained on and dried, and I know how you feel about not being able to find money because one-and-three's one-and-three in anybody's pocket, and naturally if I see it knocking around I'll get you on the blower tomorrow straight-away and tell you where you can find it."

I thought I'd go down in a fit: three green-backs as well had been washed down by the water, and more were following, lying flat at first after their fall, then getting tilted at the corners by wind and rainspots as if they were alive and wanted to get back into the dry snug drainpipe out of the terrible weather, and you can't imagine how I wished they'd be able to. Old Hitler-face didn't know what to make of it but just kept staring down and down, and I thought I'd better keep on talking, though I knew it wasn't much good now.

"It's a fact, I know, that money's hard to come by and half-crowns don't get found on bus seats or in dustbins, and I didn't see any in bed last night because I'd 'ave known about it, wouldn't I? You can't sleep with things like that in the bed because they're too hard, and anyway at first they're . . ." It took Hitler-boy a long time to catch on; they were beginning to spread over the yard a bit, reinforced by the third colour of a ten-bob note, before his hand clamped itself on to my shoulder.

III

The pop-eyed potbellied governor said to a pop-eyed potbellied Member of Parliament who sat next to his pop-eyed potbellied whore of a wife that I was his only hope for getting the Borstal Blue Ribbon Prize Cup For Long Distance Cross Country Running (All England), which I was, and it set me laughing to myself inside, and I didn't say a word to any potbellied pop-eyed bastard that might give them real hope, though I knew the governor anyway took my quietness to mean he'd got that cup already stuck on the bookshelf in his office among the few other mildewed trophies.

"He might take up running in a sort of professional way when he gets out," and it wasn't until he'd said this and I'd heard it with my own flap-tabs that I realized it might be possible to do such a thing, run for money, trot for wages on piece work at a bob a puff rising bit by bit to a guinea a gasp and retiring through old age at thirty-two because of lace-curtain lungs, a football heart, and legs like varicose beanstalks. But I'd have a wife and car and get my grinning long-distance clock in the papers and have a smashing secretary to answer piles of letters sent by tarts who'd mob me when they saw who I was as I pushed my way into Woolworth's for a packet of razor blades and a cup of tea. It was something to think about all right, and sure enough the governor knew he'd got me when he said, turning to me as if I would at any rate have to be consulted about it all: "How does this matter strike you, then, Smith, my lad?"

A line of potbellied pop-eyes gleamed at me and a row of goldfish mouths opened and wiggled gold teeth at me, so I gave them the answer they wanted because I'd hold my trump card until later. "It'd suit me fine, sir," I said.

"Good lad. Good show. Right spirit. Splendid."

"Well," the governor said, "get that cup for us today and I'll do all I can for you. I'll get you trained so that you whack every man in the Free World." And I had a picture in my brain of me running and beating everybody in the world, leaving them all behind until only I was trot-trotting across a big wide moor alone, doing a marvellous speed as I ripped between boulders and reed-clumps, when suddenly: CRACK! CRACK!—bullets that can go faster than any man running, coming from a copper's rifle planted in a tree, winged me and split my gizzard in spite of my perfect running, and down I fell.

The potbellies expected me to say something else. "Thank you, sir." I said.

Told to go, I trotted down the pavilion steps, out on to the field because the big cross-country was about to begin and the two entries from Gunthorpe had fixed themselves early at the starting line and were ready to move off like white kangaroos. The sports ground looked a treat: with big tea-tents all round and flags flying and seats for families—empty because no mam or dad had known what opening day meant—and boys still running heats for the hundred years, and lords and ladies walking from stall to stall, and the Borstal Boys Brass Band in blue uniforms; and up on the stands the brown jackets of Hucknall as well as our own grey blazers, and then the Gunthorpe lot with short sleeves rolled. The blue sky was full of sunshine and it couldn't have been a better day, and all of the big show was like something out of Ivanhoe that we'd seen on the pictures a few days before.

"Come on, Smith," Roach the sports master called to me, "we don't want you to be late for the big race, eh? Although I dare say you'd catch them up if you were." The others catcalled and grunted at this, but I took no notice and placed myself between Gunthorpe and one of the Aylesham trusties, dropped on my knees and plucked a few grass blades to suck on the way round. So the big race it was, for them, watching from the grandstand under a fluttering Union Jack, a race for the governor, that he had been waiting for, and I hoped he and all the rest of his popeyed gang were busy placing big bets on me, hundred to one to win, all the money they had in their pockets, all the wages they were going to get for the next five years, and the more they placed the happier I'd be. Because here was a dead cert going to die on the big name they'd built for him, going to go down dying with laughter whether it choked him or not. My knees felt the cool soil pressing into them, and out of my eye's corner I saw Roach lift his hand. The

Gunthorpe boy twitched before the signal was given; somebody cheered too soon; Medway bent forward; then the gun went, and I was away.

We went once around the field and then along a half-mile drive of elms, being cheered all the way, and I seemed to feel I was in the lead as we went out by the gate and into the lane, though I wasn't interested enough to find out. The five-mile course was marked by splashes of whitewash gleaming on gateposts and trunks and stiles and stones, and a boy with a waterbottle and bandage-box stood every half-mile waiting for those that dropped out or fainted. Over the first stile, without trying, I was still nearly in the lead but one; and if any of you want tips about running, never be in a hurry, and never let any of the other runners know you are in a hurry even if you are. You can always overtake on long-distance running without letting the others smell the hurry in you; and when you've used your craft like this to reach the two or three up front then you can do a big dash later that puts everybody else's hurry in the shade because you've not had to make haste up till then. I ran to a steady jog-trot rhythm, and soon it was so smooth that I forgot I was running, and I was hardly able to know that my legs were lifting and falling and my arms going in and out, and my lungs didn't seem to be working at all, and my heart stopped that wicked thumping I always get at the beginning of a run. Because you see I never race at all; I just run, and somehow I know that if I forget I'm racing and only jog-trot along until I don't know I'm running I always win the race. For when my eyes recognize that I'm getting near the end of the course—by seeing a stile or cottage corner— I put on a spurt, and such a fast big spurt it is because I feel that up till then I haven't been running and that I've used up no energy at all. And I've been able to do this because I've been thinking; and I wonder if I'm the only one in the running business with this system of forgetting that I'm running because I'm too busy thinking; and I wonder if any of the other lads are on to the same lark, though I know for a fact that they aren't. Off like the wind along the cobbled footpath and rutted lane, smoother than the flat grass track on the field and better for thinking because it's not too smooth, and I was in my element that afternoon knowing that nobody could beat me at running but intending to beat myself before the day was over. For when the governor talked to me of being honest when I first came in he didn't know what the word meant or he wouldn't have had me here in this race, trotting along in shimmy and shorts and sunshine. He'd have had me where I'd have had him if I'd been in his place: in a quarry breaking rocks until he broke his back. At least old Hitler-face the plain-clothes dick was honester than the governor, because he at any rate had had it in for me and I for him, and when my case was coming up in court a copper knocked at our front door at four o'clock in the morning and got my mother out of bed when she was paralytic tired, reminding her she had to be in court at dead on half past nine. It was the finest bit of spite I've ever heard of, but I would call it honest, the same as my mam's words were honest when she really told that copper what she thought of him and called him all the dirty names she'd ever heard of, which took her half an hour and woke the terrace up.

I trotted on along the edge of a field bordered by the sunken lane, smelling green grass and honeysuckle, and I felt as though I came from a long line of whippets trained to run on two legs, only I couldn't see a toy rabbit in front and there wasn't a collier's cosh behind to make me keep up the pace. I passed the Gunthorpe runner whose shimmy was already black with sweat and I could just see the corner of the fenced-up copse in front where the only man I had to pass to win the race was going all out to gain the half-way mark. Then he turned into a tongue of trees and bushes where I couldn't see him anymore, and I couldn't see anybody, and I knew what the loneliness of the long-distance runner running across country felt like, realizing that as far as I was concerned this feeling was the only honesty and realness there was in the world and I knowing it would be no different ever, no matter what I felt at odd times, and no matter what anybody else tried to tell me. The runner behind me must have been a long way off because it was so quiet, and there was even less noise and movement than there had been at five o'clock of a frosty winter morning. It was hard to understand, and all I knew was that you had to run, run, run, without knowing why you were running, but on you went through fields you didn't understand and into woods that made you afraid, over hills without knowing you'd been up and down, and shooting across streams that would have cut the heart out of you had you fallen into them. And the winning post was no end to it, even though crowds might be cheering you in, because on you had to go before you got your breath back, and the only time you stopped really was when you tripped over a tree trunk and broke your neck or fell into a disused well and stayed dead in the darkness forever. So I thought: they aren't going to get me on this racing lark, this running and trying to win, this jog-trotting for a bit of blue ribbon, because it's not the way to go on at all, though they swear blind that it is. You should think about nobody and go your own way, not on a course marked out for you by people holding mugs of water and bottles of iodine in case you fall and cut yourself so that they can pick you up—even if you want to stay where you are—and get you moving again.

On I went, out of the wood, passing the man leading without knowing I was going to do so. Flip-flap, flip-flap, jog-trot, jog-trot, crunchslap-crunchslap, across the middle of a broad field again, rhythmically running in my greyhound effortless fashion, knowing I had won the race though it wasn't half over, won it if I wanted it, could go on for ten or fifteen or twenty miles if I had to and drop dead at the finish of it, which would be the same, in the end, as living an honest life like the governor wanted me to. It amounted to: win the race and be honest, and on trot-trotting I went, having the time of my life, loving my progress because it did me good and set me thinking which by now I liked to do, but not caring at all when I remembered that I had to win this race as well as run it. One of the two, I had to win the race or run it, and I knew I could do both because my legs had carried me well in front—now coming to the short cut down the bramble bank and over the sunken road—and would carry me further because they seemed made of electric cable and easily alive to keep on slapping at those ruts and roots, but I'm not going to win because the only way I'd see I came in first would be if winning meant that I was going to escape the coppers after doing the biggest bank job of my life, but winning means the exact opposite, no matter how they try to kill or kid me, means running right into their white-gloved wall-barred hands and grinning mugs and staying there for the rest of my natural long life of stone-breaking anyway, but stone-breaking in the way I want to do it and not in the way they tell me.

Another honest thought that comes is that I could swing left at the next hedge of the field, and under its cover beat my slow retreat away from the sports ground winning post. I could do three or six or a dozen miles across the turf like this and cut a few main roads behind me so's they'd never know which one I'd taken; and maybe on the last one when it got dark I could thumb a lorry-lift and get a free ride north with somebody who might not give me away. But no, I said I wasn't daft didn't I? I won't pull out with only six months left, and besides there's nothing I want to dodge and run away from; I only want a bit of my own back on the In-laws and Potbellies by letting them sit up there on their big posh seats and watch me lose this race, though as sure as God made me I know that when I do lose I'll get the dirtiest crap and kitchen jobs in the months to go before my time is up. I won't be worth a threpp'ny-bit to anybody here, which will be all the thanks I get for being honest in the only way I know. For when the governor told me to be honest it was meant to be in his way not mine, and if I kept on being honest in the way he wanted and won my race for him he'd see I got the cushiest six months still left to run; but in my own way, well, it's not allowed, and if I find a way of doing it such as I've got now then I'll get what-for in every mean trick he can set his mind to. And if you look at it in my way, who can blame him? For this is war—and ain't I said so?—and when I hit him in the only place he knows he'll be sure to get his own back on me for not collaring that cup when his heart's been set for ages on seeing himself standing up at the end of the afternoon to clap me on the back as I take the cup from Lord Earwig or some such chinless wonder with a name like that. And so I'll hit him where it hurts a lot, and he'll do all he can to get his own back, tit for tat, though I'll enjoy it most because I'm hitting first, and because I planned it longer. I don't know why I think these thoughts are better than any I've ever had, but I do, and I don't care why. I suppose it took me a long time to get going on all this because I've had no time and peace in all my bandit life, and now my thoughts are coming pat and the only trouble is I often can't stop, even when my brain feels as if it's got cramp, frostbite and creeping paralysis all rolled into one and I have to give it a rest by slap-dashing down through the brambles of the sunken lane. And all this is another uppercut I'm getting in first at people like the governor, to show how—if I can—his races are never won even though some bloke always comes unknowingly in first, how in the end the governor is going to be doomed while blokes like me will take the pickings of his roasted bones and dance like maniacs around his Borstal's ruins. And so this story's like the race and once again I won't bring off a winner to suit the governor; no, I'm being honest like he told me to, without him knowing what he means, though I don't suppose he'll ever come in with a story of his own, even if he reads this one of mine and knows who I'm talking about.

I've just come up out of the sunken lane, kneed and elbowed, thumped and bramble-scratched, and the race is two-thirds over, and a voice is going like a wireless in my mind saying that when you've had enough of feeling good like the first man on earth of a frosty morning, and you've known how it is to be taken bad like the last man on earth on a summer's afternoon, then you get at last to being like the only man on earth and don't give a bogger about either good or bad, but just trot on with your slippers slapping the good dry soil that at least would never do you a bad turn. Now the words are like coming from a crystalset that's broken down, and something's happening inside the shell-case of my guts that bothers me and I don't know why or what to blame it on, a grinding near my ticker as though a bag of rusty screws is loose inside me and I shake them up every time I trot forward. Now and again I break my rhythm to feel my left shoulder-blade by swinging a right hand across my chest as if to rub the knife away that has somehow got stuck there. But I know it's nothing to bother about, that more likely it's caused by too much thinking that now and again I take for worry. For sometimes I'm the greatest worrier in the world I think (as you twigged I'll bet from me having got this story out) which is funny anyway because my mam don't know the meaning of the word so I don't take after her; though dad had a hard time of worry all his life up to when he filled his bedroom with hot blood and kicked the bucket that morning when nobody was in the house. I'll never forget it, straight I won't, because I was the one that found him and I often wished I hadn't. Back from a session on the fruit-machines at the fish-and-chip shop, jingling my three-lemon loot to a nail-dead house, as soon as I got in I knew something was wrong, stood leaning my head against the cold mirror above the mantelpiece trying not to open my eyes and see my stone-cold clock—because I knew I'd gone as white as a piece of chalk since coming in as if I'd been got at by a Dracula-vampire and even my penny-pocket winnings kept quiet on purpose.

Gunthorpe nearly caught me up. Birds were singing from the briar hedge, and a couple of thrushies flew like lightning into some thorny bushes. Corn had grown high in the next field and would be cut down soon with scythes and mowers; but I never wanted to notice much while running in case it put me off my stroke, so by the haystack I decided to leave it all behind and put on such a spurt, in spite of nails in my guts, that before long I'd left both Gunthorpe and the birds a good way off; I wasn't far now from going into that last mile and a half like a knife through margarine, but the quietness I suddenly trotted into between two pickets was like opening my eyes underwater and looking at the pebbles on a stream bottom, reminding me again of going back that morning to the house in which my old man had croaked, which is funny because I hadn't thought about it at all since it happened and even then I didn't brood much on it. I wonder why? I suppose that since I started to think on these long-distance runs I'm liable to have anything crop up and pester at my tripes and innards, and now that I see my bloody dad behind each grass-blade in my barmy runner-brain I'm not so sure I like to think and that it's such a good thing after all. I choke my phlegm and keep on running anyway and curse the Borstal-builders and their athletics—flap-pity-flap, slop-slop, crunchslap-crunchslap-crunchslap—who've maybe got their own back on me from the bright beginning by sliding magic-lantern slides into my head that never stood a chance before. Only if I take whatever comes like this in my runner's stride can I keep on keeping on like my old self and beat them back; and now I've thought on this far I know I'll win, in the crunchslap end. So anyway after a bit I went upstairs one step at a time not thinking anything about how I should find dad and what I'd do when I did. But now I'm making up for it by going over the rotten life mam led him ever since I can remember, knocking-on with different men even when he was alive and fit and she not caring whether he knew it or not, and most of the time he wasn't so blind as she thought and cursed and roared and threatened to punch her tab, and I had to stand up to stop him even though I knew she deserved it. What a life for all of us. Well, I'm not grumbling, because if I did I might just as well win this bleeding race, which I'm not going to do, though if I don't lose speed I'll win it before I know where I am, and then where would I be?

Now I can hear the sportsground noise and music as I head back for the flags and the lead-in drive, the fresh new feel of underfoot gravel going against the iron muscles of my legs. I'm nowhere near puffed despite that bag of nails that rattles as much as ever, and I can still give a big last leap like gale-force wind if I want to, but everything is under control and I know now that there ain't another long-distance cross-country running runner in England to touch my speed and style. Our doddering bastard of a governor, our half-dead gangrened gaffer is hollow like an empty petrol drum, and he wants me and my running life to give him glory, to put in him blood and throbbing veins he never had, wants his pot-bellied pals to be his witnesses as I gasp and stagger up to his winning post so's he can say: "My Borstal gets that cup, you see. I win my bet, because it pays to be honest and try to gain the prizes I offer to my lads, and they know it, have known it all along. They'll always be honest now, because I made them so." And his pals will think: "He trains his lads to live right, after all; he deserves a medal but we'll get him made a Sir"—and at this very moment as the birds come back to whistling I can tell myself I'll never care a sod what any of the chinless spineless In-laws think or say. They've seen me and they're cheering now and loud-speakers set around the field like elephant's ears are spreading out the big news that I'm well in the lead, and can't do anything else but stay there. But I'm still thinking of the Out-law death my dad died, telling the doctors to scat from the house when they wanted him to finish up in hospital (like a bleeding guinea-pig, he raved at them). He got up in bed to throw them out and even followed them down the stairs in his shirt though he was no more than skin and stick. They tried to tell him he'd want some drugs but he didn't fall for it, and only took the pain-killer that mam and I got from a herb-seller in the next street. It's not till now that I know what guts he had, and when I went into the room that morning he was lying on his stomach with the clothes thrown back, looking like a skinned rabbit, his grey head resting just on the edge of the bed, and on the floor must have been all the blood he'd had in his body, right from his toe-nails up, for nearly all of the lino and carpet was covered in it, thin and pink.

And down the drive I went, carrying a heart blocked up like Boulder Dam across my arteries, the nail-bag clamped down tighter and tighter as though in a woodwork vice, yet with my feet like birdwings and arms like talons ready to fly across the field except that I didn't want to give anybody that much of a show, or win the race by accident. I smell the hot dry day now as I run towards the end, passing a mountain-heap of grass emptied from cans hooked on to the fronts of lawnmowers pushed by my pals; I rip a piece of tree-bark with my fingers and stuff it in my mouth, chewing wood and dust and maybe maggots as I run until I'm nearly sick, yet swallowing what I can of it just the same because a little birdie whistled to me that I've got to go on living for at least a bloody sight longer yet but that for six months I'm not going to smell that grass or taste that dusty bark or trot this lovely path. I hate to have to say this but something bloody-well made me cry, and crying is a thing I haven't bloody-well done since I was a kid of two or three. Because I'm slowing down now for Gunthorpe to catch me up, and I'm doing it in a place just where the drive turns in to the sportsfield—where they can see what I'm doing, especially the governor and his gang from the grandstand, and I'm going so slow I'm almost marking time. Those on the nearest seats haven't caught on yet to what's happening and are still cheering like mad ready for when I make that mark, and I keep on wondering when the bleeding hell Gunthorpe behind me is going to nip by on to the field because I can't hold this up all day, and I think Oh Christ it's just my rotten luck that Gunthorpe's dropped out and that I'll be here for half an hour before the next bloke comes up, but even so, I say, I won't budge, I won't go for that last hundred yards if I have to sit down cross-legged on the grass and have the governor and his chinless wonders pick me up and carry me there, which is against their rules so you can bet they'd never do it because they're not clever enough to break the rules—like I would be in their place—even though they are their own. No, I'll show him what honesty means if it's the last thing I do, though I'm sure he'll never understand because if he and all them like him did it'd mean they'd be on my side which is impossible. By God I'll stick this out like my dad stuck out his pain and kicked them doctors down the stairs: if he had guts for that then I've got guts for this and here I stay waiting for Gunthorpe or Aylesham to bash that turf and go right slap-up against that bit of clothes-line stretched across the winning post. As for me, the only time I'll hit that clothes-line will be when I'm dead and a comfortable coffin's been got ready on the other side. Until then I'm a long-distance runner, crossing country all on my own no matter how bad it feels.

The Essex boys were shouting themselves blue in the face telling me to get a move on, waving their arms, standing up and making as if to run at that rope themselves because they were only a few yards to the side of it. You cranky lot, I thought, stuck at that winning post, and yet I knew they didn't mean what they were shouting, were really on my side and always would be, not able to keep their maulers to themselves, in and out of cop-shops and clink. And there they were now having the time of their lives letting themselves go in cheering me which made the governor think they were heart and soul on his side when he wouldn't have thought any such thing if he'd had a grain of sense. And I could hear the lords and ladies now from the grandstand, and could see them standing up to wave me in: "Run!" they were shouting in their posh voices. "Run!" But I was deaf, daft and blind, and stood where I was, still tasting the bark in my mouth and still blubbing like a baby, blubbing now out of gladness that I'd got them beat at last.

Because I heard a roar and saw the Gunthorpe gang throwing their coats up in the air and I felt the pat-pat of feet on the drive behind me getting closer and closer and suddenly a smell of sweat and a pair of lungs on their last gasp passed me by and went swinging on towards that rope, all shagged out and rocking from side to side, grunting like a Zulu that didn't know any better, like the ghost of me at ninety when I'm heading for that fat upholstered coffin. I could have cheered him myself: "Go on, go on, get cracking. Knot yourself up on that piece of tape." But he was already there, and so I went on, trot-trotting after him until I got to the rope, and collapsed, with a murderous sounding roar going up through my ears while I was still on the wrong side of it.

It's about time to stop; though don't think I'm not still running, because I am, one way or another. The governor at Borstal proved me right; he didn't respect my honesty at all; not that I expected him to, or tried to explain it to him, but if he's supposed to be educated then he should have more or less twigged it. He got his own back right enough, or thought he did, because he had me carting dustbins about every morning from the big full-working kitchen to the garden-bottoms where I had to empty them; and in the afternoon I spread out slops over spuds and carrots growing in the allotments. In the evenings I scrubbed floors, miles and miles of them. But it wasn't a bad life for six months, which was another thing he could never understand and would have made it grimmer if he could, and it was worth it when I look back on it, considering all the thinking I did, and the fact that the boys caught on to me losing the race on purpose and never had enough good words to say about me, or curses to throw out (to themselves) at the governor.

The work didn't break me; if anything it made me stronger in many ways, and the governor knew, when I left, that his spite had got him nowhere. For since leaving Borstal they tried to get me in the army, but I didn't pass the medical and I'll tell you why. No sooner was I out, after that final run and six-months hard, that I went down with pleurisy, which means as far as I'm concerned that I lost the governor's race all right, and won my own twice over, because I know for certain that if I hadn't raced my race I wouldn't have got this pleurisy, which keeps me out of khaki but doesn't stop me doing the sort of work my itchy fingers want to do.

I'm out now and the heat's switched on again, but the rats haven't got me for the last big thing I pulled. I counted six hundred and twenty-eight pounds and am still living off it because I did the job all on my own, and after it I had the peace to write all this, and it'll be money enough to keep me going until I finish my plans for doing an even bigger snatch, something up my sleeve I wouldn't tell to a living soul. I worked out my systems and hiding-places while pushing scrubbing-brushes around them Borstal floors, planned my outward life of innocence and honest work, yet at the same time grew perfect in the razor-edges of my craft for what I knew I had to do once free; and what I'll do again if netted by the poaching coppers.

In the meantime (as they say in one or two books I've read since, useless though because all of them ended on a winning post and didn't teach me a thing) I'm going to give this story to a pal of mine and tell him that if I do get captured again by the coppers he can try and get it put into a book or something, because I'd like to see the governor's face when he reads it, if he does, which I don't suppose he will; even if he did read it though I don't think he'd know what it was all about. And if I don't get caught the bloke I give this story to will never give me away; he's lived in our terrace for as long as I can remember, and he's my pal. That I do know.

Study and Discussion Questions

1. What are the different kinds of loneliness Smith feels in the course of the story?
2. What are the different kinds of honesty Smith talks about?
3. Who is "us"? Who is "them"? What does Smith mean when he says, "they've shown me the knife"?
4. What does the narrator take pride in?
5. "I know every minute of my life that a big boot is always likely to smash any nice picnic I might be barmy and dishonest enough to make for myself." How does this sentence express Smith's philosophy of life? Where does his outlook come from?
6. How does the description of his father's death shed light on Smith's ideas? Why does it come where it does in the story?
7. What does Smith's family do when they collect the insurance money for his father's death? How do you feel about that?
8. Why does having the "whip hand" make you dead, according to Smith?
9. What does Smith give up through his protest? What does he gain?
10. Give instances of how Smith's running and his thinking go together.

Suggestions for Writing

1. What are the differences between the image of life as a race and the image of life as a run? What does making it a race do to the running?
2. Have you ever protested something, or have you ever regretted not protesting something? Either way, write about why you did what you did when you were faced with the decision.
3. Speculate on Sillitoe's attitude toward Smith. Cite evidence from the story to support your remarks.

Critical Resources

1. Hanson, Gillan. *Understanding Allen Sillitoe.* Columbia: University of South Carolina Press, 1997.
2. *Loneliness of the Long Distance Runner.* Director Tony Richardson. British Lion Films, 1962 (104 minutes).
3. Sawkins, John. *The Long Apprenticeship: Alienation in the Work of Alan Sillitoe.* New York: Peter Lang, 2001.

POETRY

MARGARET WALKER (1915–1998)

Born in Birmingham, Alabama, Margaret Walker grew up in an intellectual environment imbued with African-American culture and history. Her father, a minister, and her mother, an accomplished musician, instilled in Walker a love of literature and poetry. After graduating from Northwestern University in 1934, she worked at the Work Projects Administration (WPA) Writer's Project in Chicago, where she developed a friendship with Richard Wright. A few years later, while teaching at Livingston College (in North Carolina), Walker received the Yale Younger Poets Award for her collection For My People *(1942), making her the first African-American woman to win such a national honor. During this time, and for the next 24 years, Walker worked on a book that would eventually ground her literary reputation. Culled from the oral stories of her grandmother, Walker published* Jubilee *in 1966—a historical epic about a black woman (and slave) who lives and perseveres through the tumultuous transition of antebellum America to the end of the Civil War and Reconstruction. One outstanding feature of Walker's work is its lyric nature, based in African folktales and the rhythmic quality of Southern sermons. And, as is characteristic of much of her writing, "For My People" (the title poem presented here) is a celebration of African-American struggle and triumph. Other works include the poetry* Ballad of the Free *(1966),* Prophets for A New Day *(1970),* October Journey *(1973),* This Is My Century *(1989), and the book-length essay* How I Wrote "Jubilee" *(1972). Walker has also published* The Daemonic Genius of Richard Wright *(1987),* On Being Female, Black and Free *(1997), and* Moral Understandings: A Feminist Study in Ethics *(1998).*

For My People   (1942)

For my people everywhere singing their slave songs repeatedly: their dirges
        and their ditties and their blues and jubilees, praying their prayers
        nightly to an unknown god, bending their knees humbly to an un-
        seen power;

For my people lending their strength to the years, to the gone years and
        the now years and the maybe years, washing ironing cooking
        scrubbing sewing mending hoeing plowing digging planting
        pruning patching dragging along never gaining never reaping
        never knowing and never understanding;

For my playmates in the clay and dust and sand of Alabama backyards
playing baptizing and preaching and doctor and jail and soldier
and school and mama and cooking and playhouse and concert
and store and hair and Miss Choomby and company;

For the cramped bewildered years we went to school to learn to know the
reasons why and the answers to and the people who and the
places where and the days when, in memory of the bitter hours
when we discovered we were black and poor and small and
different and nobody cared and nobody wondered and nobody
understood;

For the boys and girls who grew in spite of these things to be man and
woman, to laugh and dance and sing and play and drink their
wine and religion and success, to marry their playmates and bear
children and then die of consumption and anemia and lynching;

For my people thronging 47th Street in Chicago and Lenox Avenue in
New York and Rampart Street in New Orleans, lost disinherited
dispossessed and happy people filling the cabarets and taverns
and other people's pockets needing bread and shoes and milk
and land and money and something—something all our own;

For my people walking blindly spreading joy, losing time being lazy,
sleeping when hungry, shouting when burdened, drinking when
hopeless, tied and shackled and tangled among ourselves by the
unseen creatures who tower over us omnisciently and laugh;

For my people blundering and groping and floundering in the dark of
churches and schools and clubs and societies, associations and
councils and committees and conventions, distressed and
disturbed and deceived and devoured by money-hungry glory-
craving leeches, preyed on by facile force of state and fad and
novelty, by false prophet and holy believer;

For my people standing staring trying to fashion a better way from
confusion, from hypocrisy and misunderstanding, trying to
fashion a world that will hold all the people, all the faces, all the
adams and eves and their countless generations;

Let a new earth rise. Let another world be born. Let a bloody peace be
written in the sky. Let a second generation full of courage issue
forth; let a people loving freedom come to growth. Let a beauty
full of healing and a strength of final clenching be the pulsing in

our spirits and our blood. Let the martial songs be written, let the
dirges disappear. Let a race of men now rise and take control.

Study and Discussion Questions

1. Why the repetition of the phrase "for my people"? What effect does it
    have on you?
2. What is the poet doing in the final stanza?
3. What is the mood of this poem?
4. Who are Walker's people and what are their strengths?
5. Chart the historical progression in the poem.
6. Describe the way the poem appears on the page. Why do you think Mar-
    garet Walker chose this structure? What effect does it have?

Suggestions for Writing

1. What associations does the phrase "a bloody peace" bring to your mind?
2. Write a stanza for your people (even if they are Walker's people too).

Critical Resources

1. Graham, Maryemma. *Conversations with Margaret Walker.* Jackson: Uni-
    versity of Mississippi Press, 2002.
2. ———, ed. *Fields Watered with Blood: critical Essays on Margaret Walker.*
    Athens: University of Georgia Press, 2001.
3. Walker, Margaret and Roland Freeman. *Margaret Walker's "For My Peo-
    ple": A Tribute.* Jackson: University of Mississippi, 1992. Book commem-
    orates the fiftieth anniversary of the publication of "For My People," with
    photographs by Roland Freeman.

SUSAN GRIFFIN   (b. 1943)

*Susan Griffin was born in Los Angles, California, and has spent most of her life
in the same state. She graduated from San Francisco State University in 1965 with
her B.A. While working on her M.A. she published her first volume of poetry,*
Dear Sky, *in 1971, and published two more collections (as well as the Emmy
Award–winning play* Voices*) by 1976. Griffin's early poetry, a candid, radical, feminist verse that mingles the personal and the political, was a precursor to the
ground-breaking books of cultural and feminist criticism that would bring her national recognition. For Griffin, whether it is poetry or prose, the vocation of the
writer is about voicing, fervently, the injustice one sees. Her work has continually
examined the contradictions of patriarchy and its repercussions for women, the society, and the environment. And while some critics have noted that her angry and*

polemical style often undermines the integrity of her argument, others have ap-
plauded her insight and her courage to attack difficult issues. In addition to the
aforementioned works, she has written the poetry collections Like the Iris of an
Eye *(1976),* Unremembered Country: Poems *(1987), and* Bending Home: Selected and New Poems, 1976–1998 *(1998); the nonfiction works* Woman and Nature *(1978),* Rape: The Power of Consciousness *(1979),* Pornography and Silence
(1981), A Chorus of Stones: The Private Life of War *(a Pulitzer Prize finalist,*
1992), The Eros of Everyday Life: Essays on Ecology, Gender and Society
(1995), and The Book of the Courtesans: A Catalogue of Virtues *(2001). "I Like*
to Think of Harriet Tubman," first published in Like the Iris of an Eye, *illustrates*
Griffin's attempt to show the impact history has on both the personal and the po-
litical.

I Like to Think of Harriet Tubman[1]   (1976)

I like to think of Harriet Tubman.
Harriet Tubman who carried a revolver,
who had a scar on her head from a rock thrown
by a slave-master (because she
talked back), and who   5
had a ransom on her head
of thousands of dollars and who
was never caught, and who
had no use for the law
when the law was wrong,   10
who defied the law. I like
to think of her.
I like to think of her especially
when I think of the problem of
feeding children.   15

The legal answer
to the problem of feeding children
is ten free lunches every month,
being equal, in the child's real life,
to eating lunch every other day.   20
Monday but not Tuesday.
I like to think of the President

---

[1](1820?–1913), an escaped slave and leader of the Underground Railroad, which
helped others flee slavery.

eating lunch Monday, but not
Tuesday.
And when I think of the President   25
and the law, and the problem of
feeding children, I like to
think of Harriet Tubman
and her revolver.

And then sometimes   30
I think of the President
and other men,
men who practice the law,
who revere the law,
who make the law,   35
who enforce the law,
who live behind
and operate through
and feed themselves
at the expense of   40
starving children
because of the law.

Men who sit in paneled offices
and think about vacations
and tell women   45
whose care it is
to feed children
not to be hysterical
not to be hysterical as in the word
hysterikos, the greek for   50
womb suffering,
not to suffer in their
wombs,
not to care,
not to bother the men   55
because they want to think
of other things
and do not want
to take the women seriously.
I want them   60
to take women seriously.

I want them to think about Harriet Tubman,
and remember,
remember she was beat by a white man

and she lived   65
and she lived to redress her grievances,
and she lived in swamps
and wore the clothes of a man
bringing hundreds of fugitives from
slavery, and was never caught,   70
and led an army,
and won a battle,
and defied the laws
because the laws were wrong, I want men
to take us seriously.   75
I am tired wanting them to think
about right and wrong.
I want them to fear.
I want them to feel fear now
as I have felt suffering in the womb, and   80
I want them
to know
that there is always a time
there is always a time to make right
what is wrong,   85
there is always a time
for retribution
and that time
is beginning.

Study and Discussion Questions

1. Why does the speaker of the poem like to think of Harriet Tubman?
2. List the ways in which Harriet Tubman is a heroic figure in this poem.
3. List specific issues the poem raises in which the law is wrong.
4. How is Griffin subverting traditional notions of how a woman should behave?
5. What is the role of repetition in the poem? What phrases are repeated,
   and why? What effect does this have on you?
6. Griffin writes that Harriet Tubman "defied the laws/ because the laws
   were wrong." What do you think about this? When is it justified to defy a
   law? What is the definition of a law that is wrong?

Suggestion for Writing

1. Discuss a law you believe ought to be changed, why you think it has not
   been changed, and how it could be changed.
2. Is there a historical figure you like to think of? What is it about that person that appeals to you? Write a poem modeled on Susan Griffin's about

the historical figure you chose, connecting it if you can, as Griffin does, to current situations.

Critical Resources

1. Croft, Karen. "Face Time: Susan Griffin." *SFGate.com*. May 10, 2005. <http://www.sfgate.com>
2. Shima, Alan. *Skirting the Issue: Pursuing Language in the Works of Adrienne Rich, Susan Griffin and Beverly Dahlen*. Uppsala: Uppsala University Press, 1993.
3. Sturnberg, Janet. *The Writer and Her Work* New York: Norton: 2000.

ADRIENNE RICH (b. 1929)

Born in Baltimore, Maryland, Adrienne Rich grew up in an intellectual and artistic environment—her mother was a musician; her father a professor at John Hopkins University. Her poetic ability was first recognized by W. H. Auden when he selected A Change of World *for the Yale Younger Poets Award in 1951 while Rich was attending Radcliffe College. Rich would marry two years later and have three children. The experience of motherhood would have a large impact on her perception of women in society (a topic she explores in* Of Woman Born: Motherhood as Experience and Institution, *1976). While family responsibilities slowed her artistic output amidst the arrival of the 1960s, the Vietnam War, and the rise of feminism, Rich's work moved from its early formal structure to a more radical and political style, experimenting with line length, unorthodox spacing, dialogue, and longer sequencing. By the end of the 1960s and into the 1970s, Rich produced some of her best-known work (poetry as well as essays)—writing that centers on acts of "transformation." For Rich, change is inevitable, but change and transformation are not synonymous: ". . . if the imagination is to transcend and transform experience, it has to question, to challenge, to conceive of alternatives, perhaps to the very life you are living at that moment" (from her essay, "When We Dead Awaken: Writing as Re-Vision"). This process often centers on questions of sexuality and what Rich sees as a patriarchal culture that has degraded the value of women. As exemplified throughout her career, Rich continues to assert the need for writers to participate actively in both the private and public well-being of a culture. Her other works include the poetry collections* Snapshots of a Daughter-in-Law: Poems 1954–1962 *(1963),* Leaflets: Poems *(1969),* The Will to Change: Poems, 1968–1970 *(1971),* Diving into the Wreck: Poems, 1971–1972 *(1973),* Twenty-One Love Poems *(1977),* The Fact of a Doorframe: Poems Selected and New, 1950–1984 *(1984),* Dark Fields of the Republic, 1991–1995 *(1995); and the essay collections* On Lies, Secrets, and Silence: Selected Prose, 1966–1978 *(1979) and* What is Found There: Notebooks on Poetry and Politics *(1993). Her latest work of poetry is entitled* The School Among Ruins: Poems 2000–2004. *In "The Trees," Rich uses metaphor to navigate a woman's transformation.*

The Trees   (1963)

The trees inside are moving out into the forest,
the forest that was empty all these days
where no bird could sit
no insect hide
no sun bury its feet in shadow   5
the forest that was empty all these nights
will be full of trees by morning.

All night the roots work
to disengage themselves from the cracks
in the veranda floor.   10
The leaves strain toward the glass
small twigs stiff with exertion
long-cramped boughs shuffling under the roof
like newly discharged patients
half-dazed, moving   15
to the clinic doors.

I sit inside, doors open to the veranda
writing long letters
in which I scarcely mention the departure
of the forest from the house.   20
The night is fresh, the whole moon shines
in a sky still open
the smell of leaves and lichen
still reaches like a voice into the rooms.
My head is full of whispers   25
which tomorrow will be silent.

Listen. The glass is breaking.
The trees are stumbling forward
into the night. Winds rush to meet them.
The moon is broken like a mirror,   30
its pieces flash now in the crown
of the tallest oak.

Study and Discussion Questions

1. What happens in each stanza?
2. Describe the persona of the poem, her mood and state of mind, and her relation to the trees.
3. Why is she "writing long letters" in which she scarcely mentions "the departure/ of the forest from the house"?
4. Where are the trees going? And why?
5. How is this a poem about protest? What is being protested?
6. Choose a line or two or an image you especially like and discuss it in detail, looking at the word choices and listening to the rhythm and sound of the words.

Suggestions for Writing

1. Write a version of one of those letters the speaker mentions.
2. In reality, of course, trees don't pick up their roots and depart. What do you think the trees stand for?

Critical Resources:

1. *Adrienne Rich.* The Lannen Foundation, 1992 (60 minutes). For more information go to <http://www.lannan.org>. This is one film of several on Adrienne Rich's work.
2. Birkle, Carmen. *Women's Stories of the Looking Glass: Autobiographical Reflections and Self-Representations in the Poetry of Sylvia Plath, Adrienne Rich, and Audre Lorde.* Munich, Germany: Fink, 1996.
3. Charlesworth, Barbara and Albert Gelpi, eds. *Adrienne Rich's Poetry and Prose: Poems, Prose, Reviews and Criticism.* New York: Norton, 1993.
4. Rich, Adrienne. *Arts of the Possible: Essays and Conversations.* New York: Norton, 2001.
5. Sielke, Sabine. *Fashioning the Female Subject: The Intertextual Networking of Dickinson, Moore, and Rich.* Ann Arbor: University of Michigan Press, 1997.

RAYMOND R. PATTERSON (b. 1929)

Born in Harlem the son of working-class parents at the beginning of the Great Depression, Raymond Patterson grew up inheriting the fertile artistic environment of the Harlem Renaissance. As an undergraduate at Lincoln University in Pennsylvania, he served as class poet and won the Mountain Poetry Award for Best Poem. After receiving his M.A. from New York University, Patterson taught full time, first in the New York public schools then later as a professor at City College of the City

University of New York. Influenced greatly by the effusive style of Walt Whitman and the political and lyrical sounds of Langston Hughes, Patterson's first collection of poems, 26 Ways to Look at A Black Man and Other Poems *(1969), explored the black male perspective of the Civil Rights and Black Power movements of the turbulent 1950s and 1960s. In this work, and even more so in his next collection,* Elemental Blues *(1983), Patterson's verse draws from the cadences of blues music in both content and form, utilizing repetition and rhyme to accentuate the various themes and emotions of a poem. In addition to his writing and teaching, Patterson also worked to create more awareness regarding poetry, founding the Annual Langston Hughes Festival at City College in 1973—a Festival which celebrated its thirtieth anniversary in 2003. His other works include the poetry collections* Three Patterson Lyrics for Soprano and Piano *(1986) and* Dangerous River *(1990); and the essays "What's Happening in Black Poetry" (1987) and "African American Epic Poetry: The Long Foreshadowing" (1998). "At that Moment," first published in* Twenty-Six Ways of Looking at a Black Man and Other Poems, *vividly depicts, metaphorically, some repercussions of the assassination of Malcolm X.*

At That Moment   (1969)

(For Malcolm X)

When they shot Malcolm Little down
On the stage of the Audubon Ballroom,[1]
When his life ran out through bullet holes
(Like the people running out when the murder began)
His blood soaked the floor   5
One drop found a crack through the stark
Pounding thunder—slipped under the stage and began
Its journey: burrowed through concrete into the cellar,
Dropped down darkness, exploding like quicksilver
Pellets of light, panicking rats, paralyzing cockroaches—   10
Tunneled through rubble and wrecks of foundations,
The rocks that buttress the bowels of the city, flowed
Into pipes and powerlines, the mains and cables of the city:
A thousand fiery seeds.
At that moment,   15
Those who drank water where he entered ...
Those who cooked food where he passed ...

---

[1]In Harlem, in New York City.

Those who burned light while he listened . . .
Those who were talking as he went, knew he was water
Running out of faucets, gas running out of jets, power   20
Running out of sockets, meaning running along taut wires—
To the hungers of their living. It is said
Whole slums of clotted Harlem plumbing groaned
And sundered free that day, and disconnected gas and light
Went on and on and on. . . .   25
They rushed his riddled body on a stretcher
To the hospital. But the police were too late.
It had already happened.

Study and Discussion Questions

1. What is the revolutionary fantasy the poem imagines? Where in the poem does it begin? How is it revolutionary?
2. What images of Malcolm's blood does Patterson give us in the first half of the poem?
3. List all the acts Malcolm's blood performs.
4. What does the "it" in the last line of the poem refer to?
5. What is the tone of this poem?
6. Discuss the use of alliteration and of repetition of phrases in "At That Moment." What effect do these formal choices have?

Suggestions for Writing

1. What is the poet trying to say through this fantasy about the meaning and effect of Malcolm X's life and death? Is he optimistic or pessimistic?
2. Think about other assassinations in the United States in the past thirty years. What have been the political consequences of any one of or all of these murders? Would you agree with Patterson's conclusions in this poem or argue a different position?

Critical Resources:

1. "A Voice from Harlem, Raymond Patterson." *The African American Registry.* May 1, 2005. <www.aaregistry.com>. This site is a resource for African-American history with bios and poems from dozens of African-American poets and writers, including Patterson's "At That Moment."
2. Finch, Annie, ed. *An Exaltation of Forms: Contemporary Poets Celebrate the Diversity of Their Art.* Ann Arbor: University of Michigan Press, 2002. Includes a chapter by Patterson entitled "The Blues."
3. Patterson, Raymond R. "African American Epic Poetry: The Long Foreshadowing." *The Furious Flowering of African American Poetry.* Ed. Joanne Gabbin. Charlottesville: University of Virginia Press, 1999.
4. Patterson, Raymond. "Statement." *American Poets in 1976.* Indianapolis: Bobbs-Merrill, 1976, 226–34.

5. Patterson, Raymond. "What's Happening in Black Poetry?" *A Gift of Tongues: Critical Challenges in Contemporary American Poetry.* Athens: University of Georgia Press, 1987.

JO CARSON (b. 1946)

Jo Carson grew up in the lush Appalachian Mountain region of eastern Tennessee. She attended East Tennessee State University but left to pursue a writing career in New York City. She returned later, however, to complete her degrees in theater and speech. With Johnson City as her permanent residence, Carson helped found AlternateROOTS in 1976, "to support the creation and presentation of original art which is rooted in a particular community of place, tradition or spirit" (www.alternateroots.org). For Carson, this type of "cultural work" has meant going to various communities throughout the Appalachian region and organizing theatrical productions inspired by the stories and history of the people of a particular area, and then performed by members of the same community: "What is different about these projects is that they are about and out of the place they are being produced . . . these are projects close to the tradition of storytelling. . .in that the common stuff of life is revisited/revisioned in a way that gives it some other meaning than just a hard day at work . . ." (interview, www.communityarts.net). For Carson, the goal has been to raise art awareness by making it interactive and tangibly relevant to people. She has helped produce and perform over 20 community-based plays. In 1989 she published Stories I Ain't Told Nobody Yet, *a collection of writing based on the many stories she has heard throughout her career. Carson often performs these pieces in universities throughout the country and on NPR (National Public Radio). Other published works include* The Last of The "Waltz Across Texas" and Other Stories *(1993) and the plays* Daytrips *(1989),* Swamp Gravy *(1996), and* Whispering Horses *(1997). "I Cannot Remember All the Times . . ." comes from* Stories I Ain't Told Nobody Yet.

I Cannot Remember All the Times . . .   (1989)

I cannot remember all the times he hit me.
I might could count black eyes,
how many times I said I ran into doors
or fell down or stepped into the path
of any flying object except his fist.   5
Once I got a black eye playing softball.

The rest were him. Seven, eight.
I can name what of me he broke:
my nose, my arm, and four ribs
in the course of six years' marriage.   10
The ribs were after I said divorce
and in spite of a peace bond.
I spent the night in the hospital.
He did not even spend a night in jail.
The sheriff I helped elect does not   15
apply the law to family business.
He always swore he never meant to do it.
I do believe he never planned.
It was always just the day,
the way I looked at him afraid.   20
Maybe the first time he did not mean to do it,
maybe the broken ribs were for good luck.

I want to post this in ladies rooms,
write it on the tags of women's underwear,
write it on coupons to go in Tampax packages   25
because my ex-husband will want to marry again
and there is no tattoo where he can't see it
to tell the next woman who might fall in love with him.
After six months, maybe a year,
he will start with a slap you can brush off.   30
Leave when he slaps you.
When he begins to call you cunt and whore
and threatens to kill you if you try to go
it will almost be like teasing but it is not.
Keep two sets of car keys for yourself.   35
Take your children with you when you go.
If he is throwing things, he is drinking.
If he is drunk enough he cannot catch you.
A punch in the breast hurts worse than a punch in the jaw.
A hit with an object does more damage than a hit with a fist   40
unless he is so drunk he picks up a broom instead of a poker.
If you pick up the poker, he will try to get it.
If he gets it, he will hit you with it.
He probably will not kill you because you will pass out
and then, he is all the sudden sorry and he stops.   45
When he says he will not hit you again
as he drives you to the hospital,
both of you in tears and you in pain,
you have stayed much too long already.
Tell the people at the hospital the truth   50

no matter how much you think you love him.
Do not say you fell down stairs
no matter how much he swears he loves you.
He does love you, he loves you hurt
and he will hit you again.   55

Study and Discussion Questions

1. Why do you suppose Carson begins the poem with the words "I cannot remember all the times he hit me" and reinforces "I cannot remember" by
   using part of that line as the title? Why is the failure of memory important?
2. List the ways the speaker of the poem is injured by her husband in the
   first stanza. Also list the ways (a) she, (b) he, and (c) the outside world denied what was happening.
3. Comment on the shift that occurs from the first stanza to the second. What
   do you notice about whom the poem is addressed to in each stanza? What
   do you notice about the verb tense?
4. Chart the progress of the abuse as the speaker of the poem lays it out in
   the second stanza for "the next woman who might fall in love with him."
5. How does Carson pull us (especially if we are female readers) into this poem?
   What does she tell us to do—and when? How are the details important?
6. What is the tone of this poem—angry, ironic, bitter, stern, weary?
   Those are only illustrative suggestions; you can come up with your own
   characterization.
7. Trace the speaker's progress out of the abusive relationship. How does the
   structure of the poem to some extent replicate that progress?

Suggestions for Writing

1. Share this poem separately (a) with a female friend and (b) with a male
   friend. Record how each responds to the poem (you might note nonver-
   bal as well as verbal responses). Analyze the similarities and differences
   in the responses.
2. Freewrite your own initial response to the poem. You may not want to
   share this.
3. "He does love you, he loves you hurt/ and he will hit you again." What's
   love got to do with it? Discuss Carson's analysis in this poem of the relation between love and abuse—for both people involved.

Critical Resources:

1. Ballard, Sandra and Patricia Hudson, eds. *Listen Here: Women Writing in
   Appalachia.* Lexington: University Press of Kentucky, 2003.
2. Burnham, Linda Frye. "I Can Write a River: An Interview with Jo Carson." December 1999. *Community Arts Network.* May 5, 2005.
   <http://www.communityarts.net>
3. Carson, Jo. "Good Questions." *Bloodroot: Reflections on Place by Appalachian Women Writers.* Ed. Joyce Dyer. Lexington: University of Kentucky Press, 1998, 71–79.

4. Harris, Jo. "Jo Carson." *Appalachian Journal: A Regional Studies Review* 20.1 (1992): 56–67.
5. Mooney, Jennifer. "Room is Made for Whoever': Jo Carson and the Creation of Dialogical Community." *Her Words: Diverse Voices in Contemporary Appalachian Women's Poetry*. Ed. Felicia Mitchell. Knoxville: University of Tennessee Press, 2002, 50–65.

ALLEN GINSBERG (1926–1997)

Allen Ginsberg's poem "Howl," published in 1956, marked a new era in American poetry and became one of the defining texts of what has been termed the "Beat Movement" of the 1950s and 1960s. The term "beat" itself, which draws dual meaning from both the 1950s slang word for "cheated" and the religious "beatitude" (blessed), is characteristic of the kind of word-play the Beats ushered in. Along with Jack Kerouac, William Burroughs, Gregory Corso, and others, the Beats challenged what they saw as the high-brow traditionalism of American universities by eschewing accepted literary forms. By experimenting with what one might call spontaneous creation (recording the flow of thought as it comes) expressed through the emotions a writer is feeling at the time of composition, Beat writers sought to communicate the angst and frustration that would give rise to the 1960s counterculture. Ginsberg's work too follows in the more radical traditions of Walt Whitman and William Blake ("Howl" was said to be inspired by a vision he had of Blake)—sometimes mystical in their incantations, a rhythmic free-verse of multifarious images often read by Ginsberg in the form of a chant. Much of his popularity had to do with not only the political exigency of his writing and poetry readings but also his outspoken work as a political activist. While the essential Beat attributes remained with Ginsberg throughout his life, his work evolved and changed with each new decade. In addition to Howl and Other Poems *(1956),* other notable works include Kaddish and Other Poems 1958–60 *(1961),* Reality Sandwiches *(1963),* Planet News *(1968),* Scrap Leaves *(1968),* Ankor Wat *(1968),* New Year Blues *(1972),* The Fall of America: Poems of These States 1965–1971 *(1972),* Mind Breaths *(1977), and* White Shroud: Poem 1980–1985 *(1986). There are also several audio recordings available of Ginsberg reading his poetry. The poem "America," first published in* Howl and Other Poems, *is an example of Ginsberg's free-flowing style.*

America (1956)

America I've given you all and now I'm nothing.
America two dollars and twentyseven cents January 17, 1956.

I can't stand my own mind.
America when will we end the human war?
Go fuck yourself with your atom bomb.   5
I don't feel good don't bother me.
I won't write my poem till I'm in my right mind.
America when will you be angelic?
When will you take off your clothes?
When will you look at yourself through the grave?   10
When will you be worthy of your million Trotskyites?
America why are your libraries full of tears?
America when will you send your eggs to India?
I'm sick of your insane demands.
When can I go into the supermarket and buy what I need with my   15
          good looks?
America after all it is you and I who are perfect not the next world.
Your machinery is too much for me.
You made me want to be a saint.
There must be some other way to settle this argument.   20
Burroughs[1] is in Tangiers I don't think he'll come back it's sinister.
Are you being sinister or is this some form of practical joke?
I'm trying to come to the point.
I refuse to give up my obsession.
America stop pushing I know what I'm doing.   25
America the plum blossoms are falling.
I haven't read the newspapers for months, everyday somebody goes on
          trial for murder.
America I feel sentimental about the Wobblies.
America I used to be a communist when I was a kid I'm not sorry.   30
I smoke marijuana every chance I get.
I sit in my house for days on end and stare at the roses in the closet.
When I go to Chinatown I get drunk and never get laid.
My mind is made up there's going to be trouble.
You should have seen me reading Marx.   35
My psychoanalyst thinks I'm perfectly right.
I won't say the Lord's Prayer.
I have mystical visions and cosmic vibrations.
America I still haven't told you what you did to Uncle Max after he
came over from Russia.   40

I'm addressing you.
Are you going to let your emotional life be run by Time Magazine?
I'm obsessed by Time Magazine.

---

[1]William Burroughs (1914–1997), American novelist.

I read it every week.

Its cover stares at me every time I slink past the corner candystore.   45

I read it in the basement of the Berkeley Public Library.

It's always telling me about responsibility. Businessmen are serious.

      Movie producers are serious. Everybody's serious but me.

It occurs to me that I am America.

I am talking to myself again.   50

Asia is rising against me.

I haven't got a chinaman's chance.

I'd better consider my national resources.

My national resources consist of two joints of marijuana millions of genitals

      an unpublishable private literature that jetplanes 1400 miles an   55

      hour and twentyfive-thousand mental institutions.

I say nothing about my prisons nor the millions of underprivileged who live

      in my flowerpots under the light of five hundred suns.

I have abolished the whorehouses of France, Tangiers is the next to go.

My ambition is to be President despite the fact that I'm a Catholic.   60

America how can I write a holy litany in your silly mood?

I will continue like Henry Ford my strophes are as individual as his

      automobiles more so they're all different sexes.

America I will sell you strophes $2500 apiece $500 down on your

      old strophe   65

America free Tom Mooney[2]

America save the Spanish Loyalists

America Sacco & Vanzetti must not die

America I am the Scottsboro boys.[3]

America when I was seven momma took me to Communist Cell meetings   70

      they sold us garbanzos a handful per ticket a ticket costs a

      nickel and the speeches were free everybody was angelic and

      sentimental about the workers it was all so sincere you have no

      idea what a good thing the party was in 1935 Scott Nearing was a

      grand old man a real mensch Mother Bloor the Silk-strikers'   75

      Ewig-Weibliche made me cry I once saw the Yiddish orator Israel

      Amter plain.[4] Everybody must have been a spy.

America you don't really want to go to war.

America it's them bad Russians.

Them Russians them Russians and them Chinamen. And them Russians.   80

---

[2]American Wobbly, jailed on murder charges in 1916 and pardoned more than twenty years later.

[3]Nine black youths convicted on flimsy evidence, in 1931, of raping two white women.

[4]Nearing, Bloor, Amter were American leftists. Ewig-Weibliche means "the eternal feminine."

The Russia wants to eat us alive. The Russia's power mad. She wants to
    take our cars from out our garages.
Her wants to grab Chicago. Her needs a Red *Reader's Digest.* Her wants
    our auto plants in Siberia. Him big bureaucracy running our
    filling-stations.   85
That no good. Ugh. Him make Indians learn read. Him need big black
    niggers. Hah. Her make us all work sixteen hours a day. Help.
America this is quite serious.
America this is the impression I get from looking in the television set.
America is this correct?   90
I'd better get right down to the job.
It's true I don't want to join the Army or turn lathes in precision parts
    factories, I'm nearsighted and psychopathic anyway.
America I'm putting my queer shoulder to the wheel.

Study and Discussion Questions

1. Why does Ginsberg keep repeating the word "America"?
2. What is the argument the speaker is having with America?
3. Why do you think Ginsberg chooses to address his poem to America
   rather than, say, to us, about America?
4. List the qualities of America as portrayed in this poem.
5. Characterize the speaker of the poem.
6. The speaker says, "Everybody's serious but me." How does he mean that?
   Do you agree with him?
7. What does he mean in the last line about putting his "queer shoulder to
   the wheel"? Has he undergone a change of attitude during the poem?

Suggestions for Writing

1. Find a copy of Whitman's "Song of Myself," read some of it, and compare
   Ginsberg's "America" to it. You might look at line length and rhythm and
   at the two poets' sense of themselves as Americans. There is a section from
   "Song of Myself" called "A Child said, What is the Grass?" in the Growing Up and Growing Older section of this anthology which will help you
   compare form, but other sections of "Song of Myself" are more directly
   related to the poets' sense of themselves as Americans.
2. Write a series of lines, each one beginning "America," that expresses your
   own relationship to the United States.

Critical Resources

1. Ginsberg, Allen. "America." *Howl and Other Poems.* Audio CD. Fantasy,
   1998. Ginsberg reads "Howl" and other poems.
2. *The Life and Times of Allen Ginsberg.* (Documentary) Director Jerry
   Aronson. First Run Features Home Video, 1997 (82 minutes).

3. Raskin, Jonah. *American Scream: Allen Ginsberg's Howl and the Making of the Beat Generation.* Berkeley: University of California Press, 2004.
4. Schumacher, Michael. *Dharma Lion: A Critical Biography of Allen Ginsberg.* New York: St. Martin's Press, 1992.

ESSEX HEMPHILL (1957–1995)

Essex Hemphill grew up in Washington D.C., and later lived in Philadelphia. As both black and gay, Hemphill lived his life dealing with being a double minority. Although influenced early in life by the ideas of the Black Power movement of the late 1960s, Hemphill would find a more conducive sensibility in the gay liberation movement of the 1970s. As a writer and activist, he worked to create more public awareness of the African American gay male experience—a community which had been systematically silenced and oppressed by the larger African American community as well as by the predominantly white gay and lesbian community. In 1991, Hemphill edited and published Brother to Brother *as a sequel and in honor of James Beam's* In the Life *(1986)—the two together comprise the first two published anthologies of African American gay and lesbian writers. Hemphill's poetry and essays appear in both. Frequently autobiographical, his work varies from the highly political to the highly erotic and runs the spectrum of emotion from anger to love. Hemphill died of AIDS at the age of 38. His other works include the chapbooks of poetry* Earth Life *(1985) and* Conditions *(1992); and the collection of poetry and prose* Ceremonies *(1992). The poem "Baby Can You Love Me" is structured on the entreaties of a dying lover.*

Baby Can You Love Me? (1994)

Are you willing to kill me
if I ask you to?
If I'm unable to do so
are you willing to kill me?
If I can't, by my own hand,   5
if I'm unable to
for any reason
and the prospect of my life
is diminished beyond recovery;
if I can't remember my name   10
or recognize my mother
or identify you; if I can't

sleep beside you anymore
holding your stomach
in my calloused hands;   15
if I lose control of my body
and the intricate systems
I'm required to operate;
if I should become hopelessly bedridden
will you understand my unwillingness   20
to linger on? Can you be as brave
and as clearheaded as you are now,
professing that you would
love to love me?
But could you kill me,   25
if I asked you to?
Would your love
let me not linger
in my dying bed?

Study and Discussion Questions

1. Discuss your initial emotional response to this poem—to its overall effect
   and to specific parts of the poem that felt powerful to you or that jarred
   you. What is it about the way the poem is constructed that might have contributed to your response? What in your own experience contributed to
   your response to the poem?
2. Why do you think Hemphill puts the poem in the form of questions? The
   speaker of the poem is poised in relation to himself, to his illness (AIDS),
   to his audience, to his late-twentieth-century U.S. society, to his lover.
   Think of three reasons why he might choose questions rather than statements.
3. Look up definitions of love in several unabridged dictionaries. How is
   Hemphill redefining, or at least augmenting or adding to, our definition
   of love through his poem?
4. How many questions does the speaker of the poem ask? How are the
   opening and closing questions different from those they frame?
5. What verb tense(s) is this poem set in? What effect does that choice have?
6. How is "Baby Can You Love Me?" a poem of protest?

Suggestions for Writing

1. The speaker of this poem is dying of AIDS (we know this from biographical evidence and because this poem is part of a sequence of poems
   about living with AIDS). The symptoms he describes can be seen as applicable to other kinds of dying as well—from cancer, from physical
   trauma, even from old age. Does the speaker of the poem make a con-

vincing case in his request to die if and when he reaches the state he describes here? How would you feel about it if you were dying?
2. Write a response from the point of view of the person to whom Hemphill
   addresses the poem. How would he answer all these questions? What
   might be going through his mind?
3. Write an argument for or against assisted suicide, using "Baby Can You
   Love Me?" as part of the evidence for your argument.

Critical Resources

1. Glave, Thomas. "Re-Calling Essex Hemphill." *Callaloo: A Journal of
   African-American and African Arts and Letters* 23.1 (2000): 278–284.
2. Hemphill, Essex. "Does Your Mama Know About Me?" *Traps: African-
   American Men on Gender and Sexuality.* Ed. Rudolph Byrd. Bloomington: Indiana University Press, 2001.
3. ———. "Living the Word/Looking for Home." *Queer Representations:
   Reading Lives, Reading Cultures: A Center for Lesbian and Gay Studies
   Book.* Ed. Martin Duberman. New York: New York University Press, 1997.
4. *Looking For Langston.* Director Issac Julien. British Film Institute, 1989
   (49 minutes). A documentary on Langston Hughes that Hemphill helped
   produce and also appears in.
5. *Tongues United.* (Documentary) Director Marlon Riggs. MTR Production, 1996 (55 minutes). Focuses on the life and work of Essex Hemphill
   and other gay black artists.

WILLIAM BUTLER YEATS (1865–1939)

*William Butler Yeats was born in Dublin, Ireland, and studied art in college un-
til he turned to writing. It is often said that Yeats was the greatest poet of the 20th
century, even though he preferred to work within more traditional poetics of
rhyme and form in contrast to the modernist poets (such as Eliot) who were
bringing such tradition into question. Yeats' marriage to Georgie Hyde-Lees, and
her "automatic writing," ". . . in which [the] hand and pen presumably serve as
unconscious instruments for the spirit world to send information" (Artists and
Authors for Young Adults), helped him codify his interest in the occult and mysticism. He was active in Irish nationalist causes, helped found an Irish national
theater, and served as a senator of the new Irish Free State. In 1933, he carefully
shaped his many volumes of poetry into the definitive* Collected Poems *(1933).
He received the Nobel Prize for literature in 1923. One of Yeats's early poems,
"The Lake Isle of Innisfree" expresses the conflict between inner and public life
which would recur in Yeats's work.*

The Lake Isle of Innisfree[1] (1893)

I will arise and go now, and go to Innisfree,
And a small cabin build there, of clay and wattles made:
Nine bean-rows will I have there, a hive for the honeybee,
And live alone in the bee-loud glade.

And I shall have some peace there, for peace comes dropping slow,   5
Dropping from the veils of the morning to where the cricket sings;
There midnight's all a glimmer, and noon a purple glow,
And evening full of the linnet's wings.

I will arise and go now, for always night and day
I hear lake water lapping with low sounds by the shore;   10
While I stand on the roadway, or on the pavements grey,
I hear it in the deep heart's core.

Study and Discussion Questions

1. Which of the six senses—taste, hearing, touch, sight, smell, and move-ment—does Yeats evoke in this poem? Which senses are the most im-portant in the poem?
2. List all of the images—literal and figurative—in the poem. Which sense is evoked by each of these images?
3. What does the speaker of the poem want to find on the lake isle of Inn-isfree? What does he want to leave behind? Though his protest is subtle and implicit, what is he protesting?
4. What is the rhyme scheme of this poem?
5. Mark the number of syllables in each line. If you can, scan the poem, mark-ing the accented and unaccented syllables, and then dividing them into feet. (See "How Poetry Works," for a discussion of meter.) What is the pat-tern you see repeated in each stanza of "The Lake Isle of Innisfree"?
6. Note where repetition occurs in the poem. What is the effect of the repe-tition? It helps to read this and any poem aloud.
7. What do the rhyme scheme, the meter, and the use of repetition contribute to the mood of this poem? What would you say the mood of the poem is?
8. In an early draft of this poem, the first two lines were

   I will arise and go now and go to the island of Innisfree.
   And live in a dwelling of wattles, of woven wattles and wood-work made.

   How do the changes Yeats made which resulted in the later version of the poem contribute to the music and the mood of the poem?

---

[1]A small island on a lake near Yeats's childhood home in Ireland.

9. In that same early draft, the last line of the first stanza was, "And this old care shall fade." In the version he finally published, the line is, "And live alone in the bee-loud glade." Why is the second version better (if you think it is)?

10. And in the early version, there was no third stanza. How important is the final stanza of the version we have? What does it add to the vision and the meaning of the poem?

Suggestions for Writing

1. Write down some of your own sense based images of serenity or peace. Choose one of these and go there in your mind, writing a descriptive paragraph or poem vivid enough to bring your reader there.

2. Compare/contrast "The Lake Isle of Innisfree" with Yeats's later poem "Sailing to Byzantium."

Critical Resources:

1. Alexander, Claudia. "The Poetic Quest of William Butler Yeats." *Innisfree* 7 (1987), 16–22.

2. McDonald, Peter. "A Poem for All Seasons: Yeats, Meaning and the Publishing History of "The Lake of Isle Innisfree" in the 1890s." *Yearbook of English Studies* 29 (1999): 202–30.

3. Merritt, Henry. "Rising and Going: The 'Nature' of Yeats' 'The Lake Isle of Innisfree.'" *English: The Journal of the English Association* 47.188 (1998): 103–09.

4. Thornton, R. K. R. "How Far is it From Innisfree to Byzantium." *Irish Studies Review* 11.3 (2003): 285–91.

MARTÍN ESPADA (b. 1957)

Martín Espada was born and raised in Brooklyn, New York, the son of Puerto Rican immigrant and political activist Frank Espada. After working for years as a tenant lawyer for Spanish-speaking residents, Martin became a professor of English at the University of Massachusetts, Amherst. His poetry has gained national recognition for its angry condemnation of social and political injustice. Once called the Pablo Neruda of North America, Espada's revisioning of history plays a central role in his poetry—a historicity that comes from the view of the victimized, the disenfranchised, the oppressed. While Espada's anger can sometimes overwhelm his poetry, his ability to temper such anger with humor and compassion creates poetry that plays on several levels of meaning. His works include Trumpets from the Island of Their Eviction *(1987),* Rebellion Is the Circle of a Lover's Hands *(1990),* City of Coughing and Dead Radiators *(1993),* Imagine the Angels of Bread *(1996—American Book Award),* A Mayan Astronomer in

Hell's Kitchen *(2000), and* Alabanza: New and Selected Poems *(2003). He has
also published the collection of essays* Zapata's Disciple *(1998).*

Jorge the Church Janitor Finally Quits   (1990)

Cambridge, Massachusetts, 1989

No one asks
where I am from,
I must be
from the country of janitors,
I have always mopped this floor.   5
Honduras, you are a squatter's camp
outside the city
of their understanding.

No one can speak   10
my name,
I host the fiesta
of the bathroom,
stirring the toilet
like a punchbowl.
The Spanish music of my name   15
is lost
when the guests complain
about toilet paper.

What they say   20
must be true:
I am smart,
but I have a bad attitude.

No one knows
that I quit tonight,
maybe the mop   25
will push on without me,
sniffing along the floor
like a crazy squid
with stringy gray tentacles.
They will call it Jorge.   30

Study and Discussion Questions

1. If you were reading this as an essay or argument instead of a poem, what
   would you say is the point being made in each of the four stanzas? What
   are the four stages of Espada's argument?

2. What is significant about the first line of each stanza?
3. What realization/conclusion is the speaker of the poem coming to about himself? What realization or conclusion is he coming to about the "they" of the poem (and who is the "they" of the poem)?
4. How is the church janitor's name, "Jorge," correctly pronounced? How do "they" pronounce it, do you think? Why does Jorge make such a point about this?
5. List and discuss the images in the poem—the literal images and the figurative images. How does the final stanza take the imagery to a new level?
6. How does where Jorge works contribute to the irony of the poem?
7. How is "Jorge the Church Janitor Finally Quits" a poem *of* protest? How is it a poem *about* protest?

Suggestions for Writing

1. Have you ever quit a job? Why? Write a narrative, a poem, or an essay about what led to your quitting. Or, if you haven't actually quit a job, write a fantasy about doing so.
2. Compare/contrast the situation of the protagonist in "Jorge the Church Janitor Finally Quits" with the situation of the protagonist in John Updike's short story "A & P."
3. Compare/contrast Martín Espada's use of imagery in the final stanza of "Jorge the Church Janitor Finally Quits" with the final image(s) of Carolyn Forché's "The Colonel." What is the effect in each case of this move into the fantastic, sometimes called "magical realism"?

Critical Resources

1. Acosta-Belén, Edna. "Beyond Island Boundaries: Ethnicity, Gender, and Cultural Revitalization in Nuyorican Literature." *Callaloo* 15.4 (1992): 979–98.
2. Arias, Santa. "Inside the Worlds of Latino Traveling Cultures: Martin Espada's Poetry of Rebellion." *Bilingual Review* 21.3 (1996): 231–40.
3. Fink, Thomas. "Visibility and History in the Poetry of Martin Espada." *Americas Review: A Review of Hispanic Literature and Art of the USA* 25 (1999): 202–21.
4. Ratiner, Steven. *Giving their Word: Conversations with Contemporary Poets.* Amherst: University of Massachusetts Press, 2002.

JULIA ALVAREZ (b. 1950)

Julia Alvarez was born in the Dominican Republic and emigrated to the United States in 1960. In 1971 she received her B.A. in English from Middlebury College. She obtained her M.A. in Creative Writing from Syracuse University. After a decade of teaching and writing, Alvarez published her first collection of poetry, Homecoming *(1984). Although* Homecoming *is dominated by the layered sonnets*

of "33," other poems explore Alvarez's experience as a "hyphenated American."
Through vivid lyricism, Alvarez's poetry attempts to reconcile the alienation and
cultural duality that many immigrant Americans experience—especially that of
Hispanic women who must negotiate two cultures and two languages. Her novel
How the Garcia Girls Lost Their Accents *(1991) has found its place in the grow-*
ing canon of multiethnic literature. Other works include the poetry compilations
The Other Side/El Otro Lado *(1995),* Seven Trees *(1999),* The Woman I Kept to
Myself *(2004); the novels* In the Time of Butterflies *(1994),* Yo! *(1997),* In the
Name of Salome *(2001); and the essay collection* Something to Declare *(1998).*
She has also written several books for young adults. "The White House Has Dis-
invited the Poets" was written in response to the Bush Administration's cancelling
of a poetry reading at The White House after it was clear that many poets would
be reading poems protesting the U.S. invasion of Iraq.

The White House Has Disinvited the Poets   (2003)

The White House has disinvited the poets
to a cultural tea in honor of poetry
after the Secret Service got wind of a plot
to fill Mrs. Bush's ears with anti-war verse.
Were they afraid the poets might persuade   5
a sensitive girl who always loved to read,
a librarian who stocked the shelves with Poe
and Dickinson? Or was she herself afraid
to be swayed by the cooing doves and live at odds
with the screaming hawks in her family?   10

The Latina maids are putting away the cups
and the silver spoons, sad to be missing out
on *musica* they seldom get to hear
in the hallowed halls ... The valet sighs
as he rolls the carpets up and dusts the blinds.   15
Damn but a little Langston would be good
in this dreary mausoleum of a place!
Why does the White House have to be so white?
The chef from Baton Rouge is starved for verse
uncensored by Homeland Security.   20

No Poetry Until Further Notice!
Instead the rooms are vacuumed and set up
for closed-door meetings planning an attack
against the ones who always bear the brunt

of silencing: the poor, the powerless,   25
the ones who serve, those bearing poems, not arms.
So why be afraid of us, Mrs. Bush?
you're married to a scarier fellow.
We bring you the tidings of great joy
not only peace but poetry on earth.   30

Study and Discussion Questions

On February 12, 2003, there was to be a symposium on "Poetry and the American Voice" at the White House, hosted by Laura Bush. When the Bush administration learned that poetsagainstthewar.org had put out a call for "poems speaking 'for the conscience of our country,' in opposition to George Bush's plans for a 'Shock and Awe' attack on Baghdad," the symposium was cancelled (Sam Hamill, introduction to *Poets Against the War*). The Web site received 13,000 poems in six weeks, indicating not only widespread opposition to the war but also both the power of poetry as a means of protest and the power of the Internet as an organizing tool for protest.

1. What do you notice about the structure of this poem? How many stanzas, how many lines in each stanza? Why does Alvarez need three stanzas for this poem; why not two or four or one?
2. Describe what is happening in each stanza: (a) What do we learn in stanza 1? Why the questions in that stanza? (b) How does the focus shift in stanza 2? Why do you think Alvarez makes this shift? (c) How many parts does stanza 3 have? Discuss each part and its purpose and effect.
3. How is "The White House Has Disinvited the Poets" a poem *of* protest? How is it a poem *about* protest?
4. List all the people/groups represented in this well-populated poem. What role does each individual/group play?
5. Read the poem aloud and notice any sound patterns: rhymes or almost rhymes, whether inside lines or at the ends of lines; assonance, consonance, alliteration. How do line breaks work along with the sound?
6. What is the tone of this poem? Provide evidence from the poem for your opinion.
7. List what poetry can do for us, according to this poem.

Suggestions for Writing

1. Do you agree or disagree with what Alvarez's poem suggests about the importance of poetry? Argue for either side of this question, giving examples. What about songs, novels, films?
2. Write the rationale from the White House for canceling "the cultural tea in honor of poetry." You can do this as a White House spin, or you could assume that honesty is an option and write what you think are the real reasons.
3. Read Julia Alvarez's poem, "Homecoming" (Money and Work), and compare/contrast her writing style in these two poems.

4. Other poems from the poetsagainstthewar.org Web site in this anthology are Martín Espada, "Alabanza: In Praise of Local 100"; Pamela Hale, "Poem for an Iraqi Child in a Forgotten News Clip"; Katha Pollit, "Trying to Write a Poem Against the War"; and Adrienne Rich, "The School Among the Ruins." Discuss Alvarez's poem in the context of one or more of these poems.

Critical Resources

1. Alvarez, Julia. "On Finding a Latino Voice." *The Writing Life: Writers on How They Think and Work.* New York: Public Affairs, 2003.
2. Hammill, Sam ed. *Poets Against the War.* New York: Thunder's Mouth Press/Nation Books, 2003.
3. Henao, Eda. *The Colonial Subject's Search for Nation, Culture, and Identity in the Works of Julia Alvarez, Rosario Ferre and Ana Lydia Vega.* Lewiston: Edwin Mellen Press, 2003.
4. Varnes, Katherine. "Practicing for the Real Me: Form and Authenticity in the Poetry of Julia Alvarez." *Antipodas: Journal of Hispanic and Galician Studies* 10 (1998): 67–77.
5. *Women of Hope: Latinas Abriendo Camino: Twelve Ground Breaking Latina Women.* Princeton: Films for the Humanities, 1996 (29 minutes).

❀ ❀ ❀

JUDY GRAHN (b. 1940)

Judy Grahn grew up in New Mexico and has worked as a waitress, typist, sandwich maker, and meat wrapper. She has also taught in women's writing programs in New York and Berkeley, and she cofounded the Gay and Lesbian Studies Program at the New College of California in San Francisco. Grahn was a cofounder of the Women's Press Collective in 1970 in northern California. Her writings in-clude The Work of a Common Woman *(1978) and* The Queen of Wands *(1982), poetry;* Another Mother Tongue: Gay Words, Gay Worlds *(1984) and* Blood and Bread and Roses *(1986), nonfiction;* Mundane's World *(1988) a novel and* Really Reading Gertrude Stein *(1989). She has also edited two volumes of* True to Life Adventure Stories *(1978, 1980). Grahn has consistently brought a working-class perspective into feminist poetry. "A Woman Is Talking to Death" published as a chapbook in 1973, explored concepts of love, heroism, decency, re-sponsibility, and community. See also Grahn's poem "Ella, in a square apron, along Highway 80" (Money and Work) and her short story "Boys at The Rodeo" (Women and Men).*

A Woman Is Talking To Death (1973)

One

Testimony in trials that never got heard

my lovers teeth are white geese flying above me
my lovers muscles are rope ladders under my hands

we were driving home slow
my lover and I, across the long Bay Bridge, 5
one February midnight, when midway
over in the far left lane, I saw a strange scene:

one small young man standing by the rail,
and in the lane itself, parked straight across
as if it could stop anything, a large young 10
man upon a stalled motorcycle, perfectly
relaxed as if he'd stopped at a hamburger stand;
he was wearing a peacoat and levis, and
he had his head back, roaring, you
could almost hear the laugh, it 15
was so real.

"Look at that fool," I said, "in the
middle of the bridge like that," a very
womanly remark.

Then we heard the meaning of the noise 20
of metal on a concrete bridge at 50
miles an hour, and the far left lane
filled up with a big car that had a
motorcycle jammed on its front bumper, like
the whole thing would explode, the friction 25
sparks shot up bright orange for many feet
into the air, and the racket still sets
my teeth on edge.

When the car stopped we stopped parallel 30
and Wendy headed for the callbox while I
ducked across those 6 lanes like a mouse
in the bowling alley. "Are you hurt?" I said,

the middle-aged driver had the greyest black face,
"I couldn't stop, I couldn't stop, what happened?"

Then I remembered. "Somebody," I said, "was *on*　　　　　　　35
the motorcycle," I ran back,
one block? two blocks? the space for walking
on the bridge is maybe 18 inches, whoever
engineered this arrogance, in the dark
stiff wind it seemed I would
be pushed over the rail, would fall down　　　　　　　　　　40
screaming onto the hard surface of
the bay, but I did not, I found the tall young man
who thought he owned the bridge, now lying on
his stomach, head cradled in his broken arm.　　　　　　　45

He had glasses on, but somewhere he had lost
most of his levis, where were they?
and his shoes. Two short cuts on his buttocks,
that was the only mark except his thin white
seminal tubes were all strung out behind; no　　　　　　　50
child left *in* him; and he looked asleep.

I plucked wildly at his wrist, then put it
down; there were two long haired women
holding back the traffic just behind me
with their bare hands, the machines came　　　　　　　　55
down like mad bulls, I was scared, much
more than usual, I felt easily squished
like the earthworms crawling on a busy
sidewalk after the rain; *I wanted to*
leave. And met the driver, walking back.　　　　　　　　60

"The guy is dead." I gripped his hand,
the wind was going to blow us off the bridge.

"Oh my God," he said, "haven't I had enough
trouble in my life?" He raised his head,
and for a second was enraged and yelling,　　　　　　　　65
at the top of the bridge—"I was just driving
home!" His head fell down. "My God, and
now I've killed somebody."

I looked down at my own peacoat and levis,
then over at the dead man's friend, who　　　　　　　　　70

was bawling and blubbering, what they would
call hysteria in a woman. "It isn't possible"
he wailed, but it was possible, it was
indeed, accomplished and unfeeling, snoring   75
in its peacoat, and without its levis on.
He died laughing: that's a fact.

I had a woman waiting for me,
in her car and in the middle of the bridge,
I'm frightened, I said,   80
I'm afraid, he said, stay with me,
please don't go, stay with me, be
my witness—"No," I said, "I'll be your
witness—later," and I took his name
and number, "but I can't stay with you,   85
I'm too frightened of the bridge, besides
I have a woman waiting
and no license—
and no tail lights—"
So I left—   90
as I have left so many of my lovers.

we drove home
shaking, Wendy's face greyer
than any white person's I have ever seen.
maybe he beat his wife, maybe he once   95
drove taxi, and raped a lover
of mine—how to know these things?
we do each other in, that's a fact.

who will be my witness?
death wastes our time with drunkenness   100
and depression
death, who keeps us from our
lovers.
he had a woman waiting for him,
I found out when I called the number   105
days later

"Where is he" she said, "he's disappeared."
He'll be all right" I said, "*we* could
have hit the guy as easy as anybody, it
wasn't anybody's fault, they'll know that,"   110
women so often say dumb things like that,

they teach us to be sweet and reassuring,
and say ignorant things, because we don't invent
the crime, the punishment, the bridges

that same week I looked into the mirror   115
and nobody was there to testify,
how clear, an unemployed queer woman
makes no witness at all,
nobody at all was there for
those two questions: what does   120
she do, and who is she married to?

I am the woman who stopped on the bridge
and this is the man who was there
our lovers teeth are white geese flying
above us, but we ourselves are   125
easily squished.

keep the women small and weak
and off the street, and off the
bridges, that's the way, brother
one day I will leave you there,   130
as I have left you there before,
working for death.

we found out later
what we left him to.
Six big policemen answered the call,   135
all white, and no child *in* them.
they put the driver up against his car
and beat the hell out of him.
What did you kill that poor kid for?
you mutherfucking nigger.   140
that's a fact.

Death only uses violence
when there is any kind of resistance,
the rest of the time a slow
weardown will do.   145

They took him to 4 different hospitals
til they got a drunk test report to fit their
case, and held him five days in jail
without a phone call.

how many lovers have we left.   150

there are as many contradictions to the game,
as there are players.
a woman is talking to death,
though talk is cheap, and life takes a long time
to make   155
right. He got a cheesy lawyer
who had him cop a plea, 15 to 20
instead of life
Did I say life?

the arrogant young man who thought he   160
owned the bridge, and fell asleep on it
he died laughing: that's a fact.
the driver sits out his time
off the street somewhere,
does he have the most vacant of   165
eyes, will he die laughing?

Two

They don't have to lynch the women anymore

death sits on my doorstep
cleaning his revolver   170
death cripples my feet and sends me out
to wait for the bus alone,
then comes by driving a taxi.

the woman on our block with 6 young children
has the most vacant of eyes   175
death sits in her bedroom, loading
his revolver

they don't have to lynch the women
very often anymore, although
they used to—the lord and his men   180
went through the villages at night, beating &
killing every woman caught
outdoors.
the European witch trials took away
the independent people; two different villages   185

—after the trials were through that year—
had left in them, each—
one living woman:
one

What were those other women up to? had they   190
run over someone? stopped on the wrong bridge?
did they have teeth like
any kind of geese, or children
in them?

Three

This woman is a lesbian be careful   195

In the military hospital where I worked
as a nurse's aide, the walls of the halls
were lined with howling women
waiting to deliver   200
or to have some parts removed.
One of the big private rooms contained
the general's wife, who needed
a wart taken off her nose.
we were instructed to give her special attention   205
not because of her wart or her nose
but because of her husband, the general.

as many women as men die, and that's a fact.

At work there was one friendly patient, already
claimed, a young woman burnt apart with X-ray,   210
she had long white tubes instead of openings;
rectum, bladder, vagina—I combed her hair, it
was my job, but she took care of me as if
nobody's touch could spoil her.

ho ho death, ho death   215
have you seen the twinkle in the dead woman's eye?

when you are a nurse's aide
someone suddenly notices you
and yells about the patient's bed,
and tears the sheets apart so you   220

can do it over, and over
while the patient waits
doubled over in her pain
for you to make the bed *again*
and no one ever looks at you,   225
only at what you do not do
Here, general, hold this soldier's bed pan
for a moment, hold it for a year—
then we'll promote you to making his bed.
we believe you wouldn't make such messes   230

if you had to clean up after them.

that's a fantasy.
this woman is a lesbian, be careful.

When I was arrested and being thrown out
of the military, the order went out: dont anybody   235
speak to this woman, and for those three
long months, almost nobody did; the dayroom, when
I entered it, fell silent til I had gone; they
were afraid, they knew the wind would blow
them over the rail, the cops would come,   240
the water would run into their lungs.
Everything I touched
was spoiled. They were my lovers, those
women, but nobody had taught us to swim.
I drowned, I took 3 or 4 others down   245
when I signed the confession of what we
had done   together.

No one will ever speak to me again.

I read this somewhere; I wasn't there:
in WW II the US army had invented some floating   250
amphibian tanks, and took them over to
the coast of Europe to unload them,
the landing ships all drawn up in a fleet,
and everybody watching. Each tank had a
crew of 6 and there were 25 tanks.   255
The first went down the landing planks
and sank, the second, the third, the
fourth, the fifth, the sixth went down
and sank. They weren't supposed
to sink, the engineers had   260

made a mistake. The crews looked around
wildly for the order to quit,
but none came, and in the sight of
thousands of men, each 6 crewmen
saluted his officers, battened down   265
his hatch in turn and drove into the
sea, and drowned, until all 25 tanks
were gone. did they have vacant
eyes, die laughing, or what? what
did they talk about, those men,   270
as the water came in?

was the general their lover?

Four

A Mock Interrogation

Have you ever held hands with a woman?   275

Yes, many times—women about to deliver, women about to
have breasts removed, wombs removed, miscarriages, women
having epileptic fits, having asthma, cancer, women having
breast bone marrow sucked out of them by nervous or indifferent interns, women with heart condition, who were   280
vomiting, overdosed, depressed, drunk, lonely to the point
of extinction: women who had been run over, beaten up,
deserted, starved. women who had been bitten by rats; and
women who were happy, who were celebrating, who were
dancing with me in large circles or alone, women who were   285
climbing mountains or up and down walls, or trucks or roofs
and needed a boost up, or I did; women who simply wanted
to hold my hand because they liked me, some women who
wanted to hold my hand because they liked me better than
anyone.   290

These were many women?

Yes. many.

What about kissing? Have you kissed any women?

I have kissed many women.

When was the first woman you kissed with serious feeling?   295

The first woman ever I kissed was Josie, who I had loved at
such a distance for months. Josie was not only beautiful,
she was tough and handsome too. Josie had black hair and
white teeth and strong brown muscles. Then she dropped
out of school unexplained. When she came back she came   300
back for one day only, to finish the term, and there was a
child in her. She was all shame, pain, and defiance. Her eyes
were dark as the water under a bridge and no one would
talk to her, they laughed and threw things at her. In the
afternoon I walked across the front of the class and looked   305
deep into Josie's eyes and I picked up her chin with my
hand, because I loved her, because nothing like her trouble
would ever happen to me, because I hated it that she was
pregnant and unhappy, and an outcast. We were thirteen.

You didn't kiss her?   310

How does it feel to be thirteen and having a baby?

You didn't actually kiss her?

Not in fact.

You have kissed other women?

Yes, many, some of the finest women I know, I have kissed.   315
women who were lonely, women I didn't know and didn't
want to, but kissed because that was a way to say yes we are
still alive and loveable, though separate, women who recognized
a loneliness in me, women who were hurt, I confess to
kissing the top of a 55 year old woman's head in the snow in   320
Boston, who was hurt more deeply than I have ever been
hurt, and I wanted her as a very few people have wanted
me—I wanted her and me to own and control and run the
city we lived in, to staff the hospital I knew would mistreat
her, to drive the transportation system that had betrayed   325
her, to patrol the streets controlling the men who would
murder or disfigure or disrupt us, not accidently with
machines, but on purpose, because we are not allowed out
on the street alone—

Have you ever committed any indecent acts with women?   330

Yes, many. I am guilty of allowing suicidal women to die
before my eyes or in my ears or under my hands because I
thought I could do nothing, I am guilty of leaving a prostitute
who held a knife to my friend's throat to keep us from
leaving, because we would not sleep with her, we thought   335
she was old and fat and ugly; I am guilty of not loving her
who needed me; I regret all the women I have not slept with
or comforted, who pulled themselves away from me for lack
of something I had not the courage to fight for, for us, our
life, our planet, our city, our meat and potatoes, our love.   340
These are indecent acts, lacking courage, lacking a certain
fire behind the eyes, which is the symbol, the raised fist, the
sharing of resources, the resistance that tells death he will
starve for lack of the fat of us, our extra. Yes I have committed
acts of indecency with women and most of them were   345
acts of omission. I regret them bitterly.

Five

Bless this day oh cat our house

"I was allowed to go
3 places, growing up," she said—   350
"3 places, no more.
there was a straight line from my house
to school, a straight line from my house
to church, a straight line from my house
to the corner store."   355
her parents thought something might happen to her.
but nothing ever did.

my lovers teeth are white geese flying above me
my lovers muscles are rope ladders under my hands
we are the river of life and the fat of the land   360
death, do you tell me I cannot touch this woman?

if we use each other up
on each other
that's a little bit less for you
a little bit less for you, ho   365
death, ho ho death.

Bless this day oh cat our house
help me be not such a mouse

death tells the woman to stay home
and then breaks in the window.   370

I read this somewhere, I wasn't there:
In feudal Europe, if a woman committed adultery
her husband would sometimes tie her
down, catch a mouse and trap it
under a cup on her bare belly, until   375
it gnawed itself out, now are you
afraid of mice?

Six

Dressed as I am, a young man once called
me names in Spanish   380

a woman who talks to death
is a dirty traitor

inside a hamburger joint and
dressed as I am, a young man once called me
names in Spanish   385
then he called me queer and slugged me.
first I thought the ceiling had fallen down
but there was the counterman making a ham
sandwich, and there was I spread out on his
counter.   390

For God's sake I said when
I could talk, this guy is beating me up
can't you call the police or something,
can't you stop him? he looked up from
working on his sandwich, which was *my*   395
sandwich, I had ordered it. He liked
the way I looked. "There's a pay phone
right across the street" he said.

I couldn't listen to the Spanish language
for weeks afterward, without feeling the   400
most murderous of urges, the simple
association of one thing to another,
so damned simple.

The next day I went to the police station
to become an outraged citizen.   405
Six big policemen stood in the hall,
all white and dressed as they do
they were well pleased with my story, pleased
at what had gotten beat out of me, so
I left them laughing, went home fast   410
and locked my door.
For several nights I fantasized the scene
again, this time grabbing a chair
and smashing it over the bastard's head,
killing him. I called him a spic, and   415
killed him. My face healed, his didn't
no child *in* me.

now when I remember I think:
maybe *he* was Josie's baby.
all the chickens come home to roost,   420
all of them.

Seven

Death and disfiguration

One Christmas eve my lovers and I
we left the bar, driving home slow   425
there was a woman lying in the snow
by the side of the road. She was wearing
a bathrobe and no shoes, where were
her shoes? she had turned the snow
pink, under her feet. she was an Asian   430
woman, didn't speak much English, but
she said a taxi driver beat her up
and raped her, throwing her out of his
car.

what on earth was she doing there   435
on a street she helped to pay for
but doesn't own?
doesn't she know to stay home?

I am a pervert, therefore I've learned
to keep my hands to myself in public   440
but I was so drunk that night,

I actually did something loving
I took her in my arms, this woman,
until she could breathe right, and
my friends who are perverts too   445
they touched her too
we all touched her.
"You're going to be all right"
we lied. She started to cry
"I'm 55 years old" she said   450
and that said everything.

Six big policemen answered the call
no child *in* them.
they seemed afraid to touch her,
then grabbed her like a corpse and heaved her   455
on their metal stretcher into the van
crashing and clumsy.
She was more frightened than before.
they were cold and bored.
'don't leave me' she said.   460
'she'll be all right' they said.
we left, as we have left all of our lovers
as all lovers leave all lovers
much too soon to get the real loving done.

Eight

a mock interrogation   465

Why did you get into the cab with him, dressed as you are?

I wanted to go somewhere.

Did you know what the cab driver might do
if you got into the cab with him?   470

I just wanted to go somewhere.

How many times did you
get into the cab with him?

I dont remember.

If you dont remember, how do you know it happened to you?   475

Nine

Hey you death

ho and ho poor death
our lovers teeth are white geese flying above us   480
our lovers muscles are rope ladders under our hands
even though no women yet go down to the sea in ships
except in their dreams.

only the arrogant invent a quick and meaningful end
for themselves, of their own choosing.   485
everyone else knows how very slow it happens
how the woman's existence bleeds out her years,
how the child shoots up at ten and is arrested and old
how the man carries a murderous shell within him
and passes it on.   490

we are the fat of the land, and
we all have our list of casualties

to my lovers I bequeath
the rest of my life

I want nothing left of me for you, ho death   495
except some fertilizer
for the next batch of us
who do not hold hands with you
who do not embrace you
who try not to work for you   500
or sacrifice themselves or trust
or believe you, ho ignorant
death, how do you know
we happened to you?

wherever our meat hangs on our own bones   505
for our own use
your pot is so empty

death, ho death
you shall be poor

Study and Discussion Questions

1. Consider each of the nine sections of this long narrative poem:
   a. What is the "plot" of each section?
   b. Who are the characters in each section? What is the point of view in each section?
   c. What are the major images in each section?
   d. What are the main themes or issues in each section?
   e. Discuss how images, issues/themes, and characters recur from one section to another.
   f. Collectively, what is the effect of this piling up of images and events?
2. "My lover's teeth are white geese flying above me/ My lover's muscles are rope ladders under my hands"—what do these images suggest to you? What is the significance of their repetition throughout the poem?
3. What do the "six big policemen . . . all white" who appear throughout the poem, symbolize? What does the speaker mean when she says "no child *in* them"?
4. What purpose is served by the repeated use of the phrase "that's a fact"? By the use of the phrase "that's a fantasy" in section Three?
5. At the end of section Three, Grahn tells a story of 150 crewmen in amphibian tanks following orders and dying. Discuss this anecdote in relation to other historical accounts in sections Two and Five.
7. What choices do the characters within "A Woman Is Talking to Death" have? Give specific examples.
8. Discuss the interrogations in sections Four and Eight. Who is conducting the interrogations? Who is being interrogated? What change or development do you see in the narrator's responses between Four and Eight?
9. In the preface to "A Woman Is Talking to Death," Judy Grahn said that a challenge she faced with this poem was "how to discuss the criss-cross oppressions which people use against each other and which continually divide us—and how to define a lesbian life within the context of other people in the world." How does Grahn define and discuss these criss-cross oppressions specifically in the poem? Give examples.
10. Who/What is "death"? In section Nine, what is the speaker saying to death? What acts in this poem work against death? What acts work for death?
11. How does Grahn redefine in "A Woman is Talking to Death" the following concepts: courage/heroism; indecency/sin; responsibility/accountability; love and lover; witness? Point to a scene or passage is which any of these redefinitions is going on and discuss.
12. What are the specific issues that are being protested in this poem? What does "A Woman Is Talking to Death" have to say about the *process* of protest?

Suggestions for Writing

1. In her preface to "A Woman Is Talking to Death," Judy Grahn says that she did not realize when she began to write the poem that "I was also taking up the subject of heroes in a modern life which for many people is

more like a war than not, or that I would begin a redefinition for myself of the subject of love." Write a paper exploring how Grahn redefines in this poem one of the concepts listed in question 11 in the Study and Discussion Questions.

2. How does the persona/narrator of the poem begin to move out from herself to include others in her concern? Would you see "A Woman Is Talking to Death" as ultimately a poem about the power of connecting to other people? Argue for or against, citing evidence from the poem.

3. Pick one episode/story/anecdote from "A Woman Is Talking to Death" and discuss its function in the poem as a whole.

Critical Resources

1. Avi-ram, Amitai. "The Politics of the Refrain in Judy Grahn's 'A Woman is Talking to Death.'" *Women and Language* 10.2 (1987): 38–43.

2. Backus, Margot Gayle. "Judy Grahn and the Lesbian Elegy: Testimonial and Prophetic Responses to Social Death in 'A Woman is Talking to Death.'" *Journal of Women in Culture and Society* 18.4 (1993): 815–37.

3. Whitehead, Kim. *The Feminist Poetry Movement,* Jackson, Miss.: University Press of Mississippi, 1996.

Additional Poems

WALT WHITMAN (1819–1892)

To The States   (1860)

To The States or any of them, or any city of The States, *Resist much, obey little,*
Once unquestioning obedience, once fully enslaved,
Once fully enslaved, no nation, state, city, of this earth, ever afterward resumes its liberty.

JOHN GREENLEAF WHITTIER (1807–1892)

For Righteousness' Sake   (1855)

Inscribed to friends under arrest for treason against the slave power.

The age is dull and mean. Men creep,
Not walk; with blood too pale and tame

To pay the debt they owe to shame;
Buy cheap, sell dear; eat, drink, and sleep
Down-pillowed, deaf to moaning want;   5
Pay tithes for soul-insurance; keep
    Six days to Mammon, one to Cant.

In such a time, give thanks to God,
    That somewhat of the holy rage
With which the prophets in their age   10
On all its decent seemings trod,
    Has set your feet upon the lie,
That man and ox and soul and clod
    Are market stock to sell and buy!

The hot words from your lips, my own,   15
    To caution trained, might not repeat;
    But if some tares among the wheat
Of generous thought and deed were sown,
    No common wrong provoked your zeal;
The silken gauntlet that is thrown   20
    In such a quarrel rings like steel.

The brave old strife the fathers saw
    For Freedom calls for men again
    Like those who battled not in vain
For England's Charter, Alfred's law,[1]   25
    And right of speech and trial just
Wage in your name their ancient war
    With venal courts and perjured trust.

God's ways seem dark, but, soon or late,
    They touch the shining hills of day;   30
    The evil cannot brook delay,
The good can well afford to wait.
    Give ermined knaves their hour of crime;
Ye have the future grand and great,
    The safe appeal of Truth to Time!   35

---

[1]The Magna Carta (1215), charter of English liberties; Alfred the Great (849–899),
King of Wessex, instituted many reforms.

PAUL LAURENCE DUNBAR (1872–1906)

We Wear the Mask   (1896)

We wear the mask that grins and lies,
It hides our cheeks and shades our eyes,—
This debt we pay to human guile;
With torn and bleeding hearts we smile,
And mouth with myriad subtleties.   5

Why should the world be overwise,
In counting all our tears and sighs?
Nay, let them only see us, while
    We wear the mask.

We smile, but, O great Christ, our cries   10
To thee from tortured souls arise.
We sing, but oh the clay is vile
Beneath our feet, and long the mile;
But let the world dream otherwise,
    We wear the mask!   15

RALPH CHAPLIN (1887–1961)

SONG: *Solidarity Forever*   (1915)

When the union's inspiration through the workers' blood shall run,
There can be no power greater anywhere beneath the sun.
Yet what force on earth is weaker than the feeble strength of one?
But the union makes us strong.

Refrain: Solidarity forever!   5
                   Solidarity forever!
                   Solidarity forever!
                   For the union makes us strong.

Is there aught we hold in common with the greedy parasite
Who would lash us into serfdom and would crush us with his might?   10
Is there anything left for us but to organize and fight?
For the union makes us strong.

It is we who plowed the prairies; built the cities where they trade;
Dug the mines and built the workshops; endless miles of railroad laid.
Now we stand, outcast and starving, 'mid the wonders we have made;   15
But the union makes us strong.

All the world that's owned by idle drones, is ours and ours alone.
We have laid the wide foundations; built it skyward stone by stone.
It is ours, not to slave in, but to master and to own,
While the union makes us strong.   20

They have taken untold millions that they never toiled to earn.
But without our brain and muscle not a single wheel can turn.
We can break their haughty power; gain our freedom while we learn
That the union makes us strong.

In our hands is placed a power greater than their hoarded gold;   25
Greater than the might of armies, magnified a thousand-fold.
We can bring to birth the new world from the ashes of the old,
For the union makes us strong.

CLAUDE McKAY (1890–1948)

If We Must Die   (1922)

If we must die, let it not be like hogs
Hunted and penned in an inglorious spot,
While round us bark the mad and hungry dogs,
Making their mock at our accursed lot.
If we must die, O let us nobly die,   5
So that our precious blood may not be shed
In vain; then even the monsters we defy
Shall be constrained to honor us though dead!
O kinsmen! we must meet the common foe!
Though far outnumbered let us show us brave,   10
And for their thousand blows deal one deathblow!
What though before us lies the open grave?
Like men we'll face the murderous, cowardly pack,
Pressed to the wall, dying, but fighting back!

e. e. cummings (1894–1962)

i sing of Olaf glad and big   (1935)

i sing of Olaf glad and big
whose warmest heart recoiled at war:
a conscientious object-or

his wellbelovéd colonel(trig
westpointer most succinctly bred)   5
took erring Olaf soon in hand;
but—though an host of overjoyed
noncoms(first knocking on the head
him)do through icy waters roll
that helplessness which others stroke   10
with brushes recently employed
anent this muddy toiletbowl,
while kindred intellects evoke
allegiance per blunt instruments—
Olaf(being to all intents   15
a corpse and wanting any rag
upon what God unto him gave)
responds, without getting annoyed
"I will not kiss your fucking flag"

straightway the silver bird looked grave   20
(departing hurriedly to shave)
but—though all kinds of officers
(a yearning nation's blueeyed pride)
their passive prey did kick and curse
until for wear their clarion   25
voices and boots were much the worse,
and egged the firstclassprivates on
his rectum wickedly to tease
by means of skilfully applied
bayonets roasted hot with heat—   30
Olaf(upon what were once knees)
does almost ceaselessly repeat
"there is some shit I will not eat"

our president, being of which
assertions duly notified   35
threw the yellowsonofabitch
into a dungeon, where he died

Christ(of His mercy infinite)
i pray to see; and Olaf,too

preponderatingly because   40
unless statistics lie he was
more brave than me:more blond than you.

PABLO NERUDA (1904–1973)

Ode to Federico García Lorca[1]   (1935)

Translated by Donald D. Walsh

If I could weep with fear in a solitary house,
if I could take out my eyes and eat them,
I would do it for your black-draped orange-tree voice
and for your poetry that comes forth shouting.

Because for you they paint hospitals bright blue,   5
and schools and sailors' quarters grow,
and wounded angels are covered with feathers,
and nuptial fish are covered with scales,
and hedgehogs go flying to the sky:
for you tailorshops with their black skins   10
fill up with spoons and blood,
and swallow red ribbons and kiss each other to death,
and dress in white.

When you fly dressed as a peach tree,
when you laugh with a laugh of hurricaned rice,   15
when to sing you shake arteries and teeth,
throat and fingers,
I could die for how sweet you are,
I could die for the red lakes
where in the midst of autumn you live   20
with a fallen steed and a bloodied god,
I could die for the cemeteries
that pass like ash-gray rivers
with water and tombs,

---

[1]Spanish poet and playwright (1899–1936), executed by the Fascists during the Spanish Civil War.

at night, among drowned bells: 25
rivers as thick as wards
of sick soldiers, that suddenly grow
toward death in rivers with marble numbers
and rotted crowns, and funeral oils:
I could die to see you at night 30
watching the sunken crosses go by,
standing and weeping,
because before death's river you weep
forlornly, woundedly,
you weep weeping, your eyes filled 35
with tears, with tears, with tears.

If at night, wildly alone, I could
gather oblivion and shadow and smoke
above railroads and steamships,
with a black funnel, 40
biting the ashes,
I would do it for the tree in which you grow,
for the nests of golden waters that you gather,
and for the vine that covers your bones,
revealing to you the secret of the night. 45

Cities with a smell of wet onions
wait for you to pass singing raucously,
and silent sperm boats pursue you,
and green swallows nest in your hair,
and also snails and weeks, 50
furled masts and cherry trees
definitively walk about when they glimpse
your pale fifteen-eyed head
and your mouth of submerged blood.

If I could fill town halls with soot 55
and, sobbing, tear down clocks,
it would be to see when to your house
comes summer with its broken lips,
come many people with dying clothes,
come regions of sad splendor, 60
come dead plows and poppies,
come gravediggers and horsemen,
come planets and maps with blood,
come owls covered with ashes,
come masked men dragging damsels 65
pierced by great knives,

come roots, veins, hospitals,
springs, ants,
comes night with the bed where
a solitary hussar is dying among the spiders, 70
comes a rose of hatred and pins,
comes a yellowish vessel,
comes a windy day with a child,
come I with Oliverio, Norah,
Vicente Aleixandre, Delia, 75
Maruca, Malva, Marina, María Luisa, and Larco,
the Blond, Rafael, Ugarte,
Cotapos, Rafael Alberti,
Carlos, Bebé, Manolo Altolaguirre,
Molinari, 80
Rosales, Concha Méndez,
and others that slip my mind.

Come, let me crown you, youth of health
and butterflies, youth pure
as a black lightningflash perpetually free, 85
and just between you and me,
now, when there is no one left among the rocks,
let us speak simply, man to man:
what are verses for if not for the dew?
What are verses for if not for that night 90
in which a bitter dagger finds us out, for that day,
for that dusk, for that broken corner
where the beaten heart of man makes ready to die?

Above all at night,
at night there are many stars, 95
all within a river
like a ribbon next to the windows
of houses filled with the poor.

Someone of theirs has died, perhaps
they have lost their jobs in the offices, 100
in the hospitals, in the elevators,
in the mines,
human beings suffer stubbornly wounded
and there are protests and weeping everywhere:
while the stars flow within an endless river 105
there is much weeping at the windows,
the thresholds are worn away by the weeping,
the bedrooms are soaked by the weeping

that comes wave-shaped to bite the carpets.

Federico,   110
you see the world, the streets,
the vinegar,
the farewells in the stations
when the smoke lifts its decisive wheels
toward where there is nothing but some   115
separations, stones, railroad tracks.

There are so many people asking questions
everywhere.
There is the bloody blindman, and the angry one, and the
disheartened one,   120
and the wretch, the thorn tree,
the bandit with envy on his back.

That's the way life is, Federico, here you have
the things that my friendship can offer you,
the friendship of a melancholy manly man.   125
By yourself you already know many things,
and others you will slowly get to know.

W. H. AUDEN (1907–1973)

The Unknown Citizen   (1940)

(To JS/07/M/378
This Marble Monument
Is Erected by the State)

He was found by the Bureau of Statistics to be
One against whom there was no official complaint,
And all the reports on his conduct agree
That, in the modern sense of an old-fashioned word, he was a saint,
For in everything he did he served the Greater Community.   5
Except for the War till the day he retired
He worked in a factory and never got fired,
But satisfied his employers, Fudge Motors Inc.
Yet he wasn't a scab or odd in his views,
For his Union reports that he paid his dues,   10

(Our report on his Union shows it was sound)
And our Social Psychology workers found
That he was popular with his mates and liked a drink.
The Press are convinced that he bought a paper every day
And that his reactions to advertisements were normal in every way.   15
Policies taken out in his name prove that he was fully insured,
And his Health-card shows he was once in hospital but left it cured.
Both Producers Research and High-Grade Living declare
He was fully sensible to the advantages of the Instalment Plan
And had everything necessary to the Modern Man,   20
A phonograph, a radio, a car and a frigidaire.
Our researchers into Public Opinion are content
That he held the proper opinions for the time of year;
When there was peace, he was for peace; when there was war, he went.
He was married and added five children to the population,   25
Which our Eugenist says was the right number for a parent of his generation,
And our teachers report that he never interfered with their education.
Was he free? Was he happy? The question is absurd:
Had anything been wrong, we should certainly have heard.

ROBERT HAYDEN (1913–1980)

Frederick Douglass[1]   (1947)

When it is finally ours, this freedom, this liberty, this beautiful
and terrible thing, needful to man as air,
usable as earth; when it belongs at last to all,
when it is truly instinct, brain matter, diastole, systole,
reflex action; when it is finally won; when it is more   5
than the gaudy mumbo jumbo of politicians:
this man, this Douglass, this former slave, this Negro
beaten to his knees, exiled, visioning a world
where none is lonely, none hunted, alien,
this man, superb in love and logic, this man   10
shall be remembered. Oh, not with statues' rhetoric,

---

[1]Escaped slave, abolitionist, writer (1817?–1895).

not with legends and poems and wreaths of bronze alone,
but with the lives grown out of his life, the lives
fleshing his dream of the beautiful, needful thing.

LANGSTON HUGHES (1902–1967)

Harlem   (1951)

What happens to a dream deferred?

> Does it dry up
> like a raisin in the sun?
> Or fester like a sore—
> And then run?   5
> Does it stink like rotten meat?
> Or crust and sugar over—
> like a syrupy sweet?

> Maybe it just sags
> like a heavy load.   10

> *Or does it explode?*

WOLE SOYINKA (b. 1934)

Telephone Conversation   (1960)

The price seemed reasonable, location
Indifferent. The landlady swore she lived
Off premises. Nothing remained
But self-confession. 'Madam,' I warned,
'I hate a wasted journey—I am African.'   5
Silence. Silenced transmission of
Pressurized good-breeding. Voice, when it came,
Lipstick coated, long gold-rolled
Cigarette-holder pipped. Caught I was, foully.
'HOW DARK?' . . . I had not misheard . . . 'ARE YOU LIGHT   10
OR VERY DARK?' Button B. Button A. Stench
Of rancid breath of public hide-and-speak.
Red booth. Red pillar-box. Red double-tiered

Omnibus squelching tar. It *was* real! Shamed
By ill-mannered silence, surrender   15
Pushed dumbfoundment to beg simplification.
Considerate she was, varying the emphasis—
'ARE YOU DARK? OR VERY LIGHT?' Revelation came.
'You mean—like plain or milk chocolate?'
Her assent was clinical, crushing in its light   20
Impersonality. Rapidly, wave-length adjusted,
I chose. 'West African sepia'—and as afterthought,
'Down in my passport.' Silence for spectroscopic
Flight of fancy, till truthfulness clanged her accent
Hard on the mouthpiece. 'WHAT'S THAT?' conceding   25
'DON'T KNOW WHAT THAT IS.' 'Like brunette.'
'THAT'S DARK, ISN'T IT?' 'Not altogether.
Facially, I am brunette, but madam, you should see
The rest of me. Palm of my hand, soles of my feet
Are a peroxide blonde. Friction, caused—   30
Foolishly madam—by sitting down, has turned
My bottom raven black—One moment madam!'—sensing
Her receiver rearing on the thunderclap
About my ears—'Madam,' I pleaded, 'wouldn't you rather
See for yourself?'   35

RAY DUREM (1915–1963)

To the pale poets   (1962)

I know I'm not sufficiently obscure
to please the critics, nor devious enough.
Imagery escapes me.
I cannot find those mild and precious words
to clothe the carnage.   5
Blood is blood and murder's murder.
What's a lavender word for lynch?

Come, you pale poets, wan, refined, and dreamy—
here is a black woman working out her guts
in a white man's kitchen   10
for little money and no glory.
How should I tell that story?
There is a black boy, blacker still from death,
face down in the cold Korean mud.

Come on with your effervescent jive,   15
explain to him why he ain't alive.

Reword our specific discontent
into some plaintive melody,
a little whine, a little whimper,
not too much—and no rebellion,   20
God, no! Rebellion's much too corny.
You deal with finer feelings,
very subtle—an autumn leaf
hanging from a tree—
I see a body.   25

PEGGY SEEGER (b. 1935)

SONG: *I'm Gonna Be an Engineer*   (1970)

When I was a little girl, I wished I was a boy,
I tagged along behind the gang and wore my corduroys,
Everybody said I only did it to annoy
But I was gonna be an engineer.

Mamma told me, "Can't you be a lady?   5
Your duty is to make me the mother of a pearl.
Wait until you're older, dear, and maybe
You'll be glad that you're a girl."

DAINTY AS A DRESDEN STATUE.
GENTLE AS A JERSEY COW.   10
SMOOTH AS SILK, GIVES CREAMY MILK
LEARN TO COO, LEARN TO MOO,
THAT'S WHAT YOU DO TO BE A LADY NOW—

When I went to school I learned to write and how to read,
Some history, geography, and home economy.   15
And typing is a skill that every girl is sure to need,
To while away the extra time until the time to breed,
And then they had the nerve to say, "What would you like to be?"
I says, "I'm gonna be an engineer!"
    No, you only need to learn to be a lady,   20
    The duty isn't yours for to try and run the world,

An engineer could never have a baby!
Remember, dear, that you're a girl.

SHE'S SMART (FOR A WOMAN).
I WONDER HOW SHE GOT THAT WAY?   25
YOU GET NO CHOICE, YOU GET NO VOICE,
JUST STAY MUM, PRETEND YOU'RE DUMB
AND THAT'S HOW YOU COME TO BE A LADY TODAY—

Then Jimmy come along and we set up a conjugation,
We were busy every night with loving recreation.   30
I spent my day at work so HE could get his education,
Well, now he's an engineer.
 He says, "I know you'll always be a lady,
 It's the duty of my darling to love me all her life,
 Could an *engineer* look after or obey me?   35
 Remember, dear, that you're my wife."

Well, as soon as Jimmy got a job, I began again,
Then, happy at my turret-lathe a year or so, and then:
The morning that the twins were born, Jimmy says to them,
"Kids, your mother *was* an engineer."   40
 You owe it to the kids to be a lady,
 Dainty as a dishrag, faithful as a chow,
 Stay at home, you got to mind the baby,
 Remember you're a mother now.

Well, every time I turn around it's something else to do,   45
It's cook a meal, mend a sock, sweep a floor or two,
I listen in to Jimmy Young, it makes me want to spew,
I WAS GONNA BE AN ENGINEER!
 Don't I really wish that I could be a lady?
 I could do the lovely things that a lady's 'sposed to do,   50
 I wouldn't even mind, if only they would pay me,
 And I could be a person too.

WHAT PRICE—FOR A WOMAN?
YOU CAN BUY HER FOR A RING OF GOLD.
TO LOVE AND OBEY (WITHOUT ANY PAY)   55
YOU GET A COOK AND A NURSE (FOR BETTER OR WORSE)
YOU DON'T NEED A PURSE WHEN THE LADY IS SOLD.

Ah, but now that times are harder and my Jimmy's got the sack,
I went down to Vickers', they were glad to have me back,

But I'm a third-class citizen, my wages tell me that,   60
And I'm a first-class engineer.
 The boss he says, "We pay you as a lady,
 You only got the job 'cause I can't afford a man,
 With you I keep the profits high as may be,
 You're just a cheaper pair of hands."   65

YOU GOT ONE FAULT—YOU'RE A WOMAN.
YOU'RE NOT WORTH THE EQUAL PAY.
A BITCH OR A TART, YOU'RE NOTHNG BUT HEART,
SHALLOW AND VAIN, YOU GOT NO BRAIN,
YOU EVEN GO DOWN THE DRAIN LIKE A LADY TODAY—   70

Well, I listened to my mother and I joined a typing-pool,
I listened to my lover and I put him through his school,
But if I listen to the boss, I'm just a bloody fool
And an underpaid engineer!
 I been a sucker ever since I was a baby,   75
 As a daughter, as a wife, as a mother and a "dear"—
 But I'll fight them as a woman, not a lady,
 Fight them as an engineer!

MURIEL RUKEYSER (1913–1980)

Ballad of Orange and Grape   (1973)

After you finish your work
after you do your day
after you've read your reading
after you've written your say—
you go down the street to the hot dog stand,   5
one block down and across the way.
On a blistering afternoon in East Harlem in the twentieth
  century.

Most of the windows are boarded up,
the rats run out of a sack—   10
sticking out of the crummy garage
one shiny long Cadillac;
at the glass door of the drug-addiction center,
a man who'd like to break your back.

But here's a brown woman with a little girl dressed in rose and   15
      pink, too.

Frankfurters frankfurters sizzle on the steel
where the hot-dog-man leans—
nothing else on the counter
but the usual two machines,   20
the grape one, empty, and the orange one, empty,
I face him in between.
A black boy comes along, looks at the hot dogs, goes on
      walking.

I watch the man as he stands and pours   25
in the familiar shape
bright purple in the one marked ORANGE
orange in the one marked GRAPE,
the grape drink in the machine marked ORANGE
and orange drink in the GRAPE.   30
Just the one word large and clear, unmistakable, on each
      machine.

I ask him: How can we go on reading
and make sense out of what we read?—
How can they write and believe what they're writing,   35
the young ones across the street,
while you go on pouring grape into ORANGE
and orange into the one marked GRAPE—?
(How are we going to believe what we read and we write and
      we hear and we say and we do?)   40

He looks at the two machines and he smiles
and he shrugs and smiles and pours again.
It could be violence and nonviolence
it could be white and black women and men
it could be war and peace or any   45
binary system, love and hate, enemy, friend.
Yes and no, be and not-be, what we do and what we don't do.

On a corner in East Harlem
garbage, reading, a deep smile, rape,
forgetfulness, a hot street of murder,   50
misery, withered hope,
a man keeps pouring grape into ORANGE
and orange into the one marked GRAPE,
pouring orange into GRAPE and grape into ORANGE forever.

SYLVIA PLATH (1932–1963)

Daddy   (1962)

You do not do, you do not do
Any more, black shoe
In which I have lived like a foot
For thirty years, poor and white,
Barely daring to breathe or Achoo.   5

Daddy, I have had to kill you.
You died before I had time—
Marble-heavy, a bag full of God,
Ghastly statue with one gray toe
Big as a Frisco seal   10

And a head in the freakish Atlantic
Where it pours bean green over blue
In the waters off beautiful Nauset.[1]
I used to pray to recover you.
Ach, du.   15

In the German tongue, in the Polish town
Scraped flat by the roller
Of wars, wars, wars.
But the name of the town is common.
My Polack friend   20

Says there are a dozen or two.
So I never could tell where you
Put your foot, your root,
I never could talk to you.
The tongue stuck in my jaw.   25

It stuck in a barb wire snare.
Ich, ich, ich, ich,[2]
I could hardly speak.
I thought every German was you.
And the language obscene   30

---

[1]A beach on Cape Cod, Massachusetts.
[2]"I" in German.

An engine, an engine
Chuffing me off like a Jew.
A Jew to Dachau, Auschwitz, Belsen.
I began to talk like a Jew.
I think I may well be a Jew.   35

The snows of the Tyrol, the clear beer of Vienna
Are not very pure or true.
With my gipsy ancestress and my weird luck
And my Taroc[3] pack and my Taroc pack
I may be a bit of a Jew.   40

I have always been scared of *you,*
With your Luftwaffe, your gobbledygoo.
And your neat mustache
And your Aryan eye, bright blue.
Panzer-man, panzer-man, O You—   45

Not God but a swastika
So black no sky could squeak through.
Every woman adores a Fascist,
The boot in the face, the brute
Brute heart of a brute like you.   50

You stand at the blackboard, daddy,
In the picture I have of you,
A cleft in your chin instead of your foot
But no less a devil for that, no not
Any less the black man who   55

Bit my pretty red heart in two.
I was ten when they buried you.
At twenty I tried to die
And get back, back, back to you.
I thought even the bones would do.   60

But they pulled me out of the sack,
And they stuck me together with glue.
And then I knew what to do.
I made a model of you,
A man in black with a Meinkampf[4] look   65

---

[3]Tarot cards.
[4]*Mein Kampf* (1925), by Adolf Hitler, articulated his Nazi philosophy.

And a love of the rack and the screw.
And I said I do, I do.
So daddy, I'm finally through.
The black telephone's off at the root,
The voices just can't worm through.   70

If I've killed one man, I've killed two—
The vampire who said he was you
And drank my blood for a year,
Seven years, if you want to know.
Daddy, you can lie back now.   75

There's a stake in your fat black heart
And the villagers never liked you.
They are dancing and stamping on you.
They always *knew* it was you.
Daddy, daddy, you bastard, I'm through.   80

LINDA HOGAN (b. 1947)

Black Hills Survival Gathering, 1980[1]   (1981)

Bodies on fire
the monks in orange cloth
sing morning into light.

Men wake on the hill.
Dry grass blows from their hair.   5
B52's blow over their heads
leaving a cross on the ground.
Air returns to itself and silence.

Rainclouds are disappearing
with fractures of light in the distance.   10
Fierce gases forming,
the sky bending
where people arrive

---

[1]A protest by a group of Native Americans and environmentalists against development in the Black Hills of South Dakota.

on dusty roads that change
matter to energy.   15

My husband wakes.
My daughter wakes.
Quiet morning, she stands
in a pail of water
naked, reflecting light   20
and this man I love,
with kind hands
he washes her slim hips,
narrow shoulders, splashes
the skin containing   25
wind and fragile fire,
the pulse in her wrist.

My other daughter wakes
to comb warm sun across her hair.
While I make coffee I tell her   30
this is the land of her ancestors,
blood and heart.
Does her hair become a mane
blowing in the electric breeze,
her eyes dilate and darken?   35

The sun rises on all of them
in the center of light
hills that have no boundary,
the child named Thunder Horse,
the child named Dawn Protector   40
and the man
whose name would mean home in Navajo.

At ground zero
in the center of light we stand.
Bombs are buried beneath us,   45
destruction flies overhead.
We are waking
in the expanding light
the sulphur-colored grass.
A red horse standing on a distant ridge   50
looks like one burned
over Hiroshima,
silent, head hanging in sickness.
But look

she raises her head   55
and surges toward the bluing sky.

Radiant morning.
The dark tunnels inside us carry life.
Red.
Blue.   60
The children's dark hair against my breast.
On the burning hills
in flaring orange cloth
men are singing and drumming
Heartbeat.   65

JOY HARJO (b. 1951)

The Woman Hanging from the
Thirteenth Floor Window   (1983)

She is the woman hanging from the 13th floor
window. Her hands are pressed white against the
concrete moulding of the tenement building. She
hangs from the 13th floor window in east Chicago,
with a swirl of birds over her head. They could   5
be a halo, or a storm of glass waiting to crush her.

She thinks she will be set free.

The woman hanging from the 13th floor window
on the east side of Chicago is not alone.
She is a woman of children, of the baby, Carlos,   10
and of Margaret, and of Jimmy who is the oldest.
She is her mother's daughter and her father's son.
She is several pieces between the two husbands
she has had. She is all the women of the apartment
building who stand watching her, watching themselves.   15

When she was young she ate wild rice on scraped down
plates in warm wood rooms. It was in the farther
north and she was the baby then. They rocked her.

She sees Lake Michigan lapping at the shores of
herself. It is a dizzy hole of water and the rich   20

live in tall glass houses at the edge of it. In some
places Lake Michigan speaks softly, here, it just sputters
and butts itself against the asphalt. She sees
other buildings just like hers. She sees other
women hanging from many-floored windows   25
counting their lives in the palms of their hands
and in the palms of their children's hands.

She is the woman hanging from the 13th floor window
on the Indian side of town. Her belly is soft from
her children's births, her worn levis swing down below   30
her waist, and then her feet, and then her heart.
She is dangling.

The woman hanging from the 13th floor hears voices.
They come to her in the night when the lights have gone
dim. Sometimes they are little cats mewing and scratching   35
at the door, sometimes they are her grandmother's voice,
and sometimes they are gigantic men of light whispering
to her to get up, to get up, to get up. That's when she wants
to have another child to hold onto in the night, to be able
to fall back into dreams.   40

And the woman hanging from the 13th floor window
hears other voices. Some of them scream out from below
for her to jump, they would push her over. Others cry softly
from the sidewalks, pull their children up like flowers and gather
them into their arms. They would help her, like themselves.   45

But she is the woman hanging from the 13th floor window,
and she knows she is hanging by her own fingers, her
own skin, her own thread of indecision.

She thinks of Carlos, of Margaret, of Jimmy.
She thinks of her father, and of her mother.   50
She thinks of all the women she has been, of all
the men. She thinks of the color of her skin, and
of Chicago streets, and of waterfalls and pines.
She thinks of moonlight nights, and of cool spring storms.
Her mind chatters like neon and northside bars.   55
She thinks of the 4 a.m. lonelinesses that have folded
her up like death, discordant, without logical and
beautiful conclusion. Her teeth break off at the edges.
She would speak.

The woman hangs from the 13th floor window crying for   60
the lost beauty of her own life. She sees the
sun falling west over the grey plane of Chicago.
She thinks she remembers listening to her own life
break loose, as she falls from the 13th floor
window on the east side of Chicago, or as she   65
climbs back up to claim herself again.

SHERMAN ALEXIE (b. 1966)

The Powwow at the End of the World   (1996)

I am told by many of you that I must forgive and so I shall
after an Indian woman puts her shoulder to the Grand Coulee Dam
and topples it. I am told by many of you that I must forgive
and so I shall after the floodwaters burst each successive dam
downriver from the Grand Coulee. I am told by many of you   5
that I must forgive and so I shall after the floodwaters find
their way to the mouth of the Columbia River as it enters the Pacific
and causes all of it to rise. I am told by many of you that I must forgive
and so I shall after the first drop of floodwater is swallowed by that salmon
waiting in the Pacific. I am told by many of you that I must forgive   10
        and so I shall
after that salmon swims upstream, through the mouth of the Columbia
and then past the flooded cities, broken dams and abandoned reactors
of Hanford.[1] I am told by many of you that I must forgive and so I shall
after that salmon swims through the mouth of the Spokane River   15
as it meets the Columbia, then upstream, until it arrives
in the shallows of a secret bay on the reservation where I wait alone.
I am told by many of you that I must forgive and so I shall after
that salmon leaps into the night air above the water, throws
a lightning bolt at the brush near my feet, and starts the fire   20
which will lead all of the lost Indians home. I am told
by many of you that I must forgive and so I shall
after we Indians have gathered around the fire with that salmon
who has three stories it must tell before sunrise: one story will teach us
how to pray; another story will make us laugh for hours;   25
the third story will give us reason to dance. I am told by many
of you that I must forgive and so I shall when I am dancing
with my tribe during the powwow at the end of the world.

---

[1]Hanford, Washington, site of major concentration of radioactive waste from nuclear
weapons.

PAMELA HALE (b. 1968)

Poem for an Iraqi Child in a Forgotten News Clip   (2003)

I'm sorry that your mom was killed
When a missile struck your home
You were only three, and innocent.
Your mother too was innocent.

That missile came in my name,   5
Paid for by my tax dollars.
I was against the bombing, but
Not registered to vote,
Afraid to make a stand.

I have a daughter, about your age.   10
She is beautiful and strong.
Her mother is here, her father there,
But her home has never been bombed.

She makes fliers to pass out at school.   15
"No one should have to die for oil."
She scares her teachers and school counselor.
She is too young to vote.
But not afraid to make a stand.

This time, I will not stand idly by   20
While politicians propagandize and
Big corporations divvy up the booty
In advance. No.

This time I will make my voice heard,
Say the things I couldn't say before,
Support my daughter and the others when   25
They stand against another unjust war.

I am sorry for your loss.
Sorry too, for my part in it,
My apathy, my inattention.
Sorry for your loneliness and deprivation.   30
Your lost childhood. Your pain.
Sorry for the bombs that fell and fell,
For the planes that circle still.
In my name.

KATHA POLLITT (b. 1949)

Trying to Write a Poem Against the War (2003)

My daughter, who's as beautiful as the day,
hates politics: Face it, Ma,
they don't care what you think! All
passion, like Achilles,
she stalks off to her room, 5
to confide in her purple guitar and await
life's embassies. She's right,
of course: bombs will be hurled
at ordinary streets
and leaders look grave for the cameras, 10
and what good are more poems against war
the real subject of which
so often seems to be the poet's superior
more sensitivities? I could
be mailing myself to the moon 15
or marrying a palm tree,
and yet what can we do
but offer what we have?
and so I spend
this cold gray glittering morning 20
trying to write a poem against war
that perhaps may please my daughter
who hates politics
and does not care much for poetry, either.

PHILIP LEVINE (b. 1928)

They Feed They Lion (1972)

Out of burlap sacks, out of bearing butter,
Out of black bean and wet slate bread,
Out of the acids of rage, the candor of tar,
Out of creosote, gasoline, drive shafts, wooden dollies,
They Lion grow. 5
           Out of the gray hills
Of industrial barns, out of rain, out of bus ride,
West Virginia to Kiss My Ass, out of buried aunties,

Mothers hardening like pounded stumps, out of stumps,
Out of the bones' need to sharpen and the muscles' to stretch,　　　10
They Lion grow.
　　　　　Earth is eating trees, fence posts,
Gutted cars, earth is calling in her little ones,
"Come home, Come home!" From pig balls,
From the ferocity of pig driven to holiness,　　　15
From the furred ear and the full jowl come
The repose of the hung belly, from the purpose
They Lion grow.
　　　　　From the sweet glues of the trotters
Come the sweet kinks of the fist, from the full flower　　　20
Of the hams the thorax of caves,
From "Bow Down" come "Rise Up,"
Come they Lion from the reeds of shovels,
The grained arm that pulls the hands,
They Lion grow.　　　25
　　　　　From my five arms and all my hands,
From all my white sins forgiven, they feed,
From my car passing under the stars,
They Lion, from my children inherit,
From the oak turned to a wall, they Lion,　　　30
From they sack and they belly opened
And all that was hidden burning on the oil-stained earth
They feed they Lion and he comes.

DRAMA

SOPHOCLES (496?–406 B.C.)

Born into a wealthy family, Sophocles was a major figure in Athenian life, serving in civic roles (as a priest and general) and as a playwright. Well versed in Homer and other Greek poets, Sophocles first gained recognition as a tragedian after winning a drama contest, besting Aeschylus. Sophocles would go on to write more than one hundred plays in his lifetime (only seven exist today), and his work is considered, along with that of Aeschylus and Euripides, the foundation of Greek tragedy. Although clearly influenced by the elder Aeschylus, Sophocles is attributed with such theatrical innovations as the introduction of the third actor—allowing greater complexity of plot and more subtle character development. Additionally, Sophocles sought to humanize Greek mythology by focusing on the mortal nature of his characters—their indecision, their suffering, their ability to overcome. His development of the "tragic flaw" placed emphasis on human fallibility rather than fate as determined by the gods. His other surviving plays include Oedipus the King, Electra, *and* Oedipus at Colonus, *written when he was almost ninety years old.* Antigone, *a play about the daughter of Oedipus, probes questions of loyalty and standing up for what you believe is right.*

Antigone   (ca. 441 B.C.)

An English version by Dudley Fitts and Robert Fitzgerald.

Characters

ANTIGONE ⎫
⎬ *daughters of Oedipus*
ISMENE   ⎭

EURYDICE, *wife of Creon*
CREON, *King of Thebes*
HAIMON, *son of Creon*
TEIRESIAS, *a blind seer*
A SENTRY
A MESSENGER
CHORUS

Scene: *Before the palace of* CREON, *King of Thebes. A central double door, and two lateral doors. A platform extends the length of the façade, and from this platform three steps lead down into the "orchestra" or chorus-ground.*

Time: *dawn of the day after the repulse of the Argive army from the assault on Thebes.*

PROLOGUE

ANTIGONE *and* ISMENE *enter from the central door of the Palace.*

ANTIGONE: Ismene, dear sister,
      You would think that we had already suffered enough
      For the curse on Oedipus:°
      I cannot imagine any grief
      That you and I have not gone through. And now—   5
      Have they told you of the new decree of our King Creon?
ISMENE: I have heard nothing: I know
      That two sisters lost two brothers, a double death
      In a single hour; and I know that the Argive army
      Fled in the night; but beyond this, nothing.   10
ANTIGONE: I thought so. And that is why I wanted you
      To come out here with me. There is something we must do.
ISMENE: Why do you speak so strangely?
ANTIGONE: Listen, Ismene:
      Creon buried our brother Eteocles   15
      With military honors, gave him a soldier's funeral,
      And it was right that he should; but Polyneices,
      Who fought as bravely and died as miserably,—
      They say that Creon has sworn
      No one shall bury him, no one mourn for him,   20
      But his body must lie in the fields, a sweet treasure
      For carrion birds to find as they search for food.
      That is what they say, and our good Creon is coming here
      To announce it publicly; and the penalty—
      Stoning to death in the public square!   25
                         There it is,
      And now you can prove what you are:
      A true sister, or a traitor to your family.
ISMENE: Antigone, you are mad! What could I possibly do?

°Oedipus: Oedipus, father of Antigone, Ismene, Polyneices, and Eteocles, was King of Thebes. Unknowingly, he killed his father and married his mother. Upon learning what he had done, he put out his eyes and went into exile. Heirs to the throne, Polyneices and Eteocles eventually quarreled. Eteocles drove out Polyneices, but Polyneices returned to attack Thebes, and both brothers died in battle. Creon became king and ordered that Polyneices's body be left unburied.

ANTIGONE: You must decide whether you will help me or not.   30
ISMENE: I do not understand you. Help you in what?
ANTIGONE: Ismene, I am going to bury him. Will you come?
ISMENE: Bury him! You have just said the new law forbids it.
ANTIGONE: He is my brother. And he is your brother, too.
ISMENE: But think of the danger! Think what Creon will do!   35
ANTIGONE: Creon is not strong enough to stand in my way.
ISMENE: Ah sister!

> Oedipus died, everyone hating him
> For what his own search brought to light, his eyes
> Ripped out by his own hand; and Iocaste died,   40
> His mother and wife at once: she twisted the cords
> That strangled her life; and our two brothers died,
> Each killed by the other's sword. And we are left:
> But oh, Antigone,
> Think how much more terrible than these   45
> Our own death would be if we should go against Creon
> And do what he has forbidden! We are only women,
> We cannot fight with men, Antigone!
> The law is strong, we must give in to the law
> In this thing, and in worse. I beg the Dead   50
> To forgive me, but I am helpless: I must yield
> To those in authority. And I think it is dangerous business
> To be always meddling.

ANTIGONE: If that is what you think,

> I should not want you, even if you asked to come.   55
> You have made your choice, you can be what you want to be
> But I will bury him; and if I must die,
> I say that this crime is holy: I shall lie down
> With him in death, and I shall be as dear
> To him as he to me.   60
>   It is the dead,
> Not the living, who make the longest demands:
> We die for ever . . .
>   You may do as you like,
> Since apparently the laws of the gods mean nothing to you.   65

ISMENE: They mean a great deal to me; but I have no strength
> To break laws that were made for the public good.

ANTIGONE: That must be your excuse, I suppose. But as for me,
> I will bury the brother I love.

ISMENE: Antigone,   70
> I am so afraid for you!

ANTIGONE: You need not be:
> You have yourself to consider, after all.

ISMENE: But no one must hear of this, you must tell no one!
   I will keep it a secret, I promise!   75
ANTIGONE: Oh tell it! Tell everyone!
   Think how they'll hate you when it all comes out
   If they learn that you knew about it all the time!
ISMENE: So fiery! You should be cold with fear.
ANTIGONE: Perhaps. But I am doing only what I must.   80
ISMENE: But can you do it? I say that you cannot.
ANTIGONE: Very well: when my strength gives out, I shall do no more.
ISMENE: Impossible things should not be tried at all.
ANTIGONE: Go away, Ismene:
   I shall be hating you soon, and the dead will too,   85
   For your words are hateful. Leave me my foolish plan:
   I am not afraid of the danger; if it means death,
   It will not be the worst of deaths—death without
   honor.
ISMENE: Go then, if you feel that you must.   90
   You are unwise,
   But a loyal friend indeed to those who love you.

Exit into the Palace. ANTIGONE *goes off, left. Enter the* CHORUS.

PARODOS° • *Strophe° 1*

CHORUS: Now the long blade of the sun, lying
   Level east to west, touches with glory
   Thebes of the Seven Gates. Open, unlidded
   Eye of golden day! O marching light
   Across the eddy and rush of Dirce's stream,°   5
   Striking the white shields of the enemy
   Thrown headlong backward from the blaze of morning!
CHORAGOS:°   Polyneices their commander
   Roused them with windy phrases,
   He the wild eagle screaming   10
   Insults above our land,
   His wings their shields of snow,
   His crest their marshalled helms.

   Parodos: Sung by the Chorus upon entering.   Strophe: Sung by the chorus as they move from stage right to stage left.   5 Dirce's stream: Near Thebes.   8 Choragos: Leader of the Chorus.

Antistrophe° 1

CHORUS: Against our seven gates in a yawning ring
    The famished spears came onward in the night;   15
    But before his jaws were sated with our blood,
    Or pinefire took the garland of our towers,
    He was thrown back; and as he turned, great Thebes—
    No tender victim for his noisy power—
    Rose like a dragon behind him, shouting war.   20
CHORAGOS: For God hates utterly
    The bray of bragging tongues;
    And when he beheld their smiling,
    Their swagger of golden helms,
    The frown of his thunder blasted   25
    Their first man from our walls.

Strophe 2

CHORUS: We heard his shout of triumph high in the air
    Turn to a scream; far out in a flaming arc
    He fell with his windy torch, and the earth struck him.
    And others storming in fury no less than his   30
    Found shock of death in the dusty joy of battle.
CHORAGOS: Seven captains at seven gates
    Yielded their clanging arms to the god
    That bends the battle-line and breaks it.
    These two only, brothers in blood,   35
    Face to face in matchless rage,
    Mirroring each the other's death,
    Clashed in long combat.

Antistrophe 2

CHORUS: But now in the beautiful morning of victory
    Let Thebes of the many chariots sing for joy!   40
    With hearts for dancing we'll take leave of war:
    Our temples shall be sweet with hymns of praise,
    And the long night shall echo with our chorus.

Antistrophe: Sung by the chorus as they move from stage left to stage right.

SCENE I

CHORAGOS: But now at last our new King is coming:
Creon of Thebes, Menoikeus' son.
In this auspicious dawn of his reign
What are the new complexities
That shifting Fate has woven for him?   5
What is his counsel? Why has he summoned
The old men to hear him?

Enter CREON *from the Palace, center. He addresses the* CHORUS *from the top step.*

CREON: Gentlemen: I have the honor to inform you that our Ship of
State, which recent storms have threatened to destroy, has come safely
to harbor at last, guided by the merciful wisdom of Heaven. I have sum-   10
moned you here this morning because I know that I can depend upon
you: your devotion to King Laios was absolute; you never hesitated in
your duty to our late ruler Oedipus; and when Oedipus died, your loyalty was transferred to his children. Unfortunately, as you know, his two
sons, the princes Eteocles and Polyneices, have killed each other in bat-   15
tle; and I, as the next in blood, have succeeded to the full power of the
throne.

    I am aware, of course, that no Ruler can expect complete loyalty
from his subjects until he has been tested in office. Nevertheless, I say
to you at the very outset that I have nothing but contempt for the kind   20
of Governor who is afraid, for whatever reason, to follow the course
that he knows is best for the State; and as for the man who sets private
friendship above the public welfare,—I have no use for him, either. I
call God to witness that if I saw my country headed for ruin, I should
not be afraid to speak out plainly; and I need hardly remind you that I   25
would never have any dealings with an enemy of the people. No one
values friendship more highly than I; but we must remember that
friends made at the risk of wrecking our Ship are not real friends at all.

    These are my principles, at any rate, and that is why I have made the
following decision concerning the sons of Oedipus: Eteocles, who died   30
as a man should die, fighting for his country, is to be buried with full
military honors, with all the ceremony that is usual when the greatest
heroes die; but his brother Polyneices, who broke his exile to come back
with fire and sword against his native city and the shrines of his fathers'
gods, whose one idea was to spill the blood of his blood and sell his own   35
people into slavery—Polyneices, I say, is to have no burial: no man is to
touch him or say the least prayer for him; he shall lie on the plain, unburied; and the birds and the scavenging dogs can do with him whatever
they like.

This is my command, and you can see the wisdom behind it. As long   40
as I am King, no traitor is going to be honored with the loyal man. But
whoever shows by word and deed that he is on the side of the State,—
he shall have my respect while he is living, and my reverence when he
is dead.

CHORAGOS: If that is your will, Creon son of Menoikeus,   45
You have the right to enforce it: we are yours.

CREON: That is my will. Take care that you do your part.

CHORAGOS: We are old men: let the younger ones carry it out.

CREON: I do not mean that: the sentries have been appointed.

CHORAGOS: Then what is it that you would have us do?   50

CREON: You will give no support to whoever breaks this law.

CHORAGOS: Only a crazy man is in love with death!

CREON: And death it is; yet money talks, and the wisest
Have sometimes been known to count a few coins too many.

Enter SENTRY *from left.*

SENTRY: I'll not say that I'm out of breath from running, King, because   55
every time I stopped to think about what I have to tell you, I felt like
going back. And all the time a voice kept saying, "You fool, don't you
know you're walking straight into trouble?"; and then another voice:
"Yes, but if you let somebody else get the news to Creon first, it will be
even worse than that for you!" But good sense won out, at least I hope   60
it was good sense, and here I am with a story that makes no sense at all;
but I'll tell it anyhow, because, as they say, what's going to happen's going to happen, and—

CREON: Come to the point. What have you to say?

SENTRY: I did not do it. I did not see who did it. You must not punish me 65
for what someone else has done.

CREON: A comprehensive defense! More effective, perhaps,
If I knew its purpose. Come: what is it?

SENTRY: A dreadful thing . . . I don't know how to put it—

CREON: Out with it!   70

SENTRY: Well, then;
The dead man—

                    Polyneices—

Pause. The SENTRY *is overcome, fumbles for words.* CREON *waits impassively.*

                              out there—
                                        someone,—   75
New dust on the slimy flesh!

Pause. No sign from CREON.

Someone has given it burial that way, and
Gone . . .

Long pause. CREON *finally speaks with deadly control:*

CREON:　And the man who dared do this?
SENTRY:　　　　　　　　　　　　I swear I　　　　　　　　　80
Do not know! You must believe me!
　　　　　　　　　　　　　　　Listen:
The ground was dry, not a sign of digging, no,
Not a wheeltrack in the dust, no trace of anyone.
It was when they relieved us this morning: and one of them,
The corporal, pointed to it.　　　　　　　　　　　　　85
　　　　　　　　　　There it was,
The strangest—
　　　　　　Look:
The body, just mounded over with light dust: you see?
Not buried really, but as if they'd covered it　　　　　90
Just enough for the ghost's peace. And no sign
Of dogs or any wild animal that had been there.

And then what a scene there was! Every man of us　　　95
Accusing the other: we all proved the other man did it,
We all had proof that we could not have done it.
We were ready to take hot iron in our hands,
Walk through fire, swear by all the gods,
It was not I
I do not know who it was, but it was not I!　　　　100

CREON's *rage has been mounting steadily, but the* SENTRY *is too intent upon
his story to notice it.*

And then, when this came to nothing, someone said
A thing that silenced us and made us stare
Down at the ground: you had to be told the news,
And one of us had to do it! We threw the dice,
And the bad luck fell to me. So here I am,　　　　　105
No happier to be here than you are to have me:
Nobody likes the man who brings bad news.
CHORAGOS:　I have been wondering, King: can it be that the gods have
　　done this?
CREON *(Furiously)*:　Stop!　　　　　　　　　　　　110
Must you doddering wrecks
Go out of your heads entirely? "The gods!"
Intolerable!
The gods favor this corpse? Why? How had he served them?

Tried to loot their temples, burn their images,   115
Yes, and the whole State, and its laws with it!
Is it your senile opinion that the gods love to honor bad men?
A pious thought!—
                 No, from the very beginning
There have been those who have whispered together,   120
Stiff-necked anarchists, putting their heads together,
Scheming against me in alleys. These are the men,
And they have bribed my own guard to do this thing.
(Sententiously) Money!
There's nothing in the world so demoralizing as money.   125
Down go your cities,
Homes gone, men gone, honest hearts corrupted,
Crookedness of all kinds, and all for money!
(To SENTRY*)*   But you—!
I swear by God and by the throne of God,   130
The man who has done this thing shall pay for it!
Find that man, bring him here to me, or your death
Will be the least of your problems: I'll string you up
Alive, and there will be certain ways to make you
Discover your employer before you die;   135
And the process may teach you a lesson you seem to have missed:
The dearest profit is sometimes all too dear:
That depends on the source. Do you understand me?
A fortune won is often misfortune.
SENTRY: King, may I speak?   140
CREON: Your very voice distresses me.
SENTRY: Are you sure that it is my voice, and not your conscience?
CREON: By God, he wants to analyze me now!
SENTRY: It is not what I say, but what has been done, that hurts you.
CREON: You talk too much.   145
SENTRY: Maybe; but I've done nothing.
CREON: Sold your soul for some silver: that's all you've done.
SENTRY: How dreadful it is when the right judge judges wrong!
CREON: Your figures of speech
May entertain you now; but unless you bring me the man,   150
You will get little profit from them in the end.

Exit CREON *into the Palace.*

SENTRY: "Bring me the man"—!
I'd like nothing better than bringing him the man!

But bring him or not, you have seen the last of me here.
At any rate, I am safe!   155

Exit SENTRY.

ODE I • *Strophe 1*

CHORUS: Numberless are the world's wonders, but none
More wonderful than man; the stormgray sea
Yields to his prows, the huge crests bear him high;
Earth, holy and inexhaustible, is graven
With shining furrows where his plows have gone   5
Year after year, the timeless labor of stallions.

Antistrophe 1

The lightboned birds and beasts that cling to cover,
The lithe fish lighting their reaches of dim water,
All are taken, tamed in the net of his mind;
The lion on the hill, the wild horse windy-maned,   10
Resign to him; and his blunt yoke has broken
The sultry shoulders of the mountain bull.

Strophe 2

Words also, and thought as rapid as air,
He fashions to his good use; statecraft is his,
And his the skill that deflects the arrows of snow,   15
The spears of winter rain: from every wind
He has made himself secure—from all but one:
In the late wind of death he cannot stand.

Antistrophe 2

O clear intelligence, force beyond all measure!
O fate of man, working both good and evil!   20
When the laws are kept, how proudly his city stands!
When the laws are broken, what of his city then?
Never may the anarchic man find rest at my hearth,
Never be it said that my thoughts are his thoughts.

SCENE II

Re-enter SENTRY *leading* ANTIGONE.

CHORAGOS: What does this mean? Surely this captive woman
  Is the Princess, Antigone. Why should she be taken?
SENTRY: Here is the one who did it! We caught her
  In the very act of burying him.—Where is Creon?
CHORAGOS: Just coming from the house.   5

Enter CREON, *center.*

CREON: What has happened?
  Why have you come back so soon?
SENTRY *(Expansively)*:

                            O King,
  A man should never be too sure of anything:
  I would have sworn   10
  That you'd not see me here again: your anger
  Frightened me so, and the things you threatened me with;
  But how could I tell then
  That I'd be able to solve the case so soon?
  No dice-throwing this time: I was only too glad to come!   15
  Here is this woman. She is the guilty one:
  We found her trying to bury him.
  Take her, then; question her; judge her as you will.
  I am through with the whole thing now, and glad of it.
CREON: But this is Antigone! Why have you brought her here?   20
SENTRY: She was burying him, I tell you!
CREON *(Severely)*:

                        Is this the truth?
SENTRY: I saw her with my own eyes. Can I say more?
CREON: The details: come, tell me quickly!
SENTRY: It was like this: 25
  After those terrible threats of yours, King,
  We went back and brushed the dust away from the body.
  The flesh was soft by now, and stinking,
  So we sat on a hill to windward and kept guard.
  No napping this time! We kept each other awake.   30
  But nothing happened until the white round sun
  Whirled in the center of the round sky over us:
  Then, suddenly,
  A storm of dust roared up from the earth, and the sky
  Went out, the plain vanished with all its trees   35

In the stinging dark. We closed our eyes and endured it.
The whirlwind lasted a long time, but it passed;
And then we looked, and there was Antigone!
I have seen
A mother bird come back to a stripped nest, heard　　40
Her crying bitterly a broken note or two
For the young ones stolen. Just so, when this girl
Found the bare corpse, and all her love's work wasted,
She wept, and cried on heaven to damn the hands
That had done this thing.　　45
　　　　　　　　And then she brought more dust
And sprinkled wine three times for her brother's ghost.

We ran and took her at once. She was not afraid,
Not even when we charged her with what she had done.
She denied nothing.　　50
　　　　　　　　And this was a comfort to me,
And some uneasiness: for it is a good thing
To escape from death, but it is no great pleasure
To bring death to a friend.
　　　　　　　　Yet I always say　　55
There is nothing so comfortable as your own safe skin!
CREON　　*(Slowly, dangerously)*:
　　And you, Antigone,
　　You with your head hanging,—do you confess this thing?
ANTIGONE:　　I do. I deny nothing.
CREON *(To* SENTRY*)*:　　You may go.　　60
　　　　　　　　　　　　　　　(Exit SENTRY*)*
(To ANTIGONE*)* Tell me, tell me briefly:
　　Had you heard my proclamation touching this matter?
ANTIGONE:　　It was public. Could I help hearing it?
CREON:　　And yet you dared defy the law.
ANTIGONE:　　　　　　　　I dared.　　65
　　It was not God's proclamation. That final Justice
　　That rules the world below makes no such laws.

　　Your edict, King, was strong,
　　But all your strength is weakness itself against
　　The immortal unrecorded laws of God.　　70
　　They are not merely now: they were, and shall be,
　　Operative for ever, beyond man utterly.

　　I knew I must die, even without your decree:
　　I am only mortal. And if I must die
　　Now, before it is my time to die,　　75

Surely this is no hardship: can anyone
Living, as I live, with evil all about me,
Think Death less than a friend? This death of mine
Is of no importance; but if I had left my brother
Lying in death unburied, I should have suffered.   80
Now I do not.
                    You smile at me. Ah Creon,
Think me a fool, if you like; but it may well be
That a fool convicts me of folly.

CHORAGOS: Like father, like daughter: both headstrong, deaf to   85
reason!
She has never learned to yield.

CREON: She has much to learn.
The inflexible heart breaks first, the toughest iron
Cracks first, and the wildest horses bend their necks   90
At the pull of the smallest curb.
                                Pride? In a slave?
This girl is guilty of a double insolence,
Breaking the given laws and boasting of it.
Who is the man here,   95
She or I, if this crime goes unpunished?
Sister's child, or more than sister's child,
Or closer yet in blood—she and her sister
Win bitter death for this!

(*To* SERVANTS)   Go, some of you,   100
Arrest Ismene. I accuse her equally.
Bring her: you will find her sniffling in the house there.

Her mind's a traitor: crimes kept in the dark
Cry for light, and the guardian brain shudders;
But how much worse than this   105
Is brazen boasting of barefaced anarchy!

ANTIGONE: Creon, what more do you want than my death?

CREON: Nothing.
That gives me everything.

ANTIGONE: Then I beg you: kill me.   110
This talking is a great weariness: your words
Are distasteful to me, and I am sure that mine
Seem so to you. And yet they should not seem so:
I should have praise and honor for what I have done.
All these men here would praise me   115
Were their lips not frozen shut with fear of you.
(*Bitterly*) Ah the good fortune of kings,
Licensed to say and do whatever they please!

CREON: You are alone here in that opinion.

ANTIGONE: No, they are with me. But they keep their tongues in   120
  leash.
CREON: Maybe. But you are guilty, and they are not.
ANTIGONE: There is no guilt in reverence for the dead.
CREON: But Eteocles—was he not your brother too?
ANTIGONE: My brother too.   125
CREON: And you insult his memory?
ANTIGONE *(Softly)*:   The dead man would not say that I insult it.
CREON: He would: for you honor a traitor as much as him.
ANTIGONE: His own brother; traitor or not, and equal in blood.
CREON: He made war on his country. Eteocles defended it.   130
ANTIGONE: Nevertheless, there are honors due all the dead.
CREON: But not the same for the wicked as for the just.
ANTIGONE: Ah Creon, Creon,
  Which of us can say what the gods hold wicked?
CREON: An enemy is an enemy, even dead.   135
ANTIGONE: It is my nature to join in love, not hate.
CREON *(Finally losing patience)*:   Go join them, then; if you must have
  your love,
  Find it in hell!
CHORAGOS: But see, Ismene comes: 140

Enter ISMENE, *guarded.*

  Those tears are sisterly, the cloud
  That shadows her eyes rains down gentle sorrow.
CREON: You too, Ismene,
  Snake in my ordered house, sucking my blood
  Stealthily—and all the time I never knew   145
  That these two sisters were aiming at my throne!
                                                        Ismene,
  Do you confess your share in this crime, or deny it?
  Answer me.
ISMENE: Yes, if she will let me say so. I am guilty.   150
ANTIGONE *(Coldly)*:   No, Ismene. You have no right to say so.
  You would not help me, and I will not have you help me.
ISMENE: But now I know what you meant; and I am here
  To join you, to take my share of punishment.
ANTIGONE: The dead man and the gods who rule the dead   155
  Know whose act this was. Words are not friends.
ISMENE: Do you refuse me, Antigone? I want to die with you:
  I too have a duty that I must discharge to the dead.
ANTIGONE: You shall not lessen my death by sharing it.
ISMENE: What do I care for life when you are dead?   160
ANTIGONE: Ask Creon. You're always hanging on his opinions.

ISMENE: You are laughing at me. Why, Antigone?

ANTIGONE: It's a joyless laughter, Ismene.

ISMENE: But can I do nothing?

ANTIGONE: Yes. Save yourself. I shall not envy you.   165
    There are those who will praise you; I shall have honor, too.

ISMENE: But we are equally guilty!

ANTIGONE: No more, Ismene.
    You are alive, but I belong to Death.

CREON (*To the* CHORUS):   Gentlemen, I beg you to observe these girls: 170
    One has just now lost her mind; the other,
    It seems, has never had a mind at all.

ISMENE: Grief teaches the steadiest minds to waver, King.

CREON: Yours certainly did, when you assumed guilt with the
    guilty!   175

ISMENE: But how could I go on living without her?

CREON: You are.
    She is already dead.

ISMENE: But your own son's bride!

CREON: There are places enough for him to push his plow.   180
    I want no wicked women for my sons!

ISMENE: O dearest Haimon, how your father wrongs you!

CREON: I've had enough of your childish talk of marriage!

CHORAGOS: Do you really intend to steal this girl from your son?

CREON: No; Death will do that for me.   185

CHORAGOS: Then she must die?

CREON (*Ironically*):   You dazzle me.
                        —But enough of this talk!
    (*To* GUARDS) You, there, take them away and guard them well:
    For they are but women, and even brave men run   190
    When they see Death coming.

    Exeunt ISMENE, ANTIGONE, *and* GUARDS

ODE II • *Strophe 1*

CHORUS: Fortunate is the man who has never tasted God's vengeance!
    Where once the anger of heaven has struck, that house is shaken
    For ever: damnation rises behind each child
    Like a wave cresting out of the black northeast,
    When the long darkness under sea roars up   5
    And bursts drumming death upon the windwhipped sand.

Antistrophe 1

> I have seen this gathering sorrow from time long past
> Loom upon Oedipus' children: generation from generation
> Takes the compulsive rage of the enemy god.
> So lately this last flower of Oedipus' line   10
> Drank the sunlight! but now a passionate word
> And a handful of dust have closed up all its beauty.

Strophe 2

> What mortal arrogance
> Transcends the wrath of Zeus?
> Sleep cannot lull him, nor the effortless long months   15
> Of the timeless gods: but he is young for ever,
> And his house is the shining day of high Olympos.
>   All that is and shall be,
>   And all the past, is his.
> No pride on earth is free of the curse of heaven.   20

Antistrophe 2

> The straying dreams of men
> May bring them ghosts of joy:
> But as they drowse, the waking embers burn them;
> Or they walk with fixed eyes, as blind men walk.
> But the ancient wisdom speaks for our own time: 25
>   *Fate works most for woe*
>   *With Folly's fairest show.*
> Man's little pleasure is the spring of sorrow.

SCENE III

CHORAGOS: But here is Haimon, King, the last of all your sons.
   Is it grief for Antigone that brings him here,
   And bitterness at being robbed of his bride?

Enter HAIMON.

CREON: We shall soon see, and no need of diviners.

                    —Son,   5

You have heard my final judgment on that girl:
Have you come here hating me, or have you come
With deference and with love, whatever I do?
HAIMON: I am your son, father. You are my guide.
You make things clear for me, and I obey you.   10
No marriage means more to me than your continuing wisdom.
CREON: Good. That is the way to behave: subordinate
Everything else, my son, to your father's will.
This is what a man prays for, that he may get
Sons attentive and dutiful in his house,   15
Each one hating his father's enemies,
Honoring his father's friends. But if his sons
Fail him, if they turn out unprofitably,
What has he fathered but trouble for himself
And amusement for the malicious?   20
                              So you are right
Not to lose your head over this woman.
Your pleasure with her would soon grow cold, Haimon,
And then you'd have a hellcat in bed and elsewhere.
Let her find her husband in Hell!   25
Of all the people in this city, only she
Has had contempt for my law and broken it.

Do you want me to show myself weak before the people?
Or to break my sworn word? No, and I will not.
The woman dies.   30
I suppose she'll plead "family ties." Well, let her.
If I permit my own family to rebel,
How shall I earn the world's obedience?
Show me the man who keeps his house in hand,
He's fit for public authority.   35
                              I'll have no dealings
With law-breakers, critics of the government:
Whoever is chosen to govern should be obeyed—
Must be obeyed, in all things, great and small,
Just and unjust! O Haimon,   40
The man who knows how to obey, and that man only,
Knows how to give commands when the time comes.
You can depend on him, no matter how fast
The spears come: he's a good soldier, he'll stick it out.
Anarchy, anarchy! Show me a greater evil!   45
This is why cities tumble and the great houses rain down,
This is what scatters armies!
No, no: good lives are made so by discipline.
We keep the laws then, and the lawmakers,

And no woman shall seduce us. If we must lose,   50
    Let's lose to a man, at least! Is a woman stronger than we?
CHORAGOS: Unless time has rusted my wits,
    What you say, King, is said with point and dignity.
HAIMON *(Boyishly earnest)*:   Father:
    Reason is God's crowning gift to man, and you are right   55
    To warn me against losing mine. I cannot say—
    I hope that I shall never want to say!—that you
    Have reasoned badly. Yet there are other men
    Who can reason, too; and their opinions might be helpful.
    You are not in a position to know everything   60
    That people say or do, or what they feel:
    Your temper terrifies them—everyone
    Will tell you only what you like to hear.
    But I, at any rate, can listen; and I have heard them
    Muttering and whispering in the dark about this girl.   65
    They say no woman has ever, so unreasonably,
    Died so shameful a death for a generous act:
    "She covered her brother's body. Is this indecent?
    She kept him from dogs and vultures. Is this a crime?
    Death?—She should have all the honor that we can give her!"   70

This is the way they talk out there in the city.

You must believe me:
Nothing is closer to me than your happiness.
What could be closer? Must not any son
Value his father's fortune as his father does his?   75
I beg you, do not be unchangeable:
Do not believe that you alone can be right.
The man who thinks that,
The man who maintains that only he has the power
To reason correctly, the gift to speak, the soul—   80
A man like that, when you know him, turns out empty.
It is not reason never to yield to reason!

In flood time you can see how some trees bend,
And because they bend, even their twigs are safe,
While stubborn trees are torn up, roots and all.   85
And the same thing happens in sailing:
Make your sheet fast, never slacken,—and over you go,
Head over heels and under: and there's your voyage.
Forget you are angry! Let yourself be moved!
I know I am young; but please let me say this: 90
The ideal condition

Would be, I admit, that men should be right by instinct;
But since we are all too likely to go astray,
The reasonable thing is to learn from those who can teach.

CHORAGOS: You will do well to listen to him, King,   95
If what he says is sensible. And you, Haimon,
Must listen to your father.—Both speak well.

CREON: You consider it right for a man of my years and experience
to go to school to a boy?

HAIMON: It is not right   100
If I am wrong. But if I am young, and right,
What does my age matter?

CREON: You think it right to stand up for an anarchist?

HAIMON: Not at all. I pay no respect to criminals.

CREON: Then she is not a criminal?   105

HAIMON: The City would deny it, to a man.

CREON: And the City proposes to teach me how to rule?

HAIMON: Ah. Who is it that's talking like a boy now?

CREON: My voice is the one voice giving orders in this City!

HAIMON: It is no City if it takes orders from one voice.   110

CREON: The State is the King!

HAIMON: Yes, if the State is a desert.

Pause.

CREON: This boy, it seems, has sold out to a woman.

HAIMON: If you are a woman: my concern is only for you.

CREON: So? Your "concern"! In a public brawl with your father!   115

HAIMON: How about you, in a public brawl with justice?

CREON: With justice, when all that I do is within my rights?

HAIMON: You have no right to trample God's right.

CREON *(Completely out of control)*:   Fool, adolescent fool! Taken in
by a woman!   120

HAIMON: You'll never see me taken in by anything vile.

CREON: Every word you say is for her!

HAIMON *(Quietly, darkly)*:   And for you.
And for me. And for the gods under the earth.

CREON: You'll never marry her while she lives.   125

HAIMON: Then she must die.—But her death will cause another.

CREON: Another?
Have you lost your senses? Is this an open threat?

HAIMON: There is no threat in speaking to emptiness.

CREON: I swear you'll regret this superior tone of yours!   130
You are the empty one!

HAIMON: If you were not my father,

I'd say you were perverse.

CREON: You girlstruck fool, don't play at words with me!

HAIMON: I am sorry. You prefer silence.   135

CREON: Now, by God—!

I swear, by all the gods in heaven above us,
You'll watch it, I swear you shall!
(To the SERVANTS*)*   Bring her out!
Bring the woman out! Let her die before his eyes!   140
Here, this instant, with her bridegroom beside her!

HAIMON: Not here, no; she will not die here, King.
And you will never see my face again.
Go on raving as long as you've a friend to endure you.

Exit HAIMON.

CHORAGOS: Gone, gone.   145
Creon, a young man in a rage is dangerous!

CREON: Let him do, or dream to do, more than a man can.
He shall not save these girls from death.

CHORAGOS: These girls
You have sentenced them both?   150

CREON: No, you are right.
I will not kill the one whose hands are clean.

CHORAGOS: But Antigone?

CREON *(Somberly)*:   I will carry her far away
Out there in the wilderness, and lock her
Living in a vault of stone. She shall have food,   155
As the custom is, to absolve the State of her death.
And there let her pray to the gods of hell:
They are her only gods:
Perhaps they will show her an escape from death,   160
Or she may learn,
                        though late,
That piety shown the dead is pity in vain.

Exit CREON.

ODE III • *Strophe*

CHORUS: Love, unconquerable
Waster of rich men, keeper
Of warm lights and all-night vigil
In the soft face of a girl:
Sea-wanderer, forest-visitor!   5

Even the pure Immortals cannot escape you,
And mortal man, in his one day's dusk,
Trembles before your glory.

Antistrophe

Surely you swerve upon ruin
The just man's consenting heart,   10
As here you have made bright anger
Strike between father and son—
And none has conquered but Love!
A girl's glance working the will of heaven:
Pleasure to her alone who mocks us,   15
Merciless Aphrodite.

SCENE IV

CHORAGOS   *(As* ANTIGONE *enters guarded)*:
But I can no longer stand in awe of this,
Nor, seeing what I see, keep back my tears.
Here is Antigone, passing to that chamber
Where all find sleep at last.

Strophe 1

ANTIGONE: Look upon me, friends, and pity me   5
Turning back at the night's edge to say
Good-by to the sun that shines for me no longer;
Now sleepy Death
Summons me down to Acheron, that cold shore:
There is no bridesong there, nor any music.   10
CHORUS: Yet not unpraised, not without a kind of honor,
You walk at last into the underworld;
Untouched by sickness, broken by no sword.
What woman has ever found your way to death?

Antistrophe 1

ANTIGONE: How often I have heard the story of Niobe,   15
Tantalos' wretched daughter, how the stone
Clung fast about her, ivy-close: and they say
The rain falls endlessly
And sifting soft snow; her tears are never done.

I feel the loneliness of her death in mine.   20
CHORUS: But she was born of heaven, and you
    Are woman, woman-born. If her death is yours,
    A mortal woman's, is this not for you
    Glory in our world and in the world beyond?

Strophe 2

ANTIGONE: You laugh at me. Ah, friends, friends,   25
    Can you not wait until I am dead? O Thebes,
    O men many-charioted, in love with Fortune,
    Dear springs of Dirce, sacred Theban grove,
    Be witnesses for me, denied all pity,
    Unjustly judged! and think a word of love   30
    For her whose path turns
    Under dark earth, where there are no more tears.
CHORUS: You have passed beyond human daring and come at last
    Into a place of stone where Justice sits.
    I cannot tell   35
    What shape of your father's guilt appears in this.

Antistrophe 2

ANTIGONE: You have touched it at last: that bridal bed
    Unspeakable, horror of son and mother mingling:
    Their crime, infection of all our family!
    O Oedipus, father and brother!   40
    Your marriage strikes from the grave to murder mine.
    I have been a stranger here in my own land:
    All my life
    The blasphemy of my birth has followed me.
CHORUS: Reverence is a virtue, but strength   45
    Lives in established law: that must prevail.
    You have made your choice,
    Your death is the doing of your conscious hand.

Epode

ANTIGONE: Then let me go, since all your words are bitter,
    And the very light of the sun is cold to me.   50
    Lead me to my vigil, where I must have
    Neither love nor lamentation; no song, but silence.

CREON *interrupts impatiently.*

CREON: If dirges and planned lamentations could put off death,
   Men would be singing for ever.
   (To the SERVANTS*)* Take her, go!   55
   You know your orders: take her to the vault
   And leave her alone there. And if she lives or dies,
   That's her affair, not ours: our hands are clean.
ANTIGONE: O tomb, vaulted bride-bed in eternal rock,
   Soon I shall be with my own again   60
   Where Persephone welcomes the thin ghosts underground:
   And I shall see my father again, and you, mother,
   And dearest Polyneices—
   dearest indeed
   To me, since it was my hand   65
   That washed him clean and poured the ritual wine:
   And my reward is death before my time!

   And yet, as men's hearts know, I have done no wrong.
   I have not sinned before God. Or if I have,
   I shall know the truth in death. But if the guilt   70
   Lies upon Creon who judged me, then, I pray,
   May his punishment equal my own.
CHORAGOS: O passionate heart,
   Unyielding, tormented still by the same winds!
CREON: Her guards shall have good cause to regret their delaying. 75
ANTIGONE: Ah! That voice is like the voice of death!
CREON: I can give you no reason to think you are mistaken.
ANTIGONE: Thebes, and you my fathers' gods,
   And rulers of Thebes, you see me now, the last
   Unhappy daughter of a line of kings,   80
   Your kings, led away to death. You will remember
   What things I suffer, and at what men's hands,
   Because I would not transgress the laws of heaven.
   (To the GUARDS, *simply)*:   Come: let us wait no longer.

Exit ANTIGONE, *left, guarded.*

ODE IV • *Strophe 1*

CHORUS: All Danae's beauty was locked away
   In a brazen cell where the sunlight could not come:
   A small room, still as any grave, enclosed her.
   Yet she was a princess too,

And Zeus in a rain of gold poured love upon her.   5
O child, child,
No power in wealth or war
Or tough sea-blackened ships
Can prevail against untiring Destiny!

Antistrophe 1

And Dryas' son° also, that furious king,   10
Bore the god's prisoning anger for his pride:
Sealed up by Dionysos in deaf stone,
His madness died among echoes.
So at the last he learned what dreadful power
His tongue had mocked: 15
For he had profaned the revels,
And fired the wrath of the nine
Implacable Sisters° that love the sound of the flute.

Strophe 2

And old men tell a half-remembered tale
Of horror done where a dark ledge splits the sea   20
And a double surf beats on the gray shores:
How a king's new woman,° sick
With hatred for the queen he had imprisoned,
Ripped out his two sons' eyes with her bloody hands
While grinning Ares watched the shuttle plunge   25
Four times: four blind wounds crying for revenge,

Antistrophe 2

Crying, tears and blood mingled—Piteously born,
Those sons whose mother was of heavenly birth!
Her father was the god of the North Wind
And she was cradled by gales,   30
She raced with young colts on the gluttering lulls
And walked untrammeled in the open light:
But in her marriage deathless Fate found means
To build a tomb like yours for all her joy.

---

10 Dryas' son: Lycurgus, King of Thrace.   18 Implacable sisters: The nine Muses.
22 King's new woman: Reference to Eidothea, wife of King Phineas.

SCENE V

Enter blind TEIRESIAS, *led by a boy. The opening speeches of* TEIRESIAS
should be in singsong contrast to the realistic lines of CREON.

TEIRESIAS: This is the way the blind man comes, Princes, Princes,
    Lock-step, two heads lit by the eyes of one.
CREON: What new thing have you to tell us, Old Teiresias?
TEIRESIAS: I have much to tell you: listen to the prophet, Creon.
CREON: I am not aware that I have ever failed to listen.   5
TEIRESIAS: Then you have done wisely, King, and ruled well.
CREON: I admit my debt to you. But what have you to say?
TEIRESIAS: This, Creon: you stand once more on the edge of fate.
CREON: What do you mean? Your words are a kind of dread.
TEIRESIAS: Listen, Creon: 10
    I was sitting in my chair of augury, at the place
    Where the birds gather about me. They were all a-chatter,
    As is their habit, when suddenly I heard
    A strange note in their jangling, a scream, a
    Whirring fury; I knew that they were fighting,   15
    Tearing each other, dying
    In a whirlwind of wings clashing. And I was afraid.
    I began the rites of burnt-offering at the altar,
    But Hephaistos failed me: instead of bright flame,
    There was only the sputtering slime of the fat thighflesh   20
    Melting: the entrails dissolved in gray smoke,
    The bare bone burst from the welter. And no blaze!

    This was a sign from heaven. My boy described it,
    Seeing for me as I see for others.

    I tell you, Creon, you yourself have brought   25
    This new calamity upon us. Our hearths and altars
    Are stained with the corruption of dogs and carrion birds
    That glut themselves on the corpse of Oedipus' son.
    The gods are deaf when we pray to them, their fire
    Recoils from our offering, their birds of omen   30
    Have no cry of comfort, for they are gorged
    With the thick blood of the dead.
                    O my son,
    These are no trifles! Think: all men make mistakes,
    But a good man yields when he knows his course is wrong,   35
    And repairs the evil. The only crime is pride.

Give in to the dead man, then: do not fight with a corpse—
What glory is it to kill a man who is dead?
Think, I beg you:
It is for your own good that I speak as I do.   40
You should be able to yield for your own good.
CREON: It seems that prophets have made me their special province.
All my life long
I have been a kind of butt for the dull arrows
Of doddering fortune-tellers!   45
                    No, Teiresias:
If your birds—if the great eagles of God himself
Should carry him stinking bit by bit to heaven,
I would not yield. I am not afraid of pollution:
No man can defile the gods.   50
                    Do what you will,
Go into business, make money, speculate
In India gold or that synthetic gold from Sardis,
Get rich otherwise than by my consent to bury him.
Teiresias, it is a sorry thing when a wise man   55
Sells his wisdom, lets out his words for hire!
TEIRESIAS: Ah Creon! Is there no man left in the world—
CREON: To do what?—Come, let's have the aphorism!
TEIRESIAS: No man who knows that wisdom outweighs any wealth?
CREON: As surely as bribes are baser than any baseness.   60
TEIRESIAS: You are sick, Creon! You are deathly sick!
CREON: As you say: it is not my place to challenge a prophet.
TEIRESIAS: Yet you have said my prophecy is for sale.
CREON: The generation of prophets has always loved gold.
TEIRESIAS: The generation of kings has always loved brass.   65
CREON: You forget yourself! You are speaking to your King.
TEIRESIAS: I know it. You are a king because of me.
CREON: You have a certain skill; but you have sold out.
TEIRESIAS: King, you will drive me to words that—
CREON: Say them, say them!   70
Only remember: I will not pay you for them.
TEIRESIAS: No, you will find them too costly.
CREON: No doubt. Speak:
Whatever you say, you will not change my will.
TEIRESIAS: Then take this, and take it to heart!   75
The time is not far off when you shall pay back
Corpse for corpse, flesh of your own flesh.
You have thrust the child of this world into living night,
You have kept from the gods below the child that is theirs:
The one in a grave before her death, the other,   80

Dead, denied the grave. This is your crime:
And the Furies and the dark gods of Hell
Are swift with terrible punishment for you.

Do you want to buy me now, Creon?
                                Not many days,   85
And your house will be full of men and women weeping.
And curses will be hurled at you from far
Cities grieving for sons unburied, left to rot
Before the walls of Thebes.

These are my arrows, Creon: they are all for you.   90
(To BOY*)*:   But come, child: lead me home.
Let him waste his fine anger upon younger men.
Maybe he will learn at last
To control a wiser tongue in a better head.

Exit TEIRESIAS.

CHORAGOS: The old man has gone, King, but his words   95
   Remain to plague us. I am old, too,
   But I cannot remember that he was ever false.
CREON: That is true. . . . It troubles me.
   Oh it is hard to give in! but it is worse
   To risk everything for stubborn pride.   100
CHORAGOS: Creon: take my advice.
CREON: What shall I do?
CHORAGOS: Go quickly: free Antigone from her vault
   And build a tomb for the body of Polyneices.
CREON: You would have me do this?   105
CHORAGOS: Creon, yes!
   And it must be done at once: God moves
   Swiftly to cancel the folly of stubborn men.
CREON: It is hard to deny the heart! But I
   Will do it: I will not fight with destiny.   110
CHORAGOS: You must go yourself, you cannot leave it to others.
CREON: I will go.
   —Bring axes, servants:
   Come with me to the tomb. I buried her, I
   Will set her free.   115
              Oh quickly!
   My mind misgives—
   The laws of the gods are mighty, and a man must serve them
   To the last day of his life!

Exit CREON.

PAEAN • *Strophe 1*

CHORAGOS: God of many names
CHORUS: O Iacchos

                                          son
    of Kadmeian Semele
                              O born of the Thunder!   5
    Guardian of the West
                          Regent
    of Eleusis' plain
                          O Prince of maenad Thebes
    and the Dragon Field by rippling Ismenos: 10

Antistrophe 1

CHORAGOS: God of many names
CHORUS: the flame of torches
    flares on our hills
                              the nymphs of Iacchos
    dance at the spring of Castalia: 15
    From the vine-close mountain
                                          come ah come in ivy:
    Evohe evohe!° sings through the streets of Thebes

Strophe 2

CHORAGOS: God of many names
CHORUS: Iacchos of Thebes   20
    heavenly Child
                          of Semele bride of the Thunderer!
    The shadow of plague is upon us:
                                          come
    with clement feet   25
                          oh come from Parnasos
    down the long slopes
                                  across the lamenting water

Antistrophe 2

CHORAGOS: Io Fire! Chorister of the throbbing stars!
    O purest among the voices of the night!   30
    Thou son of God, blaze for us!

---

18 Evohe evohe!: "Come forth; come forth!"

CHORUS: Come with choric rapture of circling Maenads
    Who cry *Io Iacche!*
                      God of many names!

EXODOS°

Enter MESSENGER, *left.*

MESSENGER: Men of the line of Kadmos, you who live
    Near Amphion's citadel.°
                           I cannot say
Of any condition of human life "This is fixed,
This is clearly good, or bad" Fate raises up,   5
And Fate casts down the happy and unhappy alike:
No man can foretell his Fate.
                       Take the case of Creon:
Creon was happy once, as I count happiness:
Victorious in battle, sole governor of the land,   10
Fortunate father of children nobly born.
And now it has all gone from him! Who can say
That a man is still alive when his life's joy fails?
He is a walking dead man. Grant him rich,
Let him live like a king in his great house: 15
If his pleasure is gone, I would not give
So much as the shadow of smoke for all he owns.

CHORAGOS: Your words hint at sorrow: what is your news for us?

MESSENGER: They are dead. The living are guilty of their death.

CHORAGOS: Who is guilty? Who is dead? Speak!   20

MESSENGER: Haimon.
    Haimon is dead; and the hand that killed him
    Is his own hand.

CHORAGOS: His father's? or his own?

MESSENGER: His own, driven mad by the murder his father had   25
    done.

CHORAGOS: Teiresias, Teiresias, how clearly you saw it all!

MESSENGER: This is my news: you must draw what conclusions you
    can from it.

CHORAGOS: But look: Eurydice, our Queen: 30
    Has she overheard us?

Enter EURYDICE *from the Palace, center.*

EURYDICE: I have heard something, friends:

°Exodos: Concluding scene.   2 Amphion's citadel: Thebes.

As I was unlocking the gate of Pallas' shrine,
For I needed her help today, I heard a voice
Telling of some new sorrow. And I fainted   35
There at the temple with all my maidens about me.
But speak again: whatever it is, I can bear it:
Grief and I are no strangers.

MESSENGER: Dearest Lady,
I will tell you plainly all that I have seen.   40
I shall not try to comfort you: what is the use,
Since comfort could lie only in what is not true?
The truth is always best.

                              I went with Creon
To the outer plain where Polyneices was lying,   45
No friend to pity him, his body shredded by dogs.
We made our prayers in that place to Hecate
And Pluto, that they would be merciful. And we bathed
The corpse with holy water, and we brought
Fresh-broken branches to burn what was left of it,   50
And upon the urn we heaped up a towering barrow
Of the earth of his own land.

                              When we were done, we ran
To the vault where Antigone lay on her couch of stone.
One of the servants had gone ahead,   55
And while he was yet far off he heard a voice
Grieving within the chamber, and he came back
And told Creon. And as the King went closer,
The air was full of wailing, the words lost,
And he begged us to make all haste. "Am I a prophet?"   60
He said, weeping, "And must I walk this road,
The saddest of all that I have gone before?
My son's voice calls me on. Oh quickly, quickly!
Look through the crevice there, and tell me
If it is Haimon, or some deception of the gods!"   65

We obeyed; and in the cavern's farthest corner
We saw her lying:
She had made a noose of her fine linen veil
And hanged herself. Haimon lay beside her,
His arms about her waist, lamenting her,   70
His love lost under ground, crying out
That his father had stolen her away from him.

When Creon saw him the tears rushed to his eyes
And he called to him: "What have you done, child?
     Speak to me.   75

What are you thinking that makes your eyes so strange?
O my son, my son, I come to you on my knees!"
But Haimon spat in his face. He said not a word,
Staring—
                    And suddenly drew his sword   80
And lunged. Creon shrank back, the blade missed;
    and the boy,
Desperate against himself, drove it half its length
Into his own side, and fell. And as he died
He gathered Antigone close in his arms again,   85
Choking, his blood bright red on her white cheek.
And now he lies dead with the dead, and she is his
At last, his bride in the houses of the dead.

Exit EURYDICE *into the Palace.*

CHORAGOS: She has left us without a word. What can this mean?
MESSENGER: It troubles me, too; yet she knows what is best,   90
    Her grief is too great for public lamentation,
    And doubtless she has gone to her chamber to weep
    For her dead son, leading her maidens in his dirge.

Pause.

CHORAGOS: It may be so: but I fear this deep silence
MESSENGER: I will see what she is doing. I will go in.   95

Exit MESSENGER *into the Palace.*

Enter CREON *with attendants, bearing* HAIMON's *body.*

CHORAGOS: But here is the King himself: oh look at him,
    Bearing his own damnation in his arms.
CREON: Nothing you say can touch me any more.
    My own blind heart has brought me
    From darkness to final darkness. Here you see   100
    The father murdering, the murdered son—
    And all my civic wisdom!

    Haimon my son, so young, so young to die,
    I was the fool, not you; and you died for me.
CHORAGOS: That is the truth; but you were late in learning it.   105
CREON: This truth is hard to bear. Surely a god
    Has crushed me beneath the hugest weight of heaven,
    And driven me headlong a barbaric way

To trample out the thing I held most dear.

The pains that men will take to come to pain!   110

Enter MESSENGER *from the Palace.*

MESSENGER: The burden you carry in your hands is heavy,
But it is not all: you will find more in your house.
CREON: What burden worse than this shall I find there?
MESSENGER: The Queen is dead.
CREON: O port of death, deaf world,   115
Is there no pity for me? And you, Angel of evil,
I was dead, and your words are death again.
Is it true, boy? Can it be true?
Is my wife dead? Has death bred death?
MESSENGER: You can see for yourself.   120

The doors are opened, and the body of EURYDICE *is disclosed within.*

CREON: Oh pity!
All true, all true, and more than I can bear!
O my wife, my son!
MESSENGER: She stood before the altar, and her heart
Welcomed the knife her own hand guided,   125
And a great cry burst from her lips for Megareus° dead,
And for Haimon dead, her sons; and her last breath
Was a curse for their father, the murderer of her sons.
And she fell, and the dark flowed in through her closing eyes.
CREON: O God, I am sick with fear.   130
Are there no swords here? Has no one a blow for me?
MESSENGER: Her curse is upon you for the deaths of both.
CREON: It is right that it should be. I alone am guilty.
I know it, and I say it. Lead me in,
Quickly, friends.   135
I have neither life nor substance. Lead me in.
CHORAGOS: You are right, if there can be right in so much wrong.
The briefest way is best in a world of sorrow.
CREON: Let it come,
Let death come quickly, and be kind to me.   140
I would not ever see the sun again.
CHORAGOS: All that will come when it will; but we, meanwhile,
Have much to do. Leave the future to itself.
CREON: All my heart was in that prayer!

---

126 Megareus: Son of Creon, killed in the attack on Thebes.

CHORAGOS: Then do not pray any more: the sky is deaf.   145
CREON: Lead me away. I have been rash and foolish.
I have killed my son and my wife.
I look for comfort; my comfort lies here dead.
Whatever my hands have touched has come to nothing.
Fate has brought all my pride to a thought of dust.   150

As CREON *is being led into the house, the* CHORAGOS *advances and speaks directly to the audience.*

CHORAGOS: There is no happiness where there is no wisdom;
No wisdom but in submission to the gods.
Big words are always punished,
And proud men in old age learn to be wise.

Study and Discussion Questions

1. Summarize the tragedies which have befallen Antigone and Ismene prior to the opening dialogue.
2. What are the principles out of which Antigone acts? What are Ismene's principles?
3. What are Creon's stated reasons, and what are his motives, for (a) forbidding burial of Polyneices, (b) punishing the law breaker, and (c) exiling Antigone?
4. What does Creon assume everyone else's motives are?
5. How is time important to what happens in the play?
6. Under what conditions does Antigone say she would have obeyed Creon's decree?
7. Are there any hints that the gods are on Antigone's side in the conflict?
8. What is the situation of each of the main characters at the end of the play?
9. Antigone and Creon have at least four areas of conflict: youth versus age, female versus male, the individual versus the state, the religious versus the secular. Give examples from the play for each of these conflicts.

Suggestions for Writing

1. The title of a classical tragedy is usually the name of the tragic figure, whose flaw brings his or her downfall. How is the situation more complicated in this play? What would you say Antigone's flaw is? Are there other candidates for tragic hero in this play? What is the flaw of each other candidate for tragic hero you come up with?
2. Choose one choral ode and discuss its purpose and effect within the play.
3. How are Creon and Antigone alike? Analyze some passages where you see their similarities.
4. Discuss how Haimon manipulates language in his speech to his father in Scene III.

5. Is Antigone's decision to protest Creon's decree and be honest and open about her actions a case of going too far? Is she courageous and admirable or just plain crazy? Take a position and argue it using evidence from the play.

Critical Resources

1. Bloom, Harold, ed. *Sophocles: A Comprehensive Research and Study Guide.* Philadelphia: Chelsea House, 2003.
2. Foley, Helene. *Female Acts in Greek Tragedy.* Princeton, NJ: Princeton UP, 2001. (Contains a chapter entitled "Sacrificial Virgins: Antigone as Moral Agent.")
3. Goff, Barbara, ed. *History, Tragedy, Theory: Dialogues on Athenian Drama.* Austin: U of Texas P, 1995. (Contains a chapter on Antigone and contextualizes the artistic and political climate of Athens at the time Sophocles wrote the play.)
4. Zelenak, Michael. *Gender and Politics in Greek Tragedy.* New York: P. Lang, 1998. Contains an introduction about the politics of Greek tragedy, as well as a chapter on Antigone.

❀ ❀ ❀

HERBERT BIBERMAN (1900–1971)
MICHAEL WILSON (1914–1978)

Salt of the Earth *has become a landmark in American cinema both for its radical content and for the circumstances surrounding the making of the film. Filmed during the early days of the Cold War and at the peak of McCarthyism,* Salt of the Earth *concerns a fifteen-month zinc miners' strike in Silver City, New Mexico, in 1951, and the difficult struggle the mostly Mexican American miners waged in order to protect their rights as workers and as Americans. Considering the political landscape at the time, focusing on the issue of workers' rights was considered communist propaganda and deemed "un-American" by the United States Congress. And indeed, film director Herbert Biberman had been forced to appear in front of the House Un-American Activities Commission for his alleged membership in the Communist Party. He (along with nine others known as the "Hollywood Ten") spent six months in jail and was officially blacklisted from working in Hollywood again. Upon his release, Biberman set out to make* Salt of the Earth *independently with screenplay writer Michael Wilson (also blacklisted), and, in the face of intense hostility from the U.S. government and the Hollywood film industry, finished the film in 1953, working closely with the actual miners and their families of Local 890 in Silver City. Unlike other films from this same period,* Salt of the Earth *took a hard and unsentimental look at the reality of working-class struggle, exploring themes of class consciousness, women's rights, and racial and ethnic discrimination. In 1992, the Library of Congress added* Salt of the Earth *to the National Film Registry for preservation as an important historical artifact.*

Salt of the Earth   (1953)

FADE IN (before titles):

Ext., QUINTERO *backyard. Medium shot, day.*

A woman at work chopping wood. Though her back is to the Camera, we sense her weariness in toil by the set of her shoulders. A five-year-old girl is helping the woman, gathering kindling. Over this scene comes the first title. A guitar dominates the musical theme. The motif is grave, nostalgic.

Ext., QUINTERO *backyard. A series of shots, day.*

As successive titles appear, each is matched by a view of the woman at her chores. Though at no time do we see her face, we begin to gather that she is large with child. The woman carries the load of wood to an outdoor fire, staggering under its weight, the little girl following with a box of kindling. . . . The woman feeds wood into the fire, on top of which is a washtub. . . . She scrubs clothes in the tub, bowed to the work, the little girl watching. . . . She wrings out articles of clothing, hanging them on a clothesline, the little girl helping gravely.

Ext., QUINTERO *backyard. Medium close shot, day.*

As the last title fades, the woman continues hanging the wash and for the first time we see her face: a mask of suppression, a chiselled yet eroded beauty, the eyes hooded, smoldering. At the same time, though her lips do not move, we hear her voice: grave, nostalgic, cadenced, like the music of the guitar, inflecting the melody of Mexican-American speech.

WOMAN'S VOICE: How shall I begin my story that has no beginning?

Medium full shot.

The clothes billowing in the wind as the woman hangs them up.

WOMAN'S VOICE: My name is Esperanza, Esperanza Quintero. I am a miner's wife.

Ext., front of the QUINTERO *cottage. Full shot, day.*

Copyright 1999 Organa LLC, from the DVD Salt of the Earth, *"The Hollywood Ten."*

It is a small clapboard dwelling surrounded by a picket fence. Flowers are blooming outside the fence. Beyond this house similar cottages can be seen, strung out along a dirt road.°

ESPERANZA'S VOICE: This is our home. The house is not ours. But the flowers . . . the flowers are ours.

Ext., Zinc Town. Vista shot, day.

We see several small stores, a gas station, scattered frame and adobe shacks, and in deep b.g. a Catholic church.

ESPERANZA'S VOICE: This is my village. When I was a child, it was called San Marcos.

Fuller vista shot, including the mine on a hilltop.

The mine dominates the town like a volcano. Its vast cone of waste has engulfed most of the vegetation on the hill and seems to threaten the town itself.

ESPERANZA'S VOICE: The Anglos changed the name to Zinc Town. Zinc Town, New Mexico, U.S.A.

Ext., church cemetery. Medium shot, day.

An ancient graveyard beside a Catholic church.

ESPERANZA'S VOICE: Our roots go deep in this place, deeper than the pines, deeper than the mine shaft.

Ext., countryside. Long pan shot, day.

We see great scudding clouds and the jagged skyline of a mountain spur. The mountain is scarred and pitted by old diggings. The lower slope is a skirt of waste, the grey powdery residue of an abandoned mine.

ESPERANZA'S VOICE: In these arroyos my great grandfather raised cattle before the Anglos ever came.

Close shot: a sign attached to a fence.

Ext.: *Outdoor shot.* Int.: *Indoor shot.* o.s.: *Out of scene.* f.g.: *Foreground.* b.g.: *Background.* Pan.: *Panoramic, or panning, shot (camera pivots).*

It reads:

PROPERTY OF
DELAWARE ZINC, INC.

Vista shot: the zinc mine in the distance.

ESPERANZA'S VOICE: The land where the mine stands—that was owned by my husband's own grandfather.

Closer shot, featuring the mine head.

At closer range we see the head frame, power house and Administration Building.

ESPERANZA'S VOICE: Now it belongs to the company. Eighteen years my husband has given to that mine.

Int., mine. Close shot, RAMÓN QUINTERO

at work. He is lighting fuses of dynamite charges which are packed into the rock face of a narrow drift. There are a dozen such fuses. The drift is lighted only by the lamp on RAMÓN's *hat.*

ESPERANZA'S VOICE: Living half his life with dynamite and darkness.

Close-up: a fuse.

It sputters, runs.

The drift, wider angle

to include RAMÓN'S *wild face as he turns and runs. We see only a bobbing lamp and the long shadow of a man running. We see a flash of light, hear muffled thunder.*

Ext., QUINTERO *backyard. Medium shot, day.*

ESPERANZA *has paused a moment in her work, looking off toward the mine with a worried frown. Now she picks up the heavy clothes-basket and walks toward the cottage. The little* ESTELLA *is not in sight.*

ESPERANZA'S VOICE: Who can say where it began, my story? I do not know. But this day I remember as the beginning of an end.

Int., QUINTERO *kitchen. Medium shot, day.*

It is no more than a narrow passageway, dominated by an ancient wood-burning stove. There is no running water. ESPERANZA *sets the basket down beside an ironing board, picks up an iron from the stove and tests it with a moistened finger.*

ESPERANZA'S VOICE: It was my Saint's Day. I was thirty-five years old. A day of celebration. And I was seven months gone with my third child.

ESTELLA *has run into shot, presenting her mother with a rose.* ESPERANZA *pins the rose in* ESTELLA'S *hair, with a small smile, then returns to her ironing. As she irons, her face becomes more and more desolate.*

ESPERANZA'S VOICE: And on that day—I remember I had a wish . . . a thought so sinful . . .

In a convulsive gesture her fingers go to her lips. She drops the iron and hurries from the kitchen.

Int., parlor. Medium close shot at shrine.

We see only a corner of the small cramped parlor where ESPERANZA, *with bowed head and clenched hands, stands before a shrine to the Virgin.*

ESPERANZA'S VOICE: . . . a thought so evil that I prayed God to forgive me for it. I wished . . . I wished that my child would never be born. No. Not into this world.

ESPERANZA *covers her face with her hands. The little girl enters scene, stares gravely at her.*

ESTELLA: Are you sick, Mama?
ESPERANZA: No, Estellita.
ESTELLA: Are you sad? *(As* ESPERANZA *doesn't answer)* Are we going to church? For your confession?
ESPERANZA: Later. When I finish the ironing. *(She goes out.)*

Full shot: kitchen.

As ESPERANZA *starts ironing again, her son* LUÍS *enters by the back door. A handsome boy of 13, but now panting and bedraggled, he pours himself a glass of water and gulps it down.* ESPERANZA *watches him sidelong.*

ESPERANZA: Fighting again? *(No response.)* With those Anglo kids?
LUIS: Aah, they think they're tough.
ESPERANZA: But you promised you wouldn't.
LUIS *(unrepentant)*:
Papa says if an Anglo makes fun of you to let him have it.

ESPERANZA *suddenly seizes his shoulder, spinning him around as if about to slap him, crying simultaneously:*

ESPERANZA: Never mind what your papa . . .

For the first time she (and we) see that the boy's mouth is bleeding. Her anger is washed away in a wave of concern, and she picks up a cloth and wipes the blood.

ESPERANZA: Hold still . . . does it hurt?

LUIS *(pulling away)*:   Naah.

He spies a birthday cake on the drainboard, sticks his finger in the icing.

LUIS: How come the cake?

ESPERANZA *grabs the cake, puts it in the cupboard.*

ESPERANZA: Never mind. Go get your father when he comes off shift. Tell him to come straight home.

Glad to be released, the boy darts off as we:

DISSOLVE TO:

Ext., Delaware Zinc Co. mine. Long shot, day.

In deep b.g. stands the head frame of the mine. We hear one shrill blast of a steam whistle, and as this sound dies away we hear the rattling hoist and conveyor belt, punctuated occasionally by the loud crash of ore from the bucket into the crusher. In right f.g. stands the Administration Building, a long wooden bungalow.

Moving with a group of miners

striding in a body toward the Administration Building. They appear angry and determined. RAMÓN QUINTERO *is in the lead. The others are* ANTONIO MORALES, ALFREDO DÍAZ, SEBASTIAN PRIETO, JENKINS *and* KALINSKY. *They all wear tin hats and grimy work clothes.*

Another angle, featuring Administration Building

as CHIEF FOREMAN BARTON *emerges from the* SUPERINTENDENT'S *office. He wears khaki and a Stetson. Seeing the approaching miners, he moves out to intercept them.*

Group shot: BARTON *and miners.*

The miners stop as BARTON, *hands in his hip pockets, blocks their way.* BAR-
TON *is a rangy Texan with a perpetual half-smile on his lips.* RAMÓN, *the miners'
spokesman, is rugged, handsome, younger in appearance than* ESPERANZA, *although he is a year older. There is a smoldering intensity in his manner and speech.
During the following the boy* LUÍS *enters scene, coming up behind his father. The
men ignore him.*

BARTON: Hear you had a little trouble, Quintero. Defective fuse? *(*RAMÓN
    nods.) Well, you're all in one piece. So what's the beef?
RAMON: *You* know the beef. This new rule of yours, that we work alone. We're
    taking it up with the Super.
BARTON: Super's busy—with your Negotiatin' Committee.
RAMON: So much the better.

He starts off, but BARTON *blocks his path again.*

Another angle.

BARTON: Now wait a minute. Super's the one made the rule. *He* ain't gonna
    give you no helper.
RAMON: He will if he wants us to go blasting.

The other miners step forward in support of RAMÓN. *They protest excitedly,
their speeches overlapping.*

ANTONIO: Listen, Mr. Barton—there's blood in that mine. The blood of my
    friends. All because they had to work alone . . .
JENKINS: That's how ya get splattered over the rocks, when there's nobody to
    help you check your fuses . . .
ALFREDO *(breaking in):*   . . . And nobody to warn the other men to stay clear.
BARTON: Warning's the shift foreman's job.
RAMON: Foreman wants to get the ore out. Miner wants to get his brothers out.
    In one piece.
BARTON: You work alone, savvy? You can't handle the job, I'll find someone
    who can.
RAMON: Who? A scab?
BARTON: An American.

He exits. RAMÓN *stands there, taut.*

DISSOLVE TO:

Int., kitchen of QUINTERO *cottage. Full shot, evening.*

ESPERANZA *enters from the parlor with some dirty dishes followed by* ES-
TELLA, *who carries her own plate. As* ESPERANZA *picks up the coffee pot, she*
spies ESTELLA *holding a candle over the frosting of the cake on the drain-*
board.

ESTELLA: Mama, can I put the candles . . .
ESPERANZA *(a fierce whisper)*: Hush . . . not a word about the cake, hear?

Int., parlor. Full shot.

The room is small, cramped. The plaster walls are cracked and peeling. Most
of the furnishings are faded and old. Nevertheless, the cottage is tidy and gives ev-
idence of considerable care. A dilapidated couch is covered with a fine Mexican
blanket. In one corner of the room stands a shrine to the Virgin. A vase of fresh-
cut flowers stands on the mantlepiece beneath a framed portait of Benito Juárez.
The only item of splendor in the room is a high-polished radio-phonograph con-
sole. Over scene we hear a tin-panalley compost of "Western" music sung by cow-
boy entertainers.

RAMÓN *sits with* LUÍS *at a small table near the kitchen door.* ESPERANZA *en-*
ters with the coffee pot, pours his coffee. ESTELLA *follows her, climbing onto her*
father's lap.

LUIS: Papa . . . is there gonna be a strike?

RAMÓN *ignores the question, brooding.* ESPERANZA, *who would also like to*
hear an answer, watches his face as he sips his coffee.

ESPERANZA *(finally, timidly)*:   Ramón . . . I don't like to bother you . . . but the
store lady said if we don't make a payment on the radio this month, they'll
take it away.

RAMÓN'S *forehead falls against his up-raised palm, as if to say it's too much to*
bear. The little girl looks at him gravely.

ESPERANZA: We're only one payment behind. I argued with her. It isn't right.
RAMON *(softly, imploring heaven)*:   It isn't right, she says. Was it right that we
bought this . . . this instrument?

He rises, holding ESTELLA.

RAMON: But you had to have it, didn't you? It was so nice to listen to.
ESPERANZA *(quietly)*:   I listen to it. Every night. When you're out to the beer
parlor.

Ignoring this mild rebuke, RAMÓN *crosses to the radio. Camera pans with him.*
He glares at the console, mimicking an announcer's commercial.

RAMON: "No money down. Easy term payments." I tell you something: this installment plan, it's the curse of the working man.

He slams his coffee cup down on the console, sets his daughter down and goes to the kitchen. ESPERANZA *quickly polishes the console where he struck it.*

Int., kitchen. Medium close shot.

RAMÓN *strips to the waist, pours some water from the tub on the stove into a pan on the drainboard.* ESPERANZA *appears in the doorway, watching him, her heart sinking. Her fingers go to her lips in a characteristic gesture.*

ESPERANZA: Where you going?
RAMON: Got to talk to the brothers.

ESPERANZA *bites her finger, trying to hide her disappointment.* RAMÓN *bends over the pan to wash. He has not noticed the cake.* ESPERANZA *picks it up quickly, hides it in a cupboard.* RAMÓN *splashes his face and neck with water, looks up in irritation.*

RAMON: This water's cold again.
ESPERANZA: I'm sorry. The fire's gone out.

She begins to stoke the stove.

RAMON: Forget it.
ESPERANZA: Forget it? I chop wood for the stove five times a day. Every time I remember. I remember that across the tracks the Anglo miners have hot water. In pipes. And bathrooms. Inside.
RAMON *(bitterly)*:   Do you think I like living this way? What do you want of me?

He reaches for a towel. ESPERANZA *hands him one.*

ESPERANZA: But if your union . . . if you're asking for better conditions . . . why can't you ask for decent plumbing, too?

Frustrated, evasive, RAMÓN *turns away, buttoning his shirt.*

RAMON: We did. It got lost in the shuffle.
ESPERANZA: What?
RAMON *(shrugging)*:   We can't get everything at once. Right now we've got more important demands.
ESPERANZA *(timidly)*:   What's more important than sanitation?

RAMON *(flaring)*:   The safety of the men—that's more important! Five accidents this week—all because of speed-up. You're a woman, you don't know what it's like up there.

She bows her head without answering and picks up the heavy tub of water on the stove. Unassisted, she lugs it to the dishpan in the sink and fills it. RAMÓN *begins to comb his hair, adding in a more subdued tone:*

RAMON: First we got to get equality on the job. Then we'll work on these other things. Leave it to the men.

ESPERANZA *(quietly)*:   I see. The men. You'll strike, maybe, for your demands— but what the wives want, that comes later, always later.

RAMON *(darkly)*:   Now don't start talking against the union again.

ESPERANZA *(a shrug of defeat)*:   What has it got me, your union?

RAMÓN *looks at her in amazement, not with anger, but with deep concern.*

RAMON: Esperanza, have you forgotten what it was like ... before the union came? *(Points toward parlor.)* When Estella was a baby, and we couldn't even afford a doctor when she got sick? It was for our families! We met in grave-yards to build that union!

ESPERANZA *(lapsing into despair)*:   All right. Have your strike. I'll have my baby. But no hospital will take me, because I'll be a striker's wife. The store will cut off our credit, and the kids will go hungry. And we'll get behind on the payments again, and then they'll come and take away the radio ...

RAMON *(furiously)*:   Is that all you care about? That radio? Can't you think of anything except yourself?

ESPERANZA *(breaking)*:   If I think of myself it's because you never think of me. Never. Never. Never ...

Reverse angle, shooting toward parlor.

She covers her face with her hands, begins to sob violently. RAMÓN *seizes her arms, shakes her. In b.g. we see the two children, still at table.*

RAMON: Stop it! The children are watching. Stop it!

ESPERANZA *(sobbing uncontrollably)*:   Never ... never ... never!

RAMON: Aaah, what's the use?

He drops her arms abruptly, almost flinging her aside, and stalks out of the kitchen, out of the house. ESPERANZA *remains leaning against the cupboard, sobbing. Camera holds: The boy* LUÍS *rises from the table, comes to the kitchen door, looks at his mother. Then he, too, turns and leaves the house.*

QUICK DISSOLVE TO:

Ext., beer parlor, Zinc Town. Full shot, night.

The place is lighted by a neon sign. From within we hear a juke box playing er- satz Mexican music. The boy approaches the door, pauses and enters.

Int., beer parlor. Full shot, night.

It is nondescript, small, dingy, dimly lighted, indistinguishable from a hundred other small-town bars. A half dozen miners, including ANTONIO MORALES, SE- BASTIAN PRIETO, *and* ALFREDO DÍAZ *stand at the bar rail, drinking beer. The bar- tender is an Anglo. We hear:*

We know it's not safe for miners to work alone! The boss will always tell you
  things like that!

LUÍS *has reached a post near a table at the far end of the room. Four men are seated around the table:* SAL RUIZ, FRANK BARNES, CHARLEY VIDAL *and* RAMÓN—*whose back is to Camera.* SAL *is drinking coffee; the other three are drinking beer.* LUÍS *stops, and as Camera moves in on group we pick up:*

RAMON *(angrily)*: They don't work alone in other mines! Anglos *always* work in pairs. So why should I risk my life? Because I'm only a Mexican?
SAL AND CHARLEY: But that's in the demands ... we're negotiating ...
RAMON: Three months of negotiations! And nothing happens! *(Indi- cates Frank.)* Even with Brother Barnes here from the International, what've we got? *(Ticks them off.)* No raise. No seniority. No safety code. Nothing.

Reverse angle, shooting toward RAMON.

The boy LUÍS *can be seen in b.g., but everyone ignores him. During the previ- ous speech* SEBASTIAN PRIETO *and* ANTONIO MORALES *have approached the table.* ANTONIO *sets a fresh bottle of beer before* RAMÓN.

ANTONIO: Take a drink. Calm down!
RAMON *(to* FRANK, *ignoring* ANTONIO*)*: I say we gotta take action. Now.
FRANK: Rest of the men feel like you?

RAMÓN *glances over his shoulder at the standing miners.* SEBASTIAN *glances uncertainly at* ANTONIO.

ANTONIO *(firmly)*:   He speaks for all of us.

CHARLEY: Ever stop to think maybe they want us to strike?

RAMON: Don't horse *me.* Price of zinc's never been higher. They don't want no strike—not with their war boom on.

FRANK: Then why's the company hanging tough? They've signed contracts with other locals—why not this one?

RAMON *(strikes the table)*:   Because most of us here are Mexican-Americans! Because we want equality with Anglo miners—the same pay, the same conditions.

FRANK: Exactly. And equality's the one thing the bosses can't afford. The biggest club they have over the Anglo locals is, "Well—at least you get more than the Mexicans."

RAMON: Okay, so discrimination hurts the Anglo too, *but it hurts me more.* And I've had enough of it!

SAL: But you don't pull a strike when the bosses want it—so they can smash your union. You wait till you're ready, so you can win.

RAMON: Do the bosses wait? No sanitation. So my kids get sick. Does the company doctor wait? Twenty bucks. So we miss one payment on the radio I bought for my wife. Does the company store wait? "Pay—or we take it away." Why they in such a hurry, the bosses' store? They're trying to scare us, that's why—to make us afraid to move. To hang on to what we got—and like it! Well, I don't like it . . . I'm not scared . . . and I'm fed up—to here! *(His hand goes a foot over his head.)*

ANTONIO: Hey Ramón—te buscan!

With a jerk of his head he indicates LUÍS. RAMÓN *turns around, spots his son. He rises, frowning, and moves toward him.*

Two shot: RAMÓN *and* LUÍS.

RAMON *(roughly)*:   What are you doing here? *(Suddenly worried.)* Something wrong with Mama?

LUIS *(deadpan)*:   I thought maybe you forgot . . .

RAMON: Forgot what?

LUIS: It's Mama's Saint's Day.

RAMÓN *is stunned, as though from a slap across the face. At last he works up a travesty of a grin.*

RAMON: You think I forgot? I was planning a surprise . . .

RAMÓN *turns back to the men.*

Camera follows him, holding on the group.

RAMON *(chuckling)*:   What a kid. He can't wait. It's my wife's Saint's Day. I was gonna ask you, brothers—how about a mañanita,[1] huh?
AD LIBS *(eagerly)*:   Sure. What time?
The later the better . . .
Wait'll she's asleep . . .

DISSOLVE TO:

Ext., QUINTERO *cottage. Full shot night.*

No lights are visible in the cottage, or in those adjoining it. A cluster of men, women and children can be seen in the front yard, serenading by moonlight. The song is called "Las Mañanitas." Two of the men are strumming guitars.

Closer angle: The serenaders.

They include RAMÓN *and* LUÍS, ANTONIO *and* LUZ MORALES, SAL AND CON-SUELO RUIZ, CHARLEY *and* TERESA VIDAL, FRANK *and* RUTH BARNES, ALFREDO DÍAZ *and his wife,* SEBASTIAN PRIETO *and a silver-haired old lady of great dignity,* MRS. SALAZAR. *The children range from 2 to 15, and there are many of them. Except for the youngest they sing as lustily as their parents.*

Int., bedroom, QUINTERO *house. Full shot, night.*

The small bedroom is partitioned by a screen, separating the children's cots from the parents' bed. A crucifix hangs over the bed. The room is feebly lighted by one small lamp. ESPERANZA *lies in bed, an arm flung across her eyes. The sound of the singing comes faintly over scene. Camera moves in slowly on* ES-PERANZA. *Her arm falls to her side. She opens her eyes. She listens, motionless.*

Another angle: the bedroom

as ESTELLA *emerges from behind the screen and climbs onto her mother's bed, with a kind of sleepy-eyed wonder.*

---

[1]Name Day celebration.

ESTELLA: Why are they singing, Mama?

ESPERANZA: They are singing for me.

ESTELLA: Can we light the candles now? On the cake?

ESPERANZA *(smiles)*:   Yes. We will light the candles.

Suddenly she flings back the bed covers, reaches for a dressing gown and puts it on.

Ext., QUINTERO *cottage. Full shot, night.*

The lights come up in the parlor. The front door opens, revealing ESPERANZA *and* ESTELLA. *They smile, remain in the open doorway as the serenaders go into a final chorus. The song ends in laughter and applause. They swarm into the house.*

Int., parlor. Full shot, night.

A merry bedlam, with ESPERANZA *receiving her guests.* SAL RUIZ *starts up a bawdy folk song on his guitar. He is urged on by* CHARLEY VIDAL'S *wild falsetto.* ANTONIO *lugs a case of beer into the house and immediately starts uncapping it, passing foaming bottles to everyone. The women gather around* ESPERANZA, *embracing her, wishing her a happy birthday in English and Spanish. Ramón is the last to enter.*

Closer angle, featuring ESPERANZA *and* RAMÓN

confronting one another in the center of the room. RAMÓN *gazes at her in silence, repentant. She returns his gaze, for the moment oblivious of her guests, who gracefully withdraw from the situation.* ESPERANZA'S *eyes fill with tears, she smiles tremulously, and her fingers go to her lips.*

ESPERANZA: I . . . I must get dressed.

She flees from the room. RAMÓN *follows her, gesturing to men to keep on with their singing.*

Int., bedroom. Two shot: RAMÓN *and* ESPERANZA.

He puts his arms around her, tentatively. Her forehead falls against his shoulder.

ESPERANZA: I did not mean to weep again. Why should I weep for joy?

RAMON: I'm a fool.

ESPERANZA: No, no . . .

She raises her head, brushing her cheek against his.

ESPERANZA: Was it expensive, the beer?
RAMON: Antonio paid for it.
ESPERANZA: Forgive me . . . for saying you never thought of me.
RAMON (*with effort*):   I did forget. Luís told me.

Grateful for his honesty, she pulls his head down, kisses him. He returns her kiss passionately.

DISSOLVE TO:

A montage, showing

ESPERANZA *chopping wood outside her kitchen door. The carefree guitar music of the mañanita carries over scene—and* ESPERANZA *pauses in her labors, seeming to hear it again.*

ESPERANZA'S VOICE: All the next week I kept thinking about my mañanita. I had never had so nice a party . . .

The image on the screen gives way to another as ESPERANZA *recollects the occasion: we see* ESPERANZA *and* ESTELLA *blowing out the candles on the birthday cake, surrounded by their beaming guests.*

ESPERANZA'S VOICE: It was like a song running through my mind, a humming in my heart, a day-dream to lighten the long days' work . . .

Ext., QUINTERO *backyard. Close shot:* ESPERANZA

bending over a large tub, scrubbing clothes. She pauses, smiles reflectively.

ESPERANZA'S VOICE: We forgot our troubles at the mañanita—even Ramón . . .

A new image is superimposed on the screen.

Now we see RAMÓN *dancing with* CONSUELO RUIZ, *while* ESPERANZA *looks on, smiling.*

ESPERANZA'S VOICE: I couldn't dance that night—not in my condition. But I wasn't really jealous when he danced with the others . . . because it was good just to see him smile again . . .

Ext., QUINTERO *yard, clothesline. Full shot, day.*

ESPERANZA *and* LUZ *are hanging clothes and talking across the fence between them. Their two children are playing together in f.g.*

ESPERANZA'S VOICE: And then one morning I was hanging out my wash.

Another angle: the yard, shooting toward front gate.

In deep b.g. we see three women enter the MORALES *yard and approach* LUZ. *They beckon to* ESPERANZA.

ESPERANZA'S VOICE: And while we were talking the ladies came. They were a kind of delegation. It was about the sanitation, they said . . .

Closer angle: the group at fence

as ESPERANZA *comes over. Throughout this scene the two children climb up, down and sideways on the fence in an intricate little geometric dance.* LUZ *goes on hanging up her clothes. We see the delegation talking earnestly to* ESPERANZA *and* LUZ *but we hear only:*

ESPERANZA'S VOICE: The Anglo miners have bathrooms and hot running water, Consuelo said, why shouldn't we?
ESPERANZA *(sighing)*:   I know, I spoke to Ramón about it—only a week ago.
RUTH: And what did he say?
ESPERANZA: They dropped it from their demands.
CONSUELO *(sighs)*:   Es lo de siempre.[2]
TERESA *(the militant)*:   We got to make them understand—make the men face up to it. *(To* RUTH) Show her the sign.

Another angle: the group

as RUTH *lifts up a placard, hitherto unseen, which she has been holding at her side. It reads:*

WE WANT SANITATION
NOT DISCRIMINATION

CONSUELO: We'll make a lot of signs like this. Then we'll get all the wives together and go right up to the mine.

----

[2]It's always the same.

ESPERANZA: To the mine?

TERESA: Sure. Where they're negotiating. In the company office. We'll go up there and picket the place.

CONSUELO: Then both sides will see we mean business.

ESPERANZA *(thunderstruck)*:   A picket line? Of . . . of ladies?

RUTH: Sure. Why not?

LUZ *flings a pair of damp pants on the clothes line without hanging them up.*

LUZ: You can count me in.

ESPERANZA *(scandalized)*:   Luz!

LUZ: Listen, we ought to be in the wood choppers' union. Chop wood for breakfast. Chop wood to wash his clothes. Chop wood, heat the iron. Chop wood, scrub the floor. Chop wood, cook his dinner. And you know what he'll say when he gets home *(Mimics* ANTONIO*)* "What you been doing all day? Reading the funny papers?"

The women laugh softly, all except ESPERANZA.

TERESA: Come on, Esperanza—how about it? We got to.

ESPERANZA: No. No. I can't. If Ramón ever found me on a picket line . . . *(Her voice trails off).*

CONSUELO: He'd what? Beat you?

ESPERANZA: No . . . No . . .

Suddenly we hear, from far off, five short blasts of a steam whistle. The women fall silent instantly, listening. Then it comes again. Five short blasts.

Ext., mine head. Long shot, day.

We can see little puffs of steam from the whistle on the head frame, and again we hear five short blasts.

Back to the women

frozen, apprehensive. LUZ *expels the word that has already crossed their minds.*

LUZ: . . . accidente . . .

She grabs her son from off the fence and hurries with him to the gate and out on to the road. The others begin to follow, as though magnetized. The signal continues over:

A series of shots, showing

women emerging from their houses, looking off at the mine.

Women strung out along the dirt road leading to the mine.

ESPERANZA, *slowed down by her unborn child, tagging along behind, holding Estella's hand.*

Ext., mine head. Medium long shot, day.

Men are scurrying toward the head frame from all directions. Two of them carry a stretcher. At this distance the whistle blast is much louder.

Ext., Administration Office. Medium long shot, day.

The union negotiators, RUIZ, VIDAL *and* BARNES, *emerge from the company office and walk swiftly toward the mine head.* SUPERINTENDENT ALEXANDER *and two company men follow.*

Ext., road leading toward mine. Long panning shot.

An ancient, dusty ambulance, its siren wailing, bounces along the narrow road leading to the mine. The advancing women make way for it.

Ext., head frame of mine. Medium shot, at hoist.

A cluster of miners wait tensely around the hoist as the cage rises to ground level. Several miners wearing tin hats are crowded inside the cage, but their faces are so grimy we cannot make out who they are.

Medium long shot: women and children

who have stopped on a little knoll at some distance from the mine head. They are looking down at:

The mine head, from their angle.

So many men gather around the injured man or men that we can still not distinguish them. But we see a body placed on a stretcher. Two men carry it toward the waiting ambulance.

Back to women. Close group shot.

One woman breaks away and plunges down the hill. The others heave a collective sigh—a sigh of relief, anguish, compassion.

LUZ: It's Mr. Kalinsky.

Rear of ambulance. Medium shot.

A large number of miners are milling about. The injured man is lifted into the ambulance and the doors are shut. Just then MRS. KALINSKY *runs up. She pounds on the doors.*

MRS. KALINSKY *(hysterically)*:   Let me see him! Let me see him!

Several miners try to calm her. They lead her away as the ambulance starts up.

AD LIBS: Now Mrs. Kalinsky, he's gonna be all right . . . His leg's broken, that's all . . . Come on now, you can see him in the hospital . . .

The milling crowd. Another angle

as SUPERINTENDENT ALEXANDER *comes up to the chief foreman.* RAMÓN *is close by. He is dirty, sweating, furious.*

ALEXANDER: How did it happen?
BARTON: He wandered into a drift—when this fellow was blasting. *(He indicates* RAMÓN.*)*
RAMON *(seething)*:   I told you it would happen. It's bound to happen when a man works alone!
ALEXANDER *(to* RAMÓN*)*:   Why didn't you give a warning signal?
RAMON *(indicates* BARTON, *bitterly)*:   Your foreman says that's a foreman's job.
BARTON: I checked the drift just before he blasted. It was all clear The man must have been asleep or something.
RAMON: You weren't even there. You were back at the station. Kalinsky told me—
BARTON: *(softly)*:   You're a liar, Pancho. A no-good, dirty . . .

RAMÓN *lunges at him.* BARTON *fends him off.* RAMÓN *keeps boring in, but* SAL RUIZ *and* FRANK BARNES *grab him. We hear an angry bedlam.*

AD LIBS   *(in Spanish and English)*:

Déjame! I'll kill him!
Hold him! Hold him! ...
Basta, Ramón!
All right, all right. Break it up ...
ALEXANDER *(pointing at* RAMÓN*)*: You, there. Get a hold on yourself. A man's
been hurt. I'm as sorry about it as you are. Savvy?

RAMÓN *finally quiets down. By now the miners have formed a ragged phalanx
in b.g. The three union negotiators,* RAMÓN, *the* SUPERINTENDENT *and the* CHIEF
FOREMAN *form a group in f.g.* ALEXANDER *speaks to all of them.*

ALEXANDER: Accidents are costly to everyone—and to the company most of
all. *(Glances at his watch.)* And now, I see no reason to treat the occasion like
a paid holiday. Suppose we all get back to work.

He takes a couple of steps, stops, noting that no one has moved.

ALEXANDER *(an order)*:   Mr. Barton.
BARTON *(a bluff approach)*:   All right, fellows, the excitement's over. Let's get
to it.

BARTON *starts toward the mine head. But the men do not move. Faintly we hear
mutterings in Spanish from the miners' ranks.*

AD LIBS:
     ... 'hora.
     ... Sí, yo creo que sí.

Another angle, featuring ALEXANDER.

ALEXANDER *(exasperated, to* VIDAL*)*:   What are they saying?
CHARLEY: No savvy.
ALEXANDER *(turning to* FRANK*)*:   Well, Barnes? How about it? Tell them to
get back to work.
FRANK *(grinning)*:   They don't work for me. I work for them.
ALEXANDER *(sharply)*:   Ruiz?

Wider angle, shooting toward miners.

Sal RUIZ *takes his time. He lights a cigarette. Then he calls out in Spanish:*

SAL: It's up to you, brothers.

A murmur runs through the ranks, "si, si." Several miners glance at RAMÓN. *Suddenly* RAMÓN *wheels, strides toward the power house, which is adjacent to the head frame of the mine. Passing through the miner's ranks, he bellows at the top of his lungs:*

RAMON: Cente!

Ext., power house. Close shot, at door.

As the man named CENTE (VICENTE) *sticks his head out the doorway of a galvanized tin shack, we hear a yell from off scene.*

RAMON'S VOICE: Apágalo![3]

CENTE'S *head disappears.*

A control board. Close shot

containing several big industrial circuit breakers. CENTE'S *hand comes up, pulls the switch.*

Ext., head frame, featuring crusher.

The gigantic primary crusher, with rock rattling around in it, suddenly stops.

Ext., head frame: at conveyor

carrying small lumps of ore from the crusher. The belt stops.

Back to men. Full shot.

The stillness is vast and sudden. RAMÓN *walks back to the massed ranks of his fellow miners. He halts beside* ANTONIO *at the end of the file. No one else moves or speaks.*

Closer angle: the miners' ranks.

ANTONIO *nudges* RAMÓN, *indicating something o.s.* RAMÓN'S *head turns, looking off scene. One by one the heads of the other miners turn, glancing o.s.*

---

[3]Turn it off.

Medium shot: FOREMAN *and* SUPERINTENDENT

standing before the silent miners. BARTON *realizes that the men are not look-ing at him, but at something above and beyond him.* BARTON *looks over his shoul-der.* ALEXANDER *slowly follows suit.*

From their angle, long shot: the women and children

standing on the knoll above the mine. They are silent and grave. The women's skirts billow in the wind, like unfurled flags, like the tattered banners of a guerrilla band that has come to offer its services to the regular army.

FADE OUT.

FADE IN:

Close-up: a license plate.

It is a New Mexico plate, and though it is night we can make out clearly the words on the white background on the plate:

LAND OF ENCHANTMENT

Camera pulls back slowly to disclose

a cowboy boot perched on a car bumper.

Camera pulls back further, disclosing

a khaki-clad leg, a pearl-handled revolver in a holster—then the full figure of a deputy leaning on the fender of his car. He is picking his teeth with a matchstick and gazing at:

Ext., union hall, shooting past sheriff's car, night.

The car is parked provocatively near the entrance to the building. A sign over the doorway, lighted by reflectors, identifies the place as the union hall. From within we hear the muted tumult of a packed house. In near f.g. is another parked car containing several women and children.

ESPERANZA'S VOICE: That night the men held a union meeting . . . just to make the walk-out official.

Suddenly we hear a roar of applause from inside the hall. The door opens; LUÍS *and a tow-headed youngster come bounding out, run toward the car, Camera panning with them.*

ESPERANZA'S VOICE: It didn't take them long. They voted to strike—93 to 5.

We see the car door open: RUTH BARNES *and* TERESA *emerge from the front seat;* CONSUELO, *holding a sleeping infant, gets out of the back.* ESPERANZA *is the last to appear.* ESTELLA *is asleep in her arms.*

ESPERANZA'S VOICE: . . . And Teresa said now was the time for us to go in. I didn't want to . . . I had never been to a union meeting. But the others said, one go, all go . . .

We see the women coaxing ESPERANZA. *She follows them reluctantly toward the union hall.*

Full shot, night: int., union hall

as seen from the entrance. A hundred miners are packed densely on the center block of benches, facing the union officers in b.g. SAL RUIZ *is presiding;* FRANK BARNES *sits at the table beside him.* CHARLEY VIDAL *stands near the chairman, delivering an impassioned speech.*

CHARLEY VIDAL: We have many complaints, brothers, and many demands. But they all add up to one word: Equality!

Over sound track we hear the Spanish of CHARLEY'S *speech, but it is modulated to:*

ESPERANZA'S VOICE: The meeting was nearly over when we came in. Charley Vidal was making a speech. He said there was only one issue in this strike— equality. But the mine owners would stop at nothing to keep them from getting equality.

The hall. Another angle, including the women.

The men are so intent on CHARLEY VIDAL'S *speech that they do not notice the entrance of the women, who tip-toe unobtrusively to the side of the room where they take seats on the unoccupied wall bench.* ESTELLA *wakes up, blinking in the bright lights.*

The hall. Full shot, featuring CHARLEY.

ESPERANZA'S VOICE: He said the bosses would try to split the Anglo and Mexican-American workers and offer rewards to one man if he would sell out his brother . . . There was only one answer to that, Charley said—solidarity. The solidarity of working men.

CHARLEY *concludes his speech*

CHARLEY VIDAL: To all this, brothers, there is only one answer, the solidarity of working men!

He sits down to loud applause which comes up over sound track. SAL RUIZ *rises, bangs his gavel.*

Group shot: the women.

RUTH *and* TERESA *nudge* CONSUELO, *trying to get her to rise—but* CONSUELO, *frightened, clings to her sleeping infant.* RUTH *grabs the baby and* TERESA *practically pushes* CONSUELO *to her feet.*

Wider angle, shooting past SAL, *including women.*

CHARLEY VIDAL *plucks at* SAL'S *sleeve, points in the direction of the women.*

SAL: Yes? You ladies have an announcement?
CONSUELO *(haltingly):* Well—it's not an announcement, I guess. the ladies wanted me to . . .
VOICE FROM THE FLOOR: Louder!
SAL: Consuelo, will you speak from over here?

Painfully self-conscious, CONSUELO *moves toward camera in f.g. She faces the men and begins again, nervous, but trying to speak louder.*

CONSUELO: The ladies have been talking about sanitation . . . and we were thinking . . . if the issue is equality, like you say it is, then maybe we ought to have equality in plumbing too . . .

Close group shot: miners.

Some appear resentful of the women's intrusion; others seem amused. ANTONIO *whispers something to* ALFREDO. ALFREDO *laughs. Frowning,* RAMÓN *looks around at Esperanza, as he might look at a woman who entered church uncovered.*

CONSUELO'S VOICE: I mean, maybe it could be a strike demand . . . and some of the ladies thought—it might be a good idea to have a ladies auxiliary! Well, we would like to help out . . . if we can . . .

Full shot: the hall, featuring CONSUELO.

CONSUELO *hurries back to her seat. Camera holds.*

We hear mild, scattered applause, and then a male falsetto giggle sets off a wave of laughter. RUIZ *rises, grins sheepishly.*

SAL: I'm sure I can speak for all of the brothers. We appreciate the ladies offering to help, but it's getting late and I suggest we table it. The chair will entertain a motion to adjourn.
FIRST MINER *(from the floor):* Move to adjourn!
SECOND MINER: Second!
SAL: So ordered.

He brings down his gavel, and the meeting ends. Some of the miners break for the door, others begin to mill about. RUTH *and* CONSUELO *walk to the front of the hall. Now, in quick succession we see four vignettes:*

Two shot: SAL *and* CONSUELO.

He meets her near the speaker's table, flings out his arms in a helpless gesture.

SAL: Why didn't you check with me? It's embarrassing!

Two shot: RUTH *and* FRANK.

She leans across the speaker's table before FRANK *can rise and remarks acidly:*

RUTH: Why didn't you support her? You're the worst of the lot.
FRANK. But honey . . .
RUTH: Or why don't you just put a sign outside? "No dogs or women allowed!"

Another part of the hall. CHARLEY *and* TERESA.

CHARLEY: But Teresa, you can't push these things too fast.
TERESA *(fiercely):* You were pushing all right—pushing us right back in our place.

ESPERANZA *and* RAMÓN, *near doorway.*

ESPERANZA *is holding* ESTELLA, *who is asleep again.* RAMÓN *is at the rear of a group of miners filing out of the hall. As two of the miners pass Camera, we hear one say to the other:*

FIRST MINER: That's a pretty good idea—making sanitation one of the demands again.

As RAMÓN *moves into f.g., he indicates with the slightest of gestures for* ESPERANZA *to follow. She obeys.*

Ext., union hall. Medium panning shot, night.

RAMÓN *emerges from the hall, moves to a corner of the building in f.g.* ESPERANZA *joins him there in the darkness.* RAMÓN *speaks softly.*

RAMON: At least you didn't make a fool of yourself—like Consuelo.

SLOW DISSOLVE TO:

Ext., picket line. Long establishing shot.

This panorama should be as inclusive as the location site permits. Thirty or more miners march counter-clockwise on a dirt road. Beyond this elliptical picket line on either side of the road are two signs:

DELAWARE ZINC CO., INC.
KEEP OUT
MINERS ON STRIKE
WE WANT EQUALITY

Though the area is unfenced, these signs mark an imaginary boundary. But access to the mine is difficult except by way of the road. To the right of the road is a steep wooded hillside. The road skirts this hill till it reaches the mountain of waste in deep b.g., then winds uphill to the knoll on which the mine stands. To the left of the road is a railroad spur and a gully. The gully is bridged by trestles, beyond which a fork of the road leads to Zinc Town. Two sheriff's cars are parked on the road near the picket post. No women are visible in this scene.

ESPERANZA'S VOICE: And so it began—much like any other strike. There would be no settlement, the company said, till the men returned to their jobs. But their back-to-work movement didn't work.

WIPE TO:

The picket line. Closer angle.

Two open touring cars loaded with strike-breakers slowly approach the picket line. The lead car stops before this human wall. The pickets make no menacing gestures, but they are ominous in massed silence.

ESPERANZA'S VOICE: And so the company recruited a few strike-breakers from
  out of town.

We see the lead car make a U-turn and withdraw the way it came. It is followed by the second car.

ESPERANZA'S VOICE: But they usually lost their nerve when they saw the size
  of the picket line.

Another angle, featuring SHERIFF's *cars*

parked near the picket line. A half-dozen deputies stand around idly. They are khaki-clad, booted, wearing their Stetsons with the brims rolled up. They display their side-arms ostentatiously, their holsters hanging low in the fashion of story-book gunmen.

ESPERANZA'S VOICE: The Sheriff's men were always there. They stood around,
  showing off their weapons. But the men only marched, day after day, week
  after week . . .

WIPE TO:

Ext., road, outside QUINTERO *cottage. Full shot, day.*

CHARLEY VIDAL *and another miner stand in the back of a pick-up, distributing rations to* ESPERANZA *and* LUZ MORALES. *The small sacks contain beans,
corn meal, coffee, etc.*

ESPERANZA'S VOICE: At first it was a kind of unwritten rule that the women
  stay at home. The union gave us rations and we had to figure out how to feed
  our families on them . . .

Ext., picket line. Medium shot, day.

There are fewer pickets now, and the miners, weary of the monotony, march in a more leisurely fashion. We see MRS. SALAZAR *(the old lady introduced at the mañanita) standing close by the picket line. She is crocheting.* RAMÓN, *the picket captain, and other miners glance uncomfortably at her.*

ESPERANZA'S VOICE: But then one morning Mrs. Salazar went to the picket line. Her husband had been killed in a strike many years before . . . and she wanted to be there.

WIPE TO:

The picket line. Matching shot, on another day.

MRS. SALAZAR *is now marching with the men. She is still crocheting. Her expression of calm determination is unchanging.*

ESPERANZA'S VOICE: Nobody remembers just how it happened, but one day Mrs. Salazar started marching with them . . . and she kept on marching with them.

WIPE TO:

The picket post. Another angle.

We see TERESA VIDAL *standing beside an old jalopy, pouring a cup of coffee for her husband.*

ESPERANZA'S VOICE: After a while some of the women began to bring coffee for their husbands . . . and maybe a couple of tacos—because a man gets tired and hungry on picket duty . . .

WIPE TO:

The pickets. Group shot.

Several pickets gape ravenously at ANTONIO *as he bites into the tacos given him by* LUZ.

ESPERANZA'S VOICE: It was about that time the union decided maybe they'd better set up a Ladies Auxiliary after all.

WIPE TO:

The picket post. Another angle

and another day. A number of miners have turned carpenter, erecting a shack of scrap lumber and galvanized tin close by the picket line. Several women have set up a table outside the unfinished shack on which we see a pot of beans, a coffee pot, etc. ESPERANZA *is not among them.*

WIPE TO:

Ext., coffee shack. Medium shot, day.

The shack is now complete. We see RAMÓN *approach the doorway, where a woman hands him a cup of coffee. He tastes it, makes a wry face.*

ESPERANZA'S VOICE: I didn't come to the lines at first. My time was near—and besides, Ramón didn't approve. But Ramón is a man who loves good coffee. And he swore the other ladies made it taste like zinc sludge ...

WIPE TO:

Matching shot: The coffee shack, featuring ESPERANZA.

Standing in the doorway, her pregnancy is more evident than ever. But her face is alight with one of her rare smiles as she pours a cup of coffee and hands it to RAMÓN. ESTELLA *can be seen peeking out from behind her mother's skirt.*

ESPERANZA'S VOICE: So one day I made the coffee ...

Camera pans with RAMÓN *as he strolls back toward the picket line, sipping his coffee.*

Group shots at picket line.

The men are not marching now, but standing in groups on the road. KALINSKY *is among them, on crutches, his leg in a cast.* RAMÓN *takes a sheet of paper from his shirt pocket and checks it.*

RAMON: Now let's see ... who's missing? Prieto, Sebastian. Prieto?
SECOND MINER: Haven't seen him for two days.
JENKINS *(entering scene, grinning)*:   Hey, Ramón—listen to this. The chief fore-man come to me last night, said he'd make me shift foreman if I'd start a back-to-work movement. "Jenkins," he says, "why string along with them tamale eaters?" I just told him I come to like tamales fine.

The men laugh, RAMÓN *smiles, but the look he gives* JENKINS *is tinged with speculative suspicion. Just then a patrol of three miners led by* ALFREDO DIAZ *enters scene from the hillslope.* ALFREDO *reports to* RAMÓN. *He is breathing hard.*

ALFREDO: Two scabs got through on the other side of the hill. We chased the rest back.

RAMON: Recognize them?

ALFREDO *(shaking head)*:   Anglos. From out of town. But they're not miners—
I could tell that. They don't know zinc from Shinola.

RAMON: *Okay.* Take five. Get yourself some coffee.

As the three men of the patrol walk off to the coffee shack, one of the miners on the picket line calls out:

FIRST MINER: Hey, Ramón, here comes the super . . .

Ext., winding road. Long shot: pickets' angle.

On the road from Zinc Town, across the trestle, we see a shiny new Cadillac crawling along the dusty road. It draws to a stop some distance away.

Close shot: Cadillac.

SUPERINTENDENT ALEXANDER *sits at the wheel. Beside him is* GEORGE HARTWELL, *a company representative from New York.* HARTWELL *is impeccably dressed in a gabardine suit and Panama hat. He peers over* ALEXANDER'S *shoulder as the superintendent points out:*

ALEXANDER: You can get the best view of the layout from here. That's their main picket line. They have another post on the back road, and roving patrols . . .

Reverse panning shot: their angle,

showing the SHERIFF's *cars, the picket line the unfenced hill, and the mountain of waste beyond it.*

HARTWELL'S VOICE: On company property? Why don't you have them thrown off?

ALEXANDER'S VOICE: But it's all company property, Mr. Hartwell—the stores, the housing area, everything. Where do you throw them? And who does the throwing?

ALEXANDER *nods, shifts the car into gear, and they move off.*

Ext., road. Medium long shot: the moving Cadillac.

It makes the bend, comes on up the hill and stops again near the SHERIFF's *cars, which are parked some thirty paces from the picket line. The* SHERIFF *walks toward the Cadillac.*

Close shot: Cadillac

as the SHERIFF *comes up to* ALEXANDER'S *side of the car. The* SHERIFF *has the appearance and speech of a New Mexican rancher, which he is. He touches his Stetson in a gesture of respect.*

SHERIFF: Mornin'.

ALEXANDER: How's it going?

SHERIFF: Well, those new fellows you hired from out of town—we brought 'em up here in a truck this morning, but they took one look at that picket line and turned tail.

HARTWELL *(looking at pickets)*:   They don't look so rough to me.

SHERIFF *(skeptically)*:   Well, Mr. Hartwell, they've got some pretty tough hombres, specially that picket captain there—what's his name . . . Ray, Raymond something-or-other . . .

ALEXANDER: Oh yes. I know that one.

He shifts into gear and drives off. The SHERIFF *touches his Stetson courteously.*

Back to picket line.

The men are marching now, moving in a tight ellipse across the road. KALIN-SKY *hobbles along beside them on his crutches.* RAMÓN *stands in the middle of the road, facing the picket line, his back to the approaching Cadillac. He lectures the men with mock severity.*

RAMON: Now why don't you let these gentlemen pass? Don't you know who's is that car?

ANTONIO *(shouting)*:   It's the paymaster from Moscow—with our gold.

RAMON: No, no, it's the president of the company himself—come all the way out here to make Jenkins general manager. So why you acting so mean?

The miners grin as they march, one of them slapping JENKINS *on the back.*

Int., Cadillac. Two shot, through windshield.

The car is halted again, and the picket line can be seen in b.g. ALEXANDER *is used to this treatment, but* HARTWELL *is annoyed.*

HARTWELL: Aren't they going to let us pass?

ALEXANDER: Eventually. This is just a little ritual to impress us with their power.

HARTWELL: Childish.

ALEXANDER: Well, they're like children in many ways. Sometimes you have to humor them, sometimes you have to spank them—and sometimes you have to take their food away. *(Points off scene.)*. Here comes the one we were talking about.

We see RAMÓN *leave the picket line and come toward the car. He is still sipping his coffee.* ALEXANDER *chuckles.*

ALEXANDER: He's quite a character. Claims his grandfather once owned the land where the mine is now. *(Both men laugh.)*

Another angle: at car

as RAMÓN *comes up. He leans down and peers inside.*

RAMON *(politely)*:   Want to go up to your office, Mr. Alexander?

ALEXANDER *(a half-smile)*:   Naturally. You think I parked here for a cup of coffee?

RAMON: You're welcome to one.

ALEXANDER: No thanks.

RAMON *(glancing at* HARTWELL*)*:   The men would like to know who this gentleman is.

ALEXANDER: That's none of their affair.

HARTWELL *(quickly)*:   That's all right—it's no secret. My name's Hartwell. I'm from the company's Eastern office.

RAMON: You mean Delaware?

HARTWELL: No. New York.

RAMON *(with mock awe)*:   New York? You're not the Company President by any chance?

HARTWELL *(smiles faintly)*:   No.

RAMON: Too bad. The men've always wanted to get a look at the President. *(Eagerly)*. But you've come out here to settle the strike?

HARTWELL *(shrugging)*:   Well, if that's possible . . .

RAMON: It's possible. Just negotiate.

HARTWELL *(coolly, to* ALEXANDER*)*:   Are we talking to a union spokesman?

ALEXANDER: Not exactly. But I wish he were one. He knows more about mining than those pie-cards we've had to deal with.

Hartwell is unprepared for ALEXANDER'S *gambit—but a mask falls suddenly over* RAMÓN's *face.* ALEXANDER *looks at* RAMÓN, *continuing with all the sincerity he can muster.*

ALEXANDER: I mean it. I know your work record. You were in line for foreman when this trouble started—did you know that? You had a real future with this company, but you let those Reds stir you up. And now they'll sell you down the river. Why don't you wake up, Ray? *(A pause)* That's your name, isn't it, Ray?

RAMON: No. My name is Quintero. Mister Quintero.

There is a moment's silence. ALEXANDER *compresses his lips, chagrined at the rebuff.*

ALEXANDER: Are you going to let us pass—or do I have to call the Sheriff?

RAMON: There's nothing stopping you. *(He steps back, indicating)*

The road, from their angle.

The road is clear. The pickets are no longer marching, but are lined up facing each other on both sides of the road. We hear the Cadillac accelerate. It plunges forward into scene, moves on past the pickets in a cloud of dust. RAMÓN *comes into scene, moving toward the picket post. He bellows at the miners:*

RAMON: I was wrong! They don't want Jenkins for general manager—they want *me!*

The men laugh, re-form in groups on the road.

Ext., coffee shack. Medium shot.

RAMÓN, *grinning, strolls over to* ESPERANZA, *who is standing in the doorway.*

RAMON: You shoulda heard that guy. What a line! I was up for foreman, he says. Fíjate!

ESPERANZA *smiles, then suddenly winces. Her hand goes to her midriff.* RAMÓN *is alarmed.*

RAMON: What's the matter?

ESPERANZA   *(smiles again)*: It's nothing. Just a little catch . . .

She takes ESTELLA *by the hand and starts to walk down the road toward the* SHERIFF's *cars.* RAMÓN *escorts her.*

Camera pans with them. Suddenly we hear from very far off a boy's voice calling:

VOICE: Papa! Papa! . . . Over here!
RAMON *(looking back):*   Is that Luís? What's he doing? Playing hookey again?

The wooded hill. Long shot from their angle.

In a thicket of juniper far up the slope we can make out two boys: LUIS *and a comrade of the same age. They are waving their arms frantically.* RAMÓN *walks into scene in f.g., cups his hands, bellows:*

RAMON: Luís! Come down here!
LUIS *(barely audible):*   Papa! We seen 'em! Two scabs! Over there!

Closer angle: LUIS *and companion.*

SECOND BOY *(pointing):*   They're hiding in the gully. Over there!

Back to picket post.

The miners are trying to spot the scabs. They mill about restlessly, all talking at once:

AD LIBS: Qué dijo?[4]
   He's spotted two scabs . . .
   Where?
   Over in the gully . . .
   Come on, let's get 'em . . .
RAMON *(yelling):*   Hold it, brothers! You—Antonio—Alfredo—Cente—you come with me. The rest stay on the line.

The four men set off at a run on the road paralleling the railroad tracks. Camera holds. ESPERANZA *comes into scene in f.g. She calls in exasperation:*

ESPERANZA: Luís! Luís! Come back here!

ESPERANZA *walks on, passing through the picket line.*

The hillside. Long shot,

as LUÍS *and his companion run diagonally down the slope.*

---

[4]What's he saying?

The gully. Long planning shot.

Two figures scramble out of the gully.

They run toward the railroad track, cross it and head for the uphill road to the mine.

Long panning shot: RAMÓN *and his men*

running, fanning out, trying to cut off the strike-breakers. CENTE *makes for the tracks.* RAMÓN *stays on the road.* ANTONIO *and* ALFREDO *dart up the hill.*

Group shot: at SHERIFF's *cars.*

The deputies have roused themselves. The SHERIFF *smiles, gives them a sign. Four deputies climb into a sedan and drive off.*

Closer angle: the two strike-breakers

running, One of them, a blond Anglo, stops suddenly, then runs back the way he came. Camera follows the other man. He reaches the road leading up through the mountain of waste to the mine.

Back to ESPERANZA

far behind the others, but coming on steadily, walking alone, as though in a trance.

The winding road. higher up.

ANTONIO *emerges onto the road above the strike-breaker, cutting him off.*

The STRIKE-BREAKER: *shooting toward waste heap.*

He veers off the road, tries to evade his pursuers by climbing the steep pile of waste, but makes no headway in the powdery dust. Slipping, clawing, he creates a small avalanche, plunges back to the road below.

The road, near foot of waste heap.

The STRIKE-BREAKER *comes tumbling down, scrambles to his feet, runs back toward the tracks. Camera pans with him.* CENTE *suddenly appears, blocking his way. Then* RAMÓN *appears, trapping the strike-breaker on the railroad trestle. The two miners advance slowly toward him.*

Closer angle: at trestle.

The strike-breaker stands there, panting, terrified. We are close enough now to recognize him. It is SEBASTIAN PRIETO.

Reverse angle, shooting toward RAMÓN *who stops, stunned by this unexpected betrayal.*

RAMON *(panting)*:   Prieto . . . Sebastian Prieto . . .

He comes on slowly toward SEBASTIAN. *There is murder in his eyes.*

SEBASTIAN: Ramón . . . listen . . . for the love of God . . .

RAMON: You . . . you . . . I'd expect it of an Anglo, yes . . . but you . . .

SEBASTIAN: Ramón . . . listen to me . . . I'm in a jam . . . I had to get a job . . .

RAMON: You Judas . . . blood-sucker . . .

SEBASTIAN: Ramón—listen . . . my kids . . .

RAMON *(seizing his collar)*:   Tú! Traidor a tu gente! Rompehuelga! Desgraciado![5]

SEBASTIAN: My kids don't have enough to eat!

RAMON *(shaking him)*:   You think my kids have enough to eat, you rat?

SEBASTIAN: I know, it's wrong. Just let me go. I'll leave town . . . just let me go.

RAMON *(contemptuously)*:   You think I was going to work you over? I wouldn't dirty my hands with you . . .

He spits in the man's face and shoves him away. SEBASTIAN *trips on the railroad track and falls.*

Medium long shot: the trestle

as seen from the road. The SHERIFF's *car plunges into scene in f.g., skids to a stop. The deputies pile out, run toward the trestle. In the distance we see* SEBASTIAN *scramble to his feet, cross the railroad spur and retreat to the gully out of which he came.* RAMÓN *stands watching him. The deputies are almost on him before he turns. One of them seizes him by the arm. He appears to be protesting, but the men are out of ear-shot. Suddenly we see the flash of handcuffs snapped on* RAMÓN's *right wrist.* RAMÓN, *offering no resistance, holds up his left hand—but a deputy spins him around with an arm lock and snaps* RAMÓN *wrists together behind his back. It all happens very quickly, and they lead him off.*

---

[5]You! Traitor to your people! Strikebreaker! Unfortunate person/devil!

Another angle, featuring miners and boys

standing in a group now, watching the arrest. LUÍS *starts to run to his father, but* ANTONIO *holds him back.*

Medium shot: at SHERIFF*'s car.*

RAMÓN *is thrust roughly into the back seat of the car between two deputies. The other two get in front. The driver turns the car around, raising a great cloud of dust. The car speeds off. Camera pans with it, holds on* ESPERANZA *watching at the side of the road. Suddenly* ESPERANZA *winces. Her hands go to her belly, and she bends slightly, as though from a severe cramp.*

Close shot: ESPERANZA.

Her face contorted with pain, with the realization that her labor has begun. She looks around helplessly, calls:

ESPERANZA: Luís! Luís! The baby . . .

Medium long shot from her angle: LUIS *and men*

listening, paralyzed, as we hear in Spanish:

ESPERANZA'S VOICE: The baby! Get the women! Quick!

Ext., back road. Medium long shot.

The SHERIFF*'s car speeds toward us down the road, stops suddenly in a swirl of dust. This is an isolated area near the mine; no observers can be seen.*

Int., back seat of SHERIFF*'s car. Med. close shot.*

RAMÓN *sits very straight, his wrists locked behind his back. The deputy on his left is a freckled-faced youth named* KIMBROUGH. *The deputy on his right is a pale, cavernous, slack-jawed man named* VANCE. VANCE *is slowly drawing on a pigskin glove.* RAMÓN *glances at the glove. Then he looks out the window.*

RAMON *(his voice low, tremulous)*:   Why do you stop?
KIMBROUGH *(grins)*:   Wanna have a talk with you—'bout why you slugged that fellow back there.
RAMON: That's a lie. I didn't—

The gloved hand comes up, swipes RAMÓN *across the mouth.*

VANCE (*softly*):   Now you know that ain't no way to talk to a white man.

Ext., road, near picket post. Medium long shot.

We can see MRS. SALAZAR *and several other women running to meet* ESPER-ANZA. *A couple of pickets follow along.* MRS. SALAZAR *shouts back at them in Spanish:*

MRS. SALAZAR: Go back and get a blanket, you idiots! So we can carry her!

Int., SHERIFF's *car. Medium full shot.*

RAMÓN *sits tense now, awaiting the next blow. A trickle of blood runs down his chin. The two deputies in front sit like wax dummies, paying no attention to what is going on in back.*

KIMBROUGH: Hey, Vance. You said this bull-fighter was full of pepper. He don't look so peppery now.
VANCE: Oh, but he is. He's full of chile, this boy.

He drives a gloved fist into RAMÓN's *belly.* RAMÓN *gasps, his eyes bulge.*

VANCE: He likes it hot. His chiquita makes it good and hot for him—don't she, Pancho?

VANCE *strikes him in the abdomen again.* KIMBROUGH *snickers.*

Ext., road: another SHERIFF's *car near picket line. Medium shot.*

The SHERIFF *is standing there with his other two deputies when* KALINSKY *hobbles up.*

KALINSKY (*breathlessly*):   Sheriff . . . we need a doctor—quick. A lady's gonna have a baby . . .
SHERIFF: What d'ya take me for? An ambulance driver?
KALINSKY: But there's a company doctor in town. We don't have a car. If you'd just go get him . . .
SHERIFF: You kiddin'? Company doctor won't come to no picket line.

KALINSKY *clenches his fists, furious, helpless. Then he labors back toward the coffee shack. Camera pans with him. In the distance we see four men carrying* ES-PERANZA *on a folded blanket.*

Ext., coffee shack. Full shot.

MRS. SALAZAR *is walking beside the improvised stretcher. She directs the men to enter the shack.*

MRS. SALAZAR: We can't get her home . . . there isn't time. Take her inside . . .

Int., SHERIFF's *car. Close shot.*

RAMÓN *is doubled up, his head between his legs.* VANCE *pulls him erect.*

VANCE: Hold your head up, Pancho. That ain't no way to sit.
RAMON *(a mutter in Spanish)*:   I'll outlive you all, you lice.
VANCE *(softly)*:   How's that? What's that Spic talk?

He strikes RAMÓN *in the belly.* RAMÓN *gives a choked cry.*

Now the intercutting becomes very rapid. The shots are brief flashes. Close up: ESPERANZA

lying on a cot in the coffee shack, her face contorted with pain. She gasps:

ESPERANZA: God forgive me . . . wishing . . . this child would never be born.

Back to RAMÓN.

KIMBROUGH *holds up* RAMÓN's *head while* VANCE *punches him methodically.* RAMÓN *gasps in Spanish:*

RAMON: Mother of God . . . have mercy . . .

Close up: ESPERANZA.

ESPERANZA *(in Spanish)*:   Have mercy on this child . . . let this child live . . .

Close up: RAMON *biting his lip in agony.*

RAMON *(in Spanish)*:   Oh, my God . . . Esperanza . . . Esperanza . . .

RAMÓN's *voice carries over to:*

Close up: ESPERANZA.

ESPERANZA: Ramón . . .

A contraction seizes her and she screams, her scream carrying over.

Close up: RAMÓN.

Now the two images merge, and undulate, and blur, as with receding consciousness. And then darkness on the screen. We hear the feeble wail of a newborn infant.

DISSOLVE TO:

Int., Catholic church. Full shot, day.

Except for the altar lights in deep b.g. the church is in shadow. A group of five men and five women are silhouetted at the altar rail, facing the priest. We cannot immediately identify them.

ESPERANZA'S VOICE: Ramón was in the hospital for a week . . . and then in the county jail for thirty days . . . charged with assault and resisting arrest. But I made up my mind to postpone the christening till he could be there. . . .

Group shot: at altar rail

including not only the QUINTERO *family but also* ANTONIO *and* LUZ, TERESA *and* CHARLEY, RUTH *and* FRANK, SAL *and* CONSUELO. ANTONIO *holds the baby up to the priest, who makes the sign of the cross. His lips move in prayer.* RAMÓN *peers fondly at the baby over* ANTONIO'*s shoulder.*

ESPERANZA'S VOICE: . . . And so the baby was baptized the day Ramón got out of jail. Antonio was his godfather, and Teresa Vidal his godmother. We christened him Juan.

The priest sprinkles holy water over the infant's head.

WIPE TO:

Int., QUINTERO *cottage: parlor. Full shot, night.*

The same men are seated around the parlor table, playing poker. From the phonograph we hear Mexican dance music. CONSUELO *bustles in with coffee for the men.*

ESPERANZA'S VOICE: That night we had a double celebration: Juanito's christening, Ramón's homecoming.

Int., bedroom. Full shot.

The room is almost completely dark but we can make out the forms of six children sleeping crossways on the bed. The baby's crib is beside the bed.

ESPERANZA'S VOICE: And we put all the children to sleep in the bedroom, as usual. . . .

Int., kitchen. Full shot.

The five wives are gathered there, preparing sandwiches, talking.

ESPERANZA'S VOICE: And the ladies adjourned to the kitchen—as usual.

Int., parlor: at poker table.

The Camera angle is that of a standing kibitzer. RAMÓN *is nearest the kitchen. Around him clockwise sit* ANTONIO, SAL, CHARLEY *and* FRANK. SAL *is dealing the fifth card of a stud poker hand. The play is continuous and fast, a counterpoint to the more serious discussion.*

ESPERANZA'S VOICE: And the men took over the parlor—as usual.

Her voice fades, and now we hear:

CHARLEY *(throwing in matches)*:   Five thousand dollars.
FRANK: Beats.
ANTONIO: Raise you ten thousand.
CHARLEY: You dog. All right, let's see them.
ANTONIO: Aces, wired. *(Scooping up pile of matches)* Come to papa.

While CHARLEY *gathers the cards and shuffles,* FRANK *turns to* RAMÓN.

RAMON: Hear those deputies slugged 'Cente.
FRANK: Yeah. Lots of provocation lately. They figure if they can lock up the leadership on some phony riot charge, maybe they can bust the strike.

Int., kitchen. Full shot

as TERESA *reenters from the parlor.* RUTH BARNES *is tapping her foot restlessly to the radio music which continues over scene.*

RUTH: Are we gonna let them play poker all night? I want to dance.
LUZ *(roguishly)*:   With whose husband?
RUTH: With any of them—even my own.
LUZ: If you dance with my husband, you'll have to put up with this . . .

She grabs RUTH *and dances her around in a lascivious parody of* ANTONIO'*s style. The women giggle.*

ESPERANZA's *head turns at the sound of an infant's wail.*

Int., parlor: at the poker table.

FRANK *is shuffling the cards.* ESPERANZA *is seen crossing the bedroom in b.g.*

SAL *(to* RAMÓN*)*:   And another thing. Your attitude toward Anglos. If you're gonna be a leader ...

RAMON *(cutting in)*:   What attitude?

SAL: You lump them all together—Anglo workers and Anglo bosses.

RAMON *(indicating* FRANK*)*:   He's a guest in my house, isn't he?

SAL: Sure, But you want the truth? You're even suspicious of him.

RAMON: Maybe. I think he's got a few things to learn about our people.

There is a rather uneasy pause. ESPERANZA *is seen re-crossing from bedroom to kitchen, the baby in her arms.* FRANK *continues shuffling.*

FRANK: Go on. Spill it.

RAMON *(slowly)*:   Well, you're the organizer. You work out strike strategy—and most of the time you're dead right. But when you figure everything the rank-an-file's to do, down to the last detail, you don't give *us* anything to think about. You afraid we're too lazy to take initiative?

FRANK *(defensively)*:   You know I don't think that.

RAMON: Maybe not. But there's another thing . . . like when you came in tonight—*(indicates picture)* I heard you ask your wife, "Who's that? His grandfather?"

Close shot: portrait of Juárez.

RAMON'S VOICE: That's Juárez—the father of Mexico. If I didn't know a picture of George Washington, you'd say I was an awful dumb Mexican.

Back to group.

CHARLEY *(softening the blow)*:   I've never seen it fail. Try to give Ramón a friendly criticism and he throws it right back in your face.

FRANK: No. He's right. I've got a lot to learn.

ANTONIO: Now we've got that settled, deal the cards.

FRANK *deals.* SAL *grins at* FRANK.

SAL: If it makes you feel any better, he's got even less use for women.

Back to kitchen. Full shot.

ESPERANZA *sits on a stool near the stove, her back to camera and the other* *women, nursing the baby.* TERESA *and* CONSUELO *are sampling the sandwiches they have made.*

CONSUELO: What are they talking about in there?
RUTH *(from the doorway)*:   Discussing each other's weaknesses.
LUZ *(mock surprise)*:   I didn't know they had any.
RUTH *(looking o.s.)*:   Right now, Ramón's on the receiving end.
TERESA: Let's break up that game.

Back to men at poker table.

FRANK *(earnestly to* RAMÓN*)*:   If the women are shut off from life in the union . . .
ANTONIO: Bet your hand!

RUTH *enters scene with coffee for the men. The other women, save* ESPERANZA, *trail in behind her.* FRANK *is so intent on his point that he ignores* RUTH's *presence.*

FRANK: We can't think of them just as housewives—but as allies. And we've got to treat them as such.
RUTH *(snorts)*:   Look who's talking! The Great White Father, and World's Champion of Women's Rights.
FRANK: Aw, cut it out, Ruth.
RUTH *(to* RAMÓN*)*:   Me, I'm a camp follower—following this organizer from one mining camp to another—Montana, Colorado, Idaho. But did he ever think to organize the women? No. Wives don't count in the Anglo locals either.

RAMÓN *laughs.* RUTH *turns back to him.*

RUTH: Not that I like the way you treat your wife. But when Doctor Barnes gives you his cure-all for female troubles, ask him if he's tried it at home.
RAMON *(grinning)*:   Hey, Esperanza!
RUTH: Esperanza's nursing the baby.

A glow of eagerness brightens RAMÓN's *face. He flings down the cards and goes out to the kitchen. The exasperated* ANTONIO *tosses his cards aside.*

ANTONIO: There goes the game.

LUZ: Good. Consuelo, turn up the radio *(To* ANTONIO*)* Come on, Papa, on your feet.

ANTONIO *gets up and begins to dance with his wife. We mark how accurate a parody his wife made of his style.* CHARLEY *dances with* TERESA. RUTH *folds her arms, glaring at* FRANK.

Int., kitchen. Close two shot.

RAMÓN *stands beside his wife, looking over her shoulder at the suckling child. The Camera angle is such that we cannot see* JUANITO.

RAMON *(proudly)*:   Look at him . . .

RAMÓN *clenches his fists, tenses his forearms, grunts approvingly.*

RAMON: A fighter, huh?
ESPERANZA: He was born fighting. And born hungry.
RAMON: Drink, drink, Juanito. You'll never have it so good.
ESPERANZA: He'll have it good. Some day.

For a moment they say nothing, watching the baby. Then, with a sidelong worried glance:

ESPERANZA: What were they saying? About you? In there?
RAMON: They say I am no good to you.
ESPERANZA *(shrugs)*:   You are no good to me—in *jail.*
RAMON *(musing)*:   I'd lie on my cot in the cell and I couldn't sleep with the bugs and the stink and the heat. And I'd say to myself; think of something nice. Something beautiful. And then I'd think of you. And my heart would pound against the cot for love of you.

ESPERANZA *is deeply moved, but she does not show him her face.* RAMÓN*'s face becomes tense with determination.*

RAMON *(half-whispering)*:   Not just Juanito. You'll have it good too, Esperanza. We're going to win this strike.
ESPERANZA: What makes you so sure?
RAMON *(brooding)*:   Because if we lose, we lose more than a strike. We lose the union. And the men know this. And if we win, we win more than a few demands. We win . . . *(groping for words)* something bigger. Hope. Hope for our kids. Juanito can't grow strong on milk alone.

His words are shattered by a loud knock at the front door. RAMÓN *turns, listening. We hear the door open and voices indistinctly. Camera holds on* RAMÓN *and* ESPERANZA.

VOICES:
>This the Quintero place?
>What do you want?
>Got a court order . . .
>You don't get in here without a warrant.
>We got the warrant too . . .
>We don't want no trouble. All we want's the radio.

RAMÓN *goes abruptly. Camera holds on* ESPERANZA, *listening.*

KIMBROUGH'S VOICE: We don't like to break in on you like this, but this fella owns the radio store, he got himself a repossession order on this radio here.
RAMON'S VOICE: Don't touch it.
KIMBROUGH'S VOICE: I don't want no trouble, Quintero. We got orders to repossess this machine.

ESPERANZA *rises swiftly, moves toward the parlor with the baby.*

RAMON'S VOICE: I said . . . don't touch it.

Int., parlor. Full shot.

Everyone is standing. Several armed deputies stand around the radio console, ready to move it, but checked momentarily by RAMÓN. KIMBROUGH'*s right hand is on the butt of his revolver.* ESPERANZA *enters scene. In one continuous movement, she hands the baby to* CONSUELO *and blocks* RAMÓN, *clutching him, and speaking with a new-found fierceness.*

ESPERANZA: Let them take it!
RAMON: Over my dead body.
ESPERANZA: I don't want your dead body. I don't want you back in jail either.
RAMON: But it's *yours.* I won't let them . . .
ESPERANZA (*savagely, in Spanish*): Can't you see they want to start a fight so that they can lock you *all* up at one time?

Slowly, RAMÓN *goes lax, and* ESPERANZA *relaxes her hold on him. The deputies pick up the heavy console, lug it toward the front door. The* QUINTEROS' *guests are glum and silent. The deputies leave, closing the door behind them.*

RAMON (*bitterly*): What are you so sad about?

He crosses to a shelf, picks up a dusty guitar and tosses it to SAL.

RAMON: Let's hear some real music for a change.

SAL *grins. He begins to improvise as we*

DISSOLVE TO:

Ext., mine and picket post. Long panoramic shot, day.

In the distance we can see the tiny figures of the strikers maintaining their vigil on the picket line. Behind them looms the lifeless head frame of the mine.

ESPERANZA'S VOICE: But the strike did not end. Ramón was wrong. It went on and on, into the fourth month, the fifth, the sixth. The company still refused to negotiate. We couldn't buy food at the company store . . .

Ext., store window. Medium close shot, day.

A Mexican-American woman is looking at a display of canned foods in the window of a small town store.

We see a hand place a small placard in the store window. It reads: NO CREDIT TO STRIKERS. Camera moves in till the sign fills the screen, and we

WIPE TO:

ESPERANZA'S VOICE: They tried to turn people against us. They printed lies about us in their newspapers . . .

The picket line. Medium shot, day.

A dozen or so pickets march counter-clockwise in a leisurely fashion. ANTONIO *holds an unfolded newspaper which he appears to be reading to the others, but we hear:*

ESPERANZA'S VOICE: They tried to turn the Anglo miners against us. They said that all the Mexicans ought to be sent back where they came from. But the men said . . .

ESPERANZA*'s voice fades, and now we hear from the picket line:*

ANTONIO *(slapping newspaper)*:   How can I go back where I came from? The shack I was born in is buried under company property.

KALINSKY: Why don't nobody ever tell the bosses to go back where they came from?

CENTE: Wouldn't be no bosses in the state of New Mexico if they did.

ALFREDO *(dreamily)*:   Brother! Live to see the day.

ANTONIO: Jenkins ain't no boss. *(Winking)* Mean we're gonna let people like
     Jenkins stay here?
RAMON: You can't send him back to Oklahoma. It'd be inhumane.
JENKINS *(grinning)*:   But I was born in Texas.
ANTONIO AND ALFREDO *(mock horror)*:   Oh *no*.
That's even worse.

They all start laughing, pummelling JENKINS *as they march.*

WIPE TO:

An ancient jalopy. Full shot, day

*on a dirt road outside an adobe house. The car is piled high with the belong-
ings of a Mexican-American family. The mother and her children are in the car.
The man is shaking hands with the neighbors in a sad goodbye.*

ESPERANZA'S VOICE: And the seventh month came. By now the strike fund was
     nearly gone. A few families couldn't take it any longer. They packed up and
     moved away—and where they went we do not know . . .

Int., union hall. Medium shot at desk, day.

SAL *and* CHARLEY *are seated behind the desk. A number of miners stand opposite them. One by one, the miners count out money, hand it to the union officers.* RAMÓN *stands nearby, watching.*

ESPERANZA'S VOICE: And so it was decided by the union that hardship cases
     should seek work in other mines. And this was done. And the strikers who
     found jobs divided their pay with the union, so the rest of us might eat.

Int., QUINTERO *cottage. Medium shot, evening.*

The QUINTERO *family is seated at the table. Their plates are empty.* ESPER-
ANZA *picks up a bowl containing two spoonfuls of beans. She divides them
among the children.*

ESPERANZA'S VOICE: Ramón was not a hardship case. Only three children to
     feed. No—the Quintero family was not hungry all the time. Just most of the
     time.

Ext., union hall. Full shot: a truck, day.

*Two men stand in the back of the truck, handing down cases of food to the min-
ers. One of the men in the truck is a Negro. When* CHARLEY VIDAL *comes over,
the Negro leans down and shakes his hand warmly.*

ESPERANZA'S VOICE: Even so, the mine owners might have starved us out were it not for the help we got from our International in Denver, and from the other locals.... And we who thought no one outside our county knew of our troubles, or cared if they did know—found we were wrong.

Int., union hall. Close shot at desk, day.

The desk is piled high with mail. SAL *and* FRANK *are opening it. We see dollar bills, loose change, checks.*

ESPERANZA'S VOICE: Letters came. From our own people, the Spanish-speaking people of the Southwest . . . and from far away—Butte, Chicago, Birmingham, New York—messages of solidarity and the crumpled dollar bills of working men.

Camera pulls back slowly to disclose

two women at a mimeograph machine.

Camera pans slowly around the union hall, disclosing other women at work—cutting stencils, filing papers, sealing envelopes, etc. Several small children romp and climb over the benches.

ESPERANZA'S VOICE: But that was not all—we women were helping. And not just as cooks and coffee makers. A few of the men made jokes about it, but the work had to be done—so they let us stay.

Medium shot, featuring ESPERANZA

standing behind a desk, sealing envelopes. The infant JUANITO *lies on an improvised pallet beside her, hemmed in by piles of leaflets.* ESTELLA *is licking stamps.*

ESPERANZA'S VOICE: No one knew how great a change it was, till the day of the crisis . . .

Full shot: the union hall.

The SHERIFF, *a* U.S. MARSHALL, *and several deputies appear suddenly in the entrance to the hall. They cross the room to* SAL RUIZ' *desk. The* SHERIFF *is grinning broadly.*

ESPERANZA'S VOICE: That was the day when the Sheriff and the Marshall came. The Sheriff was smiling—so we knew he brought bad news.

Closer angle: group at table.

SAL *takes the paper, reads it gravely. The* SHERIFF *grins triumphantly and leaves, followed by his entourage.*

ESPERANZA'S VOICE: The company had got a court injunction ordering the strikers to stop picketing. A Taft-Hartley injunction, they called it. It meant heavy fines and jail sentences for the strikers if they disobeyed.

SAL *rises slowly, re-reading the court order as* FRANK *and* CHARLEY *join him, reading over his shoulder. Their faces express worry, defeat.*

ESPERANZA'S VOICE: A decision had to be made at once—whether to obey the order, or not.

WIPE TO:

Int., union hall. Full panning shot, night.

The hall is packed. The striking miners, as usual, occupy the center bloc of seats. But this time there are almost as many women as men in the hall. They sit with their children in the rear or on benches against the side walls.

Camera holds on FRANK BARNES, *standing at the front of the hall, addressing the miners.*

FRANK *(as* ESPERANZA'S *voice fades)*:   If we obey the court, the strike will be lost . . . the scabs would move in as soon as the pickets disappear. If we defy the court, the pickets will be arrested and the strike will be lost anyway.

Closer angle, featuring FRANK.

FRANK: So there it is brothers. The bosses have us coming and going. I just want to say this—no matter which way you decide, the International will back you up—as it's always backed you up. This is a democratic union. The decision's up to you.

Reverse angle, shooting past FRANK *at miners.*

We hear a rumble of dissatisfaction as FRANK *sits down. There is no applause. Heads huddling, the miners grapple with the dilemma.* RAMÓN *rises angrily.*

RAMON: If we give up now, if we obey this rotten Taft-Hartley law, we give up everything it's taken us fifty years to gain. There is only one answer: fight them! Fight them all!

OTHER MINERS:
How?
They'll arrest us!
We gain nothing.

Their voices fade. RAMÓN, *still on his feet, turns on his critics, lashing them. Another miner rises, extending his arms in a gesture of helplessness. Over this we hear:*

ESPERANZA'S VOICE: The men quarreled. They made brave speeches. It seemed that Brother Barnes was right—the company had them coming and going. It seemed the strike was lost.

Full shot: the union hall. Another angle.

In near f.g. CHAIRMAN RUIZ *is on his feet, pounding his gavel. In b.g. we can see* TERESA VIDAL *waving for recognition. The chair recognizes her.*

TERESA *has advanced to the speakers' table in f.g. Though obviously scared, she is not as inarticulate or halting as* CONSUELO *had been.*

TERESA: Brother Chairman, if you read the court injunction carefully you will see that it only prohibits *striking miners* from picketing. *(A pause.)* We women are not striking miners. We will take over your picket line.

We hear a stirring, then a raucous male laugh.

TERESA: Don't laugh. *We* have a solution. You have none. Brother Quintero was right when he said we'll lose fifty years of gains if we lose this strike. Your wives and children too. But this we promise—if the women take your places on the picket line, the strike will *not* be broken, and no scabs will take your jobs.

There is silence in the hall now. TERESA *starts to walk back to her seat when* SAL's *voice checks her.*

SAL: If that's a motion . . . only members of the union can make a motion.

SAL *glances at* CHARLEY VIDAL, *who sits beside him.* CHARLEY *hesitates.* TERESA *glares at her husband.* CHARLEY *takes a deep breath, yells:*

CHARLEY: I so move!
VOICE *(from the floor)*:   Second!
SAL *(uneasy)*:   You've heard the motion. The floor is open for debate.
MINER: If we allow our *women* to help us, we'll be the joke of the whole labor movement!

ANOTHER MINER: Look, brother, our women are ours, our country-women! Why shouldn't they help us?

The hall. Another angle.

We see miners with their heads together in heated argument, grimaces and gestures of disapproval, individual miners rising to address the chair.

Another angle, featuring LUZ MORALES.

Eyes flashing, she addresses the men.

ESPERANZA'S VOICE: And Luz asked which was worse, to hide behind a woman's skirt, or go down on his knees before the boss?

Another angle, featuring GONZALES.

GONZALES: We haven't counted enough on our women. The bosses haven't counted on them at all.

Another angle, featuring CHARLEY VIDAL.

CHARLEY: Will the bosses win *now* because we have no unity between the men and their wives and sisters?

Another angle, featuring a miner and his wife.

A husky miner named JOSÉ SÁNCHEZ *can be seen goading his wife to speak. The frightened woman finally obeys.*

ESPERANZA'S VOICE: And Carlotta Sánchez said she didn't think picketing was proper for ladies. It wasn't nice. Maybe even a sin.

Another angle, featuring GONZALES *and* RAMÓN.

GONZALES: I say give the sisters a chance ...

GONZALES' *voice fades, and* RAMÓN *rises, glancing angrily at* GONZALES, *and begins to speak.*

RAMON: And what will happen when the cops come, and beat our women up? Will we stand there? Watch them? No. We'll take over anyway, and we'll be right back where we are now. Only worse. Even *more* humiliated. Brothers, I beg you—don't allow this.

RAMÓN *sits down. There is scattered applause from the men. Someone calls the question.*

Reverse angle, shooting toward chairman.

SAL *(rapping his gavel):* All right. The question's been called. You brothers know what you're voting on—that the sisters of the auxiliary take over the picket line. All those in favor will so signify . . .
TERESA'S VOICE *(a bellow):* Brother Chairman! A point of order!

Wider angle, shooting toward TERESA *and* ESPERANZA.

TERESA *nudges* ESPERANZA. *She rises shyly. It seems that* ESPERANZA'S *stage fright will leave her mute—but at last she finds her voice:*

ESPERANZA: I don't know anything . . . about these questions of parliament. But you men are voting on something the *women* are to do, or not to do. So I think it's only fair the women be allowed to vote—especially if they have to do the job.

We hear cries of approval from the women's section, intermingled with shouted objections from some men.

Group shot: at chairman's table.

SAL *has to make a ruling, but he seems undecided. He glances at* CHARLEY. CHARLEY *winks, nods. He glances at* FRANK. FRANK *grins and nods.* SAL *clears his throat.*

SAL: Brothers . . . and sisters. It would be unconstitutional to permit women to vote at a union meeting. *(Male applause.)* If there's no objection, we could adjourn this meeting . . . *(There are cries of protest from men and women alike. He holds up his hand.)* No, wait, wait . . . and reconvene this meeting as a community mass meeting with every adult entitled to a vote!
VOICE: I so move!
SECOND VOICE: Second!
SAL: All those in favor will raise their hands. *(Most of the hands are raised.)* Now those opposed . . . *(Only a few hands are raised.)* The ayes have it! Now, every adult is entitled to a vote!
WOMEN'S VOICES: Question! Question! Call the question!
SAL *(grinning):* Those in favor that the sisters take over the picket line will so signify by raising their hands.

The hall. Full panning shot from SAL's *angle.*

An overwhelming majority of the women are voting for the plan. About a third of the men raise their hands—but some of them lower their arms when nudged angrily by their neighbors. Tellers move through the hall counting hands. Camera holds on RAMÓN, *who is practically sitting on his hands. He frowns at:*

ESPERANZA, *from his angle,*

her eyes averted, but her hand defiantly up.

Back to chairman.

The tellers approach SAL, *whisper the affirmative vote. He adds the totals, then pounds his gavel.*

SAL: Okay. All those opposed?

Full panning shot: as before.

Most of the women sit with their fingers intertwined, as though in prayer. A few weaker sisters raise their hands uncertainly. Their neighbors nudge them. The hands come down again. Camera pans to the men as the tellers count. We see a forest of raised hands. Some miners are frantically holding up both arms.

Back to chairman. Medium shot.

The tellers give SAL *their figures.* SAL's *face is grave, reveals nothing. He rises, announces quietly:*

SAL: The motion has carried—a hundred and three to eight-five. *(No applause.)*

Reverse angle. Full panning shot.

A profound stillness has settled over the hall. The men turn in their places, looking at their womenfolk with doubt, apprehension, expectancy. Camera pans to the women who line the side wall. They look at each other with a breathless wonder as the full import of their undertaking dawns on them.

FADE OUT.

FADE IN:

Ext., picket line. Long panoramic shot, morning.

This panorama should be as sweeping a vista as the first scene of the picket line. We get the sense of women streaming toward the picket post from four points of the compass. Some arrive in ancient cars, others walk by way of the road or foot paths or the railroad tracks. There are so many women on the line that even though they march two abreast they overlap the road.

ESPERANZA'S VOICE: And so they came, the women . . . they rose before dawn and they came, wives, daughters, grandmothers. They came from Zinc Town and the hills beyond, from other mining camps, ten, twenty, thirty miles away . . .

Closer view: the picket line.

The women march in an orderly, determined fashion. There is no gaiety. TERESA *and* MRS. SALAZAR *are in charge. They are as bold and self-assured as two drill sergeants. Most of the women are dressed for the occasion—wearing shirts, jeans and sneakers or saddle shoes.*

ESPERANZA'S VOICE: By sun-up there were a hundred on the line. And they kept coming—women we had never seen before, women who had nothing to do with the strike. Somehow they heard about a women's picket line—and they came.

Medium long shot: miners on hillside.

On the steep wooded slope above the picket post the varsity squats on its collective haunches. The men smoke, watching the picket line with mingled awe and apprehension.

ESPERANZA'S VOICE: And the men came too. They looked unhappy. I think they were afraid. Afraid the women wouldn't stand fast—or maybe afraid they would.

The hillside. Another angle, higher up the slope.

Several miners stand here with their families. They, too, look unhappy. JENKINS *and his wife are among them.*

ESPERANZA'S VOICE: But not all the women went to the picket post. Some were forbidden by their husbands. *(A pause.)* I was one of these.

Close group shot: the QUINTERO *family*

standing apart from the others, near a clump of juniper. LUÍS *stands beside his father, whose uneasy frown is directed at the picket line.* ESTELLA *stands beside her mother, who holds the baby* JUANITO *in her arms.* ESPERANZA *keeps gazing at the picket line off scene, never at* RAMÓN.

ESPERANZA: It's not fair . . . I should be there with them. After all, I'm the one
   who got the women the vote.
RAMON *(stubbornly)*:   No.
ESPERANZA: But the motion passed. It's . . . it's not democratic of you to . . .
RAMON *(interrupting)*:   The union don't run my house. *(After a long pause.)*
   Those Anglo dames stirred you up to make fools of yourselves—but you don't
   see any of *them* down there.
ESPERANZA *(squinting, peering)*:   Yes, I do. There's Ruth Barnes.
RAMON: She's the organizer's wife. She's got to be there.
ESPERANZA: No, she *wants* to be there. *(Looking off)* And there's Mrs.
   Kalinsky.
RAMON *(pointing off scene)*:   There's Jenkins' wife. You don't see her on no
   picket line.
ESPERANZA *(quietly)*:   Anglo husbands can also be backward.
RAMON: Can be *what?*
ESPERANZA: Backward.

He glances quizzically at her. She keeps staring at:

The picket line from their angle.

ESPERANZA'S VOICE *(plaintively)*:   Can't I even put in an appearance?
RAMON'S VOICE: In heaven's name, woman, with a baby in your arms?

Back to family group.

ESPERANZA: The baby likes to be walked. It helps him burp.

RAMÓN *shakes his head. He looks off at:*

The SHERIFF*'s convoy. Long shot.*

Some fifty paces beyond the picket line we can see two open trucks and two sheriff's cars. The trucks are loaded with men.

Ext., SHERIFF*'s car. Medium shot.*

SUPERINTENDENT ALEXANDER, CHIEF FOREMAN BARTON, *the* SHERIFF *and the deputy* VANCE *are standing beside the car.* ALEXANDER *is in a petulant mood, but the* SHERIFF *and* VANCE *seem amused by the situation. Three pretty Mexican-American girls pass by on their way to the picket line.* VANCE *whistles at them. As they move out of the scene* VANCE *calls:*

VANCE: Hey, girls! Wait a minute! Don't you wanta see my pistol?

ALEXANDER: Shut up. *(As the* SHERIFF *chuckles)* What's so amusing? They're flaunting a court order.

SHERIFF *(grins)*:   Not so sure about that. Letter of the Law, you know. All the injunction says is no picketing by miners.

ALEXANDER *(furious)*:   Whose side are you on anyway?

SHERIFF: Now don't get excited, Mr. Alexander. They'll scatter like a covey of quail.

BARTON *(impatiently)*:   Well, let's get at it—before another hundred dames show up.

SHERIFF *(rouses himself, calls)*:   All right, boys.

Wider angle: the convoy.

Drivers and deputies climb into the cab of each truck. BARTON, VANCE *and two other deputies get into the lead car.* VANCE *holds up his tear gas gun.*

VANCE: What about these?

SHERIFF: Forget it. They'll scatter like quail.

BARTON *starts the motor. He waves at the truck drivers and the other sheriff's car. They wave back. The convoy starts up, gathering speed rapidly.*

Full shot: miners on the hillslope.

They spring to their feet, tense.

Full shot: the picket line.

The women stop marching, turn in unison to face the oncoming convoy.

Full panning shot: the convoy

hurtling toward the picket line.

Close shot: faces of miners.

They groan involuntarily.

Close shot: faces of women pickets,

steady, unflinching.

The SHERIFF's *car from their angle,*

horn blowing, speeding directly at them, looming bigger, closer.

Full shot: the picket line.

At the last split second, BARTON *jams on his brakes, and the car skids. The women have not moved.*

Close shot: women and car.

The car skids into the picket line. A woman is swiped by the front fender, flung onto the road.

Full shot: the picket line.

We hear a collective gasp from the women. Then they scream. Two women run to their injured sister. The others swarm around the car. The deputies are trying to get the doors open. The women begin to rock the car. Finally the deputies manage to get out. They flail the women with their fists, their gun stocks. But there are four women to each deputy, and they cling to the men, grabbing at their weapons.

Medium shot: the first truck.

The Anglo scabs standing in the back of the truck react in fear and consternation. But they stay where they are.

Medium long shot: miners on hillside.

A group of them start coming down the hill. We can see CHARLEY *and* FRANK *gesturing, trying to restrain them—but the miners come on.*

Back to the picket post.

VANCE *kicks out at woman who is trying to tear off his cartridge-belt, sends her sprawling. He backs off, panic-stricken, and fires a tear gas shell into a mass of women pickets. The exploding shell disperses them momentarily. The women fan out, coughing and choking.*

The picket post, shooting from hill above.

At MRS. SALAZAR's *command, the women form into two platoons; the larger group remains on the road, blocking the convoy, despite the fact that other deputies open fire with tear gas; but another line has formed at the side of the road, facing the miners bent on entering the fray.*

Closer angle: the second picket line.

As the miners coming down the slope reach the road, MRS. SALAZAR *waves them back angrily, yells in Spanish:*

MRS. SALAZAR: Get back! Get back! Stay out of this!

FIRST MINER *(desperately)*:   But they're beating up my wife!

WOMEN *(simultaneously in English and Spanish)*:   It'll be worse if you get in it.
Then they'll start shooting . . .
They'll throw you in jail!
We can take care of ourselves . . .
You're not needed here . . .
Get back! Get back!

The men fall back, nonplussed by the vehemence of the women.

Back to picket post. Long shot from hillside.

Other deputies have come running from the rear of the convoy to support the four outnumbered deputies. The scabs remain in their trucks. But the wind is blowing the wrong way, and the tear gas drifts back toward the trucks. The scabs begin to cough. A couple of them jump over the tailgate of the first truck and run. That starts a panicky rout. Other scabs tumble out of the trucks and run back down the road to escape the tear gas.

Close group shot: the QUINTERO *family*

staring at the action. ESPERANZA *can't stand it any longer. She hands the baby to* RAMÓN *and is gone before he realizes her intent.*

His view: ESPERANZA

running diagonally down the slope toward the picket post. In the distance we see deputies still battling the women. The deputies seem to have lost their heads. They lash out viciously at any woman who confronts them, in a vain attempt to scatter the women and clear the road.

Closer angle: the picket post.

LUZ MORALES *is climbing* VANCE's *back, clinging to his arms. Another woman clutches at his gun hand, trying to prevent him from drawing his pistol.* ESPERANZA *comes running up. She stops for a second, slips off her right shoe.* VANCE *knocks the other woman down, pulls his revolver from his holster.* ESPERANZA *whacks him over the wrist with her shoe, knocking the weapon out of his hand.* LUZ *digs into his hair with both hands.*

Back to RAMÓN *on hillside,*

helpless, speechless, holding the baby. Suddenly he runs out of scene. LUÍS *grabs* ESTELLA's *hand, follows.*

Another part of the hill: the lower slope.

CHARLEY *and* FRANK *are watching the action.* RAMÓN *comes running into scene.*

RAMON: Why are you standing there? Do something!
CHARLEY *(looking o.s.)*:   Relax.
RAMON: But women are getting hurt! We've gotta take over!
CHARLEY: They're doing all right.
FRANK *(grins, looks at baby)*:   Anyway, looks like you've got your hands full.

Completely frustrated, RAMÓN *looks down at the tiny bundle in his arms. Then he looks off at:*

The picket post: long shot from RAMON's *angle.*

We can see BARTON *calling his men off. He jumps in the car, turns it around. Several deputies climb aboard as he drives off. The others retreat on foot, leaving the two abandoned trucks. The women re-form their lines, and begin to sing "The Union Is Our Leader."*

DISSOLVE TO:

Int., QUINTERO *cottage. Full shot: parlor, late afternoon.*

RAMÓN *paces the floor fretfully, puffing on a cigarette. The baby crib is in a corner, and Juanito is wailing.* ESTELLA *tries to match her father's caged-lion stride.*

ESTELLA: Papa, I'm hungry.
RAMON *(a growl)*:   So'm I:

LUÍS *enters from the front door.* RAMÓN *glares at him.*

RAMON: Where's your mama?
LUIS: She's coming. Charley Vidal gave her a lift.

The boy starts off, then turns back again, his eyes glowing.

LUIS: Boy! Did you see the way Mama whopped that deputy with her shoe?
   Knocked the gun right out ...
RAMON *(thundering)*:   I don't want you hanging around there, hear?

We hear the sound of a chugging truck outside. RAMÓN *goes to the window, peers out.*

Ext., road outside QUINTERO *cottage. Medium shot.*

The union pick-up, full of women, stops at the gate. ESPERANZA *and* LUZ *sit beside* CHARLEY *in the cab. They get out. All the women are laughing and smiling.*

Int., parlor. Full shot

as ESPERANZA *enters. She is dirty, be-draggled, and bone-tired—but there is a new light in her eyes, and when she smiles she grins.*

RAMON *(hoping for the worst)*:   You all right?
ESPERANZA: Sure.

She kisses him lightly on the cheek, kisses ESTELLA *and* LUÍS, *crosses immediately to the crib, glances at* JUANITO *and enters the kitchen. Camera pans with her.* RAMÓN *follows slowly, halts in the kitchen doorway.*

RAMON: Must've been some experience for you, huh?
ESPERANZA *(from kitchen)*:   Yes.
RAMON: I guess you got enough today to last a lifetime, huh?
ESPERANZA *(from kitchen)*:   I'm going back tomorrow.

She emerges from the kitchen with the baby's bottle, crosses to the crib.

The infant's wailing ceases abruptly. Ramón comes over, scowling.

RAMON: You might get hurt. *(No response)* Listen, if you think I'm gonna play nursemaid from now on, you're crazy . . . I've had these kids all day!
ESPERANZA *(simply)*:   I've had them since the day they were born.

She exits to the kitchen. RAMÓN *trails after her.*

Int., kitchen. Medium shot.

ESPERANZA *works swiftly, putting pots and pans on the stove, preparing supper, etc.* RAMÓN *continues to scowl at her.*

RAMON: I'm telling you. I don't stay home with these kids tomorrow.
ESPERANZA *(calmly)*:   Okay. Then, tomorrow, I take the kids with me to the picket line.

DISSOLVE TO:

Ext., picket line. Full panning shot, day.

There are fewer women on the line than on the first day, but they march with the same assurance and discipline as before. A good half of them crochet as they march.

ESPERANZA'S VOICE: And so I came back the next day—and every day for the next month . . .

Camera pans

past the picket line to the coffee shack, moves on to pick up a group of small children playing near the road.

ESPERANZA'S VOICE: I kept Juanito in the coffee shack, and when the weather was good and there was peace on the line I brought his crib outside. Estella played with the little ones, and Luís . . .

Camera swish pans

to a clump of juniper on the hillside in deep b.g. We can make out Luís, crouching there with several cronies, apparently plotting something.

ESPERANZA'S VOICE: . . . Luís was in school.

Camera swish pans

to another part of the hill, closer to the picket post. RAMÓN *can be seen reclining on the slope with several cronies. The men appear moody and depressed.*

ESPERANZA'S VOICE: Ramón came every day and sat on the hillside, just watching. The ladies—well, they criticized Ramón for not keeping the kids.

Back to picket post. Full shot.

In b.g. women are crocheting, chatting as they march. The baby's crib, sheathed in mosquito netting, lies on a table outside coffee shack in f.g. ESPERANZA *is changing the baby's diaper.* MRS. SALAZAR *and* TERESA *are talking to her.*

WIPE TO:

Another angle.

Trucks and SHERIFF's *cars can be seen parked near the picket line. The scabs and deputies stand in the trucks, jeering at the marching women.*

ESPERANZA'S VOICE: For a while the Sheriff's men left us alone. But then it started again. They cursed us, insulted us, called us foul names. It started again.

WIPE TO:

The picket post. Wider angle

as a moving truck loaded with scabs tries to force its way through the living wall of women. The women try to push the truck back. They cling to it, and the scabs lean down and beat them off. The truck lurches forward, striking a woman and flinging her onto the road.

Several other women have opened the hood of the truck. They rip out ignition wires. The truck stalls.

WIPE TO:

The picket post. Long shot.

The truck is gone. Four deputies wearing gas masks are firing tear gas shells into the picket line. The women retreat, fan out in a great arc.

ESPERANZA'S VOICE: They used tear gas again. This time the wind was against us.

Another angle, shooting toward hillslope.

ESPERANZA *and* ESTELLA *can be seen running up the slope away from the gas.* ESPERANZA *carries the baby.*

ESPERANZA'S VOICE: When that happened we spread out, as we had planned, and I took the baby away from the danger, as we had planned.

Back to picket post. Medium long shot.

Instead of tear gas enveloping the picket line, the picket line envelops the drifting gas, re-forms again downwind.

ESPERANZA'S VOICE: But they couldn't break our line. They couldn't break it . . .

DISSOLVE TO:

Full shot: the road, below picket post,

where a small army of scabs and deputies is gathered. The scabs stand sheepishly beside the trucks. The SHERIFF, BARTON, *and several deputies are gazing off at the picket line. They are no longer amused. The superintendent's Cadillac enters scene, coming up the road. It rolls to a stop near the Sheriff's party.*

Close group shot: at car.

ALEXANDER *(to* SHERIFF*)*:   Well?

SHERIFF *(hopelessly)*:   I've tried everything but shootin' 'em down.

ALEXANDER: You haven't tried locking them up!

SHERIFF *(doubtfully)*:   You want 'em *all* arrested?

ALEXANDER: No, just the ring leaders. The fire-eaters. And the ones with big families . . . *(to Barton)* Barton—where's that boy?

BARTON *(waves, shouts)*:   Hey, you—c'mere.

SEBASTIAN PRIETO, *the fingerman, leaves a group of deputies in b.g. and comes over. The* SHERIFF *glances at him with contempt, then starts toward the picket line,* PRIETO *and the deputies moving with him.*

The picket line. Full shot

as they approach the line. The women keep on marching. ESPERANZA *is among them, carrying the baby.*

SHERIFF *(shouting at them)*:   Awright, girls—I'm gonna give you a choice—you can go home or you can go to jail. No ifs, ands or buts. Git off the picket line or git arrested.

Silence. The women keep on marching. The SHERIFF *turns to* SEBASTIAN.

SHERIFF: Okay. Point 'em out.

SEBASTIAN *(a furtive mumble)*:   That one—Teresa Vidal. She's the leader.

KIMBROUGH *walks over to the line, grabs* TERESA's *arm as she marches by.*

Closer angle, featuring KIMBROUGH *and* TERESA.

KIMBROUGH: You're under arrest. Home or the hoosegow—what's it gonna be?

Several of the women stop marching. MRS. KALINSKY *picks up a stick. They approach* KIMBROUGH *menacingly.*

TERESA: Keep marching sisters. Let's show some discipline.

MRS. KALINSKY: But Teresa, we . . .

TERESA: They'll charge us with resisting arrest. Keep marching!

She jerks loose from KIMBROUGH *and walks alone toward the trucks.*

Back to SHERIFF's *group. Medium shot*

as SEBASTIAN *fingers other women the deputies walk off one by one to arrest them.*

SEBASTIAN: And Mrs. Salazar . . . the old one. And Chana Díaz—that one, in the blue dress. And Luz Morales, the little one, shaking her fist . . . and Mrs. Kalinsky, the Anglo . . . and Ruth Barnes, she's the organizer's wife . . .

The picket line. Medium shot

as the women are plucked off the line, one by one. They do not resist. We can see ESPERANZA *still marching. She seems to clutch the baby more tightly to her.* ESTELLA *tags along beside her mother.*

Reverse angle, shooting toward trucks.

The back of one truck is already filled with women, and the other is filling rapidly.

Two shot: SHERIFF *and* SEBASTIAN.

SEBASTIAN: . . . And Lala Alvarez, the pretty one over there. And that one.
SHERIFF *(irritably)*: With the baby?
SEBASTIAN *(a sly grin)*: She's Ramón Quintero's wife. He don't like her being here at all.

The SHERIFF *hesitates a moment, his eyes narrowed in thought, then gives* VANCE *the nod.* VANCE *approaches the line.*

Medium shot: at picket line.

VANCE *plucks at* ESPERANZA's *sleeve. She stops for a second, frightened, wavering. The women remaining on the line call out to her:*

AD LIBS *(in Spanish)*: We'll take the baby, Esperanza . . .
Don't worry about Juanito . . . We'll keep Estella too . . .

VANCE *pulls at her arm again.* ESPERANZA *stiffens with a sudden fierceness.*

ESPERANZA: No. The baby stays with me. *(She stoops down to* ESTELLA.*)* Go to Papa. You stay with Papa, hear?

Head high, carrying the baby, ESPERANZA *walks off toward the waiting trucks. The little girl watches her go, bereft, perplexed.*

Ext., hillside. Close shot: RAMÓN.

He comes to his feet, tense with anxiety.

Ext., picket line. Long panning shot from his angle.

Suddenly ESTELLA *breaks away from the picket line and runs after her mother.* ESPERANZA *is climbing into the back of the second truck, which is now full.* ES- TELLA *jumps onto the tailgate and a woman pulls her up. We hear motors start- ing. The trucks pull off slowly. At the same instant we hear* TERESA's *clear voice, singing "Solidarity Forever." The other women join her. The chorus swells. Cam- era holds on the receding trucks, and the singing fades. Now the Camera pans slowly back to the picket line. There are only a handful of women remaining. But from somewhere we hear the song again. Camera pans on, holds on a view of the wooded hillside. Suddenly we see twenty or more women coming down the slope with* CONSUELO RUIZ *in the lead. They are singing, these reserves, coming to re- plenish the gaps in the line.*

SLOW DISSOLVE TO:

Int., county jail: two cells. Full shot, night.

Over the dissolve we hear the rhythmic clank of tin cups against steel bars. Lights come up slowly to reveal two adjacent jail cells packed with women. All are standing, for there is no room to sit down. The women in f.g. bang on the bars, and all of them chant rhythmically in Spanish:

WOMEN:
Queremos comida . . .
Queremos camas . . .
Queremos baños . . .
Queremos comida . . .[6]

Reverse two shot: TURNKEY *and* VANCE

as seen from the cell. The two deputies are leaning back in their chairs against a blank wall opposite the cells. The deafening chant is driving the turnkey to dis-

---

[6]We want food . . . we want beds . . . we want baths . . .

traction. He puts his hands to his ears. Suddenly he rises and comes over, holding up his hands for quiet. VANCE *follows.*

TURNKEY: Now listen! Please, girls! Be quiet! Listen! *(The din subsides.)* I've told you ten times. We don't have no food. We don't have no beds. We don't have no baths. So please—*please*—*shut up!*

VANCE *grins at* LUZ MORALES, *whose face can be seen behind the bars in close foreground. He reaches out, chucks her under the chin.* LUZ *scratches at his hand, and he withdraws it. The chant is resumed.*

Int., rear of cell. Close group shot.

The one cot in the cell is occupied by ESTELLA *and the infant* JUANITO. JUANITO *is crying.* ESPERANZA *hovers worriedly over him, trying to get him a take a nippled bottle, which he rejects.*

ESPERANZA *(to* TERESA*)*: He can't drink this milk. It'll make him sick. He's on a formula. *(In a panic of guilt)* I was a fool! I shouldn't have kept him with me.

TERESA: Don't you worry. We'll get some action.

She moves off to the front of the cell, calling for quiet.

Front of cell, featuring TERESA.

The women stop their clamor for a moment. TERESA *calls out to* VANCE:

TERESA: The baby can't drink this store milk. We want his formula!

VANCE *(puzzled)*: You want what?

RUTH: The formula, the formula . . .

The women begin banging away with their cups again taking up the chant:

WOMEN: We want the formula! We want the formula!

VANCE *winces at the noise.*

Int., court house hallway. Medium shot, night.

RAMÓN *can be seen coming slowly up the hall.* LUÍS *trails behind him.* RAMÓN *walks like a man in enemy territory. From off scene the sound of the women's chant carries over: "We want the formula . . ."*

The hall. Another angle.

RAMÓN *is passing a door marked:* OFFICE OF THE DISTRICT ATTOR-NEY. *The door is slightly ajar.* RAMÓN *stops, turns back, looks inside.*

Int., district attorney's office from RAMÓN'*s angle.*

All that can be seen in RAMÓN'*s cone of vision is a desk across the room. The D.A.'s feet are on the desk. He is in his shirt sleeves, but wearing his hat.* ALEXAN-DER *sits on the corner of the desk.* HARTWELL *and the* SHERIFF *wander in and out of scene, pacing the floor.*

D.A.: Well, you can get the J.P. to swear out peace bonds. Or heist the bail high enough so you can keep 'em in jail.

SHERIFF *(exasperated)*: *Keep* 'em? What am I supposed to do—feed 'em outa my own pocket?

Back to hallway. RAMÓN *and* LUIS.

RAMÓN'*s hand is half-raised to the door-knob. It falls to his side. He listens.*

D.A.'S VOICE: What I want to know, Mr. Hartwell, is when you gonna settle this thing. You won't negotiate with 'em. What are you after, anyway?

Medium shot: HARTWELL *from* RAMÓN'*s angle.*

HARTWELL *(pacing)*: The company has other mines. You've got to see the larger picture. Once these people get out of hand . . .

Without noticing RAMÓN, *but conscious of the need to keep what he is saying confidential,* HARTWELL *has moved to the door and closed it, cutting off the rest of his sentence.*

Back to RAMÓN,

frustrated in his desire to hear more. Just then VANCE *rounds a corner in b.g. and enters scene, walking toward Camera. He stops short, seeing* RAMÓN. *For a moment they stare at one another.* VANCE *looks scared, despite the fact that he is armed and within his own bastille.*

VANCE: What you doin' here? Ain't you seen enough of me?

RAMON *(scarcely audible)*: I come for my kids. They're in your jail.

VANCE *warily brushes past* RAMÓN *and opens the office door, gesturing for the* SHERIFF. *During the few moments the door is open, we hear:*

D.A.'S VOICE: But you've played every trump in your hand and they're not dead yet.
HARTWELL'S VOICE: Not every trump.
D.A.'S VOICE: Such as what?

The SHERIFF *comes out, closing the door behind him, cutting off the inside conversation again.*

VANCE: I can't shut them dames up. They keep yellin' about the formula.
SHERIFF: The what?
VANCE: Formula for the baby or somethin'. *(Indicates* RAMÓN*)* His kid.

The SHERIFF *glances at* RAMÓN *and stalks off down the hall.* VANCE *follows.*

Int., jail corridor, shooting toward cells,

as the SHERIFF *and* VANCE *enter. The women's clamor is as loud as ever. The* SHERIFF *holds up his hands for quiet.*

SHERIFF: Now look here. I got you some milk for the baby. So what's all the belly-achin' about?
AD LIB: It's no good, the milk ... Queremos la formula ... The baby has a formula ... If Juanito gets sick you'll be responsible ...
SHERIFF *(exasperated)*:   I'm not running a drug store. You girls got nobody but yourselves to blame and you can be home with your families in an hour. All you have to do is sign a pledge that you won't go back to the picket line.
MANY VOICE *(in English and Spanish)*:   Don't sign nothin' for the stinker. No, no deals, no deals ... Make him get the formula.

They start banging on the bars again. The SHERIFF *turns angrily to* VANCE.

SHERIFF: Where'd that fellow go?

VANCE *takes a few steps, shouts around a corner, beckoning.*

VANCE: Hey, Pancho, c'mere!

RAMÓN *enters scene, walking slowly into f.g.* LUÍS *tags along behind. The women fall silent abruptly. It is very still.*

Close group shot: at cell door.

The SHERIFF *motions to the turnkey to unlock one of the cells. He obeys.*

SHERIFF: Awright. Where's the baby? And the little girl?

ESPERANZA *brings the baby from the rear of the cell.* ESTELLA *squeezes past the tightly packed women, joins her mother.* RAMÓN *and* ESPERANZA *gaze at one another with deep poignancy, unsmiling. He holds out his hands. She gives the baby to him.* ESTELLA *looks up at her mother.* ESPERANZA *nods, gives her a little push.* ESTELLA *walks outside.* LUÍS *takes her hand. The father and his children walk off slowly, out of scene. The women watch them go. The turnkey locks the cell again. Suddenly they start banging on the bars.*

VOICES:
Queremos comida . . .
Queremos camas . . .
Queremos baos . . .
Queremos comida . . .

                                                        DISSOLVE TO:

Ext., QUINTERO *back yard. Full shot, day.*

The shot matches the earlier scene of LUZ *and* ESPERANZA—*but now* RAMÓN *and* ANTONIO *are hanging out the wash.* ESTELLA *and the little* MORALES *boy are there.* RAMÓN *sees them playing in the baskets.*

RAMON: Will you kids get out of those baskets!

There are two large wicker baskets besides the fence: one contains JUANITO, *the other a mountain of damp clothes. As he works,* ANTONIO *calls from across the fence:*

ANTONIO *(in Spanish)*:   How goes it?
RAMON *(in Spanish)*:   It never ends.

He snaps out a damp undershirt, hangs it up. Suddenly he explodes:

RAMON: Three hours! Just to heat enough water to wash this stuff! *(A pause. He goes on working.)* I tell you something. If this strike is ever settled—which I doubt—I don't go back to work unless the company installs hot running water for us. *(Another pause.)* It should've been a union demand from the beginning.
ANTONIO: Yeah.

We hear the baby wail. RAMÓN *walks over to the basket, puts the nipple of the bottle back in* JUANITO's *mouth. Then he resumes his chores.* ANTONIO *muses as he works.*

ANTONIO: It's like Charley Vidal says—there's two kinds of slavery, wage slavery and domestic slavery. The Woman Question, he calls it.

RAMON: The woman . . . *question?*

ANTONIO: Question, question—the problem, what to do about 'em.

RAMON *(cautious)*:   So? What does he want to do about 'em?

ANTONIO: He says give 'em equality. Equality in jobs, equality in the home.
Also sex equality.

RAMÓN *(a long pause)*:   What do you mean—sex equality?

ANTONIO: You know . . . *(Leers, shifts into Spanish.)* What's good for the goose
is good for the gander.

Close shot: RAMÓN

*with a clothespin in his mouth, mulling over this concept. His imagination runs
away with him. He scowls thoughtfully.*

ANTONIO'S VOICE: He's some organizer, that Charley. He can organize a wife
right out of your home.

RAMÓN *bites viciously on a clothespin and hangs up a pair of diapers.*

DISSOLVE TO:

Int., QUINTERO *kitchen. Medium shot, night.*

*There are two large tubs on the cluttered drainboard—one of soapy water, one
of rinse water.* RAMÓN *is washing the dishes.* LUÍS *is drying them.* RAMÓN *is sweaty
and sullen.* LUÍS *is bored and impatient.*

LUIS: Papa, can't I leave now? There's a meeting of the Junior Shop Stewards . . .

RAMON: The what!

LUIS: The Junior Shop Stewards. There's lots of ways we can help.

RAMON *(exploding)*:   Don't I have enough troubles without them shipping you
off to reform school?

LUIS *(earnestly)*:   But, Papa—you need all the help you can get.

RAMON: You've got to help around the house!

LUIS: But you've got me doing everything. Mama never used to make me dry
the . . .

RAMON *(cutting him off)*:   You should have helped her without being asked.

*At that moment we hear the raucous braying of an automobile horn from out-
side.* LUÍS *dashes into the parlor.* RAMÓN *stands there scrubbing a greasy dish.
Now we hear gay laughter, and then, in Spanish:*

CHARLEY'S VOICE: Buenas noches!
ESPERANZA'S VOICE: Hasta mañana, Charley.

Int., parlor. Full shot: shooting toward front door.

RAMÓN *enters scene f.g., stops. The front door bursts open,* ESPERANZA *enters. She embraces* LUÍS. *He grins, responding with a shy, awkward hug.* ESPERANZA *looks at* RAMÓN. *Her face is aglow. She looks younger and heartier than we have ever seen her. She comes quickly into close foreground, embracing* RAMÓN. *He puts his arms around her—but stiffly, withholding himself. She looks up at him lovingly.*

RAMON: How do you feel?
ESPERANZA: I'm okay. But it's nice to be home.
RAMON: Four nights. How did you sleep?
ESPERANZA: We raised such a fuss they finally brought cots in. *(She laughs; her hand goes to her throat.)* I nearly lost my voice, yelling so much. *(Suddenly)* How's Estellita? And the baby? *(She goes out.)*
RAMON *(following her)*:
   They're asleep.

Int., bedroom. Medium shot.

The bedroom is dark. ESPERANZA *and* RAMÓN *are only moving shadows. Dimly we see her hovering over the crib.* RAMÓN *whispers.*

RAMON: Did you have to sign a pledge? Not to go back to the line?
ESPERANZA *(a whisper)*: No, no . . . we wouldn't do it.

From off scene we hear a knock at the front door. ESPERANZA *crosses the dark room to answer it,* RAMÓN *following.*

RAMON *(a whisper)*: But if you go back they'll lock you up again.
ESPERANZA *(whispering)*: No, no . . . the Sheriff had enough of us. We drove him crazy. *(She goes out.)*

Int., parlor. Full shot.

ESPERANZA *opens the front door, admitting three women:* TERESA, RUTH *and* CONSUELO. *They enter beaming, excited.*

TERESA: It's all set. Consuelo's squad can take the day off tomorrow. We're taking over.
ESPERANZA *(ushering them in)*: Good. Come in, we'll work it out. Sit down, sit down.

The three women sit down on the couch. ESPERANZA *crosses to the dining table to get a chair for herself.* RAMÓN *is standing there.*

Two shot: RAMÓN *and* ESPERANZA.

He is the stern patriarch now. As she reaches for the chair he says, sotto voce:

RAMON: We've got to have a talk, you and me.
ESPERANZA: All right, but later. I've got a meeting now.
RAMON *(suppressed outrage)*:   A meeting?
ESPERANZA: Yes. To plan for the picket line tomorrow.

She walks off with her chair. Camera holds on RAMÓN. *He is burning. We hear:*

ESPERANZA'S VOICE: Now—let's see . . . who's available?
TERESA'S VOICE: Chana's husband is out of town—on that delegation to see the governor. And Anita Gonzales' husband, too . . .
CONSUELO'S VOICE: And six or seven others—Lala's husband and Mariana's . . .

RAMÓN *looks like he's about to explode.*

Int., parlor. Full shot.

As RAMÓN *strides toward the front door, we hear:*

RUTH: And there's a whole bunch of men going on a fuel hunting expedition—thirty or forty of them—so their wives are out too.
ESPERANZA: But we can ask them to keep our kids, so the rest of us can . . .

RAMÓN *exits, slamming the door loudly behind him. The women react with a what's-eating-him look.* TERESA *turns sympathetically to* ESPERANZA.

TERESA: What are you going to do about him, Esperanza?
CONSUELO: It's time he was house broken. Maybe if a delegation of us talked to him . . .
ESPERANZA *(deeply upset)*:   No, no . . . I have to work it out with him myself.

DISSOLVE TO:

Int., beer parlor. Full shot: the bar, night.

Seven miners are seated on stools at the bar, drinking beer. These are the disconsolate ones—the defeated and the perplexed, the traditionalist hold-outs and the unwilling baby-sitters. An atmosphere of gloom pervades the place. Their backs are to Camera, but seated from left to right they are: JENKINS, ANTONIO, *two unidentified miners (whom we have seen around the picket line),* CENTE CAVAZOS, JOSÉ SANCHEZ *and* RAMÓN. *The bartender, an Anglo, is a beefy, easy-going fellow with a friendly manner. He sets fresh beers before a couple of miners, but no money changes hands. We see the bartender mark something on a tab at the register. Camera moves on to the next miner, an Anglo, leaning moodily on his elbow.*

ANGLO MINER: I got a friend, he's got a friend in the Bureau of Mines. Know what he says? They ain't never gonna open up that mine again.
FOURTH MINER: How come?
ANGLO MINER *(as Camera moves past him)*:   He says the ore's played out. So help me.
'CENTE: Could be.

Camera holds on RAMÓN. *There's a whiskey glass and a bottle of beer before him. Ramón is in a sodden blue funk.*

RAMON: Bull. Lotta bull. That's a rich mine. I know.

He drinks off his whiskey, chases it down with beer, then stares moodily at the empty glass.

RAMON: But what's the difference? They'll never settle with us. Never.

Suddenly we hear an excited shout:

ANTONIO'S VOICE: Hey! Hey! What d'ya know!

Full shot: miners at bar.

ANTONIO *holds up a magazine, stabbing a picture with his finger.*

ANTONIO: It's him! It's him! El Presidente! The President of the Company.

All the miners except RAMÓN *get off their stools and come over, looking at the picture.*

ANTONIO: Listen to this: *(reading)* "MAN OF DISTINCTION. J. Hamilton Miller, financier, Business executive, Board Chairman of Continental Factors, and president of Delaware Zinc Incorporated. An enthusiastic sportsman and expert marksman, Mr. Miller manages to find time every year for an African safari. He leaves this month for Kenya, where he hopes to bag his thirteenth lion!"

There is a long silence. The men stare at the portrait—with hatred, with despair. ANTONIO *rips the page out of the magazine.*

ANTONIO: I'm gonna frame this. *(Turning)* Hey, Ramón—look.

RAMÓN *just grunts with disgust. He sips his beer.*

RAMON *(absently)*:   Got to look at the larger picture.

A pall falls over the group again. The miners return to their bar stools.

Close moving shot (as before).

JENKINS *(starting into space)*:   How do you like that? The guy is a lion hunter.
ANTONIO: What d'you expect him to hunt—rabbits?
FOURTH MINER: Man, oh man, I'd sure like to get me some venison.
'CENTE: I ain't tasted meat in four weeks. *(Suddenly)* How about it, Ramón?
   Let's take off for a couple of days, huh?
RAMON *(after a long pause)*:   Why ask me? Am I runnin' this strike? If you
   want permission to go over the hill, go ask the Ladies Auxiliary.

He drains his beer, rises and stalks off.

DISSOLVE TO:

Full shot, night: int., QUINTERO *bedroom,*

dimly lit by one small lamp. ESPERANZA *appears to be asleep.* RAMÓN *enters,
crosses to the bed and sits down heavily. He begins to remove his shoes. Camera
moves in.* ESPERANZA's *eyes come open, in the way of one who has been wide
awake. Without moving she says in quiet reproach:*

ESPERANZA: I waited up till midnight.
RAMON *(not looking at her)*:   You weren't waiting for *me.*
ESPERANZA: That meeting only lasted ten minutes. *(A pause. Then quietly)* The
   first night I'm home, and you run to the beer parlor. What is it? Can't you bear
   the sight of me?
RAMON *(fierce whisper)*:   Be still . . .
ESPERANZA: But you wanted to talk. Tell me.

He rises suddenly and goes out. ESPERANZA *slips out of bed, flings on a
dressing gown.*

Int., kitchen. Medium shot, night.

RAMÓN *has a cup and is pouring coffee from the pot on the stove.* ESPERANZA
enters scene, stands in the doorway.

ESPERANZA: Tell me.

RAMON *(not looking at her)*:   We can't go on this way. I just can't . . . go on living with you. Not this way.

ESPERANZA *(softly)*:   No. We can't go on this way. We can't go back to the old way either.

RAMÓN *sips his coffee, glares at her.*

RAMON: The *old way?* What's your "new way"? What's it mean? Your "right" to neglect your kids?

He goes abruptly to the parlor. ESPERANZA *stands there a moment, then slowly follows him.*

Int., parlor. Full shot.

RAMÓN *goes to a closet, gets a rifle and a box of shells off the shelf. He sits down on the edge of a chair and begins to clean the rifle with an oily rag.* ESPERANZA *enters scene, watching him. There is a long silence.*

ESPERANZA: Where are you going?

RAMON: Hunting.

ESPERANZA: When?

RAMON: Sun up.

ESPERANZA: Alone?

RAMON: No.

ESPERANZA *(after a pause)*:   Ramón—you can't.

RAMON: Why not? I'm not needed here.

ESPERANZA: But you *are* needed. Especially now—with most of the other men away. You're captain of the stand-by squad.

RAMON *(bitterly)*:   Sure, the standby squad. Stand-by for the funeral.

ESPERANZA: Whose funeral? We're doing all right. There hasn't been a scab near the picket line for three days.

RAMON: And you know why? Because the company knows they can starve us out—even if it takes another two, three months. What's it to them if the mine's shut down a little longer?

ESPERANZA: It's a lot to them. They'd do anything to open that mine.

RAMON: Aah! They've got other mines. You don't see the larger picture. *(A pause.)* They've got millions. Millions. They can outlast us, and they know it.

ESPERANZA: You mean you're ready to give up?

RAMON *(flaring)*:   Who said anything about giving up? I'll never go back to the company on my knees. Never.

He pulls back the bolt of the rifle, inserts a cartridge, tests the bolt.

ESPERANZA: You want to go down fighting, is that it? *(He shrugs.)* I don't want to go down fighting. I want to win.

No response. She walks over to him, Camera following.

ESPERANZA: Ramón . . . we're not getting weaker. We're stronger than ever before. *(He snorts with disgust.) They're* getting weaker. They thought they could
break our picket line. And they failed. And now they can't win unless they
pull off something big, and pull it off fast.

RAMON: Like what?

ESPERANZA: I don't know. But I can feel it coming. It's like . . . like a lull before the storm. Charley Vidal says . . .

RAMON   *(exploding)*: Charley Vidal says! *(He rises, flinging rifle aside.)* Don't
throw Charley Vidal up to me!

ESPERANZA: Charley's my friend. I need friends. *(She looks at him strangely.)*
Why are you afraid to have me as your friend?

RAMON: I don't know what you're talking about.

ESPERANZA: No, you don't. Have you learned nothing from this strike? Why
are you afraid to have me at your side? Do you still think you can have dignity only if I have none?

RAMON: You talk of dignity? After what you've been doing?

ESPERANZA: Yes. I talk of dignity. The Anglo bosses look down on you, and
you hate them for it. "Stay in your place, you dirty Mexican"—that's what
they tell you. But why must you say to me, "Stay in *your* place." Do you feel
better having someone lower than you?

RAMON: Shut up, you're talking crazy.

But ESPERANZA *moves right up to him, speaking now with great passion.*

ESPERANZA: Whose neck shall I stand on, to make me feel superior? And what
will I get out of it? I don't want anything lower than I am. I'm low enough already. I want to rise. And push everything up with me as I go . . .

RAMON *(fiercely)*:   Will you be still?

ESPERANZA: *(shouting)*:   And if you can't understand this you're a fool—because you can't win this strike without me! You can't win *anything* without
me!

He seizes her shoulder with one hand, half raises the other to slap her. ESPER-
ANZA's *body goes rigid. She stares straight at him, defiant and unflinching.* RAMÓN
drops his hand.

ESPERANZA: That would be the old way. Never try it on me again—never.

She crosses to the doorway, then turns back.

ESPERANZA: I am going to bed now. Sleep where you please—but not with me.

She goes out.

FADE OUT.

FADE IN:

Ext., picket post. Full shot, early morning.

Dispirited and shivering, the women march, hunched against the wind. Near the coffee shack is an oil drum in which a wood fire is burning. TERESA, *the picket captain, walks toward* ESPERANZA.

TERESA *closely watches* ESPERANZA's *dejected face.*

Two shot: at oil drum.

The two women warm their hands over the fire. TERESA *muses:*

TERESA: So they had a little taste of what its like to be a woman. . . . and they run away.

ESPERANZA: With Ramón it's . . . pride. I spoke out of the bitterness in me. And he was hurt.

ESPERANZA *stares at the fire.* TERESA *looks at her with deep sympathy.*

TERESA: Anything worth learning is a hurt. These changes come with pain . . . for other husbands too . . . not just Ramón.

DISSOLVE TO:

Ext., mountain landscape. Long panning shot, day.

A vista of wild and lonely beauty. A cold wind rustles the junipers and pine of a steep boulder-strewn arroyo. The deer hunters can be seen walking up a narrow trail in single file. They are bunched together, save for RAMÓN, *who lags behind.*

Medium panning shot, featuring RAMÓN.

He walks slowly up the trail into f.g., brooding. As he walks he hears ESPER-ANZA's *voice of the preceding night, hauntingly.*

ESPERANZA'S VOICE: You mean you're ready to give up? *(Pause)* I don't want to go down fighting. I want to win. *(Pause)* Have you learned nothing from this strike? *(Pause)* I can feel it coming. It's like a lull before the storm. *(Pause)* And now they can't win unless they pull off something big and pull it off fast.

A shot is heard ringing through the arroyo. It pulls RAMÓN *up short. He calls to the other men, suddenly:*

RAMON:　Brothers, we've got to go back!

Ext., picket post: Wide angle at drum, including truck.

CHARLEY *is at the wheel, Sal besides him. The truck stops near the oil drum.* CHARLEY *leans out, calls urgently.*

CHARLEY:　Esperanza! Where's Ramón?
ESPERANZA *(dully)*:　Ramón?
SAL:　Did he go hunting with the others?
CHARLEY *(as* ESPERANZA *nods)*:　Where? Where can we find him? Do you know?
ESPERANZA:　No.

During this exchange several women have left the picket line and come over.

SAL *(muttering bitterly)*:　Deer hunters! Deserters, that's what they are.
TERESA:　Something wrong? *(Insistently)* Charley, tell us.
CHARLEY *(reluctantly)*:　Company's got an eviction order.

DISSOLVE TO:

Series of shots: Large close shot of young woman crying: "EVICTION!" "EVICTION!" Large close shot young boy crying "EVICTION! EVICTION! EVICTION!" Woman at clothesline hearing the call and leaving. Woman at kitchen door calling out "Where?" and leaving. Truck on road stops. Man runs in, calls, "EVICTION! At the QUINTERO *place." Car on road is stopped by several women; they pile in, the car pulls away. Shots of people walking, by twos and by groups, finally passing the car in which are seated* ALEXANDER *and* HARTWELL.

ALEXANDER *(to a perturbed* HARTWELL*)*:　Don't worry. Quintero's gone hunting with the others. Evict him first; the rest will be easy. Let their neighbors watch. Scare some sense into them.

DISSOLVE TO:

Ext., road and company housing. Long shot.

The SHERIFF's *convoy is drawn up outside a row of company houses. We can see deputies milling about in the front yard of one of the cottages, and a cluster of women watching them from outside the fence.*

Ext., cottage: closer angle.

It is the QUINTERO *place. The* SHERIFF *stands in the front yard, directing oper-*
ations. His deputies are lugging furniture out of the house. They dump it in the yard
or at the side of the road. Several of them emerge from the front door with the QUIN-
TEROS' *bed.* ESPERANZA, LUZ *and a dozen other women silently watch the evic-*
tion from outside the fence. MRS. SALAZAR *is there with a bevy of kids (including*
Juanito whom she holds in her arms). The only man present is the parish priest.

Ext., main road, Zinc Town. Long panning shot.

We pick up JENKINS' *car loaded with the stand-by squad roaring toward the*
housing area. The car passes the store, the church, the school. As the car comes into
f.g., and moves on out of scene, Camera holds on the school playground. In the
distance we see LUÍS *beckoning to a number of his companions. The boys set off*
at a run up the road.

Back to company housing. Group shot: women

featuring ESPERANZA *and* LUZ.

LUZ: Can't we do something?

No answer from ESPERANZA. *She moves toward the front gate. Other women*
follow her. Camera pans with them. Just then the deputy KIMBROUGH *comes*
through the gate carrying a lamp and a vase. He dumps them onto the road. The
vase breaks. He shoves ESPERANZA *roughly away from the gate.*

KIMBROUGH: All right, girls—get back, get back.

Reverse angle: shooting past convoy

as JENKINS' *car swerves around the tail of the convoy, comes on up the road,*
stops near the cottage. RAMÓN *and the others pile out. They join the throng of*
women. RAMÓN *carries his rifle purposefully.*

Group shot: women and priest

watching the deputies as RAMÓN *comes to* ESPERANZA'*s side. She sees him.*
Her face lights up. RAMÓN'*s eyes meet hers for a moment. He is unsmiling. Then*
he looks away at:

The deputies, from his angle,

dumping the precious accumulations of a lifetime onto the road: the shrine, a
kewpie doll, a faded photograph.

Close shot: portrait of Juarez.

It falls in the dust. The frame breaks.

Back to watchers, featuring RAMÓN,

 his face working in hatred and anger. ESPERANZA *is beside him now. He brings the barrel of his rifle up as if to level it. She glances at him in terror. Suddenly* RAMÓN *goes slack; the shadow of defeat crosses his face. With an abrupt movement he thrusts the rifle on* MRS. SALAZAR—*who takes it, blinking with surprise.*

 Ext., cottage. Full shot from their angle.

 Four deputies are emerging from the front door burdened with the ancient iron stove. Camera pans away from them, holds on the fence separating the QUINTERO *and* MORALES *yards. Now we see* LUÍS *and his cronies pop up from behind the fence. Each boy holds a grass-tailed clod. They let fly. Camera swish pans back to the porch—and we see two of the clods hit their target, spattering the deputies with dirt. One deputy drops his corner of the stove, and it crashes down the steps. Several other deputies take off after the boys, leaving the gate unguarded. The* SHERIFF *yells:*

SHERIFF: Never mind them brats! Come on—get the work done.

 Reverse angle, featuring tenants.

 Other women, children and old men are arriving on the scene. There are now over twenty women watching the eviction but there is no excitement, no talk.

 Closer angle, featuring RAMÓN *and* ESPERANZA.

 RAMÓN *is calmer now, but alert, planning, thinking. He looks around at their gathering forces—not yet impressive, but growing every moment. He almost smiles with slow realization.*

RAMON *(half to himself):* This is what we've been waiting for.
ESPERANZA *(anxious, puzzled):* What are you saying?
RAMON: This means they've given up trying to break the picket line. *(A pause.)* Now we can *all* fight together—all of us.

 Suddenly he draws ESPERANZA *close, whispers something in her ear. She nods, turns swiftly to several other women, huddles with them a moment.*

 Camera pans with the women as they enter the yard, swooping down to pick up household belongings on their way.

Ext., front yard. Full shot.

Other women, seeing what ESPERANZA *and her sisters are up to, swiftly join them in the yard, begin to pick up furniture and carry it back into the house by way of the rear door. Deputies emerging from the house, loaded down with furniture and bric-a-brac, find themselves passing women loaded with objects they have just deposited in the yard. One of the deputies stops in close f.g., staring at the women in slack-jawed bafflement.* RAMÓN *glances at* MRS. SALAZAR. *He winks.* MRS. SALAZAR *smiles. It is the first time we have seen her smile.*

Back to yard, featuring sheriff.

His deputies are hopelessly dispersed. Half of them are chasing the boys, while the furniture-moving contingent is out-numbered by women crowding into the yard. The SHERIFF *wheels right and left in helpless exasperation. He spots* RAMÓN *near the front fence, strides over to him.*

SHERIFF *(bellowing)*:   Now see here, Quintero! These women are obstructin' justice. You make 'em behave, savvy?

RAMON: I can't do nothing, sheriff. You know how it is—they won't listen to a man any more.

SHERIFF *(blustering)*:   You want me to lock 'em up again?

RAMON *(smiles)*:   You want 'em *in* your lock-up again?

The SHERIFF *stalks off, fuming.*

Ext., road and yard. Full shot.

More women keep arriving all the time. Several small fry, imitating their mothers, run into the yard, pick up lamps, pots, pans, etc., and return them to the house.

A side road. Medium long shot.

Two cars pull up and stop near the convoy. CONSUELO RUIZ *and six other women get out, approach the cottage.*

The yard. Full shot.

From off scene we hear the blast of an automobile horn, while from the middle of the yard the sheriff bellows at his men:

SHERIFF: Form a cordon! Keep 'em away from the house! Form a cordon!

Ext., road. Medium long shot: past convoy.

Two other cars pull up at the tail of the convoy. FRANK BARNES *and a half-dozen miners get out, hurry toward the* QUINTERO *cottage.*

Back to yard. Full shot.

By now the sheriff's men have reassembled and are forming a cordon, from the porch steps to the front gate, permitting no one else to enter the yard. Four deputies pick up the QUINTEROS' *bed and begin to carry it toward the truck. When they reach the gate they find it blocked by the six new miners and four of* RAMÓN's *stand-by squad. The deputies stop, ease their burden to the ground. Just then we hear a klaxon from o.s. Everyone turns to see:*

Another convoy. Long panning shot.

The union truck is in the lead. CHARLEY VIDAL *is at the wheel, and the back of the truck is loaded with a dozen miners. Following it are a half-dozen miners' cars. The union convoy rolls past the parked* SHERIFF's *convoy, draws to a stop in f.g. The miners tumble out, move in a body toward the gate of the* QUINTERO *cottage. They are all big men, and their faces are grim and determined. We count 15, 20, 25, 30 of them.*

Close group shot: miners at gate looking at their approaching brothers. AL-FREDO *nudges* GONZALES.

ALFREDO: Hey! The guys from the open pit . . .
GONZALES: And the guys from the mill.

Ext., cottage and yard. Full shot (boom shot if possible).

RAMÓN, ESPERANZA *and other women and children re-emerge from the house, stop on the porch in a compact mass. Facing them outside the gate are forty miners. The deputies are in between. They stir nervously, glancing from side to side. No one says anything. A heavy stillness falls over the yard. Now we see other women and children closing in at the side fence: then* LUÍS *and a half-dozen other boys appear at the opposite fence. The* SHERIFF *is in dead center of this shot. Without realizing it, he makes a full turn of 360, looking at his adversaries.*

His angle. Slow panning shot.

The SHERIFF's *forces are completely surrounded by over a hundred men, women and children. Appearing on the surrounding hills, on every side, are other miners, other women, other kids—massed, impassive.*

Full shot: the SHERIFF

turning, staring at the massed power against him. With an abrupt, frustrated gesture the SHERIFF *waves to his men to follow and walks out the gate. The miners break ranks to let him pass. When the last deputy has left the yard the men close ranks and face the convoy. Still there is no voice, no sound save the starting motors.*

The road and yard. Full shot

as seen from the porch, Shooting past the miners outside the gate. The convoy lurches into motion. The men watch it till the last car has passed. Then they turn to face the women, who enter scene f.g., moving down the steps, meeting the men in the yard. Suddenly someone laughs and then there is a release in laughter running through the crowd, and we hear half-whispered, awed comment.

AD LIBS   *(English and Spanish)*: We stopped them . . . It took all we had, but we stopped them . . . When we heard about it at the mill, we just walked off . . . Did you see their faces? . . .

The receding convoy. Long panning shot.

The convoy approaches a crossroad a quarter of a mile downhill from the QUINTERO *house. We see a Cadillac parked there at the corner. The lead car of the convoy stops and the* SHERIFF *gets out. He walks over to the Cadillac.*

Close shot: at Cadillac.

ALEXANDER *and* HARTWELL *are sitting there. The* SHERIFF *starts to speak, then closes his mouth again. He indicates his empty trucks with a helpless gesture.*

SHERIFF: Got any more ideas?
ALEXANDER *(defensively, passing the buck)*:   I don't make policy.

He looks at HARTWELL. HARTWELL *puffs on a cigarette. After a long pause he says:*

HARTWELL: I'll talk to New York. Maybe we better settle this thing. *(Another puff)* For the present.

Back to QUINTERO *yard. Full shot.*

Part of the milling throng has already dispersed; those who remain are carrying the last of the QUINTEROS' *possessions back into the house. We see* LUÍS *jump the fence and run toward his mother in f.g. She gives him a fierce hug.*

Medium shots at front gate.

RAMÓN *approaches* MRS. SALAZAR. *He takes the baby from her arms.* ES-TELLA *enters the gate, dragging the portrait of Juárez. Solemnly she lifts up the portrait.* RAMÓN *takes it. He walks back toward the porch,* ESTELLA *at his side.*

The yard, shooting from the porch.

ESPERANZA *and* LUÍS *stand on the porch steps in f.g. Reaching them,* RAMÓN *turns, looks back at his friends, some of whom are still in the yard. They seem to be waiting for him to speak.*

ESPERANZA'S VOICE: We did not know then that we had won the strike. But our hearts were full. And when Ramón said.
RAMON (*Simply*):   Thanks . . . sisters . . . and brothers.

The people smile softly. A few of them lift their hands in a wave of acknowl-edgment. They begin to leave.

Close up shot: the QUINTERO *family on porch.*

RAMÓN *holds the baby in the crook of his arm. He hands the portrait of Juárez to* LUÍS. *The boy gazes at it with respect, wipes the dust off it, and readjusts the torn frame.* RAMÓN *heaves a long sigh. Unsmiling, he looks off at the receding convoy.* ESPERANZA *watches him.*

There is a pause. Still not looking at her, RAMÓN *says haltingly:*

RAMON: Esperanza . . . thank you . . . for your dignity.

ESPERANZA's *eyes fill with tears.*

RAMON: You were right. Together we can push everything up with us as we go.
ESPERANZA'S VOICE: Then I knew we had won something they could never take away—something I could leave to our children—and they, the salt of the earth, would inherit it.

ESPERANZA *places her hand in* RAMÓN's. *With the children they walk into the house.*

FADE OUT.

Study and Discussion Questions

1. How does the opening of *Salt of the Earth* establish the point of view of the film? What is that point of view? Why is point of view important?
2. Discuss the first scene in terms of the interplay between scene description and spoken words.
3. What do we learn about the situation of Esperanza and her family, both currently and historically, in the opening scenes?
4. How does this story define being American? How might it bring your definitions of what an American is into question?
5. Why is the radio important to Esperanza? How does it become a symbol in the film?
6. Discuss the choice to have Esperanza narrate the story through voice-overs. What effect does this have on how we see the events? How would the story be different if, say, Ramón had narrated it?
7. Discuss the relationship between Esperanza and Ramón. Show how that relationship changes as the story develops.
8. Discuss Ramón as a character. What are his strengths? What are his weaknesses? How does he change, grow, and develop during *Salt of the Earth?*
9. The screenplay shows the mine owners pitting the Anglo and the Mexican American workers against each other. What does this reveal about power in America and about how social class, race/ethnicity, and power interact?
10. List some of the company's tactics to break the strike. What assumptions are these tactics based on?
11. How do the men initially react to the women's demands? How are the men blind to the work women do? Find instances in the text.
12. Outline the stages of the women's participation in the strike.
13. Discuss the union meeting to deal with the court order forbidding the miners to picket. Esperanza's voice-over calls this "the day of the crisis." How is this scene a turning point in the film, both in terms of the relations between workers and mine owners and between the women and the men?
14. The sheriffs in a strike situation are supposed to be neutral. Do you feel the law is neutral in *Salt of the Earth?* How do the police officers affect and fit into the various power relationships in the story?
15. Note instances of support from workers outside the zinc miners' strike.
16. List instances of gender role reversal in the second half of *Salt of the Earth.*
17. Why does the screenplay pair the scenes of Ramón being beaten by the police with Esperanza's labor? How does this pairing contribute to the other statements about gender and about men's and women's work?
18. List the ways in which the women are depicted as heroes in the traditional sense of the word *heroic*. Are our ideas about what constitutes heroism redefined in the course of the film?
19. The night Esperanza gets back from jail and Ramón gets back from the bar can be seen as the crisis point in their relationship. Discuss the issues between them that the scene brings up.
20. Consider the eviction scene, which is the final scene of *Salt of the Earth.* Why and how do the workers triumph? How does this scene resolve the gender conflicts as well?

21. Hartwell, the company agent, says, "Maybe we better settle this thing. For the present." What does that statement by management suggest about the place of this story in the larger struggle for workers' rights?
22. What does the phrase *salt of the earth* mean? Look up the history and usage of the saying.
23. *Salt of the Earth* fits well into the Protest section of *Literature and Society* since it is about a workers' strike. How is a labor strike a form of protest? (That is not all that it is, of course.) Why do the zinc miners in *Salt of the Earth* go on strike? Are they justified in doing so? What would have happened if they hadn't stood up for their rights? When do you think workers are justified in calling a strike?

Suggestions for Writing

1. Write a paper about *Salt of the Earth* focusing on the parallels between the workers' struggle with the mine owners for dignity and equality and the women's struggle with the men for dignity and equality.
2. See the film *Salt of the Earth*. Choose a scene and study the way the screenplay is translated into the visual medium.
3. Consider the extensive use of Spanish (without subtitles) in the film version of *Salt of the Earth*. There is some Spanish in the screenplay as well. How does this make the average non-foreign-language speaking American feel? Why do you think the Bieberman, the director, chose to do this?
4. Write a screenplay for a scene in your life. Remember that in addition to dialogue you need to describe everything that you want the viewers to see as well as provide instructions for camera angles and shots.
5. Choose a scene in the screenplay and rewrite it as a scene in prose fiction. What are the differences between writing a screenplay and writing a story? What do you gain and what do you lose in each form?
6. Research the 1951 strike in Silver City, New Mexico, on which *Salt of the Earth* is based.
7. Property and land ownership are important background to this story. Research land disputes between indigenous people and settlers/companies/governments in American history. Discuss what you find in relation to land ownership issues in *Salt of the Earth*.
8. Research the history of labor unions in the United States. What is the purpose of a labor union? What are some laws concerning labor/management relations, including the Taft-Hartley Act mentioned in *Salt of the Earth*. Use what you have learned to discuss the zinc miners' strike—what the workers and their families do, what the mine owners do.

Critical Resources

1. Biberman, Herbert. *Salt of the Earth: The Story of a Film*. Boston: Beacon, 1965.

2. Dittmar, Linda. "The Articulating Self: Difference as Resistance in *Black Girl, Ramparts of Clay* and *Salt of the Earth*." *Multiple Voices in Feminist Film Criticism*. Ed. Linda Dittmar et al. Minneapolis: U of Minnesota P, 1994.

3. Pfaelzer, Jean. "Salt of the Earth: Women, Class, and the Utopian Imagination." *Legacy:* 16.1 (1999): 120–31.

4. Riambau, Esteve and Casimiro Torreiro. "This Film Is Going to Make History: An Interview with Rosaura Revueltas." *Cineaste: America's Leading Magazine on the Art and Politics of the Cinema* 19.2 (1992). (Revueltas played the role of Esperanza in the film.)

5. *Salt of the Earth*. Director Herbert Biberman. Independent Production Corporation/International Union of Mine, Mill & Smelter Workers, 1954 (92 minutes).

NONFICTION

HENRY DAVID THOREAU (1817–1862)

"I went to the woods to live life to the fullest . . ." And so begins Henry David Thoreau's germinal work Walden, or Life in the Woods. *The book itself embodies many of the fundamental precepts of American Transcendentalism—a school of thought, led by Ralph Waldo Emerson, that stressed the human's intuitive ability to "transcend" the rational world of science and society in order to discover higher truths about life. Centered in Concord, Massachusetts, Thoreau's birthplace and home for most of his life, the Transcendentalists would have a large impact on Thoreau's world-view. In 1833, Thoreau was accepted to Harvard after barely passing the entrance exams. He went on to study math, the classics, and the natural sciences, graduating with honors in 1837. At about the same time, Thoreau met and developed a friendship with Emerson, who encouraged Thoreau to keep a daily journal and to write. Emerson employed Thoreau for some time writing for the Transcendentalist journal* The Dial, *giving him an opportunity to publish his own writings as well as cultivate his own developing thought. In 1845, Thoreau "left for the woods" and built a small cabin on the shore of Walden Pond (2 miles from any neighbor), where he lived for "2 years, 2 months and 2 days" writing and sustaining himself by fishing and growing his own food. It was here that Thoreau began to find his voice, writing about nature and speculating about the individual's relation to society.* Walden, or Life in the Woods *was finally published in 1854, after several years of crafting and revision. It is a difficult work to classify, incorporating naturalist essays, philosophical tracts, and social criticism—but Thoreau brings these disparate elements under the broad umbrella of transcendental thought, exploring such themes as humanity's relationship to nature, the individual's duty to self and fellow humans, and the importance of following one's desired path in life as dictated by the individual and not societal norms. Indeed, these themes run throughout Thoreau's writing. In recent years, scholars have focused more on Thoreau's style in relation to his philosophy—his use of hyperbole and puns; his construction of proverb-like arguments, enhanced by irony; and his candid, often humorous, precision of language. In addition to his massive 40-volume journal, his other works include* A Week on the Concord and Merrimack Rivers *(1849) and* A Yankee in Canada, with Anti-Slavery and Reform Papers *(1866). Though much of his work has been published posthumously, "Civil Disobedience" (published in 1849) is an essay written by Thoreau after being jailed for refusing to pay taxes to a Massachusetts state legislature that supported slavery. Like* Walden, *"Civil Disobedience" has continually roused successive generations to utilize nonviolent means for cultural change, influencing such leaders as Mahatma Gandhi in India and Martin Luther King, Jr. in the United States.*

Civil Disobedience   (1849)

I heartily accept the motto,—"That government is best which governs least;"[1] and I should like to see it acted up to more rapidly and systematically. Carried out, it finally amounts to this, which also I believe,—"That government is best which governs not at all;" and when men are prepared for it, that will be the kind of government which they will have. Government is at best but an expedient; but most governments are usually, and all governments are sometimes, inexpedient. The objections which have been brought against a standing army, and they are many and weighty, and deserve to prevail, may also at last be brought against a standing government. The standing army is only an arm of the standing government. The government itself, which is only the mode which the people have chosen to execute their will, is equally liable to be abused and perverted before the people can act through it. Witness the present Mexican war,[2] the work of comparatively a few individuals using the standing government as their tool; for, in the outset, the people would not have consented to this measure.

This American government,—what is it but a tradition, though a recent one, endeavoring to transmit itself unimpaired to posterity, but each instant losing some of its integrity? It has not the vitality and force of a single living man; for a single man can bend it to his will. It is a sort of wooden gun to the people themselves; and, if ever they should use it in earnest as a real one against each other, it will surely split. But it is not the less necessary for this; for the people must have some complicated machinery or other, and hear its din, to satisfy that idea of government which they have. Governments show thus how successfully men can be imposed on, even impose on themselves, for their own advantage. It is excellent, we must all allow; yet this government never of itself furthered any enterprise, but by the alacrity with which it got out of its way. *It* does not keep the country free. *It* does not settle the West. *It* does not educate. The character inherent in the American people has done all that has been accomplished; and it would have done somewhat more, if the government had not sometimes got in its way. For government is an expedient by which men would fain succeed in letting one another alone; and, as has been said, when it is most expedient, the governed are most let alone by it. Trade and commerce, if they were not made of India rubber, would never manage to bounce over the obstacles which legislators are continually putting in their way; and, if one were to judge these men wholly by the effects of their actions, and not partly by their intentions, they would deserve to be classed and punished with those mischievous persons who put obstructions on the railroads.

But, to speak practically and as a citizen, unlike those who call themselves no-government men, I ask for, not at once no government, but *at once* a better

---

[1]On the masthead of the *United States Magazine and Democratic Review.*
[2]1846–1848; begun with the annexation of Texas by the United States; seen by many critics as an attempt to extend slavery to the West.

government. Let every man make known what kind of government would command his respect, and that will be one step toward obtaining it.

After all, the practical reason why, when the power is once in the hands of the people, a majority are permitted, and for a long period continue, to rule, is not because they are most likely to be in the right, nor because this seems fairest to the minority, but because they are physically the strongest. But a government in which the majority rule in all cases cannot be based on justice, even as far as men understand it. Can there not be a government in which majorities do not virtually decide right and wrong, but conscience?—in which majorities decide only those questions to which the rule of expediency is applicable? Must the citizen ever for a moment, or in the least degree, resign his conscience to the legislator? Why has every man a conscience, then? I think that we should be men first, and subjects afterward. It is not desirable to cultivate a respect for the law, so much as for the right. The only obligation which I have a right to assume, is to do at any time what I think right. It is truly enough said, that a corporation has no conscience; but a corporation of conscientious men is a corporation *with* a conscience. Law never made men a whit more just; and, by means of their respect for it, even the well-disposed are daily made the agents of injustice. A common and natural result of an undue respect for law is, that you may see a file of soldiers, colonel, captain, corporal, privates, powder-monkeys and all, marching in admirable order over hill and dale to the wars, against their wills, aye, against their common sense and consciences, which makes it very steep marching indeed, and produces a palpitation of the heart. They have no doubt that it is a damnable business in which they are concerned; they are all peaceably inclined. Now, what are they? Men at all? or small moveable forts and magazines, at the service of some unscrupulous man in power? Visit the Navy Yard, and behold a marine, such a man as an American government can make, or such as it can make a man with its black arts, a mere shadow and reminiscence of humanity, a man laid out alive and standing, and already, as one may say, buried under arms with funeral accompaniments, though it may be

> "Not a drum was heard, nor a funeral note,
> As his corse to the ramparts we hurried;
> Not a soldier discharged his farewell shot
> O'er the grave where our hero we buried."[3]

The mass of men serve the State thus, not as men mainly, but as machines, with their bodies. They are the standing army, and the militia, jailers, constables, *posse comitatus,* &c. In most cases there is no free exercise whatever of the judgment or of the moral sense; but they put themselves or a level with wood and earth and stones; and wooden men can perhaps be manufactured that will serve the purpose as well. Such command no more respect than men of straw, or a lump of dirt. They have the same sort of worth only as horses and dogs. Yet such

---

[3]From "The Burial of Sir John Moore at Corunna," by Charles Wolfe.

as these even are commonly esteemed good citizens. Others, as most legislators, politicians, lawyers, ministers, and office-holders, serve the State chiefly
with their heads; and, as they rarely make any moral distinctions, they are as
likely to serve the devil, without intending it, as God. A very few, as heroes, patriots, martyrs, reformers in the great sense, and *men,* serve the State with their
consciences also, and so necessarily resist it for the most part; and they are commonly treated by it as enemies. A wise man will only be useful as a man, and
will not submit to be "clay," and "stop a hole to keep the wind away,"[4] but leave
that office to his dust at least:—

> "I am too high-born to be propertied,
> To be a secondary at control,
> Or useful serving-man and instrument
> To any sovereign state throughout the world."[5]

He who gives himself entirely to his fellow-men appears to them useless and
selfish; but he who gives himself partially to them is pronounced a benefactor
and philanthropist.

How does it become a man to behave toward this American government today? I answer that he cannot without disgrace be associated with it. I cannot for
an instant recognize that political organization as *my* government which is the
slave's government also.

All men recognize the right of revolution; that is, the right to refuse allegiance
to and to resist the government, when its tyranny or its inefficiency are great and
unendurable. But almost all say that such is not the case now. But such was the
case, they think, in the Revolution of '75. If one were to tell me that this was a
bad government because it taxed certain foreign commodities brought to its
ports, it is most probable that I should not make an ado about it, for I can do
without them: all machines have their friction; and possibly this does enough
good to counterbalance the evil. At any rate, it is a great evil to make a stir about
it. But when the friction comes to have its machine, and oppression and robbery
are organized, I say, let us not have such a machine any longer. In other words,
when a sixth of the population of a nation which has undertaken to be the refuge
of liberty are slaves, and a whole country is unjustly overrun and conquered by
a foreign army, and subjected to military law, I think that it is not too soon for
honest men to rebel and revolutionize. What makes this duty the more urgent is
the fact, that the country so overrun is not our own, but ours is the invading army.

Paley,[6] a common authority with many on moral questions, in his chapter on
the "Duty of Submission to Civil Government," resolves all civil obligation into
expediency; and he proceeds to say, "that so long as the interest of the whole society requires it, that is, so long as the established government cannot be resisted

---

[4]From William Shakespeare, *Hamlet,* V, i, 236–37.
[5]From William Shakespeare, *King John,* V, ii, 79–82.
[6]William Paley (1743–1805), British philosopher.

or changed without public inconveniency, it is the will of God that the established government be obeyed, and no longer."—"This principle being admitted, the justice of every particular case of resistance is reduced to a computation of the quantity of the danger and grievance on the one side, and of the probability and expense of redressing it on the other." Of this, he says, every man shall judge for himself. But Paley appears never to have contemplated those cases to which the rule of expediency does not apply, in which a people, as well as an individual, must do justice, cost what it may. If I have unjustly wrested a plank from a drowning man, I must restore it to him though I drown myself. This, according to Paley, would be inconvenient. But he that would save his life, in such a case, shall lose it. This people must cease to hold slaves, and to make war on Mexico, though it cost them their existence as a people.

In their practice, nations agree with Paley; but does any one think that Massachusetts does exactly what is right at the present crisis?

"A drab of state, a cloth-o'-silver slut,
To have her train borne up, and her soul trail in the dirt."[7]

Practically speaking, the opponents to a reform in Massachusetts are not a hundred thousand politicians at the South, but a hundred thousand merchants and farmers here, who are more interested in commerce and agriculture than they are in humanity, and are not prepared to do justice to the slave and to Mexico, *cost what it may.* I quarrel not with far-off foes, but with those who, near at home, co-operate with, and do the bidding of those far away, and without whom the latter would be harmless. We are accustomed to say, that the mass of men are unprepared; but improvement is slow, because the few are not materially wiser or better than the many. It is not so important that many should be as good as you, as that there be some absolute goodness somewhere; for that will leaven the whole lump. There are thousands who are *in opinion* opposed to slavery and to the war, who yet in effect do nothing to put an end to them; who, esteeming themselves children of Washington and Franklin, sit down with their hands in their pockets, and say that they know not what to do, and do nothing; who even postpone the question of freedom to the question of free-trade, and quietly read the prices-current along with the latest advices from Mexico, after dinner, and, it may be, fall asleep over them both. What is the price-current of an honest man and patriot to-day? They hesitate, and they regret, and sometimes they petition; but they do nothing in earnest and with effect. They will wait, well disposed, for others to remedy the evil, that they may no longer have it to regret. At most, they give only a cheap vote, and a feeble countenance and God-speed, to the right, as it goes by them. There are nine hundred and ninety-nine patrons of virtue to one virtuous man; but it is easier to deal with the real possessor of a thing than with the temporary guardian of it.

---

[7]From Cyril Tourneur, *The Revenger's Tragedie* (1607), IV, iv, 71–72.

All voting is a sort of gaming, like chequers or backgammon, with a slight moral tinge to it, a playing with right and wrong, with moral questions; and betting naturally accompanies it. The character of the voters is not staked. I cast my vote, perchance, as I think right; but I am not vitally concerned that that right should prevail. I am willing to leave it to the majority. Its obligation, therefore, never exceeds that of expediency. Even voting *for the right* is *doing* nothing for it. It is only expressing to men feebly your desire that it should prevail. A wise man will not leave the right to the mercy of chance, nor wish it to prevail through the power of the majority. There is but little virtue in the action of masses of men. When the majority shall at length vote for the abolition of slavery, it will be because they are indifferent to slavery, or because there is but little slavery left to be abolished by their vote. *They* will then be the only slaves. Only *his* vote can hasten the abolition of slavery who asserts his own freedom by his vote.

I hear of a convention to be held at Baltimore, or elsewhere, for the selection of a candidate for the Presidency, made up chiefly of editors, and men who are politicians by profession; but I think, what is it to any independent, intelligent, and respectable man what decision they may come to, shall we not have the advantage of his wisdom and honesty, nevertheless? Can we not count upon some independent votes? Are there not many individuals in the country who do not attend conventions? But no: I find that the respectable man, so called, has immediately drifted from his position, and despairs of his country, when his country has more reason to despair of him. He forthwith adopts one of the candidates thus selected as the only *available* one, thus proving that he is himself *available* for any purposes of the demagogue. His vote is of no more worth than that of any unprincipled foreigner or hireling native, who may have been bought. Oh for a man who is a *man,* and, as my neighbor says, has a bone in his back which you cannot pass your hand through! Our statistics are at fault: the population has been returned too large. How many *men* are there to a square thousand miles in this country? Hardly one. Does not America offer any inducement for men to settle here? The American has dwindled into an Odd Fellow,—one who may be known by the development of his organ of gregariousness, and a manifest lack of intellect and cheerful self-reliance; whose first and chief concern, on coming into the world, is to see that the alms-houses are in good repair; and, before yet he has lawfully donned the virile garb, to collect a fund for the support of the widows and orphans that may be; who, in short, ventures to live only by the aid of the mutual insurance company, which has promised to bury him decently.

It is not a man's duty, as a matter of course, to devote himself to the eradication of any, even the most enormous wrong; he may still properly have other concerns to engage him; but it is his duty, at least, to wash his hands of it, and, if he gives it no thought longer, not to give it practically his support. If I devote myself to other pursuits and contemplations, I must first see, at least, that I do not pursue them sitting upon another man's shoulders. I must get off him first, that he may pursue his contemplations too. See what gross inconsistency is tolerated. I have heard some of my townsmen say, "I should like to have them order me out to help put down an insurrection of the slaves, or to march to Mexico,—see if I would go;" and yet these very men have each, directly by their allegiance, and so indirectly, at least, by their money, furnished a substitute. The soldier is applauded who refuses to serve in an unjust war by those who do not refuse to sustain the unjust government which makes the war; is applauded by those whose own act and authority he disregards and sets at nought; as if the State were penitent to that degree that it hired one to scourge it while it sinned, but not to that degree that it left off sinning for a moment. Thus, under the name of order and civil government, we are all made at last to pay homage to and support our own meanness. After the first blush of sin, comes its indifference; and from immoral it becomes, as it were, *un*moral, and not quite unnecessary to that life which we have made.

The broadest and most prevalent error requires the most disinterested virtue to sustain it. The slight reproach to which the virtue of patriotism is commonly liable, the noble are most likely to incur. Those who, while they disapprove of the character and measures of a government, yield to it their allegiance and support, are undoubtedly its most conscientious supporters, and so frequently the most serious obstacles to reform. Some are petitioning the State to dissolve the Union, to disregard the requisitions of the President. Why do they not dissolve it themselves,—the union between themselves and the State,—and refuse to pay their quota into its treasury? Do not they stand in the same relation to the State, that the State does to the Union? And have not the same reasons prevented the State from resisting the Union, which have prevented them from resisting the State?

How can a man be satisfied to entertain an opinion merely, and enjoy *it?* Is there any enjoyment in it, if his opinion is that he is aggrieved? If you are cheated out of a single dollar by your neighbor, you do not rest satisfied with knowing that you are cheated, or with saying that you are cheated, or even with petitioning him to pay you your due; but you take effectual steps at once to obtain the full amount, and see that you are never cheated again. Action from principle,— the perception and the performance of right,—changes things and relations; it is essentially revolutionary, and does not consist wholly with any thing which was. It not only divides states and churches, it divides families; aye, it divides the *individual,* separating the diabolical in him from the divine.

Unjust laws exist: shall we be content to obey them, or shall we endeavor to amend them, and obey them until we have succeeded, or shall we transgress them at once? Men generally, under such a government as this, think that they ought to wait until they have persuaded the majority to alter them. They think that, if they should resist, the remedy would be worse than the evil. But it is the fault of the government itself that the remedy *is* worse than the evil. *It* makes it worse. Why is it not more apt to anticipate and provide for reform? Why does it not cherish its wise minority? Why does it cry and resist before it is hurt? Why does it not encourage its citizens to be on the alert to point out its faults, and *do* better than it would have them? Why does it always crucify Christ, and excommunicate Copernicus and Luther, and pronounce Washington and Franklin rebels?

One would think, that a deliberate and practical denial of its authority was the only offense never contemplated by government; else, why has it not assigned its definite, its suitable and proportionate penalty? If a man who has no property refuses but once to earn nine shillings for the State, he is put in prison for a period unlimited by any law that I know, and determined only by the discretion of those who placed him there; but if he should steal ninety times nine shillings from the State, he is soon permitted to go at large again.

If the injustice is part of the necessary friction of the machine of government, let it go, let it go: perchance it will wear smooth,—certainly the machine will wear out. If the injustice has a spring, or a pulley, or a rope, or a crank, exclusively for itself, then perhaps you may consider whether the remedy will not be worse than the evil; but if it is of such a nature that it requires you to be the agent of injustice to another, then, I say, break the law. Let your life be a counter friction to stop the machine. What I have to do is to see, at any rate, that I do not lend myself to the wrong which I condemn.

As for adopting the ways which the State has provided for remedying the evil, I know not of such ways. They take too much time, and a man's life will be gone. I have other affairs to attend to. I came into this world, not chiefly to make this a good place to live in, but to live in it, be it good or bad. A man has not every thing to do, but something; and because he cannot do *every thing*, it is not necessary that he should do *something* wrong. It is not my business to be petitioning the governor or the legislature any more than it is theirs to petition me; and, if they should not hear my petition, what should I do then? But in this case the State has provided no way; its very Constitution is the evil. This may seem to be harsh and stubborn and unconciliatory; but it is to treat with the utmost kindness and consideration the only spirit that can appreciate or deserves it. So is all change for the better, like birth and death which convulse the body.

I do not hesitate to say, that those who call themselves abolitionists should at once effectually withdraw their support, both in person and property, from the government of Massachusetts, and not wait till they constitute a majority of one, before they suffer the right to prevail through them. I think that it is enough if they have God on their side, without waiting for that other one. Moreover, any man more right than his neighbors, constitutes a majority of one already.

I meet this American government, or its representative the State government, directly, and face to face, once a year, no more, in the person of its tax-gatherer; this is the only mode in which a man situated as I am necessarily meets it; and it then says distinctly, Recognize me; and the simplest, the most effectual, and, in the present posture of affairs, the indispensablest mode of treating with it on this head, of expressing your little satisfaction with and love for it, is to deny it then. My civil neighbor, the tax-gatherer, is the very man I have to deal with,—for it is, after all, with men and not with parchment that I quarrel,—and he has voluntarily chosen to be an agent of the government. How shall he ever know well what he is and does as an officer of the government, or as a man, until he is obliged to consider whether he shall treat me, his neighbor, for whom he has respect, as a neighbor and well-disposed man, or as a maniac and disturber of the peace, and see if he can get over this obstruction to his neighborliness without a ruder and more impetuous thought or speech corresponding with his action? I know this well, that if one thousand, if one hundred, if ten men whom I could name,—if ten *honest* men only,–aye, if *one* HONEST man, in this State of Mass-achusetts, *ceasing to hold slaves,* were actually to withdraw from this copartner-ship, and be locked up in the county jail therefor, it would be the abolition of slavery in America. For it matters not how small the beginning may seem to be: what is once well done is done for ever. But we love better to talk about it: that we say is our mission. Reform keeps many scores of newspapers in its service, but not one man. If my esteemed neighbor, the State's ambassador,[8] who will de-vote his days to the settlement of the question of human rights in the Council Chamber, instead of being threatened with the prisons of Carolina, were to sit down the prisoner of Massachusetts, that State which is so anxious to foist the sin of slavery upon her sister,—though at present she can discover only an act of inhospitality to be the ground of a quarrel with her,—the Legislature would not wholly waive the subject the following winter.

Under a government which imprisons any unjustly, the true place for a just man is also a prison. The proper place to-day, the only place which Massachu-setts has provided for her freer and less desponding spirits, is in her prisons, to be put out and locked out of the State by her own act, as they have already put themselves out by their principles. It is there that the fugitive slave, and the Mex-ican prisoner on parole, and the Indian come to plead the wrongs of his race, should find them; on that separate, but more free and honorable ground, where the State places those who are not *with* her but *against* her,—the only house in a slave-state in which a free man can abide with honor. If any think that their in-fluence would be lost there, and their voices no longer afflict the ear of the State, that they would not be as an enemy within its walls, they do not know by how much truth is stronger than error, nor how much more eloquently and effectively he can combat injustice who has experienced a little in his own person. Cast your whole vote, not a strip of paper merely, but your whole influence. A minority is powerless while it conforms to the majority; it is not even a minority then; but it is irresistible when it clogs by its whole weight. If the alternative is to keep all just men in prison, or give up war and slavery, the State will not hesitate which to choose. If a thousand men were not to pay their tax-bills this year, that would not be a violent and bloody measure, as it would be to pay them, and enable the State to commit violence and shed innocent blood. This is, in fact, the definition of a peaceable revolution, if any such is possible. If the tax-gatherer, or any other public officer, asks me, as one has done, "But what shall I do?" my answer is, "If you really wish to do any thing, resign your office." When the subject has refused allegiance, and the officer has resigned his office, then the revolution is accom-plished. But even suppose blood should flow. Is there not a sort of blood shed

---

[8]Samuel Hoar (1778–1856), sent by the state of Massachusetts to South Carolina to help black sailors from Massachusetts who were taken from their ships there, was evicted from Charleston by the South Carolina legislature.

when the conscience is wounded? Through this wound a man's real manhood and immortality flow out, and he bleeds to an everlasting death. I see this blood flowing now.

I have contemplated the imprisonment of the offender, rather than the seizure of his goods,—though both will serve the same purpose,—because they who assert the purest right, and consequently are most dangerous to a corrupt State, commonly have not spent much time in accumulating property. To such the State renders comparatively small service, and a slight tax is wont to appear exorbitant, particularly if they are obliged to earn it by special labor with their hands. If there were one who lived wholly without the use of money, the State itself would hesitate to demand it of him. But the rich man—not to make any invidious comparison—is always sold to the institution which makes him rich. Absolutely speaking, the more money, the less virtue; for money comes between a man and his objects, and obtains them for him; and it was certainly no great virtue to obtain it. It puts to rest many questions which he would otherwise be taxed to answer; while the only new question which it puts is the hard but superfluous one, how to spend it. Thus his moral ground is taken from under his feet. The opportunities of living are diminished in proportion as what are called the "means" are increased. The best thing a man can do for his culture when he is rich is to endeavour to carry out those schemes which he entertained when he was poor. Christ answered the Herodians according to their condition. "Show me the tribute-money," said he;—and one took a penny out of his pocket;—If you use money which has the image of Caesar on it, and which he has made current and valuable, that is, *if you are men of the State,* and gladly enjoy the advantages of Caesar's government, then pay him back some of his own when he demands it; "Render therefore to Caesar that which is Caesar's, and to God those things which are God's,"—leaving them no wiser than before as to which was which; for they did not wish to know.

When I converse with the freest of my neighbors, I perceive that, whatever they may say about the magnitude and seriousness of the question, and their regard for the public tranquility, the long and the short of the matter is, that they cannot spare the protection of the existing government, and they dread the consequences of disobedience to it to their property and families. For my own part, I should not like to think that I ever rely on the protection of the State. But, if I deny the authority of the State when it presents its tax-bill, it will soon take and waste all my property, and so harass me and my children without end. This is hard. This makes it impossible for a man to live honestly and at the same time comfortably in outward respects. It will not be worth the while to accumulate property; that would be sure to go again. You must hire or squat somewhere, and raise but a small crop, and eat that soon. You must live within yourself, and depend upon yourself, always tucked up and ready for a start, and not have many affairs. A man may grow rich in Turkey even, if he will be in all respects a good subject of the Turkish government. Confucius said,—"If a State is governed by the principles of reason, poverty and misery are subjects of shame; if a State is not governed by the principles of reason, riches and honors are the subjects of shame." No: until I want the protection of Massachusetts to be extended to me in some distant southern port, where my liberty is endangered, or until I am bent solely on building up an estate at home by peaceful enterprise, I can afford to refuse allegiance to Massachusetts, and her right to my property and life. It costs me less in every sense to incur the penalty of disobedience to the State, than it would to obey. I should feel as if I were worth less in that case.

Some years ago, the State met me in behalf of the church, and commanded me to pay a certain sum toward the support of a clergyman whose preaching my father attended, but never I myself. "Pay it," it said, "or be locked up in the jail." I declined to pay. But, unfortunately, another man saw fit to pay it. I did not see why the schoolmaster should be taxed to support the priest, and not the priest the schoolmaster; for I was not the State's schoolmaster, but I supported myself by voluntary subscription. I did not see why the lyceum should not present its tax-bill, and have the State to back its demand, as well as the church. However, at the request of the selectmen, I condescended to make some such statement as this in writing:—"Know all men by these presents, that I, Henry Thoreau, do not wish to be regarded as a member of any incorporated society which I have not joined." This I gave to the town-clerk; and he has it. The State, having thus learned that I did not wish to be regarded as a member of that church, has never made a like demand on me since; though it said that it must adhere to its original presumption that time. If I had known how to name them, I should then have signed off in detail from all the societies which I never signed on to; but I did not know where to find a complete list.

I have paid no poll-tax for six years. I was put into a jail once on this account, for one night; and, as I stood considering the walls of solid stone, two or three feet thick, the door of wood and iron, a foot thick, and the iron grating which strained the light, I could not help being struck with the foolishness of that institution which treated me as if I were mere flesh and blood and bones, to be locked up. I wondered that it should have concluded at length that this was the best use it could put me to, and had never thought to avail itself of my services in some way. I saw that, if there was a wall of stone between me and my townsmen, there was a still more difficult one to climb or break through, before they could get to be as free as I was. I did not for a moment feel confined, and the walls seemed a great waste of stone and mortar. I felt as if I alone of all my townsmen had paid my tax. They plainly did not know how to treat me, but behaved like persons who are underbred. In every threat and in every compliment there was a blunder; for they thought that my chief desire was to stand the other side of that stone wall. I could not but smile to see how industriously they locked the door on my meditations, which followed them out again without let or hinderance, and *they* were really all that was dangerous. As they could not reach me, they had resolved to punish my body; just as boys, if they cannot come at some person against whom they have a spite, will abuse his dog. I saw that the State was half-witted, that it was timid as a lone woman with her silver spoons, and that it did not know its friends from its foes, and I lost all my remaining respect for it, and pitied it.

Thus the State never intentionally confronts a man's sense, intellectual or moral, but only his body, his senses. It is not armed with superior wit or honesty, but with superior physical strength. I was not born to be forced. I will breathe after my own fashion. Let us see who is the strongest. What force has a multitude? They only can force me who obey a higher law than I. They force me to become like themselves. I do not hear of *men* being *forced* to live this way or that by masses of men. What sort of life were that to live? When I meet a government which says to me, "Your money or your life," why should I be in haste to give it my money? It may be in a great strait, and not know what to do: I cannot help that. It must help itself, do as I do. It is not worth the while to snivel about it. I am not responsible for the successful working of the machinery of society. I am not the son of the engineer. I perceive that, when an acorn and a chestnut fall side by side, the one does not remain inert to make way for the other, but both obey their own laws, and spring and grow and flourish as best they can, till one, perchance, overshadows and destroys the other. If a plant cannot live according to its nature, it dies; and so a man.

The night in prison was novel and interesting enough. The prisoners in their shirt-sleeves were enjoying a chat and the evening air in the door-way, when I entered. But the jailer said, "Come, boys, it is time to lock up;" and so they dispersed, and I heard the sound of their steps returning into the hollow apartments. My room-mate was introduced to me by the jailer, as "a first-rate fellow and a clever man." When the door was locked, he showed me where to hang my hat, and how he managed matters there. The rooms were whitewashed once a month; and this one, at least, was the whitest, most simply furnished, and probably the neatest apartment in the town. He naturally wanted to know where I came from, and what brought me there; and, when I had told him, I asked him in my turn how he came there, presuming him to be an honest man, of course; and, as the world goes, I believe he was. "Why," said he, "they accuse me of burning a barn; but I never did it." As near as I could discover, he had probably gone to bed in a barn when drunk, and smoked his pipe there; and so a barn was burnt. He had the reputation of being a clever man, had been there some three months waiting for his trial to come on, and would have to wait as much longer; but he was quite domesticated and contented, since he got his board for nothing, and thought that he was well treated.

He occupied one window, and I the other; and I saw, that if one stayed there long, his principal business would be to look out the window. I had soon read all the tracts that were left there, and examined where former prisoners had broken out, and where a grate had been sawed off, and heard the history of the various occupants of that room; for I found that even here there was a history and a gossip which never circulated beyond the walls of the jail. Probably this is the only house in the town where verses are composed, which are afterward printed in a circular form, but not published. I was shown quite a long list of verses which were composed by some young men who had been detected in an attempt to escape, who avenged themselves by singing them.

I pumped my fellow-prisoner as dry as I could, for fear I should never see him again; but at length he showed me which was my bed, and left me to blow out the lamp.

It was like travelling into a far country, such as I had never expected to behold, to lie there for one night. It seemed to me that I never had heard the town-clock strike before, nor the evening sounds of the village; for we slept with the windows open, which were inside the grating. It was to see my native village in the light of the middle ages, and our Concord was turned into a Rhine stream, and visions of knights and castles passed before me. They were the voices of old burghers that I heard in the streets. I was an involuntary spectator and auditor of whatever was done and said in the kitchen of the adjacent village-inn,—a wholly new and rare experience to me. It was a closer view of my native town. I was fairly inside of it. I never had seen its institutions before. This is one of its peculiar institutions; for it is a shire town. I began to comprehend what its inhabitants were about.

In the morning, our breakfasts were put through the hole in the door, in small oblong-square tin pans, made to fit, and holding a pint of chocolate, with brown bread, and an iron spoon. When they called for the vessels again, I was green enough to return what bread I had left; but my comrade seized it, and said that I should lay that up for lunch or dinner. Soon after, he was let out to work at haying in a neighboring field, whither he went every day, and would not be back till noon; so he bade me good-day, saying that he doubted if he should see me again.

When I came out of prison,—for some one interfered, and paid the tax,—I did not perceive that great changes had taken place on the common, such as he observed who went in a youth, and emerged a tottering and gray-headed man; and yet a change had to my eyes come over the scene,—the town, and State, and country,—greater than any that mere time could effect. I saw yet more distinctly the State in which I lived. I saw to what extent the people among whom I lived could be trusted as good neighbors and friends; that their friendship was for summer weather only; that they did not greatly purpose to do right; that they were a distinct race from me by their prejudices and superstitions, as the Chinamen and Malays are; that, in their sacrifices to humanity, they ran no risks, not even to their property; that, after all, they were not so noble but they treated the thief as he had treated them, and hoped, by a certain outward observance and a few prayers, and by walking in a particular straight though useless path from time to time, to save their souls. This may be to judge my neighbors harshly; for I believe that most of them are not aware that they have such an institution as the jail in their village.

It was formerly the custom in our village, when a poor debtor came out of jail, for his acquaintances to salute him, looking through their fingers, which were crossed to represent the grating of a jail window, "How do ye do?" My neighbors did not thus salute me, but first looked at me, and then at one another, as if I had returned from a long journey. I was put into jail as I was going to the shoemaker's to get a shoe which was mended. When I was let out the next morning, I proceeded to finish my errand, and, having put on my mended shoe, joined a huckleberry party, who were impatient to put themselves under my conduct; and in half an hour,—for the horse was soon tackled,—was in the midst of a huckleberry field, on one of our highest hills, two miles off; and then the State was nowhere to be seen.

This is the whole history of "My Prisons."[9]

I have never declined paying the highway tax, because I am as desirous of being a good neighbor as I am of being a bad subject; and, as for supporting schools, I am doing my part to educate my fellow-countrymen now. It is for no particular item in the tax-bill that I refuse to pay it. I simply wish to refuse allegiance to the State, to withdraw and stand aloof from it effectually. I do not care to trace the course of my dollar, if I could, till it buys a man, or a musket to shoot one with,—the dollar is innocent,—but I am concerned to trace the effects of my allegiance. In fact, I quietly declare war with the State, after my fashion, though I will still make what use and get what advantage of her I can, as is usual in such cases.

If others pay the tax which is demanded of me, from a sympathy with the State, they do but what they have already done in their own case, or rather they abet injustice to a greater extent than the State requires. If they pay the tax from a mistaken interest in the individual taxed, to save his property or prevent his going to jail, it is because they have not considered wisely how far they let their private feelings interfere with the public good.

This, then, is my position at present. But one cannot be too much on his guard in such a case, lest his action be biassed by obstinacy, or an undue regard for the opinions of men. Let him see that he does only what belongs to himself and to the hour.

I think sometimes, Why, this people mean well; they are only ignorant; they would do better if they knew how: why give your neighbors this pain to treat you as they are not inclined to? But I think, again, this is no reason why I should do as they do, or permit others to suffer much greater pain of a different kind. Again, I sometimes say to myself, When many millions of men, without heat, without ill-will, without personal feeling of any kind, demand of you a few shillings only, without the possibility, such is their constitution, of retracting or altering their present demand, and without the possibility, on your side, of appeal to any other millions, why expose yourself to this overwhelming brute force? You do not resist cold and hunger, the winds and the waves, thus obstinately; you quietly submit to a thousand similar necessities. You do not put your head into the fire. But just in proportion as I regard this as not wholly a brute force, but partly a human force, and consider that I have relations to those millions as to so many millions of men, and not of mere brute or inanimate things, I see that appeal is possible, first and instantaneously, from them to the Maker of them, and, secondly, from them to themselves. But, if I put my head deliber-

---

[9]Reference to *Le Mie Prigioni* (1832), prison memoirs of Silvio Pellico.

ately into the fire, there is no appeal to fire or to the Maker of fire, and I have only myself to blame. If I could convince myself that I have any right to be satisfied with men as they are, and to treat them accordingly, and not according, in some respects, to my requisitions and expectations of what they and I ought to be, then, like a good Mussulman and fatalist, I should endeavor to be satisfied with things as they are, and say it is the will of God. And, above all, there is this difference between resisting this and a purely brute or natural force, that I can resist this with some effect; but I cannot expect, like Orpheus, to change the nature of the rocks and trees and beasts.

I do not wish to quarrel with any man or nation. I do not wish to split hairs, to make fine distinctions, or set myself up as better than my neighbors. I seek rather, I may say, even an excuse for conforming to the laws of the land. I am but too ready to conform to them. Indeed I have reason to suspect myself on this head; and each year, as the tax-gatherer comes round, I find myself disposed to review the acts and position of the general and state governments, and the spirit of the people, to discover a pretext for conformity. I believe that the State will soon be able to take all my work of this sort out of my hands, and then I shall be no better a patriot than my fellow-countrymen. Seen from a lower point of view, the Constitution, with all its faults, is very good; the law and the courts are very respectable; even this State and this American government are, in many respects, very admirable and rare things, to be thankful for, such as a great many have described them; but seen from a point of view a little higher, they are what I have described them; seen from a higher still, and the highest, who shall say what they are, or that they are worth looking at or thinking of at all?

However, the government does not concern me much, and I shall bestow the fewest possible thoughts on it. It is not many moments that I live under a government, even in this world. If a man is thought-free, fancy-free, imagination-free, that which is *not* never for a long time appearing *to be* to him, unwise rulers or reformers cannot fatally interrupt him.

I know that most men think differently from myself; but those whose lives are by profession devoted to the study of these or kindred subjects, content me as little as any. Statesmen and legislators, standing so completely within the institution, never distinctly and nakedly behold it. They speak of moving society, but have no resting-place without it. They may be men of a certain experience and discrimination, and have no doubt invented ingenious and even useful systems, for which we sincerely thank them; but all their wit and usefulness lie within certain not very wide limits. They are wont to forget that the world is not governed by policy and expediency. Webster never goes behind government, and so cannot speak with authority about it. His words are wisdom to those legislators who contemplate no essential reform in the existing government; but for thinkers, and those who legislate for all time, he never once glances at the subject. I know of those whose serene and wise speculations on this theme would soon reveal the limits of his mind's range and hospitality. Yet, compared with the cheap professions of most reformers, and the still cheaper wisdom and eloquence of politicians in general, his are almost the only sensible and valuable words, and we thank Heaven for him. Comparatively, he is always strong, original, and, above all, practical. Still his quality is not wisdom, but prudence. The lawyer's truth is not Truth, but consistency, or a consistent expediency. Truth is always in harmony with herself, and is not concerned chiefly to reveal the justice that may consist with wrong-doing. He well deserves to be called, as he has been called, the Defender of the Constitution. There are really no blows to be given by him but defensive ones. He is not a leader, but a follower. His leaders are the men of '87.[10] "I have never made an effort," he says, "and never propose to make an effort; I have never countenanced an effort, and never mean to countenance an effort, to disturb the arrangement as originally made, by which the various States came into the Union." Still thinking of the sanction which the Constitution gives to slavery, he says, "Because it was a part of the original compact,—let it stand." Notwithstanding his special acuteness and ability, he is unable to take a fact out of its merely political relations, and behold it as it lies absolutely to be disposed of by the intellect,—what, for instance, it behoves a man to do here in America to-day with regard to slavery, but ventures, or is driven, to make some such desperate answer as the following, while professing to speak absolutely, and as a private man,—from which what new and singular code of social duties might be inferred?—"The manner," says he, "in which the government of those States where slavery exists are to regulate it, is for their own consideration, under their responsibility to their constituents, to the general laws of propriety, humanity, and justice, and to God. Associations formed elsewhere, springing from a feeling of humanity, or any other cause, have nothing whatever to do with it. They have never received any encouragement from me, and they never will."

They who know of no purer sources of truth, who have traced up its stream no higher, stand, and wisely stand, by the Bible and the Constitution, and drink at it there with reverence and humility; but they who behold where it comes trickling into this lake or that pool, gird up their loins once more, and continue their pilgrimage toward its fountain-head.

No man with a genius for legislation has appeared in America. They are rare in the history of the world. There are orators, politicians, and eloquent men, by the thousand; but the speaker has not yet opened his mouth to speak, who is capable of settling the much-vexed questions of the day. We love eloquence for its own sake, and not for any truth which it may utter, or any heroism it may inspire. Our legislators have not yet learned the comparative value of free-trade and of freedom, of union, and of rectitude, to a nation. They have no genius or talent for comparatively humble questions of taxation and finance, commerce and manufactures and agriculture. If we were left solely to the wordy wit of legislators in Congress for our guidance, uncorrected by the seasonable experience and the effectual complaints of the people, America would not long retain her

---

[10]Those who wrote the Constitution.

rank among the nations. For eighteen hundred years, though perchance I have no right to say it, the New Testament has been written; yet where is the legislator who has wisdom and practical talent enough to avail himself of the light which it sheds on the science of legislation?

The authority of government, even such as I am willing to submit to,—for I will cheerfully obey those who know and can do better than I, and in many things even those who neither know nor can do so well,—is still an impure one: to be strictly just, it must have the sanction and consent of the governed. It can have no pure right over my person and property but what I concede to it. The progress from an absolute to a limited monarchy, from a limited monarchy to a democracy, is a progress toward a true respect for the individual. Is a democracy, such as we know it, the last improvement possible in government? Is it not possible to take a step further towards recognizing and organizing the rights of man? There will never be a really free and enlightened State, until the State comes to recognize the individual as a higher and independent power, from which all its own power and authority are derived, and treats him accordingly. I please myself with imagining a State at last which can afford to be just to all men, and to treat the individual with respect as a neighbor; which even would not think it inconsistent with its own repose, if a few were to live aloof from it, not meddling with it, nor embraced by it, who fulfilled all the duties of neighbors and fellowmen. A State which bore this kind of fruit, and suffered it to drop off as fast as it ripened, would prepare the way for a still more perfect and glorious State, which also I have imagined, but not yet anywhere seen.

Study and Discussion Questions

1. What is wrong, according to Thoreau, with the very concept of government?
2. How does Thoreau characterize and what is his objection to a standing army?
3. Define *expediency*. Define *justice*.
4. What two injustices supported by the U.S. government is Thoreau protesting?
5. What is Thoreau's opinion of majority rule?
6. How do we support and help maintain government policies, according to Thoreau?
7. In Thoreau's philosophy, where does responsibility reside?
8. How does Thoreau tell us he personally protests injustice?
9. What does Thoreau say about his night in jail?
10. How does Thoreau feel about his home town after spending a night in its jail?
11. Someone else pays Thoreau's tax and he is let out of jail; a couple of hours later he is picking berries in a field. Does this undermine his argument, or is this irrelevant?
12. How is Thoreau "free"? Give some examples from the essay.
13. What are the lower, higher, and highest points of view to which Thoreau refers?
14. Where, according to Thoreau, ought power ultimately be located?

Suggestions for Writing

1. List some ways in which Thoreau's position in "Civil Disobedience" is idealistic and ways in which it is practical. Would you say he is more idealistic or more practical? Why?
2. Early in "Civil Disobedience," Thoreau says, "The only obligation which I have a right to assume is to do at any time what I think right." Do you agree with him or not? Take an example from your own experience to support your argument.
3. Take Thoreau's position and apply it to a current issue of conscience, expediency, and justice.
4. "Under a government which imprisons any unjustly, the true place for a just man is also a prison," writes Thoreau. What rights would *you* be willing to go to prison to defend?

Critical Resources:

1. Lauter, Paul. *Walden; and Civil Disobedience: The Complete Texts with Introduction, Historical Contexts, Critical Essays.* Boston: Houghton-Mifflin, 2000.
2. Myerson, Joel, ed. *The Cambridge Companion to Henry David Thoreau.* New York: Cambridge UP, 1995.
3. Rosenweld, Lawrence A. "The Theory, Practice and Influence of Thoreau's Civil Disobedience." *A Historical Guide to HD Thoreau.* Ed. William E. Cain. New York: Oxford UP, 2000.
4. Schneider, Richard, ed. *Approaches to Teaching Thoreau's Walden and Other Works.* New York: Modern Language Association, 1996. (Contains several essays on "Civil Disobedience.")

HARRIET JACOBS (1813–1897)

Harriet Ann Jacobs was born into slavery. Her mother died when Jacobs was six years old, and Jacobs was taken in by her owner, Margaret Horniblow, who taught her how to read and write. Horniblow died six years later, and Jacobs was put in the custody of Dr. James Norcom (Dr. Flint in the narrative). After resisting years of sexual harassment from Norcom, she was sent to his plantation as punishment. Knowing that her children might suffer for her defiance, she escaped and hid in a secret cubby-hole in the roof of her grandmother's (a freed slave) house for the next seven years. When the opportunity finally arrived, Jacobs escaped to New York, where she met the abolitionist Lydia Maria Child, who would help her publish Incidents in the Life of a Slave Girl *under the pseudonym Linda Brent. As Jacobs wrote in the preface to the first edition, she wanted "to arouse the women of the North to a realizing sense of the condition of women in the South, still in bondage, suffering what I suffered, and most of them far worse." At the time, most slave narratives were written from the male perspective (e.g., Frederick Douglass's* Narrative of the Life of Frederick Douglass: An American Slave*); Jacobs's account exposed to the world the plight of female slaves (the selling of their children as punishment, the sexual abuse by slave owners). The genre of the slave narrative served as an important catalyst for the beginning of the Civil War.*

FROM *Incidents in the Life of a Slave Girl*   (1861)

V

THE TRIALS OF GIRLHOOD

During the first years of my service in Dr. Flint's family, I was accustomed to share some indulgences with the children of my mistress. Though this seemed to me no more than right, I was grateful for it, and tried to merit the kindness by the faithful discharge of my duties. But I now entered on my fifteenth year—a sad epoch in the life of a slave girl. My master began to whisper foul words in my ear. Young as I was, I could not remain ignorant of their import. I tried to treat them with indifference or contempt. The master's age, my extreme youth, and the fear that his conduct would be reported to my grandmother, made him bear this treatment for many months. He was a crafty man, and resorted to many means to accomplish his purposes. Sometimes he had stormy, terrific ways, that made his victims tremble; sometimes he assumed a gentleness that he thought must surely subdue. Of the two, I preferred his stormy moods, although they left me trembling. He tried his utmost to corrupt the pure principles my grandmother had instilled. He peopled my young mind with unclean images, such as only a vile monster could think of. I turned from him with disgust and hatred. But he was my master. I was compelled to live under the same roof with him—where I saw a man forty years my senior daily violating the most sacred commandments of nature. He told me I was his property; that I must be subject to his will in all things. My soul revolted against the mean tyranny. But where could I turn for protection? No matter whether the slave girl be as black as ebony or as fair as her mistress. In either case, there is no shadow of law to protect her from insult, from violence, or even from death; all these are inflicted by fiends who bear the shape of men. The mistress, who ought to protect the helpless victim, has no other feelings towards her but those of jealousy and rage. The degradation, the wrongs, the vices, that grow out of slavery, are more than I can describe. They are greater than you would willingly believe. Surely, if you credited one half the truths that are told you concerning the helpless millions suffering in this cruel bondage, you at the north would not help to tighten the yoke. You surely would refuse to do for the master, on your own soil, the mean and cruel work which trained blood-hounds and the lowest class of whites do for him at the south.

Every where the years bring to all enough of sin and sorrow; but in slavery the very dawn of life is darkened by these shadows. Even the little child, who is accustomed to wait on her mistress and her children, will learn, before she is twelve years old, why it is that her mistress hates such and such a one among the slaves. Perhaps the child's own mother is among those hated ones. She listens to violent outbreaks of jealous passion, and cannot help understanding what is the cause. She will become prematurely knowing in evil things. Soon she will learn to tremble when she hears her master's footfall. She will be compelled to realize that she is no longer a child. If God has bestowed beauty upon her, it will prove her greatest curse. That which commands admiration in the white woman only hastens the degradation of the female slave. I know that some are too much brutalized by slavery to feel the humiliation of their position; but many slaves feel it most acutely, and shrink from the memory of it. I cannot tell how much I suffered in the presence of these wrongs, nor how I am still pained by the retrospect. My master met me at every turn, reminding me that I belonged to him, and swearing by heaven and earth that he would compel me to submit to him. If I went out for a breath of fresh air, after a day of unwearied toil, his footsteps dogged me. If I knelt by my mother's grave, his dark shadow fell on me even there. The light heart which nature had given me became heavy with sad forebodings. The other slaves in my master's house noticed the change. Many of them pitied me; but none dared to ask the cause. They had no need to inquire. They knew too well the guilty practices under that roof; and they were aware that to speak of them was an offence that never went unpunished.

I longed for some one to confide in. I would have given the world to have laid my head on my grandmother's faithful bosom, and told her all my troubles. But Dr. Flint swore he would kill me, if I was not as silent as the grave. Then, although my grandmother was all in all to me, I feared her as well as loved her. I had been accustomed to look up to her with a respect bordering upon awe. I was very young, and felt shamefaced about telling her such impure things, especially as I knew her to be very strict on such subjects. Moreover, she was a woman of a high spirit. She was usually very quiet in her demeanor, but if her indignation was once roused, it was not very easily quelled. I had been told that she once chased a white gentleman with a loaded pistol, because he insulted one of her daughters. I dreaded the consequences of a violent outbreak; and both pride and fear kept me silent. But though I did not confide in my grandmother, and even evaded her vigilant watchfulness and inquiry, her presence in the neighborhood was some protection to me. Though she had been a slave, Dr. Flint was afraid of her. He dreaded her scorching rebukes. Moreover, she was known and patronized by many people; and he did not wish to have his villainy made public. It was lucky for me that I did not live on a distant plantation, but in a town not so large that the inhabitants were ignorant of each other's affairs. Bad as are the laws and customs in a slaveholding community, the doctor, as a professional man, deemed it prudent to keep up some outward show of decency.

O, what days and nights of fear and sorrow that man caused me! Reader, it is not to awaken sympathy for myself that I am telling you truthfully what I suffered in slavery. I do it to kindle a flame of compassion in your hearts for my sisters who are still in bondage, suffering as I once suffered.

I once saw two beautiful children playing together. One was a fair white child; the other was her slave, and also her sister. When I saw them embracing each other, and heard their joyous laughter, I turned sadly away from the lovely sight. I foresaw the inevitable blight that would fall on the little slave's heart. I knew how soon her laughter would be changed to sighs. The fair child grew up to be a still fairer woman. From childhood to womanhood her pathway was blooming with flowers, and overarched by a sunny sky. Scarcely one day of her life had been clouded when the sun rose on her happy bridal morning.

How had those years dealt with her slave sister, the little playmate of her childhood? She, also, was very beautiful; but the flowers and sunshine of love were not for her. She drank the cup of sin, and shame, and misery, whereof her persecuted race are compelled to drink.

In view of these things, why are ye silent, ye free men and women of the north? Why do your tongues falter in maintenance of the right? Would that I had more ability! But my heart is so full, and my pen is so weak! There are noble men and women who plead for us, striving to help those who cannot help themselves. God bless them! God give them strength and courage to go on! God bless those, every where, who are laboring to advance the cause of humanity!

XVII

THE FLIGHT

"$300 REWARD! Ran away from the subscriber, an intelligent, bright, mulatto girl, named Linda, 21 years of age. Five feet four inches high. Dark eyes, and black hair inclined to curl; but it can be made straight. Has a decayed spot on a front tooth. She can read and write, and in all probability will try to get to the Free States. All persons are forbidden, under penalty of the law, to harbor or employ said slave. $150 will be given to whoever takes her in the state, and $300 if taken out of the state and delivered to me, or lodged in jail.

DR. FLINT"

XXI

THE LOOPHOLE OF RETREAT

A small shed had been added to my grandmother's house years ago. Some boards were laid across the joists at the top, and between these boards and the roof was a very small garret, never occupied by any thing but rats and mice. It was a pent roof, covered with nothing but shingles, according to the southern custom for such buildings. The garret was only nine feet long and seven wide. The highest part was three feet high, and sloped down abruptly to the loose board floor. There was no admission for either light or air. My uncle Phillip, who was a carpenter, had very skilfully made a concealed trap-door, which communicated with the storeroom. He had been doing this while I was waiting in the swamp. The storeroom opened upon a piazza. To this hole I was conveyed as soon as I entered the house. The air was stifling; the darkness total. A bed had been spread on the floor. I could sleep quite comfortably on one side; but the slope was so sudden that I could not turn on the other without hitting the roof. The rats and mice ran over my bed; but I was weary, and I slept such sleep as the wretched may, when a tempest has passed over them. Morning came. I knew it only by the noises I heard; for in my small den day and night were all the same. I suffered for air even more than for light. But I was not comfortless. I heard the voices of my children. There was joy and there was sadness in the sound. It made my tears flow. How I longed to speak to them! I was eager to look on their faces; but there was no hole, no crack, through which I could peep. This continued darkness was oppressive. It seemed horrible to sit or lie in a cramped position day after day, without one gleam of light. Yet I would have chosen this, rather than my lot as a slave, though white people considered it an easy one; and it was so compared with the fate of others. I was never cruelly overworked; I was never lacerated with the whip from head to foot; I was never so beaten and bruised that I could not turn from one side to the other; I never had my heel-strings cut to prevent my running away; I was never chained to a log and forced to drag it about, while I toiled in the fields from morning till night; I was never branded with hot iron, or torn by bloodhounds. On the contrary, I had always been kindly treated, and tenderly cared for, until I came into the hands of Dr. Flint. I had never wished for freedom till then. But though my life in slavery was comparatively devoid of hardships, God pity the woman who is compelled to lead such a life!

My food was passed up to me through the trap-door my uncle had contrived; and my grandmother, my uncle Phillip, and aunt Nancy would seize such opportunities as they could, to mount up there and chat with me at the opening. But of course this was not safe in the daytime. It must all be done in darkness. It was impossible for me to move in an erect position, but I crawled about my den for exercise. One day I hit my head against something, and found it was a gimlet. My uncle had left it sticking there when he made the trap-door. I was as rejoiced as Robinson Crusoe could have been at finding such a treasure. It put a lucky thought into my head. I said to myself, "Now I will have some light. Now I will see my children." I did not dare to begin my work during the daytime, for fear of attracting attention. But I groped round; and having found the side next the street, where I could frequently see my children, I stuck the gimlet in and waited for evening. I bored three rows of holes, one above another; then I bored out the interstices between. I thus succeeded in making one hole about an inch long and an inch broad. I sat by it till late into the night, to enjoy the little whiff of air that floated in. In the morning I watched for my children. The first person I saw in the street was Dr. Flint. I had a shuddering, superstitious feeling that it was a bad omen. Several familiar faces passed by. At last I heard the merry laugh of children, and presently two sweet little faces were looking up at me, as though they knew I was there, and were conscious of the joy they imparted. How I longed to *tell* them I was there!

My condition was now a little improved. But for weeks I was tormented by hundreds of little red insects, fine as a needle's point, that pierced through my skin, and produced an intolerable burning. The good grandmother gave me herb teas and cooling medicines, and finally I got rid of them. The heat of my den was intense, for nothing but thin shingles protected me from the scorching summer's sun. But I had my consolations. Through my peeping-hole I could watch the children, and when they were near enough, I could hear their talk. Aunt Nancy brought me all the news she could hear at Dr. Flint's. From her I learned that the doctor had written to New York to a colored woman, who had been born and raised in our neighborhood, and had breathed his contaminating atmosphere. He offered her a reward if she could find out any thing about me. I know not what was the nature of her reply; but he soon after started for New York in haste, saying to his family that he had business of importance to transact. I peeped at him as he passed on his way to the steamboat. It was a satisfaction to have miles of land and water between us, even for a little while; and it was a still greater satisfaction to know that he believed me to be in the Free States. My little den seemed less dreary than it had done. He returned, as he did from his former journey to New York, without obtaining any satisfactory information. When he passed our house next morning, Benny[1] was standing at the gate. He had heard them say that he had gone to find me, and he called out, "Dr. Flint, did you bring my mother home? I want to see her." The doctor stamped his foot at him in a rage, and exclaimed, "Get out of the way, you little damned rascal! If you don't, I'll cut off your head."

Benny ran terrified into the house, saying, "You can't put me in jail again. I don't belong to you now." It was well that the wind carried the words away from the doctor's ear. I told my grandmother of it, when we had our next conference at the trap-door; and begged of her not to allow the children to be impertinent to the irascible old man.

---

[1] Her son, whose father, Mr. Sands, is white.

Autumn came, with a pleasant abatement of heat. My eyes had become accustomed to the dim light, and by holding my book or work in a certain position near the aperture I contrived to read and sew. That was a great relief to the tedious monotony of my life. But when winter came, the cold penetrated through the thin shingle roof, and I was dreadfully chilled. The winters there are not so long, or so severe, as in northern latitudes; but the houses are not built to shelter from cold, and my little den was peculiarly comfortless. The kind grandmother brought me bed-clothes and warm drinks. Often I was obliged to lie in bed all day to keep comfortable; but with all my precautions, my shoulders and feet were frostbitten. O, those long, gloomy days, with no object for my eye to rest upon, and no thoughts to occupy my mind, except the dreary past and the uncertain future! I was thankful when there came a day sufficiently mild for me to wrap myself up and sit at the loophole to watch the passers by. Southerners have the habit of stopping and talking in the streets, and I heard many conversations not intended to meet my ears. I heard slave-hunters planning how to catch some poor fugitive. Several times I heard allusions to Dr. Flint, myself, and the history of my children, who, perhaps, were playing near the gate. One would say, "I wouldn't move my little finger to catch her, as old Flint's property," Another would say, "I'll catch *any* nigger for the reward. A man ought to have what belongs to him, if he *is* a damned brute." The opinion was often expressed that I was in the Free States. Very rarely did any one suggest that I might be in the vicinity. Had the least suspicion rested on my grandmother's house, it would have been burned to the ground. But it was the last place they thought of. Yet there was no place, where slavery existed, that could have afforded me so good a place of concealment.

Dr. Flint and his family repeatedly tried to coax and bribe my children to tell something they had heard said about me. One day the doctor took them into a shop, and offered them some bright little silver pieces and gay handkerchiefs if they would tell where their mother was. Ellen[2] shrank away from him, and would not speak; but Benny spoke up, and said, "Dr. Flint, I don't know where my mother is. I guess she's in New York; and when you go there again, I wish you'd ask her to come home, for I want to see her; but if you put her in jail, or tell her you'll cut her head off, I'll tell her to go right back."

XXIX

PREPARATIONS FOR ESCAPE

I hardly expect that the reader will credit me, when I affirm that I lived in that little dismal hole, almost deprived of light and air, and with no space to move my limbs, for nearly seven years. But it is a fact; and to me a sad one, even now;

---

[2]Her daughter.

for my body still suffers from the effects of that long imprisonment, to say nothing of my soul. Members of my family, now living in New York and Boston, can testify to the truth of what I say.

Countless were the nights that I sat late at the little loophole scarcely large enough to give me a glimpse of one twinkling star. There, I heard the patrols and slave-hunters conferring together about the capture of runaways, well knowing how rejoiced they would be to catch me.

Season after season, year after year, I peeped at my children's faces, and heard their sweet voices, with a heart yearning all the while to say, "Your mother is here." Sometimes it appeared to me as if ages had rolled away since I entered upon that gloomy, monotonous existence. At times, I was stupefied and listless; at other times I became very impatient to know when these dark years would end, and I should again be allowed to feel the sunshine, and breathe the pure air.

After Ellen left us, this feeling increased. Mr. Sands had agreed that Benny might go to the north whenever his uncle Phillip could go with him; and I was anxious to be there also, to watch over my children, and protect them so far as I was able. Moreover, I was likely to be drowned out of my den, if I remained much longer; for the slight roof was getting badly out of repair, and uncle Phillip was afraid to remove the shingles, lest some one should get a glimpse of me. When storms occurred in the night, they spread mats and bits of carpet, which in the morning appeared to have been laid out to dry; but to cover the roof in the daytime might have attracted attention. Consequently, my clothes and bedding were often drenched; a process by which the pains and aches in my cramped and stiffened limbs were greatly increased. I revolved various plans of escape in my mind, which I sometimes imparted to my grandmother, when she came to whisper with me at the trap-door. The kind-hearted old woman had an intense sympathy for runaways. She had known too much of the cruelties inflicted on those who were captured. Her memory always flew back at once to the sufferings of her bright and handsome son, Benjamin, the youngest and dearest of her flock. So, whenever I alluded to the subject, she would groan out, "O, don't think of it, child. You'll break my heart." I had no good old aunt Nancy now to encourage me; but my brother William and my children were continually beckoning me to the north.

And now I must go back a few months in my story. I have stated that the first of January was the time for selling slaves, or leasing them out to new masters. If time were counted by heart-throbs, the poor slaves might reckon years of suffering during that festival so joyous to the free. On the New Year's day preceding my aunt's death, one of my friends, named Fanny, was to be sold at auction, to pay her master's debts. My thoughts were with her during all the day, and at night I anxiously inquired what had been her fate. I was told that she had been sold to one master, and her four little girls to another master, far distant; that she had escaped from her purchaser, and was not to be found. Her mother was the old Aggie I have spoken of. She lived in a small tenement belonging to my grandmother, and built on the same lot with her own house. Her dwelling was searched and watched, and that brought the patrols so near me that I was obliged to keep very close in my den. The hunters were somehow eluded; and not long afterwards Benny accidentally caught sight of Fanny in her mother's hut. He told his grandmother, who charged him never to speak of it, explaining to him the frightful consequences; and he never betrayed the trust. Aggie little dreamed that my grandmother knew where her daughter was concealed, and that the stooping form of her old neighbor was bending under a similar burden of anxiety and fear; but these dangerous secrets deepened the sympathy between the two old persecuted mothers.

My friend Fanny and I remained many weeks hidden within call of each other; but she was unconscious of the fact. I longed to have her share my den, which seemed a more secure retreat than her own; but I had brought so much trouble on my grandmother, that it seemed wrong to ask her to incur greater risks. My restlessness increased. I had lived too long in bodily pain and anguish of spirit. Always I was in dread that by some accident, or some contrivance, slavery would succeed in snatching my children from me. This thought drove me nearly frantic, and I determined to steer for the North Star at all hazards. At this crisis, Providence opened an unexpected way for me to escape. My friend Peter came one evening, and asked to speak with me. "Your day has come, Linda," said he. "I have found a chance for you to go to the Free States. You have a fortnight to decide." The news seemed too good to be true; but Peter explained his arrangements, and told me all that was necessary was for me to say I would go. I was going to answer him with a joyful yes, when the thought of Benny came to my mind. I told him the temptation was exceedingly strong, but I was terribly afraid of Dr. Flint's alleged power over my child, and that I could not go and leave him behind. Peter remonstrated earnestly. He said such a good chance might never occur again; that Benny was free, and could be sent to me; and that for the sake of my children's welfare I ought not to hesitate a moment. I told him I would consult with uncle Phillip. My uncle rejoiced in the plan, and bade me go by all means. He promised, if his life was spared, that he would either bring or send my son to me as soon as I reached a place of safety. I resolved to go, but thought nothing had better be said to my grandmother till very near the time of departure. But my uncle thought she would feel it more keenly if I left her so suddenly. "I will reason with her," said he, "and convince her how necessary it is, not only for your sake, but for hers also. You cannot be blind to the fact that she is sinking under her burdens." I was not blind to it. I knew that my concealment was an ever-present source of anxiety, and that the older she grew the more nervously fearful she was of discovery. My uncle talked with her, and finally succeeded in persuading her that it was absolutely necessary for me to seize the chance so unexpectedly offered.

The anticipation of being a free woman proved almost too much for my weak frame. The excitement stimulated me, and at the same time bewildered me. I made busy preparations for my journey, and for my son to follow me. I resolved to have an interview with him before I went, that I might give him cautions and advice, and tell him how anxiously I should be waiting for him at the north.

Grandmother stole up to me as often as possible to whisper words of counsel. She insisted upon my writing to Dr. Flint, as soon as I arrived in the Free States, and asking him to sell me to her. She said she would sacrifice her house, and all she had in the world, for the sake of having me safe with my children in any part of the world. If she could only live to know *that* she could die in peace. I promised the dear old faithful friend that I would write to her as soon as I arrived, and put the letter in a safe way to reach her; but in my own mind I resolved that not another cent of her hard earnings should be spent to pay rapacious slaveholders for what they called their property. And even if I had not been unwilling to buy what I had already a right to possess, common humanity would have prevented me from accepting the generous offer, at the expense of turning my aged relative out of house and home, when she was trembling on the brink of the grave.

I was to escape in a vessel; but I forbear to mention any further particulars. I was in readiness, but the vessel was unexpectedly detained several days. Meantime, news came to town of a most horrible murder committed on a fugitive slave, named James. Charity, the mother of this unfortunate young man, had been an old acquaintance of ours. I have told the shocking particulars of his death, in my description of some of the neighboring slaveholders. My grandmother, always nervously sensitive about runaways, was terribly frightened. She felt sure that a similar fate awaited me, if I did not desist from my enterprise. She sobbed, and groaned, and entreated me not to go. Her excessive fear was somewhat contagious, and my heart was not proof against her extreme agony. I was grievously disappointed, but I promised to relinquish my project.

When my friend Peter was apprised of this, he was both disappointed and vexed. He said, that judging from our past experience, it would be a long time before I had such another chance to throw away. I told him it need not be thrown away; that I had a friend concealed near by, who would be glad enough to take the place that had been provided for me. I told him about poor Fanny, and the kind-hearted, noble fellow, who never turned his back upon any body in distress, white or black, expressed his readiness to help her. Aggie was much surprised when she found that we knew her secret. She was rejoiced to hear of such a chance for Fanny, and arrangements were made for her to go on board the vessel the next night. They both supposed that I had long been at the north, therefore my name was not mentioned in the transaction. Fanny was carried on board at the appointed time, and stowed away in a very small cabin. This accommodation had been purchased at a price that would pay for a voyage to England. But when one proposes to go to fine old England, they stop to calculate whether they can afford the cost of the pleasure; while in making a bargain to escape from slavery, the trembling victim is ready to say, "Take all I have, only don't betray me!"

The next morning I peeped through my loophole, and saw that it was dark and cloudy. At night I received news that the wind was ahead, and the vessel had not sailed. I was exceedingly anxious about Fanny, and Peter too, who was running a tremendous risk at my instigation. Next day the wind and weather remained the same. Poor Fanny had been half dead with fright when they carried her on board, and I could readily imagine how she must be suffering now. Grandmother came often to my den, to say how thankful she was I did not go. On the third morning she rapped for me to come down to the storeroom. The poor old sufferer was breaking down under her weight of trouble. She was easily flurried now. I found her in a nervous, excited state, but I was not aware that she had forgotten to lock the door behind her, as usual. She was exceedingly worried about the detention of the vessel. She was afraid all would be discovered, and then Fanny, and Peter, and I, would all be tortured to death, and Phillip would be utterly ruined, and her house would be torn down. Poor Peter! If he should die such a horrible death as the poor slave James had lately done, and all for his kindness in trying to help me, how dreadful it would be for us all! Alas, the thought was familiar to me, and had sent many a sharp pang through my heart. I tried to suppress my own anxiety, and speak soothingly to her. She brought in some allusion to aunt Nancy, the dear daughter she had recently buried, and then she lost all control of herself. As she stood there, trembling and sobbing, a voice from the piazza called out, "Whar is you, aunt Marthy?" Grandmother was startled, and in her agitation opened the door, without thinking of me. In stepped Jenny, the mischievous housemaid, who had tried to enter my room, when I was concealed in the house of my white benefactress. "I's bin huntin ebery whar for you, aunt Marthy," said she. "My missis wants you to send her some crackers." I had slunk down behind a barrel, which entirely screened me, but I imagined that Jenny was looking directly at the spot, and my heart beat violently. My grandmother immediately thought what she had done, and went out quickly with Jenny to count the crackers locking the door after her. She returned to me, in a few minutes, the perfect picture of despair. "Poor child!" she exclaimed, "my carelessness has ruined you. The boat ain't gone yet. Get ready immediately, and go with Fanny. I ain't got another word to say against it now; for there's no telling what may happen this day."

Uncle Phillip was sent for, and he agreed with his mother in thinking that Jenny would inform Dr. Flint in less than twenty-four hours. He advised getting me on board the boat, if possible; if not, I had better keep very still in my den, where they could not find me without tearing the house down. He said it would not do for him to move in the matter, because suspicion would be immediately excited; but he promised to communicate with Peter. I felt reluctant to apply to him again, having implicated him too much already; but there seemed to be no alternative. Vexed as Peter had been by my indecision, he was true to his generous nature, and said at once that he would do his best to help me, trusting I should show myself a stronger woman this time.

He immediately proceeded to the wharf, and found that the wind had shifted, and the vessel was slowly beating down stream. On some pretext of urgent necessity, he offered two boatmen a dollar apiece to catch up with her. He was of lighter complexion than the boatmen he hired, and when the captain saw them coming so rapidly, he thought officers were pursuing his vessel in search of the runaway slave he had on board. They hoisted sails, but the boat gained upon them, and the indefatigable Peter sprang on board.

The captain at once recognized him. Peter asked him to go below, to speak about a bad bill he had given him. When he told his errand, the captain replied, "Why, the woman's here already; and I've put her where you or the devil would have a tough job to find her."

"But it is another woman I want to bring," said Peter. "*She* is in great distress, too, and you shall be paid any thing within reason, if you'll stop and take her."

"What's her name?" inquired the captain.

"Linda," he replied.

"That's the name of the woman already here," rejoined the captain. "By George! I believe you mean to betray me."

"O!" exclaimed Peter, "God knows I wouldn't harm a hair of your head. I am too grateful to you. But there really *is* another woman in great danger. Do have the humanity to stop and take her!"

After a while they came to an understanding. Fanny, not dreaming I was any where about in that region, had assumed my name, though she called herself Johnson. "Linda is a common name," said Peter, "and the woman I want to bring is Linda Brent."

The captain agreed to wait at a certain place till evening, being handsomely paid for his detention.

Of course, the day was an anxious one for us all. But we concluded that if Jenny had seen me, she would be too wise to let her mistress know of it; and that she probably would not get a chance to see Dr. Flint's family till evening, for I knew very well what were the rules in that household. I afterwards believed that she did not see me; for nothing ever came of it, and she was one of those base characters that would have jumped to betray a suffering fellow being for the sake of thirty pieces of silver.

I made all my arrangements to go on board as soon as it was dusk. The intervening time I resolved to spend with my son. I had not spoken to him for seven years, though I had been under the same roof, and seen him every day, when I was well enough to sit at the loophole. I did not dare to venture beyond the storeroom; so they brought him there, and locked us up together, in a place concealed from the piazza door. It was an agitating interview for both of us. After we had talked and wept together for a little while, he said, "Mother, I'm glad you're going away. I wish I could go with you. I knew you was here; and I have been *so* afraid they would come and catch you!"

I was greatly surprised, and asked him how he had found it out.

He replied, "I was standing under the eaves, one day, before Ellen went away, and I heard somebody cough up over the wood shed. I don't know what made me think it was you, but I did think so. I missed Ellen, the night before she went away; and grandmother brought her back into the room in the night; and I thought maybe she'd been to see *you,* before she went, for I heard grandmother whisper to her, 'Now go to sleep; and remember never to tell.'"

I asked him if he ever mentioned his suspicions to his sister. He said he never did; but after he heard the cough, if he saw her playing with other children on that side of the house, he always tried to coax her round to the other side, for fear they would hear me cough, too. He said he had kept a close lookout for Dr. Flint, and if he saw him speak to a constable, or a patrol, he always told grandmother. I now recollected that I had seen him manifest uneasiness, when people were on that side of the house, and I had at the time been puzzled to conjecture a motive for his actions. Such prudence may seem extraordinary in a boy of twelve years, but slaves, being surrounded by mysteries, deceptions, and dangers, early learn to be suspicious and watchful, and prematurely cautious and cunning. He had never asked a question of grandmother, or uncle Phillip, and I had often heard him chime in with other children, when they spoke of my being at the north.

I told him I was now really going to the Free States, and if he was a good, honest boy, and a loving child to his dear old grandmother, the Lord would bless him, and bring him to me, and we and Ellen would live together. He began to tell me that grandmother had not eaten any thing all day. While he was speaking, the door was unlocked, and she came in with a small bag of money, which she wanted me to take. I begged her to keep a part of it, at least, to pay for Benny's being sent to the north; but she insisted, while her tears were falling fast, that I should take the whole. "You may be sick among strangers," she said, "and they would send you to the poorhouse to die." Ah, that good grandmother!

For the last time I went up to my nook. Its desolate appearance no longer chilled me, for the light of hope had risen in my soul. Yet, even with the blessed prospect of freedom before me, I felt very sad at leaving forever that old homestead, where I had been sheltered so long by the dear old grandmother; where I had dreamed my first young dream of love; and where, after that had faded away, my children came to twine themselves so closely round my desolate heart. As the hour approached for me to leave, I again descended to the storeroom. My grandmother and Benny were there. She took me by the hand, and said, "Linda, let us pray." We knelt down together, with my child pressed to my heart, and my other arm round the faithful, loving old friend I was about to leave forever. On no other occasion has it ever been my lot to listen to so fervent a supplication for mercy and protection. It thrilled through my heart, and inspired me with trust in God.

Peter was waiting for me in the street. I was soon by his side, faint in body, but strong of purpose. I did not look back upon the old place, though I felt that I should never see it again.

Study and Discussion Questions

1. What are some of the effects of living as a slave that Jacobs describes in this excerpt from her narrative?
2. Jacobs relates feelings common to people who are abused—shame, fear, anger, confusion. How does the social structure that Jacobs was in have a particular impact on her sense of self in this situation?
3. Why does Jacobs beg her grandmother not to "allow the children to be impertinent" to Dr. Flint?

4. To whom, and for what purpose, is Jacobs writing? How do her audience and her purpose shape the language she uses? Jacobs wrote her narrative under a pen name, Linda Brent. Why do you think she chose to do this?
5. How might the excerpt here be different if it were written for other former slaves?
6. Of her seven years hiding in the garret, Jacobs writes, "My body still suffers from the effects of that long imprisonment, to say nothing of my soul." In what way do you think her "soul" still suffers?

Suggestions for Writing

1. Write a journal entry Jacobs might have written one day while hiding in the garret. Write a journal entry Jacobs might have written on the boat heading north.
2. Research Harriet Jacobs's role in the abolitionist movement and write a paper about her life once she went north.
3. Compare/contrast Jacobs's narrative with a slave narrative written by a man, for example Frederick Douglass's. How did gender create different circumstances for slaves?

Critical Resources

1. Jacobs, Harriet and John S. Jacobs. *Incidents in the Life of A Slave Girl, Written by Herself, Harriet Jacobs. With a True Tale of Slavery by John S. Jacobs.* Ed. Nell Irvin Painter. New York: Penguin, 2000. This edition contains the narrative of John S. Jacobs, Harriet's brother.
2. McKay, Nellie, ed. *Incidents in the Life of a Slave Girl: Contexts, Criticisms.* New York: Norton, 2001.
3. Yellin, Jean. *Harriet Jacobs: A Life.* New York: Civitas, 2004.
4. Zafar, Rafia, ed. *Harriet Jacobs and Incidents in the Life of a Slave Girl: New Critical Essays.* Cambridge and New York: Cambridge UP, 1996.

THOMAS S. WHITECLOUD (1914–1972)

Thomas S. Whitecloud was born in New York City. His mother was of European descent and his father a Chippewa Indian who graduated from Yale Law School. As a young boy, Whitecloud's father decided to leave his family and return to the Lac du Flambeau Reservation in Wisconsin, where he grew up. Though Whitecloud continued to live with his mother, he spent periods of time living on the reservation. He attended a number of different public and federal Indian schools and worked miscellaneous jobs, including truck driving, farm work, and boxing, until he finally found his milieu at the University of Redlands. Although Whitecloud considered writing and studying literature, he instead opted to study medicine. He received his M.D. in the early 1940s, then served as a surgeon in Europe during

World War II. After the war, he worked as an Indian Service doctor in various states until establishing a private practice in Texas. At the time of his death, White-cloud had several works (essays and poetry) in manuscript form. "Blue Winds Dancing," published his senior year in college, is considered Whitecloud's most notable work.

Blue Winds Dancing   (1938)

There is a moon out tonight. Moon and stars and clouds tipped with moonlight. And there is a fall wind blowing in my heart. Ever since this evening, when against a fading sky I saw geese wedge southward. They were going home. . . . Now I try to study, but against the pages I see them again, driving southward. Going home.

Across the valley there are heavy mountains holding up the night sky, and beyond the mountains there is home. Home, and peace, and the beat of drums, and blue winds dancing over snow fields. The Indian lodge will fill with my people, and our gods will come and sit among them. I should be there then. I should be at home.

But home is beyond the mountains, and I am here. Here where fall hides in the valleys, and winter never comes down from the mountains. Here where all the trees grow in rows; the palms stand stiffly by the roadsides, and in the groves the orange trees line in military rows, and endlessly bear fruit. Beautiful, yes; there is always beauty in order, in rows of growing things! But it is the beauty of captivity. A pine fighting for existence on a windy knoll is much more beautiful.

In my Wisconsin, the leaves change before the snows come. In the air there is the smell of wild rice and venison cooking; and when the winds come whispering through the forests, they carry the smell of rotting leaves. In the evenings, the loon calls, lonely; and birds sing their last songs before leaving. Bears dig roots and eat late fall berries, fattening for their long winter sleep. Later, when the first snows fall, one awakens in the morning to find the world white and beautiful and clean. Then one can look back over his trail and see the tracks following. In the woods there are tracks of deer and snowshoe rabbits, and long streaks where partridges slide to alight. Chipmunks make tiny footprints on the limbs; and one can hear squirrels busy in hollow trees, sorting acorns. Soft lake waves wash the shores, and sunsets burst each evening over the lakes, and make them look as if they were afire.

That land which is my home! Beautiful, calm—where there is no hurry to get anywhere, no driving to keep up in a race that knows no ending and no goal. No classes where men talk and talk, and then stop now and then to hear their own words come back to them from the students. No constant peering into the maelstrom of one's mind; no worries about grades and honors; no hysterical preparing for life until that life is half over; no anxiety about one's place in the thing they call Society.

I hear again the ring of axes in deep woods, the crunch of snow beneath my feet. I feel again the smooth velvet of ghost-birch bark. I hear the rhythm of the drums. . . . I am tired. I am weary of trying to keep up this bluff of being civilized. Being civilized means trying to do everything you don't want to, never doing anything you want to. It means dancing to the strings of custom and tradition; it means living in houses and never knowing or caring who is next door. These civilized white men want us to be like them—always dissatisfied, getting a hill and wanting a mountain.

Then again, maybe I am not tired. Maybe I'm licked. Maybe I am just not smart enough to grasp these things that go to make up civilization. Maybe I am just too lazy to think hard enough to keep up.

Still, I know my people have many things that civilization has taken from the whites. They know how to give; how to tear one's piece of meat in two and share it with one's brother. They know how to sing—how to make each man his own songs and sing them; for their music they do not have to listen to other men singing over a radio. They know how to make things with their hands, how to shape beads into design and make a thing of beauty from a piece of birch bark.

But we are inferior. It is terrible to have to feel inferior; to have to read reports of intelligence tests, and learn that one's race is behind. It is terrible to sit in classes and hear men tell you that your people worship sticks of wood—that your gods are all false, that the Manitou forgot your people and did not write them a book.

I am tired. I want to walk again among the ghost-birches. I want to see the leaves turn in autumn, the smoke rise from the lodgehouses, and to feel the blue winds. I want to hear the drums; I want to hear the drums and feel the blue whispering winds.

There is a train wailing into the night. The trains go across the mountains. It would be easy to catch a freight. They will say he has gone back to the blanket; I don't care. The dance at Christmas. . . .

A bunch of bums warming at a tiny fire talk politics and women and joke about the Relief and the WPA[1] and smoke cigarettes. These men in caps and overcoats and dirty overalls living on the outskirts of civilization are free, but they pay the price of being free in civilization. They are outcasts. I remember a sociology professor lecturing on adjustment to society; hobos and prostitutes and criminals are individuals who never adjusted, he said. He could learn a lot if he came and listened to a bunch of bums talk. He would learn that work and a woman and a place to hang his hat are all the ordinary man wants. These are all he wants, but other men are not content to let him want only these. He must be taught to want radios and automobiles and a new suit every spring. Progress would stop if he did not want these things. I listen to hear if there is any talk of communism or socialism in the hobo jungles. There is none. At best there is a

---

[1]Works Progress Administration, Federal government agency established in 1935 to create jobs for the unemployed.

sort of disgusted philosophy about life. They seem to think there should be a better distribution of wealth, or more work, or something. But they are not rabid about it. The radicals live in the cities.

I find a fellow headed for Albuquerque, and talk road-talk with him. "It is hard to ride fruit cars. Bums break in. Better to wait for a cattle car going back to the Middle West, and ride that." We catch the next east-bound and walk the tops until we find a cattle car. Inside, we crouch near the forward wall, huddle, and try to sleep. I feel peaceful and content at last. I am going home. The cattle car rocks. I sleep.

Morning and the desert. Noon and the Salton Sea, lying more lifeless than a mirage under a somber sun in a pale sky. Skeleton mountains rearing on the skyline, thrusting out of the desert floor, all rock and shadow and edges. Desert. Good country for an Indian reservation. . . .

Yuma and the muddy Colorado. Night again, and I wait shivering for the dawn.

Phoenix. Pima country. Mountains that look like cardboard sets on a forgotten stage. Tucson. Papago country. Giant cacti that look like petrified hitchhikers along the highways. Apache country. At El Paso my road-buddy decides to go on to Houston. I leave him, and head north to the mesa country. Las Cruces and the terrible Organ Mountains, jagged peaks that instill fear and wondering. Albuquerque. Pueblos along the Rio Grande. On the boardwalk there are some Indian women in colored sashes selling bits of pottery. The stone age offering its art to the twentieth century. They hold up a piece and fix the tourists with black eyes until, embarrassed, he buys or turns away. I feel suddenly angry that my people should have to do such things for a living. . . .

Santa Fe trains are fast, and they keep them pretty clean of bums. I decide to hurry and ride passenger coaltenders. Hide in the dark, judge the speed of the train as it leaves, and then dash out, and catch it. I hug the cold steel wall of the tender and think of the roaring fire in the engine ahead, and of the passengers back in the dining car reading their papers over hot coffee. Beneath me there is blur of rails. Death would come quick if my hands should freeze and I fall. Up over the Sangre De Cristo range, around cliffs and through canyons to Denver. Bitter cold here, and I must watch out for Denver Bob. He is a railroad bull who has thrown bums from fast freights. I miss him. It is too cold, I suppose. On north to the Sioux country.

Small towns lit for the coming Christmas. On the streets of one I see a beam-shouldered young farmer gazing into a window filled with shining silver toasters. He is tall and wears a blue shirt buttoned, with no tie. His young wife by his side looks at him hopefully. He wants decorations for his place to hang his hat to please his woman. . . .

Northward again. Minnesota, and great white fields of snow; frozen lakes, and dawn running in dusk without noon. Long forests wearing white. Bitter cold, and one night the northern lights. I am nearing home.

I reach Woodruff at midnight. Suddenly I am afraid, now that I am but twenty miles from home. Afraid of what my father will say, afraid of being looked on as a stranger by my own people. I sit by a fire and think about myself and all the other young Indians. We just don't seem to fit in anywhere—certainly not among the whites, and not among the older people. I think again about the learned sociology professor and his professing. So many things seem to be clear now that I am away from school and do not have to worry about some man's opinion of my ideas. It is easy to think while looking at dancing flames.

Morning. I spend the day cleaning up, and buying some presents for my family with what is left of my money. Nothing much, but a gift is a gift, if a man buys it with his last quarter. I wait until evening, then start up the track toward home.

Christmas Eve comes in on a north wind. Snow clouds hang over the pines, and the night comes early. Walking along the railroad bed, I feel the calm peace of snowbound forests on either side of me. I take my time; I am back in a world where time does not mean so much now. I am alone; alone but not nearly so lonely as I was back on the campus at school. Those are never lonely who love the snow and the pines; never lonely when the pines are wearing white shawls and snow crunches coldly underfoot. In the woods I know there are the tracks of deer and rabbit; I know that if I leave the rails and go into the woods I shall find them. I walk along feeling glad because my legs are light and my feet seem to know that they are home. A deer comes out of the woods just ahead of me, and stands silhouetted on the rails. The North, I feel, has welcomed me home. I watch him and am glad that I do not wish for a gun. He goes into the woods quietly, leaving only the design of his tracks in the snow. I walk on. Now and then I pass a field, white under the night sky, with houses at the far end. Snow comes from the chimneys of the houses, and I try to tell what sort of wood each is burning by the smoke; some burn pine, others aspen, others tamarack. There is one from which comes black coal smoke that rises lazily and drifts out over the tops of the trees. I like to watch houses and try to imagine what might be happening in them.

Just as a light snow begins to fall, I cross the reservation boundary; somehow it seems as though I have stepped into another world. Deep woods in a white-and-black winter night. A faint trail leading to the village.

The railroad on which I stand comes from a city sprawled by a lake—a city with a million people who walk around without seeing one another; a city sucking the life from all the country around; a city with stores and police and intellectuals and criminals and movies and apartment houses; a city with its politics and libraries and zoos.

Laughing, I go into the woods. As I cross a frozen lake I begin to hear the drums. Soft in the night the drums beat. It is like the pulse beat of the world. The white line of the lake ends at a black forest, and above the trees the blue winds are dancing.

I come to the outlying houses of the village. Simple box houses, etched black in the night. From one or two windows soft lamp light falls on the snow. Christmas here, too, but it does not mean much; not much in the way of parties and presents. Joe Sky will get drunk. Alex Bodidash will buy his children red mittens and a new sled. Alex is a Carlisle man, and tries to keep his home up to white standards. White standards. Funny that my people should be ever falling farther behind. The more they try to imitate whites the more tragic the result. Yet they want us to be imitation white men. About all we imitate well are their vices.

The village is not a sight to instill pride, yet I am not ashamed; one can never be ashamed of his own people when he knows they have dreams as beautiful as white snow on a tall pine.

Father and my brother and sister are seated around the table as I walk in. Father stares at me for a moment, then I am in his arms, crying on his shoulder. I give them the presents I have brought, and my throat tightens as I watch my sister save carefully bits of red string from the packages. I hide my feelings by wrestling with my brother when he strikes my shoulder in token of affection. Father looks at me, and I know he has many questions, but he seems to know why I have come. He tells me to go on alone to the lodge, and he will follow.

I walk along the trail to the lodge, watching the northern lights forming in the heavens. White waving ribbons that seem to pulsate with the rhythm of the drums. Clean snow creaks beneath my feet, and a soft wind sighs through the trees, singing to me. Everything seems to say "Be happy! You are home now—you are free. You are among friends—we are your friends; we, the trees, and the snow, and the lights." I followed the trail to the lodge. My feet are light, my heart seems to sing to the music, and I hold my head high. Across white snow fields blue winds are dancing.

Before the lodge door I stop, afraid. I wonder if my people will remember me. I wonder—"Am I Indian, or am I white?" I stand before the door a long time. I hear the ice groan on the lake, and remember the story of the old woman who is under the ice, trying to get out, so she can punish some runaway lovers. I think to myself, "If I am white I will not believe that story; if I am Indian, I will know that there is an old woman under the ice." I listen for a while, and I know that there is an old woman under the ice. I look again at the lights, and go in.

Inside the lodge there are many Indians. Some sit on benches around the walls, others dance in the center of the floor around a drum. Nobody seems to notice me. It seems as though I were among a people I have never seen before. Heavy women with long black hair. Women with children on their knees—small children that watch with intent black eyes the movements of the dancers, whose small faces are solemn and serene. The faces of the old people are serene, too, and their eyes are merry and bright. I look at the old men. Straight, dressed in dark trousers and beaded velvet vests, wearing soft moccasins. Dark, lined faces intent on the music. I wonder if I am at all like them. They dance on, lifting their feet to the rhythm of the drums, swaying lightly, looking upward. I look at their eyes, and am startled at the rapt attention to the rhythm of the music.

The dance stops. The men walk back to the walls, and talk in low tones or with their hands. There is little conversation, yet everyone seems to be sharing some secret. A woman looks at a small boy wandering away, and he comes back to her.

Strange, I think, and then remember. These people are not sharing words—they are sharing a mood. Everyone is happy. I am so used to white people that it seems strange so many people could be together without someone talking.

These Indians are happy because they are together, and because the night is beautiful outside, and the music is beautiful. I try hard to forget school and white people, and be one of these—my people. I try to forget everything but the night, and it is a part of me; that I am one with my people and we are all a part of something universal. I watch eyes, and see now that the old people are speaking to me. They nod slightly, imperceptibly, and their eyes laugh into mine. I look around the room. All the eyes are friendly; they all laugh. No one questions my being here. The drums begin to beat again, and I catch the invitation in the eyes of the old men. My feet begin to lift to the rhythm, and I look out beyond the walls into the night and see the lights. I am happy. It is beautiful. I am home.

Study and Discussion Questions

1. What are some of the things that draw Whitecloud back home?
2. What are his major criticisms of "civilization"?
3. Depression-era social criticism often focuses on poverty, on unequal distribution of material wealth. How does Whitecloud's social criticism go further?
4. What does Whitecloud find to admire, and to connect with, among the "bums"?
5. What are some of the signs that Whitecloud is not fully at one with the people of his village?
6. Why is the essay titled "Blue Winds Dancing"? Why "blue"? Why "dancing"?

Suggestions for Writing

1. Explain, using evidence from the essay, why you think Whitecloud will, or will not, return to school after Christmas. Will his protest remain merely verbal?
2. Have you experienced anything at all like what Whitecloud describes? Has going to college alienated you in any way from your family or community? If so, discuss how your experience is similar to and different from his.
3. Does Whitecloud idealize life on the reservation? Are there any hints in the essay that all is not well there?

Critical Resources

1. Fleck, Richard. *Critical Perspectives on Native American Fiction.* Washington, D.C.: Three Continents, 1993.
2. Lopez, Ken. *Native American Literature.* Hadley, MA: Ken Lopez, Bookseller, 1994.
3. Wiget, Andrew. ed. *Dictionary of Native American Literature.* New York: Garland, 1994.

❀ ❀ ❀

MARTIN LUTHER KING, JR. (1929–1968)

*Martin Luther King, Jr. was born in Atlanta, Georgia, attended segregated schools,
and enrolled at Morehouse College at age fifteen. Despite his religious upbringing (his father was a Baptist minister), King questioned the over-zealous Christianity of his father and developed his own brand of Christian belief and earned
a Ph.D. in theology at Boston University. In 1954, King was appointed pastor of
a church in Montgomery, Alabama, and the next year, spurred by Rosa Parks's refusal to give up her bus seat to a white man, he led a boycott by African Americans of segregated buses. Two years later he became president of the new civil
rights organization, the Southern Christian Leadership Conference, which would
be instrumental in the Civil Rights Movement of the 1960s and the end of legal
segregation. In 1963, he led a massive march (250,000 people) on Washington,
D.C., where he delivered this speech, "I Have a Dream." The following year, at the
age of 35, he was awarded the Nobel Prize for Peace for his commitment to nonviolent protest. In both his passionate speeches and his writing, King's style appealed to the conscience of various classes of people through the crafting of
rational arguments supported by potent metaphors. King was assassinated in
Memphis, Tennessee, in 1968 after giving a speech in support of striking sanitation
workers. His books include* Stride Toward Freedom *(1958),* Why We Can't Wait
(1964), and Trumpet of Conscience *(1968).*

I Have a Dream   (1963)

I am happy to join with you today[1] in what will go down in history as the greatest demonstration for freedom in the history of our nation.

Fivescore years ago, a great American, in whose symbolic shadow we stand
today, signed the Emancipation Proclamation. This momentous decree came as
a great beacon light of hope to millions of Negro slaves who had been seared in
the flames of withering injustice. It came as a joyous daybreak to end the long
night of their captivity.

But one hundred years later, the Negro still is not free; one hundred years
later, the life of the Negro is still sadly crippled by the manacles of segregation
and the chains of discrimination; one hundred years later, the Negro lives on a
lonely island of poverty in the midst of a vast ocean of material prosperity; one
hundred years later, the Negro is still languished in the corners of American society and finds himself in exile in his own land.

---

[1] August 28, 1963, at a civil rights demonstration in Washington, D.C.

So we've come here today to dramatize a shameful condition. In a sense we've come to our nation's capital to cash a check. When the architects of our republic wrote the magnificent words of the Constitution and the Declaration of Independence, they were signing a promissory note to which every American was to fall heir. This note was the promise that all men, yes, black men as well as white men, would be guaranteed the unalienable rights of life, liberty, and the pursuit of happiness.

It is obvious today that America has defaulted on this promissory note in so far as her citizens of color are concerned. Instead of honoring this sacred obligation, America has given the Negro people a bad check; a check which has come back marked "insufficient funds." We refuse to believe that there are insufficient funds in the great vaults of opportunity of this nation. And so we've come to cash this check, a check that will give us upon demand the riches of freedom and the security of justice.

We have also come to this hallowed spot to remind America of the fierce urgency of now. This is no time to engage in the luxury of cooling off or to take the tranquilizing drug of gradualism. Now is the time to make real the promises of democracy; now is the time to rise from the dark and desolate valley of segregation to the sunlit path of racial justice; now is the time to lift our nation from the quicksands of racial injustice to the solid rock of brotherhood; now is the time to make justice a reality for all God's children. It would be fatal for the nation to overlook the urgency of the moment. This sweltering summer of the Negro's legitimate discontent will not pass until there is an invigorating autumn of freedom and equality.

Nineteen sixty-three is not an end, but a beginning. And those who hope that the Negro needed to blow off steam and will now be content, will have a rude awakening if the nation returns to business as usual.

There will be neither rest nor tranquility in America until the Negro is granted his citizenship rights. The whirlwinds of revolt will continue to shake the foundations of our nation until the bright day of justice emerges.

But there is something that I must say to my people who stand on the warm threshold which leads into the palace of justice. In the process of gaining our rightful place we must not be guilty of wrongful deeds.

Let us not seek to satisfy our thirst for freedom by drinking from the cup of bitterness and hatred. We must forever conduct our struggle on the high plane of dignity and discipline. We must not allow our creative protest to degenerate into physical violence. Again and again we must rise to the majestic heights of meeting physical force with soul force.

The marvelous new militancy which has engulfed the Negro community must not lead us to a distrust of all white people, for many of our white brothers, as evidenced by their presence here today, have come to realize that their destiny is tied up with our destiny and they have come to realize that their freedom is inextricably bound to our freedom. This offense we share mounted to storm the battlements of injustice must be carried forth by a biracial army. We cannot walk alone.

And as we walk, we must make the pledge that we shall always march ahead. We cannot turn back. There are those who are asking the devotees of civil rights, "When will you be satisfied?" We can never be satisfied as long as the Negro is the victim of the unspeakable horrors of police brutality.

We can never be satisfied as long as our bodies, heavy with fatigue of travel, cannot gain lodging in the motels of the highways and the hotels of the cities. We cannot be satisfied as long as the Negro's basic mobility is from a smaller ghetto to a larger one.

We can never be satisfied as long as our children are stripped of their self-hood and robbed of their dignity by signs stating "for whites only." We cannot be satisfied as long as a Negro in Mississippi cannot vote and a Negro in New York believes he has nothing for which to vote. No, we are not satisfied, and we will not be satisfied until justice rolls down like waters and righteousness like a mighty stream.

I am not unmindful that some of you have come here out of excessive trials and tribulation. Some of you have come fresh from narrow jail cells. Some of you have come from areas where your quest for freedom left you battered by the storms of persecution and staggered by the winds of police brutality. You have been the veterans of creative suffering. Continue to work with the faith that un-earned suffering is redemptive.

Go back to Mississippi; go back to Alabama; go back to South Carolina; go back to Georgia; go back to Louisiana; go back to the slums and ghettos of the northern cities, knowing that somehow this situation can, and will be changed. Let us not wallow in the valley of despair.

So I say to you, my friends, that even though we must face the difficulties of today and tomorrow, I still have a dream. It is a dream deeply rooted in the American dream that one day this nation will rise up and live out the true meaning of its creed—we hold these truths to be self-evident, that all men are created equal.

I have a dream that one day on the red hills of Georgia, sons of former slaves and sons of former slave-owners will be able to sit down together at the table of brotherhood.

I have a dream that one day, even the state of Mississippi, a state sweltering with the heat of injustice, sweltering with the heat of oppression, will be trans-formed into an oasis of freedom and justice.

I have a dream my four little children will one day live in a nation where they will not be judged by the color of their skin but by content of their character. I have a dream today!

I have a dream that one day, down in Alabama, with its vicious racists, with its governor having his lips dripping with the words of interposition and nullifi-cation, that one day, right there in Alabama, little black boys and black girls will be able to join hands with little white boys and white girls as sisters and broth-ers. I have a dream today!

I have a dream that one day every valley shall be exalted, every hill and moun-tain shall be made low, the rough places shall be made plain, and the crooked places shall be made straight and the glory of the Lord will be revealed and all flesh shall see it together.

This is our hope. This is the faith that I go back to the South with.

With this faith we will be able to hew out of the mountain of despair a stone of hope. With this faith we will be able to transform the jangling discords of our nation into a beautiful symphony of brotherhood.

With this faith we will be able to work together, to pray together, to struggle together, to go to jail together, to stand up for freedom together, knowing that we will be free one day. This will be the day when all of God's children will be able to sing with new meaning—"my country 'tis of thee; sweet land of liberty; of thee I sing; land where my fathers died, land of the pilgrim's pride; from every mountain side, let freedom ring"—and if America is to be a great nation, this must become true.

So let freedom ring from the prodigious hilltops of New Hampshire.

Let freedom ring from the mighty mountains of New York.

Let freedom ring from the heightening Alleghenies of Pennsylvania.

Let freedom ring from the snow-capped Rockies of Colorado.

Let freedom ring from the curvaceous slopes of California.

But not only that.

Let freedom ring from Stone Mountain of Georgia.

Let freedom ring from Lookout Mountain of Tennessee.

Let freedom ring from every hill and molehill of Mississippi, from every mountainside, let freedom ring.

And when we allow freedom to ring, when we let it ring from every village and hamlet, from every state and city, we will be able to speed up that day when all of God's children—black men and white men, Jews and Gentiles, Catholics and Protestants—will be able to join hands and to sing in the words of the old Negro spiritual, "Free at last, free at last; thank God Almighty, we are free at last."

Study and Discussion Questions

1. What does King mean by the metaphor of the promissory note and the "bad check"?
2. King has two audiences, white Americans and black Americans. What is he saying to each audience and what is directed to both?
3. How does King define the American Dream in this speech?
4. List the parts of *King's* dream.
5. How is the last of the paragraphs that begin "I have a dream" different from the preceding ones?

Suggestions for Writing

1. Gather some examples of the way King uses repetition in this speech. What effect does the repetition have? Read the speech aloud.

2. How much civil rights progress has been made in the years since King made this speech? Give examples of what has changed and what has not.
3. Should ministers and other religious leaders be politically active? Argue for or against.
4. Write a paper comparing/contrasting "I Have a Dream" with King's 1967 speech, "A Time to Break Silence" in the "Peace and War" section.

Critical Resources

1. Hansen, Drew. *The Dream: Martin Luther King and the Speech that Inspired a Nation.* New York: Ecco, 2003.
2. *I Have a Dream.* (Documentary) Maljack Productions, Inc. 1986 (28 minutes). Contains video footage of speech.
3. Leff, Michael and Fred J. Kauffeld, eds. *Texts in Context: Critical Dialogues on Significant Episodes in American Political Rhetoric: With Newly Edited Speech Texts by Anna E. Dickinson and Martin Luther King Jr.* Davis, CA: Hermagoras, 1989.
4. Miller, Keith. *Voice of Deliverance: The Language of Martin Luther King and Its Sources.* New York: Free Press, 1992.
5. Schlueter, Nathan. *One Dream or Two? Justice in America and in the Thought of Martin Luther King Jr.* Lanham, MD: Lexington, 2002.

VARIETIES OF PROTEST: PAPER TOPICS

1. Discuss the imagery of anger and protest in one or more works. (Suggestions: Alexie, "The Powwow at the End of the World"; Rich, "The Trees"; Patterson, "At That Moment"; Levine, "They Feed They Lion")
2. Discuss one or more works that are themselves protests in spite of the fact that they are about protests that may seem to fail. (Suggestions: Melville, "Bartleby, The Scrivener"; Zoline, "The Heat Death of the Universe"; cummings, "i sing of Olaf glad and big")
3. Discuss one or more works that deal with protests motivated more by personal conviction than by desire for change in one's life, that is, where the impetus for the protest originates in idealism rather than pragmatism. (Suggestions: Thoreau, "Civil Disobedience"; Sophocles, *Antigone*)
4. "Nothing so aggravates an earnest person as passive resistance," says the narrator of "Bartleby, The Scrivener." Discuss the effec-

tiveness of passive resistance as a tactic in one or more works. (Suggestions: Melville, "Bartleby, The Scrivener"; Thoreau, "Civil Disobedience"; King, "I Have A Dream")

5. Discuss one or more works that deal either with protest around an issue of concern to you, or a kind of protest you might consider engaging in.

6. Compare the dynamics of individual protest versus group protest using two works. (Suggestions: McPherson, "A Loaf of Bread"; Sophocles, *Antigone;* Sillitoe, "The Loneliness of the Long-distance Runner"; the screenplay *Salt of the Earth*)

7. Discuss one or more works in which the act of protest clearly grows out of the immediate circumstances of a character's life. (Suggestions: Zoline, "The Heat Death of the Universe"; Jacobs, *Incidents in the Life of a Slave Girl;* Carson, "I Cannot Remember All the Times . . ."; Whitecloud, "Blue Winds Dancing")

8. Select one of the works in this section, state what the writer's stance is toward the issue that is the subject of the work, and analyze the way in which the writer uses formal techniques to make her or his point. How effective are these techniques? (Suggestions: King, "I Have a Dream"; Zoline, "Heat Death of the Universe; Alvarez, "The White House Has Disinvited the Poets"; the screenplay *Salt of the Earth*)

9. Beyond marching in a demonstration or refusing to pay one's taxes, there are many ingenious ways to engage in acts of protest represented in the works here. Select and analyze one or more works about a form of protest that particularly interests you. (Suggestions: Seeger, "I'm Gonna Be An Engineer"; Grahn, "A Woman Is Talking to Death"; Whitecloud, "Blue Winds Dancing"; Fisher, "A Drop In the Bucket"; Sillitoe, "The Loneliness of the Long-distance Runner"; Espada, "Jorge the Church Janitor Finally Quits")

10. Discuss the use of humor in effective protest writing. (Suggestions: Ginsberg, "America"; Auden, "The Unknown Citizen"; Soyinka, "Telephone Conversation")

11. Discuss attitudes toward the appropriateness of violence as a means of protest in one or more works. (Suggestions: Harjo, "The Woman Hanging from the Thirteenth Floor Window"; Plath, "Daddy"; Hughes, "Harlem"; Steinbeck, from *The Grapes of Wrath;* King, "I Have a Dream")

12. Discuss attitudes toward the appropriateness of violence as a *response* to protest. (Suggestions: Grahn, "A Woman Is Talking to Death"; Sophocles, *Antigone;* the screenplay *Salt of the Earth*)

13. What do you think are the most important characteristics that make for effective protest literature or visual art? List these characteristics and discuss, using examples from several texts. Or choose one text you find particularly powerful and discuss what makes it effective.

HOW FICTION WORKS

A good way to begin discussing fiction might be to look at some. The following is more a sketch than a fully developed short story, but it raises a number of important questions about how fiction works.

PAULETTE CHILDRESS WHITE

Alice

Alice. Drunk Alice. Alice of the streets. Of the party. Of the house of dark places. From whom without knowing I hid love all my life behind remembrances of her house where I went with Momma in the daytime to borrow things, and we found her lounging in the front yard on a dirty plastic lawn chair drinking warm beer from the can in a little brown bag where the flies buzzed in and out of the always-open door of the house as we followed her into the cool, dim rank-smelling rooms for what it was we'd come. And I fought frowns as my feet caught on the sticky gray wooden floor but looked up to smile back at her smile as she gave the dollar or the sugar or the coffee to Momma who never seemed to notice the floor or the smell or Alice.

Alice, tall like a man, with soft wooly hair spread out in tangles like a feathered hat and her face oily and her legs ashy, whose beauty I never quite believed because she valued it so little but was real. Real like wild flowers and uncut grass, real like the knotty sky-reach of a dead tree. Beauty of warm brown eyes in a round dark face and of teeth somehow always white and clean and of lips moist and open, out of which rolled the voice and the laughter, deep and breathless, rolling out the strong and secret beauty of her soul.

Alice of the streets. Gentle walking on long legs. Close-kneed. Careful. Stopping sometimes at our house on her way to unknown places and other people. She came wearing loose, flowered dresses and she sat in our chairs rubbing the too-big knees that sometimes hurt, and we gathered, Momma, my sisters and I, to hear the beautiful bad-woman talk and feel the rolling laughter, always sure that she left more than she came for. I accepted the tender touch of her hands on my hair or my face or my arms like favors I never returned. I clung to the sounds of her words and the light of her smiles like stolen fruit.

Alice, mother in a house of dark places. Of boys who fought each other and ran cursing through the wild back rooms where I did not go alone but sometimes with Alice when she caught them up and knuckled their heads and made them cry or hugged them close to her saying funny things to tease them into laughter. And of the oldest son, named for his father, who sat twisted into a wheelchair by sunny windows in the front where she stayed with him for hours giving him her love, filling him with her laughter and he sat there—his words strained, difficult but soft and warm like the sun from the windows.

Alice of the party. When there was not one elsewhere she could make one of the evenings when her husband was not storming the dim rooms in drunken fits or lying somewhere in darkness filling the house with angry grunts and snores before the days he would go to work. He sat near her drinking beer with what company was there—was always sure to come—greedy for Alice and her husband, who leaned into and out of each other, talking hard and laughing loud and telling lies and being real. And there were rare and wondrously wicked times when I was caught there with Daddy who was one of the greedy ones and could not leave until the joy-shouting, table-slapping arguments about God and Negroes, the jumping up and down, the bellowing "what about the time" talks, the boasting and reeling of people drunk with beer and laughter and the ache of each other was over and the last ones sat talking sad and low, sick with themselves and too much beer. I watched Alice growing tired and ill and thought about the boys who had eaten dinners of cake and soda pop from the corner store, and I struggled to despise her for it against the memory of how, smiling they'd crept off to their rooms and slept in peace. And later at home, I, too, slept strangely safe and happy, hugging the feel of that sweet fury in her house and in Alice of the party.

Alice, who grew older as I grew up but stayed the same while I grew beyond her, away from her. So far away that once, on a clear early morning in the spring, when I was eighteen and smart and clean on my way to work downtown in the high-up office of my government job, with eyes that would not see I cut off her smile and the sound of her voice calling my name. When she surprised me on a clear spring morning, on her way somewhere or from somewhere in the streets and I could not see her beauty, only the limp flowered dress and the tangled hair and the face puffy from too much drinking and no sleep, I cut off her smile. I let my eyes slide away to say without speaking that I had grown beyond her. Alice, who had no place to grow in but was deep in the soil that fed me.

It was eight years before I saw Alice again and in those eight years Alice had buried her husband and one of her boys and lost the oldest son to the county hospital where she traveled for miles to take him the sun and her smiles. And she had become a grandmother and a member of the church and cleaned out her house and closed the doors. And in those eight years I had married and become the mother of sons and did not always keep my floors clean or my hair combed or my legs oiled and I learned to like the taste of beer and how to talk bad-woman talk. In those eight years life had led me to the secret laughter.

Alice, when I saw her again, was in black, after the funeral of my brother, sitting alone in an upstairs bedroom of my mother's house, her face dusted with brown powder and her gray-streaked hair brushed back into a neat ball and her wrinkled hands rubbing the tight-stockinged, tumor-filled knees and her eyes quiet and sober when she looked at me where I stood at the top of the stairs. I had run upstairs to be away from the smell of food and the crowd of comforters come to help bury our dead when I found Alice sitting alone in black and was afraid to smile remembering how I'd cut off her smile when I thought I had grown beyond her and was afraid to speak because there was too much I wanted to say.

Then Alice smiled her same smile and spoke my name in her same voice and rising slowly from the tumored knees said, "Come on in and sit with me." And for the very first time I did.

Let's begin with a deceptively simple question: Who's telling the story? Although Paulette Childress White's name appears above the title, we cannot easily know whether White is recounting her own experiences or instead writing a fictional account of a fictional "I" who knew a fictional "Alice." Were the teller of the story (the "I") an obvious lunatic, say, or a creature from another galaxy, we might deduce that this "I" isn't the author Paulette Childress White; but since we cannot be certain, we can simply avoid the question by calling the voice telling the story the narrator.

The choice of narrator is central in any piece of fiction. Had Alice herself narrated, for example, we readers might have seen things quite differently—more emphasis, perhaps, on those painful knees; physical description of the present narrator (let's call her June) rather than of Alice; and, most important, Alice's thoughts rather than those of her young friend.

White also might have chosen to avoid an "I" or first-person narrator altogether, by telling the story instead in a disembodied voice that described, perhaps dispassionately, what happened to two individuals, Alice and June, each referred to in the third person, that is, as "she." By choosing the narrator she did, White has made the story at least as much about June as about Alice. And if we look more carefully—at the sixth sentence in the story, for example, where we find the phrase "without knowing"—we can be even more precise and say that the narrator is not June as she was growing up, knowing Alice, but rather an older June *remembering* her changing relationship to Alice. Thus, through her choice and construction of narrator, White has made this a story about what a young woman growing up learned, though unaware of it at the time, from her encounters with a woman named Alice.

Having understood the function of the particular narrator White has created, we can see more clearly that this seemingly rambling sketch has a plot. Plot is not simply a sequence of events but a web of relationships between those events. Central to most plots is conflict of some kind and early on the story establishes a conflict between two different attitudes toward Alice, "Alice . . . from whom without knowing I hid love all my life behind remembrances of her house." The narrator can still see the "dirty plastic lawn chair," Alice drinking "warm beer from the can in a little brown bag," the flies buzzing, the "cool, dim rank-smelling rooms," but also, "her smile." Drawn to Alice's warmth, energy, and love, yet repelled by the sloppiness she cannot understand, June has strongly conflicting feelings toward this "beautiful bad-woman." As a child, June is at once attracted and made nervous by Alice's relaxed sensuality. She sees Alice's lapses as mother and homemaker not as evidence of the great burden her situation places on her, or as natural consequences of her engaging spontaneity, but as a moral failing. She observes that Alice's sons eat dinners of "cake and soda pop from the corner store," but also how happy they seem, and has to "struggle to despise her." At eighteen, dressed up and on the way to the government job she is so proud of, June runs into a bedraggled Alice and snubs her, refuses to return her smile. Eight years later, confident, settled, herself an overburdened mother, but also attuned now to "the secret laughter," she sees Alice again, and for the first time fully appreciates, understands, and loves her. So while we have a character sketch of Alice, the plot centers around June.

"Alice" has a rather simple plot, but White makes the story rich with emotion through her use of language, her style. The sixth sentence of the first paragraph, for example, through its length, its rhythm, its easy flow, helps create a mood of dream-like remembering, as the adult narrator gathers her past impressions of Alice. White also effectively uses many well-chosen details to create a picture of Alice: her "too-big knees that sometimes hurt," her "teeth somehow always white and clean," her "lips moist and open," the warm beer she drank "from the can in a little brown bag," and later "her limp flowered dress" and "tangled hair."

White also uses comparisons, or similes, to help us understand June's feelings toward Alice. To say that Alice's beauty is "real like wild flowers and uncut grass, real like the knotty sky-reach of a dead tree" is to communicate very concisely something rather complicated. When the narrator says "I clung to the sounds of her words and the light of her smiles like stolen fruit," we can readily imagine her ambivalence. By the time we reach the end, when June was "afraid to speak because there was too much I wanted to say," White doesn't have to *tell* us what June wanted to say because she has already shown us—made us share those feelings.

Something else shown rather than told is the social dimension of "Alice," the relationship of its characters and their situations to their society and to such social categories as gender, race, and class. That Paulette Childress White is a woman may be obvious; that she is black and working class may be less obvious; but consideration of these facts can help us see more in the story. Perhaps above all else, "Alice" portrays a relationship between two *women*. For all her spirit and energy, Alice is worn down by the responsibility of caring for a husband and sons, including one in a wheelchair, responsibilities that fall on her because she is a woman in a society that assigns nurturing to women. In rejecting Alice, June may be rejecting what she fears will be her own fate as a married woman. The government job she holds so proudly (and it is on the way to this job that she so cruelly snubs Alice) represents her hope that she might avoid that fate. Later, a mother herself, experiencing many of the pressures of that role (her own floors are not always clean; now she, too, relaxes with a beer sometimes), June has a fuller and more sympathetic understanding of Alice, "who had no place to grow in," and also a grateful understanding of how much the example of Alice's strength nurtured her as she was growing up. So the reconciliation at the end is more than just a reconciliation between two people; it is a reconciliation between two women, who have a special understanding because of the difficulties and, most important, the joys (that "secret laughter") that they share.

The ending of "Alice" represents a reconciliation also between two *black* people or, put another way, between June and the black working-class community toward which she felt so ambivalent while growing up. This may be subtler than the feminism of the story, but there is enough evidence, especially in the descriptions of Alice in the second paragraph, for us to infer that the characters are black and working-class, even without knowing that the author is. Though White never spells this out, the poverty, and the many losses Alice experiences—a son and husband dead, another son in the county hospital—are surely related in some way to her status as an African-American in a racist society. And just as that government job represents June's hope for escape from the suffering she sees in her community (government jobs were among the few possible avenues out of poverty for African-Americans in recent decades), her reconciliation with Alice at the end represents a reconciliation with her community, a fuller acceptance of her roots and of herself.

Now this might seem like "reading things into the story." But we interpret whenever we read and think about fiction. Other readings of "Alice" are of course possible; the point, if we want to share our interpretations with others, is to offer evidence. Our interpretations will inevitably depend not only on what the author has written but on who we are. A racist and sexist reader of "Alice," for example, might see it as a story about the eternal laziness of black women: Alice drinks too much, neglects her children and her housekeeping responsibilities, creates her own problems; June has a chance to better herself (the government gives her a job, after all) but eventually becomes just like Alice. This, too, is a reading of the story, though a quite perverse reading, one that seems to ignore a great deal of what White has written, perhaps most of all her efforts to make Alice so sympathetic a character.

We can never say with any finality that one reading is the correct reading, but with an understanding of the ways writers work to shape our responses, a community of readers, through discussion, through argument, can begin to distinguish a careful and persuasive reading from one that simply ignores what the author has written. The following more general discussion of how fiction works is designed to help.*

---

*Paulette Childress White (b. 1948) grew up and went to high school in Detroit, Michigan. She began art school, but could not afford to continue. She married and she wrote poems and stories while raising children, eventually publishing her poetry, which includes *Love Poem to a Black Junkie* (1975) and *The Watermelon Dress* (1984). "Alice," her first published story, appeared in *Essence* in 1977.

POINT OF VIEW

A writer attempts to shape our responses to characters and events by telling a story from a particular angle or perspective, much as a film maker, through positioning of the camera, shapes our responses to a film. In fiction, as the discussion of "Alice" suggested, a writer's construction of a narrator—that is, the **point of view**—is central to our experience as readers.

Narrators are commonly categorized as either nonparticipant or participant narrators. A **nonparticipant narrator** always speaks in the third person, referring to characters by name and as "he" or "she," never as "I." This kind of narrative voice may develop a personality of its own (humorous, solemn, ironic) but does not belong to any character in the fictional world it creates. A nonparticipant narrator may comment on the action in the story but does not participate in it.

Nonparticipant narrators are usually labeled according to how much they know, how much they tell us. An **omniscient narrator** knows not only what is happening everywhere but what everyone is thinking. Such a narrator can provide us with broad overviews ("Smithville has been for decades the dullest town in the state"), can describe events involving various characters ("While Joe slept peacefully, his younger brother, across town, was buying a gun"), and can dip into the minds of any number of characters to tell us their thoughts ("Carol wondered whether her investigation of Joe's murder would lead to a front page story"). An omniscient narrator is an artifice—no individual could know so much—but an artifice that readers adapt to quickly and that writers find an extremely flexible instrument for storytelling.

A **limited omniscient narrator** (or **selective omniscient narrator**) is also a third-person narrator, a disembodied voice, but one that has access to the inner thoughts of only one character and focuses on the experiences and perceptions of that single character, sometimes a character in the thick of the story's action, sometimes one on the periphery, more observer than actor. Since in reality we have immediate access to the thoughts of only one person, ourself, the limited omniscient point of view can often give us a strong sense of intimacy, an identification with the character through whose consciousness events are filtered. If the narrative, or a section of it, consists entirely of this character's thoughts, as if spoken aloud to himself or herself, then we have an **interior monologue;** and if these thoughts are presented not as a logical sequence of statements but as a seeming jumble of thought fragments and sensory perceptions in an effort to create a strong sense of the character's inner reality, then we have **stream of consciousness** writing. (Both the interior monologue and stream of consciousness writing, by the way, can also be used with participant narrators.)

A third type of nonparticipant narrator is the **objective narrator,** a third-person narrator that describes characters from the outside only, never revealing their thoughts. Since readers want and need to know what characters are thinking, the burden on this kind of "fly-on-the-wall" narrator, as it is often called, is to describe characters' appearance, speech, and actions in a way that enables us to *infer* their thoughts. An objective narrator is sometimes also called a **dramatic narrator,** since *dialogue*—what characters say—often becomes, as in drama, the key element in revealing their thoughts.

A **participant narrator** is a character in the story as well as the teller of the story. Such a narrator describes a fictional world of which he or she is a part and therefore, like the narrator of "Alice," says "I." This "I" may be central to the action, or may be a minor character, more witness than actor. Like the limited omniscient narrator, the first-person participant narrator enters into the mind of only one character, himself or herself. Use of a participant narrator can mean a loss of flexibility; all that the writer can present directly to the reader are the words of a single character. But a participant narrator can also create a certain intimacy and drama; as we read we may feel as if a person (rather than a disembodied voice, as with a nonparticipant narrator) is speaking directly to us.

When a writer reveals to us what a character is thinking, how a character sees the world, we develop an attitude toward that character's thinking. Depending on the writer's language, the nature and logic of that character's views, their relation to events and other characters in the story, we may identify with that character and find his or her views sensible, reasonable, and persuasive, or we may feel distant from that character and question those views. When we have a participant narrator, often a child or other innocent, and we understand the implications of what is happening better than that narrator does, we have a **naive narrator.** If the narrator, whether naive or deliberately deceptive, comes to conclusions we as readers know are wrong, we can speak of an **unreliable narrator.**

A writer can put distance between us and a participant narrator quite quickly. Fyodor Dostoevsky's novel *Notes from Underground* opens like this: "I am a sick man. . . . I am a spiteful man. I am an unattractive man." Then, a few paragraphs later, after describing his nasty, spiteful behavior as a government official, the narrator tells us: "I was lying when I said just now that I was a spiteful official. I was lying from spite." Whether we decide this narrator is toying with us or insane (or both), it doesn't take much talk like this to alienate us from him. Though the entire novel is narrated by this character, from his point of view, though we see only what he chooses to show us and have access to no one's thoughts but his, we scarcely identify with him. Instead we watch him from an emotional distance, with morbid fascination.

A nonparticipant narrator can also distance us from the character whose thoughts are revealed. "After the Party," a short story by Tess Slesinger, begins like this:

> Mrs. Colborne had given three cocktail parties a week in honor of various celebrities, ever since her nervous breakdown back in 1930. The doctor had told her then, when she was convalescing, that she must get interested in something; he suggested dancing (she felt she was too old), social work (but she shuddered, she had had dreadful experiences, really dreadful), writing a novel, going round the world, being psychoanalyzed in Vienna, studying

economics in London, taking a course in sculpture, endowing a hospital, adopting a baby, breeding dogs, Christian Science (he was very broad), collecting early clocks, marrying again (oh dear no, Mrs. Colborne said, that was as bad as social work), starting a publishing house, running an interior decorating shop, moving to the country, or learning to hand-paint china.

The entire story is told from Mrs. Colborne's point of view. Though we have ample access to her thoughts, we don't really *share* them. Slesinger has quickly and deftly led us to see Mrs. Colborne in a way that she does not see herself, that is, to see her as foolish.

With participant narrators and with limited omniscient, nonparticipant narrators, writers shape our attitude toward events and characters not only by controlling distance between reader and character but also by the choice of *which* character's thoughts to reveal, and when. A story, say, of a domestic dispute culminating in a woman leaving her husband would obviously look very different from her point of view than from his; unless there were significant distancing we would tend to sympathize with the character through whose eyes we saw events most often. A good way to begin figuring out the significance of point of view in a work of fiction is to ask yourself the following: What attitude is the writer trying to create toward the character whose thoughts are revealed? And how would the story be different if narrated from a different point of view?

PLOT

A **plot** is a sequence of fictional events arranged in a meaningful pattern. A fictional plot is usually based on or driven by **conflict,** that is, opposition or antagonism between two elements. There may be conflict between two individuals, between two groups of people, between an individual and society, even between two tendencies within an individual. Conflict in a work of fiction is often complex and may consist of two or more constituent conflicts, whether sequentially or simultaneously.

We can often gain much insight into the meaning of a story by looking at the shape of its plot. A happy ending, for example, can have very different implications than an unhappy ending. A happy ending can tie everything together neatly, and help us forget whatever conflict set the plot in motion; an unhappy ending can be messier, leaving conflicts unresolved, questions unanswered, problems continuing. The social criticism of Alan Sillitoe's story "The Loneliness of the Long-distance Runner," for example, would be seriously undermined if, at the end, its troubled, angry, rebellious working-class hero were to get a good job, become a success, move up the social ladder, and settle down as a happy, comfortable, well-fed family man. We needn't go so far as this hero does in condemning happy endings (he calls the few books he's read "useless" because "all of them ended on a winning post and didn't teach me a thing") but we can see the potential diminishment of life's complexity in simplistic happy endings. In a different story, however, an upbeat ending might strengthen the story's social criticism by suggesting there is an alternative to accommodation and despair.

Not just the ending of a story but the whole sequencing of events helps shape its meaning. Imagine a plot about a married couple, Sue and Al, which consists of three major incidents: they fight at home over a trivial matter; Sue has an angry dispute at work with a coworker over a minor misunderstanding; Al goes to a bar and drinks heavily. A great deal, of course, would depend on point of view and other matters, but we can probably make the following comparisons with some confidence. If the sequence of events were Al's drinking, then the quarrel at home, then Sue's blow-up at work, we might assume (in the absence of evidence to the contrary) a certain causality—that Al's drinking led to the quarrel, which upset Sue and made her testy at work; we might have a story, then, about the evils of drink. If, instead, the sequence were Sue's dispute at work, then the fight at home, then Al's drinking in the bar, we might infer that Sue's difficulties at work led to her fight with Al, which in turn led to his drinking—a story, perhaps, about the toll jobs can take on people, or, with an antifeminist slanting, a story about what happens when women work outside the home. Alternatively, if the fight came first, say at breakfast, and then simultaneously Sue went off to trouble at work and Al went off to whiskey in the bar, we might have a story about the difficulties of marriage and the unhappiness it can cause for both partners.

Staying with this last time sequence—the fight at home, then work and drink simultaneously—we might speculate on what difference the *order of narration* might make. Were the drinking to come last, we might expect (assuming, say, an omniscient narrator that revealed Sue's and Al's thoughts similarly) to sympathize more fully with Al than with Sue, as the story would come to a close with him alone in the bar with his thoughts. On the other hand, were the story to end with Sue, frustrated and miserable at work, we might see it more as her story than his.

Use of **flashback,** in which the chronological flow of a narrative is interrupted to narrate a scene that occurred earlier, might change our relative sympathy toward the two characters in other ways. Suppose that we read first about Sue's dispute at work, then, in a flashback, read about the fight between Al and Sue earlier that morning, and then, finally, read about Al's drinking after the fight. While the story might devote equal time to Al's drinking and Sue's difficulties at work, we would read about Al's drinking with knowledge of its cause (the fight at breakfast) and thus with more sympathy, while we would read about Sue's testiness at work *without* knowledge of its cause (for this knowledge would only come later in the story) and possibly just think her an irritable person. On the other hand, if the story began with Al's drinking, flashed back to the fight at breakfast, and then moved on to the fight's repercussions for Sue at work, we would probably sympathize more fully with her. And since Sue and Al are, after all, fighting, it certainly matters with whom we sympathize.

These are just a few of the ways that plot structure can shape our attitudes toward characters and events in fiction. Other and more complicated kinds of plot are obviously possible, including plots without discernible causality, the point of which might be that what happens to us in life is random and meaningless. (We'd certainly get bored reading more than a few stories with such plots.) Sometimes, too, parallels and contrasts between incidents, rather than links of causality, can be the key to a story's meaning. But however a work of fiction is structured, a good step toward understanding its meanings is to chart its plot.

CHARACTER

Characterization, the means a writer uses to reveal what a character is like, can take many forms. With an omniscient or limited omniscient narrator, a writer can describe a character directly: "Harry Smythe was too confident for his own good. . . ." But with a participant narrator, characterization can be more complicated: "I have always been an honest person. . . . Albert, who got the promotion that rightfully was mine, is a sneak and a hypocrite." As readers we would have to weigh assertions like these against other evidence.

Writers cannot only tell but also show us what their characters are like. We can come to know characters through what they do, or don't do: bravery or cowardice, for example, or generosity or selfishness are easily demonstrated through action. We can learn about characters through what they say and, if we are privy to their thoughts, through what they think. In addition, we can learn about them from what *other* characters say and think about them. And, of course, a combination of elements can reveal character; we may, for example, understand characters' hypocrisy only by observing the discrepancy between their actions and their words. Finally, we can sometimes find clues to what characters are like in incidental ways, through their appearance, perhaps, or even their name; in fiction, unlike life, someone named Knightly (as in Jane Austen's novel *Emma*) is likely to be of noble character, while someone named Jesse B. Simple (as in Langston Hughes's sketches) will, ironically, probably turn out to be a sophisticated social critic.

Fictional characters are usually seen as either **major** or **minor characters.** Major characters are at the center of the plot and usually drawn in detail; minor characters are peripheral and may be sketched in less detail. The most important character in a work of fiction we call the **protagonist,** and if the primary conflict is between that character and another, we call the latter the **antagonist.** Major characters tend to be complex (or "round," to use novelist E. M. Forster's term); minor characters may be simpler, one dimensional, or "flat." Major characters, because they often have conflicting tendencies within them, are more likely to be *dynamic,* to change somehow in the course of a work of fiction; minor characters, too simply drawn to embody conflict, tend to be *static.*

Discussion of flat characters leads to the issue of **stereotypes.** In short fiction, even the central character may not be very fully developed. Consequently, we will often find characters outlined quickly, based on a single defining trait and sometimes on commonly held assumptions about particular kinds of individuals: the lonely spinster, the manly hunter, the mad scientist, and so on. Stereotyping can be useful, for it allows a writer to sketch a character in a few quick strokes, with confidence that most readers will fill in the details in a predictable way. But since we tend to see fiction as representative, as embodying in specific characters general truths about human beings, such stereotyped characters can also reinforce our worst prejudices, particularly about oppressed groups in society. It is one thing for a writer to portray an accountant as dull or a professor as absentminded, and quite another to use such stereotypes as the shrewish wife or the dumb blue-collar worker or the lazy welfare recipient. Of course writers often create characters _against_ type, as, for example, in Kate Chopin's "The Story of an Hour," in which traditional assumptions about a devoted wife are proven quite wrong.

LANGUAGE AND TONE

A careful look, sentence by sentence, at the language of a work of fiction—the words chosen and the way they are put together—can often help us understand what that work means. Writers work to make language serve their purposes, to produce the effects they desire, and what is distinctive about the language of a writer or a work we call **style.**

One aspect of style, one important use of language in fiction, is the **metaphor.** In James Baldwin's story "Sonny's Blues," the narrator, a school teacher in Harlem, uses metaphor to describe the boys in his class, boys without much future: "they were growing up with a rush and their heads bumped abruptly against the low ceiling of their actual possibilities." The implicit comparison or metaphor (an _explicit_ comparison is called a **simile**) is between (1) growing up, through no fault of your own, with little chance of success; and (2) bumping your head on a low ceiling as you grow taller. It makes vivid and real, in few words, the painful nature of the trap these boys are in.

Metaphors are one way writers use language to shape our attitude toward characters and events, that is, one way they establish **tone.** The tone of the quote from "Sonny's Blues" is primarily sympathetic. There are other kinds of tone. The novel _Maggie: A Girl of the Streets,_ by Stephen Crane, begins like this:

> A very little boy stood upon a heap of gravel for the honor of Rum Alley. He was throwing stones at howling urchins from Devil's Row, who were circling madly about the heap and pelting at him.
>   His infantile countenance was livid with fury. His small body was writhing in the delivery of great, crimson oaths.

The tone here is mocking; Crane is making fun of the almost grotesque spectacle he is describing. The "honor" being fought for is the honor of "Rum Alley," fought for not by knights or soldiers but by "howling urchins." Crane's language is **ironic,** in that he is saying one thing (that the boys are fighting for honor) and meaning another (that Rum Alley is hardly the place to find honor).

Irony often joins with comedy and also scorn, as in the tone of the following passage, the opening of "Slave on the Block," a story by Langston Hughes:

> They were people who went in for Negroes—Michael and Anne—the Carraways. But not in the social-service, philanthropic sort of way, no. They saw no use in helping a race that was already too charming and naive and lovely for words. Leave them unspoiled and just enjoy them, Michael and Anne felt. So they went in for the Art of Negroes—the dancing that had such jungle life about it, the songs that were so simple and fervent, the poetry that was so direct, so real. They never tried to influence that art, they only bought it and raved over it, and copied it. For they were artists, too.

Hughes, like Crane, is making fun of his characters, though with far less sympathy. Hughes does not need to spell out his attitude toward the Carraways; his language creates a distinct tone of mockery. "They saw no use in helping a race that was already too charming and naive and lovely for words." Both through their actions (buying art) and what are implicitly their thoughts ("too . . . lovely for words") we see the superficiality and phoniness of the Carraways' admiration for black people. By the time we get to the last sentence ("they were artists, too") its irony comes through with clarity and force.

Tone serves a different function in the opening of "Dotson Gerber Resurrected," a short story by Hal Bennett:

> We saw the head of Mr. Dotson Gerber break ground at approximately nine o'clock on a bright Saturday morning in March out near our collard patch, where Poppa had started to dig a well and then filled it in. Of course, none of us knew then that the shock of red hair and part of a head sprouting from the abandoned well belonged to Mr. Dotson Gerber, who'd been missing from his farm since early last fall.

Here the language is deliberately matter-of-fact. Bennett wants us to accept this unlikely event as real, so his narrator describes it very simply, flatly, as if there were no reason in the world not to believe it. The narrator moves quickly past the fantastic part, the head breaking ground, to a series of quite ordinary details—the time, the day, the month, and so on. He draws us in further, toward acceptance of this bizarre event, by starting the second sentence with "Of course." This not only sustains the matter-of-factness of his tone, but also says to us that he's not the type who'd try to put one over on us—he'd never claim they *recognized* the head.

The opening of *The American* (1877), a novel by Henry James, illustrates another use of language, and a very different style:

> On a brilliant day in May, in the year 1868, a gentleman was reclining at his ease on the great circular divan which at that period occupied the cen-

tre of the Salon Carré, in the Museum of the Louvre. The commodious ottoman has since been removed, to the extreme regret of all weak-kneed lovers of the fine arts; but the gentleman in question had taken serene possession of its softest spot, and, with his head thrown back and his legs outstretched, was staring at Murillo's beautiful moon-borne Madonna in profound enjoyment of his posture.

James's language here creates a strong sense of social class. It is not just the scene described that does this, but the way it is described, the implicit assumption that the reader understands, without explanation, references to "the Salon Carré" and "Murillo's . . . moon-borne Madonna," references most familiar in James's day to a small class of people who could afford to travel to Paris. The length and the slow pace of the sentences, too, suggest a world of refined leisure; their stately rhythms surround the reader with the sense of a stable, established aristocratic order.

Compare this now to the opening of *Waiting for Nothing,* Tom Kromer's autobiographical novel about a young man, jobless and hungry, during the Great Depression:

> It is night. I am walking along this dark street, when my foot hits a stick. I reach down and pick it up. I finger it. It is a good stick, a heavy stick. One sock from it would lay a man out.

The difference here lies not just in the setting, the street rather than the Louvre, but in the language used to describe the scene. The words are everyday words, mostly of one syllable (unlike James's), and expressions such as "this dark street" and "sock" are colloquial rather than formal English. The sentences are short and grammatically simple; their broken rhythms create a sense of almost reflex behavior, a focus on immediate survival, unlike the leisurely, contemplative atmosphere James's language creates.

These are just a few of the ways the particular language of a work of fiction shapes our reading experience. Slow down and examine a passage or two as you read—perhaps an opening passage or one that somehow grabs you—and see if you can figure out what the writer is up to.

SETTING

The time and place—the setting—of a work of fiction may seem initially like background but in fact can have a profound effect upon character and plot. To go back to Paulette Childress White's "Alice" for a moment, Alice's house, the *place* where much of the story is set, is so powerfully visualized it might almost be a character in its own right. Or rather, in the narrator's memory of her early years, Alice and her house are in some sense inextricably intertwined. *Time* is also important in "Alice" in that, though a very short story, possibly twenty years pass from opening to closing memory, from young child following behind her mother memories to snubbing Alice on the street at age eighteen to reconciling with Alice as an adult woman when the narrator is twenty-six.

Similarly, Tillie Olsen's short story "I Stand Here Ironing" covers sixteen or seventeen years of the first person narrator's memory, from the birth of her daughter to the present where she stands ironing. But there's another aspect of time as setting that becomes important here and in many works of fiction is helpful to an understanding of the story. What is the *time period* in which the action takes place? Olsen's story begins in the economically deprived days of the Great Depression (the 1930s), which create conditions of poverty which in turn affect the narrrator's parenting which in turn affect the narrative plot.

The time of day or season of the year is another aspect of setting that can affect the tone or atmosphere of a story. *Waiting for Nothing,* by Tom Kromer, is also set during the Great Depression and the homeless narrator's plight is underlined by Kromer's choice to set the story at night in a city. The setting is a motivating factor for the narrator, who needs somehow to acquire enough money to pay for a meal and a place to sleep that night.

Two other categories of fiction we have included examples of in *Literature and Society* have a special relationship to setting: science fiction and graphic texts. Science fiction is a genre that can almost be defined by its interest in setting, whether in extrapolating into the future and creating a future setting as Ray Bradbury does in his story "August 2026: There Will Come Soft Rains" (Peace and War), or in creating an alien planet and/or culture as Octavia Butler does in her story, "Bloodchild" (Growing Up and Growing Older). A third science fiction story, Pamela Zoline's "The Heat Death of the Universe," is set in a suburban house in the late 1950s/early 1960s, but that house becomes a very odd, surreal place.

In graphic or visual texts, setting becomes a much more clearly foregrounded part of the narrative, both in the sense of time passing that the movement from frame to frame provides and in the visual representation of setting instead of verbal description of setting that we are used to in fiction. Harvey Pekar's "Hypothetical Quandary" (Money and Work) from *American Splendor shows* us the main character and his working-class neighborhood. And to read Marjane Satrapi's "The Dowry" (Peace and War) from her graphic memoir *Persepolis* means we need to focus on what goes on visually and in words within each frame as well as pay attention to how verbal and visual elements flow from one frame to the next.

Setting—time and place—establishes conditions that affect the characters either directly or indirectly, either immediately or in their past. What is the nature and the quality of the *tension* between character and setting in a work of fiction or memoir? Setting often has an impact on a character's motivation, and character motivations frequently activate the plot. Writers also use setting to establish a mood or atmosphere in the narrative which affects not only the characters but also you, the reader.

THEME AND SYMBOL

Fiction is specific. It tells of specific characters in specific places doing specific things. But, if it is to interest us very much, it should also be in some sense general, with implications beyond the confines of the imaginary world it creates. What we can abstract from the specifics of a work of fiction—its central idea or statement, what it is *about*—we call its **theme.** Since fiction is often complex and open ended, formulating the theme of a work of fiction is not simple. One reader might argue that "Alice" is basically about appreciating, when adults, people we did not appreciate when we were children. Another might see its theme as the ultimate connectedness of all women. Trying to distill a theme from a work of fiction raises important questions about its essential meaning and is therefore an important step in coming to understand it.

This complex embodiment of the general in the specific is also the basis of literary symbolism. A **symbol** is an object (or person, setting, event) that suggests meanings beyond its literal meaning in a work of literature. Some symbols are widely used and conventional, such as a rose to symbolize love, a physical wound to symbolize an emotional one; some are specific to a particular work. Generally, a symbol, especially a nonconventional symbol, is open ended; that is, we cannot give it one precise meaning. Much of the value of symbols in fiction lies in their open enedeness, their complexity, but also in their economy and in the emotional power of indirection, that is, of suggesting without saying. In Alan Sillitoe's novella "The Loneliness of the Long-distance Runner" (Protest), running itself becomes a powerful and complex symbol. What is the difference, the story asks, between a run and a race? But the symbolic resonance of long-distance running is only part of what Sillitoe's story is about.

Symbols appear often in fiction, but it is very easy to overemphasize their importance, treating a story as if it were a puzzle, its solution the discovery and explanation of symbols. Most things in fiction are *not* symbolic. Writers usually highlight their symbols, whether through repetition or positioning, and a predominantly symbolic interpretation of most works of fiction makes sense only if it fits together with and enriches interpretation based on character, plot, and point of view. Interpretations which reduce everything to abstraction and symbolism ignore the essential value of fiction as the complex and multilayered representation of lived human experience.

Symbolism returns us to the question of what "correctness" in interpreting fiction means. There is no perfect or even best interpretation of a story; no amount of care, persistence, and intelligence in examining plot, character, point of view, or symbolism will lead us to an ultimate interpretation. Fictional texts cannot have meanings totally independent of readers; the act of reading is, in a sense, an interaction between story and reader; jointly they create its meaning.

Thus fiction can have different meanings for different individuals, cultures, or eras. In the eyes of some critics, Herman Melville's novel *Billy Budd* sanctions

Captain Vere's hanging of the naive hero Billy, who has impulsively struck and unintentionally killed an evil man; they see as its theme the necessity of enforcing the law. But for others, the novel is about the utter injustice of this hanging, the essential difference between justice and law. For some readers, Mark Twain's *The Adventures of Huckleberry Finn* is a deeply racist novel; for others, it is a profound attack on racism. And in any number of classic novels and stories, recent feminist critics have found the theme of men's and women's roles where earlier readers have found studies of money or science or war.

However, this does not mean that anything goes, that any reaction represents a valid interpretation. Interpretation, as opposed to reaction, should be rooted in evidence. Informed by an understanding of how fiction works, the pleasures of reading multiply.

HOW POETRY WORKS

If I read a book and it makes my whole body so cold no fire can ever warm me, I know that it is poetry. If I feel physically as if the top of my head were taken off, I know that it's poetry.

Emily Dickinson

As imagination bodies forth
The forms of things unknown, the poet's pen
Turns them to shapes and gives to airy nothing
a local habitation and a name.

William Shakespeare

Poetry is "imaginary gardens with real toads in them."

Marianne Moore

Poetry is the spontaneous overflow of powerful feelings
. . . emotion recollected in tranquility.

William Wordsworth

The figure a poem makes. It begins in delight and ends in wisdom. . . . Like a piece of ice on a hot stove, the poem must ride on its own melting.

Robert Frost

Poetry is not a turning loose of emotion, but an escape from emotion; it is not the expression of personality, but an escape from personality.

T. S. Eliot

. . . a door opens, a door shuts. In between you
have had a glimpse: a garden, a person, a rainstorm, a dragonfly, a heart, a city. . . . So a poem
takes place.

Sylvia Plath

A poem should not mean but be.
    Archibald Macleish

Blood is blood and murder's murder.
What's a lavender word for lynch?
Come, you pale poets, wan refined and dreamy—
here is a black woman working out her guts
in a white man's kitchen
for little money and no glory.
How should I tell that story?

Ray Durem

I have always maintained that the writer's task has nothing
to do with mystery or magic, and that the poet's, at least,
must be a personal effort for the benefit of all. The closest
thing to poetry is a loaf of bread or a ceramic dish or a
piece of wood lovingly carved, even if by clumsy hands.

Pablo Neruda

A poem is not its words or images, any more than a
symphony is its notes or a river its drops of water.
Poetry depends on the moving relations within
itself. It is an art that lives in time, expressing and
evoking the moving relation between the individual
consciousness and the world. The work that a poem
does is a transfer of human energy, and I think
human energy may be defined as consciousness, the
capacity to make change in existing conditions.

Muriel Rukeyser

Poems are like dreams; in them you put what you don't know you know.

Adrienne Rich

WHAT IS POETRY?

Read through the luxuriant array of definitions of poetry at the beginning of this chapter written by poets from William Shakespeare to Adrienne Rich. Poetry is imaginative, as both Shakespeare and Rich remark. A poem is concerned with emotion though, as William Wordsworth and T. S. Eliot suggest, it is emotion shaped, controlled, and contained in form. A poem often says something significant; it attempts to achieve beauty. Of course, what is significant and beautiful is open to discussion and may change with time and place, culture, social class, gender, and race, as Ray Durem suggests. Poetry is generally more concentrated than prose. A word can stand for a phrase, a phrase for a sentence, a line for a paragraph. If you try to paraphrase a poem, "translate" it into prose, your translation will tend to be longer and looser than the poem itself. Poetry is melodic and rhythmic, as concerned with sound as it is with content. Historically connected to music, song, and dance, poetry has often been an integral part of ritual, from the Elysian mysteries of Hellenic Greece to the celebration of the Catholic Mass. A good bit of the Bible is poetry, including the Old Testament love poem "The Song of Solomon" (Women and Men). Indeed, we consider song lyrics poetry and have included examples of blues, rap, labor, and popular songs.

Poetry is specific, particular, and concrete rather than abstract. William Carlos Williams remarked, "No ideas but in things" ("Paterson"). Wallace Stevens, in his "Miscellaneous Notebooks," agrees that universality, if it is to be achieved at all, will be achieved through focusing on the particular: "Imagination applied to the whole world is vapid in comparison to imagination applied to a detail." Poetry is concerned with ideas and insights, but it usually expresses these through sense-oriented language, through images of sight, sound, touch, smell, taste, and movement. Thus Robert Frost, in his essay "The Figure a Poem Makes," sums up his discussion of what and how a poem is with this metaphor: "Like a piece of ice on a hot stove, the poem must ride on its own melting." This image is a conceptual concept—condensed, vivid, experiential, hard to forget. Poetry is often built around images, representations of sensory experience. For T. S. Eliot, the image is an "objective correlative" of a complex combination of idea and emotion. Milton in the seventeenth century wrote that the language of poetry is "simple, sensuous and impassioned." For Muriel Rukeyser, poetry is composed of time, connections of human energy, and the capacity for personal and social change; for another poet of passion and politics, Pablo Neruda, poetry is "a personal effort for the benefit of all" and he expresses that idea through three images—a loaf of bread, a ceramic dish, and a lovingly even if clumsily carved piece of wood. Poetry is playful and often joyful in its use of language, even if the mood of the poem is somber. Sound is an essential dimension of poetry. Stevens writes, "above all else, poetry is words . . . words, above everything else, are, in poetry, sound" ("The Noble Rider and the Sound of Words"). And Frost writes, "If it is a wild tune, it is a poem." Poetry is mysterious and often seems more connected to the subconscious than does prose. Perhaps this is what Adrienne Rich means when she says "poems are like dreams"—like dreams because the concentrated language of poetry can short-circuit or disrupt the usual relations of syntax, or because poetry is more associative than strictly logical.

KINDS OF POETRY

Though poetry ranges from limerick to epic, generally there is agreement about three major categories of poetry: *lyric, dramatic,* and *narrative.*

A **lyric poem** is fairly short and subjective, expressing the emotions and thoughts of one person, the speaker of the poem. Originally written to be sung to the accompaniment of a lyre, lyrics are often strongly melodic. Hymn, song, sonnet, ode, elegy, pastoral, and perhaps haiku are all types of lyrics. Following is a late-nineteenth-century example of a lyric poem, Christina Rossetti's "A Birthday," in which the melodic element is very clear and striking.

A Birthday

My heart is like a singing bird
  Whose nest is in a watered shoot;
My heart is like an apple-tree
  Whose boughs are bent with thickset fruit;

My heart is like a rainbow shell   5
  That paddles in a halcyon sea;
My heart is gladder than all these
  Because my love is come to me.

Raise me a dais of silk and down;
  Hang it with vair and purple dyes;   10
Carve it in doves and pomegranates,
  And peacocks with a hundred eyes;

Work it in gold and silver grapes,
  In leaves and silver fleurs-de-lys;
Because the birthday of my life   15
  Is come, my love is come to me.

But a lyric poem need not be so celebratory as "A Birthday." Edna St. Vincent Millay's four-line lyric "Grown-up" is a rueful recognition that adult life is not so exciting achieved as it was anticipated.

Grown-up

Was it for this I uttered prayers,
And sobbed and cursed and kicked the stairs,
That now, domestic as a plate,
I should retire at half-past eight?

Though entirely different in mood and in rhythmic sound pattern, what both these lyrics have in common is that they express, through specific image and event, an individual state of mind.

Dramatic poetry employs dramatic form or elements of dramatic technique, such as the **dramatic monologue** of T. S. Eliot's "The Love Song of J. Alfred Prufrock," which assumes an audience and draws that audience into the poem in the opening lines: "Let us go then, you and I,/ When the evening is spread out against the sky." Poems that have more characters than simply the lyric speaker of the poem, and poems that use dialogue between characters or that stress conflict between characters, whether the characters directly speak or not, such as Wole Soyinka's "Telephone Conversation" or Patricia Smith's "Undertaker," may be dramatic poems. Drama itself, plays, may incorporate poetry. See Sophocles' "Antigone," Shakespeare's "Othello," and Marc Kaminsky's "In the Traffic of a Targeted City."

A **narrative poem** tells a story. It may be short or long, simple or complex. **Epics,** long poems that tell the story of a hero and/or of a nation or race—Homer's *Odyssey,* for example—are narrative poems. Judy Grahn's "A Woman Is Talking to Death" includes lyric and dramatic elements but is finally more a narrative poem, a contemporary epic, with a number of smaller stories in the form of flashbacks set inside one framing story. **Ballads,** poems which tell a story in a form historically intended to be sung, are also narrative poems. Bruce Springsteen's "My Hometown" is an example of a contemporary ballad meant to be sung. Susan Griffin's "This Is the Story of the Day in the Life of a Woman Trying" (the title makes her narrative intent clear), Carolyn Forché's "The Colonel," and Essex Hemphill's "June 25" are narrative poems which are also examples of **prose poems,** poems which are not written in lines yet retain the intensity of image and language characteristic of poetry. A prose poem, by the way, might just as easily be a lyric or dramatic poem.

Though many poems can be classified as lyric, dramatic, or narrative, much modern and contemporary poetry merges types or lives on the boundaries between them. So, although it is helpful to know that these three types of poetry exist and what their major characteristics are, it doesn't do to see them as rigid categories into which poems must fit. As Wallace Stevens once wrote, "All poetry is experimental poetry." The word "poet" itself comes from a Greek word that means "maker" or "creator." Poets are constantly experimenting or, as Ezra Pound remarked, "making it new," and in the process invigorating language and perception.

IMAGERY

An **image** is a literal and particular representation of an experience or object perceived through the senses. It is presented in language in such a way that we can see, hear, smell, taste, or touch it, or feel it move in our imagination. Images in poetry may be literal or figurative, such as similies or metaphors. The following example is of literal imagery:

Several things could happen in this poem.
Plums could appear, on a pewter plate.
A dead red hare, hung by one foot.
A vase of flowers. Three shallots.

A man could sing, in a burgundy robe   5
with a gold belt tied in a square knot.
Someone could untie the knot.
A woman could toss a gold coin.

In these opening stanzas of Martha Collins's "Several Things," the poet presents us with a handful of images on which she will work a number of changes in the course of the poem. She also shares with us her sense of the playfulness of poetry, its imaginative creative quality, the process by which one makes a poem from images. A number of our senses are engaged in these lines. In "plums could appear, on a pewter plate," we see the plums, red, purple, or almost black, against the dull silver color of the plate. It could be that our sense of touch is evoked, if we have ever handled the cold, heavy smoothness of pewter. Perhaps our sense of taste is stimulated by the memory of a tartly sweet, ripe plum. The image "A man could sing, in a burgundy robe/ with a gold belt tied in a square knot" evokes our sense of hearing as we imagine the man singing. More directly, the burgundy robe is richly visual and reminds us of the plums in the preceding stanza. The "gold belt tied in a square knot" is particularly visual, and our eyes move, like a camera, from the man as a whole to the belt at his waist—which in the next line someone (perhaps the woman tossing a gold coin) unties. As you will see when you read the entire poem, "Several Things" was originally inspired by a recipe.

Also concerned in part with food, the following two stanzas from John Keats's long poem "The Eve of St. Agnes" practically knock you over with their lush sensuality:

The Eve of St. Agnes

And still she slept an azure-lidded sleep,
In blanched linen, smooth, and lavender'd.
While he from forth the closet brought a heap
Of candied apple, quince, and plum, and gourd;
With jellies soother than the creamy curd,   5
And lucent syrops, tinct with cinnamon;
Manna and dates, in argosy transferr'd
From Fez; and spiced dainties, every one,
From silken Samarcand to cedar'd Lebanon.

These delicates he heap'd with glowing hand   10
On golden dishes and in baskets bright
Of wreathed silver: sumptuous they stand
In the retired quiet of the night,
Filling the chilly room with perfume light.—
'And now, my love, my seraph fair, awake!   15
'Thou art my heaven, and I thine eremite:
'Open thine eyes, for meek St. Agnes' sake,
'Or I shall drowse beside thee, so my soul doth ache.'

Even though this poem was first published in 1820 and contains a number of
words we might need to look up in the dictionary, still the imagery evoking the
senses of sight, smell, taste, touch, and, through its absence, sound—is, even on
first reading, as seductive as the scene. Try listing which sense or senses each image in the first stanza evokes. You might also try a short "sense-based" poem of
your own, using two or three of the senses. If the idea of writing a whole poem
seems too intimidating, try a series of loosely connected lines, each one containing a single image based on one sense—sound, perhaps, or taste or touch.

Moving from the elaboration to economy, look at Ezra Pound's compact
poem "In a Station of the Metro," which presents us with two images we are
meant to hold in our minds simultaneously:

In a Station of the Metro

The apparition of these faces in the crowd;
Petals on a wet, black bough.

That's it. Pound defined an image as "an intellectual and emotional complex in
a instant of time." Here he gives us an insight that might be paraphrased in this
way: "I was standing in a subway station one night and it occurred to me that
the white and somewhat ghostly faces of people waiting for the train looked the

way apple blossoms look against a tree branch after a rainstorm." Paraphrasing a poem is often a useful first step in understanding the literal meaning of a poem, but the paraphrase clearly doesn't have the economical power of the poem itself.

We are fortunate in the case of this poem to have what the poet himself said about it. What follows is not a paraphrase, which is a prose rendering of a completed poem, but Pound's description of the process by which the poem was created:

> Three years ago in Paris I got out of a "metro" train at La Concorde, and saw suddenly a beautiful face, and then another and another, and then a beautiful child's face, and then another beautiful woman, and I tried all that day to find words for what this had meant to me, and I could not find any words that seemed to me worthy, or as lovely as that sudden emotion. And that evening, as I went home along the Rue Raynouard, I was still trying, and I found, suddenly, the expression. I do not mean that I found words, but there came an equation ... not in speech, but in little splotches of color. It was just that—a "pattern," or hardly a pattern, if by "pattern" you mean something with a "repeat" in it. But it was a word, the beginning, for me, of a language in color. . . .
>
> The "one-image poem" is a form of super-position, that is to say it is one idea set on top of another. I found it useful in getting out of the impasse in which I had been left by my metro emotion. I wrote a thirty-line poem, and destroyed it because it was what we call work "of second intensity." Six months later I made a poem half that length; a year later I made the following *hokku* [haiku]-like sentence:—
>
> The apparition of these faces in the crowd;
> Petals on a wet, black bough.
>
> I dare say it is meaningless unless one has drifted into a certain vein of thought. In a poem of this sort one is trying to record the precise instant when a thing outward and objective transforms itself, or darts into a thing inward and subjective.

Pound and other early-twentieth-century poets such as H. D. (Hilda Doolittle), T. S. Eliot, Carl Sandburg, Amy Lowell, D. H. Lawrence, and William Carlos Williams were part of the Imagist Movement, which flourished in the second decade of this century. In rebellion against what they saw as the conventionality and fatigue of late-nineteenth-century poetry, the Imagists published three anthologies that, as it turned out, revolutionized modern poetry. Their major objectives were to (1) use the language of common speech but always to employ the exact word; (2) avoid clichés; (3) create rhythms as expressions of mood; that is, rather than use strict forms such as the sonnet, they preferred free verse, in which the rhythm of the poem arises organically from the mood and emotion of the poem; (4) allow absolute freedom in choice of subject—a red wheelbarrow was just as appropriately poetic as Keats's "lucent syrops, tinct with cinnamon";

(5) present an image—concretely, definitely, sensually, clearly, even harshly if necessary; (6) work for concentration and economy, which they felt were the essence of poetry; and (7) suggest rather than tell. The Imagists were influenced by the economy and emphasis on image of Japanese and Chinese poetry, especially forms like the **haiku** (or *hokku*), a poem of seventeen syllables in three lines of five, seven, and five syllables, the intent of which is to create a picture that evokes emotion and often a spiritual insight. Though two lines instead of three, and two syllables over the official seventeen, "In a Station of the Metro" is heavily influenced by the haiku form. The Imagists also found poetic models in Greek lyricists such as Sappho and in the vers libre (free verse) of French Symbolist poets such as Mallarme, Rimbaud, and Baudelaire. The Imagists lasted barely ten years as an organized movement or school of poetry, but perhaps because their number included several of the major modern poets, their example and theory are still a major force in contemporary British and American poetry.

FIGURATIVE LANGUAGE

Look back for a minute at Christina Rossetti's "A Birthday." The first two stanzas of the poem are built from a series of three similes. Her heart, she writes, is *like* a singing bird, like an apple tree, like a rainbow shell. A **simile** is a direct comparison or stated similarity between apparently unrelated things, and similes, like metaphors, are figurative images. The signal of a simile is the presence of "like" or "as." If we say, "her thoughts were like clouds passing across a clear blue sky," we are connecting two unrelated things—thoughts and clouds—and further we are suggesting or implying that the human mind is like the sky. This simile asks the reader to think about her own memory or experience of seeing clouds moving across a clear blue sky and then to apply that memory to "thoughts." Often a simile gives us a clearer sense of something unfamiliar or less easy to describe by comparing it to something with which we are more familiar. Given the context, the image "clouds passing across a clear blue sky" could suggest a breezy summer day, dynamic but serene—or it might suggest a coming storm.

Let's look at another complete poem, Langston Hughes's "Harlem," which is built mostly on a series of five similes.

Harlem

What happens to a dream deferred?

Does it dry up
like a raisin in the sun?
Or fester like a sore—
And then run?

5

Does it stink like rotten meat?
Or crust and sugar over—
Like a syrupy sweet?

Maybe it just sags
like a heavy load.   10

Or does it explode?

Written in the early 1950s, "Harlem" (part of Hughes's book-length poetic
sequence *Montage of a Dream* Deferred) is an attempt to present the mood of
a community the way "clouds passing across a clear blue sky" might present one
person's state of mind. The concept Hughes explores here is the "dream deferred," the American dream of justice and equality for all, which for African-
Americans has been postponed far too long. Hughes's opening question, "What
happens to a dream deferred?" is answered by a series of similes, several also in
the form of questions, each of which expands and deepens our sense of the controlling phrase, "a dream deferred." The deferred dream, Hughes writes, is like
a dried-up raisin, like a festering sore, like stinking, rotten meat, like a sugary,
dried-up sweet, like a sagging load. In the last line, *"Or does it explode?"* Hughes
only implies the final simile, leaving the particular form of the explosion (vol-
canic? atomic? "riot-ic"?) up to our imaginations. The rhetorical effect of the implied simile here is, oddly, more powerful and frightening than if Hughes had
given it to us directly. Note also that in "Harlem" all of our senses are engaged—
sight, touch, smell, hearing, taste, and motion. We'll come back to this poem in
the section on sound.

A **metaphor,** also a figurative image, is a simile with "like" or "as" left out.
That is, one thing is compared to or identified with another by being spoken of
as though it *were* that object. In "A Woman Is Talking to Death," Judy Grahn
writes: "My lovers teeth are white geese flying above me/ My lovers muscles are
rope ladders under my hands." Vivid, strong, perhaps even harsh in the Imagists'
sense, Grahn deliberately avoids here a soft, vague romanticism in speaking
about love. Metaphor can also work through negatives, as when Edna St. Vincent Millay defines love by what it is not.

Love is not all: it is not meat nor drink
Nor slumber nor a roof against the rain;
Nor yet a floating spar to men that sink
And rise and sink and rise and sink again

A poem built entirely on one extended metaphor is Ted Hughes's "The
Lovepet," which presents love as a stray and starving animal a man and woman
have adopted. On the image level of the poem, which is also the literal level, the
lovepet gradually and voraciously eats the couple out of house and home and

more. On the conceptual level, the poem charts the disintegration of a marriage.
Here is one section of "The Lovepet":

It ate the faces of their children
They gave it their photograph albums they gave it their records
It ate the color of the sun
They gave it a thousand letters they gave it money
It ate their future complete it waited for them   5
Staring and starving
They gave it screams it had gone too far
It ate into their brains
It ate the roof
It ate lonely stone it ate wind crying famine   10
It went furiously off.

Related to simile and metaphor but less easy to identify is the **symbol**, usually an image that stands for or suggests something else, often an abstract idea
or complex of ideas. There are three types or levels of symbol: archetypal, cultural, and personal. *Archetypal symbols* are the most universally recognizable
and are often, though not always, grounded in natural images: the cycle of the
seasons, the rising and setting of the sun, water, desert and mountains, birth and
death. We can see metaphor becoming a complex symbol in Shakespeare's Sonnet #73, in which three images—autumn trees, twilight, and a dying fire—convey the poet's sense of aging.

LXXIII

That time of year thou mayst in me behold
When yellow leaves, or none, or few, do hang
Upon those boughs which shake against the cold.
Bare ruin'd choirs, where late the sweet birds sang.
In me thou see'st the twilight of such day   5
As after sunset fadeth in the west;
Which by and by black night doth take away,
Death's second self, that seals up all in rest.
In me thou see'st the glowing of such fire,
That on the ashes of his youth doth lie,   10
As the death-bed whereon it must expire,
Consum'd with that which it was nourish'd by.
  This thou perceiv'st, which makes thy love more strong,
  To love that well which thou must leave ere long.

Different cultures each have powerful and richly evocative histories, spiritual
beliefs, literatures, and physical or geographical realities. All of these have

symbolic resonance for people raised in or familiar with a particular culture. *Cultural symbols* are therefore less universal and more grounded in a specific cultural legacy and may not travel across cultures as symbolic. For example, a Native American coyote trickster figure may not carry the same set of symbolic meanings to a reader in a culture without either coyotes or trickster figures. Or to take another example, the symbolic resonances of Mary, mother of Jesus, in the title of a Yeats poem ("The Mother of God"), don't work for a person raised in an Islamic or Buddhist tradition. Different historical periods, even in one's own native culture, may also have culturally based images which contemporary readers might miss. Symbolic images, of course, appear outside of literature. The eagle on the back of a quarter is, for example, a symbol for the United States. It is not an archetypal symbol like twilight or autumn in Shakespeare's sonnet but a symbol specific to U.S. culture. See if you can make a list of images that you think might have symbolic resonance that are specific to your own culture.

Personal symbols are even more specific and limited. The poet needs to take an image specific to his or her own experience and give it enough context and power in the poem to lift it to the level of a symbol others can understand. In "City-Life," D. H. Lawrence turns the image of a fish hook into a symbol for the situation of twentieth-century factory workers. Philip Levine's "They Feed They Lion" (Protest) is a powerful and layered symbolic poem filled with separate images that variously work on all three levels: archetypal, cultural, and personal. Here are the first and last stanzas of Levine's poem:

Out of burlap sacks, out of bearing butter,
Out of black bean and wet slate bread,
Out of the acids of rage, the candor of tar,
Out of creosote, gasoline, drive shafts, wooden dollies,
They Lion grow.

and the final stanza:

   From my five arms and all my hands,
From all my white sins forgiven, they feed,
From my car passing under the stars,
They Lion, from my children inherit,
From the oak turned to a wall, they Lion,
From they sack and they belly opened
And all that was hidden burning on the oil-stained earth
They feed they Lion and he comes.

Of course, even though there are many images in the poem, the Lion is the controlling image and symbol. Who or what is the Lion? Levine, who grew up in working-class Detroit, wrote this poem after the 1968 riots in that industrial city.

Perhaps **personification,** which gives human qualities or attributes to animals, ideas, or inanimate objects, is a technique that Levine is using in "They Feed They

Lion," though we think not: His Lion is bigger than human. Ted Hughes's "The Lovepet," discussed earlier, is not an example of personification either, because the animal, though it stands for a human emotion, love, retains animal qualities. On the other hand, John Donne's seventeenth-century poem "The Sun Rising" is an example of personification because it makes the sun into a silly, interfering busybody who demonstrates his skewed sense of priorities by bringing an end to the night the poet has been spending with his beloved. Here is the first stanza:

> Busy old fool, unruly sun.
> Why dost thou thus,
> Through windows, and through curtains call on us?
> Must to thy motions lovers' seasons run?
> Saucy pedantic wretch, go chide
> Late school-boys, and sour prentices,
> Go tell court-huntsmen, that the King will ride
> Call country ants to harvest offices;
> Love, all alike, no season knows, nor clime,
> Nor hours, days, months, which are the rags of time.

The poem is a speech—"go away, please"—addressed to the sun, who is not only personified but also made symbolic of time passing. Personification also structures Theodore Roethke's "Dolor," a portrait in shades of gray of a bureaucratic age. Unlike Donne's poem, Roethke's describes rather than addresses the objects personified. "I have known," he writes, and "I have seen. . . ." Here is the whole poem:

Dolor

I have known the inexorable sadness of pencils,
Neat in their boxes, dolor of pad and paper-weight,
All the misery of manila folders and mucilage,
Desolation in immaculate public places,
Lonely reception room, lavatory, switchboard,   5
The unalterable pathos of basin and pitcher,
Ritual of multigraph, paper-clip, comma,
Endless duplication of lives and objects.
And I have seen dust from the walls of institutions,
Finer than flour, alive, more dangerous than silica,   10
Sift, almost invisible, through long afternoons of tedium,
Dropping a fine film on nails and delicate eyebrows,
Glazing the pale hair, the duplicate grey standard faces.

Roethke deliberately mixes up people and objects in this poem. He endows the objects with human attributes and emotions: Pencils are sad, manila folders miserable, public places desolate. People, on the other hand, are objectified. Their

"duplicate grey standard faces," like statues, collect dust through the "long afternoons of tedium." The use of personification of objects and objectification of
persons in "Dolor" makes a poignant and powerful statement about what it is
like to work in an office and what it is like to live in an age of office work.
Roethke wrote this poem in the 1940s. What details might we add if we wanted
to bring the poem up to date on office work in the early twenty-first century?
Even though some of Roethke's details may be obsolete, does his poem still
catch the essential nature of office work? How about the symbolic resonance of
the office—as a symbol for the relationship of human beings to their work in
the modern age or even as a symbol for human existence in the modern age?

THE SOUND OF A POEM

Poetry is as much an oral as it is a visual form. It is meant to be read aloud and
to be heard. The history of poetry—from ritual chants through Homeric epics
to medieval lyrics sung to musical accompaniment, to the recorded performances of June Jordan and Joy Harjo with choral or musical backup—is a history of words spoken and sung. Only comparatively recently in human history
has poetry reached its audience primarily as a written form. Even today, poets
generally perform their work, giving poetry readings and making recordings of
their poems. For the past fifteen or twenty years, there has been a lively resur-
gence of poetry as oral performance. The rise of slam poetry competitions,
where the performance is an important as the poem itself, and the audience
votes a winner on the spot, is one example. Rap, or hiphop, is another example
of verbal performance art, here words wedded to music. Poetry readings as a
rallying point for protest on social issues have a long tradition and are again on
the rise. A recent example is the Poets Against the War Web site, which spon-
sored more than 200 poetry readings nationwide on the same date in February
2003 to protest the United States entering into war with Iraq. Throughout history, poems have been set to music; alternatively, song lyrics can reach the level
of poetry and be usefully studied as poems, though we need to keep the music
in mind as an important dimension of the lyrics. It is almost always helpful in
understanding a poem on the page to hear how the poet reads the poem, what
words he or she emphasizes, where the pauses come, what kind of mood comes
across in the tone of voice.

Often we do not have access to the poet's own voice (certainly we don't with
pre-twentieth-century poets like Shakespeare or Donne), but poetry is written
in such a way as to give us cues about how to read the poem ourselves. The visual arrangement of lines on the page, where the lines break, where the **stanzas**
(poetic paragraphs) begin and end, how punctuation is used all tell us very specifically how to translate the poem from sight into sound. Where, for example, do
we pause, and for how long? The end of a **line,** even if there is no punctuation
there, calls for a small, sometimes almost imperceptible pause. A comma asks for

a slightly longer pause, a semicolon slightly longer, a colon or a dash slightly longer than a semicolon; and a period or a question mark asks for a full pause. A stanza break emphasizes a pause. Here is Langston Hughes's "Harlem" again.

Harlem

What happens to a dream deferred?

> Does it dry up
> like a raisin in the sun?
> Or fester like a sore—
> And then run?   5
> Does it stink like rotten meat?
> Or crust and sugar over—
> like a syrupy sweet?

> Maybe it just sags
> like a heavy load.   10

> *Or does it explode?*

The way the words, lines, and stanzas are arranged in this poem tells you how to read it. The first line, "What happens to a dream deferred?" is set off and emphasized in three ways. First, it is a stanza by itself, which is like a one-sentence paragraph in prose—a separate unit of meaning that the writer wants to emphasize. Second, it is a complete grammatical unit, a question. Third, it is set off from the rest of the poem because it is three spaces closer to the left margin. Because the whole question is contained in one line, it is read as one breath unit, with no breaks.

The second stanza of "Harlem" consists of four similes, all in the form of questions. Note how Hughes asks you to read the similes in a way that varies the rhythm and makes them more interesting than if he had used the same format four times in a row.

Does it dry up
like a raisin in the sun?

Because there is no punctuation after "up," the pause between lines is quite short, and because Hughes chose to break the sentence into two lines, the words "dry up" are emphasized. The last word or phrase in a line generally has the most resonance. The second simile

Or fester like a sore—
And then run?

asks for a substantially longer pause between lines, signaled by the dash. Hughes varies this again in the following simile, "Does it stink like rotten meat?" in which the question is in one line, has no pause, and therefore moves more quickly. The fourth simile ("or crust and sugar over—/ like a syrupy sweet") then slows the reader down again, picking up the form used in the second simile, the dash at the end of the line.

Hughes then moves to a stanza of two lines, still one simile but this time not phrased as a question.

Maybe it just sags
like a heavy load.

If you read those two lines aloud, you will see that putting the verb "sags" at the end of the line emphasizes the word and gives it more force. Try reading it as a sentence with no pause, then again as two lines the way the poet has directed you to.

Finally, "Harlem" ends with a one-line question, *"Or does it explode?"* Hughes emphasizes this possibility by making it the last line of the poem, by putting it in italics, and by making it the only one-line stanza except for the first—"What happens to a dream deferred?"—thus visually relating those two lines, the question and that particular answer, in our minds. "Harlem" is clearly a political poem, a warning about what could happen if a whole group's dreams continue to be denied. However, Hughes manages, through his visual and sound structure, to argue in a way that makes most readers more likely to listen than if he had come right out and stated his point bluntly. Putting the explosion in the form of a question, with its rising inflection, startles the reader initially less than if the poet had used a declarative form, and also leaves the question hanging in the air, asking for an answer.

When a **line** is a grammatical unit, a sentence or a clause, it is called an **end-stopped line.** When the grammatical unit spills over onto another line, it is called an **enjambed line.** The line is one of the most important tools of a free verse poet—and most poets writing in English since the early twentieth century Imagists are free verse poets. Where a poet breaks the lines determines the shape and the sound of the poem and often, as a result, the mood and meaning of the poem. To test this, take any poem in *Literature and Society* and change the line breaks; then note how that can change the poem. Here's another line exercise: Take a piece of prose—anything, even a newspaper article or instructions on how to work your new hair dryer—and make a poem from it simply by how you break the lines. This is, by the way, called a "found poem."

Rhyme, Resonance, and Repetition

Let us consider the sounds of words and the sound patterns that poets build between words to establish a mood, convey an emotion, and make connections between images and ideas. The sound patterns of a poem are sometimes obvious and sometimes subtle, but if you look for them you will find them. Read the poem aloud, more than once; listen and look for the patterns your ear hears and your eye sees on the page. Write a list of everything you notice about the sound of the poem. How do the sounds and the sound patterns parallel and reinforce the images, ideas, and theme of the poem? You may have the beginnings of an essay here, but we're getting ahead of ourselves. First let's think about rhyme, resonance, and repetition.

How much **rhyme** is used, where it is used, and how it is used has varied considerably in the history of poetry. Rhyme was not too important in English poetry before Chaucer in the fourteenth century, and it is used considerably less strictly in twentieth-century free verse poetry than in poetry of the three centuries preceding our own.

A good example of the strict use of **end rhyme** is in Shakespeare's Sonnet #73 quoted earlier, "That time of year thou mayst in me behold." A **sonnet** is a fourteen-line poem, generally written in iambic pentameter (see the section on meter), that follows a set **rhyme scheme,** a pattern in the rhymes at the end of lines. The traditional **Shakespearean** or **English sonnet** has three **quatrains** or groups of four lines, followed by a **couplet,** or two-line unit which carries the poem's conclusion. The rhyme scheme is usually *abab* for the first quatrain, *cdcd* for the second, *efef* for the third, and *gg* for the final couplet. Each letter of the alphabet identifies a particular rhyme, so each quatrain in this type of sonnet has two rhymes in alternating lines and, in addition, the two lines of the final couplet rhyme. The couplet often comments on or sums up the poem.

Another type of sonnet is the **Italian** or **Petrarchan sonnet,** divided into one octave of eight lines, usually rhyming *abbaabba,* and a sestet of six lines, rhyming *cdecde, cdccdc,* or *cdedce.* Often the octave raises a question or presents a narrative and the sestet answers the question or interprets the narrative to make a more abstract point. Milton's "On the Late Massacre in Piemont" is an Italian sonnet.

The sonnet has remained popular and a number of twentieth century poets do sonnet variations. Any time you come across a fourteen-line poem, it is worthwhile to investigate its sonnet affiliations. Another strict poetic form which still attracts contemporary poets, though less often than the sonnet, is the **villanelle,** a French form composed of five tercets (three-line stanzas) and a final quatrain (a four-line stanza) and built around two recurring rhymes. We've included three examples of villanelle: Elizabeth Bishop's "One Art," Jay Parini's "After the Terror," and Dylan Thomas's "Do Not Go Gentle Into That Good Night."

Twentieth-century poets are not particularly wedded to strict rhyme schemes like the sonnet or villanelle and tend more often to write in **free verse,** a cadenced rhythmic form that varies from poem to poem, arising organically from the subject, images, issues, and mood of a particular poem in the process of creation. Still, a number of modern and contemporary poets do use end rhyme, though sometimes more subtly and less strictly than pre-twentieth-century poets. Let's look again at Ezra Pound's haiku-like poem, this time paying attention not to the images but to the sounds.

In a Station of the Metro

The apparition of these faces in the crowd;
Petals on a wet, black bough.

The end of each line, "crowd" and "bough," are examples of **assonance** or repetition of similar vowel sounds (here, "ow") in stressed syllables, though the consonants differ. The last word in the title of this poem, "Metro," *almost* rhymes with "crowd" and "bough." When the rhyming words have almost the same sound, a **slant rhyme** has occurred. It should be clear from this example that sound patterns can't be found just by looking at the poem; it needs to be read aloud so that the ear can hear the rhymes.

Rhyme happens inside lines as well as at the end of lines. Even more subtle than slant rhyme, **internal rhyme** can give a poem much of its musical quality. In Pound's poem, "station" (the title is part of the poem) and "faces" rhyme because of the long "a" sound, and "apparition" repeats the "tion" (shun) sound in "station." The hard "t" sound recurs in "station," "metro," "petals," and "wet." We can also see (and hear) Pound making use of **alliteration** or repetition of initial letters of a word, most often consonants. Here "black bough" is an example of alliteration.

If a poem is working the way a poet wants it to, these sound patterns or *resonance* help carry and reinforce the meaning and feeling of the poem. Read these last five lines of Marge Piercy's poem "The woman in the ordinary," about a young woman on the verge of breaking out of her rut to become whatever it is she has the potential to become.

In her bottled up is a woman peppery as curry,
a yam of a woman of butter and brass,
compounded of acid and sweet like a pineapple,
like a handgrenade set to explode,
like goldenrod ready to bloom.

Though this poem does not rely on end rhyme at all, notice how the images and the meaning of the poem are reinforced in these lines by various devices of sound. The images are spicy and bold: curry, peppery; brass, acid—examples of internal rhyme. Piercy uses an abundance of alliteration with "p" and "b" sounds—bottled, peppery, butter, brass, pineapple, explode, bloom. "P" and "b" are called "plosive" sounds because, in order to make them, you must close your lips and blow the air that carries the sound forcefully at the closed lips, "exploding" them open. Try it. Piercy's use of literally explosive sounds reinforces her explosively growing images and theme. Another pattern in these lines, not quite so striking, is the use of nasal sounds like "m" and "n" in such words as woman, yam, compounded, pineapple, handgrenade, bloom. You might want to think about what effect this second pattern of sound has and how it works together with the pattern of plosives.

Other frequently repeated sounds in the passage from "the woman in the ordinary" include the liquid "l" and "r." Keats's repetition of the liquid "l" in the
two stanzas from "The Eve of St. Agnes" quoted earlier has much to do with the
luscious, luxurious effect of that poem. "S" is a sibilant sound, and a number of
"s" words together make a hissing sound. Langston Hughes employs in
"Harlem" many "s" words—raisin, sun, fester, sore, stink, crust, sugar, syrupy,
sweet, sags—that make an ominous hissing undercurrent (rather like the burning fuse of a bomb) to his other major sound in "Harlem," the hard sound of air
stopped behind the teeth in "d" and "t"—dream deferred, dry, rotten, load, explode. We have **onomatopoeia** when a word imitates a natural sound, for example, if "a snake hissed and its passing rustled the grass." In this sentence, the word
"hissed" imitates the sound it stands for and is strictly onomatopoetic; all the
other "s" sounds reinforce the hissing and also imitate the slithering sound the
snake makes as (we hope) it slides away. Although Piercy's and Hughes's uses
of sound to reinforce sense are not always strictly onomatopoetic, they extend
our sense of the possibilities of that probably too narrowly defined term.

A poet can repeat whole phrases or lines to achieve a desired effect. Christina
Rossetti's "A Birthday," quoted in full earlier, uses *repetition* in three ways. In the
first stanza, every other line begins "My heart is. . . ." The first three pairs of lines
are similes; the fourth concludes: "My heart is gladder than all these/ Because
my love is come to me." In the second stanza, Rossetti uses an imperative verb
form three times—hang it, carve it, work it—and though the particular verb
changes, the imperative form is repeated. Finally, in the last two lines of the second stanza, she picks up a phrase from the end of her first stanza, so that both
stanzas end with the same phrase, "my love is come to me," emphasizing what
is, after all, the occasion for this joyful poem.

Producing a very different effect from that of Rossetti's poem is Muriel
Rukeyser's "Waiting for Icarus," which uses repetition throughout. The poem is
a contemporary retelling of the Greek myth about the young man, Daedalus,
who borrowed his father's wings and flew disastrously close to the sun—but from
the point of view of the woman who waits for him on the shore. Of course, the
woman is absent in the original myth, and that is part of Rukeyser's point. Read
the poem in the "Women and Men" section, noting that all the lines in the first
stanza (ten) begin with "He said . . ." and all the lines in the second stanza (seven)
begin with "I remember." Here is the final stanza:

> I have been waiting all day, or perhaps longer.
> I would have liked to try those wings myself.
> It would have been better than this.

"Waiting for Icarus" moves from what the speaker of the poem remembers "he"
(the young man) said to what she remembers "they" (the other girls, her mother)
said to, finally, a tentative assertion of her own voice and identity in the last three
lines of the poem. These three lines, it should be noted, are the only ones to which
the poet puts a period. And though the rest of each line in the poem is varied

enough so that the poem itself remains interesting, the initial repetition in each line is meant to be monotonous, to replicate the boredom of waiting, of being a passive spectator and listener rather than part of the action. Here's an exercise: Try writing a short poem, say of five to twelve lines, in which you use a sound pattern to create a mood.

Meter

The rhythmic and recurrent pattern of stressed and unstressed syllables in a poem is called its **meter.** Each unit of this pattern, which will have either two or three syllables, is called a **foot.** The number of feet in a line of poetry gives you the meter. In English, the most frequently used foot is **iambic,** which has two syllables, with the accent on the second (˘ ´). The most common poetic line in English is **iambic pentameter,** composed of five iambs, or ten syllables in a pattern of alternating unstressed and stressed syllables. The first quatrain of Shakespeare's Sonnet #73 is in iambic pentameter, composed of five **iambs.** Read the lines out loud, then mark the stressed syllables with an accent mark, a slash mark over the syllable: (´).

> That time of year thou mayst in me behold
> When yellow leaves, or none, or few, do hang
> Upon those boughs which shake against the cold.
> Bare ruin'd choirs, where late the sweet birds sang:

A particular type of iambic pentameter is **blank verse** or *unrhymed iambic pentameter,* which we can see in these opening four lines of Robert Frost's "Mending Wall." With one exception, the meter is entirely iambic, that is, a two-syllable foot made up of an unstressed syllable followed by a stressed syllable.

Something there is that doesn't love a wall,

That sends the frozen-ground-swell under it

And spills the upper boulders in the sun,

And makes gaps even two can pass abreast.

Unrelieved iambic pentameter can be tedious, and we see some variation in Frost's lines. The opening begins with another kind of two syllable foot, a **trochee,** which is a stressed syllable followed by an unstressed. Whatever the dominant meter is, however, names the line. As well as in lyric poems, blank verse is frequently used in dramatic poems and in poetic drama. It is, for example, characteristic of Shakespearean drama. Look at some of the longer speeches in *Othello* (Women and Men).

Iambic pentameter is the meter most natural to the English language. Whenever the foot or accentual pattern varies from iambic or the line length (how many feet in the line) varies from pentameter, there is a noticeable effect. Shorter lines speed up a poem, causing abruptness or possibly exhilaration, while a longer line might create a more leisurely, solemn, or grand mood. An iambic line (unstressed/stressed) which includes a trochaic foot (stressed/unstressed) can emphasize a particular word by varying the normal pattern.

Following is a list of terms used to describe the most common patterns in English poetry:

FOOT	EXAMPLE
iamb/iambic (˘ ´)	ĕx-plóde
trochee/trochaic (´ ˘)	wrít-ĕr
spondee/spondaic (´ ´)	húm-drúm
anapest/anapestic (˘ ˘ ´)	ăf-tĕr-nóon
dactyl/dactylic (´ ˘ ˘)	týpe-wrĭt-ĕr

LINE LENGTH

monometer: one foot
dimeter: two feet
trimeter: three feet
tetrameter: four feet
pentameter: five feet
hexameter: six feet
heptameter: seven feet
octameter: eight feet

Scansion

To scan a poem is to divide the lines into feet and mark the unstressed and stressed syllables. We can simply mark the stressed syllables with an accent (´) or we can mark both stressed and unstressed syllables, putting an upside-down horseshoe (ŭ) over the unstressed syllable. In this way we can determine what the overall meter of the poem is. Keep in mind that scansion is not an exact science and that generally what you will be getting is an approximation.

Look at this first stanza of Theodore Roethke's sixteen-line poem "My Papa's Waltz."

The whĭskey ŏn your breath

Could makĕ ă small boy dízzy̆;

But Ĭ hung ŏn likĕ death:

Sŭch waltzĭng wăs nŏt easy.

If we read these four lines aloud and put the accents where they would be in ordinary speech, it is not too hard to mark which syllables are stressed and which
are unstressed. It is helpful to begin by looking at a two- or three-syllable word.
We know, for example, that "whiskey" is stressed on the first syllable, and this
gives us a clue as to how to stress the surrounding syllables. The pattern here is
the most commonly found pattern in English, iambic. There are three iambs in
the first line, and also in the third. The second and fourth lines each contain three
iambs, plus an extra unstressed syllable at the end, which isn't counted. Overall,
the meter of this poem is iambic trimeter. The lines move regularly and quickly,
rather like the breathless waltzing (in three-quarter time) that the poet is describing. The trimeter or count of three replicates the time of a waltz; the iambic
pattern replicates the waltz's rise and fall.

   Poets quite deliberately choose the meter of a poem to fit the theme and
mood. Look at the very different first two lines of "Dolor," another poem by
Theodore Roethke.

Ĭ hăve knówn thĕ ĭnéxŏrăblĕ sádnĕss ŏf péncils,

Néat ĭn thĕir bóxĕs, dólŏr ŏf pád ănd pápĕr-wèight

In this thirteen-line poem (the whole poem is quoted earlier in this chapter),
Roethke alternates between anapestic (˘ ˘ ´) and dactylic (´ ˘ ˘) lines. The first
line has four anapestic feet with an extra unstressed syllable at the end. The second line has a dactyl, a trochee, a dactyl, a trochee, and a dactyl, adding up to
five feet. Roethke alternates between anapestic tetrameter and dactylic pentameter in "Dolor." But when you've said that, what have you got besides a
mouthful of terminology? What scanning this poem can tell you is that Roethke
is primarily using a longer foot (of three syllables rather than the two he employs
in "My Papa's Waltz") and that this longer foot, combined with the longer line
(four or five feet in "Dolor" instead of three as in "My Papa's Waltz"), gives this
poem a longer, slower, more drawn out, and perhaps more mournful rhythm.
That each line reverses the previous one (unstressed then stressed syllables in
the first line; stressed followed by unstressed in the second) makes reading the
poem laborious work for the reader, in contrast to the fast and easy, spinning,
dancing rhythm of "My Papa's Waltz." Roethke's choice of meter in "Dolor" fits
precisely the mood and subject of that poem, the tedium of office work.

A NOTE ON TONE

A poem might be joyful, gloomy, bitter, celebratory, angry, ironic, distanced, intimate, playful, comic, or something else. The **tone** or mood of a poem is both our
sense of the attitude or emotion of the poet and the mood the poem evokes in
us. We are all more or less skilled at picking up mood when someone speaks to

us. In a piece of writing we cannot hear the speaker's tone of voice, in the literal sense of that phrase, so we must rely on other clues: the sound of the poem, the images, the statement the poem makes, and/or the story it tells. A consideration of tone and mood is quite helpful in interpreting a poem. Ask yourself what the writer's attitude is toward the subject of the poem, toward the audience, toward the persona or speaker of the poem. In the two foregoing Theodore Roethke poems, the meter gave us valuable evidence to back up our sense of the quite different tones of "Dolor" and "My Papa's Waltz."

THE SPEAKER OF THE POEM

The speaker of a poem is not identical to the poet. Often the poet creates a **persona** (from the Latin for "mask") who speaks the poem in the first person ("I"). This is usually a single character, like Prufrock in T. S. Eliot's "The Love Song of J. Alfred Prufrock," or the unnamed woman, weary of waiting, in Muriel Rukeyser's "Waiting for Icarus." Gwendolyn Brooks's short poem about a group of high school dropouts has a communal *persona*.

We Real Cool

The Pool Players.
Seven at the Golden Shovel.

We real cool. We
Left school. We

Lurk late. We
Strike straight. We

Sing sin. We
Thin gin. We

Jazz June. We
Die soon.

5

In "We Real Cool," the speaker(s) of the poem are clearly not identical with the poet. We know there are seven of them. Because they have "left school," we suspect that they are adolescents. And we can probably assume, because this poem was written in 1960, that the seven are male if they are hanging out at a pool hall. In fact, Brooks confirms this in comments on the poem.

There are many cases, however, in which the speaker of the poem is less clearly differentiated from the poet, as in Roethke's "My Papa's Waltz," which is written as though it were the poet's memory of his own childhood. In the second half of the twentieth century, with the rise of *confessional poetry* (e.g., Plath), *Beat poetry* (e.g., Ginsberg), and the *lyric narrative poem* (e.g., Grahn, Griffin), the voice in the poem often seems quite close to that of the poet. However, as a general rule, it is safest, in thinking and writing about poetry (or fiction), to assume that the speaker of a poem (or the first-person narrator of a story), however autobiographical the material, is a *creation* of the writer and, like the setting, sound, images, and mood, is a result of choices the writer has made in the service of the whole effect she or he is working to create. Think, for example, about a story you might tell someone about an event in your own day; the "I" narrator and main character of your story is somewhat of a character as well as being you.

To whom is the poem spoken? The speaker of John Donne's "The Sun Rising" is addressing himself to the rising sun, which he personifies as a "busy old fool." In Roethke's "My Papa's Waltz," the speaker of the poem is talking to his father or, more probably, to his memory of his father. Langston Hughes's "Harlem" seems to be addressed directly to the reader. The series of questions that make up the poem is a series of rhetorical hooks that snag our attention. Many poems, primarily descriptive, don't seem addressed to anyone specific. For example, Marge Piercy's "The woman in the ordinary" describes a person; Ezra Pound's "In a Station of the Metro" describes a scene.

THE WORLD OF THE POEM

The speaker of a poem doesn't exist in a vacuum but is in interaction or tension with the world of the poem. Like a story, a poem has a setting that may be physical, social, or both. It is often helpful to list or to describe the characteristics of a poem's world. Following is Adrienne Rich's Poem XI from *Twenty-one Love Poems*.

XI.

Every peak is a crater. This is the law of volcanoes,
making them eternally and visibly female.
No height without depth, without a burning core,
though our straw soles shred on the hardened lava.
I want to travel with you to every sacred mountain   5
smoking within like the sibyl stooped over her tripod,
I want to reach for your hand as we scale the path,
to feel your arteries glowing in my clasp,
never failing to note the small, jewel-like flower
unfamiliar to us, nameless till we rename her,   10
that clings to the slowly altering rock—

that detail outside ourselves that brings us to ourselves,
was here before us, knew we would come, and sees beyond us.

Poem XI is about a journey, a mode in which writers since Homer have expressed the tension between self and world. What is the relation or the tension here between the speaker of the poem and the world of the poem? The physical setting of this poem is the slope of a volcano. There appear to be two people in the poem, two women who are climbing the sides of the volcano. The two people on this journey seem to be in harmony. If they were fighting with each other all the way up the mountain, the tone and meaning of the poem would be quite different.

We can see the particular quality and degree of the tension between speaker and physical setting in the line "though our straw soles shred on the hardened lava." The journey is arduous and wearing but not dangerous or life-threatening. Because the travelers are women and the volcano is redefined as female in the first two lines, we might guess that this is a journey of self-discovery. How do we know that the two people in the poem are women? Because the poet, Adrienne Rich, is female we assume, given the absence of any evidence to the contrary, that the speaker of the poem is also female. And because everything that is given gender in the poem is female—the volcano, the sibyl, the "small, jewel-like flower"—we can assume that the speaker's traveling companion is also female. In fact, this is an intensely female poem, and *Twenty-one Love Poems* is a series of poems about a relationship between two women, so the context of the poem— that it is part of a sequence—also gives us clues.

The journey of the poem is both physical and metaphysical. The two travelers are climbing the volcano; they are also learning about themselves, noting "the detail outside ourselves that brings us to ourselves." There is a carefully wrought tension in this poem between opposites: Peak is set against crater, height against depth, straw soles against hardened lava, the flower against the "the slowly altering rock" to which it clings. The poem is a journey from duality to unity, toward a place where inside and outside meet. The process of this journey is in part accomplished through perception and language. The central mystery of the poem, "the small, jewel-like flower/ unfamiliar to us," is given meaning through language, is "nameless till we rename her." Not all poems demonstrate so clearly the importance of setting and the relation between setting and speaker; nevertheless, this is almost always a useful area to explore in reading and writing about a poem.

THE WORLD AND THE POEM

Not only is there a set of dynamic relations or tensions within a poem, but, like any other work of literature, a poem is in a certain tension with the time, place, and person who produced it and with the time, place, and person who reads it.

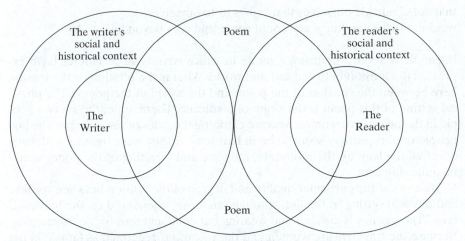

"A poem is not its words or images, any more than a symphony is its notes or a river its drops of water. Poetry depends on the moving relations within itself. It is an art that lives in time, expressing and evoking the moving relation between the individual consciousness and the world. The work that a poem does is a transfer of human energy, and I think human energy may be defined as consciousness, the capacity to make change in existing conditions."

Muriel Rukeyser

A diagram of that set of relations might look something like these overlapping circles.

Though a poem, like any work of literature, should be able to stand on its own, knowing something about the writer can deepen our understanding and enjoyment of the poem. The important social, political, and philosophical issues of the poet's era, what writers might have influenced her or him, what kind of poetry was customarily written at that time, and where in the writing career of the poet this particular poem was written are factors that enhance our understanding of the poem. Similarly, our interpretation of a poem and the resonance a poem has for us have something to do with who we are and when and where and how we are living. If you are male and eighteen years old, you might have a different emotional response to Gwendolyn Brooks's "We Real Cool" than if you are thirty-five years old and female. You might read the poem differently depending on whether you are black or white, middle class or working class, American or Australian. We come to a poem with all the baggage of our personal biography and the beliefs of our community and historical period.

Does this imply that a poem means anything we want it to mean? Or that all the analytical tools previously discussed are unimportant? No, what it means is simply that a poem is multidimensional and living. More than anything else, it is a communication, across space and time, between the person who wrote it and the person who reads it. "You can tear a poem apart to see what makes it technically tick," writes Dylan Thomas,

> and say to yourself, when the works are laid out before you, the vowels, the consonants, the rhymes and rhythms, "Yes, this is *it*. This is why the

poem moves me so. It is because of the craftsmanship." But you're back again where you began. You're back with the mystery of having been moved by words. The best craftsmanship always leaves holes and gaps in the works of the poem so that something that is *not* in the poem can creep, crawl, flash, or thunder in.

Perhaps the best way to learn how to read a poem is to write some poetry, enough to learn through experience that poetic craft is a matter of making choices and that writing well is a combination of sweat, skill, and luck out of which, sometimes, something magical happens.

APPENDIX: EXPLICATING A POEM

The following questions will help you as you begin your study of a poem. (You might also invent or be given questions specific to a particular poem). Answering these **explication** questions should provide useful information and a set of notes that will help you not only discuss the poem in class but write a detailed and convincing paper about it.

1. What is your personal response to the poem when you first read it, when you read it later, when you hear it read? Is there any specific image, line, word, sound, or section of the poem that particularly strikes you, even if you can't say why at this time? Does the poem remind you of anything in your own life?

2. What is in fact happening in the poem? Is there a story, a scene, a picture? Don't worry about the theme or the symbolism of the poem until you notice what is straightforwardly and literally happening in the poem.

3. Look up in a large dictionary (a) any words in the poem you don't know and (b) any words that seem important in the poem (even if you think you know what they mean) because such words may have secondary meanings that you aren't familiar with but which the poet is also evoking. This could change your understanding of the poem.

4. Is there a *persona* or speaker/character in the poem? Who is he or she? What specific clues are there in the poem that tell you what he or she is like? Even if the speaker of the poem simply seems to be the poet, characterize what you come to know about that voice.

5. Describe the world of the poem, the "setting," both physical and social.

6. Discuss the relation or tension between speaker and world in the poem. Is it comfortable or uncomfortable? Does any change take place?

7. Experience the images in the poem, which are based on the senses of sight, sound, taste, touch, smell, and movement. List the images. Are there a number of discrete images or one extended image? Do the images form a pattern? Image and sound are the heart of poetry. Detailed work on this question on imagery and the one on sound that follows will provide you with solid evidence for your interpretation of the poem.

8. Pay attention to the sound of the poem. Read it out loud. If you can find a recording of the poet reading his or her poem, listen to that. Notice patterns of rhyme, rhythm, and repetition in repeated use of certain vowels or consonants. List any patterns you find.

9. Consider the effect of the line breaks, especially in free verse poems. Pay attention to the stanza structure of the poem and its effect. Describe the visual effect of the poem on the page. How do these factors contribute to mood and meaning?

10. How does the title comment on or extend the poem? Also notice any additional material, such as an epigraph or footnotes. Why are they there?

11. Pay attention to the beginning and the ending of the poem. Why does the poet begin here? Why end there?

12. What is the mood or tone of the poem? What do you think creates that mood or tone—the images, the sounds, the speaker's attitude? How is the mood achieved? What emotions does the poem cause you to feel?

13. Finally, what does the poem "mean"? Notice that this is not the first question to ask about a poem but almost the last. If you are writing an explication or other type of analytical essay on the poem, your thesis or interpretation of the poem will be supported by the evidence you have gathered answering the previous twelve questions.

14. You could now locate this poem—in relation to other poems by the same poet, to other poems written in the same historical period/place, and to historical issues and/or events contemporary with the poem. This question may move you into the realm of the research paper.

HOW DRAMA WORKS

As we did in "How Fiction Works," let's begin with an example, this time the opening of Arthur Miller's 1949 play, *Death of a Salesman*. The passage we examine represents only about 5 percent of the whole play, but it lays the groundwork for much of what is to come and illustrates a number of important general points about how drama works. Turn now to page 730 and read carefully as far as the italicized sentence on page 734 that begins "*On* WILLY's *last line ...*" Then return to this page and continue reading.

After the play's title and list of characters, we encounter the *stage directions*, which clearly set drama apart from other literary genres. Much fiction, for example, is written entirely in the past tense ("It was a dark and stormy night ..."), but the stage directions of a play are in the present tense ("*A melody is heard ...*")—a hint of the immediacy of drama, even drama on the page rather than on stage. In general, stage directions are aimed primarily at people putting on the play. Descriptions of the set, fairly elaborate in this case, can help someone design and build that set. Physical descriptions of characters (Willy is "*past sixty years of age, dressed quietly*") can help in the selection of actors, in the design of their costumes, and in the acting. Psychological descriptions of characters ("*Linda ... has developed an iron repression of her exceptions to Willy's behavior*") can help actors conceptualize their roles, speak their lines, and hold and move their faces and their bodies.

But stage directions are also essential to *readers* of a play. It is often tempting to skim through or skip over stage directions, especially if they are long, and get right to the dialogue, to "the play itself." But if, instead, we read stage directions carefully, and try to visualize what an actual performance of the play might look like, we will come much closer to the experience of seeing such a performance and perhaps even capture some of its excitement.

A close look at the opening of *Death of a Salesman* should suggest how important stage directions can be for readers. The directions begin with stark contrast: the flute music, "*telling of grass and trees and the horizon,*" against the "*towering, angular shapes*" of the apartment buildings with their "*angry glow of orange.*" The "*small, fragile-seeming home*" is surrounded by "*a solid vault of apartment houses.*" This creates a sense of entrapment, of external, rather ominous forces closing in on a peaceful but vulnerable center, much as Willy Loman's dream and life, we learn later, are the victims of forces beyond his control.

The set described seems to *suggest* a home rather than reproduce one realistically on stage. There is some furniture, but no fixtures; the setting is largely transparent; walls can be walked through. Willy's "*imaginings*" of the past are to be acted out at the front of the stage, with actors stepping freely through walls; but to portray the "*present*," actors will treat the wall-lines as solid walls and enter and exit only through a door. The stage directions suggest—and the play bears this out—that Willy will live much of his life in his imagination and that stage action will flow smoothly between imaginary scenes and scenes of present "reality." What is done quite easily in fiction—movement back and forth between actual experience and what takes place only in a character's mind—can be more difficult in drama, and Miller has created a rather complex scheme for doing the job.

Seeing the play in performance, we would quickly get used to the idea that walls are not always walls and that the same actors can represent both the present and the past, both external reality and the world inside Willy's head. Reading the play is both more difficult and easier than seeing it. Visualizing what is on the page takes effort, but our imagination, if aroused, is even more flexible than Miller's set.

The stage directions in a play represent the writer's only real chance to speak directly to readers. The rest of the play consists simply of what characters say, in other words, of dialogue. Though stage directions contain narrative elements ("*She is taking off his shoes*"), basically there is no narrator in drama. The story is not told, the plot is not related by one controlling voice, or more than one alternating, as in fiction. The story, in a sense, seems to tell itself. We watch and listen to what characters are doing and saying if we *see* a play; we read what seems like a transcript of what characters are doing and saying if we *read* a play.

In fiction, a narrator may prepare us for the main action by quickly summarizing events that have led up to it and by relating the personal histories of its main characters. But in drama, we generally have only the characters' own words. (Miller helps us a little with his description in the opening stage directions of Linda and Willy's relationship, but this is very brief and, of course, in performance, would not be spoken.) The action of *Death of a Salesman* begins in the middle of things—Willy has just dragged himself into the house—but we quickly learn a great deal about him and his family. The dialogue, especially in early scenes, not only moves the action forward, but also provides us with important information about the characters.

We learn, among other things, that Willy is having trouble with his job. He's getting tired and finding it difficult to keep his mind on the present. His boss, son of the man he once worked for, is younger and doesn't appreciate him. Willy is concerned that one of his sons, Biff, a young man of great promise back in high school, is now a farm hand, a failure in his father's eyes. More than concerned, he's angry, and yet he also loves Biff and is proud of him. Deeply conflicted in his feelings toward Biff, Willy refers to him as "a lazy bum" and then, a moment later, insists that "there's one thing about Biff—he's not lazy." We suspect Willy has been counting on his son's life somehow to compensate for his own, and though we haven't yet met Biff, we can imagine that the pressure of Willy's expectations has taken its toll on him.

Willy is frustrated, rude, and irritable; he snaps repeatedly at Linda, his wife. When she buys American cheese, instead of the usual Swiss, he takes it as a personal affront, an attack on his authority and dignity. Linda worries about him and seems to do everything in her power to calm and comfort him, downplaying his problems ("Maybe it's your glasses"), offering suggestions and criticism only gently, suffering his rudeness *"with infinite patience."* Unlike Willy, she's not concerned about her son's income and status so much as about his feelings; she just wants Biff and Willy to get along with each other.

Willy cares very much about money and status, yet has little of either, and seems ashamed of his son. He is trapped, as is Linda, and escapes into *"reminiscences,"* which is just what the staging dramatizes—the sense of external forces closing like a trap, and the contrast between a difficult present and memories of an idealized past. So by the time that Willy complains, near the end of the scene, of being "boxed . . . in" by the apartments around him, the full significance of his words should be clear, as should the irony of his talk of living in "the greatest country in the world."

In a short scene, which lasts perhaps ten minutes on stage, we've learned a great deal (much more, indeed, than has been spelled out here), not only about several characters in the play, but about some of the conflicts that will drive the plot: conflict between Willy and Biff, conflict between memory and present reality, conflict between Willy and his world. So even though the title of the play has more or less already told us what ultimately happens to Willy, we arrive at the transition to the next scene (*"Biff and Happy raise themselves up in their beds"*) eager to learn what happens next and rather well informed about the people it will happen to.

DRAMA ON STAGE AND ON THE PAGE

A good way to begin a more general discussion of how drama works is to pursue further the difference between seeing and reading a play. Perhaps the most striking thing about a play performed on stage is the presence of live actors. Lines spoken aloud have an impact that words on the page do not; this is why we often read aloud, whether to others or to ourselves, passages that we find especially moving or meaningful. Anger, despair, or delight in an actor's voice can communicate emotion to us in a way that words on a page cannot. And actors can move as well as speak. In many of Shakespeare's plays, heroes and villains flash their swords and daggers. Even from the back row, live theater can be impressive.

A set described in written stage directions is usually described only once, but a set on stage stands continuously before us, constantly shaping our responses. In plays from other cultures and historical periods, a set (as well as props and costumes) can help draw us in to that place and time. The use of space itself, even on the barest stage, can also affect us in important ways. We may notice, when reading, that stage directions place two lovers physically far apart as they discuss their problems, but it is quite another thing to see half the width of the stage gaping between them for the duration of the scene, making tangible the emotional distance they are feeling. Visual impact is essential to drama on stage.

The presence of an audience also makes drama seen different from drama read. Dramatic performance is a communal art; its roots are in religion and ritual. To a large extent, members of the audience experience a play not as separate individuals, but as a community, even if a community of strangers. Anyone who has seen a funny movie alone in a theater, or nearly alone, has no doubt felt the emptiness of the surrounding seats, the absence of a community of viewers. The kind of collective response we experience when we see a play is what we miss when we read a play.

Live drama also excites an audience because each performance is, in some sense, unique, its success uncertain. Will the actors remember all their lines? Will this be an exceptional performance? Will the audience, through its response, perhaps even inspire the actors to their best performance ever? The effect of the audience may be more obvious, say, at a rock concert; an audience may communicate its pleasure or displeasure to the actors more conspicuously at a comic than at a tragic play; but even when the audience's response is subtle, it does influence the actors' performance and helps shape the theatrical event. When we read a play, on the other hand, our response is ours alone.

The point, of course, is not that we shouldn't bother to read drama, but that we need to keep the nature of live drama in mind as we do read. When possible, we ought to read plays—or at least key scenes, or lines—aloud, preferably with others but alone if necessary, so we can feel the sound of a human voice speaking lines meant to be spoken. And if we have the chance, and the money, we ought to see live performances of plays we are reading.

But there are certain advantages to reading rather than seeing a play. If we care, for example, about the playwright's intentions, the printed text is usually a more objective guide than any performance. A performance, after all, is an interpretation, and even the most elaborately detailed stage directions cannot fully spell out how a playwright envisions the play on stage. The stage directions of *Death of a Salesman* say nothing, for example, about Willy Loman's height, and the play would be different if he were 5' 2" than if he were a foot taller. A director cannot avoid interpreting; even casting Willy Loman as a man of average height would represent one interpretation rather than another. Occasionally a playwright directs his or her own play, and such a rare production is usually paid special attention. But short of that, the play in print probably represents the closest we can come to the original voice of its author.

Reading can also provide a good first approach to a difficult play. The rich language, dense with meaning, of Shakespeare's *Othello* or Synge's *Riders to the Sea,* can take time to assimilate, and most of us need the help of footnotes to understand an English very different from today's. But even with plays that do not seem difficult at first glance, plays in which the language is conversational—*The Piano Lesson* or *Death of a Salesman,* or much of *In the Traffic of a Targeted City,* for example—reading allows us to stop the action and think over what's been happening, something impossible to do in a theater. Though reading a play may afford us a less intense emotional experience than seeing that play performed, it may offer a fuller intellectual experience; we may feel less, but we are more likely to understand what we feel.

The fact that most plays are written to be performed shapes the texts we read in ways that may not be obvious. Theater audiences need to be kept awake and interested; if they find a play dull, it may close quickly, a serious blow to the playwright, who may then find it difficult to get future plays produced. So plays generally have strong plots and often rely rather heavily on suspense. Fiction, by contrast, can easily digress from the main line of action to develop a mood or dwell on the subtleties of a character's psyche. But in most drama, plot is central, and events must keep unfolding in order to move that plot forward.

Playwrights face other constraints when constructing their plots that writers of fiction do not face. Plot in drama is generally linear; since audiences see events on stage one after another, they tend to assume that these events take place in that same order. Flashbacks, common in fiction, are more difficult to manage in drama—thus the complicated stage directions at the start in *Death of a Salesman* and in Kaminsky's *In the Traffic of a Targeted City,* which has two settings—New York City in the 1980s and Hiroshima in 1945. Since sets can be expensive and take some effort to change (though modern technology has made this easier), plays that use realistic sets usually do not take place, for example, on mountain tops or at sea, and tend to avoid frequent changes of location. For similar reasons of practicality, realistic plays usually avoid scenes that directly involve animals or small children. In fiction, the stroke of a pen can put thirty people in a room, talking and eating hors d'oeuvres. But in drama, the limited size of the stage, and of the budget (not to mention the trouble an audience might have understanding an individual character speaking against the chatter of the others), makes this quite difficult. None of the many constraints that performance puts on playwriting are absolute, of course, but they help to explain why playwrights so often write scenes of two or three or four characters in a room together talking.

CHANGING STAGE CONVENTIONS

In different historical periods, playwrights have faced different constraints within which they had to work. Or, to put it in positive terms, they have found different technical devices available to them for creating dramatic reality. If a dramatic technique or device—the **soliloquy,** for example, in which a character, alone on stage, speaks his or her private thoughts aloud to the audience—is widely used in a particular period and has become accepted and readily understood by audiences, we call it a **convention.** Theatrical conventions have changed over the years, and what may have seemed to audiences in one period like a perfectly clear and reasonable way of depicting reality on the stage may seem artificial and perhaps even confusing to audiences in another. Though we may feel uncomfortable with dramatic conventions that differ significantly from those of our own time, in order to understand and appreciate what we read, we should know something about them.

Classical Greek theater, in particular the fifth-century B.C. theater of Sophocles' *Antigone*, was very different from the theater of today. Plays were performed outdoors, in a large semicircular amphitheater, before an audience of tens of thousands. Actors stood in front of a painted scene building, wearing oversized masks that made them visible to a large audience and functioned as megaphones to project their voices. In the **orchestra,** a circular area between the actors and the audience, stood the **chorus,** fifteen men who, between scenes, danced solemnly and chanted commentary on the main action. Key events, such as Antigone's burial of her brother and, later, her own death, often took place offstage and were reported by messengers. The time a play covered was, by convention, usually less than a day, often only a few hours; plots were constructed around a short period of intense action, the prelude to which audiences already knew or learned about indirectly.

The Elizabethan theater, for which Shakespeare wrote, used a roofed stage that projected into an audience of perhaps two thousand. Nearly surrounding the stage and stacked up in balconies and galleries in a rather compact building, the members of the audience were all physically quite close to the actors, so that conventions such as the **aside** (in which a character speaks directly to the audience, unheard by the other actors on stage), as well as the soliloquy, seemed quite natural. There were few props and no scenery. For the most part, characters on stage created a sense of place through their words, as in *Othello,* when Montano, Governor of Cyprus, opens a scene by asking a man standing on a small upper stage, "What from the cape can you discern at sea?" The absence of scenery allowed for rapid shifting of scene from place to place. Together with rather free manipulation of time—minutes or weeks could elapse between scenes, and even years between acts—this created great flexibility and made possible considerable complexity of plot.

The **realistic theater,** which began in the nineteenth century in Europe, attempted to reproduce as faithfully as possible the reality of daily life as it might appear to an observer. The **box set** of the realistic stage consisted of a rectangular room with one wall missing so that the audience could see in. The room was fully furnished, and every effort was made, down to the smallest detail, to make the room appear like an actual room. In line with the desired illusion that the members of the audience were invisible observers of real life, characters never addressed the audience in soliloquies or asides and spoke in what seemed to be the language of everyday life, not in the poetry of Sophocles' or Shakespeare's noble personages. Events were linked together with discernibly credible causality, for plots, like sets and characters, had, above all, to maintain the appearance of reality.

Theater in the twentieth century has been characterized primarily by the variety of its conventions. Some plays, like August Wilson's *A Piano Lesson* or Susan Glaspell's *Trifles,* staged with attention to physical detail, have tried to imitate surface reality directly; others, like "Krapp's Last Tape," an example of absurdist theater, performed on bare or almost bare stages, have called upon the audience to imagine physical settings; and still others, like *Death of a Salesman* and *In the Traffic of a Targeted City,* taking a middle course, have used props and sets as much to suggest as to construct the physical environment of the play's action. Most twentieth-century plays use actors in a realistic way. But in Bertolt Brecht's epic theater, *Three Penny Opera* or *Mother Courage,* to take two examples, a number of techniques—songs, text projected onto the stage area, self-consciously theatrical acting—are used in order to break down the illusion of reality so that the audience will not become absorbed in events on stage but will instead think critically about them. Twentieth-century playwrights tend to draw on whatever conventions suit their dramatic purposes.

It is tempting to view theatrical conventions we are accustomed to, particularly realistic conventions, as somehow less artificial, more natural than those we are not used to, such as the soliloquies and asides in *Othello* or the Chorus in *Antigone.* But how natural is it, after all, for a group of actors in a boxlike room on a stage to hold private conversations and pretend not to be aware that the audience is watching? One might very well argue that Shakespearean actors, who openly acknowledge the presence of the audience by addressing it in asides and soliloquies, are behaving more naturally than actors in realistic drama. While different conventions have different implications—they shape what a playwright can and cannot do, and how it is to be done—*all* conventions are artificial. Those we are accustomed to tend to be transparent; we do not even notice them most of the time. But unfamiliar conventions can easily seem artificial, even foolish. We will get the most out of the drama we read if we ask ourselves the same question about all conventions: How does the playwright use them to shape the meaning of the play?

PLOT AND CHARACTER

An essential element in plays, whatever their conventions, is **plot.** The plot of a play, like the plot of a work of fiction, is a sequence of events arranged in a meaningful pattern. The plot of many plays follows a traditional pattern: **exposition,** in which characters, relationships, setting are introduced; then **rising action,** in which matters begin getting complicated, conflict develops; then **climax,** a turning point or moment of decision, when dramatic intensity peaks; then **falling action,** in which the consequences of the climactic events unfold; and, finally,

denouement, in which action comes to a meaningful end. This pattern is followed more closely in *Antigone* and *Othello* than, say, in "Krapp's Last Tape" or in *In the Traffic of a Targeted City;* we often might want to look for this pattern to help us understand how plays are structured, but we should not insist on finding it. A play might have multiple plots or a **subplot,** a second plot that, though connected, is also clearly subordinated to the main plot. Shakespeare's plays usually contain a subplot and an approach to writing about such a play could be to look at the subplot and note how it illuminates or is in tension with the main plot.

Events that have occurred before the moment at which the play's action begins can also serve as a sort of second plot that complicates the meaning of the main plot. The past events that Willy Loman's onstage reminiscences gradually reveal in *Death of a Salesman* provide an often painful contrast with the events unfolding in the present and help us understand their significance. The story of the piano that forms the material and symbolic center of August Wilson's *The Piano Lesson* lurks in the memories of the brother and sister who each are struggling to possess it. The hero of "Krapp's Last Tape" replays tape-recorded journal entries he made as a younger man, so that past and present plot are interwoven in meaningful ways. In Susan Glaspell's *Trifles,* past events prove especially significant. These past events are neither acted on stage nor narrated on tape; they are merely described by various characters and revealed through objects left behind, but they make themselves felt very strongly in the present. The bold action Mrs. Hale and Mrs. Peters take at the end of the play is very much inspired by the boldness of Minnie Foster in the story they have pieced together of her actions in the past. Of course, plotting can get much more complicated than this, but the point to emphasize again is that plot consists not simply of events but of their meaningful arrangement. A step toward understanding that meaning can be to ask how a play would be different if the same events were arranged differently for an audience, that is, fashioned into a different plot.

It is difficult to imagine plot in drama without **character,** and in much drama, as in much fiction, what happens to characters grows out of what kind of people they are. It is not uncommon in fiction, particularly in long works of fiction that trace the entire life of a central character, for plot to shape character significantly; the central figure, from childhood on perhaps, goes through a number of formative experiences that help determine what kind of person he or she becomes. But drama usually begins in the middle of things; characters have already become more or less what they are, and their interactions, perhaps with external events as well as with each other, set a plot in motion. A character's nature may be gradually *revealed* over the course of a play, but it is unlikely to change fundamentally.

Characters in drama, like characters in fiction, can be **major characters** (most central to the plot, fully developed, complex) or **minor characters** (on the periphery, sketchily drawn, rather one-dimensional); original characters (generally, they are major not minor characters) or **stock characters** (that is, easily recognized "types"); and **protagonist** (the main character, the hero) or **antagonist** (opponent to the protagonist). Categorization is not always easy, though; critics still debate, for example, whether Antigone or Creon is the protagonist of Sophocles' *Antigone,* and it is hard to pin the label "protagonist" on any single character in *In the Traffic of a Targeted City.*

Though stage directions and the list of characters (the **dramatis personae**) at the start of a play may sometimes describe characters for a reader directly, most characterization in drama—far more so than in fiction—is indirect. Character in drama can be revealed through what characters say, through what they do, through what others say to and about them, and, sometimes, through what they say to audiences in soliloquies and asides. As readers, we need to compare and carefully evaluate all sorts of revelations of character, including such clues as physical appearance and even name (Krapp, or Loman, or Boy Willie, for example).

TRAGEDY AND COMEDY

Tragedy is defined by character as well as by plot. Generally, tragedy involves a hero or protagonist of great social importance, such as a king or prince, who, often because of a flaw such as excessive pride, makes a decision and acts in a way that ultimately brings about his or her death. The hero usually dies after gaining new understanding that comes too late to alter the hero's fate. Othello, out of naiveté and perhaps pride, among other things, allows himself to be deceived by Iago, and his belief that Desdemona has betrayed him drives him to murder her; and then, after he has come to understand the truth, to kill himself. In *Antigone,* the matter is more complicated, for while Antigone may be flawed by zealousness and does die, Creon is flawed as well but, unlike Antigone, comes to a new understanding before the end. Which character we view as protagonist (and thus as tragically flawed) may have less to do with the structure of the play itself than with where our individual sympathies lie, whether with the ruler Creon or with the rebel Antigone. In the 1904 play *Riders to the Sea,* Irish playwright John Synge focuses on Maurya, an aging woman who is in the process of losing the last of her several sons to the sea, which is an everpresent force of nature in the lives of this peasant population of the Aran Islands off the coast of Ireland. Fate is the ocean and the necessity to go to it to make a living. However, the tragic hero, Maurya, doesn't die or, as far as we can tell, have a tragic flaw, though you may disagree. In *Death of a Salesman,* Arthur Miller tries to make what he called "the common man" the subject of tragedy. "I don't say he's a great man," Willy's wife Linda says at one point, ". . . but he's a human being, and a terrible thing is happening to him. So attention must be paid." But whether Willy Loman achieves the stature we tend to associate with tragedy, or whether he is more pathetic than tragic, is certainly open to question.

Comedy, generally, differs from tragedy in that its hero is more likely to be a young lover than an old noble; it ends in a marriage or other joyful event, not death; its overall mood is playful, not somber; and it appeals to our intellect more than to our emotions. Though many plays fit one of these definitions quite well, most modern plays squirm uncomfortably if we try to force them into the comic or the tragic mold. While *Othello* and other tragedies make use of **comic relief,** humorous interludes that provide escape from and also an intensifying contrast to the overall mood of tragedy, modern plays sometimes mix comic elements much more thoroughly with the material of tragedy. Krapp, old, alone, compulsively eating bananas and playing his tapes, is at once funny and pathetic, a combination not uncommon in the **Theater of the Absurd.** Absurdist plays like those of Samuel Beckett portray human existence as meaningless, hopeless, irrational and the individual as ultimately isolated and alienated. Yet these plays are often grotesquely funny, their humor in stark contrast to the horror of their underlying message. Though the mood, the hero, and the structure of many recent plays may be difficult to categorize as simply tragic or comic, tragic and comic elements are central to most drama; and the concepts of tragedy and comedy can often provide a useful starting point for the analysis of a play. Often containing both tragic and comic elements, **epic theater,** developed in the 1930s by Bertolt Brecht, sought to make drama more effective as social criticism by destroying the illusion of reality that a play usually worked to create. The audience's absorption into the world of a play, its identification with characters on stage, Brecht believed, deadened their critical faculties. Through the overtly theatrical techniques he employed (no doubt more effective for theater audiences than for readers), he strove to create what he called an "alienation effect" in order to keep audiences distanced from events on stage, so that they might be compelled to ask themselves how the world could be different. Epic, as well as absurdist, theater techniques have been absorbed into the possibilities available to modern and contemporary drama and often appear in plays of social protest.

DRAMA AND SOCIAL CRITICISM

Plays often picture human suffering in various forms, but they differ considerably in what they suggest about the causes and the necessity of such suffering. Tragedy has traditionally portrayed suffering as part of the nature of things. Though the action of a flawed protagonist may precipitate disaster, we come to believe that such disaster is inevitable. Modern readers may look to the psychology of Creon or Antigone for explanations, but for Sophocles' original audiences, fate (that is, the gods) played an essential role in bringing catastrophe. As the daughter of Oedipus, Antigone shares his curse, for, as the Chorus explains, "Where once the anger of heaven has struck, that house is shaken/ For ever." And while Shakespeare's Iago may be acting without help from the gods, once he has set his powerful traps, Othello's fate seems almost inescapable; the structure and feel of *The Tragedy of Othello, The Moor of Venice* are also of inevitability.

What women and men see when they look at the same scene, whether a woman who may have killed her husband should be brought to justice, and just what justice means, are questions which underlie the solving of a murder mystery in Susan Glaspell's play *Trifles*. This is drama of social criticism and can lead to intense debates about the relative power and status of men and women. Social criticism is implicit in several of the plays included here, in which social conditions or issues are a foregrounded part of the dramatic tension. Wakako Yamauchi's *And the Soul Shall Dance* focuses on the situation of Japanese-American immigrants and their American-born children in mid-twentieth-century U.S.A. *In the Traffic of a Targeted City* juxtaposes life in New York City in the 1980s with the day the atomic bomb fell in Hiroshima; the same two actors move between the two settings and play all the characters, sometimes reading from actual memoirs of Hiroshima survivors. The antique carved piano of August Wilson's *The Piano Lesson,* center of that play's dramatic conflict, is a complex symbol of the legacy of slavery and the lack of economic opportunity for African-Americans in the twentieth century.

Twentieth-century drama of social criticism has worked in various ways to suggest that change is necessary and possible. *Salt of the Earth,* a screenplay for a film rather than a play for the stage, tracks the trajectory of a strike by Mexican-American zinc miners in New Mexico, dramatizing the political effectiveness of gender, ethnic, and worker solidarity against the power of corporate money. Though in some ways departing from the realistic theater, *Death of a Salesman,* too, can be read as social criticism; the play may end with the death of its protagonist, but it need not be understood as tragedy of inevitability. For Willy is the victim of the flawed society that produced him. He has swallowed whole an American dream that could never deliver what it promised and he suffers for his misplaced faith in a business world that discards him when he proves unprofitable. "Business is business," Howard explains coldly as he fires Willy. Like other cultural productions, drama and film can be counted on to embody a perspective on the social order, be it critical or uncritical, consistent or perhaps contradictory; and though we may disagree about what that perspective is, trying to understand it is an essential part of reading and interpreting drama.

FILM

Film can usefully be compared with drama, though it also shares certain characteristics with fiction, poetry (when it is more lyrical than narrative), and nonfiction (most notably in documentary film). Indeed, film is generally divided into three types: **fiction film, documentary film,** and **avante garde film.** Fiction film tells a made-up story, and quite a few films work from screenplays adapted from novels or short stories. A documentary film may have either a plot or an argument and is based on fact. Avante garde film is often impressionistic, less narrative, and of the three types most often like lyric poetry. Like drama in performance, film creates an image to be seen and heard by an audience, though generally what is seen plays the more important role in film and what is heard (in particular, the dialogue) plays the more important role in drama. Like drama, film—however "real" it may seem—also relies on conventions, such as the use of music (romantic, ominous, lighthearted, and so on) to help create a mood even when no conceivable source for that music exists within the world of the film. Unlike drama, though, film does not have to choose between variety and surface realism in settings; film can shift rapidly and repeatedly to new physical locations, thus combining, in a sense, the flexibility of the Elizabethan stage with the faithful reproduction of appearances of the realistic stage.

Film shares with fiction rather than with drama the ability to embody point of view, for the camera, in some ways like the narrator in a work of fiction, continuously controls what we see and how we see it. A scene, for example, of a Civil War battle shot from a distance (a **long shot**) might lead us to concentrate on the question of which side is winning, while a **close-up** of the face of one soldier in that battle might instead emphasize fear and suffering, that is, the human cost of war. And a **zoom shot** that began at a distance and gradually moved in to focus on one face might make a point about the relationship between these two aspects of war.

Camera angle as well as distance can shape a viewer's response to a film. A scene of a political leader delivering an impassioned speech, for example, if shot fairly close and from a low angle (so that the viewer looked up at the politician), might create an image, perhaps a menacing one, of great personal power. On the other hand, a scene of a person sitting alone in a room, if shot from a high angle (looking down), might create an image of weakness and vulnerability. Film can also shape a viewer's response through **cutting,** that is, through instantaneous changes from one perspective or scene to another (made by attaching together pieces of film shot separately). In a scene, for example, of a disagreement over a raise between a manager and a low-paid employee, a quick cut to a shot of the manager's diamond pinky ring might help us take sides. Similarly, repeated cutting back and forth (or **crosscutting**) between a husband watching television and a wife scrubbing pots and pans would make an unmistakable point.

There is obviously a great deal more to say about the wide variety of techniques available to filmmakers (and most introductory film books explore the technical side of filmmaking in detail, including the genre of animated film, which includes the environmentally conscious films of the great Japanese animator, Hayao Miyazaki), but it is also worth noting that in general making films is business, usually big business. A Hollywood film costs millions of dollars to produce and millions more to advertise, so artistic considerations easily give way to commercial ones. The romantic image of the artist aflame with a vision and beholden only to his or her muse bears little resemblance to the work of a Hollywood filmmaker hoping to sell a film to a mass audience. Consequently, some of the best as well as the most innovative American films today come from "independent" filmmakers, working with small budgets and outside Hollywood. *Salt of the Earth* (Varieties of Protest) is not only an independent film; it is a film made under difficult political and economic conditions by a director (Martin Bieberman) and a screenwriter (Michael Wilson) who had been banned from working in Hollywood by Senator McCarthy's Committee on Unamerican Activities in 1950. The film is based on an actual zinc miners' strike, and a number of the actors in the film were miners and other local people involved in the strike.

Look at the opening scenes of *Salt of the Earth*. Reflecting the greater importance of the visual dimension in film, the scene directions in the screenplay are extensive, as much like narration in fiction as like stage directions in drama. The screenplay opens:

FADE IN (before titles)

Ext., Quintero Backyard. Medium Shot, Day.

A woman at work chopping wood. Though her back is to the Camera, we sense her weariness in toil by the set of her shoulders. A five-year-old girl is helping the woman, gathering kindling. Over this scene comes the first title.

A Guitar dominates the musical theme. The motif is grave, nostalgic.

We are given a setting and situation (a family, poor and hardworking); the actors in relation to the camera; and a mood through physical cues ("the set of her shoulders") and music—a guitar, "grave, nostalgic."

Before any dialogue occurs we meet Esperanza, our protagonist, in a **voiceover** which accompanies increasingly panoramic shots of her house, her village ("it was called San Marcos. . . . The Anglos changed the name to Zinc Town"), and the mine which "dominates the town like a volcano" (the scene directions). The camera then moves to close-ups of the mine and of Ramón, Esperanza's husband, at work setting off a dynamite charge underground, and then back to the Quintero's backyard, kitchen, parlor. One dramatic juxtaposition is a close shot of a sign attached to a fence: PROPERTY OF DELAWARE ZINC, INC. with Esperanza's voice: "The land where the mine stands—that was owned by my husband's own grandfather."

"How shall I begin my story that has no beginning?" are the opening words of Esperanza's voiceover. She tells us in deceptively simple language about herself, her family, her history in this place "before the Anglos ever came." We see and hear how hard she works for her family, her worry about her husband's dangerous job, her pride and dignity. The voice-over ends with the seven months pregnant Esperanza praying for forgiveness that she has "wished that my child would never be born. Not into this world." The voice of Esperanza over both close and panoramic camera shots gives us a lot of information about the history behind the current situation which will power the plot of the film. It also gives us a first person perspective, an intimate relationship and instant sympathy with Esperanza, who seems to be speaking directly to us, telling us her story.

The scenes immediately following introduce us to Ramón leading a contingent of workers to protest poor safety conditions in the mine, which initiates the conflict between workers and mine owners that will form one thread of the film's plot. The conversation between Ramón and Esperanza at home shows that there are both love and problems in this marriage, some of them economic and some

cultural. Ramón pooh-poohs Esperanza's request to include a union contract demand for running water in the company owned houses (though in the next scene
in the bar he repeats her concerns as though they were his own), and he forgets
that it is her name day (similar in importance to a birthday). Reminded by his
son, he organizes a party for her later that night and, more importantly, honestly
confesses to Esperanza that he had forgotten until their son reminded him. This
then is the second thread of plot: As the workers strike for equal rights, the miners and their wives, and especially Ramón and Esperanza, move toward a more
equal gender relationship. Throughout the film, these two movements are intertwined, moving together through the stages of narrative and dramatic plot: exposition, rising action, climax, falling action, denouement.

A NOTE ON TELEVISION

Television uses many of the same techniques as film, though we find, for example, fewer long shots and more close-ups on television because of the smaller size
of the screen. Like film, television is shaped significantly by commercial considerations; network executives, and thus everyone else involved, watch the ratings
very closely. Creators of television series face numerous external constraints.
Each episode of a series will be the same length and must be divided into segments of more or less prescribed length; the segments end at moments of excitement or suspense so that viewers will keep watching despite commercial
interruption. Major characters in a series cannot die, no matter how much danger they find themselves in, if they are to appear again the following week; and
writers have to come up with twenty-six episodes a year. So it is not surprising
that many series—even those that begin with great promise—settle quickly into
tired formulas.

   From time to time plays are produced for television. As with film versions of
plays, some of these consist simply of a stage performance recorded on video-
tape or film, and they offer a convenient way of seeing a play. Others move the
play off the stage, outdoors if a scene calls for it; they keep the original dialogue
but use the camera as expressively as in any film or television show. In plays
made for television by independent video artists and in other productions that
depart from the weekly routine, we can sometimes glimpse the still largely un-
tapped potential of the medium.

How Nonfiction Works

You might be asking yourself why nonfiction is included in an anthology called *Literature and Society*. What is literature, and is nonfictional prose literature? Literature can be defined in evaluative terms, as writing that achieves a certain level of excellence regardless of its form. But how do we decide what is excellent and what is not; and, further, who decides? Literature has also been defined as writing that is imaginative or "creative," rather than factual. But imagination can take many forms, not all of them clearly or entirely poetic, fictional, or dramatic. The speaker in Judy Brady's "I Want a Wife" imagines herself out of the role of wife, with which she is obviously intimately familiar, and into the role of possessor of a wife—one whose social expectations might include having a wife to cook and clean up after her, to bear and raise her children, to act as hostess and secretary, and, in general, to make her life easier. Clearly a work of imagination, "I Want a Wife" is just as clearly not a story, a poem, or a play but a satiric essay. While literary nonfiction has a long and distinguished history—think of Daniel Defoe, Henry Thoreau, Virginia Woolf, James Baldwin—only in the past few years has the wide range of literary nonfictional writing been gathered into a newly named genre: **creative nonfiction.** Creative nonfiction loosely includes autobiography, memoir, personal essay, biography, nature writing, meditative writing, sermons, personal essays. Creative nonfiction is distinguished by (1) its allegiance to truthfulness, to an authenticity grounded in fact, and (2) its literary nature, its use of images, stories, and sentences meant to last. Thus, many works of creative nonfiction use techniques we have already become acquainted with in the sections "How Fiction Works," "How Poetry Works," and "How Drama Works": narration, plot, point of view, figurative language, dramatic scenes, voice, atmosphere, setting, dialogue, character sketches and character development, and sense-based and rhythmic language. Literature, it seems to us, includes any writing that (1) takes itself seriously as writing and persuades its readers to take it seriously, and (2) pays decided attention to matters of language and of form, being as concerned with how it says something as with what is said. Two further considerations, more open to disagreement and debate, are that literature should move us in some way, have an emotional effect on us, and that it should have lasting value.

The typical news story in the daily paper is very probably not literature. It is ephemeral, not meant to last. It is written to a formula—who, what, where, when, how, and maybe if there's space, why—and even if the individual reporter is a good writer, one task of the news editor is to smooth out flair and originality and to shape that individual voice into a style consistent with the rest of the paper's writing. Editorial and feature writing are, of course, another matter, and Meridel Le Sueur's "Women on the Breadlines" is an example of reportage that we can be reasonably secure in calling literature. Written during the Great Depression as an exposé to bring the situation of unemployed women to the attention of a nation focused on finding jobs for men, the piece uses fictional devices such as narration, character sketch, and setting; poetic devices such as metaphor and simile; and dramatic devices such as dialogue and scene to construct an essay that both informs and persuades.

> So we sit hour after hour, day after day, waiting for a job to come in. There are many women for a single job. A thin sharp woman sits inside a wire cage looking at a book. For four hours we have watched her looking at that book. She has a hard little eye. In the small bare room there are half a dozen women sitting on the benches waiting. Many come and go. Our faces are all familiar to each other, for we wait here every day.

This paragraph early in Le Sueur's essay provides a setting and begins to introduce us to some of the people who inhabit that setting. The description of the "small bare room" and the women in it, including the first-person narrator who is both a participant and an observer, is written in such a way as to evoke a particular atmosphere or mood—of tedium, endurance, passivity, and perhaps a growing desperation. What makes "Women on the Breadlines" an essay rather than a story is Le Sueur's emphasis on developing an idea and an argument. Throughout she mixes narration with persuasion, using the characters, anecdotes, and atmosphere as evidence for her argument that women too are out of work and suffering, that their invisibility is in part due to their socialization as women and is mirrored in media, government, and popular ignorance of their condition. After telling us about one woman, Bernice, who has lived on crackers for weeks, she writes, "A woman will shut herself up in a room until it is taken away from her, and eat a cracker a day and be as quiet as a mouse so there are no social statistics concerning her." The individual women Le Sueur describes in vivid detail serve as representative types. She continually moves from the particular to the general, from the specific to the abstract, each detail a piece of evidence in the construction and development of her thesis. This method of argument is already clear in her opening sentences: "I am sitting in the city free employment bureau. It's the women's section. We have been sitting here now for four hours. We sit here every day, waiting for a job. There are no jobs."

Although Le Sueur's rhetorical intent breaks through her narration often enough to make classifying this piece as an essay not too difficult, some prose lives quite congenially and unrepentantly on the line between fiction and nonfiction. Richard Wright's "The Man Who Went to Chicago" has been variously classified as fiction and nonfiction during its publishing history. Published by Wright as a separate fictional piece in the 1940s, it finally ended up in an expanded version as part of *American Hunger,* the posthumously published second volume of his autobiography. Writing about his experience with several different jobs in Chicago during the Depression, Wright sometimes lets his narration launch him into an impassioned argument against American racism. Is this essay, memoir, or autobiographical fiction? How much did Wright shape, combine, and rearrange events, details, and characters? How much is "truth" and how much "fiction"? The question of truth also arises with Maxine Hong Kingston's "No Name Woman," the first of five sections of *The Woman Warrior,* her account of growing up Chinese-American. This book won the National Book Critics Circle award as best work of nonfiction in 1976, yet the piece consists of "stories" spiraling out of other "stories." We bring up these examples not in order to confuse but to suggest that although labeling and categorizing can be useful, they also have their limits. Writers are adventurers and explorers who constantly cross and expand the mapped boundaries of form. This fact is nowhere clearer than in nonfictional prose, a category that seems to include everything in literary prose left over after we have separated out works of fiction and drama.

TYPES OF NONFICTIONAL PROSE

It is possible to name and describe two broad categories of nonfictional prose— *narrative nonfictional prose* and *rhetorical nonfictional prose*—though the dividing lines are fuzzy, and a work of nonfictional prose may succeed in being both at once. **Narrative nonfictional prose** recounts an event or sequence of events. It moves in time, either in simple chronological sequence or in a more complex pattern as does Joy Harjo's memory layered personal essay, "Three Generations of Native American Women's Birth Experience." **Diaries** and **journals** are most often simple chronologies of events and introspection recorded sequentially. A diary is usually more intimate, personal, and private, whereas a journal tends to be a more public form, as much concerned with the world as it is with the self writing. The **letters** people write to friends and acquaintances are often narrative, and collections of letters, especially by well-known people, are often published and read with interest. **Epistles,** on the other hand, are more formal and public letters, written by individuals or groups and addressing philosophical or political issues. Internet **blogs** are fast taking up some of the personal writing terrain of diaries and journals. There are at least two differences: (1) Diaries and journals, whether or not they were eventually published, tended at the time of writing to be for oneself and not a public; blogs of course are posted and instantly available to as large a community of readers as wishes to log on; (2) the corollary of having an immediate community of readers is that readers can instantly respond to the writing by writing to the writer. On the one hand, this changes the isolated and meditative nature we've often associated with diaries and journals. Journals, diaries, letters, epistles, and most recently blogs, e-mails, and instant message conversations have also, as forms, been utilized by fiction writers to construct their fictional narratives.

Perhaps the most varied and enjoyable forms of narrative nonfictional prose are **autobiography** and **memoir.** Where autobiography tells the "whole" story of the life of the writer, usually though not always chronologically, memoir focuses on some aspect of the writer's life or a period in the writer's life. We have included several such selections—Richard Wright's "The Man Who Went to Chicago," Studs Terkel's oral history interview with steelworker Mike Lefevre, Black Elk's "The Butchering at Wounded Knee," Maxine Hong Kingston's "No Name Woman," Thomas Whitecloud's "Blue Winds Dancing," excerpts from Harriet Jacobs's *Incidents in the Life of a Slave Girl,* Audre Lorde's *Zami,* Dorothy Allison's "Gun Crazy," and Marjane Satrapi's **graphic memoir,** *Persepolis.* Each of these works narrates and meditates upon an event or series of events crucial in retrospect in the life of the writer—from Kingston's and Lorde's memories of the beginning of puberty, to Black Elk's description of the defeat of his people, to Dorothy Allison's memory of growing up poor in the South, to Satrapi's visual and prose account of fleeing Iran as a teenager during the Islamic Revolution during the 1980s. To say that the mode of writing (or in the case of the oral history, talking) in these autobiographical selections is primarily narrative does not mean that there is no persuasive intent in the writing. Harriet Jacobs, for example, hoped that by describing her own considerable suffering as a slave, she would move her white readers to support the antislavery cause. Thomas Whitecloud's description of leaving white "civilization" and going home to his people contains some cogent criticisms—both through direct statement and through comparison with his Chippewa relatives and their community—of mainstream United States in the 1930s.

Rhetoric is the art and skill of persuasion, and **rhetorical nonfictional prose** presents facts and ideas in such a way as to persuade a reader of the truth, or at least the likelihood, of the writer's position. Just as persuasion may be found in narrative nonfictional prose, so narrative elements are often part of rhetorical nonfictional prose. Image, anecdote, character sketch, and descriptions of places may contribute to the development of an idea or an argument. The earlier discussion of Meridel Le Sueur's "Women on the Breadlines" points out how she uses a variety of narrative techniques to move her readers closer to the position she is advocating. "Women on the Breadlines" is a **journalistic essay,** an example of reportage that goes beyond the simple reporting of events to take and support a position. You can read editorial and feature essays in newspapers and periodicals to find contemporary examples of this mode of writing.

Alongside narrative and rhetorical writing are two other modes of nonfictional prose: the **descriptive** and the **expository.** Descriptive writing tells readers what a person or object or place looks like or feels, smells, tastes, or sounds like. This kind of writing can easily slide into poetry; the border between a short piece of descriptive prose using sound and imagery to evoke a place, event, or person and a prose poem which does the same is very tenuous. Expository writing, on the other hand, explains; it provides readers with information—how a watch works, what "neurosis" means, how to read nonfictional prose. In writing considered literature, a work that is exclusively descriptive or expository is less usual;

description most often appears in the service of narration and exposition in the service of persuasion. So we find it more useful to talk of descriptive and expository *elements* in nonfictional writing.

Whether narrative or rhetorical, most nonnarrative nonfictional prose pieces could also be called **essays,** a term originating in a French verb meaning "to try" or "to attempt." The essay can be divided into the **informal essay,** relatively more personal or subjective, more tentative, not meant to be the last word on a subject, relaxed in tone and form, often more dependent on the techniques of fiction, poetry, and drama; and the **formal essay,** more dignified and serious in tone, more objective and distanced from reader and subject, more formally structured. Scientific treatises, much traditional historical writing, and a good deal of literary criticism are written in the more formal mode. An informal essay which is at least partly using the writer's experience as evidence for his or her thesis is often called a **personal essay.** Most of the essays included in this anthology can be classed as informal. Some examples of personal essays included in *Literature and Society* are Joy Harjo's "Three Generations of Native American Women's Birth Experience," Dorothy Allison's "A Question of Class," Richard Rodriguez's "Huck Finn, Dan Quayle, and the Value of Acceptance," Henry David Thoreau's "Civil Disobedience," and Thomas Whitecloud's "Blue Winds Dancing." Your own papers about literature are usually essays and, depending on your temperament, your topic, and your teacher's guidelines, may lie anywhere on the spectrum from informal to formal.

STRATEGIES OF NONFICTIONAL PROSE

The passage by Virginia Woolf on "Shakespeare's Sister," Henry David Thoreau's "Civil Disobedience," and Judy Brady's "I Want a Wife" are examples of **political essays;** each writer has a definite position for (or against) which she or he is arguing. Woolf uses the method of comparison and contrast to imagine what the chances of becoming a writer would have been for a young woman in Shakespeare's time. "Let me imagine, since facts are so hard to come by, what would have happened had Shakespeare had a wonderfully gifted sister, called Judith, let us say." In "Civil Disobedience," Thoreau mixes personal narration (the story of how he went to jail for not paying his taxes) with an argument about why it is immoral to pay taxes when they will be used for immoral purposes— in this case, to support war and the institution of slavery. Then Thoreau moves to the next level of his argument to try to persuade each of us to know what our convictions are and to act out of them. One way of characterizing Thoreau's rhetorical method is as concentric circles of argument, each one opening out into a further level of abstraction, but with a kernel of personal narration at the very center to anchor his theorizing. In a sense, the form of Thoreau's writing reflects his ethics—no one else can tell us what is right; each person must act (and write) out of personal experience and conviction.

Brady's much shorter essay uses humor as a strategy to keep us reading in the face of any initial resistance we might have to her topic. The relentless repetition of the phrase "I want a wife," combined with vivid detail from her own and observed experience as a wife, carries us along with the writer so that by the time she concludes, "My god, who wouldn't want a wife?" we are inclined to agree with her. Brady's use of repetition as a rhetorical strategy is more common in oral than in written forms and is a technique we encounter frequently in poetry (and song). Repetition often is used in **sermons** and **speeches** because repeating important ideas or emotions is crucial to retention of content when the audience doesn't have a text that it can reread. In addition, repetition creates in spoken prose a rhythm that in turn creates a mood shared communally, holding an audience's attention and moving it toward a particular conclusion. The Reverend Martin Luther King, Jr.'s powerful and moving speeches were influenced by the rhetorical form of the sermon, especially as it developed in the African-American church. His two speeches included here, "I Have a Dream," and "A Time to Break Silence," as well as Sojourner Truth's "Ain't I a Woman," are examples of particularly effective oral rhetoric. The reader of the text of a speech needs to remember that, like poetry, a speech is meant to be heard and that reading some or all of it aloud can be an aid to understanding. Whereas much modern writing envisions an individual reader, speeches, like drama, imagine a communal audience. In any piece of writing, and especially in any rhetorical piece of writing, it is useful to think about the audience the writer had in mind. In considering a speech, its time and place and occasion can be crucial in your interpretation of its meaning. For example, Sojourner Truth's redefinition of "woman" makes more sense when you know that she was a black working-class woman in the middle of the nineteenth century speaking to an audience primarily of middle-class white women and men about women's place and women's rights.

Like any other piece of writing, a work of nonfictional prose needs to be able to stand on its own and make sense to us as a separate entity. However, an essay, like a poem, a story, or a play, may be in part working out of or challenging a literary, philosophical, or political tradition, or be responding to contemporary social or biographical events. Researching and keeping in mind historical factors such as the time, place, and occasion of a piece of writing, literary factors such as its place in the writer's overall work, and biographical factors such as what else was going on in the writer's life at that time can provide a valuable context for the text itself. Especially in the case of rhetorical nonfictional prose, it is useful to discover, if we can, what other writers have said or were saying about the same subject, for often an essay will be a response to another essay or a contribution to an argument being carried on by a number of people in a given period.

In reading and writing about nonfictional prose, it may make sense to look for the **theme** of the work if the piece is primarily narrative or to look for the **thesis** of the work if it is primarily rhetorical or persuasive. What does the work as a whole add up to? What was the writer's intent or purpose in writing it? What is your response to the work, and do you think yours is the response the writer wanted? How does the writer develop either the theme or the thesis? What are its stages? What are its elements? What does the writer use to build an argument, present an idea, provide an experience for us to share?

One of the best ways to understand any type of writing is to attempt (or essay) it yourself, to experience the craft of writing in that mode from the inside. This is true of fiction, poetry, and drama, though with the last you might content yourself with a short scene rather than a whole play. In essaying creative nonfiction, you might try writing a short autobiographical sketch, centered perhaps on one significant incident in your life, as Dorothy Allison does in "Gun Crazy" or as Marjane Satrapi does in "The Dowry." Or you could tell a part of your life story from the perspective created by a particular focus, such as social class, race, or gender or sexual preference, as Kingston, Lorde, Allison, Black Elk, Whitecloud, Wright, Avicolli, and Jacobs do. Or you could argue your position on a topic by using an anecdote or extended image or metaphor to present your main point, as Audre Lorde does with the image of the morter and pestle in her story about the onset of puberty in *Zami*. Our chapter "Literature and the Writing Process" is constructed to help train you in a variety of approaches to a particular type of writing—nonfictional prose that has a literary text as its subject. The twenty-one works of creative nonfiction included in *Literature and Society* can stimulate your thinking about social issues as well as serve as models for your own writing—about literature, ideas, beliefs, and life experiences.

CREDITS

1972, 1974.) Reprinted by permission of The New Press. www.thenewpress.com.

Dylan Thomas, "Do Not Go Gentle Into That Good Night" from *The Poems of Dylan Thomas.* Copyright 1952 by Dylan Thomas. Reprinted with the permission of New Directions Publishing Corp.

Henry David Thoreau, *Civil Disobedience.* Public domain.

Jean Toomer, "Fern" from *Cane.* Copyright 1923 by Boni & Liveright. Copyright renewed 1951 by Jean Toomer. Reprinted with the permission of Liveright Publishing Corporation.

B. Traven, "Assembly Line" from *The Night Visitor and Other Stories* (New York: Hill & Wang, 1966). Copyright © 1966 by B. Traven. Copyright renewed 1994 by R.E. Lujan.

Sojourner Truth, "Ain't I a Woman" from Miriam Schneir (ed.), *Feminism: The Essential Historical Writings* (New York: Random House). Public domain.

Marina Tsvetayeva, "A white low sun," translated by David McDuff, from Jon Silkin, *The Penguin Book of First World War Poetry* (London: Penguin, 1979). Reprinted with the permission of the translator.

John Updike, "Ex-Basketball Player" from *The Carpentered Hen and Other Tame Creatures.* (New York: Alfred A. Knopf, 1957). Copyright © 1982 by John Updike. Used by permission of Alfred A. Knopf, a division of Random House, Inc. "A&P" from *Pigeon Feathers and Other Stories* (New York: Alfred A. Knopf, 1962). Copyright © 1962 and renewed 1990 by John Updike. Used by permission of Alfred A. Knopf, a division of Random House, Inc.

Alma Luz Villanueva, "Crazy Courage" from *Desire.* (Tempe: Bilingual Press/Editorial Bilingue, 1998). Reprinted by permission.

Tino Villanueva, "Not Knowing, in Aztlan" from *Shaking Off the Dark* (Houston: Arte Publico Press, 1984). Copyright © 1984 by Tino Villanueva. Reprinted with the permission of the author.

Alice Walker, "Everyday Use" from *In Love and Trouble: Stories of Black Women.* Copyright © 1973 by Alice Walker. Reprinted with the permission of Harcourt, Inc.

Margaret Walker, "Lineage" and "For My People" from *This is My Century: New and Collected Poems.* Copyright 1987 by Margaret Walker. Reprinted with the permission of The University of Georgia Press.

Bruce Weigl, "Song of Napalm" from *Monkey Wars* (Athens: University of Georgia Press, 1985). Copyright © 1985 by Bruce Weigl. Reprinted with the permission of the author.

Thomas S. Whitecloud, "Blue Winds Dancing" from *Scribner's Magazine* CIII, no. 2 (February 1938). Reprinted with the permission of Scribner, an imprint of Simon & Schuster Adult Publishing Group, from *Scribner's Magazine, Vol.* CIII, No. 2, February 1938 by Charles Scribner's Sons; copyright renewed © 1966.

Walt Whitman, "We Two Boys Together Clinging," "To a Stranger," "To The States," "The Dying Veteran," "I Saw in Louisiana a Live-Oak Growing," and "A child said *What is the grass?"* excerpt from *Leaves of Grass.* Public domain.

John Greenleaf Whittier, "For Righteousness' Sake." Public domain.

William Carlos Williams, "To a Poor Old Woman" and "The Young Housewife" from *Collected Poems, Volume I: 1909–1939.* Copyright 1938 by New Directions Publishing Corporation. Reprinted with the permission of the publishers.

August Wilson, *The Piano Lesson* (Penguin/Plume, 1990). copyright © 1988, 1990 by August Wilson. Used by permission of Dutton Signet, a division of Penguin Group (USA) Inc.

INDEX OF AUTHORS
AND TITLES

INDEX OF FIRST LINES
OF POEMS

Index of Literary Terms